LITERATURE

TEXAS

Language and Literacy

PEARSON

Upper Saddle River, New Jersey
Boston, Massachusetts
Chandler, Arizona
Glenview, Illinois

Cover: (C) ©Steve Satushek/Stone/Getty Images, (R) ©Don Farrall/Getty Images, (C) ©Datacraft/imagenavi/Getty Images, (Bkgd) ©Peter Griffith/Getty Images, (C) ©Jan Greune/LOOK/Getty Images

Acknowledgments appear on pages R88–R91, which constitute an extension of this copyright page.

Copyright © 2011 Pearson Education, Inc., or its affiliates. All Rights Reserved. Printed in the United States of America. This publication is protected by copyright, and permission should be obtained from the publisher prior to any prohibited reproduction, storage in a retrieval system, or transmission in any form or by any means, electronic, mechanical, photocopying, recording, or likewise. For information regarding permissions, write to Pearson Curriculum Group Rights & Permissions, One Lake Street, Upper Saddle River, New Jersey 07458.

Pearson, Prentice Hall, and Pearson Prentice Hall are trademarks, in the U.S. and/or other countries, of Pearson Education, Inc., or its affiliates.

SAT is a registered trademark of the College Entrance Examination Board. ACT is a trademark owned by ACT, Inc.

Wikipedia® is a registered trademark of the Wikimedia Foundation, Inc., ‹http://www.wikimediafoundation.org›.

iPod® and Mac® are registered trademarks of Apple, Inc.

Use of the trademarks implies no relationship, sponsorship, endorsement, sale, or promotion on the part of Pearson Education, Inc., or its affiliates.

ISBN-13: 978-0-13-368443-8
ISBN-10:   0-13-368443-1

2 3 4 5 6 7 8 9 10 VO63 14 13 12 11 10

Texas Program Advisors

Pearson wishes to thank the following educators for their ongoing advice in the development of Prentice Hall Literature Texas. *Their valuable insights have helped ensure that this Literature series meets the needs of Texas students and their teachers.*

Tina Mercer Blanchard
Pearce Middle School
Austin, Texas

Debra Born
Tomball Junior High School
Tomball, Texas

Francine Burris
Arlington High School
Arlington, Texas

Dana Davis
Irving High School
Irving, Texas

Sandra Garcia
Dr. Joaquin G. Cigarroa Middle School
Laredo, Texas

Juanita Leticia Garza
Dr. Leonides G. Cigarroa High School
Laredo, Texas

Lupita Cipriano Gonzalez
Dr. Joaquin G. Cigarroa Middle School
Laredo, Texas

Michael Guevara
Alamo Heights High School
San Antonio, Texas

Becky Holditch
Deerpark Middle School
Austin, Texas

Elaine Loughlin
Palo Duro High School
Amarillo, Texas

Yvonne E. Martin, M.Ed.
Hendrickson High School
Pflugerville, Texas

Elaine Lunday McNeill
Canyon Middle School
New Braunfels, Texas

Deborah A. Merritt
Valley View Middle School
El Paso, Texas

Donna L. Meyer
McCullough Junior High School
The Woodlands, Texas

Judith Waldene Nevil
Irving High School
Irving, Texas

Mona A. Robinson
Pasadena Memorial High School
Pasadena, Texas

Shawna Robinson
Dulles High School
Sugar Land, Texas

Amanda Sanchez
Valley Verde Early College High School
El Paso, Texas

Crystal Anne Sliva
Sam Rayburn High School
Pasadena, Texas

Nora Elia Soria
Dr. Leonides G. Cigarroa High School
Laredo, Texas

Molly H. Swetts
Central High School
San Angelo, Texas

Linda Taylor
W.W. Samuell High School
Dallas, Texas

Loran J. Termine, Ed.S.
Magnolia Junior High School
Magnolia, Texas

Kelley Tucker
West Texas Middle School
Stinnett, Texas

Sue Tull
Secondary ELA Coordinator
Sugar Land, Texas

Kristina "Kasey" Turner
Galena Park High School
Houston, Texas

Valerie Vannaman
Eastwood Middle School
El Paso, Texas

Cheryl Vinson
Irving High School
Irving, Texas

Joyce Wascom
Dr. Ralph H. Poteet High School
Mesquite, Texas

Christine Zittel
Klein High School
Klein, Texas

Contributing Authors

The contributing authors guided the direction and philosophy of Pearson Prentice Hall Literature. *Working with the development team, they helped to build the pedagogical integrity of the program and to ensure its relevance for today's teachers and students.*

Grant Wiggins, Ed.D., is the President of Authentic Education in Hopewell, New Jersey. He earned his Ed.D. from Harvard University and his B.A. from St. John's College in Annapolis. Wiggins consults with schools, districts, and state education departments on a variety of reform matters; organizes conferences and workshops; and develops print materials and Web resources on curricular change. He is the coauthor, with Jay McTighe, of *Understanding by Design* and *The Understanding by Design Handbook*, the award-winning and highly successful materials on curriculum published by ASCD. His work has been supported by the Pew Charitable Trusts, the Geraldine R. Dodge Foundation, and the National Science Foundation.

Jeff Anderson has worked with struggling writers and readers in Texas and across the U.S. for almost 20 years. Anderson's specialty is the integration of grammar and editing instruction into the processes of reading and writing. He has published two books, *Mechanically Inclined: Building Grammar, Usage, and Style into Writer's Workshop* and *Everyday Editing: Inviting Students to Develop Skill and Craft in Writer's Workshop* as well as a DVD, *The Craft of Grammar.* Anderson's work has appeared in *English Journal.* Anderson won the NCTE Paul and Kate Farmer Award for his *English Journal* article on teaching grammar in context.

Sharon Vaughn, Ph.D., teaches at the University of Texas at Austin. She is the previous Editor-in-Chief of the *Journal of Learning Disabilities* and the Coeditor of *Learning Disabilities Research and Practice.* She is the recipient of the American Education Research Association SIG Award for Outstanding Researcher. Vaughn's work focuses on effective practices for enhancing reading outcomes for students with reading difficulties. She is the author of more than 100 articles and numerous books designed to improve research-based practices in the classroom.

Kelly Gallagher is a full-time English teacher at Magnolia High School in Anaheim, California. He is the former co-director of the South Basin Writing Project at California State University, Long Beach. Gallagher wrote *Reading Reasons: Motivational Mini-Lessons for the Middle and High School; Deeper Reading: Comprehending Challenging Texts 4-12;* and *Teaching Adolescent Writers.* Gallagher won the Secondary Award of Classroom Excellence from the California Association of Teachers of English—the state's top English teacher honor.

William G. Brozo, Ph.D., is a Professor of Literacy at George Mason University in Fairfax, Virginia. He has taught reading and language arts in junior and senior high school and is the author of numerous texts on literacy development. Dr. Brozo's work focuses on building capacity among teacher leaders, enriching the literate culture of schools, enhancing the literate lives of boys, and making teaching more responsive to the needs of all students. His recent publications include *Bright Beginnings for Boys: Engaging Young Boys in Active Literacy* and *The Adolescent Literacy Inventory.* Brozo is an Expert Reviewer on the Texas Adolescent Literacy Academies Advisory Board.

Jim Cummins, Ph.D., is a Professor in the Modern Language Centre at the University of Toronto. A well-known educator, lecturer, and author, Cummins focuses his research on bilingual education and the academic achievement of culturally diverse students. He is the author of numerous publications, including *Negotiating Identities: Education for Empowerment in a Diverse Society.* Cummins coined the acronyms *BICS* and *CALP* to help differentiate the type of language ability students need for success in learning a new language.

Harvey Daniels, Ph.D., has been a classroom teacher, writing project director, author, and university professor. "Smokey" serves as an international consultant to schools, districts, and educational agencies. He is known for his work on student-led book clubs, as recounted in *Literature Circles: Voice and Choice in Book Clubs & Reading Groups* and *Mini Lessons for Literature Circles.* Recent works include *Subjects Matter: Every Teacher's Guide to Content-Area Reading* and *Content Area Writing: Every Teacher's Guide.*

Sheridan Blau, Ph.D., is Professor of Education and English at the University of California, Santa Barbara, where he directs th e South Coast Writing Project and the Literature Institute for Teachers. He has served in senior advisory roles for such groups as the National Board for Professional Teaching Standards, the College Board, and the American Board for Teacher Education. Blau served for twenty years on the National Writing Project Advisory Board and Task Force, and is a former president of NCTE. Blau is the author of *The Literature Workshop: Teaching Texts and Their Readers*, which was named by the Conference on English Education as the 2004 Richard Meade Award winner for outstanding research in English education.

Jane Feber is the author of *Creative Book Reports* and *Active Word Play*. A classroom teacher for 35 years, Feber currently teaches language arts at Mandarin Middle School in Jacksonville, Florida, where she serves as department chair. Feber plays an active role in the Florida Council of Teachers of English. She was the 2006 recipient of NCTE's Edwin A. Hoey Award and received the Gladys Prior Award for Teaching Excellence. In 2008, she was the National Middle School Association's Teacher of the Year.

Danling Fu, Ph.D., is Professor of Language and Culture in the College of Education at the University of Florida. She researches and provides inservice training to public schools nationally, focusing on literacy instruction for new immigrant students. Fu's books include *My Trouble is My English* and *An Island of English* addressing English language learners in the secondary schools. She has authored chapters in the Handbook of Adolescent Literacy Research and in Adolescent Literacy: Turning Promise to Practice.

Sharroky Hollie, Ph.D., is an assistant professor at California State University, Dominguez Hills, and an urban literacy visiting professor at Webster University, St. Louis. Hollie's work focuses on professional development, African American education, and second language methodology. He is a contributing author in two texts on culturally and linguistically responsive teaching. He is the Executive Director of the Center for Culturally Responsive Teaching and Learning and the cofounding director of the Culture and Language Academy of Success, an independent charter school in Los Angeles.

Dr. Donald J. Leu, Ph.D., teaches at University of Connecticut and holds a joint appointment in Curriculum and Instruction and Educational Psychology. He directs the New Literacies Research Lab and is a member of the Board of Directors of the International Reading Association. Leu studies the skills required to read, write, and learn with Internet technologies. His research has been funded by groups including the U.S. Department of Education, the National Science Foundation, and the Bill & Melinda Gates Foundation.

Doug Buehl is a teacher, author, and national literacy consultant. He taught in the Madison Metropolitan School District, Madison, Wisconsin, for 33 years. Buehl is the author of *Classroom Strategies for Interactive Learning* and coauthor of *Reading and the High School Student: Strategies to Enhance Literacy* and *Strategies to Enhance Literacy and Learning in Middle School Content Area Classrooms*. He was a member of the IRA Commission on Adolescent Literacy, and served on the task force that drafted the National Standards for Middle and High School Literacy Coaches.

Jon Scieszka founded GUYS READ, a nonprofit literacy initiative for boys, to call attention to the problem of getting boys connected with reading. In 2008, he was named the first U.S. National Ambassador for Young People's Literature by the Library of Congress. Scieszka taught from first grade to eighth grade for ten years in New York City, drawing inspiration from his students to write *The True Story of the 3 Little Pigs!*, *The Stinky Cheese Man,* the *Time Warp Trio* series of chapter books, and the *Trucktown* series of books for beginning readers.

Maria V. Balderrama, Ph.D., is a Professor at California State University, San Bernardino's College of Education. She is a bilingual, multicultural educator and researcher with more than 25 years in public education. Professor Balderrama's experiences include work with diverse youth, their families, teachers, and school administrators. Her most recent book is *Teacher Performance Expectations for Educating English Learners* (with L. T. Díaz-Rico). Her work is widely recognized for its contributions to the field.

Arnetha F. Ball, Ph.D., is a Professor at Stanford University. Her areas of expertise include language and literacy studies of diverse student populations, research on writing instruction, and teacher preparation for working with diverse populations. She is the author of *African American Literacies Unleashed* with Dr. Ted Lardner, and *Multicultural Strategies for Education and Social Change.*

Unit Authors

An award-winning contemporary author hosts each unit in each level of Pearson Prentice Hall Literature. Serving as a guide for your students, these authors introduce literary concepts, answer questions about their work, and discuss their own writing processes, using their works as models. Following are the featured unit authors for Grade 9.

Elizabeth McCracken
(b. 1966)
Unit 1: Fiction and Nonfiction Elizabeth McCracken is highly qualified as a guide for this unit, having written prize-winning fiction and nonfiction. Her first novel, *The Giant's House*, was a finalist for the National Book Award. Her nonfiction includes pieces on Charles Dickens's *Bleak House* and Victor Hugo's *The Hunchback of Notre Dame* and the personal essay "Desiderata." In both genres, she creates a lively and engaging voice.

Pat Mora
(b. 1942)
Unit 4: Poetry Pat Mora, the guide for the poetry unit, has won acclaim for both writing and teaching poetry. Her many verse collections include *Agua Santa: Holy Water, Borders, Chants, Communion*, and *My Own True Name: New and Selected Poems for Young Adults*. Among the prizes given to her verse are the Southwest Book Award and the Pellicer-Frost Bi-national Poetry Award.

Wayson Choy
(b. 1939)
Unit 2: Short Stories Known for his novel *The Jade Peony*, which won Canada's Trillium Book Award, and for its sequel, *All That Matters*, Wayson Choy is also devoted to the short-story form. The seed for *The Jade Peony* was a much-anthologized short story of the same name. Another story received the Best American Short Stories Award. His writing has been praised by *Maclean's* magazine for its "exquisite grace."

Gary L. Blackwood
(b. 1945)
Unit 5: Drama Though famous for his award-winning fiction and nonfiction for young adults, Gary L. Blackwood is a perfect guide for the drama unit. He has had half a dozen stage plays produced, including his dramatization of his novel *The Shakespeare Stealer*, performed at the Kennedy Center in Washington, D.C., and at other well-known theaters. Mr. Blackwood has also taught classes and workshops in playwriting.

Rebecca Walker
(b. 1969)
Unit 3: Types of Nonfiction Rebecca Walker is the ideal guide for the nonfiction unit. Her essays and articles have appeared in many magazines and publications, and her books are taught in high schools and colleges in the U.S. and Canada. When she was twenty-five, Ms. Walker was named by *Time* magazine as one of the fifty influential American leaders under the age of forty. She has received awards for both her writing and her work as an advocate for young women.

Coach Dean Smith
(b. 1931)
and John Kilgo
(b. 1935)
Unit 6: Themes in Literature: Heroism Coach Dean Smith is ideally suited as a guide for this unit on heroes. Throughout his career with the University of North Carolina basketball team, he was known as much for developing the character of his players as he was for his 879 career victories. With John Kilgo, a distinguished sportswriter, Smith wrote about his philosophy in *The Carolina Way*.

Contents in Brief

Each unit addresses a Big Question to enrich exploration of literary concepts and reading strategies.

UNIT 1

Can *truth* change?

Fiction and Nonfiction

Focus on the TEKS

TEXAS

TEXAS
PHLitOnline
www.PHLitOnline.com

- Big Question video
- Illustrated vocabulary words
- Interactive vocabulary games
- Big Question Tunes

UNIT 1

Can *truth* change?

TEKS at a Glance

This page provides a quick look at some of the skills you will learn and practice in Unit 1. The abbreviations listed after each skill refer to the Texas Essential Knowledge and Skills. Additional skills listed are not required TEKS but support the knowledge statement indicated. You will find a more detailed description of your language arts standards throughout this book.

Reading/Comprehension Skills

Make Predictions	RC-9(A)
Author's Purpose	RC-9(A); RC-9(B)

Reading

Vocabulary Development

Prefixes: *fore-, con-*	(1)(A)
Suffixes: *-ate, -tion*	(1)(A)
Narration: Autobiographical Narrative	(1)(E)
Roots: *-fin-, -term-*	(1)(A)
Using a Dictionary, Glossary, and Thesaurus	(1)(E)

Additional Skills

Big Question Vocabulary	(1)
Suffixes: *-able, -ive*	(1)

Comprehension of Literary Texts

Literary Essay	(6)
Plot	(5)(A)
Comparing Points of View	(5)(C)
Voice	(6)
Character	(5)(B)
Comparing Themes Across Genres	(2)(A)

Comprehension of Informational Texts

Analyze Ideas and Organizational Patterns	(9)(C)
Analyze Graphical Sources	(11)(B)

Media Literacy

On Your Own	(12)(A)

Listening and Speaking

Interview	(24)(A); (25)
Retelling	(25)
Giving and Following Oral Instructions	(24)(B)

Writing

Critique	(15)(A)(v)
Narration: Autobiographical Narrative	(13)(A); (14)(A); (13)(C); (13)(D); (13)(E)
Essay, Poem, Dialogue, or Script	(13)(A)
Multimedia Presentation	(15)(D)
Character Profile	(15)(A)(v)
Exposition: Problem-and-Solution Essay	(13)(A); (13)(B); (15)(A)(i);(ii);(iii);(iv);(v)

Additional Skills

Writing About the Big Question	(15)
Anecdote	(15)
Timed Writing	(15)

Oral and Written Conventions

Common and Proper Nouns	(18)(A)
Narration: Autobiographical Narrative	(18)(A); (18)(B)(i)
Personal, Reflexive, and Reciprocal Pronouns	(17)(A)(iii)
Exposition: Problem-and-Solution Essay	(17)(A)(iii); (19)

Additional Skills

Abstract and Concrete Nouns	(17)
Revising to Correct Use of Possessive Nouns	(13)(D)
Relative, Interrogative, and Indefinite Pronouns	(17)
Revising Pronoun-Antecedent Agreement	(13)(D)

Research

Learning Log	(21)(B); (21)(C)
Exposition: Problem-and-Solution Essay	(21)(A)

UNIT

2

GENRE FOCUS ▸ **Short Stories**

Focus on the TEKS

(5) Reading/ Comprehension of Literary Text/Fiction
(1)(A) Reading/ Vocabulary Development
RC-9(B) Reading/ Comprehension Skills

(7) Reading/ Comprehension of Literary Text/Sensory Language
RC-9(B) Reading/ Comprehension Skills

(11)(A) Reading/ Comprehension of Informational Text/ Procedural Text

TEXAS

TEXAS
PHLitOnline
www.PHLitOnline.com

- Big Question video
- Illustrated vocabulary words
- Interactive vocabulary games
- Big Question Tunes

UNIT

2

THE BIG Q Is conflict *necessary?*

TEKS at a Glance

This page provides a quick look at some of the skills you will learn and practice in Unit 2. The abbreviations listed after each skill refer to the Texas Essential Knowledge and Skills. Additional skills listed are not required TEKS but support the knowledge statement indicated. You will find a more detailed description of your language arts standards throughout this book.

Reading/Comprehension Skills

Make Inferences	**RC-9(B)**
Cause and Effect	**RC-9(A)**

Reading

Vocabulary Development

Suffixes: *-esque, -ant, -ity, -ous*	**(1)(A)**
Roots: *-bene-, -jec(t)-*	**(1)(A)**
Word Origins and Derivations	**(1)(A); (1)(E)**

Additional Skills

Big Question Vocabulary	**(1)**
Prefixes: *de-, inter-*	**(1)**

Comprehension of Literary Text

Conflict	**(5)**
Irony	**(7)**
Comparing Plot Development	**(5)(A)**
Characterization	**(5)(B)**
Dialogue and Dialect	**(5)**
Point of View	**(5)(C)**
Comparing Elements of Fiction	**(5)**

Comprehension of Informational Text

Analyze Procedural Texts	**(11)(A)**
Analyze Summary and Critique	**(9)(A)**

Media Literacy

On Your Own	**(12)(B)**

Listening and Speaking

Oral Presentation	**(25)**
Debate	**(24)(C)**
Dialogue	**(24)(A)**
Deliver and Evaluate Presentations	**(24)(A); (24)(C); (25)**

Writing

Literary Text: Short Story	**(14)(A); (13)(D); (13)(E)**
Written Presentation	**(13)(A)**
Expository Text: Cause-and-Effect Essay	**(13)(A); (13)(D); (13)(E); (15)(A)(i);(ii);(iv);(v)**

Additional Skills

Writing About the Big Question	**(15)**
Alternative Ending	**(15)(C)**
News Report	**(15)(C)**
Timed Writing	**(15)**
Informal Letter	**(15)**

Oral and Written Conventions

Subjunctive Mood	**(17)(B)**
Verbs: Active and Passive Voice	**(17)(A)(i)**
Expository Text: Cause-and-Effect Essay	**(19)**

Additional Skills

Regular Verbs	**(17)**
Irregular Verbs	**(17)**
Revising Inconsistent Verb Tenses	**(13)(D)**
Revising to Correct Faulty Subject-Verb Agreement	**(13)(D)**

Research

Oral Presentation	**(23)(C)**
Debate	**(23)(A)**
Literary Text: Short Story	**(23)(E)**
Informative Brochure	**(20)(A)**

GENRE FOCUS ▸ # Types of Nonfiction

Focus on the TEKS

RC-9(A); RC-9(B) Reading/ Comprehension Skills **(6)** Reading/ Comprehension of Literary Text/Literary Nonfiction

(8) Reading/ Comprehension of Informational Text/ Culture and History **(9)** Reading/ Comprehension of Informational Text/ Expository Text

(9)(D) Reading/ Comprehension of Informational Text/ Expository Text **(11)(B)** Reading/ Comprehension of Informational Text/ Procedural Text **(12)(C)** Reading/ Media Literacy

TEXAS

TEXAS
PHLitOnline
www.PHLitOnline.com

- Big Question video
- Illustrated vocabulary words
- Interactive vocabulary games
- Big Question Tunes

UNIT 3

TEKS at a Glance

This page provides a quick look at some of the skills you will learn and practice in Unit 3. The abbreviations listed after each skill refer to the Texas Essential Knowledge and Skills. Additional skills listed are not required TEKS but support the knowledge statement indicated. You will find a more detailed description of your language arts standards throughout this book.

Reading/Comprehension Skills

Main Idea	RC-9(A); RC-9(B)
Comparing Biographical Writing	RC-9(B)

Reading

Vocabulary Development

Roots: *-potens-, -sum-, -cred-, -duc-/-duct-*	(1)(A)
Producing Analogies	(1)(C)

Additional Skills

Big Question Vocabulary	(1)
Roots: *-viv-, -dur-, -nov-, -temp-*	(1)

Comprehension of Literary Texts

Literary Essay	(6)
Comparing Humorous Writing	(5); (6)

Comprehension of Informational Texts

Author's Style	(9)
Main Idea	(8)
Expository Text	(9)
Connect and Synthesize Ideas	(9)(D); (11)(B)
Persuasive Text	(10)
Analyze Persuasion	(10)(A)
Persuasive Speech	(10)(B)
Analyze Evidence	(10)(A); (10)(B)

Media Literacy

Analyze Media Messages	(12)(B)
On Your Own	(12)(B)

Listening and Speaking

Panel Discussion	(24)(A); (26)
Persuasive Presentation	(24)(C); (25)
Television News Report	(25)

Writing

Book Jacket Copy	(16)
Script for a Public Service Announcement	(14)(C)
Work-Related Text: Business Letter	(13)(C); (15)(B)(i);(ii)
Abstract	(15)
Essay	(15)
Persuasive Text: Editorial	(16)(A); (B); (C); (D); (E)

Additional Skills

Writing About the Big Question	(15)
Revising to Combine Choppy Sentences	(13)(C)
Revising to Create Parallelism	(13)(C)

Oral and Written Conventions

Work-Related Text: Business Letter	(18)(A); (19)
Persuasive Text: Editorial	(19)

Additional Skills

Direct and Indirect Objects	(17)
Predicate Nominatives and Predicate Adjectives	(17)
Adjectives	(17)
Adverbs	(17)

Research

Journal Entries	(20)(B); (22)(B)

GENRE FOCUS

Poetry

Focus on the TEKS

TEXAS

UNIT 4

THE BIG ? How does *communication* change us?

TEKS at a Glance

This page provides a quick look at some of the skills you will learn and practice in Unit 4. The abbreviations listed after each skill refer to the Texas Essential Knowledge and Skills. Additional skills listed are not required TEKS but support the knowledge statement indicated. You will find a more detailed description of your language arts standards throughout this book.

Reading/Comprehension Skills

Read Fluently	RC-9(A)
Paraphrase	RC-9(A)

Reading

Vocabulary Development

Prefixes: *ana-, mono-, pre-, im-*	(1)(A)
Literary Text: Poem	(1)(E)
Connotation and Denotation	(1)(B); (1)(E)

Additional Skills

Big Question Vocabulary	(1)
Roots: *-fer-, -vert-*	(1)
Suffixes: *-ment, -ion*	(1)

Comprehension of Literary Text

Figurative Language	(7)
Sound Devices	(3)
Comparing Imagery	(3)
Narrative Poetry	(3)
Rhyme and Meter	(3)
Comparing Forms of Lyric Poetry	(3); (5)(D)

Comprehension of Informational Text

Analyze the Clarity of Objectives	(11)(A)
Summarize Text: Controlling Idea and Details	(8); (9)(A)

Media Literacy

Report	(12)(B)
Comparing Media Coverage	(12)(A)
On Your Own	(12)(B)

Listening and Speaking

Informal Presentation	(25)
Formal Presentation	(25)
Panel Discussion	(26)

Writing

Choose a Genre	(13)(A)
Editorial	(16)(D); (E)
Literary Text: Poem	(14)(B); (13)(C); (13)(D); (13)(E)
Poem	(14)(B)
Expository Text: Interpretative Response	(13)(A); (13)(E); (15)(C)(i);(ii);(iii)

Additional Skills

Writing About the Big Question	(1)
Timed Writing	(15)
Revising to Strengthen Use of Poetic Techniques	(13)(C)

Oral and Written Conventions

Infinitives	(17)(A)(i)
Expository Text: Interpretative Response	(19)

Additional Skills

Prepositions	(17)
Prepositional Phrases	(17)
Appositive Phrases	(17)
Using Quotations	(18)

GENRE
FOCUS ▶ # Drama

Focus on the TEKS

(1)(A); (1)(B)
Reading/Vocabulary
Development
(4) Reading/
Comprehension of
Literary Text/Drama
(5)(B) Reading/
Comprehension of
Literary Text/Fiction
(7) Reading/
Comprehension of
Literary Text/Sensory
Language
RC-9(A) Reading/
Comprehension Skills
(9)(A) Reading/
Comprehension of
Informational Text/
Expository Text

**(12)(A);
(12)(C)** Reading/
Media Literacy

 **Focus on the TEKS**

(2)(A) Reading/ Comprehension of Literary Text/Theme and Genre

WRITE GUY
Jeff Anderson, M.Ed.

Drama Selection

(4) Reading/ Comprehension of Literary Text/Drama **(5)(D)** Reading/ Comprehension of Literary Text/Fiction **(1)(A)** Reading/ Vocabulary Development

www.PHLitOnline.com

- Big Question video
- Illustrated vocabulary words
- Interactive vocabulary games
- Big Question Tunes

UNIT 5

Do our *differences* define us?

 **Focus on the TEKS**

TEKS at a Glance

This page provides a quick look at some of the skills you will learn and practice in Unit 5. The abbreviations listed after each skill refer to the Texas Essential Knowledge and Skills. Additional skills listed are not required TEKS but support the knowledge statement indicated. You will find a more detailed description of your language arts standards throughout this book.

Reading/Comprehension Skills

Summarize	RC-9(A)

Additional Skills

Draw Conclusions	RC-9

Reading

Vocabulary Development

Prefixes: *trans-, pro-*	(1)(A)
Connotation and Denotation	(1)(B)
Roots: *-nym-, -nom-*	(1)(A)
Borrowed and Foreign Words	(1)(D); (1)(E)

Additional Skills

Big Question Vocabulary	(1)
Roots: *-loque-*	(1)
Prefixes: *en-, ambi-*	(1)

Comprehension of Literary Texts

Dialogue and Stage Directions	(4)
Figurative Language	(7)
Dramatic Speeches	(4); (5)(B)
Dramatic Irony	(4)
Tragedy and Motive	(4)
Comparing Archetypal Themes	(2)(A)
Comedy	(4)
Comparing Satire	(7)

Comprehension of Informational Texts

Critical Thinking: Analyze	(9)(A); (5)(D)
Evaluate Sources	(9)(C)

Media Literacy

Film Review	(12)(B)
Analyze Media Coverage	(12)(A); (12)(C)
Evaluate Formality and Tone	(12)(D)
On Your Own	(12)(D)

Listening and Speaking

Staged Performance	(24)(B)
Mock Trial	(26)

Writing

Editorial	(16)(A)
Persuasive Letter	(16)(B); (16)(C)
Multimedia Presentation	(15)(D)
Literary Text: Script	(14)(C); (13)(D); (13)(E)
Script	(14)(C)
Research Writing: Research Report	(15)(D); (13)(E)

Additional Skills

Timed Writing	(15)

Oral and Written Conventions

Participles and Participle Phrases	(17)(A)(i)
Gerunds and Gerund Phrases	(17)(A)(i)
Literary Text: Script	(19)
Restrictive and Nonrestrictive Clauses	(17)(A)(ii); (18)(B)(ii)
Research Writing: Research Report	(18)(A); (19)

Additional Skills

Revising to Combine Sentences Using Adverb Clauses	(13)(D)

Research

Annotated Flow Chart	(21)(B); (21)(C); (22)(B); (23)(C)
Multimedia Presentation	(21)(C)
Informational Chart	(20)(B); (21)(A)
Evaluate Sources	(22)(B)
Research Writing: Research Report	(20)(A); (20)(B); (21)(A); (22)(A);(B);(C); (23)(A);(B);(C);(D);(E)

UNIT 6

THE BIG Q: Do *heroes* have responsibilities?

GENRE FOCUS

Themes in Literature: Heroism

Focus on the TEKS

(5)(A); (5)(D) Reading/Comprehension of Literary Text/Fiction
(2)(C) Reading/Comprehension of Literary Text/Theme and Genre

(2)(C) Reading/Comprehension of Literary Text/Theme and Genre
RC-9(A) Reading/Comprehension Skills

(9)(B) Reading/Comprehension of Informational Text/Expository Text

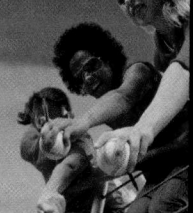

TEXAS

PHLitOnline
www.PHLitOnline.com

- Big Question video
- Illustrated vocabulary words
- Interactive vocabulary games
- Big Question Tunes

UNIT 6

THE BIG ? Do *heroes* have responsibilities?

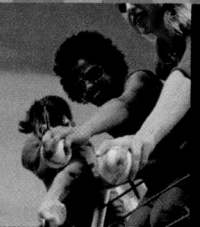

TEXAS

TEKS at a Glance

This page provides a quick look at some of the skills you will learn and practice in Unit 6. The abbreviations listed after each skill refer to the Texas Essential Knowledge and Skills. Additional skills listed are not required TEKS but support the knowledge statement indicated. You will find a more detailed description of your language arts standards throughout this book.

Reading/Comprehension Skills

Compare and Contrast	RC-9(A)

Reading

Vocabulary Development

Connotation and Denotation	(1)(B)
Roots: *-min-, -spect-*	(1)(A)
Writing Workshop: Procedural Document: Instructions	(1)(E)
Idioms, Jargon, and Technical Terms	(1)(C)

Additional Skills

Big Question Vocabulary	(1)
Prefixes: *be-, dis-*	(1)
Roots: *-merg-, -fer-*	(1)

Comprehension of Literary Texts

Epic	(5)(A)
Historical and Cultural Setting	(2)(C)
Critical Thinking: Analyze	(5)(D)
Comparing Literary Influences	(2)(B)
Protagonist and Antagonist	(5)(B)
Comparing Influences on Contemporary Literature	(2)(B)

Additional Skills

Epic Simile	(2)
Philosophical Assumptions	(2)

Comprehension of Informational Texts

Evaluate Opinions	(9)(B)
Analyze Author's Purpose	(8)

Media Literacy

Media Analysis	(12)(D)
On Your Own	(12)(D)

Listening and Speaking

Conversation	(26); (25)
Debate	(26); (24)(C)
Idioms, Jargon, and Technical Terms	(25)
Delivering Technical Presentations	(24)(A); (25)

Writing

Everyday Epic	(14)(A)
Biography	(9)(A)
Procedural Document: Instructions	(15)(B)(i);(ii); (13)(D); (13)(E)
Expository Text: Comparison-and-Contrast Essay	(13)(A); (15)(A)(i);(ii);(iii); (13)(D); (13)(E)

Additional Skills

Timed Writing	(15)
Revising to Correct Fragments and Run-ons	(13)(D)
Journal Entries	(15)(C)
Letter	(15)

Oral and Written Conventions

Simple and Compound Sentences	(17)(C)
Complex and Compound-Complex Sentences	(17)(C)
Procedural Document: Instructions	(19)
Commas and Dashes	(18)(B)(ii);(iii)
Expository Text: Comparison-and-Contrast Essay	(19)

Additional Skills

Revising to Correct Fragments and Run-ons	(13)(C)
Colons, Semicolons, and Ellipsis Points	(18)
Using a Variety of Sentence Structures	(13)(C)

Research

Oral Report	(20)(A); (21)(B); (23)(C); (23)(D)
Media Analysis	(23)(C)

How to Use This Book

How is this book organized?

- There are six units, each focusing on a specific genre.
- Each unit has a Big Question to get you thinking about important ideas and to guide your reading.

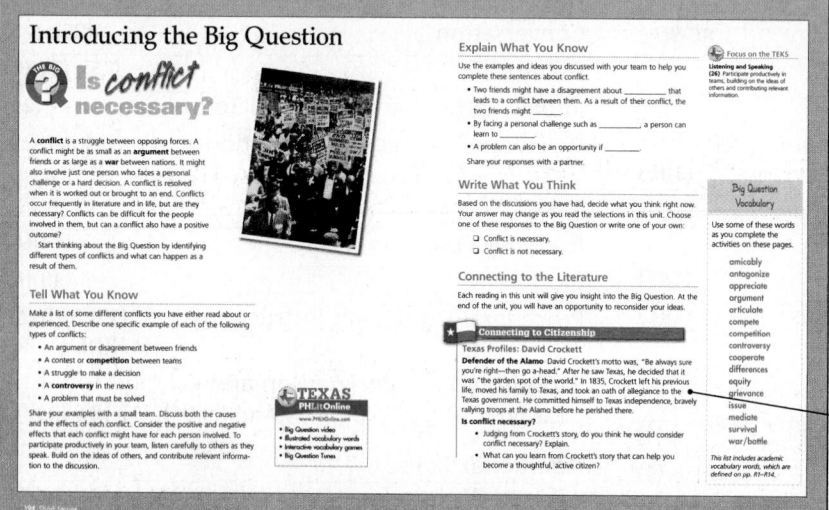

◀ At the beginning of the unit—**Introducing the Big Question** provides a reading focus for the entire unit. Use **academic vocabulary** to think, talk, and write about this question.

Explore the lives of influential Texans and discuss the qualities that contribute to responsible citizenship through **Connecting to Citizenship**.

At the end of the unit— **Applying the Big Question** gives you an opportunity to reflect on what you have read and learned. See how your ideas about the Big Question have deepened or changed as a result of your work throughout the unit. ▶

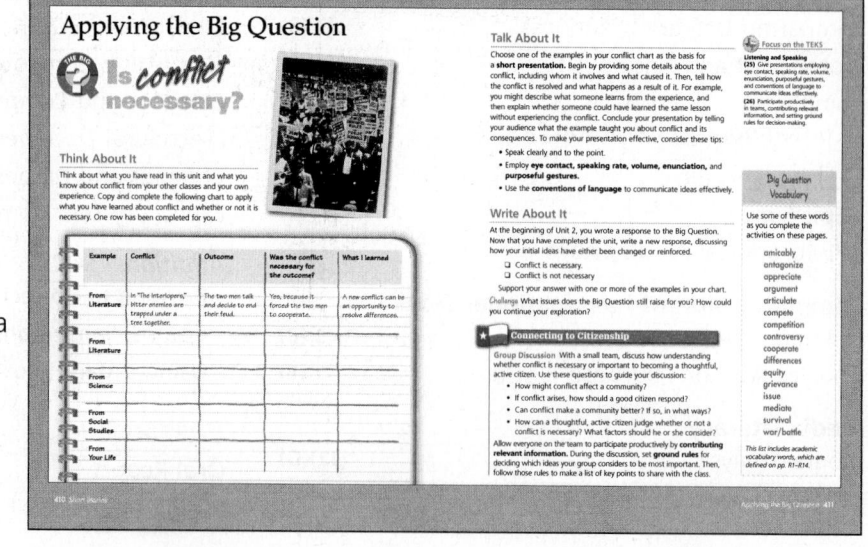

How are the literary selections organized?

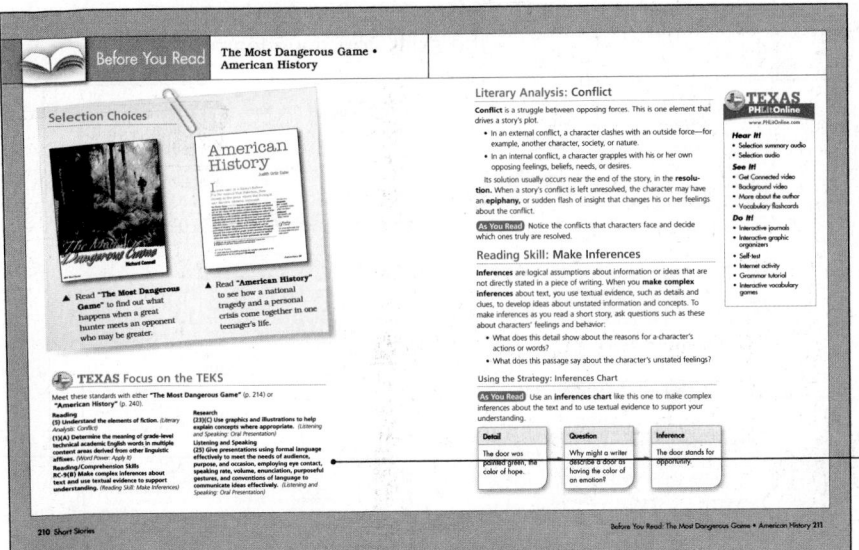

◀ **Before You Read** introduces two selection choices that both teach the same skills. Your teacher will help you choose the selection that is right for you.

Focus on the TEKS provides a listing of the Texas Essential Knowledge and Skills that are the focus for the lesson.

Writing About the Big Question is a quick-writing activity that helps you connect the Big Question to the selection you are about to read.

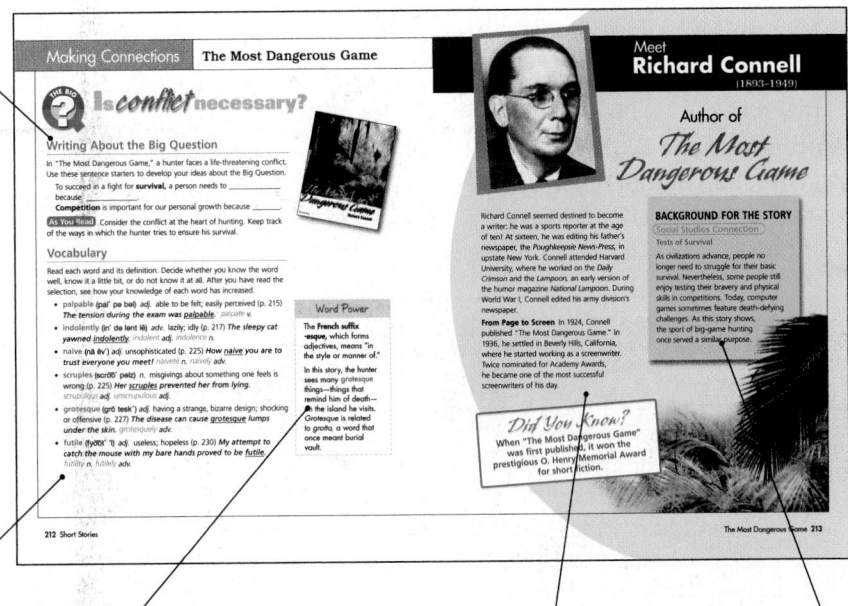

Vocabulary and Word Power introduce important selection vocabulary words and teach you about prefixes, suffixes, and roots.

Meet the Author and Background teach you about the author's life and provide information that will help you understand the selection.

After You Read helps you practice the skills you have learned. ▼

Critical Thinking questions help you reflect on what you have read and apply the Big Question to the selection.

Monitor your progress by completing **After You Read** activities.

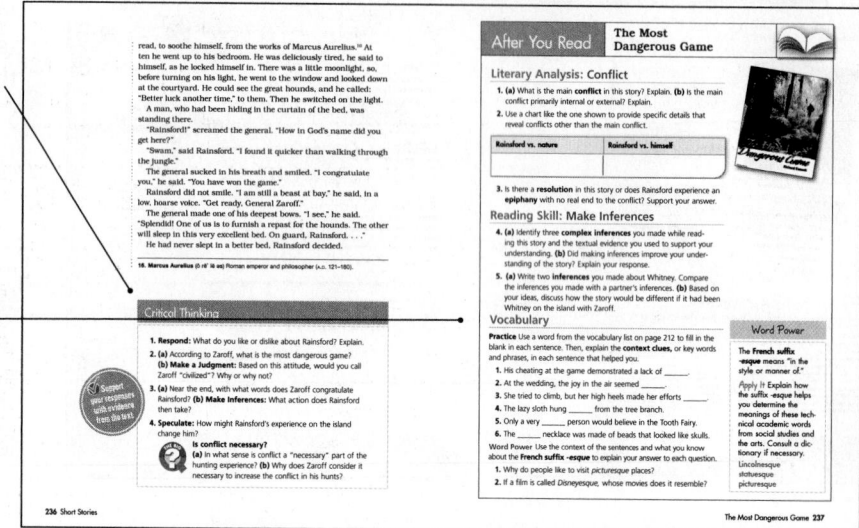

Integrated Language Skills provides instruction and practice for important grammar skills.

Projects and activities help you deepen your understanding of the selection while strengthening your **writing, listening, speaking, and research skills.**

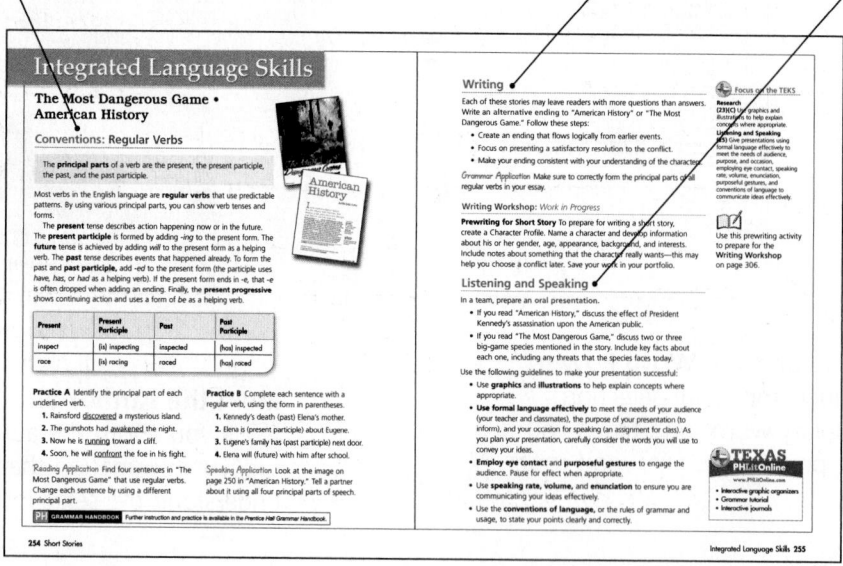

What special features will I find in this book?

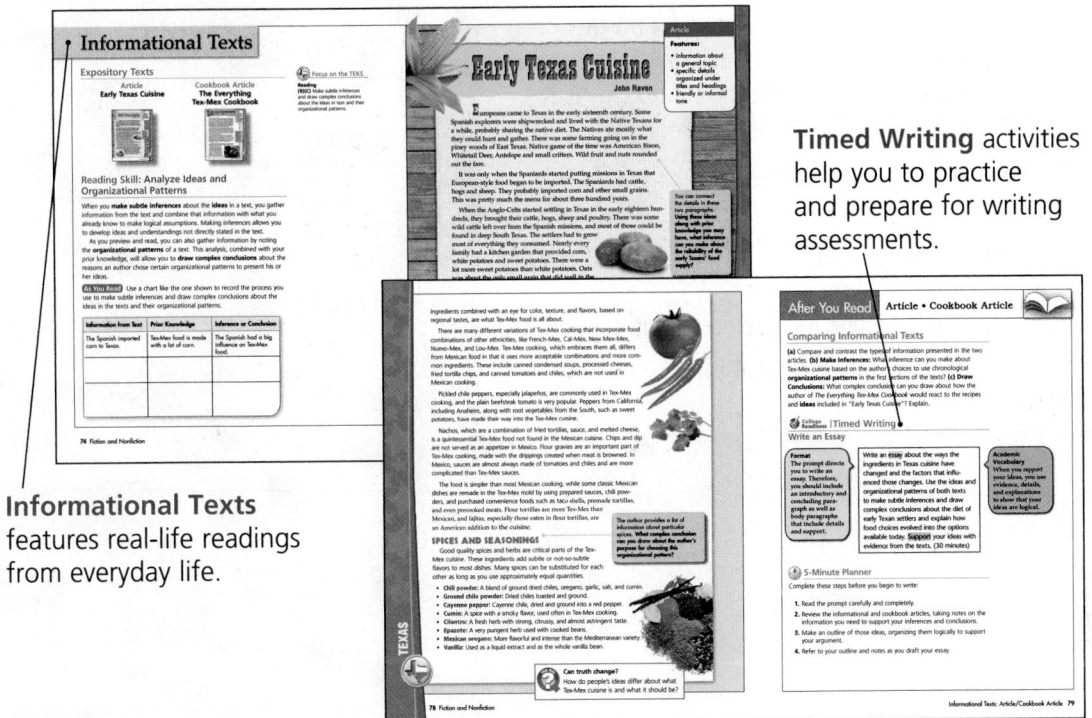

Timed Writing activities help you to practice and prepare for writing assessments.

Informational Texts features real-life readings from everyday life.

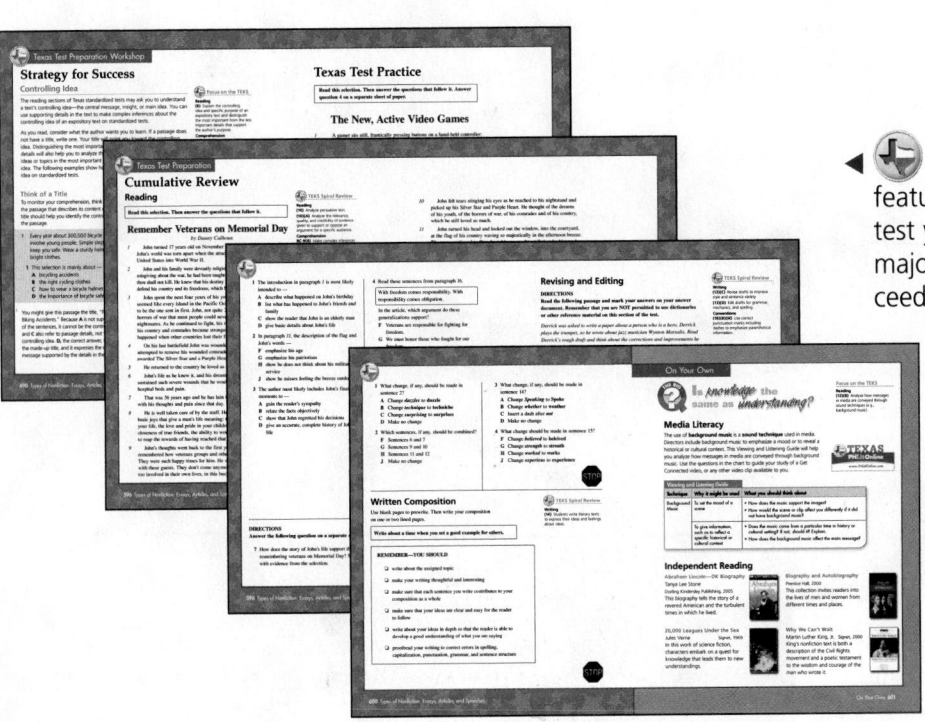

◀ **Texas Test Preparation** features throughout the book test your knowledge of all major TEKS to help you succeed on standardized tests.

On Your Own
Further explore the Big Question through media and independent reading.

Media Literacy Handbook

INTRODUCTION: Today, messages are transmitted across a variety of media modes, such as film, television, radio, and the Internet. As you interact with these messages each day—in images, advertisements, movies, and an array of different contexts—it is important to consider the potential influence of the medium.

- What is the intention of the message?
- How is it communicated?
- How do specific elements of the medium—such as color, image, or font—help convey the message?
- Why might the creator of the message have selected this medium?

These are the key issues of media literacy, the study of messages in the media and their impact.

Camera Shots and Angles

Filmmakers create camera shots and sequences to help them tell stories. Some shots capture an entire scene; others zoom in on specific characters.

Special Effects

Filmmakers use special effects to create on-screen illusions that bring the imagination to life.

Questions About Film Techniques

- What effect is created by the choice of camera angle shown in the image at left? Choose another camera angle and explain how that shot might convey a different message than the one shown here.

- Study the images above. In what way does the use of special effects make the film better for viewers?

LEARN MORE: Complete the Media Literacy section of the On Your Own pages and the Media Literacy Workshops.

Focus and Framing
A sharp focus captures all details in a photographic image. A softer focus lessens the amount of detail that can be seen. The framing of elements within a photograph directs the eye toward a portion of the image.

Lighting and Shadow
Lighting techniques are used in photography to enhance mood and direct the viewer's focus.

Special Techniques

Most images you see today have been manipulated or changed in some way. Even a small change—such as an added graphic element or a difference in shading—can alter the mood of an image.

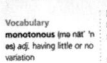

Three Skeleton Key

George G. Toudouze

Vocabulary
monotonous (mə nät′ 'n əs) adj. having little or no variation

My most terrifying experience? Well, one does have a few in thirty-five years of service in the Lights, although it's mostly monotonous routine work—keeping the light in order, making out the reports.

When I was a young man, not very long in the service, there was an opening in a lighthouse newly built off the coast of Guiana,[1] on a small rock twenty miles or so from the mainland. The pay was high, so in order to reach the sum I had set out to save before I married, I volunteered for service in the new light.

1. **Guiana** (gē an′ ə) region on the northern coast of South America.

Three Skeleton Key, the small rock on which the light stood, bore a bad reputation. It earned its name from the story of the three convicts who, escaping from Cayenne[2] in a stolen dugout canoe, were wrecked on the rock during the night, managed to escape the sea but eventually died of hunger and thirst. When they were discovered, nothing remained but three heaps of bones, picked clean by the birds. The story was that the three skeletons, gleaming with phosphorescent light,[3] danced over the small rock, screaming. . . .

2. **Cayenne** (kī en′) capital city of French Guiana.
3. **phosphorescent** (fäs′ fə res′ ənt) light a glowing light produced by certain natural chemical reactions.

Reading Check
What is especially dangerous about the waters surrounding Three Skeleton Key?

1148 Themes in Literature: Heroism

Three Skeleton Key 1149

Questions About Graphics and Photos

- What would be the effect if the image at left used a different focus?
- In what way does the use of color and light create mood in the photo at left?
- What special techniques were applied to the original photograph shown above? What effect does the use of special techniques create?

LEARN MORE: Answer Critical Viewing questions and complete the Media Literacy Workshops.

Persuasive Techniques
Advertisements use carefully selected visual elements to appeal to the viewer's emotions.

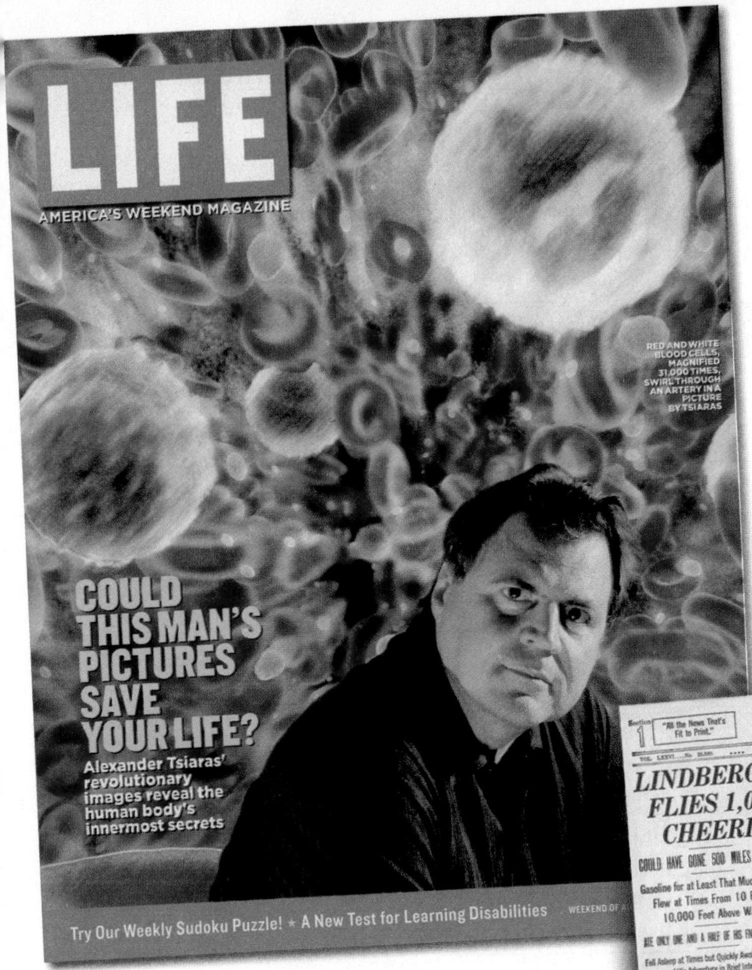

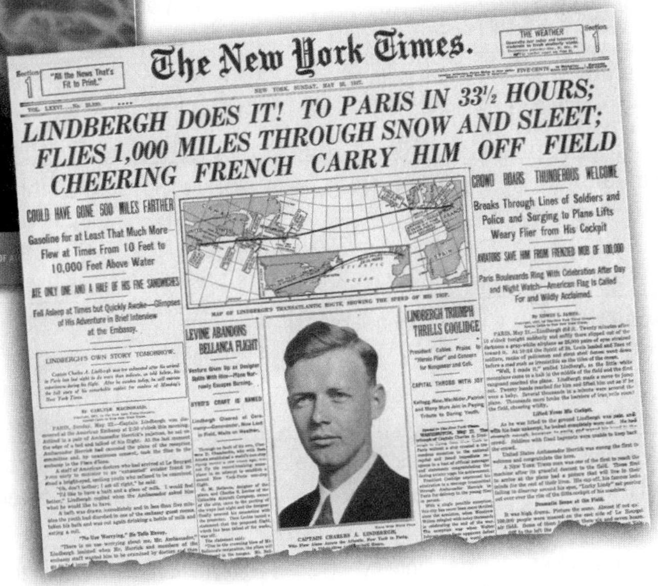

The New York Times.

"All the News That's Fit to Print."

LINDBERGH DOES IT! TO PARIS IN 33½ HOURS; FLIES 1,000 MILES THROUGH SNOW AND SLEET; CHEERING FRENCH CARRY HIM OFF FIELD

COULD HAVE GONE 500 MILES FARTHER

Gasoline for at Least That Much More—Flew at Times From 10 Feet to 10,000 Feet Above Water

ATE ONLY ONE AND A HALF OF HIS FIVE SANDWICHES

Fell Asleep at Times but Quickly Awoke—Glimpses of His Adventure in Brief Interview at the Embassy.

CROWD ROARS THUNDEROUS WELCOME

Breaks Through Lines of Soldiers and Police and Surging to Plane Lifts Weary Flier from His Cockpit

AVIATORS SAVE HIM FROM FRENZIED MOB OF 100,000

Paris Boulevards Ring With Celebration After Day and Night Watch—American Flag Is Called For and Wildly Acclaimed.

LINDBERGH'S OWN STORY TOMORROW.

LEVINE ABANDONS BELLANCA FLIGHT

LINDBERGH TRIUMPH THRILLS COOLIDGE

CAPTAIN CHARLES A. LINDBERGH.

Text and Graphics

Newspaper and magazine layouts are constructed to capture the eye and quickly convey the important ideas of a story. The use of type fonts, images, and page space direct the eye to portions of the printed page.

Questions About Print Media

- What image or graphic dominates the advertisement at left? How does the image make the advertisement more effective?
- Which of the above grabs your attention: the image or the text on the magazine cover? Explain.
- What do you notice first on the newspaper's front page? What overall effect does the use of type size and fonts create?

LEARN MORE: See the Media Literacy section of the On Your Own pages and the Media Literacy Workshops.

Building Academic Vocabulary

Academic Vocabulary

Academic vocabulary is the language you encounter in textbooks and on standardized tests. Understanding these words and using them in your classroom discussions and writing will help you communicate your ideas clearly and effectively. The words listed in this chart appear throughout your literature book.

Word	Definition	Related Words	Word in Context
ambiguous (am BIHG yoo uhs) *adj.*	having more than one meaning	ambiguity	The story's uncertain ending was ambiguous.
appreciate (uh PREE shee ayt) *v.*	be aware of; the value of	appreciative appreciating	Once I read Frost's poem, I learned to appreciate his use of symbols.
argument (AHR gyuh muhnt) *n.*	persuasive message	argue argumentative	The argument in the essay is well supported.
articulate (ahr TIHK yuh layt) *v.*	express an idea clearly	articulating articulated	The writer was able to articulate his ideas clearly.
articulate (ahr TIHK yuh liht) *adj.*	able to express clearly	articulating articulated	It is important to be articulate when giving a speech.
assumption (uh SUHMP shuhn) *n.*	something taken for granted	assume assuming	My assumption that the character was telling the truth proved wrong.
character (KAR ihk tuhr) *n.*	qualities that make a person unique	characteristic characteristically	Jenny's character became clear through her actions and words.
circumstance (SUR kuhm stans) *n.*	situation; event	circumstantial	In that circumstance, I would have done the same thing as that character.
clarify (KLAR uh fy) *v.*	make something more clear or understandable	clarification	More details were needed to clarify the writer's ideas about pollution.
compete (kuhm PEET) *v.*	battle against; try to win	competition competitor	The two characters compete in a battle of wits.

> **Ordinary Language:**
> I **like** poems with strong rhymes and rhythms.
>
> **Academic Language:**
> I **appreciate** poems with strong rhymes and rhythms.

Word	Definition	Related Words	Word in Context
competition (kom puh TIHSH uhn) *n.*	rivalry; act of competing	compete competitor	There seemed to be a competition between the mother and daughter.
comprehend (kom prih HEHND) *v.*	understand	comprehension	It was easy to comprehend the character's motives.
comprehension (kom prih HEHN shuhn) *n.*	act of understanding something	comprehend	My comprehension of the poem was hampered by the use of archaic language.
concept (KON sehpt) *n.*	idea; notion	conceive conceptualize	The concept of freedom is explored in this essay.
context (KON tehkst) *n.*	surrounding text; situation	contextual	In this context, the word *democracy* takes on new meaning.
controversy (KON truh vur see) *n.*	discussion of a question in which opposing opinions clash	controversial	The essayist explores the controversy that brewed in the heartland.
convince (kuhn VIHNS) *v.*	persuade by argument or evidence	convincing	The writer tries to convince her audience to change their ways.
credible (KREHD uh buhl) *adj.*	believable	creed credibility	I found the story's plot to be credible.
defend (dih FEHND) *v.*	protect against attack	defense	The writer tries to defend his notions about fairness.
determine (dih TUR muhn) *v.*	cause something to happen in a certain way	determination	The character's actions determine his fate.
differentiate (dihf uh REHN shee ayt) *v.*	see or express what makes two or more things different from each other	differ different	In this essay, the writer differentiates between students and scholars.
discriminate (dihs KRIHM uh nayt) *v.*	see the differences between things; act against someone because of prejudice	discrimination	The character was unable to discriminate between loyal and disloyal friends.

Ordinary Language:
In this essay, I will **talk about** the story's theme.

Academic Language:
In this essay, I will **discuss** the story's theme.

Word	Definition	Related Words	Word in Context
discuss (dihs KUHS) *v.*	talk about; write about	discussion	Discuss your ideas in your response.
identify (y DEHN tuh fy) *v.*	say who someone or something is	identification	I will identify three key factors in the story's success.
illuminate (ih LOO muh nayt) *v.*	light up; make something clearer	illumination	Here is my attempt to illuminate my ideas.
imitate (IHM uh tayt) *v.*	copy the actions of another	imitation imitator	The poet imitates the sounds of a rooster through onomatopoeia.
informed (ihn FORMD) *v.*	gave someone information	inform information	The character informed his teacher that he had finished his test.
interpret (ihn TUR priht) *v.*	understand or explain the meaning of something	interpretor interpretation	How do you interpret the title of this poem?
interpretation (ihn tur pruh TAY shuhn) *n.*	explanation of the meaning of something	interpretor interpret	My interpretation of the theme differs from that of my friend.
involvement (ihn VOLV muhnt) *n.*	state of being; included in something	involve	The character's involvement in sports propels the plot.
perspective (puhr SPEHK tihv) *n.*	point of view		The story is told from the perspective of a three-year-old.
speculate (SPEHK yuh layt) *v.*	think about or make up theories about a subject; guess at	speculative	Speculate about the author's reasons for setting this story in the tundra.
standard (STAN duhrd) *n.*	idea or thing to which other things are compared	standardize	Shakespeare sets the standard by which many playwrights are judged.
standard (STAN duhrd) *adj.*	normal; average	standardize substandard	It is standard practice for stories to center on conflict.
unique (yoo NEEK) *adj.*	one of a kind	uniqueness	The poet has a unique style.
verify (VEHR uh fy) *v.*	make sure something is true; confirm	verification	You should verify the facts before you accept them.

Increasing Your Word Knowledge

Increase your word knowledge and chances of success by taking an active role in developing your vocabulary. Here are some tips for you.

To own a word, follow these steps:

Steps to Follow	Model
1. Learn to identify the word and its basic meaning.	The word *examine* means "to look at closely."
2. Take note of the word's spelling.	*Examine* begins and ends with an *e*.
3. Practice pronouncing the word so that you can use it in conversation.	The *e* on the end of the word is silent. Its second syllable gets the most stress.
4. Visualize the word and illustrate its key meaning.	When I think of the word *examine*, I visualize a doctor checking a patient's health.
5. Learn the various forms of the word and its related words.	*Examination* and *exam* are forms of the word *examine*.
6. Compare the word with similar words.	*Examine, peruse,* and *study* are synonyms.
7. Contrast the word with similar words.	When you *peruse* materials, you do a more casual kind of examination. *Study* is often used to describe preparing for a test.
8. Use the word in various contexts.	"I'd like to *examine* the footprints more closely." "I will *examine* the use of imagery in this poem."

Building Your Speaking Vocabulary

Language gives us the ability to express ourselves. The more words you know, the better able you will be to get your points across. There are two main aspects of language: reading and speaking. Using the steps above will help you to acquire a rich vocabulary. Follow these steps to help you learn to use this rich vocabulary in discussions, speeches, and conversations.

Steps	Tip
1. Practice pronouncing the word.	Become familiar with pronunciation guides to allow you to sound out unfamilar words. Listening to audio books as you read the text will help you learn prounciations of words.
2. Learn word forms.	Dictionaries often list forms of words following the main word entry. Practice saying word families aloud: "generate," "generated," "generation," "regenerate," "generator."
3. Translate your thoughts.	Restate your own thoughts and ideas in a variety of ways, to inject formality or to change your tone, for example.
4. Hold discussions.	With a classmate, practice using academic vocabulary words in discussions about the text. Choose one term to practice at a time, and see how many statements you can create using that term.
5. Tape-record yourself.	Analyze your word choices by listening to yourself objectively. Note places your word choice could be strengthened or changed.

Literary Map of Texas

Palo Duro Canyon
● Amarillo

● Littlefield
● Lubbock

Wichita Falls ⑥

Paris ●

④ Richardson
● Dallas

⑬ Karna

⑫ El Paso

⑤ Indian Creek

⑧ McGregor

② Eddy

① Austin

Big Bend National Park

San Antonio ⑦

Houston ③

Wharton ⑨

● Galvestor

⑪ Crystal City

Corpus Christi ●

⑩ Brownsville

This map shows some of the writers who make up the rich literary history of Texas. Writers whose works appear in this book are listed below in red.

① Austin
Susan Wittig Albert
J. Frank Dobie
O. Henry

② Eddy
Roy Bedichek

③ Houston
James Lee Burke
Sherry Garland
Barbara Jordan
Marie Delgado Travis

④ Richardson
Deborah Crombie

⑤ Indian Creek
Katherine Anne Porter

⑥ Wichita Falls
Larry McMurtry

⑦ San Antonio
Sandra Cisneros
Olga Samples Davis
Naomi Shihab Nye
John Phillip Santos

⑧ McGregor
Teresa Paloma Acosta

⑨ Wharton
Horton Foote

⑩ Brownsville
Americo Paredes

⑪ Crystal City
Tomás Rivera

⑫ El Paso
Pat Mora

⑬ Karnack
Lady Bird Johnson

𝒩

Texas at a Glance

Nickname: The Lone Star State
Motto: Friendship
Slogan: Texas: It's like a whole other country.
State Small Mammal: Nine-banded Armadillo
State Large Mammal: Longhorn

State Bird: Mockingbird
State Flower: Bluebonnet
State Tree: Pecan
Capital: Austin
Area: Largest state in the contiguous United States; 2nd largest overall

Fun Facts:

- At the top of the Capitol Dome in Austin stands one of the most famous Texas statues, the Goddess of Liberty. The statue, placed atop the Dome in 1888, weighs almost 3,000 pounds! Because the statue stands 15 feet, 7 1/2 inches tall, it makes the Texas Capitol Building taller than the U.S. Capitol.

- The original 31 walnut desks are still used in the Capitol's Senate chamber. Now, microphones extend from where the inkwells used to be!

- Bell County, Texas, native Miriam Ferguson was the first woman elected to the office of governor in the United States. Ferguson was the governor of Texas from 1925 to 1927 and again from 1933 to 1935.

- The Lone Star State has four national forests (Angelina, Davy Crockett, Sabine, and Sam Houston), two national parks (Big Bend and Guadalupe Mountains), two national recreation areas (Amistad and Lake Meredith), one national seashore (Padre Island), one national preserve (the Big Thicket), and one national monument (Alibates Flint Quarries).

- The monarch butterfly is the official state insect of Texas. It is the only species of butterfly that does not hibernate. Instead it migrates as the seasons change.

- The official dish of Texas is chili.

THE BIG **?**

Can *truth* change?

Fiction and Nonfiction

Unit 1

PHLitOnline

www.PHLitOnline.com

Hear It!
- Selection summary audio
- Selection audio
- Big Question Tunes

See It!
- Penguin author video
- Big Question video
- Get Connected videos
- Background videos
- More about the authors
- Illustrated vocabulary words
- Vocabulary flashcards

Do It!
- Interactive journals
- Interactive graphic organizers
- Grammar tutorials
- Interactive vocabulary games
- Test practice

1

Introducing the Big Question

 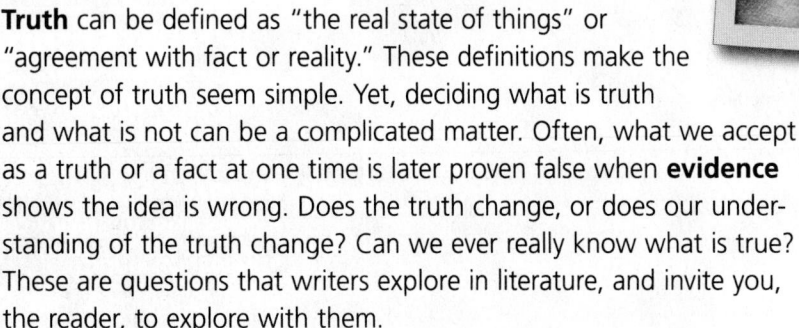 Can *truth* change?

Truth can be defined as "the real state of things" or "agreement with fact or reality." These definitions make the concept of truth seem simple. Yet, deciding what is truth and what is not can be a complicated matter. Often, what we accept as a truth or a fact at one time is later proven false when **evidence** shows the idea is wrong. Does the truth change, or does our understanding of the truth change? Can we ever really know what is true? These are questions that writers explore in literature, and invite you, the reader, to explore with them.

Start thinking about the Big Question by identifying different types of truths or facts.

Tell What You Know

Make a list of a few statements that you think express truths. Give one specific example of each of the following types of truths, and explain how you know that each statement is true.

- a historical fact
- a scientific fact
- an assumption about how people interact with each other
- a truth about choices people can make in life
- a truth about what will happen in the future

Join a small team in your class and share your examples with your teammates. As you discuss each example, participate productively by building on the ideas of others and by contributing information that is relevant. Try to **convince** your teammates that each statement is a truth and not an opinion. Listen attentively as your teammates explain their examples. Consider which of their points seem **credible** and which do not.

TEXAS
PHLitOnline
www.PHLitOnline.com
- Big Question video
- Illustrated vocabulary words
- Interactive vocabulary games
- Big Question Tunes

Explain What You Know

Use the examples and ideas you discussed with your partner to help you complete these sentences about truth.

- The difference between a fact about history and an opinion about history is that _____.
- Scientific facts can be disproved if _____.
- We can **speculate** about future truths based on _____.

Share your responses with a partner.

Write What You Think

Based on your discussions, decide what you think right now. Your answer may change as you read the selections in this unit. Choose one of these responses to the Big Question or write one of your own:

- ❑ Truth can change.
- ❑ Truth cannot change.

Connecting to the Literature

Each reading in this unit will give you insight into the Big Question. At the end of the unit, you will have an opportunity to see how your ideas have changed.

Connecting to Citizenship

Texas Profiles: Sam Rayburn

Speaker of the House Sam Rayburn was a Texas Congressman who took his oath of office in 1913, and served for 48 years. For a time, he was Speaker of the House of Representatives. Rayburn was on the Interstate and Foreign Commerce Committee, which regulates commerce with foreign countries and between states. As a member of this committee, he helped pass the Truth in Securities Act. This act helped the public to get more information about investments they made in publicly traded securities.

Can truth change?

- How might having more information help people make sound investments?
- What can you learn from Rayburn's story that can help you become a thoughtful and active citizen?

Focus on the TEKS

Listening and Speaking
(26) Participate productively in teams, building on the ideas of others and contributing relevant information.

Big Question Vocabulary

Use some of these words as you complete the activities on these pages.

assumption
belief
circumstance
context
convince
credible
distort
evidence
manipulate
perceive
perspective
skeptics
speculate
truth
verify

This list includes academic vocabulary words, which are defined on pp. R1–R14.

Can *truth* change?

Fiction and nonfiction show us truth in different ways.

TEXAS
PHLitOnline

www.PHLitOnline.com

- Penguin author video
- Interactive journals
- Interactive graphic organizers
- Selection audio
- Self-test

What Are Fiction and Nonfiction?
by Elizabeth McCracken

This is how I learned the difference between fiction and nonfiction.

On my 15th birthday I walked into the local public library and demanded a job and wonder of wonders they gave me one. Good thing: most of the jobs my friends had (waitress, camp counselor, ice cream scooper) required eye contact and good balance. I had a terrific knowledge of the alphabet, and a need *not* to look people in the eye. In other words, I was a born shelver.

On-the-Job Training

Fiction is prose writing that tells about imaginary characters and events; **nonfiction** is prose writing that presents information and ideas about real people, places, events, or objects.

My beat was Fiction A–SM, which was in the hallway leading from the circulation desk to the reference room. The library building was old and weird and made of lots of little rooms. Books had to be shelved where they could. Fiction SM–Z, for instance, was in the front room. The majority of shelf space was devoted to nonfiction, the way it is in most libraries.

"Nonfiction was bossy."

At first I wasn't interested in nonfiction. Nonfiction was bossy. Cookbooks, history books, and auto repair manuals told you what happened or they told you what to do. You had to believe it because it was true. How could that compare to my beloved Fiction A–SM? Let's face it: I wasn't even interested in Fiction SM–Z. I shelved novels and short story collections, books with black and white skulls on the spine (mysteries) or yellow and red Young Adult stickers.

I was very slow because I kept stopping to read. Somewhere in there, I decided to write a book myself, a novel that one day would be shelved in Fiction A–SM. The only problem was what to write about: I'd had a dull, happy life.

After a while I got faster, and they gave me an additional section to shelve: New Nonfiction. It turned out that I *liked* history books (the 900s), collections of essays (800s), biographies (shelved according to subject), even cookbooks (600s).

Fictional Characters With Nonfictional Cars

These books made me want to write, too. I could make up characters and then look up what kind of cars they'd drive, what kind of food they'd eat, what kind of clothes they'd wear. Even now, the first thing I do when I start a short story or a novel is to read a nonfiction book on the same subject.

Fiction is a piece of truth that turns lies to meaning.

from *Skin*
— Dorothy Allison

Meet
Elizabeth McCracken (b. 1966)

Author of *The Giant's House* and "Desiderata"

Elizabeth McCracken, who was a librarian before she became a full-time writer, says she misses working in the library. Her dual identity as novelist and librarian serves her well in her first novel, *The Giant's House* (1996), which depicts a relationship between a librarian and the world's tallest teenager. In explaining her fascination with eccentric characters, she has said, "I believe that most people are extraordinary."

> ### Did You Know?
> McCracken confesses that "there are probably more times than I care to admit when I giggle happily at something I've written."

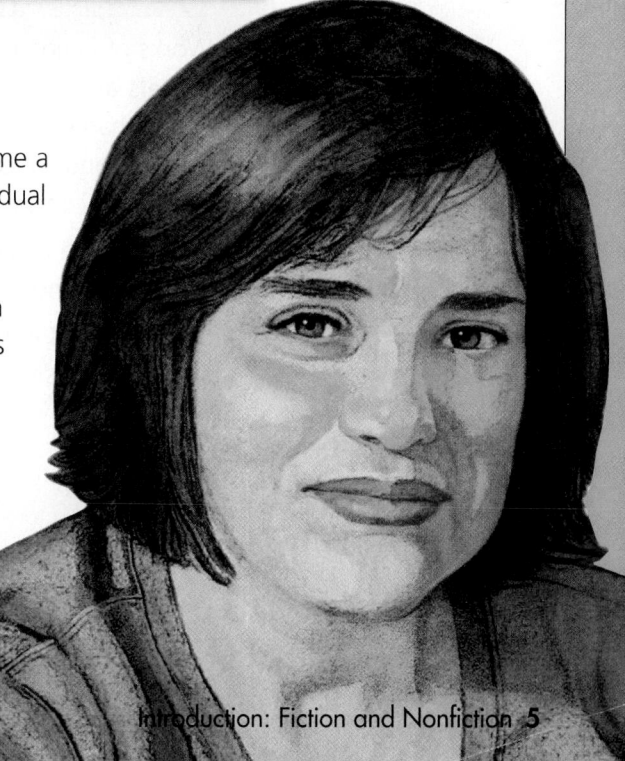

Exploring Fiction and Nonfiction

Characteristics of Fiction

All works of fiction, no matter how long, short, simple, or complex, share certain elements.

- Fiction features **characters,** invented people who experience a series of events, called the **plot.** Characters always face a **conflict,** or problem, that sets the plot in motion.
- It occurs in a time and place, or **setting.** The setting may be real or imaginary.
- Fiction is told, or narrated, from the **point of view** of a character who may or may not be part of the story.
- It includes a **theme,** a message or an insight about life.

CALVIN AND HOBBES ©1994 Watterson. Reprinted with permission of UNIVERSAL PRESS SYNDICATE. All Rights Reserved.

Types of Fiction

Works of fiction can be categorized by length and complexity.

Novels are long works of fiction that are usually presented in segments called chapters. Novels often feature several characters, take place in multiple settings, and concern more than one conflict. In addition to the main plot, a novel may contain **subplots,** or separate, related stories.

Novellas are works of fiction that are longer than short stories but shorter than novels.

Short stories are works of fiction that are brief enough to be read in one sitting. Short stories usually focus on one main plot that is driven by a single main conflict.

Characteristics of Nonfiction

Works of nonfiction share several characteristics.
- Nonfiction presents facts, describes true-life experiences, or discusses ideas from the author's point of view, or **perspective.**
- Nonfiction is written for a specific **audience,** or group of readers. It also addresses a clear **purpose,** or reason for writing.
- **Tone,** the author's attitude toward the subject or reader, is displayed through the writer's word choice and style.
- Often, nonfiction reflects the **cultural** and **historical contexts** in which the author is writing.

Focus on the TEKS

(6) Analyze how literary essays interweave personal examples and ideas with factual information.

Types of Nonfiction

Nonfiction can be divided into **literary nonfiction** and **informational text.**

Literary nonfiction interweaves personal examples and ideas with factual information to explain, present a perspective, or describe a situation or event. Examples include literary essays, diaries, and biographies.

Informational text includes the following types of writing:

Expository text informs or explains. Examples include essays and reports.

Persuasive text presents evidence to support or oppose an argument in order to convince the reader of the author's propositions. Examples include editorials and political speeches.

Procedural text provides data that can be used to solve a problem or perform a task. Examples include instructions and consumer publications.

 TEKS Check

Think of a short story and a literary essay that you have read. Use the chart to determine each work's specific type.

	Title	Questions for Analysis	Specific Type
Fiction: Short Story		• How long is the text? • How complex are the **plot** and **characters**?	
Nonfiction: Literary Essay		• What is the purpose of the text? • How does the author interweave **personal examples** with facts?	

Elizabeth McCracken Introduces
The Giant's House

My fiction often starts with a photograph: I stare, I get obsessed, I start to make things up.

Inspired by a World Record

My favorite book when I was a kid was *The Guinness Book of World Records,* and every year the same picture appeared in the front: the world's tallest man, Robert Pershing Wadlow, who grew to be 8'11". The picture showed him with his father and little brother; Robert Wadlow's hair brushed the ceiling of their house.

Other than being enormous, he was ordinary looking. He wore glasses and a suit. His ears stuck out a little. There was a little chart of his ages and heights. For instance, when he was in kindergarten he was more than six feet tall.

Maybe that picture meant something to me because I was always the shortest kid in school, and that seemed something like being the tallest, but mostly I liked how ordinary it was. If you were that tall, you'd have to work hard to be ordinary. People wouldn't want to let you be normal. No matter what your real personality was, all people would see would be *tall*. They'd keep telling you that you *weren't* normal, and soon you might think the same thing.

My Main Characters and Their Conflicts

I did a little research on Robert Wadlow when I started *The Giant's House,* but mostly I wanted to make things up, to get to know *my* **characters:** James Carlson Sweatt, the World's Tallest Man, and the people who knew him.

I decided to tell the story from the **point of view** of Peggy, the town librarian, because I needed someone who would always be struggling to see both sides of James—the enormous body that needed a lot of help to get through the ordinary-sized world, and the regular, teenaged-sized personality that needed conversation and music and company.

That's the narrator's **conflict** in the book, just as James's struggle is simply to live as best as he can, considering his size.

from

THE GIANT'S HOUSE

Elizabeth McCracken

James took out books on astronomy, ornithology:[1] sciences at once about tininess and height. He approached the desk with books he'd liked and asked for more—he knew it was easier to find more books with a good example in hand.

Then one day, in the first months of 1955—I remember looking over his head at some awful persistent Christmas decoration Astoria had stuck to the ceiling—he came to me without books. His height had become unwieldy; he reached out to touch walls as he walked, sometimes leaving marks way above where the other teenage boys smudged their hands. "I want books about people like me," he said.

I thought I knew what he was talking about, but I wanted to be cautious. "What exactly about you?" I asked. I made myself think of all the things he could have meant: Boy Scouts, basketball players. Never jump to conclusions when trying to answer a reference question. Interview the patron.

---

1. **astronomy, ornithology** Astronomy is the study of the stars and planets. Ornithology is the study of birds.

Fiction
Setting McCracken quickly establishes the time setting of her narrative—early 1955.

Reading
Check

What kind of books does James ask the librarian to find?

"Tall people," he said.

"Tall people? Just tall people in general?"

"Very tall people. Like me," he said, clearly exasperated with my playing dumb. "What they do."

"Okay," I told him. "Try the card catalog. Look in the big books on the table—see those books?" I pointed. "Those are books of subject headings for the card catalog. Look under words that you think describe your topic." James was used to me doing this: I gave directions but would not pull the books off the shelf for him. My job was to show people—even people I liked—how to use the library, not to use it for them. "Dig around," I said. "Try height, try stature. Then look in the catalog for books."

He nodded, leaned on the desk, and pushed off.

An hour later he headed out the door.

"Did you find what you needed?" I asked.

Elizabeth McCracken
Author's Insight
"Card catalogs have been replaced by computer catalogs. I miss them, even though computers are more efficient in almost every way."

▶ **Critical Viewing**
What details in this picture convey what it is like to do research in a library? **[Connect]**

"Did you find what you needed?" I asked.

"There isn't anything," he said. "There was one book that sort of was about it, but I couldn't find it on the shelf."

"There's something," I told him. "Come back. We'll look for it together."

That night after closing, I hunted around myself. The only thing under *stature* was a book about growth and nutrition. I tried our two encyclopedias under height and found passing references. Not much.

In truth, my library was a small-town place, and this was a specialized topic. Still, I was certain I could find more. I got that familiar mania—there is information somewhere here, and I can find it, I have to. A good librarian is not so different from a prospector, her whole brain a divining rod. She walks to books and stands and wonders: here? Is the answer here? The same blind faith in finding, even when hopeless. If someone caught me when I was in the throes of tracking something elusive, I would have told them: but it's out there. I can feel it. God *wants* me to find it.

That night I wandered the reference department, eyed the bindings of the encyclopedias, dictionaries, atlases. James was so big I almost expected to locate him in the gazetteer.² I set my hands upon our little card catalog, curled my fingers in the curved handles of the drawers. Then I went to the big volumes of subject headings.

Looking under *height* and *stature* turned up nothing; *anthropometry* was not quite right. Then I realized the word I was looking for: *Giant*.

Giant described him. *Giant*, I knew, would lead me to countless things—not just the word, located in indexes and catalogs and encyclopedias, but the idea of Giant, the knowledge that the people that James wanted to read about, people who could be described as like him, were not just tall but giants. I sat in a spindle-backed chair in the reference room, waiting for a minute. Then I checked the volume of the Library of Congress headings. *Giants. See also: dwarfs.*

We did not have a book, but I found several encyclopedia entries. Nowadays I could just photocopy; but that night I wrote down the page and volume numbers, thinking I could not bear to tell him the word to look under. Most of the very tall people mentioned in the encyclopedia had worked in the circus as professional giants, so I went to our books on the circus.

The photographs showed enormous people. Not just tall, though of course they were that, often with an ordinary person posed beside them. The tall people looked twice as big as the ambas-

---

2. **gazetteer** (gaz´ ə tir´) *n.* dictionary or index of geographical names.

Vocabulary
elusive (ē l͞o͞o´ siv) *adj.* hard to grasp or retain mentally

Elizabeth McCracken
Author's Insight
"I love the word *anthropometry,* which means 'the measuring of human beings.'"

Reading Check

What word does the librarian use to direct her search?

▶ **Critical Viewing**
Why might a card catalog like the one shown seem rich with possibility to a librarian like Peggy? **[Speculate]**

Fiction
Characters Real-life details about Anna Swann, Byrne, and Jack Earle make these characters more vivid.

sador from the normal-sized, as if they were an entirely different race. The books described weak stomachs and legs and bones. Sometimes what made them tall showed in their faces: each feature looked like something disturbed in an avalanche, separate from the others, in danger of slipping off.

Anna Swann, the Nova Scotia Giantess, married Captain Bates, the Kentucky Giant. As a young woman at Barnum's Dime Museum in New York, Miss Swann had been in two fires; in the second she had to be lifted out by a crane. No ordinary over-the-shoulder rescue for a woman better than seven feet tall. She and her husband retired to Ohio, to a specially made house. Their church installed an extra-large pew.

Byrne, the Irish Giant, lived in fear of a certain doctor who lusted after his skeleton; he imagined the doctor's giant kettle ready to boil his bones.

Jack Earle was over seven feet tall, traveled with the circus for years; after his retirement he wrote poetry.

I took comfort in Anna Swann and her husband. They were solid-looking people. Respectable. They'd had two children, though neither survived. The book described them as *in love*, and you could believe that from the pictures: their complementary heights

were just a lovely coincidence to their love affair. I found myself that late night a little jealous of Anna Swann and her handsome, bearded captain.

The books said that giants tended to exaggerate their heights for exhibition purposes. I did not know it then, but every person I read about was shorter than James grew to be.

The worst book was called *Medical Curiosities*. I say worst now. That is hindsight. The night I looked, I thought, in fact, that it was the best book—not because it was good or even accurate, but because it had the most pages on the subject I was researching. I found it under the subject heading *Abnormalities, human*. A terrible phrase, and one I knew I could not repeat to James. It was a late-nineteenth-century medical book, described two-headed people and parasitic twins and dwarfs. And giants. Not exactly information, but interesting: giants who had enormous or usual appetites; ones who grew throughout their lives or only after adolescence; professional giants and private citizens.

So I took that book, and the circus books, marked the pertinent places with the old catalog cards I used for scrap, and set them aside. Ready for him, so that he did not have to look in the index, or wander through the pages at all.

Elizabeth McCracken
Author's Insight
"I can't remember whether I've seen this book or I made it up. There are definitely books with this title, but did I have one in mind? Who knows!"

Vocabulary
pertinent (purt´ 'n ənt) *adj.* relevant; having a connection to the matter at hand

Reading Check
Under what subject heading does the librarian finally find information that will be useful to James?

◄ **Critical Viewing**
Does this picture make great height look appealing or not? Use details from this photograph in your answer. **[Support]**

"Your tall friend is here," Astoria said to me the next week. I was in my office, reading reviews. "He's looking for you."

James waited for me at the circ desk. "You said we could—"

"I looked," I said. I'd stowed the books beneath the shelf. "Try these out."

He took them to the big table in the front room. Read them. He made the sturdy chair, the same chair I'd sat in the night before, seem tiny.

Afterward he came up to me.

"How were they?" I asked. "Would you like to take them home?"

He shook his head.

"No," he said. "Thanks."

"Nothing useful here at all?"

"No," he said.

I tried to catch his eye. "Close?"

"Close. I guess." He pointed at *Medical Curiosities*. "I guess that's close."

I picked up the book and opened it to where the marker was, but he'd moved it to another page. A line drawing of a double-bodied baby looked up at me. Horrible. I snapped the book shut.

"I meant medical books," he said. "But new ones. Ones that say what goes wrong. How to cure it."

"Cures," I said. "Oh." Cures for giants? No such thing. No cure for height. Only preventive medicine. I said it as a question. "Cures? For tall people?"

"Yes," he said.

All I wanted was for him to explain it to me. It seemed presumptuous to come to any conclusions myself. I knew what he was talking about. I did. But what he wanted, I couldn't help him with.

Darla, the shelver, came rattling up with her metal cart. "Shelve these?" she said, pointing at the books. The catalog cards I'd used stuck out from the pages; James had lined them up, like a pack of cards he'd shuffled into them. "Hi, Jim," she said.

"Hi." He squinted down at her.

She stared at me; I waited for her to get back to shelving.

Fiction
Plot Peggy's attempts at research finally cause James to reveal his real quest.

Elizabeth McCracken
Author's Insight
"Earlier in the book, James comes to the library to learn how to do card and other magic tricks."

"Cures," I said. "Oh." Cures for giants? No such thing. No cure for height. Only preventive medicine.

◄ **Critical Viewing**
What advantages and disadvantages might James have in the physical space of a library? **[Connect]**

MODEL SELECTION

"Peggy. Shelve them, or not?"

"Not yet," I said. She sighed and pushed the cart off.

James stood in silence on the other side of the desk. He looked ready to leave.

"You mean how to stop growing," I said.

"Yes." Now he looked at me. "Medicine, or operations, or something."

"I'm not sure we have anything here," I said. That was a lie. I knew we didn't. "A medical library somewhere, perhaps. Or a university library. But really—" I started pulling the bookmarks from the books. I tried to sound gentle. "Really, you should ask your doctor."

"I have," he said. "I've asked a lot of doctors."

Fiction
Novel The end of this excerpt hints that the plot of the novel *The Giant's House* includes conflicts beyond Peggy's search for library books on height.

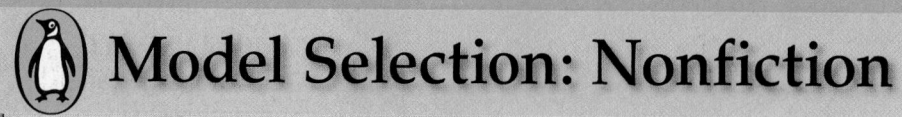

Elizabeth McCracken Introduces "Desiderata"

I write fiction naturally, but most of my nonfiction comes out of an assignment. In the case of "Desiderata," someone at my publishing house was putting together a Web site and asked me to write a **personal essay,** with an **informal tone.** My **audience,** of course, would be anyone who visited the site, and my **purpose** was to make them want to read my novel *The Giant's House.*

How to Find Subjects for Writing: Snooping

Personally, I find myself boring, but other people interest me. In other words, I'm a snoop. I like to read through other people's mail, flip through other people's photo albums, eavesdrop on other people's phone conversations. Best of all: my family's mail, my family's conversations.

I'm the youngest in my family, and it shows: I'm a bratty kid sister, always sneaking in places, always wondering what happened before I showed up. My parents were married for thirteen years before I was born! My brother was alive for two and a half years! No fair! I want to know everything, and what I don't know I'll make up.

Finding Inspiration in a Shopping List

I couldn't figure out exactly what to write about for the Web site until I looked at my grandmother's shopping list, which was taped to my computer screen. So that's what I decided to write about.

My nosiness is probably what made me a writer. I was lucky enough to have been born into a family of sentimental packrats, and before I could even read, my relatives were showing me photographs and telling me stories. I liked to hear *The Little Engine That Could,* but even better I liked to hear the story of my mother and her twin sister and their first exchange of birthday presents. They gave each other an American flag and a balloon on a stick.

The essay itself was my way of getting all that ephemera—stuff that's doomed to disappear or degrade, things that were never meant to last—in some kind of order.

Desiderata

Elizabeth McCracken

Desiderata, I learned in library science school, were the items you needed for an archive to make it useful. Useful, not complete, because there is no such thing as a complete archive. There's always a letter out there you want and need, either in someone else's collection or in an attic or just unfound. You need and want things you don't even know exist. That's how collections work.

I come from a family strong on documents. I have a small archive myself. My grandfather McCracken was a genealogist—I have his history of the McCrackens, a lovely compilation of research on early ancestors and personal remembrances of his own relatives. His wife, my grandmother, wrote stories and poems; I have copies of those, and remember once opening a drawer full of letters she wrote to God, part prayer and part daily correspondence to Someone dear. I have my grandmother Jacobson's collection of family letters; she had 11 brothers and sisters, some who wrote often and some just now and then. I have diplomas of relatives I never met. I have diaries and laundry lists. I love anything written by a relative, any evidence of what they really thought.

And I read these documents fairly regularly. Besides letters from her family, my grandmother also saved letters from Martha,

Elizabeth McCracken
Author's Insight
"The minute I heard the word 'desiderata' I knew I would try to use it in my writing. It appears in *The Giant's House,* too."

Elizabeth McCracken
Author's Insight
"My grandfather edited a magazine called *The American Genealogist* for years."

her children's nanny. My mother, who says she had the happiest childhood on record, remembers Martha and her letters as lovely and slightly daffy. Her twin sister, my aunt Carolyn, remembers the letters and the woman as dark and Dickensian,[1] longing for a time that never really existed. I'd always assumed that the truth was somewhere in the middle, but I have the letters and now know that Martha was, at best, weird. She wrote to my travelling grandmother that the twins—The Dollies, she called them—didn't miss her at all. She reported that she took them out to her mother's farm, and couldn't understand why the girls were so upset to be served for dinner the chicken they'd met earlier. She reported on The Dollies' toilet training as if it were grand opera, and the Dollies heroines who wanted only, desperately, to triumph.

I'm glad to know this, I think. Certainly, it's a whole different Martha than the one I knew from my mother's stories. I know Martha now because of all that she reveals of herself, not knowing she was doing it, in her letters.

Still, there are many frustrations to family papers. First of all, you may learn things you don't want to know. For instance: some of my grandmother's sisters wanted to sue the widow of one of their brothers. Even in letters from the litigious[2] sisters themselves, this comes across as merely petty and vindictive. There are letters that can break your heart: my Aunt Edna, writing to my grandmother, lamented how poor her health was, how the doctors told her to slow down; I know from the dates that Edna died two weeks later, of a heart attack.

But the major frustration is how incomplete everything is, how incomplete *people* are if you try to meet them this way. The great-aunt who wanted to sue only happened to write it down; maybe she gave up the idea. Maybe she was suffering otherwise—her life was continually tragic in small ways, I know that. Some of the great-aunts I barely know, because they barely wrote. Or rather, I *think* they barely wrote—my grandmother saved every letter some years, and selected letters others. Perhaps those great-aunts simply never made it into the collection.

And then there's my grandmother Jacobson herself. She was a wonderful and complex woman, an attorney and small business-person who died at home at the age of 90. The pieces of paper I have from her don't conjure her up at all. Her diary (which I don't

Vocabulary
vindictive (vin dik´ tiv)
adj. revengeful; inclined to seek vengeance

---

1. **Dickensian** of or relating to English novelist Charles Dickens (1812–1870).
2. **litigious** (li tij´ əs) *adj.* given to carrying out lawsuits; quarrelsome.

own but have read) is a very careful record of daily events, nothing more. She doesn't detail worries or doubts, and the fact is she was a worried and somewhat doubtful person. I think she knew that we'd read it, eventually, and didn't want to tell us in her diary anything she hadn't told us already.

One piece of paper I do have: a post-it note from late in her life, which she used to mark a recipe in *The Jewish Cookbook*. It says:

> coffee
> bananas
> bread
> milk
> wax beans?

and then, in the corner, written diagonally and underlined,

> *lottery ticket.*

I know that this dates to a time when she was both worried about money and had become very serious about luck. I don't know how superstitious she'd previously been, but about two years before she died, she began to see luck good and bad, in everything: she read her horoscope, her children's horoscope, the horoscope of everyone who might touch her life that day. She believed in fortune cookies. She told her own fortune playing solitaire. And she bought lottery tickets, not so much because she believed she might win but because not playing meant she did not believe that sudden good things could happen. She was a businessperson, after all: she knew what a bad investment that weekly dollar was.

I love that little green piece of paper. *Desideratum* to me, though less than ephemera[3] to anyone else.

I could tell dozens of other stories from the pages of family papers: my aunt Blanche's pell-mell record of taking care of her favorite sister, Elizabeth, who was dying of Alzheimer's; Blanche has that disease herself now, and you can see the early signs in these notes. My great-uncles' cheery letters from Europe during World War II. A letter my brother wrote to my grandmother when I was four and he was six, thanking her for a gift and then recording that I was resisting writing a thank-you note myself.

Here's a last story. My father's parents were, when I knew them, quiet people. I know now that my version of them is different

---

Nonfiction
Exposition The actual text from her grandmother's note helps the author show the kinds of pieces she has collected. Later, she explains how she finds meaning in them.

Elizabeth McCracken
Author's Insight
"Four of my grandmother's brothers served overseas. Their mother died five hours after the last, my great-uncle Gerald, came back to the family house."

There are letters that can break your heart...

Reading Check
What is the author's major frustration in regard to her collection of family papers?

---

3. ephemera (e fem´ ər ə) *n.* something, often printed material, meant to last for only a short time.

▲ Critical Viewing
Are letters and photos like this one meaningful to society as a whole or just to individuals and families? Explain.
[Make a Judgment]

from anyone else's, but they were my grandparents and I never questioned who I understood them to be. After their deaths, I inherited a cherry chest-of-drawers from their house. I owned this imposing piece of furniture for a few years before I lifted some paper lining from one of the drawers and found a letter. Part of a letter, actually, written by my grandfather to my grandmother before their marriage.

It was one of the most beautiful love letters I've ever read, full of delight for her person and for their love together. It was passionate and thrilled and almost disbelieving of his great fortune, to have found her. I never imagined my grandfather, my quiet careful grandfather, was the sort of man who'd write any kind of love letter, never mind this kind. Wrong again. And my grandmother had saved it for more than fifty years. I wondered whether she took it out and reread it from time to time, or whether she'd forgotten where she'd put it.

My parents were out of town that weekend, and as it happened I'd agreed to pick them up at the airport. I brought the letter to give to my father—if it meant that much to me, I couldn't imagine what it would mean to him. And so, sitting on a bench in Logan,[4] I gave it to him. "Look what I found," I said.

"Oh," he said, perfectly pleased but not surprised. "Another letter. I'll put it with the others."

Turns out there were many more—my grandparents had written each other several times a day during their courtship. Which makes it, of course, a happier story.

My question is: was that letter more a *desideratum* for me, or my father? He had the collection, I didn't. Sometimes I regret giving it to him. I've forgotten the exact words my grandfather used, but it doesn't seem right to ask for someone else's love letter back. Someday I'll see it again, I know. Meanwhile, I need it and desire it. I need and desire everything that belongs to my family, and in some ways, I think, that's what I do with my days, writing fiction. I am writing love letters to diaries and post-it notes and telegrams and birthday cards. I am writing love letters to love letters.

It was one of the most beautiful love letters I've ever read...

---

4. **Logan** Boston's Logan International Airport, named for General Edward Lawrence Logan.

Critical Thinking

1. **Respond:** Do you feel sympathy for James in *The Giant's House*? Explain.

2. **(a)** What information about his condition does James hope to find? **(b) Make Inferences:** What is James's attitude toward his plight?

3. **(a)** Note two points at which the narrator, Peggy, refers to her training as a librarian. **(b) Analyze:** Do Peggy's efforts for James meet her criteria for being a good librarian? Explain.

4. **(a) Speculate:** Complete a chart like the one shown to formulate a plan that James could use to learn more about his condition today. **(b) Evaluate:** Consult with a classmate to identify which of the resources you listed might be the most valuable.

Research Question	Possible Source

5. **(a)** In "Desiderata," what frustrations does McCracken experience in "meeting" people through family papers? **(b) Speculate:** Based on this essay, why do you think McCracken became a writer of **fiction?**

Can truth change?
(a) In *The Giant's House,* why do James's and Peggy's perspectives affect their views of his height? **(b)** In "Desiderata," does the truth about McCracken's ancestors change as she learns more about them? Why or why not?

Fiction and Nonfiction Review

1. How does the **setting** of *The Giant's House* affect James's problem?

2. In her **nonfiction** essay "Desiderata," is McCracken's primary **purpose** to persuade, to inform, or to reflect? Explain.

Research the Author

McCracken was a librarian before she became a writer. Use the Internet and library resources to find more McCracken works reflecting her interest in libraries and research. Share your findings in an **oral presentation.**

- Summarize works by McCracken on library work and research.
- Include accurate quotes from McCracken's writings.

The Washwoman • New Directions

Selection Choices

▲ Read **"The Washwoman"** to see how community affects a household.

▲ Read **"New Directions"** to see how a woman makes a life for herself despite great challenges.

 TEXAS Focus on the TEKS

Meet these standards with either **"The Washwoman"** (p. 26) or **"New Directions"** (p. 36).

Reading

(6) Analyze how literary essays interweave personal examples and ideas with factual information to explain, present a perspective, or describe a situation or event. (*Literary Analysis: Literary Essay*)

(1)(A) Determine the meaning of grade-level technical academic English words in multiple content areas derived from Latin or other linguistic affixes. (*Word Power: Apply It*)

Reading/Comprehension Skills

RC-9(A) Reflect on understanding to monitor comprehension. (*Reading Skill: Make Predictions*)

Oral and Written Conventions

(18)(A) Use conventions of capitalization.
(*Conventions: Common Nouns and Proper Nouns*)

Listening and Speaking

(24)(A) Listen responsively to a speaker by taking notes that highlight the speaker's ideas for critical reflection and by asking questions related to the content for clarification and elaboration. (*Listening and Speaking: Interview*)

(25) Give presentations employing eye contact, speaking rate, volume, enunciation, and purposeful gestures to communicate ideas effectively. (*Listening and Speaking: Interview*)

Literary Analysis: Literary Essay

A **literary essay** is a short piece of nonfiction that tells a story about a real person or event. Authors of literary essays interweave **personal examples and ideas** with **factual information** to achieve specific purposes. For example, an author may wish to explain, present an opinion or perspective, or describe a situation or an event. By incorporating personal and factual information, authors are able to build complete, multi-dimensional pictures in their readers' minds.

Using the Strategy: Analysis Chart

As You Read Use a chart like the one shown to analyze how the literary essay interweaves personal examples and ideas with factual information to explain, present a perspective, or describe a situation or event.

Detail	Type	Purpose(s)
washwoman lived on Krochmalna Street	factual information	explain, decribe a situation

Reading Skill: Make Predictions

A **prediction** is an informed idea about what might happen later in a literary essay. Predictions are based on details in the text and your own experience. When you verify predictions, you read on to see if the prediction is correct. Making and verifying predictions is one way to **monitor your comprehension** as you read.

As You Read Pause periodically to reflect on your understanding. Monitor your comprehension by **asking questions** and making predictions. Finally, verify the accuracy of those predictions as you continue reading.

TEXAS
PHLitOnline

www.PHLitOnline.com

Hear It!
- Selection summary audio
- Selection audio

See It!
- Get Connected video
- Background video
- More about the author
- Vocabulary flashcards

Do It!
- Interactive journals
- Interactive graphic organizers
- Self-test
- Internet activity
- Grammar tutorial
- Interactive vocabulary games

 Can *truth* change?

Writing About the Big Question

In "The Washwoman," a Jewish family learns to appreciate a Christian washwoman whose son has abandoned her. Use these sentence starters to develop your ideas about the Big Question.

A mother's relationship with her son can sometimes be **distorted** because of _____. They could gain **insight** into each other's **perspective** by _____.

As You Read Look for the ways that the washwoman's relationships change over time.

Vocabulary

Read each word and its definition. Decide whether you know the word well, know it a little bit, or do not know it at all. After you read, see how your knowledge of each word has increased.

- **forebears** (fôr´ berz) *n.* ancestors (p. 27) *His forebears started the family business.*

- **accumulated** (ə kyoom´ yoo lāt´ id) *v.* piled up, collected, or gathered together, especially over a period of time (p. 27) *We have accumulated a large stack of newspapers in our living room. accumulate v. accumulation n. cumulative adj*

- **rancor** (raŋ´ kər) *n.* bitter hate (p. 28) *The rivals fumed with rancor for each other.*

- **atonement** (ə tōn´ mənt) *n.* act of making up for a wrongdoing or an injury (p. 28) *He volunteered at a nursing home as atonement for his misbehavior. atone v.*

- **obstinacy** (äb´ stə nə sē) *n.* stubbornness (p. 30) *The child refused to clean up, and she was punished for her obstinacy. obstinate adj.*

- **pious** (pī´ əs) *adj.* having or showing religious devotion (p. 31) *The pious man went to church every week. piety n. impious adj.*

Word Power

The **Old English prefix fore-** means "earlier" or "in front of."

In this story, the washwoman comes from generations of "peasant forebears," or ancestors who lived long before her.

Meet
Isaac Bashevis Singer
(1904–1991)

Author of

The Washwoman

Storytelling always had an important place in Isaac Bashevis Singer's life. He grew up in the city of Warsaw in what now is Poland. Singer's father was a rabbi, a teacher of the Jewish faith and laws. Advice-seekers streamed through the family home, telling their stories as the fascinated young Singer listened and observed.

"Life Itself Is a Story" Fleeing persecution against Jews, Singer left Poland for New York City in 1935. In New York, Singer began to make a name for himself as a writer. He set many of his tales in the world of European Jewry he had left. Ironically, as he wrote, World War II devastated that world. Villages like the one of his birth were wiped off the face of the earth even as Singer brought them to life on the page.

Did You Know?
Isaac Bashevis Singer won the Nobel Prize for Literature in 1978.

BACKGROUND FOR THE ESSAY

Social Studies Connection
Jews in Poland

"The Washwoman" takes place in the early twentieth century in what is now Poland. Centuries earlier, many Jewish people had settled there, drawn by the promise of religious tolerance. By Singer's time, Poland had been conquered by other countries. Yet, Poland's Jews held on to their traditions, continuing to speak Yiddish, a language blending German with Hebrew and other languages.

The Washwoman

Isaac Bashevis Singer

The Oldest Inhabitant, 1876, Julian Alden Weir, Butler Institute of American Art, Youngstown, Ohio

O̲ur home had little contact with Gentiles.[1] The only Gentile in the building was the janitor. Fridays he would come for a tip, his "Friday money." He remained standing at the door, took off his hat, and my mother gave him six groschen.[2]

Besides the janitor there were also the Gentile washwomen who came to the house to fetch our laundry. My story is about one of these.

She was a small woman, old and wrinkled. When she started washing for us, she was already past seventy. Most Jewish women of her age were sickly, weak, broken in body. All the old women in our street had bent backs and leaned on sticks when they walked. But this washwoman, small and thin as she was, possessed a strength that came from generations of peasant forebears. Mother would count out to her a bundle of laundry that had accumulated over several weeks. She would lift the unwieldy pack, load it on her narrow shoulders, and carry it the long way home. She lived on Krochmalna Street too, but at the other end, near the Wola section. It must have been a walk of an hour and a half.

She would bring the laundry back about two weeks later. My mother had never been so pleased with any washwoman. Every piece of linen sparkled like polished silver. Every piece was neatly ironed. Yet she charged no more than the others. She was a real find. Mother always had her money ready, because it was too far for the old woman to come a second time.

Laundering was not easy in those days. The old woman had no faucet where she lived but had to bring in the water from a pump. For the linens to come out so clean, they had to be scrubbed thoroughly in a washtub, rinsed with washing soda, soaked, boiled in an enormous pot, starched, then ironed. Every piece was handled ten times or more. And the drying! It could not be done outside because thieves would steal the laundry. The wrung-out wash had to be carried up to the attic and hung on clotheslines. In the winter it would become as brittle as glass and almost break when touched. And there was always a to-do with other housewives and washwomen who wanted the attic clothesline for their own use. Only God knows all the old woman had to endure each time she did a wash!

---

1. **Gentiles** (jen′ tĭls) *n.* any persons not Jewish; here, specifically Christians.
2. **groschen** (grō′ shən) *n.* Austrian cent or penny.

Literary Analysis
Literary Essay
In the first three paragraphs, how does the author interweave personal ideas with factual information to explain and describe a situation?

Vocabulary
forebears (fôr′ berz′) *n.* ancestors

accumulated (ə kyōōm′ yōō lāt′ id) *v.* piled up, collected, or gathered together, especially over a period of time

▲ **Iron, end of 19th century**

Reading Check

According to Singer, what is the washwoman's physical appearance?

She could have begged at the church door or entered a home for the penniless and aged. But there was in her a certain pride and love of labor with which many Gentiles have been blessed. The old woman did not want to become a burden, and so she bore her burden. •

My mother spoke a little Polish, and the old woman would talk with her about many things. She was especially fond of me and used to say I looked like Jesus. She repeated this every time she came, and Mother would frown and whisper to herself, her lips barely moving, "May her words be scattered in the wilderness."

The woman had a son who was rich. I no longer remember what sort of business he had. He was ashamed of his mother, the washwoman, and never came to see her. Nor did he ever give her a groschen. The old woman told this without rancor. One day the son was married. It seemed that he had made a good match. The wedding took place in a church. The son had not invited the old mother to his wedding, but she went to the church and waited at the steps to see her son lead the "young lady" to the altar.

The story of the faithless son left a deep impression on my mother. She talked about it for weeks and months. It was an affront not only to the old woman but to the entire institution of motherhood. Mother would argue, "Nu, does it pay to make sacrifices for children? The mother uses up her last strength, and he does not even know the meaning of loyalty."

And she would drop dark hints to the effect that she was not certain of her own children: Who knows what they would do some day? This, however, did not prevent her from dedicating her life to us. If there was any delicacy in the house, she would put it aside for the children and invent all sorts of excuses and reasons why she herself did not want to taste it. She knew charms that went back to ancient times, and she used expressions she had inherited from generations of devoted mothers and grandmothers. If one of the children complained of a pain, she would say, "May I be your ransom and may you outlive my bones!" Or she would say, "May I be the atonement for the least of your fingernails." When we ate she used to say, "Health and marrow in your bones!" The day before the new moon she gave us a kind of candy that was said to prevent parasitic worms. If one of us had something in his eye, Mother would lick the eye clean with her tongue. She also fed us rock candy against coughs, and from time to time she would take us to be blessed against the evil eye. This did not prevent her from studying *The Duties of the Heart, The Book of the Covenant,* and other serious philosophic works.

Vocabulary
rancor (raŋ´ kər)
n. bitter hate

Literary Analysis
Literary Essay
In this paragraph, how does the author interweave personal examples with factual information to present a perspective and describe a situation?

Vocabulary
atonement (ə tōn´ mənt)
n. act of making up for a wrongdoing or an injury

But to return to the washwoman. That winter was a harsh one. The streets were in the grip of a bitter cold. No matter how much we heated our stove, the windows were covered with frostwork and decorated with icicles. The newspapers reported that people were dying of the cold. Coal became dear. The winter had become so severe that parents stopped sending children to cheder,[3] and even the Polish schools were closed.

On one such day the washwoman, now nearly eighty years old, came to our house. A good deal of laundry had accumulated during the past weeks. Mother gave her a pot of tea to warm herself, as well as some bread. The old woman sat on a kitchen chair trembling and shaking, and warmed her hands against the teapot. Her fingers were gnarled from work, and perhaps from arthritis too. Her fingernails were strangely white. These hands spoke of the stubbornness of mankind, of the will to work not only as one's strength permits but beyond the limits of one's power. Mother counted and wrote down the list: men's undershirts, women's vests, long-legged drawers, bloomers, petticoats, shifts, featherbed covers, pillowcases, sheets, and the men's fringed garments. Yes, the Gentile woman washed these holy garments as well.

▲ **Critical Viewing**
How does this picture of a neighborhood in Poland compare with how you imagine Singer's neighborhood to look? **[Compare]**

Reading Check
How did the winter weather affect the neighborhood?

---

3. cheder (khā′ dər) *n.* religious school.

Reading Skill
Make Predictions
What prediction can you
make based on these
details about the cold
and the washwoman's
absence?

The bundle was big, bigger than usual. When the woman placed it on her shoulders, it covered her completely. At first she swayed, as though she were about to fall under the load. But an inner obstinacy seemed to call out: No, you may not fall. A donkey may permit himself to fall under his burden, but not a human being, the crown of creation.

It was fearful to watch the old woman staggering out with the enormous pack, out into the frost, where the snow was dry as salt and the air was filled with dusty white whirlwinds, like goblins dancing in the cold. Would the old woman ever reach Wola?

She disappeared, and Mother sighed and prayed for her.

Usually the woman brought back the wash after two or, at the most, three weeks. But three weeks passed, then four and five, and nothing was heard of the old woman. We remained without linens. The cold had become even more intense. The telephone wires were now as thick as ropes. The branches of the trees looked like glass. So much snow had fallen that the streets had become uneven, and sleds were able to glide down many streets as on the slopes of a hill. Kindhearted people lit fires in the streets for vagrants[4] to warm themselves and roast potatoes in, if they had any to roast.

A**t first she swayed, as though she were about to fall under the load.**

For us the washwoman's absence was a catastrophe. We needed the laundry. We did not even know the woman's address. It seemed certain that she had collapsed, died. Mother declared she had had a premonition, as the old woman left our house that last time, that we would never see our things again. She found some old torn shirts and washed and mended them. We mourned, both for the laundry and for the old, toil-worn woman who had grown close to us through the years she had served us so faithfully. •

More than two months passed. The frost had subsided, and then a new frost had come,

---

4. **vagrants** (vā´ grənts) *n.* people who wander from place to place, especially those without regular jobs.

a new wave of cold. One evening, while Mother was sitting near the kerosene lamp mending a shirt, the door opened and a small puff of steam, followed by a gigantic bundle, entered. Under the bundle tottered the old woman, her face as white as a linen sheet. A few wisps of white hair straggled out from beneath her shawl. Mother uttered a half-choked cry. It was as though a corpse had entered the room. I ran toward the old woman and helped her unload her pack. She was even thinner now, more bent. Her face had become more gaunt, and her head shook from side to side as though she were saying no. She could not utter a clear word, but mumbled something with her sunken mouth and pale lips.

After the old woman had recovered somewhat, she told us that she had been ill, very ill. Just what her illness was, I cannot remember. She had been so sick that someone had called a doctor, and the doctor had sent for a priest. Someone had informed the son, and he had contributed money for a coffin and for the funeral. But the Almighty had not yet wanted to take this pain-racked soul to Himself. She began to feel better, she became well, and as soon as she was able to stand on her feet once more, she resumed her washing. Not just ours, but the wash of several other families too.

"I could not rest easy in my bed because of the wash," the old woman explained. "The wash would not let me die."

"With the help of God you will live to be a hundred and twenty," said my mother, as a benediction.

"God forbid! What good would such a long life be? The work becomes harder and harder . . . my strength is leaving me . . . I do not want to be a burden on anyone!" The old woman muttered and crossed herself, and raised her eyes toward heaven.

Fortunately there was some money in the house and Mother counted out what she owed. I had a strange feeling: the coins in the old woman's washed-out hands seemed to become as worn and clean and pious as she herself was. She blew on the coins and tied them in a kerchief. Then she left, promising to return in a few weeks for a new load of wash.

Reading Skill
Make Predictions
Was your earlier prediction about the old woman accurate? Why or why not?

◄ **Critical Viewing**
What do you think it would be like to wash clothes using a washboard and tub like these? **[Speculate]**

Vocabulary
pious (pī´ əs) *adj.* having or showing religious devotion

✓ Reading Check
Why does the washwoman do other people's laundry?

But she never came back. The wash she had returned was her last effort on this earth. She had been driven by an indomitable will to return the property to its rightful owners, to fulfill the task she had undertaken.

And now at last her body, which had long been no more than a shard[5] supported only by the force of honesty and duty, had fallen. Her soul passed into those spheres where all holy souls meet, regardless of the roles they played on this earth, in whatever tongue, of whatever creed. I cannot imagine paradise without this Gentile washwoman. I cannot even conceive of a world where there is no recompense for such effort.

---

5. **shard** (shärd) *n.* fragment or broken piece.

Critical Thinking

Support your responses with evidence from the text.

1. **Respond:** Why do you think the washwoman gives so much and asks so little in return?

2. **(a)** Which job does the washwoman perform for Singer's family? **(b) Connect:** Which laborious obstacles to doing the job well does Singer describe?

3. **(a)** What prevents the washwoman from returning to the family for several months? **(b) Draw Conclusions:** What does the washwoman's eventual return tell you about her character? Explain.

4. **(a)** What specific information about the washwoman's personal life does the author include? **(b) Speculate:** What other kinds of information about the washwoman might the author have chosen to include but left out? **(c) Analyze:** Based on this essay, explain why an author might choose to include some details and omit others in a text.

Can truth change?
(a) How would you describe the character of the washwoman at the beginning of the story and then at the end? **(b)** How do her relationships grow?

After You Read | The Washwoman

Literary Analysis: Literary Essay

1. (a) In this **literary essay,** what difficulties does the washwoman face? **(b)** How does she respond to those challenges? **(c)** What inspirational lesson does the author take away from the story?

2. (a) Use a chart like the one shown to record six details—two **personal examples,** two **personal ideas,** and two **facts**—that Singer includes about his mother, the washwoman, or the washwoman's son. **(b)** How does the interweaving of these details help to describe the characters and their situations?

Mother	Washwoman	Washwoman's Son

Reading Skill: Make Predictions

3. List three **predictions** that you made while reading "The Washwoman." Then, trade papers with a partner and discuss the accuracy of your predictions and the details you used to make them. Finally, discuss which details in the essay helped you to verify your predictions.

Vocabulary

Practice Use a word from the vocabulary list on page 24 to replace each underlined word or phrase with its opposite.

1. The former enemies have put their old <u>friendship</u> behind them.

2. The actor's <u>flexibility</u> made him difficult to direct.

3. She inherited the family trade from her <u>children</u>.

4. Running extra laps was his <u>reward</u> for being late to practice.

5. My son has <u>given away</u> a large pile of clothing in his room.

6. The old woman was <u>disrespectful of her religion</u>.

Word Power Use the context of the sentences and what you know about the **Old English prefix** *fore-* to explain your answer to each question.

1. Where does the <u>foreword</u> of a book appear?

2. If something is <u>foreseen</u>, is it a surprise?

Word Power

The **Old English prefix** *fore-* means "earlier" or "in front of."

Apply It Explain how the prefix *fore-* helps you determine the meanings of these technical academic words from science and the arts. Consult a dictionary if necessary.

forecast
forerunner
forehead

Can *truth* change?

Writing About the Big Question

In "New Directions," Mrs. Annie Johnson finds herself on her own with two young children. Use these sentence starters to develop your ideas about the Big Question.

The **truth** about a person can change as a result of _____.

We see things differently as **circumstances** change because _____.

(**As You Read**) Look for the ways Annie Johnson's situation changes over time, and decide whether she really has set off in a new direction.

Vocabulary

Read each word and its definition. Decide whether you know the word well, know it a little bit, or do not know it at all. After you read, see how your knowledge of each word has increased.

- **conceded** (kən sēd´ əd) *v.* admitted as true or valid; acknowledged (p. 36) *Julie <u>conceded</u> that she had made an awful mistake.* concede *v.* concession *n.*

- **amicably** (am´ i kə blē) *adv.* in a friendly way (p. 36) *Luckily, they settled their disagreements <u>amicably</u> before the problem escalated into something violent.* amicable *adj.*

- **meticulously** (mə tik´ yo͞o ləs lē) *adv.* very carefully and precisely (p. 37) *She <u>meticulously</u> applied her makeup.* meticulous *adj.*

- **balmy** (bäm´ ē) *adj.* having the qualities of balm; soothing, mild, pleasant (p. 38) *It was a <u>balmy</u> spring day with sunshine and a warm breeze.* balm *n.* balminess *n.*

- **ominous** (äm´ ə nəs) *adj.* threatening (p. 38) *The sound of the thunder seemed <u>ominous</u>.* ominously *adv.* omen *n.*

- **unpalatable** (un pal´ it ə bəl) *adj.* distasteful; unpleasant (p. 38) *She thought changing soiled diapers was her most <u>unpalatable</u> chore.* palate *n.* palatable *adj.*

Word Power

The **Latin prefix con-** means "with" or "together."

If a person **concedes**, he or she yields to or gives in. In the story, Annie Johnson's husband *concedes* that their marriage is not going to work.

Meet
Maya Angelou
(b. 1928)

Author of
New Directions

Maya Angelou's life is a story of overcoming hardships and succeeding. She was raised in rural, segregated Arkansas. In 1940, she moved to San Francisco, where she worked as a waitress, cook, and dancer. In the 1950s, Angelou went to New York, where she discovered her talents as a writer.

"I am human, and nothing human can be alien to me." Angelou wrote these words, and she lives by them. She went on to become a poet, a playwright, an editor, an actress, a director, and a teacher. Her many literary honors include a nomination for a Pulitzer Prize. She also read one of her poems at President Bill Clinton's inauguration in January 1993.

BACKGROUND FOR THE ESSAY

Social Studies Connection
Limited Options

In the early 1900s, job opportunities were limited for many Americans—particularly African Americans like Annie Johnson, the main character in "New Directions." At that time, the most common jobs available for African American women were cleaning, child care, and household labor. For women who had families, caring for someone else's household was an extra burden.

DID YOU KNOW?
Angelou's first name is Marguerite. Her brother gave her the nickname Maya when she was a child.

New Directions

Maya Angelou

Literary Analysis
Literary Essay
In the first three paragraphs, how does the author interweave personal ideas with factual information to explain and describe a situation?

Vocabulary
conceded (kən sēd´ əd)
v. admitted as true or valid; acknowledged

amicably (am´ i kə blē)
adv. in a friendly way

In 1903 the late Mrs. Annie Johnson of Arkansas found herself with two toddling sons, very little money, a slight ability to read and add simple numbers. To this picture add a disastrous marriage and the burdensome fact that Mrs. Johnson was a Negro.

When she told her husband, Mr. William Johnson, of her dissatisfaction with their marriage, he conceded that he too found it to be less than he expected, and had been secretly hoping to leave and study religion. He added that he thought God was calling him not only to preach but to do so in Enid, Oklahoma. He did not tell her that he knew a minister in Enid with whom he could study and who had a friendly, unmarried daughter. They parted amicably, Annie keeping the one-room house and William taking most of the cash to carry himself to Oklahoma.

Annie, over six feet tall, big-boned, decided that she would not go to work as a domestic and leave her "precious babes" to anyone else's care. There was no possibility of being hired at the town's cotton gin or lumber mill, but maybe there was a way to make the two factories work for her. In her words, "I looked up the road I was going and back the way I come, and since I wasn't satisfied, I decided to step off the road and cut me a new path." She told herself that she wasn't a fancy cook but that she could "mix groceries well enough to scare hungry away and from starving a man."

She made her plans meticulously and in secret. One early evening to see if she was ready, she placed stones in two five-gallon pails and carried them three miles to the cotton gin. She rested a little, and then, discarding some rocks, she walked in the darkness to the saw mill five miles farther along the dirt road. On her way back to her little house and her babies, she dumped the remaining rocks along the path.

That same night she worked into the early hours boiling chicken and frying ham. She made dough and filled the rolled-out pastry with meat. At last she went to sleep.

The next morning she left her house carrying the meat pies, lard, an iron brazier,[1] and coals for a fire. Just before lunch she appeared in an empty lot behind the cotton gin. As the dinner noon bell rang, she dropped the savors into boiling fat and the aroma rose and floated over to the workers who spilled out of the gin, covered with white lint, looking like specters.

Most workers had brought their lunches of pinto beans and biscuits or crackers, onions and cans of sardines, but they were tempted by the hot meat pies which Annie ladled out of the fat. She wrapped them in newspapers, which soaked up the grease, and offered them for sale at a nickel each. Although business was slow, those first days Annie was determined. She balanced her appearances between the two hours of activity.

---

1. **brazier** (brā′ zhər) *n.* A brazier is a pan or bowl that holds burning coals or charcoal as a heat source for cooking. In some braziers, food is placed on a grill directly over the flames. Johnson uses hers to heat a pot of boiling fat so that she can deep-fry her pies.

Vocabulary
meticulously (mə tik′ yoo ləs lē) *adv.* very carefully and precisely

Reading Skill
Make Predictions
What prediction might you make about Annie's plans? Why?

As the dinner noon bell rang, she dropped the savors into boiling fat and the aroma rose...

◀ **Critical Viewing**
Judging from this photograph, why do you think Annie Johnson felt that lumber workers would want to buy her pies? **[Draw Conclusions]**

Vocabulary

balmy (bäm´ ē) *adj.* having the qualities of balm; soothing, mild, pleasant

ominous (äm´ ə nəs) *adj.* threatening

unpalatable (un pal´ it ə bəl) *adj.* distasteful; unpleasant

Literary Analysis
Literary Essay
In this section, how does the author interweave personal examples with factual information to present a perspective and describe a situation?

So, on Monday if she offered hot fresh pies at the cotton gin and sold the remaining cooled-down pies at the lumber mill for three cents, then on Tuesday she went first to the lumber mill presenting fresh, just-cooked pies as the lumbermen covered in sawdust emerged from the mill.

For the next few years, on balmy spring days, blistering summer noons, and cold, wet, and wintry middays, Annie never disappointed her customers, who could count on seeing the tall, brown-skin woman bent over her brazier, carefully turning the meat pies. When she felt certain that the workers had become dependent on her, she built a stall between the two hives of industry and let the men run to her for their lunchtime provisions.

She had indeed stepped from the road which seemed to have been chosen for her and cut herself a brand-new path. In years that stall became a store where customers could buy cheese, meal, syrup, cookies, candy, writing tablets, pickles, canned goods, fresh fruit, soft drinks, coal, oil, and leather soles for worn-out shoes.

Each of us has the right and the responsibility to assess the roads which lie ahead, and those over which we have traveled, and if the future road looms ominous or unpromising, and the roads back uninviting, then we need to gather our resolve and, carrying only the necessary baggage, step off that road into another direction. If the new choice is also unpalatable, without embarrassment, we must be ready to change that as well.

Critical Thinking

1. **Respond:** What do you admire about Annie Johnson? Explain.

2. **(a)** Why does Annie Johnson have to find a source of income? **(b)** Why does she decide against a job as a domestic? **(c) Make Inferences:** What does Annie Johnson's decision suggest about the kind of mother she is?

3. **(a)** What does Annie Johnson decide to do to earn a living? **(b) Evaluate:** How would you describe Annie Johnson's abilities as a businessperson? Explain your response.

4. **(a)** What details in the text show that Annie Johnson's business grows? **(b) Draw Conclusions:** What does her achievement suggest about the human spirit in general?

Support your responses with evidence from the text.

Can truth change?
(a) How does the truth of Annie's life change? **(b)** Do you think taking a "new direction" in life is worth the risk of failure? Explain.

Literary Analysis: Literary Essay

1. (a) In this **literary essay,** what problem sets the story in motion?
(b) How is the problem overcome?

2. (a) Use a chart like the one shown to record six details—two
personal examples, two **personal ideas,** and two **facts**—that
Angelou includes about Annie Johnson or her husband. **(b)** How
does the interweaving of these details help to describe the characters and their situations?

Annie Johnson	Annie Johnson's Husband

Reading Skill: Make Predictions

3. Write three **predictions** that you made while reading "New
Directions." Then, trade papers with a partner and discuss the
accuracy of your predictions and the details you used to make
them. Finally, discuss which details in the essay helped you to verify
your predictions.

Vocabulary

Practice Use a word from the vocabulary list on page 34 to replace
each underlined word or phrase with its opposite.

1. When people act in a friendly manner, they behave <u>viciously</u>.

2. Some people think that spinach is <u>delicious</u>.

3. The rumble of a volcano is an <u>encouraging</u> sound.

4. You can avoid mistakes on tests by checking your work <u>carelessly</u>.

5. Ralph finally <u>did not admit</u> his participation in the prank.

6. A <u>chilly</u> wind was blowing on that summer day.

Word Power Use the context of the sentences and what you know
about the **Latin prefix con-** to explain your answer to each question.

1. What does it mean if something is <u>concentrated</u>?

2. How does a person <u>contend</u> with problems?

Word Power

The **Latin prefix con-**
means "with" or
"together."

Apply It Explain how
the prefix con- helps
you determine the
meanings of these
technical academic
words from science
and social studies.
Consult a dictionary if
necessary.

concavity
concentric
confederate

Integrated Language Skills

The Washwoman • New Directions

Conventions: Common Nouns and Proper Nouns

A **common noun** names any one of a class of people, places, or things. A **proper noun** names a specific person, place, or thing. Proper nouns are always **capitalized.**

Type	Common Noun	Proper Noun
person	student	Deana Johnson
place	city	Raleigh-Durham
thing	novel	*A Separate Peace*

Some nouns can be either common or proper, depending on how they are used. Look at these examples:

My **mom** made us brownies for dessert.
May I please have another brownie, **Mom?**

The **president** must sign a bill before it becomes a law.
The bill was signed by **President** Roosevelt.

Practice A Copy and read each of the following sentences. Draw one line under each common noun and two lines under each proper noun.

1. "The Washwoman" is a story by Isaac Bashevis Singer.
2. Singer's mother studied books, such as *The Duties of the Heart.*
3. The setting of the story is Poland, where Singer grew up.
4. The washwoman has a large effect on the family.

Reading Application In "The Washwoman," find one sentence with a proper noun and a common noun.

Practice B Rewrite each of the sentences below, replacing one common noun with a proper noun in each. Be sure to use proper conventions of capitalization.

1. The woman in the story started a business cooking food.
2. Her husband moved to a new state.
3. She and her two baby sons were on their own in a new state.
4. The lumber workers bought food from her.

Writing Application Using the following sentence as a model, write two more sentences that include both common and proper nouns: *Annie hoped to name her business Johnson's Pies.* Use proper conventions of capitalization in your sentences.

PH GRAMMAR HANDBOOK Further instruction and practice are available in the *Prentice Hall Grammar Handbook.*

Writing

Both selections involve strong women dealing with life's circumstances. Write an **anecdote,** a brief narrative, about a person you know and respect. For example, you might describe something admirable that the person did and what you learned from it.

- Before you draft, note what you respect about the person. This is the controlling impression your anecdote will convey.

- Describe a specific event that illustrates the characteristics you admire in your subject.

- Use significant details to support the message you want to convey.

Grammar Application If you include proper nouns in your anecdote, be sure to use proper conventions of capitalization.

Writing Workshop: *Work in Progress*

Prewriting for Autobiographical Narrative For an essay you may write later, list three or four vivid memories, describing the visual picture you see in your mind for each one. Develop the scene in your mind by adding details related to other senses. Include what you heard, smelled, and felt. Make notes about the weather and the temperature, the setting, and the taste, if there is one. Save this Memory List in your writing portfolio.

Listening and Speaking

With a partner, role-play an **interview** featuring the main character in the selection you read. For example, plan an interview between the washwoman and a reporter or between Annie Johnson and a potential employer. If necessary, refresh your memory by rereading the selection.

Follow these steps to complete the assignment:

- Generate and ask relevant questions that are open-ended and that cannot be answered simply with a yes or a no, in order to demonstrate your knowledge of the subject matter.

- Listen carefully to what your partner says in the interview.

- Respond to your partner by **taking notes** that highlight his or her main ideas. Reflect critically on these points and **ask questions** for clarification or elaboration.

- To make your delivery more effective, speak clearly and to the point. Employ appropriate **eye contact, speaking rate, volume, enunciation,** and **purposeful gestures.**

- After the role play, evaluate each other's work for the quality of the techniques used.

 Focus on the TEKS

Conventions
(18)(A) Use conventions of capitalization.

Listening and Speaking
(24)(A) Listen responsively to a speaker by taking notes that highlight the speaker's ideas for critical reflection and by asking questions related to the content for clarification and elaboration.

(25) Give presentations employing eye contact, speaking rate, volume, enunciation, and purposeful gestures to communicate effectively.

Use this prewriting activity to prepare for the **Writing Workshop** on page 94.

www.PHLitOnline.com

- Interactive graphic organizers
- Grammar tutorial
- Interactive journals

Selection Choices

▲ Read **"Sonata for Harp and Bicycle"** to see how a man solves a ghostly problem.

▲ Read **"The Cask of Amontillado"** to see how a man seeks revenge.

TEXAS Focus on the TEKS

Meet these standards with either **"Sonata for Harp and Bicycle"** (p. 46) or **"The Cask of Amontillado"** (p. 60).

Reading
(5)(A) Analyze non-linear plot development (e.g., foreshadowing). (Literary Analysis: Plot)

(1)(A) Determine the meaning of grade-level technical academic English words in multiple content areas derived from Latin affixes. (Word Power: Apply It)

Reading/Comprehension Skills
RC-9(A) Reflect on understanding to monitor comprehension (e.g., asking questions). (Reading Skill: Make Predictions)

Writing
(15)(A)(v) Write an analytical essay that includes relevant information. (Writing: Critique)

Listening and Speaking
(25) Give presentations using informal language effectively to meet the needs of audience, purpose, and occasion, employing eye contact, speaking rate, volume, enunciation, and purposeful gestures to communicate ideas effectively. (Listening and Speaking: Retelling)

Literary Analysis: Plot

Plot development is the sequence of events in a story. It is structured around a **conflict,** or problem, and it can be divided into these parts:

- **Exposition:** characters and setting are introduced
- **Rising Action:** central conflict begins
- **Climax:** high point of intensity in the conflict is reached
- **Falling Action:** conflict's intensity lessens
- **Resolution:** conflict concludes and loose ends are tied up

When writers reveal events in the order in which they occur, they are using **linear plot development.** If a section of a narrative interrupts the sequence of events, the writer has employed **non-linear plot development. Foreshadowing** is the use of clues to hint at events that will happen later in a story. Foreshadowing creates **suspense,** a feeling of tension.

As You Read Analyze **linear and non-linear plot development.** Make a list of details that may foreshadow future events in the story.

Reading Skill: Make Predictions

Monitor your comprehension by making and verifying predictions. A **prediction** is an idea you develop about what will happen later in a narrative. It is based on details in the text combined with your own experience. When reading, **make and verify predictions.** If a prediction turns out to be wrong, evaluate your reasoning by **asking questions:** *Did you misread details? Did the author purposely create false expectations in order to surprise you later in the story?*

Revise, or change, your prediction based on your evaluation.

Using the Strategy: Predictions Map

As You Read Use a map like this to reflect on your understanding. Monitor your comprehension by recording and analyzing your predictions.

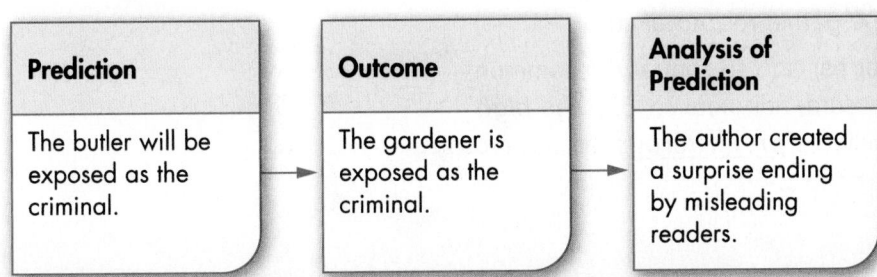

Prediction	Outcome	Analysis of Prediction
The butler will be exposed as the criminal.	The gardener is exposed as the criminal.	The author created a surprise ending by misleading readers.

TEXAS
PHLitOnline
www.PHLitOnline.com

Hear It!
- Selection summary audio
- Selection audio

See It!
- Get Connected video
- Background video
- More about the author
- Vocabulary flashcards

Do It!
- Interactive journals
- Interactive graphic organizers
- Self-test
- Internet activity
- Grammar tutorial
- Interactive vocabulary games

Can *truth* change?

Writing About the Big Question

In "**Sonata for Harp and Bicycle**," miscommunication leads to tragedy and a curse on a building. Use these sentence starters to develop your ideas about the Big Question:

You can change your own fate by _____.

Evidence can change our **beliefs** because _____.

As You Read Look for the ways the main character takes charge of his life to change the truth of his situation.

Vocabulary

Read each word and its definition. Decide whether you know the word well, know it a little bit, or do not know it at all. After you have read the selection, see how your knowledge of each word has increased.

- **encroaching** (en krōch´ iŋ) *adj.* intruding (p. 47) *The encroaching weeds are taking over the lawn.* encroach v. encroachment n.

- **tantalizingly** (tan´ tə līz´ iŋ lē) *adv.* in a teasing way (p. 48) *He held the ball tantalizingly out of reach.* tantalize v. tantalizing adj.

- **furtive** (fur´ tiv) *adj.* sneaky; hidden (p. 50) *With a furtive wink, he let his best friends in on the joke.* furtively adv.

- **menacing** (men´ əs iŋ) *adj.* threatening (p. 51) *The menacing cat stalked the little bird.* menace v. menace n.

- **reciprocate** (ri sip´ rə kāt´) *v.* return (p. 52) *Because Julio invited Mary to the party, she decided to reciprocate the offer by asking him to the game.* reciprocal adj.

- **preposterous** (prē päs´ tər əs) *adj.* so contrary to common sense as to be laughable; absurd; ridiculous (p. 53) *The high ticket prices for the show were preposterous.* preposterously adv.

Word Power

The Latin **suffix -*ate*** means "to become or form," and it often indicates the word is a verb.

In this story, the main character **reciprocates** the love of his admirer, forming a reciprocal or shared relationship.

Meet
Joan Aiken
(1924–2004)

Author of
Sonata for Harp and Bicycle

The daughter of an American poet, Conrad Aiken, and a Canadian mother, Jessie MacDonald, Joan Aiken was born in England and grew up there. She lived with her family in an eerie old house, an experience that helped foster her fascination with mystery and the unexplained. Her mother's second husband was another writer, Martin Armstrong. Not surprisingly, Aiken knew when she was very young that she would become a writer someday.

The "Family Trade" Aiken began writing when she was five and published her first story at sixteen. After spending some time working in London for a magazine, an advertising agency, and the United Nations, she decided to pursue what she called "the family trade." Her many literary works include novels, poems, plays, and stories for both children and adults.

BACKGROUND FOR THE ESSAY
Music Connection
Sonata

A sonata (sə nät′ ə) is a musical composition in several movements, or parts. Sonatas are often written for solo piano or for piano and another instrument. In titling her story "Sonata for Harp and Bicycle," Joan Aiken playfully suggests a musical structure that will, like a sequence of chords, be resolved harmoniously at the end.

Did You Know?
Aiken did not attend a school until she was twelve. Before then, she was taught at home.

Sonata for Harp and Bicycle

Joan Aiken

"No one is allowed to remain in the building after five o'clock," Mr. Manaby told his new assistant, showing him into the little room that was like the inside of a parcel.

"Why not?"

"Directorial policy," said Mr. Manaby. But that was not the real reason.

Gaunt and sooty, Grimes Buildings lurched up the side of a hill toward Clerkenwell.[1] Every little office within its dim and crumbling exterior owned one tiny crumb of light—such was the proud boast of the architect—but toward evening the crumbs were collected as by an immense vacuum cleaner, absorbed and demolished, yielding to an uncontrollable mass of dark that came tumbling in through windows and doors to take their place. Darkness infested the building like a flight of bats returning willingly to roost.

"Wash hands, please. Wash hands, please," the intercom began to bawl in the passages at a quarter to five. Without much need of prompting, the staff hustled like lemmings along the corridors to green- and blue-tiled washrooms that mocked with an illusion of cheerfulness the encroaching dusk.

"All papers into cases, please," the voice warned, five minutes later. "Look at your desks, ladies and gentlemen. Any documents left lying about? Kindly put them away. Desks must be left clear and tidy. Drawers must be shut."

A multitudinous shuffling, a rustling as of innumerable bluebottle flies might have been heard by the attentive

---

1. **Clerkenwell** district of London.

Vocabulary
encroaching
(en krōch´ iŋ) *adj.*
intruding

Reading Check

What is the new assistant told about being in the building after five o'clock?

ear after this injunction, as the employees of Moreton Wold and Company thrust their papers into cases, hurried letters and invoices into drawers, clipped statistical abstracts together and slammed them into filing cabinets, dropped discarded copy into wastepaper baskets. Two minutes later, and not a desk throughout Grimes Buildings bore more than its customary coating of dust.

"Hats and coats on, please. Hats and coats on, please. Did you bring an umbrella? Have you left any shopping on the floor?" At three minutes to five the homegoing throng was in the lifts[2] and on the stairs; a clattering, staccato-voiced flood darkened momentarily the great double doors of the building, and then as the first faint notes of St. Paul's[3] came echoing faintly on the frosty air, to be picked up near at hand by the louder chimes of St. Biddulph's-on-the-Wall, the entire premises of Moreton Wold stood empty.

"But why is it?" Jason Ashgrove, the new copywriter, asked his secretary one day. "Why are the staff herded out so fast? Not that I'm against it, mind you; I think it's an admirable idea in many ways, but there is the liberty of the individual to be considered, don't you think?"

"Hush!" Miss Golden, the secretary, gazed at him with large and terrified eyes. "You mustn't ask that sort of question. When you are taken onto the Established Staff you'll be told. Not before."

"But I want to know now," Jason said in discontent. "Do you know?"

"Yes, I do," Miss Golden answered tantalizingly. "Come on, or we shan't have finished the Oat Crisp layout by a quarter to." And she stared firmly down at the copy in front of her, lips folded, candyfloss hair falling over her face, lashes hiding eyes like peridots,[4] a girl with a secret.

Jason was annoyed. He rapped out a couple of rude and witty rhymes which Miss Golden let pass in a withering silence.

"What do you want for your birthday, Miss Golden? Sherry? Fudge? Bubble bath?"

"I want to go away with a clear conscience about Oat Crisps," Miss Golden retorted. It was not true; what she chiefly wanted was Mr. Jason Ashgrove, but he had not realized this yet.

"Come on, don't tease! I'm sure you haven't been on the Established Staff all that long," he coaxed her. "What happens when one is taken on, anyway? Does the Managing Director have us up for a confidential chat? Or are we given a little book called *The Awful Secret of Grimes Buildings?*"

---

2. **lifts** *n.* British term for elevators.
3. **St. Paul's** famous church in London.
4. **peridots** (per´ i däts´) *n.* yellowish-green gems.

Literary Analysis
Plot
What problem is introduced in Jason's conversation with Miss Golden?

Vocabulary
tantalizingly (tan´ tə līz´ iŋ lē) *adv.* in a teasing way

Miss Golden wasn't telling. She opened her drawer and took out a white towel and a cake of rosy soap.

"Wash hands, please! Wash hands, please!"

Jason was frustrated. "You'll be sorry," he said. "I shall do something desperate."

"Oh no, you mustn't!" Her eyes were large with fright. She ran from the room and was back within a couple of moments, still drying her hands.

"If I took you out for a coffee, couldn't you give me just a tiny hint?"

Side by side Miss Golden and Mr. Ashgrove ran along the green-floored passages, battled down the white marble stairs among the hundred other employees from the tenth floor, the nine hundred from the floors below.

He saw her lips move as she said something, but in the clatter of two thousand feet the words were lost.

"—fire escape," he heard, as they came into the momentary hush of the carpeted entrance hall. And "—it's to do with a bicycle. A bicycle and a harp."

"I don't understand."

Now they were in the street, chilly with the winter dusk smells of celery on carts, of swept-up leaves heaped in faraway parks, and cold layers of dew sinking among the withered evening primroses in the bombed areas. London lay about them wreathed in twilit mystery and fading against the barred and smoky sky. Like a ninth wave the sound of traffic overtook and swallowed them.

"Please tell me!"

But, shaking her head, she stepped onto a scarlet homebound bus and was borne away from him.

Jason stood undecided on the pavement, with the crowds dividing around him as around the pier of a bridge. He scratched his head, looked about him for guidance.

An ambulance clanged, a taxi hooted, a drill stuttered, a siren wailed on the river, a door slammed, a brake squealed, and close beside his ear a bicycle bell tinkled its tiny warning.

A bicycle, she had said. A bicycle and a harp.

Jason turned and stared at Grimes Buildings.

Somewhere, he knew, there was a back way in, a service entrance. He walked slowly past the main doors, with their tubs of

Reading Skill
Make Predictions
Which text clue leads you to predict that a romance will develop between Jason and Miss Golden? Explain.

Reading Check

What question does Jason Ashgrove want Miss Golden to answer?

furtive (fur´ tiv) *adj.*
sneaky; hidden

Literary Analysis
Plot
How do Jason's
actions increase the
suspense of the
narrative?

▼ **Critical Viewing**
What advantages would
patrolling corridors on a
bicycle offer as opposed
to patrolling on foot?
[Evaluate]

snowy chrysanthemums, and up Glass Street. A tiny furtive wedge
of darkness beckoned him, a snicket, a hacket, an alley carved into
the thickness of the building. It was so narrow that at any moment,
it seemed, the overtopping walls would come together and squeeze
it out of existence.

Walking as softly as an Indian, Jason passed through it, slid by
a file of dustbins,[5] and found the foot of the fire escape. Iron treads
rose into the mist, like an illustration to a Gothic[6] fairy tale.

He began to climb.

When he had mounted to the ninth story he paused for breath. It
was a lonely place. The lighting consisted of a dim bulb at the foot
of every flight. A well of gloom sank beneath him. The cold fingers
of the wind nagged and fluttered at the tails of his jacket, and he
pulled the string of the fire door and edged inside.

Grimes Buildings were triangular, with the street forming the
base of the triangle, and the fire escape the point. Jason could
see two long passages coming toward him, meeting at an acute
angle where he stood. He started down the left-hand one, tiptoeing
in the cavelike silence. Nowhere was there any sound, except for
the faraway drip of a tap. No night watchman would stay in the
building; none was needed. Burglars gave the place a wide berth.

Jason opened a door at random; then
another. Offices lay everywhere about him,
empty and forbidding. Some held lipstick-
stained tissues, spilled powder, and
orange peels; others were still foggy with
cigarette smoke. Here was a Director's
suite of rooms—a desk like half an acre
of frozen lake, inch-thick carpet, roses,
and the smell of cigars. Here
was a conference room
with scattered squares of
doodled blotting paper.
All equally empty.

He was not sure
when he first began
to notice the bell.
Telephone, he thought
at first, and then he
remembered that all
the outside lines were
disconnected at five. And

---

5. **dustbins** *n.* British term for garbage cans.
6. **Gothic** *adj.* mysterious.

this bell, anyway, had not the regularity of a telephone's double ring: there was a tinkle, and then silence; a long ring, and then silence; a whole volley of rings together, and then silence.

Jason stood listening, and fear knocked against his ribs and shortened his breath. He knew that he must move or be paralyzed by it. He ran up a flight of stairs and found himself with two more endless green corridors beckoning him like a pair of dividers.

Another sound now: a waft of ice-thin notes, riffling up an arpeggio[7] like a flurry of snowflakes. Far away down the passage it echoed. Jason ran in pursuit, but as he ran the music receded. He circled the building, but it always outdistanced him, and when he came back to the stairs he heard it fading away to the story below.

He hesitated, and as he did so heard again the bell; the bicycle bell. It was approaching him fast, bearing down on him, urgent, menacing. He could hear the pedals, almost see the shimmer of an invisible wheel. Absurdly, he was reminded of the insistent clamor of an ice-cream vendor, summoning children on a sultry Sunday afternoon.

There was a little fireman's alcove beside him, with buckets and pumps. He hurled himself into it. The bell stopped beside him, and then there was a moment while his heart tried to shake itself loose in his chest. He was looking into two eyes carved out of expressionless air; he was held by two hands knotted together out of the width of dark.

"Daisy, Daisy?" came the whisper. "Is that you, Daisy? Have you come to give me your answer?"

Jason tried to speak, but no words came.

"It's not Daisy! Who are you?" The sibilants[8] were full of threat. "You can't stay here. This is private property."

He was thrust along the corridor. It was like being pushed by a whirlwind—the fire door opened ahead of him without a touch, and he was on the openwork platform, clutching the slender railing. Still the hands would not let him go.

"How about it?" the whisper mocked him. "How about jumping? It's an easy death compared with some."

Jason looked down into the smoky void. The darkness nodded to him like a familiar.[9]

"You wouldn't be much loss, would you? What have you got to live for?"

Literary Analysis
Plot
What earlier details foreshadowed this mysterious ringing?

Vocabulary
menacing (men´ əs iŋ) *adj.* threatening

> *He hesitated, and as he did so heard again the bell; the bicycle bell.*

Reading Check

What makes the ringing sound that Jason hears inside the Grimes Buildings?

---

7. arpeggio (är pej´ ō) *n.* notes of a chord played one after the other instead of together.
8. sibilants (sib´ əl əntz) *n.* hissing sounds.
9. a familiar *n.* a spirit.

Miss Golden, Jason thought. She would miss me. And the syllables Berenice Golden lingered in the air like a chime. Drawing on some unknown deposit of courage he shook himself loose from the holding hands and ran down the fire escape without looking back.

Next morning when Miss Golden, crisp, fragrant, and punctual, shut the door of Room 492 behind her, she stopped short of the hat-pegs with a horrified gasp.

"Mr. Ashgrove, your hair!"

"It makes me look more distinguished, don't you think?" he said.

It had indeed this effect, for his impeccable dark cut had turned to a stippled silver which might have been envied by many a diplomat.

▶ Critical Viewing
The harp is an important part of this mystery. Describe the sound you think this instrument would make.
[Speculate]

"How did it happen? You've not—" her voice sank to a whisper—"you've not been in Grimes Buildings after dark?"

"Miss Golden—Berenice," he said earnestly. "Who was Daisy? Plainly you know. Tell me the story."

"Did you see him?" she asked faintly.

"Him?"

"William Heron—The Wailing Watchman. Oh," she exclaimed in terror, "I can see you did. Then you are doomed—doomed!"

"If I'm doomed," said Jason, "let's have coffee, and you tell me the story quickly."

"It all happened over fifty years ago," said Berenice, as she spooned out coffee powder with distracted extravagance. "Heron was the night watchman in this building, patrolling the corridors from dusk to dawn every night on his bicycle. He fell in love with a Miss Bell who taught the harp. She rented a room—this room—and gave lessons in it. She began to reciprocate his love, and they used to share a picnic supper every night at eleven, and she'd stay on a while to keep him company. It was an idyll,[10] among the fire buckets and the furnace pipes.

Vocabulary
reciprocate (ri sip´ rə kāt´) v. return

10.idyll (ī´ dəl) n. romantic scene, usually in the country.

"On Halloween he had summoned up the courage to propose to her. The day before he had told her he was going to ask her a very important question, and he came to the Buildings with a huge bunch of roses and a bottle of wine. But Miss Bell never turned up.

"The explanation was simple. Miss Bell, of course, had been losing a lot of sleep through her nocturnal romance, and so she used to take a nap in her music room between seven and ten, to save going home. In order to make sure that she would wake up, she persuaded her father, a distant relative of Graham Bell,[11] to attach an alarm-waking fixture to her telephone which called her every night at ten. She was too modest and shy to let Heron know that she spent those hours in the building, and to give him the pleasure of waking her himself.

"Alas! On this important evening the line failed, and she never woke up. The telephone was in its infancy at that time, you must remember.

"Heron waited and waited. At last, mad with grief and jealousy, having called her home and discovered that she was not there, he concluded that she had betrayed him; he ran to the fire escape, and cast himself off it, holding the roses and the bottle of wine.

"Daisy did not long survive him but pined away soon after. Since that day their ghosts have haunted Grimes Buildings, he vainly patrolling the corridors on his bicycle, she playing her harp in the room she rented. But they never meet. And anyone who meets the ghost of William Heron will himself, within five days, leap down from the same fatal fire escape."

She gazed at him with tragic eyes.

"In that case we must lose no time," said Jason, and he enveloped her in an embrace as prompt as it was ardent. Looking down at the gossamer hair sprayed across his pin-stripe, he added, "Just the same it is a preposterous situation. Firstly, I have no intention of jumping off the fire escape—" here, however, he repressed a shudder as he remembered the cold, clutching hands of the evening before—"and secondly, I find it quite nonsensical that those two inefficient ghosts have spent fifty years in this building without coming across each other. We must remedy the matter, Berenice. We must not begrudge our new-found happiness to others."

He gave her another kiss so impassioned that the electric typewriter against which they were leaning began chattering to itself in a frenzy of enthusiasm.

He fell in love with a Miss Bell who taught the harp.

Literary Analysis
Plot
How does this new information foreshadow later events and increase the suspense of the narrative?

Reading Skill
Make Predictions
What do you think Jason might do to "remedy the matter"?

Vocabulary
preposterous (prē päs´ tər əs) *adj.* so contrary to common sense as to be laughable; absurd; ridiculous

Reading Check
According to Berenice, what happens to anyone who meets the ghost of William Heron?

---

11. Graham Bell Alexander Graham Bell (1847–1922), the inventor of the telephone.

"This very evening," he went on, looking at his watch, "we will put matters right for that unhappy couple and then, if I really have only five more days to live, which I don't for one moment believe, we will proceed to spend them together, my bewitching Berenice, in the most advantageous manner possible."

She nodded, spellbound.

"Can you work a switchboard?" he added. She nodded again. "My love, you are perfection itself. Meet me in the switchboard room then, at ten this evening. I would say, have dinner with me, but I shall need to make one or two purchases and see an old R.A.F.[12] friend. You will be safe from Heron's curse in the switchboard room if he always keeps to the corridors."

"I would rather meet him and die with you," she murmured.

"My angel, I hope that won't be necessary. Now," he said, sighing, "I suppose we should get down to our day's work."

Strangely enough the copy they wrote that day, although engendered from such agitated minds, sold more packets of Oat Crisps than any other advertising matter before or since.

That evening when Jason entered Grimes Buildings he was carrying two bottles of wine, two bunches of red roses, and a large canvas-covered bundle. Miss Golden, who had concealed herself in the switchboard room before the offices closed for the night, eyed these things with surprise.

"Now," said Jason, after he had greeted her, "I want you first to ring our own extension."

"No one will reply, surely?"

"I think she will reply."

Sure enough, when Berenice rang Extension 170 a faint, sleepy voice, distant and yet clear, whispered, "Hullo?"

"Is that Miss Bell?"

"Yes."

Berenice went a little pale. Her eyes sought Jason's and, prompted by him, she said formally, "Switchboard here, Miss Bell. Your ten o'clock call."

"Thank you," the faint voice said. There was a click and the line went blank.

"Excellent," Jason remarked. He unfastened his package and slipped its straps over his shoulders. "Now plug into the intercom."

Berenice did so, and then said, loudly and clearly, "Attention. Night watchman on duty, please. Night watchman on duty. You have

Reading Skill
Make Predictions
What do you predict Jason will do with the two bunches of roses? Why?

---

12. **R.A.F.** Royal Air Force.

an urgent summons to Room 492. You have an urgent summons to Room 492." The intercom echoed and reverberated through the empty corridors, then coughed itself to silence.

"Now we must run. You take the roses, sweetheart, and I'll carry the bottles."

Together they raced up eight flights of stairs and along the passages to Room 492. As they neared the door a burst of music met them—harp music swelling out, sweet and triumphant. Jason took a bunch of roses from Berenice, opened the door a little way, and gently deposited them, with a bottle, inside the door. As he closed it again Berenice said breathlessly, "Did you see anyone?"

"No," he said. "The room was too full of music." She saw that his eyes were shining.

They stood hand in hand, reluctant to move away, waiting for they hardly knew what. Suddenly the door opened again. Neither Berenice nor Jason, afterward, would speak of what they saw but each was left with a memory, bright as the picture on a Salvador Dali[13] calendar, of a bicycle bearing on its saddle a harp, a bottle of wine, and a bouquet of red roses, sweeping improbably down the corridor and far, far away.

---

13. **Salvador Dali** (sal′ və dôr′ dä′ lē) (1904–1989) modern artist famous for his unusual pictures.

Reading Check
What is Jason carrying as he enters the Grimes Buildings?

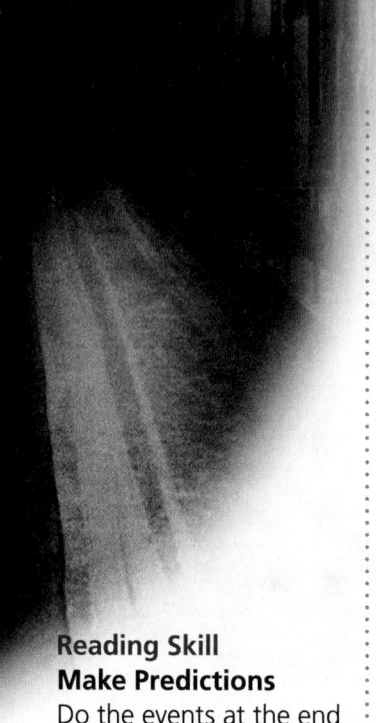

"We can go now," Jason said.

He led Berenice to the fire door, tucking the bottle of Médoc in his jacket pocket. A black wind from the north whistled beneath them as they stood on the openwork platform, looking down.

"We don't want our evening to be spoiled by the thought of a curse hanging over us," he said, "so this is the practical thing to do. Hang onto the roses." And holding his love firmly, Jason pulled the rip cord of his R.A.F. friend's parachute and leaped off the fire escape.

A bridal shower of rose petals adorned the descent of Miss Golden, who was possibly the only girl to be kissed in midair in the district of Clerkenwell at ten minutes to midnight on Halloween.

Reading Skill
Make Predictions
Do the events at the end of the story verify your predictions? Why or why not?

Critical Thinking

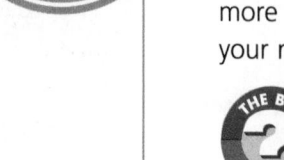

Support your responses with evidence from the text.

1. **Respond:** If you were Jason, would you try to solve the mystery of the Grimes Buildings? Explain.

2. **(a)** What three important objects does Miss Golden mention to Jason as they leave the Grimes Buildings at five o'clock?
   (b) Connect: How does he use this information?

3. **(a)** What physical change has happened to Jason that Miss Golden sees the next day? **(b) Analyze:** What evidence suggests that his encounter in the closed building has caused the change?

4. **(a)** What actions does Jason take to avoid the curse that awaits those who see Heron's ghost? **(b) Make Inferences:** Who is more concerned about the curse—Jason or Miss Golden? Support your response with evidence from the story.

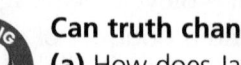

Can truth change?
(a) How does Jason react to the news of the curse?
(b) How do his actions help change the "truth"?

After You Read

Sonata for Harp and Bicycle

Literary Analysis: **Plot**

1. Using a chart like this one, identify two key events in the **rising action,** one that marks the **climax,** and two in the **falling action.** Trade charts with a partner and discuss why you chose these events.

2. (a) Identify a detail that **foreshadows** Jason's decision to enter the building after hours. **(b)** Analyze that event and explain why Aiken may have chosen to include this foreshadowing clue.

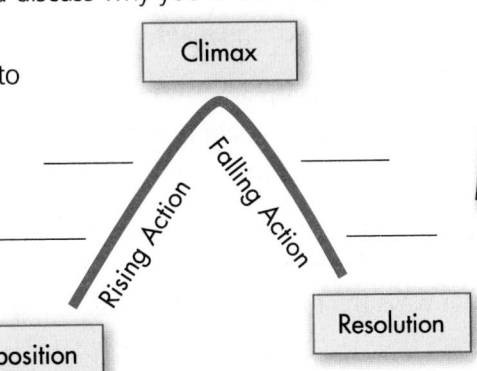

Reading Skill: **Make Predictions**

3. (a) What **questions** did you ask when Jason entered the Grimes Buildings after closing and heard a bicycle bell? **(b)** What **prediction** did you make at this point the story?

4. Was your prediction **verified** by later story events? Explain.

Vocabulary

Practice An **analogy** shows the relationship between pairs of words. Use a word from the vocabulary list on page 44 to complete each analogy. For each case, your choice should create a word pair that matches the relationship between the first two words.

1. angry : shout :: _____ : whisper
2. steal : take :: _____ : give
3. hopelessly : far :: _____ : near
4. ending : concluding :: _____ : infringing
5. criticizing : praising :: _____ : comforting
6. funny : serious :: _____ : reasonable

Word Power Use the context of the sentences and what you know about the **suffix -ate** to explain your answer to each question.

1. What does someone do if they *participate* in an activity?
2. If a question is *complicated*, is it easy?

Word Power

The **suffix -*ate*** means "to become or form."

Apply It Explain how the Latin suffix -*ate* helps you determine the meanings of these technical academic words from social studies and science. Use a dictionary if necessary.

evaporate
immigrate
incorporate

Can *truth* change?

Writing About the Big Question

In "The Cask of Amontillado," a wronged man seeks revenge. Use these sentence starters to develop your ideas about the Big Question.

The **truth** about a person can be discovered when _____.

It can either be **verified** by _____ or **distorted** by _____.

(As You Read) Look for the ways the main character takes charge of his life.

Vocabulary

Read each word and its definition. Decide whether you know the word well, know it a little bit, or do not know it at all. After you have read the selection, see how your knowledge of each word has increased.

- **precluded** (prē klōōd′ id) *v.* prevented (p. 61) *When his injury precluded any chance of victory, the fans lost hope.* preclude *v.* include *v.*

- **retribution** (re′ trə byōō′ shən) *n.* payback; punishment for a misdeed (p. 61) *He wanted retribution for an insult he had received.* tribute *n.*

- **afflicted** (ə flikt′ əd) *v.* suffering or sickened (p. 63) *The old man was afflicted with a rare type of pneumonia.* affliction *n.* afflict *v.*

- **explicit** (eks plis′ it) *adj.* clearly stated (p. 63) *I could not ignore her explicit refusal.* explicate *v.*

- **recoiling** (ri koil′ iŋ) *v.* staggering back (p. 65) *Wendy, recoiling in horror, shrieked at the rattlesnake in her path.* recoil *v.* recoil *n.*

- **subsided** (səb sīd′ əd) *v.* settled down; became less active or intense (p. 67) *As we walked away from the beach, the sound of the waves subsided.* subside *v.* subsidiary *n.*

Word Power

The Latin **suffix -*tion*** means "the act of." It usually indicates the word is a noun.

In this story, the main character seeks **retribution**, or the act of revenge.

Meet
Edgar Allan Poe
(1809–1849)

Author of
The Cask of Amontillado

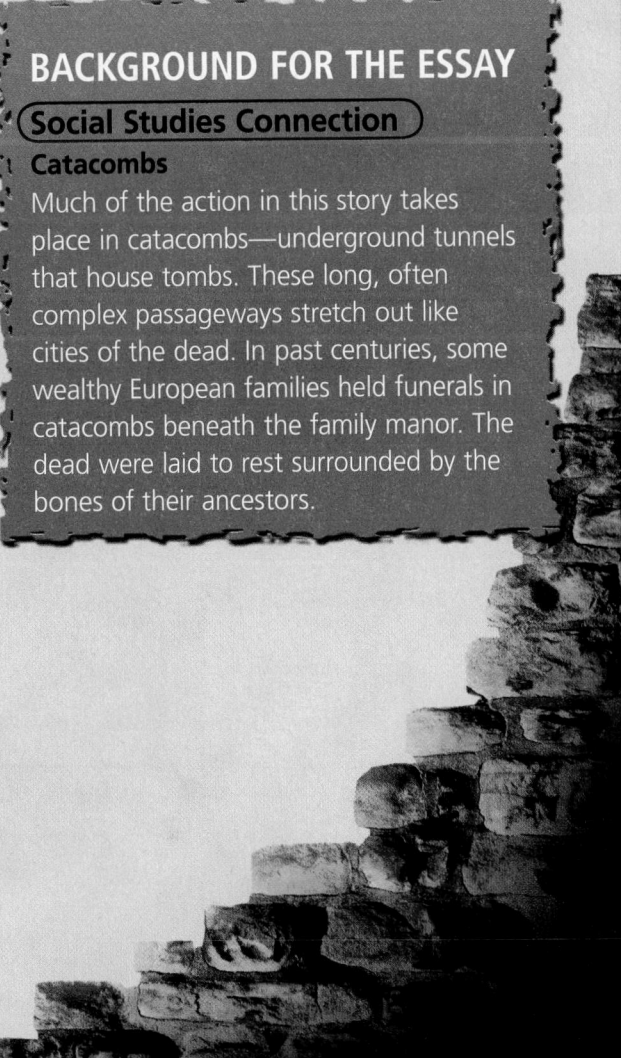

One of the first great American storytellers, Edgar Allan Poe made the most of a short, tragic life. Orphaned at the age of three, Poe was raised by foster parents, the Allans, from whom he took his middle name. The Allans were good to Poe and gave him an education, but he had to leave college when his foster father refused to pay Poe's gambling debts. Poe found some happiness when he married Virginia Clemm. However, her early death from tuberculosis in 1847 caused Poe to become increasingly antisocial. In 1849, he was discovered in a delirious condition on a Baltimore street, and three days later he was dead.

An Inspiration to Later Generations
Like few others, Poe blazed trails for future writers. His work helped to define the short story, and his dark imagination helped establish the genre of horror literature now popularized by writers like Stephen King.

BACKGROUND FOR THE ESSAY
(Social Studies Connection)
Catacombs
Much of the action in this story takes place in catacombs—underground tunnels that house tombs. These long, often complex passageways stretch out like cities of the dead. In past centuries, some wealthy European families held funerals in catacombs beneath the family manor. The dead were laid to rest surrounded by the bones of their ancestors.

Did You Know?
Poe invented the genre of the detective story with his tale "The Murders in the Rue Morgue."

The Cask of Amontillado [1]

Edgar Allan Poe

The thousand injuries of Fortunato I had borne as I best could, but when he ventured upon insult I vowed revenge. You, who so well know the nature of my soul, will not suppose, however, that I gave utterance to a threat. At *length* I would be avenged; this was a point definitely settled—but the very definitiveness with which it was resolved precluded the idea of risk. I must not only punish but punish with impunity.[2] A wrong is unredressed when retribution overtakes its redresser. It is equally unredressed when the avenger fails to make himself felt as such to him who has done the wrong.

It must be understood that neither by word nor deed had I given Fortunato cause to doubt my good will. I continued, as was my wont, to smile in his face, and he did not perceive that my smile *now* was at the thought of his immolation.[3]

---

1. **Amontillado** (ə män′ tə ya′ dō) *n.* a pale, dry sherry.
2. **impunity** (im pyōō′ nə tē′) *n.* freedom from consequences.
3. **immolation** (im′ ə lā′ shən) *n.* destruction.

Vocabulary
precluded (prē klōōd′ id) *v.* prevented
retribution (re′ trə byōō′ shən) *n.* payback; punishment for a misdeed

Reading Check
Why does the narrator vow revenge on Fortunato?

Reading Skill
Make Predictions
What role do you predict Fortunato's "weak point" will play in the narrator's revenge?

He had a weak point—this Fortunato—although in other regards he was a man to be respected and even feared. He prided himself on his connoisseurship[4] in wine. Few Italians have the true virtuoso[5] spirit. For the most part their enthusiasm is adopted to suit the time and opportunity, to practice imposture upon the British and Austrian millionaires. In painting and gemmary, Fortunato, like his countrymen, was a quack, but in the matter of old wines he was sincere. In this respect I did not differ from him materially; I was skillful in the Italian vintages myself, and bought largely whenever I could.

It was about dusk, one evening during the supreme madness of the carnival season, that I encountered my friend. He accosted me with excessive warmth, for he had been drinking much. The man wore motley.[6] He had on a tight-fitting parti-striped dress, and his head was surmounted by the conical cap and bells. I was so pleased to see him that I thought I should never have done wringing his hand.

I said to him, "My dear Fortunato, you are luckily met. How remarkably well you are looking today. But I have received a pipe[7] of what passes for Amontillado, and I have my doubts."

"How?" said he. "Amontillado? A pipe? Impossible! And in the middle of the carnival!"

"I have my doubts," I replied: "and I was silly enough to pay the full Amontillado price without consulting you in the matter. You were not to be found, and I was fearful of losing a bargain."

"Amontillado!"

"I have my doubts."

"Amontillado!"

"And I must satisfy them."

"Amontillado!"

"As you are engaged, I am on my way to Luchesi. If any one has a critical turn it is he. He will tell me—"

"Luchesi cannot tell Amontillado from sherry."

"And yet some fools will have it that his taste is a match for your own."

"Come, let us go."

---

4. **connoisseurship** (kän´ ə sʉr´ ship) *n.* expert judgment.
5. **virtuoso** (vʉr´ choo ō´ sō) *adj.* masterly skill in a particular field.
6. **motley** (mät´ lē) *n.* a clown's multicolored costume.
7. **pipe** (pīp) *n.* large barrel, holding approximately 126 gallons.

"Whither?"

"To your vaults."

"My friend, no; I will not impose upon your good nature. I perceive you have an engagement. Luchesi—"

"I have no engagement—come."

"My friend, no. It is not the engagement, but the severe cold with which I perceive you are afflicted. The vaults are insufferably damp. They are encrusted with niter."

"Let us go, nevertheless. The cold is merely nothing. Amontillado! You have been imposed upon. And as for Luchesi, he cannot distinguish sherry from Amontillado."

Thus speaking, Fortunato possessed himself of my arm; and putting on a mask of black silk and drawing a *roquelaure*[8] closely about my person, I suffered him to hurry me to my palazzo.

There were no attendants at home; they had absconded to make merry in honor of the time. I had told them that I should not return until the morning, and had given them explicit orders not to stir from the house. These orders were sufficient, I well knew, to insure their immediate disappearance, one and all, as soon as my back was turned.

I took from their sconces two flambeaux, and giving one to Fortunato, bowed him through several suites of rooms to the archway that led into the vaults. I passed down a long and winding staircase, requesting him to be cautious as he followed. We came at length to the foot of the descent, and stood together upon the damp ground of the catacombs of the Montresors.

The gait of my friend was unsteady, and the bells upon his cap jingled as he strode.

"The pipe," he said.

"It is farther on," said I; "but observe the white webwork which gleams from these cavern walls."

He turned towards me, and looked into my eyes with two filmy orbs that distilled the rheum of intoxication.

"Niter?" he asked, at length.

"Niter," I replied. "How long have you had that cough?"

---

8. *roquelaure* (räk´ ə lôr) *n.* knee-length cloak.

Vocabulary
afflicted (ə flikt´ əd) *v.* suffering or sickened

Vocabulary
explicit (eks plis´ it) *adj.* clearly stated

It was about dusk, one evening during the supreme madness of the carnival season, that I encountered my friend.

Reading Check
What common interest does the narrator share with Fortunato?

"Ugh! ugh! ugh!—ugh! ugh! ugh!—ugh! ugh! ugh!—ugh! ugh! ugh!—ugh! ugh! ugh!"

My poor friend found it impossible to reply for many minutes.

"It is nothing," he said, at last.

"Come," I said, with decision, "we will go back; your health is precious. You are rich, respected, admired, beloved; you are happy, as once I was. You are a man to be missed. For me it is no matter. We will go back; you will be ill, and I cannot be responsible. Besides, there is Luchesi—"

"Enough," he said; "the cough is a mere nothing; it will not kill me. I shall not die of a cough."

"True—true," I replied; "and, indeed, I had no intention of alarming you unnecessarily—but you should use all proper caution. A draft of this Médoc will defend us from the damps."

Here I knocked off the neck of a bottle which I drew from a long row of its fellows that lay upon the mold.

"Drink," I said, presenting him the wine.

He raised it to his lips with a leer. He paused and nodded to me familiarly, while his bells jingled.

"I drink," he said "to the buried that repose around us."

"And I to your long life."

He again took my arm, and we proceeded.

"These vaults," he said, "are extensive."

"The Montresors," I replied, "were a great and numerous family."

"I forget your arms."

"A huge human foot d'or, in a field azure; the foot crushes a serpent rampant whose fangs are imbedded in the heel."

"And the motto?"

"*Nemo me impune lacessit.*"[9]

"Good!" he said.

The wine sparkled in his eyes and the bells jingled. My own fancy grew warm with the Médoc. We had passed through long walls of piled skeletons, with casks and puncheons[10] intermingling, into the inmost recesses of the catacombs. I paused again, and this time I made bold to seize Fortunato by an arm above the elbow.

---

9. ***Nemo me impune lacessit*** Latin for "No one attacks me with impunity."
10. **puncheons** (pun′ chənz) *n.* large barrels.

Literary Analysis
Plot
What fate does this conversation foreshadow for Fortunato?

▼ **Casks for storing wine**

"The niter!" I said; "see, it increases. It hangs like moss upon the vaults. We are below the river's bed. The drops of moisture trickle among the bones. Come, we will go back ere it is too late. Your cough—"

"It is nothing," he said; "let us go on. But first, another draft of the Médoc."

I broke and reached him a flagon of De Grâve. He emptied it at a breath. His eyes flashed with a fierce light. He laughed and threw the bottle upwards with a gesticulation I did not understand.

I looked at him in surprise. He repeated the movement—a grotesque one.

"You do not comprehend?" he said.

"Not I," I replied.

"Then you are not of the brotherhood."

"How?"

"You are not of the masons."[11]

"Yes, yes," I said; "yes, yes."

"You? Impossible! A mason?"

"A mason," I replied.

"A sign," he said, "a sign."

"It is this," I answered, producing from beneath the folds of my *roquelaure* a trowel.

"You jest," he exclaimed, recoiling a few paces. "But let us proceed to the Amontillado."

"Be it so," I said, replacing the tool beneath the cloak and again offering him my arm. He leaned upon it heavily. We continued our route in search of the Amontillado. We passed through a range of low arches, descended, passed on, and descending again, arrived at a deep crypt, in which the foulness of the air caused our flambeaux rather to glow than flame.

At the most remote end of the crypt there appeared another less spacious. Its walls had been lined with human remains,

---

11. **masons** *n.* the Freemasons, an international secret society.

Literature Connection

Poe and the Gothic Tradition

The literary genre known as gothic fiction emerged in England in the late 1700s in works like *Castle of Otranto* (1765) by Horace Walpole and *The Mysteries of Udolpho* (1794) by Ann Radcliffe. The word *gothic* was originally used to describe a style of building that was common in the late Middle Ages. To writers in the eighteenth century, the cold chambers and secret passages of such buildings suggested mystery and dark tales of vengeance and passion.

Edgar Allan Poe translated the imagery and atmosphere of British gothic fiction to an American landscape, pioneering an American gothic tradition. Contemporary writers like Stephen King and Anne Rice, as well as countless filmmakers, carry on that tradition today.

Connect to the Literature

What qualities of gothic fiction do you find in "The Cask of Amontillado"? Explain.

Vocabulary
recoiling (ri koil´ iŋ) *v.* staggering back

Reading Check

Where does Montresor bring Fortunato?

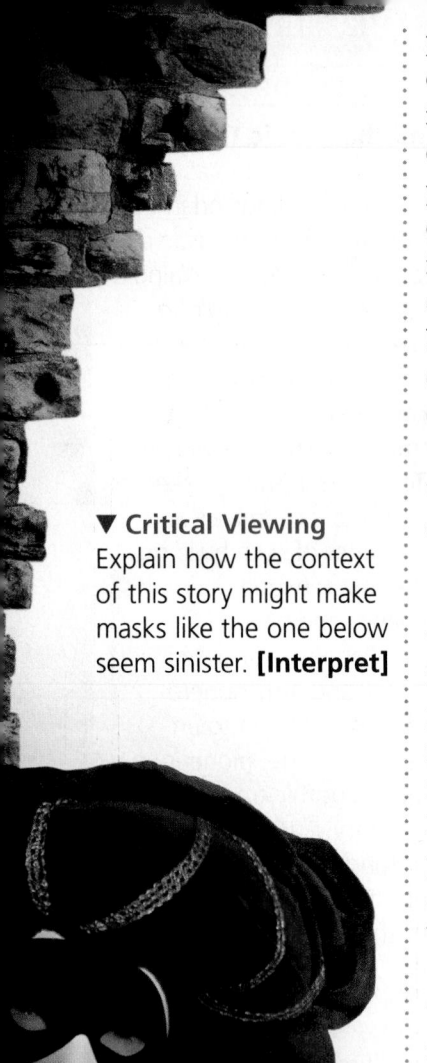

▼ **Critical Viewing**
Explain how the context of this story might make masks like the one below seem sinister. **[Interpret]**

piled to the vault overhead, in the fashion of the great catacombs of Paris. Three sides of this interior crypt were still ornamented in this manner. From the fourth side the bones had been thrown down, and lay promiscuously upon the earth, forming at one point a mound of some size. Within the wall thus exposed by the displacing of the bones, we perceived a still interior crypt or recess, in depth about four feet, in width three, in height six or seven. It seemed to have been constructed for no especial use within itself, but formed merely the *interval* between two of the colossal supports of the roof of the catacombs, and was backed by one of their circumscribing walls of solid granite.

It was in vain that Fortunato, uplifting his dull torch, endeavored to pry into the depth of the recess. Its termination the feeble light did not enable us to see.

"Proceed," I said: "herein is the Amontillado. As for Luchesi—"

"He is an ignoramus," interrupted my friend, as he stepped unsteadily forward, while I followed immediately at his heels. In an instant he had reached the extremity of the niche, and finding his progress arrested by the rock, stood stupidly bewildered. A moment more and I had fettered him to the granite. In its surface were two iron staples, distant from each other about two feet, horizontally. From one of these depended a short chain, from the other a padlock. Throwing the links about his waist, it was but the work of a few seconds to secure it. He was too much astounded to resist. Withdrawing the key I stepped back from the recess.

"Pass your hand," I said, "over the wall; you cannot help feeling the niter. Indeed, it is very damp. Once more let me implore you to return. No? Then I must positively leave you. But I must first render you all the little attentions in my power."

"The Amontillado!" ejaculated my friend, not yet recovered from his astonishment.

"True," I replied; "the Amontillado."

As I said these words I busied myself among the pile of bones of which I have before spoken. Throwing them aside, I soon uncovered a quantity of building stone and mortar. With these materials and with the aid of my trowel, I began vigorously to wall up the entrance of the niche.

I had scarcely laid the first tier of the masonry when I discovered that the intoxication of Fortunato had in a great measure worn off. The earliest indication I had of this was a low moaning cry from the depth of the recess. It was not the cry of a drunken man. There was then a long and obstinate silence. I laid the second tier, and the third, and the fourth; and then I heard the furious vibrations of the chain. The noise lasted for several minutes, during which, that I might hearken to it with the more satisfaction, I ceased my labors and sat down upon the bones. When at last the clanking subsided, I resumed the trowel, and finished without interruption the fifth, the sixth, and the seventh tier. The wall was now nearly upon a level with my breast. I again paused, and holding the flambeaux over the masonwork, threw a few feeble rays upon the figure within.

A succession of loud and shrill screams, bursting suddenly from the throat of the chained form, seemed to thrust me violently back. For a brief moment I hesitated, I trembled. Unsheathing my rapier, I began to grope with it about the recess; but the thought of an instant reassured me. I placed my hand upon the solid fabric of the catacombs, and felt satisfied. I reapproached the wall; I replied to the yells of him who clamored. I reechoed, I aided, I surpassed them in volume and in strength. I did this, and the clamorer grew still.

It was now midnight, and my task was drawing to a close. I had completed the eighth, the ninth, and the tenth tier. I had finished a portion of the last and the eleventh; there remained but a single stone to be fitted and plastered in. I struggled with its weight; I placed it partially in its destined position. But now there came from out the niche a low laugh that erected the hairs upon my head. It was succeeded by a sad voice, which I had difficulty in recognizing as that of the noble Fortunato. The voice said—

"Ha! ha! ha!—he! he! he!—a very good joke, indeed—an excellent jest. We will have many a rich laugh about it at the palazzo—he! he! he!—over our wine—he! he! he!"

"The Amontillado!" I said.

"He! he! he!—he! he! he!—yes, the Amontillado. But is it not getting late? Will not they be awaiting us at the palazzo, the Lady Fortunato and the rest? Let us be gone."

"Yes," I said, "let us be gone."

"For the love of God, Montresor!"

Vocabulary
subsided (səb sīd´ əd) *v.*
settled down; became less active or intense

Reading Skill
Make Predictions
Does this scene in which Montresor imprisons Fortunato verify your earlier predictions? Explain.

Reading Check
How does Fortunado become locked in the chains so easily?

It was now midnight, and my task was drawing to a close.

"Yes," I said, "for the love of God!"

But to these words I hearkened in vain for a reply. I grew impatient. I called aloud—

"Fortunato!"

No answer. I called again—

"Fortunato!"

No answer still. I thrust a torch through the remaining aperture and let it fall within. There came forth in return only a jingling of the bells. My heart grew sick; it was the dampness of the catacombs that made it so. I hastened to make an end of my labor. I forced the last stone into its position; I plastered it up. Against the new masonry I reerected the old rampart of bones. For the half of a century no mortal has disturbed them. *In pace requiescat!*[12]

12. *In pace requiescat!* Latin for "May he rest in peace!"

Critical Thinking

Support your responses with evidence from the text.

1. **Respond:** At what point in the story do you find Montresor most disturbing? Explain.

2. **(a)** How does Montresor describe Fortunato's strengths and weaknesses early in the story? **(b) Analyze:** Which character traits make Fortunato easy prey for Montresor?

3. **(a)** What specific steps does Montresor take to ensure that his plan works? **(b) Interpret:** Why does Montresor keep urging Fortunato to turn back?

4. **(a) Support:** Why does Montresor feel he has the right to punish Fortunato? **(b) Assess:** Does Montresor express any regret or ever question whether this punishment is fair, just, or rational?
(c) Draw Conclusions: What does your answer tell you about Montresor's character?

Can truth change?
Montresor acts as both victim and judge in this story. Do you think that Montresor sees the truth and acts appropriately? Explain.

Literary Analysis: Plot

1. Using a chart like this one, identify two key events in the **rising action,** one that marks the **climax,** and two in the **falling action.** Trade charts with a partner and discuss why you chose these events.

2. (a) Identify a statement or event that **foreshadows** Fortunato's fate. **(b)** Analyze that event and explain why Poe may have chosen to include this foreshadowing clue.

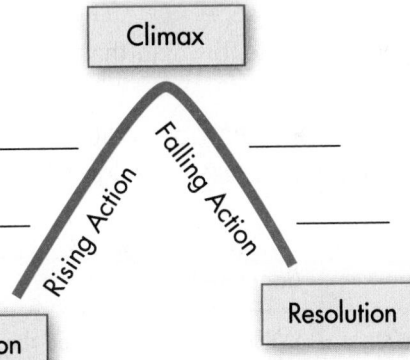

Climax

Rising Action

Falling Action

Resolution

Exposition

Reading Skill: Make Predictions

3. (a) What **questions** did you ask after reading about Montresor's and Fortunato's shared interest in wine? **(b)** What **prediction** did you make based on this information? **(c)** What details helped you make your prediction?

4. Was your prediction **verified** by later story events? Explain.

Vocabulary

Practice An **analogy** shows the relationship between pairs of words. Use a word from the vocabulary list on page 58 to complete each analogy. For each case, your choice should create a word pair that matches the relationship between the first two words.

1. conversation: dialogue :: _____ : revenge

2. harmed : helped :: _____ : allowed

3. delicious : food :: _____ : instructions

4. graceful : awkward :: _____ : increased

5. humor : laughing :: disgust : _____

6. enormous : gigantic :: troubled : _____

Word Power Use the context of the sentences and what you know about the **suffix -tion** to explain your answer to each question.

1. What is audience *participation?*

2. If you make a *contribution* to a cause, what have you done?

Word Power

The **suffix -tion** means "the act of."

Apply It Explain how the Latin suffix *-tion* helps you determine the meanings of these technical academic words from science and social studies. Use a dictionary if necessary.

conservation
compensation
nationalization

Integrated Language Skills

Sonata for Harp and Bicycle •
The Cask of Amontillado

Conventions: Abstract and Concrete Nouns

A **concrete noun** names a person, place, or thing that can be seen or recognized through any of the five senses.

An **abstract noun** names an idea, an action, a condition, or a quality—something that cannot be recognized through the senses.

Abstract Noun	Concrete Noun
Fortunato discovered Montresor's *intention,* but it was too late.	William Heron patrolled the halls on a *bicycle.*

Practice A Tell whether the underlined word in each sentence is a concrete noun or an abstract noun. Then, use the word in an original sentence about the story.

1. Mr. Manaby instructed Jason, the new <u>assistant</u>, to leave at five.
2. What went on in the building after five was a <u>mystery</u> to Jason.
3. He did not seem to have <u>fear</u> of the curse.
4. He wanted to know why he could not stay later at the <u>office</u>.
5. He found answers by taking a tremendous <u>risk</u>.

Reading Application In "Sonata for Harp and Bicycle," find one sentence with a concrete noun and one with an abstract noun.

Practice B Identify an abstract and a concrete noun in each sentence. Then, use one of the words in an original sentence.

1. Montresor held vengeance in his heart.
2. He lured Fortunato to the catacombs with a falsehood.
3. The men were supposedly on the search for a cask of wine.
4. Instead, Fortunato met a horrid fate in a remote crypt.
5. Montresor felt no remorse after placing the chain around Fortunato.

Writing Application Using these two sentences as models, write two more sentences that follow the pattern of presenting and describing nouns: *The wine sparkled in his eyes and bells jingled. The joy glowed on his face and his keys jangled.*

PH **GRAMMAR HANDBOOK** Further instruction and practice are available in the *Prentice Hall Grammar Handbook.*

Writing

Each of these stories presents readers with a compelling plot. Write a **critique** analyzing and evaluating the suspense and the ending of either "Sonata for Harp and Bicycle" or "The Cask of Amontillado."

- Before you draft, list the qualities a suspenseful story should have. Then, list the qualities that make a satisfactory ending for you.
- Use your lists to evaluate the suspense, the ending of the story, and the author's use of stylistic devices.
- Support your critique with **relevant information.** As you write this **analytical essay,** consult your lists, using them as evidence.

Grammar Application As you draft, carefully consider your noun choices. Use abstract nouns when you are describing ideas or qualities and concrete nouns when you are discussing physical things.

Writing Workshop: *Work in Progress*

Prewriting for Autobiographical Narrative Review the Memory List in your writing portfolio. For each scene description, write how you reacted in the situation. Save this Reaction Work in your writing portfolio.

Listening and Speaking

With a partner, **retell** one of the stories from another point of view. You might tell "Sonata for Harp or Bicycle" from the ghost's point of view or from Miss Golden's point of view. You might tell "The Cask of Amontillado" from Fortunato's point of view. If you need to refresh your memory, reread your chosen selection for clues about your new narrator's perspective.

Follow these steps to complete the assignment.

- Identify an audience, the group of people who will hear your retelling, and consider the type of information that will be suitable for them.
- Use **informal language** effectively to **meet the needs of your audience, purpose, and occasion.** Also keep in mind which words and expressions are appropriate for the narrator's character.
- As you speak, **use eye contact and purposeful gestures** to communicate ideas effectively.
- Vary your intonation and **adjust your speaking rate, volume, and enunciation** to reflect the emotions of the narrator.
- Ask your partner to evaluate your presentation.

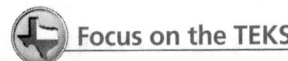 Focus on the TEKS

Writing
(15)(A)(v) Write an analytical essay that includes relevant information.

Listening and Speaking
(25) Give presentations using informal language effectively to meet the needs of audience, purpose, and occasion, employing eye contact, speaking rate, volume, enunciation, and purposeful gestures to communicate ideas effectively.

Use this prewriting activity to prepare for the **Writing Workshop** on page 94.

www.PHLitOnline.com

- Interactive graphic organizers
- Grammar tutorial
- Interactive journals

Strategy for Success

Ask Questions

Asking questions as you read selections on Texas standardized reading tests will help you to monitor your own comprehension. If you can ask and answer questions about the text easily, keep reading ahead. If asking and answering your own questions is difficult, slow your reading rate, and re-read passages that prove challenging. Then, check your understanding by asking questions.

The types of questions you ask depends on the type of text you are reading. If you are reading a story, you might ask about the plot or about what will happen next. If you are reading informational text, you might ask how information is related or why the author has included specific information. The following examples show how you can use the strategy of asking questions on standardized tests.

 Focus on the TEKS

Comprehension
RC-9(A) Reflect on understanding to monitor comprehension (e.g., asking questions).

Ask About Foreshadowing

When you see foreshadowing in a story, ask yourself what might happen later in the story. Check your answer as you read.

1 The sun shone brightly. Mya smiled. "Nothing could go wrong on a day like today!" she said. She had no idea just how mistaken she was.

1 Which of the following foreshadows Mya's difficult day?
 A *The sun shone brightly.*
 B *Mya smiled.*
 C *"Nothing could go wrong on a day like today!"*
 D *She had no idea just how mistaken she was.*

A, B, and **C** all describe the character's current situation and how she feels. Only **D** suggests that the situation may change later in the story. The correct answer is **D.**

Ask About Information

Ask yourself why the author has included certain information. What might be the topic of this passage?

1 Scorpions' feeding habits differ significantly from those of other arachnids. Although scorpions do not have regular jaws, they are able to chew their food as they digest it.

2 The topic of this passage is —
 F arachnids that eat plants
 G the eating habits of scorpions
 H arachnid-eating scorpions
 J physical characteristics of arachnids

F, H, and **J** are not related to the text. The passage hints at the importance of scorpions' eating habits, so that could be a topic for the article. The answer is **G.**

Texas Test Practice

Read this selection. Then answer the questions that follow it.

The Spelling Specialist

1   I out-spelled my older sister Annie in the school spelling bee when I was in third grade and she was in fourth, and she's never forgotten it. After that she entered every contest I did, just to prove she could win. By the time I started ninth grade at the high school where Annie was a sophomore, the competition had died down a little. But that was before I became the alternate for our academic bowl.

2   Annie was already on the team and had been nominated as the captain. "My sister will be a fine alternate," she told the others, "but for competitions, you'll be glad I'm on the team. I've won almost every contest we've entered."

3   As an alternate, I had to sit on the sidelines during competitions, watching Annie and the others pressing their buzzers to answer difficult questions in science, art, math, and history. I watched enviously.

4   Then Annie arrived at practice with an announcement that would change everything. "They're introducing a new question category," Annie told us, "and you'll never guess what it is: spelling."

5   Smiling, Annie turned to me. "So now we need a spelling specialist on the team, and only one person here can spell better than I can. I think it's time she took my place on the regular team."

1 The primary conflict in the story is between —
   A Annie and the academic bowl team
   B Annie and the narrator
   C the narrator and her jealousy
   D the competing teams

2 The statement "But that was before I became the alternate for our academic bowl" foreshadows —
   F the sisters' cooperation
   G a return to competitiveness
   H the team's success
   J a new question category

3 Annie suggests replacing herself on the team because —
   A she has to give up her position
   B she does not want to be captain
   C her replacement has been on the team longer
   D she believes that the change will help the team

4 Paragraph 5 suggests that —
   F the narrator will be envious
   G Annie will be angry
   H the team will fail
   J the sisters will stop competing

Informational Texts

Expository Texts

Article
Early Texas Cuisine

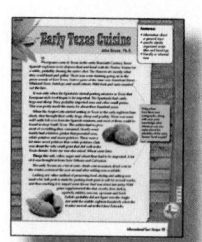

Cookbook Article
**The Everything
Tex-Mex Cookbook**

Focus on the TEKS

Reading
(9)(C) Make subtle inferences
and draw complex conclusions
about the ideas in text and their
organizational patterns.

Reading Skill: Analyze Ideas and Organizational Patterns

When you **make subtle inferences** about the **ideas** in a text, you gather
information from the text and combine that information with what you
already know to make logical assumptions. Making inferences allows you
to develop ideas and understandings not directly stated in the text.

As you preview and read, you can also gather information by noting
the **organizational patterns** of a text. This analysis, combined with your
prior knowledge, will allow you to **draw complex conclusions** about the
reasons an author chose certain organizational patterns to present his or
her ideas.

As You Read Use a chart like the one shown to record the process you
use to make subtle inferences and draw complex conclusions about the
ideas in the texts and their organizational patterns.

Information from Text	Prior Knowledge	Inference or Conclusion
The Spanish probably imported corn from Mexico.	Tex-Mex food is made with a lot of corn.	The Spanish had a big influence on Tex-Mex food.

Early Texas Cuisine

John Raven

Features:

- information about a general topic
- specific details organized under titles and headings
- friendly or informal tone

Europeans came to Texas in the early sixteenth century. Some Spanish explorers were shipwrecked and lived with the Native Texans for a while, probably sharing the native diet. The Natives ate mostly what they could hunt and gather. There was some farming going on in the piney woods of East Texas. Native game of the time was American Bison, Whitetail Deer, Antelope and small critters. Wild fruit and nuts rounded out the fare.

It was only when the Spaniards started putting missions in Texas that European-style food began to be imported. The Spaniards had cattle, hogs and sheep. They probably imported corn and other small grains. This was pretty much the menu for about three hundred years.

When the Anglo-Celts started settling in Texas in the early eighteen hundreds, they brought their cattle, hogs, sheep and poultry. There was some wild cattle left over from the Spanish missions, and most of those could be found in deep South Texas. The settlers had to grow most of everything they consumed. Nearly every family had a kitchen garden that provided corn, white potatoes and sweet potatoes. There were a lot more sweet potatoes than white potatoes. Oats was about the only small grain that did well in the Texas climate. Some rye was also raised. Wheat came later.

> You can connect the details in these two paragraphs. **Using these ideas along with prior knowledge you may have, what inference can you make about the reliability of the early Texans' food supply?**

Things like salt, coffee, sugar and wheat flour had to be imported. A lot of it was brought in from New Orleans and Galveston.

The early Texans ate a lot of corn—fresh corn in season, dried corn in the winter, cornmeal the year around after milling was available.

Lacking any other method of preserving food, drying and salting was used a lot. Salt pork is made by packing fresh pork in salt for several weeks, and then smoking it to impart some flavor. Beef was dried into jerky. Wild game supplemented the diet, mostly deer, turkey, squirrels, rabbits, raccoon, opossum and fowl. Buffalo probably did not figure into the Anglo diet until the middle eighteen hundreds when the frontier moved out to the Llano Estacado.

TEXAS

Corn Cookery:

This subhead indicates that the author is moving from discussing general cuisine to a specific food—corn.
By analyzing this organizational pattern, what complex conclusion can you draw about the importance of corn to early Texan cuisine?

The simplest method of eating corn is just to pull back the husk and take a bite, that is providing it's early in the season and the corn is still tender. Dried corn could be boiled and eaten that way, or it could be ground into meal and made into corn mush or corn cakes or corn bread.

Corn mush is simple food. Just stir some cornmeal into boiling water and cook it down until it thickens, add some butter, sugar or honey and a little milk, and you have a delicious hot breakfast. Omit the butter, sugar and milk and cut back on the water enough to make a thick batter, and you can fry it into Johnny cakes or bake it on a clean garden implement for hoe cakes.

For corn bread, you have to have a leavening agent, like baking powder or baking soda and buttermilk, to make it rise.

The Native Texans learned to soak dried corn in lime water to make hominy which can be ground into *masa*, a type of corn flour, a staple of Tex-Mex cooking.

Cornmeal comes in white or yellow. Either is acceptable. You can find some blue cornmeal in New Mexico and Arizona, and it's really blue. No matter the color, if you can find cornmeal that's been stone ground, it just seems to be better.

The recipes that follow go back quite a few years. As with many old recipes, it is assumed that the cook knows his or her way around a kitchen of the day. They don't exactly waste words with step-by-step directions.

Cornmeal Mush (from 1830)

½ cup Cornmeal
2-¾ cups Water
¾ teaspoon Salt

Sprinkle cornmeal into boiling water, stirring constantly. Add salt and cook for about half an hour. Serve with sugar and cream.

Indian Cornmeal Cake (from 1830)

1-½ cups Yellow Cornmeal
1 teaspoon Salt
½ cup Flour
3 teaspoons Rosewater (Vanilla)
1-⅔ cups Sugar
1 teaspoon Cinnamon
1 cup Butter
8 Eggs

Mix the sugar, butter and eggs. Mix the cornmeal and salt together, and combine with the sugar, butter and egg mixture. Add vanilla and cinnamon and mix well. Pour into a floured cake pan and bake in a moderate oven.

TEXAS

Can truth change?

How did immigration affect the essence of Texan cuisine?

Cookbook Article

Features:

- background information
- general information about the cuisine
- lists of specialized tools and ingredients involved in the cuisine

The Everything TEX-MEX COOKBOOK

Linda Larsen

ORIGINS OF TEX-MEX

Mexican cooking is an ancient cuisine that stretches back thousands of years. It is a combination of native Indian and Spanish foods and recipes brought to the country by the Conquistadors. There's even a bit of French, Austrian, and Italian influence! Before Spain invaded Mexico, there was no wheat, cattle, pigs, butter, rice, almonds, or walnuts in the cuisine. That means before the Conquistadors, Mexican cooking did not use pork, beef, cheese, or rice, but was based on corn, tomatoes, squash, beans, game, and pumpkins. The food was very healthy and mostly vegetarian. The Spanish invasion greatly expanded the Mexican cuisine, which even used indigenous animals like the armadillo and iguana.

This cuisine came to the United States in the 1800s, when Spaniards and Mexicans arrived in Texas to work on the ranches and settle in the cities. These immigrants found Indians eating regional foods and crops such as rabbits, deer, pumpkins, and cactus. The huge ranches of western Texas added beef products to the cuisine, along with recipes and entire meals cooked over a fire: campfire cooking, smoking, and barbecue. This was simple food made of available and inexpensive, sometimes free, ingredients.

As Tex-Mex cooking spread across the country, chili was introduced at the Chicago World's Fair in 1893, and tamales became a popular street food in Chicago during the Depression. During this time the term itself was considered something of an insult, mocking Mexican dishes that were "Americanized" with lots of cheese, instant rice, and cheap cuts of meat. Even today it's easy to find food advertised as "Tex-Mex" characterized by large combination platters of overcooked food covered in yellow cheese and all tasting the same.

A CUISINE IS BORN

As other cultures discovered Tex-Mex cooking, it lost its junk-food status. The French, Brazilians, and even countries in the Middle East adopted the flavors and textures and added their own twists.

What didn't change is that the most important foods in Tex-Mex cooking are tomatoes, beef, beans, chiles, and corn. In fact, corn is so deeply embedded in the culture that many of the names for foods made of corn come directly from the Aztec language—for example, *tamal* (tamale) and *tlaxcalli* (tortilla). Tex-Mex cooking is an Americanized form of Mexican cooking, but with its own twists added from other cultures.

Preview the article by reading the headings and the bulleted list. **Use this information to make subtle inferences about the text's organizational pattern. What inferences can you make about how the content will be presented?**

The author points out that the ingredients used were mostly inexpensive. **Combining this idea with what you may already know about the early West, what inference can you make about the food budgets of early Texans?**

TEXAS

Ingredients combined with an eye for color, texture, and flavors, based on regional tastes, are what Tex-Mex food is all about.

There are many different variations of Tex-Mex cooking that incorporate food combinations of other ethnicities, like French-Mex, Cal-Mex, New Mex-Mex, Nuevo-Mex, and Lou-Mex. Tex-Mex cooking, which embraces them all, differs from Mexican food in that it uses more acceptable combinations and more common ingredients. These include canned condensed soups, processed cheeses, fried tortilla chips, and canned tomatoes and chiles, which are not used in Mexican cooking.

Pickled chile peppers, especially jalapeños, are commonly used in Tex-Mex cooking, and the plain beefsteak tomato is very popular. Peppers from California, including Anaheim, along with root vegetables from the South, such as sweet potatoes, have made their way into the Tex-Mex cuisine.

Nachos, which are a combination of fried tortillas, sauce, and melted cheese, are a quintessential Tex-Mex food not found in the Mexican cuisine. Chips and dip are not served as an appetizer in Mexico. Flour gravies are an important part of Tex-Mex cooking, made with the drippings created when meat is browned. In Mexico, sauces are almost always made of tomatoes and chiles and are more complicated than Tex-Mex sauces.

The food is simpler than most Mexican cooking, while some classic Mexican dishes are remade in the Tex-Mex mold by using prepared sauces, chili powders, and purchased convenience foods such as taco shells, premade tortillas, and even precooked meats. Flour tortillas are more Tex-Mex than Mexican, and fajitas, especially those eaten in flour tortillas, are an American addition to the cuisine.

SPICES AND SEASONINGS

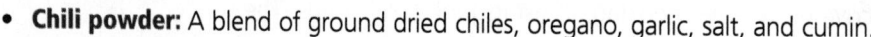

Good quality spices and herbs are critical parts of the Tex-Mex cuisine. These ingredients add subtle or not-so-subtle flavors to most dishes. Many spices can be substituted for each other as long as you use approximately equal quantities.

The author provides a list of information about particular spices. **What complex conclusion can you draw about the author's purpose for choosing this organizational pattern?**

- **Chili powder:** A blend of ground dried chiles, oregano, garlic, salt, and cumin.
- **Ground chile powder:** Dried chiles toasted and ground.
- **Cayenne pepper:** Cayenne chile, dried and ground into a red pepper.
- **Cumin:** A spice with a smoky flavor, used often in Tex-Mex cooking.
- **Cilantro:** A fresh herb with strong, citrussy, and almost astringent taste.
- **Epazote:** A very pungent herb used with cooked beans.
- **Mexican oregano:** More flavorful and intense than the Mediterranean variety.
- **Vanilla:** Used as a liquid extract and as the whole vanilla bean.

Can truth change?

How do people's ideas differ about what Tex-Mex cuisine is and what it should be?

TEXAS

Comparing Informational Texts

(a) Compare and contrast the types of information presented in the two articles. **(b) Make Inferences:** What inference can you make about Tex-Mex cuisine based on the author's choices to use chronological **organizational patterns** in the first sections of the texts? **(c) Draw Conclusions:** What complex conclusion can you draw about how the author of *The Everything Tex-Mex Cookbook* would react to the recipes and **ideas** included in "Early Texas Cuisine"? Explain.

 College Readiness | Timed Writing

Write an Essay

Format
The prompt directs you to write an essay. Therefore, you should include introductory and concluding paragraphs as well as body paragraphs that include details and support.

Write an essay about the ways the ingredients in Texas cuisine have changed and the factors that influenced those changes. Use the ideas and organizational patterns of both texts to make subtle inferences and draw complex conclusions about the diet of early Texan settlers and explain how their food choices are the forerunners of the food options available today. Support your ideas with evidence from the texts. (30 minutes)

Academic Vocabulary
When you *support* your ideas, you use evidence, details, and explanations to show that your ideas are logical.

 ## 5-Minute Planner

Complete these steps before you begin to write:

1. Read the prompt carefully and completely.
2. Review the informational and cookbook articles, taking notes on the information you need to support your inferences and conclusions.
3. Make an outline of those ideas, organizing them logically to support your argument.
4. Refer to your outline and notes as you draft your essay.

Comparing Literary Works

Comparing Points of View

The **narrator's point of view** is the perspective from which a story is told. Often, **a work of fiction is shaped by the narrator's point of view.**

- **First-person point of view:** The narrator is a character who participates in the action and uses the first-person pronouns *I* and *me*.

- **Third-person point of view:** The narrator is not a character in the story but a voice outside it. The narrator uses the third-person pronouns *he, she, him, her, they*, and *them* to refer to all characters. There are two kinds of third-person points of view. In the **third-person omniscient point of view,** the narrator knows everything, including the thoughts of all the characters. In the **third-person limited point of view,** the narrator sees and reports things through one character's eyes.

The narrator's point of view can shape not only what kind of information is revealed to the reader, but can also affect the reliability of the information. As you read, consider how the details the narrator shares may be influenced by his or her attitudes and experiences.

(As You Read) Complete a Venn diagram like this one to analyze and compare the way in which the works of fiction are shaped by the narrators' different points of view.

Focus on the TEKS

Reading
(5)(C) Analyze the way in which a work of fiction is shaped by the narrator's point of view.

Checkouts   The Girl Who Can

Uses
third-person
pronouns

**TEXAS
PHLitOnline**
www.PHLitOnline.com

- Vocabulary flashcards
- Interactive journals
- More about the authors
- Selection audio
- Interactive graphic organizers

Can *truth* change?

Writing About the Big Question

Although the characters in these stories seem sure of certain things, when circumstances change, new possibilities—and new questions—emerge. Use these sentence starters to develop your ideas about the Big Question.

People may have **assumptions** about others or themselves based on _____.

Those **beliefs** can be changed when _____.

Meet the Authors

Cynthia Rylant (b. 1954)
Author of "Checkouts"

Cynthia Rylant spent four years as a child living with her grandparents in a small town in West Virginia. With no public library and little money to buy books, she started reading comic books. Once in college, she discovered great literature, but she did not consider becoming a writer until she took a job as a librarian and began reading children's books.

Writing About Her Life In her work, Rylant draws upon her experiences as a young adult. "The best writing," she says, "is that which is most personal, most revealing." She has written many award-winning stories, poems, and novels.

Ama Ata Aidoo (b. 1942)

Author of "The Girl Who Can"

Ama Ata Aidoo was born in Ghana, Africa, where her father was a village chief. He wanted his daughter to have a Western education and sent her to a university in Cape Coast, Ghana. Aidoo earned her bachelor's degree in English and later taught at universities in Ghana and the United States.

Works and Themes Aidoo has written plays, short stories, poetry, and novels. Her fiction, written in English, often explores the conflicts between Western and African cultures and the roles of women in modern society.

Checkouts

Cynthia Rylant

Her parents had moved her to Cincinnati, to a large house with beveled glass[1] windows and several porches and the history her mother liked to emphasize. You'll love the house, they said. You'll be lonely at first, they admitted, but you're so nice you'll make friends fast. And as an impulse tore at her to lie on the floor, to hold to their ankles and tell them she felt she was dying, to offer anything, anything at all, so they might allow her to finish growing up in the town of her childhood, they firmed their mouths and spoke from their chests and they said, It's decided.

They moved her to Cincinnati, where for a month she spent the greater part of every day in a room full of beveled glass windows, sifting through photographs of the life she'd lived and left behind. But it is difficult work, suffering, and in its own way a kind of art, and finally she didn't have the energy for it anymore, so she emerged from the beautiful house and fell in love with a bag boy at the supermarket. Of course, this didn't happen all at once, just like that, but in the sequence of things that's exactly the way it happened.

She liked to grocery shop. She loved it in the way some people love to drive long country roads, because doing it she could think and relax and wander. Her parents wrote up the list and handed it to her and off she went without complaint to perform what they regarded as a great sacrifice of her time and a sign that she was indeed a very nice girl. She had never told them how much she loved grocery shopping, only that she was "willing" to do it. She had an intuition which told her that her parents were not safe for sharing such strong, important facts about herself. Let them think they knew her.

---

1. **beveled** (bev´ əld) **glass** *n.* glass having angled or slanted edges.

Once inside the supermarket, her hands firmly around the handle of the cart, she would lapse into a kind of reverie and wheel toward the produce. Like a Tibetan monk in solitary meditation, she calmed to a point of deep, deep happiness; this feeling came to her, reliably, if strangely, only in the supermarket.

Then one day the bag boy dropped her jar of mayonnaise and that is how she fell in love.

He was nervous—first day on the job—and along had come this fascinating girl, standing in the checkout line with the unfocused stare one often sees in young children, her face turned enough away that he might take several full looks at her as he packed sturdy bags full of food and the goods of modern life. She interested him because her hair was red and thick, and in it she had placed a huge orange bow, nearly the size of a small hat. That was enough to distract him, and when finally it was her groceries he was packing, she looked at him and smiled and he could respond only by busting her jar of mayonnaise on the floor, shards of glass and oozing cream decorating the area around his feet.

She loved him at exactly that moment, and if he'd known this perhaps he wouldn't have fallen into the brown depression he fell into, which lasted the rest of his shift. He believed he must have looked the fool in her eyes, and he envied the sureness of everyone around him: the cocky cashier at the register, the grim and harried store manager, the bland butcher, and the brazen bag boys who smoked in the warehouse on their breaks. He wanted a second chance. Another chance to be confident and say witty things to her as he threw tin cans into her bags, persuading her to allow him to help her to her car so he might learn just a little about her, check out the floor of the

Then one day the bag boy dropped her jar of mayonnaise and that is how she fell in love.

Literary Analysis
Point of View
How does the use of pronouns in this paragraph show that this story is being told from the third-person point of view?

Vocabulary
reverie (rev′ ə rē) *n.* dreamy thinking and imagining

Literary Analysis
Point of View
Whose thoughts and feelings are expressed in this paragraph?

Reading Check
At first, why does the girl fascinate the boy?

Literary Analysis
Point of View
What does the narrator reveal about the boy's regrets?

car for signs of hobbies or fetishes and the bumpers for clues as to beliefs and loyalties.

But he busted her jar of mayonnaise and nothing else worked out for the rest of the day.

Strange, how attractive clumsiness can be. She left the supermarket with stars in her eyes, for she had loved the way his long nervous fingers moved from the conveyor belt to the bags, how deftly (until the mayonnaise) they had picked up her items and placed them in her bags. She had loved the way the hair kept falling into his eyes as he leaned over to grab a box or a tin. And the tattered brown shoes he wore with no socks. And the left side of his collar turned in rather than out.

The bag boy seemed a wonderful contrast to the perfectly beautiful house she had been forced to accept as her home, to the history she hated, to the loneliness she had become used to, and she couldn't wait to come back for more of his awkwardness and dishevelment.

Vocabulary
dishevelment
(di shev′ əl ment) *n.*
disorder; messiness

Strange, how attractive clumsiness can be.

Incredibly, it was another four weeks before they saw each other again. As fate would have it, her visits to the supermarket never coincided with his schedule to bag. Each time she went to the store, her eyes scanned the checkouts at once, her heart in her mouth. And each hour he worked, the bag boy kept one eye on the door, watching for the red-haired girl with the big orange bow.

Yet in their disappointment these weeks there was a kind of ecstasy. It is reason enough to be alive, the hope you may see again some face which has meant something to you. The anticipation of meeting the bag boy eased the girl's painful transition into her new and jarring life in Cincinnati. It provided for her an anchor amid all that was impersonal and unfamiliar, and she spent less time on thoughts of what she had left behind as she concentrated on what might lie ahead. And for the boy, the long and often tedious hours at the supermarket which provided no challenge other than that of showing up the following workday . . . these hours became possibilities of mystery and romance for him as he watched the electric doors for the girl in the orange bow.

And when finally they did meet up again, neither offered a clue to the other that he, or she, had been the object of obsessive thought for weeks. She spotted him as soon as she came into the store, but she kept her eyes strictly in front of her as she pulled out a cart and wheeled it toward the produce. And he, too, knew the instant she came through the door—though the orange bow was gone, replaced by a small but bright yellow flower instead—and he never once turned his head in her direction but watched her from the corner of his vision as he tried to swallow back the fear in his throat.

It is odd how we sometimes deny ourselves the very pleasure we have longed for and which is finally within our reach. For

Literary Analysis
Point of View
Which details in this paragraph suggest the story is told from the omniscient point of view? Explain.

some perverse reason she would not have been able to articulate, the girl did not bring her cart up to the bag boy's checkout when her shopping was done. And the bag boy let her leave the store, pretending no notice of her.

This is often the way of children, when they truly want a thing, to pretend that they don't. And then they grow angry when no one tried harder to give them this thing they so casually rejected, and they soon find themselves in a rage simply because they cannot say yes when they mean yes. Humans are very complicated. (And perhaps cats, who have been known to react in the same way, though the resulting rage can only be guessed at.)

The girl hated herself for not checking out at the boy's line, and the boy hated himself for not catching her eye and saying hello, and they most sincerely hated each other without having ever exchanged even two minutes of conversation.

Eventually—in fact, within the week—a kind and intelligent boy who lived very near her beautiful house asked the girl to a movie and she gave up her fancy for the bag boy at the supermarket. And the bag boy himself grew so bored with his job that he made a desperate search for something better and ended up in a bookstore where scores of fascinating girls lingered like honeybees about a hive. Some months later the bag boy and the girl with the orange bow again crossed paths, standing in line with their dates at a movie theater, and, glancing toward the other, each smiled slightly, then looked away, as strangers on public buses often do, when one is moving off the bus and the other is moving on.

Vocabulary
perverse (pər vʉrs´) *adj.* different from what is considered right or reasonable

Literary Analysis
Point of View
How does the narrator's point of view shape this paragraph?

Support your responses with evidence from the text.

Critical Thinking

1. **Respond:** Are you disappointed that the girl and boy do not get together during the story? Why or why not?

2. **(a)** What do the boy and girl think about while they are apart? **(b) Make Inferences:** How do you think the two characters feel when they see each other at the movie theater?

3. **Draw Conclusions:** Does the experience described in the story seem like a missed opportunity or a necessary outcome? Explain.

4. **(a) Summarize:** Why do the boy and girl never act on their feelings? **(b) Make a Judgment:** Do you agree that "humans are very complicated"? Explain, using details from the story.

Can truth change?
How does the way in which the boy and the girl think of each other change during the course of the selection? Explain why you think these changes occur.

The Girl Who Can

Ama Ata Aidoo

They say that I was born in Hasodzi; and it is a very big village in the central region of our country, Ghana. They also say that when all of Africa is not choking under a drought, Hasodzi lies in a very fertile lowland in a district known for its good soil. Maybe that is why any time I don't finish eating my food, Nana says, "You Adjoa, you don't know what life is about . . . you don't know what problems there are in this life . . ."

As far as I could see, there was only one problem. And it had nothing to do with what I knew Nana considered as "problems," or what Maami thinks of as "the problem." Maami is my mother. Nana is my mother's mother. And they say I am seven years old. And my problem is that at this seven years of age, there are things I can think in my head, but which, maybe, I do not have the proper language to speak them out with. And that, I think, is a very serious problem because it is always difficult to decide whether to keep quiet and not say any of the things that come into my head, or say them and get laughed at. Not that it is easy to get any grown-up to listen to you, even when you decide to take the risk and say something serious to them.

Take Nana. First, I have to struggle to catch her attention. Then I tell her something I had taken a long time to figure out. And then you know what always happens? She would at once stop whatever she is doing and, mouth open, stare at me for a very long time. Then, bending and turning her head slightly, so that one ear comes down towards me, she'll say in that voice: "Adjoa, you say what?" After I have repeated whatever I had said, she would either, still in that voice, ask me "never, never, but NEVER to repeat THAT," or she would immediately burst out laughing. She would laugh and laugh and laugh, until tears run down her cheeks and she would stop whatever she is doing and wipe away the tears with the hanging edges of her cloth. And she would continue laughing until she is completely tired. But then, as soon as another person comes by, just to make sure she doesn't forget whatever it was I had said, she would repeat it to her. And then, of course, there would be two old people laughing and screaming with tears running down their faces. Sometimes this show continues until there are three, four or even more of such laughing and screaming tear-faced grownups. And all that performance for whatever I'd said? I find something quite confusing in all this. That is, no one ever explains to me why sometimes I shouldn't repeat some things I say; while at other times, some other things I say would not only be all right, but would be considered so funny they would be repeated so many times for so many people's enjoyment. You see how neither way of hearing me out can encourage me to express my thoughts too often?

◀ **Critical Viewing**
Describe the feelings the girl in the photograph expresses. **[Interpret]**

Vocabulary
fertile (furt´ 'l) *adj.* rich in nutrients that promote growth

Literary Analysis
Point of View
Which pronouns in this paragraph show that this story is being told from the first-person point of view?

Reading Check

What does the narrator say is her problem?

Like all this business to do with my legs. I have always wanted to tell them not to worry. I mean Nana and my mother. It did not have to be an issue for my two favorite people to fight over. I didn't want to be told not to repeat it or for it to be considered so funny that anyone would laugh at me until they cried. After all, they were my legs . . . When I think back on it now, those two, Nana and my mother must have been discussing my legs from the day I was born. What I am sure of is that when I came out of the land of sweet, soft silence into the world of noise and comprehension, the first topic I met was my legs.

Vocabulary
comprehension
(käm´ prē hen´ shen) *n.*
understanding

That discussion was repeated very regularly.

Nana: "Ah, ah, you know, Kaya, I thank my God that your very first child is female. But Kaya, I am not sure about her legs. Hm . . . hm . . . hm . . ."

And Nana would shake her head.

Maami: "Mother, why are you always complaining about Adjoa's legs? If you ask me . . ."

Nana: "They are too thin. And I am not asking you!"

Nana has many voices. There is a special one she uses to shut everyone up.

"Some people have no legs at all," my mother would try again with all her small courage.

▼ **Critical Viewing**
Might these mothers and children have relationships similar to those between Adjoa and her elders? Explain.
[Connect]

"But Adjoa has legs," Nana would insist; "except that they are too thin. And also too long for a woman. Kaya, listen. Once in a while, but only once in a very long while, somebody decides — nature, a child's spirit mother, an accident happens, and somebody gets born without arms, or legs, or both sets of limbs. And then let me touch wood; it is a sad business. And you know, such things are not for talking about every day. But if any female child decides to come into this world with legs, then they might as well be legs."

"What kind of legs?" And always at that point, I knew from her voice that my

mother was weeping inside. Nana never heard such inside weeping. Not that it would have stopped Nana even if she had heard it. Which always surprised me. Because, about almost everything else apart from my legs, Nana is such a good grown-up. In any case, what do I know about good grown-ups and bad grown-ups? How could Nana be a good grown-up when she carried on so about my legs? All I want to say is that I really liked Nana except for that.

Nana: "As I keep saying, if any woman decides to come into this world with her two legs, then she should select legs that have meat on them: with good calves. Because you are sure such legs would support solid hips. And a woman must have solid hips to be able to have children."

"Oh, Mother." That's how my mother would answer. Very, very quietly. And the discussion would end or they would move on to something else.

Sometimes, Nana would pull in something about my father:

How, "Looking at such a man, we have to be humble and admit that after all, God's children are many . . ."

How, "After one's only daughter had insisted on marrying a man like that, you still have to thank your God that the biggest problem you got later was having a granddaughter with spindly legs that are too long for a woman, and too thin to be of any use."

The way she always added that bit about my father under her breath, she probably thought I didn't hear it. But I always heard it. Plus, that is what always shut my mother up for good, so that even if I had not actually heard the words, once my mother looked like even her little courage was finished, I could always guess what Nana had added to the argument.

"Legs that have meat on them with good calves to support solid hips . . . to be able to have children."

So I wished that one day I would see, for myself, the legs of any woman who had had children. But in our village, that is not easy. The older women wear long wrap-arounds[1] all the time. Perhaps if they let me go bathe in the river in the evening, I could have checked. But I never had the chance. It took a lot of begging just to get my mother and Nana to let me go splash around in the shallow end of the river with my friends, who were other little girls like me. For proper baths, we used the small bathhouse behind our hut. Therefore, the only naked female legs I have ever really seen are those of other little girls like me, or older girls in the school. And those of my mother and Nana: two pairs of legs which must surely belong to the approved kind; because Nana gave birth to my mother

---

1. **wrap-arounds** (rap´ ə roundz´) *n.* a type of garment that is open down the side and is wrapped around the body.

Literary Analysis
Point of View
How does the narrator's point of view shape what what is said about Nana in this paragraph?

Vocabulary
humble (hum´ bəl) *adj.* modest; having humility

When I think back on it now, those two, Nana and my mother must have been discussing my legs from the day I was born.

Reading Check

According to the narrator, which topic makes the mother weep inside?

and my mother gave birth to me. In my eyes, all my friends have got legs that look like legs, but whether the legs have got meat on them to support the kind of hips that . . . that I don't know.

According to the older boys and girls, the distance between our little village and the small town is about five kilometers. I don't know what five kilometers mean. They always complain about how long it is to walk to school and back. But to me, we live in our village, and walking those kilometers didn't matter. School is nice. School is another thing Nana and my mother discussed often and appeared to have different ideas about. Nana thought it would be a waste of time. I never understood what she meant. My mother seemed to know—and disagreed. She kept telling Nana that she—that is, my mother—felt she was locked into some kind of darkness because she didn't go to school. So that if I, her daughter, could learn to write and read my own name and a little besides—perhaps be able to calculate some things on paper—that would be good. I could always marry later and maybe . . .

Nana would just laugh. "Ah, maybe with legs like hers, she might as well go to school."

Running with our classmates on our small sports field and winning first place each time never seemed to me to be anything about which to tell anyone at home. This time it was different. I don't know how the teachers decided to let me run for the junior section of our school in the district games. But they did.

When I went home to tell my mother and Nana, they had not believed it at first. So Nana had taken it upon herself to go and "ask into it properly." She came home to tell my mother that it was really true. I was one of my school's runners.

"Is that so?" exclaimed my mother. I know her. Her mouth moved as though she was going to tell Nana, that, after all, there was a secret about me she couldn't be expected to share with anyone. But then Nana herself looked so pleased, out of surprise, my mother shut her mouth up. In any case, since the first time they heard the news, I have often caught Nana staring at my legs with a strange look on her face, but still pretending like she was not looking. All this week, she has been washing my school uniform herself. That is a big surprise. And she didn't stop at that,

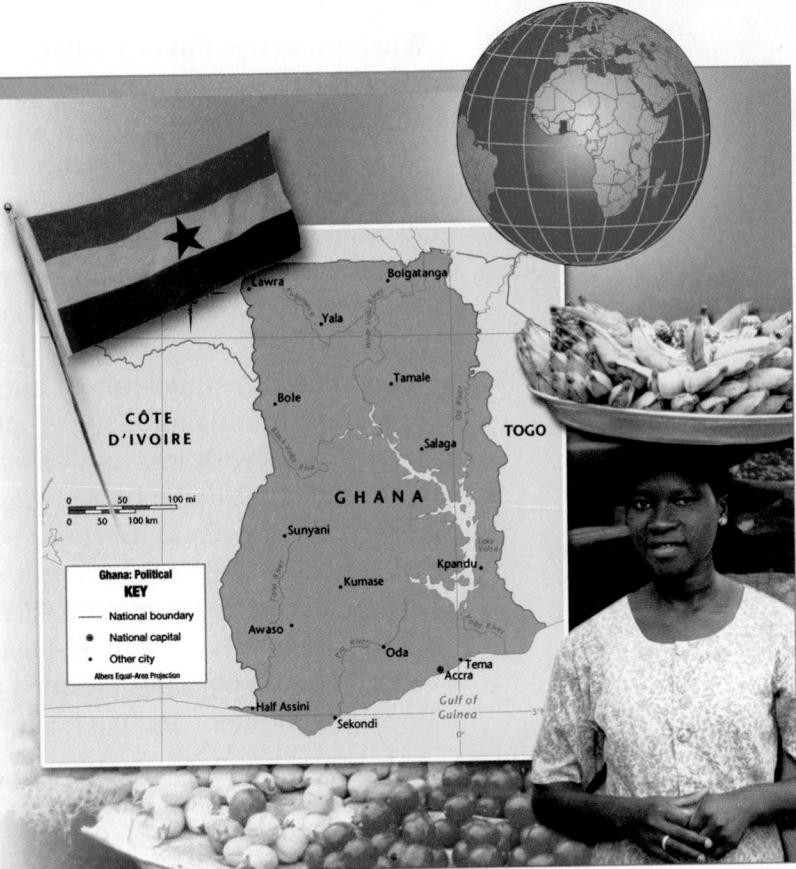

Social Studies Connection

Country Profile: Ghana

Location: southern coast of West Africa bordering the Atlantic Ocean

Climate: tropical; wet in the south and dry in the north

Terrain: low fertile plains and plateaus

Population: 20.2 million

Connect to the Literature

Adjoa says that she lives in a fertile lowland of central Ghana. What benefits and challenges might this region's climate and terrain present for a runner like Adjoa?

she even went to Mr. Mensah's house and borrowed his charcoal pressing iron. Each time she came back home with it and ironed and ironed and ironed the uniform, until, if I had been the uniform, I would have said aloud that I had had enough.

Wearing my school uniform this week has been very nice. At the parade, on the first afternoon, its sheen caught the rays of the sun and shone brighter than anybody else's uniform. I'm sure Nana saw that too, and must have liked it. Yes, she has been coming into town with us every afternoon of this district sports week. Each afternoon, she has pulled one set of fresh old cloth from the big brass bowl to wear. And those old clothes are always so stiffly starched, you can hear the cloth creak when she passes by. But she walks way behind us schoolchildren. As though she was on her own way to some place else.

Yes, I have won every race I ran for my school, and I have won the cup for the best all-round junior athlete. Yes, Nana said that she didn't care if such things are not done. She would do it. You know what she did? She carried the gleaming cup on her back. Like they do with babies, and other very precious things. And this time, not taking the trouble to walk by herself.

Reading Check

After learning about her running talent, what does Nana do with the narrator's uniform?

When we arrived in our village, she entered our compound to show the cup to my mother before going to give it back to the headmaster.

Oh, grown-ups are so strange. Nana is right now carrying me on her knee, and crying softly. Muttering, muttering, muttering that: "saa, thin legs can also be useful . . . thin legs can also be useful . . ." that "even though some legs don't have much meat on them, to carry hips . . . they can run. Thin legs can run . . . then who knows? . . ."

I don't know too much about such things. But that's how I was feeling and thinking all along. That surely, one should be able to do other things with legs as well as have them because they can support hips that make babies. Except that I was afraid of saying that sort of thing aloud. Because someone would have told me never, never, but NEVER to repeat such words. Or else, they would have laughed so much at what I'd said, they would have cried.

It's much better this way. To have acted it out to show them, although I could not have planned it.

As for my mother, she has been speechless as usual.

Oh, grown-ups are so strange.

Critical Thinking

Support your responses with evidence from the text.

1. **Respond:** Do you sympathize with the narrator? Explain.

2. **(a)** Why does Nana criticize the narrator's legs?
   (b) Draw Conclusions: How does this criticism reveal Nana's fears for the narrator's future? Explain.

3. **(a)** What are Nana's feelings about the narrator going to school?
   (b) Compare and Contrast: How do the mother's feelings about school differ from Nana's? **(c) Make Generalizations:** Based on these details, what kind of lives do you think many women in Ghana are expected to lead?

4. **(a) Make Inferences:** After Adjoa is chosen for the games, why does Nana keep staring at her legs? **(b) Draw Conclusions:** Why does Nana iron Adjoa's school uniform so carefully?

5. **(a) Analyze:** At the end of the story, Adjoa says it was much better to "have acted it out to show them." What has she "acted out"? **(b) Evaluate:** Was it "better," as Adjoa says? Explain.

 **Can truth change?**
Do the narrator's legs mean the same thing to her and her family at the end of the selection as they do at the beginning? Use details to support your answer.

Comparing Points of View

1. Use a chart like the one shown to note the actions, thoughts, and feelings of the listed characters in both stories.

Checkouts	Actions	Thoughts	Feelings
Girl			
Boy			
The Girl Who Can	Actions	Thoughts	Feelings
Nana			
Adjoa			

2. **(a)** Which details from your chart show that the **third-person omniscient point of view** in "Checkouts" gives readers insight into the inner lives of all the characters? Explain. **(b)** Which details show that the **first-person point of view** in "The Girl Who Can" lets the reader understand the narrator best of all? Explain.

 College Readiness | Timed Writing

Writing to Compare Points of View

Compare and contrast the girl in "Checkouts" and the narrator in "The Girl Who Can." In an essay, analyze the way in which the works of fiction are shaped by the narrators' points of view, and explain how that influence affects your attitude toward each girl. (30 minutes)

 5-Minute Planner

1. Read the prompt carefully and completely.
2. Organize your ideas by answering these questions:
   - Who are the narrators in the two stories?
   - How do you know what each girl is thinking?
   - Do both narrators seem equally reliable? Why or why not?
3. Reread the prompt, and then draft your essay.

Literary Text: Autobiographical Narrative

Defining the Form An **autobiographical narrative** is a story that describes real events in the writer's life and shares the lessons or wisdom the writer gained from the experiences. You might use elements of autobiographical narration in letters, journals, or persuasive essays.

Assignment Write an autobiographical narrative about an event that taught you a valuable lesson. Include the following elements in your story:

✔ a sequence of events and specific details that engage your audience and suit your purpose

✔ a well-developed *conflict,* or problem, and *resolution*

✔ a range of *literary strategies* (such as *suspense*) and *devices* (such as *foreshadowing*) to enhance the plot

✔ your thoughts, feelings, or views about the significance of events

✔ error-free grammar, including correct use of possessive nouns

To preview the criteria on which your autobiographical narrative may be judged, see the rubric on page 99.

 Focus on the TEKS

Writing
(13)(A) Plan a first draft.
(14)(A) Write an engaging story with a well-developed conflict and resolution, and a range of literary strategies (e.g., suspense) and devices to enhance the plot.

Reading
(1)(E) Use a dictionary (printed or electronic) to confirm the meanings of words.

📖 **Writing Workshop:** *Work in Progress*

Review the work you did on pages 41 and 71.

Prewriting/Planning Strategy

Structure the sequence. Begin planning the development of your **conflict** and **resolution** by creating a detailed record of events on a timeline like the one shown. Write the first incident related to your subject and record subsequent incidents in the order in which they occurred. Consider the significance of each event as you plan your first draft.

Reading-Writing Connection

To get a feel for auto-biographical narratives, read "My English" by Julia Alvarez on page 114.

Timeline

Event 2: Dad took off training wheels.

Event 4: Improved riding. Tried other activities.

Apply It!

Event 1: Dreamed of riding bike with no training wheels.

Event 3: Rode two-wheeled bike and fell.

Painting a Picture with Words

Word choice is the specific language a writer uses to tell a story. By choosing the right words, you can make the people, places, and events you describe as real for your reader as they are for you, which makes for an engaging story.

Choosing Details Remember that your readers can see only what you show them with words. As you write, do not just list events; use details to show readers what happened and how it felt. Add life to your story with precise descriptions. The chart below gives a range of tips that will help you elaborate further on an idea.

Story Element	Elaboration Tip
Experience	Explain its main effect on you.
Time and Place	Describe impressions using sensory details.
Suspense	Add details that raise the tension and heighten the story's problem.
Main Events of Story	Include thoughts or feelings that occurred to you at the time of the events.
Story Outcome	Consider other possible outcomes of events.

Avoiding Vague Language An engaging story not only describes an event; it makes readers feel as if they were there. To be sure that your readers understand what you are trying to communicate, avoid words that are vague. Instead, use language that creates a clear image in readers' minds.

Vague: There was a *beautiful* tree in the playground.

Precise: In the playground stood an *old oak* tree with *thick branches that stretched at least twenty feet in every direction.*

Vague: It was a *hot* day.

Precise: It was the kind of day *when the sun is so bright that it hurts your eyes and the sidewalk scorches your feet if you walk barefoot.*

Evaluating Word Choice Check your writing to be sure you have used precise words. If you find that a word you are using does not capture the meaning you are trying to communicate, use a **thesaurus** to find a more precise word. Then, check a printed or an electronic **dictionary** to confirm the meaning of the new word and be sure that you are using it correctly.

Drafting Strategies

Identify your main point. As you draft, think about why this experience matters. Clearly state the main problem you faced and what it taught you. Then, organize your ideas to highlight the significance of that main point.

Pace the action. Details and description add substance to your essay, but be sure that every detail you include has a clear purpose and keeps the audience engaged in your story. To maintain interest, employ these **literary strategies** and **devices** to enhance your plot:

- Emphasize the central **conflict** that sets the narrative in motion by introducing and then developing it with specific details.

- Create **suspense** by withholding some details until later in the story or using **foreshadowing** to make the reader want to read on.

- Describe what you learned in a well-developed **resolution**, using concrete details to illustrate your ideas.

Use a graphic organizer like this to help you decide which details to include in your narrative and the most effective time to reveal them.

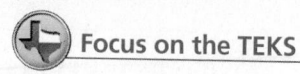 **Focus on the TEKS**

Writing
(13)(C) Revise drafts to improve sentence variety after rethinking how well questions of purpose, audience, and genre have been addressed.

(14)(A) Write an engaging story with a well-developed conflict and resolution, and a range of literary strategies (e.g., suspense) and devices to enhance the plot.

Detail	Purpose	Best Use of Detail
I put my good-luck penny in my pocket the first time I rode without training wheels, but it fell out while I was riding.	This detail shows that it was courage and hard work, not luck, that helped me ride without training wheels.	Tell that I put the penny in my pocket early in the narrative. Delay revealing that it fell out until the end, when I explain what I learned.

Revising Strategy

Improve sentence variety. Even though your narrative is about you, avoid beginning every sentence with *I*. Circle the first word in each sentence in your draft. Then, keeping in mind your audience, your purpose, and the genre in which you are writing, revise your draft. Vary your sentence beginnings to make your story more interesting.

WRITE GUY
Jeff Anderson, M.Ed.

What Do You Notice?

Author's Perspective

Read the following sentences from Isaac Bashevis Singer's "The Washwoman" several times.

Mother uttered a half-choked cry. It was as though a corpse had entered the room. I ran toward the old woman and helped her unload her pack.

Discuss your ideas about the passage with a partner. Note ways in which Singer shows his perspective without using *I* repeatedly. Consider ways you can show your perspective without overusing *I*.

Model: Revising to Vary Sentence Beginnings

The first time I   ,I was five years old
~~(I)was five years old when I first tried~~ to ride a two-wheeled bike∧.

                              S   I had loved riding my bike,
~~(I)had loved riding my bike~~ s∧ince I was three, ∧ but I had always ridden

              The thought of riding   frightened me
with training wheels. ~~(I)was afraid to ride~~ without the training wheels∧.

Revising to Correct Use of Possessive Nouns

Possessive nouns show to whom places or things belong. A possessive noun is usually formed by adding an apostrophe and an *s* ('s) to a noun.

Noun	Possessive Noun
the homework of the *student*	the *student's* homework

Because they modify other nouns, possessive nouns function in sentences as adjectives.

Forming Possessive Nouns Correctly

Singular Nouns

- Add an apostrophe and an *s* to show the possessive case of most singular nouns.

    the radiator of the car ⟶ the car's radiator

- When a singular noun ends in *s,* you may still be able to add an apostrophe and *s.* However, if the apostrophe and *s* make the word difficult to pronounce, the apostrophe may be used alone.

    the sleeve of the dress ⟶ the dress's sleeve
    the poetry of Burns ⟶ Burns' poetry

Plural Nouns

- Add an apostrophe to show the possessive case of plural nouns ending in *s* or *es: the representatives'* decision.

- Add an apostrophe and *s* to show the possessive case of plural nouns that do not end in *s* or *es: the men's* books.

Compound Nouns

- Add an apostrophe and *s* to the last word of a compound noun: the *Prime Minister's* visit.

- Add only an apostrophe if the last word of a compound noun ends in *s: the House of Representatives'* decision.

> **PH GRAMMAR HANDBOOK**
>
> Further instruction and practice are available in the *Prentice Hall Grammar Handbook.*

Grammar in Your Writing

Review the draft of your autobiographical narrative, highlighting all the possessive nouns. Check that you have used singular possessives and plural possessives correctly and that you have used appropriate punctuation. Correct any errors you find.

Student Model: Jonathan Chan, Royersford, PA

 Focus on the TEKS

Writing
(13)(D) Edit drafts for grammar, mechanics, and spelling.
(13)(E) Publish written works for appropriate audiences.
Conventions
(18)(A) Use conventions of capitalization.
(18)(B)(i) Use correct punctuation marks including quotation marks to indicate sarcasm.

True Friend

Late one Thursday night in July, my sister and I were packing for our upcoming trip to youth camp. This was my first time attending the camp, but it would be my older sister Phoebe's third experience. Everything was running smoothly until my mother called from downstairs, "Don't forget to grab a sleeping bag from my closet!" Our mother never dreamed such a simple statement would start a desperate dash by both of us to seize the most coveted sleeping bag in our household.

The night-sky blue, extra long, brand new, one hundred percent fleece sleeping bag with a built-in pillow was one-of-a-kind. By comparison, the old sleeping bag, with a broken zipper and a small hole forming at the bottom, looked even worse. Phoebe and I reached for the beautiful new bag at the exact same moment. Insulting remarks sailed from our lips as we each grabbed it. Our stomps and yells attracted our parents to the fight scene. I began to argue that I had reached the bag first, when my sister simply let go, returned to her room, and slammed the door. She was so thoroughly angry we did not speak again that night.

As the weekend progressed, our relationship did not improve. Even worse, she had shared the story with her friends. Phoebe's words were so moving, they convinced her friends to embark on a personal voyage to "get me." As a result, I spent the getaway with a target on my back.

As the skinny new kid at the camp, terror struck my heart when I heard a rumor about the plot against me. By Sunday morning, the plan, "Operation Little Brother," was all set. My sister's friends were on a mission.

I was shooting hoops in the gym that morning when my sister's friends appeared. I looked frantically for an escape but was quickly surrounded. The assailants closed to within inches of me when a familiar voice echoed through the emptiness of the open gymnasium. My sister walked calmly between her friends and me and said, "Do not bother him or you will feel the wrath of Phoebe." I was in awe. With this statement, "Operation Little Brother" came to an abrupt end. The sister I was feuding with had just saved me. Her friends never bothered me again.

On the trip home I asked her to explain her unlikely action. She simply replied, "I still don't like you, but I would dislike myself even more if I ever abandoned a friend in trouble." Since then, I have often modeled my actions to emulate my sister's behavior that day. I have learned that even when I am angry, I must stand up for my friends. My sister has taught me many things, but the most important lesson is how to be a true friend.

The detailed description of the sleeping bag helps to establish the conflict.

Here, the conflict intensifies.

Jonathan uses specific details to paint a picture of the problem he faces.

The dialogue helps to convey the drama of the moment and make the characters interesting and believable.

Jonathan concludes by drawing an important lesson from his experience.

Editing and Proofreading

Edit your draft for errors in grammar and mechanics, such as the conventions of capitalization. Use a printed or electronic dictionary to check correct spellings.

Focus on Punctuation: Review your work to be sure you have used quotation marks correctly to indicate dialogue as well as sarcasm or irony.

Publishing and Presenting

Consider ways to publish your written work for appropriate audiences:

Present an oral narrative. Mark up a copy of your autobiographical narrative, underlining any thoughts or conversations that you believe your audience would enjoy. As you present to your classmates, emphasize those passages. Be sure to pace the presentation of actions to accommodate changes in time or mood. When you are done, gracefully accept your classmates' applause and praise.

Post your essay in class or online. Create an online blog or a bulletin board display of the narratives written by you and your classmates. Have each writer supply a short comment about the event or idea that inspired his or her writing.

Reflecting on Your Writing

Writer's Journal Jot down your answers to this question:

How did writing about the event help you to understand it?

Rubric for Self-Assessment

Find evidence in your writing to address each category. Then, use the rating scale to grade your event.

Spiral Review

Earlier in the unit, you learned about **common and proper nouns** (p. 40) and **abstract and concrete nouns** (p. 70). Check the capitalization of the common and proper nouns in your narrative. Review your essay to be sure you have chosen your concrete and abstract nouns carefully.

Written Composition Criteria	Rating Scale
	not very very
Focus and Coherence: How central are you to the action of the story?	1 2 3 4
Organization: How clear is the narrative's plot? How well are literary strategies and devices used to enhance the plot?	1 2 3 4
Development of Ideas: How developed are your conflict and resolution?	1 2 3 4
Conventions: How correct is your grammar, especially your use of possessive nouns?	1 2 3 4
Voice: How engaging are the details and language of the story?	1 2 3 4

Before You Read

from A White House Diary • My English

Selection Choices

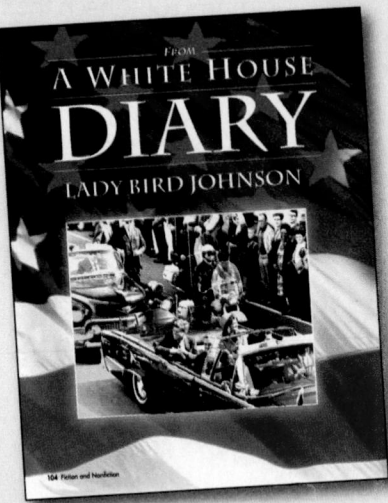

▲ Read **from A White House Diary** to learn first-hand what happened on the day a president was assassinated.

▲ Read **"My English"** to learn how a Spanish-speaking child makes English her language.

 TEXAS Focus on the TEKS

Meet these standards with either **A White House Diary** (p. 104) or **"My English"** (p. 114).

Reading
(6) Understand the varied features of literary nonfiction and provide evidence from the text to support understanding. Analyze how literary essays interweave personal examples and ideas with factual information to explain or present a perspective on a situation or event. (Literary Analysis: Voice; Spiral Review: Literary Essay)

(1)(A) Determine the meaning of grade-level technical academic English words in multiple content areas derived from Greek and other linguistic roots. (Word Power: Apply It)

Reading/Comprehension Skills
RC-9(B) Make complex inferences about text and use textual evidence to support understanding. (Reading Skill: Author's Purpose)

Oral and Written Conventions
(17)(A)(iii) Use and understand reciprocal pronouns. (Conventions: Personal, Reflexive, and Reciprocal Pronouns)

Writing
(13)(A) Plan a first draft by selecting the correct genre for conveying the intended meaning to multiple audiences. (Writing: Essay, Poem, Dialogue, or Script)

(15)(D) Produce a multimedia presentation with graphics, images, and sound that conveys a distinctive point of view and appeals to a specific audience. (Research and Technology: Multimedia Presentation)

Literary Analysis: Voice

Voice is the way a writer sounds on the page. For example, the writer's voice in a work can be smooth and sophisticated, choppy and blunt, or breathless and full of wonder. Voice is a result of several elements:

- **Word choice:** the kinds of words the writer uses
- **Attitude:** the way the writer feels about his or her subject
- **Sentence structure:** the arrangement of words in sentences

In autobiographical writing, the author tells all or part of his or her life story. The details the author includes show what he or she notices, thinks, and feels about events. One feature of autobiographical writing is that the voice of the author usually reflects his or her personality and way of speaking. For readers, voice can also affect the tone and credibility of the text.

As You Read Jot down elements that express the writer's voice.

Reading Skill: Author's Purpose

An **author's purpose** is his or her main reason for writing. An author can write for a general purpose, such as to inform, to entertain, or to persuade. He or she may also write for a **specific purpose,** such as to expose a particular problem in society. To get the most out of what you read, preview the text before you read. Look for textual evidence that will enable you to **make inferences** about the author's purpose.

- Notice information or ideas conveyed in the title.
- Look for any organizing features, such as subheads.
- Identify the subject of photos, illustrations, or diagrams.

Using the Strategy: Author's Purpose Map

As You Read First preview the text, using an organizer like the one shown to jot down inferences you make about the author's specific purpose. Later, as you read the full text, confirm whether your inferences are correct.

Text Feature	Inferences About Purpose

TEXAS
PHLitOnline
www.PHLitOnline.com

Hear It!
- Selection summary audio
- Selection audio

See It!
- Get Connected video
- Background video
- More about the author
- Vocabulary flashcards

Do It!
- Interactive journals
- Interactive graphic organizers
- Self-test
- Internet activity
- Grammar tutorial
- Interactive vocabulary games

Can *truth* change?

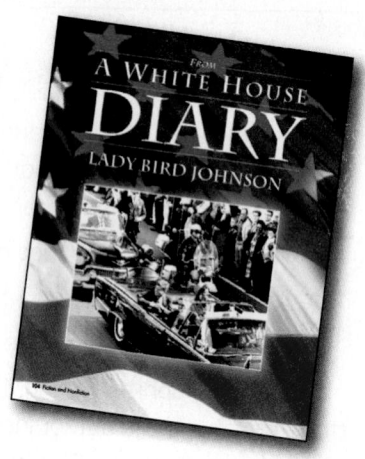

Writing About the Big Question

In this passage from *A White House Diary,* Lady Bird Johnson recalls details about the day President John F. Kennedy was assassinated. Use these sentence starters to develop your ideas about the Big Question.

Abrupt changes in **circumstances** can _____.

Accepting the **truth** of these changes can be difficult because _____.

As You Read Look for details that show how the author's feelings and attitudes shift as a result of her eyewitness observations during these historic days.

Vocabulary

Read each word and its definition. Decide whether you know the word well, know it a little bit, or do not know it at all. After you read, see how your knowledge of each word has increased.

- **tumultuous** (too mul´ choo əs) *adj.* greatly disturbed; in an uproar (p. 107) *The year we moved cross-country was a tumultuous one for the whole family. tumult n.*

- **implications** (im´ pli kā´ shənz) *n.* indirect results (p. 108) *He did not think about the implications of his decision to change jobs. implicate v. imply v.*

- **confines** (kän´ fīnz) *n.* boundaries or bounded region; border; limit (p. 109) *Please, stay within the confines of this yard. confine v. confinement n. confined adj.*

- **desolate** (des´ ə lit) *adj.* forlorn; wretched (p. 109) *Living alone on a desolate mountain top would make most people feel lonely. desolate v. desolation n.*

- **poignant** (pɔin´ yənt) *adj.* emotionally touching (p. 109) *The moment of farewell is often very poignant. poignancy n.*

- **immaculate** (i mak´ yə lit) *adj.* perfectly correct; without a flaw, fault, or error (p. 109) *My mother kept an immaculate house, with nothing out of place. immaculately adv.*

Word Power

The root **-fin-**, meaning "end," comes to English through the **Middle French** word *finer,* meaning "to limit."

In this selection, the author describes the **confines** of a plane, emphasizing the tight, enclosed space on board the aircraft.

Meet
Lady Bird Johnson
(1912–2007)

Author of

A WHITE HOUSE
DIARY

Texas-born Claudia Alta Taylor received her nickname when a nurse said the two-year-old was "as pretty as a lady bird." A graduate of the University of Texas, Lady Bird met and married Lyndon Johnson, then a young congressional aide, in 1934. Even though she was a shy woman, Lady Bird was a valued advisor and effective campaigner for her husband, who said that voters "would happily have elected her over me."

Living History When President Kennedy was assassinated, Vice President Lyndon Johnson became president, and Lady Bird became First Lady of the United States. In this role, she made many contributions to her husband's agenda, including the launch of Head Start, a project that makes early childhood education available to all children.

BACKGROUND FOR THE MEMOIR
History Connection
The Assassination of JFK

President John F. Kennedy was a young, vibrant, and popular leader who had been elected in 1960. His assassination on November 22, 1963, was a stunning and unforgettable event. As the news media reported the tragedy, people wept openly in the streets. A mournful nation agreed with Lyndon B. Johnson, JFK's successor, when he said, "We have suffered a loss that cannot be weighed."

DID YOU KNOW?
In 1982, Lady Bird Johnson founded the National Wildflower Research Center in Austin, Texas.

FROM

A WHITE HOUSE
DIARY

LADY BIRD JOHNSON

Dallas, Friday, November 22, 1963

It all began so beautifully. After a drizzle in the morning, the sun came out bright and clear. We were driving into Dallas. In the lead car were President and Mrs. Kennedy, John and Nellie Connally,[1] a Secret Service[2] car full of men, and then our car with Lyndon and me and Senator Ralph Yarborough.

The streets were lined with people—lots and lots of people—the children all smiling, placards, confetti, people waving from windows. One last happy moment I had was looking up and seeing Mary Griffith leaning out of a window waving at me. (Mary for many years had been in charge of altering the clothes which I purchased at Neiman-Marcus.)

Then, almost at the edge of town, on our way to the Trade Mart for the Presidential luncheon, we were rounding a curve, going down a hill, and suddenly there was a sharp, loud report. It sounded like a shot. The sound seemed to me to come from a building on the right above my shoulder. A moment passed, and then two more shots rang out in rapid succession. There had been such a gala air about the day that I thought the noise must come from firecrackers—part of the celebration. Then the Secret Service men were suddenly down in the lead car. Over the car radio system, I heard "Let's get out of here!" and our Secret Service man, Rufus Youngblood, vaulted over the front seat on top of Lyndon, threw him to the floor, and said, "Get down."

---

1. **John and Nellie Connally** John Connally, then governor of Texas, and his wife, Nellie.
2. **Secret Service** division of the U.S. Treasury Department, responsible for protecting the president.

Reading Skill
Author's Purpose
What does this sub-head tell you about the author's purpose in this part of the diary?

Literary Analysis
Voice
What do the details about firecrackers tell you about the writer's attitude toward the events she describes?

Reading Check
What was Lady Bird Johnson's last happy moment on this day?

November 22, 1963

President John F. Kennedy and his wife, Jackie, arrive in Dallas, Texas.

November 22, 1963

The President, First Lady, and Texas Governor Connally ride through Dallas.

November 22, 1963

President Kennedy smiles at the crowd in his last moments.

from A White House Diary **105**

Senator Yarborough and I ducked our heads. The car accelerated terrifically—faster and faster. Then, suddenly, the brakes were put on so hard that I wondered if we were going to make it as we wheeled left and went around the corner. We pulled up to a building. I looked up and saw a sign, "HOSPITAL." Only then did I believe that this might be what it was. Senator Yarborough kept saying in an excited voice, "Have they shot the President? Have they shot the President?" I said something like, "No, it can't be."

As we ground to a halt—we were still the third car—Secret Service men began to pull, lead, guide, and hustle us out. I cast one last look over my shoulder and saw in the President's car a bundle of pink, just like a drift of blossoms, lying on the back seat. It was Mrs. Kennedy lying over the President's body.

The Secret Service men rushed us to the right, then to the left, and then onward into a quiet room in the hospital—a very small room. It was lined with white sheets, I believe.

People came and went—Kenny O'Donnell, the President's top aide, Congressman Homer Thornberry, Congressman Jack Brooks. Always there was Rufe right there and other Secret Service agents—Emory Roberts, Jerry Kivett, Lem Johns, and Woody Taylor. People spoke of

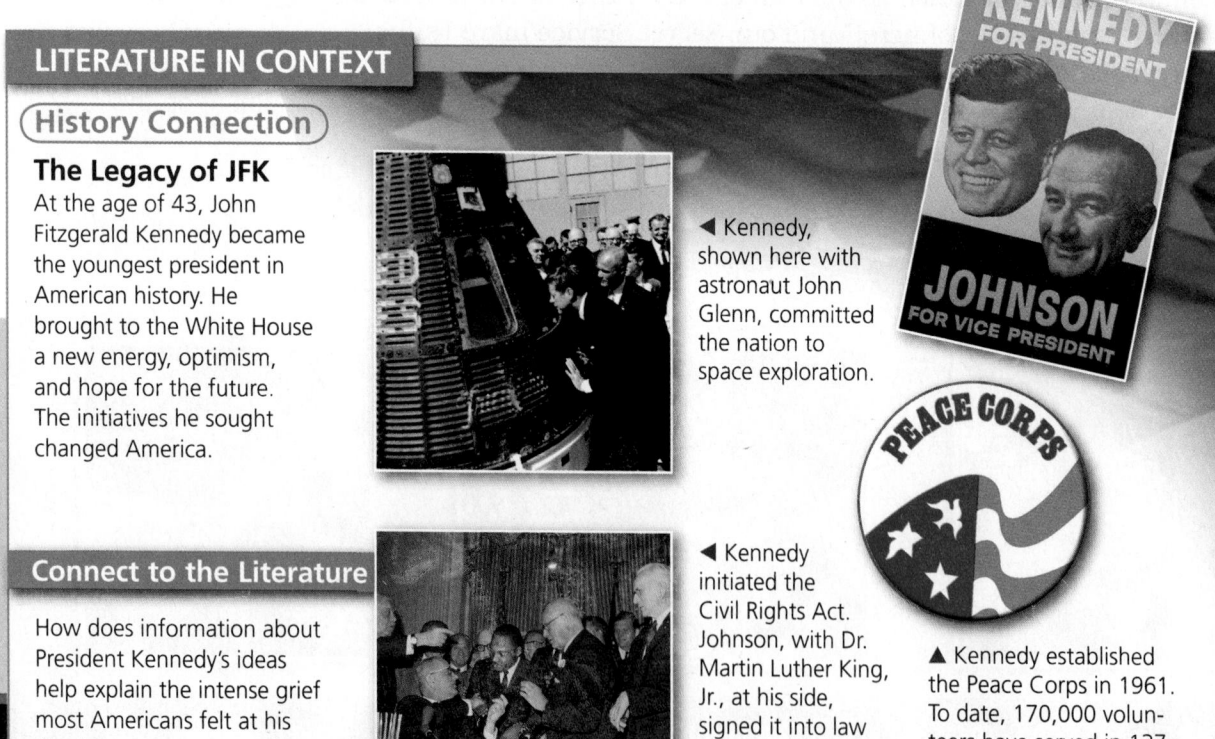

LITERATURE IN CONTEXT

History Connection

The Legacy of JFK
At the age of 43, John Fitzgerald Kennedy became the youngest president in American history. He brought to the White House a new energy, optimism, and hope for the future. The initiatives he sought changed America.

◀ Kennedy, shown here with astronaut John Glenn, committed the nation to space exploration.

Connect to the Literature

How does information about President Kennedy's ideas help explain the intense grief most Americans felt at his death?

◀ Kennedy initiated the Civil Rights Act. Johnson, with Dr. Martin Luther King, Jr., at his side, signed it into law in 1965.

▲ Kennedy established the Peace Corps in 1961. To date, 170,000 volunteers have served in 137 countries.

how widespread this might be. There was talk about where we would go—to the plane, to our house, back to Washington.

Through it all Lyndon was remarkably calm and quiet. He suggested that the Presidential plane ought to be moved to another part of the field. He spoke of going back out to the plane in unmarked black cars. Every face that came in, you searched for the answer. I think the face I kept seeing the answer on was the face of Kenny O'Donnell, who loved President Kennedy so much.

It was Lyndon who spoke of it first, although I knew I would not leave without doing it. He said, "You had better try to see Jackie and Nellie." We didn't know what had happened to John.

I asked the Secret Service if I could be taken to them. They began to lead me up one corridor and down another. Suddenly I found myself face to face with Jackie in a small hallway. I believe it was right outside the operating room. You always think of someone like her as being insulated, protected. She was quite alone. I don't think I ever saw anyone so much alone in my life. I went up to her, put my arms around her, and said something to her. I'm sure it was something like "God, help us all," because my feelings for her were too tumultuous to put into words.

And then I went to see Nellie. There it was different, because Nellie and I have gone through so many things together since 1938. I hugged her tight and we both cried and I said, "Nellie, John's going to be all right." And Nellie said, "Yes, John's going to be all right." Among her many other fine qualities, she is also strong.

I turned and went back to the small white room where Lyndon was. Mac Kilduff, the President's press man on this trip, and Kenny O'Donnell were coming and going. I think it was from Kenny's face that I first knew the truth and from Kenny's voice that I first heard

▼ **Critical Viewing**
What do the photographs below show about how mood can change? **[Interpret]**

Spiral Review
Literary Essay In the third paragraph, how does the author interweave personal ideas and examples with factual information to explain and present her perspective on a situation?

Vocabulary
tumultuous
(tōō mul´ chōō əs) *adj.*
greatly disturbed; in an uproar

Reading Check

Where were the Johnsons taken after the shots were fired?

Dealey Plaza

This is the site of JFK's assassination.

November 22, 1963

Spectators drop to the ground moments after shots are fired at President Kennedy.

November 22, 1963

Mourners lay flowers along the street, weeping for their fallen president.

from A White House Diary **107**

▼ **Critical Viewing**
The middle photograph shows Lyndon Johnson being sworn in as president. How do you think he felt at that moment? Why? **[Analyze]**

Vocabulary
implications
(im´ pli kā´ shənz) *n.*
indirect results

the words "The President is dead." Mr. Kilduff entered and said to Lyndon, "Mr. President."

It was decided that we would go immediately to the airport. Hurried plans were made about how we should get to the cars and who was to ride in which car. Our departure from the hospital and approach to the cars was one of the swiftest walks I have ever made.

We got in. Lyndon told the agents to stop the sirens. We drove along as fast as we could. I looked up at a building and there, already, was a flag at half-mast. I think that was when the enormity of what had happened first struck me.

When we got to the field, we entered *Air Force One*[3] for the first time. There was a TV set on and the commentator was saying, "Lyndon B. Johnson, now President of the United States." The news commentator was saying the President had been shot with a 30-30 rifle. The police had a suspect. They were not sure he was the assassin.

On the plane, all the shades were lowered. We heard that we were going to wait for Mrs. Kennedy and the coffin. There was a telephone call to Washington—I believe to the Attorney General.[4]

It was decided that Lyndon should be sworn in here as quickly as possible, because of national and world implications, and because we did not know how widespread this was as to intended victims. Judge Sarah Hughes, a Federal Judge in Dallas—and I am glad it was she— was called and asked to come in a hurry to administer the oath.

---

3. *Air Force One* name of the airplane officially assigned to transport the president of the United States.
4. **Attorney General** chief law officer of the nation, head of the U.S. Department of Justice; at the time, the position was held by Robert Kennedy, JFK's brother.

November 22, 1963

Vice President Johnson responds to the news of Kennedy's death.

November 22, 1963

Lyndon B. Johnson is sworn in as the thirty-sixth U.S. president.

November 22, 1963

The coffin of John F. Kennedy is removed from Air Force One.

Mrs. Kennedy had arrived by this time, as had the coffin. There, in the very narrow confines of the plane—with Jackie standing by Lyndon, her hair falling in her face but very composed, with me beside him, Judge Hughes in front of him, and a cluster of Secret Service people, staff, and Congressmen we had known for a long time around him—Lyndon took the oath of office.

It's odd the little things that come to your mind at times of utmost stress, the flashes of deep compassion you feel for people who are really not at the center of the tragedy. I heard a Secret Service man say in the most desolate voice—and I hurt for him: "We never lost a President in the Service." Then, Police Chief Curry of Dallas came on the plane and said, "Mrs. Kennedy, believe me, we did everything we possibly could." That must have been an agonizing moment for him.

We all sat around the plane. The casket was in the corridor. I went in the small private room to see Mrs. Kennedy, and though it was a very hard thing to do, she made it as easy as possible. She said things like, "Oh, Lady Bird, we've liked you two so much. . . . Oh, what if I had not been there. I'm so glad I was there."

I looked at her. Mrs. Kennedy's dress was stained with blood. One leg was almost entirely covered with it and her right glove was caked, it was caked with blood—her husband's blood. Somehow that was one of the most poignant sights—that immaculate woman exquisitely dressed, and caked in blood.

I asked her if I couldn't get someone in to help her change and she said, "Oh, no. Perhaps later I'll ask Mary Gallagher but not right now." And then with almost an element of fierceness—if a person

Vocabulary

confines (kän' fīnz) *n.* boundaries or bounded region; border; limit

desolate (des' ə lit) *adj.* forlorn; wretched

poignant (poin' yənt) *adj.* emotionally touching

immaculate (i mak' yə lit) *adj.* perfectly correct; without a flaw, fault, or error

Reading Skill
Author's Purpose
What is the writer's purpose in including the comments of the Secret Service man?

Reading Check

How did Mrs. Johnson first know that the President was dead?

November 22, 1963

President Johnson prepares to make his first address to a grieving nation.

November 25, 1963

John F. Kennedy, Jr., salutes his father's coffin.

A Nation Mourns

The flag on the White House is lowered to half-mast.

from A White House Diary **109**

that gentle, that dignified, can be said to have such a quality—she said, "I want them to see what they have done to Jack."

I tried to express how we felt. I said, "Oh, Mrs. Kennedy, you know we never even wanted to be Vice President and now, dear God, it's come to this." I would have done anything to help her, but there was nothing I could do, so rather quickly I left and went back to the main part of the airplane where everyone was seated.

The flight to Washington was silent, each sitting with his own thoughts. One of mine was a recollection of what I had said about Lyndon a long time ago—he's a good man in a tight spot. I remembered one little thing he had said in that hospital room—"Tell the children to get a Secret Service man with them."

Finally we got to Washington, with a cluster of people waiting and many bright lights. The casket went off first, then Mrs. Kennedy, and then we followed. The family had come to join her. Lyndon made a very simple, very brief, and, I think, strong statement to the people there. Only about four sentences. We got in helicopters, dropped him off at the White House, and I came home in a car with Liz Carpenter.[5]

---

5. **Liz Carpenter** Mrs. Johnson's press secretary.

The flight to Washington was silent, each sitting with his own thoughts.

Support your responses with evidence from the text.

Critical Thinking

1. **Respond:** What do you admire most about Mrs. Johnson? Explain.

2. **(a)** What does Mrs. Kennedy say when Mrs. Johnson offers to find someone to help her change her clothes?
   (b) Interpret: What does Mrs. Kennedy mean? **(c) Analyze:** Why do you think Mrs. Johnson reports this detail?

3. **(a)** What comment about her husband does Mrs. Johnson recall on the flight back to Washington? **(b) Make Inferences:** What character traits does this comment suggest President Johnson possesses? Explain. **(c) Support:** Which details from the selection show that Mrs. Johnson possesses similar character traits?

4. **Evaluate:** Do you think Mrs. Johnson effectively expresses what it felt like to live through this historic incident? Explain.

   Can truth change?
   How do the events of November 22, 1963, change what Lady Bird Johnson thinks of as her everyday reality?

Literary Analysis: Voice

1. (a) Complete a chart like the one shown to find examples of Johnson's word choice, attitude, and sentence structure.

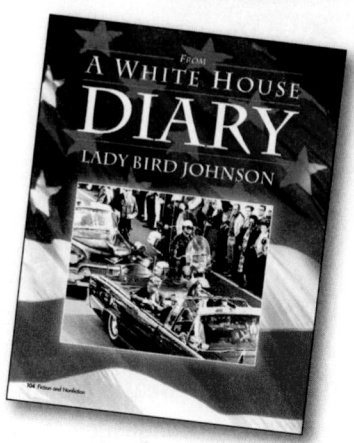

Voice		
Word Choice	**Attitude**	**Sentence Structure**

(b) Using examples from your chart, describe Johnson's **voice.**

2. (a) What factual details about Lyndon Johnson are emphasized in Lady Bird Johnson's autobiographical writing? **(b)** What are two personal examples and ideas that reflect Mrs. Johnson's unique perspective?

Reading Skill: Author's Purpose

3. Review the notes you made in your preview of the excerpt. Which of your ideas about the **author's purpose** were confirmed as you read the selection? Which were not? Explain.

4. (a) What general purpose do you think Mrs. Johnson had in writing this portion of *A White House Diary*? Explain. **(b)** What more specific purpose do you think she had? Explain.

Vocabulary

Practice An **analogy** shows the relationship between pairs of words. To complete each analogy, use a word from the vocabulary list on page 102. For each case, your choice should create a word pair that matches the relationship between the first two words given.

1. weak : strong :: calm : _____
2. rain : flood :: choice : _____
3. laughter : humorous :: sadness : _____
4. troubled : carefree :: _____ : delighted
5. steep : precipitous :: _____ : perfect
6. vital : necessary :: _____ : bounds

Word Power Use the context of the sentences and what you know about the **root -fin-** to explain your answer to each question.

1. If you have a *definite* opinion, are you uncertain?
2. Do you think of the *infinity* of space as limitless?

Word Power

The root **-fin-**, meaning "end," comes to English through the **Middle French** word *finer*, meaning "to limit."

Apply It Explain how the root *-fin-* helps you determine the meanings of these technical academic words from science and the arts. Consult a dictionary if necessary.

definition
finale
refinery

Can *truth* change?

Writing About the Big Question

In "My English," Alvarez describes how her view of her place in the world changes as she learns English. Use these sentence starters to develop your ideas about the Big Question.

Learning a language can affect our **perspective** because_____.

We may make **assumptions** about people from other cultures because _____.

As You Read Look for details that show how the author's confidence in herself changes as she learns English.

Vocabulary

Read each word and its definition. Decide whether you know the word well, know it a little bit, or do not know it at all. After you read, see how your knowledge of each word has increased.

- **bilingual** (bī liŋ´ gwəl) *adj.* using two languages (p. 114) *The bilingual student speaks Spanish and English.* linguistics *n.*

- **countenance** (koun´ tə nəns) *n.* face (p. 116) *The child's overjoyed countenance showed her relief at being home.*

- **ponderously** (pän´ dər əs lē) *adv.* in a labored, boring, and serious way (p. 117) *The telemarketer ponderously explained the rules of the service contract.* ponderous *adj.* ponder *v.*

- **enumerated** (ē nōō´ mər āt id) *v.* named one by one; specified, as in a list (p. 118) *Joel enumerated the names of video games he likes to play.* enumerate *v.* enumerable *adj.* numeral *n.*

- **interminably** (in tʉr´ mi nə blē) *adv.* endlessly (p. 119) *To the tired audience, the speaker seemed to go on interminably.* interminable *adj.* terminal *adj.* terminal *n.* terminate *v.*

- **accentuated** (ak sen´ chōō āt id) *v.* emphasized; heightened the effect of (p. 119) *Her new haircut accentuated her graceful neck.* accentuate *v.* accent *n.*

Word Power

The root *-term-*, meaning "limit or end," comes from the **Greek** word *terma*, meaning "boundary."

The teacher in this essay does not make the class diagram sentences interminably, or in a way that has no end.

Meet
Julia Alvarez
(b. 1950)

Author of
My English

When her family fled the Dominican Republic and returned to New York, Julia Alvarez was ten years old, and Spanish was her primary language. Painfully aware of not fitting in, Julia took refuge in reading and making up stories. She says, "I landed, not in the United States, but in the English language. That became my new home."

"I write to find out who I am." Alvarez attended Middlebury College, where she won several poetry awards. She later earned a master's degree in creative writing from Syracuse University. Alvarez says that writing is "a way to understand yourself." Her writing has been praised for its humor, sensitivity, and insight.

Did You Know?

One of Julia Alvarez's books, *In the Time of the Butterflies*, was made into a film starring Salma Hayek.

BACKGROUND FOR THE AUTOBIOGRAPHY

Social Studies Connection
Alvarez's Two Nationalities

Julia Alvarez, the author of "My English," was born in New York but spent her early years in the Dominican Republic, a small Caribbean nation. An independent state since 1844, the Dominican Republic has often struggled with foreign conquest, political unrest, and dictatorship. Alvarez's family was forced to return to New York in 1960 because her father had participated in a movement against the brutal Dominican dictator Raphael Trujillo.

My English

Julia Alvarez

Spiral Review
Literary Essay In this paragraph, how does the author interweave personal examples and ideas with factual information to explain and present her perspective on a situation?

Vocabulary
bilingual (bī lin´ gwəl)
adj. using two languages

Mami and Papi used to speak it when they had a secret they wanted to keep from us children. We lived then in the Dominican Republic, and the family as a whole spoke only Spanish at home, until my sisters and I started attending the Carol Morgan School, and we became a bilingual family. Spanish had its many tongues as well. There was the castellano[1] of Padre[2] Joaquín from Spain, whose lisp we all loved to imitate. Then the educated español my parents' families spoke, aunts and uncles who were always correcting us children, for we spent most of the day with the maids

---

1. **castellano** (că´ stā yä´ nō) *Spanish for "Castilian," the most widely spoken dialect of the Spanish language.*
2. **Padre** (pä´ drā) *"Father" (Spanish), a form of address for a Roman Catholic priest.*

and so had picked up their "bad Spanish." Campesinas,[3] they spoke a lilting, animated campuno,[4] ss swallowed, endings chopped off, funny turns of phrases. This campuno was my true mother tongue, not the Spanish of Calderón de la Barca or Cervantes or even Neruda,[5] but of Chucha and Iluminada and Gladys and Ursulina from Juncalito and Licey and Boca de Yuma and San Juan de la Maguana.[6] Those women yakked as they cooked, they storytold, they gossiped, they sang—boleros, merengues, canciones, salves.[7] Theirs were the voices that belonged to the rain and the wind and the teeny, teeny stars even a small child could blot out with her thumb.

Besides all these versions of Spanish, every once in a while another strange tongue emerged from my papi's mouth or my mami's lips. What I first recognized was not a language, but a tone of voice, serious, urgent, something important and top secret being said, some uncle in trouble, someone divorcing, someone dead. *Say it in English so the children won't understand.* I would listen, straining to understand, thinking that this was not a different language but just another and harder version of Spanish. *Say it in English so the children won't understand.* From the beginning, English was the sound of worry and secrets, the sound of being left out.

I could make no sense of this "harder Spanish," and so I tried by other means to find out what was going on. I knew my mother's face by heart. When the little lines on the corners of her eyes crinkled, she was amused. When her nostrils flared and she bit her lips, she was trying hard not to laugh. She held her head down, eyes glancing up, when she thought I was lying. Whenever she spoke that gibberish English, I translated the general content by watching the Spanish expressions on her face.

LITERATURE IN CONTEXT

Social Studies Connection

The Dominican Republic
The Dominican Republic occupies the eastern portion of the Caribbean island of Hispaniola, which it shares with the Republic of Haiti. Located about 600 miles southeast of Florida, this area was one of the landing points of Christopher Columbus's first voyage in 1492. The dominant language and culture are Spanish.

Connect to the Literature

Considering the distance between the Dominican Republic and the United States, why do you think knowing both Spanish and English would be useful?

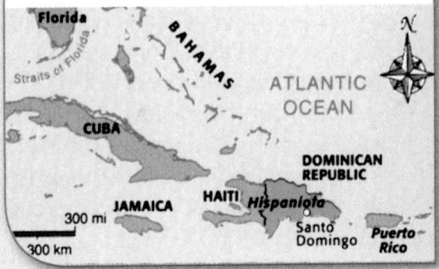

Reading Check

According to Alvarez, how does English sound?

---

3. **Campesinas** (căm pä sē′ näs) simple rural women; peasant women (Spanish).
4. **campuno** (căm pōō′ nō) Spanish dialect spoken in rural areas of the Dominican Republic.
5. **Calderón de la Barca** (căl de rôn′ dā lä bär′ cä) . . . **Cervantes** (ser vän′ tes) . . . **Neruda** (nā rōō′ dä) important literary figures.
6. **Juncalito** (hōōn cä lē′ tō) . . . **Licey** . . . **Boca de Yuma** (bō′ cä dā yōō′ mä) . . . **San Juan de la Maguana** (sän hwän′ dā lä mä gwä′ nä) small rural villages in the Dominican Republic.
7. **boleros** (bō ler′ ōs) . . . **merengues** (me reŋ′ gās) . . . **canciones** (căn sē ō′ nes) . . . **salves** (säl′ ves) Spanish and Latin American songs and dances.

Soon, I began to learn more English, at the Carol Morgan School. That is, when I had stopped gawking. The teacher and some of the American children had the strangest coloration: light hair, light eyes, light skin, as if Ursulina had soaked them in bleach too long, to' deteñío.[8] I did have some blond cousins, but they had deeply tanned skin, and as they grew older, their hair darkened, so their earlier paleness seemed a phase of their acquiring normal color. Just as strange was the little girl in my reader who had a *cat* and a *dog*, that looked just like un gatito y un perrito. Her mami was *Mother* and her papi *Father*. Why have a whole new language for school and for books with a teacher who could speak it teaching you double the amount of words you really needed?

Butter, butter, butter, butter. All day, one English word that had particularly struck me would go round and round in my mouth and weave through all the Spanish in my head until by the end of the day, the word did sound like just another Spanish word. And so I would say, "Mami, please pass la mantequilla." She would scowl and say in English, "I'm sorry, I don't understand. But would you be needing some butter on your bread?" ●

Why my parents didn't first educate us in our native language by enrolling us in a Dominican school, I don't know. Part of it was that Mami's family had a tradition of sending the boys to the States to boarding school and college, and she had been one of the first girls to be allowed to join her brothers. At Abbot Academy,[9] whose school song was our lullaby as babies ("Although Columbus and Cabot[10] never heard of Abbot, it's quite the place for you and me"), she had become quite Americanized. It was very important, she kept saying, that we learn our English. She always used the possessive pronoun: *your* English, an inheritance we had come into and must wisely use. Unfortunately, my English became all mixed up with our Spanish.

Mix-up, or what's now called Spanglish, was the language we spoke for several years. There wasn't a sentence that wasn't colonized by an English word. At school, a Spanish word would suddenly slide into my English like someone butting into line. Teacher, whose face I was learning to read as minutely as my mother's, would scowl but no smile played on her lips. Her pale skin made her strange countenance hard to read, so that I often misjudged how much I could get away with. Whenever I made a

8. **to' deteñío** (tō dā tān yē ō) all washed out; completely colorless (Spanish).
9. **Abbot Academy** boarding school for girls in Andover, Massachusetts; merged in 1973 with the neighboring boys' school, Phillips Academy.
10. **Cabot** (kab ət) John Cabot, (1450–1499) Italian explorer who sailed in the service of England and was the first European to discover the coast of North America in 1497.

Literary Analysis
Voice
Which words and phrases here convey the writer's uncertainty about English and her unwillingness to learn it?

Vocabulary
countenance
(koun´tə nəns) *n.* face

mistake, Teacher would shake her head slowly, "In English, YU-LEE-AH, there's no such word as *columpio*. Do you mean a *swing*?"

I would bow my head, humiliated by the smiles and snickers of the American children around me. I grew insecure about Spanish. My native tongue was not quite as good as English, as if words like *columpio* were illegal immigrants trying to cross a border into another language. But Teacher's discerning grammar-and-vocabulary-patrol ears could tell and send them back.

Soon, I was talking up an English storm. "Did you eat English parrot?" my grandfather asked one Sunday. I had just enlisted yet one more patient servant to listen to my rendition of "Peter Piper picked a peck of pickled peppers" at breakneck pace. "Huh?" I asked impolitely in English, putting him in his place. *Cat got your tongue? No big deal! So there! Take that! Holy Toledo!* (Our teacher's favorite "curse word.") *Go jump in the lake! Really dumb. Golly. Gosh.* Slang, clichés, sayings, hotshot language that our teacher called, ponderously, idiomatic expressions. Riddles, jokes, puns, conundrums. *What is yellow and goes click-click? Why did the chicken cross the road? See you later, alligator.* How wonderful to call someone an alligator and not be scolded for being disrespectful. In fact, they were supposed to say back, *In a while, crocodile.*

There was also a neat little trick I wanted to try on an English-speaking adult at home. I had learned it from Elizabeth, my smart-alecky friend in fourth grade, whom I alternately worshiped and resented. I'd ask her a question that required an explanation, and she'd answer, "Because . . ." "Elizabeth, how come you didn't go to Isabel's birthday party?" "Because . . ." "Why didn't you put your name in your reader?" "Because . . ." I thought that such a cool way to get around having to come up with answers. So, I practiced saying it under my breath, planning for the day I could use it on an unsuspecting English-speaking adult.

One Sunday at our extended family dinner, my grandfather sat down at the children's table to chat with us. He was famous, in fact, for the way he could carry on adult conversations with his grandchildren. He often spoke to us in English so that we could practice speaking it outside the classroom. He was a Cornell[11] man, a United Nations representative from our country. He gave speeches in English. Perfect English, my mother's phrase. That

---

11. **Cornell** Cornell University in Ithaca, New York.

Literary Analysis
Voice
How would you describe the author's voice, based on her examples of idiomatic expressions?

Vocabulary
ponderously
(pän´ dər əs lē) *adv.*
in a labored, boring, and serious way

Cat got your tongue?

See you later, alligator.

In a while, crocodile.

Reading Check
Which language did Alvarez learn to speak first—English or Spanish?

Sunday, he asked me a question. I can't even remember what it was because I wasn't really listening but lying in wait for my chance. "Because . . .," I answered him. Papito waited a second for the rest of my sentence and then gave me a thumbnail grammar lesson, "*Because* has to be followed by a clause."

"Why's that?" I asked, nonplussed.[12]

"Because," he winked. "Just because."

A beginning wordsmith, I had so much left to learn; sometimes it was disheartening. Once Tío[13] Gus, the family intellectual, put a speck of salt on my grandparents' big dining table during Sunday dinner. He said, "Imagine this whole table is the human brain. Then this teensy grain is all we ever use of our intelligence!" He enumerated geniuses who had perhaps used two grains, maybe three: Einstein, Michelangelo, da Vinci, Beethoven. We children believed him. It was the kind of impossible fact we thrived on, proving as it did that the world out there was not drastically different from the one we were making up in our heads.

Later, at home, Mami said that you had to take what her younger brother said "with a grain of salt." I thought she was still referring to Tío Gus's demonstration, and I tried to puzzle out what she was saying. Finally, I asked what she meant. "Taking what someone says with a grain of salt is an idiomatic expression in English," she explained. It was pure voodoo is what it was—what later I learned poetry could also do: a grain of salt could symbolize both the human brain and a condiment for human nonsense. And it could be itself, too: a grain of salt to flavor a bland plate of American food.

When we arrived in New York, I was shocked. A country where everyone spoke English! These people must be smarter, I thought. Maids, waiters, taxi drivers, doormen, bums on the street, all spoke this difficult language. It took some time before I understood that Americans were not necessarily a smarter, superior race. It was as natural for them to learn their mother tongue as it was for a little Dominican baby to learn Spanish. It came with "mother's milk," my mother explained, and for a while I thought a mother tongue was a mother tongue because you got it from your mother's milk along with proteins and vitamins.

Soon it wasn't so strange that everyone was speaking in English instead of Spanish. I learned not to hear it as English, but as sense. I no longer strained to understand, I understood. I relaxed in this second language. Only when someone with a heavy southern or

Vocabulary
enumerated
(ē nōō´ mər āt id) *v.*
named one by one;
specified, as in a list

Reading Skill
Author's Purpose
Why do you think the writer includes these details about Mami's comments?

"Taking what someone says **with a grain of salt** *is an idiomatic expression in English," she explained.*

---

12. **nonplussed** (nän plŭst´) *v.* confused; baffled.
13. **Tío** (tē´ ō) "Uncle" (Spanish).

British accent spoke in a movie, or at church when the priest droned his sermon—only then did I experience that little catch of anxiety. I worried that I would not be able to understand, that I wouldn't be able to "keep up" with the voice speaking in this acquired language. I would be like those people from the Bible we had studied in religion class, whom I imagined standing at the foot of an enormous tower[14] that looked just like the skyscrapers around me. They had been punished for their pride by being made to speak different languages so that they didn't understand what anyone was saying.

But at the foot of those towering New York skyscrapers, I began to understand more and more—not less and less—English. In sixth grade, I had one of the first in a lucky line of great English teachers who began to nurture in me a love of language, a love that had been there since my childhood of listening closely to words. Sister Maria Generosa did not make our class interminably diagram sentences from a workbook or learn a catechism[15] of grammar rules. Instead, she asked us to write little stories imagining we were snowflakes, birds, pianos, a stone in the pavement, a star in the sky. What would it feel like to be a flower with roots in the ground? If the clouds could talk, what would they say? She had an expressive, dreamy look that was accentuated by the wimple[16] that framed her face.

Supposing, just supposing . . . My mind would take off, soaring into possibilities, a flower with roots, a star in the sky, a cloud full of sad, sad tears, a piano crying out each time its back was tapped, music only to our ears.

---

14. **enormous tower** a reference to the Tower of Babel in Genesis 11:1–9. According to Genesis, early Babylonians tried to build a tower to heaven, but they were thwarted when God caused them to speak many languages rather than one.
15. **catechism** (kat´ ə kiz´ əm) *n.* short book written in question-and-answer format.
16. **wimple** (wim´ pəl) *n.* cloth worn around the head, neck, and chin by some nuns.

▼ **Critical Viewing**
Based on these photographs, why do you think Alvarez might have found New York to be both intimidating and exciting? **[Analyze]**

Vocabulary
interminably
(in tur´ mi nə blē) *adv.* endlessly

accentuated
(ak sen´ chōō āt id) *v.* emphasized; heightened the effect of

Reading Check
To what city does Alvarez's family relocate?

Literary Analysis
Voice
Which words and phrases in these paragraphs give the author's voice a poetic quality?

Sister Maria stood at the chalkboard. Her chalk was always snapping in two because she wrote with such energy, her whole habit[17] shaking with the swing of her arm, her hand tap-tap-tapping on the board. "Here's a simple sentence: 'The snow fell.'" Sister pointed with her chalk, her eyebrows lifted, her wimple poked up. Sometimes I could see wisps of gray hair that strayed from under her headdress. "But watch what happens if we put an adverb at the beginning and a prepositional phrase at the end: 'Gently, the snow fell on the bare hills.'"

I thought about the snow. I saw how it might fall on the hills, tapping lightly on the bare branches of trees. Softly, it would fall on the cold, bare fields. On toys children had left out in the yard, and on cars and on little birds and on people out late walking on the streets. Sister Marie filled the chalkboard with snowy print, on and on, handling and shaping and moving the language, scribbling all over the board until English, those verbal gadgets, those tricks and turns of phrases, those little fixed units and counters, became a charged, fluid mass that carried me in its great fluent waves, rolling and moving onward, to deposit me on the shores of my new homeland. I was no longer a foreigner with no ground to stand on. I had landed in the English language.

---

17. **habit** (hab´ it) *n.* robe or dress worn by some nuns.

I was no longer a foreigner with no ground to stand on. I had landed in the English language.

Support your responses with evidence from the text.

Critical Thinking

1. **Respond:** After reading her account of her early life, what question would you like to ask Julia Alvarez? Explain.

2. **(a)** When Alvarez was young, at what times did her parents speak English at home? **(b) Make Inferences:** Why do you think Alvarez says that English was the "sound of being left out"?

3. **(a)** What method does Sister Maria Generosa use to teach Alvarez English? **(b) Analyze:** How does this method differ from the way she was taught at the Carol Morgan School? **(c) Assess:** Which method does Alvarez prefer? Why?

4. **Evaluate:** How well do you think Alvarez succeeds in portraying the growth of her relationship with the English language?

   Can truth change?
   How do Alvarez's ideas about English change as she learns the language?

Literary Analysis: Voice

1. (a) Complete a chart like the one shown to find examples of Alvarez's word choice, attitude, and sentence structure.
(b) Using examples from your chart, describe Alvarez's **voice** in this work of nonfiction.

Voice		
Word Choice	**Attitude**	**Sentence Structure**

2. (a) What factual details about learning English are emphasized in this example of autobiographical writing? **(b)** What are two personal examples and ideas that reflect her individual perspective?

Reading Skill: Author's Purpose

3. Review the notes you made in your preview of "My English." Which of your ideas about the **author's purpose** were confirmed as you read the selection? Which were not? Explain.

4. (a) What general purpose do you think Alvarez had in writing this essay? Explain. **(b)** What more specific purpose or purposes do you think she had for writing? Support your answer.

Vocabulary

Practice An **analogy** shows the relationship between pairs of words. To complete each analogy, use a word from the vocabulary list on page 112. For each case, your choice should create a word pair that matches the relationship between the first two words given.

1. happily : sadly :: _____ : quickly

2. bipartisan : party :: _____ : language

3. frame : photograph :: _____ : expression

4. counted : tally :: _____ : list

5. terrific : great :: _____ : highlighted

6. boldly : meekly :: _____ : lightly

Word Power Use the context of the sentences and what you know about the **root -term-** to explain your answer to each question.

1. If you are *determined*, are you likely to quit?

2. If a worker is *terminated*, has he or she been fired?

Word Power

The root **-term-**, meaning "limit," comes from the **Greek** word *terma*, meaning "boundary."

Apply It Explain how the root *-term-* helps you determine the meanings of these technical academic words from social studies. Consult a dictionary if necessary.

term of office
termination
determine

Integrated Language Skills

from A White House Diary • My English

Conventions: Personal, Reflexive, and Reciprocal Pronouns

A **pronoun** takes the place of a noun. A **personal pronoun** refers to the person speaking (first person), the person spoken to (second person), or the person or thing spoken about (third person).

Reflexive pronouns end in *-self* or *-selves* and are used to indicate that someone or something performs an action to, for, or upon himself, herself, or itself.

Reciprocal pronouns indicate that a feeling or action is mutual, or shared by two (*each other*) or more (*one another*) subjects.

	First Person	Second Person	Third Person
Personal Pronouns	**Singular:** I, me, my, mine **Plural:** we, us, our, ours	**Singular:** you, your, yours **Plural:** you, your, yours	**Singular:** he, she, him her, his, hers, it, its **Plural:** they, them, their, theirs
Reflexive Pronouns	**Singular:** myself **Plural:** ourselves	**Singular:** yourself **Plural:** yourselves	**Singular:** himself, herself, itself **Plural:** themselves
Reciprocal Pronouns	each other (shared by two) one another (shared by more than two)		

Practice A Read the sentences and identify the function of each pronoun as personal, reflexive, or reciprocal.

1. At first, Lady Bird Johnson was herself unsure of what had happened.
2. Lady Bird and Nellie consoled each other.
3. If you were alive in 1963, you would still remember the events of November 22.

Speaking Application Tell a partner about an important day in your life. Use personal and reciprocal pronouns in your telling.

Practice B Rewrite each sentence using at least one reciprocal pronoun. Make sure your sentences have the same meanings as the originals.

1. Alvarez did not resemble the character in her book. The character did not resemble her, either.
2. Grandfather sat with the children. The children sat with grandfather.

Writing Application Using this sentence as a model, write two sentences that include both personal and reciprocal pronouns: *Julia Alvarez writes about her parents speaking English to each other.*

PH GRAMMAR HANDBOOK Further instruction and practice are available in the *Prentice Hall Grammar Handbook*.

Writing

Both selections deal with the experience of going through a tough time. Write about an event of importance to you. As the first step in planning your draft, **select the correct genre** for conveying your intended meaning to multiple audiences: your peers and your teacher. For example, you may write an **essay,** a **poem,** a **dialogue,** or a **script.** Then, consider these questions:

- What specific words and images does this event call to mind?
- Has this subject always been important to you? Why or why not?
- How does this subject influence your outlook on the world?

Grammar Application Use personal, reflexive, and reciprocal pronouns correctly in your writing.

Writing Workshop: *Work in Progress*

Prewriting for Problem-Solution Essay Think of issues that concern people in your school or community. Jot down several problems you think can be solved. As you write, use a narrative format, describing events in the order they occured. Circle one and write a statement of a possible solution. Put these Problem Notes in your writing portfolio.

Research and Technology

Each of these selections is based on actual historical events. Using presentation software, produce a **multimedia presentation** for your class about one of these two topics suggested by the reading:

- Changes to the role of first lady over time
- Immigration to the United States since 1800, the reasons people left their home countries, and what they sought in the United States

Follow these steps to complete the assignment:

- Choose your topic and conduct research to learn more.
- Decide upon a distinctive point of view from which you will present your information.
- Consider your specific audience and what they will want and need to know about your subject.
- Identify the main idea and key points of your presentation.
- Choose appropriate media such as **graphics, images, and sounds** that convey your **distinctive point of view** and appeal to your specific **audience.** Use graphics and illustrations to explain concepts when appropriate.

 Focus on the TEKS

Conventions
(17)(A)(iii) Use and understand reciprocal pronouns in the context of reading, writing, and speaking.

Writing
(13)(A) Plan a first draft by selecting the correct genre for conveying the intended meaning to multiple audiences.

(15)(D) Produce a multimedia presentation with graphics, images, and sound that conveys a distinctive point of view and appeals to a specific audience.

Use this prewriting activity to prepare for the **Writing Workshop** on page 172.

www.PHLitOnline.com

- Interactive graphic organizers
- Grammar tutorial
- Interactive journals

Before You Read

The Secret Life of Walter Mitty • Uncle Marcos

Selection Choices

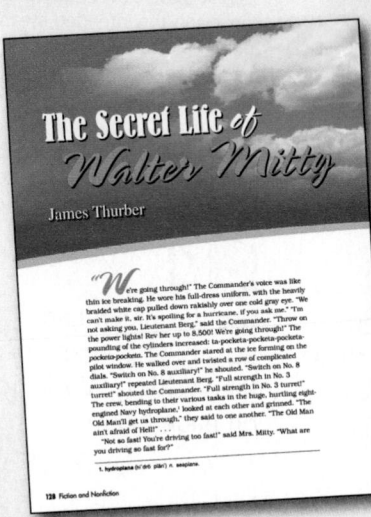

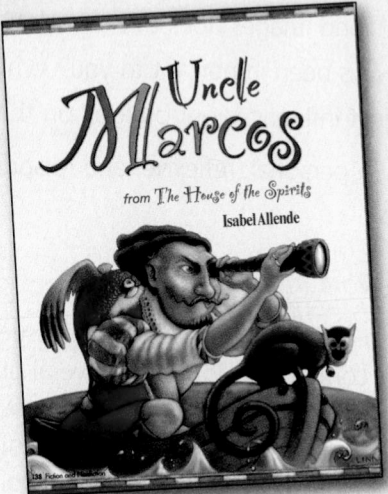

▲ Read **"The Secret Life of Walter Mitty"** to learn how a man lives an imaginary life of adventure in his own mind.

▲ Read **"Uncle Marcos"** to learn about an eccentric uncle's fabulously memorable life.

 TEXAS Focus on the TEKS

Meet these standards with either **"The Secret Life of Walter Mitty"** (p. 128) or **"Uncle Marcos"** (p. 138).

Reading
(5)(B) Analyze how authors develop complex yet believable characters in works of fiction through a range of literary devices. (Literary Analysis: Character)

Reading/Comprehension Skills
RC-9(A) Reflect on understanding to monitor comprehension (e.g., asking questions). (Reading Skill: Author's Purpose)

RC-9(B) Make complex inferences about text. (Reading Skill: Author's Purpose)

Writing
(15)(A)(v) Write an analytical essay that includes relevant information. (Writing: Character Profile)

Research
(21)(B) Organize information gathered from multiple sources to create a variety of forms (e.g., learning logs). (Research and Technology: Learning Log)

(21)(C) Summarize researched information. (Research and Technology: Learning Log)

Literary Analysis: Character

A **character** is a person or an animal who takes part in the action of a literary work. Authors develop complex yet believable characters in works of fiction through a range of literary devices and strategies. You can learn about a character through the character's words and actions, the author's narration, and what others say about the character.

- A **round character** is complex, showing many different qualities— revealing faults as well as virtues. In contrast, a **flat character** is one-dimensional, showing a single trait.
- A **dynamic character** develops, changes, and learns something during the course of a story—unlike a **static character,** who remains the same.

The main character of a story tends to be a round character and is usually dynamic. The main character's development and growth are often central to a story's plot and theme.

As You Read Jot down the literary devices and strategies the author uses to develop characters that are complex yet believable.

Reading Skill: Author's Purpose

An **author's purpose** is his or her main reason for writing. In fiction, the specific purpose is often conveyed by the story's theme. Pause periodically while reading and **reflect** on your understanding. **Ask questions** to **make inferences** about the story's details and events. Use the following questions as models:

- *What significance might this event have?*
- *Why does the author include this detail?*

Use the inferences you make to determine the author's purpose.

Using the Strategy: Author's Purpose Map

As You Read Use a chart like the one shown to reflect on your understanding. Record your **questions** and inferences about story details and events. Then, identify the author's purpose based on your findings.

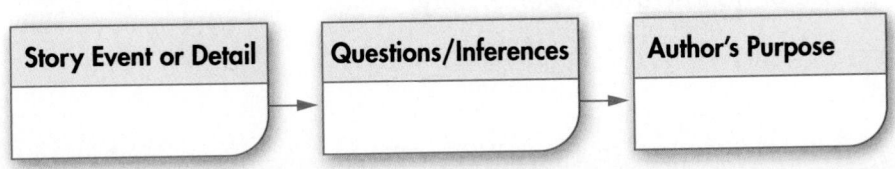

Story Event or Detail	Questions/Inferences	Author's Purpose

TEXAS
PHLitOnline
www.PHLitOnline.com

Hear It!
- Selection summary audio
- Selection audio

See It!
- Get Connected video
- Background video
- More about the author
- Vocabulary flashcards

Do It!
- Interactive journals
- Interactive graphic organizers
- Self-test
- Internet activity
- Grammar tutorial
- Interactive vocabulary games

Can *truth* change?

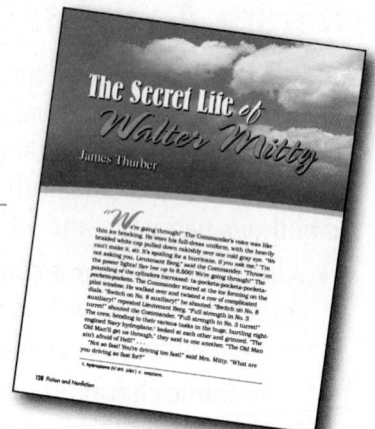

Writing About the Big Question

In "The Secret Life of Walter Mitty," Mitty lives two lives: the one dominated by his wife and the one of his imagination. Use these sentence starters to develop your ideas about the Big Question.

Compared to our everyday life, the life of our imagination is _____.

Truth can change in our imagination because _____.

As You Read Look for details in the text that show how important Mitty's imagination is in his daily life.

Vocabulary

Read each word and its definition. Decide whether you know the word well, know it a little bit, or do not know it at all. After you read, see how your knowledge of each word has increased.

- **distraught** (di strôt´) *adj.* very troubled or confused (p. 130) *She was <u>distraught</u> over losing her wallet.*

- **insolent** (in´ sə lənt) *adj.* boldly disrespectful (p. 130) *Her <u>insolent</u> words offended the guests.* *insolence n. insolently adv.*

- **insinuatingly** (in sin´ yo͞o āt´ iŋ lē) *adv.* suggesting indirectly (p. 131) *My friend looked at me <u>insinuatingly</u>, as if she thought I had taken the money from her purse.* *insinuate v. insinuation n.*

- **pandemonium** (pan´ də mō´ nē əm) *n.* any place or scene of wild disorder, noise, or confusion (p. 132) *When the band left the stage, the crowd erupted into <u>pandemonium</u>.*

- **derisive** (di rī´ siv) *adj.* showing contempt or ridicule (p. 134) *With a <u>derisive</u> laugh, the bully pushed the little boy off the swing.* *derision n. deride v.*

- **inscrutable** (in skro͞ot´ ə bəl) *adj.* baffling; mysterious (p. 134) *No one has ever solved the puzzle of his <u>inscrutable</u> personality.*

Word Power

The **Latin suffix -able** means "can or will" or "capable of being."

Thurber closes the story by describing Mitty as **inscrutable** to the end. The word choice indicates that Mitty is able to remain mysterious to the last moment.

Meet
James Thurber
(1894–1961)

Author of
The Secret Life of
Walter Mitty

James Thurber was a rare writer who expressed his comic genius in both words and pictures. He wrote stories, plays, essays, and poems, and he was also a great cartoonist. Born in Ohio, he joined the staff of *The New Yorker* magazine in 1927. "The Secret Life of Walter Mitty" was published in that magazine in 1939, becoming an instant success.

Humor and Anxiety Many of Thurber's stories and sketches grew directly out of his own life. As he put it, "Humor is a kind of emotional chaos told about calmly and quietly in retrospect." Thurber's characters try to stand up to the surprises of the modern world. Whether they succeed or fail, they always strike readers as authentic and very funny.

BACKGROUND FOR THE STORY

Science Connection

Reality and Imagination

Psychologists say that a person's thoughts are often a series of seemingly unconnected reflections. An event in the real world can prompt unpredictable mental responses, such as memories, snippets of songs, or daydreams. In Thurber's story, random events cause Walter Mitty's thoughts to jump back and forth between his exciting "secret" life and his humdrum everyday existence.

Did You Know?

Thurber offered a Hollywood producer $10,000 not to make a movie about Walter Mitty. The movie was made anyway in 1947. A new version is scheduled to be released in 2010.

The Secret Life of Walter Mitty

James Thurber

"We're going through!" The Commander's voice was like thin ice breaking. He wore his full-dress uniform, with the heavily braided white cap pulled down rakishly over one cold gray eye. "We can't make it, sir. It's spoiling for a hurricane, if you ask me." "I'm not asking you, Lieutenant Berg," said the Commander. "Throw on the power lights! Rev her up to 8,500! We're going through!" The pounding of the cylinders increased: ta-pocketa-pocketa-pocketa-*pocketa-pocketa*. The Commander stared at the ice forming on the pilot window. He walked over and twisted a row of complicated dials. "Switch on No. 8 auxiliary!" he shouted. "Switch on No. 8 auxiliary!" repeated Lieutenant Berg. "Full strength in No. 3 turret!" shouted the Commander. "Full strength in No. 3 turret!" The crew, bending to their various tasks in the huge, hurtling eight-engined Navy hydroplane,[1] looked at each other and grinned. "The Old Man'll get us through," they said to one another. "The Old Man ain't afraid of Hell!" . . .

"Not so fast! You're driving too fast!" said Mrs. Mitty. "What are you driving so fast for?"

---

1. hydroplane (hī′drō plān′) *n.* seaplane.

"Hmm?" said Walter Mitty. He looked at his wife, in the seat beside him, with shocked astonishment. She seemed grossly unfamiliar, like a strange woman who had yelled at him in a crowd. "You were up to fifty-five," she said. "You know I don't like to go more than forty. You were up to fifty-five." Walter Mitty drove on toward Waterbury in silence, the roaring of the SN202 through the worst storm in twenty years of Navy flying fading in the remote, intimate airways of his mind. "You're tensed up again," said Mrs. Mitty. "It's one of your days. I wish you'd let Dr. Renshaw look you over."

Walter Mitty stopped the car in front of the building where his wife went to have her hair done. "Remember to get those overshoes while I'm having my hair done," she said. "I don't need overshoes," said Mitty. She put her mirror back into her bag. "We've been all through that," she said, getting out of the car. "You're not a young man any longer." He raced the engine a little. "Why don't you wear your gloves? Have you lost your gloves?" Walter Mitty reached in a pocket and brought out the gloves. He put them on, but after she had turned and gone into the building and he had driven on to a red light, he took them off again. "Pick it up, brother!" snapped a cop as the light changed, and Mitty hastily pulled on his gloves and lurched ahead. He drove around the streets aimlessly for a time, and then he drove past the hospital on his way to the parking lot.

Reading Skill
Author's Purpose
Pause to reflect. What does the phrase "intimate airways of his mind" suggest about the author's purpose in writing this story?

Reading Check

Why is Mrs. Mitty upset?

The Secret Life of Walter Mitty **129**

Vocabulary
distraught (di strôt´)
adj. very troubled
or confused

Someone handed him a fountain pen.

Literary Analysis
Character
What device or strategy does the author use here to help develop Walter Mitty as a complex, mul-tidimensional character?

Vocabulary
insolent (in´ sə lənt)
adj. boldly disrespectful

. . . "It's the millionaire banker, Wellington McMillan," said the pretty nurse. "Yes?" said Walter Mitty, removing his gloves slowly. "Who has the case?" "Dr. Renshaw and Dr. Benbow, but there are two specialists here, Dr. Remington from New York and Mr. Pritchard-Mitford from London. He flew over." A door opened down a long, cool corridor and Dr. Renshaw came out. He looked distraught and haggard. "Hello, Mitty," he said. "We're having the devil's own time with McMillan, the millionaire banker and close personal friend of Roosevelt. Obstreosis of the ductal tract.[2] Tertiary. Wish you'd take a look at him." "Glad to," said Mitty.

In the operating room there were whispered introductions: "Dr. Remington, Dr. Mitty. Mr. Pritchard-Mitford, Dr. Mitty." "I've read your book on streptothricosis," said Pritchard-Mitford, shaking hands. "A brilliant performance, sir." "Thank you," said Walter Mitty. "Didn't know you were in the States, Mitty," grumbled Remington. "Coals to Newcastle,[3] bringing Mitford and me up here for tertiary." "You are very kind," said Mitty. A huge, complicated machine, connected to the operating table, with many tubes and wires, began at this moment to go pocketa-pocketa-pocketa. "The new anesthetizer is giving way!" shouted an intern. "There is no one in the East who knows how to fix it!" "Quiet, man!" said Mitty, in a low, cool voice. He sprang to the machine, which was now going pocketa-pocketa-queep-pocketa-queep. He began fingering delicately a row of glistening dials. "Give me a fountain pen!" he snapped. Someone handed him a fountain pen. He pulled a faulty piston out of the machine and inserted the pen in its place. "That will hold for ten minutes," he said. "Get on with the operation." A nurse hurried over and whispered to Renshaw, and Mitty saw the man turn pale. "Coreopsis has set in," said Renshaw nervously. "If you would take over, Mitty?" Mitty looked at him and at the craven figure of Benbow, who drank, and at the grave, uncertain faces of the two great specialists. "If you wish," he said. They slipped a white gown on him; he adjusted a mask and drew on thin gloves; nurses handed him shining . . .

"Back it up, Mac! Look out for that Buick!" Walter Mitty jammed on the brakes. "Wrong lane, Mac," said the parking-lot attendant, looking at Mitty closely. "Gee. Yeh," muttered Mitty. He began cautiously to back out of the lane marked "Exit Only." "Leave her sit there," said the attendant. "I'll put her away." Mitty got out of the car. "Hey, better leave the key." "Oh," said Mitty, handing the man the ignition key. The attendant vaulted into the car, backed it up with insolent skill, and put it where it belonged.

---

2. **obstreosis of the ductal tract** Thurber has invented this and other medical terms.
3. **coals to Newcastle** The proverb "bringing coals to Newcastle" means bringing things to a place unnecessarily—Newcastle, England, was a coal center and so did not need coal brought to it.

They're so cocky, thought Walter Mitty, walking along Main Street; they think they know everything. Once he had tried to take his chains off, outside New Milford, and he had got them wound around the axles. A man had had to come out in a wrecking car and unwind them, a young, grinning garageman. Since then Mrs. Mitty always made him drive to a garage to have the chains taken off. The next time, he thought, I'll wear my right arm in a sling; they won't grin at me then. I'll have my right arm in a sling and they'll see I couldn't possibly take the chains off myself. He kicked at the slush on the sidewalk. "Overshoes," he said to himself, and he began looking for a shoe store. •

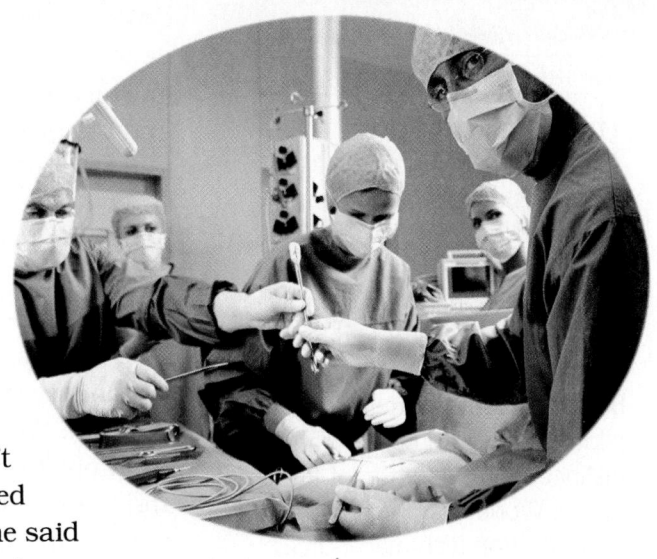

When he came out into the street again, with the overshoes in a box under his arm, Walter Mitty began to wonder what the other thing was his wife had told him to get. She had told him, twice, before they set out from their house for Waterbury. In a way he hated these weekly trips to town—he was always getting something wrong. Kleenex, he thought, Squibb's, razor blades? No. Toothpaste, toothbrush, bicarbonate, carborundum, initiative and referendum?[4] He gave it up. But she would remember it. "Where's the what's-its-name?" she would ask. "Don't tell me you forgot the what's-its-name." A newsboy went by shouting something about the Waterbury trial.

. . . "Perhaps this will refresh your memory." The District Attorney suddenly thrust a heavy automatic at the quiet figure on the witness stand. "Have you ever seen this before?" Walter Mitty took the gun and examined it expertly. "This is my Webley-Vickers 50.80," he said calmly. An excited buzz ran around the courtroom. The Judge rapped for order. "You are a crack shot with any sort of firearms, I believe?" said the District Attorney, insinuatingly. "Objection!" shouted Mitty's attorney. "We have shown that the defendant

---

4. carborundum (kär´ bə run´ dəm), **initiative** (i ni´ shē ə tiv) **and referendum** (ref´ ə ren´ dəm) Thurber is purposely making a nonsense list; *carborundum* is a hard substance used for scraping, *initiative* is a process by which citizens may introduce ideas for laws, and *referendum* is a process by which citizens may vote on laws.

▲ **Critical Viewing**
Describe a situation that might make Walter Mitty daydream about being a surgeon like the one shown. **[Hypothesize]**

Vocabulary
insinuatingly
(in sin´ yoo āt´ iŋ lē)
adv. suggesting indirectly

Reading Check

Why does Mitty say that next time he will wear his arm in a sling?

The Royal Air Force

Although he is American, Mitty fantasizes about being a brave and handsome English officer, a bomber pilot in the Royal Air Force (RAF). The RAF was officially formed in 1918 and distinguished itself in numerous air battles during World War I. RAF pilots would earn even greater distinction in the Battle of Britain during World War II. The reference to "Von Richtman's circus" recalls one of the RAF's finest moments—the shooting down in 1918 of Baron Manfred von Richthofen, also known as "The Red Baron," who was Germany's greatest fighter pilot.

Connect to the Literature

What elements of life in the RAF would Mitty enjoy?

Vocabulary
pandemonium
(pan´ də mō´ nē əm)
n. any place or scene
of wild disorder,
noise, or confusion

could not have fired the shot. We have shown that he wore his right arm in a sling on the night of the fourteenth of July." Walter Mitty raised his hand briefly and the bickering attorneys were stilled. "With any known make of gun," he said evenly, "I could have killed Gregory Fitzhurst at three hundred *feet with my left hand.*" Pandemonium broke loose in the courtroom. A woman's scream rose above the bedlam and suddenly a lovely, dark-haired girl was in Walter Mitty's arms. The District Attorney struck at her savagely. Without rising from his chair, Mitty let the man have it on the point of the chin. "You miserable cur!" . . .

"Puppy biscuit," said Walter Mitty. He stopped walking and the buildings of Waterbury rose up out of the misty courtroom and surrounded him again. A woman who was passing laughed. "He said 'Puppy biscuit,'" she said to her companion. "That man said 'Puppy biscuit' to himself." Walter Mitty hurried on. He went into an A. & P., not the first one he came to but a smaller one farther up the street. "I want some biscuit for small, young dogs," he said to the clerk. "Any special brand, sir?" The greatest pistol shot in the world thought a moment. "It says 'Puppies Bark for It' on the box," said Walter Mitty.

His wife would be through at the hairdresser's in fifteen minutes, Mitty saw in looking at his watch, unless they had trouble drying it; sometimes they had trouble drying it. She didn't like to get to the hotel first;

she would want him to be there waiting for her as usual. He found a big leather chair in the lobby, facing a window, and he put the overshoes and the puppy biscuit on the floor beside it. He picked up an old copy of *Liberty* and sank down into the chair. "Can Germany Conquer the World Through the Air?" Walter Mitty looked at the pictures of bombing planes and of ruined streets.

. . . "The cannonading has got the wind up in young Raleigh,[5] sir," said the sergeant. Captain Mitty looked up at him through tousled hair. "Get him to bed," he said wearily. "With the others. I'll fly alone." "But you can't, sir," said the sergeant anxiously. "It takes two men to handle that bomber and the Archies[6] are pounding hell out of the air. Von Richtman's circus[7] is between here and Saulier." "Somebody's got to get that ammunition dump," said Mitty. "I'm going over. Spot of brandy?" He poured a drink for the sergeant and one for himself. War thundered and whined around the dugout and battered at the door. There was a rending of wood and splinters flew through the room. "A bit of a near thing," said Captain Mitty carelessly. "The box barrage is closing in," said the sergeant. "We only live once, Sergeant," said Mitty, with his faint, fleeting smile. "Or do we?" He poured another brandy and tossed it off. "I never see a man could hold his brandy like you, sir," said the sergeant. "Begging your pardon, sir." Captain Mitty stood up and strapped on his huge Webley-Vickers automatic. "It's forty kilometers through hell, sir," said the sergeant. Mitty finished one last brandy. "After all," he said softly, "what isn't?" The pounding of the cannon increased; there was the rat-tat-tatting of machine guns, and from somewhere came the menacing pocketa-pocketa-pocketa of the new flame-throwers. Walter Mitty walked to the door of the dugout humming "Auprés de Ma Blonde."[8] He turned and waved to the sergeant. "Cheerio!" he said. . . .

Something struck his shoulder. "I've been looking all over this hotel for you," said Mrs. Mitty. "Why do you have to hide in this old chair? How did you expect me to find you?" "Things close in," said Walter Mitty vaguely. "What?" Mrs. Mitty said. "Did you get the what's-its-name? The puppy biscuit? What's in that box?" "Overshoes," said Mitty. "Couldn't you have put them on in the store?" "I

"We only live once, Sergeant," said Mitty, with his faint, fleeting smile.

Reading
Check

What triggers Mitty's daydream about being a military Captain?

---

5. **has got the wind up in young Raleigh** has made young Raleigh nervous.
6. **Archies** slang term for antiaircraft guns.
7. **Von Richtman's circus** a fictional German airplane squadron.
8. **"Auprès de Ma Blonde"** (ō prā′ də mä blôn′ də) "Next to My Blonde," a popular French song.

Vocabulary
derisive (di rī´siv) *adj.*
showing contempt
or ridicule

Literary Analysis
Character
How do Walter Mitty's
responses in this
paragraph show him
to be a complex yet
believable character?

Vocabulary
inscrutable (in skrōōt´
ə bəl) *adj.* baffling;
mysterious

was thinking," said Walter Mitty. "Does it ever occur to you that I am sometimes thinking?" She looked at him. "I'm going to take your temperature when I get you home," she said.

They went out through the revolving doors that made a faintly derisive whistling sound when you pushed them. It was two blocks to the parking lot. At the drugstore on the corner she said, "Wait here for me. I forgot something. I won't be a minute." She was more than a minute. Walter Mitty lighted a cigarette. It began to rain, rain with sleet in it. He stood up against the wall of the drugstore, smoking. . . . He put his shoulders back and his heels together. "To hell with the handkerchief," said Walter Mitty scornfully. He took one last drag on his cigarette and snapped it away. Then, with that faint, fleeting smile playing about his lips, he faced the firing squad; erect and motionless, proud and disdainful, Walter Mitty the Undefeated, inscrutable to the last.

Critical Thinking

1. **Respond:** Do you feel sorry for Walter Mitty? Why or why not?

2. **(a)** What distraction jars Mitty out of his first daydream?
   (b) Compare and Contrast: Explain how Mitty's behavior in this daydream differs from his behavior in real life.

3. **(a)** In the "real world," what tasks are Mitty and his wife carrying out? **(b) Make Inferences:** What deeds is Mitty attempting to accomplish in his fantasy life? **(c) Compare and Contrast:** How do the tasks of his daily life compare to those of his fantasy life?

4. **(a) Make Inferences:** Which aspects of Mitty's personality trigger his final daydream? **(b) Draw Conclusions:** In what ways is this daydream a comment on his fate in real life?

5. **(a) Evaluate:** Do Mitty's daydreams help him in any way or do they hurt him? **(b) Discuss:** Share your responses with a small group and discuss the differences and similarities among them. **(c) Reflect:** How has your evaluation grown or changed as a result of this discussion?

Can truth change?
How does Walter Mitty rely on daydreams to change the truth of his everyday life?

✓ Support
your responses
with evidence
from the text.

Literary Analysis: Character

1. Mitty wants to be like the heroes in his daydreams. **(a)** Using a chart like the one shown, identify one detail from each of Mitty's daydreams and the quality that each detail reveals.

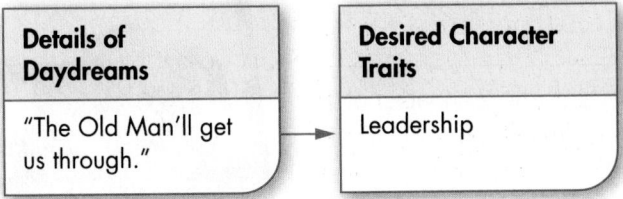

Details of Daydreams		Desired Character Traits
"The Old Man'll get us through."	→	Leadership

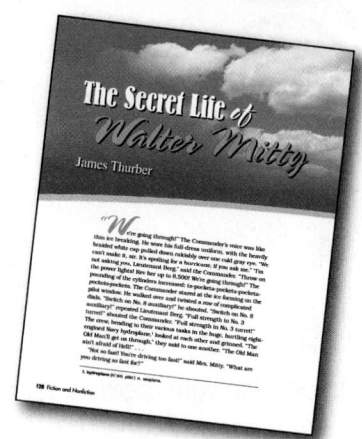

(b) What literary devices and strategies does the author use to develop Mitty as a complex yet believable **character?**

2. Review the characters of Walter and Mrs. Mitty. **(a)** Determine whether each character is round or flat. Explain your responses. **(b)** Determine whether each character is static or dynamic. Explain.

Reading Skill: Author's Purpose

3. (a) What specific **purpose** might James Thurber have had for creating the character of Walter Mitty? **(b)** Identify three details from the story that support your responses. **(c)** What **complex inferences** did you make about these details that helped you determine Thurber's purpose?

Vocabulary

Practice Review the vocabulary list for "The Secret Life of Walter Mitty" on page 126. Then, decide whether each of the following statements is true or false. Explain your answers.

1. Someone who is *distraught* is likely to behave in a calm manner.

2. Coaches encourage their players to be *insolent*.

3. *Inscrutable* handwriting is difficult to interpret.

4. If you speak *insinuatingly*, you say exactly what you mean.

5. A *derisive* comment shows great kindness.

6. *Pandemonium* might result if you gave unlimited candy to kindergarten students.

Word Power Use the context of sentences and what you know about the **Latin suffix -able** to explain your answer to each question.

1. Should you give up when facing an *achievable* goal?

2. If two bicycles are *comparable*, are they much alike?

Word Power

The **Latin suffix -able** means "can or will" or "capable of being."

Apply It Explain how the suffix -able helps you determine the meanings of these words. Consult a dictionary if necessary.

unpalatable
interminable
portable

 Can *truth* change?

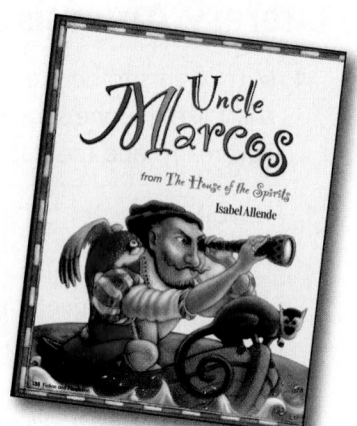

Writing About the Big Question

In "Uncle Marcos," the narrator describes the fantastic escapades of an uncle who is not satisfied with the ordinary. Use these sentence starters to develop your ideas about the Big Question.

A person who **believes** strongly in impractical and impossible things may _____.

Manipulating the **truth** can be _____ because _____.

As You Read Look for details that show how Uncle Marcos created his own realities.

Vocabulary

Read each word and its definition. Decide whether you know the word well, know it a little bit, or do not know it at all. After you read, see how your knowledge of each word has increased.

- **pallid** (pal′ id) *adj.* pale (p. 139) *The flu gave him a weak and pallid appearance.* *pallidness n. pallidly adv. pallor n.*

- **impassive** (im pas′ iv) *adj.* showing no emotion (p. 141) *She wanted to cry, but her face remained impassive as she watched her daughter leave for college.* *passive adj.*

- **conspicuous** (kən spik′ yo͞o əs) *adj.* attracting attention by being unexpected, unusual or outstanding (p. 141) *Renee felt conspicuous in her red coat and hat.* *inconspicuous adj.*

- **disconsolately** (dis kän′ sə lit lē) *adv.* very unhappily (p. 144) *He gazed disconsolately as his friends drove to the game without him.* *disconsolate adj. consolation n. console v.*

- **pertinent** (pʉrt′ 'n ənt) *adj.* relevant; to the point (p. 146) *Your outrageous comments are not at all pertinent to our discussion.* *pertinence n. impertinent adj.*

- **unrequited** (un ri kwīt′ id) *adj.* not returned or repaid (p. 146) *Romance novels sometimes describe the sadness of unrequited love.*

Word Power

The **Latin suffix -ive** means "of, belonging to, or quality of."

In this story, Uncle Marcos cannot believe that any woman could remain **impassive** when listening to a barrel organ. He thinks the organ must surely evoke the quality of passion.

Meet
Isabel Allende
(b. 1942)

Author of

Uncle Marcos

The daughter of diplomats, Isabel Allende grew up in the South American country of Chile. Her uncle was the Chilean president Salvador Allende. When his government was overthrown in 1973, Allende fled to Venezuela. She lived there in exile until 1988, when she moved to California.

Family and Fiction "Uncle Marcos" is excerpted from Allende's first novel, *The House of the Spirits*, which was inspired by her own remarkable family. Allende's family stories, however, are usually told with large helpings of imagination. She delights in blending the real and the imaginary. Allende once summed up her profession by quoting her granddaughter. Asked what it means to have a great imagination, the child replied, "You can remember what never happened."

BACKGROUND FOR THE STORY

(Literature Connection)
Magical Realism

Imagine a world in which people float in the air and rain falls continuously for years. Such fantastic details fill stories and novels by a group of writers, including Isabel Allende, who are called magical realists. Works of magical realism blend fantastic details with realistic ones to stretch the boundaries of readers' imaginations.

Did You Know?
Allende's first novel,
The House of the Spirits, began as a letter to her 100-year-old grandfather.

Uncle Marcos

from The House of the Spirits

Isabel Allende

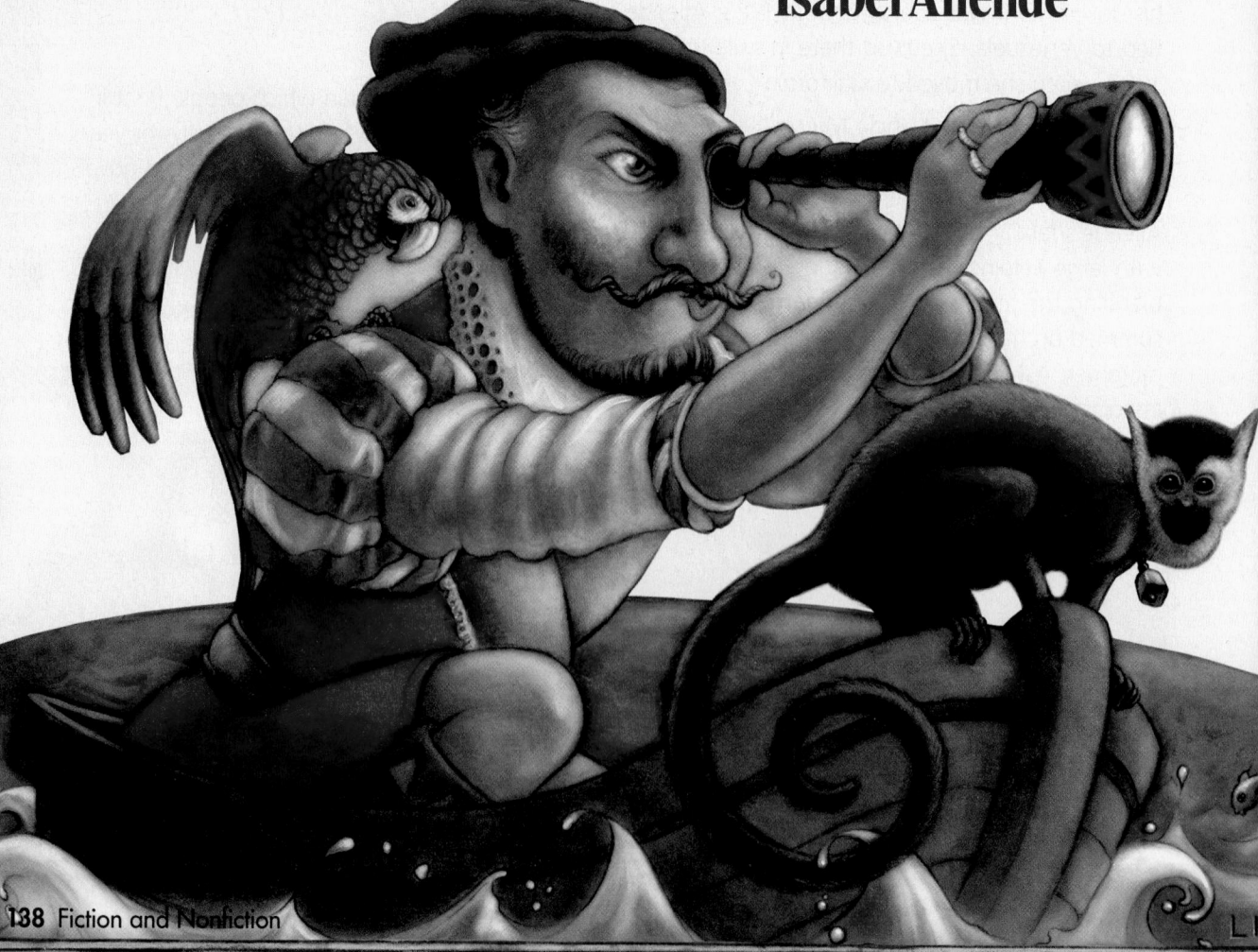

*I*t had been two years since Clara had last seen her Uncle Marcos, but she remembered him very well. His was the only perfectly clear image she retained from her whole childhood, and in order to describe him she did not need to consult the daguerreotype[1] in the drawing room that showed him dressed as an explorer leaning on an old-fashioned double-barreled rifle with his right foot on the neck of a Malaysian tiger, the same triumphant position in which she had seen the Virgin standing between plaster clouds and pallid angels at the main altar, one foot on the vanquished devil. All Clara had to do to see her uncle was close her eyes and there he was, weather-beaten and thin, with a pirate's mustache through which his strange, sharklike smile peered out at her. It seemed impossible that he could be inside that long black box that was lying in the middle of the courtyard.

Each time Uncle Marcos had visited his sister Nivea's home, he had stayed for several months, to the immense joy of his nieces and nephews, particularly Clara, causing a storm in which the sharp lines of domestic order blurred. The house became a clutter of trunks, of animals in jars of formaldehyde,[2] of Indian lances and sailor's bundles. In every part of the house people kept tripping over his equipment, and all sorts of unfamiliar animals appeared that had traveled from remote lands only to meet their death beneath Nana's irate broom in the farthest corners of the house. Uncle Marcos's manners were those of a cannibal, as Severo put it. He spent the whole night making incomprehensible movements in the drawing room; later they turned out to be exercises designed to perfect the mind's control over the body and to improve digestion. He performed alchemy[3] experiments in the kitchen, filling the house with fetid smoke and ruining pots and pans with solid substances that stuck to their bottoms and were impossible to

Vocabulary
pallid (pal′ id) *adj.* pale

Reading Check

What happens to the order of the house when Uncle Marcos visits?

---

1. **daguerreotype** (də ger′ ō tīp′) *n.* early type of photograph.
2. **formaldehyde** (fôr mal′ də hīd′) *n.* solution used as a preservative.
3. **alchemy** (al′ kə mē) *n.* early form of chemistry with philosophic and magical associations.

remove. While the rest of the household tried to sleep, he dragged his suitcases up and down the halls, practiced making strange, high-pitched sounds on savage instruments, and taught Spanish to a parrot whose native language was an Amazonic dialect. During the day, he slept in a hammock that he had strung between two columns in the hall, wearing only a loincloth that put Severo in a terrible mood but that Nivea forgave because Marcos had convinced her that it was the same costume in which Jesus of Nazareth had preached. Clara remembered perfectly, even though she had been only a tiny child, the first time her Uncle Marcos came to the house after one of his voyages. He settled in as if he planned to stay forever. After a short time, bored with having to appear at ladies' gatherings where the mistress of the house played the piano, with playing cards, and with dodging all his relatives' pressures to pull himself together and take a job as a clerk in Severo del Valle's law practice, he bought a barrel organ and took to the streets with the hope of seducing his Cousin Antonieta and entertaining the public in the bargain. The machine was just a rusty box with wheels, but he painted it with seafaring designs and gave it a fake ship's smokestack. It ended up looking like a coal stove. The organ played either a military march or a waltz, and in between turns of the handle the parrot, who had managed to learn Spanish although he had not lost his foreign accent, would draw a crowd with his piercing shrieks. He also plucked slips of paper from a box with his beak, by way of selling fortunes to the curious. The little pink, green, and blue papers were so clever that they always divulged the exact secret wishes of the customers. Besides fortunes there were little balls of sawdust to amuse the children. The idea of the organ was a last desperate attempt to win the hand of Cousin Antonieta after more conventional means of courting her had failed. Marcos thought no

▲ Barrel organ

> The organ played either a military march or a waltz...

woman in her right mind could remain impassive before a barrel-organ serenade. He stood beneath her window one evening and played his military march and his waltz just as she was taking tea with a group of female friends. Antonieta did not realize the music was meant for her until the parrot called her by her full name, at which point she appeared in the window. Her reaction was not what her suitor had hoped for. Her friends offered to spread the news to every salon[4] in the city, and the next day people thronged the downtown streets hoping to see Severo del Valle's brother-in-law playing the organ and selling little sawdust balls with a motheaten parrot, for the sheer pleasure of proving that even in the best of families there could be good reason for embarrassment. In the face of this stain to the family reputation, Marcos was forced to give up organ grinding and resort to less conspicuous ways of winning over his Cousin Antonieta, but he did not renounce his goal. In any case, he did not succeed, because from one day to the next the young lady married a diplomat who was twenty years her senior; he took her to live in a tropical country whose name no one could recall, except that it suggested negritude,[5] bananas, and palm trees, where she managed to recover from the memory of that suitor who had ruined her seventeenth year with his military march and his waltz. Marcos sank into a deep depression that lasted two or three days, at the end of which he announced that he would never marry and that he was embarking on a trip around the world. He sold his organ to a blind man and left the parrot to Clara, but Nana secretly poisoned it with an overdose of cod-liver oil, because no one could stand its lusty glance, its fleas, and its harsh, tuneless hawking of paper fortunes and sawdust balls. ●

That was Marcos's longest trip. He returned with a shipment of enormous boxes that were piled in the far courtyard, between the chicken coop and the woodshed, until the winter was over. At the first signs of spring he had them transferred to the parade grounds, a huge park where people would gather to watch the soldiers file by on Independence Day, with the goosestep they had learned from the Prussians. When the crates were opened, they were found to contain

---

4. **salon** (sə län´) *n.* regular gathering of distinguished guests that meets in a private home.
5. **negritude** (neg´ rə tōōd´) *n.* blacks and their cultural heritage.

Vocabulary
impassive (im pas´ iv)
adj. showing no emotion

Literary Analysis
Character How does Uncle Marcos's behavior suggest that he is a complex yet believable character?

Vocabulary
conspicuous
(kən spik´ yōō əs) *adj.* attracting attention by being unexpected, unusual or outstanding

Reading Check

What does Uncle Marcos do with the barrel organ?

loose bits of wood, metal, and painted cloth. Marcos spent two weeks assembling the contents according to an instruction manual written in English, which he was able to decipher thanks to his invincible imagination and a small dictionary. When the job was finished, it turned out to be a bird of prehistoric dimensions, with the face of a furious eagle, wings that moved, and a propeller on its back. It caused an uproar. The families of the oligarchy[6] forgot all about the barrel organ, and Marcos became the star attraction of the season. People took Sunday outings to see the bird; souvenir vendors and strolling photographers made a fortune. Nonetheless, the public's interest quickly waned. But then Marcos announced that as soon as the weather cleared he planned to take off in his bird and cross the mountain range. The news spread, making this the most talked-about event of the year. The contraption lay with its stomach on terra firma,[7] heavy and sluggish and looking more like a wounded duck than like one of those newfangled airplanes they were starting to produce in the United States. There was nothing in its appearance to suggest that it could move, much less take flight across the snowy peaks. Journalists and the curious flocked to see it. Marcos smiled his immutable[8] smile before the avalanche of questions and posed for photographers without offering the least technical or scientific explanation of how he hoped to carry out his plan. People came from the provinces to see the sight. Forty years later his great-nephew Nicolás, whom Marcos did not live to see, unearthed the desire to fly that had always existed in the men of his lineage. Nicolás was interested in doing it for commercial reasons, in a gigantic hot-air sausage on which would be printed an advertisement for carbonated drinks. But when Marcos announced his plane trip, no one believed that his contraption could be put to any practical use. The appointed day dawned full of clouds, but so many people had turned out that Marcos did not want to disappoint them. He showed up punctually at the appointed spot and did not once look up at the sky, which was growing darker and darker with thick gray clouds. The astonished crowd filled all the nearby streets, perching on rooftops and the balconies of the nearest houses and squeezing into the park.

▼ Critical Viewing
In this story, a man builds a flying machine. Which character traits might you find in someone who would try to do this? [Speculate]

6. **oligarchy** (äl´ i gär´ kē) *n.* government ruled by a few.
7. **terra firma** (ter´ a fʉr´ ma) *n.* Latin term meaning "firm earth; solid ground."
8. **immutable** (im myo͞ot´ ə bəl) *adj.* never changing.

No political gathering managed to attract so many people until half a century later, when the first Marxist candidate attempted, through strictly democratic channels, to become President. Clara would remember this holiday as long as she lived. People dressed in their spring best, thereby getting a step ahead of the official opening of the season, the men in white linen suits and the ladies in the Italian straw hats that were all the rage that year. Groups of elementary-school children paraded with their teachers, clutching flowers for the hero. Marcos accepted their bouquets and joked that they might as well hold on to them and wait for him to crash, so they could take them directly to his funeral. The bishop himself, accompanied by two incense bearers, appeared to bless the bird without having been asked, and the police band played happy, unpretentious music that pleased everyone. The police, on horseback and carrying lances, had trouble keeping the crowds far enough away from the center of the park, where Marcos waited dressed in mechanic's overalls, with huge racer's goggles and an explorer's helmet. He was also equipped with a compass, a telescope, and several strange maps that he had traced himself based on various theories of Leonardo da Vinci and on the polar knowledge of the Incas.[9] Against all logic, on the second try the bird lifted off without mishap and with a certain elegance, accompanied by the creaking of its skeleton and the roar of its motor. It rose flapping its wings and disappeared into the clouds, to a send-off of applause, whistlings, handkerchiefs, drumrolls, and the sprinkling of holy water. All that remained on earth were the comments of the amazed crowd below and a multitude of experts, who attempted to provide a reasonable explanation of the miracle. Clara continued to stare at the sky long after her uncle had become invisible. She thought she saw him ten minutes later, but it was only a migrating sparrow. After three days the initial euphoria that had accompanied the first airplane flight in the country died down and no one gave the episode another thought, except for Clara, who continued to peer at the horizon.

9. **Leonardo da Vinci** (lē′ ə när′ dō də vin′ chē) . . . **Incas** Leonardo da Vinci (1452–1519) was an Italian painter, sculptor, architect, and scientist. The Incas were Native Americans who dominated ancient Peru until the Spanish conquest.

Reading Skill
Author's Purpose
Pause to reflect. What does the statement "Clara would remember this holiday as long as she lived" suggest about the author's purpose in writing this story?

Against all logic, on the second try the bird lifted off without mishap...

Reading Check
Where does Uncle Marcos plan to fly in his flying machine?

Vocabulary
disconsolately
(dis kän´ sə lit lē) *adv.*
very unhappily

After a week with no word from the flying uncle, people began to speculate that he had gone so high that he had disappeared into outer space, and the ignorant suggested he would reach the moon. With a mixture of sadness and relief, Severo decided that his brother-in-law and his machine must have fallen into some hidden crevice of the cordillera,[10] where they would never be found. Nivea wept disconsolately and lit candles to San Antonio, patron of lost objects. Severo opposed the idea of having masses said, because he did not believe in them as a way of getting into heaven, much less of returning to earth, and he maintained that masses and religious vows, like the selling of indulgences, images, and scapulars,[11] were a dishonest business. Because of his attitude, Nivea and Nana had the children say the rosary,[12] behind their father's back for nine days. Meanwhile, groups of volunteer explorers and mountain climbers tirelessly searched peaks and passes, combing every accessible stretch of land until they finally returned in triumph to hand the family the mortal remains of the deceased in a sealed black coffin. The intrepid traveler was laid to rest in a grandiose funeral. His death made him a hero and his name was on the front page of all the papers for several days. The same multitude that had gathered to see him off the day he flew away in his bird paraded past his coffin. The entire family wept as befit the occasion, except for Clara, who continued to watch the sky with the patience of an astronomer. One week after he had been buried, Uncle Marcos, a bright smile playing behind his pirate's mustache, appeared in person in the doorway of Nivea and Severo del Valle's house. Thanks to the surreptitious[13] prayers of the women and children, as he himself admitted, he was alive and well and in full possession of his faculties, including his sense of humor. Despite the noble lineage of his aerial maps, the flight had been a failure. He had lost his airplane and had to return on foot, but he had not broken any bones and his adventurous spirit was intact. This confirmed the family's eternal devotion to San Antonio, but was not taken as a warning by future generations, who also tried to fly, although by different means. Legally, however, Marcos was a corpse. Severo del Valle was obliged to use all his legal ingenuity to bring his brother-in-law back to life and the full rights of citizenship. When the coffin was pried open in the presence of the appropriate authorities, it was found to contain a bag of sand. This discovery ruined the

Reading Skill
Author's Purpose
What do the narrator's observations about Marcos suggest about the author's purpose?

Literary Analysis
Character
Which details in this passage indicate that Marcos has changed since the beginning of the story?

---

10. **cordillera** (kôr´ dil yer´ ə) *n.* system or chain of mountains.
11. **indulgences, images, and scapulars** (skap´ yə lərz) Indulgences are pardons for sins; images are pictures or sculptures of religious figures; scapulars are garments worn by Roman Catholics as tokens of religious devotion.
12. **say the rosary** use a set of beads to say prayers.
13. **surreptitious** (sʉr´ əp tish´ əs) *adj.* secretive.

reputation, up till then untarnished, of the volunteer explorers and mountain climbers, who from that day on were considered little better than a pack of bandits.

● Marcos's heroic resurrection made everyone forget about his barrel-organ phase. Once again he was a sought-after guest in all the city's salons and, at least for a while, his name was cleared. Marcos stayed in his sister's house for several months. One night he left without saying goodbye, leaving behind his trunks, his books, his weapons, his boots, and all his belongings. Severo, and even Nivea herself, breathed a sigh of relief. His visit had gone on too long. But Clara was so upset that she spent a week walking in her sleep and sucking her thumb. The little girl, who was only seven at the time, had learned to read from her uncle's storybooks and been closer to him than any other member of the family because of her prophesying powers. Marcos maintained that his niece's gift could be a source of income and a good opportunity for him to cultivate his own clairvoyance.[14] He believed that all human beings possessed this ability, particularly his own family, and that if it did not function well it was simply due to a lack of training. He bought a crystal ball in the Persian bazaar, insisting that it had magic powers and was from the East (although it was later found to be part of a buoy from a fishing boat), set it down on a background of black velvet, and announced that he could tell people's fortunes, cure the evil eye, and improve the quality of dreams, all for the modest sum of five centavos.[15] His first customers were the maids from around the neighborhood. One of them had been accused of stealing, because her employer had misplaced a valuable ring. The crystal ball revealed the exact location of the object in question: it had rolled beneath a wardrobe. The next day there was a line outside the front door of the house. There were coachmen, storekeepers, and milkmen; later a few municipal employees and distinguished ladies made a discreet appearance, slinking along the side walls of the house to keep from being recognized. The customers were received by Nana, who ushered them into the

After a week with no word from the flying uncle, people began to speculate that he had gone so high that he had disappeared into outer space...

Reading Check

What power does Marcos believe Clara holds?

---

14. **clairvoyance** (klĕr voi´ əns) *n.* supposed ability to perceive unseen things.
15. **centavos** (sen tä´ vōs) *n.* coins equal to 1/100 of a *cruzeiro,* the basic monetary unit of Brazil.

waiting room and collected their fees. This task kept her busy throughout the day and demanded so much of her time that the family began to complain that all there ever was for dinner was old string beans and jellied quince.[16] Marcos decorated the carriage house with some frayed curtains that had once belonged in the drawing room but that neglect and age had turned to dusty rags. There he and Clara received the customers. The two divines wore tunics "color of the men of light," as Marcos called the color yellow. Nana had dyed them with saffron powder, boiling them in pots usually reserved for rice and pasta. In addition to his tunic, Marcos wore a turban around his head and an Egyptian amulet around his neck. He had grown a beard and let his hair grow long and he was thinner than ever before. Marcos and Clara were utterly convincing, especially because the child had no need to look into the crystal ball to guess what her clients wanted to hear. She would whisper in her Uncle Marcos's ear, and he in turn would transmit the message to the client, along with any improvisations of his own that he thought pertinent. Thus their fame spread, because all those who arrived sad and bedraggled at the consulting room left filled with hope.

Unrequited lovers were told how to win over indifferent hearts, and the poor left with foolproof tips on how to place their money at the dog tracks. Business grew so prosperous that the waiting room was always packed with people, and Nana began to suffer dizzy spells from being on her feet so many hours a day. This time Severo had no need to intervene to put a stop to his brother-in-law's venture, for both Marcos and Clara, realizing that their unerring guesses could alter the fate of their clients, who always followed their advice to the letter, became frightened and decided that this was a job for swindlers. They abandoned their carriage-house oracle and split the profits, even though the only one who had cared about the material side of things had been Nana. •

Of all the del Valle children, Clara was the one with the greatest interest in and stamina for her uncle's stories. She could repeat each and every one of them. She knew by heart words from several dialects of the Indians, was acquainted with their customs, and could describe the exact way in which they pierced their lips and earlobes with wooden shafts, their initiation rites, the names of the most poisonous snakes, and the appropriate antidotes for each. Her uncle was so eloquent that the child could feel in her own skin the burning sting of snakebites, see reptiles slide across the carpet between the legs of the jacaranda[17] room divider, and hear the shrieks of macaws behind the drawing-room drapes. She did

Vocabulary
pertinent (pʉrt´ 'n ənt)
adj. relevant; to the point
unrequited (un ri
kwīt´ id) *adj.* not
returned or repaid

Literary Analysis
Character
What device or strategy does the author use here to help develop Clara as a complex, multidimensional character?

---

16. **quince** (kwins) hard, gold or greenish-yellow apple-shaped fruit.
17. **jacaranda** (jak´ ə ran´ də) type of tropical American tree.

not hesitate as she recalled Lope de Aguirre's search for El Dorado,[18] or the unpronounceable names of the flora and fauna her extraordinary uncle had seen; she knew about the lamas who take salt tea with yak lard and she could give detailed descriptions of the opulent women of Tahiti, the rice fields of China, or the white prairies of the North, where the eternal ice kills animals and men who lose their way, turning them to stone in seconds. Marcos had various travel journals in which he recorded his excursions and impressions, as well as a collection of maps and books of stories and fairy tales that he kept in the trunks he stored in the junk room at the far end of the third courtyard. From there they were hauled out to inhabit the dreams of his descendants, until they were mistakenly burned half a century later on an infamous pyre.

Now Marcos had returned from his last journey in a coffin. He had died of a mysterious African plague that had turned him as yellow and wrinkled as a piece of parchment. When he realized he was ill, he set out for home with the hope that his sister's ministrations and Dr. Cuevas's knowledge would restore his health and youth, but he was unable to withstand the sixty days on ship and died at the latitude of Guayaquil,[19] ravaged by fever and hallucinating about musky women and hidden treasure. The captain of the ship, an Englishman by the name of Longfellow, was about to throw him overboard wrapped in a flag, but Marcos, despite his savage appearance and his delirium, had made so many friends on board and seduced so many women that the passengers prevented him from doing so, and Longfellow

---

18. **Lope de Aguirre's** (lō′ pā dā ä gēr′ rās) . . . **El Dorado** Lope de Aguirre was a Spanish adventurer (1518–1561) in colonial South America who searched for a legendary country called El Dorado, which was supposedly rich in gold.
19. **Guayaquil** (gwī′ ä kēl′) seaport in western Ecuador.

LITERATURE IN CONTEXT

Humanities Connection

Magical Realists
The literary movement known as Magical Realism is most closely associated with the wonder-filled novels and short stories of a group of twentieth-century Latin American authors. Isabel Allende is an important writer in this group. The great Argentinian writer Jorge Luis Borges is another. His style often combines realistic characters and events with details that seem to come out of dreams and myths. Gabriel García Márquez of Colombia is often considered the central figure of the movement. His works chronicle the lives of passionate and sympathetic characters who experience miraculous happenings and strange, unearthly events.

Connect to the Literature

What elements of "Uncle Marcos" confirm that it belongs to the literary movement known as Magical Realism?

Reading Check
Who loves hearing Marcos's stories the most?

was obliged to store the body side by side with the vegetables of the Chinese cook, to preserve it from the heat and mosquitoes of the tropics until the ship's carpenter had time to improvise a coffin. At El Callao[20] they obtained a more appropriate container, and several days later the captain, furious at all the troubles this passenger had caused the shipping company and himself personally, unloaded him without a backward glance, surprised that not a soul was there to receive the body or cover the expenses he had incurred.

Later he learned that the post office in these latitudes was not as reliable as that of far-off England, and that all his telegrams had vaporized en route. Fortunately for Longfellow, a customs lawyer who was a friend of the del Valle family appeared and offered to take charge, placing Marcos and all his paraphernalia in a freight car, which he shipped to the capital to the only known address of the deceased: his sister's house. . . .

20. **El Callao** (kə yä′ ō) seaport in western Peru.

Critical Thinking

✓ Support your responses with evidence from the text.

1. **Respond:** Which of Uncle Marcos's adventures would you most like to share with him? Why?

2. **(a)** What does Uncle Marcos do to try to win the hand of Cousin Antonieta? **(b) Connect:** Is her reaction what Uncle Marcos expects? Use details from the text to explain.

3. **(a)** What does Uncle Marcos make from the materials he brings back in "enormous boxes"? **(b) Make Inferences:** What do you think motivates Uncle Marcos to undertake this project?

4. **(a) Compare and Contrast:** Compare and contrast Clara's reaction to her uncle's disappearance with those of the others. **(b) Interpret:** What does Clara's reaction show about her personality and her relationship to Uncle Marcos? Explain.

5. **(a) Draw Conclusions:** What life lessons can people learn from the character of Uncle Marcos? **(b) Discuss:** Share your responses with a group and discuss similarities and differences among them. **(c) Reflect:** How has the discussion affected your response?

THE BIG **Q**

Can truth change?

(a) How is Uncle Marcos's reality different from that of the narrator and other characters? **(b)** Which reality do you think is truer? Defend your answers.

Literary Analysis: Character

1. (a) Using a chart like the one shown, list at least three of Uncle Marcos's projects or adventures. Then, identify a character trait that each project or adventure reveals.

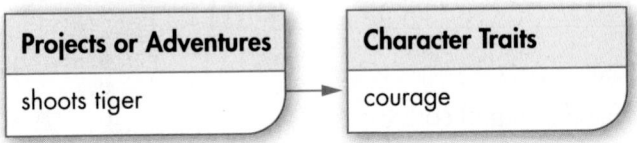

Projects or Adventures	Character Traits
shoots tiger	courage

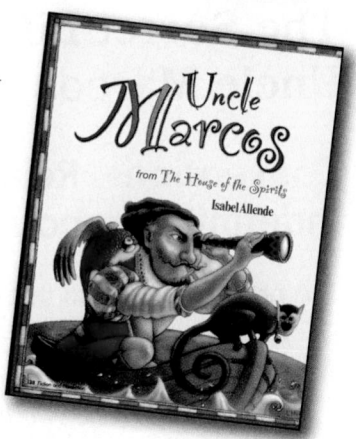

(b) What literary devices and strategies does the author use to develop Uncle Marcos as a complex yet believable **character?**

2. Review the characters of Clara and Uncle Marcos. **(a)** Determine whether each character is round or flat. Explain your responses. **(b)** Explain whether each character is static or dynamic.

Reading Skill: Author's Purpose

3. (a) What specific **purpose** might Isabel Allende have had for creating the character of Uncle Marcos? **(b)** Identify three details from the story that support your responses. **(c)** What **complex inferences** did you make about these details that helped you determine Allende's purpose?

Vocabulary

Practice Review the vocabulary list for "Uncle Marcos" on page 136. Then, decide whether each of the following statements is true or false. Explain your answers.

1. Something that looks *pallid* is full of color.

2. Sighing *disconsolately* is a good way to express enthusiasm.

3. *Unrequited* love is symbolized by a wedding.

4. Standing on your head in public would be considered *conspicuous*.

5. A *pertinent* detail has absolutely nothing to do with the topic.

6. You can easily read the mood of an *impassive* person.

Word Power Use the context of the sentences and what you know about the **Latin suffix -ive** to explain your answer to each question.

1. Do *permissive* parents allow their children their freedom?

2. If people are *cooperative*, will they refuse to work together?

Word Power

The **Latin suffix -ive** means "of, belonging to, or quality of."

Apply It Explain how the suffix -ive helps you determine the meanings of these words. Consult a dictionary if necessary.

sedative
collective
festive

Integrated Language Skills

The Secret Life of Walter Mitty • Uncle Marcos

Conventions: Relative, Interrogative, and Indefinite Pronouns

A **pronoun** is a word that stands for a noun.

- A **relative pronoun** begins a subordinate clause and connects it to another idea in the sentence. The five most common relative pronouns are *that, which, who, whom,* and *whose*.
- An **interrogative pronoun** is used to begin a question. The five interrogative pronouns are *what, which, who, whom,* and *whose*.
- **Indefinite pronouns** refer to people, places, or things, often without specifying which ones.

Indefinite Pronouns					
Singular				**Plural**	**Singular or Plural**
another	either	much	one	both	all most
anybody	everybody	neither	other	few	any none
anyone	everyone	nobody	somebody	many	more some
anything	everything	no one	someone	others	
each	little	nothing	something	several	

Practice A Identify the pronouns in each sentence as being relative, interrogative, or indefinite.

1. No one knew about Mitty's daydreams.
2. Who doesn't daydream occasionally?
3. Mitty was a courageous pilot who saved his crew from certain death.
4. Mitty, whose wife was getting her hair done, waited quietly in the hotel.

Reading Application Find examples of sentences in "The Secret Life of Walter Mitty" that use a relative, an interrogative, and an indefinite pronoun.

Practice B Complete each sentence by adding a relative, an interrogative, or an indefinite pronoun.

1. Has _____ heard Uncle Marcos's stories?
2. People _____ listen to him find him hard to believe.
3. The adventures _____ Uncle Marcos had sometimes embarrassed his family.
4. _____ of them were surprised by his flying.

Writing Application Use this sentence as a model to write five new sentences. Substitute the underlined word or words with the same part of speech. *Many of them came from a country that is in Asia.*

PH GRAMMAR HANDBOOK Further instruction and practice are available in the *Prentice Hall Grammar Handbook*.

Writing

 **Focus on the TEKS**

Writing
(15)(A)(v) Write an analytical essay that includes relevant information.
Research
(21)(B) Organize information gathered from multiple sources to create a variety of forms (e.g., learning logs).
(21)(C) Summarize researched information.

Both of these selections present memorable characters who entertain readers. Using details from the story you read, write a **character profile.** If you read "The Secret Life of Walter Mitty," analyze one of the heroic personalities in Mitty's daydreams. If you read "Uncle Marcos," analyze Uncle Marcos.

- Begin by jotting down **relevant information**—details that capture the character's appearance, personality, and achievements.
- Decide on a single impression to convey about the character.
- Organize and present details so that they all contribute to the precise impression you have chosen.
- Maintain a consistent tone and focus throughout the analytical essay.

Grammar Application Check your character profile to be sure that you have used relative, interrogative, and indefinite pronouns correctly.

Writing Workshop: *Work in Progress*

Prewriting for Problem-Solution Essay Review the Problem Notes in your writing portfolio. To build on this work, provide three specific examples of the problem. Then, list three examples to show how your solution would work. Put these Problem/Solution Notes in your writing portfolio.

Use this prewriting activity to prepare for the **Writing Workshop** on page 172.

Research and Technology

Literature often suggests great topics for further research. Use **multiple sources** to research one of the topics below. Then, organize the information you gather from these sources in a **learning log,** a written record of information you learn about a topic. In your learning log, **summarize** the information you researched. When your log is complete, compare your findings to details and descriptions in the story you read.

- If you read "The Secret Life of Walter Mitty," research scientific facts and theories about daydreams. Record your research in a learning log. Decide whether Mitty's daydreams reflect the facts you have learned about such dreams.
- If you read "Uncle Marcos," research the history of human flight. Look for historic details that can be compared to the descriptions of flight given in the story. Record your research in a learning log. Decide if Allende's description of flight is realistic or fantastic.

 **TEXAS**
PHLitOnline
www.PHLitOnline.com

- Interactive graphic organizers
- Grammar tutorial
- Interactive journals

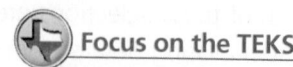

Strategy for Success

Analyze Author's Purpose

The reading sections of the PSAT, the SAT, and the Texas standardized tests ask you to examine the author's purpose for writing—whether to entertain, to persuade, or to inform. The author may not state a purpose directly, but you can reflect—including asking questions—and make complex inferences about text to help you identify the author's purpose on standardized tests.

As you read, infer what the author is trying to do. For example, does the text simply share information, or does the text support an opinion that the author would like you to accept? The following examples show how you can ask questions to infer the author's purpose on standardized tests.

Focus on the TEKS

Reading/Comprehension Skills RC-9(A) Reflect on understanding to monitor comprehension (e.g., asking questions, summarizing and synthesizing, making connections, creating sensory images).

RC-9(B) Make complex inferences about text and use textual evidence to support understanding.

Identify Persuasion

Ask yourself if the author wants you to do something or to accept an opinion.

15 Why are freshmen not allowed to run for student council? They are as much a part of our high school as the older students, and they have more spirit. It is time for a change in policy.

1. The purpose of the paragraph is to argue that freshmen
   (A) should be allowed to run for student council
   (B) are as much a part of the school as older students
   (C) have plenty of school spirit
   (D) do not seem enthusiastic
   (E) are better than older students

Choices **B** and **C** are supporting details. Choices **D** and **E** are not supported by the text. Choice **A** is correct. The author states this issue and gives an opinion about it.

Identify Informational Text

Does the text include facts but not opinions? Is its focus on informing, not entertaining? If so, you can infer that it is informational text.

15 Adult clownfish can flit easily through anemone tentacles. Baby clownfish must gradually become immune to anemone stings.

2. The purpose of the passage is to
   (A) entertain with a story about anemones and clownfish
   (B) explain how clownfish adapt to anemones
   (C) describe the sting of anemone tentacles
   (D) persuade readers that anemones are unsafe
   (E) explain the life cycle of a clownfish

The author is not telling a story or trying to persuade, so choices **A** and **D** are incorrect. Choices **C** and **E** are not discussed. The correct answer is choice **B**.

SAT/PSAT Practice

Questions 1–4 are based on the following passage.

A mound of soft soil in the middle of your lawn could be a warning sign that your yard
has been invaded by a colony of red imported fire ants. If their colony is disturbed—
accidentally or not—these ants respond aggressively, attacking with painful stings.

Line   Ants of similar size that are native to Texas are considerably less aggressive; most
5 of them rarely sting and will run away from any disturbance. In other ways, however,
it can be difficult to distinguish them from red imported fire ants. The most common
native species of ant looks almost identical, except that a few ants in the native colony
are larger workers with square-shaped heads.

Red imported fire ants, originally from South America, were accidentally introduced
10 into the United States, most likely in the holds of ships. They arrived in Texas in the
1950s and quickly spread across two-thirds of the state in the east as well as some
urban areas in the west. The ants are persistent; with almost any type of pesticide, the
ants will still invade again, possibly as soon as after the next rain.

However, scientists are currently researching cost-effective, environmentally sound
15 ways to better manage red imported fire ants. One joint project between the University
of Texas and the United States Department of Agriculture (USDA) is studying a parasitic
fly that can kill fire ants. Other possibilities for natural pesticides include mites and fungi.

1. The purpose of lines 4–8 is to
(A) compare types of ants in Texas
(B) explain how fire ants were imported
(C) give a warning about fire-ant stings
(D) describe native ants in Texas
(E) persuade readers to learn about ants

2. The author's comment, "the ants will still invade
again, possibly as soon as after the next rain" is
an example of
(A) the author's personal opinion
(B) an entertaining note about fire ants
(C) support for the author's position
(D) factual information about fire ants
(E) a story about fire ants

3. The purpose of lines 14–17 is to
(A) convince readers to support the USDA's
efforts to control fire ants
(B) explain current research related to
controlling fire ants
(C) amuse the reader with descriptions of
unusual methods of fire-ant control
(D) show readers that fire ants are a serious
problem
(E) compare possible solutions to the fire-ant
problem

4. The purpose of the passage is to
(A) compare native and imported ants
(B) explain why fire ants came to Texas
(C) persuade readers to control fire ants
(D) inform readers about red imported fire ants
in Texas
(E) encourage readers to try natural pesticides
for ants

Informational Texts

Procedural Texts

Schedule
Pascack Valley Line Train Schedule

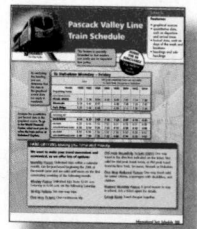

Brochure
Texas State Railroad

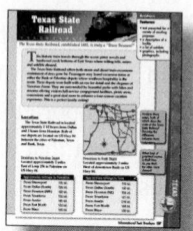

Focus on the TEKS

Reading
(11)(B) Analyze factual, quantitative, or technical data presented in multiple graphical sources.

Reading Skill: Analyze Graphical Sources

Many informational texts, especially procedural texts, include **graphical sources.** These sources include charts, tables, graphs, maps, and illustrations that are designed to allow readers to easily access and use details and information. To analyze data presented in graphical sources, begin by identifying the type of data presented:

- **Factual data** is general information or details.
- **Quantitative data** uses measurements, such as weight, and times.
- **Technical data** presents scientific or specialized knowledge.

Next, note how the data is organized and what, if any, text features are present to help you navigate the source. Finally, consider how the various pieces of information presented relate to one another and how the different pieces can be utilized.

As You Read Use a chart like this to help you analyze the **factual, quantitative,** and **technical data** in the **multiple graphical sources** presented here. For each type of graphical source listed, give an example of data from each text.

Text Feature/Organizational Pattern	Schedule	Brochure
Headings in tables and charts	"To Hoboken Monday—Friday"	
Rows and columns in tables and charts		
Symbols in maps		

Pascack Valley Line Train Schedule

NJ TRANSIT
The Way To Go. ®

This feature is specially formatted so that readers can easily see an important fare policy.

AVOID THE $5 SURCHARGE
Buy before you board

Features:
- graphical sources
- quantitative data, such as departure and arrival times
- factual data, such as days of the week and locations
- headings and sub-headings

By analyzing this heading, you can determine that the data in this graphical source does not apply to weekends.

Analyze the quantitative and factual data in this graphical source. To go to the World Financial Center, what must you do when the train arrives at Hoboken? Explain.

To Hoboken Monday – Friday

TRAINS Departing from:	AM		Off-peak roundtrip fares are not valid to New York, Secaucus or Hoboken					
	1600	1602	1604	1606	1608	1610	1612	1614
METRO-NORTH STATION PEARL RIVER	5 15	5 38	6 04	6 35	6 45	7 05	7 24	7 38
Montvale	5 18	5 41	6 07		6 48	7 08	7 28	7 41
Park Ridge	5 20	5 43	6 09		6 50	7 11	7 30	7 44

Arriving at:								
HOBOKEN	6 14	6 37	7 07	7 18	7 49	8 07	8 19	8 41
via PATH	6 24	6 44	7 14	7 32	8 01	8 19	8 31	8 49
arrive World Trade Center	6 34	6 54	7 25	7 43	8 12	8 30	8 42	9 00
via FERRY	6 30	6 50	7 16	7 32	7 56	8 20	8 28	8 52
arrive World Financial Center	6 40	7 00	7 26	7 42	8 06	8 30	8 38	9 02

FARE OPTIONS saving you time and money

We want to make your travel convenient and economical, so we offer lots of options:

Monthly Passes Unlimited trips within a calendar month; can be purchased beginning the 20th of the month prior and are valid until noon on the first commuting weekday of the following month.

Weekly Passes Unlimited trips from 12:01 a.m. Saturday to 6:00 a.m. on the following Saturday.

10-Trip Tickets Ten one-way trips.

One-Way Tickets One continuous trip.

Off-Peak Roundtrip Tickets (ORT) One-way travel in the direction indicated on the ticket. Not valid for AM peak travel to/via, or PM peak travel from/via New York, Secaucus, Newark or Hoboken.

One-Way Reduced Tickets One-way travel valid for senior citizens, passengers with disabilities, and children.

Student Monthly Passes A good reason to stay in school. Ask a ticket agent for details.

Group Rates Travel cheaper together.

The main headings draw the reader's attention to important information.

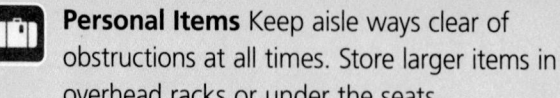

KNOW BEFORE YOU GO

Personal Items Keep aisle ways clear of obstructions at all times. Store larger items in the overhead racks or under the seats.

Pets Only service animals accompanying customers with disabilities or their trainers, police dogs and small pets in carry-on travel cages are allowed on-board NJ TRANSIT trains.

Smoking Smoking is not allowed on any trains, in any stations, or on any platforms.

Electronic Devices and Cell Phones Listen or speak at a volume that does not disturb other passengers.

Bicycles You can bring collapsible bicycles on all trains at all times. Standard frame bicycles are permitted in accessible cars only except aboard weekday peak period trains or on major holidays. NJ TRANSIT conductors may use their judgment based on crowding and capacity, to make exceptions. Note that a customer with a disability is given priority over a customer with a bicycle.

Symbols are a kind of graphical source. Analyze these symbols along with the factual data in the text.

WE'RE ACCESSIBLE AT MANY STATIONS

Stations with this symbol are accessible to customers using mobility assist devices. For assistance on or off the train, please inform the train crew. Customers traveling from Hoboken, please arrive 15 minutes before your scheduled train departure and notify an NJ TRANSIT representative for assistance.

Pascack Valley Line

- SPRING VALLEY ♿
- Nanuet ♿
- Pearl River
- Montvale ♿
- Park Ridge
- Woodcliff Lake
- Hillsdale
- Westwood ♿
- Emerson
- Oradell
- River Edge
- North Hackensack
- Anderson Street
- Essex Street ♿
- Teterboro
- Wood-Ridge
- Secaucus Junction ♿
- HOBOKEN ♿

Here, factual data is presented in a graphical source—a map. **Analyze the graphical source. What factual information does the icon next to some of the stops provide?**

THE BIG ?

Can truth change?
Which parts of this train schedule might change from time to time?

Texas State Railroad

Brochure

Features:
- graphical sources
- attraction history and highlights
- text presented for a variety of reading purposes

The Texas State Railroad, established 1881, is truly a "Texas Treasure!"

This historic train travels through the scenic piney woods and hardwood creek bottoms of East Texas where rolling hills, nature and wildlife abound.

The Texas State Railroad offers both steam and diesel train excursions reminiscent of days gone by. Passengers may board excursion trains at either the Rusk or Palestine depots where southern hospitality is the norm. These depots were built with an eye for detail and the elegance of Victorian charm. They are surrounded by beautiful parks with lakes and streams offering visitors full-service campground facilities, picnic areas, concessions and a great deal more to enhance a four-season vacation experience. This is a perfect family outing!

Location

The Texas State Railroad is located approximately 2 1/2 hours from Dallas and 3 hours from Houston. Both of our depots are located on US Hwy 84 between the cities of Palestine, Texas and Rusk, Texas.

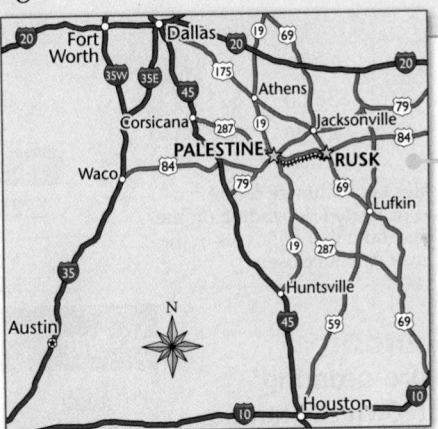

This map is a graphical source. **Analyze its factual data. What information does it provide?**

These charts give mileage from various Texas cities to the train depots. **Analyze the quantitative data presented in these graphical sources. How would this data be helpful to visitors?**

Directions to Palestine Depot
Located approximately 2 miles East of Loop 256 in Palestine on US Hwy 84.

Approximate mileage to Palestine	
From Shreveport	135 mi.
From Dallas (South)	120 mi.
From Houston (NW)	150 mi.
From Texarkana	156 mi.
From Austin	185 mi.
From Fort Worth	134 mi.
From Waco	100 mi.

Directions to Rusk Depot
Located approximately 3 miles West of downtown Rusk on US Hwy 84.

Approximate mileage to Rusk	
From Shreveport	110 mi.
From Dallas (South)	145 mi.
From Houston (NE)	150 mi.
From Texarkana	131 mi.
From Austin	210 mi.
From Fort Worth	160 mi.
From Waco	130 mi.

TEXAS

Schedule and Fares

Celebrate the spirit of Texas, with a ride on the historic Texas State Railroad. Round trips depart either the Rusk or the Palestine depots at 11 a.m., with return at 3:30 p.m. Each trip takes 1 1/2 hours each way with a 1 1/2 hour lunch layover at the opposite train depot for a total 4 1/2 hour experience. There are a variety of lunch options. Ask the reservation office for details.

PLEASE NOTE: schedule, price, engines and equipment are subject to change without notice.

> This chart presents fares. **Analyze the factual and quantitative data in this graphical source. Think about whom you might take on this train trip, which train you would take, and what the total fare would be.**

Fares

Fares are for regular excursions departing from either Palestine or Rusk Depots.

Diesel Fares

	Adult	Child
General Seating	$34.00	$17.00
Climate Controlled**	$38.00	$19.00

Steam Fares

	Adult	Child
General Seating	$38.00	$21.00
Climate Controlled**	$42.00	$23.00

*Prices do not include sales tax.**Climate controlled seating is air conditioned or heated depending on the current temperature. Please note that windows in the climate controlled cars must remain closed.

First Class Car Information

First Class Car – Coming Soon

Enjoy a first-class ride in the Governor's Car.

MKT Caboose	
$325	Rent caboose with up to 8 people in your party.
$100 upgrade	Upgrade comes with food and beverages, including gourmet cheese and crackers, fruit tray, delicious chocolate confections, sodas and coffee.

Cab Ride	
$225	Must be 18 years or older.

Brown Bag Lunch
Save money by pre-ordering!

Pre-order your brown bag lunches when you reserve your train tickets to avoid the lines when you arrive at the opposite depot for lunch. Our fresh sandwiches are made daily on a delicious hoagie with several choices of meat and cheeses.

> This table presents factual and quantitative data. **Analyze this graphical source. What items are in every sack lunch?**

Type	Sandwich choice	Included in sack lunch	Cost
Adult hoagie style sandwich	Roast beef & swiss, Ham & cheddar, Turkey & cheddar	Chips, pickle, cookie, and a bottle of water	$8
Child sandwich on white bread	Ham & cheddar, Turkey & cheddar	Chips, fruit roll-up, and a bottle of water	$5.50
Child	Peanut butter & jelly	Chips, fruit roll-up, and a bottle of water	$5

THE BIG ?

Can truth change?
What true data in the brochure's graphical sources might change? What true data probably will not change?

TEXAS

Comparing Informational Texts

(a) Summarize the data presented in the maps and charts of the schedule and the brochure. **(b) Analyze:** How does the map in the schedule differ from the map in the brochure? **(c) Analyze:** Which text's graphical sources are easier to use? Explain.

 **College Readiness** | **Timed Writing**

Write an Explanatory Essay

> **Format**
> The prompt directs you to write an explanatory essay. Therefore, be sure your response clearly explains and addresses the situation as it is described in the prompt.

Analyze the information in the Texas State Railroad brochure, especially the quantitative and factual data in its graphical sources. Use your analysis to write an essay that explains how a Dallas family (two adults, two children) should plan a visit. Be sure to explain the following:

- directions and mileage from Dallas to Palestine (including approximate departure and return times)
- fares and lunch costs calculated for the family, based on your preferences (20 minutes)

> **Academic Vocabulary**
> When you *calculate*, you use mathematics to compute an amount.

5-Minute Planner

Complete these steps before you begin to write:

1. Read the prompt carefully and completely.
2. Analyze the chart to find the mileage to Palestine from Dallas. Analyze data in the maps to make notes about each step of the route. Analyze other data to figure out departure and return times.
3. Analyze data in the Fares and Brown Bag Lunch charts to price the excursion and the food of your choice for each family member. **TIP** Be sure to check your math!
4. Add any other data that you think the family needs to know.
5. Refer to your notes as you draft your essay.

Comparing Literary Works

Comparing Themes Across Genres

Theme is the central message or insight about life that is conveyed in a short story, an essay, or another literary work. Sometimes it is explicit, or stated directly. More often, it is implicit—or expressed indirectly—through the words and actions of the characters or the events of a story. The way theme is developed depends in part on the **genre,** or form, of the work.

- **Nonfiction:** In nonfiction literature, such as essays or articles, the theme is usually stated explicitly, as a main idea or thesis. The thesis statement frequently appears at the beginning of the work.

- **Fiction and poetry:** In fiction and poetry, the theme is often implicit. Readers can figure out the implied theme by looking at story events, the words and actions of characters, and patterns of related images and ideas called *motifs.*

The **context,** or time and place, in which the author is writing, can also affect the expression of a theme. For example, an author living in a culture that values technology might express a theme differently from an author whose culture is not technologically advanced. As you analyze a work, keep in mind its cultural, historical, or contemporary contexts.

The topic of the following selections is the environment. "If I Forget Thee, Oh Earth . . ." is a short story, and *Silent Spring* is nonfiction.

As You Read Complete a Venn diagram to analyze how the genres of these texts with similar themes shape meaning.

Focus on the TEKS

Reading
(2)(A) Analyze how the genre of texts with similar themes shapes meaning.

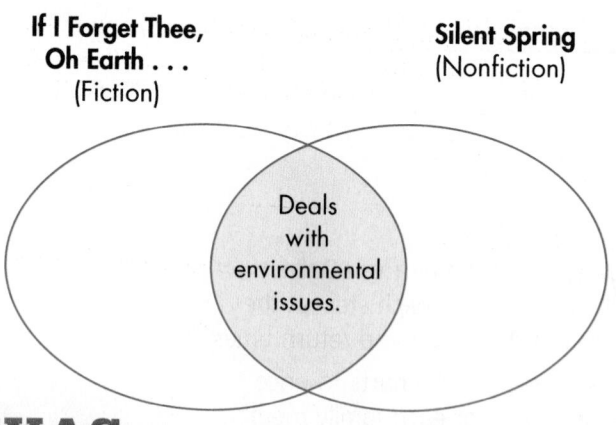

If I Forget Thee, Oh Earth . . .
(Fiction)

Silent Spring
(Nonfiction)

Deals with environmental issues.

TEXAS
PHLitOnline
www.PHLitOnline.com

- Vocabulary flashcards
- Interactive journals
- More about the authors
- Selection audio
- Interactive graphic organizers

Can *truth* change?

Writing About the Big Question

Some people feel that the condition of Earth is a constant, unchangeable truth. Use these sentence starters to develop your ideas about the Big Question.

I **speculate** that in 100 years, Earth will be _____.

My **assumptions** are based on _____.

Meet the Authors

Arthur C. Clarke (1917–2008)

Author of "If I Forget Thee, Oh Earth . . ."

Born in England, Arthur C. Clarke was both a writer and a scientist. He wrote his first science-fiction stories during his teens, and he later published more than fifty works of fiction and nonfiction.

A True Scientist Although best known for his science fiction, Clarke was a serious scientist as well. In 1945, he published a technical article called "Extra-Terrestrial Relays" in which he established the principles of the satellite communications system we have today.

Rachel Carson (1907–1964)

Author of *Silent Spring*

Even as a young girl, Rachel Carson thought of herself as a writer, and she entered college to pursue that goal. Once there, she renewed an interest in nature and switched her major to marine biology. She later earned a master's degree in zoology.

Environmental Activist Carson had long been worried about the overuse of pesticides. "Everything which meant most to me as a naturalist was being threatened," she said, and she felt that the most important thing she could do was publicize the facts. *Silent Spring* became one of the most influential environmental books ever written. Carson died of cancer before she witnessed the major impact of her book.

"If I Forget Thee, Oh Earth..."

Arthur C. Clarke

Literary Analysis

Theme What information about Marvin's environment appears in this description of the Farmlands?

Vocabulary

purged (pʉrjd) v. cleansed

When Marvin was ten years old, his father took him through the long, echoing corridors that led up through Administration and Power, until at last they came to the uppermost levels of all and were among the swiftly growing vegetation of the Farmlands. Marvin liked it here: it was fun watching the great, slender plants creeping with almost visible eagerness toward the sunlight as it filtered down through the plastic domes to meet them. The smell of life was everywhere, awakening inexpressible longings in his heart: no longer was he breathing the dry, cool air of the residential levels, purged of all smells but the faint tang of ozone.[1] He wished he could stay here for a little while, but Father would not let him. They went onward until they had reached the entrance to the Observatory, which he had never visited: but they did not stop, and Marvin knew

---

1. **ozone** (ō′ zōn′) n. form of oxygen with a sharp odor.

with a sense of rising excitement that there could be only one goal left. For the first time in his life, he was going Outside.

There were a dozen of the surface vehicles, with their wide balloon tires and pressurized cabins, in the great servicing chamber. His father must have been expected, for they were led at once to the little scout car waiting by the huge circular door of the airlock. Tense with expectancy, Marvin settled himself down in the cramped cabin while his father started the motor and checked the controls. The inner door of the lock slid open and then closed behind them: he heard the roar of the great air pumps fade slowly away as the pressure dropped to zero. Then the "Vacuum" sign flashed on, the outer door parted, and before Marvin lay the land which he had never yet entered.

He had seen it in photographs, of course: he had watched it imaged on television screens a hundred times. But now it was lying all around him, burning beneath the fierce sun that crawled so slowly across the jet-black sky. He stared into the west, away from the blinding splendor of the sun—and there were the stars, as he had been told but had never quite believed. He gazed at them for a long time, marveling that anything could be so bright and yet so tiny. They were intense unscintillating points, and suddenly he remembered a rhyme he had once read in one of his father's books:

Twinkle, twinkle, little star,
How I wonder what you are.

Well, he knew what the stars were. Whoever asked that question must have been very stupid. And what did they mean by "twinkle"? You could see at a glance that all the stars shone with the same steady, unwavering light. He abandoned the puzzle and turned his attention to the landscape around him.

They were racing across a level plain at almost a hundred miles an hour, the great balloon tires sending up little spurts of dust behind them. There was no sign of the Colony: in the few minutes while he had been gazing at the stars, its domes and radio towers had fallen below the horizon. Yet there were other indications of man's presence, for about a mile ahead Marvin could see the curiously shaped structures clustering round the head of a mine. Now and then a puff of vapor would emerge from a squat smokestack and would instantly disperse.

They were past the mine in a moment: Father was driving with a reckless and exhilarating skill as if—it was a strange thought to come into a child's mind—he were trying to escape from something. In a few minutes they had reached the edge of the plateau on which the Colony had been built. The ground fell sharply away beneath them in a dizzying slope whose lower stretches were lost in shadow.

Literary Analysis
Theme What do the words "burning beneath the fierce sun" suggest about what Marvin is observing?

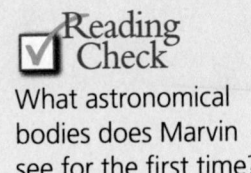

Reading Check
What astronomical bodies does Marvin see for the first time?

(Science Connection)

International Space Station
In Arthur C. Clarke's story, a space colony is all that remains of the human species. If the idea of a space colony seems implausible, consider the fact that a small colony is being developed directly over your head in the form of an International Space Station. Sixteen nations are contributing scientific and technological resources to build the Station, which has been under construction since 1998. The Space Station will be used for experiments and research, and it will also provide insight into the way humans can learn to live and work in outer space. The first astronaut crew arrived at the Station in November of 2000, and since then, people have lived and worked continuously at the Station, more than 200 miles above Earth.

Connect to the Literature

How do you think the astronauts' feelings about living in outer space compare to Marvin's feelings?

Ahead, as far as the eye could reach, was a jumbled wasteland of craters, mountain ranges, and ravines. The crests of the mountains, catching the low sun, burned like islands of fire in a sea of darkness: and above them the stars still shone as steadfastly as ever.

There could be no way forward—yet there was. Marvin clenched his fists as the car edged over the slope and started the long descent. Then he saw the barely visible track leading down the mountainside, and relaxed a little. Other men, it seemed, had gone this way before.

Night fell with a shocking abruptness as they crossed the shadow line and the sun dropped below the crest of the plateau. The twin searchlights sprang into life, casting blue-white bands on the rocks ahead, so that there was scarcely need to check their speed. For hours they drove through valleys and past the foot of mountains whose peaks seemed to comb the stars, and sometimes they emerged for a moment into the sunlight as they climbed over higher ground.

And now on the right was a wrinkled, dusty plain, and on the left, its ramparts and terraces rising mile after mile into the sky, was a wall of mountains that marched into the distance until its peaks sank from sight below the rim of the world. There was no sign that men had ever explored this land, but once they passed the skeleton of a crashed rocket, and beside it a stone cairn[2] surmounted by a metal cross.

It seemed to Marvin that the mountains stretched on forever: but at last, many hours later, the range ended in a towering, precipitous headland[3] that rose steeply from a cluster of little hills. They drove down into a shallow valley that curved in a great arc toward the far side of the mountains: and as they did so, Marvin slowly realized that something very strange was happening in the land ahead.

The sun was now low behind the hills on the right: the valley before them should be in total darkness. Yet it was awash with a cold white radiance that came spilling over the crags beneath which they were driving. Then, suddenly, they were out in the open plain, and the source of the light lay before them in all its glory.

---

2. cairn (kern) *n.* a cone-shaped pile of stones built as a monument.
3. precipitous headland (prē sip´ ə təs hed´ land´) *n.* steep cliff that juts out over water.

It was very quiet in the little cabin now that the motors had stopped. The only sound was the faint whisper of the oxygen feed and an occasional metallic crepitation as the outer walls of the vehicle radiated away their heat. For no warmth at all came from the great silver crescent that floated low above the far horizon and flooded all this land with pearly light. It was so brilliant that minutes passed before Marvin could accept its challenge and look steadfastly into its glare, but at last he could discern the outlines of continents, the hazy border of the atmosphere, and the white islands of cloud. And even at this distance, he could see the glitter of sunlight on the polar ice.

It was beautiful, and it called to his heart across the abyss of space. There in that shining crescent were all the wonders that he had never known—the hues of sunset skies, the moaning of the sea on pebbled shores, the patter of falling rain, the unhurried benison of snow. These and a thousand others should have been his rightful heritage, but he knew them only from the books and ancient records, and the thought filled him with the anguish of exile.

Why could they not return? It seemed so peaceful beneath those lines of marching cloud. Then Marvin, his eyes no longer blinded by the glare, saw that the portion of the disk that should have been in darkness was gleaming faintly with an evil phosphorescence[4] and he remembered. He was looking upon the funeral pyre of a world—upon the radioactive aftermath of Armageddon.[5] Across a quarter of a million miles of space, the glow of dying atoms was still visible, a perennial reminder of the ruinous past. It would be centuries yet before that deadly glow died from the rocks and life could return again to fill that silent, empty world.

And now Father began to speak, telling Marvin the story which until this moment had meant no more to him than the fairy tales he had once been told. There were many things he could not understand: it was impossible for him to picture the glowing, multicolored pattern of life on the planet he had never seen. Nor could he comprehend the forces that had destroyed it in the end, leaving the Colony, preserved by its isolation, as the sole survivor. Yet he could share the agony of those final days, when the Colony had learned at last that never again would the supply ships come flaming down through the stars with gifts from home. One by one the radio stations had ceased to call: on the shadowed globe the lights of the cities had dimmed and died, and they were alone at last, as no men had ever been alone before, carrying in their hands the future of the race.

---

4. **phosphorescence** (fäs´ fə res´ əns) *n.* emission of light resulting from exposure to radiation.
5. **Armageddon** (är´ mə ged´ 'n) *n.* in the Bible, the place where the final battle between good and evil is to be fought.

Literary Analysis
Theme Which details in these paragraphs provide an insight into what Marvin and others in his colony have lost?

Vocabulary
perennial (pə ren´ ē əl) *adj.* happening over and over; perpetual

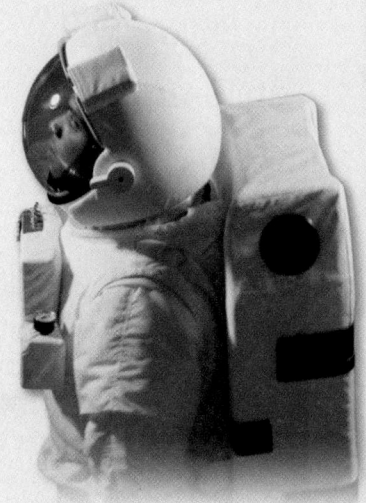

Reading Check
What does Marvin notice in a portion of the disk?

Literary Analysis
Theme Is the theme of this selection implicit or explicit? How might the genre of the selection have shaped the selection's meaning?

Yet one day—how far ahead?—his children's children would return to claim their heritage.

Support your responses with evidence from the text.

Then had followed the years of despair, and the long-drawn battle for survival in their fierce and hostile world. That battle had been won, though barely: this little oasis of life was safe against the worst that Nature could do. But unless there was a goal, a future toward which it could work, the Colony would lose the will to live, and neither machines nor skill nor science could save it then.

So, at last, Marvin understood the purpose of this pilgrimage. He would never walk beside the rivers of that lost and legendary world, or listen to the thunder raging above its softly rounded hills. Yet one day—how far ahead?—his children's children would return to claim their heritage. The winds and the rains would scour the poisons from the burning lands and carry them to the sea, and in the depths of the sea they would waste their venom until they could harm no living things. Then the great ships that were still waiting here on the silent, dusty plains could lift once more into space, along the road that led to home.

That was the dream: and one day, Marvin knew with a sudden flash of insight, he would pass it on to his own son, here at this same spot with the mountains behind him and the silver light from the sky streaming into his face.

He did not look back as they began the homeward journey. He could not bear to see the cold glory of the crescent Earth fade from the rocks around him, as he went to rejoin his people in their long exile.

Critical Thinking

1. **Respond:** How do you think you would handle Marvin's situation? Explain.

2. **(a)** At the end of the story, what does Marvin realize?
   (b) Draw Conclusions: What was the purpose of Marvin's trip with his father?

3. **(a) Make Inferences:** What evidence from the text indicates that the story is set on the moon? **(b) Analyze:** How does the choice of setting make the story more realistic?

4. **(a) Make Inferences:** How did Earth come to be destroyed?
   (b) Speculate: What suggestions do you think Clarke might have offered today to prevent a situation like this from occurring?

   Can truth change?
   How does the truth about the moon and Earth shift for Marvin after his trip with his father?

from Silent Spring

Rachel Carson

There was once a town in the heart of America where all life seemed to live in harmony with its surroundings. The town lay in the midst of a checkerboard of prosperous farms, with fields of grain and hillsides of orchards where, in spring, white clouds of bloom drifted above the green fields. In autumn, oak and maple and birch set up a blaze of color that flamed and flickered across a backdrop of pines. Then foxes barked in the hills and deer silently crossed the fields, half hidden in the mists of the fall mornings.

Along the roads, laurel, viburnum and alder, great ferns and wildflowers delighted the traveler's eye through much of the year. Even in winter the roadsides were places of beauty, where

Literary Analysis
Theme Which details in this paragraph paint a picture of the beauty and energy of nature? Explain.

countless birds came to feed on the berries and on the seed heads of the dried weeds rising above the snow. The countryside was, in fact, famous for the abundance and variety of its bird life, and when the flood of migrants was pouring through in spring and fall people traveled from great distances to observe them. Others came to fish the streams, which flowed clear and cold out of the hills and contained shady pools where trout lay. So it had been from the days many years ago when the first settlers raised their houses, sank their wells, and built their barns.

Then a strange blight crept over the area and everything began to change. Some evil spell had settled on the community: mysterious maladies swept the flocks of chickens; the cattle and sheep sickened and died. Everywhere was a shadow of death. The farmers spoke of much illness among their families. In the town the doctors had become more and more puzzled by new kinds of sickness appearing among their patients. There had been several sudden and unexplained deaths, not only among adults but even among children, who would be stricken suddenly while at play and die within a few hours.

There was a strange stillness. The birds, for example— where had they gone? Many people spoke of them, puzzled and disturbed. The feeding stations in the backyards were deserted. The few birds seen anywhere were moribund; they trembled violently and could not fly. It was a spring without voices. On the mornings that had once throbbed with the dawn chorus of robins, catbirds, doves, jays, wrens, and scores of other bird voices there was now no sound; only silence lay over the fields and woods and marsh.

On the farms the hens brooded, but no chicks hatched. The farmers complained that they were unable to raise any pigs—the litters were small and the young survived only a few days. The apple trees were coming into bloom but no bees droned among the blossoms, so there was no pollination and there would be no fruit.

The roadsides, once so attractive, were now lined with browned and withered vegetation as though swept by fire. These, too, were silent, deserted by all living things. Even

▶ **Critical Viewing** What details in this picture indicate that a "strange blight" may have affected this area? **[Connect]**

Vocabulary
blight (blīt) *n.* something that destroys or prevents growth
maladies (mal´ ə dēz) *n.* diseases

Vocabulary
moribund (môr´ i bund´) *adj.* slowly dying

the streams were now lifeless. Anglers[1] no longer visited them, for all the fish had died.

In the gutters under the eaves and between the shingles of the roofs, a white granular powder still showed a few patches; some weeks before it had fallen like snow upon the roofs and the lawns, the fields and streams.

No witchcraft, no enemy action had silenced the rebirth of new life in this stricken world. The people had done it themselves.

This town does not actually exist, but it might easily have a thousand counterparts in America or elsewhere in the world. I know of no community that has experienced all the misfortunes I describe. Yet every one of these disasters has actually happened somewhere, and many real communities have already suffered a substantial number of them. A grim specter has crept upon us almost unnoticed, and this imagined tragedy may easily become a stark reality we all shall know.

The people had done it themselves.

1. **anglers** (aŋ' glərz) *n.* people who fish with a line and hook.

Critical Thinking

1. **Respond:** What—if anything—do you find most troubling about the environmental problems described in this excerpt? Explain.

2. **(a)** What is the condition of life at the beginning of this excerpt? **(b) Analyze:** How does the condition of life change as the narrative continues?

Support your responses with evidence from the text.

3. **(a)** What happens to the farm animals and the vegetation? **(b) Make Inferences:** What causes this sudden change?

4. **(a)** What information about the town does Carson reveal at the end of the excerpt? **(b) Speculate:** Would the narrative be more effective if the town was real? Why or why not?

5. **(a)** According to Carson, who caused the environmental problems? **(b) Speculate:** What suggestions do you think Carson would make to people today?

Can truth change?
How do you think Carson would respond to the question, *Can truth change?*

Comparing Themes Across Genres

1. Use a chart like the one shown to analyze the themes expressed in "If I Forget Thee, Oh Earth . . ." and the excerpt from *Silent Spring.* First, list important details from each selection and what you think the details mean. Use this information to state the theme of the selection.

Details from "If I Forget Thee, Oh Earth..."	What They Mean	Theme
Details from *Silent Spring*	**What They Mean**	**Theme**

2. (a) Using your chart, explain how the themes in the two selections are similar. **(b)** Compare how the genres of these texts shape how the meaning of each text is expressed.

 College Readiness | Timed Writing

Writing to Compare Themes Across Genres

Write an essay in which you compare your reactions to the way "If I Forget Thee, Oh Earth . . ." and the excerpt from *Silent Spring* each explore their similar themes. In your response, consider how the genre of each selection affects your reading experience. (25 minutes)

🕐 5-Minute Planner

1. Read the prompt carefully and completely.

2. Jot down your answers to these questions to help organize your thoughts:

- Do you feel more affected by the experiences of the character Marvin or by the words of Rachel Carson, the author of *Silent Spring*?

- Which genre do you find more effective in shaping meaning and expressing the theme of a work—fiction or nonfiction? Why?

- Why do you think an author would choose one genre over another when conveying a theme?

3. Decide on a structure for your essay. Plan what points you will cover in each paragraph.

4. Reread the prompt, and then draft your essay.

Expository Text: Problem-and-Solution Essay

Some forms of expository writing engage us in the issues of our daily lives. A problem-and-solution essay is a type of analytical essay in which an author analyzes a problem and then proposes a possible solution. You might use this type of writing in letters, memos, proposals, or editorials.

Assignment Write an analytical problem-and-solution essay of sufficient length about an issue that confronts your school or community. Your essay should feature the following elements:

✔ effective *introductory and concluding paragraphs*

✔ a *controlling idea or thesis* supported by *relevant information,* including facts, statistics, and details

✔ language appropriate to your audience and purpose, including *rhetorical devices* and *transitions between paragraphs*

✔ an *organizing structure* appropriate to your purpose and audience as well as the context in which you are writing

✔ error-free grammar, including correct use of pronouns

To preview the criteria on which your problem-and-solution essay may be judged, see the rubric on page 179.

 Writing Workshop: *Work in Progress*

Review the work you did on pages 123 and 151.

 Focus on the TEKS

Writing

(13)(A) Plan a first draft by determining appropriate topics through a range of strategies (e.g., background reading, personal interests) and developing a thesis or controlling idea.

(15)(A)(iii) Write an analytical essay of sufficient length that includes a controlling idea or thesis.

Research

(21)(A) Follow the research plan to compile data from authoritative sources in a manner that identifies the major issues and debates within the field of inquiry.

Reading-Writing Connection

To get a feel for the use of problem-and-solution structure in a speech, read "First Inaugural Address" by Franklin Delano Roosevelt on page 552.

WRITE GUY
Jeff Anderson, M.Ed.

What Do You Notice?

Powerful Diction

Read the following sentences from Rachel Carson's *Silent Spring* several times.

A grim specter has crept upon us almost unnoticed, and this imagined tragedy may easily become a stark reality we all shall know.

What do you notice about the passage? Discuss your observations with a partner. Then, discuss Carson's diction, or word choice. Consider how you might use vivid word choices in your own writing.

Prewriting/Planning Strategies

Plan the first draft of your problem-and-solution essay by determining an **appropriate topic** using one of these strategies:

- **Use Background Reading** Review local newspapers and magazines for items about issues and problems in your community. List problems for which you can imagine practical solutions, and select one as your topic.

- **Consider Personal Interests** Complete the following sentence starters and jot down any ideas that come to mind. Then, choose one of the issues generated by the sentence starters as your topic.

> **I am personally intersted in helping _____.**
> **I am personally interested in the problem of _____.**
> **I am concerned because people my age face _____.**
> **I am concerned about the issue of _____.**

Develop a thesis. Once you have chosen an appropriate topic, develop your **thesis, or controlling idea**—a statement that describes the problem you are exploring. All the information you include in your essay will be related to your thesis.

Create a problem profile. Using your thesis as a starting point, create a profile like the one shown to help you focus your essay.

Problem Profile
Thesis/Problem: Litter is creating an unsafe and unsightly environment.
Who is affected? Everyone on Earth
What causes the problem?   Lack of: • responsibility   • environmental education   • sense of ownership
What are the possible solutions? Stiffer fines, more policing, more environmental education, volunteer trash pickup

Follow a research plan. Once you have clearly defined the problem, decide upon a plan to collect the details and information you will need to start your draft. You should investigate all sides of the issue you are discussing in order to anticipate readers' concerns. Therefore, make sure your plan identifies the **major issues and debates** within your field of inquiry. Follow your research plan to compile data from **authoritative sources.**

TEXAS
PHLitOnline
www.PHLitOnline.com
- Author video: Writing Process
- Author video: Rewards of Writing

Drafting Strategies

Use rhetorical devices. The use of rhetorical devices will help engage your audience and convey your meaning in a memorable way. To draft an **effective introductory paragraph,** consider one of these devices for starting your essay:

- **Personal example:** Provide a detail from your own experience.
- **Anecdote:** Give a factual account of how the problem has already affected others.
- **Scenario:** Present a hypothetical but realistic picture of future consequences if the problem is not addressed.

Similarly, consider using a rhetorical device to end your essay. An **effective concluding paragraph** will make a lasting impression on your audience.

Plan an organizing structure. Use a **graphic organizer** like this one to structure your ideas in a sustained and persuasive way. Use your notes to plan an organizing structure for your essay that is appropriate to your **purpose** and **audience** as well as the **context** in which you are writing.

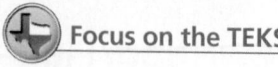
Focus on the TEKS

Reading
(1)(E) Use a dictionary or glossary to determine or confirm the meanings of words and phrases.

Writing
(13)(B) Structure ideas in a sustained and persuasive way (e.g., using graphic organizers) and develop drafts in open-ended situations that include rhetorical devices used to convey meaning.
(15)(A)(i);(ii);(iv);(v) Write an analytical essay that includes effective introductory and concluding paragraphs; rhetorical devices; an organizing structure appropriate to purpose, audience, and context; relevant information and valid inferences.

Conventions
(19) Spell correctly, including using various resources to determine correct spellings.

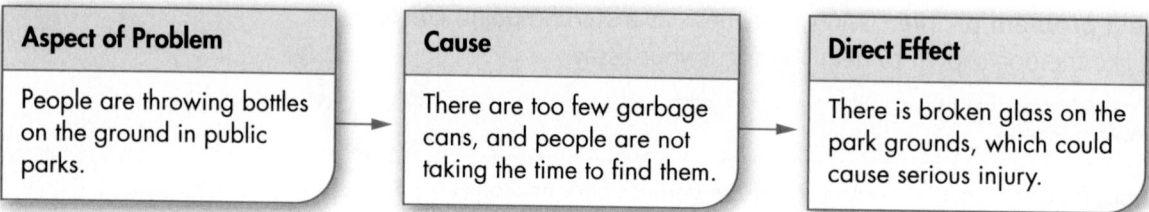

Aspect of Problem	Cause	Direct Effect
People are throwing bottles on the ground in public parks.	There are too few garbage cans, and people are not taking the time to find them.	There is broken glass on the park grounds, which could cause serious injury.

Select relevant information. To support your ideas, use only **relevant information** from which you can make **valid inferences.** You cannot "prove" your solution in advance, but you can persuade the audience that your proposal is likely to work by using the following types of evidence.

- **Statistics:** Provide relevant numerical data.
- **Expert opinions:** Include the advice of those who have training or experience related to your topic problem. Integrate quotations and citations from experts to support the evidence.
- **Comparable situations:** Describe other real-life difficulties that were resolved by actions similar to the ones you propose.

Anticipate readers' concerns. Anticipate arguments that you might get from people with differing opinons. Mention these concerns and provide well-supported answers that explain why your solution is best.

Consult dictionaries and glossaries. Use various resources to determine correct spellings and to determine or confirm the meanings of any words and phrases you don't know.

Elizabeth McCracken

On Word Choice

One of the best things about writing my novel *Niagara Falls All Over Again,* which tells the story of a comedy team, was that I could watch videotapes of old TV shows and movies, and claim that I was working. My favorite tapes were old episodes of a show that my beloved comic duo, Abbott and Costello, hosted once a month. This passage is basically just a description of what I saw when I was "working," watching *The Colgate Comedy Hour.*

"Write about your most beloved obsessions."
—Elizabeth McCracken

from *Niagara Falls All Over Again*

We broke into television as the once-a-month hosts of a weekly hour-long live variety show. By 1951, our movie career was mostly over, and we were back where we'd begun, except famous, rich, and middle-aged: a thin man and a fat man on a stage, willing to do anything for a laugh. We were shameless. We insulted the band leader, we knocked down scenery on purpose, we tried to crack each other up. We broke props we'd need later, just so we could improvise first about the breakage, and then about the lack of props. Our old wheezing vaudeville jokes were new again, thanks to the postwar baby boom: the country was full of brand-new people with blissfully unsophisticated senses of humor. You could see Rocky search for the red light that told us which camera was paying attention, doing a slow burn and then saying, "Watch me, camera two," and tipping his hat. . . .

I have a weakness for repetition, both straight repeats (like all the We's) and slight variations, like *break, broke.*

Some writers say, Avoid adverbs. It's true that some people use adverbs to do the work that verbs and adjectives should do, but I use *blissfully* here as a joke—most people wouldn't see a lack of sophistication as *blissful.*

He's wearing a bowler hat. I draw my characters' clothing when I write (though I'm a very poor artist). I know them better if I know what they wear.

Revising Strategies

Support your generalizations. Review your essay to be certain that the details you have used support or explain your thesis, or controlling idea. Your essay should be of sufficient length to adequately cover your topic, but should not contain information that is not directly related to your thesis. Use the following strategy to revise your paragraphs:

1. Highlight your thesis, the general statement in which you summarize the main idea of your essay.

2. Underline the sentences that develop and support this idea.

3. Eliminate any sentences that do not support your thesis or that simply restate it.

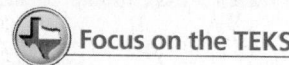
Focus on the TEKS

Writing
(13)(C) Revise drafts to improve word choice after rethinking how well questions of purpose, audience, and genre have been addressed.
(13)(E) Revise final draft in response to feedback from peers
(15)(A) Write an analytical essay of sufficient length.

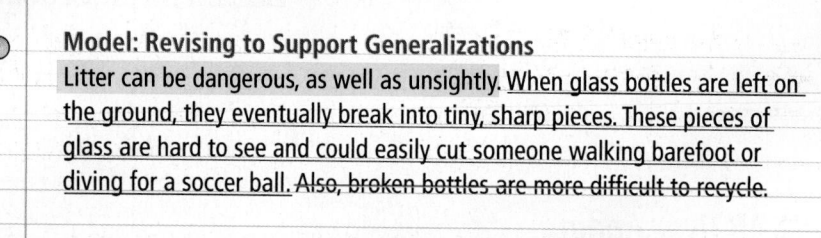

Model: Revising to Support Generalizations

Litter can be dangerous, as well as unsightly. When glass bottles are left on the ground, they eventually break into tiny, sharp pieces. These pieces of glass are hard to see and could easily cut someone walking barefoot or diving for a soccer ball. Also, broken bottles are more difficult to recycle.

Revise your word choice. Review your draft as if you were a member of your target audience. Find specialized or technical terms that need to be defined. Look for vocabulary that seems too difficult or easy for your readers. Then, revise your draft to improve word choice, adjusting your language so that it is appropriate for your **purpose, audience,** and **genre.** Use resources and reference materials to select more effective and precise language.

General Audience	Target Audience of Experts
Another way to fight fatigue is to exercise.	Another way to raise low levels of blood sugar is to get more exercise.

Peer Feedback

Exchange drafts with a partner. Review each other's work, circling words that are either too specialized and technical or too simple and basic for your target audiences. Use reference materials such as a dictionary or thesaurus to suggest more effective and precise language. Then, revise your final draft in response to the feedback from your peer. Consider your partner's comments and replace inappropriate terms with language that better suits your readers' experience and knowledge levels.

Revising Pronoun-Antecedent Agreement

Pronouns are words that take the place of nouns. **Antecedents** are the nouns that the pronouns refer to.

Identifying Errors in Pronoun-Antecedent Agreement Pronouns "disagree" with their antecedents when they are mismatched in number, person, or gender. A pronoun should agree with its antecedent in number:

Incorrect: *Anne and Natasha* reminded *her* parents.
Correct: *Anne and Natasha* reminded *their* parents. (plural)

Incorrect: *Neither Carl nor Jeff* remember *their* ID number.
Correct: *Neither Carl nor Jeff* remembers *his* ID number. (singular)

A pronoun should agree with its antecedent in person:

Incorrect: When a *person* hurries, *you* may fall.
Correct: When *a person* hurries, *he or she* may fall. (third-person singular)
Correct: When *people* hurry, *they* may fall. (third-person plural)

A pronoun should agree with its antecedent in gender:

> **PH GRAMMAR HANDBOOK**
>
> Further instruction and practice are available in the *Prentice Hall Grammar Handbook*.

Gender of Third-Person Singular Pronouns

Masculine	Feminine	Neuter
he, him, his, himself	she, her, hers, herself	it, its, itself

Fixing Errors in Pronoun-Antecedent Agreement To correct errors, first identify the antecedent of each pronoun. As you work through each paragraph of your draft, consider the following:

1. **For compound antecedents joined by *and*, use a plural personal pronoun.**

2. **For singular antecedents joined by *or* or *nor*, use a singular personal pronoun.**

3. **Check every occurrence of the pronoun *you* to make sure that you have not made a shift in person.**

Grammar in Your Writing

Review the introductory and concluding paragraphs in your draft. Underline each antecedent and circle each pronoun. Check the marked words for pronoun-antecedent agreement and fix any errors.

Student Model: Carly Armstrong, Rowlett, TX

 Focus on the TEKS

Writing
(13)(D) Edit drafts for grammar, mechanics, and spelling.
(13)(E) Publish written work for appropriate audiences.
Conventions
(19) Spell correctly, including using various resources to check correct spellings.

Underwater Earthquakes

Boom! Snap! Whoosh! Crash! These sounds were what millions of people woke up to in 2004. Under the deep, blue water of the Indian Ocean, an underwater earthquake struck, causing vibrations all around the world. Lasting six to eight minutes, this was one of the longest lasting earthquakes in history. This underwater earthquake mostly affected Thailand and Indonesia, devastating many people. "Why should we care? We are on the other side of the world," you may say. We should all care because people lost their loved ones and historic landmarks were destroyed. These earthquakes cause huge tidal waves that rise and demolish buildings, homes, and many great memories, replacing them with tragic ones.

What can be done to prevent these storms? The answer is nothing. But we can do something to help the people and businesses that were destroyed, by joining groups to earn money to rebuild the lives of those who lost everything. Also, those who live in "storm central" should move to a safer place that does not threaten their lives.

Another problem that occurs with underwater earthquakes is floods. With the high tidal waves, you should definitely get to higher ground as soon as possible, because most likely the whole surrounding area will be underwater. If you do not leave, there is no telling what diseases you could get from the polluted water.

Last, but most definitely not least, most electricity often goes out after earthquakes. With no electricity, there is no way to contact anyone for help if you are in trouble. It would be best to always have a land-line or a cell phone in your home in case you are put in danger and have no power. Also with these earthquakes, there is a shortage of clean water. So if you stay, you should not drink tap water unless it is boiled, until the government says it is safe.

There are so many problems caused by an underwater earthquake, and several solutions for each problem, so families should select the solution that promises the best outcome. Every family needs to decide what is best for them. Earthquakes can be disastrous, and people may lose some physical belongings, but keeping a family safe should be the priority. Being prepared and making wise choices is always the best solution.

In the introductory paragraph, Carly provides a general statement of the problem.

Here, Carly introduces general solutions to the problem.

In these paragraphs, Carly proposes several specific solutions.

In the concluding paragraph, Carly makes a general statement, summarizing the solutions introduced in the essay.

Editing and Proofreading

Edit your draft for errors in grammar and mechanics, such as punctuation. Use various resources such as printed or electronic dictionaries and glossaries to check correct spellings.

Focus on Spelling: As you proofread, circle any words that you are not sure how to spell, frequently misspell, or seldom use. Then, use reference resources, such as a dictionary or a thesaurus, to confirm the correct spelling. Follow these steps to find spellings in a dictionary:

- **Check the first letters of a word.** Think of homophones for that sound.
- **Check the other letters.** Once you spell the first sound correctly, try sounding out the rest of the word. Look for likely spellings in the dictionary. If you do not find your word, look for more unusual spellings of the sound.

Spiral Review

Earlier in this unit, you learned about **personal, reflexive and reciprocal pronouns** (p. 122) and **relative, interrogative and indefinite pronouns** (p. 150). Check your essay to be sure that you have used these pronouns correctly.

Publishing and Presenting

Consider ways to publish your written work for appropriate audiences:

Send a letter. Send your essay to the appropriate official, agency, or organization. Use traditional mail or e-mail. When you receive a response, share it with your classmates in a presentation. Save both the essay and response in your portfolio.

Make a speech. Deliver your essay as a speech to a group from your school or a community that shares your concerns about the problem. Then, lead a question-and-answer session.

Reflecting on Your Writing

Writer's Journal Jot down your answers to this question.

How did writing about the problem help you to understand it?

Rubric for Self-Assessment

Find evidence in your writing to address each category. Then, use the rating scale to grade your work.

Written Composition Criteria	Rating Scale			
	not very			*very*
Focus and Coherence: How relevant is the information used to support the thesis?	1	2	3	4
Organization: How appropriate is your organizing structure to your audience, purpose, and context?	1	2	3	4
Development of Ideas: How effective are your introductory and concluding paragraphs?	1	2	3	4
Conventions: How correct is your use of pronouns?	1	2	3	4
Voice: How appropriate is your language to your audience and purpose?	1	2	3	4

Applying the Big Question

THE BIG Q? Can *truth* change?

Think About It

Think about what you have read in this unit and what you know about the concept of truth from your other classes and your own experience. Copy and complete the following chart to apply what you have learned about the truth and whether or not it can change. One row has been completed for you.

Example	A statement of truth or fact	Evidence	How it could change or why it could not	What I learned
From Literature	In "The Cask of Amontillado," Fortunato insults Montresor.	Montresor reports this.	If Fortunato narrated the story, he might say he never insulted Montresor.	The truth can change, depending on who tells it.
From Literature				
From Science				
From Social Studies				
From Your Life				
In the Media				

Talk About It

Choose one of the examples in your truth chart as the basis for a **comparison of media coverage.** The example should involve an event that has been covered in the news media. Then, select several newspaper articles, television news programs, documentaries, blogs, and Internet sources about the event, and compare and contrast coverage of the event in the various media sources you chose. Follow these steps:

- Make notes about which details are presented.
- Determine whether the reporter tells the story from all sides or just one side.
- Look for the use of words that distort the facts of the story.

Organize your findings and share them with your class in an **oral presentation.** Conclude by explaining what you learned about whether different media presentations can change the truth.

Write About It

At the beginning of Unit 1, you wrote a response to the Big Question. Now that you have completed the unit, see how your understanding has deepened. Write a new response, discussing how your initial ideas have either been changed or reinforced.

- ❏ Truth can change.
- ❏ Truth cannot change.
- ❏ My own response: _____.

Support your answer with one or more of the examples in your chart.

Challenge What issues does this question still raise for you? How could you continue your exploration?

Connecting to Citizenship

Group Discussion With a small team, discuss how knowing whether truth can change is important to becoming a good citizen. Use these questions to guide your discussion:

- What truths might change concerning a community?
- What truths should every good citizen know?
- How does knowing the truth help you to become an active and thoughtful citizen?

Allow everyone on the team to **participate productively** by building on the ideas of others and contributing relevant information.

Focus on the TEKS

Reading
(12)(C) Compare and contrast coverage of the same event in various media (e.g., newspapers, television, documentaries, blogs, Internet).

Listening and Speaking
(26) Participate productively in teams, building on the ideas of others and contributing relevant information.

Big Question Vocabulary

Use some of these words as you complete the activities on these pages.

assumption
belief
circumstance
context
convince
credible
distort
evidence
manipulate
perceive
perspective
skeptics
speculate
truth
verify

This list includes academic vocabulary words, which are defined on pp. R1–R14.

Using a Dictionary, Glossary, and Thesaurus

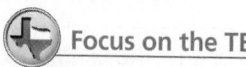 **Focus on the TEKS**

Reading
(1)(E) Use a dictionary, a glossary, or a thesaurus (printed or electronic) to determine or confirm the meanings of words and phrases, including their denotations and their etymology.

Dictionaries, glossaries, and thesauri are available in printed and electronic formats. They can be used to determine or confirm the meanings of words and phrases, including their **denotations,** or literal meanings, and **etymologies,** or histories.

A **dictionary** lists and defines words. Dictionaries also include each entry's part of speech. Pronunciations are shown with phonetic symbols. Abbreviations are used to explain etymologies. The entry shown here uses *ME* for *Middle English*, *OFr.* for *Old French*, *L* for *Latin*, and *Gr* for *Greek*.

Dictionary

> **poet** (pō´ət) *n.* [ME < OFr. *poete* < L *poeta* < Gr *poietes*, one who makes, poet < *poiein*, to make: see POEM] **1.** a person who writes poems or verses **2.** a person who displays imaginative power and beauty of thought, language, etc.

A **glossary** is an alphabetical list of words and phrases that pertain to a particular subject. It includes the pronunciation, part of speech, and denotation of each entry. For example, the glossary on pages R1–R14 includes words taught in this book.

Glossary

> **serve** (surv) *v.* work for; be useful for

A **thesaurus** is a list of synonyms. You can use it to find the exact word to fit your meaning and to vary your word selection so that you can avoid repeating words.

Thesaurus

> **teaching** *n.* teaching, education, schooling, instruction, tuition, coaching, tutoring
> *v.* teach, educate, instruct, give information, give lessons in, school, edify

Practice A Look up each word in the glossary on pages R1–R14. Determine and write the meaning, or denotation, of these words and phrases.

1. allotment
2. momentous
3. disputed fact
4. poignant
5. arduous battle
6. potential hero

Practice B Use a dictionary to answer these questions about denotations (meanings), etymologies, pronunciations, and parts of speech.

1. What is the etymology of the word *integrity?*

2. Can *wane* be properly used as a noun? If so, what is its denotation, or meaning?

3. What word can be used to replace *agitate* in this sentence? "Jonathan began to *agitate* the fish tank."

4. What is the adverb form of the word *dire?*

5. What is the etymology of the phrase *through the mill?*

6. Does the vowel sound in *fray* sound like the vowel in *at, ate,* or *car?*

7. What is the denotation, or meaning, of the phrase *flow chart?*

8. What word can be used to replace *adverse* in this sentence? "Are you *adverse* to leaving early?"

Activity Work with a team of classmates. Write a sentence about a story you know, and pass your sentence to another student. Then, use a thesaurus to find words with similar meanings to those in the sentence. Change the sentence you receive by replacing one word with a synonym. See how long you can keep passing the sentence and coming up with new words while keeping the original sentence's meaning.

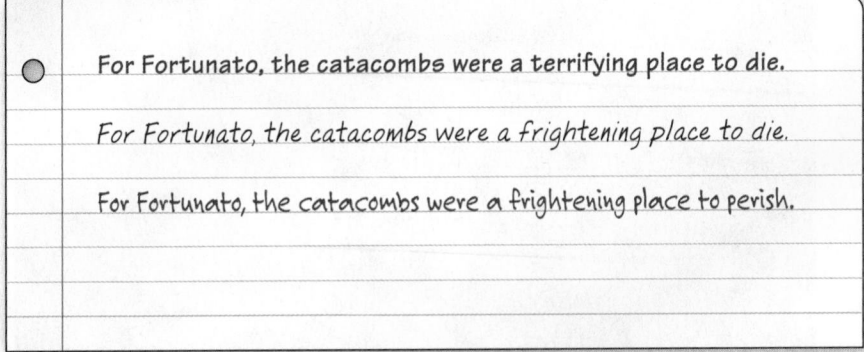

For Fortunato, the catacombs were a terrifying place to die.

For Fortunato, the catacombs were a frightening place to die.

For Fortunato, the catacombs were a frightening place to perish.

Teamwork

Look up these words and phrases in a dictionary: *feint, insignia, pommel horse.* Write each term's pronunciation, etymology, and denotation, or meaning. Study each pronunciation and practice saying it. Then, compare your pronunciations with those of a small team of classmates. If you disagree, review the pronunciation key in the dictionary, and decide who is correct.

Giving and Following Oral Instructions

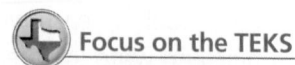

Focus on the TEKS

Listening and Speaking (24)(B) Follow and give complex oral instructions to perform specific tasks, answer questions, solve problems, and complete processes.

You can give and follow oral directions to perform specific tasks, answer questions, solve problems, and complete processes.

Learn the Skills

Use the strategies to complete the activity on p. 185.

Give clear instructions. Explain complex processes in easy-to-follow steps. Ask questions to be sure that your audience understands.

Listen attentively. When you follow instructions, listen carefully. Repeat the steps to the instructor to show that you understand. If you are confused, ask the instructor to explain.

Use instructions for different purposes. Give and follow complex oral directions for each of the following purposes. Work with a partner to complete these practice exercises.

- **Perform specific tasks.** Draw a design using only straight lines. Do not let your partner see your drawing. Then, give your partner step-by-step instructions for drawing the design. Finally, compare your drawings to see how well the instructions were given and followed.

- **Answer questions.** Ask your partner how to get from school to a place he or she knows well. Follow your partner's instructions by tracing the route on a map.

- **Solve problems.** Name a problem you face, such as staying organized or managing your time. Ask your partner for instructions that will help you solve this problem. Report back to your partner after you have followed the instructions.

- **Complete processes.** Give instructions for completing a process you have learned in school, such as solving an equation.

Practice the Skills

Use what you've learned in this workshop to perform the following task.

ACTIVITY: Give Complex Oral Instructions

Choose a specific task or process that would help your classmates solve a problem that they face. Give complex oral instructions that tell the class how to perform this task. Answer the following questions in your presentation.

- What are you teaching your classmates to do?
- How could your directions help your classmates solve a problem?
- What materials will your classmates need to follow the directions?
- How will your classmates know when they have completed the process correctly?
- What are the steps in the task or process?

As your classmates make their presentations, follow their directions. Use the Presentation Checklist below to analyze their presentations, and let your classmates use the checklist to analyze your presentation.

Presentation Checklist

Presentation Content
Does the presentation meet all of the requirements of the activity?
Check all that apply.
- ❏ It gives listeners instructions to complete a task or process.
- ❏ It helps listeners solve a problem.
- ❏ It answers the questions outlined in the activity assignment.

Presentation Delivery
Did the speaker give the instructions clearly? Check all that apply.
- ❏ The speaker gave instructions in logical, easy-to-follow steps.
- ❏ The speaker asked questions to check that the audience understood the steps.
- ❏ The speaker gave clear answers to questions asked by the audience.

After your presentation, ask your classmates to tell you how they rated you on the Presentation Checklist. While your classmates give their instruction presentations, follow their instructions and use the checklist to rate them. As a group, discuss which presentations were the easiest to follow and why.

Cumulative Review
Reading

Read this selection. Then answer the questions that follow it.

TEKS Spiral Review

Reading
(1)(E) Use a dictionary or a glossary to determine or confirm the meanings of words and phrases, including their connotations and denotations.
(5)(B) Analyze how authors develop complex yet believable characters in works of fiction through a range of literary devices, including character foils.
(5)(C) Analyze the way in which a work of fiction is shaped by the narrator's point of view.
Comprehension
RC-9(A) Reflect on understanding to monitor comprehension.

from The Window
by Jeanette Ingold

1   We drive a long while after leaving the Dallas airport, first over highway and then back roads, and then I'm inside a house and still chilly. Aunt Emma puts a bundlely sweater on my shoulders and I hear a furnace coming roaring on. "Cold November," says Uncle Abe. "We'll have heat in just a few minutes."

2   I can't stop a shiver.

3   "Em," says Abe, "guess we've got another cold-blooded one," and I think he's saying that I'm mean, but he's not.

4   Gabriel says, "Your Uncle Abe means thin-blooded. Emma always wants the heat up."

5   The house smells of cooking, onion and broccoli and meats layered one meal into the next, nice smells, but smells.

6   And of flowers, but not sweet ones like my roommate's at the hospital. I ask Aunt Emma what kind and she says marigolds. "About the last, I guess. We could get frost any night now."

7   "Most people plant marigolds to keep deer away," says Gabriel, "that's how bad they smell. But Em likes them."

8   "An honest smell," says Aunt Emma, "and they're easy to grow." Her answer starts another question. It seems to hang in the air: This Mandy, does she grow easy?

9   No, I want to shout. I don't grow easy. I'm trying the best I can and messing up terribly and I don't see how the three of you are going to make anything any better.

10   No, I want to shout. Don't you read? It's never easy to raise a child, not even for the people whose job it's supposed to be. Mothers grow children. Not great-aunts and old uncles.

11   No, I want to shout. Stare at me, in this bundlely sweater. I don't even know quite where to look, now that you're silent and your voices don't tell me where you are. Do I look easy to grow?

12   "May I see my room, please?" I ask.

13   Again that silence. I'd said, May I see. You'd think I'd know better, would have learned these last weeks what see and look do to people who can, when they hear the words said in front of someone who can't. When someone who can't says them herself.

14   "Certainly," answers Aunt Emma. She laughs, an embarrassed little laugh. "Actually, we have a choice for you. About what room you want, I mean. There's one here on this floor…"

15   "Aren't your bedrooms all upstairs?"

16   I know they are. Mom had a picture of this house, though she'd never been in it. "My mother's house," she'd say, when she'd find me looking at it. "Your grandmother's."

17   Again that embarrassed little laugh. "Yes," Aunt Emma says, "but there's a little room down here, a study, that we thought you could…"

18   "Whose study?"

19   "Well, your uncle Abe's, but…"

20   "I don't need it," he breaks in. "I can work perfectly well upstairs. Lots of space in my bedroom for a desk."

21   I ask, "What's the other choice?" I know what they're doing, trying to give me a room where I won't have to climb steps. But I'm blind, not crippled.

22   "The other one is on the second floor," says Emma, "but it's so tiny…"

23   It's Uncle Gabriel who interrupts this time. "Actually, there's another choice," he says. "Nobody's using the attic room, nobody has for years. It's not much bigger, but…"

24   "Let me see it, please."

25   I am not going to stop saying see just to spare their feelings. It's what I mean. And what do they want me to say, anyway? Let me feel the attic, please? Smell the attic? Choose it for my bedroom without learning one thing about it first?

26   It's Gabriel who puts my hand on his arm and walks me to the staircase. I run the tip of my long cane side to side. The bare treads are wood and very wide, worn to rounded edges.

27   "It's a long flight," he says.

28   I start up on my own, as rapidly as I can go and not hesitating once, even when I'm thinking, don't fall on my face. And I do it right.

29   I wait for the others. Aunt Emma comes up wheezing. I've made her climb the steps faster than she usually does. Abe doesn't come up at all.

30   "The attic?" I ask. "How do we get there?"

1 Read the following dictionary entry for the word *tread*.

tread \tred\ *n* **1.** a mark (as a footprint) **2.** manner of stepping **3.** the part of a tire that makes contact with a road **4.** the upper horizontal part of a step

Which of these definitions matches the word *tread* as it is used in paragraph 26 of the story?

A Definition 1

B Definition 2

C Definition 3

D Definition 4

2 Mandy's response in paragraph 21 reveals that she is —

F only trying to be polite

G afraid to sleep downstairs

H upset that her relatives think she is weak

J hoping to explore other parts of the house

3 It is reasonable to predict that Mandy will choose —

A the second-floor room

B her uncle's study

C the attic room

D the small room downstairs

4 The narrator can best be described as —

F fiercely independent

G shy and awkward

H anxious to please

J carefree and content

5 Why does Aunt Emma give an "embarrassed little laugh" when Mandy uses the word *see*?

A She thinks Mandy is trying to make a joke.

B She is concerned about what Mandy is feeling.

C She is worried that Mandy will not like her room.

D She is uncomfortable about Mandy's blindness.

6 Why does the author choose to tell this story from a first-person point of view?

F to help readers understand what it is like to be blind

G to show how relatives react to meeting for the first time

H to let the reader see every character's thoughts

J to fully describe the surroundings of the story

DIRECTIONS
Answer the following question on a separate sheet of paper.

7 How does Mandy's unique point of view shape how details in the story are portrayed? Support your answer with evidence from the selection.

Revising and Editing

TEKS Spiral Review

Writing
(17)(A)(iii) Use and understand the function of the following parts of speech in the context of reading and writing: reciprocal pronouns (e.g., each other, one another).
(18)(A) Use conventions of capitalization.

DIRECTIONS
Read the following passage and mark your answers on your answer document. Remember that you are NOT permitted to use dictionaries or other reference material on this section of the text.

Grace wrote this report about a famous author from Texas. Read Grace's paper and think about the corrections and improvements she should make. When you finish, answer the questions that follow.

Katherine Anne Porter

(1) Katherine Anne Porter was a Texan author of short stories. (2) She was well-known for her strong-willed personality, independent spirit, and skilled writing about life's difficulties.

(3) Porter was born in 1890 in the town of indian creek, Texas. (4) When she was two years old, her mother died, so Porter was raised by her grandmother. (5) As a result, from early childhood she had to be strong and independent. (6) Perhaps this is why her writing focused on the harsh realities of life.

(7) In her early twenties, she moved frequently, taking various jobs such as actress, singer, and secretary. (8) Then, in 1917, she was hired for her first writing job: society columnist for the Fort Worth *Critic*. (9) In 1919, she abandoned society writing and began to write fiction instead. (10) She moved to Greenwich Village in New York City to focus on her writing.

(11) In New York, Porter published her first story in *Century* magazine. (12) She continued to publish stories in magazines that let them write exactly the way she wanted to. (13) Porter became known for her perfect prose about hardship, betrayal, and justice.

(14) Porter's first book, *Flowering Judas,* was a short story collection. (15) It was published in 1930. (16) However, her work did not become popular until ten years later, when she published her second book, *Pale Horse, Pale Rider.* (17) It was soon followed by her third book, *The Leaning Tower and Other Stories.*

(18) Porter also wrote a novel, *Ship of Fools.* It was published in 1962. (19) She was inspired by a trip she had taken to Germany during the time of World War II. (20) In the novel, she wrote about what might lead people to be unkind to each other. (21) In 1966, her book *Collected Stories* won a Pulitzer Prize. (22) After a long and successful career as a writer, Porter died in 1980 at the age of ninety.

1 What change, if any, should be made in sentence 3?

  A Change *born* to **borned**

  B Change *indian creek* to **Indian Creek**

  C Delete the comma after *creek*

  D Make no change

2 What change should be made in sentence 12?

  F Change *them* to **it**

  G Change *magazines* to **Magazines**

  H Add a comma after *stories*

  J Change *them* to **her**

3 What change, if any, should be made in sentence 20?

  A Change *lead* to **led**

  B Insert a comma after *wrote*

  C Change *each other* to **one another**

  D Make no change

4 What change, if any, should be made in sentence 21?

  F Change *Stories* to **stories**

  G Change *Pulitzer* to **pulitzer**

  H Insert a comma after *Stories*

  J Make no change

Written Composition

Use blank pages to prewrite. Then write your composition on one or two lined pages.

TEKS Spiral Review

Writing
(14)(A) Write literary texts to express ideas and feelings about real or imagined people, events, and ideas. Write an engaging story.

> Write a composition about a time you overcame a difficulty.

REMEMBER—YOU SHOULD

❑ write about the assigned topic

❑ make your writing thoughtful and interesting

❑ make sure that each sentence you write contributes to your composition as a whole

❑ make sure that your ideas are clear and easy for the reader to follow

❑ write about your ideas in depth so that the reader is able to develop a good understanding of what you are saying

❑ proofread your writing to correct errors in spelling, capitalization, punctuation, grammar, and sentence structure

Can *truth* change?

Focus on the TEKS

Reading
(12)(A) Compare and contrast how information is communicated by visual images versus non-visual texts.

Media Literacy

Visual images and **non-visual texts** communicate information differently. Compare and contrast the background information before each selection in this unit and the Background videos. How do they communicate information differently? How might the differences between visual images and non-visual text change the truth of a message? Use the chart below to analyze the visuals as you view the Background videos or other video clips available to you.

Viewing and Listening Guide

Visual image	What it is	What you should think about
Photograph	A still image recorded by a camera	• What information do the photographs reveal that you could not learn from text alone? • How could an art director change or manipulate photographs? Why might the director do that?
Video Clip	A short segment of video footage	• Why would a director choose this clip? Does it set a tone? Is it visually appealing? • Could text alone have conveyed the same information as effectively? Why or why not?

Independent Reading

The Red Badge of Courage, Adapted Classic
Stephen Crane
Prentice Hall, 2000
In this novel, soldier Henry Fleming discovers truths about fear and courage while the Civil War rages around him.

Up Close: Rachel Carson
Ellen Levine
Viking, 2007
This biography tells the story of one woman's struggle to protect the beauty of nature for us all.

A Separate Peace
John Knowles
Macmillan, 1959
Envy leads two friends to confront difficult truths and unpleasant realities.

Six Characters in Search of an Author
Luigi Pirandello
Signet Classics, 1970
This twentieth-century play reveals a variety of fundamental truths about the human condition.

Short Stories

www.PHLitOnline.com

Hear It!
- Selection summary audio
- Selection audio
- Big Question Tunes

See It!
- Penguin author video
- Big Question video
- Get Connected videos
- Background videos
- More about the authors
- Illustrated vocabulary words
- Vocabulary flashcards

Do It!
- Interactive journals
- Interactive graphic organizers
- Grammar tutorials
- Interactive vocabulary games
- Test practice

193

Introducing the Big Question

Is *conflict* necessary?

A **conflict** is a struggle between opposing forces. A conflict might be as small as an **argument** between friends or as large as a **war** between nations. It might also involve just one person who faces a personal challenge or a hard decision. A conflict is resolved when it is worked out or brought to an end. Conflicts occur frequently in literature and in life, but are they necessary? Conflicts can be difficult for the people involved in them, but can a conflict also have a positive outcome?

Start thinking about the Big Question by identifying different types of conflicts and what can happen as a result of them.

Tell What You Know

Make a list of some different conflicts you have either read about or experienced. Describe one specific example of each of the following types of conflicts:

- An argument or disagreement between friends
- A contest or **competition** between teams
- A struggle to make a decision
- A **controversy** in the news
- A problem that must be solved

Share your examples with a small team. Discuss both the causes and the effects of each conflict. Consider the positive and negative effects that each conflict might have for each person involved. To participate productively in your team, listen carefully to others as they speak. Build on the ideas of others, and contribute relevant information to the discussion.

TEXAS
PHLitOnline
www.PHLitOnline.com

- Big Question video
- Illustrated vocabulary words
- Interactive vocabulary games
- Big Question Tunes

Explain What You Know

Use the examples and ideas you discussed with your team to help you complete these sentences about conflict.

- Two friends might have a disagreement about _____ that leads to a conflict between them. As a result of their conflict, the two friends might _____.
- By facing a personal challenge such as _____, a person can learn to _____.
- A problem can also be an opportunity if _____.

Share your responses with a partner.

Write What You Think

Based on the discussions you have had, decide what you think right now. Your answer may change as you read the selections in this unit. Choose one of these responses to the Big Question or write one of your own:

- ❏ Conflict is necessary.
- ❏ Conflict is not necessary.

Connecting to the Literature

Each reading in this unit will give you insight into the Big Question. At the end of the unit, you will have an opportunity to reconsider your ideas.

Connecting to Citizenship

Texas Profiles: David Crockett

Defender of the Alamo David Crockett's motto was, "Be always sure you're right—then go a-head." After he saw Texas, he decided that it was "the garden spot of the world." In 1835, Crockett left his previous life, moved his family to Texas, and took an oath of allegiance to the Texas government. He committed himself to Texas independence, bravely rallying troops at the Alamo before he perished there.

Is conflict necessary?

- Judging from Crockett's story, do you think he would consider conflict necessary? Explain.
- What can you learn from Crockett's story that can help you become a thoughtful, active citizen?

Focus on the TEKS

Listening and Speaking (26) Participate productively in teams, building on the ideas of others and contributing relevant information.

Big Question Vocabulary

Use some of these words as you complete the activities on these pages.

amicably
antagonize
appreciate
argument
articulate
compete
competition
controversy
cooperate
differences
equity
grievance
issue
mediate
survival
war/battle

This list includes academic vocabulary words, which are defined on pp. R1–R14.

 # Introduction: Short Stories

THE BIG ?

Is *conflict* necessary?

Conflicts in short stories reflect conflicts in the world.

TEXAS PHLitOnline

www.PHLitOnline.com

- Penguin author video
- Interactive journals
- Interactive graphic organizers
- Selection audio
- Self-test

What Is a Short Story?

by Wayson Choy

Your life, like mine, is surrounded by all kinds of stories. We collect them, and we tell them. Think how you are always hungry for stories that inspire or scare you, that make you thoughtful about important things, or remind you, in fresh ways, of your present or past.

In fact, everyone's life is an assemblage of short stories—like the kind that writers create to enhance our understanding of our own decisive moments and revelations.

Short Stories Deepen Our Awareness

More than just entertainment, a fine **short story** will always focus on a fragment of truth that matters to you. Such a story often relates a brief incident, to create a unity—a harmony of details—that will expose you to a deeper experience of life. The climax of a good short story can flash inside you like a bolt of lightning or gently glow like a candle. In fact, the light a fine story gives to you can linger for a lifetime.

For example, when I first read Shirley Jackson's "The Lottery," I came to realize that ordinary people—like you or me—can willfully take part in chilling, horrific events. And when I first read Truman Capote's "A Christmas Memory," his story made me think in new ways about a family member who loved me when I was very young, and who was now gone. Like me, you may discover that short stories can powerfully disturb and awaken you.

The Best Stories Say, *You Are Not Alone*

But what makes a short story a good one? The passage here by the famous writer Somerset Maugham recalls Edgar Allan Poe's idea that a good story—like those collected in this unit—will "sparkle, excite or impress." Isn't that what your own favorite stories do for you?

The short story is a work of fiction created from the writer's imagination and personal vision. If you surrender to the writer's **narrative voice**—that enchanted moment when you begin to hear a storytelling voice—you will be transported into another world. And always, the best short stories will say to the deepest part of you . . . *You are not alone.*

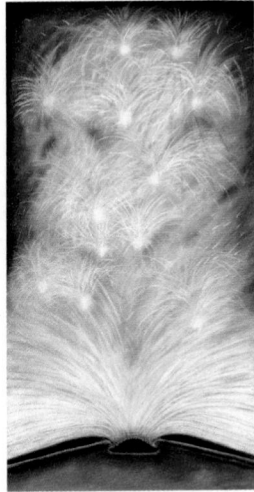

It is not hard to state what Poe meant by a good short story: it is a piece of fiction, dealing with a single incident, material or spiritual, that can be read at a sitting; it is original, it must sparkle, excite or impress; and it must have a unity of effect or impression.

from **"Credo of a Storyteller"**
—W. Somerset Maugham

Meet
Wayson Choy (b. 1939)

Author of "The Jade Peony"

In his books, Wayson Choy deals with a theme arising from the immigrant experience—the conflicts between generations and cultures. In *The Jade Peony,* he tells how members of the Chen family must balance their allegiance to the past and their dreams for the future in order to form their own identities. Choy published this novel, which he developed from his story "The Jade Peony," when he was in his late fifties. He taught for many years at Humber College, Toronto, Canada.

Did You Know?
Late in life, Choy learned from a former babysitter that he had been adopted.

Exploring Short Stories

Elements of Short Stories

A **short story** is a brief work of fiction meant to be read in one sitting. Due to its length, a short story must be compact, accomplishing its purpose in relatively few words.

The following are some of the key elements of a short story:

Plot A short story's **plot** is its series of events. Throughout the plot, events unfold, build to a climax (or high point), and are then brought to a conclusion during the resolution. There are two methods of plot development:

- Authors use **linear plot development** when they reveal events in the order in which they occur.
- Authors use **non-linear plot development** when they interrupt the sequence of events in a plot. Flashbacks, sub-plots, and parallel plots can be used within non-linear plots.

Conflict The plot of a short story usually focuses on a **conflict,** or struggle. There are two main types of conflict in literature:

- An **external conflict** is a struggle between two characters, between an individual and a group, or between a character and a force of nature.
- An **internal conflict** is a struggle within the mind of one character.

Character The **characters** in a story are the personalities who participate in the action. Usually, story characters are human beings, but they can also be animals or even objects. Writers use these methods of characterization to develop complex yet believable characters:

- describing characters' appearances, words, and actions
- showing characters interacting with one another
- sharing characters' thoughts and feelings

Setting The **setting** of a story is the time and place of the action.

- The time of a setting can be past, present, or future, and it may also include a specific year, season, or hour of day.
- Place can refer to the **cultural** or **historical setting** as well as to a specific geographic location in a country, town, or community.

In some stories, the setting not only provides a backdrop for the action, but can also shape the characters, plot, and conflict. For example, cultural expectations may cause characters to take specific actions. The setting can also help create a **mood**—the atmosphere of the story.

Symbol A **symbol** is a person, place, or object that has a literal meaning and also stands for something larger, such as an idea or an emotion. Symbols may be particular to a specific literary work or universal.

Theme The **theme** of a short story is its central message or insight into life. This message may be stated or implied.

- A **stated theme** is expressed directly by the author.
- An **implied theme** is suggested indirectly through the experiences of the characters or through the events and the setting of the work.

 **TEKS Check**

 Focus on the TEKS

Reading
(5)(A) Analyze non-linear plot development and compare it to linear plot development.

Recall a short story, a movie, or a television drama you know that used non-linear plot development (e.g., flashbacks, foreshadowing, sub-plots, parallel plot structures). Use a chart like this one to analyze the non-linear plot development and compare it to linear plot development.

Compare Non-Linear and Linear Plot Development	
List the title of a work that uses non-linear plot development.	
List an example of non-linear plot development in that work (e.g., a flashback).	
How would that work have been different if it had used linear plot development?	

Wayson Choy Introduces
"The Jade Peony"

During World War II, while my immigrant parents worked all hours, I was cared for by Chinatown's village elders in Vancouver, Canada. These elders told me such vivid myths involving ghosts, magic amulets, hissing dragons, and talking foxes, that I dreamed one day that I would tell my own tales.

Finding Inspiration

As a student, when I was assigned to write a story based on the color "pink"—I was stuck. My aunt recalled that rare jades were pink in tone, and that afternoon, another aunt mentioned how the peonies were flowering in her garden.

Suddenly, something magical happened: the two ideas came together. My imagination glimpsed a wrinkled hand passing a carved pink jade into a boy's small palm. After imagining these **characters,** the first words of "The Jade Peony" came to me: "When Grandmama died at 83 . . ."

Themes: Questions that Haunt You

After some research and a dozen revisions, I realized that I had been focusing on life and dying, and the realities of love between generations. Years later, I understood that there were **themes,** meanings and questions —*hauntings*—that had attached themselves to my story. For example, how many kinds of love were there? Were spirits real? And was dying the end of everything? One theme came to possess me: *Love has no rules.* Therefore, I now write believing that I, and my readers, will continue to discover similar meanings.

Symbol: What Does the Jade Peony Mean?

But I wondered why I came up with the jade peony—what, as a **symbol,** did the amulet stand for? I realized it has many layers of meaning, related to love and memory. I thought of the jade left to me by my mother and father, just as you might think about some important legacy left to you by a friend or a family member. I also thought of the apron my mother last wore before she was rushed to the hospital. Whenever I think of that apron, I see my dead mother alive again, a vivid ghost standing over her stove to feed us all. Finally, I, as a writer created the symbol of the jade peony to make the people I love come alive again.

the Jade Peony[1]

Wayson Choy

When Grandmama died at 83 our whole household held its breath. She had promised us a sign of her leaving, final proof that her present life had ended well. My parents knew that without any clear sign, our own family fortunes could be altered, threatened. My stepmother looked endlessly into the small cluttered room the ancient lady had occupied. Nothing was touched; nothing changed. My father, thinking that a sign should appear in Grandmama's garden, looked at the frost-killed shoots and cringed: *no, that could not be it.*

My two older teenage brothers and my sister, Liang, age 14, were embarrassed by my parents' behavior. What would all the white people in Vancouver[2] think of us? We were Canadians now, *Chinese-Canadians,* a hyphenated reality that my parents could never accept. So it seemed, for different reasons, we all held our breath waiting for *something.*

Wayson Choy
Author's Insight
"With references to signs and threatened fortunes, I wanted to create a ghostly mystery about the grandmother's dying."

Reading Check

What had Grandmama promised her family?

---

1. **Jade Peony** (jād pē´ ə nē) jade is a hard, dense gemstone; a peony is a common garden flower, the Chinese variety of which produces large, single blossoms in early summer.
2. **Vancouver** (van ko͞o´ vər) large city in the province of British Columbia, Canada.

Short Stories
Plot Choy establishes a conflict around Grandmama's refusal to go to the hospital.

I was eight when she died. For days she had resisted going into the hospital . . . *a cold, just a cold* . . . and instead gave constant instruction to my stepmother and sister on the boiling of ginseng roots mixed with bitter extract.[3] At night, between wracking coughs and deadly silences, Grandmama had her back and chest rubbed with heated camphor[4] oil and sipped a bluish decoction[5] of an herb called Peacock's Tail. When all these failed to abate her fever, she began to arrange the details of her will. This she did with my father, confessing finally: "I am too stubborn. The only cure for old age is to die."

My father wept to hear this. I stood beside her bed; she turned to me. Her round face looked darker, and the gentleness of her eyes, the thin, arching eyebrows, seemed weary. I brushed the few strands of gray, brittle hair from her face; she managed to smile at me. Being the youngest, I had spent nearly all my time with her and could not imagine that we would ever be parted. Yet when she spoke, and her voice hesitated, cracked, the somber shadows of her room chilled me. Her wrinkled brow grew wet with fever, and her small body seemed even more diminutive.

"I—I am going to the hospital, Grandson." Her hand reached out for mine. "You know, Little Son, whatever happens I will never leave you." Her palm felt plush and warm, the slender, old fingers boney and firm, so magically strong was her grip that I could not imagine how she could ever part from me. Ever.

Her hands were magical. My most vivid memories are of her hands: long, elegant fingers, with impeccable nails, a skein[6] of fine, barely-seen veins, and wrinkled skin like light pine. Those hands were quick when she taught me, at six, simple tricks of juggling, learnt when she was a village girl in Southern Canton;[7] a troupe of actors had stayed on her father's farm. One of them, "tall and

▼ Critical Viewing
How does this image of Chinatown reflect the blending of cultures that can happen when people immigrate to a new country? **[Analyze]**

---

3. **ginseng** (jin´ seŋ´) *n.* **roots . . . bitter extract** ginseng is a Chinese herb known for its healing properties; bitter extract is a liquid made from bitter plants or herbs.
4. **camphor** (kam´ fər) *n.* thick substance made from the bark and wood of the camphor tree.
5. **decoction** (dē käk´ shən) *n.* substance extracted by boiling.
6. **skein** (skān) *n.* something that resembles coiled yarn or thread.
7. **Canton** (kan tän´) major port city in southeastern China.

pale as the whiteness of petals," fell in love with her, promising to return. In her last years his image came back like a third being in our two lives. He had been magician, acrobat, juggler, and some of the things he taught her she had absorbed and passed on to me through her stories and games. But above all, without realizing it then, her hands conveyed to me the quality of their love.

Most marvelous for me was the quick-witted skill her hands revealed in making windchimes for our birthdays: windchimes in the likeness of her lost friend's only present to her, made of bits of string and scraps, in the center of which once hung a precious jade peony. This wondrous gift to her broke apart years ago, in China, but Grandmama kept the jade pendant[8] in a tiny red silk envelope, and kept it always in her pocket, until her death.

These were not ordinary, carelessly made chimes, such as those you now find in our Chinatown[9] stores, whose rattling noises drive you mad. But making her special ones caused dissension in our family, and some shame. Each one that she made was created from a treasure trove of glass fragments and castaway costume jewelry, in the same way that her first windchime had been made. The problem for the rest of the family was in the fact that Grandmama looked for these treasures wandering the back alleys of Keefer and Pender Streets,[10] peering into our neighbors' garbage cans, chasing away hungry, nervous cats and shouting curses at them.

"All our friends are laughing at us!" Older Brother Jung said at last to my father, when Grandmama was away having tea at Mrs. Lim's.

"We are not poor," Oldest Brother Kiam declared, "Yet she and Sek-Lung poke through those awful things as if—" he shoved me in frustration and I stumbled against my sister, "—they were beggars!"

"She will make Little Brother crazy!" Sister Liang said. Without warning, she punched me sharply in the back; I jumped. "You see, look how *nervous* he is!"

I lifted my foot slightly, enough to swing it back and kick Liang in the shin. She yelled and pulled back her fist to punch me again. Jung made a menacing move towards me.

"Stop this, all of you!" My father shook his head in exasperation. How could he dare tell the Grand Old One, his aging mother, that what was somehow appropriate in a poor village in China, was an abomination here. How could he prevent me, his youngest, from accompanying her? If she went walking into those alleyways

Vocabulary
dissension (di sen´ shən) *n.* difference of opinion; disagreement

Wayson Choy
Author's Insight "Here I wanted to show how the wind chimes were symbolically important to some family members but provoked a lot of conflict and inner turmoil among the others."

Vocabulary
abomination (ə bäm´ ə nā´ shən) *n.* anything hateful and disgusting

Reading Check

From whom did Grandmama learn juggling?

---

8. **pendant** (pen´ dənt) *n.* hanging ornament, as on a necklace.
9. **Chinatown** (chī´ nə toun´) *n.* Chinese quarter of any city outside of China; in this case, of Vancouver.
10. **Keefer and Pender Streets** principal streets of Vancouver's Chinatown.

alone she could well be attacked by hoodlums. "She is not a beggar looking for food. She is searching for—for. . . ."

My stepmother attempted to speak, then fell silent. She, too, seemed perplexed and somewhat ashamed. They all loved Grandmama, but she was *inconvenient*, unsettling.

As for our neighbors, most understood Grandmama to be harmlessly crazy, others that she did indeed make lovely toys but for what purpose? *Why?* they asked, and the stories she told me, of the juggler who smiled at her, flashed in my head.

Finally, by their cutting remarks, the family did exert enough pressure so that Grandmama and I no longer openly announced our expeditions. Instead, she took me with her on "shopping trips," ostensibly for clothes or groceries, while in fact we spent most of our time exploring stranger and more distant neighborhoods, searching for splendid junk: jangling pieces of a vase, cranberry glass fragments embossed with leaves, discarded glass beads from Woolworth[11] necklaces. . . . We would sneak them all home in brown rice sacks, folded into small parcels, and put them under her bed. During the day when the family was away at school or work, we brought them out and washed every item in a large black pot of boiling lye[12] and water, dried them quickly, carefully, and returned them, sparkling, under her bed.

Our greatest excitement occurred when a fire gutted the large Chinese Presbyterian Church, three blocks from our house. Over the still-smoking ruins the next day, Grandmama and I rushed precariously over the blackened beams to pick out the stained glass that glittered in the sunlight. Small figure bent over, wrapped against the autumn cold in a dark blue quilted coat, happily gathering each piece like gold, she became my spiritual playmate: "There's a good one! *There!*"

Hours later, soot-covered and smelling of smoke, we came home with a carton full of delicate fragments, still early enough to steal them all into the house and put the small box under her bed. "These are special pieces," she said, giving the box a last push, "because they come from a sacred place." She slowly got up and I saw, for the first time, her hand begin to shake. But then, in her joy, she embraced me. Both of our hearts were racing, as if we were two dreamers. I buried my face in her blue quilt, and for a moment, the whole world seemed silent.

"My juggler," she said, "he never came back to me from Honan[13] . . . perhaps the famine. . . ." Her voice began to quake. "But I shall have my sacred windchime . . . I shall have it again."

Short Stories
Character Choy uses the search for windchime materials to establish a sense of the pact between the old woman and her grandson.

11. **Woolworth** a variety store belonging to the chain founded by Frank Woolworth in 1879.
12. **lye** (lī) *n.* substance derived from wood ashes, commonly used in making soap or for washing.
13. **Honan** (hō′ nän′) province in east central China.

One evening, when the family was gathered in their usual places in the parlor, Grandmama gave me her secret nod: a slight wink of her eye and a flaring of her nostrils. There was *trouble* in the air. Supper had gone badly, school examinations were due, father had failed to meet an editorial deadline at the *Vancouver Chinese Times*. A huge sigh came from Sister Liang.

"But it is useless this Chinese they teach you!" she lamented, turning to Stepmother for support. Silence. Liang frowned, dejected, and went back to her Chinese book, bending the covers back.

"Father," Oldest Brother Kiam began, waving his bamboo brush in the air, "you must realize that this Mandarin only confuses us. We are Cantonese[14] speakers. . . ."

"And you do not complain about Latin, French or German in your English school?" Father rattled his newspaper, a signal that his patience was ending.

"But, Father, those languages are *scientific*," Kiam jabbed his brush in the air. "We are now in a scientific, logical world."

Father was silent. We could all hear Grandmama's rocker.

"What about Sek-Lung?" Older Brother Jung pointed angrily at me. "He was sick last year, but this year he should have at least started Chinese school, instead of picking over garbage cans!"

"He starts next year," Father said, in a hard tone that immediately warned everyone to be silent. Liang slammed her book.

Grandmama went on rocking quietly in her chair. She complimented my mother on her knitting, made a remark about the "strong beauty" of Kiam's brushstrokes which, in spite of himself, immensely pleased him. All this babbling noise was her family torn and confused in a strange land: everything here was so very foreign and scientific.

The truth was, I was sorry not to have started school the year before. In my innocence I had imagined going to school meant certain privileges worthy of all my brothers' and sister's complaints. The fact that my lung infection in my fifth and sixth years, mistakenly diagnosed as TB,[15] earned me some reprieve, only made me long for school the more. Each member of the family took turns on Sunday, teaching me or annoying me. But it was the countless hours I spent with Grandmama that were my real education. Tapping me on my head she would say, "Come, Sek-Lung, we have *our* work," and we would walk up the stairs to her small crowded room. There, in the midst of her antique shawls, the old ancestral

"**B**ut I shall have my sacred windchime... I shall have it again."

Vocabulary
reprieve (ri prēv´)
n. temporary relief; postponement of a penalty

Reading Check

What "treasures" do the old woman and her grandson find among the ruins of the church?

---

14. **Mandarin** (man´ də rin) **. . . Cantonese** (kan´ tə nēz´) Mandarin is the most commonly spoken form of Chinese; Cantonese is a variety of Chinese spoken in some parts of China, including the cities of Canton and Hong Kong, and by most Chinese immigrants.

15. **TB** (tē´ bē´) *n.* abbreviation for tuberculosis, a contagious disease that begins in the lungs.

calligraphy and multi-colored embroidered hangings, beneath the mysterious shelves of sweet herbs and bitter potions, we would continue doing what we had started that morning: the elaborate windchime for her death.

"I can't last forever," she declared, when she let me in on the secret of this one. "It will sing and dance and glitter," her long fingers stretched into the air, pantomiming the waving motion of her ghost chimes; "My spirit will hear its sounds and see its light and return to this house and say goodbye to you."

Deftly she reached into the carton she had placed on the chair beside me. She picked out a fish-shape amber piece, and with a long needle-like tool and a steel ruler, she scored[16] it. Pressing the blade of a cleaver against the line, with the fingers of her other hand, she lifted up the glass until it cleanly *snapped* into the exact shape she required. Her hand began to tremble, the tips of her fingers to shiver, like rippling water.

"You see that, Little One?" She held her hand up. "That is my body fighting with Death. He is in this room now."

My eyes darted in panic, but Grandmama remained calm, undisturbed, and went on with her work. Then I remembered the glue and uncorked the jar for her. Soon the graceful ritual movements of her hand returned to her, and I became lost in the magic of her task: she dabbed a cabalistic[17] mixture of glue on one end and skillfully dropped the braided end of a silk thread into it. This part always amazed me: the braiding would slowly, *very* slowly, *unknot*, fanning out like a prized fishtail. In a few seconds the clear, homemade glue began to harden as I blew lightly over it, welding to itself each separate silk strand.

Each jam-sized pot of glue was precious; each large cork had been wrapped with a fragment of pink silk. I remember this part vividly, because each cork was treated to a special rite. First we went shopping in the best silk stores in Chinatown for the perfect square of silk she required. It had to be a deep pink, a shade of color blushing toward red. And the tone had to match — as closely as possible — her precious jade carving, the small peony of white

---

▲ **Critical Viewing**
How does this image of a windchime compare to the ones Grandmama likes to make? **[Compare and Contrast]**

Wayson Choy
Author's Insight "I want to establish these realistic details—a pot of glue, a cork—so that what happens near the end with the appearance of an albino cat is rooted in the real."

16. **scored** (skôrd) *v.* put a notch or groove in.
17. **cabalistic** (kab′ ə lis′ tik) *adj.* relating to a secret or mystical belief or practice.

and light-red jade, her most lucky possession. In the center of this semi-translucent carving, no more than an inch wide, was a pool of pink light, its veins swirling out into the petals of the flower.

"This color is the color of my spirit," she said, holding it up to the window so I could see the delicate pastel against the broad strokes of sunlight. She dropped her voice, and I held my breath at the wonder of the color. "This was given to me by the young actor who taught me how to juggle. He had four of them, and each one had a center of this rare color, the color of Good Fortune." The pendant seemed to pulse as she turned it: "Oh, Sek-Lung! He had white hair and white skin to *his toes*! It's *true*, I saw him bathing." She laughed and blushed, her eyes softened at the memory. The silk had to match the pink heart of her pendant: the color was magical for her, to hold the unraveling strands of her memory. . . .

It was just six months before she died that we really began to work on her last windchime. Three thin bamboo sticks were steamed and bent into circlets; 30 exact lengths of silk thread, the strongest kind, were cut and braided at both ends and glued to stained glass. Her hands worked on their own command, each hand racing with a life of its own: cutting, snapping, braiding, knotting. . . . Sometimes she breathed heavily and her small body, growing thinner, sagged against me. *Death*, I thought, *He is in this room*, and I would work harder alongside her. For months Grandmama and I did this every other evening, a half dozen pieces each time. The shaking in her hand grew worse, but we said nothing. Finally, after discarding hundreds, she told me she had the necessary 30 pieces. But this time, because it was a sacred chime, I would not be permitted to help her tie it up or have the joy of raising it. "Once tied," she said, holding me against my disappointment, "not even I can raise it. Not a sound must it make until I have died."

"What will happen?"

"Your father will then take the center braided strand and raise it. He will hang it against my bedroom window so that my ghost may see it, and hear it, and return. I must say goodbye to this world properly or wander in this foreign land forever."

"You can take the streetcar!" I blurted, suddenly shocked that she actually meant to leave me. I thought I could hear the clear-chromatic chimes, see the shimmering colors on the wall: I fell against her and cried, and there in my crying I knew that she would die. I can still remember the touch of her hand on my head, and the smell of her thick woolen sweater pressed against my face. "I will always be with you, Little Sek-Lung, but in a different way . . . you'll see."

Short Stories

Symbol In this passage, Choy connects the windchime with Grandmama's spirit, both in youth and old age.

Short Stories

Plot With this discussion of the death, the author starts to bring the story full circle, back to the beginning discussion of "signs."

Reading Check

What does Grandmama say is the color of her spirit?

Months went by, and nothing happened. Then one late September evening, when I had just come home from Chinese School, Grandmama was preparing supper when she looked out our kitchen window and saw a cat—a long, lean white cat—jump into our garbage pail and knock it over. She ran out to chase it away, shouting curses at it. She did not have her thick sweater on and when she came back into the house, a chill gripped her. She leaned against the door: "That was not a cat," she said, and the odd tone of her voice caused my father to look with alarm at her. "I can not take back my curses. It is too late." She took hold of my father's arm: "It was all white and had pink eyes like sacred fire."

My father started at this, and they both looked pale. My brothers and sister, clearing the table, froze in their gestures.

"The fog has confused you," Stepmother said. "It was just a cat."

But Grandmama shook her head, for she knew it was a sign. "I will not live forever," she said. "I am prepared."

The next morning she was confined to her bed with a severe cold. Sitting by her, playing with some of my toys, I asked her about the cat: "Why did father jump at the cat with the pink eyes? He didn't see it, you did."

"But he and your mother know what it means."

"What?"

"My friend, the juggler, the magician, was as pale as white jade, and he had pink eyes." I thought she would begin to tell me one of her stories, a tale of enchantment or of a wondrous adventure, but she only paused to swallow; her eyes glittered, lost in memory. She took my hand, gently opening and closing her fingers over it. "Sek-Lung," she sighed, "*he* has come back to me."

Then Grandmama sank back into her pillow and the embroidered flowers lifted to frame her wrinkled face. I saw her hand over my own, and my own began to tremble. I fell fitfully asleep by her side. When I woke up it was dark and her bed was empty. She had been taken to the hospital and I was not permitted to visit.

A few days after that she died of the complications of pneumonia. Immediately after her death my father came home and said nothing to us, but walked up the stairs to her room, pulled aside the drawn lace curtains of her window and lifted the windchimes to the sky.

I began to cry and quickly put my hand in my pocket for a handkerchief. Instead, caught between my fingers, was the small, round firmness of the jade peony. In my mind's eye I saw Grandmama smile and heard, softly, the pink center beat like a beautiful, cramped heart.

Short Stories

Character Grandmama's and the father's similar reactions to the white cat emphasize the understanding, both personal and cultural, that they share.

After You Read | The Jade Peony

Critical Thinking

1. **Respond:** What do you think of the relationship between Sek-Lung and his grandmother? Explain.

2. **(a)** Who gave the grandmother her first windchime? **(b) Make Inferences:** Why do you think the making of windchimes was such a meaningful activity in the grandmother's later years?

3. **(a) Compare and Contrast:** How do Sek-Lung's reactions to his grandmother's activities differ from those of the other family members? **(b) Analyze:** How do you explain these differing attitudes?

4. **Make Inferences:** How is the making of the grandmother's last windchime different for her and for her family?

Is conflict necessary?
(a) In this story, what conflicts does Sek-Lung face? **(b)** Does Sek-Lung grow from these challenges? Explain your answer.

Short Story Review

1. Consider the setting, plot, and characters in "The Jade Peony." Which do you think is the most important element in this **short story**? Support your answer with details from the story.

2. **(a)** What is the underlying theme, or message, of this story?
(b) Complete a chart like the one shown to examine details in the story. List events, actions, or descriptions that seem important. Then, complete the rest of the chart. **(c)** Discuss your ideas with a partner.

What It Says	What It Means	Why It Is Important

Research the Author

Like Sek-Lung, Wayson Choy is both Chinese and Canadian. Use Internet and print sources to create an **oral presentation** discussing Choy's insights into his dual heritage. Follow these steps:

- Read biographical articles and interviews with Choy. Write notes to connect and explain Choy's comments.

- Provide an analysis for your audience that reflects a logical progression of ideas.

Selection Choices

The Most Dangerous Game
Richard Connell

214 Short Stories

▲ Read **"The Most Dangerous Game"** to find out what happens when a great hunter meets an opponent who may be greater.

American History

Judith Ortiz Cofer

I once read in a *Ripley's Believe It or Not* column that Paterson, New Jersey, is the place where the Straight and Narrow (streets) intersect.

The Puerto Rican tenement known as El Building was one block up from Straight. It was, in fact, the corner of Straight and Market; not "at" the corner, but the corner. At almost any hour of the day, El Building was like a monstrous jukebox, blasting out salsas¹ from open windows as the residents, mostly new immigrants just up from the island, tried to drown out whatever they were currently enduring with loud music. But the day that President Kennedy was shot there was a *profound* silence in El Building; even the abusive tongues of viragoes,² the cursing of the unemployed, and the screeching of small children had been somehow muted. President Kennedy was a saint to these people. In fact, soon his photograph would be hung alongside the Sacred Heart and over the spiritist altars that many women kept in their apartments. He would

1. **salsas** (säl' səs) songs written in a particular Latin American musical style.
2. **viragoes** (vi rä' göz) fierce, irritable women who often shout.

◄ Critical Viewing
In what ways does this painting illustrate the narrator's description of the neighborhood in the first paragraph? **[Compare]**

Vocabulary
tenement
(ten' ə mənt)
n. apartment house, often run-down

profound
(prō found') adj
deep; intense

☑ Reading Check
On what memorable day in history does this story take place?

American History 241

▲ Read **"American History"** to see how a national tragedy and a personal crisis come together in one teenager's life.

 TEXAS Focus on the TEKS

Meet these standards with either **"The Most Dangerous Game"** (p. 214) or **"American History"** (p. 240).

Reading
(5) Understand the elements of fiction. *(Literary Analysis: Conflict)*

(1)(A) Determine the meaning of grade-level technical academic English words in multiple content areas derived from other linguistic affixes. *(Word Power: Apply It)*

Reading/Comprehension Skills
RC-9(B) Make complex inferences about text and use textual evidence to support understanding. *(Reading Skill: Make Inferences)*

Research
(23)(C) Use graphics and illustrations to help explain concepts where appropriate. *(Listening and Speaking: Oral Presentation)*

Listening and Speaking
(25) Give presentations using formal language effectively to meet the needs of audience, purpose, and occasion, employing eye contact, speaking rate, volume, enunciation, purposeful gestures, and conventions of language to communicate ideas effectively. *(Listening and Speaking: Oral Presentation)*

Literary Analysis: Conflict

Conflict is a struggle between opposing forces. This is one element that drives a story's plot.

- In an external conflict, a character clashes with an outside force—for example, another character, society, or nature.
- In an internal conflict, a character grapples with his or her own opposing feelings, beliefs, needs, or desires.

Its solution usually occurs near the end of the story, in the **resolution.** When a story's conflict is left unresolved, the character may have an **epiphany,** or sudden flash of insight that changes his or her feelings about the conflict.

As You Read Notice the conflicts that characters face and decide which ones truly are resolved.

Reading Skill: Make Inferences

Inferences are logical assumptions about information or ideas that are not directly stated in a piece of writing. When you **make complex inferences** about text, you use textual evidence, such as details and clues, to develop ideas about unstated information and concepts. To make inferences as you read a short story, ask questions such as these about characters' feelings and behavior:

- What does this detail show about the reasons for a character's actions or words?
- What does this passage say about the character's unstated feelings?

Using the Strategy: Inferences Chart

As You Read Use an **inferences chart** like this one to make complex inferences about the text and to use textual evidence to support your understanding.

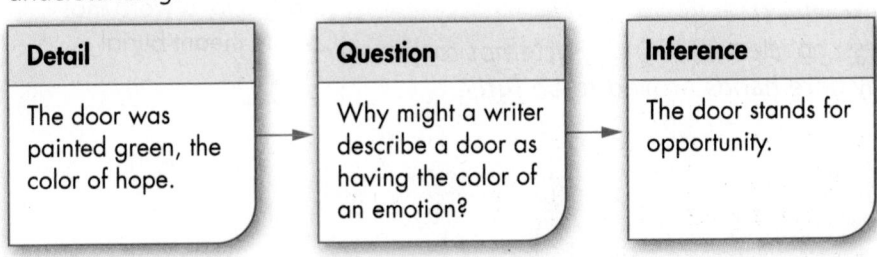

Detail	Question	Inference
The door was painted green, the color of hope.	Why might a writer describe a door as having the color of an emotion?	The door stands for opportunity.

TEXAS
PHLitOnline
www.PHLitOnline.com

Hear It!
- Selection summary audio
- Selection audio

See It!
- Get Connected video
- Background video
- More about the author
- Vocabulary flashcards

Do It!
- Interactive journals
- Interactive graphic organizers
- Self-test
- Internet activity
- Grammar tutorial
- Interactive vocabulary games

Is *conflict* necessary?

Writing About the Big Question

In "The Most Dangerous Game," a hunter faces a life-threatening conflict. Use these sentence starters to develop your ideas about the Big Question.

To succeed in a fight for **survival,** a person needs to _____ because _____.

Competition is important for our personal growth because _____.

As You Read Consider the conflict at the heart of hunting. Keep track of the ways in which the hunter tries to ensure his survival.

Vocabulary

Read each word and its definition. Decide whether you know the word well, know it a little bit, or do not know it at all. After you have read the selection, see how your knowledge of each word has increased.

- **palpable** (pal´ pə bəl) *adj.* able to be felt; easily perceived (p. 215) *The tension during the exam was* <u>palpable</u>. *palpate v.*

- **indolently** (in´ də lənt lē) *adv.* lazily; idly (p. 217) *The sleepy cat yawned* <u>indolently</u>. *indolent adj. indolence n.*

- **naive** (nä ēv´) *adj.* unsophisticated (p. 225) *How* <u>naive</u> *you are to trust everyone you meet! naiveté n. naively adv.*

- **scruples** (scr\overline{oo}´ pəlz) *n.* misgivings about something one feels is wrong (p. 225) *Her* <u>scruples</u> *prevented her from lying. scrupulous adj. unscrupulous adj.*

- **grotesque** (grō tesk´) *adj.* having a strange, bizarre design; shocking or offensive (p. 227) *The disease can cause* <u>grotesque</u> *lumps under the skin. grotesquely adv.*

- **futile** (fy\overline{oo}t´ 'l) *adj.* useless; hopeless (p. 230) *My attempt to catch the mouse with my bare hands proved to be* <u>futile</u>. *futility n. futilely adv.*

Word Power

The **French suffix -esque,** which forms adjectives, means "in the style or manner of."

In this story, the hunter sees many **grotesque** things—things that remind him of death—on the island he visits. *Grotesque* is related to *grotto,* a word that once meant burial vault.

Meet
Richard Connell
(1893–1949)

Author of
The Most Dangerous Game

Richard Connell seemed destined to become a writer: he was a sports reporter at the age of ten! At sixteen, he was editing his father's newspaper, the *Poughkeepsie News-Press,* in upstate New York. Connell attended Harvard University, where he worked on the *Daily Crimson* and the *Lampoon,* an early version of the humor magazine *National Lampoon.* During World War I, Connell edited his army division's newspaper.

From Page to Screen In 1924, Connell published "The Most Dangerous Game." In 1936, he settled in Beverly Hills, California, where he started working as a screenwriter. Twice nominated for Academy Awards, he became one of the most successful screenwriters of his day.

BACKGROUND FOR THE STORY

Social Studies Connection

Tests of Survival

As civilizations advance, people no longer need to struggle for their basic survival. Nevertheless, some people still enjoy testing their bravery and physical skills in competitions. Today, computer games sometimes feature death-defying challenges. As this story shows, the sport of big-game hunting once served a similar purpose.

Did You Know?

When "The Most Dangerous Game" was first published, it won the prestigious O. Henry Memorial Award for short fiction.

The Most Dangerous Game

Richard Connell

"**O**ff there to the right—somewhere—is a large island," said Whitney. "It's rather a mystery—"

"What island is it?" Rainsford asked.

"The old charts call it 'Ship-Trap Island,'" Whitney replied. "A suggestive name, isn't it? Sailors have a curious dread of the place. I don't know why. Some superstition—"

"Can't see it," remarked Rainsford, trying to peer through the dank tropical night that was palpable as it pressed its thick warm blackness in upon the yacht.

"You've good eyes," said Whitney, with a laugh, "and I've seen you pick off a moose moving in the brown fall bush at four hundred yards, but even you can't see four miles or so through a moonless Caribbean[1] night."

"Not four yards," admitted Rainsford. "Ugh! It's like moist black velvet."

"It will be light in Rio," promised Whitney. "We should make it in a few days. I hope the jaguar guns have come from Purdey's. We should have some good hunting up the Amazon. Great sport, hunting."

"The best sport in the world," agreed Rainsford.

"For the hunter," amended Whitney. "Not for the jaguar."

"Don't talk rot, Whitney," said Rainsford. "You're a big-game hunter, not a philosopher. Who cares how a jaguar feels?"

---

1. **Caribbean** (kar´ ə bē´ ən) the Caribbean Sea, a part of the Atlantic Ocean, bounded by the north coast of South America, Central America, and the West Indies.

◄ **Critical Viewing**
Based on the details in this image, what do you think this story will be about? **[Speculate]**

Vocabulary
palpable (pal´ pə bəl)
adj. able to be felt; easily perceived

Reading Check

What do Rainsford and Whitney see from the ship?

"Perhaps the jaguar does," observed Whitney.

"Bah! They've no understanding."

"Even so, I rather think they understand one thing—fear. The fear of pain and the fear of death."

"Nonsense," laughed Rainsford. "This hot weather is making you soft, Whitney. Be a realist. The world is made up of two classes— the hunters and the huntees. Luckily, you and I are the hunters. Do you think we've passed that island yet?"

"I can't tell in the dark. I hope so."

"Why?" asked Rainsford.

"The place has a reputation—a bad one."

"Cannibals?" suggested Rainsford.

"Hardly. Even cannibals wouldn't live in such a God-forsaken place. But it's gotten into sailor lore, somehow. Didn't you notice that the crew's nerves seemed a bit jumpy today?"

"They were a bit strange, now you mention it. Even Captain Nielsen—"

"Yes, even that tough-minded old Swede, who'd go up to the devil himself and ask him for a light. Those fishy blue eyes held a look I never saw there before. All I could get out of him was: 'This place has an evil name among sea-faring men, sir.' Then he said to me, very gravely: 'Don't you feel anything?'—as if the air about us was actually poisonous. Now, you mustn't laugh when I tell you this—I did feel something like a sudden chill.

"There was no breeze. The sea was as flat as a plate-glass window. We were drawing near the island then. What I felt was a—a mental chill; a sort of sudden dread."

"Pure imagination," said Rainsford. "One superstitious sailor can taint the whole ship's company with his fear."

"Maybe. But sometimes I think sailors have an extra sense that tells them when they are in danger. Sometimes I think evil is a tangible thing—with wave lengths, just as sound and light have. An evil place can, so to speak, broadcast vibrations of evil. Anyhow, I'm glad we're getting out of this zone. Well, I think I'll turn in now, Rainsford."

"I'm not sleepy," said Rainsford. "I'm going to smoke another pipe on the afterdeck."

"Good night, then, Rainsford. See you at breakfast."

"Right. Good night, Whitney." •

There was no sound in the night as Rainsford sat there, but the muffled throb of the engine that drove the yacht swiftly through the darkness, and the swish and ripple of the wash of the propeller.

Rainsford, reclining in a steamer chair, indolently puffed on his favorite brier. The sensuous drowsiness of the night was on him. "It's so dark," he thought, "that I could sleep without closing my eyes; the night would be my eyelids—"

An abrupt sound startled him. Off to the right he heard it, and his ears, expert in such matters, could not be mistaken. Again he heard the sound, and again. Somewhere, off in the blackness, someone had fired a gun three times.

Rainsford sprang up and moved quickly to the rail, mystified. He strained his eyes in the direction from which the reports had come, but it was like trying to see through a blanket. He leaped upon the rail and balanced himself there, to get greater elevation; his pipe, striking a rope, was knocked from his mouth. He lunged for it; a short, hoarse cry came from his lips as he realized he had reached too far and had lost his balance. The cry was pinched off short as the blood-warm waters of the Caribbean Sea closed over his head.

Vocabulary
indolently (in´ də lənt lē)
adv. lazily; idly

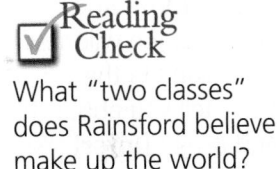

Reading Check

What "two classes" does Rainsford believe make up the world?

He struggled up to the surface and tried to cry out, but the wash from the speeding yacht slapped him in the face and the salt water in his open mouth made him gag and strangle. Desperately he struck out with strong strokes after the receding lights of the yacht, but he stopped before he had swum fifty feet. A certain cool-headedness had come to him; it was not the first time he had been in a tight place. There was a chance that his cries could be heard by someone aboard the yacht, but that chance was slender, and grew more slender as the yacht raced on. He wrestled himself out of his clothes, and shouted with all his power. The lights of the yacht became faint and ever-vanishing fireflies; then they were blotted out entirely by the night.

Rainsford remembered the shots. They had come from the right, and doggedly he swam in that direction, swimming with slow, deliberate strokes, conserving his strength. For a seemingly endless time he fought the sea. He began to count his strokes; he could do possibly a hundred more and then—

Rainsford heard a sound. It came out of the darkness, a high screaming sound, the sound of an animal in an extremity of anguish and terror.

He did not recognize the animal that made the sound; he did not try to; with fresh vitality he swam toward the sound. He heard it again; then it was cut short by another noise, crisp, staccato.

"Pistol shot," muttered Rainsford, swimming on.

Ten minutes of determined effort brought another sound to his ears—the most welcome he had ever heard—the muttering and growling of the sea breaking on a rocky shore. He was almost on the rocks before he saw them; on a night less calm he would have been shattered against them. With his remaining strength he dragged himself from the swirling waters. Jagged crags appeared to jut into the opaqueness, he forced himself upward, hand over hand. Gasping, his hands raw, he reached a flat place at the top. Dense jungle came down to the very edge of the cliffs. What perils that tangle of trees and underbrush might hold for him did not concern Rainsford just then. All he knew was that he was safe from his enemy, the sea, and that utter weariness was on him. He flung himself down at the jungle edge and tumbled headlong into the deepest sleep of his life. ●

When he opened his eyes he knew from the position of the sun that it was late in the afternoon. Sleep had given him new vigor; a sharp hunger was picking at him. He looked about him, almost cheerfully.

"Where there are pistol shots, there are men. Where there are men, there is food," he thought. But what kind of men, he wondered, in so forbidding a place? An unbroken front of snarled and ragged jungle fringed the shore.

He saw no sign of a trail through the closely knit web of weeds and trees; it was easier to go along the shore, and Rainsford floundered along by the water. Not far from where he had landed, he stopped.

Some wounded thing, by the evidence a large animal, had thrashed about in the underbrush; the jungle weeds were crushed down and the moss was lacerated; one patch of weeds was stained crimson. A small, glittering object not far away caught Rainsford's eye and he picked it up. It was an empty cartridge.

"A twenty-two," he remarked. "That's odd. It must have been a fairly large animal too. The hunter had his nerve with him to tackle it with a light gun. It's clear that the brute put up a fight. I suppose the first three shots I heard was when the hunter flushed his quarry and wounded it. The last shot was when he trailed it here and finished it."

Reading Skill
Make Inferences
What inferences does Rainsford make based on the evidence of pistol shots?

Reading Check

As Rainsford swims for shore, what sounds does he hear coming out of the darkness?

He examined the ground closely and found what he had hoped to find—the print of hunting boots. They pointed along the cliff in the direction he had been going. Eagerly he hurried along, now slipping on a rotten log or a loose stone, but making headway; night was beginning to settle down on the island.

Bleak darkness was blacking out the sea and jungle when Rainsford sighted the lights. He came upon them as he turned a crook in the coast line, and his first thought was that he had come upon a village, for there were many lights. But as he forged along he saw to his great astonishment that all the lights were in one enormous building—a lofty structure with pointed towers plunging upward into the gloom. His eyes made out the shadowy outlines of a palatial château;[2] it was set on a high bluff, and on three sides of it cliffs dived down to where the sea licked greedy lips in the shadows.

"Mirage," thought Rainsford. But it was no mirage, he found, when he opened the tall spiked iron gate. The stone steps were real enough; the massive door with a leering gargoyle[3] for a knocker was real enough; yet about it all hung an air of unreality.

He lifted the knocker, and it creaked up stiffly, as if it had never before been used. He let it fall, and it startled him with its booming loudness. He thought he heard steps within; the door remained closed. Again Rainsford lifted the heavy knocker, and let it fall. The door opened then, opened as suddenly as if it were on a spring, and Rainsford stood blinking in the river of glaring gold light that poured out. The first thing Rainsford's eyes discerned was the largest man Rainsford had ever seen—a gigantic creature, solidly made and black-bearded to the waist. In his hand the man held a long-barreled revolver, and he was pointing it straight at Rainsford's heart.

Out of the snarl of beard two small eyes regarded Rainsford.

"Don't be alarmed," said Rainsford, with a smile which he hoped was disarming. "I'm no robber. I fell off a yacht. My name is Sanger Rainsford of New York City."

The menacing look in the eyes did not change. The revolver pointed as rigidly as if the giant were a statue. He gave no sign that he understood Rainsford's words, or that he had even heard them. He was dressed in uniform, a black uniform trimmed with gray astrakhan.[4]

"I'm Sanger Rainsford of New York," Rainsford began again. "I fell off a yacht. I am hungry."

The man's only answer was to raise with his thumb the hammer of his revolver. Then Rainsford saw the man's free hand go to his forehead in a military salute, and he saw him click his heels together and stand at attention. Another man was coming down

Reading Skill
Make Inferences
Using the textual evidence in this scene to support your understanding, what complex inferences can you make about the two men Rainsford meets?

---

2. **palatial** (pə lā′ shəl) **château** (sha tò») a mansion as luxurious as a palace.
3. **gargoyle** (gär′ goil′) *n.* strange and distorted animal form projecting from a building.
4. **astrakhan** (as′ trə kən) *n.* loosely curled fur made from the skins of very young lambs.

the broad marble steps, an erect, slender man in evening clothes. He advanced to Rainsford and held out his hand.

In a cultivated voice marked by a slight accent that gave it added precision and deliberateness, he said: "It is a very great pleasure and honor to welcome Mr. Sanger Rainsford, the celebrated hunter, to my home."

Automatically Rainsford shook the man's hand.

"I've read your book about hunting snow leopards in Tibet, you see," explained the man. "I am General Zaroff."

Rainsford's first impression was that the man was singularly handsome; his second was that there was an original, almost bizarre quality about the general's face. He was a tall man past middle age, for his hair was a vivid white; but his thick eyebrows and pointed military mustache were as black as the night from which Rainsford had come. His eyes, too, were black and very bright. He had high cheek bones, a sharp-cut nose, a spare, dark face, the face of a man used to giving orders, the face of an aristocrat. Turning to the giant in uniform, the general made a sign. The giant put away his pistol, saluted, withdrew.

"Ivan is an incredibly strong fellow," remarked the general, "but he has the misfortune to be deaf and dumb. A simple fellow, but, I'm afraid, like all his race, a bit of a savage."

"Is he Russian?"

"He is a Cossack," said the general, and his smile showed red lips and pointed teeth. "So am I."

"Come," he said, "we shouldn't be chatting here. We can talk later. Now you want clothes, food, rest. You shall have them. This is a most restful spot."

Ivan had reappeared, and the general spoke to him with lips that moved but gave forth no sound.

"Follow Ivan, if you please, Mr. Rainsford," said the general. "I was about to have my dinner when you came. I'll wait for you. You'll find that my clothes will fit you, I think."

It was to a huge, beam-ceilinged bedroom with a canopied bed big enough for six men that Rainsford followed the silent giant. Ivan laid out an evening suit, and Rainsford, as he put it on, noticed that it came from a London tailor who ordinarily cut and sewed for none below the rank of duke.

The dining room to which Ivan conducted him was in many ways remarkable. There was a medieval magnificence about it; it suggested a baronial hall of feudal times with its oaken panels,

LITERATURE IN CONTEXT

History Connection

Cossacks

Ivan and Zaroff are Cossacks, members of a people from southern Russia who also made up a special Russian military unit. As a group, Cossacks were famous for their fierceness, and the soldiers enjoyed a privileged status. Because of their elite position, these soldiers were also fiercely independent. When the czar—the ruler of Russia—was overthrown in the Russian Revolution of 1917, Cossacks like Zaroff were executed or forced into exile. As a Cossack, Zaroff is unwilling to acknowledge that the rules of ordinary people apply to him.

Connect to the Literature

What traits does Zaroff exhibit that might be due, in part, to his having been a Cossack?

◀ **Czar Nicholas II, overthrown in the Russian Revolution of 1917**

Reading Check

What type of building does Rainsford encounter on the island he reaches?

The Most Dangerous Game **221**

its high ceiling, its vast refectory table where twoscore men could sit down to eat. About the hall were the mounted heads of many animals—lions, tigers, elephants, moose, bears; larger or more perfect specimens Rainsford had never seen. At the great table the general was sitting, alone.

"You'll have a cocktail, Mr. Rainsford," he suggested. The cocktail was surpassingly good; and, Rainsford noted, the table appointments were of the finest—the linen, the crystal, the silver, the china.

They were eating *borsch*, the rich, red soup with whipped cream so dear to Russian palates. Half apologetically General Zaroff said: "We do our best to preserve the amenities of civilization here. Please forgive any lapses. We are well off the beaten track, you know. Do you think the champagne has suffered from its long ocean trip?"

Literary Analysis
Conflict Explain how Rainsford's discomfort in this passage is both an internal and an external conflict.

"Not in the least," declared Rainsford. He was finding the general a most thoughtful and affable host, a true cosmopolite.[5] But there was one small trait of the general's that made Rainsford uncomfortable. Whenever he looked up from his plate he found the general studying him, appraising him narrowly.

"Perhaps," said General Zaroff, "you were surprised that I recognized your name. You see, I read all books on hunting published in English, French, and Russian. I have but one passion in my life, Mr. Rainsford, and it is the hunt."

"You have some wonderful heads here," said Rainsford as he ate a particularly well cooked filet mignon. "That Cape buffalo is the largest I ever saw."

"Oh, that fellow. Yes, he was a monster."

"Did he charge you?"

"Hurled me against a tree," said the general. "Fractured my skull. But I got the brute."

"I've always thought," said Rainsford, "that the Cape buffalo is the most dangerous of all big game."

For a moment the general did not reply; he was smiling his curious red-lipped smile. Then he said slowly: "No. You are wrong, sir. The Cape buffalo is not the most dangerous big game." He sipped his wine. "Here in my preserve on this island," he said in the same slow tone, "I hunt more dangerous game."

Rainsford expressed his surprise. "Is there big game on this island?"

The general nodded. "The biggest."

"Really?"

"Oh, it isn't here naturally, of course. I have to stock the island."

"What have you imported, general?" Rainsford asked. "Tigers?"

The general smiled. "No," he said. "Hunting tigers ceased to

---

5. **cosmopolite** (käz mäp´ ə līt´) *n.* person at home in all parts of the world.

interest me some years ago. I exhausted their possibilities, you see. No thrill left in tigers, no real danger. I live for danger, Mr. Rainsford."

The general took from his pocket a gold cigarette case and offered his guest a long black cigarette with a silver tip; it was perfumed and gave off a smell like incense.

"We will have some capital hunting, you and I," said the general. "I shall be most glad to have your society."

"But what game—" began Rainsford.

"I'll tell you," said the general. "You will be amused, I know. I think I may say, in all modesty, that I have done a rare thing. I have invented a new sensation. May I pour you another glass of port, Mr. Rainsford?"

"Thank you, general."

The general filled both glasses, and said: "God makes some men poets. Some He makes kings, some beggars. Me He made a hunter. My hand was made for the trigger, my father said. He was a very rich man with a quarter of a million acres in the Crimea,[6] and he was an ardent sportsman. When I was only five years old he gave me a little gun, specially made in Moscow for me, to shoot sparrows with. When I shot some of his prize turkeys with it, he did not punish me; he complimented me on my marksmanship. I killed my first bear in the Caucasus[7] when I was ten. My whole life has been one prolonged hunt. I went into the army—it was expected of noblemen's sons—and for a time commanded a division of Cossack cavalry, but my real interest was always the hunt. I have hunted every kind of game in every land. It would be impossible for me to tell you how many animals I have killed."

The general puffed at his cigarette.

"After the debacle[8] in Russia I left the country, for it was imprudent for an officer of the Czar to stay there. Many noble Russians lost everything. I, luckily, had invested heavily in American securities, so I shall never have to open a tea room in Monte Carlo or drive a taxi in Paris. Naturally, I continued to hunt—grizzlies in your Rockies, crocodiles in the Ganges, rhinoceroses in East Africa. It was in Africa that the Cape buffalo hit me and laid me up for six months. As soon as I recovered I started for the Amazon to hunt jaguars, for I had heard they were unusually cunning. They weren't." The Cossack sighed. "They were no match at all for a hunter with his wits about him, and a high-

---

6. **Crimea** (krī mē´ ə) region in southwestern Ukraine extending into the Black Sea.
7. **Caucasus** (kô´ kə səs) mountain range between the Black and Caspian seas.
8. **debacle** (di bä´ kəl) *n.* bad defeat (Zaroff is referring to the Russian Revolution of 1917, a defeat for upper-class Russians like himself).

"Here in my preserve on this island," he said in the same slow tone, "I hunt more dangerous game."

**Spiral Review
Character**
How does the use of dialogue help to develop the character of Zaroff?

**Reading Skill
Make Inferences**
Using the textual evidence about Zaroff's life presented in this paragraph, what complex inference can you make about how the general feels concerning hunting?

Reading Check
Why does Zaroff recognize Rainsford's name?

powered rifle. I was bitterly disappointed. I was lying in my tent with a splitting headache one night when a terrible thought pushed its way into my mind. Hunting was beginning to bore me! And hunting, remember, had been my life. I have heard that in America business men often go to pieces when they give up the business that has been their life."

"Yes, that's so," said Rainsford.

The general smiled. "I had no wish to go to pieces," he said. "I must do something. Now, mine is an analytical mind, Mr. Rainsford. Doubtless that is why I enjoy the problems of the chase."

"No doubt, General Zaroff."

"So," continued the general, "I asked myself why the hunt no longer fascinated me. You are much younger than I am, Mr. Rainsford, and have not hunted as much, but you perhaps can guess the answer."

"What was it?"

"Simply this: hunting had ceased to be what you call 'a sporting proposition.' It had become too easy. I always got my quarry. Always. There is no greater bore than perfection."

The general lit a fresh cigarette.

Literary Analysis
Conflict How was the "tragic moment" Zaroff refers to the sign of an internal conflict?

"No animal had a chance with me any more. That is no boast; it is a mathematical certainty. The animal had nothing but his legs and his instinct. Instinct is no match for reason. When I thought of this it was a tragic moment for me, I can tell you."

Rainsford leaned across the table, absorbed in what his host was saying.

"It came to me as an inspiration what I must do," the general went on.

"And that was?"

The general smiled the quiet smile of one who has faced an obstacle and surmounted it with success. "I had to invent a new animal to hunt," he said.

"A new animal? You're joking."

"Not at all," said the general. "I never joke about hunting. I needed a new animal. I found one. So I bought this island, built this house, and here I do my hunting. The island is perfect for my purpose—there are jungles with a maze of trails in them, hills, swamps—"

"But the animal, General Zaroff?"

"Oh," said the general, "it supplies me with the most exciting hunting in the world. No other hunting compares with it for an instant. Every day I hunt, and I never grow bored now, for I have a quarry with which I can match my wits."

Rainsford's bewilderment showed in his face.

"I wanted the ideal animal to hunt," explained the general. "So I said: 'What are the attributes of an ideal quarry?' And the answer was, of course: 'It must have courage, cunning, and, above all, it must be able to reason.'"

"But no animal can reason," objected Rainsford.

"My dear fellow," said the general, "there is one that can."

"But you can't mean—" gasped Rainsford.

"And why not?"

"I can't believe you are serious, General Zaroff. This is a grisly joke."

"Why should I not be serious? I am speaking of hunting."

"Hunting? General Zaroff, what you speak of is murder."

The general laughed with entire good nature. He regarded Rainsford quizzically. "I refuse to believe that so modern and civilized a young man as you seem to be harbors romantic ideas about the value of human life. Surely your experiences in the war—"

"Did not make me condone cold-blooded murder," finished Rainsford stiffly.

Laughter shook the general. "How extraordinarily droll you are!" he said. "One does not expect nowadays to find a young man of the educated class, even in America, with such a naive, and, if I may say so, mid-Victorian point of view.[9] It's like finding a snuff-box in a limousine. Ah, well, doubtless you had Puritan ancestors. So many Americans appear to have had. I'll wager you'll forget your notions when you go hunting with me. You've a genuine new thrill in store for you, Mr. Rainsford."

"Thank you, I'm a hunter, not a murderer."

"Dear me," said the general, quite unruffled, "again that unpleasant word. But I think I can show you that your scruples are quite ill founded."

"Yes?"

"Life is for the strong, to be lived by the strong, and, if need be, taken by the strong. The weak of the world were put here to give the strong pleasure. I am strong. Why should I not use my gift? If I wish to hunt, why should I not? I hunt the scum of the earth—sailors from tramp ships—lascars,[10] blacks, Chinese, whites, mongrels—a thoroughbred horse or hound is worth more than a score of them."

"But they are men," said Rainsford hotly.

"Precisely," said the general. "That is why I use them. It gives me pleasure. They can reason, after a fashion. So they are dangerous."

"But where do you get them?"

The general's left eyelid fluttered down in a wink. "This island is called Ship-Trap," he answered. "Sometimes an angry god of the

9. **mid-Victorian point of view** a point of view emphasizing proper behavior and associated with the time of Queen Victoria of England (1819–1901).
10. **lascars** (lasʹ kərz) n. Indian or East Indian sailors, employed on European ships.

Literary Analysis
Conflict What does Rainsford suddenly understand about Zaroff?

Vocabulary
naive (nä ēvʹ) *adj.* unsophisticated

scruples (skro͞oʹ pəlz) *n.* misgivings about something one feels is wrong

Reading Check

What does Zaroff do to ease his boredom with hunting?

high seas sends them to me. Sometimes, when Providence is not so kind, I help Providence a bit. Come to the window with me."

Rainsford went to the window and looked out toward the sea.

"Watch! Out there!" exclaimed the general, pointing into the night. Rainsford's eyes saw only blackness, and then, as the general pressed a button, far out to sea Rainsford saw the flash of lights.

The general chuckled. "They indicate a channel," he said, "where there's none: giant rocks with razor edges crouch like a sea monster with wide-open jaws. They can crush a ship as easily as I crush this nut." He dropped a walnut on the hardwood floor and brought his heel grinding down on it. "Oh, yes," he said, casually, as if in answer to a question, "I have electricity. We try to be civilized here."

"Civilized? And you shoot down men?"

Reading Skill
Make Inferences
Based on the textual evidence in this description, what complex inference can you make about the method Zaroff uses to lure his quarry to the island?

A trace of anger was in the general's black eyes, but it was there for but a second, and he said, in his most pleasant manner: "Dear me, what a righteous young man you are! I assure you I do not do the thing you suggest. That would be barbarous. I treat these visitors with every consideration. They get plenty of good food and exercise. They get into splendid physical condition. You shall see for yourself tomorrow."

"What do you mean?"

"We'll visit my training school," smiled the general. "It's in the cellar. I have about a dozen pupils down there now. They're from the Spanish bark San Lucar that had the bad luck to go on the rocks out there. A very inferior lot, I regret to say. Poor specimens and more accustomed to the deck than to the jungle."

He raised his hand, and Ivan, who served as waiter, brought thick Turkish coffee. Rainsford, with an effort, held his tongue in check.

"It's a game, you see," pursued the general blandly. "I suggest to one of them that we go hunting. I give him a supply of food and an excellent hunting knife. I give him three hours' start. I am to follow, armed only with a pistol of the smallest caliber and range. If my quarry eludes me for three whole days, he wins the game. If I find him"—the general smiled—"he loses."

"Suppose he refuses to be hunted?"

Literary Analysis
Conflict Is Zaroff's statement that his captives do not have to participate in the hunt true? Explain.

"Oh," said the general, "I give him his option, of course. He need not play the game if he doesn't wish to. If he does not wish to hunt, I turn him over to Ivan. Ivan once had the honor of serving as official knouter[11] to the Great White Czar, and he has his own ideas of sport. Invariably, Mr. Rainsford, invariably they choose the hunt."

"And if they win?"

The smile on the general's face widened. "To date I have not lost," he said.

---

11. **knouter** (nout´ ər) *n.* someone who beats criminals with a leather whip, or knout.

Then he added, hastily: "I don't wish you to think me a braggart, Mr. Rainsford. Many of them afford only the most elementary sort of problem. Occasionally I strike a tartar.[12] One almost did win. I eventually had to use the dogs."

"The dogs?"

"This way, please. I'll show you."

The general steered Rainsford to a window. The lights from the windows sent a flickering illumination that made grotesque patterns on the courtyard below, and Rainsford could see moving about there a dozen or so huge black shapes; as they turned toward him, their eyes glittered greenly.

"A rather good lot, I think," observed the general. "They are let out at seven every night. If anyone should try to get into my house—or out of it—something extremely regrettable would occur to him." He hummed a snatch of song from the Folies Bergère.[13]

"And now," said the general, "I want to show you my new collection of heads. Will you come with me to the library?"

"I hope," said Rainsford, "that you will excuse me tonight, General Zaroff. I'm really not feeling at all well."

"Ah, indeed?" the general inquired solicitously. "Well, I suppose that's only natural, after your long swim. You need a good, restful night's sleep. Tomorrow you'll feel like a new man, I'll wager. Then we'll hunt, eh? I've one rather promising prospect—"

Rainsford was hurrying from the room.

"Sorry you can't go with me tonight," called the general. "I expect rather fair sport—a big, strong black. He looks resourceful—Well good night, Mr. Rainsford; I hope you have a good night's rest."

The bed was good, and the pajamas of the softest silk, and he was tired in every fiber of his being, but nevertheless Rainsford could not quiet his brain with the opiate of sleep. He lay, eyes wide open. Once he thought he heard stealthy steps in the corridor outside his room. He sought to throw open the door; it would not

12. **tartar** (tärt´ ər) *n.* stubborn, violent person.
13. **Folies** (fô´ lē) **Bergère** (ber zher') musical theater in Paris.

▲ **Critical Viewing**
Why might Zaroff have used dogs like these on his hunts? **[Connect]**

Vocabulary
grotesque (grō tesk´) *adj.* having a strange, bizarre design; shocking or offensive

Reading Skill
Make Inferences
What kind of heads do you think Zaroff wants to show Rainsford? Explain.

Reading Check

Who are the "pupils" in Zaroff's cellar?

open. He went to the window and looked out. His room was high up in one of the towers. The lights of the château were out now, and it was dark and silent, but there was a fragment of sallow moon, and by its wan light he could see, dimly, the courtyard; there, weaving in and out in the pattern of shadow, were black, noiseless forms; the hounds heard him at the window and looked up, expectantly, with their green eyes. Rainsford went back to the bed and lay down. By many methods he tried to put himself to sleep. He had achieved a doze when, just as morning began to come, he heard, far off in the jungle, the faint report of a pistol. •

General Zaroff did not appear until luncheon. He was dressed faultlessly in the tweeds of a country squire. He was solicitous about the state of Rainsford's health.

"As for me," sighed the general, "I do not feel so well. I am worried, Mr. Rainsford. Last night I detected traces of my old complaint."

To Rainsford's questioning glance the general said: "Ennui. Boredom."

Then, taking a second helping of crêpes suzette, the general explained: "The hunting was not good last night. The fellow lost his head. He made a straight trail that offered no problems at all. That's the trouble with these sailors; they have dull brains to begin with, and they do not know how to get about in the woods. They do excessively stupid and obvious things. It's most annoying. Will you have another glass of Chablis, Mr. Rainsford?"

Literary Analysis
Conflict How does Rainsford's statement about wishing to leave make his internal conflict an external one?

"General," said Rainsford firmly, "I wish to leave this island at once."

The general raised his thickets of eyebrows; he seemed hurt. "But, my dear fellow," the general protested, "you've only just come. You've had no hunting—"

"I wish to go today," said Rainsford. He saw the dead black eyes of the general on him, studying him. General Zaroff's face suddenly brightened.

He filled Rainsford's glass with venerable Chablis from a dusty bottle.

"Tonight," said the general, "we will hunt—you and I."

Rainsford shook his head. "No, general," he said. "I will not hunt."

Reading Skill
Make Inferences
What complex inference can you make about the hunting trip Zaroff is suggesting?

The general shrugged his shoulders and delicately ate a hothouse grape. "As you wish, my friend," he said. "The choice rests entirely with you. But may I not venture to suggest that you will find my idea of sport more diverting than Ivan's?"

He nodded toward the corner to where the giant stood, scowling, his thick arms crossed on his hogshead of chest.

"You don't mean—" cried Rainsford.

"My dear fellow," said the general, "have I not told you I always mean what I say about hunting? This is really an inspiration. I drink to a foeman worthy of my steel—at last."

The general raised his glass, but Rainsford sat staring at him.

"You'll find this game worth playing," the general said enthusiastically. "Your brain against mine. Your woodcraft against mine. Your strength and stamina against mine. Outdoor chess! And the stake is not without value, eh?"

"And if I win—" began Rainsford huskily.

"I'll cheerfully acknowledge myself defeated if I do not find you by midnight of the third day," said General Zaroff. "My sloop will place you on the mainland near a town."

The general read what Rainsford was thinking.

"Oh, you can trust me," said the Cossack. "I will give you my word as a gentleman and a sportsman. Of course you, in turn, must agree to say nothing of your visit here."

"I'll agree to nothing of the kind," said Rainsford.

"Oh," said the general, "in that case— But why discuss that now? Three days hence we can discuss it over a bottle of Veuve Cliquot, unless—"

The general sipped his wine.

Then a businesslike air animated him. "Ivan," he said to Rainsford, "will supply you with hunting clothes, food, a knife. I suggest you wear moccasins; they leave a poorer trail. I suggest too that you avoid the big swamp in the southeast corner of the island. We call it Death Swamp. There's quicksand there. One foolish fellow tried it. The deplorable part of it was that Lazarus followed him. You can imagine my feelings, Mr. Rainsford. I loved Lazarus; he was the finest hound in my pack. Well, I must beg you to excuse me now. I always take a siesta after lunch. You'll hardly have time for a nap, I fear. You'll want to start, no doubt. I shall not follow till dusk. Hunting at night is so much more exciting than by day, don't you think? Au revoir,[14] Mr. Rainsford, au revoir."

General Zaroff, with a deep, courtly bow, strolled from the room.

From another door came Ivan. Under one arm he carried khaki hunting clothes, a haversack of food, a leather sheath containing a long-bladed hunting knife; his right hand rested on a cocked revolver thrust in the crimson sash about his waist. . . .

Rainsford had fought his way through the bush for two hours. "I must keep my nerve. I must keep my nerve," he said through tight teeth.

---

14. Au (ō´) **revoir** (rə vwär´) French for "until we meet again."

"My dear fellow," said the general, "have I not told you I always mean what I say about hunting?"

Reading Check

What two suggestions does Zaroff give Rainsford before they begin the hunt?

He had not been entirely clear-headed when the château gates snapped shut behind him.

His whole idea at first was to put distance between himself and General Zaroff, and, to this end, he had plunged along, spurred on by the sharp rowels of something very like panic. Now he had got a grip on himself, had stopped, and was taking stock of himself and the situation.

He saw that straight flight was futile; inevitably it would bring him face to face with the sea. He was in a picture with a frame of water, and his operations, clearly, must take place within that frame.

"I'll give him a trail to follow," muttered Rainsford, and he struck off from the rude paths he had been following into the trackless wilderness. He executed a series of intricate loops; he doubled on his trail again and again, recalling all the lore of the fox hunt, and all the dodges of the fox. Night found him leg-weary, with his hands

Vocabulary
futile (fyo͞ot′ 'l) *adj.*
useless; hopeless

▼ **Critical Viewing**
How does this picture support Rainsford's thought that straight flight through the jungle is futile? **[Support]**

and face lashed by the branches, on a thickly wooded ridge. He knew it would be insane to blunder on through the dark, even if he had the strength. His need for rest was imperative and he thought: "I have played the fox, now I must play the cat of the fable." A big tree with a thick trunk and outspread branches was nearby, and, taking care to leave not the slightest mark, he climbed up into the crotch, and stretching out on one of the broad limbs, after a fashion, rested. Rest brought him new confidence and almost a feeling of security. Even so zealous a hunter as General Zaroff could not trace him there, he told himself; only the devil himself could follow that complicated trail through the jungle after dark. But, perhaps, the general was a devil—

An apprehensive night crawled slowly by like a wounded snake, and sleep did not visit Rainsford, although the silence of a dead world was on the jungle. Toward morning when a dingy gray was varnishing the sky, the cry of some startled bird focused Rainsford's attention in that direction. Something was coming through the bush, coming slowly, carefully, coming by the same winding way Rainsford had come. He flattened himself down on the limb, and through a screen of leaves almost as thick as tapestry, he watched. The thing that was approaching was a man.

It was General Zaroff. He made his way along with his eyes fixed in utmost concentration on the ground before him. He paused, almost beneath the tree, dropped to his knees and studied the ground. Rainsford's impulse was to hurl himself down like a panther, but he saw the general's right hand held something metallic—a small automatic pistol.

The hunter shook his head several times, as if he were puzzled. Then he straightened up and took from his case one of his black cigarettes; its pungent incense-like smoke floated up to Rainsford's nostrils.

Rainsford held his breath. The general's eyes had left the ground and were traveling inch by inch up the tree. Rainsford froze there, every muscle tensed for a spring. But the sharp eyes of the hunter stopped before they reached the limb where Rainsford lay; a smile spread over his brown face. Very deliberately he blew a smoke ring into the air; then he turned his back on the tree and walked carelessly away, back along the trail he had come. The swish of the underbrush against his hunting boots grew fainter and fainter.

The pent-up air burst hotly from Rainsford's lungs. His first thought made him feel sick and numb. The general could follow a trail through the woods at night; he could follow an extremely difficult trail; he must have uncanny powers; only by the merest chance had the Cossack failed to see his quarry.

Reading Skill
Make Inferences
What textual evidence in the description of Zaroff's searching the tree might lead you to make the inference that he knows Rainsford is there?

Reading Check
On the first night of the hunt, where does Rainsford attempt to hide from Zaroff?

Rainsford's second thought was even more terrible. It sent a shudder of cold horror through his whole being. Why had the general smiled? Why had he turned back?

Rainsford did not want to believe what his reason told him was true, but the truth was as evident as the sun that had by now pushed through the morning mists. The general was playing with him! The general was saving him for another day's sport! The Cossack was the cat; he was the mouse. Then it was that Rainsford knew the full meaning of terror.

"I will not lose my nerve. I will not."

He slid down from the tree, and struck off again into the woods. His face was set and he forced the machinery of his mind to function. Three hundred yards from his hiding place he stopped where a huge dead tree leaned precariously on a smaller, living one. Throwing off his sack of food, Rainsford took his knife from its sheath and began to work with all his energy.

The job was finished at last, and he threw himself down behind a fallen log a hundred feet away. He did not have to wait long. The cat was coming again to play with the mouse. ●

Following the trail with the sureness of a bloodhound, came General Zaroff. Nothing escaped those searching black eyes, no crushed blade of grass, no bent twig, no mark, no matter how faint, in the moss. So intent was the Cossack on his stalking that he was upon the thing Rainsford had made before he saw it. His foot touched the protruding bough that was the trigger. Even as he touched it, the general sensed his danger and leaped back with the agility of an ape. But he was not quite quick enough; the dead tree, delicately adjusted to rest on the cut living one, crashed down and struck the general a glancing blow on the shoulder as it fell; but for his alertness, he must have been smashed beneath it. He staggered, but he did not fall; nor did he drop his revolver. He stood there, rubbing his injured shoulder, and Rainsford, with fear again gripping his heart, heard the general's mocking laugh ring through the jungle.

"Rainsford," called the general, "if you are within the sound of my voice, as I suppose you are, let me congratulate you. Not many men know how to make a Malay mancatcher. Luckily, for me, I too have hunted in Malacca. You are proving interesting, Mr. Rainsford. I am going now to have my wound dressed; it's only a slight one. But I shall be back. I shall be back."

When the general, nursing his bruised shoulder, had gone, Rainsford took up his flight again. It was flight now, a desperate, hopeless flight, that carried him on for some hours. Dusk came, then darkness, and still he pressed on. The ground grew softer

Literary Analysis
Conflict Who seems to be winning the conflict at this point in the story? Explain.

History Connection

World War I Trenches

When Rainsford digs himself in, he is drawing on his experiences as a soldier. During World War I (1914–1918), European armies on both sides dug hundreds of miles of deep, narrow ditches. The soldiers lived in these trenches, from where they would charge the enemy's trenches.

◀ Soldiers' equipment included masks to protect them from mustard gas and other chemical weapons.

LIFE IN THE TRENCHES

- Throughout the war, approximately seven thousand British soldiers were killed, wounded, or disabled every day while serving in the trenches.

- Soldiers living in trenches were plagued by lice, rats, beetles, and frogs.

- The trenches smelled terrible due to dead bodies, overflowing latrines, and unwashed men.

A single pair of trench rats could produce as many as 880 offspring in one year. ▼

Connect to the Literature

Rainsford says his time in the trenches was "placid" compared to his experience on the island. How does this information about trenches clarify his fear?

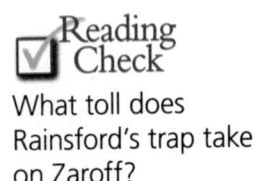

under his moccasins; the vegetation grew ranker, denser; insects bit him savagely. Then, as he stepped forward, his foot sank into the ooze. He tried to wrench it back, but the muck sucked viciously at his foot as if it were a giant leech. With a violent effort, he tore his foot loose. He knew where he was now. Death Swamp and its quicksand.

His hands were tight closed as if his nerve were something tangible that someone in the darkness was trying to tear from his grip. The softness of the earth had given him an idea. He stepped back from the quicksand a dozen feet or so, and, like some huge prehistoric beaver, he began to dig.

Rainsford had dug himself in in France when a second's delay meant death. That had been a placid pastime compared to his digging now. The pit grew deeper; when it was above his shoulders, he climbed out and from some hard saplings cut stakes and

Reading Check

What toll does Rainsford's trap take on Zaroff?

The Most Dangerous Game **233**

sharpened them to a fine point. These stakes he planted in the bottom of the pit with the points sticking up. With flying fingers he wove a rough carpet of weeds and branches and with it he covered the mouth of the pit. Then, wet with sweat and aching with tiredness, he crouched behind the stump of a lightning-charred tree.

He knew his pursuer was coming; he heard the padding sound of feet on the soft earth, and the night breeze brought him the perfume of the general's cigarette. It seemed to Rainsford that the general was coming with unusual swiftness; he was not feeling his way along, foot by foot. Rainsford, crouching there, could not see the general, nor could he see the pit. He lived a year in a minute. Then he felt an impulse to cry aloud with joy, for he heard the sharp crackle of the breaking branches as the cover of the pit gave way; he heard the sharp scream of pain as the pointed stakes found their mark. He leaped up from his place of concealment. Then he cowered back. Three feet from the pit a man was standing, with an electric torch in his hand.

"You've done well, Rainsford," the voice of the general called. "Your Burmese tiger pit has claimed one of my best dogs. Again you score. I think, Mr. Rainsford, I'll see what you can do against my whole pack. I'm going home for a rest now. Thank you for a most amusing evening."

At daybreak Rainsford, lying near the swamp, was awakened by a sound that made him know that he had new things to learn about fear. It was a distant sound, faint and wavering, but he knew it. It was the baying of a pack of hounds.

Rainsford knew he could do one of two things. He could stay where he was and wait. That was suicide. He could flee. That was postponing the inevitable. For a moment he stood there, thinking. An idea that held a wild chance came to him, and, tightening his belt, he headed away from the swamp.

The baying of the hounds drew nearer, then still nearer, nearer, ever nearer. On a ridge Rainsford climbed a tree. Down a watercourse, not a quarter of a mile away, he could see the bush moving. Straining his eyes, he saw the lean figure of General Zaroff; just ahead of him Rainsford made out another figure whose wide shoulders surged through the tall jungle weeds; it was the giant Ivan, and he seemed pulled forward by some unseen force; Rainsford knew that Ivan must be holding the pack in leash.

They would be on him any minute now. His mind worked frantically. He thought of a native trick he had learned in Uganda. He slid down the tree. He caught hold of a springy young sapling and to it he fastened his hunting knife, with the blade pointing down the trail; with a bit of wild grapevine he tied back the sapling. Then he ran for his life. The hounds raised their voices as they hit the fresh scent. Rainsford knew now how an animal at bay feels. ●

He had to stop to get his breath. The baying of the hounds stopped abruptly, and Rainsford's heart stopped too. They must have reached the knife.

He shinnied excitedly up a tree and looked back. His pursuers had stopped. But the hope that was in Rainsford's brain when he climbed died, for he saw in the shallow valley that General Zaroff was still on his feet. But Ivan was not. The knife, driven by the recoil of the springing tree, had not wholly failed.

"Nerve, nerve, nerve!" he panted, as he dashed along. A blue gap showed between the trees dead ahead. Ever nearer drew the hounds. Rainsford forced himself on toward that gap. He reached it. It was the shore of the sea. Across a cove he could see the gloomy gray stone of the château. Twenty feet below him the sea rumbled and hissed. Rainsford hesitated. He heard the hounds. Then he leaped far out into the sea. . . .

When the general and his pack reached the place by the sea, the Cossack stopped. For some minutes he stood regarding the blue-green expanse of water. He shrugged his shoulders. Then he sat down, took a drink of brandy from a silver flask, lit a perfumed cigarette, and hummed a bit from *Madame Butterfly*.[15]

General Zaroff had an exceedingly good dinner in his great paneled dining hall that evening. With it he had a bottle of Pol Roger and half a bottle of Chambertin. Two slight annoyances kept him from perfect enjoyment. One was the thought that it would be difficult to replace Ivan; the other was that his quarry had escaped him; of course the American hadn't played the game—so thought the general as he tasted his after-dinner liqueur. In his library he

---

15. *Madame Butterfly* an opera by Giacomo Puccini.

Literary Analysis
Conflict What new internal conflict does the sound of the baying dogs create for Rainsford?

Reading Check
What does Rainsford do when he reaches the edge of the cliff?

read, to soothe himself, from the works of Marcus Aurelius.[16] At ten he went up to his bedroom. He was deliciously tired, he said to himself, as he locked himself in. There was a little moonlight, so, before turning on his light, he went to the window and looked down at the courtyard. He could see the great hounds, and he called: "Better luck another time," to them. Then he switched on the light.

A man, who had been hiding in the curtain of the bed, was standing there.

"Rainsford!" screamed the general. "How in God's name did you get here?"

"Swam," said Rainsford. "I found it quicker than walking through the jungle."

The general sucked in his breath and smiled. "I congratulate you," he said. "You have won the game."

Rainsford did not smile. "I am still a beast at bay," he said, in a low, hoarse voice. "Get ready, General Zaroff."

The general made one of his deepest bows. "I see," he said. "Splendid! One of us is to furnish a repast for the hounds. The other will sleep in this very excellent bed. On guard, Rainsford. . . ."

He had never slept in a better bed, Rainsford decided.

---

16. **Marcus Aurelius** (ô rē´ lē əs) Roman emperor and philosopher (A.D. 121–180).

Critical Thinking

Support your responses with evidence from the text.

1. **Respond:** What do you like or dislike about Rainsford? Explain.

2. **(a)** According to Zaroff, what is the most dangerous game? **(b) Make a Judgment:** Based on this attitude, would you call Zaroff "civilized"? Why or why not?

3. **(a)** Near the end, with what words does Zaroff congratulate Rainsford? **(b) Make Inferences:** What action does Rainsford then take?

4. **Speculate:** How might Rainsford's experience on the island change him?

Is conflict necessary?
(a) In what sense is conflict a "necessary" part of the hunting experience? **(b)** Why does Zaroff consider it necessary to increase the conflict in his hunts?

After You Read

The Most Dangerous Game

Literary Analysis: Conflict

1. **(a)** What is the main **conflict** in this story? Explain. **(b)** Is the main conflict primarily internal or external? Explain.

2. Use a chart like the one shown to provide specific details that reveal conflicts other than the main conflict.

Rainsford vs. nature	Rainsford vs. himself

3. Is there a **resolution** in this story or does Rainsford experience an **epiphany** with no real end to the conflict? Support your answer.

Reading Skill: Make Inferences

4. **(a)** Identify three **complex inferences** you made while reading this story and the textual evidence you used to support your understanding. **(b)** Did making inferences improve your understanding of the story? Explain your response.

5. **(a)** Write two **inferences** you made about Whitney. Compare the inferences you made with a partner's inferences. **(b)** Based on your ideas, discuss how the story would be different if it had been Whitney on the island with Zaroff.

Vocabulary

Practice Use a word from the vocabulary list on page 212 to fill in the blank in each sentence. Then, explain the **context clues,** or key words and phrases, in each sentence that helped you.

1. His cheating at the game demonstrated a lack of _____.

2. At the wedding, the joy in the air seemed _____.

3. She tried to climb, but her high heels made her efforts _____.

4. The lazy sloth hung _____ from the tree branch.

5. Only a very _____ person would believe in the Tooth Fairy.

6. The _____ necklace was made of beads that looked like skulls.

Word Power Use the context of the sentences and what you know about the **French suffix -esque** to explain your answer to each question.

1. Why do people like to visit *picturesque* places?

2. If a film is called *Disneyesque,* whose movies does it resemble?

Word Power

The **French suffix -esque** means "in the style or manner of."

Apply It Explain how the suffix -esque helps you determine the meanings of these technical academic words from social studies and the arts. Consult a dictionary if necessary.

Lincolnesque
statuesque
Romanesque

Is *conflict* necessary?

Writing About the Big Question

In "American History," a teenage girl wrestles with personal feelings while the adults around her try to grasp a tragic historic event. Use these sentence starters to develop your ideas about the Big Question.

For both individuals and countries, historic events often involve conflict because _____.

Fighting the same **battle** allows people to overlook the **differences** among them because _____.

As You Read Think about how Elena prioritizes the thoughts that compete for her attention.

Vocabulary

Read each word and its definition. Decide whether you know the word well, know it a little bit, or do not know it at all. After you read, see how your knowledge of each word has increased.

- **tenement** (ten´ ə mənt) *n.* apartment house, often run-down (p. 241) *Many families lived in the large tenement.*

- **profound** (prō found´) *adj.* deep; intense (p. 241) *Mia felt profound sorrow when her dog died.* *profoundly adv.*

- **discreet** (di skrēt´) *adj.* careful about one's actions; prudent; keeping silent or preserving confidences (p. 244) *Please, be discreet when you talk to the press about our agreement.* *discreetly adv. discretion n. indiscreet adj. indiscretion n.*

- **vigilant** (vij´ ə lənt) *adj.* watchful (p. 245) *The bodyguard kept a vigilant eye on the candidate.* *vigil n. vigilance n.*

- **elation** (ē lā´ shən) *n.* exultant joy or pride; high spirits (p. 249) *She danced with elation when she saw the new puppy.* *elate v. elated adj.*

- **dilapidated** (də lap´ ə dāt´ əd) *adj.* broken down (p. 250) *The old furniture was dilapidated and worn.*

Word Power

The **Anglo-French suffix -ant** is often used to form adjectives. It usually means "performing an action."

In this story, a mother is **vigilant** about her daughter. She watches closely—keeps vigil—to make sure her daughter focuses on the right things.

Meet
Judith Ortiz Cofer
(b. 1952)

Author of
American History

Judith Ortiz Cofer spent her childhood in two different cultures. Born in Puerto Rico, she moved with her parents to Paterson, New Jersey, when she was four years old. She grew up mostly in Paterson, but she also spent time in Puerto Rico with her *abuela* (grandmother).

The Art of Storytelling It was from her grandmother that Ortiz Cofer learned the art of storytelling. "When my *abuela* sat us down to tell a story," she says, "we learned something from it, even though we always laughed. That was her way of teaching." In her own work, Ortiz Cofer teaches readers about the richness and difficulty of coming of age in two cultures at once.

BACKGROUND FOR THE STORY
History Connection
The Kennedy Assassination

On November 22, 1963, President John F. Kennedy was shot and killed in Dallas, Texas, and the United States was plunged into mourning. Most people who lived through that time can still remember where they were when they heard the news. Kennedy's assassination and the nation's grief defined a generation. Key events in "American History" take place on that fateful day.

Did You Know?
Ortiz Cofer teaches for Operation Homecoming, a writing program for U.S. military personnel.

American History

Judith Ortiz Cofer

I once read in a *Ripley's Believe It or Not* column that Paterson, New Jersey, is the place where the Straight and Narrow (streets) intersect.

The Puerto Rican tenement known as El Building was one block up from Straight. It was, in fact, the corner of Straight and Market; not "at" the corner, but *the* corner. At almost any hour of the day, El Building was like a monstrous jukebox, blasting out *salsas*[1] from open windows as the residents, mostly new immigrants just up from the island, tried to drown out whatever they were currently enduring with loud music. But the day President Kennedy was shot there was a profound silence in El Building; even the abusive tongues of *viragoes*,[2] the cursing of the unemployed, and the screeching of small children had been somehow muted. President Kennedy was a saint to these people. In fact, soon his photograph would be hung alongside the Sacred Heart and over the spiritist altars that many women kept in their apartments. He would

---

1. *salsas* (säl´ ses) songs written in a particular Latin American musical style.
2. *viragoes* (vi rä´ gōz) fierce, irritable women who often shout.

Vocabulary
tenement
(ten´ ə mənt)
n. apartment house, often run-down

profound
(prō found´) *adj.*
deep; intense

Reading Check

On what memorable day in history does this story take place?

◀ **Critical Viewing**
In what ways does this painting illustrate the narrator's description of the neighborhood in the first paragraph? **[Compare]**

become part of the hierarchy of martyrs they prayed to for favors that only one who had died for a cause would understand. •

On the day that President Kennedy was shot, my ninth grade class had been out in the fenced playground of Public School Number 13. We had been given "free" exercise time and had been ordered by our P.E. teacher, Mr. DePalma, to "keep moving." That meant that the girls should jump rope and the boys toss basketballs through a hoop at the far end of the yard. He in the meantime would "keep an eye" on us from just inside the building.

It was a cold gray day in Paterson. The kind that warns of early snow. I was miserable, since I had forgotten my gloves, and my knuckles were turning red and raw from the jump rope. I was also taking a lot of abuse from the black girls for not turning the rope hard and fast enough for them.

"Hey, Skinny Bones, pump it, girl. Ain't you got no energy today?" Gail, the biggest of the black girls who had the other end of the rope, yelled, "Didn't you eat your rice and beans and pork chops for breakfast today?"

The other girls picked up the "pork chops" and made it into a refrain: "pork chop, pork chop, did you eat your pork chop?" They entered the double ropes in pairs and exited without tripping or missing a beat. I felt a burning on my cheeks and then my glasses fogged up so that I could not manage to coordinate the jump rope with Gail. The chill was doing to me what it always did, entering my bones, making me cry, humiliating me. I hated the city, especially in winter. I hated Public School Number 13. I hated my skinny flat-chested body, and I envied the black girls who could jump rope so fast that their legs became a blur. They always seemed to be warm while I froze.

There was only one source of beauty and light for me that school year. The only thing I had anticipated at the start of the semester. That was seeing Eugene. In August, Eugene and his family had moved into the only house on the block that had a yard and trees. I could see his place from my window in El Building. In fact, if I sat on the fire escape I was literally suspended above Eugene's backyard. It was my favorite spot to read my library books in the summer. Until that August the house had been occupied by an old Jewish couple. Over the years I had become part of their family, without their knowing it, of course. I had a view of their kitchen and their backyard, and though I could not hear what they said, I knew when they were arguing, when one of them was sick, and many other things. I knew all this by watching them at mealtimes. I could see their kitchen table, the sink, and the stove. During good times, he sat at the table and read his newspapers while she

▶ Critical Viewing
In what ways is this school scene similar to your school? In what ways is it different?
[Compare and Contrast]

Reading Skill
Make Inferences
Using the textual evidence in this paragraph, what complex inference can you make about how the narrator feels toward Eugene?

fixed the meals. If they argued, he would leave and the old woman would sit and stare at nothing for a long time. When one of them was sick, the other would come and get things from the kitchen and carry them out on a tray. The old man had died in June. The last week of school I had not seen him at the table at all. Then one day I saw that there was a crowd in the kitchen. The old woman had finally emerged from the house on the arm of a stocky, middle-aged woman, whom I had seen there a few times before, maybe her daughter. Then a man had carried out suitcases. The house had stood empty for weeks. I had had to resist the temptation to climb down into the yard and water the flowers the old lady had taken such good care of.

By the time Eugene's family moved in, the yard was a tangled mass of weeds. The father had spent several days mowing, and

Reading Check

Who is Eugene, and how does the narrator become aware of him?

There was only one source of beauty and light for me that school year.

▲ Critical Viewing
Which description from
the selection does
this painting suggest?
[Connect]

Vocabulary
discreet (di skrēt′)
adj. careful about
one's actions; prudent;
keeping silent or
preserving confidences

when he finished, from where I sat, I didn't see the red, yellow, and purple clusters that meant flowers to me. I didn't see this family sit down at the kitchen table together. It was just the mother, a red-headed tall woman who wore a white uniform—a nurse's, I guessed it was; the father was gone before I got up in the morning and was never there at dinner time. I only saw him on weekends when they sometimes sat on lawn chairs under the oak tree, each hidden behind a section of the newspaper; and there was Eugene. He was tall and blond, and he wore glasses. I liked him right away because he sat at the kitchen table and read books for hours. That summer, before we had even spoken one word to each other, I kept him company on my fire escape.

Once school started I looked for him in all my classes, but P. S. 13 was a huge, overpopulated place and it took me days and many discreet questions to discover that Eugene was in honors classes for all his subjects; classes that were not open to me because English was not my first language, though I was a straight A student. After much maneuvering, I managed "to run into him" in the hallway where his locker was—on the other side of the building from mine—and in study hall at the library, where he first seemed to notice me but did not speak; and finally, on the way home after school one day when I decided to approach him directly, though my stomach was doing somersaults.

I was ready for rejection, snobbery, the worst. But when I came up to him, practically panting in my nervousness, and blurted out: "You're Eugene. Right?" he smiled, pushed his glasses up on his nose, and nodded. I saw then that he was blushing deeply. Eugene liked me, but he was shy. I did most of the talking that day. He nodded and smiled a lot. In the weeks that followed, we walked home together. He would linger at the corner of El Building for a few minutes then walk down to his two-story house. It was not until Eugene moved into that house that I noticed that El Building blocked most of the sun, and that the only spot that got a little sunlight during the day was the tiny square of earth the old woman had planted with flowers.

I did not tell Eugene that I could see inside his kitchen from my bedroom. I felt dishonest, but I liked my secret sharing of his evenings, especially now that I knew what he was reading since we chose our books together at the school library.

One day my mother came into my room as I was sitting on the windowsill staring out. In her abrupt way she said: "Elena, you are acting 'moony.' " *Enamorada* [3] was what she really said, that is—like a girl stupidly infatuated. Since I had turned fourteen . . . my mother had been more vigilant than ever. She acted as if I was going to go crazy or explode or something if she didn't watch me and nag me all the time about being a *señorita* [4] now. She kept talking about virtue, morality, and other subjects that did not interest me in the least. My mother was unhappy in Paterson, but my father had a good job at the blue jeans factory in Passaic and soon, he kept assuring us, we would be moving to our own house there. Every Sunday we drove out to the suburbs of Paterson, Clifton, and Passaic, out to where people mowed grass on Sundays in the summer, and where children made snowmen in the winter from pure white snow, not like the gray slush of Paterson which seemed to fall from the sky in that hue. I had learned to listen to my parents' dreams, which were spoken in Spanish, as fairy tales, like the stories about life in the island paradise of Puerto Rico before I was born. I had been to the island once as a little girl, to grandmother's funeral, and all I remembered was wailing women in black, my mother becoming hysterical and being given a pill that

---

3. **Enamorada** (ā nä´ mō rä´ dä) Spanish for "enamored; lovesick."
4. **señorita** (se´ nyð rē´ tä) *n.* Spanish for "young lady."

Literary Analysis
Conflict What internal conflict does the narrator experience as she prepares to approach Eugene?

Vocabulary
vigilant (vij´ ə lənt) *adj.* watchful

Reading Check
According to her mother, how does Elena seem to feel about Eugene?

made her sleep two days, and me feeling lost in a crowd of strangers all claiming to be my aunts, uncles, and cousins. I had actually been glad to return to the city. We had not been back there since then, though my parents talked constantly about buying a house on the beach someday, retiring on the island—that was a common topic among the residents of El Building. As for me, I was going to go to college and become a teacher.

But after meeting Eugene I began to think of the present more than of the future. What I wanted now was to enter that house I had watched for so many years. I wanted to see the other rooms where the old people had lived, and where the boy spent his time. Most of all, I wanted to sit at the kitchen table with Eugene like two adults, like the old man and his wife had done, maybe drink some coffee and talk about books. I had started reading *Gone with the Wind*. I was enthralled by it, with the daring and the passion of the beautiful girl living in a mansion, and with her devoted parents and the slaves who did everything for them. I didn't believe such a world had ever really existed, and I wanted to ask Eugene some questions since he and his parents, he had told me, had come up from Georgia, the same place where the novel was set. His father worked for a company that had transferred him to Paterson. His mother was very unhappy, Eugene said, in his beautiful voice that rose and fell over words in a strange, lilting way. The kids at school called him "the hick" and made fun of the way he talked. I knew I was his only friend so far, and I liked that, though I felt sad for him sometimes. "Skinny Bones" and the "Hick" was what they called us at school when we were seen together. ●

The day Mr. DePalma came out into the cold and asked us to line up in front of him was the day that President Kennedy was shot. Mr. DePalma, a short, muscular man with slicked-down black hair, was the science teacher, P.E. coach, and disciplinarian at P. S. 13. He was the teacher to whose homeroom you got assigned if you were a troublemaker, and the man called out to break up playground fights, and to escort violently angry teenagers to the office. And Mr. DePalma was the man who called your parents in for "a conference."

That day, he stood in front of two rows of mostly black and Puerto Rican kids, brittle from their efforts to "keep moving" on a November day that was turning bitter cold. Mr. DePalma, to our complete shock, was crying. Not just silent adult tears, but really sobbing. There were a few titters from the back of the line where I stood shivering.

"Listen," Mr. DePalma raised his arms over his head as if he were about to conduct an orchestra. His voice broke, and he covered his

Spiral Review
Character
In this paragraph, how does the author develop both Elena and Eugene as complex yet believable characters?

Literary Analysis
Conflict What external conflict does Eugene experience at school?

face with his hands. His barrel chest was heaving. Someone giggled behind me.

"Listen," he repeated, "something awful has happened." A strange gurgling came from his throat, and he turned around and spat on the cement behind him.

"Gross," someone said, and there was a lot of laughter.

"The president is dead, you idiots. I should have known that wouldn't mean anything to a bunch of losers like you kids. Go home." He was shrieking now. No one moved for a minute or two, but then a big girl let out a "Yeah!" and ran to get her books piled up with the others against the brick wall of the school building. The others followed in a mad scramble to get to their things before somebody caught on. It was still an hour to the dismissal bell.

A little scared, I headed for El Building. There was an eerie feeling on the streets. I looked into Mario's drugstore, a favorite hangout for the high school crowd, but there were only a couple of old Jewish men at the soda bar talking with the short order cook in tones that sounded almost angry, but they were keeping their voices low. Even the traffic on one of the busiest intersections in Paterson—Straight Street and Park Avenue—seemed to be moving slower. There were no horns blasting that day. At El Building, the usual little group of unemployed men were not hanging out on the front stoop making it difficult for women to enter the front door. No music spilled out from open doors in the hallway. When I walked into our apartment, I found my mother sitting in front of the grainy picture of the television set.

She looked up at me with a tear-streaked face and just said: "*Dios mío*,"[5] turning back to the set as if it were pulling at her eyes. I went into my room.

Though I wanted to feel the right thing about President Kennedy's death, I could not fight the

---

5. *Dios mío* (dē´ ōs mē´ ō) Spanish for "My God!"

Reading Skill
Make Inferences
What textual evidence in Elena's description of her walk home might lead you to make the inference that people feel anguish over the assassination of the president?

◀ **Critical Viewing**
What lines in the story help you to understand this image? **[Connect]**

Reading
Check
How does Mr. DePalma's reaction to the news of Kennedy's assassination differ from the students' reaction?

feeling of elation that stirred in my chest. Today was the day I was to visit Eugene in his house. He had asked me to come over after school to study for an American history test with him. We had also planned to walk to the public library together. I looked down into his yard. The oak tree was bare of leaves and the ground looked gray with ice. The light through the large kitchen window of his house told me that El Building blocked the sun to such an extent that they had to turn lights on in the middle of the day. I felt ashamed about it. But the white kitchen table with the lamp hanging just above it looked cozy and inviting. I would soon sit there, across from Eugene, and I would tell him about my perch just above his house. Maybe I should.

In the next thirty minutes I changed clothes, put on a little pink lipstick, and got my books together. Then I went in to tell my mother that I was going to a friend's house to study. I did not expect her reaction.

"You are going out *today?*" The way she said "today" sounded as if a storm warning had been issued. It was said in utter disbelief. Before I could answer, she came toward me and held my elbows as I clutched my books.

"*Hija*,[6] the president has been killed. We must show respect. He was a great man. Come to church with me tonight."

She tried to embrace me, but my books were in the way. My first impulse was to comfort her, she seemed so distraught, but I had to meet Eugene in fifteen minutes.

"I have a test to study for, Mama. I will be home by eight."

"You are forgetting who you are, *Niña*.[7] I have seen you staring down at that boy's house. You are heading for humiliation and

---

6. *Hija* (ē´ hä) Spanish for "daughter."
7. *Niña* (nē´ nyä) Spanish for "child."

Vocabulary
elation (ē lā´ shən) *adj.* exultant joy or pride; high spirits

Literary Analysis
Conflict On the evening of the assassination, how do Elena's plans conflict with her mother's?

Reading Check

How does Elena feel about studying with Eugene?

"*Hija*, the president has been killed. We must show respect. He was a great man."

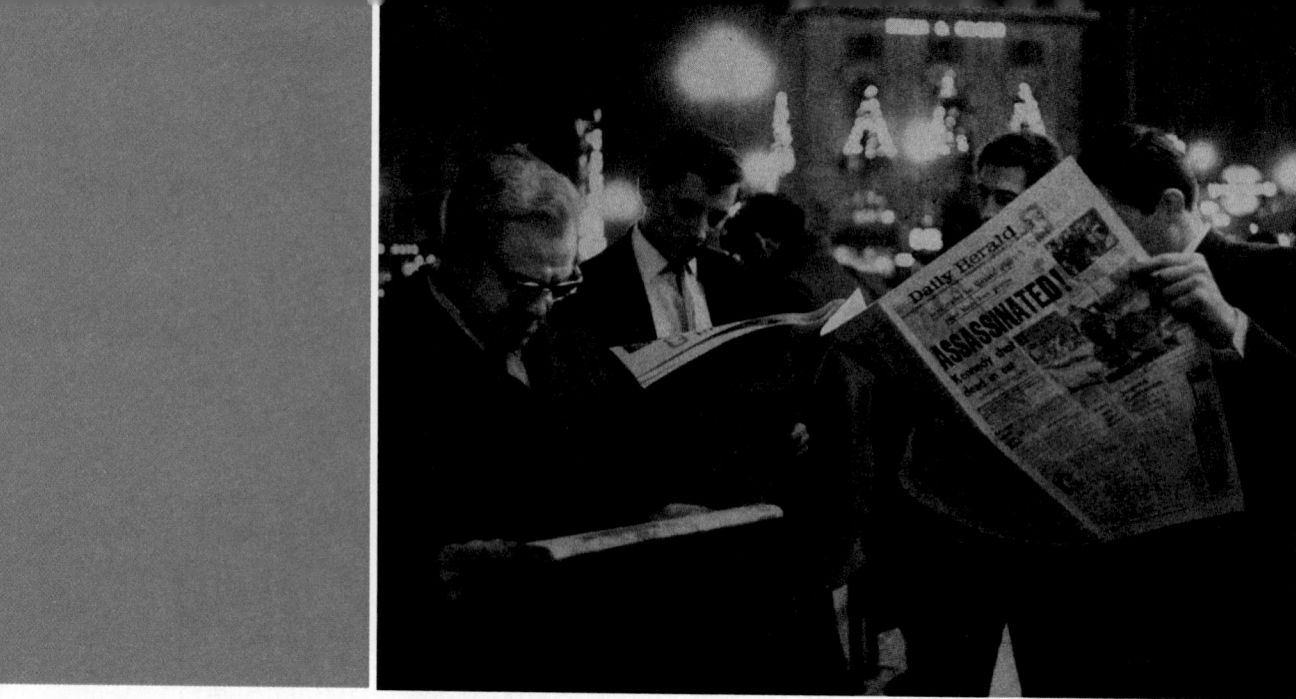

▲ **Critical Viewing**
What is striking about
this image? **[Respond]**

Vocabulary
dilapidated (də lap´ə
dāt´ əd) *adj.* broken
down

Reading Skill
Make Inferences
Based on textual evidence
in the description of the
woman's face, what
complex inference can
you make about what
she was doing before
Elena arrived?

pain." My mother said this in Spanish and in a resigned tone
that surprised me, as if she had no intention of stopping me from
"heading for humiliation and pain." I started for the door. She sat in
front of the TV holding a white handkerchief to her face. •

I walked out to the street and around the chain-link fence that
separated El Building from Eugene's house. The yard was neatly
edged around the little walk that led to the door. It always amazed
me how Paterson, the inner core of the city, had no apparent logic
to its architecture. Small, neat, single residences like this one could
be found right next to huge, dilapidated apartment buildings like El
Building. My guess was that the little houses had been there first,
then the immigrants had come in droves, and the monstrosities
had been raised for them—the Italians, the Irish, the Jews, and
now us, the Puerto Ricans and the blacks. The door was painted a
deep green: *verde*, the color of hope, I had heard my mother say it:
Verde-Esperanza.[8]

I knocked softly. A few suspenseful moments later the door
opened just a crack. The red, swollen face of a woman appeared.
She had a halo of red hair floating over a delicate ivory face—the
face of a doll—with freckles on the nose. Her smudged eye makeup made her look unreal to me, like a mannequin seen through a
warped store window.

"What do you want?" Her voice was tiny and sweet-sounding, like
a little girl's, but her tone was not friendly.

"I'm Eugene's friend. He asked me over. To study." I thrust out my
books, a silly gesture that embarrassed me almost immediately.

---

8. **Verde-Esperanza** (ver´ dā es pā rän´ zä) Spanish for "green-hope."

"You live there?" She pointed up to El Building, which looked particularly ugly, like a gray prison with its many dirty windows and rusty fire escapes. The woman had stepped halfway out and I could see that she wore a white nurse's uniform with "St. Joseph's Hospital" on the name tag.

"Yes. I do."

She looked intently at me for a couple of heartbeats, then said as if to herself, "I don't know how you people do it." Then directly to me: "Listen. Honey. Eugene doesn't want to study with you. He is a smart boy. Doesn't need help. You understand me. I am truly sorry if he told you you could come over. He cannot study with you. It's nothing personal. You understand? We won't be in this place much longer, no need for him to get close to people—it'll just make it harder for him later. Run back home now."

I couldn't move. I just stood there in shock at hearing these things said to me in such a honey-drenched voice. I had never heard an accent like hers, except for Eugene's softer version. It was as if she were singing me a little song.

"What's wrong? Didn't you hear what I said?" She seemed very angry, and I finally snapped out of my trance. I turned away from the green door, and heard her close it gently.

Our apartment was empty when I got home. My mother was in someone else's kitchen, seeking the solace she needed. Father would come in from his late shift at midnight. I would hear them talking softly in the kitchen for hours that night. They would not discuss their dreams for the future, or life in Puerto Rico, as they often did; that night they would talk sadly about the young widow and her two children, as if they were family. For the next few days, we would observe *luto*[9] in our apartment; that is, we would practice restraint and silence—no loud music or laughter. Some of the women of El Building would wear black for weeks.

That night, I lay in my bed trying to feel the right thing for our dead president. But the tears that came up from a deep source inside me were strictly for me. When my mother came to the door, I pretended to be sleeping. Sometime during the night, I saw from my bed the streetlight come on. It had a pink halo around it. I went to my window and pressed my face to the cool glass. Looking up

---

9. *luto* (lo͞oʹ tō) Spanish for "mourning."

Literary Analysis
Conflict How do Eugene's mother's comments change the story's conflict?

The door was painted a deep green: verde, the color of hope, I had heard my mother say it: *Verde-Esperanza.*

Reading Check

How does Eugene's mother react to Elena's visit to their house?

at the light I could see the white snow falling like a lace veil over its face. I did not look down to see it turning gray as it touched the ground below.

Critical Thinking

Support your responses with evidence from the text.

1. **Respond:** What would you like to say to Elena? Explain.

2. **(a)** In the first paragraph, what words does Elena use to describe her building? **(b)** How does she describe Eugene's house from her fire escape? **(c) Compare and Contrast:** Based on these descriptions, explain the contrast in Elena's feelings toward her own home and Eugene's house.

3. **(a)** What subject is Elena going to study with Eugene? **(b) Interpret:** What other reasons might Ortiz Cofer have for calling this story "American History"?

4. **(a) Analyze:** Where is Elena's mother and what is she doing when Elena returns from Eugene's house? **(b) Analyze:** In the last scene of the story, why does Elena say that her tears are just for herself?

Is conflict necessary?
(a) For Elena, which problem in the story—the national one or the personal one—is more important? **(b)** Are these conflicts necessary for Elena's personal growth and understanding of the world? Explain your response.

Literary Analysis: Conflict

1. (a) What is the main **conflict** in this story? Explain. **(b)** Is the main conflict primarily internal or external? Explain your response.

2. Use a chart like the one shown to provide specific details that reveal conflicts other than the main conflict.

Elena vs. another person	Elena vs. herself

3. (a) What realization about life's disappointments does Elena come to at the end of the story? **(b)** Does this **epiphany** lead to a clear **resolution?** Support your answer with details from the story.

Reading Skill: Make Inferences

4. (a) Identify three **complex inferences** you made while reading this story and the textual evidence you used to support your understanding. **(b)** Did making inferences improve your understanding of the story? Explain your response.

5. (a) Discuss with a partner two inferences you made about characters' responses to President Kennedy's assassination. **(b)** Based on your inferences, discuss how the story would be different if Elena had tried to visit Eugene on a different day.

Vocabulary

Practice Use a word from the "American History" vocabulary list on page 238 to fill in the blank in each sentence. Then, explain the **context clues,** or key words and phrases, in each sentence that helped you.

1. During the blackout, the guard was more _____ than usual.

2. The _____ car had no wheels and was covered in rust.

3. She felt a _____ sense of pride as she graduated with honors.

4. The serene garden contrasted with the bustling _____.

5. We shouted with _____ when our team won the game.

6. I remained _____, even though I was desperate to tell the secret.

Word Power Use the context of the sentences and what you know about the **Anglo-French suffix -ant** to explain your answer to each question.

1. Would it be easy to get along with a *compliant* person?

2. Why is a baby *reliant* upon her parents?

Word Power

The **Anglo-French suffix -ant** often means "performing an action."

Apply It Explain how the suffix -*ant* helps you determine the meanings of these technical academic words from science. Consult a dictionary if necessary.

defoliant
pollutant
retardant

Integrated Language Skills

The Most Dangerous Game • American History

Conventions: Regular Verbs

The **principal parts** of a verb are the present, the present participle, the past, and the past participle.

Most verbs in the English language are **regular verbs** that use predictable patterns. By using various principal parts, you can show verb tenses and forms.

The **present** tense describes action happening now or in the future. The **present participle** is formed by adding -ing to the present form. The **future** tense is achieved by adding *will* to the present form as a helping verb. The **past** tense describes events that happened already. To form the past and **past participle,** add -ed to the present form (the participle uses *have, has*, or *had* as a helping verb). If the present form ends in -e, that -e is often dropped when adding an ending. Finally, the **present progressive** shows continuing action and uses a form of *be* as a helping verb.

Present	Present Participle	Past	Past Participle
inspect	(is) inspecting	inspected	(has) inspected
race	(is) racing	raced	(has) raced

Practice A Identify the principal part of each underlined verb.

1. Rainsford <u>discovered</u> a mysterious island.
2. The gunshots had <u>awakened</u> the night.
3. Now he is <u>running</u> toward a cliff.
4. Soon, he can <u>confront</u> the foe in his fight.

Reading Application Find four sentences in "The Most Dangerous Game" that use regular verbs. Change each sentence by using a different principal part.

Practice B Complete each sentence with a regular verb, using the form in parentheses.

1. Kennedy's death (past) Elena's mother.
2. Elena is (present participle) about Eugene.
3. Eugene's family has (past participle) next door.
4. Elena is (present participle) with him after school.

Speaking Application Look at the image on page 250 in "American History." Tell a partner about it using all four principal parts of speech.

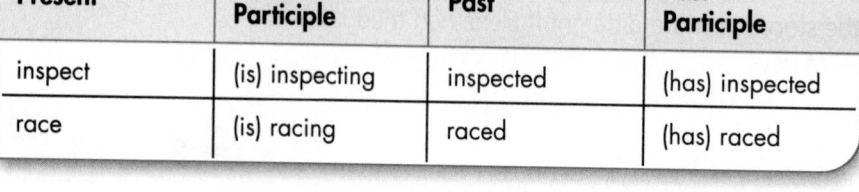

PH GRAMMAR HANDBOOK Further instruction and practice are available in the *Prentice Hall Grammar Handbook.*

Writing

Each of these stories may leave readers with more questions than answers. Write an **alternative ending** to "American History" or "The Most Dangerous Game." Follow these steps:

- Create an ending that flows logically from earlier events.
- Focus on presenting a satisfactory resolution to the conflict.
- Make your ending consistent with your understanding of the characters.

Grammar Application Make sure to correctly form the principal parts of all regular verbs in your essay.

Writing Workshop: *Work in Progress*

Prewriting for Short Story To prepare for writing a short story, create a Character Profile. Name a character and develop information about his or her gender, age, appearance, background, and interests. Include notes about something that the character really wants—this may help you choose a conflict later. Save your work in your portfolio.

Listening and Speaking

In a team, prepare an **oral presentation.**

- If you read "American History," discuss the effect of President Kennedy's assassination upon the American public.
- If you read "The Most Dangerous Game," discuss two or three big-game species mentioned in the story. Include key facts about each one, including any threats that the species faces today.

Use the following guidelines to make your presentation successful:

- Use **graphics** and **illustrations** to help explain concepts where appropriate.
- **Use formal language effectively** to meet the needs of your audience (your teacher and classmates), the purpose of your presentation (to inform), and your occasion for speaking (an assignment for class). As you plan your presentation, carefully consider the words you will use to convey your ideas.
- **Employ eye contact** and **purposeful gestures** to engage the audience. Pause for effect when appropriate.
- Use **speaking rate, volume,** and **enunciation** to ensure you are communicating your ideas effectively.
- Use the **conventions of language,** or the rules of grammar and usage, to state your points clearly and correctly.

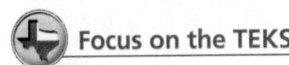 **Focus on the TEKS**

Research
(23)(C) Use graphics and illustrations to help explain concepts where appropriate.
Listening and Speaking
(25) Give presentations using formal language effectively to meet the needs of audience, purpose, and occasion, employing eye contact, speaking rate, volume, enunciation, purposeful gestures, and conventions of language to communicate ideas effectively.

Use this prewriting activity to prepare for the **Writing Workshop** on page 306.

TEXAS
PHLitOnline
www.PHLitOnline.com

- Interactive graphic organizers
- Grammar tutorial
- Interactive journals

The Gift of the Magi • The Interlopers

Selection Choices

▲ Read **"The Gift of the Magi"** to learn what happens when a husband and wife with little money seek the perfect present for each other.

▲ Read **"The Interlopers"** to see how lifelong enemies react when they become each other's only hope for survival.

 TEXAS Focus on the TEKS

Meet these standards with either **"The Gift of the Magi"** (p. 260) or **"The Interlopers"** (p. 270).

Reading
(7) Explain the role of irony in literary works.
(Literary Skill: Irony)

Reading/Comprehension Skills
RC-9(B) Make complex inferences about text and use textual evidence to support understanding. *(Reading Skill: Make Inferences)*

Research
(23)(A) Marshal evidence in support of a clear thesis statement and related claims. *(Listening and Speaking: Debate)*

Listening and Speaking
(24)(C) Evaluate the effectiveness of a speaker's main and supporting ideas. *(Listening and Speaking: Debate)*

Literary Analysis: Irony

Irony is a contradiction between appearance and reality—it is the difference between what is expected and what actually happens.

In **situational irony,** something happens in the story that contradicts the expectations of a character or the reader. For example, a runner who trains hard would be expected to do well in a race. It would be ironic if she trained so hard that she overslept and missed the race.

A surprise ending often presents a situational irony. The turn of events may be startling, but writers using irony usually build clues into the story that make the ending logical, just the same.

The role of ironies and surprise endings in literary works is to help convey the story's theme, or message.

As You Read Watch for surprises and make notes about what each one may mean. Use your notes to explain the role of irony in the literary work.

Reading Skill: **Make Inferences**

When you **make inferences,** you formulate logical assumptions based on details in a text. In addition to what the author tells you, you can also use your own prior knowledge and experience to make inferences. As you learn, watch movies and plays, and observe the world every day, you gather knowledge and experiences.

- When you read something new, look for ways in which the characters and situations resemble ones you have seen before.
- Then, apply that knowledge and experience to make inferences.

Using the Strategy: Inferences Chart

As You Read Use a flow chart like this one to make complex inferences as you read and to record the **textual evidence** that supports your understanding.

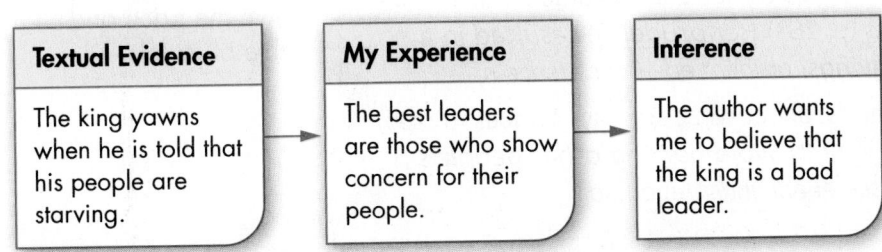

TEXAS
PHLitOnline
www.PHLitOnline.com

Hear It!
- Selection summary audio
- Selection audio

See It!
- Get Connected video
- Background video
- More about the author
- Vocabulary flashcards

Do It!
- Interactive journals
- Interactive graphic organizers
- Self-test
- Internet activity
- Grammar tutorial
- Interactive vocabulary games

Is *conflict* necessary?

Writing About the Big Question

In "The Gift of the Magi," Jim and Della want to exchange Christmas presents, but money is an issue. Use these sentence starters to develop your ideas about the Big Question.

When money is tight, it may be hard to show you **appreciate** others because _____. To resolve this problem, you might _____ or _____.

As You Read Think about the similarities in the ways that Della and Jim try to overcome their Christmastime conflict.

Vocabulary

Read each word and its definition. Decide whether you know the word well, know it a little bit, or do not know it at all. After you read, see how your knowledge of each word has increased.

- **instigates** (in´ stə gāts´) *v.* urges on; stirs up (p. 261) *When he is not watched carefully, he instigates trouble.* instigation *n.*

- **depreciate** (dē prē´ shē āt´) *v.* reduce in value (p. 262) *Items that do not depreciate are good investments.* depreciation *n.*

- **cascade** (kas kād´) *n.* a small steep waterfall; anything suggesting such a waterfall (p. 262) *Her hair flowed down her back like a cascade.* cascade *v.* cascading *v.*

- **faltered** (fôl´ tərd) *v.* acted hesitantly; showed uncertainty (p. 262) *The manager faltered in her decision to hire the inexperienced worker.* falter *v.*

- **prudence** (proō´ dəns) *n.* a sensible and careful attitude that makes you avoid some risks (p. 263) *Her prudence resulted in a substantial amount of savings.* prudent *adj.* imprudence *n.*

- **discreet** (di skrēt´) *adj.* careful about what one says or does (p. 265) *Being discreet is a good way to avoid hurting other people's feelings.* discretion *n.* indiscreet *adj.* indiscretion *adj.*

Word Power

The **Latin prefix *de-*** has various meanings, including "down."

In this story, Della's hair is said to **depreciate** a queen's treasures. Her hair is so lovely that, by comparison, it brings down the price and value of jewels.

Meet
O. Henry
(1862–1910)

Author of
The Gift of the Magi

William Sydney Porter, better known as O. Henry, dropped out of school at sixteen to work in his uncle's drugstore. In 1882, he left his home in North Carolina to seek his fortune in Texas. He worked on a ranch, then at a bank, and eventually started writing sketches. He became a reporter, columnist, and cartoonist for the *Houston Post*.

Writing Stories in Prison In 1896, Porter was jailed for his involvement in a bank scandal. While in prison, he began writing stories. When he was released, Porter changed his name to O. Henry, moved to New York City, and developed into one of America's most celebrated writers of short fiction.

Did You Know?
Since 1919, the O. Henry Awards for short fiction have been given to the best short stories written each year.

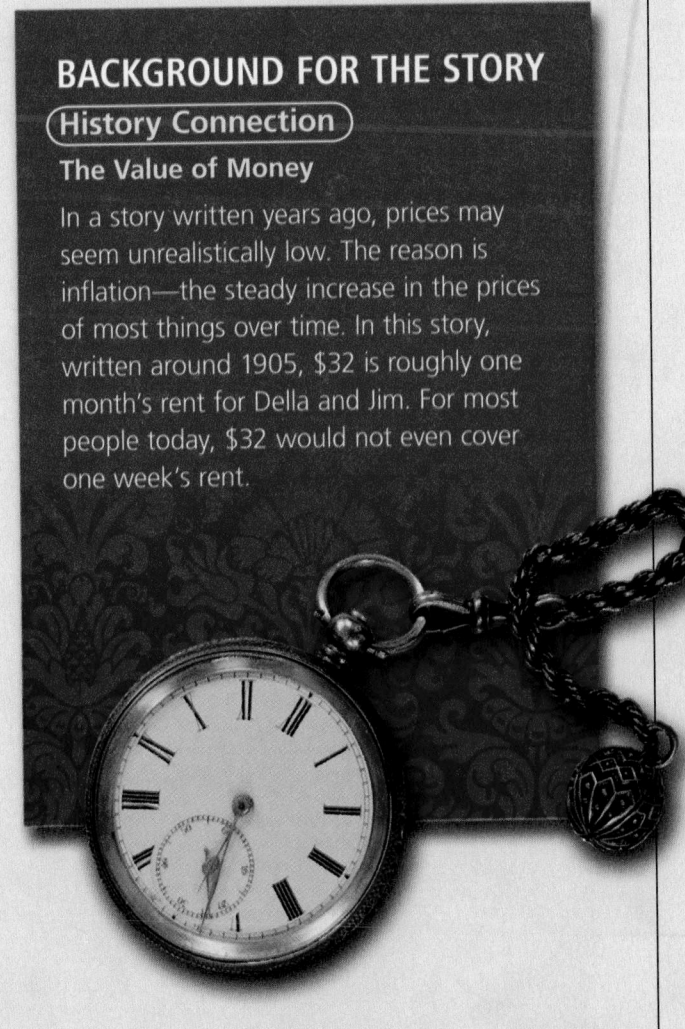

BACKGROUND FOR THE STORY
History Connection
The Value of Money

In a story written years ago, prices may seem unrealistically low. The reason is inflation—the steady increase in the prices of most things over time. In this story, written around 1905, $32 is roughly one month's rent for Della and Jim. For most people today, $32 would not even cover one week's rent.

The Gift of the Magi

℘ O. HENRY ℘

One dollar and eighty-seven cents. That was all. And sixty cents of it was in pennies. Pennies saved one and two at a time by bulldozing the grocer and the vegetable man and the butcher until one's cheeks burned with the silent imputation of parsimony[1] that such close dealing implied. Three times Della counted it. One dollar and eighty-seven cents. And the next day would be Christmas.

There was clearly nothing to do but flop down on the shabby little couch and howl. So Della did it. Which instigates the moral reflection that life is made up of sobs, sniffles, and smiles, with sniffles predominating.

While the mistress of the home is gradually subsiding from the first stage to the second, take a look at the home. A furnished flat at $8 per week. It did not exactly beggar description,[2] but it certainly had that word on the lookout for the mendicancy squad.[3]

In the vestibule below was a letter-box into which no letter would go, and an electric button from which no mortal finger could coax a ring. Also appertaining thereunto was a card bearing the name "Mr. James Dillingham Young."

The "Dillingham" had been flung to the breeze during a former period of prosperity when its possessor was being paid $30 per week. Now, when the income was shrunk to $20, the letters of "Dillingham" looked blurred, as though they were thinking seriously of contracting to a modest and unassuming D. But whenever Mr. James Dillingham Young came home and reached his flat above he was called "Jim" and greatly hugged by Mrs. James Dillingham Young, already introduced to you as Della. Which is all very good.

Della finished her cry and attended to her cheeks with the powder rag. She stood by the window and looked out dully at a gray cat walking a gray fence in a gray backyard. Tomorrow would be Christmas Day, and she had only $1.87 with which to buy

---

1. **imputation** (im´ pyoo tā´ shən) **of parsimony** (pär´ sə mō´ nē) accusation of stinginess.
2. **beggar description** make description seem inadequate or useless.
3. **it certainly . . . mendicancy** (men´ di kən´ sē) **squad** it would have been noticed by the police who arrest beggars.

Vocabulary
instigates (in´ stə gāts´)
v. urges on; stirs up

Reading Skill
Make Inferences Based on the textual evidence in this paragraph, what complex inference can you make about the kind of person Jim would like to be?

Reading Check

How much money does Della have to buy a present for Jim?

▲ **Critical Viewing**
How do you think Della felt in a street like this one as she approached Madame Sofronie's shop? **[Analyze]**

Vocabulary
depreciate (dē prē´ shē āt´) *v.* reduce in value

cascade (kas kād´) *n.* a small steep waterfall; anything suggesting such a waterfall

faltered (fôl´ tərd) *v.* acted hesitantly; showed uncertainty

Jim a present. She had been saving every penny she could for months, with this result. Twenty dollars a week doesn't go far. Expenses had been greater than she had calculated. They always are. Only $1.87 to buy a present for Jim. Her Jim. Many a happy hour she had spent planning for something nice for him. Something fine and rare and sterling—something just a little bit near to being worthy of the honor of being owned by Jim.

There was a pier glass between the windows of the room. Perhaps you have seen a pier glass in an $8 flat. A very thin and very agile person may, by observing his reflection in a rapid sequence of longitudinal strips, obtain a fairly accurate conception of his looks. Della, being slender, had mastered the art.

Suddenly she whirled from the window and stood before the glass. Her eyes were shining brilliantly, but her face had lost its color within twenty seconds. Rapidly she pulled down her hair and let it fall to its full length.

Now, there were two possessions of the James Dillingham Youngs in which they both took a mighty pride. One was Jim's gold watch that had been his father's and his grandfather's. The other was Della's hair. Had the Queen of Sheba lived in the flat across the airshaft, Della would have let her hair hang out the window some day to dry just to depreciate Her Majesty's jewels and gifts. Had King Solomon been the janitor, with all his treasures piled up in the basement, Jim would have pulled out his watch every time he passed, just to see him pluck at his beard from envy.

So now Della's beautiful hair fell about her rippling and shining like a cascade of brown waters. It reached below her knee and made itself almost a garment for her. And then she did it up again nervously and quickly. Once she faltered for a minute and stood still while a tear or two splashed on the worn red carpet.

On went her old brown jacket; on went her old brown hat. With a whirl of skirts and with the brilliant sparkle still in her eyes, she fluttered out the door and down the stairs to the street.

Where she stopped the sign read: "Mme. Sofronie. Hair Goods of All Kinds." One flight up Della ran, and collected herself, panting. Madame, large, too white, chilly, hardly looked the "Sofronie."

"Will you buy my hair?" asked Della.

"I buy hair," said Madame. "Take yer hat off and let's have a sight at the looks of it."

Down rippled the brown cascade.

"Twenty dollars," said Madame, lifting the mass with a practiced hand.

"Give it to me quick," said Della.

Oh, and the next two hours tripped by on rosy wings. Forget the hashed metaphor. She was ransacking the stores for Jim's present.

She found it at last. It surely had been made for Jim and no one else. There was no other like it in any of the stores, and she had turned all of them inside out. It was a platinum fob chain simple and chaste in design, properly proclaiming its value by substance alone and not by meretricious ornamentation—as all good things should do. It was even worthy of The Watch. As soon as she saw it she knew that it must be Jim's. It was like him. Quietness and value—the description applied to both. Twenty-one dollars they took from her for it, and she hurried home with the 87 cents. With that chain on his watch Jim might be properly anxious about the time in any company. Grand as the watch was he sometimes looked at it on the sly on account of the old leather strap that he used in place of a chain. •

When Della reached home her intoxication gave way a little to prudence and reason. She got out her curling irons and lighted the gas and went to work repairing the ravages made by generosity added to love. Which is always a tremendous task, dear friends—a mammoth task.

Within forty minutes her head was covered with tiny, close-lying curls that made her look wonderfully like a truant schoolboy. She looked at her reflection in the mirror long, carefully, and critically.

Cultural Connection

Watch Fob Chain

A fob chain is central to the plot of "The Gift of the Magi." The word *fob* probably entered the English language from the German dialect word *fuppe*, meaning "pocket." Before the wristwatch became common, a man would carry a pocket watch that fit in a special vest pocket. To keep the watch from falling or becoming lost, it was fastened to the vest by means of a strap or chain (sometimes with an ornament, or a fob, at the end) that was attached to a pin with a locking clasp, making it secure. Sometimes, as pictured here, a chain's finely detailed metalwork elevated the piece to a work of art.

Connect to the Literature

A pocket watch was often handed down from father to son, as was Jim Young's in O. Henry's story. Why might this fact alone make a fob chain and watch precious to its owner despite its modest cash value?

Vocabulary
prudence (prōō´ dəns)
n. a sensible and careful attitude that makes you avoid some risks

Reading Check

What does Della sell for twenty dollars?

"If Jim doesn't kill me," she said to herself, "before he takes a second look at me, he'll say I look like a Coney Island[4] chorus girl. But what could I do—oh! what could I do with a dollar and eighty-seven cents?"

At 7 o'clock the coffee was made and the frying-pan was on the back of the stove hot and ready to cook the chops.

Jim was never late. Della doubled the fob chain in her hand and sat on the corner of the table near the door that he always entered. Then she heard his step on the stair away down on the first flight, and she turned white for just a moment. She had a habit of saying little silent prayers about the simplest everyday things, and now she whispered: "Please God, make him think I am still pretty."

The door opened and Jim stepped in and closed it. He looked thin and very serious. Poor fellow, he was only twenty-two—and to be burdened with a family! He needed a new overcoat and he was without gloves.

Jim stopped inside the door, as immovable as a setter at the scent of quail. His eyes were fixed upon Della, and there was an expression in them that she could not read, and it terrified her. It was not anger, nor surprise, nor disapproval, nor horror, nor any of the sentiments that she had been prepared for. He simply stared at her fixedly with that peculiar expression on his face.

Della wriggled off the table and went for him.

"Jim, darling," she cried, "don't look at me that way. I had my hair cut off and sold it because I couldn't have lived through Christmas without giving you a present. It'll grow out again—you won't mind, will you? I just had to do it. My hair grows awfully fast. Say 'Merry Christmas!' Jim, and let's be happy. You don't know what a nice—what a beautiful, nice gift I've got for you."

"You've cut off your hair?" asked Jim, laboriously, as if he had not arrived at that patent fact yet even after the hardest mental labor.

"Cut it off and sold it," said Della. "Don't you like me just as well, anyhow? I'm me without my hair, ain't I?"

Jim looked about the room curiously.

"You say your hair is gone?" he said, with an air almost of idiocy.

> "...I couldn't have lived through Christmas without giving you a present."

---

4. **Coney** (kō´ nē) **Island** beach and amusement park in Brooklyn, New York.

"You needn't look for it," said Della. "It's sold, I tell you—sold and gone, too. It's Christmas Eve, boy. Be good to me, for it went for you. Maybe the hairs of my head were numbered," she went on with a sudden serious sweetness, "but nobody could ever count my love for you. Shall I put the chops on, Jim?"

Out of his trance Jim seemed quickly to wake. He enfolded his Della. For ten seconds let us regard with discreet scrutiny some inconsequential object in the other direction. Eight dollars a week or a million a year—what is the difference? A mathematician or a wit would give you the wrong answer. The Magi brought valuable gifts, but that was not among them. This dark assertion will be illuminated later on.

Jim drew a package from his overcoat pocket and threw it upon the table.

"Don't make any mistake, Dell," he said, "about me. I don't think there's anything in the way of a haircut or a shave or a shampoo that could make me like my girl any less. But if you'll unwrap that package you may see why you had me going a while at first."

White fingers and nimble tore at the string and paper. And then an ecstatic scream of joy; and then, alas! a quick feminine change to hysterical tears and wails, necessitating the immediate employment of all the comforting powers of the lord of the flat.

For there lay The Combs—the set of combs, side and back, that Della had worshipped for long in a Broadway window. Beautiful combs, pure tortoise shell, with jeweled rims—just the shade to wear in the beautiful vanished hair. They were expensive combs, she knew, and her heart had simply craved and yearned over them without the least hope of possession. And now, they were hers, but the tresses that should have adorned the coveted adornments were gone.

But she hugged them to her bosom, and at length she was able to look up with dim eyes and a smile and say: "My hair grows so fast, Jim!"

And then Della leaped up like a little singed cat and cried, "Oh, oh!"

Jim had not yet seen his beautiful present. She held it out to him eagerly upon her open palm. The dull precious metal seemed to flash with a reflection of her bright and ardent spirit.

Vocabulary
discreet (di skrēt´) *adj.* careful about what one says or does

Literary Analysis
Irony What role does irony play in the situation described here?

Reading Check

How does Jim react to Della's newly cut hair?

Literary Analysis
Irony
Explain why the ending is a surprise to both the characters and the reader.

"Isn't it a dandy, Jim? I hunted all over town to find it. You'll have to look at the time a hundred times a day now. Give me your watch. I want to see how it looks on it."

Instead of obeying, Jim tumbled down on the couch and put his hands under the back of his head and smiled.

"Dell," said he, "let's put our Christmas presents away and keep 'em a while. They're too nice to use just at present. I sold the watch to get the money to buy your combs. And now suppose you put the chops on."

The Magi, as you know, were wise men—wonderfully wise men— who brought gifts to the Babe in the manger. They invented the art of giving Christmas presents. Being wise, their gifts were no doubt wise ones, possibly bearing the privilege of exchange in case of duplication. And here I have lamely related to you the uneventful chronicle of two foolish children in a flat who most unwisely sacrificed for each other the greatest treasures of their house. But in a last word to the wise of these days let it be said that of all who give gifts these two were the wisest. Of all who give and receive gifts, such as they are wisest. Everywhere they are wisest. They are the magi.

Critical Thinking

1. **Respond:** If you were Jim or Della, how would you feel about the gift you received? Explain your response.

2. **(a)** What does Della do to get money for Jim's present?
   (b) Make Inferences: What does her action suggest about her character?

Support your responses with evidence from the text.

3. **(a)** How does Jim react when he first sees that Della has cut her hair? **(b) Analyze:** Why does Della misunderstand Jim's reaction?

4. **Draw Conclusions:** O. Henry says of these "two foolish children" that they were "the wisest." How do you think he would define wisdom? Explain your response.

Is conflict necessary?
(a) What internal conflict occurs for both Jim and Della? **(b)** Do you think that this is a necessary conflict? Explain.

Literary Analysis: Irony

1. (a) Identify **irony** in the story by using a chart like the one shown. In the first box, note the outcome that Jim and Della expect when they present their gifts to each other. In the second box, describe what actually happens.

What Characters Expect	→	What Actually Happens

(b) Explain the role of irony in this literary work.

2. (a) Which details in the story make its surprise ending seem like a logical outcome of events? **(b)** Why do you think surprise endings are such a popular device in literature and movies?

Reading Skill: Make Inferences

3. (a) What inferences do you think O. Henry intended readers to make about the characters of Jim and Della? **(b)** What evidence in the text supports your inferences?

4. In what ways do your prior knowledge and experience of characters like Jim and Della help you **make complex inferences** about them? Use **evidence** from the text to support your understanding.

Vocabulary

Practice Explain why each statement below is true or false.

1. One who *instigates* conflict might be called a "problem-solver."

2. After six years of hard use, a car will *depreciate* in value.

3. Only a *discreet* person should be trusted with a secret.

4. It is a sign of *prudence* to drive a car before you have your license.

5. In a fireworks display, a shell might create a sparkling *cascade*.

6. The horse *faltered* in the home stretch and won as a result.

Word Power Use the context of the sentences and what you know about the **Latin prefix de-** to explain your answer to each question.

1. If you were to *depress* a friend, would he feel better?

2. What happens to food when people *devour* it?

Word Power

The **Latin prefix de-** has various meanings, including "down."

Apply It Explain how the prefix *de-* helps you determine the meanings of these words. Consult a dictionary if necessary.

debilitate
deacidify
declassify

Is *conflict* necessary?

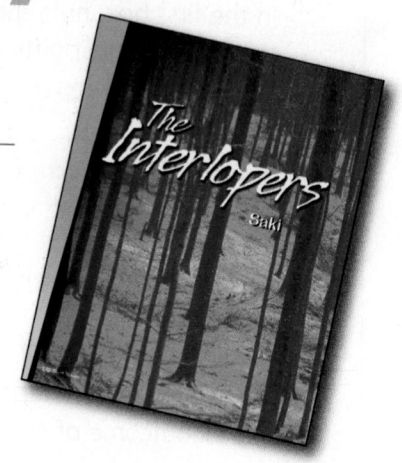

Writing About the Big Question

In "The Interlopers," men from feuding families face a situation that makes them rethink their hatred for each other. Use these sentence starters to develop your ideas about the Big Question.

In a longtime feud, the people involved may struggle to resolve their **issues amicably** because _____.

Those in **competition** often **antagonize** each other because

_____.

As You Read Consider the men's reasons for continuing the feud and their reasons for ending it.

Vocabulary

Read each word and its definition. Decide whether you know the word well, know it a little bit, or do not know it at all. After you read, see how your knowledge of each word has increased.

- **precipitous** (prē sip´ ə təs) *adj.* steep; sheer (p. 272) *At the edge of the cliff, you will face a <u>precipitous</u> drop. precipice n.*

- **acquiesced** (ak´ wē est´) *v.* agreed quietly without protest or enthusiasm (p. 272) *The boy sullenly <u>acquiesced</u> to the demand that he take out the garbage. acquiescence n.*

- **feud** (fyo͞od) *n.* a long and violent quarrel, especially between clans or families, often characterized by killing (p. 272) *The <u>feud</u> between the Hatfields and the McCoys lasted for almost 30 years. feud v.*

- **disputed** (di spyo͞ot´ id) *adj.* contested; argued about (p. 272) *The <u>disputed</u> border between the yards had been a source of conflict for many years. dispute n. dispute v.*

- **condolences** (kən dō´ lən səz) *n.* expressions of sympathy with another in grief (p. 274) *The mourners shared their <u>condolences</u>.*

- **interlopers** (in´ tər lō´ pərz) *n.* people who intrude or meddle in other peoples' business or lives (p. 275) *Even though we had been invited to the party, we felt like unwelcome <u>interlopers</u>.*

Word Power

The **Latin prefix *inter-*** means "between."

This is the story of **interlopers**, describing those who leap or intrude into each other's affairs and find themselves unwelcome.

Meet
Saki (1870–1916)

Author of
The Interlopers

Saki is the pen name of the British writer H. H. Munro. Munro was born in Burma and sent at age two to live in England. As a young adult, he returned to Burma to serve in the police force. However, poor health forced him to return to England, where he began work as a journalist.

Talent and Tragedy In 1904, Munro published a collection of short stories entitled *Reginald*. He went on to write several more collections of stories and two novels. The abrupt ending of Saki's own life was as shocking as one of his plot twists: When World War I broke out, he enlisted in the British army and was killed fighting in France.

BACKGROUND FOR THE STORY

Social Studies Connection

Family Feuds

A feud is a bitter, prolonged fight, typically between families or clans, that may continue for years or even generations. The brutality of a feud can make for gripping drama, as it does in "The Interlopers."

Did You Know?
Munro's pen name is thought to have been taken from a character in *The Rubaiyat*, by Persian poet Omar Khayyam.

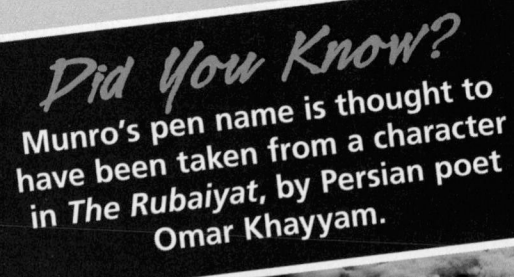

The Interlopers

Saki

*I*n a forest of mixed growth somewhere on the eastern spurs of the Carpathians,[1] a man stood one winter night watching and listening, as though he waited for some beast of the woods to come within the range of his vision, and, later, of his rifle. But the game for whose presence he kept so keen an outlook was none that figured in the sportsman's calendar as lawful and proper for the chase: Ulrich von Gradwitz (ool rik fôn gräd´ vitz) patrolled the dark forest in quest of a human enemy.

---

1. Carpathians (kär pā´ thē ənz) mountains in central Europe.

Reading Check
Where does the story take place?

Vocabulary

precipitous (prē´ sip ə təs) *adj.* steep; sheer

acquiesced (ak´ wē est´) *v.* agreed quietly without protest or enthusiasm

feud (fyo͞od) *n.* a long and violent quarrel, especially between clans or families

disputed (di spyo͞ot´ əd) *adj.* contested; argued about

Reading Skill

Make Inferences What complex inferences does the textual evidence in this paragraph help you to make about these characters?

Reading Skill

Make Inferences How does your knowledge of feuds help you make an inference about the reason Ulrich hopes to meet Znaeym?

The forest lands of Gradwitz were of wide extent and well stocked with game; the narrow strip of precipitous woodland that lay on its outskirt was not remarkable for the game it harbored or the shooting it afforded, but it was the most jealously guarded of all its owner's territorial possessions. A famous lawsuit, in the days of his grandfather, had wrested it from the illegal possession of a neighboring family of petty landowners; the dispossessed party had never acquiesced in the judgment of the Courts, and a long series of poaching affrays[2] and similar scandals had embittered the relationships between the families for three generations. The neighbor feud had grown into a personal one since Ulrich had come to be head of his family; if there was a man in the world whom he detested and wished ill to it was Georg Znaeym (gà´ ôrg znä´ im), the inheritor of the quarrel and the tireless game-snatcher and raider of the disputed border-forest. The feud might, perhaps, have died down or been compromised if the personal ill will of the two men had not stood in the way; as boys they had thirsted for one another's blood, as men each prayed that misfortune might fall on the other, and this wind-scourged winter night Ulrich had banded together his foresters to watch the dark forest, not in quest of four-footed quarry, but to keep a lookout for the prowling

thieves whom he suspected of being afoot from across the land boundary. The roebuck which usually kept in the sheltered hollows during a storm wind, were running like driven things tonight, and there was movement and unrest among the creatures that were wont to sleep through the dark hours. Assuredly there was a disturbing element in the forest, and Ulrich could guess the quarter from whence it came.

He strayed away by himself from the watchers whom he had placed in ambush on the crest of the hill, and wandered far down the steep slopes amid the wild tangle of undergrowth, peering through the tree trunks and listening through the whistling and skirling of the wind and the restless beating of the branches for

---

2. **poaching** (pōch´ iŋ) **affrays** (ə fràz´) disputes about hunting on someone else's property.

sight or sound of the marauders. If only on this wild night, in this dark, lone spot, he might come across Georg Znaeym, man to man, with none to witness—that was the wish that was uppermost in his thoughts. And as he stepped round the trunk of a huge beech he came face to face with the man he sought.

The two enemies stood glaring at one another for a long silent moment. Each had a rifle in his hand, each had hate in his heart and murder uppermost in his mind. The chance had come to give full play to the passions of a lifetime. But a man who has been brought up under the code of a restraining civilization cannot easily nerve himself to shoot down his neighbor in cold blood and

without word spoken, except for an offense against his hearth and honor. And before the moment of hesitation had given way to action a deed of Nature's own violence overwhelmed them both. A fierce shriek of the storm had been answered by a splitting crash over their heads, and ere they could leap aside a mass of falling beech tree had thundered down on them. Ulrich von Gradwitz found himself stretched on the ground, one arm numb beneath him and the other held almost as helplessly in a tight tangle of forked branches, while both legs were pinned beneath the fallen mass.

His heavy shooting-boots had saved his feet from being crushed to pieces, but if his fractures were not as serious as they might have been, at least it was evident that he could not move from his present position till someone came to release him. The descending twigs had slashed the skin of his face, and he had to wink away some drops of blood from his eyelashes before he could take in a general view of the disaster. At his side, so near that under ordinary circumstances he could almost have touched him, lay Georg Znaeym, alive and struggling, but obviously as helplessly pinioned down as himself. All round them lay a thick-strewn wreckage of splintered branches and broken twigs.

Relief at being alive and exasperation at his captive plight brought a strange medley of pious thank-offerings and sharp

*T*he two enemies stood glaring at one another for a long silent moment.

Literary Analysis
Irony Each character wishes harm to the other. What role does irony play in the author's description of how the wish is fulfilled?

What happens to the two men when the tree falls?

curses to Ulrich's lips. Georg, who was nearly blinded with the blood which trickled across his eyes, stopped his struggling for a moment to listen, and then gave a short, snarling laugh.

"So you're not killed, as you ought to be, but you're caught, anyway," he cried; "caught fast. Ho, what a jest, Ulrich von Gradwitz snared in his stolen forest. There's real justice for you!"

And he laughed again, mockingly and savagely.

"I'm caught in my own forest land," retorted Ulrich. "When my men come to release us you will wish, perhaps, that you were in a better plight than caught poaching on a neighbor's land, shame on you."

Georg was silent for a moment; then he answered quietly:

"Are you sure that your men will find much to release? I have men, too, in the forest tonight, close behind me, and *they* will be here first and do the releasing. When they drag me out from under these branches it won't need much clumsiness on their part to roll this mass of trunk right over on the top of you. Your men will find you dead under a fallen beech tree. For form's sake I shall send my condolences to your family."

"It is a useful hint," said Ulrich fiercely. "My men had orders to follow in ten minutes' time, seven of which must have gone by already, and when they get me out—I will remember the hint. Only as you will have met your death poaching on my lands I don't think I can decently send any message of condolence to your family."

"Good," snarled Georg, "good. We fight this quarrel out to the

Literary Analysis
Irony What role does irony play in the author's description of Georg's joy over catching Ulrich?

Vocabulary
condolences (kən dōˊ lən səz) *n.* expressions of sympathy with another in grief

death, you and I and our foresters, with no cursed interlopers to come between us. Death and damnation to you, Ulrich von Gradwitz."

"The same to you, Georg Znaeym, forest-thief, game-snatcher."

Both men spoke with the bitterness of possible defeat before them, for each knew that it might be long before his men would seek him out or find him; it was a bare matter of chance which party would arrive first on the scene.

Both had now given up the useless struggle to free themselves from the mass of wood that held them down; Ulrich limited his endeavors to an effort to bring his one partially free arm near enough to his outer coat pocket to draw out his wine flask. Even when he had accomplished that operation it was long before he could manage the unscrewing of the stopper or get any of the liquid down his throat. But what a heaven-sent draft it seemed! It was an open winter, and little snow had fallen as yet, hence the captives suffered less from the cold than might have been the case at that season of the year; nevertheless, the wine was warming and reviving to the wounded man, and he looked across with something like a throb of pity to where his enemy lay, just keeping the groans of pain and weariness from crossing his lips.

"Could you reach this flask if I threw it over to you?" asked Ulrich suddenly; "there is good wine in it, and one may as well be as comfortable as one can. Let us drink, even if tonight one of us dies."

▲ **Critical Viewing**
What are some dangers the characters might face in a setting like this one? **[Analyze]**

Vocabulary
interlopers (in´ tər lō´ pərz) *n.* people who intrude or meddle in other peoples' business or lives

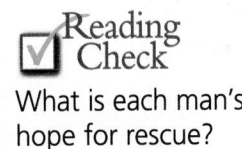
Reading Check

What is each man's hope for rescue?

The Interlopers **275**

"No, I can scarcely see anything; there is so much blood caked round my eyes," said Georg, "and in any case I don't drink wine with an enemy."

Ulrich was silent for a few minutes, and lay listening to the weary screeching of the wind. An idea was slowly forming and growing in his brain, an idea that gained strength every time that he looked across at the man who was fighting so grimly against pain and exhaustion. In the pain and languor that Ulrich himself was feeling the old fierce hatred seemed to be dying down.

"Neighbor," he said presently, "do as you please if your men come first. It was a fair compact. But as for me, I've changed my mind. If my men are the first to come you shall be the first to be helped, as though you were my guest. We have quarreled like devils all our lives over this stupid strip of forest, where the trees can't even stand upright in a breath of wind. Lying here tonight, thinking, I've come to think we've been rather fools; there are better things in life than getting the better of a boundary dispute. Neighbor, if you will help me to bury the old quarrel I—I will ask you to be my friend."

Reading Skill
Make Inferences What inference can you make about what Georg is considering during this long silence?

Georg Znaeym was silent for so long that Ulrich thought, perhaps, he had fainted with the pain of his injuries. Then he spoke slowly and in jerks.

"How the whole region would stare and gabble if we rode into the market square together. No one living can remember seeing a Znaeym and a von Gradwitz talking to one another in friendship. And what peace there would be among the forester folk if we ended our feud tonight. And if we choose to make peace among our people there is none other to interfere, no interlopers from outside . . . You would come and keep the Sylvester night beneath my roof, and I would come and feast on some high day at your castle . . . I would never fire a shot on your land, save when you invited me as a guest; and you should come and shoot

Literary Analysis
Irony What is surprising about this new meaning of interlopers?

with me down in the marshes where the wildfowl are. In all the countryside there are none that could hinder if we willed to make peace. I never thought to have wanted to do other than hate you all my life, but I think I have changed my mind about things too, this last half-hour. And you offered me your wine flask . . . Ulrich von Gradwitz, I will be your friend."

For a space both men were silent, turning over in their minds the wonderful changes that this dramatic reconciliation would bring about. In the cold, gloomy forest, with the wind tearing in fitful gusts through the naked branches and whistling round the tree trunks, they lay and waited for the help that would now bring release and succor to both parties. And each prayed a private prayer that his men might be the first to arrive, so that he might be the first to show honorable attention to the enemy that had become a friend. •

Presently, as the wind dropped for a moment, Ulrich broke silence.

"Let's shout for help," he said; "in this lull our voices may carry a little way."

"They won't carry far through the trees and undergrowth," said Georg, "but we can try. Together, then."

The two raised their voices in a prolonged hunting call.

"Together again," said Ulrich a few minutes later, after listening in vain for an answering halloo.

"I heard something that time, I think," said Ulrich.

"I heard nothing but the pestilential wind," said Georg hoarsely.

There was silence again for some minutes, and then Ulrich gave a joyful cry.

"I can see figures coming through the wood. They are following in the way I came down the hillside."

Both men raised their voices in as loud a shout as they could muster.

"They hear us! They've stopped. Now they see us. They're running down the hill toward us," cried Ulrich.

"How many of them are there?" asked Georg.

"I can't see distinctly," said Ulrich; "nine or ten."

"Then they are yours," said Georg; "I had only seven out with me."

Literary Analysis
Irony What role does irony play in the author's description of the two men's cooperation?

I n the cold, gloomy forest, with the wind tearing in fitful gusts through the naked branches and whistling round the tree trunks...

Reading Check

What do the men agree to do?

Literary Analysis
Irony In what way does the story's surprise ending make the title ironic?

"They are making all the speed they can, brave lads," said Ulrich gladly.

"Are they your men?" asked Georg. "Are they your men?" he repeated impatiently as Ulrich did not answer.

"No," said Ulrich with a laugh, the idiotic chattering laugh of a man unstrung with hideous fear.

"Who are they?" asked Georg quickly, straining his eyes to see what the other would gladly not have seen.

"*Wolves.*"

Critical Thinking

Support your responses with evidence from the text.

1. **Respond:** With whom did you sympathize: Ulrich, Georg, neither, or both? Explain your response.

2. **(a)** Whose family won possession of the disputed land in the lawsuit? **(b) Make Inferences:** Why does Georg not consider himself a poacher?

3. **(a)** In what condition does the fallen tree leave each man? **(b) Draw Conclusions:** Why do the men decide finally to end their feud?

4. **(a) Evaluate:** Considering the cause of their predicament, do you think the two men deserved their fate? Why or why not?
   (b) Discuss: Share your ideas with a partner and then explain how your answer has grown or changed.

Is conflict necessary?
(a) How long has the controversy between Ulrich and Georg been going on? **(b)** Why does it take special courage for Ulrich and Georg to consider the conflict no longer "necessary"?

Literary Analysis: Irony

1. (a) Identify **irony** in the story by using a chart like the one shown. In the first box, note the outcome that Ulrich and Georg expect when they first confront each other in the forest. In the second box, describe what actually happens.

What Characters Expect	What Actually Happens

(b) Explain the role of irony in this literary work.

2. (a) Which nuances, or subtle details, in "The Interlopers" make its surprise ending seem like a logical outcome of events?
(b) Is the ending certain, or is it ambiguous and open to many interpretations? Explain your response.

Reading Skill: Make Inferences

3. (a) What inferences do you think Saki intended readers to make about the characters of Ulrich and Georg? **(b)** What evidence in the text supports your inferences?

4. In what ways do your prior knowledge and experience of characters help you to **make complex inferences** about Ulrich and Georg? Use **evidence** from the text to support your understanding.

Vocabulary

Practice Explain why each statement is true or false.

1. A beach generally has a *precipitous* slope down to the water.

2. It is proper to express *condolences* to one who has suffered a loss.

3. *Interlopers* are people who are always welcome.

4. A *feud* between powerful families could endanger a community.

5. People involved in a *disputed* matter enjoy each other's company.

6. If protesters did not obey a curfew, they would have *acquiesced*.

Word Power Use the context of the sentences and what you know about the **Latin prefix *inter-*** to explain your answer to each question.

1. Does an *international* crisis affect more than one country?

2. Where is an *intertidal* zone located?

Word Power

The **Latin prefix *inter-*** means "between."

Apply It Explain how the prefix *inter-* helps you determine the meanings of these words. Consult a dictionary if necessary.

interaction
intermission
interstate

Integrated Language Skills

The Gift of the Magi • The Interlopers

Conventions: Irregular Verbs

Irregular verbs form their principal parts in a variety of ways.

Regular verbs form the present participle by adding *-ing* to the present form. They form the past and past participle by adding *-ed* to the present form. **Irregular verbs** also form the present participle by adding *-ing* to the present form. However, they form the past and past participle in a variety of ways. Here are a few of the most common examples:

Present	Past	Past Participle
be (am, is, are)	was, were	(has) been
buy	bought	(has) bought
choose	chose	(has) chosen
come	came	(has) come
give	gave	(has) given
go	went	(has) gone
have	had	(has) had
see	saw	(has) seen
sell	sold	(has) sold
speak	spoke	(has) spoken
take	took	(has) taken
write	wrote	(has) written

Practice A Use the correct form of each verb in parentheses.

1. O. Henry has (write) a great story.
2. Della (sell) her hair and (buy) Jim a watch fob.
3. Jim (choose) a set of combs for Della.
4. By the end, the husband and wife have (speak) of their love and have (see) its power.

Reading Application Find five irregular verbs that appear in "The Gift of the Magi." Write the principal parts of each.

Practice B Revise each sentence by correcting the mistakes in the principal parts of verbs.

1. In the forest, Ulrich speaked to himself.
2. Georg has chose to trespass on my land.
3. Suddenly, Ulrich seen Georg, rifle in hand.
4. What cause for hatred have these men gave?

Writing Application Rewrite the following sentence, replacing the underlined words with correct forms of these phrases: take cover, be afraid, speak quietly, write wills. *While they waited for the wolves, they became friends.*

PH GRAMMAR HANDBOOK Further instruction and practice are available in the *Prentice Hall Grammar Handbook*.

Writing

Both of these selections present conflicts that have ironic endings. Write a brief **news report** about the experiences characters faced in either story.

- First, gather facts by asking the questions *Who? What? Where? When? Why?* and *How?* Decide which facts to present in your lead. Write an opening paragraph or lead that summarizes events and grabs the reader's interest.
- Integrate characters' quotations into the report. Be sure to show how the quotes support your ideas.
- Read your lead paragraph to a classmate. Revise or eliminate any part that is not clear or that does not make your reader curious.
- Add several more paragraphs, providing details that tell the rest of the story.

Grammar Application Make sure to form the principal parts of irregular verbs correctly.

Writing Workshop: *Work in Progress*

Prewriting for Short Story Using the Character Profile from your portfolio, write a letter from your character to a best friend, telling about an important event. Describe the event in detail and show why it is important in the character's life. Save this letter in your portfolio.

Listening and Speaking

Participate productively with a small team to present a **debate.**

- If you read "The Gift of the Magi," debate whether sacrifice is the best expression of love.
- If you read "The Interlopers," debate which character is entitled to the disputed land.

Follow these steps to complete the assignment:

- With your team, **marshal evidence** that supports a clear thesis statement and related claims. Look for specific ways in which the story supports your argument. Find events, quotations from dialogue, and other textual evidence. Do additional research to find outside evidence, such as statistics or quotations from experts, to back up your ideas.
- **Anticipate opposing arguments** by considering what the other side may say. Be ready with a response and evidence to support it.
- **Evaluate the effectiveness** of each speaker's main and supporting ideas by considering how they affected you. As a class, decide which team, as a whole, was more persuasive.

 Focus on the TEKS

Research
(23)(A) Marshal evidence in support of a clear thesis statement and related claims.
Listening and Speaking
(24)(C) Evaluate the effectiveness of a speaker's main and supporting ideas.

Use this prewriting activity to prepare for the **Writing Workshop** on page 306.

TEXAS
PHLitOnline
www.PHLitOnline.com
- Interactive graphic organizers
- Grammar tutorial
- Interactive journals

Strategy for Success

Make Inferences

Comprehension Skills
RC-9(B) Make complex inferences about text.

The reading sections of Texas standardized tests ask you to make inferences about what you read. Authors may leave some concepts in a text unstated. To help you understand what is left unsaid, you can use textual evidence to make complex inferences about text on standardized tests.

To use this strategy on standardized tests, look for details and clues in the text. For example, an author may not state that a character feels cheerful, but may instead describe a character's wide smile. Considering how situations or characters are similar to those you have experienced can help you make inferences. The following examples show how you can make inferences on standardized tests.

Use Character Clues

Examine characters' actions to infer what they are feeling or thinking. Textual evidence like this provides strong support for inferences.

1　Mrs. Ng's porcelain vase slipped through Monica's fingers and smashed on the parquet floor. Monica bent down, both to pick up the pieces and to avoid looking into Mrs. Ng's eyes.

　1 Monica's attitude could best be described as —
　　A embarrassed
　　B carefree
　　C disrespectful
　　D infuriated

The reader can reasonably infer that Monica does not want to meet Mrs. Ng's eyes because she is embarrassed about dropping Mrs. Ng's vase. **B, C,** and **D** are not supported by the text. **A** is correct.

Use Your Experience

You can infer the unstated meaning of a situation if it reminds you of something you have seen or experienced.

1　We each had a bucket to fill with fresh-picked blueberries. That night, when I gave Dad my half-empty bucket, he made me stick out my tongue. "Aha!" he said.

　2 Why does the narrator's father say "Aha!" when he sees the tongue?
　　F He thinks the narrator has not picked many blueberries.
　　G He knows the narrator has been eating blueberries.
　　H He knows the narrator has spilled the bucket of berries.
　　J He wants to eat berries from the narrator's bucket.

F, H, and **J** are not supported by the details in the passage. You can infer that the father sees that the narrator's tongue has turned blue from eating blueberries, so **G** is correct.

Texas Test Practice

Read this selection. Then answer the questions that follow it.

The Lawn Mower

1   Marco hated mowing the lawn on Saturday mornings. Repeatedly turning the mower's starter, he reflected that having a malfunctioning lawn mower was bad enough without having to deal with Mr. Boone.

2   Mr. Boone often passed by on his morning walk. "Hi, Marco!" he would say brightly. "Having trouble with the mower?" Marco would shrug and wrestle with the starter. Chatting would not get the grass cut faster.

3   One Saturday, as dark clouds formed on the horizon, Marco was trying unsuccessfully to fix the mower before the storm began. Mr. Boone rounded the corner as usual. "Hi, Marco!" he said cheerily. "Still having trouble with your mower?"

4   Marco threw down his screwdriver. Who would stop to chat before a storm? "I can't talk!" he called. "I'll never start the mower in time!"

5   Mr. Boone sighed and walked up the driveway. "Marco," he said, "I'm a mechanic, and I've fixed lots of these. Will you let me look at it?"

6   Sheepishly, Marco stepped back and watched Mr. Boone examine the mower. Mr. Boone said, "The connection is loose. I'll tighten it—give it a try." Marco turned the starter key, and the mower sprang to life.

7   "Thanks, Mr. Boone!" Marco called over the noise.

---

1 Marco shrugs in answer to Mr. Boone's question because he —

   A enjoys mowing the lawn
   B is not interested in talking
   C is too tired to talk
   D does not know the answer

2 Based on paragraph 4, the reader can infer that Marco feels —

   F happy to see Mr. Boone
   G frightened of the storm
   H irritated by Mr. Boone
   J grateful for help

3 Mr. Boone asks about the mower mainly because —

   A he thinks he can fix it
   B he owns a similar mower
   C he wants to distract Marco
   D he admires Marco's lawn

4 Marco watches "sheepishly" because —

   F he has to become a mechanic
   G he is in a hurry to mow
   H he has misjudged Mr. Boone
   J he feels overwhelmed

Informational Texts

Procedural Texts

Consumer Safety Guide
Beach Safety Guide

Technical Instructions
Rock Climbing Equipment and Techniques

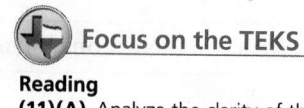

Focus on the TEKS

Reading
(11)(A) Analyze the clarity of the objectives of procedural texts.

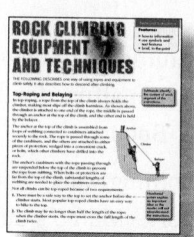

Reading Skills: Analyze Procedural Texts

The objectives, or goals, of a procedural text are to provide instructions and give important information to help people perform specific tasks. Procedural texts should be clear and functional. To **analyze the clarity of the objectives of a procedural text,** look at how the text identifies the steps in a process and the order in which those steps should be completed. Also consider procedural texts' features, such as subheads and illustrations, which may help make the information presented in instructions clear to readers. Finally, ask yourself to identify the objective, or goal, of the procedural text. If the objective is clear to you, consider how the text and the features support your understanding. If the objective is not clear, consider how the text and features might be improved.

As You Read Use a chart like the one below to analyze how text features help to clarify each text's objectives. Then, write two paragraphs, each analyzing the clarity of the objectives of one of the procedural texts.

Text Features	Description	Clarifies objectives by...
Subheads	Boldfaced words that identify the main idea of each section	
Highlighted text	Boldfaced, italicized, uppercase, or colored words that emphasize important information	
Charts, graphs, maps	Graphic organizers that present information in a clear, easy-to-understand form	
Illustrations and diagrams	Pictures or graphic organizers that show ideas described in the text	
Captions	Brief information that describes illustrations, diagrams, or other graphic organizers	

Features:

- essential information
- symbols and text features
- brief sentences

BEACH SAFETY GUIDE
HIGH SURF SIGN

WARNING

HIGH SURF
CAN CAUSE SERIOUS
INJURIES OR DROWNING
IF IN DOUBT, DON'T GO OUT

The word *warning* is in bold black lettering on an orange background. **How does this text feature help to clarify the objective of this procedural text?**

A simple picture clearly illustrates the danger.

WARNING LEVEL: *DANGEROUS*...a potential for loss of *life* or *limb* exists.

CONDITION: Large powerful waves are generated by winds and storms at sea, sometimes thousands of miles from the Hawaiian Islands. Seasonal high surf occurs on all shores of Oahu. Typically, shorelines facing North, East and West receive high surf during winter months. Shores facing Southeast and Southwest receive high surf during summer months. Surf on the North shore may reach heights of twenty-five feet plus—on the West shore, *fifteen* feet plus!

INSTRUCTIONS: If you're uncertain of your abilities, don't go into the ocean during high surf; heed all posted high surf warnings!

The uppercase red letters in each heading make it clear to readers that they are reading important information.

BEACH SAFETY GUIDE
STRONG CURRENT SIGN

> **WARNING**
>
> **STRONG CURRENT**
>
> **YOU COULD BE SWEPT AWAY FROM SHORE AND COULD DROWN**
>
> **IF IN DOUBT, DON'T GO OUT**

A specific warning message is stated briefly and clearly. The most important words are printed in the largest letters.

WARNING LEVEL: *DANGEROUS...a potential for loss of life or limb exists.*

CONDITION: These are swift moving channels of water against which it is difficult to swim. Strong currents frequently accompany high surf and rapid tide changes and can be recognized as a turbulent channel of water between areas where waves are breaking.

The text is divided by subheads. **How do these bold red subheads help clarify the objectives of this text?**

INSTRUCTIONS: When caught in a strong current—Try to keep a level head. Don't panic! Wave one or both hands in the air, and scream or call for help. Swim diagonally to the current, not against it.

OCEAN SAFETY TIPS:

The tips reinforce warnings and instructions and clear up any misunderstandings readers might have.

- Swim in Lifeguarded Areas.
- Never Swim Alone.
- Don't Dive Into Unknown Water or Into Shallow Breaking Waves.
- Ask a Lifeguard About <u>Beach and Surf Conditions</u> Before Swimming.
- If You Are Unable to Swim Out of a Strong Current, Signal for Help.
- Rely on Your Swimming Ability Rather Than a Flotation Device.
- Look For, Read and Obey All <u>Beach Safety Signs and Symbols</u>.
- If In Doubt, Just Stay Out!

Is conflict necessary?

How do the signs and instructions help swimmers distiguish between safe and dangerous swimming conditions?

ROCK CLIMBING EQUIPMENT AND TECHNIQUES

Technical Instructions

Features:
- how-to information
- use symbols and text features
- brief, to-the-point

THE FOLLOWING DESCRIBES one way of using ropes and equipment to climb safely. It also describes how to descend after climbing.

Top-Roping and Belaying

Subheads identify the content of each segment of the instructions.

In top-roping, a rope from the top of the climb always holds the climber, making most slips off the climb harmless. As shown below, the climber is attached to one end of the rope, the middle is passed through an anchor at the top of the climb, and the other end is held by the belayer.

The anchor at the top of the climb is assembled from loops of webbing connected to carabiners attached securely to the rock. The rope is passed through some of the carabiners, and the others are attached to either pieces of protection, wedged into a convenient crack, or bolts, which other climbers have drilled into the rock.

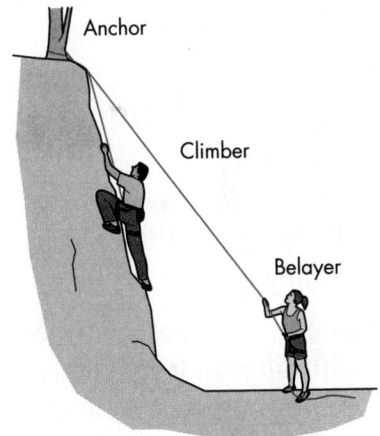

Anchor

Climber

Belayer

The anchor's carabiners with the rope passing through are suspended below the top of the climb to prevent the rope from rubbing. When bolts or protection are far from the top of the climb, substantial lengths of webbing are needed to place the carabiners correctly.

Not all climbs can be top-roped because of two requirements:

1. There must be a safe way to the top to set the anchor before the climber starts. Most popular top-roped climbs have an easy way to hike to the top.

2. The climb may be no longer than half the length of the rope; when the climber starts, the rope must cross the full length of the climb twice.

Numbered points explain an important idea so the reader will not misunderstand the instructions.

The belayer stops the rope with a belay device attached to his harness if the climber slips. The belay device makes it easy to apply enough friction to stop a falling climber. If there is some danger of the belayer being lifted into the air, he can be anchored down.

The belayer must keep the slack in the rope to a minimum since when a climber slips, any slack must be taken up before the rope can stop the fall. To take up this slack, the belayer pulls the rope downward as the climber climbs. While doing this, the belayer must never release the rope fully to ensure the climber could never fall far.

Rappeling

Rappeling is a scheme for lowering yourself with the rope. As shown above, the center of the rope is passed through an anchor at the top of the climb. The person descending wears a harness and attaches himself to the rope with a belay device, which he uses to control his descent.

Unlike climbing, it is best to be nearly horizontal while rappeling. In this position, the body is pointing more directly at the rock, giving the feet better friction and leading to more control.

Starting a rappel is the most difficult part. It is very disconcerting to switch from standing to being supported completely by the rope. Moreover, it is necessary to get below the anchor before

the rope can help. If the anchor is below the top of the climb, climbing down is necessary.

Once everybody has descended, the rope is recovered by pulling it through the anchor. The anchor cannot be recovered, but this is not usually a problem. In many cases, other climbers have placed a permanent anchor at the top, often a pair of bolts drilled into the rock connected to a ring with some chains. Another possibility is to use the base of a tree as an anchor. Since the rope is under little tension when it is pulled through the anchor, this abrades the rope and tree only slightly, and can be done occasionally.

A single rope can only be used to descend half a rope-length, but two ropes can be tied together to rappel a full rope-length. This is useful, for example, when descending a multi-pitch lead climb via the same route used for the ascent. The belay stations, usually spaced a full rope-length, can be used as rappel anchors. Three or more ropes cannot be used to rappel in this manner, since doing so would require rappeling past a knot and pulling a knot through the anchor, which are generally impossible.

Anchor

The instructions include illustrations and labels. **How do these text features help to clarify the objectives of this procedural text?**

Instructions outline the sequence of steps necessary to complete the task safely.

Is conflict necessary?
THE BIG ?
Climbers face a conflict between enjoying a climb and risking their lives. How do the technical instructions give climbers options for reducing risks?

Comparing Informational Texts

(a) Compare and contrast the way the consumer safety guide and the technical instructions use text features to clarify their **objectives.**

(b) Analyze: Compare the clarity of the objectives of the procedural texts. Which text has clearer objectives? Provide evidence from the texts to support your response.

 **College Readiness** | Timed Writing

Write a Speech

Format and Audience
The prompt directs you to write a brief speech for your community. Your remarks should be several paragraphs long and should address the concerns of your audience.

People are often injured when they take unintentional risks. Write a brief speech for your community, urging people to observe safety signs and to follow equipment instructions exactly. Use information in the signs and technical instructions to support your ideas. (25 minutes)

Academic Vocabulary
When you *support* your ideas, you use details and examples to show that your ideas are reasonable and correct.

 5-Minute Planner

Complete these steps before you begin to write:

1. Read the prompt carefully and completely. Look for key words and instructions that tell what you should include in your speech.

2. Review the signs and technical instructions. Consider the importance of the details presented, including the sequence of the information and procedures.

3. Jot down the main ideas you'll cover in outline form.

4. Use your outline to organize your ideas as you write. **TIP** New ideas may occur to you as you write. Include them, but first check your outline and make sure you've put them in the best place.

Comparing Literary Works

Comparing Plot Development

Plot is the sequence of events in a narrative. Often, authors follow a **linear plot development.** They tell about events in the order in which they occur. Sometimes, however, authors use **non-linear plot development.** Events are not revealed in the order in which they occur, but in some other sequence that the writer chooses.

One technique or device an author may use in non-linear plot development is flashback. A **flashback** is a scene within a story that interrupts the sequence of events to reveal something that happened at an earlier time.

The two selections that follow provide examples of linear and non-linear plot development. Compare and contrast the use of linear plot development in "The Man to Send Rain Clouds" with the use of non-linear plot development in "A Walk to the Jetty."

As You Read Fill in the events of each story on timelines like the ones shown. You can use your completed timelines to analyze non-linear plot development and to compare it to linear plot development.

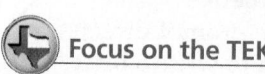

Focus on the TEKS

Reading
(5)(A) Analyze non-linear plot development (e.g., foreshadowing) and compare it to linear plot development.

"The Man to Send Rain Clouds"

Grandfather dies

"A Walk to the Jetty"

last day on Antigua, 10:00—walk to the jetty

PHLitOnline
www.PHLitOnline.com

- Vocabulary flashcards
- Interactive journals
- More about the authors

- Selection audio
- Interactive graphic organizers

Is *conflict* necessary?

Writing About the Big Question

The characters in these stories are caught up in events that cause them emotional conflict. Complete this sentence:

When events in our lives force us to analyze our decisions and actions, we _____.

Meet the Authors

Leslie Marmon Silko (b. 1948)

Author of "The Man to Send Rain Clouds"

Storytelling has always been an important part of Leslie Marmon Silko's life. Raised on the Laguna Pueblo reservation in New Mexico, she grew up listening to tribal stories told by her great-grandmother and great aunts. She has said that the oral tradition is "a collective memory and depends upon the whole community."

The Old and the New In her stories, novels, and poems, Silko explores what life is like for Native Americans in today's world. Many of her works capture the contrast between traditional values and beliefs and elements of modern life.

Jamaica Kincaid (b. 1949)

Author of "A Walk to the Jetty"

Jamaica Kincaid was born Elaine Potter Richardson on Antigua, an island in the Caribbean. Although she grew up in a loving home, she yearned to be on her own and set off all alone for a new life in New York.

Building a New Life After a series of unskilled jobs and an unsuccessful attempt to get a college degree, Richardson found success writing articles for teen magazines. More success followed with the publication of her autobiographical novels *Annie John* and *Lucy.* "A Walk to the Jetty" is the conclusion to *Annie John.*

THE MAN TO SEND RAIN CLOUDS

LESLIE MARMON SILKO

They found him under a big cottonwood tree. His Levi jacket and pants were faded light blue so that he had been easy to find. The big cottonwood tree stood apart from a small grove of winterbare cottonwoods which grew in the wide, sandy arroyo.[1] He had been dead for a day or more, and the sheep had wandered and scattered up and down the arroyo. Leon and his brother-in-law, Ken, gathered the sheep and left them in the pen at the sheep camp before they returned to the cottonwood tree. Leon waited under the tree while Ken drove the truck through the deep sand to the edge of the arroyo. He squinted up at the sun and unzipped his jacket—it sure was hot for this time of year. But high and northwest the blue mountains were still in snow. Ken came sliding down the low, crumbling bank about fifty yards down, and he was bringing the red blanket.

Before they wrapped the old man, Leon took a piece of string out of his pocket and tied a small gray feather in the old man's long white hair. Ken gave him the paint. Across the brown wrinkled forehead he drew a streak of white and along the high cheekbones he drew a strip of blue paint. He paused and watched Ken throw pinches of corn meal and pollen into the wind that fluttered the small gray feather. Then Leon painted with yellow under the old man's broad nose, and finally, when he had painted green across the chin, he smiled.

"Send us rain clouds, Grandfather." They laid the bundle in the back of the pickup and covered it with a heavy tarp before they started back to the pueblo.

They turned off the highway onto the sandy pueblo road. Not long after they passed the store and post office they saw Father Paul's car coming toward them. When he recognized their faces he slowed his car and waved for them to stop. The young priest rolled down the car window.

"Did you find old Teofilo?" he asked loudly.

Leon stopped the truck. "Good morning, Father. We were just out to the sheep camp. Everything is O.K. now."

"Thank God for that. Teofilo is a very old man. You really shouldn't allow him to stay at the sheep camp alone."

"No, he won't do that any more now."

"Well, I'm glad you understand. I hope I'll be seeing you at Mass[2] this week—we missed you last Sunday. See if you can get old Teofilo to come with you." The priest smiled and waved at them as they drove away.

---

1. **arroyo** (ə rȯiʹ ō) *n.* a dry gully or hollow in the earth's surface.
2. **Mass** (mas) *n.* church service celebrated by Roman Catholics.

Literary Analysis
Plot Development
Which words in this passage signal to the reader that this part of the story is told using linear plot development?

Reading Check

How do Leon and Ken prepare the old man's body before they move it?

Louise and Teresa were waiting. The table was set for lunch, and the coffee was boiling on the black iron stove. Leon looked at Louise and then at Teresa.

"We found him under a cottonwood tree in the big arroyo near sheep camp. I guess he sat down to rest in the shade and never got up again." Leon walked toward the old man's bed. The red plaid shawl had been shaken and spread carefully over the bed, and a new brown flannel shirt and pair of stiff new Levi's were arranged neatly beside the pillow. Louise held the screen door open while Leon and Ken carried in the red blanket. He looked small and shriveled, and after they dressed him in the new shirt and pants he seemed more shrunken.

It was noontime now because the church bells rang the Angelus.[3] They ate the beans with hot bread, and nobody said anything until after Teresa poured the coffee.

Ken stood up and put on his jacket. "I'll see about the gravediggers. Only the top layer of soil is frozen. I think it can be ready before dark."

Leon nodded his head and finished his coffee. After Ken had been gone for a while, the neighbors and clanspeople came quietly to embrace Teofilo's family and to leave food on the table because the gravediggers would come to eat when they were finished.

The sky in the west was full of pale yellow light. Louise stood outside with her hands in the pockets of Leon's green army jacket that was too big for her. The funeral was over, and the old men had taken their candles and medicine bags[4] and were gone. She waited until the body was laid into the pickup before she said anything to Leon. She touched his arm, and he noticed that her hands were still dusty from the corn meal that she had sprinkled around the old man. When she spoke, Leon could not hear her.

"What did you say? I didn't hear you."

"I said that I had been thinking about something."

"About what?"

"About the priest sprinkling holy water for Grandpa. So he won't be thirsty."

Leon stared at the new moccasins that Teofilo had made for the ceremonial dances in the summer. They were nearly hidden by the red blanket. It was getting colder, and the wind pushed gray dust down the narrow pueblo road. The sun was approaching the long mesa where it disappeared during the winter. Louise stood there shivering and watching his face. Then he zipped up his jacket and opened the truck door. "I'll see if he's there."

Literary Analysis
Plot Development
Which clues in this paragraph tell you that this part of the story is told using linear plot development?

---

3. **Angelus** (anʹ jə ləs) *n.* bell rung at morning, noon, and evening to announce a prayer.
4. **medicine bags** bags containing objects that were thought to have special powers.

Ken stopped the pickup at the church, and Leon got out: and then Ken drove down the hill to the graveyard where people were waiting. Leon knocked at the old carved door with its symbols of the Lamb.[5] While he waited he looked up at the twin bells from the king of Spain with the last sunlight pouring around them in their tower.

The priest opened the door and smiled when he saw who it was. "Come in! What brings you here this evening?"

The priest walked toward the kitchen, and Leon stood with his cap in his hand, playing with the earflaps and examining the living room—the brown sofa, the green armchair, and the brass lamp that hung down from the ceiling by links of chain. The priest dragged a chair out of the kitchen and offered it to Leon.

"No thank you, Father. I only came to ask you if you would bring your holy water to the graveyard."

The priest turned away from Leon and looked out the window at the patio full of shadows and the dining-room windows of the nuns' cloister[6] across the patio. The curtains were heavy, and the light

---

5. **the Lamb** Jesus Christ, as the sacrificial Lamb of God.
6. **cloister** (kloıs´ tər) *n.* place devoted to religious seclusion.

▲ **Critical Viewing**
How does the scene depicted in this painting compare to the images described in the story?
[Compare and Contrast]

☑ Reading Check
What do the old men take with them when the funeral is over?

The Man to Send Rain Clouds **295**

Vocabulary
penetrated (pen´ i trāt´
əd) *v.* broke through

from within faintly penetrated; it was impossible to see the nuns inside eating supper. "Why didn't you tell me he was dead? I could have brought the Last Rites[7] anyway."

Leon smiled. "It wasn't necessary, Father."

The priest stared down at his scuffed brown loafers and the worn hem of his cassock. "For a Christian burial it was necessary."

His voice was distant, and Leon thought that his blue eyes looked tired.

"It's O.K. Father, we just want him to have plenty of water."

The priest sank down into the green chair and picked up a glossy missionary magazine. He turned the colored pages full of lepers and pagans[8] without looking at them.

"You know I can't do that, Leon. There should have been the Last Rites and a funeral Mass at the very least."

Leon put on his green cap and pulled the flaps down over his ears. "It's getting late, Father. I've got to go."

When Leon opened the door Father Paul stood up and said, "Wait." He left the room and came back wearing a long brown overcoat. He followed Leon out the door and across the dim churchyard to the adobe steps in front of the church. They both stooped to fit through the low adobe entrance. And when they started down the hill to the graveyard only half of the sun was visible above the mesa.

The priest approached the grave slowly, wondering how they had managed to dig into the frozen ground; and then he remembered that this was New Mexico, and saw the pile of cold loose sand beside the hole. The people stood close to each other with little clouds of steam puffing from their faces. The priest looked at them and saw a pile of jackets, gloves, and scarves in the yellow, dry tumbleweeds that grew in the graveyard. He looked at the red blanket, not sure that Teofilo was so small, wondering if it wasn't some perverse Indian trick—something they did in March to ensure a good harvest—wondering if maybe old Teofilo was actually at sheep camp corraling the sheep for the night. But there he was, facing into a cold dry wind and squinting at the last sunlight, ready to bury a red wool blanket while the faces of his parishioners were in shadow with the last warmth of the sun on their backs.

His fingers were stiff, and it took him a long time to twist the lid off the holy water. Drops of water fell on the red blanket and soaked into dark icy spots. He sprinkled the grave and the water disappeared almost before it touched the dim, cold sand; it reminded him of something—he tried to remember what it was,

Vocabulary
perverse (pər vʉrs´) *adj.*
deviating from what is
considered right

---

7. **Last Rites** religious ceremony for a dying person or for someone who has just died.
8. **pagans** (pā´ gənz) *n.* people who are not Christians, Muslims, or Jews.

because he thought if he could remember he might understand this. He sprinkled more water; he shook the container until it was empty, and the water fell through the light from sundown like August rain that fell while the sun was still shining, almost evaporating before it touched the wilted squash flowers.

HE SPRINKLED THE GRAVE AND THE WATER DISAPPEARED ALMOST BEFORE IT TOUCHED THE DIM, COLD SAND...

The wind pulled at the priest's brown Franciscan robe[9] and swirled away the corn meal and pollen that had been sprinkled on the blanket. They lowered the bundle into the ground, and they didn't bother to untie the stiff pieces of new rope that were tied around the ends of the blanket. The sun was gone, and over on the highway the eastbound lane was full of headlights. The priest walked away slowly. Leon watched him climb the hill, and when he had disappeared within the tall, thick walls, Leon turned to look up at the high blue mountains in the deep snow that reflected a faint red light from the west. He felt good because it was finished, and he was happy about the sprinkling of the holy water; now the old man could send them big thunderclouds for sure.

Literary Analysis
Plot Development
What effect does the linear plot development—the conveying of each detail as it occurs—in this paragraph have on you as a reader?

9. **Franciscan** (fran sis´ kən) **robe** robe worn by a member of the Franciscan religious order, founded in 1209 by Saint Francis of Assisi.

Critical Thinking

1. **Respond:** What did you find most interesting about this story?

2. **(a)** What do Leon and Ken find at the beginning of the story?
   (b) Make Inferences: Why does Leon avoid telling Father Paul about Teofilo?

3. **Make Inferences:** What insight into the Pueblo people does Father Paul gain during the ceremony?

4. **(a) Draw Conclusions:** What do Leon's thoughts after Teofilo's burial reveal about his views of death?
   (b) Compare and Contrast: What does the ending reveal about the contrasts between Pueblo and Christian beliefs?

 **Is conflict necessary?**
Why does Father Paul decide that the conflict over modern and traditional death rituals is not "necessary"?

Support your responses with evidence from the text.

From
A Walk to the Jetty
from Annie John

Jamaica Kincaid

My mother had arranged with a stevedore[1] to take my trunk to the jetty ahead of me. At ten o'clock on the dot, I was dressed, and we set off for the jetty. An hour after that, I would board a launch that would take me out to sea, where I then would board the ship. Starting out, as if for old time's sake and without giving it a thought, we lined up in the old way: I walking between my mother and my father. I loomed way above my father and could see the top of his head. We must have made a strange sight: a grown girl all dressed up in the middle of a morning, in the middle of the week, walking in step in the middle between her two parents, for people we didn't know stared at us. It was all of half an hour's walk from out house to the jetty, but I was passing through most of the years of my life. We passed by the house where Miss Dulcie, the seamstress that I had been apprenticed to for a time, lived, and just as I was passing by, a wave of bad feelings for her came over me, because I suddenly remembered that the months I spent with her all she had me do was sweep the floor, which was always full of threads and pins and needles, and I never seemed to sweep it clean enough to please her. Then she would send me to the store to buy buttons or thread,

Vocabulary
apprenticed
(ə pren´ tist) *v.* assigned to work a specified length of time in a craft or trade in return for instruction

---

1. **stevedore** (stē və dôr) *n.* person whose job is loading and unloading ships.

though I was only allowed to do this if I was given a sample of the button or thread, and then she would find fault even though they were an exact match of the samples she had given me. And all the while she said to me, "A girl like you will never learn to sew properly, you know." At that time, I don't suppose I minded it, because it was customary to treat the first-year apprentice with such scorn, but now I placed on the dustheap of my life Miss Dulcie and everything that I had had to do with her.

We were soon on the road that I had taken to school, to church, to Sunday school, to choir practice, to Brownie meetings, to Girl Scout meetings, to meet a friend. I was five years old when I first walked on this road unaccompanied by someone to hold my hand. My mother had placed three pennies in my little basket, which was a duplicate of her bigger basket, and sent me to the chemist's shop to buy a pennyworth of senna leaves, a pennyworth of eucalyptus leaves, and a pennyworth of camphor.[2] She then instructed me on what side of the road to walk, where to make a turn, where to cross, how to look carefully before I crossed, and if I met anyone that I knew to politely pass greetings and keep on my way. I was wearing a freshly ironed yellow dress that had printed on it scenes of acrobats flying through the air and swinging on a trapeze. I had just had a bath, and after it, instead of powdering me with my baby-smelling talcum powder, my mother had, as a special favor, let me use her own talcum powder, which smelled quite perfumy and came in a can that had painted on it people going out to dinner in nineteenth century London and was called Mazie. How it pleased me to walk out the door and bend my head down to sniff at myself and see that I smelled just like my mother. I went to the chemist's shop, and he had to come from behind the counter and bend down to hear what it was that I wanted to buy, my voice was so little and timid then. I went back just the way I had come, and when I walked into the yard and presented my basket with its three packages to my mother, her eyes filled with tears and she swooped me up and held me high in the air and said that I was wonderful and good and that there would never be anybody better. If I had just conquered Persia, she couldn't have been more proud of me.

We passed by our church—the church in which I had been christened and received and had sung in the junior choir. We passed by a house in which a girl I used to like and was sure I

---

2. **chemist's shop... camphor** (kam′ fər) A chemist's shop is a British term for a pharmacy. The items mentioned are small amounts of plant matter to be used in remedies.

▲ Antigua, Annie John's home, is about 14 miles long and 11 miles wide, covering 108 square miles.

Literary Analysis
Plot Development
Analyze the non-linear plot development in the second paragraph of the short story. What device is used to tell the story of Annie's visit to the chemist's shop?

couldn't live without had lived. Once, when she had mumps, I went to visit her against my mother's wishes, and we sat on her bed and ate the cure of roasted, buttered sweet potatoes that had been placed on her swollen jaws, held there by a piece of white cloth. I don't know how, but my mother found out about it, and I don't know how, but she put an end to our friendship. Shortly after, the girl moved with her family across the sea to somewhere else. We passed the doll store, where I would go with my mother when I was little and point out the doll I wanted that year for Christmas. We passed the store where I bought the much-fought-over shoes I wore to church to be received in. We passed the bank. On my sixth birthday, I was given, among other things, the present of a sixpence.[3] My mother and I then went to this bank, and with the sixpence I opened my own savings account. I was given a little gray book with my name in big letters on it, and in the balance column it said "6d." Every Saturday morning after that, I was given a sixpence—later a shilling, and later a two-and-sixpence—and I would take it to the bank for deposit. I had never been allowed to withdraw even a farthing from my bank account until just a few weeks before I was to leave; then the whole account was closed out, and I received from the bank the sum of six pounds ten shillings and two and a half pence.

We passed the office of the doctor who told my mother three times that I did not need glasses, that if my eyes were feeling weak a glass of carrot juice a day would make them strong again. This happened when I was eight. And so every day at recess I would run to my school gate and meet my mother, who was waiting for me with a glass of juice from carrots she had just grated and then squeezed, and I would drink it and then run back to meet my chums. I knew there was nothing at all wrong with my eyes, but I had recently read a story in The Schoolgirl's Own Annual in which the heroine, a girl a few years older than I was then, cut such a figure to my mind with the way she was always adjusting her small, round, horn-rimmed glasses that I felt I must have a pair exactly like them. When it became clear that I didn't need glasses, I began to complain about the glare of the sun being too much for my eyes, and I walked around with my hands shielding them—especially in my mother's presence. My mother then bought me a pair of sunglasses with the exact horn-rimmed frames I wanted, and how I enjoyed the gestures of blowing on the lenses, wiping them with the hem of my uniform, adjusting the glasses when they slipped

Literary Analysis
Plot Development
Analyze the non-linear development in this paragraph. What events occur outside the natural order of the narration?

---

3. **sixpence** *n.* monetary unit in the British commonwealth, worth six pennies (not of the same value as the pennies in United States currency). A shilling is worth two sixpence, and a pound is worth twenty shillings. A farthing is a "fourthing": one fourth of a penny.

down my nose, and just removing them from their case and putting them on. In three weeks, I grew tired of them and they found a nice resting place in a drawer, along with some other things that at one time or another I couldn't live without.

We passed the store that sold only grooming aids, all imported from England. This store had in it a large porcelain dog—white, with black spots all over and a red ribbon of satin tied around its neck. The dog sat in front of a white porcelain bowl that was always filled with fresh water, and it sat in such a way that it looked as if it had just taken a long drink. When I was a small child, I would ask my mother, if ever we were near this store, to please take me to see the dog, and I would stand in front of it, bent over slightly, my hands resting on my knees, and stare at it and stare at it. I thought this dog more beautiful and more real than any actual dog I had ever seen or any actual dog I would ever see. I must have outgrown my interest in the dog, for when it disappeared I never asked what became of it. We passed the library, and if there was anything on this walk that I might have wept over leaving, this most surely would have been the thing. My mother had been a member of the library long before I was born. And since she took me everywhere with her when I was quite little, when she went to the library she took me along there, too. I would sit in her lap very quietly as she read books that she did not want to take home with her. I could not read the words yet, but just the way they looked on the page was interesting to me.

Once, a book she was reading had a large picture of a man in it, and when I asked her who he was she told me that he was Louis Pasteur[4] and that the book was about his life. It stuck in my mind, because she said it was because of him that she boiled my milk to purify it before I was allowed to drink it, that it was his idea, and that that was why the process was called pasteurization. One of the things I had put away in my mother's old trunk in which she kept all my childhood things was my library card. At that moment, I owed sevenpence in overdue fees.

As I passed by all the places, it was as if I were in a dream, for I didn't notice the people coming and going in and out of them. I didn't feel my feet touch ground. I didn't even feel my own body—I just saw these places as if they were hanging in the air, not having top or bottom, and as if I had gone in and out of them all in the same moment. The sun was bright; the sky was blue and just above my head. We then arrived at the jetty.

My heart now beat fast, and no matter how hard I tried, I couldn't keep my mouth from falling open and my nostrils from spreading

---

Literary Analysis
Plot Development
Analyze the non-linear plot development in this paragraph. What details does the writer give to establish this flashback to the library?

Reading Check

What does Annie remember when she passes the doctor's office?

---

4. **Louis Pasteur** (Pas tur′) French chemist and bacteriologist (1822–1895) who developed pasteurization, a process for using heat to kill disease-causing bacteria in milk.

Hughie Lee-Smith, *"Vista II"*, 1987 (detail), oil on canvas. Art © Estate of Hughie Lee-Smith / Licensed by VAGA, New York, NY

▲ **Critical Viewing**
How does this image reflect the mood of the story?
[Interpret]

to the ends of my face. My old fear of slipping between the boards of the jetty and falling into the dark-green water where the dark-green eels lived came over me. When my father's stomach started to go bad, the doctor had recommended a walk every evening right after he ate his dinner. Sometimes he would take me with him. When he took me with him, we usually went to the jetty, and there he would sit and talk to the night watchman about cricket[5] or some other thing that didn't interest me, because it was not personal; they didn't talk about their wives, or their children, or their parents, or about any of their likes and dislikes. They talked about things in such a strange way, and I didn't see what they found funny, but sometimes they made each other laugh so much that their guffaws would bound out to sea and send back an echo. I was always sorry when we got to the jetty and saw that the night watchman on duty was the one he enjoyed speaking to; it was like being locked up in a book filled with numbers and diagrams and what-ifs. For the thing about not being able to understand and enjoy what they were saying was I had nothing to take my mind off my fear of slipping in between the boards of the jetty.

Now, too, I had nothing to take my mind off what was happening to me. My mother and my father—I was leaving them forever. My home on an island—I was leaving it forever. What to make of everything? I felt a familiar hollow space inside. I felt I was being held down against my will. I felt I was burning up from head to toe. I felt that someone was tearing me up into little pieces as they floated out into nothing in the deep blue sea. I didn't know whether to laugh or cry. I could see that it would be better not to think too clearly about any one thing. The launch was being made ready to take me, along with some other passengers, out to the ship that was anchored in the sea. My father paid our fares, and we joined a line of people waiting to board. My mother checked my bag to make sure that I had my passport, the money she had given me, and a sheet of paper placed between some pages in my Bible on which were written the names of the relatives—people I had not known existed—with whom I would live in England. Across from the jetty was a wharf, and some stevedores were loading and unloading barges. I don't know why seeing that struck me so, but suddenly a wave of strong feeling came over me, and my heart swelled with a great gladness as the words "I shall never see this again" spilled outside me. But then, just as quickly, my heart shriveled up and the words "I shall never see this again" stabbed at me. I don't know what stopped me from falling in a heap at my parents' feet.

---

5. cricket *n.* British game, similar to baseball.

When we were all on board, the launch headed out to sea. Away from the jetty, the water became the customary blue, and the launch left a wide path in it that looked like a road. I passed by sounds and smells that were so familiar that I had long ago stopped paying any attention to them. But now here they were, and the ever-present "I shall never see this again" bobbed up and down inside me. There was the sound of the seagull diving down into the water and coming up with something silverfish in its mouth. There was the smell of the sea and the sight of small pieces of rubbish floating around in it. There were boards filled with fishermen coming in early. There was the sound of their voices as they shouted greetings to each other. There was the hot sun, there was the blue sea, there was the blue sky. Not very far away, there was the white sand of the shore, with the run-down houses all crowded in next to each other, for in some places only poor people lived near the shore. I was seated in the launch between my parents, and when I realized that I was gripping their hands tightly I glanced quickly to see if they were looking at me with scorn, for I felt sure that they must have known of my never-see-this-again feelings. But instead my father kissed me on the forehead and my mother kissed me on the mouth, and they both gave over their hands to me, so that I could grip them as much as I wanted. I was on the verge of feeling that it had all been a mistake, but I remembered that I wasn't a child anymore, and that now when I made up my mind about something I had to see it through. At that moment, we came to the ship, and that was that.

The goodbyes had to be quick, the captain said. My mother introduced herself to him and then introduced me. She told him to keep an eye on me, for I had never gone this far away from home on my own. She gave him a letter to pass on to the captain of the next ship that I would board in Barbados[6]. They walked me to my cabin, a small space that I would share with someone else—a woman I did not know. I had never before slept in a room with someone I did not know. My father kissed me goodbye and told me to be good and to write home often. After he said this, he looked at me, then looked at the floor and swung his left foot, then looked at me again. I could see that he wanted to say something else, something that he had never said to me before, but then he just turned and walked away. My mother said, "Well," and then she threw her arms around me. Big tears streamed down her face, and it must have been that— for I could not bear to see my mother cry—which started me crying, too. She then tightened her arms around me and held me to her

---

6. **Barbados** (bär bā′ dōs) easternmost island in the West Indies; southeast of Antigua.

I passed by sounds and smells that were so familiar that I had long ago stopped paying any attention to them.

Reading
Check

Where is Annie John going after leaving the island?

Vocabulary

raked (rákt) *v.* scratched or scraped, as with a rake

stupor (stō̄′ per) *n.* mental dullness or insensibility

Literary Analysis
Plot Development
Is the author using linear plot development or non-linear plot development for the final paragraphs of the story? How do you know?

close, so that I felt that I couldn't breathe. With that, my tears dried up and I was suddenly on my guard. "What does she want now?" I said to myself. Still holding me close to her, she said, in a voice that raked across my skin, "It doesn't matter what you do or where you go, I'll always be your mother and this will always be your home."

I dragged myself away from her and backed off a little, and then I shook myself, as if to wake myself out of a stupor. We looked at each other for a long time with smiles on our faces, but I know the opposite of that was in my heart. As if responding to some invisible cue, we both said, at the very same moment, "Well." Then my mother turned around and walked out the cabin door. I stood there for I don't know how long, and then I remembered that it was customary to stand on deck and wave to your relatives who were returning to shore. From the deck, I could not see my father, but I could see my mother facing the ship, her eyes searching to pick me out. I removed from my bag a red cotton handkerchief that she had earlier given me for this purpose, and I waved it wildly in the air. Recognizing me immediately she waved back just as wildly, and we continued to do this until she became just a dot in the matchbox-size launch swallowed up in the big blue sea.

I went back to my cabin and lay down on my berth. Everything trembled as if it had a spring at its very center. I could hear the small waves lap-lapping around the ship. They made an unexpected sound, as if a vessel filled with liquid had been placed on its side and now was slowly emptying out.

Critical Thinking

Support your responses with evidence from the text.

1. **Respond:** Was Annie right to leave her home? Explain.

2. **(a)** What is Annie doing as the story opens? **(b) Analyze:** If this story used linear plot development, what would be the first event the narrator told about? **(c) Draw Conclusions:** What do you think is the author's purpose in using a non-linear plot development?

3. **(a)** What information do the flashbacks give? **(b) Interpret:** What two journeys does Annie make in this story? Explain.

4. **(a)** What does Annie's mother tell her on the ship when they hug? **(b) Compare and Contrast:** How does Annie's relationship with her mother compare to her relationship with her father?

   Is conflict necessary?
   (a) What is the main conflict in this story? **(b)** Was there any way for Annie to avoid it? Explain.

Comparing Plot Development

1. Using a chart like the following one, list three events from each of the stories to illustrate the **linear** or **non-linear plot development.**

	Event	Event	Event
"The Man to Send Rain Clouds" (linear)			
"A Walk to the Jetty" (non-linear)			

2. (a) Would "The Man to Send Rain Clouds" have been as effective if it had used a non-linear plot development? Explain. **(b)** Would "A Walk to the Jetty" have been as effective if it had used a linear plot development? Explain.

 College Readiness |Timed Writing

Writing to Compare Plot Development

Compare the linear plot development of "The Man to Send Rain Clouds" with the non-linear plot development of "A Walk to the Jetty." In a brief essay, discuss how these types of developments affect the reader's experiences with the stories. (25 minutes)

 5-Minute Planner

1. Read the prompt carefully and completely.

2. Think about these questions and jot down your answers.

- What kinds of information does Jamaica Kincaid give in the flashbacks in "A Walk to the Jetty"?

- What kinds of information does Silko give in "The Man to Send Rain Clouds" that is best told with linear plot development?

3. Think about your organization. Will you use a block organization or a point-by-point organization to compare the plot development of the two stories?

4. Make a brief outline of your ideas. Use the outline as you write.

5. Reread the prompt, and then draft your essay.

Literary Text: Short Story

Focus on the TEKS

Writing
(14)(A) Write an engaging story with a well-developed conflict and resolution, interesting and believable characters, and a range of literary strategies (e.g., dialogue, suspense) and devices to enhance the plot.

Defining the Form Stories are one of the oldest and most familiar forms of literature. A traditional **short story** is a brief fictional narrative composed of plot, setting, and characters. You might use elements of this type of writing in science fiction, mysteries, and autobiographies.

Assignment Write an engaging short story that presents characters in a specific setting and involved in a specific conflict that is resolved. Include these elements:

✔ a well-developed *conflict* and *resolution*

✔ a *range of literary strategies,* such as *dialogue* and *suspense,* and devices to enhance the plot

✔ *interesting* and *believable characters*

✔ details that establish a particular setting

✔ error-free grammar, including correct use of verbs

To preview the criteria on which your short story may be judged, see the rubric on page 311.

 Writing Workshop: *Work in Progress*

Review the work you did on pages 255 and 281.

Prewriting/Planning Strategy

Develop characters. Use a chart like the one shown to help you think about each character and the conflict he or she might face. Match a character with a conflict to begin brainstorming a story. Then, take time to consider how you would have the conflict play out in the character's life.

Potential Characters	Potential Conflicts
A business man	loses family heirloom
An elderly woman	wins lottery
A teenage girl	cheats on exam
A mechanic	loses job
A sports player	moves to a new town

Apply It!

Reading-Writing Connection

To get the feel for short stories, read "American History" by Judith Ortiz Cofer (p. 240) and "The Gift of the Magi" by O. Henry (p. 260).

Developing the Plot

The organization of a story includes several elements, which are often presented in a particular order. The building blocks of a story's plot are:

Exposition: introduction of the characters, setting, and basic situation

Inciting Incident: introduction of a central conflict

Rising Action: development of the **conflict,** or main problem

Climax: the high point of interest or suspense

Falling Action: winding down of the conflict

Resolution: general insight about or change in the characters

Decide who and what your story is about. Think about the characters, the setting, and the basic situation. Then, introduce these elements in the exposition of your story.

Develop the conflict, or problem. Consider your main character and his or her feelings about the basic situation of the story. Ask yourself:

- How does he or she react to the situation?
- How does his or her reaction lead to the development of the conflict?
- What circumstances add to the character's actions?

Use your answers to plan the inciting incident and rising action.

Employ literary strategies and devices to enhance the plot. After the development of the inciting incident and rising action, think about the most interesting and effective way for the conflict to be played out and resolved. Decide what will be the high point of anxiety or the possible turning point in the conflict. Consider employing **suspense** to enhance your plot. By holding back information, you create tension and keep the audience wanting to know what will happen next. Use these considerations to construct the climax of your story.

Develop the resolution, or what will happen in the end. Everything that happens after the climax simply wraps up loose ends. This part of the story is also a place where you can express the lesson of the story. You might present this insight both indirectly through the events and directly through narration. Think about what your character learned through the conflict and use that knowledge to express the insight he or she gained.

Having a clear plan for your plot will allow you to write a story with a well-developed conflict and resolution.

Drafting Strategies

Develop interesting and believable characters. An audience will be able to relate to characters who are in unusual, even extraordinary, circumstances, as long as those characters are well-crafted. Use direct and indirect characterization to let your readers get to know the personalities in your short story and to enhance the plot.

- **Direct characterization:** A narrator describes a character.
- **Indirect characterization:** The writer hints at a character by revealing the character's appearance, actions, words, and feelings and by showing how others react to the character.

Write realistic dialogue. Another strategy to enhance the **plot** and develop your characters in a believable way is to have them speak realistically. When dialogue is used effectively as a literary strategy, it does not sound stiff and unnatural. It should sound like people speaking to one another. Read your dialogue aloud. Listen and decide whether your dialogue sounds natural.

Show, don't tell. Use descriptions, dialogue, movements, gestures, and characters' interior monologues to make the setting and events vivid for your readers. Do not simply report that a street was noisy—provide details that help readers hear the commotion. For example, you might write that the character thought "How can I possibly think with all these blaring horns?" Additionally, you can add sensory details—words that appeal to the senses of sight, smell, taste, touch, and hearing.

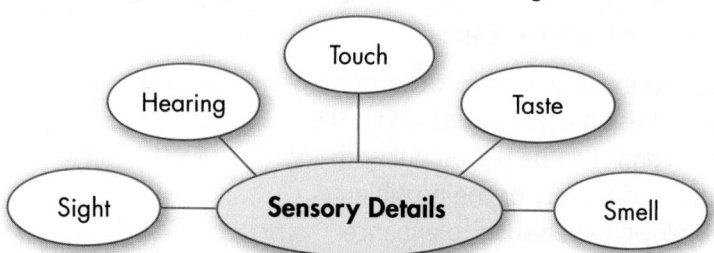

Revising Strategies

Maintain an effective sequence of events. Every detail in your story should deepen your portrayal of the characters or increase the tension of the conflict. Review your draft, noting any interruptions to the momentum of your plot. Consider modifying or deleting such interruptions.

Use active language. To create dynamic sentences, choose the active voice instead of the passive voice. Make sure that the subjects in your sentences perform the actions.

- **Passive Voice:** The problem was solved by Curtis.
- **Active Voice:** Curtis solved the problem.

 **Focus on the TEKS**

Write
(14)(A) Write an engaging story with interesting and believable characters, and a range of literary strategies (e.g., dialogue) to enhance the plot.

WRITE GUY
Jeff Anderson, M.Ed.

What Do You Notice?

Vivid Word Choice

Read the following sentence from Saki's short story "The Interlopers" several times.

A fierce shriek of the storm had been answered by a splitting crash over their heads, and ere they could leap aside a mass of falling beech tree had thundered down on them.

Discuss your ideas about the passage with a partner. Consider how you could use a style similar to Saki's when choosing the details that describe and convey your story's conflict and climax.

Revising Inconsistent Verb Tenses

A **tense** is a form of a verb that expresses the time of an action. The six verb tenses are present, present perfect, past, past perfect, future, and future perfect. Inconsistent use of verb tenses causes confusion in a story.

Uses of Past Perfect and Future Perfect Tense	
Past action or condition completed before another	I had been to the museum before it was remodeled.
Future action or condition completed before another	I will have seen that movie before it will be on television.
Continuing past action interrupted by another	I had been on the telephone when you rang the doorbell.
Continuing future action interrupted by another	By the time I graduate, I will have been in school for thirteen years.

Identifying Inconsistent Verb Tenses Inconsistent verb tense occurs when a sentence begins in one tense and incorrectly switches to another. Shifts in tense should always reflect a logical sequence.

Incorrect: I *will be* on time today, and I *was* on time tomorrow.
Correct: I *was* on time today, and I *will be* on time tomorrow.
Perfect tenses can clarify a sequence of actions.

Unclear: By the time she *will arrive*, we *will start* the meeting.
Clear: By the time she *arrives*, we *will have started* the meeting.

Fixing Errors Scan your draft for shifts in tense.

1. **Identify the reason for each shift.** Correct unnecessary shifts.

2. **Determine which actions happened first.** When two actions occur at different times in the past, use the past perfect tense for the earlier action. When two actions will occur at different times in the future, use the future perfect tense for the earlier action.

Grammar in Your Writing

Review a passage of your draft that includes both narrative and dialogue. Underline any shifts in tense that you find. Be sure that the shift represents a clear and logical time order. Fix any inconsistent tenses.

Student Model: Randy Hays, Clackamas, OR

 Focus on the TEKS

Writing
(13)(D) Edit drafts for grammar, mechanics, and spelling.
(13)(E) Publish written work for appropriate audiences.
Research
(23)(E) Use a style manual (e.g., *Modern Language Association, Chicago Manual of Style*) to format written materials.

The Oil Slick

The Oil Slick is a place where I play baseball with a bunch of friends. We call the field the "Oil Slick" because a boat carrying gallons of oil once sailed by. The boat sprang a leak, polluting the water around it. The Oil Slick also has a big hole in the outfield. . . .

My nickname is Giant. It suits me because I am the tallest player on the team. . . . I only know the nicknames of the others on my team. They're called Ant, Dash, Rip, X-Ray, Target, Eye, Animal, Uno, and Cover. . . .

This morning, I headed out to the Oil Slick, ready to play. However, before we started, Uno held a meeting. "As you know," he said, "there is a hole in the out-field."

"Who can tell me why the hole is there?" There was silence until Uno spoke again. "That's what I thought," he said. "Some people say there's treasure buried on this field. Somebody probably tried to dig for it, and they left that hole behind. I thought maybe we should dig, too, but then I figured that'd be stupid. It's probably just a rumor. We wouldn't find anything, diggin' holes."

Silence again until someone shouted. "Let's play already!" Everyone went to their positions and the game started. . . .

Rip hit the ball and it flew past the right-fielder, Eye. Concentrating on the ball, Eye ran toward the hole. He didn't know when to stop and he fell. . . .

We all ran and looked down the hole. Nobody had ever bothered to really look before, and it was deep, much deeper than we thought. Hoping to find Eye, we jumped in. . . .

When we saw what the hole truly was we forgot about Eye. We had expected dirt, rocks—the usual stuff you'd find in a hole. Instead, we saw smooth walls, stretching into the distance. All this time, without ever suspecting it, we had been playing above a maze of tunnels. . . .

We headed down the tunnel to our right. . . .These weren't ordinary tunnels. They had the names of famous baseball players carved right into the walls. Then, we noticed something strange. There were other, different words painted on the wall and what they said scared us all: "Your friend is here. Don't try to find him. Or else."

We continued through the tunnels until we emerged in a room which . . . had a sign that said, "You Found Him." Sure enough, there was Eye, leaning against a wall. He saw us and shouted, "Go! Now!"

But it was too late. A door slammed shut and we were trapped. Then, we heard a familiar voice. "You saw the warnings, but you didn't stop. Now you are trapped and the treasure is mine!". . .

Randy starts the story with a detailed description of an interesting setting.

Quirky nicknames help to make the characters interesting and believable.

Randy uses dialogue to introduce the mystery of the hole in the field—the source of the story's conflict. Notice the correct use of punctuation to show the character's direct words.

Randy develops the conflict further here.

Editing and Proofreading

Edit your draft for errors in grammar and mechanics, such as punctuation. Use various resources, such as printed and electronic dictionaries, to check correct spellings.

Focus on Spelling: Often, suffixes cause no spelling change to the base word. Sometimes, though, final *e*'s are dropped or final *y*'s change to *i*. The final consonant in a word may change as well, as in *suspend-suspension*. Some changes occur when the internal spelling of the base word changes, as in *maintain-maintenance*.

Confirm Dialogue Formatting: Use a style manual (e.g., *Modern Language Association, Chicago Manual of Style*) to check whether you have formatted and punctuated the dialogue in your story correctly.

Spiral Review
Earlier in this unit, you learned about **regular verbs** (p. 254) and **irregular verbs** (p. 280). Check your short story to be sure that you have formed the principal parts of verbs correctly.

Publishing and Presenting

Consider ways to publish your written work for appropriate audiences:

Deliver an oral presentation. Read your story aloud to your classmates. Get feedback from your classmates and make necessary revisions.

Design an online anthology. Work with your class to design and build an online anthology of your original stories. Advertise the online anthology in your school.

Reflecting on Your Writing

Writer's Journal Jot down your answers to this question:
What did writing a short story teach you about fiction?

Rubric for Self-Assessment

Find evidence in your writing to address each category. Then, use the rating scale to grade your work.

Written Composition Criteria	Rating Scale
	not very / very
Focus and Coherence: How well-chosen are the details that establish your particular setting?	1 2 3 4
Organization: How well-organized and well-developed are the actions that make up your conflict and resolution?	1 2 3 4
Development of Ideas: How well are literary strategies, such as dialogue and suspense, and other devices used to develop and enhance your plot?	1 2 3 4
Conventions: How correct is your grammar, especially your use of verb tenses?	1 2 3 4
Voice: How interesting and believable are your characters?	1 2 3 4

Before You Read

Rules of the Game •
The Necklace

Selection Choices

▲ Read **"Rules of the Game"** to learn how a daughter's success leads to a new set of problems with her mother.

▲ Read **"The Necklace"** to see the lasting effects of a woman's desire for social acceptance.

 TEXAS Focus on the TEKS

Meet these standards with either **"Rules of the Game"** (p. 316) or **"The Necklace"** (p. 332).

Reading
(5)(B) Analyze how authors develop complex yet believable characters in works of fiction through a range of literary devices. *(Literary Analysis: Characterization)*

(1)(A) Determine the meaning of grade-level technical academic English words in multiple content areas derived from Latin roots. *(Word Power: Apply It)*

Reading/Comprehension Skills
RC-9(A) Reflect on understanding to monitor comprehension (e.g., making connections).
(Reading Skill: Cause and Effect)

Oral and Written Conventions
(17)(B) Identify and use the subjunctive mood to express doubts, wishes, and possibilities.
(Conventions: Subjunctive Mood)

Writing
(13)(A) Plan a first draft by selecting the correct genre for conveying the intended meaning to multiple audiences. *(Writing: Written Presentation)*

Research
(20) Ask open-ended research questions.
(Research and Technology: Informative Brochure)

(20)(A) Brainstorm. *(Research and Technology: Informative Brochure)*

Literary Analysis: Characterization

Characterization is the development of characters in a work. Writers develop complex yet believable characters through a range of literary devices, including characterization. A **character** is a person, an animal, or even an object that participates in the action and experiences the events of a literary work.

- **Direct characterization:** The writer (speaking through a narrator) explains a character.
- **Indirect characterization:** The writer hints at a character through the actions, words, and thoughts of the character and others.

Using the Strategy: Characterization Chart

As You Read Use a characterization chart like this one to analyze how each author develops his or her characters.

Story Details	What They Show About the Character
Narrator's comments	
Character's thoughts, words, and actions	
Character's appearance	
What others say or think about the character	

Reading Skill: Cause and Effect

A **cause** is an event, action, or feeling that produces a result. An **effect** is the result produced. A single cause may produce several effects. For example, a poor student starts to do well in school. Her success results in greater self-esteem. Effects, in turn, may become causes. For example, that same student's new confidence may lead her to audition for a play.

As You Read **Reflect on your understanding to monitor your comprehension** of the story events. Jot down your answers to the following questions to **make connections** between causes and effects in the text.

- What happened?
- Why did it happen?
- What happens as a result?
- Does that result cause something else to happen?

TEXAS
PHLitOnline
www.PHLitOnline.com

Hear It!
- Selection summary audio
- Selection audio

See It!
- Get Connected video
- Background video
- More about the author
- Vocabulary flashcards

Do It!
- Interactive journals
- Interactive graphic organizers
- Self-test
- Internet activity
- Grammar tutorial
- Interactive vocabulary games

Is *conflict* necessary?

Writing About the Big Question

In "Rules of the Game," a girl learns some important life lessons while working to master chess. Use these sentence starters to develop your ideas about the Big Question:

Competition can cause internal conflicts because _____.

Overcoming conflict while playing a game can help us **battle** through other real-life struggles because _____.

As You Read Look for ways in which Waverly starts treating her mother like a chess opponent.

Vocabulary

Read each word and its definition. Decide whether you know the word well, know it a little bit, or do not know it at all. After you read, see how your knowledge of each word has increased.

- **pungent** (pun´ jənt) *adj.* producing a sharp smell (p. 318) *We could smell the <u>pungent</u> Indian spices as we walked into the apartment.* pungency *n.* pungently *adv.*

- **benevolently** (bə nev´ ə lənt lē) *adv.* in a well-meaning way (p. 322) *The helpful officer smiled <u>benevolently</u> at the children.* benevolent *adj.* benevolence *n.*

- **retort** (ri tôrt´) *n.* sharp or clever reply (p. 322) *Her quick <u>retort</u> silenced her critic.* retort *v.*

- **prodigy** (präd´ ə jē) *n.* person who is amazingly talented or intelligent, especially a child of unusual genius (p. 324) *The six-year-old concert pianist was a <u>prodigy</u>.*

- **malodorous** (mal ō´ dər əs) *adj.* having a bad smell (p. 325) *The bag was filled with <u>malodorous</u> garbage.* malodorously *adv.* malodorousness *n.* odor *n.*

- **concessions** (kən sesh´ ənz) *n.* things given or granted as privileges (p. 326) *I had to make a lot of <u>concessions</u> to get my brother to give me his game tickets.* concede *v.* concessionary *adj.*

Word Power

The **Latin root -*bene*-** means "well."

In this story, an elderly man who is playing chess in the park smiles **benevolently** at Waverly. His smile shows that he wishes her well.

Meet
Amy Tan
(b. 1952)

Author of
Rules of the Game

As a child, Amy Tan did not imagine that she would become a successful novelist. Her parents, who had emigrated from China to the San Francisco Bay area, wanted her to become a doctor. Doubting her abilities in science, Tan instead majored in English in college. She went on to become a successful business writer.

Finding Herself in Fiction When she reached her mid-thirties, Tan began writing stories. While she was surprised by the pleasure writing fiction gave her, she was even more surprised by the content of her work. Tan had tried to play down her ethnicity, but in her fiction, she found herself exploring the experiences of Chinese American women. In 1985, Tan wrote "Rules of the Game," which she later included in her best-selling first novel, *The Joy Luck Club.*

BACKGROUND FOR THE STORY

Social Studies Connection

The Game of Chess

A game of strategy, chess resembles a battle between two armies, each led by a figurehead king and a powerful queen. Chess may have started in India. After it spread to Persia (present-day Iran), Arab invaders introduced it to other lands. Today, it is played throughout the world.

Did You Know?

When she was eight years old, Tan's essay "What the Library Means to Me" won first prize in a local contest.

Rules of the Game

from The Joy Luck Club

Amy Tan

I was six when my mother taught me the art of invisible strength. It was a strategy for winning arguments, respect from others, and eventually, though neither of us knew it at the time, chess games.

"Bite back your tongue," scolded my mother when I cried loudly, yanking her hand toward the store that sold bags of salted plums. At home, she said, "Wise guy, he not go against wind. In Chinese we say, Come from South, blow with wind—poom!—North will follow. Strongest wind cannot be seen."

The next week I bit back my tongue as we entered the store with the forbidden candies. When my mother finished her shopping, she quietly plucked a small bag of plums from the rack and put it on the counter with the rest of the items.

My mother imparted her daily truths so she could help my older brothers and me rise above our circumstances. We lived in San Francisco's Chinatown. Like most of the other Chinese children who played in the back alleys of restaurants and curio shops, I didn't think we were poor. My bowl was always full, three five-course meals every day, beginning with a soup full of mysterious things I didn't want to know the names of.

We lived on Waverly Place, in a warm, clean, two-bedroom flat that sat above a small Chinese bakery specializing in steamed pastries and dim sum. In the early morning, when the alley was still quiet, I could smell fragrant red beans as they were cooked down to a pasty sweetness. By daybreak, our flat was heavy with the odor of fried sesame balls and sweet curried chicken crescents. From my bed, I would listen as my father got ready for work, then locked the door behind him, one-two-three clicks.

At the end of our two-block alley was a small sandlot playground with swings and slides well-shined down the middle with use. The play area was bordered by wood-slat benches where old-country people sat cracking roasted watermelon seeds with their golden teeth and scattering the husks to an impatient gathering of gurgling pigeons. The best playground, however, was the dark alley itself. It was crammed with daily mysteries and adventures. My brothers and I would peer into the medicinal herb shop, watching old Li dole out onto a stiff sheet of white paper the right amount of insect shells, saffron-colored seeds and pungent leaves for his ailing customers. It was said that he once cured a woman dying of an ancestral curse that had eluded the best of American doctors. Next to the pharmacy was a printer who specialized in gold-embossed wedding invitations and festive red banners.

Farther down the street was Ping Yuen Fish Market. The front window displayed a tank crowded with doomed fish and turtles struggling to gain footing on the slimy green-tiled sides. A hand-written sign informed tourists, "Within this store, is all for food, not for pet." Inside, the butchers with their bloodstained white smocks deftly gutted the fish while customers cried out their orders and shouted, "Give me your freshest," to which the butchers always protested, "All are freshest." On less crowded market days, we would inspect the crates of live frogs and crabs which we were warned not to poke, boxes of dried cuttlefish, and row upon row of iced prawns, squid, and slippery fish. The sanddabs made me shiver each time; their eyes lay on one flattened side and reminded me of my mother's story of a careless girl who ran into a crowded street and was crushed by a cab. "Was smash flat," reported my mother.

At the corner of the alley was Hong Sing's, a four-table cafe with a recessed stairwell in front that led to a door marked "Tradesmen." My brothers and I believed the bad people emerged from this door at night. Tourists never went to Hong Sing's,

Vocabulary
pungent (puń jənt) *adj.* producing a sharp smell

Literary Analysis
Characterization
What does this quotation reveal about the narrator's mother?

ONE WAY

END

WAVERLY

天后廟街

since the menu was printed only in Chinese. A Caucasian man with a big camera once posed me and my playmates in front of the restaurant. He had us move to the side of the picture window so the photo would capture the roasted duck with its head dangling from a juice-covered rope. After he took the picture, I told him he should go into Hong Sing's and eat dinner. When he smiled and asked me what they served, I shouted, "Guts and duck's feet and octopus gizzards!" Then I ran off with my friends, shrieking with laughter as we scampered across the alley and hid in the entryway grotto of the China Gem Company, my heart pounding with hope that he would chase us.

My mother named me after the street that we lived on: Waverly Place Jong, my official name for important American documents. But my family called me Meimei [mā′ mā′], "Little Sister," I was the youngest, the only daughter. Each morning before school, my mother would twist and yank on my thick black hair until she had formed two tightly wound pigtails. One day, as she struggled to weave a hard-toothed comb through my disobedient hair, I had a sly thought.

I asked her, "Ma, what is Chinese torture?" My mother shook her head. A bobby pin was wedged between her lips. She wetted her palm and smoothed the hair above my ear, then pushed the pin in so that it nicked sharply against my scalp.

"Who say this word?" she asked without a trace of knowing how wicked I was being. I shrugged my shoulders and said, "Some boy in my class said Chinese people do Chinese torture."

"Chinese people do many things," she said simply. "Chinese people do business, do medicine, do painting. Not lazy like American people. We do torture. Best torture." ●

My older brother Vincent was the one who actually got the chess set. We had gone to the annual Christmas party held at the First Chinese Baptist Church at the end of the alley. The missionary ladies had put together a Santa bag of gifts donated by members of another church. None of the gifts had names on them. There were separate sacks for boys and girls of different ages.

One of the Chinese parishioners had donned a Santa Claus costume and a stiff paper beard with cotton balls glued to it. I think the only children who thought he was the real thing were too young to know that Santa Claus was not Chinese. When my turn came up, the Santa man asked me how old I was. I thought it was a trick question; I was seven according to the American formula and eight by the Chinese calendar. I said I was born on March 17, 1951. That seemed to satisfy him. He then solemnly asked if I had been a very,

Literary Analysis
Characterization
What does Mrs. Jong's response to the accusation that Chinese people do torture reveal about her personality?

Reading Check
What gift does Vincent receive at the Christmas party?

very good girl this year and did I believe in Jesus Christ and obey my parents. I knew the only answer to that. I nodded back with equal solemnity.

Having watched the other children opening their gifts, I already knew that the big gifts were not necessarily the nicest ones. One girl my age got a large coloring book of biblical characters, while a less greedy girl who selected a small box received a glass vial of lavender toilet water. The sound of the box was also important. A ten-year-old boy had chosen a box that jangled when he shook it. It was a tin globe of the world with a slit for inserting money. He must have thought it was full of dimes and nickels, because when he saw that it had just ten pennies, his face fell with such undisguised disappointment that his mother slapped the side of his head and led him out of the church hall, apologizing to the crowd for her son who had such bad manners he couldn't appreciate such a fine gift.

As I peered into the sack, I quickly fingered the remaining presents, testing their weight, imagining what they contained. I chose a heavy, compact one that was wrapped in shiny silver foil and a red satin ribbon. It was a twelve-pack of Life Savers and I spent the rest of the party arranging and rearranging the candy tubes in the order of my favorites. My brother Winston chose wisely as well. His present turned out to be a box of intricate plastic parts; the instructions on the box proclaimed that when they were properly assembled he would have an authentic miniature replica of a World War II submarine.

Vincent got the chess set, which would have been a very decent present to get at a church Christmas party except it was obviously used and, as we discovered later, it was missing a black pawn and a white knight. My mother graciously thanked the unknown benefactor, saying, "Too good. Cost too much." At which point, an old lady with fine white, wispy hair nodded toward our family and said with a whistling whisper, "Merry, merry Christmas."

When we got home, my mother told Vincent to throw the chess set away. "She not want it. We not want it," she said, tossing her head stiffly to the side with a tight, proud smile. My brothers had deaf ears. They were already lining up the chess pieces and reading from the dog-eared instruction book. ●

I watched Vincent and Winston play during Christmas week. The chess board seemed to hold elaborate secrets waiting to be untangled. The chessmen were more powerful than Old Li's magic herbs that cured ancestral curses. And my brothers wore such serious faces that I was sure something was at stake that was greater than avoiding the tradesmen's door to Hong Sing's.

Literary Analysis
Characterization
In this paragraph, how does the author develop Waverly as a complex yet believable character?

Reading Skill
Cause and Effect
Monitor your comprehension. Reflect on your understanding to make a connection between the events of the Christmas party and the events of Christmas week.

"Let me! Let me!" I begged between games when one brother or the other would sit back with a deep sigh of relief and victory, the other annoyed, unable to let go of the outcome. Vincent at first refused to let me play, but when I offered my Life Savers as replacements for the buttons that filled in for the missing pieces, he relented. He chose the flavors: wild cherry for the black pawn and peppermint for the white knight. Winner could eat both. As our mother sprinkled flour and rolled out small doughy circles for the steamed dumplings that would be our dinner that night, Vincent explained the rules, pointing to each piece. "You have sixteen pieces and so do I. One king and queen, two bishops, two knights, two castles, and eight pawns. The pawns can only move forward one step, except on the first move. Then they can move two. But they can only take men by moving crossways like this, except in the beginning, when you can move ahead and take another pawn."

"Why?" I asked as I moved my pawn. "Why can't they move more steps?"

"Because they're pawns," he said.

"But why do they go crossways to take other men? Why aren't there any women and children?"

"Why is the sky blue? Why must you always ask stupid questions?" asked Vincent. "This is a game. These are the rules. I didn't make them up. See. Here. In the book." He jabbed a page with a pawn in his hand. "Pawn. P-A-W-N. Pawn. Read it yourself."

My mother patted the flour off her hands. "Let me see book," she said quietly. She scanned the pages quickly, not reading the foreign English symbols, seeming to search deliberately for nothing in particular.

"This American rules," she concluded at last. "Every time people come out from foreign country, must know rules. You not know, judge say, Too bad, go back. They not telling you why so you can use their way go forward. They say, Don't know why, you find out yourself. But they knowing all the time. Better you take it, find out why yourself." She tossed her head back with a satisfied smile.

I found out about all the whys later. I read the rules and looked up all the big words in a dictionary. I borrowed books from the Chinatown library. I studied each chess piece, trying to absorb the power each contained.

Literary Analysis
Characterization
What do you learn about Vincent based on this conversation?

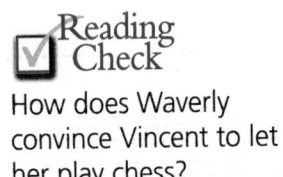

Reading Check
How does Waverly convince Vincent to let her play chess?

Endgame

Endgame describes a tense period in a chess game when the end seems close at hand. With fewer pieces left, lines of attack and defense become clearer to both players. Mistakes are magnified in an endgame, when victory and defeat can be determined by a single ill-considered move. In this story, Waverly develops a keen awareness of the strategies needed to secure a victory in the endgame.

Connect to the Literature

Why might it be difficult for a young beginning chess player like Waverly to master the endgame?

Vocabulary

benevolently (bə nev´ ə lənt lē) *adv.* in a well-meaning way

retort (ri tôrt´) *n.* sharp or clever reply

I learned about opening moves and why it's important to control the center early on; the shortest distance between two points is straight down the middle. I learned about the middle game and why tactics between two adversaries are like clashing ideas; the one who plays better has the clearest plans for both attacking and getting out of traps. I learned why it is essential in the endgame to have foresight, a mathematical understanding of all possible moves, and patience; all weaknesses and advantages become evident to a strong adversary and are obscured to a tiring opponent. I discovered that for the whole game one must gather invisible strengths and see the endgame before the game begins.

I also found out why I should never reveal "why" to others. A little knowledge withheld is a great advantage one should store for future use. That is the power of chess. It is a game of secrets in which one must show and never tell.

I loved the secrets I found within the sixty-four black and white squares. I carefully drew a handmade chessboard and pinned it to the wall next to my bed, where at night I would stare for hours at imaginary battles. Soon I no longer lost any games or Life Savers, but I lost my adversaries. Winston and Vincent decided they were more interested in roaming the streets after school in their Hopalong Cassidy cowboy hats. •

On a cold spring afternoon, while walking home from school, I detoured through the playground at the end of our alley. I saw a group of old men, two seated across a folding table playing a game of chess, others smoking pipes, eating peanuts, and watching. I ran home and grabbed Vincent's chess set, which was bound in a cardboard box with rubber bands. I also carefully selected two prized rolls of Life Savers. I came back to the park and approached a man who was observing the game.

"Want to play?" I asked him. His face widened with surprise and he grinned as he looked at the box under my arm.

"Little sister, been a long time since I play with dolls," he said, smiling benevolently. I quickly put the box down next to him on the bench and displayed my retort.

Lau Po, as he allowed me to call him, turned out to be a much better player than my brothers. I lost many games and many Life Savers. But over the weeks, with each diminishing roll of candies,

I added new secrets. Lau Po gave me the names. The Double Attack from the East and West Shores. Throwing Stones on the Drowning Man. The Sudden Meeting of the Clan. The Surprise from the Sleeping Guard. The Humble Servant Who Kills the King. Sand in the Eyes of Advancing Forces. A Double Killing Without Blood.

There were also the fine points of chess etiquette. Keep captured men in neat rows, as well-tended prisoners. Never announce "Check" with vanity, lest someone with an unseen sword slit your throat. Never hurl pieces into the sandbox after you have lost a game, because then you must find them again, by yourself, after apologizing to all around you. By the end of the summer, Lau Po had taught me all he knew, and I had become a better chess player.

A small weekend crowd of Chinese people and tourists would gather as I played and defeated my opponents one by one. My mother would join the crowds during these outdoor exhibition games. She sat proudly on the bench, telling my admirers with proper Chinese humility, "Is luck."

A man who watched me play in the park suggested that my mother allow me to play in local chess tournaments. My mother smiled graciously, an answer that meant nothing. I desperately wanted to go, but I bit back my tongue. I knew she would not let me play among strangers. So as we walked home I said in a small voice that I didn't want to play in the local tournament. They would have American rules. If I lost, I would bring shame on my family.

"Is shame you fall down nobody push you," said my mother.

During my first tournament, my mother sat with me in the front row as I waited for my turn. I frequently bounced my legs to unstick them from the cold metal seat of the folding chair. When my name was called, I leapt up. My mother unwrapped something in her lap. It was her chang, a small tablet of red jade which held the sun's fire. "Is luck," she whispered, and tucked it into my dress pocket. I turned to my opponent, a fifteen-year-old boy from Oakland. He looked at me, wrinkling his nose.

As I began to play, the boy disappeared, the color ran out of the

By the end of summer, Lau Po had taught me all he knew . . .

Reading Skill
Cause and Effect
What does Waverly anticipate would be the effect of her expressing her desire to play in local chess tournaments?

Reading
Check

How does Waverly's mother respond to Waverly's admirers in the park?

room, and I saw only my white pieces and his black ones waiting on the other side. A light wind began blowing past my ears. It whispered secrets only I could hear.

"Blow from the South," it murmured. "The wind leaves no trail." I saw a clear path, the traps to avoid. The crowd rustled. "Shhh! Shhh!" said the corners of the room. The wind blew stronger. "Throw sand from the East to distract him." The knight came forward ready for the sacrifice. The wind hissed, louder and louder. "Blow, blow, blow. He cannot see. He is blind now. Make him lean away from the wind so he is easier to knock down."

"Check," I said, as the wind roared with laughter. The wind died down to little puffs, my own breath. ●

My mother placed my first trophy next to a new plastic chess set that the neighborhood Tao society had given to me. As she wiped each piece with a soft cloth, she said, "Next time win more, lose less."

"Ma, it's not how many pieces you lose," I said. "Sometimes you need to lose pieces to get ahead."

"Better to lose less, see if you really need."

At the next tournament, I won again, but it was my mother who wore the triumphant grin.

"Lost eight piece this time. Last time was eleven. What I tell you? Better off lose less!" I was annoyed, but I couldn't say anything.

I attended more tournaments, each one farther away from home. I won all games, in all divisions. The Chinese bakery downstairs from our flat displayed my growing collection of trophies in its window, amidst the dust-covered cakes that were never picked up. The day after I won an important regional tournament, the window encased a fresh sheet cake with whipped-cream frosting and red script saying, "Congratulations, Waverly Jong, Chinatown Chess Champion." Soon after that, a flower shop, headstone engraver, and funeral parlor offered to sponsor me in national tournaments. That's when my mother decided I no longer had to do the dishes. Winston and Vincent had to do my chores.

"Why does she get to play and we do all the work," complained Vincent.

"Is new American rules," said my mother. "Meimei play, squeeze all her brains out for win chess. You play, worth squeeze towel."

By my ninth birthday, I was a national chess champion. I was still some 429 points away from grand-master status, but I was touted as the Great American Hope, a child prodigy and a girl to boot. They ran a photo of me in *Life* magazine next to a quote in which Bobby Fischer[1] said, "There will never be a woman grand

Reading Skill
Cause and Effect
Monitor your comprehension. Reflect on your understanding to make a connection between Waverly's mindset and the outcome of the match.

Literary Analysis
Characterization
What do Waverly's mother's comments here reveal indirectly about her ambitions for Waverly?

Vocabulary
prodigy (präd´ ə jē) *n.* person who is amazingly talented or intelligent, especially a child of unusual genius

master." "Your move, Bobby," said the caption.

The day they took the magazine picture I wore neatly plaited braids clipped with plastic barrettes trimmed with rhinestones. I was playing in a large high school auditorium that echoed with phlegmy coughs and the squeaky rubber knobs of chair legs sliding across freshly waxed wooden floors. Seated across from me was an American man, about the same age as Lau Po, maybe fifty. I remember that his sweaty brow seemed to weep at my every move. He wore a dark, malodorous suit. One of his pockets was stuffed with a great white kerchief on which he wiped his palm before sweeping his hand over the chosen chess piece with great flourish.

In my crisp pink-and-white dress with scratchy lace at the neck, one of two my mother had sewn for these special occasions, I would clasp my hands under my chin, the delicate points of my elbows poised lightly on the table in the manner my mother had shown me for posing for the press. I would swing my patent leather shoes back and forth like an impatient child riding on a school bus. Then I would pause, suck in my lips, twirl my chosen piece in midair as if undecided, and then firmly plant it in its new threatening place, with a triumphant smile thrown back at my opponent for good measure.

---

1. **Bobby Fischer** (1943–2008), this American chess prodigy attained the top rank of grandmaster in 1958.

Vocabulary
malodorous
(mal ō′ dər əs) *adj.*
having a bad smell

Reading Check

Why does Waverly no longer have to do her chores?

I no longer played in the alley of Waverly Place. I never visited the playground where the pigeons and old men gathered. I went to school, then directly home to learn new chess secrets, cleverly concealed advantages, more escape routes.

But I found it difficult to concentrate at home. My mother had a habit of standing over me while I plotted out my games. I think she thought of herself as my protective ally. Her lips would be sealed tight, and after each move I made, a soft "Hmmmmph" would escape from her nose.

"Ma, I can't practice when you stand there like that," I said one day. She retreated to the kitchen and made loud noises with the pots and pans. When the crashing stopped, I could see out of the corner of my eye that she was standing in the doorway. "Hmmmmph!" Only this one came out of her tight throat.

My parents made many concessions to allow me to practice. One time I complained that the bedroom I shared was so noisy that I couldn't think. Thereafter, my brothers slept in a bed in the living room facing the street. I said I couldn't finish my rice; my head didn't work right when my stomach was too full. I left the table with half-finished bowls and nobody complained. But there was one duty I couldn't avoid. I had to accompany my mother on Saturday market days when I had no tournament to play. My mother would proudly walk with me, visiting many shops, buying very little. "This my daughter Wave-ly Jong," she said to whoever looked her way.

One day, after we left a shop I said under my breath, "I wish you wouldn't do that, telling everybody I'm your daughter." My mother stopped walking. Crowds of people with heavy bags pushed past us on the sidewalk, bumping into first one shoulder, then another.

"Aiii-ya. So shame be with mother?" She grasped my hand even tighter as she glared at me.

I looked down. "It's not that, it's just so obvious. It's just so embarrassing."

"Embarrass you be my daughter?" Her voice was cracking with anger.

"That's not what I meant. That's not what I said."

"What you say?"

I knew it was a mistake to say anything more, but I heard my voice speaking. "Why do you have to use me to show off? If you

Vocabulary
concessions (kən sesh´ ənz) *n.* things given or granted as privileges

Reading Skill
Cause and Effect
Monitor your comprehension. Reflect on your understanding to make a connection between Waverly's success at chess and her family life. Explain.

want to show off, then why don't you learn to play chess?" My mother's eyes turned into dangerous black slits. She had no words for me, just sharp silence.

I felt the wind rushing around my hot ears. I jerked my hand out of my mother's tight grasp and spun around, knocking into an old woman. Her bag of groceries spilled to the ground.

"Aii-ya! Stupid girl!" my mother and the woman cried. Oranges and tin cans careened down the sidewalk. As my mother stooped to help the old woman pick up the escaping food, I took off.

I raced down the street, dashing between people, not looking back as my mother screamed shrilly, "Meimei! Meimei!" I fled down an alley, past dark curtained shops and merchants washing the grime off their windows. I sped into the sunlight, into a large street crowded with tourists examining trinkets and souvenirs. I ducked into another dark alley, down another street, up another alley. I ran until it hurt and I realized I had nowhere to go, that I was not running from anything. The alleys contained no escape routes.

My breath came out like angry smoke. It was cold. I sat down on an upturned plastic pail next to a stack of empty boxes, cupping my chin with my hands, thinking hard. I imagined my mother, first walking briskly down one street or another looking for me, then giving up and returning home to await my arrival. After two hours, I stood up on creaking legs and slowly walked home.

The alley was quiet and I could see the yellow lights shining from our flat like two tiger's eyes in the night. I climbed the sixteen steps to the door, advancing quietly up each so as not to make any warning sounds. I turned the knob; the door was locked. I heard a chair moving, quick steps, the locks turning—click! click! click!—and then the door opened.

"About time you got home," said Vincent. "Boy, are you in trouble."

He slid back to the dinner table. On a platter were the remains of a large fish, its fleshy head still connected to bones swimming upstream in vain escape. Standing there waiting for my punishment, I heard my mother speak in a dry voice.

"We not concerning this girl. This girl not have concerning for us."

Nobody looked at me. Bone chopsticks clinked against the insides of bowls being emptied into hungry mouths.

I walked into my room, closed the door, and lay down on my bed. The room was dark, the ceiling filled with shadows from the dinnertime lights of neighboring flats.

> *My mother had a habit of standing over me while I plotted out my games.*

Reading Check

What do Waverly and her mother argue about at the market?

In my head, I saw a chessboard with sixty-four black and white squares. Opposite me was my opponent, two angry black slits. She wore a triumphant smile. "Strongest wind cannot be seen," she said.

Her black men advanced across the plane, slowly marching to each successive level as a single unit. My white pieces screamed as they scurried and fell off the board one by one. As her men drew closer to my edge, I felt myself growing light. I rose up into the air and flew out the window. Higher and higher, above the alley, over the tops of tiled roofs, where I was gathered up by the wind and pushed up toward the night sky until everything below me disappeared and I was alone.

I closed my eyes and pondered my next move.

Spiral Review
Irony
What role does irony play in the thoughts Waverly expresses in this paragraph?

"Strongest wind cannot be seen."

Critical Thinking

Support your responses with evidence from the text.

1. **Respond:** Which character did you find most realistic? Explain.

2. **(a)** Early in the story, what happens when Waverly asks for a bag of salted plums? **(b) Connect:** What happens when she stops asking? **(c) Make Inferences:** How does Waverly later apply that strategy to her desire to play chess competitively?

3. **(a)** How does Mrs. Jong teach Waverly rules of behavior? **(b) Connect:** How does Waverly translate these rules into strategies for winning at chess? **(c) Draw Conclusions:** How does she use these rules against her mother?

4. **Speculate:** Who do you think will "win" the game between Waverly and her mother? Explain.

5. **Take a Position:** Was Waverly right in challenging her mother's actions and attitude? Explain why or why not.

Is conflict necessary?
(a) Is it necessary for Waverly to oppose her mother at the market? **(b)** How do their personal and cultural differences make it "necessary" for Waverly to see her mother on the other side of the chess board?

Literary Analysis: Characterization

1. Describe the character of Waverly. Then, analyze how the author develops her as a **complex yet believable character** through a range of literary devices.

2. **(a)** Is the conversation in which Waverly and Mrs. Jong discuss Chinese torture an example of direct characterization or indirect characterization? Explain your response. **(b)** What do you learn about Mrs. Jong's character from this exchange?

Reading Skill: Cause and Effect

3. Use a chart like the one shown to reflect on your understanding and **make connections** between the causes and effects in this story. **(a)** Note two causes for Waverly's success with chess. **(b)** List three effects of her success.

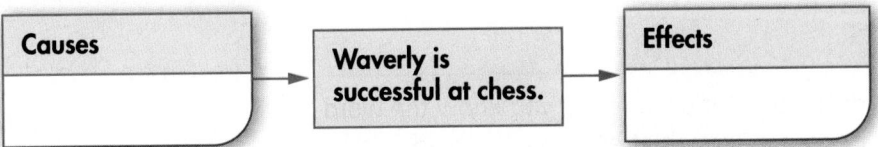

Causes		Effects
	Waverly is successful at chess.	

4. **(a)** Why does Mrs. Jong give Waverly special privileges? **(b)** How do these privileges affect Waverly and her relationship with her mother? Use details from the text to explain your response.

Vocabulary

Practice Tell whether each sentence below makes sense. Use the meaning of the italicized vocabulary word to explain your answer.

1. The *pungent* scent of the baking pie drew the hungry crowd.
2. The girl was wary when the lady *benevolently* distributed cookies.
3. The audience was bored by the comedian's brilliant *retort*.
4. He gave his wife a bottle of expensive, *malodorous* perfume.
5. During play rehearsals, Mom made some *concessions* regarding my homework.
6. With his average talent, the violin *prodigy* amazed no one.

Word Power Use the context of the sentences and what you know about the **Latin root -bene-** to explain your answer to each question.

1. Would you appreciate what a *benefactor* would do for you?
2. What are some of the *benefits* of exercise?

Word Power

The **Latin root -bene-** means "well."

Apply It Explain how the root -bene- helps you determine the meanings of these technical academic words from social studies. Consult a dictionary if necessary.

benign
benediction
beneficiary

Is *conflict* necessary?

Writing About the Big Question

In "The Necklace," a woman is jealous of people with greater wealth and social standing. Use these sentence starters to develop your ideas about the Big Question.

Jealousy can lead to many conflicts because_____.

Learning to **appreciate** who we are and what we have can help us avoid conflict because _____.

As You Read Consider how a jealous attitude creates both internal and external conflict.

Vocabulary

Read each word and its definition. Decide whether you know the word well, know it a little bit, or do not know it at all. After you read, see how your knowledge of each word has increased.

- **rueful** (rōō′ fəl) *adj.* feeling sorrow or regret (p. 333) *With a rueful sigh, she picked up the pieces of the broken dish.* rue *v.*

- **resplendent** (ri splen′ dənt) *adj.* shining brightly (p. 336) *The winner's face was resplendent as he accepted the prize.* splendor *n.* splendid *adj.*

- **dejection** (dē jek′ shən) *n.* lowness of spirits; depression (p. 339) *I suffered dejection when I lost the spelling bee.* deject *v.* dejected *adj.*

- **fortitude** (fôrt′ ə tōōd′) *n.* the strength to bear misfortune and pain (p. 340) *Lucy met each problem with fortitude and a sense of humor.* forte *n.*

- **disheveled** (di shev′ əld) *adj.* untidy (p. 341) *Val's disheveled hair showed that it was very windy outside.* dishevel *v.*

- **profoundly** (prō found′ lē) *adv.* deeply (p. 342) *We were all profoundly moved by the long-lost brothers' reunion.* profound *adj.*

Word Power

The **Latin root -jec(t)-** means "to throw."

In this story, the Loisels feel **dejection.** A problem has made them feel gloomy; literally, it has thrown them down emotionally.

Meet
Guy de Maupassant
(1850–1893)

Author of
The Necklace

Perhaps the best-known short-story writer in the world, Guy de Maupassant (gē´ də mō pä sän´) wrote tales that are realistic and pessimistic, and often offer surprise endings.

Friendship with Writers Following his army service, Maupassant settled in Paris, where he began to develop his skills as a writer, guided by the famous French author Gustave Flaubert. Maupassant also joined a circle of writers led by French novelist Emile Zola. With Zola's encouragement, Maupassant published his first short story, "Ball of Fat," in 1880. The story earned him immediate fame and freed him to write full time. "The Necklace" is perhaps his most widely read story.

BACKGROUND FOR THE STORY

Social Studies Connection

European Society

During the nineteenth century, the old social order in Europe changed. Previously, society had been divided into two main classes: nobles, who owned land, and peasants, who farmed it. However, as industry spread, a new middle class emerged and people could rise—or sink—in social position. Some sought to own material goods as a mark of higher social standing.

Did You Know?
Maupassant wrote more than 300 short stories, six novels, and other books.

The Necklace

Guy de Maupassant

*S*he was one of those pretty, charming young women who are born, as if by an error of Fate, into a petty official's family.

She had no dowry,[1] no hopes, not the slightest chance of being appreciated, understood, loved, and married by a rich and distinguished man; so she slipped into marriage with a minor civil servant at the Ministry of Education.

Unable to afford jewelry, she dressed simply: but she was as wretched as a déclassée, for women have neither caste nor breeding—in them beauty, grace, and charm replace pride of birth. Innate refinement, instinctive elegance, and suppleness of wit give them their place on the only scale that counts, and these qualities make humble girls the peers of the grandest ladies.

She suffered constantly, feeling that all the attributes of a gracious life, every luxury, should rightly have been hers. The poverty of her rooms—the shabby walls, the worn furniture, the ugly upholstery—caused her pain. All these things that another woman of her class would not even have noticed, tormented her and made her angry. The very sight of the little Breton girl who cleaned for her awoke rueful thoughts and the wildest dreams in her mind. She dreamt of thick-carpeted reception rooms with Oriental hangings, lighted by tall,

---

1. **dowry** (dou′ rē) *n.* property that a woman brought to her husband at marriage.

Literary Analysis
Characterization
In the first two paragraphs, what literary devices does the author use to develop the young woman as a complex yet believable character? Explain.

Vocabulary
rueful (rōō′ fəl) *adj.* feeling sorrow or regret

Reading Check
Why does the woman suffer constantly?

The Necklace **333**

bronze torches, and with two huge footmen in knee breeches, made drowsy by the heat from the stove, asleep in the wide armchairs. She dreamt of great drawing rooms upholstered in old silks, with fragile little tables holding priceless knick-knacks, and of enchanting little sitting rooms redolent of perfume, designed for tea-time chats with intimate friends—famous, sought-after men whose attentions all women longed for.

When she sat down to dinner at her round table with its three-day-old cloth, and watched her husband opposite her lift the lid of the soup tureen and exclaim, delighted: "Ah, a good homemade beef stew! There's nothing better . . ." she would visualize elegant dinners with gleaming silver amid tapestried walls peopled by knights and ladies and exotic birds in a fairy forest; she would think of exquisite dishes served on gorgeous china, and of gallantries whispered and received with sphinx-like smiles while eating the pink flesh of trout or wings of grouse.

She had no proper wardrobe, no jewels, nothing. And those were the only things that she loved—she felt she was made for them. She would have so loved to charm, to be envied, to be admired and sought after.

She had a rich friend, a schoolmate from the convent she had attended, but she didn't like to visit her because it always made her so miserable when she got home again. She would weep for whole days at a time from sorrow, regret, despair, and distress.

Then one evening her husband arrived home looking triumphant and waving a large envelope.

"There," he said, "there's something for you."

She tore it open eagerly and took out a printed card which said:

"The Minister of Education and Madame Georges Ramponneau [ma dam´ zhôrzh ram pə nō´] request the pleasure of the company of M. and Mme. Loisel [lwa zel´] at an evening reception at the Ministry on Monday, January 18th."

Instead of being delighted, as her husband had hoped, she tossed the invitation on the table and muttered, annoyed:

"What do you expect me to do with that?"

"Why, I thought you'd be pleased, dear. You never go out and this would be an occasion for you, a great one! I had a lot of trouble getting it. Everyone wants an invitation; they're in great demand and there are only a few reserved for the employees. All the officials will be there."

She looked at him, irritated, and said impatiently:

"I haven't a thing to wear. How could I go?"

Literary Analysis
Characterization
What does the husband's comment in this paragraph reveal indirectly about his character?

Reading Skill
Cause and Effect
Why do visits to her rich friend always fill the young woman with despair?

It had never even occurred to him. He stammered:

"But what about the dress you wear to the theater? I think it's lovely. . . ."

He fell silent, amazed and bewildered to see that his wife was crying. Two big tears escaped from the corners of her eyes and rolled slowly toward the corners of her mouth. He mumbled:

"What is it? What is it?"

But, with great effort, she had overcome her misery; and now she answered him calmly, wiping her tear-damp cheeks:

"It's nothing. It's just that I have no evening dress and so I can't go to the party. Give the invitation to one of your colleagues whose wife will be better dressed than I would be."

He was overcome. He said:

"Listen, Mathilde [ma tēld´], how much would an evening dress cost—a suitable one that you could wear again on other occasions, something very simple?"

She thought for several seconds, making her calculations and at the same time estimating how much she could ask for without eliciting an immediate refusal and an exclamation of horror from this economical government clerk.

At last, not too sure of herself, she said:

"It's hard to say exactly but I think I could manage with four hundred francs."

He went a little pale, for that was exactly the amount he had put aside to buy a rifle so that he could go hunting the following summer near Nanterre, with a few friends who went shooting larks around there on Sundays.

However, he said:

"Well, all right, then. I'll give you four hundred francs. But try to get something really nice." •

As the day of the ball drew closer, Madame Loisel seemed depressed, disturbed, worried—despite the fact that her dress was ready. One evening her husband said:

"What's the matter? You've really been very strange these last few days."

And she answered:

"I hate not having a single jewel, not one stone, to wear. I shall look so dowdy.[2] I'd almost rather not go to the party."

Reading Skill
Cause and Effect
The husband is surprised by his wife's reaction to the party invitation. Reflect on your understanding and make connections to determine what cause is connected to this effect.

> She had no proper wardrobe, no jewels, nothing. And those were the only things that she loved—she felt she was made for them.

Reading Check

What does Monsieur Loisel give up to make his wife happy?

---

2. **dowdy** (dou´dē) *adj.* shabby.

He suggested:

"You can wear some fresh flowers. It's considered very chic[3] at this time of year. For ten francs you can get two or three beautiful roses."

That didn't satisfy her at all.

"No . . . there's nothing more humiliating than to look poverty-stricken among a lot of rich women."

Then her husband exclaimed:

"Wait—you silly thing! Why don't you go and see Madame Forestier [fôr əs tyā´] and ask her to lend you some jewelry. You certainly know her well enough for that, don't you think?"

She let out a joyful cry.

"You're right. It never occurred to me."

The next day she went to see her friend and related her tale of woe.

Madame Forestier went to her mirrored wardrobe, took out a big jewel case, brought it to Madame Loisel, opened it, and said:

"Take your pick, my dear."

Her eyes wandered from some bracelets to a pearl necklace, then to a gold Venetian cross set with stones, of very fine workmanship. She tried on the jewelry before the mirror, hesitating, unable to bring herself to take them off, to give them back. And she kept asking:

"Do you have anything else, by chance?"

"Why yes. Here, look for yourself. I don't know which ones you'll like."

All at once, in a box lined with black satin, she came upon a superb diamond necklace, and her heart started beating with overwhelming desire. Her hands trembled as she picked it up. She fastened it around her neck over her high-necked dress and stood there gazing at herself ecstatically.

Hesitantly, filled with terrible anguish, she asked:

"Could you lend me this one—just this and nothing else?"

"Yes, of course."

She threw her arms around her friend's neck, kissed her ardently, and fled with her treasure.

The day of the party arrived. Madame Loisel was a great success. She was the prettiest woman there—resplendent, graceful, beaming, and deliriously happy. All the men looked at her, asked who she was, tried to get themselves introduced to her. All the minister's aides wanted to waltz with her. The minister himself noticed her.

Literary Analysis
Characterization
What does Madame Loisel's comment reveal indirectly about her attitudes and values?

Vocabulary
resplendent (ri splen´ dənt) *adj.* shining brightly

---

3. **chic** (shēk) *adj.* fashionable.

She danced enraptured—carried away, intoxicated with pleasure, forgetting everything in this triumph of her beauty and the glory of her success, floating in a cloud of happiness formed by all this homage, all this admiration, all the desires she had stirred up—by this victory so complete and so sweet to the heart of a woman. ●

When she left the party, it was almost four in the morning. Her husband had been sleeping since midnight in a small, deserted

▲ **Critical Viewing**
What key part of the story could this image illustrate? **[Connect]**

Reading Check

How does Madame Loisel feel at the ball?

▲ **Critical Viewing**
What details in this painting suggest the setting of the story?
[Connect]

sitting room, with three other gentlemen whose wives were having a wonderful time.

He brought her wraps so that they could leave and put them around her shoulders—the plain wraps from her everyday life whose shabbiness jarred with the elegance of her evening dress. She felt this and wanted to escape quickly so that the other women, who were enveloping themselves in their rich furs, wouldn't see her.

Loisel held her back.

"Wait a minute. You'll catch cold out there. I'm going to call a cab."

But she wouldn't listen to him and went hastily downstairs. Outside in the street, there was no cab to be found; they set out to look for one, calling to the drivers they saw passing in the distance.

They walked toward the Seine,[4] shivering and miserable. Finally, on the embankment, they found one of those ancient nocturnal broughams[5] which are only to be seen in Paris at night, as if they were ashamed to show their shabbiness in daylight.

---

4. **Seine** (sān) river flowing through Paris.
5. **broughams** (brōōmz) *n.* horse-drawn carriages.

It took them to their door in the Rue des Martyrs, and they went sadly upstairs to their apartment. For her, it was all over. And he was thinking that he had to be at the Ministry by ten.

She took off her wraps before the mirror so that she could see herself in all her glory once more. Then she cried out. The necklace was gone; there was nothing around her neck.

Her husband, already half undressed, asked:

"What's the matter?"

She turned toward him in a frenzy:

"The . . . the . . . necklace—it's gone."

He got up, thunderstruck.

"What did you say? . . . What! . . . Impossible!"

And they searched the folds of her dress, the folds of her wrap, the pockets, everywhere. They didn't find it.

He asked:

"Are you sure you still had it when we left the ball?"

"Yes. I remember touching it in the hallway of the Ministry."

"But if you had lost it in the street, we would have heard it fall. It must be in the cab."

"Yes, most likely. Do you remember the number?"

"No. What about you—did you notice it?"

"No."

They looked at each other in utter dejection. Finally Loisel got dressed again.

"I'm going to retrace the whole distance we covered on foot," he said, "and see if I can't find it."

And he left the house. She remained in her evening dress, too weak to go to bed, sitting crushed on a chair, lifeless and blank.

Her husband returned at about seven o'clock. He had found nothing.

He went to the police station, to the newspapers to offer a reward, to the offices of the cab companies—in a word, wherever there seemed to be the slightest hope of tracing it.

She spent the whole day waiting, in a state of utter hopelessness before such an appalling catastrophe.

Loisel returned in the evening, his face lined and pale; he had learned nothing.

"You must write to your friend," he said, "and tell her that you've broken the clasp of the necklace and that you're getting it mended. That'll give us time to decide what to do."

He brought her wraps so that they could leave and put them around her shoulders—the plain wraps from her everyday life...

Vocabulary
dejection (di jek´ shən) *n.* lowness of spirits; depression

Literary Analysis
Characterization
What do the Loisels' actions after the necklace is lost reveal about their individual characters?

Reading Check

When does Madame Loisel discover the necklace is missing?

Reading Skill
Cause and Effect
Reflect on your under-
standing to monitor
your comprehension.
What connections can
you make between
the borrowing of the
necklace and the
couple's visit to the
jeweler?

She wrote the letter at his dictation.

By the end of the week, they had lost all hope.

Loisel, who had aged five years, declared:

"We'll have to replace the necklace."

The next day they took the case in which it had been kept and went to the jeweler whose name appeared inside it. He looked through his ledgers:

"I didn't sell this necklace, madame. I only supplied the case."

Then they went from one jeweler to the next, trying to find a necklace like the other, racking their memories, both of them sick with worry and distress.

In a fashionable shop near the Palais Royal, they found a diamond necklace which they decided was exactly like the other. It was worth 40,000 francs. They could have it for 36,000 francs.

They asked the jeweler to hold it for them for three days, and they stipulated that he should take it back for 34,000 francs if the other necklace was found before the end of February.

Loisel possessed 18,000 francs left him by his father. He would borrow the rest.

He borrowed, asking a thousand francs from one man, five hundred from another, a hundred here, fifty there. He signed promissory notes,[6] borrowed at exorbitant rates, dealt with usurers and the entire race of moneylenders. He compromised his whole career, gave his signature even when he wasn't sure he would be able to honor it, and horrified by the anxieties with which his future would be filled, by the black misery about to descend upon him, by the prospect of physical privation and moral suffering, went to get the new necklace, placing on the jeweler's counter 36,000 francs.

When Madame Loisel went to return the necklace, Madame Forestier said in a faintly waspish tone:

"You could have brought it back a little sooner! I might have needed it."

She didn't open the case as her friend had feared she might. If she had noticed the substitution, what would she have thought? What would she have said? Mightn't she have taken Madame Loisel for a thief? ●

Madame Loisel came to know the awful life of the poverty-stricken. However, she resigned herself to it with unexpected fortitude. The crushing debt had to be paid. She would pay it. They dismissed the maid; they moved into an attic under the roof.

She came to know all the heavy household chores, the loathsome work of the kitchen. She washed the dishes, wearing

Vocabulary
fortitude
(fôrt´ ə to͞od´) *n.* the
strength to bear
misfortune and pain

---

6. **promissory** (präm´ i sôr´ ē) **notes** written promises to pay back borrowed money.

down her pink nails on greasy casseroles and the bottoms of saucepans. She did the laundry, washing shirts and dishcloths which she hung on a line to dry; she took the garbage down to the street every morning, and carried water upstairs, stopping at every floor to get her breath. Dressed like a working-class woman, she went to the fruit store, the grocer, and the butcher with her basket on her arm, bargaining, outraged, contesting each sou[7] of her pitiful funds.

Every month some notes had to be honored and more time requested on others.

Her husband worked in the evenings, putting a shopkeeper's ledgers in order, and often at night as well, doing copying at twenty-five centimes a page.

And it went on like that for ten years.

After ten years, they had made good on everything, including the usurious rates and the compound interest.

Madame Loisel looked old now. She had become the sort of strong woman, hard and coarse, that one finds in poor families. Disheveled, her skirts askew, with reddened hands, she spoke in a loud voice, slopping water over the floors as she washed them. But sometimes, when her husband was at the office, she would sit down by the window and muse over that party long ago when she had been so beautiful, the belle of the ball.

How would things have turned out if she hadn't lost that necklace? Who could tell? How strange and fickle life is! How little it takes to make or break you!

Then one Sunday when she was strolling along the Champs Elysées[8] to forget the week's chores for a while, she suddenly caught sight of a woman taking a child for a walk. It was Madame Forestier, still young, still beautiful, still charming.

Madame Loisel started to tremble. Should she speak to her? Yes, certainly she should. And now that she had paid everything back, why shouldn't she tell her the whole story?

She went up to her.

"Hello, Jeanne."

The other didn't recognize her and was surprised that this plainly dressed woman should speak to her so familiarly. She murmured:

"But . . . madame! . . . I'm sure . . . You must be mistaken."

"No, I'm not. I am Mathilde Loisel."

She had become the sort of strong woman, hard and coarse, that one finds in poor families.

Vocabulary
disheveled
(di shev´ əld) *adj.* untidy

Reading Skill
Cause and Effect
What causes Madame Loisel to tremble at the sight of Madame Forestier?

Reading Check

How has Madame Loisel's appearance changed?

---

7. sou (sōō) *n.* former French coin, worth very little; the centime (sän» tèm«), mentioned later, was also of little value.
8. Champs Elysées (shän zā lē zā´) fashionable street in Paris.

Her friend gave a little cry.

"Oh! Oh, my poor Mathilde, how you've changed!"

"Yes, I've been through some pretty hard times since I last saw you and I've had plenty of trouble—and all because of you!"

"Because of me? What do you mean?"

"You remember the diamond necklace you lent me to wear to the party at the Ministry?"

"Yes. What about it?"

"Well, I lost it."

"What are you talking about? You returned it to me."

"What I gave back to you was another one just like it. And it took us ten years to pay for it. You can imagine it wasn't easy for us, since we were quite poor. . . . Anyway, I'm glad it's over and done with."

Madame Forestier stopped short.

"You say you bought a diamond necklace to replace that other one?"

"Yes. You didn't even notice then? They really were exactly alike." And she smiled, full of a proud, simple joy.

Madame Forestier, profoundly moved, took Mathilde's hands in her own.

"Oh, my poor, poor Mathilde! Mine was false. It was worth five hundred francs at the most!"

**Spiral Review
Irony**
What role does
irony play in the
conclusion
of this story?

Critical Thinking

1. **Respond:** Do you feel sorry for Madame Loisel at the end of the story? Why or why not?

2. **(a)** As the story begins, why is Madame Loisel unhappy with her life? **(b) Make Inferences:** Do you think the author wants readers to sympathize with her unhappiness? Explain your response.

3. **(a)** How does Monsieur Loisel respond to Madame Loisel's disappointment? **(b) Compare and Contrast:** How is Monsieur Loisel different from his wife? Use details from the text to explain.

4. **(a) Interpret:** How does the change in Madame Loisel's appearance illustrate the internal and external conflicts of the story? **(b) Draw Conclusions:** What is the effect of this change?

Is conflict necessary?
(a) What external conflict is proven unnecessary by the end of the story? **(b)** Could a change in Madame Loisel's attitude have prevented her internal conflict?

Support
your responses
with evidence
from the text.

Literary Analysis: **Characterization**

1. Describe Madame Loisel's character. Then, analyze how the author develops her as a **complex yet believable character** through a range of literary devices.

2. (a) Is the conversation on the day of the ball in which the Loisels discuss Madame's attire an example of indirect characterization or direct characterization? Explain your response. **(b)** What do you learn about both Monsieur and Madame Loisel's characters from this exchange?

Reading Skill: **Cause and Effect**

3. Reflect on your understanding. Use a chart like the one shown to **make connections** between the **causes and effects** in this story. Note two causes for and two effects of Madame Loisel's decision to borrow the necklace from Madame Forestier.

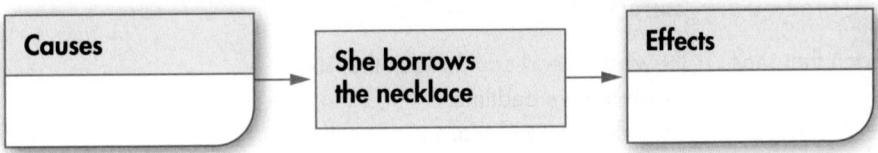

Causes		She borrows the necklace		Effects

4. Does Madame Loisel cause her own suffering? Explain.

Vocabulary

Practice Tell whether each sentence below makes sense. Use the meaning of the italicized vocabulary word to explain your answer.

1. With a *rueful* smile, she described the fun she had had at the fair.

2. The tired campers were *resplendent* as they hiked in the rain.

3. Alan went to the interview *disheveled* and wearing a new suit.

4. The class was *profoundly* moved by the story of the heroic dog.

5. One of my grandfather's greatest qualities is his *fortitude*.

6. With great *dejection,* the family celebrated the engagement.

Word Power Use the context of the sentences and what you know about the **Latin root *-jec(t)-*** to explain your answer to each question.

1. Why might a player be *ejected* from a basketball game?

2. Could you challenge an idea by raising an *objection* to it?

Word Power

The **Latin root *-jec(t)-*** means "to throw."

Apply It Explain how the root *-jec(t)-* helps you determine the meanings of these technical academic words from science. Consult a dictionary if necessary.

project
reject
trajectory
inject

Integrated Language Skills

Rules of the Game • The Necklace

Conventions: Subjunctive Mood

The **subjunctive mood** is used to express doubts, wishes, and possibilities. It shows that what is being expressed is not now true, and may never be true.

The subjunctive mood is often used in clauses beginning with *if* and *that*. *That* clauses in the subjunctive mood frequently follow verbs such as *ask, wish, demand, insist, prefer, suggest,* and *require*.

To form the subjunctive mood of a third-person singular verb in the present tense, drop the usual *–s* or *–es* ending. In the present tense, the subjunctive form of the verb *be* is *be*. In the past tense, the subjunctive form of *be* is *were*.

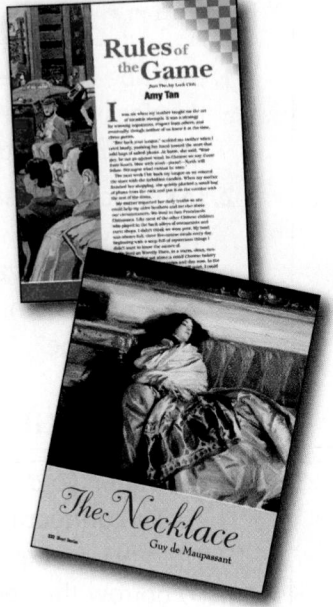

Incorrect	Correct
If I *was* taller, I could reach that shelf. I wish it *was* bedtime.	If I *were* taller, I could reach that shelf. I wish it *were* bedtime.
The rules demand that everyone *is* quiet during the test.	The rules demand that everyone *be* quiet during the test.
The guide insists that each tourist boards the bus.	The guide insists that each tourist *board* the bus.

Practice A In each sentence, identify the verb that is in the subjunctive mood.

1. The host asked that everyone be quiet during the chess tournament.

2. Waverly might win fewer matches if her mother were less supportive.

3. Mrs. Jong demands that Waverly accompany her to the market.

Speaking Application With a partner, discuss a topic about which you have doubts. In your discussion, use at least two sentences with verbs in the subjunctive mood.

Practice B Complete each sentence by adding a verb in the subjunctive mood.

1. Madame Loisel practically demands that her husband _____ her a gown.

2. She behaves as if social standing _____ more important than love.

3. Her husband suggests that she _____ some jewelry from a friend.

Writing Application Write a brief paragraph about a wish, a doubt, or a possibility. Use the subjunctive mood in at least two sentences in your paragraph.

PH GRAMMAR HANDBOOK Further instruction and practice are available in the *Prentice Hall Grammar Handbook*.

Writing

Each of these stories deals with people learning lessons. Think about a lesson that you could teach the characters in "The Necklace" or "Rules of the Game." Plan and develop a **written presentation** about your ideas.

- Make notes about an issue that the characters face. Consider what you might teach them and how best to convey your ideas.
- Based on your audience, purpose, and point of view as an outsider, choose an **appropriate genre** and text structure. For example, you might write an essay, or you might tell a story with a moral.
- As you revise, check that your presentation is organized logically. Add transitions where needed to improve the flow of ideas.

Grammar Application Make sure to use the subjunctive mood correctly in your essay to express doubts, wishes, and possibilities.

Writing Workshop: *Work in Progress*

Prewriting for Cause-and-Effect Essay It often is easier to see effects than to understand causes. In fact, much of science is the attempt to find causes for known effects. For a cause-and-effect essay you may write, list ten effects for which you do not know the cause. Put this "What's the Cause?" list into your writing portfolio.

Research and Technology

The characters in these stories need facts in order to succeed. With a few classmates, make an **informative brochure.**

- If you read "The Necklace," make a brochure about the qualities and uses of diamonds.
- If you read "Rules of the Game," make a brochure about the history, rules, and strategies of chess.

Follow these steps to complete the assignment:

- **Brainstorm** with your team to formulate **open-ended research questions.** Then, use a variety of print and electronic sources to answer the questions your team has asked.
- Organize your coverage. Plan the sections for the brochure. Choose which ideas are most important, and use illustrations to convey some information (for example, you might include diagrams of chess moves).
- Design your brochure. Add visual elements but avoid a "cluttered" look. If possible, use computer software to lay out your brochure.

 Focus on the TEKS

Conventions
(17)(B) Identify and use the subjunctive mood to express doubts, wishes, and possibilities.
Research
(20) Ask open-ended research questions.
(20)(A) Brainstorm.
Writing
(13)(A) Plan a first draft by selecting the correct genre for conveying meaning to multiple audiences.

Use this prewriting activity to prepare for the **Writing Workshop** on page 402.

TEXAS PHLitOnline
www.PHLitOnline.com

- Interactive graphic organizers
- Grammar tutorial
- Interactive journals

Selection Choices

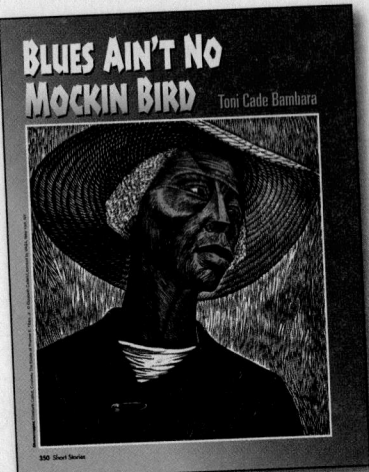

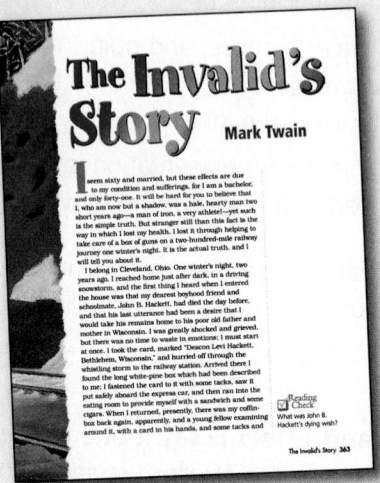

▲ Read **"Blues Ain't No Mockin Bird"** to find out what happens when two photographers clash with a woman who does not want them to film her property.

▲ Read **"The Invalid's Story"** to see how a master humorist takes what otherwise would be a somber train ride and makes it comical.

 TEXAS Focus on the TEKS

Meet these standards with either **"Blues Ain't No Mockin Bird"** (p. 350) or **"The Invalid's Story"** (p. 362).

Reading

(5)(B) Analyze how authors develop complex yet believable characters in works of fiction through a range of literary devices. *(Literary Analysis: Dialogue and Dialect)*

(5)(C) Analyze the way in which a work of fiction is shaped by the narrator's point of view. *(Spiral Review: Point of View)*

(1)(A) Determine the meanings of grade-level technical academic English words in multiple content areas derived from Latin affixes. *(Word Power: Apply It)*

Reading/Comprehension Skills

RC-9(A) Reflect on understanding to monitor comprehension (e.g., making connections). *(Reading Skill: Cause and Effect)*

Oral and Written Conventions

(17)(A)(i) Use and understand the function of more complex active and passive tenses in the context of reading, writing, and speaking. *(Conventions: Verbs: Active and Passive Voice)*

Listening and Speaking

(24)(A) Listen responsively to a speaker by asking questions related to the content for clarification and elaboration. *(Listening and Speaking: Dialogue)*

Literary Analysis: Dialogue and Dialect

Dialogue is a conversation between or among characters in a literary work. In prose, dialogue is usually set off by quotation marks, and a new paragraph indicates a change in speaker. Authors use dialogue for these purposes:

- to develop complex yet believable characters
- to reveal character traits and relationships
- to advance the action of the plot and develop the conflict
- to add variety, color, and realism to narratives

To make characters and settings vivid, authors may write dialogue reflecting characters' dialect. **Dialect** is a way of speaking that is common to people of a region or group. The words, pronunciations, and grammar of a dialect differ from those of the standard form of a language.

As You Read Analyze how the author develops complex yet believable characters through the devices of dialogue and dialect.

Reading Skill: Cause and Effect

A **plot** is a series of causes and effects. A **cause** is an event, an action, or a feeling that produces a result. An **effect** is the result produced. To **monitor your comprehension** while reading, reflect on your understanding and visualize the action to analyze cause and effect.

- Use text details to picture the setting, characters, and action.
- Use the details of your mental picture to help you **make connections** between actions and events.

Using the Strategy: Cause-and-Effect Flow Chart

As You Read Reflect on your understanding to monitor your comprehension. Use a flow chart like this one to make connections between the causes and effects in the text.

Event (Cause)	Mental Picture	Event (Effect)
Steve turned on the sprinkler.	Matt on lawn Jaime on porch Sprinkler on lawn	Matt got wet; Jaime just laughed.

TEXAS
PHLitOnline
www.PHLitOnline.com

Hear It!
- Selection summary audio
- Selection audio

See It!
- Get Connected video
- Background video
- More about the author
- Vocabulary flashcards

Do It!
- Interactive journals
- Interactive graphic organizers
- Self-test
- Internet activity
- Grammar tutorial
- Interactive vocabulary games

Is *conflict* necessary?

Writing About the Big Question

In "Blues Ain't No Mockin Bird," an elderly woman finds it necessary to fight with people who threaten something important to her. Use these sentence starters to develop your ideas about the Big Question.

People will **battle** to protect _____ because _____.

Personal feelings and **issues** spark conflicts between people because _____.

As You Read Compare the responses of the various characters to the situation that antagonizes Granny, and look for the successful resolution of the conflict.

Vocabulary

Read each word and its definition. Decide whether you know the word well, know it a little bit, or do not know it at all. After you read, see how your knowledge of each word has increased.

- **ladle** (lād´ 'l) *n.* a long-handled, cuplike spoon for dipping out liquids (p. 351) *The waiter used a ladle to put soup into my bowl.* *ladle v.*

- **raggedy** (rag´ i dē) *adj.* torn and in bad condition (p. 354) *I always wear raggedy old clothes to work in the garden. ragged adj.*

- **stalks** (stôks) *v.* walks in a stiff, haughty, or grim manner (p. 355) *An angry man stalks out of the room in a huff. stalk n. stalker n.*

- **formality** (fôr mal´ ə tē) *n.* attention to established rules or customs (p. 356) *His formality conveyed respect for his guests. formal adj. formalize v. informal adj.*

- **reckless** (rek´ lis) *adj.* careless; rash (p. 356) *Reckless driving is a serious offense. recklessly adv. recklessness n.*

- **reels** (rēlz) *n.* frames or spools on which thread, wire, tape, film, or a net is wound (p. 357) *The movies were stored on large metal reels in a temperature-controlled room. reel v.*

Word Power

The **Latin suffix *-ity*** forms nouns from adjectives. It means "the quality of showing a certain characteristic."

This story describes someone who dislikes the **formality** of the title *Miss.* She thinks it has a "too formal" quality.

Author of
BLUES AIN'T NO MOCKIN BIRD

Toni Cade Bambara was a social activist and a writer of short stories, a novel, plays, television scripts, and documentaries. She started writing when she was in kindergarten and had her first story published when she was a senior in college.

"I write because I must," Bambara said. "If there were no more presses, no more publishing houses, I'd still be writing." She was equally devoted to social change and worked to improve the condition of African Americans. Her writing echoes that concern. Her stories are often praised for their vivid portrayals of the daily lives of African Americans in the twentieth century.

BACKGROUND FOR THE STORY

(Science Connection)

Hawks

Hawks are large, predatory birds. They are fiercely territorial, and they often keep the same mate for life. Usually, hawks hunt rabbits, squirrels, and other birds. However, in rural areas they may kill and eat chickens. For a poor rural family like the one in this story, defending the family's flock of chickens from hawks is a matter of survival. Sometimes, when a farmer kills a hawk that has attacked his chickens, he displays it to frighten off other hawks.

DID YOU KNOW?

Bambara was born Miltona Cade but added *Bambara* after discovering it on her great-grandmother's sketchbook. *Bambara* is also the name of an African tribe known for its textiles.

BLUES AIN'T NO MOCKIN BIRD

Toni Cade Bambara

Sharecropper, Elizabeth Catlett, Courtesy The Estate of Thurlow E. Tibbs, Jr., © Elizabeth Catlett/Licensed by VAGA, New York, NY.

The puddle had frozen over, and me and Cathy went stompin in it. The twins from next door, Tyrone and Terry, were swingin so high out of sight we forgot we were waitin our turn on the tire. Cathy jumped up and came down hard on her heels and started tap-dancin. And the frozen patch splinterin every which way underneath kinda spooky. "Looks like a plastic spider web," she said. "A sort of weird spider, I guess, with many mental problems." But really it looked like the crystal paperweight Granny kept in the parlor. She was on the back porch, Granny was, making the cakes drunk. The old ladle dripping rum into the Christmas tins, like it used to drip maple syrup into the pails when we lived in the Judson's woods, like it poured cider into the vats when we were on the Cooper place, like it used to scoop buttermilk and soft cheese when we lived at the dairy.

"Go tell that man we ain't a bunch of trees."

"Ma'am?"

"I said to tell that man to get away from here with that camera." Me and Cathy look over toward the meadow where the men with the station wagon'd been roamin around all mornin. The tall man with a huge camera lassoed to his shoulder was buzzin our way.

"They're makin movie pictures," yelled Tyrone, stiffenin his legs and twistin so the tire'd come down slow so they could see.

"They're makin movie pictures," sang out Terry.

"That boy don't never have anything original to say," say Cathy grown-up.

By the time the man with the camera had cut across our neighbor's yard, the twins were out of the trees swingin low and Granny was onto the steps, the screen door bammin soft and scratchy against her palms. "We thought we'd get a shot or two of the house and everything and then—"

"Good mornin," Granny cut him off. And smiled that smile.

"Good mornin," he said, head all down the way Bingo does when you yell at him about the bones on the kitchen floor. "Nice place you got here, aunty. We thought we'd take a—"

"Did you?" said Granny with her eyebrows. Cathy pulled up her socks and giggled.

Literary Analysis
Dialogue and Dialect
Which features of the title and opening paragraph show that this story is written in dialect?

Vocabulary
ladle (lād′ 'l) *n.* a long-handled, cuplike spoon for dipping out liquids

◀ **Critical Viewing**
As you read, compare Granny with the woman in the illustration.
[Compare and Contrast]

Reading Skill
Cause and Effect
Which details in the text help you to visualize the effect that the camera crew has on Granny?

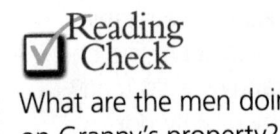
What are the men doing on Granny's property?

"Nice things here," said the man, buzzin his camera over the yard. The pecan barrels, the sled, me and Cathy, the flowers, the printed stones along the driveway, the trees, the twins, the toolshed.

"I don't know about the thing, the it, and the stuff," said Granny, still talkin with her eyebrows. "Just people here is what I tend to consider."

Camera man stopped buzzin. Cathy giggled into her collar.

"Mornin, ladies," a new man said. He had come up behind us when we weren't lookin. "And gents," discoverin the twins givin him a nasty look. "We're filmin for the county," he said with a smile. "Mind if we shoot a bit around here?"

"I do indeed," said Granny with no smile. Smilin man was smiling up a storm. So was Cathy. But he didn't seem to have another word to say, so he and the camera man backed on out the yard, but you could hear the camera buzzin still. "Suppose you just shut that machine off," said Granny real low through her teeth, and took a step down off the porch and then another.

"Now, aunty," Camera said, pointin the thing straight at her.

"Your mama and I are not related."

Smilin man got his notebook out and a chewed-up pencil. "Listen," he said movin back into our yard, "we'd like to have a statement from you . . . for the film. We're filmin for the county, see. Part of the food stamp campaign. You know about the food stamps?"

Granny said nuthin.

"Maybe there's somethin you want to say for the film. I see you grow your own vegetables," he smiled real nice. "If more folks did that, see, there'd be no need—"

Granny wasn't sayin nuthin. So they backed on out, buzzin at our clothesline and the twins' bicycles, then back on down to the meadow. The twins were danglin in the tire, lookin at Granny. Me and Cathy were waitin, too, cause Granny always got somethin to say. She teaches steady with no let-up. "I was on this bridge one time," she started off. "Was a crowd cause this man was goin to jump, you understand. And a minister was there and the police and some other folks. His woman was there, too."

"What was they doin?" asked Tyrone.

"Tryin to talk him out of it was what they was doin. The minister talkin about how it was a mortal sin, suicide. His woman takin bites out of her own hand and not even knowin it, so nervous and cryin and talkin fast."

"So what happened?" asked Tyrone.

"So here comes . . . this person . . . with a camera, takin pictures of the man and the minister and the woman. Takin pictures of the

Literary Analysis
Dialogue and Dialect What does the dialogue between Granny and the film crew show about their attitudes toward each other?

▶ Critical Viewing
Does this vegetable garden seem like one Granny would tend? Why or why not?
[Connect]

man in his misery about to jump, cause life so bad and people been messin with him so bad. This person takin up the whole roll of film practically. But savin a few, of course."

"Of course," said Cathy, hatin the person. Me standin there wonderin how Cathy knew it was "of course" when I didn't and it was *my* grandmother.

After a while Tyrone say, "Did he jump?"

"Yeh, did he jump?" say Terry all eager. And Granny just stared at the twins till their faces swallow up the eager and they don't even care any more about the man jumpin. Then she goes back onto the porch and lets the screen door go for itself. I'm lookin to Cathy to finish the story cause she knows Granny's whole story before me even. Like she knew how come we move so much and Cathy ain't but a third cousin we picked up on the way last Thanksgivin visitin. But she knew it was on account of people drivin Granny crazy till she'd get up in the night and start packin. Mumblin and

Reading Check

How does Granny respond when "Smilin" asks her to make a statement?

Vocabulary
raggedy (rag´ i dē)
adj. torn and in
bad condition

packin and wakin everybody up sayin, "Let's get on away from here before I kill me somebody." Like people wouldn't pay her for things like they said they would. Or Mr. Judson bringin us boxes of old clothes and raggedy magazines. Or Mrs. Cooper comin in our kitchen and touchin everything and sayin how clean it all was. Granny goin crazy, and Granddaddy Cain pullin her off the people, sayin, "Now, now, Cora." But next day loadin up the truck, with rocks all in his jaw, madder than Granny in the first place.

"I read a story once," said Cathy soundin like Granny teacher. "About this lady Goldilocks who barged into a house that wasn't even hers. And not invited, you understand. Messed over the

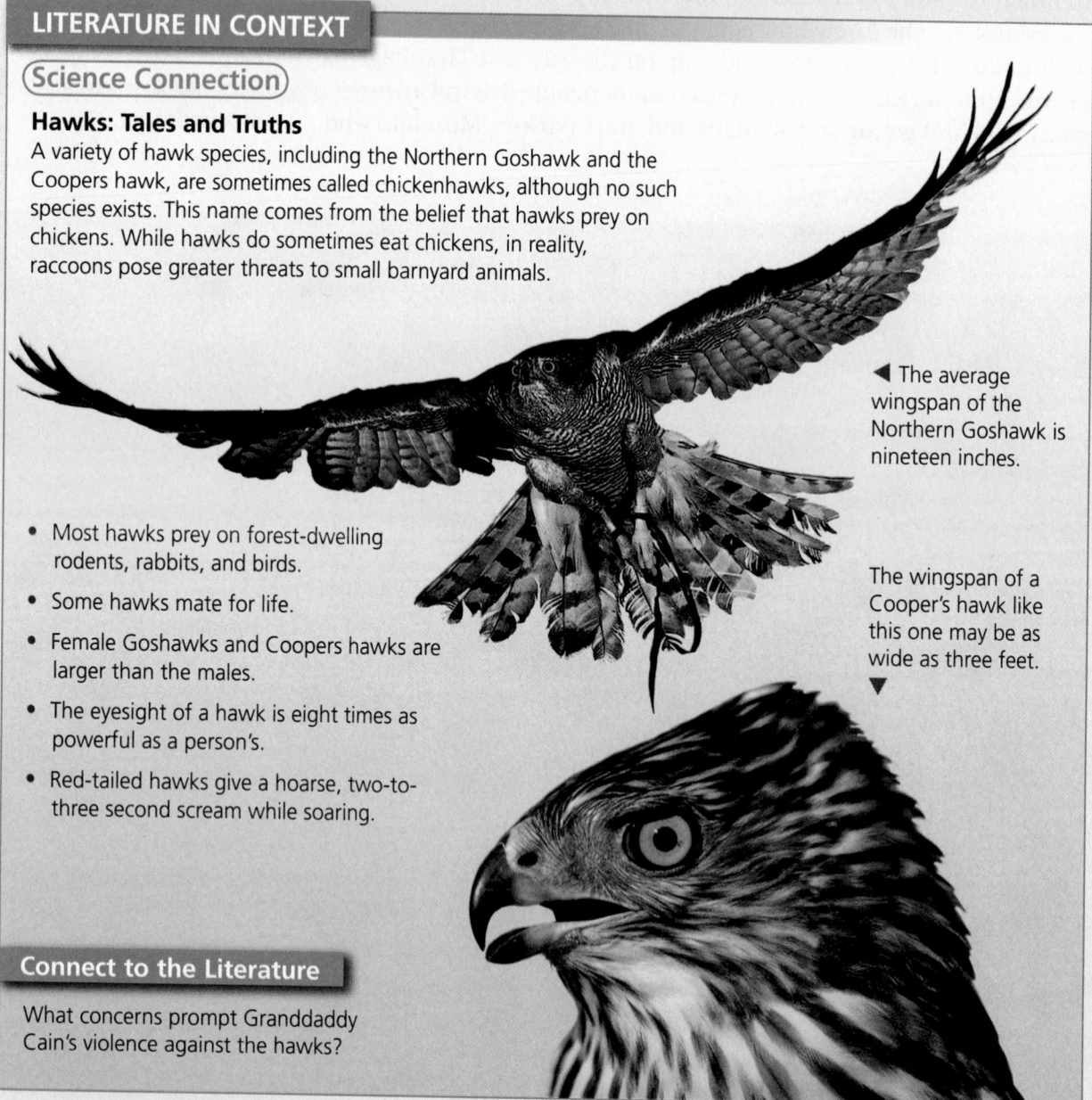

LITERATURE IN CONTEXT

Science Connection

Hawks: Tales and Truths

A variety of hawk species, including the Northern Goshawk and the Coopers hawk, are sometimes called chickenhawks, although no such species exists. This name comes from the belief that hawks prey on chickens. While hawks do sometimes eat chickens, in reality, raccoons pose greater threats to small barnyard animals.

◀ The average wingspan of the Northern Goshawk is nineteen inches.

- Most hawks prey on forest-dwelling rodents, rabbits, and birds.
- Some hawks mate for life.
- Female Goshawks and Coopers hawks are larger than the males.
- The eyesight of a hawk is eight times as powerful as a person's.
- Red-tailed hawks give a hoarse, two-to-three second scream while soaring.

The wingspan of a Cooper's hawk like this one may be as wide as three feet.
▼

Connect to the Literature

What concerns prompt Granddaddy Cain's violence against the hawks?

people's groceries and broke up the people's furniture. Had the nerve to sleep in the folks' bed."

"Then what happened?" asked Tyrone. "What they do, the folks, when they come in to all this mess?"

"Did they make her pay for it?" asked Terry, makin a fist. "I'd've made her pay me."

I didn't even ask. I could see Cathy actress was very likely to just walk away and leave us in mystery about this story which I heard was about some bears.

"Did they throw her out?" asked Tyrone, like his father sounds when he's bein extra nasty-plus to the washin-machine man.

"Woulda," said Terry. "I woulda gone upside her head with my fist and—"

"You woulda done whatcha always do—go cry to Mama, you big baby," said Tyrone. So naturally Terry starts hittin on Tyrone, and next thing you know they tumblin out the tire and rollin on the ground. But Granny didn't say a thing or send the twins home or step out on the steps to tell us about how we can't afford to be fightin amongst ourselves. She didn't say nuthin. So I get into the tire to take my turn. And I could see her leanin up against the pantry table, staring at the cakes she was puttin up for the Christmas sale, mumblin real low and grumpy and holdin her forehead like it wanted to fall off and mess up the rum cakes. •

Behind me I hear before I can see Granddaddy Cain comin through the woods in his field boots. Then I twist around to see the shiny black oilskin cuttin through what little left there was of yellows, reds, and oranges. His great white head not quite round cause of this bloody thing high on his shoulder, like he was wearin a cap on sideways. He takes the shortcut through the pecan grove, and the sound of twigs snapping overhead and underfoot travels clear and cold all the way up to us. And here comes Smilin and Camera up behind him like they was goin to do somethin. Folks like to go for him sometimes. Cathy say it's because he's so tall and quiet and like a king. And people just can't stand it. But Smilin and Camera don't hit him in the head or nuthin. They just buzz on him as he stalks by with the chicken hawk slung over his shoulder, squawkin, drippin red down the back of the oilskin. He passes the porch and stops a second for Granny to see he's caught the hawk at last, but she's just starin and mumblin, and not at the hawk. So he nails the bird to the toolshed door, the hammerin crackin through the eardrums. And the bird flappin himself to death and droolin down the door to paint the gravel in the driveway red, then brown, then black. And the two men movin up on tiptoe like they was invisible or we were blind, one.

Literary Analysis
Dialogue and Dialect
What does the idiom "gone upside her head" probably mean?

Vocabulary
stalks (stôks) v. walks in a stiff, haughty, or grim manner

Reading Check
What does Granddaddy do with the hawk?

Vocabulary
formality (fôr mal′ ə tē)
n. attention to estab-
lished rules or customs
reckless (rek′ lis) *adj.*
careless; rash

"Get them persons out of my flower bed, Mister Cain," say Granny moanin real low like at a funeral.

"How come your grandmother calls her husband 'Mister Cain' all the time?" Tyrone whispers all loud and noisy and from the city and don't know no better. Like his mama, Miss Myrtle, tell us never mind the formality as if we had no better breeding than to call her Myrtle, plain. And then this awful thing—a giant hawk—come wailin up over the meadow, flyin low and tilted and screamin, zigzaggin through the pecan grove, breakin branches and hollerin, snappin past the clothesline, flyin every which way, flyin into things reckless with crazy.

"He's come to claim his mate," say Cathy fast, and ducks down. We all fall quick and flat into the gravel driveway, stones scrapin my face. I squinch my eyes open again at the hawk on the door, tryin to fly up out of her death like it was just a sack flown into by mistake. Her body holdin her there on that nail, though. The mate beatin the air overhead and clutchin for hair, for heads, for landin space.

Reading Skill
Cause and Effect
Monitor your
comprehension. Reflect
on your understanding
and make a connection
between the arrival of
the hawk and the actions
of the film crew in this
paragraph.

The camera man duckin and bendin and runnin and fallin, jigglin the camera and scared. And Smilin jumpin up and down swipin at the huge bird, tryin to bring the hawk down with just his raggedy ole cap. Granddaddy Cain straight up and silent, watchin the circles of the hawk, then aimin the hammer off his wrist. The giant bird fallin, silent and slow. Then here comes Camera and Smilin all big and bad now that the awful screechin thing is on its back and broken, here they come. And Granddaddy Cain looks up at them like it was the first time noticin, but not payin them too much mind cause he's listenin, we all listenin, to that low groanin music comin from the porch. And we figure any minute, somethin in my back tells me any minute now, Granny gonna bust through that screen with somethin in her hand and murder on her mind. So Granddaddy say above the buzzin, but quiet, "Good day, gentlemen." Just like that. Like he'd invited them in to play cards and they'd stayed too long and all the sandwiches were gone and Reverend Webb was droppin by and it was time to go.

They didn't know what to do. But like Cathy say, folks can't stand Granddaddy tall and silent and like a king. They can't neither. The smile the men smilin is pullin the mouth back and showin the teeth. Lookin like the wolf man, both of them. Then Granddaddy holds his hand out—this huge hand I used to sit in when I was a baby and he'd carry me through the house to my mother like I was a gift on a tray. Like he used to on the trains. They called the other men just waiters. But they spoke of Granddaddy separate and said, The Waiter. And said he had engines in his feet and motors in his hands and couldn't no train throw him off and couldn't nobody turn him round. They were big enough for motors, his hands were. He held that one hand out all still and it gettin to be not at all a hand but a person in itself.

"He wants you to hand him the camera," Smilin whispers to Camera, tiltin his head to talk secret like they was in the jungle or somethin and come upon a native that don't speak the language. The men start untyin the straps, and they put the camera into that great hand speckled with the hawk's blood all black and crackly now. And the hand don't even drop with the weight, just the fingers move, curl up around the machine. But Granddaddy lookin straight at the men. They lookin at each other and everywhere but at Granddaddy's face.

"We filmin for the county, see," say Smilin. "We puttin together a movie for the food stamp program . . . filmin all around these parts. Uhh, filmin for the county."

"Can I have my camera back?" say the tall man with no machine on his shoulder, but still keepin it high like the camera was still there or needed to be. "Please, sir."

Then Granddaddy's other hand flies up like a sudden and gentle bird, slaps down fast on top of the camera and lifts off half like it was a calabash[1] cut for sharing.

"Hey," Camera jumps forward. He gathers up the parts into his chest and everything unrollin and fallin all over. "Whatcha tryin to do? You'll ruin the film." He looks down into his chest of metal **reels** and things like he's protectin a kitten from the cold.

"You standin in the misses' flower bed," say Granddaddy. "This is our own place."

The two men look at him, then at each other, then back at the mess in the camera man's chest, and they just back off. One sayin over and over all the way down to the meadow, "Watch it, Bruno. Keep ya fingers off the film." Then Granddaddy picks up the hammer and jams it into the oilskin pocket, scrapes his boots, and goes into the house. And you can hear the squish of his boots

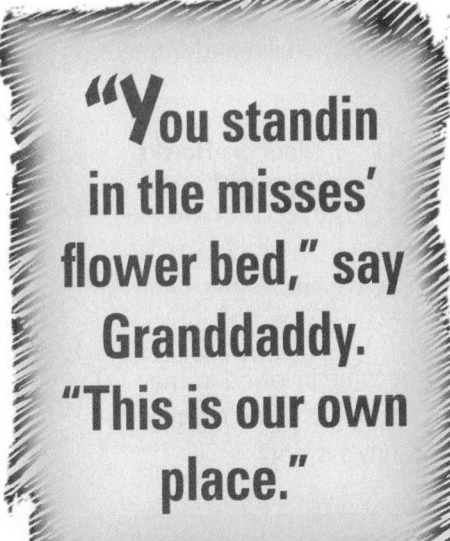

"You standin in the misses' flower bed," say Granddaddy. "This is our own place."

---

1. **calabash** (kal´ ə bash´) *n.* large gourd-like fruit.

Spiral Review
Point of View
Analyze the way in which this work of fiction is shaped by the narrator's point of view.

Vocabulary
reels (rēlz) *n.* frames or spools on which thread, wire, tape, film, or a net is wound

Reading Check
How does Granddaddy Cain react to the camera men's visit?

headin through the house. And you can see the funny shadow he throws from the parlor window onto the ground by the string-bean patch. The hammer draggin the pocket of the oilskin out so Granddaddy looked even wider. Granny was hummin now—high not low and grumbly. And she was doin the cakes again, you could smell the molasses from the rum.

"There's this story I'm goin to write one day," say Cathy dreamer. "About the proper use of the hammer."

"Can I be in it?" Tyrone say with his hand up like it was a matter of first come, first served.

"Perhaps," say Cathy, climbin onto the tire to pump us up. "If you there and ready."

Critical Thinking

Support your responses with evidence from the text.

1. **Respond:** Which character would you most like to meet? Why?

2. **(a)** Why are the photographers filming in the area?
   (b) Make Inferences: What message does Granny give the men through her speech and actions?

3. Make a chart like the one shown. **(a) Compare:** In the first column, write the ways that Camera and Smilin are like the hawks. **(b) Connect:** In the second column, write the ways that Granddaddy's actions are like the actions of the male hawk. **(c) Discuss:** Share your chart with a partner, and discuss your responses. Then, in the third column, explain whether you think the hawks represent Granddaddy and Granny, Smilin and Camera, or both pairs.

Hawks and Camera and Smilin	Hawks and Granddaddy	What the Hawks Represent

Is conflict necessary?
(a) Why does Granddaddy become involved in the story's conflict? **(b)** Why is his way of handling the conflict successful, when Granny's is not?

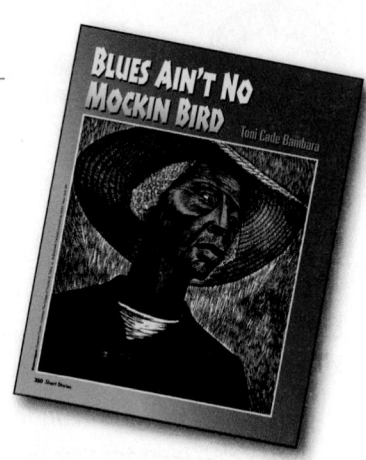

Literary Analysis: Dialogue and Dialect

1. Identify one example of **dialogue** that indicates the tension is increasing between Granny and the filmmakers.

2. Identify one example of dialogue that shows Granny is tough.

3. **(a)** Explain how the spelling and grammar used in the following passage indicate that it is an example of **dialect.** "Granny always got somethin to say. She teaches steady with no let-up." **(b)** Rewrite the passage in Standard English. **(c)** Explain how the use of dialect makes the characters and setting more complex and believable.

Reading Skill: Cause and Effect

4. **(a)** What is the **cause** of Granddaddy's decision to disassemble the men's camera? **(b)** What is the **effect** of Granddaddy's action on the cameramen? **(c)** What is the **effect** on Granny?

5. **Reflect on your understanding.** Which details in the story help you explain the causes and effects of Granddaddy's decision?

Vocabulary

Practice In vocabulary study, **analogies** show the relationships between pairs of words. Use a word from the "Blues Ain't No Mockin Bird" vocabulary list on page 348 to complete each analogy. In each, your choice should create a word pair that matches the relationship between the first two words given. Explain the relationship that the pairs in each set share.

1. solution : intelligent :: accident : _____

2. sportsmanship : game :: _____ : ceremony

3. fork : meat :: _____ : soup

4. frowns : scowls :: walks : _____

5. powerful : weak :: unworn : _____

6. carton : eggs :: _____ : film

Word Power Use the context of the sentences and what you know about the **Latin suffix -ity** to explain your answer to each question.

1. If a plan is referred to as a *possibility,* might it be used?

2. When people take a *sensitivity* training class, what do they learn?

Word Power

The **Latin suffix -ity** forms nouns from adjectives. It means "the quality of showing a certain characteristic."

Apply It Explain how the suffix -ity helps you determine the meanings of these technical academic words from science. Consult a dictionary if necessary.

elasticity
gravity
visibility

Is *conflict* necessary?

Writing About the Big Question

In "The Invalid's Story," the two main characters try to resolve a problem but do not have all the facts. Use these sentence starters to develop your ideas about the Big Question.

Lack of information can lead to a humorous conflict because _____.

It can also lead to serious **issues** and sometimes **controversy** because

_____.

As You Read Look for ways in which the lack of information makes the problem more intense—and funnier—as time passes.

Vocabulary

Read each word and its definition. Decide whether you know the word well, know it a little bit, or do not know it at all. After you read, see how your knowledge of each word has increased.

- **prodigious** (prō dij′ əs) *adj.* enormous (p. 364) *The Grand Canyon is a prodigious natural wonder.* *prodigiously adv. prodigiousness n.*

- **deleterious** (del′ ə tir′ ē əs) *adj.* harmful to health or well-being (p. 365) *Too much sun can be deleterious to one's skin.* *deleteriously adv. deleteriousness n.*

- **ominous** (äm′ ə nəs) *adj.* threatening (p. 365) *The black storm clouds coming from the West were ominous.* *ominously adv. ominousness n. omen n.*

- **judicious** (jōō dish′ əs) *adj.* showing good judgment (p. 366) *Her decision to stay indoors during the storm was judicious.* *judiciously adv. judiciousness n. judge n. judge v.*

- **placidly** (plas′ id lē) *adv.* calmly; quietly (p. 366) *He smiled placidly, content with his own thoughts.* *placid adj. placidity n.*

- **desultory** (des′ əl tôr′ ē) *adj.* random (p. 367) *They wandered through the park in a desultory way, with no clear destination.* *desultorily adv.*

Word Power

The **Latin suffix -ous** (or **-ious** or **-uous**) forms adjectives. It means "like" or "pertaining to."

In this story, the narrator talks about "an **ominous** stillness." The stillness feels like an omen, something that foretells a future danger.

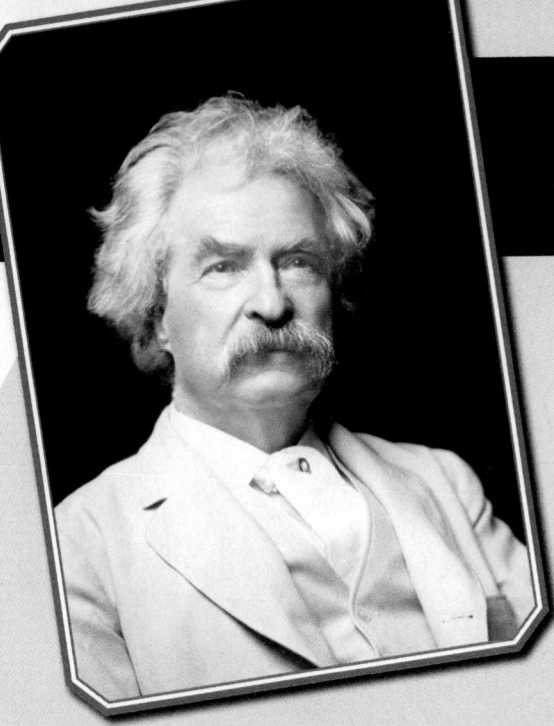

Meet
Mark Twain
(1835–1910)

Author of
The Invalid's Story

Born Samuel Clemens, Mark Twain grew up in the Mississippi River town of Hannibal, Missouri. He worked as a riverboat pilot, printer, prospector, reporter, and at many other jobs. Primarily, however, Clemens was a writer of comic stories, sketches, and novels. The most famous humorist of his day, he traveled the world entertaining people with his witty lectures.

"By the mark—twain" was a cry heard on the riverboats of Clemens's youth. It meant that the water was two fathoms deep—deep enough for a riverboat to pass unharmed. Harkening back to his youth working on those boats, Clemens took the name Mark Twain at age twenty-seven. Under that name, he wrote some of the most beloved fiction in American literature.

BACKGROUND FOR THE STORY

(History Connection)

Nineteenth-Century Train Travel

In the late nineteenth century, when this story takes place, trains were the fastest way to travel and transport cargo. Nonetheless, train cars in which people with cargo had to travel were uncomfortable. The cars were poorly ventilated boxes on wheels, and had only small windows.

Did You Know?
Mark Twain was the first writer to turn himself into a business. He even trademarked his name!

The Invalid's Story

Mark Twain

I seem sixty and married, but these effects are due to my condition and sufferings, for I am a bachelor, and only forty-one. It will be hard for you to believe that I, who am now but a shadow, was a hale, hearty man two short years ago—a man of iron, a very athlete!—yet such is the simple truth. But stranger still than this fact is the way in which I lost my health. I lost it through helping to take care of a box of guns on a two-hundred-mile railway journey one winter's night. It is the actual truth, and I will tell you about it.

I belong in Cleveland, Ohio. One winter's night, two years ago, I reached home just after dark, in a driving snowstorm, and the first thing I heard when I entered the house was that my dearest boyhood friend and schoolmate, John B. Hackett, had died the day before, and that his last utterance had been a desire that I would take his remains home to his poor old father and mother in Wisconsin. I was greatly shocked and grieved, but there was no time to waste in emotions; I must start at once. I took the card, marked "Deacon Levi Hackett, Bethlehem, Wisconsin," and hurried off through the whistling storm to the railway station. Arrived there I found the long white-pine box which had been described to me; I fastened the card to it with some tacks, saw it put safely aboard the express car, and then ran into the eating room to provide myself with a sandwich and some cigars. When I returned, presently, there was my coffin-box back again, apparently, and a young fellow examining around it, with a card in his hands, and some tacks and

Spiral Review
Point of View
Analyze the way in which this work of fiction is shaped by the narrator's point of view.

Reading Check

What was John B. Hackett's dying wish?

a hammer! I was astonished and puzzled. He began to nail on his card, and I rushed out to the express car, in a good deal of a state of mind, to ask for an explanation. But no—there was my box, all right, in the express car; it hadn't been disturbed. [The fact is that without my suspecting it a prodigious mistake had been made. I was carrying off a box of guns which that young fellow had come to the station to ship to a rifle company in Peoria, Illinois, and he had got my corpse.] Just then the conductor sang out "All aboard," and I jumped into the express car and got a comfortable seat on a bale of buckets. The expressman was there, hard at work—a plain man of fifty, with a simple, honest, good-natured face, and a breezy, practical heartiness in his general style. As the train moved off a stranger skipped into the car and set a package of peculiarly mature and capable Limburger cheese[1] on one end of my coffin-box—I mean my box of guns. That is to say, I know now that it was Limburger cheese, but at that time I never had heard of the article in my life, and of course was wholly ignorant of its character. Well, we sped through the wild night, the bitter storm raged on, a cheerless misery stole over me, my heart went down, down, down! The old expressman made a brisk remark or two about the tempest and the arctic weather, slammed his sliding doors to, and bolted them, closed his window down tight, and then went bustling around, here and there and yonder, setting things to rights, and all the time contentedly humming "Sweet By and By" in a low tone, and flatting a good deal. Presently I began to detect a most evil and searching odor stealing about on the frozen air. This depressed my spirits still more, because of course I attributed it to my poor departed friend. There was something infinitely saddening about his calling himself to my remembrance in this dumb, pathetic way, so it was hard to

Vocabulary
prodigious (prō dij´ əs) *adj.* enormous

▶ **Critical Viewing**
This potbellied stove would have been found in a train car in the late 1800s. What challenges did train travel pose at that time in history? **[Analyze]**

---

1. Limburger cheese cheese with a strong odor.

keep the tears back. Moreover, it distressed me on account of the old expressman, who, I was afraid, might notice it. However, he went humming tranquilly on, and gave no sign; and for this I was grateful. Grateful, yes, but still uneasy; and soon I began to feel more and more uneasy every minute, for every minute that went by that odor thickened up the more, and got to be more and more gamy and hard to stand. Presently, having got things arranged to his satisfaction, the expressman got some wood and made up a tremendous fire in his stove. This distressed me more than I can tell, for I could not but feel that it was a mistake. I was sure that the effect would be **deleterious** upon my poor departed friend. Thompson—the expressman's name was Thompson, as I found out in the course of the night—now went poking around his car, stopping up whatever stray cracks he could find, remarking that it didn't make any difference what kind of a night it was outside, he calculated to make us comfortable, anyway. I said nothing, but I believed he was not choosing the right way. Meantime he was humming to himself just as before; and meantime, too, the stove was getting hotter and hotter, and the place closer and closer. I felt myself growing pale and qualmish,[2] but grieved in silence and said nothing. Soon I noticed that the "Sweet By and By" was gradually fading out; next it ceased altogether, and there was an **ominous** stillness. After a few moments Thompson said—

"Pfew! I reckon it ain't no cinnamon't I've loaded up thish-year stove with!"

He gasped once or twice, then moved toward the cof—gun-box, stood over that Limburger cheese part of a moment, then came back and sat down near me, looking a good deal impressed. After a contemplative pause, he said, indicating the box with a gesture—

"Friend of yourn?"

"Yes," I said with a sigh.

"He's pretty ripe, ain't he!"

> **"Pfew! I reckon it ain't no cinnamon't I've loaded up thish-year stove with!"**

Nothing further was said for perhaps a couple of minutes, each being busy with his own thoughts; then Thompson said, in a low awed voice—

"Sometimes it's uncertain whether they're really gone or not— seem gone, you know—body warm, joints limber—and so, although you think they're gone, you don't really

---

2. **qualmish** (kwäm´ ish) *adj.* suddenly sick.

Vocabulary
deleterious (del´ ə tir´ ē əs) *adj.* harmful to health or well-being

Vocabulary
ominous (äm´ ə nəs) *adj.* threatening

Reading Skill
Cause and Effect
When you picture this scene, what details explain the cause of Thompson's gasp?

Reading Check
What does the narrator say depressed his spirits?

know. I've had cases in my car. It's perfectly awful, becuz you don't know what minute they'll rise up and look at you!" Then, after a pause, and slightly lifting his elbow toward the box,—"But he ain't in no trance! No, sir, I go bail for him!" •

We sat some time, in meditative silence, listening to the wind and the roar of the train; then Thompson said, with a good deal of feeling:

"Well-a-well, we've all got to go, they ain't no getting around it. Man that is born of woman is of few days and far between, as Scriptur'[3] says. Yes, you look at it any way you want to, it's awful solemn and cur'us: they ain't nobody can get around it; all's got to go—just everybody, as you may say. One day you're hearty and strong"—here he scrambled to his feet and broke a pane and stretched his nose out at it a moment or two, then sat down again while I struggled up and thrust my nose out at the same place, and this we kept on doing every now and then—"and next day he's cut down like the grass, and the places which knowed him then knows him no more forever, as Scriptur' says. Yes'ndeedy, it's awful solemn and cur'us; but we've all got to go, one time or another; they ain't no getting around it."

There was another long pause; then—

"What did he die of?"

I said I didn't know.

"How long has he ben dead?"

It seemed judicious to enlarge the facts to fit the probabilities; so I said:

"Two or three days."

But it did no good: for Thompson received it with an injured look which plainly said, "Two or three years, you mean." Then he went right along, placidly ignoring my statement, and gave his views at considerable length upon the unwisdom of putting off burials too long. Then he lounged off toward the box, stood a moment, then came back on a sharp trot and visited the broken pane, observing:

"'Twould 'a' ben a durn sight better, all around, if they'd started him along last summer."

Thompson sat down and buried his face in his red silk handkerchief, and began to slowly sway and rock his body like one who is doing his best to endure the almost unendurable. By this

Vocabulary

judicious (jōō dish´ əs) *adj.* showing good judgment

placidly (plas´ id lē) *adv.* calmly; quietly

...he scrambled to his feet and broke a pane and stretched his nose out at it a moment or two...

---

3. **Scriptur'** scripture; the Bible.

time the fragrance—if you may call it fragrance—was just about suffocating, as near as you can come at it. Thompson's face was turning gray: I knew mine hadn't any color left in it. By and by Thompson rested his forehead in his left hand, with his elbow on his knee, and sort of waved his red handkerchief toward the box with his other hand, and said:

"I've carried a many a one of 'em—some of 'em considerable overdue, too—but, lordy, he just lays over 'em all!—and does it easy. Cap, they was heliotrope[4] to him!"

This recognition of my poor friend gratified me, in spite of the sad circumstances, because it had so much the sound of a compliment.

Pretty soon it was plain that something had got to be done. I suggested cigars. Thompson thought it was a good idea. He said:

"Likely it'll modify him some."

We puffed gingerly along for a while, and tried hard to imagine that things were improved. But it wasn't any use. Before very long, and without any consultation, both cigars were quietly dropped from our nerveless fingers at the same moment. Thompson said, with a sigh:

"No, Cap, it don't modify him worth a cent. Fact is, it makes him worse, becuz it appears to stir up his ambition. What do you reckon we better do, now?"

I was not able to suggest anything: indeed, I had to be swallowing and swallowing all the time, and did not like to trust myself to speak. Thompson fell to maundering, in a **desultory** and low-spirited way, about the miserable experiences of this night: and he got to referring to my poor friend by various titles—sometimes military ones, sometimes civil ones; and I noticed that as fast as my poor friend's effectiveness grew, Thompson promoted him accordingly—gave him a bigger title. Finally he said:

"I've got an idea. Suppos'n' we buckle down to it and give the Colonel a bit of a shove toward t'other end of the car?—about ten foot, say. He wouldn't have so much influence, then, don't you reckon?"

I said it was a good scheme. So we took in a good fresh breath at the broken pane, calculating to hold it till we got through: then we went there and bent over that deadly cheese and took a grip on the box. Thompson nodded "All ready," and then we threw ourselves forward with all our might: but Thompson slipped, and slumped down with his nose on the cheese, and his breath got loose. He gagged and gasped, and floundered up and made a break for the door, pawing the air and saying hoarsely, "Don't hender me!—

---

4. **heliotrope** (hē′ lē ə trōp′) *n.* a sweet-smelling plant.

Literary Analysis
Dialogue and Dialect Which features of Thompson's speech in this passage reflect a particular dialect?

Vocabulary
desultory
(des′ əl tôr′ ē)
adj. random

Reading Check

How do the men use the window to lessen the effect of the odor?

Limburger Cheese

The foul stench that torments the narrator and Thompson comes from a package of Limburger cheese. This cheese was first made in Belgium and is now made in Germany and in the United States. It is notorious for its strong odor. The cheese is made from cow's milk and is "ripened" for about three months under specially controlled conditions. This ripening process gives Limburger cheese its distinctive smell and flavor. The cheese continues to ripen during shipping and its odor can become extremely intense.

Connect to the Literature

Why do you think the narrator and Thompson are so confused about the source of the smell in the train car?

gimme the road! I'm a-dying; gimme the road!" Out on the cold platform I sat down and held his head awhile, and he revived. Presently he said:

"Do you reckon we started the Gen'rul any?"

I said no: we hadn't budged him.

"Well, then, that idea's up the flume. We got to think up something else. He's suited wher' he is, I reckon; and if that's the way he feels about it, and has made up his mind that he don't wish to be disturbed, you bet he's a-going to have his own way in the business. Yes, better leave him right wher' he is, long as he wants it so; becuz he holds all the trumps, don't you know, and so it stands to reason that the man that lays out to alter his plans for him is going to get left."

But we couldn't stay out there in that mad storm; we should have frozen to death. So we went in again and shut the door, and began to suffer once more and take turns at the break in the window. By and by, as we were starting away from a station where we had stopped a moment Thompson pranced in cheerily, and exclaimed:

"We're all right, now! I reckon we've got the Commodore this time. I judge I've got the stuff here that'll take the tuck out of him."

It was carbolic acid. He had a carboy of it. He sprinkled it all around everywhere; in fact he drenched everything with it, rifle-box, cheese and all. Then we sat down, feeling pretty hopeful. But it wasn't for long. You see the two perfumes began to mix, and then—well, pretty soon we made a break for the door; and out there Thompson swabbed his face with his bandanna and said in a kind of disheartened way:

"It ain't no use. We can't buck agin him. He just utilizes everything we put up to modify him with, and gives it his own flavor and plays it back on us. Why, Cap, don't you know, it's as much as a hundred times worse in there now than it was when he first got a-going. I never did see one of 'em warm up to his work so, and take such a dumnation interest in it. No, sir, I never did, as long as I've ben on the road: and I've carried a many a one of 'em, as I was telling you."

We went in again after we were frozen pretty stiff; but my, we couldn't stay in, now. So we just waltzed back and forth, freezing, and thawing, and stifling, by turns. In about an hour we stopped at another station; and as we left it Thompson came in with a bag, and said—

"Cap, I'm a-going to chance him once more—just this once; and if we don't fetch him this time, the thing for us to do, is to just throw up the sponge and withdraw from the canvass. That's the way I put it up." ●

He had brought a lot of chicken feathers, and dried apples, and leaf tobacco, and rags, and old shoes, and sulphur, and asafetida, and one thing or another: and he piled them on a breadth of sheet iron in the middle of the floor, and set fire to them.

When they got well started, I couldn't see, myself, how even the corpse could stand it. All that went before was just simply poetry to that smell—but mind you, the original smell stood up out of it just as sublime as ever—fact is, these other smells just seemed to give it a better hold: and my, how rich it was! I didn't make these reflections there—there wasn't time—made them on the platform. And breaking for the platform, Thompson got suffocated and

Reading Skill
Cause and Effect
Monitor your comprehension. Reflect on your understanding by making a connection between the odor and the fire.

But we couldn't stay out there in that mad storm; we should have frozen to death.

fell: and before I got him dragged out, which I did by the collar, I was mighty near gone myself. When we revived, Thompson said dejectedly:

"We got to stay out here, Cap. We got to do it. They ain't no other way. The Governor wants to travel alone, and he's fixed so he can outvote us."

And presently he added:

"And don't you know, we're pisoned. It's our last trip, you can make up your mind to it. Typhoid fever is what's going to come of this. I feel it a-coming right now. Yes, sir, we're elected, just as sure as you're born."

We were taken from the platform an hour later, frozen and insensible, at the next station, and I went straight off into a virulent fever, and never knew anything again for three weeks. I found out, then, that I had spent that awful night with a harmless box of rifles and a lot of innocent cheese; but the news was too late to save me; imagination had done its work, and my health was permanently shattered; neither Bermuda nor any other land can ever bring it back to me. This is my last trip; I am on my way home to die.

Reading Skill
Cause and Effect
Monitor your comprehension by making a connection between the odor and the narrator's health.

Critical Thinking

1. **Respond:** Did you find this story entertaining? Explain.

2. **(a)** What do the men believe is creating the awful smell? **(b) Connect:** What is actually creating the smell? **(c) Compare and Contrast:** In what ways does the contrast between what they think is true and what is really true contribute to the humor?

3. Make a chart with three columns. **(a) Compare:** In the first column, write a list of sad details in the story. **(b) Connect:** In the second column, write the details that add humor to the story. **(c) Discuss and Analyze:** Share your chart with a partner and discuss your responses. Then, in the third column, explain whether you think the story is sad, funny, or both.

Is conflict necessary?
(a) For the story to be funny, why is it critical that the narrator doesn't have all the information? **(b)** If this conflict were avoided, what would be the effect on the story?

Support your responses with evidence from the text.

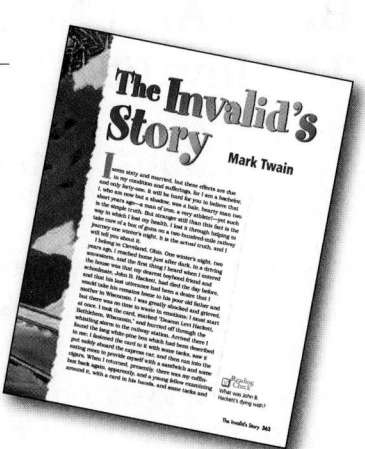

Literary Analysis: Dialogue and Dialect

1. Identify one example of **dialogue** in the story that indicates the smell is increasing. Explain your choice.

2. Identify an example of dialogue that shows that Thompson and the narrator do not know each other well. Explain your choice.

3. (a) In what way do the spelling, grammar, and words used in the following passage indicate that it is an example of **dialect?**

"No, Cap, it don't modify him worth a cent. Fact is, it makes him worse, becuz it appears to stir up his ambition. What do you reckon we better do, now?"

(b) Rewrite the passage in Standard English. **(c)** Explain how the use of dialect makes the characters and setting more complex and believable.

Reading Skill: Cause and Effect

4. (a) What is the **cause** of the smell in the express car? **(b)** What **effect** does the smell have on Thompson and the narrator?

5. Reflect on your understanding. Which details in the story help you to explain why the characters are mistaken about the smell?

Vocabulary

Practice In vocabulary study, **analogies** show the relationships between pairs of words. Use a word from the vocabulary list for "The Invalid's Story" on page 360 to complete each analogy so that the relationship in the second pair of words matches the relationship in the first pair. Explain the relationship that the pairs in each item share.

1. comedy : humorous :: measles : _____

2. graceful : clumsy :: _____ : foolish

3. tiny : small :: _____ : large

4. systematic : reliable :: _____ : unpredictable

5. violently : angry :: _____ : content

6. praise : joyful :: warning : _____

Word Power Use the context of the sentences and what you know about the **Latin suffix -ous** (or **-ious** or **-uous**) to explain your answer to each question.

1. If a sport is *hazardous,* could you be seriously hurt playing it?

2. How do most people react to *ridiculous* events?

Word Power

The **Latin suffix -ous** (or **-ious** or **-uous**) means "like" or "pertaining to."

Apply It Explain how the suffix -ous helps you determine the meanings of these technical academic words from science. Consult a dictionary if necessary.

porous
erroneous
nutritious

Integrated Language Skills

Blues Ain't No Mockin Bird • The Invalid's Story

Conventions: Active and Passive Verb Tenses

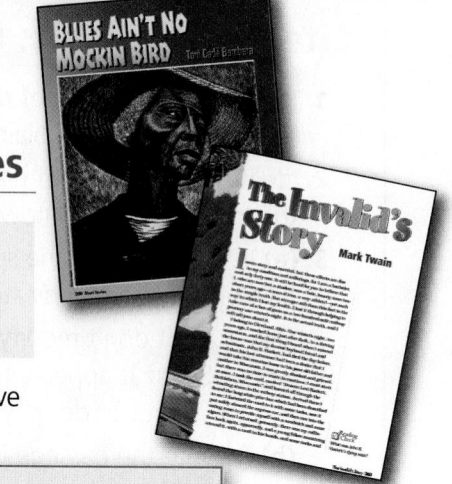

A verb in the **active voice** expresses an action done **by** its subject.

A verb in the **passive voice** expresses an action done **to** its subject.

The "voice" of a verb tells whether the subject *performs* an action (active voice) or *receives* an action (passive voice).

Active Voice	Passive Voice
Bambara and Twain have written stories about memorable conflicts. (The subjects, *Bambara* and *Twain*, perform the action of the verb, *have written*.)	Stories about memorable conflicts have been written by Bambara and Twain. (The subject, *stories*, receives the action of the verb, *have been written*.)

Use active verb tenses—and active voice—for lively, direct writing. Use passive verb tenses—and passive voice—to de-emphasize the performer of the action or when the performer is unknown.

Practice A Read each sentence and identify its verb or verb phrase. Identify each verb's or verb phrase's voice and tense as *active* or *passive*.

1. The story about the man on the bridge was told to send a message.
2. She watches them in angry silence.
3. Granddaddy Cain greets Camera and Smilin.
4. The film was pulled from the camera.

Speaking Application Read the sentences in Practice A to a partner. If a verb is in the active tense, replace it with a verb in the passive tense. If a verb is in the passive tense, replace it with a verb in the active tense. Discuss the function of each verb and the effect of each change with your partner.

Practice B Rewrite the following sentences using active voice and tenses. You may need to add words to indicate who performed the action.

1. The cheese had been placed on the box.
2. "The Invalid's Story" was written by Mark Twain.
3. The coffin was sent to Wisconsin by train.
4. A foul odor was detected by the narrator.

Writing Application Look at the image on page 369 of "The Invalid's Story." Write four sentences based on this image, using active voice and tenses twice and passive voice and tenses twice. Describe the function of the active and passive voice in your sentences.

PH GRAMMAR HANDBOOK Further instruction and practice is available in the *Prentice Hall Grammar Handbook*.

Writing

These two selections incorporate dialogue that reveals each character's unique personality traits. Write an **informal letter** from the point of view of a character in "Blues Ain't No Mockin Bird" or "The Invalid's Story." Choose a character that is not the narrator.

- Before writing, list the personality traits of your character.
- Write to a friend or relative, describing the story events and their significance from your character's point of view.
- Refer to your list as you write. Make sure that your details and language are consistent with the traits that you listed.

Grammar Application Check your letter to be sure that you have used active and passive voice and verb tenses appropriately.

Writing Workshop: *Work in Progress*

Prewriting for Cause-and-Effect Essay Review the "What's the Cause?" list in your writing portfolio. Highlight the effect that interests you the most. Then, list several questions to help you define the cause for this effect. Save this list in your writing portfolio.

Listening and Speaking

In both of these stories, dialogue and dialect are important elements. With a partner, prepare and deliver a **dialogue.**

- If you read "Blues Ain't No Mockin Bird," have Camera and Smilin discuss their experience with Granny and Granddaddy.
- If you read "The Invalid's Story," have the narrator discuss his "shattered" health with a doctor.

Follow these steps to complete the assignment:

- Decide what the dialogue will reveal about the story events and the personalities of the speakers.
- As you outline a "plot," decide how the dialogue should begin and end. Choose at least one important, dramatic event (for example, a character re-enacting an important moment from the story).
- Use language that is appropriate to the characters' situations and personalities, but be polite.

Listen responsively to each team's presentation. If something in the dialogue is not clear to you, or if you would like to hear more from a particular character, **ask questions** related to the content of each dialogue for **clarification** and **elaboration.**

Focus on the TEKS

Conventions
(17)(A)(i) Use and understand the function of more complex active and passive tenses in the context of reading, writing, and speaking.

Listening and Speaking
(24)(A) Listen responsively to a speaker by asking questions related to the content for clarification and elaboration.

Use this prewriting activity to prepare for the **Writing Workshop** on page 402.

- Interactive graphic organizers
- Grammar tutorial
- Interactive journals

Strategy for Success

Make Connections

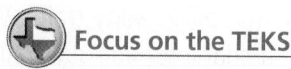
Focus on the TEKS

Comprehension
RC-9(A) Reflect on understanding to monitor comprehension (e.g., asking questions, making connections).

To excel on the reading sections of the ACT and the Texas standardized tests, you must monitor your own comprehension to be sure you understand what you read. One way to do this is to make connections as you read. For example, you might notice cause-and-effect relationships between events, actions, and observations in the text. You can make connections as you read passages on standardized tests by asking questions and analyzing chains of events.

To make connections, ask questions about what is happening in a text as you read. To uncover cause-and-effect relationships, look for chains of events, each causing the next. The following examples show how you make connections on standardized tests.

Ask Questions

Ask yourself what caused events, actions, or observations in the text. Consider whether there is one cause or if there are several causes.

1   Chameleons do not change color just on a whim. Not only do they change to reflect sunlight, but they also use color to adjust body temperature and communicate mood.

1. Chameleons change color for all of the following reasons EXCEPT:
    A. to show individuality.
    B. to reflect sunlight.
    C. to regulate temperature.
    D. to demonstrate moods.

B, C, and **D** are all listed in the passage as reasons chameleons change color. **A** is not a cause of chameleons' color changes, so it must be the correct answer.

Identify Chains of Events

Examine the chain of events. Something that is an effect of one cause may, in turn, cause something else to happen.

1   In the strong winds of the hurricane, a large tree fell across the road and blocked the passage of cars.

2. What is the direct cause of the blocked road?
    F. the strong winds
    G. the hurricane
    H. the fallen tree
    J. the passing cars

F and **G** are part of the chain of events but are not the direct cause. **J** is not related to the blocked road. The fallen tree is the effect of the strong winds and is also the cause of the blocked road, so **H** is correct.

ACT Practice

DIRECTIONS: The passage in this test is followed by several questions. After reading the passage, choose the best answer to each question and fill in the corresponding oval on your answer document. You may refer to the passage as often as necessary.

NATURAL SCIENCES

Sinkholes range in size from uneven indentations in the ground to huge craters in the earth. Regardless of size, they are formed by processes that begin long before the first signs are visible above ground.

The soil of a sinkhole falls in because of a hole, or void, in the rock
5 deep beneath it. Gradually, soil close to the void begins to move into the hole in the rock, which in turn leaves a space in the soil. Eventually, the empty space in the soil grows so big that the soil collapses—making the sinkhole visible from the surface.

While the soil may take only a short time to collapse, the original hole
10 in the rock is formed by water over hundreds of years. The water slowly dissolves minerals in the rock, which is gradually worn away.

Water stability is so crucial that even seasonal changes such as freezing, thawing, drought, and rain can increase the chance of sinkholes. Human activities such as removing soil can also destabilize the ground. If structures
15 are too heavy or if ground is disturbed by vibrations, sinkholes may occur more suddenly. Even sinkholes themselves, if left open, may collect water, grow larger, and increase the chance of sinkholes nearby.

1. What is the reason the soil of a sinkhole eventually collapses?
  A. Water washes the soil away.
  B. Heavy objects loosen the soil.
  C. The empty space gets too big.
  D. The rock becomes too weak.

2. The void in the underground rock is caused by:
  F. freezing and thawing on land.
  G. water wearing down the rock.
  H. a crater in the earth.
  J. a space in the soil.

3. According to the passage, removing soil will:
  A. repair sinkholes in the area.
  B. destabilize the ground.
  C. weaken the rock underground.
  D. strengthen the soil.

4. Sinkholes can be accelerated by all of the following EXCEPT:
  F. disturbances to the ground.
  G. other sinkholes nearby.
  H. stable water levels.
  J. vibrations.

Informational Texts

Expository Texts

Focus on the TEKS

Reading
(9)(A) Distinguish between a summary that captures the main ideas and elements of a text and a critique that takes a position and expresses an opinion.

Student Guide
The House on Mango Street

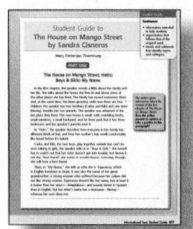

Blog Entry
The House on Mango Street

Reading Skill: Analyze Summary and Critique

A **summary** is a short description or restatement of the main ideas and elements of a text. A **critique** takes a position and expresses an opinion about a text. It may not always be immediately obvious whether an author writing about a piece of literature or nonfiction is critiquing or summarizing that work.

It is valuable to be able to **distinguish between summaries and critiques** because the authors of each type of text have different purposes. The author of a summary is attempting to present an unbiased statement of the facts, while the author of a critique is trying to persuade you that a particular position is valid. Distinguishing between these types of texts will help you to recognize when an author is attempting to influence your thinking.

The following texts include a summary and a critique of Sandra Cisneros's *The House on Mango Street* in the forms of a student guide and a blog entry.

As You Read Use checklists to analyze each of the texts and determine whether each is a summary or a critique.

Question	Summary	Critique
Does the introduction present an argument or express an opinion?	❏ No	❏ Yes
Does the text restate ideas?	❏ Yes	❏ No
Does the text present and support new ideas?	❏ No	❏ Yes
Does the text outline the content of another text?	❏ Yes	❏ No
Is the author trying to convince readers of something?	❏ No	❏ Yes
Is the author simply providing information?	❏ Yes	❏ No

Student Guide

Features:
- information intended to help students
- organization that follows that of the original work
- heads and subheads that identify topics and subtopics

Student Guide to
The House on Mango Street by Sandra Cisneros

Mary Patterson Thornburg

PART ONE

The House on Mango Street; Hairs; Boys & Girls; My Name

In the first chapter, the speaker reveals a little about her family and her life. She talks about the house she lives in and about some of the other places she has lived. The family has moved numerous times and, at the same time, has been growing, until now there are four children: the speaker has two brothers (Carlos and Kiki) and one sister (Nenny), besides her two parents. The speaker was ashamed of the last place they lived. This new house is small, with crumbling bricks, small windows, a small backyard, and no front yard, but it has three bedrooms and the speaker's parents own it.

In "Hairs," the speaker describes how everyone in her family has different kinds of hair, and how her mother's hair smells comfortably like bread before it's baked.

Carlos and Kiki, the two boys, play together outside but can't be seen talking to girls, the speaker tells us in "Boys & Girls." She herself has to watch out that her sister doesn't get into trouble, but Nenny is not the "best friend" she wants or would choose. Someday, though, she will have a best friend.

Then, in "My Name," she tells us who she is: Esperanza, which in English translates to hope; it was also the name of her great-grandmother, a strong woman who suffered because her culture did not like strong women. Esperanza doesn't like her name, but at least it is better than her sister's—Magdalena—and sounds better in Spanish than in English. But her sister's name has a nickname—Nenny—whereas her own does not.

> The author gives information about the content of the first chapter of *The House on Mango Street*. **Does the author present an opinion or take a position in this paragraph?**

PART TWO

Cathy Queen of Cats; Our Good Day; Laughter; Gil's Furniture Bought & Sold; Meme Ortiz; Louie, His Cousin & His Other Cousin

A girl named Cathy, one of Esperanza's neighbors, tells Esperanza about the neighborhood. She says she'll be Esperanza's friend for a few days, but then her family is moving. Cathy says she's related to the Queen of France, and someday her family will inherit some property, but for now they have to move because the neighborhood is going downhill.

Cathy has warned Esperanza about the two girls across the street, but in "Our Good Day" Esperanza decides to be their friend anyway. She gives the two girls (Lucy and Rachel) some money because they are all going in together to buy a bicycle from a neighborhood boy. Cathy leaves, and Esperanza, Lucy, and Rachel take a ride on their new, wobbly bicycle.

In "Laughter," Esperanza says she and Nenny don't look alike, but that there are likenesses between them deeper than looks.

The girls visit a neighborhood second-hand store ("Gil's Furniture…"). Nenny asks the owner about a music box, and he opens the lid and lets them listen. Nenny asks how much it costs, but the storeowner says it's not for sale.

Cathy has moved, and a boy called Meme Ortiz moves into her house. There's a backyard with a large tree in it. The children hold the First Annual Tarzan Jumping Contest in this tree, and Meme wins, breaking both arms.

> Here the author discusses a particular incident from the novel. **Does the author express new ideas or restate main ideas and events from the novel?**

Is conflict necessary?
How do the conflicts described in *The House on Mango Street* relate to the conflicts of real-life children and teens?

Features:
- subject line and author's name
- time and date of posting
- focus on a particular subject or topic

Boston Bibliophile

FRIDAY, JULY 18

The House on Mango Street,
by Sandra Cisneros

The House on Mango Street is one of those books I looked at in bookstores probably dozens of times before I finally read it; I'm sorry it took me so long.

A collection of short stories comprising a larger narrative, it's a little gem of a story of a young girl coming of age in a poor neighborhood. Each chapter is an individual story or vignette of young Esperanza's neighbors and friends, little episodes from her life. The young narrator shows different facets of her own personality through each portrait—a sense of humor, a sense of outrage, hope, optimism, sadness, pity, pride, shame, and compassion:

> *One day I'll own my own house, but I won't forget who I am or where I came from. Passing bums will ask, Can I come in? I'll offer them the attic, ask them to stay, because I know how it is to be without a house.*
>
> *Some days after dinner, guests and I will sit in front of a fire. Floorboards will squeak upstairs. The attic grumble.*
>
> *Rats? they'll ask.*
>
> *Bums, I'll say, and I'll be happy.*

> This first paragraph provides various types of information. **How might this paragraph help you distinguish whether this blog is a summary or a critique?**

This passage shows her hopes for herself (bettering her lot in life, owning her own home, having friends over for dinner parties by a fireplace— an idyllic middle class life), as well as her naiveté—maybe her homeless friends upstairs would like to come down, too.

The simplicity and openness of Esperanza's tone in this and other passages belies the book's serious undercurrents. Though the individual vignettes have an innocent charm, themes of desperation and fear run throughout, through stories of her neighbors and friends, many of them women, trapped, by poverty, by abuse, by illness, by a lack of education, or by a lack of imagination. By the end of the book we come to understand that she uses her writing as a means of escape, and so there is hope.

> Here, the author discusses the themes of the book.

The House on Mango Street is a lovely, sweet book for teens and adults about what it means to grow up and find meaning in life. I'd recommend it for just about anyone.

POSTED BY MARIE AT 8:07 PM

> Here, the author discusses the book as a whole. **How might this paragraph help you distinguish whether this text is a summary or a critique?**

Is conflict necessary?
According to the blog writer, how does Esperanza's writing help her to escape the conflicts that surround her?

Comparing Informational Texts

(a) Analyze: Compare the selections to distinguish between the summary and the critique. Explain your response. **(b)** Compare and contrast the texts, evaluating how well each author achieved his or her purpose for writing.

 College Readiness | Timed Writing

Write an Analysis

> **Essay**
> An essay should include an introduction with a thesis, details to support your position, and a conclusion. A short essay should be only a few paragraphs long.

Write a short essay in which you analyze the positions and opinions expressed in the critique of *The House on Mango Street*. In your essay, evaluate whether the author's opinions are supported by details provided in the text. If you find that an opinion is not well supported, give suggestions for how the author could have better supported his or her position. Provide evidence from the text to support your response. (30 minutes)

> **Academic Vocabulary**
> When you *evaluate* something, you express your opinion about it. You should provide support for your opinion by explaining your thinking process and supporting your ideas with textual evidence.

 ## 5-Minute Planner

Complete these steps before you begin to write:

1. Read the prompt carefully and completely.
2. Determine which text you will evaluate, and review it. **TIP** Be sure you only include information from the text you choose for your analysis.
3. Record the main opinion expressed in the critique and the evidence the author uses to support that opinion.
4. Consider whether you agree with the opinion and why. Take into consideration the amount of support the author includes for the opinion, and jot down additional support that could make the argument more convincing.
5. Make a brief outline of your essay before you begin drafting.

Comparing Elements of Fiction

Works of literature can have two levels of meaning. The basic level is literal—the text means exactly what it says. In some works, however, the text suggests a more abstract meaning. Authors use the following elements of fiction to give their stories and longer works a secondary, abstract level meaning.

- A **symbol** is a person or thing that represents both itself and a larger idea. For example, a dove can be a symbol of peace, and a voyage can represent the journey of life. Symbolism is the use of symbols to convey an idea.

- An **allegory** is a story or poem in which every element has parallel literal and symbolic meanings. For example, in an allegory about a sailor crossing the ocean, the sailor could represent all people; storms at sea could represent life's troubles; and sails could represent the help of friends. To appreciate an allegory, consider both levels of meaning.

Only one of the following stories is an allegory, but both use symbols.

As You Read Complete a chart like the one shown. Afterward, **draw conclusions** to determine which story uses symbols to enhance the meaning, and which is a true allegory.

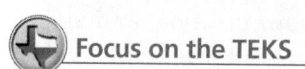

Focus on the TEKS

Reading
(5) Understand and draw conclusions about the elements of fiction.

	The Scarlet Ibis	The Golden Kite, the Silver Wind
Symbol	rotting brown petals	city wall shaped like a club
Meaning	the end of summer	a community's desire to protect itself
Possible Role in Allegory		

PHLitOnline

www.PHLitOnline.com

- Vocabulary flashcards
- Interactive journals
- More about the authors
- Selection audio
- Interactive graphic organizers

Is *conflict* necessary?

Writing About the Big Question

In both of these stories, **competitiveness** leads to conflict. Complete these sentences to develop your ideas about the Big Question:

Some people like to **compete** because _____.

To prevent a **competition** from turning into a conflict, you might _____.

Meet the Authors

James Hurst (b. 1922)

Author of "The Scarlet Ibis"

James Hurst grew up along the coast of North Carolina, a place of quiet landscapes and violent storms. After studying chemical engineering and opera and serving in the army during World War II, Hurst took a job at a New York bank. For thirty-four years, he worked as a banker and spent his evenings writing stories.

Creating Symbolism "The Scarlet Ibis," published in 1960, is Hurst's best-known story. Hurst has said that he "wanted [the ibis] to represent [the character of Doodle]—not Doodle's physical self, but his spirit."

Ray Bradbury (b. 1920)

Author of "The Golden Kite, the Silver Wind"

Born in Waukegan, Illinois, Ray Bradbury grew up in Arizona and California. He has been writing for more than sixty years and has published more than 500 stories. His work has earned him many honors, including the World Fantasy Award for lifetime achievement and the Grand Master Award from the Science Fiction Writers of America.

Writing to Entertain Bradbury is best known for his works of fantasy and science fiction. "I write for fun," Bradbury has said. "I don't see myself as a philosopher. That's awfully boring. . . . My goal is to entertain myself and others."

The Scarlet Ibis

James Hurst

▶ **Critical Viewing**
What could you infer about the childhood of someone living in the location pictured? **[Interpret]**

Literary Analysis
Elements of Fiction
What details about the flowers, weeds, and the oriole nest in the opening paragraph symbolize death?

It was in the clove of seasons, summer was dead but autumn had not yet been born, that the ibis lit in the bleeding tree. The flower garden was stained with rotting brown magnolia petals and ironweeds grew rank amid the purple phlox. The five o'clocks by the chimney still marked time, but the oriole nest in the elm was untenanted and rocked back and forth like an empty cradle. The last graveyard flowers were blooming, and their smell drifted across the cotton field and through every room of our house, speaking softly the names of our dead.

It's strange that all this is still so clear to me, now that the summer has long since fled and time has had its way. A grindstone stands where the bleeding tree stood, just outside the kitchen door, and now if an oriole sings in the elm, its song seems to die up in the leaves, a silvery dust. The flower garden is prim, the house a gleaming white, and the pale fence across the yard stands straight and spruce. But sometimes (like right now), as I sit in the cool, green-draped parlor, the grindstone begins to turn, and time with all its changes is ground away—and I remember Doodle.

Doodle was just about the craziest brother a boy ever had. Of course, he wasn't a crazy crazy like old Miss Leedie, who was in love with President Wilson and wrote him a letter every day, but was a nice crazy, like someone you meet in your dreams. He was born when I was six and was, from the outset, a disappointment. He seemed all head, with a tiny body which was red and shriveled like an old man's. Everybody thought he was going to die—everybody

except Aunt Nicey, who had delivered him. She said he would live because he was born in a caul[1] and cauls were made from Jesus' nightgown. Daddy had Mr. Heath, the carpenter, build a little mahogany coffin for him. But he didn't die, and when he was three months old Mama and Daddy decided they might as well name him. They named him William Armstrong, which was like tying a big tail on a small kite. Such a name sounds good only on a tombstone.

I thought myself pretty smart at many things, like holding my breath, running, jumping, or climbing the vines in Old Woman Swamp, and I wanted more than anything else someone to race to Horsehead Landing, someone to box with, and someone to perch with in the top fork of the great pine behind the barn, where across the fields and swamps you could see the sea. I wanted a brother. But Mama, crying, told me that even if William Armstrong lived, he would never do these things with me. He might not, she sobbed, even be "all there." He might, as long as he lived, lie on the rubber sheet in the center of the bed in the front bedroom where the white marquisette curtains billowed out in the afternoon sea breeze, rustling like palmetto fronds.[2]

It was bad enough having an invalid brother, but having one who possibly was not all there was unbearable, so I began to make plans to kill him by smothering him with a pillow. However, one afternoon as I watched him, my head poked between the iron posts of the foot of the bed, he looked straight at me and grinned. I skipped through the rooms, down the echoing halls, shouting, "Mama, he smiled. He's all there! He's all there!" and he was.

---

1. caul (kôl) n. membrane enclosing a baby at birth.
2. palmetto (pal met′ ō) fronds (frändz) n. palm leaves.

Literary Analysis
Elements of Fiction In what ways does the caul symbolize life and hope?

It's strange that all this is still so clear to me, now that the summer has long since fled and time has had its way.

Reading Check
Who is Doodle?

Scarlet Ibis

Found mostly in the South American tropics, the strikingly beautiful scarlet ibis is a wading bird with long legs, a long, slender neck, black-tipped wings, and a wingspan of more than three feet. It seldom appears in the United States north of Florida and would be an unexpected and dramatic sight to the people of coastal North Carolina.

Connect to the Literature

Why would the discovery of a scarlet ibis in coastal North Carolina, the setting of this story, be unexpected and dramatic?

When he was two, if you laid him on his stomach, he began to try to move himself, straining terribly. The doctor said that with his weak heart this strain would probably kill him, but it didn't. Trembling, he'd push himself up, turning first red, then a soft purple, and finally collapse back onto the bed like an old worn-out doll. I can still see Mama watching him, her hand pressed tight across her mouth, her eyes wide and unblinking. But he learned to crawl (it was his third winter), and we brought him out of the front bedroom, putting him on the rug before the fireplace. For the first time he became one of us.

As long as he lay all the time in bed, we called him William Armstrong, even though it was formal and sounded as if we were referring to one of our ancestors, but with his creeping around on the deerskin rug and beginning to talk, something had to be done about his name. It was I who renamed him. When he crawled, he crawled backwards, as if he were in reverse and couldn't change gears. If you called him, he'd turn around as if he were going in the other direction, then he'd back right up to you to be picked up. Crawling backward made him look like a doodle-bug, so I began to call him Doodle, and in time even Mama and Daddy thought it was a better name than William Armstrong. Only Aunt Nicey disagreed. She said caul babies should be treated with special respect since they might turn out to be saints. Renaming my brother was perhaps the kindest thing I ever did for him, because nobody expects much from someone called Doodle.

Although Doodle learned to crawl, he showed no signs of walking, but he wasn't idle. He talked so much that we all quit listening to what he said. It was about this time that Daddy built him a go-cart and I had to pull him around. At first I just paraded him up and down the piazza, but then he started crying to be taken out into the yard and it ended up by my having to lug him wherever I went. If I so much as picked up my cap, he'd start crying to go with me and Mama would call from wherever she was, "Take Doodle with you."

He was a burden in many ways. The doctor had said that he mustn't get too excited, too hot, too cold, or too tired and that he must always be treated gently. A long list of don'ts went with him, all of which I ignored once we got out of the house. To discourage his coming with me, I'd run with him across the ends of the cotton rows and careen him around corners on two wheels. Sometimes I accidentally turned him over, but he never told Mama. His skin was very sensitive, and he had to wear a big straw hat whenever he went out. When the going got rough and he had to cling to the sides of the go-cart, the hat slipped all the way down over his ears. He was a sight. Finally, I could see I was licked. Doodle was my brother and he was going to cling to me forever, no matter what I did, so I dragged him across the burning cotton field to share with him the only beauty I knew, Old Woman Swamp. I pulled the go-cart through the saw-tooth fern, down into the green dimness where the palmetto fronds whispered by the stream. I lifted him out and set him down in the soft rubber grass beside a tall pine. His eyes were round with wonder as he gazed about him, and his little hands began to stroke the rubber grass. Then he began to cry.

"For heaven's sake, what's the matter?" I asked, annoyed.

"It's so pretty," he said. "So pretty, pretty, pretty."

After that day Doodle and I often went down into Old Woman Swamp. I would gather wildflowers, wild violets, honeysuckle, yellow jasmine, snakeflowers, and water lilies, and with wire grass we'd weave them into necklaces and crowns. We'd bedeck ourselves with our handiwork and loll about thus beautified, beyond the touch of the everyday world. Then when the slanted rays of the sun burned orange in the tops of the pines, we'd drop our jewels into the stream and watch them float away toward the sea.

There is within me (and with sadness I have watched it in others) a knot of cruelty borne by the stream of love, much as our blood sometimes bears the seed of our destruction, and at times I was mean to Doodle. One day I took him up to the barn loft and showed him his casket, telling him how we all had believed he would die. It was covered with a film of Paris green[3] sprinkled to kill the rats, and screech owls had built a nest inside it.

Doodle studied the mahogany box for a long time, then said, "It's not mine."

"It is," I said. "And before I'll help you down from the loft, you're going to have to touch it."

"I won't touch it," he said sullenly.

"Then I'll leave you here by yourself," I threatened, and made as if I were going down.

Doodle was frightened of being left. "Don't go leave me, Brother," he cried, and he leaned toward the coffin. His hand, trembling, reached out, and when he touched the casket he screamed. A screech owl flapped out of the box into our faces, scaring us and covering us with Paris green. Doodle was paralyzed, so I put him on my shoulder and carried him down the ladder, and even when we were outside in the bright sunshine, he clung to me, crying, "Don't leave me. Don't leave me."

---

3. Paris green poisonous green powder used chiefly as an insecticide.

Literary Analysis
Elements of Fiction
Which details in this paragraph symbolize life and beauty?

Reading Check

What does the narrator force Doodle to touch?

When Doodle was five years old, I was embarrassed at having a brother of that age who couldn't walk, so I set out to teach him. We were down in Old Woman Swamp and it was spring and the sick-sweet smell of bay flowers hung everywhere like a mournful song. "I'm going to teach you to walk, Doodle," I said.

He was sitting comfortably on the soft grass, leaning back against the pine. "Why?" he asked.

I hadn't expected such an answer. "So I won't have to haul you around all the time."

"I can't walk, Brother," he said.

"Who says so?" I demanded.

"Mama, the doctor—everybody."

"Oh, you can walk," I said, and I took him by the arms and stood him up. He collapsed onto the grass like a half-empty flour sack. It was as if he had no bones in his little legs.

"Don't hurt me, Brother," he warned.

"Shut up. I'm not going to hurt you. I'm going to teach you to walk." I heaved him up again, and again he collapsed.

This time he did not lift his face up out of the rubber grass. "I just can't do it. Let's make honeysuckle wreaths."

"Oh yes you can, Doodle," I said. "All you got to do is try. Now come on," and I hauled him up once more.

It seemed so hopeless from the beginning that it's a miracle I didn't give up. But all of us must have something or someone to be proud of, and Doodle had become mine. I did not know then that pride is a wonderful, terrible thing, a seed that bears two vines, life and death. Every day that summer we went to the pine beside the stream of Old Woman Swamp, and I put him on his feet at least a hundred times each afternoon. Occasionally I too became discouraged because it didn't seem as if he was trying, and I would say, "Doodle, don't you want to learn to walk?"

He'd nod his head, and I'd say, "Well, if you don't keep trying, you'll never learn." Then I'd paint for him a picture of us as old men, white-haired, him with a long white beard and me still pulling him around in the go-cart. This never failed to make him try again.

Finally one day, after many weeks of practicing, he stood alone for a few seconds. When he fell, I grabbed him in my arms and hugged him, our laughter pealing through the swamp like a ringing bell. Now we knew it could be done. Hope no longer hid in the dark palmetto thicket but perched like a cardinal in the lacy toothbrush tree, brilliantly visible. "Yes, yes," I cried, and he cried it too, and the grass beneath us was soft and the smell of the swamp was sweet.

With success so imminent, we decided not to tell anyone until he could actually walk. Each day, barring rain, we sneaked into Old

Vocabulary
imminent (im´ ə nənt)
adj. likely to happen soon

Woman Swamp, and by cotton-picking time Doodle was ready to show what he could do. He still wasn't able to walk far, but we could wait no longer. Keeping a nice secret is very hard to do, like holding your breath. We chose to reveal all on October eighth, Doodle's sixth birthday, and for weeks ahead we mooned around the house, promising everybody a most spectacular surprise. Aunt Nicey said that, after so much talk, if we produced anything less tremendous than the Resurrection,[4] she was going to be disappointed.

At breakfast on our chosen day, when Mama, Daddy, and Aunt Nicey were in the dining room, I brought Doodle to the door in the go-cart just as usual and had them turn their backs, making them cross their hearts and hope to die if they peeked. I helped Doodle up, and when he was standing alone I let them look. There wasn't a sound as Doodle walked slowly across the room and sat down at his place at the table. Then Mama began to cry and ran over to him, hugging him and kissing him. Daddy hugged him too, so I went to Aunt Nicey, who was thanks praying in the doorway, and began to waltz her around. We danced together quite well until she came down on my big toe with her brogans, hurting me so badly I thought I was crippled for life.

Doodle told them it was I who had taught him to walk, so everyone wanted to hug me, and I began to cry.

"What are you crying for?" asked Daddy, but I couldn't answer. They did not know that I did it for myself; that pride, whose slave I was, spoke to me louder than all their voices, and that Doodle walked only because I was ashamed of having a crippled brother.

Two Boys in a Punt, 1915–Cover Illustration, *Popular Magazine,* N.C. Wyeth (1882–1945), Private Collection, Photography courtesy of Brandywine River Museum.

◀ **Critical Viewing**
What can you tell about the brothers' relationship from the illustration and the details in the story? **[Interpret]**

"I'm going to teach you to walk, Doodle," I said.

Reading Check
What surprise do the boys present?

---

4. **the Resurrection** (rez´ ə rek´ shən) the rising of Jesus Christ from the dead after his death and burial.

Within a few months Doodle had learned to walk well and his go-cart was put up in the barn loft (it's still there) beside his little mahogany coffin. Now, when we roamed off together, resting often, we never turned back until our destination had been reached, and to help pass the time, we took up lying. From the beginning Doodle was a terrible liar and he got me in the habit. Had anyone stopped to listen to us, we would have been sent off to Dix Hill.

My lies were scary, involved, and usually pointless, but Doodle's were twice as crazy. People in his stories all had wings and flew wherever they wanted to go. His favorite lie was about a boy named Peter who had a pet peacock with a ten-foot tail. Peter wore a golden robe that glittered so brightly that when he walked through the sunflowers they turned away from the sun to face him. When Peter was ready to go to sleep, the peacock spread his magnificent tail, enfolding the boy gently like a closing go-to-sleep flower, burying him in the gloriously iridescent, rustling vortex.[5] Yes, I must admit it. Doodle could beat me lying.

Doodle and I spent lots of time thinking about our future. We decided that when we were grown we'd live in Old Woman Swamp and pick dog-tongue for a living. Beside the stream, he planned, we'd build us a house of whispering leaves and the swamp birds would be our chickens. All day long (when we weren't gathering dog-tongue) we'd swing through the cypresses on the rope vines, and if it rained we'd huddle beneath an umbrella tree and play stickfrog. Mama and Daddy could come and live with us if they wanted to. He even came up with the idea that he could marry Mama and I could marry Daddy. Of course, I was old enough to know this wouldn't work out, but the picture he painted was so beautiful and serene that all I could do was whisper Yes, yes.

Once I had succeeded in teaching Doodle to walk, I began to believe in my own infallibility and I prepared a terrific development program for him, unknown to Mama and Daddy, of course. I would teach him to run, to swim, to climb trees, and to fight. He, too, now believed in my infallibility, so we set the deadline for these accomplishments less than a year away, when, it had been decided, Doodle could start to school.

That winter we didn't make much progress, for I was in school and Doodle suffered from one bad cold after another. But when spring came, rich and warm, we raised our sights again. Success lay at the end of summer like a pot of gold, and our campaign got off to a good start. On hot days, Doodle and I went down to Horsehead Landing and I gave him swimming lessons or showed him how to row a boat. Sometimes we descended into the cool

---

5. **vortex** (vôr′ teks′) *n.* rushing whirl, drawing in all that surrounds it.

greenness of Old Woman Swamp and climbed the rope vines or boxed scientifically beneath the pine where he had learned to walk. Promise hung about us like the leaves, and wherever we looked, ferns unfurled and birds broke into song.

That summer, the summer of 1918, was blighted. In May and June there was no rain and the crops withered, curled up, then died under the thirsty sun. One morning in July a hurricane came out of the east, tipping over the oaks in the yard and splitting the limbs of the elm trees. That afternoon it roared back out of the west, blew the fallen oaks around, snapping their roots and tearing them out of the earth like a hawk at the entrails of a chicken. Cotton bolls were wrenched from the stalks and lay like green walnuts in the valleys between the rows, while the cornfield leaned over uniformly so that the tassels touched the ground. Doodle and I followed Daddy out into the cotton field, where he stood, shoulders sagging, surveying the ruin. When his chin sank down onto his chest, we were frightened, and Doodle slipped his hand into mine. Suddenly Daddy straightened his shoulders, raised a giant knuckly fist, and with a voice that seemed to rumble out of the earth itself began cursing heaven, hell, the weather, and the Republican Party. Doodle and I, prodding each other and giggling, went back to the house, knowing that everything would be all right.

And during that summer, strange names were heard through the house: Chateau-Thierry, Amiens, Soissons, and in her blessing at the supper table, Mama once said, "And bless the Pearsons, whose boy Joe was lost at Belleau Wood."[6]

So we came to that clove of seasons. School was only a few weeks away, and Doodle was far behind schedule. He could barely clear the ground when climbing up the rope vines and his swimming was certainly not passable. We decided to double our efforts, to make that last drive and reach our pot of gold. I made him swim until he turned blue and row until he couldn't lift an oar. Wherever we went, I purposely walked fast, and although he kept up, his face turned red and his eyes became glazed. Once, he could go no further, so he collapsed on the ground and began to cry.

"Aw, come on, Doodle," I urged. "You can do it. Do you want to be different from everybody else when you start school?"

"Does it make any difference?"

"It certainly does," I said. "Now, come on," and I helped him up.

As we slipped through dog days, Doodle began to look feverish, and Mama felt his forehead, asking him if he felt ill. At night he didn't sleep well, and sometimes he had nightmares, crying out until I touched him and said, "Wake up, Doodle. Wake up."

Literary Analysis
Elements of Fiction
What conclusion can you draw about the symbolic meaning of the "blighted" summer?

Success lay at the end of summer like a pot of gold...

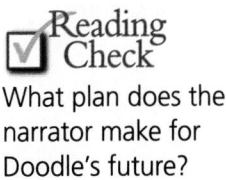
Reading Check
What plan does the narrator make for Doodle's future?

---

6. **Chateau-Thierry** (shä′ tō′ tē er′ ē), **Amiens** (à myan′), **Soissons** (swä sôn′), . . . **Belleau** (be lō′) **Wood** places in France where battles were fought during World War I.

▼ **Critical Viewing**
How would you react if this exotic bird—an ibis—showed up in your backyard? **[Relate]**

Vocabulary
precariously (pri ker´ ē əs lē) *adv.* insecurely

It was Saturday noon, just a few days before school was to start. I should have already admitted defeat, but my pride wouldn't let me. The excitement of our program had now been gone for weeks, but still we kept on with a tired doggedness. It was too late to turn back, for we had both wandered too far into a net of expectations and had left no crumbs behind.

Daddy, Mama, Doodle, and I were seated at the dining-room table having lunch. It was a hot day, with all the windows and doors open in case a breeze should come. In the kitchen Aunt Nicey was humming softly. After a long silence, Daddy spoke. "It's so calm, I wouldn't be surprised if we had a storm this afternoon."

"I haven't heard a rain frog," said Mama, who believed in signs, as she served the bread around the table.

"I did," declared Doodle. "Down in the swamp."

"He didn't," I said contrarily.

"You did, eh?" said Daddy, ignoring my denial.

"I certainly did," Doodle reiterated, scowling at me over the top of his iced-tea glass, and we were quiet again.

Suddenly, from out in the yard, came a strange croaking noise. Doodle stopped eating, with a piece of bread poised ready for his mouth, his eyes popped round like two blue buttons. "What's that?" he whispered.

I jumped up, knocking over my chair, and had reached the door when Mama called, "Pick up the chair, sit down again, and say excuse me."

By the time I had done this, Doodle had excused himself and had slipped out into the yard. He was looking up into the bleeding tree. "It's a great big red bird!" he called.

The bird croaked loudly again, and Mama and Daddy came out into the yard. We shaded our eyes with our hands against the hazy glare of the sun and peered up through the still leaves. On the topmost branch a bird the size of a chicken, with scarlet feathers and long legs, was perched precariously. Its wings hung down loosely, and as we watched, a feather dropped away and floated slowly down through the green leaves.

"It's not even frightened of us," Mama said.

"It looks tired," Daddy added. "Or maybe sick."

Doodle's hands were clasped at his throat, and I had never seen him stand still so long. "What is it?" he asked.

Daddy shook his head. "I don't know, maybe it's—"

At that moment the bird began to flutter, but the wings were uncoordinated, and amid much flapping and a spray of flying feathers, it tumbled down, bumping through the limbs of the bleeding tree and landing at our feet with a thud. Its long, graceful neck jerked twice into an S, then straightened out, and the bird was still. A white veil came over the eyes and the long white beak unhinged. Its legs were crossed and its clawlike feet were delicately curved at rest. Even death did not mar its grace, for it lay on the earth like a broken vase of red flowers, and we stood around it, awed by its exotic beauty.

"It's dead," Mama said.

"What is it?" Doodle repeated.

"Go bring me the bird book," said Daddy.

I ran into the house and brought back the bird book. As we watched, Daddy thumbed through its pages. "It's a scarlet ibis," he said, pointing to a picture. "It lives in the tropics—South America to Florida. A storm must have brought it here."

Sadly, we all looked back at the bird. A scarlet ibis! How many miles it had traveled to die like this, in our yard, beneath the bleeding tree.

"Let's finish lunch," Mama said, nudging us back toward the dining room.

"I'm not hungry," said Doodle, and he knelt down beside the ibis.

"We've got peach cobbler for dessert," Mama tempted from the doorway.

Doodle remained kneeling. "I'm going to bury him."

"Don't you dare touch him," Mama warned. "There's no telling what disease he might have had."

"All right," said Doodle. "I won't."

Daddy, Mama, and I went back to the dining-room table, but we watched Doodle through the open door. He took out a piece of string from his pocket and, without touching the ibis, looped one end around its neck. Slowly, while singing softly "Shall We Gather at the River," he carried the bird around to the front yard and dug a hole in the flower garden, next to the petunia bed. Now we were watching him through the front window, but he didn't know it. His awkwardness at digging the hole with a shovel whose handle was twice as long as he was made us laugh, and we covered our mouths with our hands so he wouldn't hear.

When Doodle came into the dining room, he found us seriously eating our cobbler. He was pale and lingered just inside the screen door. "Did you get the scarlet ibis buried?" asked Daddy.

Doodle didn't speak but nodded his head.

"Go wash your hands, and then you can have some peach cobbler," said Mama.

"I'm not hungry," he said.

Literary Analysis
Elements of Fiction
In what ways are the bird's uncoordinated movements similar to Doodle's? Explain.

On the topmost branch a bird the size of a chicken, with scarlet feathers and long legs, was perched precariously.

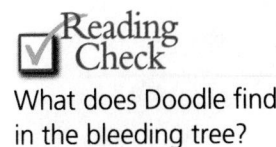
Reading Check

What does Doodle find in the bleeding tree?

"Dead birds is bad luck," said Aunt Nicey, poking her head from the kitchen door. "Specially red dead birds!"

As soon as I had finished eating, Doodle and I hurried off to Horsehead Landing. Time was short, and Doodle still had a long way to go if he was going to keep up with the other boys when he started school. The sun, gilded with the yellow cast of autumn, still burned fiercely, but the dark green woods through which we passed were shady and cool. When we reached the landing, Doodle said he was too tired to swim, so we got into a skiff and floated down the creek with the tide. Far off in the marsh a rail was scolding, and over on the beach locusts were singing in the myrtle trees. Doodle did not speak and kept his head turned away, letting one hand trail limply in the water.

After we had drifted a long way, I put the oars in place and made Doodle row back against the tide. Black clouds began to gather in the southwest, and he kept watching them, trying to pull the oars a little faster. When we reached Horsehead Landing, lightning was playing across half the sky and thunder roared out, hiding even the sound of the sea. The sun disappeared and darkness descended, almost like night. Flocks of marsh crows flew by, heading inland to their roosting trees, and two egrets, squawking, arose from the oyster-rock shallows and careened away.

Doodle was both tired and frightened, and when he stepped from the skiff he collapsed onto the mud, sending an armada of fiddler crabs rustling off into the marsh grass. I helped him up, and as he wiped the mud off his trousers, he smiled at me ashamedly. He had failed and we both knew it, so we started back home, racing the storm. We never spoke (What are the words that can solder cracked pride?), but I knew he was watching me, watching for a sign of mercy. The lightning was near now, and from fear he walked so close behind me he kept stepping on my heels. The faster I walked, the faster he walked, so I began to run. The rain was coming, roaring through the pines, and then, like a bursting Roman candle, a gum tree ahead of us was shattered by a bolt of lightning. When the deafening peal of thunder had died, and in the moment before the rain arrived, I heard Doodle, who had fallen behind, cry out, "Brother, Brother, don't leave me! Don't leave me!"

The knowledge that Doodle's and my plans had come to naught was bitter, and that streak of cruelty within me awakened. I ran as fast as I could, leaving him far behind with a wall of rain dividing us. The drops stung my face like nettles, and the wind flared the wet glistening leaves of the bordering trees. Soon I could hear his voice no more.

Literary Analysis
Elements of Fiction
What conclusion can you draw about the symbolic meaning of the "black clouds"?

I hadn't run too far before I became tired, and the flood of childish spite evanesced as well. I stopped and waited for Doodle. The sound of rain was everywhere, but the wind had died and it fell straight down in parallel paths like ropes hanging from the sky. As I waited, I peered through the downpour, but no one came. Finally I went back and found him huddled beneath a red nightshade bush beside the road. He was sitting on the ground, his face buried in his arms, which were resting on his drawn-up knees. "Let's go, Doodle," I said.

He didn't answer, so I placed my hand on his forehead and lifted his head. Limply, he fell backwards onto the earth. He had been bleeding from the mouth, and his neck and the front of his shirt were stained a brilliant red.

"Doodle! Doodle!" I cried, shaking him, but there was no answer but the ropy rain. He lay very awkwardly, with his head thrown far back, making his vermilion neck appear unusually long and slim. His little legs, bent sharply at the knees, had never before seemed so fragile, so thin.

I began to weep, and the tear-blurred vision in red before me looked very familiar. "Doodle!" I screamed above the pounding storm and threw my body to the earth above his. For a long long time, it seemed forever, I lay there crying, sheltering my fallen scarlet ibis from the heresy[7] of rain.

---

7. heresy (her´ ə sē) *n.* idea opposed to the beliefs of a religion or philosophy.

Literary Analysis
Elements of Fiction
How are the details about the blood as well as Doodle's position beneath the bush similar to what happened to the scarlet ibis?

Critical Thinking

1. **Respond:** Do you blame the narrator for Doodle's death? Explain.

2. **(a)** Why does the narrator cry when everyone congratulates him for teaching Doodle to walk? **(b) Analyze:** What do the narrator's tears reveal about his conflicted, or mixed, feelings?

3. **(a)** What does Doodle do with the dead ibis?
   (b) Compare and Contrast: How does Doodle's reaction to the dead bird compare to those of his family members? Support your answer with details from the text. **(c) Make Inferences:** What do you think motivates Doodle to treat the ibis as he does?

Is conflict necessary?
As a child, the narrator sets demanding, competitive goals for Doodle. **(a)** Why do you think Doodle strives for these goals even though he does not have a competitive nature? **(b)** In what way do those goals reflect the conflict that the narrator feels about Doodle?

Support your responses with evidence from the text.

The Golden Kite, the Silver Wind

Ray Bradbury

▼ **Critical Viewing**
How are the leader in this painting and the Mandarin in the story both similar and different? **[Compare and Contrast]**

Background "The Golden Kite, the Silver Wind" was written during the Cold War, a period of intense rivalry between the United States and the former Soviet Union that shaped world politics in the second half of the twentieth century. During this time, each action by one country—the creation of a weapon, the launching of a satellite—was countered by a reaction from the other country. As you read, think about the parallels between the story events and the conflicts of the Cold War.

"In the shape of a pig?" cried the Mandarin.[1]

"In the shape of a pig," said the messenger, and departed.

"Oh, what an evil day in an evil year," cried the Mandarin. "The town of Kwan-Si, beyond the hill, was very small in my childhood. Now it has grown so large that at last they are building a wall."

"But why should a wall two miles away make my good father sad and angry all within the hour?" asked his daughter quietly.

"They build their wall," said the Mandarin, "in the shape of a pig! Do you see? Our own city wall is built in the shape of an orange. That pig will devour us, greedily!"

"Ah."

They both sat thinking.

Life was full of symbols and omens. Demons lurked everywhere, Death swam in the wetness of an eye, the turn of a gull's wing meant rain, a fan held so, the tilt of a roof, and, yes, even a city wall was of immense importance. Travelers and tourists, caravans, musicians, artists, coming upon these two towns, equally judging the portents,[2] would say, "The city

---

1. **Mandarin** (man´ də rin) *n.* a high official of China; here, the ruling leader.
2. **portents** (pôr´ tents´) *n.* things that are thought to be signs of events to come; omens.

shaped like an orange? No! I will enter the city shaped like a pig and prosper, eating all, growing fat with good luck and prosperity!"

The Mandarin wept. "All is lost! These symbols and signs terrify. Our city will come on evil days."

"Then," said the daughter, "call in your stonemasons and temple builders. I will whisper from behind the silken screen and you will know the words."

The old man clapped his hands despairingly. "Ho, stonemasons! "Ho, builders of towns and palaces!"

The men who knew marble and granite and onyx and quartz came quickly. The Mandarin faced them most uneasily, himself waiting for a whisper from the silken screen behind his throne. At last the whisper came.

"I have called you here," said the whisper.

"I have called you here," said the Mandarin aloud, "because our city is shaped like an orange, and the vile city of Kwan-Si has this day shaped theirs like a ravenous pig—"

Here the stonemasons groaned and wept. Death rattled his cane in the outer courtyard. Poverty made a sound like a wet cough in the shadows of the room.

"And so," said the whisper, said the Mandarin, "you raisers of walls must go bearing trowels and rocks and change the shape of our city!"

The architects and masons gasped. The Mandarin himself gasped at what he had said. The whisper whispered. The Mandarin went on: "And you will change our walls into a club which may beat the pig and drive it off!"

The stonemasons rose up, shouting. Even the Mandarin, delighted at the words from his mouth, applauded, stood down from his throne. "Quick!" he cried. "To work!"

When his men had gone, smiling and bustling, the Mandarin turned with great love to the silken screen. "Daughter," he whispered, "I will embrace you." There was no reply. He stepped around the screen, and she was gone.

Such modesty, he thought. She has slipped away and left me with a triumph, as if it were mine.

The news spread through the city; the Mandarin was acclaimed. Everyone carried stone to the walls. Fireworks were set off and the demons of death and poverty did not linger, as all worked together. At the end of the month the wall had been changed. It was now a mighty bludgeon with which to drive pigs, boars, even lions, far away. The Mandarin slept like a happy fox every night.

Literary Analysis
Elements of Fiction
What qualities do the people believe the image of a pig symbolizes?

Vocabulary
ravenous (rav´ ə nəs)
adj. wildly hungry

Life was full of symbols and omens.

Reading Check

Who whispers to the king from behind a silken screen?

"I would like to see the Mandarin of Kwan-Si when the news is learned. Such pandemonium and hysteria; he will likely throw himself from a mountain! A little more of that wine, oh Daughter-who-thinks-like-a-son."

But the pleasure was like a winter flower; it died swiftly. That very afternoon the messenger rushed into the courtroom. "Oh, Mandarin, disease, early sorrow, avalanches, grasshopper plagues, and poisoned well water!"

The Mandarin trembled.

"The town of Kwan-Si," said the messenger, "which was built like a pig and which animal we drove away by changing our walls to a mighty stick, has now turned triumph to winter ashes. They have built their city's walls like a great bonfire to burn our stick!"

The Mandarin's heart sickened within him, like an autumn fruit upon an ancient tree. "Oh, gods! Travelers will spurn us. Tradesmen, reading the symbols, will turn from the stick, so easily destroyed, to the fire, which conquers all!"

"No," said a whisper like a snowflake from behind the silken screen.

"No," said the startled Mandarin.

"Tell my stonemasons," said the whisper that was a falling drop of rain, "to build our walls in the shape of a shining lake."

The Mandarin said this aloud, his heart warmed.

"And with this lake of water," said the whisper and the old man, "we will quench the fire and put it out forever!"

The city turned out in joy to learn that once again they had been saved by the magnificent Emperor of ideas. They ran to the walls and built them nearer to this new vision, singing, not as loudly as before, of course, for they were tired, and not as quickly, for since it had taken a month to rebuild the wall the first time, they had had to neglect business and crops and therefore were somewhat weaker and poorer.

There then followed a succession of horrible and wonderful days, one in another like a nest of frightened boxes.

"Oh, Emperor," cried the messenger, "Kwan-Si has rebuilt their walls to resemble a mouth with which to drink all our lake!"

"Then," said the Emperor, standing very close to his silken screen, "build our walls like a needle to sew up that mouth!"

"Emperor!" screamed the messenger. "They make their walls like a sword to break your needle!"

The Emperor held, trembling, to the silken screen. "Then shift the stones to form a scabbard to sheathe that sword!"[3]

---

3. **scabbard** (skab´ ərd) **to sheathe** (shēth) **that sword!** case to hold the blade of the sword.

Literary Analysis
Elements of Fiction
In what ways does the "winter flower" describe the fleeting pleasure the Mandarin feels?

Vocabulary
spurn (spʉrn) v. reject with contempt or disdain

"Mercy," wept the messenger the following morn, "they have worked all night and shaped their walls like lightning which will explode and destroy that sheath!"

Sickness spread in the city like a pack of evil dogs. Shops closed. The population, working now steadily for endless months upon the changing of the walls, resembled Death himself, clattering his white bones like musical instruments in the wind. Funerals began to appear in the streets, though it was the middle of summer, a time when all should be tending and harvesting. The Mandarin fell so ill that he had his bed drawn up by the silken screen and there he lay, miserably giving his architectural orders. The voice behind the screen was weak now, too, and faint, like the wind in the eaves.

"Kwan-Si is an eagle. Then our walls must be a net for that eagle. They are a sun to burn our net. Then we build a moon to eclipse their sun!"

Like a rusted machine, the city ground to a halt.

At last the whisper behind the screen cried out:

"In the name of the gods, send for Kwan-Si!"

Upon the last day of summer the Mandarin Kwan-Si, very ill and withered away, was carried into our Mandarin's courtroom by four starving footmen. The two mandarins were propped up, facing each other. Their breaths fluttered like winter winds in their mouths. A voice said:

"Let us put an end to this."

The old men nodded.

"This cannot go on," said the faint voice. "Our people do nothing but rebuild our cities to a different shape every day, every hour. They have no time to hunt, to fish, to love, to be good to their ancestors and their ancestors' children."

"This I admit," said the mandarins of the towns of the Cage, the Moon, the Spear, the Fire, the Sword and this, that, and other things.

"Carry us into the sunlight," said the voice.

The old men were borne out under the sun and up a little hill. In the late summer breeze a few very thin children were flying dragon kites in all the colors of the sun, and frogs and grass, the color of the sea and the color of coins and wheat.

The first Mandarin's daughter stood by his bed.

"See," she said.

"Those are nothing but kites," said the two old men.

"But what is a kite on the ground?" she said. "It is nothing. What does it need to sustain it and make it beautiful and truly spiritual?"

"The wind, of course!" said the others.

"And what do the sky and the wind need to make them beautiful?"

Like a rusted machine, the city ground to a halt.

Reading Check

What kind of wall does the daughter suggest should be built to defeat Kwan-Si's sun?

Literary Analysis
Elements of Fiction
What conclusion can you draw about the symbolic meaning of the relationship between the kite and the wind?

"A kite, of course—many kites, to break the monotony, the sameness of the sky. Colored kites, flying!"

"So," said the Mandarin's daughter. "You, Kwan-Si, will make a last rebuilding of your town to resemble nothing more nor less than the wind. And we shall build like a golden kite. The wind will beautify the kite and carry it to wondrous heights. And the kite will break the sameness of the wind's existence and give it purpose and meaning. One without the other is nothing. Together, all will be beauty and cooperation and a long and enduring life."

Whereupon the two mandarins were so overjoyed that they took their first nourishment in days, momentarily were given strength, embraced, and lavished praise upon each other, called the Mandarin's daughter a boy, a man, a stone pillar, a warrior, and a true and unforgettable son. Almost immediately they parted and hurried to their towns, calling out and singing, weakly but happily.

And so, in time, the towns became the Town of Golden Kite and the Town of the Silver Wind. And harvestings were harvested and business tended again, and the flesh returned, and disease ran off like a frightened jackal. And on every night of the year the inhabitants in the Town of the Kite could hear the good clear wind sustaining them. And those in the Town of the Wind could hear the kite singing, whispering, rising, and beautifying them.

"So be it," said the Mandarin in front of his silken screen.

Critical Thinking

1. **Respond:** Do you think the Mandarin's daughter gave her father good advice? Explain.

2. **(a) Interpret:** How do the townspeople react to the repeated directions to rebuild? **(b) Analyze Cause and Effect:** How does the competition between the towns affect the people's health and well-being? Explain. **(c) Evaluate:** Should the people have continued to follow the Mandarin as a leader?

3. **(a) Evaluate:** Why are walls built as a kite and the wind more effective for a peaceful and harmonious relationship between the two towns? **(b) Draw Conclusions:** What lesson does this story teach for today's world?

Is conflict necessary?
(a) Why do the two Mandarins feel that their cities must compete in wall-building? **(b)** To end their conflict, what must the Mandarins realize is more important than this competition? Explain your answer.

Support your responses with evidence from the text.

Comparing Elements of Fiction

1. Use a chart like the one shown to analyze how the characters, events, and setting in "The Golden Kite, the Silver Wind" could be **symbols** for leaders and world events during the Cold War.

Symbol	Qualities	Meaning
Mandarin	Leader of his town; worried about losing business and reputation	Leader of a nation who wants to stay on top
Mandarin's daughter		
Walls		

2. (a) In "The Scarlet Ibis," what does the ibis symbolize? **(b)** Which details support your conclusion? Explain.

3. Based on your understanding and analysis of the symbolism in the stories, which of these selections is an allegory? Explain.

 College Readiness | Timed Writing

Writing to Compare Elements of Fiction

Write an essay in which you compare the use of symbolism in "The Scarlet Ibis" and "The Golden Kite, the Silver Wind." Use details from the texts to support your response. (30 minutes)

 5-Minute Planner

1. Read the prompt carefully and completely.

2. Gather your ideas by jotting down answers to these questions:
  • What message or lesson does the author of each story express?
  • How do both authors use symbols to develop a message?

3. Decide how you will structure your essay and draft a quick outline.

4. Reread the prompt, and then draft your essay.

Expository Text: Cause-and-Effect Essay

Defining the Form Whether the subject is human nature or weather patterns, cause-and-effect reasoning explains why things happen. A **cause-and-effect essay** analyzes relationships between or among events, explaining how one causes another. You may use elements of this type of writing in science or history reports, and health articles, for example.

Assignment Write an analytical cause-and-effect essay of sufficient length to explain an event or a condition that interests you. Include these elements:

✔ *effective introductory* and *concluding paragraphs* and *a variety of sentence structures*

✔ an *organizing structure* appropriate to purpose, audience, and context

✔ smooth *transitions* in sentences and between paragraphs

✔ a clear analysis of a cause-and-effect relationship

✔ *relevant information* in the form of facts, examples, reasons, and *valid inferences* that support your assertions

✔ error-free grammar, including correct subject-verb agreement

To preview the criteria on which your cause-and-effect essay may be judged, see the rubric on page 409.

 Writing Workshop: *Work in Progress*

Review the work you did on pages 345 and 373.

WRITE GUY
Jeff Anderson, M.Ed.

What Do You Notice?

Sentence Structure

Read and re-read this passage from Elizabeth McCracken's "Desiderata."

I could tell dozens of other stories from the pages of family papers: my aunt Blanche's pell-mell record of taking care of her favorite sister, Elizabeth, who was dying of Alzheimer's; Blanche has that disease herself now, and you can see the early signs in these notes. My great-uncles' cheery letters from Europe during World War II.

Jot down what you notice about the passage. Then, consider how you might use examples to affect the audience of your own essay.

Focus on the TEKS

Writing
(15)(A)(i);(ii);(iv);(v) Write an analytical essay of sufficient length that includes effective introductory and concluding paragraphs and a variety of sentence structures; rhetorical devices, and transitions between paragraphs; an organizing structure appropriate to purpose, audience, and context; and relevant information and valid inferences.
(13)(A) Plan a first draft by determining appropriate topics through a range of strategies (background reading, personal interests).

Reading-Writing Connection

To get a feel for cause-and-effect essays, read the excerpt from *Silent Spring* by Rachel Carson on page 167.

Prewriting/Planning Strategies

To plan a first draft, first determine an appropriate topic. Choose from among a range of strategies such as the ones on this page to get started.

Examine current events through background reading. One way to begin looking for topics is to do background reading. Scan newspapers or magazines for headlines that interest you. Use a three-column chart to speculate about possible causes and effects: In the middle column, write the event; in the left column, write the possible causes; in the right column, note possible effects. Notice how the event listed in the chart is both an effect of the causes listed in the left column as well as a cause of the effects listed in the right column.

Causes	Event	Effects
• practice, focus • individual performance	Team wins championship	• increased fan interest • harder to buy tickets • revenue for city

List and freewrite. Your **personal interests** may also lead you to topic ideas. Jot down any interesting events that come to mind from the worlds of business, science, technology, the arts, nature, politics, or sports. Then, circle the item that most intrigues you. Freewrite for three minutes about that topic. As you write, note any causes and effects that come to mind. You can develop your topic from ideas you uncover in your freewriting.

Categorize to narrow your topic. Your essay must be of sufficient length to cover your subject. You may find that your subject is too broad to manage in the scope of a single essay. To **determine an appropriate topic,** consider the strategy of breaking your subject into smaller categories. For example, if your topic is about a record-breaking sports event, you might create categories such as "key player," "great coach," or "new equipment." Choose a more focused topic that interests you from your list of categories.

Chart causes and effects. Using an index card or a self-sticking note, write the central event or circumstance that is your subject. Decide if you want to explore the causes that produced the event or the effects the event produced. In either case, write those factors on separate cards or notes. Write key details related to each cause or effect on the cards or notes. Then, arrange the cards or notes in a logical sequence.

TEXAS
PHLitOnline
www.PHLitOnline.com
• Author video: Writing Process
• Author video: Rewards of Writing

Drafting Strategies

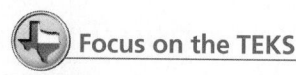 **Focus on the TEKS**

Writing
(13)(B) Structure ideas in a sustained way (e.g., using graphic organizers).

(15)(A)(i);(iv);(v) Write an analytical essay that includes effective introductory and concluding paragraphs; an organizing structure appropriate to purpose, audience, and context; and relevant information and valid inferences.

Conventions
(19) Spell correctly, including using various resources to determine correct spellings.

Choose an appropriate organizing structure. To be effective, your **introductory paragraph** should introduce your topic and show why it is important. Your **concluding paragraph** should summarize your analysis.

When organizing the body of your essay, consider your purpose, audience, and context. Choose an organizing structure that will help readers understand your ideas. Here are two possibilities for organization:

- **Chronological order** is particularly valuable when describing a sequence of causes and effects. You can start with the cause and then continue by describing its effects. You could also start with the effect and then go back through its causes one at a time.

- **Order of importance** organizes points from least important to most important. This pattern is especially effective when you are presenting a series of effects produced by a single cause.

Use logical and relevant information. As you draft your essay, avoid opinions, unsupported assertions, and trivial details. Rely instead on facts, statistics, and examples to support **valid inferences.**

- **Unsupported assertion:** Members of the royal family probably liked the color purple more than any other color.

- **Convincing support:** According to a primary source historical document, members of the royal family believed the color purple symbolized power and prosperity.

Use the TRI method. Follow these steps to **structure your ideas** in a sustained way.

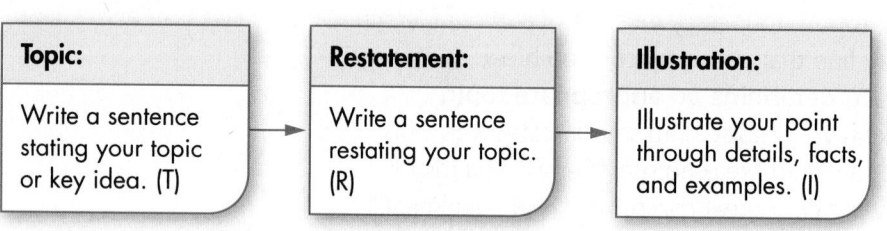

Topic:	Restatement:	Illustration:
Write a sentence stating your topic or key idea. (T)	Write a sentence restating your topic. (R)	Illustrate your point through details, facts, and examples. (I)

Once you feel comfortable with the TRI pattern, you can shift the sequence to suit your information and add variety to your writing.

Example: Originally, the color purple was associated with royalty. **(T)** Only kings, queens, and members of the nobility wore purple-colored clothing. **(R)** In England, Queen Elizabeth I actually made a law prohibiting anyone except herself and her relatives from wearing purple. **(I)**

Consult dictionaries and glossaries. Use various resources to determine correct spellings and the meanings of any words and phrases you do not know.

Wayson Choy
On Showing Cause and Effect

An origami butterfly sits on my computer to remind me that just as a butterfly must first go through various stages, my first draft will be "re-created" many times before it can take flight. During that process, I keep in mind that a sense of cause and effect is as important in fiction as in nonfiction. So, I hone the action and dialogue "to show, not tell about" the causes and effects in my characters' lives. The following draft from my novel *All That Matters* demonstrates how I do that.

I aim for "showing, not telling."
—Wayson Choy

from *All That Matters*

    I had given up a late afternoon soccer practice to do some serious studying ∧for Mr. Eades's first English test. There were plenty of others like us, books opened, eyes focused. Jenny pointed to the library seat ∧across from hers, and her eyes said, *No fooling around!* ~~Truth was, she took her English studies more seriously than she took me. It was frustrating. I just wanted to be with her. She was always in charge.~~

    ∧As she pushed my books across the table, I thought that she and I should have, two months ago, declared ourselves an official couple, especially after our fifth double date together. But Jenny didn't want that.

    ∧"Too showy," she had told me. "Maybe after we graduate. Next year."

    ∧She folded both our school sweaters together and neatly draped them over one of the empty chairs.

I needed to expand this account with more details to show causes and effects in the relationship between the narrator and his girlfriend, Jenny.

These two sentences tell that Jenny is an in-control girl who takes charge of the narrator. But I wanted to show it through dialogue and actions.

The act of folding the sweaters symbolizes Jenny's shaping of the relationship.

Revising Strategies

Clarify cause-and-effect relationships. Review your entire draft, focusing on the causes and effects you have presented. With two highlighters, use one color to mark phrases that show causes and the other to mark those that demonstrate effects. Use **transitional words** and phrases to make links clear within sentences and between paragraphs. You may also need to add details to strengthen connections or eliminate causes or effects that do not support your main point.

Model: Revising to Clarify Cause and Effect

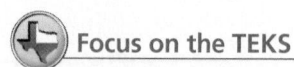
Focus on the TEKS

Writing
(13)(C) Revise drafts to improve sentence variety after rethinking how well questions of purpose, audience, and genre have been addressed.
(13)(E) Revise final draft in response to feedback from teacher.
(15)(A)(i);(ii) Write an analytical essay that includes a variety of sentence structures and transitions between paragraphs.

> Our class scored in the top five percent on standardized tests.
>   **, but mostly**
> We took some practice tests. ~~Mostly~~ we focused on learning to
>   **Because we could read well, we**
> read and understand what we read. ~~We~~ were able to do well
> on the test.

This writer adds transitional words and phrases to clarify the cause-and-effect relationships.

Apply It!

Employ a variety of sentence structures. Rethink how well you have addressed your **purpose, audience,** and **genre:** *Do your sentences not only convey information, but also present ideas in a way that will maintain your audience's interest?*

To evaluate the sentences in your writing, count the number of sentences with fewer than six words in them, and record the number in the margin. If you find too many short sentences, revise your draft to improve sentence variety. Look for places to combine short sentences using the following strategies:

- Combine two sentences using subordinating clauses that start with conjunctions such as *after, although, despite, if,* and *whenever.* Use subordinating conjunctions to show a relationship between ideas.

- Use coordinating conjunctions such as *and, but, or, nor, for, so,* and *yet* to combine ideas of equal importance.

Teacher Feedback

Ask your teacher to read your draft, and then have a discussion about your work. He or she may discuss the clarity of the cause-and-effect relationships presented throughout your essay. In response, revise sentences, omit or add transitions, or reorder paragraphs to improve the logical flow of your ideas as needed in your final draft.

Revising to Correct Faulty Subject-Verb Agreement

For a subject and verb to agree, they must agree in number.

Identifying Errors in Subject-Verb Agreement Agreement errors may occur with compound subjects, subjects joined by *or* or *nor*, and indefinite pronouns as subjects. Below, subjects are underlined and verbs italicized.

Compound Subject:
The <u>coach and the captain</u> *is going* *are going* to attend.

Subject Joined by *Or* or *Nor*:
Either <u>Jason or his brother</u> *are bringing* *is bringing* the snacks.

Indefinite Pronoun as Subject:
<u>Everybody</u> who supports our ideas *are helping* *is helping*.

If a plural subject is joined to a singular subject by *or* or *nor*, the verb should agree with the subject that is closer to it.

Correct: <u>Either the coach or the co-captains</u> *are going* to speak.

Correct: <u>Either the co-captains or the coach</u> *is going* to speak.

Indefinite Pronouns	
Always Singular	anybody, anyone, anything, each, either, every, everybody, everyone, everything, neither, nobody, no one, nothing, somebody, someone, something
Always Plural	both, few, many, others, several
Singular or Plural	all, any, more, most, none, some

Fixing Errors To correct subject and verb agreement, follow these steps:

1. **Identify whether the subject in a sentence is singular or plural.**
2. **Select the matching form of the verb:**
   - For compound subjects joined by *and*, use plural verb forms.
   - For singular subjects joined by *or* or *nor*, use singular verb forms.
   - When the subject is an indefinite pronoun, use the appropriate verb form. Use the chart on this page for guidance.

PH GRAMMAR HANDBOOK

Further instruction and practice are available in the *Prentice Hall Grammar Handbook*.

Grammar in Your Writing

Scan several paragraphs in your draft and underline all compound subjects and indefinite pronouns. In each case, make sure that the verb form you have used agrees with the subject.

Student Model: Candace Fielder, Pearland, TX

Writing
(13)(D) Edit drafts for grammar, mechanics, and spelling.
(13)(E) Publish written work for appropriate audiences.
Conventions
(19) Spell correctly, including using various resources to check correct spellings.

Tornadoes

Tornadoes are some of nature's most violent storms. They are thought to be cyclonically rotating columns of air that connect to a cumulonimbus or cumulus cloud and Earth. However, this definition is debated among scientists today who disagree over whether or not a storm has to touch down to Earth to be considered a tornado. Most tornadoes occur in the United States due to the warm, moist air going north from the Gulf of Mexico and colliding with the northern cold air moving south across the Great Plains. The wind speed of most tornadoes can vary from 40 to 110 miles per hour.

In some circumstances, storm systems can create a tornado family or a tornado outbreak. In a tornado family, one storm will produce numerous tornadoes. When there is no break between tornadoes in a tornado family, it then becomes a tornado outbreak. This results in one storm producing several tornadoes.

A favorable environment for a tornado is a higher temperature and humidity in the lower atmosphere and a cooler temperature and higher wind speed in the upper atmosphere. This kind of situation mainly occurs before a cold front and a low-pressure system. The beginning formation of a tornado is a reaction from a storm updraft, a current of warm air that rises through the thunderstorm, and the winds. This interaction results in the updraft rotating in the middle levels of the atmosphere, also known as a mesocyclone, and gives the thunderstorm more energy.

There are many different types of tornadoes, each varying in size, shape, color, sound, and rotation. They also can vary in length, lasting a few seconds to a few hours. Scientists use Doppler radar to measure the radial direction and velocity of tornadoes in storms from up to 100 miles away. Technology has improved in tornado prediction and warnings. Prior to the 1950s, news of a possible tornado would reach the weather center after the tornado had already hit. Today, with the help of weather radar, weather centers can send out tornado warnings and watches to affected areas.

A tornado rarely hits without causing damage. An area affected by a tornado could be without power for days. Tornadoes can destroy cities, homes, buildings, and take lives. According to the National Weather Service, in 2006, 66 people died from tornadoes. The National Oceanic and Atmospheric Administration's National Severe Storms Laboratory stated that in 1999, 78 tornadoes touched down across Oklahoma and Kansas, resulting in 46 dead and 800 injured, more than 8,000 homes damaged or destroyed, and property damage of nearly $1.5 billion. Not only is there damage to homes and property, but tornadoes cause injury or loss of family members on which no dollar value can be placed.

Candace builds interest by acknowledging that there are differing opinions on the topic.

The author uses the phrase "this results in" to clarify the cause-and-effect relationship being discussed.

Candace takes the knowledge level of her audience into account and provides explanations of scientific concepts.

The author provides relevant information in the form of facts and statistics taken from reputable sources.

Editing and Proofreading

Edit your draft for errors in grammar and mechanics, or punctuation. Use various resources, such as printed and electronic dictionaries and glossaries, to check correct spellings.

Focus on Sentence Clarity: Ensure that your sentences are clear by checking that the subjects agree with the verbs. In addition, read each sentence to be sure that each one expresses a complete thought.

Publishing and Presenting

Consider ways to publish your work for appropriate audiences:

Present your essay—live or in a video you post online. Use photographs, charts, and diagrams to help you explain the topic of your article. Include definitions of any challenging or specialized vocabulary your audience will need to know in order to understand the information. Ask friends in the audience or your online viewers to provide feedback on your presentation.

Submit your essay for publication. If your essay focuses on a matter of local interest, send it to your school or community newspaper.

Reflecting on Your Writing

Writer's Journal Jot down your answer to this question:
How did writing about the topic help you understand it?

Rubric for Self-Assessment

Find evidence in your writing to address each category. Then, use the rating scale to grade your work.

Written Composition Criteria	Rating Scale
	not very very
Focus and Coherence: How relevant is the information you use to validate your inferences?	1 2 3 4
Organization: How appropriate is your organizational structure to your purpose, audience, and context?	1 2 3 4
Development of Ideas: How smooth are the transitions within your sentences and between your paragraphs?	1 2 3 4
Conventions: How correct is your grammar, especially your subject-verb agreement?	1 2 3 4
Voice: How effective are your introductory and concluding paragraphs, and how varied are your sentence structures?	1 2 3 4

Spiral Review
Earlier in this unit, you learned about **subjunctive mood** (p. 344) and **active and passive tenses** (p. 372). Check your essay to be sure that you have used verb forms correctly.

Applying the Big Question

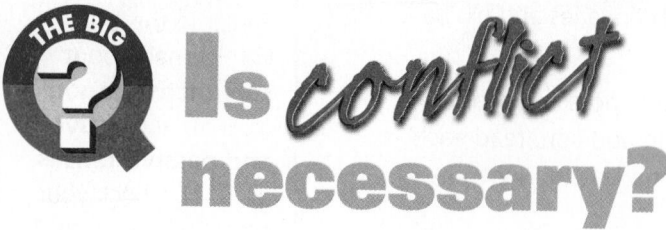 **Is** *conflict* **necessary?**

Think About It

Think about what you have read in this unit and what you know about conflict from your other classes and your own experience. Copy and complete the following chart to apply what you have learned about conflict and whether or not it is necessary. One row has been completed for you.

Example	Conflict	Outcome	Was the conflict necessary for the outcome?	What I learned
From Literature	In "The Interlopers," bitter enemies are trapped under a tree together.	The two men talk and decide to end their feud.	Yes, because it forced the two men to cooperate.	A new conflict can be an opportunity to resolve differences.
From Literature				
From Science				
From Social Studies				
From Your Life				

Talk About It

Choose one of the examples in your conflict chart as the basis for a **short presentation.** Begin by providing some details about the conflict, including whom it involves and what caused it. Then, tell how the conflict is resolved and what happens as a result of it. For example, you might describe what someone learns from the experience, and then explain whether someone could have learned the same lesson without experiencing the conflict. Conclude your presentation by telling your audience what the example taught you about conflict and its consequences. To make your presentation effective, consider these tips:

- Speak clearly and to the point.
- Employ **eye contact, speaking rate, volume, enunciation,** and **purposeful gestures.**
- Use the **conventions of language** to communicate ideas effectively.

Write About It

At the beginning of Unit 2, you wrote a response to the Big Question. Now that you have completed the unit, write a new response, discussing how your initial ideas have either been changed or reinforced.

- ❏ Conflict is necessary.
- ❏ Conflict is not necessary

Support your answer with one or more of the examples in your chart.

Challenge What issues does the Big Question still raise for you? How could you continue your exploration?

★ Connecting to Citizenship

Group Discussion With a small team, discuss how an understanding of conflict and its effects could help someone become a thoughtful, active citizen. Use these questions to guide your discussion:

- How might conflict affect a community?
- If conflict arises, how should a good citizen respond?
- Can conflict make a community better? If so, in what ways?
- How can a thoughtful, active citizen judge whether or not a conflict is necessary? What factors should he or she consider?

Allow everyone on the team to participate productively by **contributing relevant information.** During the discussion, set **ground rules** for deciding which ideas your group considers to be most important. Then, follow those rules to make a list of key points to share with the class.

 Focus on the TEKS

Listening and Speaking
(25) Give presentations employing eye contact, speaking rate, volume, enunciation, purposeful gestures, and conventions of language to communicate ideas effectively.

(26) Participate productively in teams, contributing relevant information, and setting ground rules for decision-making.

Big Question Vocabulary

Use some of these words as you complete the activities on these pages.

amicably

antagonize

appreciate

argument

articulate

compete

competition

controversy

cooperate

differences

equity

grievance

issue

mediate

survival

war/battle

This list includes academic vocabulary words, which are defined on pp. R1–R14.

Vocabulary Workshop

Word Origins and Derivations

The words that make up the English language come from a variety of sources. A word's **origin,** or source, is shown in its etymology. A word's **etymology** identifies the language in which the word first appeared and tells how its spelling and meaning have changed over time. The following excerpt from a dictionary entry shows the etymology of the word *make*.

Focus on the TEKS

Reading
(1)(A) Determine the meanings of grade-level technical academic English words in multiple content areas (e.g., science, mathematics, social studies, the arts) derived from Latin, Greek, or other linguistic roots and affixes.

(1)(E) Use a dictionary (printed or electronic) to determine the meanings of words, including their etymology.

Sample Dictionary Entry

Middle English (Dictionaries usually list abbreviations at the front or back of the book.)

The Middle English source word

> **make** (māk) *vt.* [ME *maken* < OE *macian*, akin to Ger *machen* < IE base **mag-*, to knead, press, stretch > MASON, Gr *magis*, kneaded mass, paste, dough, *mageus*, kneader]

This symbol means "derived from."

Many English words are derived from word parts originally found in Latin, Greek, and other languages. This means that you can trace the origins of certain English words back to roots (word bases or stems) and affixes (parts added to the beginnings or ends of words) of other languages. Many times, the root or affix from which an English word is derived can still be seen in the modern English word, as in these examples:

Derivative Language	Root Word	Root Word Meaning	Modern English Word	Modern English Word Meaning
Latin	-bene-	"well" "good"	bene volent	"doing or inclined to do good"
Latin	-jec(t)-	"to throw"	de ject	"to cast down or dishearten"

Practice A The terms below are from **multiple content areas.** They have all been derived from Latin, Greek, or other linguistic **roots.** Use the information provided about their roots to determine the meanings of these **technical academic English words and phrases.** Then, use a **dictionary** to confirm the meanings of these words and phrases and to determine their **etymologies,** or origins.

TEXAS
PHLitOnline
www.PHLitOnline.com

• Illustrated vocabulary words
• Interactive vocabulary games
• Vocabulary flashcards

The **Greek root** **-graph-** means "to write."

1. graphite
2. geography
3. graphic artist

The **Latin root** **-pater-** means "father."

4. patriarch
5. patron of the arts
6. patriot

The **Old English root** **-writh-** means "to twist."

7. wreath
8. wrestling match
9. wrist

Practice B Affixes are letters that are affixed, or added, to the beginnings or ends of words. The following words from **multiple content areas** have affixes derived from Latin, Greek, and other languages. Use the information provided about Latin, Greek, and other linguistic **affixes** to determine the meanings of these **technical academic English words and phrases.** Then, use a **dictionary** to confirm the meanings of these words and phrases and to determine their **etymologies,** or origins.

The **Greek affix -ik(os)** means "of or relating to; characteristic of."

1. graphic artist
2. Eurocentric
3. domestic

The **Latin affix sub-** means "under, below, behind."

4. subtraction
5. subordinate character
6. subplot

The **Old English affix -ly** means "in the manner specified."

7. consistently
8. frequently
9. typically

Activity Prepare a note card for each of these words: *derive, choice, tantalize, window, curfew.* Use a dictionary to determine the meaning of each word. Then, record some details about the word's etymology, including notes about how older words from other languages influenced its meaning. Finally, write a sentence using the word.

Teamwork
Work with three classmates to research these words. Determine each word's meaning as well as its etymology, or origin.
arachnid
atlas
encyclopedia
gigantic
hectometer
lunar
ocean
typhoon
volcano

Word:
Word's etymology:
Modern word's meaning:
Sentence:

Deliver and Evaluate Presentations

Improving your own skills as a presenter will help you to evaluate others' presentations. Similarly, improving your skills as an evaluator will help you to improve your own presentations.

Learn the Skills

Use the skills on these pages to complete the following activity. Plan a short, informal presentation and deliver your presentation to a team. Then, listen to and evaluate your teammates' presentations.

Plan your speech. Ask yourself these questions as you plan.

- Who is my **audience?** How will my speech meet their needs?

- What is my **purpose?** How will my speech meet this purpose?

- What is the **occasion?** How will my speech be appropriate?

- Should I use **technical language** or **formal language** for this audience, purpose, and occasion, or is **informal language** more appropriate?

- Have I included effective **main and supporting ideas?**

Communicate effectively. Keep your **audience, purpose,** and **occasion** in mind as you deliver your presentation. Speak at a volume loud enough to be heard by your audience. Enunciate, or speak clearly. As you talk, use an appropriate speaking rate, and pause for effect as necessary. Communicate your ideas by using conventions of language, such as correct grammar and word usage. To engage your listeners, use purposeful gestures and eye contact.

Listen responsively. When you are listening to a presentation, **take notes** to summarize, synthesize, or highlight the speaker's ideas. If you do not understand a speaker's points, **ask questions** to clarify the content. Ask the speaker to elaborate if you would like to hear more. Later, reflect on your notes and on the answers to your questions as you critique the presentation.

Focus on the TEKS

Listening and Speaking
(24)(A) Listen responsively to a speaker by taking notes that summarize, synthesize, or highlight the speaker's ideas for critical reflection and by asking questions related to the content for clarification and elaboration.
(24)(C) Evaluate the effectiveness of a speaker's main and supporting ideas.
(25) Give presentations using informal, formal, and technical language effectively to meet the needs of audience, purpose, and occasion, employing eye contact, speaking rate (e.g., pauses for effect), volume, enunciation, purposeful gestures, and conventions of the language to communicate ideas effectively.

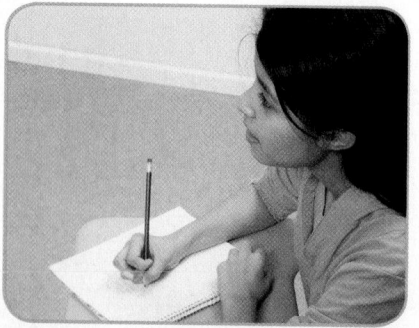

Evaluate the speaker's effectiveness. When evaluating a speaker, ask yourself whether his or her main and supporting ideas are **effective** and clear. Consider what you have learned about speaking from listening to this presentation, and consider how the presentation could be improved.

Practice the Skills

Use what you've learned in this workshop to complete the following activity.

ACTIVITY: Formal Presentation

Prepare and deliver a formal expository presentation for your class.
- Choose a topic that is appropriate for your audience (the class), purpose (informing the class), and occasion (a formal presentation in school).
- Organize your speech logically using effective main and supporting ideas.
- Use formal language to suit your audience and purpose.
- If you are presenting on a technical topic, explain any technical language that your audience might not understand.
- Preview the Evaluation Checklist to anticipate how your audience will evaluate your presentation.

Use the Evaluation Checklist to plan your own presentation and to evaluate the other speakers' presentations.

Evaluation Checklist

Speech Content
Rate the speaker's content on a scale of 1 (very poor) to 5 (very good) for each of these items. Explain your ratings.

- met the needs of the audience   Rating: _____
- met the needs of the purpose   Rating: _____
- met the needs of the occasion   Rating: _____
- used effective main ideas   Rating: _____
- used effective supporting ideas   Rating: _____

Speech Delivery
Rate the speaker's delivery on a scale of 1 (very poor) to 5 (very good) for each of these items. Explain your ratings.

- Formal language   Rating: _____
- Eye contact   Rating: _____
- Effective speaking rate   Rating: _____
- Pauses for effect   Rating: _____
- Appropriate volume   Rating: _____
- Enunciation   Rating: _____
- Purposeful gestures   Rating: _____
- Conventions of language   Rating: _____

Listen attentively to the other presentations by taking notes for critical reflection and by asking questions for clarification and elaboration. After the presentations, discuss which elements of the presentations were most effective.

Cumulative Review

DIRECTIONS Read the two selections and the viewing and representing piece. Then answer the questions that follow.

What Happened During the Ice Storm

by Jim Heynen

1   One winter there was a freezing rain. "How beautiful!" people said when things outside started to shine with ice. But the freezing rain kept coming. Tree branches glistened like glass. Then broke like glass. Ice thickened on the windows until everything outside blurred. Farmers moved their livestock into the barns, and most animals were safe. But not the pheasants. Their eyes froze shut.

2   Some farmers went ice-skating down the gravel roads with clubs to harvest pheasants that sat helplessly in the roadside ditches. The boys went out into the freezing rain to find pheasants too. They saw dark spots along a fence. Pheasants, all right. Five or six of them. The boys slid their feet along slowly, trying not to break the ice that covered the snow. They slid up close to the pheasants. The pheasants pulled their heads down between their wings. They couldn't tell how easy it was to see them huddled there.

3   The boys stood still in the icy rain. Their breath came out in slow puffs of steam. The pheasants' breath came out in quick little white puffs. Some of them lifted their heads and turned them from side to side, but they were blindfolded with ice and didn't flush. The boys had not brought clubs, or sacks, or anything but themselves. They stood over the pheasants, turning their own heads, looking at each other, each expecting the other to do something. To pounce on a pheasant, or to yell "Bang!" Things around them were shining and dripping with icy rain. The barbed-wire fence. The fence posts. The broken stems of grass. Even the grass seeds. The grass seeds looked like the little yolks inside gelatin whites. And the pheasants looked like unborn birds glazed in egg white. Ice was hardening on the boys' caps and coats. Soon they would be covered with ice too.

4   Then one of the boys said, "Shh." He was taking off his coat, the thin layer of ice splintering in flakes as he pulled his arms from the sleeves. But the inside of the coat was dry and warm. He covered two of the crouching pheasants with his coat, rounding the back of it over them like a shell. The other boys did the same. They covered all the helpless pheasants. The small gray hens and the larger brown cocks. Now the boys felt the rain soaking through their shirts and freezing. They ran across the slippery fields, unsure of their footing, the ice clinging to their skin as they made their way toward the blurry lights of the house.

TEKS Spiral Review

Reading

(2)(A) Analyze how the genre of texts with similar themes shapes meaning.

(5) Make inferences and draw conclusions about the elements of fiction.

(6) Analyze how literary essays interweave personal examples and ideas with factual information to explain, present a perspective, or describe a situation or event.

(7) Explain the role of irony, sarcasm, and paradox in literary works.

(12) Use comprehension skills to analyze how words, images, graphics, and sounds work together in various forms to impact meaning.

Comprehension

RC-9(B) Make complex inferences about text.

In the Presence of Dolphins

by Toni G. Frohoff

1   I have laughed underwater many times while swimming in the company of free-ranging dolphins. It's the type of laughter that erupts from my heart. And I have been met with the same shining eye by my dolphin companions as I have during my finest moments of friendship.

2   As I swim I am surrounded by dolphins—above me, below me, to either side. While some exchange places as they swim, others remain nearby, maintaining eye contact. "I am lost again as I am waking…" This phrase, written by Jim Carroll, keeps running through my mind as I recall the feeling of being in the midst of dolphins. The experience is surreal, yet my senses are more alive than ever. The dolphins' bodies around me feel somewhat protective, almost like a huge, flowing hand, supporting and guiding me gently. Their vocalizations come from every direction and I sometimes feel them on and inside of my body as their echolocation explores me. As I swim along, young dolphins occasionally dart in and out of our group, eyeing me most directly as they swim by. Their carefree exuberance is contagious and I know that I am in bliss.

3   I do not look forward as I swim. I feel safe in the presence of these exquisitely beautiful animals. But am I? As I swim up to the surface to take a breath of air, I look up and find myself staring straight ahead into a living wall of very large barracudas. I wonder why the dolphins have escorted me here. If I were to carefully construct a practical (or cosmic) joke, I could not have done it better myself. At this time in my life, I am unusually nervous when encountering even lone barracudas, who in these parts are very curious.

4   As I begin to initiate my panicky retreat, my instinct to flee is interrupted. I look around and see that several of the dolphins are still around me; they have remained at my side. They do not appear nervous at all and the barracudas do not seem particularly interested in any of us. Soon, calmed, I swim back toward our boat with my dolphin escorts. This experience has helped me ever since, when studying marine life in the company of extraordinarily curious or large barracudas and sharks. It was my first lesson in relying on the behavior of "predatory" animals rather than their reputation in determining my safety in their presence. I feel as if I was given a great gift—taught an invaluable lesson.

5   As a scientist, I cannot say whether or not this occurrence was incidental. However, after years of being in the presence of dolphins, I have learned most profoundly that science does not always have the capacity to address some of life's most important wonders. I find solace in the knowledge that I am not simply a scientist—I am also an animal, a member of the genus and species *Homo sapiens.* Therefore, I cannot dismiss the very personal nature of my interactions with these incredibly lovely beings. I cannot forget the many lessons that I have learned from them, inadvertently or otherwise. I cannot, and will not, put aside what my senses tell me is rare and wonderful. How ironic that it is from being in the presence of another species that I have learned how to be more "human."

GO ON

Wagging Tales

OCTOBER $2.75

the magazine for dog enthusiasts

What I Learned from My Dog

 10 Amazing Life Lessons

Going Off-Leash

 Making New Friends at the Dog Park

Good Breeding

Finding the Right Dog for You

Rescued!

 Real-Life Canine Heroism

1 Which quotation from the story best expresses the resolution?
  A *They slid up close to the pheasants.*
  B *The boys stood still in the icy rain.*
  C *To pounce on a pheasant, or to yell "Bang!"*
  D *They covered all the helpless pheasants.*

2 In paragraph 2, the pheasants pull their heads down between their wings because they are trying to —
  F hide
  G sleep
  H stay warm
  J look threatening

3 In paragraph 3, the author shows that the boys and pheasants —
  A can help each other
  B are afraid of each other
  C respond differently to the wintery weather
  D are affected by the rain in similar ways

4 The story's end is ironic because the rest of the story leads readers to believe that the boys will —
  F run away in the icy rain
  G observe the pheasants
  H attack the pheasants
  J feel sorry for the pheasants

5 Read this sentence from paragraph 3.

  If I were to carefully construct a practical (or cosmic) joke, I could not have done it better myself.

  What ironic situation is the author referring to in this quote?
  A The dolphins have taught her how to swim.
  B She never enjoyed nature before swimming with her new friends.
  C She felt safe with the dolphins but they led her to barracudas.
  D Dolphins seem to be friendly creatures.

6 Which word is closest in meaning to *vocalizations* as it is used in paragraph 2?
  F voice-like sounds
  G protective radar
  H jarring music
  J sweet singing

7 The narrator describes her encounter with barracudas by —
  A providing only objective facts
  B including only her own emotions
  C contrasting her emotions with the animals' actions
  D telling the story from the animals' point of view

GO ON

8 Which theme do **both** selections address?

  F Animals can teach people life lessons.

  G Animals in trouble deserve compassion.

  H Predatory animals are not always frightening.

  J Animals deserve to be treated as humans.

9 The boys in "What Happened During the Ice Storm" are similar to the dolphins in "In the Presence of Dolphins" in that **both** —

  A struggle with their environments

  B wait for someone in the group to act first

  C provide protection for another species

  D appear to be uncertain

Use the visual representation on page 418 to answer questions 10–11.

10 The magazine's publishers probably intend for the cover photograph to illustrate the —

  F importance of spending time outdoors

  G enjoyment of spending time with a dog

  H challenges of owning a dog

  J difficulty of training a dog

11 The article "Rescued!" is most likely intended to —

  A teach readers how to give first aid

  B inspire readers with stories of dogs rescuing people

  C help readers protect dogs

  D persuade readers that dogs are always courageous

DIRECTIONS

Answer the following questions on a separate sheet of paper.

12 In "What Happened During the Ice Storm," which details suggest why the boys pitied the pheasants? Support your answer with evidence from the selection.

13 In what way does the author of "In the Presence of Dolphins" see the dolphins as similar to human friends? Support your answer with evidence from the selection.

14 How do the humans' interactions with animals lead humans to epiphanies, or flashes of insight, in both "What Happened During the Ice Storm" and "In the Presence of Dolphins"? Support your answer with details from **both** selections.

Is *conflict* necessary?

Focus on the TEKS

Reading
(12)(B) Analyze how messages in media are conveyed through visual and sound techniques (e.g., sequencing).

Media Literacy

In video media, messages are conveyed through **visual and sound techniques** such as **sequencing.** Images and sounds are sequenced, or put in a specific order, to express a message or emphasize an idea. Consider how these techniques might emphasize or convey a conflict. This chart will help you analyze sequencing as you view video media such as the *Wayson Choy: Meet the Author* video.

TEXAS
PHLitOnline
www.PHLitOnline.com

Viewing and Listening Guide

Technique	What it is	What you should think about
Visual Sequencing	The order of a set of images in a video	• Why are the images in this specific order? Do they emphasize details? Do they help viewers follow words or sounds? • Should any images be removed from the sequence? Why or why not?
Audio (Sound) Sequencing	The order of a set of sounds in a video	• How does the director use sounds? Does a voice narrate? Are there special sounds such as music? • Why might the sequence of sounds in a video enhance an audience's viewing experience?

Independent Reading

To Kill a Mockingbird
Harper Lee
Warner Books, 1960

In this classic novel, a young girl comes of age while her father fights for justice in an unjust world.

Literature of the Expanding Frontier
Prentice Hall, 1999

This collection of stories, poems, songs, and personal accounts captures the spirits of the people who faced adversity on America's western frontier.

The Sherlock Holmes Mysteries
Sir Arthur Conan Doyle
Signet, 1985

Detective Sherlock Holmes matches wits with a variety of criminals in this collection of mystery stories.

The Sea-Wolf and Selected Stories
Jack London
Signet, 1964

A conflict of views between a captain and a crewman plays out against the backdrop of unforgiving natural forces.

THE BIG Q?

Is knowledge the same as understanding?

Types of Nonfiction

TEXAS

PHLitOnline

www.PHLitOnline.com

Hear It!
- Selection summary audio
- Selection audio
- Big Question Tunes

See It!
- Penguin author video
- Big Question video
- Get Connected videos
- Background videos
- More about the authors
- Illustrated vocabulary words
- Vocabulary flashcards

Do It!
- Interactive journals
- Interactive graphic organizers
- Grammar tutorials
- Interactive vocabulary games
- Test practice

Introducing the Big Question

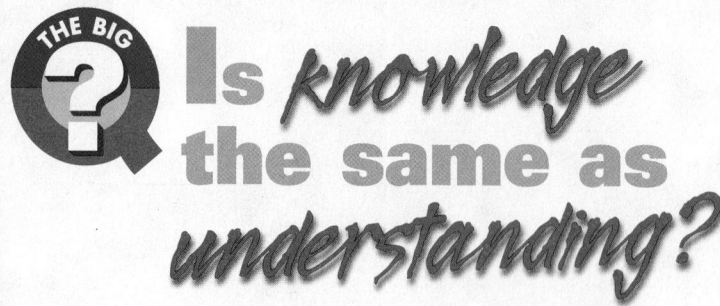 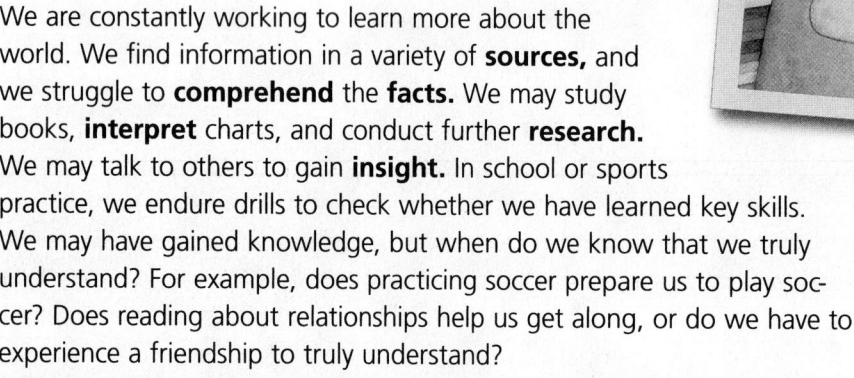

Is *knowledge the same as understanding?*

We are constantly working to learn more about the world. We find information in a variety of **sources,** and we struggle to **comprehend** the **facts.** We may study books, **interpret** charts, and conduct further **research.** We may talk to others to gain **insight.** In school or sports practice, we endure drills to check whether we have learned key skills. We may have gained knowledge, but when do we know that we truly understand? For example, does practicing soccer prepare us to play soccer? Does reading about relationships help us get along, or do we have to experience a friendship to truly understand?

Begin thinking about the Big Question by analyzing what you know and how you know it.

Tell What You Know

List topics that you have knowledge about and also understand. Describe an example from each of these categories.

- a grandparent or older adult you know well
- a concept you have learned in school
- a speech you have read over and over
- an argument you have had that still bothers you
- something you have read about but also experienced
- the memory of an important event in your life

Share your list with a small team of classmates. Discuss any differences you discover when you compare ideas about the differences between knowledge and understanding of these topics. Participate productively in the team by:

- listening while others speak
- building on the ideas of others
- contributing relevant information to the discussion

TEXAS
PHLitOnline
www.PHLitOnline.com
- Big Question video
- Illustrated vocabulary words
- Interactive vocabulary games
- Big Question Tunes

Explain What You Know

Use the ideas you discussed with your team to help complete these sentences about knowledge and understanding.

- Spending time with someone helps you know _____.
- When something important happens in your life, your knowledge _____. You may understand _____.
- The best way to learn certain subjects may be _____, but for other concepts it may be _____.
- Your knowledge of yourself leads you to _____.

Discuss your ideas with your team.

Write What You Think

Based on the discussions you have had, decide how you would respond to the Big Question. Your answer may change as you read the selections in this unit. Choose one of these responses or write one of your own.

- ❏ Understanding comes only after you have knowledge.
- ❏ I often understand things without knowing all the facts about them first.

Connecting to the Literature

Each reading in this unit will give you insight into the Big Question. At the end of the unit, you will have an opportunity to see how your ideas have changed.

 ★ **Connecting to Citizenship**

Texas Profiles: Charles Goodnight

Wealthy Cattleman, Trailblazer Charles Goodnight had only six months of formal schooling, yet he became one of the wealthiest cattlemen of the American West. After fighting in the Civil War for the Confederacy, Goodnight joined other ranchers in gathering up cattle that had been roaming free during the war. Goodnight and his partner, Oliver Loving, blazed the Goodnight-Loving Trail from Belknap, Texas, to Fort Sumner, New Mexico.

Is knowledge the same as understanding?

- How does Goodnight's story show that sometimes understanding is as important as knowledge acquired in formal education?
- What can you learn from Goodnight's story that can help you become a thoughtful, active citizen?

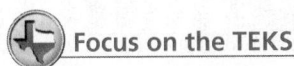 **Focus on the TEKS**

Listening and Speaking
(26) Participate productively in teams, building on the ideas of others and contributing relevant information.

Big Question Vocabulary

Use some of these words as you complete the activities on these pages.

ambiguous
comprehend
concept
clarify
connection
fact
feeling
information
insight
instinct
interpret
research
senses/sensory
sources
statistics

This list includes academic vocabulary words, which are defined on pp. R1–R14.

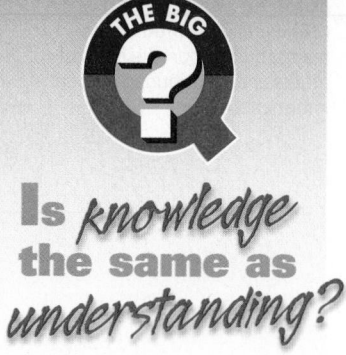

Is *knowledge* the same as *understanding?*

Nonfiction can help readers gather knowledge and build understanding.

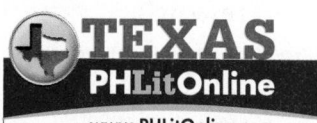

PHLitOnline

www.PHLitOnline.com

- Penguin author video
- Interactive journals
- Interactive graphic organizers
- Selection audio
- Self-test

What Is Nonfiction?

by Rebecca Walker

I have written both **articles,** brief nonfiction pieces often found in periodicals, and **essays,** nonfiction works of greater literary value in which authors express their emotions and thoughts. While I appreciate both forms, I am partial to the essay.

Comparing Articles and Essays

The essay allows for the sharing of personal experience, the expression of emotion, and the subsequent creation of a subtle intimacy between author and reader. Some of the best essays are akin to life-changing conversations between parent and child, or teacher and student. Even after the author has died, her voice can reach through time to transform the reader.

While essays and articles both give accountings of real life, articles tend to be more objective in tone. They focus on the what, when, where, and why of a particular situation, rather than on what the author feels about the answers to any of these questions. Although the author undoubtedly has a point of view, he or she strives for an objective rendering of fact.

An essay draws the reader into the author's world, pointing, suggesting, persuading. An article observes and presents, and leaves the reader to make up her own mind.

Essays That Engage and Challenge the Reader

I have always loved essays in which the author uses his personal experience to challenge the reader to think about the world in a different way. By sharing intimate details of his private life, the author invites the reader to empathize with him and, as a result, to support his conclusions.

Because I believe that most human beings change their feelings long before they change their minds, it seems undeniable that the creation of this emotional link is vital to one's impact as an author.

For example, in 1881 Frederick Douglass forwarded the abolitionist cause by sensitizing readers to the plight of enslaved African-Americans in his deeply personal essay "My Escape from Slavery." And in 1929 Virginia Woolf convinced readers that women deserved autonomy by sharing her own longing for a modest space and small income in *A Room of One's Own.*

These are just two of the authors and essays that affected the consciousness of entire generations, prompting not just individual enlightenment, but larger political reform. I admire the way these authors used their own lives as the basis for the theories they espoused. In essence they ask the reader: Shouldn't society be constructed to ensure my happiness, too?

Intellectual freedom depends upon material things. Poetry depends upon intellectual freedom. And women have always been poor, not for two hundred years merely, but from the beginning of time. Women have had less intellectual freedom than the sons of Athenian slaves. . . . That is why I have laid so much stress on money and a room of one's own.

from *A Room of One's Own*
—Virginia Woolf

Meet
Rebecca Walker (b. 1969)

Author of "Before Hip-Hop Was Hip-Hop"

When she was twenty-five, Rebecca Walker was named by *Time* magazine as one of fifty influential American leaders under the age of forty. Her essays and articles have appeared in many magazines and publications, and her books are taught in high schools and colleges in the United States and Canada. She has received awards for both her writing and her work as an advocate for young women

As Walker's essay "Before Hip-Hop Was Hip-Hop" shows, she has a lively interest in youth culture.

Did You Know?
In 1992, Walker co-founded the Third Wave Foundation, dedicated to empowering women aged 15–30 through scholarship grants and project funding.

Exploring Types of Nonfiction

Essays, Articles, and Speeches

Nonfiction is writing that is based on facts about real people, places, things, or events. Nonfiction works include the following types:

- An **essay** examines and discusses a focused topic, often including the writer's personal viewpoint.
- An **article** provides information about a topic, a person, or an event.
- A **speech**—written to be read aloud—presents a topic and may persuade, inform, explain, or entertain.

PEANUTS, reprinted by permission of United Features Syndicate, Inc.

The writer contributes more than information to nonfiction.

- **Style** is the particular way a writer uses language. Style reflects an author's personality. Factors that contribute to an author's style include *level of formality,* use of *figurative language, diction*—or word choice—, *sentence patterns,* and *methods of organization.*
- **Tone** is the author's attitude toward both the subject and the readers or listeners. In conversation, you can hear a speaker's tone in the way words and phrases are spoken. When reading, you can "hear" tone in an author's choice of words and details. The tone of a literary work can often be described with a single word, such as *pompous, playful, serious, personal, sarcastic,* or *friendly.*
- **Perspective** is the viewpoint or opinion an author expresses about the subject, either directly or indirectly. Bias occurs when a writer makes a one-sided presentation (for example, by ignoring relevant facts or by using emotional language that unfairly sways readers' feelings).
- **Purpose** is the author's reason for writing. Common purposes are to inform, to persuade, to honor, to entertain, to explain, and to warn.

Categories of Nonfiction

There are two broad categories of nonfiction.

- **Literary Nonfiction** interweaves personal examples and ideas with factual information to explain, present a perspective, or describe a situation or event. Autobiographies, biographies, and personal narratives are types of literary nonfiction.
- **Informational Texts** explain or convey information for a specific purpose. Brochures, advertisements, and news articles are types of informational texts.

Nonfiction can also be categorized by the author's purpose.

- **Narrative** essays and texts tell a story of actual events or an individual's life experiences.
- **Reflective** essays and texts express the writer's thoughts and feelings in response to a personal experience or to an idea.
- **Descriptive** essays and texts convey an impression about a person, an object, or an experience by presenting details relating to sight, sound, smell, touch, or taste.
- **Expository** essays and texts provide information or discuss ideas.
- **Persuasive** essays and texts attempt to convince readers to take a specific course of action or adopt the writer's viewpoint.
- **Procedural** essays and texts give instructions for performing specific tasks, answering questions, solving problems, or completing processes.

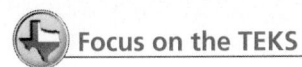
Focus on the TEKS
Reading
(9) Analyze expository text.
(10) Analyze persuasive text.

TEKS Check

Use a graphic organizer like the one shown to analyze expository and persuasive text. Begin by giving an example of each type of nonfiction. Describe the author's purpose and how that purpose was met. Then, think about the elements of each work and categorize the work as either literary nonfiction or as informational text.

Nonfiction Type	Title of Example	Author's Specific Purpose	Literary Nonfiction or Informational Text?
expository			
persuasive			

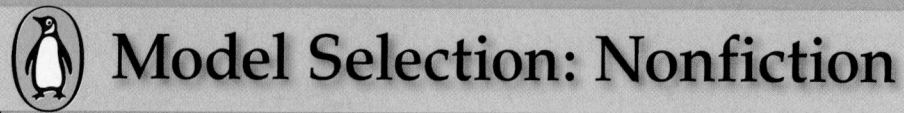

Rebecca Walker Introduces "Before Hip-Hop Was Hip-Hop"

Writing is a lonely profession. A typical day for most writers does not include the lively banter enjoyed by those who work in brightly lit offices and interact in meeting rooms, elevators, and cafeterias.

A Portrait of the Writer at Work

We sit, usually completely alone, in our grand or modest workspaces, maybe with a cat or dog at our feet, a cup of tea or a bottle of water by the mousepad.

   More often than not we work in silence, or maybe to the low hum of the television or the repetitive drone of a particularly evocative piece of music. We begin with a blank screen or piece of paper. If we are lucky, we have had some thought we find worthy, but more often we have not, and spend the next hours willing insight to dawn.

Purpose, Diction, and Level of Formality

Once we have a **purpose** and a direction, then the next bit of work begins: the arduous hunt for the **diction,** the words that can adequately express our still largely unborn revelation. Now we are looking for a feeling, a **tone** that will both track our thought and unlock its emotive power.

   The choices we make in those moments—with what **level of formality** we will address the reader, what type of language we will employ, what **narrative structure** we will devise—all these and more create an experience. The result, like what you are reading right now, is a kind of literary transmission of the writer's soul, a revelation of the distinct imprint of her mind.

My Essay: A Perspective on Hip-Hop Culture

To face this hard and solitary work I must feel that I have something relevant to say. For instance, hip-hop culture is not often seen as a reflection of the deeply humanitarian impulses of urban youth. And yet I was there at its birth, I can testify to its noble roots. While writing the following essay I wondered, "If I don't tell this story, who will?"

Before Hip-Hop was Hip-Hop

Rebecca Walker

If you ask most kids today about hip-hop, they'll spit out the names of recording artists they see on TV: Eminem, P. Diddy, J. Lo, Beyonce. They'll tell you about the songs they like and the clothes they want to buy. They'll tell you about the indisputable zones of hip-hop like "EO" (East Orange, New Jersey), the "ATL" (Atlanta, Georgia), and the "West Side" (Los Angeles, California), neighborhoods they feel they know because they've seen them in all the glossiest, "flossiest" music videos. Hip-hop is natural to these kids, like air or water, just there, a part of the digital landscape that streams through their lives.

Rebecca Walker
Author's Insight
"I chose to include slang to give the essay more flavor and authenticity. I wanted the reader to experience the language we created, not just read about it."

I watch this cultural sea change with fascination. It astounds me that hip-hop has grown into a global industry, a force that dominates youth culture from Paris to Prague, Tokyo to Timbuktu. I can't believe that in small, all-white towns like Lincoln, Nebraska, high school boys wear their clothes in the latest "steelo": pants sagging off their waists, sports jerseys hanging to their knees, baseball hats cocked to one side. Even in the pueblos of Mexico, where mariachi bands and old school crooners still rule, it is hip-hop that sells cars, sodas, and children's toys on TV.

The vast empire of hip-hop amazes me because I knew hip-hop before it was hip-hop. I was there when it all began.

Way back then, in what today's ninth graders might call the ancient eighties, there was no MTV or VH-1. We found out about music by listening to the radio, flipping through the stacks at the record store, or buying "mix tapes" from local deejays at two dollars apiece. Back then, we carried combs in our back pockets and clipped long strands of feathers to the belt loops of our designer jeans. We wore our names in cursive gold letters around our necks or in big brass letters on our belt buckles. We picked up words and inverted them, calling something that we thought was really cool, "hot," and something that had a whole lot of life, "def."

We didn't know a whole new language was rolling off our tongues as we flipped English upside down and pulled some Spanish and even a few words from Africa into our parlance. We didn't know that young people for years to come would recycle our fashions and sample the bass lines from our favorite tracks. We thought we were just being kids and expressing ourselves, showing the grown-ups we were different from them in a way that was safe and fun. In fact we were at the epicenter[1] of one of America's most significant cultural revolutions, making it happen. Who knew?

Not me.

When I moved from Washington, D.C., to the Bronx the summer before seventh grade, I had one box of records, mostly albums I had ordered from the Columbia Record Club. In 1982, if you promised to buy a record a month for one whole year, the Club sent you eight records for a penny. I had Bruce Springsteen's "The River," REO Speedwagon's "The Letter," "Belladonna" by Stevie Nicks. I had "Stairway to Heaven," by Led Zeppelin and the soundtrack from the movie *Saturday Night Fever*, which I played so

Rebecca Walker
Author's Insight
"In college I learned that scholars believe the word *hip* comes from *hipi*, a word in the West African language Wolof. *Hipi* means 'someone with his eyes open, aware of what is going on.'"

We found out about music by listening to the radio, flipping through the stacks at the record store ...

---

1. **epicenter** (epʹi sentʹ ər) *n.* focal or central point.

many times I thought my mother would go crazy from listening to me belt out the lyrics with those lanky, swanky Bee Gees.

Along with my albums I had loads of 45s, what today we would call singles, little records with just two songs on them, that I bought at the record store near my school for just a dollar a piece. I had Chaka Khan's "I'm Every Woman," and Luther Vandross' "Never Too Much," and Chuck Brown and Soul Searcher's big hit, "Bustin' Loose." I had Michael Jackson's "Rock with You" and even Aretha Franklin's cover of "You Make Me Feel Like a Natural Woman," which I sang along to in the mornings as I styled my hair.

If you had asked me then about rap music I would have shrugged my shoulders and looked at you like you were crazy. Rap music? What's that?

But then I started seventh grade and my whole world turned upside down. At Public School 141, I went to classes with kids from all over the Bronx. There were kids whose families came from Puerto Rico and the Dominican Republic, and kids whose families came from Russia and China. There were kids who were African-American and kids who were Irish-American, kids who were Italian-American and kids who were Greek-American. There

▲ **Critical Viewing** What details in this image suggest the powerful effects music can have on a person? **[Connect]**

Nonfiction Perspective Details of Walker's music preferences make it easier to understand how she sees her classmates and the world.

Reading Check

What changed in Walker's life the summer before seventh grade?

were kids whose families were poor, kids whose families were well off, and kids whose families were somewhere in between. Some were Jewish, and others devout Catholics. Some were Muslim. Some of the Asian kids were even Buddhist.

The charge created by so many different elements coming together was palpable. The school crackled with energy, and as you can imagine, things weren't always smooth. There were some pretty entrenched cliques, and a few vicious fights in the schoolyard. But there was also so much "flavor." You could hear Spanish spoken with a thick "Nuyorican" accent to a kid wearing a "yamulke." A seemingly reserved Asian-American girl would get out of her parents' car, wait for them to drive off, and then unzip her coat to reveal a fire engine red Adidas sweatsuit. A guy in a preppy, button-down shirt would "sport" gold chains with pendants of every denomination: the Jewish Star of David, the Arabic lettering for Allah, and a shiny gold cross. He was everything, that was his "steelo," and everyone gave him "props" for it.

When I got to 141, I felt like a blank canvas. Nothing had prepared me for the dynamism, the screaming self-expression of the place and its students. For the first few weeks I secretly studied the habits of the seventh, eighth and ninth graders with whom I walked the halls and shared the cafeteria. I was transfixed by the way they infused their words with attitude and drama, moving their hands and heads as they spoke. I was captivated by the way many of them walked and ran and joked with each other with confidence and bravado. I noted what they wore and how they wore it: the razor sharp creases of their Jordache jeans, the spotless sneakers with the laces left loose and untied.

Slowly, I began to add some of what I saw into my "look." I convinced my grandmother to buy me a name chain to wear around my neck, and my stepmother to buy me dark dyed designer jeans. I bought my first pair of Nike sneakers, red, white and blue Air Cortez's, with money I saved from my allowance.

One by one, I started to make friends—Diane, Loida, James, Jesus, Maya. When James and Jesus weren't making fun of me for being so "square," they took me to parties on the Grand Concourse, the big boulevard lined with old apartment buildings and department stores that ran through the Bronx. The parties were incredible, filled with young people who didn't drink, smoke or fight, but who just wanted to dance and laugh and ooh and ahhh over the "scratching" sounds and funky beats the DJ's coaxed out of their turntables.

A lot of the kids at the parties were "breakers" or "poppers and lockers," which meant they could breakdance, a style of movement

Vocabulary
palpable (pal´ pə bəl) *adj.* able to be touched, felt, or handled; tangible

entrenched (en trencht´) *adj.* securely established; unmovable

Vocabulary
bravado (brə vä´ dō) *n.* pretended courage or defiant confidence

Nonfiction Description By naming brands, Walker layers on details of the personal style she longed to achieve.

Reading Check
What examples does Walker give to show the "flavor" of her school?

that blends the Brazilian martial art of Capoeira with a dance called the Robot, and incorporates classical dance moves as well. The "breakers" moved in "crews" that competed against each other. Standing in a circle we watched as members of the different groups "moonwalked" into the center, and then hurled themselves to the floor, spinning on their heads, kicking their legs into the air, and making elaborate hand gestures, each more intricate and acrobatic than the last. Everyone at the party who wasn't "breaking" was a judge by default, and we registered our scores by clapping and yelling.

When Loida and Diane weren't "capping on" or making fun of my clothes, they were "hipping" me to Kiss 98.7 and WBLS, the radio stations that had started to slip some of the songs we liked into their rotation. Songs like "Planet Rock" by Soul Sonic Force and "Take Me Home" by Lisa Lisa and the Cult Jam. After school and on the weekends, they took me to the street vendors that sold the accessories we all coveted: the big knockoff Porsche sunglasses everybody wanted but not everybody could afford, and the heavy gold chains people collected around their necks like so many pieces of string. Loida and Diane also took me around the city on the bus, familiarizing me with the routes of the M1 and M3 and M7, showing me all the different neighborhoods like Little Italy and Chinatown, Bed-Stuy and Harlem.

I remember looking out the big sliding glass windows of the bus at the lines drawn in concrete and glass and thinking that while the world outside seemed so divided, inside, in my circle, among my friends, those lines didn't seem to exist. Loida was Dominican and Diane was Puerto Rican. Our friend Mary was Irish-American, and Lisa was Italian-American. Maya's family was from Haiti. Julius was Russian-American. We were different ages, with different likes and dislikes, but we were united in our love of hip-hop. We loved the "dope"[2] beats, the ever changing and ever expanding lexicon, the outrageous dance moves, the cocky swagger, the feeling that we were part of something dynamic and "fresh"[3] that was bigger than any one of us. That world, that other realm that we created on the streets and in our minds, that streamed from the radio in the privacy of our bedrooms and coursed between us as we talked on the phone, that was where we lived.

That was where we felt free.

Looking back on it now, I can see that hip-hop was born of the diversity I found at 141. Unlike the hip-hop of today, it didn't come pre-packaged from a marketing department with millions of dollars

---

2. dope (dōp) *adj.* slang term meaning "great; irresistible."
3. fresh (fresh) *adj.* slang term meaning "new."

Nonfiction
Purpose Walker's extensive descriptions here and throughout are meant to explain and inform.

Vocabulary
lexicon (lek´ si kän´) *n.* the special vocabulary of a particular subject

We were different ages, with different likes and dislikes, but we were united in our love of hip-hop.

to spend. Our hip-hop was the product of a bunch of kids from a bunch of different places trying to talk to each other, trying to create a common language that could cut through the many languages people spoke at home. Intuitively, kids were making a community where there was none; we were affirming our sameness in a world that seemed to only emphasize our difference. That desire to come together irrespective of superficial differences and sometimes in celebration of them, was what gave hip-hop authenticity, that was what kept it honest and as crucial to our well being as food. It's what kept it real.

I can't say much about hip-hop today, but I can say that old hip-hop, original hip-hop, changed my life forever. I only lived in the "Boogie Down Bronx" for a year, but those twelve months gave me so much. I learned that art could bring people together and make them forget their differences. I learned how good it could feel to move with a "posse," a group of friends who had my back no

Rebecca Walker
Author's Insight
"I always liked this upbeat nickname for the Bronx, because it suggests dancing and having fun— not usually what this borough is known for."

matter what. I learned that I could express myself and communicate with others through what I wore and how I walked and what music I liked. I learned that it doesn't take money or a special degree to transform the grit and drive and hardness of the city into something beautiful.

Loyalty. Community. Self-confidence. Creativity. Hip-hop taught me more about real life than anything I learned that year in class.

I hope when kids today look at shiny videos by their favorite hip-hop artists, they will see through the expensive cars and exotic locations, the women in skimpy outfits and the men trying to approximate a "gangsta" lean. I hope they will remember that hip-hop was born without a formula and without a lot of expensive props or violent undertones. I hope they will marvel at the fact that in the early days of hip-hop, young people were making it up as they went along, following their hearts, following what felt good. I hope they will think about what it takes to create culture that is unique and transcendent and honest, and I hope they begin to dream about creating a new world for themselves.

I hope hip-hop inspires them to make their own revolution.

> I hope they will think about what it takes to create culture that is unique and transcendent and honest . . .

Critical Thinking

1. **Respond:** What did you enjoy most about Walker's descriptions of hip-hop culture during her youth? Explain.

2. **(a)** According to Walker, why did PS 141 "crackle" with energy?
(b) Analyze Cause and Effect: In what ways did hip-hop help Walker and her friends bridge differences?

3. **(a) Compare and Contrast:** What differences does Walker find between the music of her youth and today's hip-hop?
(b) Take a Position: Do you think Walker's judgment is fair or biased? Explain your answer.

4. **(a) Draw Conclusions:** Why was it so important for Walker and her friends to define themselves through dress, special language, dance, and music? **(b) Generalize:** What do teenagers use today to express themselves?

Is knowledge the same as understanding?
(a) What knowledge does Walker gain from learning about hip-hop? **(b)** How does that knowledge influence her understanding of her school, her culture, and herself?

Types of Nonfiction Review

1. **(a)** Is the **tone** of Walker's **essay** personal or impersonal? **(b)** What other adjectives appropriately describe her tone? **(c)** Which details in the first three paragraphs support your answers?

2. **(a)** Use a chart like this one to analyze Walker's **style,** noting passages that support your ideas. **(b)** In a small group, discuss the examples and develop a one-sentence description of Walker's writing style.

Level of Formality	Word Choice	Sentence Patterns

Research the Author

Organize information gathered from library and Internet sources to create a **popular culture timeline** of Walker's life. Follow these steps:

- Identify key events in Walker's life in order. Include text and images.
- Add details about music and fashion at the time of each event.
- Present your timeline to the class.

Selection Choices

▲ Read **"A Celebration of Grandfathers"** to be reminded of the strength and wisdom of the older people in our lives.

▲ Read **"On Summer"** to glimpse life when it is lived to the fullest.

 TEXAS Focus on the TEKS

Meet these standards with either **"A Celebration of Grandfathers"** (p. 444) or **"On Summer"** (p. 456).

Reading
(9) Analyze expository text and provide evidence from the text to support understanding. (Literary Analysis: Author's Style)

(6) Analyze how literary essays interweave personal examples and ideas with factual information to explain and present a perspective on a situation or event. (Spiral Review: Literary Essay)

Reading/Comprehension Skills
RC-9(A) Reflect on understanding to monitor comprehension (e.g., asking questions). (Reading Skill: Main Idea)

RC-9(B) Make complex inferences about text and use textual evidence to support understanding. (Reading Skill: Main Idea)

Writing
(16) Write persuasive texts. (Writing: Book Jacket Copy)

Listening and Speaking
(24)(A) Listen responsively to a speaker by taking notes that summarize the speaker's ideas for critical reflection and by asking questions related to the content for clarification and elaboration. (Listening and Speaking: Panel Discussion)

Literary Analysis: Author's Style

An **author's style** is his or her unique way of using language. Some elements that contribute to an author's style are

- **Diction:** the words the author uses
- **Syntax:** the arrangement of words in sentences
- **Tone:** the author's attitude toward the audience or subject

A writer's diction and syntax might be described as *formal* or *informal, technical* or *ordinary,* or *sophisticated* or *down-to-earth.* His or her tone might be described as *serious, playful,* or *harsh.* An author's style affects the writer's ability to communicate ideas with readers.

As You Read Find evidence from the text that reflects the author's diction, syntax, and tone. Note how these elements contribute to his or her style.

Reading Skill: Main Idea

The **main, or controlling, idea** is the central message, insight, or opinion in a work of nonfiction. Supporting details give further information about the controlling idea. These details can include facts, statistics, quotations, or anecdotes. To identify the controlling idea and supporting details in a work, preview the text and generate questions. Before you read, consider questions such as:

- Why did the author choose this title?
- How might events in the author's life influence his or her attitude?
- What does the author want me to know?

Using the Strategy: Main Idea Chart

As You Read Pause periodically to reflect on your understanding. **Monitor your comprehension** by generating and asking questions. Then, find details that answer the questions and **use your answers to make complex inferences** about the controlling idea of the text. On a chart like this one, record the questions you ask, the answers you find, and the inferences you make about the main, or **controlling, idea.**

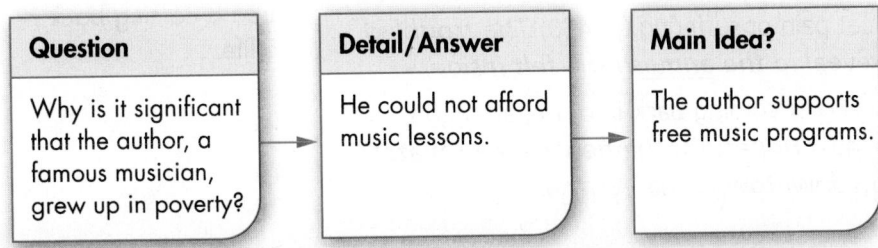

Question	Detail/Answer	Main Idea?
Why is it significant that the author, a famous musician, grew up in poverty?	He could not afford music lessons.	The author supports free music programs.

Hear It!
- Selection summary audio
- Selection audio

See It!
- Get Connected video
- Background video
- More about the author
- Vocabulary flashcards

Do It!
- Interactive journals
- Interactive graphic organizers
- Self-test
- Internet activity
- Grammar tutorial
- Interactive vocabulary games

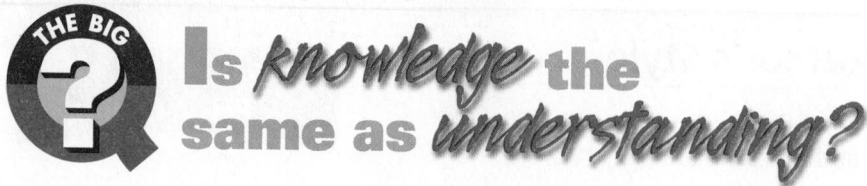

Is *knowledge* the same as *understanding?*

A Celebration of
Grandfathers

Rudolfo A. Anaya

Writing About the Big Question

"A Celebration of Grandfathers" explains how the author's grandfather and people of his generation lived and what they valued. Use these sentence starters to develop your ideas about the Big Question.

Knowing what people do and how they live can give **insight** into who they are because _____.

People of different ages often **interpret** ideas and events differently because _____.

(As You Read) Look for details that help you understand the author's grandfather.

Vocabulary

Read each word and its definition. Decide whether you know the word well, know it a little bit, or do not know it at all. After you read, see how your knowledge of each word has increased.

- **nurturing** (nʉr´ chər iŋ) *n.* the raising of; promoting the development of (p. 445) *Nurturing their children is the most important job of parents. nurture n. nurture v.*

- **perplexes** (pər pleks´ əz) *v.* confuses or puzzles (p. 445) *His odd behavior perplexes them. perplex v. perplexing adj. perplexity n.*

- **absurdity** (ab sʉr´ də tē) *n.* something ridiculous or nonsensical (p. 445) *To our surprise, our reasonable request was treated as an absurdity. absurd adj. absurdly adv.*

- **permeate** (pʉr´ mē āt´) *v.* spread or flow throughout (p. 446) *It didn't take long for the odor to permeate the entire apartment. permeation n. permeable adj. permeating v.*

- **anguish** (aŋ´ gwish) *n.* great pain or suffering (p. 450) *The troubled expression on her face revealed the anguish she felt inside.*

- **revival** (ri vī´ vəl) *n.* a bringing or coming back into use, attention, or being after a decline (p. 451) *Hopefully, the new movie theater will spark a revival of the downtown area. revive v.*

Word Power

The **Latin root -viv-** means "to live."

In this selection, the author describes the **revival** of the valley where his grandfather lived. The word suggests that the area is coming back to life.

Meet
Rudolfo A. Anaya
(b. 1937)

Author of
A Celebration of
Grandfathers

Born in New Mexico, Rudolfo A. Anaya is considered the founder of modern Chicano literature. His first novel, *Bless Me, Ultima*, was praised for its depiction of the culture and history of New Mexico. Today, it is widely accepted as a classic of American literature.

A Storytelling Tradition "I am an oral storyteller," Anaya explains, "but now I do it on the printed page." Anaya's storytelling reflects his interest in the folk tales of his native Hispanic culture, which combines Spanish, Mexican, and Central American influences. Anaya has won a number of awards, including a PEN Center West Award for his 1992 novel *Albuquerque*. He is currently a professor of English at the University of New Mexico.

BACKGROUND FOR THE ESSAY
History Connection
New Mexican Culture
Native Americans occupied present-day New Mexico before the Spanish arrived in the late 1500s. The area remained under Spanish and then Mexican rule until 1848, when the United States gained control of it. Since then, people from all over the world have settled in New Mexico. As a result, the region has become a kind of cultural crossroads.

Did You Know?
As a teenager, Anaya was paralyzed after he dove into an irrigation ditch and fractured two vertebrae in his neck. He recovered, but the ordeal forever changed his outlook on life.

A Celebration of Grandfathers **443**

A Celebration of Grandfathers

Rudolfo A. Anaya

▲ Critical Viewing
As you read, consider which aspects of the man in this picture resemble the description of the elders in the essay. **[Compare and Contrast]**

"Buenos días le de Dios, abuelo."[1] God give you a good day, grandfather. This is how I was taught as a child to greet my grandfather, or any grown person. It was a greeting of respect, a cultural value to be passed on from generation to generation, this respect for the old ones.

The old people I remember from my childhood were strong in their beliefs, and as we lived daily with them we learned a wise path of life to follow. They had something important to share with the young, and

---

1. Buenos días le de Dios, abuelo (bwā′ nəs dē′ äs lā dā dē′ ōs ä bwā lō)

when they spoke the young listened. These old abuelos and abuelitas[2] had worked the earth all their lives, and so they knew the value of nurturing, they knew the sensitivity of the earth. The daily struggle called for cooperation, and so every person contributed to the social fabric, and each person was respected for his contribution.

The old ones had looked deep into the web that connects all animate and inanimate forms of life, and they recognized the great design of the creation.

These *ancianos*[3] from the cultures of the Río Grande, living side by side, sharing, growing together, they knew the rhythms and cycles of time, from the preparation of the earth in the spring to the digging of the acequias[4] that brought the water to the dance of harvest in the fall. They shared good times and hard times. They helped each other through the epidemics and the personal tragedies, and they shared what little they had when the hot winds burned the land and no rain came. They learned that to survive one had to share in the process of life.

Hard workers all, they tilled the earth and farmed, ran the herds and spun wool, and carved their saints and their kachinas[5] from cottonwood late in the winter nights. All worked with a deep faith which perplexes the modern mind.

Their faith shone in their eyes; it was in the strength of their grip, in the creases time wove into their faces. When they spoke, they spoke plainly and with few words, and they meant what they said. When they prayed, they went straight to the source of life. When there were good times, they knew how to dance in celebration and how to prepare the foods of the fiestas.[6] All this they passed on to the young, so that a new generation would know what they had known, so the string of life would not be broken. ●

Today we would say that the old abuelitos lived authentic lives.

Newcomers to New Mexico often say that time seems to move slowly here. I think they mean they have come in contact with the inner strength of the people, a strength so solid it causes time itself to pause. Think of it. Think of the high, northern New Mexico villages, or the lonely ranches on the open llano.[7] Think of the Indian pueblo[8] which lies as solid as rock in the face of time. Remember the old people whose eyes seem like windows that peer into a distant past that makes absurdity of our contemporary

---

2. **abuelitas** (ä bwä lē´ täs) *n.* Spanish for *grandmothers.*
3. *ancianos* (än cē ä´ nōs) *n.* Spanish for *old people; ancestors.*
4. **acequias** (ä sä kē´ əs) *n.* Spanish for *irrigation ditches.*
5. **kachinas** (kə chē´ nəz) *n.* Spanish for *small wooden dolls, representing the spirit of an ancestor or a god.*
6. **fiestas** (fē es´ təz) *n.* Spanish for *celebrations; feasts.*
7. **llano** (yä´ nō) *n.* Spanish for *plain.*
8. **pueblo** (pweb´ lō) *n.* Spanish for *village or town.*

Literary Analysis
Author's Style
What is the author's tone as he discusses the *ancianos?*

Vocabulary
nurturing (nʉr´ chər iŋ) *n.* the raising of; promoting the development of

perplexes (pər pleks´ əz) *v.* confuses or puzzles

absurdity (ab sʉr´ də tē) *n.* something ridiculous or nonsensical

Reading Check
What work did the *ancianos* do?

world. That is what one feels when one encounters the old ones and their land, a pausing of time.

We have all felt time stand still. We have all been in the presence of power, the knowledge of the old ones, the majestic peace of a mountain stream or an aspen grove or red buttes rising into blue sky. We have all felt the light of dusk permeate the earth and cause time to pause in its flow.

I felt this when first touched by the spirit of Ultima, the old *curandera*[9] who appears in my first novel, *Bless Me, Ultima*. This is how the young Antonio describes what he feels:

> When she came the beauty of the llano unfolded before my eyes, and the gurgling waters of the river sang to the hum of the turning earth. The magical time of childhood stood still, and the pulse of the living earth pressed its mystery into my living blood. She took my hand, and the silent, magic powers she possessed made beauty from the raw, sun-baked llano, the green river valley, and the blue bowl which was the white sun's home. My bare feet felt the throbbing earth, and my body trembled with excitement. Time stood still . . .

At other times, in other places, when I have been privileged to be with the old ones, to learn, I have felt this inner reserve of strength upon which they draw. I have been held motionless and speechless by the power of curanderas. I have felt the same power when I hunted with Cruz, high on the Taos [tä´ ōs] mountain, where it was more than the incredible beauty of the mountain bathed in morning light, more than the shining of the quivering aspen, but a connection with life, as if a shining strand of light connected the particular and the cosmic. That feeling is an epiphany of time, a standing still of time.

But not all of our old ones are curanderos or hunters on the mountain. My grandfather was a plain man, a farmer from Puerto de Luna[10] on the Pecos River. He was probably a descendent of those people who spilled over the mountain from Taos, following the Pecos River in search of farmland. There in that river valley he settled and raised a large family.

Bearded and walrus-mustached, he stood five feet tall, but to me as a child he was a giant. I remember him most for his silence. In the summers my parents sent me to live with him on his farm, for I was to learn the ways of a farmer. My uncles also lived in that valley, the valley called Puerto de Luna, there where only the flow of

Vocabulary
permeate (pʉr´ mē āt´) *v.* spread or flow throughout

Literary Analysis
Author's Style How does Anaya's use of Spanish words add to his message of being connected to his culture?

Spiral Review
Literary Essay In these paragraphs, how does the author interweave personal examples and ideas with factual information to explain a situation and present a perspective on that situation?

---

9. *curandera* (kōō rän dā´ rä) *n.* Spanish for *medicine woman*.
10. Puerto de Luna (pwer´ tō dā lōō´ nə) *n.* Port of the Moon, the name of a town.

the river and the whispering of the wind marked time. For me it was a magical place.

I remember once, while out hoeing the fields, I came upon an anthill, and before I knew it I was badly bitten. After he had covered my welts with the cool mud from the irrigation ditch, my grandfather calmly said: "Know where you stand." That is the way he spoke, in short phrases, to the point. •

One very dry summer, the river dried to a trickle, there was no water for the fields. The young plants withered and died. In my sadness and with the impulses of youth I said, "I wish it would rain!" My grandfather touched me, looked up into the sky and whispered, "Pray for rain." In his language there was a difference. He felt connected to the cycles that brought the rain or kept it from us. His prayer was a meaningful action, because he was a participant with the forces that filled our world, he was not a bystander.

A young man died at the village one summer. A very tragic death. He was dragged by his horse. When he was found I cried, for the boy was my friend. I did not understand why death had come to one so young. My grandfather took me aside and said: "Think of the death of the trees and the fields in the fall. The leaves fall, and everything rests, as if dead. But they bloom again in the spring. Death is only this small transformation in life."

These are the things I remember, these fleeting images, few words.

I remember him driving his horse-drawn wagon into Santa Rosa in the fall when he brought his harvest produce to sell in the town. What a tower of strength seemed to come in that small man huddled on the seat of the giant wagon. One click of his tongue and the horses obeyed, stopped or turned as he wished. He never raised his whip. How unlike today when so much teaching is done with loud words and threatening hands.

Woodcutter and Burro (**"El Lenador"**), 1934, Tom Lea, on long-term loan to the New Mexico Museum of Art from the U.S. General Services Administration, Works Project Administration. Photograph by Blair Clark.

▲ **Critical Viewing**
How does the farmer in this painting compare with your image of the author's grandfather? **[Compare and Contrast]**

 Reading Check

Why did Anaya's parents send him to stay with his grandfather in the summer?

Reading Skill
Main Idea Using the textual evidence in the paragraph that begins, "We were all. . . " as support for your understanding, what inference can you make about the author's main, or controlling, idea?

▼ Critical Viewing
Why do you think a writer like Anaya might find this New Mexican landscape inspiring? **[Speculate]**

I would run to greet the wagon, and the wagon would stop. "Buenos días le de Dios, abuelo," I would say. This was the prescribed greeting of esteem and respect. Only after the greeting was given could we approach these venerable old people. "Buenos días te de Dios, mi hijo,"[11] he would answer and smile, and then I could jump up on the wagon and sit at his side. Then I, too, became a king as I rode next to the old man who smelled of earth and sweat and the other deep aromas from the orchards and fields of Puerto de Luna.

We were all sons and daughters to him. But today the sons and daughters are breaking with the past, putting aside los abuelitos. The old values are threatened, and threatened most where it comes to these relationships with the old people. If we don't take the time to watch and feel the years of their final transformation, a part of our humanity will be lessened.

I grew up speaking Spanish, and oh! how difficult it was to learn English. Sometimes I would give up and cry out that I couldn't learn. Then he would say, "Ten paciencia."[12] Have patience.

---

11. mi hijo (mē ē′ hō) *n.* Spanish for *my son.*
12. Ten paciencia (ten pä sē en′ sē ä) *n.* Spanish for *Have patience.*

Paciencia, a word with the strength of centuries, a word that said that someday we would overcome. *Paciencia*, how soothing a word coming from this old man who could still sling hundred-pound bags over his shoulder, chop wood for hours on end, and hitch up his own horses and ride to town and back in one day.

"You have to learn the language of the Americanos,"[13] he said. "Me, I will live my last days in my valley. You will live in a new time, the time of the gringos."[14]

A new time did come, a new time is here. How will we form it so it is fruitful? We need to know where we stand. We need to speak softly and respect others, and to share what we have. We need to pray not for material gain, but for rain for the fields, for the sun to nurture growth, for nights in which we can sleep in peace, and for a harvest in which everyone can share. Simple lessons from a simple man. These lessons he learned from his past which was as deep and strong as the currents of the river of life, a life which could be stronger than death. •

---

13. **Americanos** (ä mer´ ē kä´ nōs) *n.* Spanish for *Americans*.
14. **gringos** (griŋ´ gōs) *n.* Spanish for *foreigners; North Americans*.

Literary Analysis
Author's Style How does the author's repetition of the phrase "We need" add urgency to his message?

Reading Check

Why does Anaya's grandfather tell him that he must learn English?

LITERATURE IN CONTEXT

Cultural Connection

Anaya's Best-Known Work

In this essay, Anaya quotes from his novel *Bless Me, Ultima*. First published in 1972, the novel tells the story of a young boy, Antonio, who lives with his family in Guadalupe, New Mexico. Ultima, who is respected for her healing powers and her knowledge of the uses of plants, comes to live with Antonio's family. Ultima takes the boy under her wing and teaches him about the plants and trees of the area. She also teaches him some important lessons about life.

Connect to the Literature

Based on what you know about Anaya's writing, how would you expect him to describe the bond between people and the land? Explain your answer.

Vocabulary
anguish (aŋ´ gwish) *n.*
great pain or suffering

He was a man; he died. Not in his valley, but nevertheless cared for by his sons and daughters and flocks of grandchildren. At the end, I would enter his room which carried the smell of medications and Vicks, the faint pungent odor of urine, and cigarette smoke. Gone were the aroma of the fields, the strength of his young manhood. Gone also was his patience in the face of crippling old age. Small things bothered him; he shouted or turned sour when his expectations were not met. It was because he could not care for himself, because he was returning to that state of childhood, and all those wishes and desires were now wrapped in a crumbling old body.

"Ten paciencia," I once said to him, and he smiled. "I didn't know I would grow this old," he said. "Now, I can't even roll my own cigarettes." I rolled a cigarette for him, placed it in his mouth and lit it. I asked him why he smoked, the doctor had said it was bad for him. "I like to see the smoke rise," he said. He would smoke and doze, and his quilt was spotted with little burns where the cigarettes dropped. One of us had to sit and watch to make sure a fire didn't start.

I would sit and look at him and remember what was said of him when he was a young man. He could mount a wild horse and break it, and he could ride as far as any man. He could dance all night at a dance, then work the acequia the following day. He helped neighbors, they helped him. He married, raised children. Small legends, the kind that make up everyman's life.

He was 94 when he died. Family, neighbors, and friends gathered; they all agreed he had led a rich life. I remembered the last years, the years he spent in bed. And as I remember now, I am reminded that it is too easy to romanticize old age. Sometimes we forget the pain of the transformation into old age, we forget the natural breaking down of the body. Not all go gentle into the last years, some go crying and cursing, forgetting the names of those they loved the most, withdrawing into an internal anguish few of us can know. May we be granted the patience and care to deal with our ancianos.

For some time we haven't looked at these changes and needs of the old ones. The American image created by the mass media is an image of youth, not of old age. It is the beautiful and the young who are praised in this society. If analyzed carefully, we see that same damaging thought has crept into the way society views the old. In response to the old, the mass media have just created old people who act like the young. It is only the healthy, pink-cheeked, outgoing, older persons we are shown in the media. And they are always selling something, as if an entire generation of old people were salesmen in their lives. Commercials show very lively old men, who must always be in excellent health according to the new myth, selling insurance policies or real estate as they are out golfing; older women selling coffee or toilet paper to those just married. That image does not illustrate the real life of the old ones.

Real life takes into account the natural cycle of growth and change. My grandfather pointed to the leaves falling from the tree. So time brings with its transformation the often painful, wearing-down process. Vision blurs, health wanes; even the act of walking carries with it the painful reminder of the autumn of life. But this process is something to be faced, not something to be hidden away by false images. Yes, the old can be young at heart, but in their own way, with their own dignity. They do not have to copy the always-young image of the Hollywood star.

Real life takes into account the natural cycle of growth and change.

My grandfather wanted to return to his valley to die. But by then the families of the valley had left in search of a better future. It is only now that there seems to be a return to the valley, a revival. The new generation seeks its roots, that value of love for the land moves us to return to the place where our ancianos formed the culture.

I returned to Puerto de Luna last summer, to join the community in a celebration of the founding of the church. I drove by my grandfather's home, my uncles' ranches, the neglected adobe[15] washing down into the earth from whence it came. And I wondered, how might the values of my grandfather's generation live in our own? What can we retain to see us through these hard times? I

15. **adobe** (ə dō′ bē) *n.* sun-dried clay brick.

Vocabulary
revival (ri vī′ vəl) *n.* a bringing or coming back into use, attention, or being after a decline

Reading Check
What happens to Anaya's grandfather?

was to become a farmer, and I became a writer. As I plow and plant my words, do I nurture as my grandfather did in his fields and orchards? The answers are not simple.

"They don't make men like that anymore," is a phrase we hear when one does honor to a man. I am glad I knew my grandfather. I am glad there are still times when I can see him in my dreams, hear him in my reverie. Sometimes I think I catch a whiff of that earthy aroma that was his smell, just as in lonely times sometimes I catch the fragrance of Ultima's herbs. Then I smile. How strong these people were to leave such a lasting impression.

So, as I would greet my abuelo long ago, it would help us all to greet the old ones we know with this kind and respectful greeting: "Buenos días le de Dios."

How strong these people were to leave such a lasting impression.

Critical Thinking

1. Respond: Which part of the essay is most powerful to you? Explain your response.

2. (a) What qualities of old people does Anaya remember from his childhood? **(b) Analyze:** How are these qualities different from the images that Anaya says have been created by American mass media?

3. (a) What does Anaya's grandfather say is the "new time" in which Anaya will live? **(b) Make Inferences:** What does the author imply about what this "new time" will bring for his people?

 Support your responses with evidence from the text.

4. (a) Draw Conclusions: What opinion does Anaya offer on the way people should be treated as they grow old?
(b) Take a Position: Do you agree with him? Explain.
(c) Discuss: Share your answers with a partner. Then, explain how your answer has grown or changed as a result of the discussion.

 **Is knowledge the same as understanding?**
(a) What insights do the quotations from Anaya's grandfather give you into his family's values and character? **(b)** How do these insights strengthen your understanding?

Literary Analysis: **Author's Style**

1. At several points in his essay, Anaya strings together sentences that are structured in the same way, as in this example: "When they spoke, they spoke plainly and with few words, and they meant what they said. When they prayed, they went straight to the source of life. When there were good times, they knew how to dance in celebration. . . ." What effect does this aspect of the author's **syntax** create? Explain your response.

2. Use a chart like the one shown to record examples of the **diction** and **tone** Anaya uses. Then, based on his diction and tone, write three adjectives in the center of the chart that describe his **style.**

Rudolfo A. Anaya

Diction	Style	Tone

Reading Skill: **Main Idea**

3. **(a)** List three details that you used as **textual evidence** to **make complex inferences** about the **main, or controlling, idea** of Anaya's essay. **(b)** State the controlling idea of the essay in your own words.

4. Explain how Anaya supports his controlling idea with details.

Vocabulary

Practice Determine whether each sentence below is true or false. Use the meaning of the italicized word to explain your reasoning.

1. A poor instruction manual is one that *perplexes* its readers.

2. It is a compliment to have a business idea labeled "an *absurdity.*"

3. To prevent a stain, allow ink to *permeate* the fabric.

4. Comforting someone in *anguish* is a kind action.

5. *Nurturing* a plant involves watering and feeding it.

6. The closing performance of a play would be a *revival.*

Word Power Use the context of the sentences and what you know about the **Latin root -viv-** to explain your answer to each question.

1. Do most people *survive* an embarrassing moment?

2. Is a *vivid* experience one you're likely to soon forget?

Word Power

The **Latin root -viv-** means "to live."

Apply It Explain how the root -viv- helps you determine the meanings of these words. You may consult a dictionary if necessary.

convivial
vivacious
revive

Is *knowledge* **the same as** *understanding?*

Writing About the Big Question

In "On Summer," Lorraine Hansberry's growing understanding of life has changed her feelings about summer. Use these sentence starters to develop your ideas about the Big Question.

Learning the **facts** of people's lives may change how we **comprehend** them because _____.

When we make a **connection** with something, our **feelings** toward it may change because _____.

As You Read Look for details that tell about Hansberry's feelings toward summer.

Vocabulary

Read each word and its definition. Decide whether you know the word well, know it a little bit, or do not know it at all. After you read, see how your knowledge of each word has increased.

- **aloofness** (ə lōōf´ nəs) *n.* emotional distance (p. 456) *His aloofness made him appear unfriendly. aloof adj. aloofly adv.*

- **melancholy** (mel´ ən käl´ ē) *adj.* sad; gloomy (p. 456) *The rain set a melancholy mood. melancholy n. melancholic adj.*

- **bias** (bī´ əs) *n.* mental leaning or inclination; partiality (p. 457) *For years, John has had a bias toward Italian restaurants. bias v. biased adj.*

- **duration** (doo rā´ shən) *n.* the time that a thing continues or lasts (p. 457) *To sleep better at night, decrease the duration of your afternoon nap. durable adj. durability n. endure v.*

- **pretentious** (prē ten´ shəs) *adj.* grand in a showy way (p. 460) *His pretentious manner only impressed those who had just met him. pretentiousness n.*

- **apex** (ā´ peks´) *n.* highest point; peak (p. 460) *Playing in the World Series was the apex of his baseball career.*

Word Power

The **Latin root** *-dur-* means "to harden," "to hold out," or "to last."

In this story, the narrator describes the long **duration** of a summer day. She means that it seems to last for a very long time.

Meet
Lorraine Hansberry
(1930–1965)

Author of

On Summer

Lorraine Hansberry grew up on the South Side of Chicago, where her father prospered as a real-estate broker. At the time, many white people closed their neighborhoods, refusing to sell or rent property to African Americans. Hansberry's father fought this practice, taking his case all the way to the Supreme Court, where he won.

A Pioneering Playwright As her father fought to integrate Chicago's neighborhoods, Hansberry laid claim to territories of the imagination. With the 1959 production of her play *A Raisin in the Sun*, she became the first African American woman to have a drama produced on Broadway.

BACKGROUND FOR THE ESSAY
Social Studies Connection
The Great Migration
Beginning in the early 1900s, hundreds of thousands of African Americans left the rural South for northern cities. They fled discrimination and the floods and pests that threatened their livelihood as farmers. Many left relatives behind and, like Hansberry's Chicago family, journeyed south in summertime to visit.

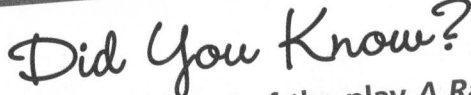

A Broadway revival of the play *A Raisin in the Sun* won Tony awards for Phylicia Rashad and Audra McDonald in 2004.

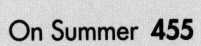

On Summer

Lorraine Hansberry

Vocabulary
aloofness (ə lo͞of´ nəs)
n. emotional distance
melancholy
(mel´ ən käl´ ē) *adj.*
sad; gloomy

It has taken me a good number of years to come to any measure of respect for summer. I was, being May-born, literally an "infant of the spring" and, during the later childhood years, tended, for some reason or other, to rather worship the cold aloofness of winter. The adolescence, admittedly lingering still, brought the traditional passionate commitment to melancholy autumn—and all that. For the longest kind of time I simply thought that *summer* was a mistake.

In fact, my earliest memory of anything at all is of waking up in a darkened room where I had been put to bed for a nap on a summer's afternoon, and feeling very, very hot. I acutely disliked the feeling then and retained the bias for years. It had originally been a matter of the heat but, over the years, I came actively to associate displeasure with most of the usually celebrated natural features and social by-products of the season: the too-grainy texture of sand; the too-cold coldness of the various waters we constantly try to escape into, and the icky-perspiry feeling of bathing caps.

It also seemed to me, esthetically[1] speaking, that nature had got inexcusably carried away on the summer question and let the whole thing get to be rather much. By duration alone, for instance, a summer's day seemed maddeningly excessive; an utter overstatement. Except for those few hours at either end of it, objects always appeared in too sharp a relief against backgrounds; shadows too pronounced and light too blinding. It always gave me the feeling of walking around in a motion picture which had been too artsily-craftsily exposed. Sound also had a way of coming to the ear without that muting influence, marvelously common to winter, across patios or beaches or through the woods. I suppose I found it too stark and yet too intimate a season.

My childhood Southside summers were the ordinary city kind, full of the street games which other rememberers have turned into fine ballets these days and rhymes that anticipated what some people insist on calling modern poetry:

> Oh, Mary Mack, Mack, Mack
> All dressed in black, black, black
> With the silver buttons, buttons, buttons
> All down her back, back, back
> She asked her mother, mother, mother
> For fifteen cents, cents, cents
> To see the elephant, elephant, elephant
> Jump the fence, fence, fence
> Well, he jumped so high, high, high
> 'Til he touched the sky, sky, sky
> And he didn't come back, back, back
> 'Til the Fourth of Ju-ly, ly, ly!

Evenings were spent mainly on the back porches where screen doors slammed in the darkness with those really very special summertime sounds. And, sometimes, when Chicago nights got too steamy, the whole family got into the car and went to the park and slept out in the

---

1. **esthetically** (es thet´ ik lē) *adv.* artistically.

Literary Analysis
Author's Style How would you describe Hansberry's tone as she explains her childhood feelings about summer?

Vocabulary
bias (bī´ əs) *n.* mental leaning or inclination; partiality

duration (doo rā´ shən) *n.* the time that a thing continues or lasts

Literary Analysis
Author's Style What effect does the use of the made-up word "artsily-craftsily" create?

Reading Check
Identify one thing the author dislikes about summer.

**Literary Analysis
Author's Style** How does Hansberry's repeated use of the word *and* to begin sentences emphasize the flow and abundance of her memories?

**Spiral Review
Literary Essay** In this paragraph, how does the author interweave personal examples and ideas with factual information to explain a situation and present a perspective on that situation?

**Reading Skill
Main Idea** Here the author shares anecdotes about her trips to Tennessee. Using this textual evidence as support for your understanding, what inference can you make about the author's main, or controlling, idea?

open on blankets. Those were, of course, the best times of all because the grownups were invariably reminded of having been children in rural parts of the country and told the best stories then. And it was also cool and sweet to be on the grass and there was usually the scent of freshly cut lemons or melons in the air. And Daddy would lie on his back, as fathers must, and explain about how men thought the stars above us came to be and how far away they were. I never did learn to believe that anything could be as far away as *that*. Especially the stars.

My mother first took us south to visit her Tennessee birthplace one summer when I was seven or eight, I think. I woke up on the back seat of the car while we were still driving through some place called Kentucky and my mother was pointing out to the beautiful hills on both sides of the highway and telling my brothers and my sister about how her father had run away and hidden from his master in those very hills when he was a little boy. She said that his mother had wandered among the wooded slopes in the moonlight and left food for him in secret places. They were very beautiful hills and I looked out at them for miles and miles after that wondering who and what a *master* might be.

I remember being startled when I first saw my grandmother rocking away on her porch. All my life I had heard that she was a great beauty and no one had ever remarked that they meant a half century before. The woman that I met was as wrinkled as a prune and could hardly hear and barely see and always seemed to be thinking of other times. But she could still rock and talk and even make wonderful cupcakes which were like cornbread, only sweet. She was captivated by automobiles and, even though it was well into the Thirties,[2] I don't think she had ever been in one before we came down and took her driving. She was a little afraid of them and could not seem to negotiate the windows, but she loved driving. She died the next summer and that is all that I remember about her, except that she was born in slavery and had memories of it and they didn't sound anything like *Gone With the Wind*.[3]

Like everyone else, I have spent whole or bits of summers in many different kinds of places since then: camps and resorts in the Middle West and New York State; on an island; in a tiny Mexican village; Cape Cod, perched atop the Truro bluffs at Longnook Beach that Millay wrote about; or simply strolling the streets of Provincetown[4] before the hours when the parties begin.

And, lastly, I do not think that I will forget days spent, a few summers ago, at a beautiful lodge built right into the rocky cliffs

---

2. **Thirties** the 1930s.
3. *Gone With the Wind* novel set in the South during the Civil War period.
4. **Provincetown** resort town at the northern tip of Cape Cod, Massachusetts.

of a bay on the Maine coast. We met a woman there who had lived a purposeful and courageous life and who was then dying of cancer. She had, characteristically, just written a book and taken up painting. She had also been of radical viewpoint all her life; one of those people who energetically believe that the world *can* be changed for the better and spend their lives trying to do just that. And that was the way she thought of cancer; she absolutely refused to award it the stature of tragedy, a devastating instance of the brooding doom and inexplicability[5] of the absurdity of human destiny, etc., etc. The kind of characterization given, lately, as we all know, to far less formidable foes in life than cancer.

But for this remarkable woman it was a matter of nature in imperfection, implying, as always, work for man to do. It was an *enemy*, but a palpable one with shape and effect and source; and if it existed, it could be destroyed. She saluted it accordingly, without despondency, but with a lively, beautiful and delightfully ribald anger. There was one thing, she felt, which would prove equal to its relentless ravages and that was the genius of man. Not his mysticism, but man with tubes and slides and the stubborn human notion that the stars are very much within our reach.

---

5. **inexplicability** (in eks´ pli kə bil´ ə tē) *n.* condition of being unexplainable.

▼ **Critical Viewing**
How does this illustration of the Maine coast add to the description in the essay? **[Connect]**

Reading Check
Whom does Hansberry visit in Tennessee?

Vocabulary
pretentious (prē ten´ shəs) *adj.* grand in a showy way
apex (ā´ peks´) *n.* highest point; peak

The last time I saw her she was sitting surrounded by her paintings with her manuscript laid out for me to read, because, she said, she wanted to know what a *young person* would think of her thinking; one must always keep up with what *young people* thought about things because, after all, they were *change.*

Every now and then her jaw set in anger as we spoke of things people should be angry about. And then, for relief, she would look out at the lovely bay at a mellow sunset settling on the water. Her face softened with love of all that beauty and, watching her, I wished with all my power what I knew that she was wishing: that she might live to see at least one more *summer.* Through her eyes I finally gained the sense of what it might mean; more than the coming autumn with its pretentious melancholy; more than an austere and silent winter which must shut dying people in for precious months; more even than the frivolous spring, too full of too many false promises, would be the gift of another summer with its stark and intimate assertion of neither birth nor death but life at the apex; with the gentlest nights and, above all, the longest days.

I heard later that she did live to see another summer. And I have retained my respect for the noblest of the seasons.

Critical Thinking

1. **Respond:** How do Hansberry's ideas about summer compare with your own? Make a list of the reasons why you like and dislike summer. Discuss your answers with a partner. Then, explain how your answer has grown or changed as a result of the discussion.

2. **(a)** When does Hansberry first visit her grandmother?
   (b) Make Inferences: Why do you think she includes the section about her grandmother in her essay? Which details led you to this idea?

3. **(a)** When does Hansberry's attitude toward summer begin to change? **(b) Interpret:** At the essay's end, Hansberry calls summer "the noblest of seasons." What do you think she means by this phrase?

4. **Evaluate:** How clearly do you think Hansberry explains the way her feelings about summer have changed? Explain.

   Is knowledge the same as understanding?
   (a) In what way has Hansberry's knowledge of summer stayed the same? **(b)** How has her understanding of summer changed? Use details from the text to explain your response.

Literary Analysis: Author's Style

1. What one word might you use to describe the overall **tone** of "On Summer"? Explain your answer.

2. Review the last two paragraphs of "On Summer." Use a chart like the one shown to record examples of the **diction** and **tone** Hansberry uses in describing her associations with summer. Then, based on her diction and tone in these paragraphs, write three adjectives in the center of the chart to describe Hansberry's **style.**

Diction	→	Style	←	Tone

Reading Skill: Main Idea

3. (a) List three details that you used as **textual evidence** to **make complex inferences** about the **main, or controlling, idea** of Hansberry's essay. **(b)** State the controlling idea of the essay in your own words.

4. Explain how Hansberry supports her controlling idea with details.

Vocabulary

Practice Determine whether each sentence below is true or false. Use the meaning of the italicized word to explain your reasoning.

1. Greeting a close friend with *aloofness* shows respect.

2. Cheerful songs might change someone's *melancholy* mood.

3. A *pretentious* politician is likely to be unpopular with many voters.

4. One must climb a mountain to reach its *apex*.

5. If a man has a *bias* toward cats, he feels neutral about them.

6. If we stay for the *duration* of the game, we will leave at halftime.

Word Power Use the context of sentences and what you know about the **Latin root -dur-** to explain your answer to each question.

1. If a manufacturer claims an item is *durable*, would you expect it to wear out quickly?

2. When a thief is caught *during* a robbery, has he or she been caught in the act?

Word Power

The **Latin root -dur-** means "to harden," "to hold out," or "to last."

Apply It Explain how the root -dur- helps you determine the meanings of these words. You may consult a dictionary if necessary.

obdurate
endure
duress

Integrated Language Skills

A Celebration of Grandfathers • On Summer

Conventions: Direct and Indirect Objects

> A **direct object** is a noun or pronoun that *receives* the action of an action verb. An **indirect object** appears with a direct object and names the person or thing that something is *given to* or *done for.*

You can determine whether a word is a direct object by asking *Whom?* or *What?* after an action verb. You can tell whether a word is an indirect object by asking *To or for whom?* or *To or for what?* An indirect object can only appear between a subject and a direct object.

Example	Explanation
The family bought **an old house.**	*House* is a direct object—answers the question *Bought what?*
The rain pelted **the campers.**	*Campers* is a direct object—answers the question *Pelted whom?*
I wrote my **brother letters.**	*Brother* is an indirect object—answers the question *Wrote to whom?* *Letters* is a direct object—answers the question *Wrote what?*

Practice A Identify the direct and indirect objects in each sentence.

1. The author greeted his grandfather.
2. His grandfather usually gave him very good advice.
3. Rudolfo Anaya always showed his grandfather respect.
4. Grandfather drove the huge wagon to market with the produce.

Reading Application In the first paragraph of "A Celebration of Grandfathers," find a sentence that uses both a direct and an indirect object.

Practice B For each item, write an original sentence using the word or phrase as directed by the information in parentheses.

1. winter (as a direct object)
2. Maine coast (as a direct object in a question)
3. author (as an indirect object), manuscript (as a direct object)
4. grandmother (as an indirect object), gift (as a direct object)

Writing Application Use this sentence starter to write three sentences about summer that include indirect objects (IO) and direct objects (DO):
I gave (IO)/(DO).

PH GRAMMAR HANDBOOK Further instruction and practice are available in the *Prentice Hall Grammar Handbook.*

Writing

Both of these selections describe the admiration the main characters have for someone older than they are. Think of an older person whom you admire. Write a few paragraphs of **book jacket copy** for a biography of that person. Book jackets often provide a brief introduction to a subject to entice and persuade people to read more.

- Include some important highlights of the person's life.
- Choose specific details that will make the reader want to know more.

Grammar Application Make sure to use direct and indirect objects correctly in your copy.

Writing Workshop: *Work in Progress*

Prewriting for Business Letter For a business letter you may write, list consumer items that have not lived up to your expectations. Note what has been disappointing about each one. Then, choose one item and consider the kinds of information a company representative would need to know. Jot down three questions that need to be answered for the reader to understand your complaint. Save this Questions List in your portfolio.

Listening and Speaking

In a small team, hold a **panel discussion** on one of these topics.

- If you read "A Celebration of Grandfathers," discuss Anaya's claim that "the American image created by the mass media is an image of youth, not old age." To get started, think about the age of most people in television and films. Decide what images are conveyed by these actors.

- If you read "On Summer," discuss the pros and cons of each season of the year. To prepare, consider what you like about your favorite season, as well as what others might dislike about the season.

Follow these steps to complete the assignment:

- Prepare notes to use during the discussion. These will help keep you on track, enabling you to speak clearly and to the point.
- During the team discussion, **participate productively** by **building on the ideas of others and contributing relevant information** to support your points.
- **Listen responsively to other speakers** on the panel by **taking notes** that summarize their ideas for critical reflection. Review these notes. Then, ask questions related to the content of what was said for **clarification** and **elaboration.**

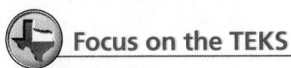 **Focus on the TEKS**

Writing
(16) Write persuasive texts.
Listening and Speaking
(24)(A) Listen responsively to a speaker by taking notes that summarize the speaker's ideas for critical reflection and by asking questions related to the content for clarification and elaboration.
(26) Participate productively in teams, building on the ideas of others and contributing relevant information.

Use this prewriting activity to prepare for the **Writing Workshop** on page 512.

www.PHLitOnline.com

- Interactive graphic organizers
- Grammar tutorial
- Interactive journals

Selection Choices

▲ Read **"Single Room, Earth View"** to get an understanding of the startling experience of traveling in space.

▲ Read **"The News"** to learn how TV news gives us a different, and more chaotic, view of the world than a newspaper can.

 TEXAS Focus on the TEKS

Meet these standards with either **"Single Room, Earth View"** (p. 468) or **"The News"** (p. 478).

Reading
(9) Analyze expository text. (Literary Analysis: Expository Text)

(8) Explain the controlling idea of an expository text. (Reading Skill: Main Idea)

Writing
(14)(C) Write a script with an explicit theme and details that contribute to a definite mood or tone. (Writing: Script for a Public Service Announcement)

Research
(20)(B) Formulate a plan for engaging in research on a complex, multi-faceted topic. (Research and Technology: Journal Entries)

(22)(B) Evaluate the relevance of information to the topic and determine the reliability, validity, and accuracy of sources (including Internet sources) by examining their authority and objectivity. (Research and Technology: Journal Entries)

Literary Analysis: Expository Text

An **expository text** is a piece of nonfiction that presents information or discusses ideas. An expository writer may use a variety of techniques to provide support, depth, and context to the ideas being discussed.

- **Description:** including **imagery**—language that appeals to the senses—and **figurative language**—such as simile and metaphor.
- **Comparison and contrast:** showing similarities and differences between two or more ideas, people, events, or things.
- **Cause and effect:** explaining the relationship between events, actions, or situations by showing how one can result from another.

As You Read Analyze expository texts by noting the techniques each writer uses to develop his or her ideas.

Reading Skill: Main Idea

The **main, or controlling, idea** is the central message, insight, or opinion in a work of nonfiction. The supporting details are the pieces of evidence a writer uses to prove his or her point. To identify and explain the controlling idea of an expository text, follow these steps:

- Note the **cultural and historical or contemporary contexts**—the time and place in which the author is writing—and consider how they might affect what the author chooses to write about.
- Note key details to decide what the controlling idea might be.
- If a detail does not seem to support that controlling idea, reread the passage to be sure that you have not misinterpreted it.
- If necessary, revise your assumptions about the controlling idea.

Using the Strategy: Cluster Diagram

As You Read Record the controlling idea and details on a cluster diagram like this one to help you explain the controlling idea of the text.

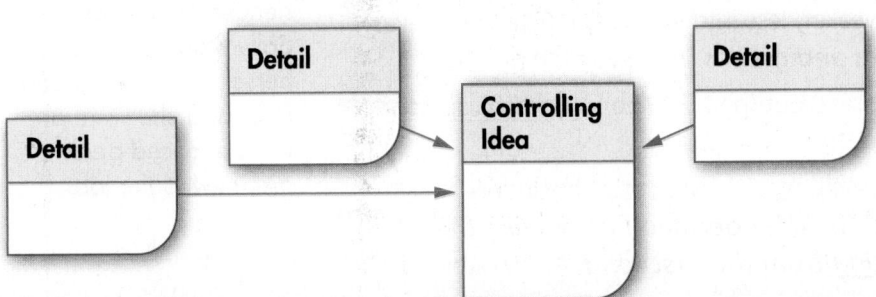

TEXAS
PHLitOnline
www.PHLitOnline.com

Hear It!
- Selection summary audio
- Selection audio

See It!
- Get Connected video
- Background video
- More about the author
- Vocabulary flashcards

Do It!
- Interactive journals
- Interactive graphic organizers
- Self-test
- Internet activity
- Grammar tutorial
- Interactive vocabulary games

Is *knowledge* the same as *understanding?*

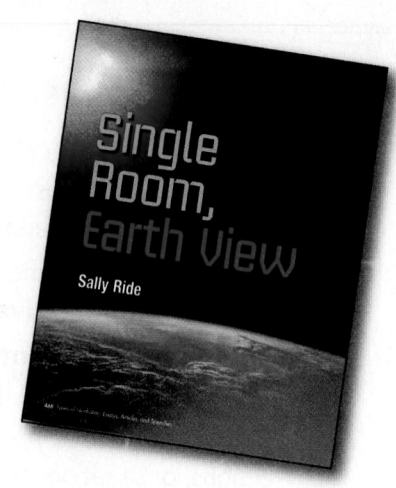

Writing About the Big Question

In "Single Room, Earth View," astronaut Sally Ride explains what it is like to see Earth from the space shuttle. Use these sentence starters to develop your ideas about the Big Question.

Looking at Earth from space may change how we **comprehend** the world because _____.

Analyzing familiar **concepts** from a different perspective can help us understand them better because _____.

As You Read Look for a way in which the writer's knowledge grows into understanding while traveling in space for the first time.

Vocabulary

Read each word and its definition. Decide whether you know the word well, know it a little bit, or do not know it at all. After you read, see how your knowledge of each word has increased.

- **articulate** (är tik´ yōo lit) *adj.* able to express oneself clearly and easily (p. 469) *The candidate is an <u>articulate</u> public speaker.* *articulate v. articulately adv. articulation n.*

- **surreal** (sər rē´ əl) *adj.* strange, like something from a dream (p. 470) *The party was a <u>surreal</u> mixture of men in business suits and punk rockers.* *surrealism n.*

- **novice** (näv´ is) *adj.* new to an activity; inexperienced (p. 470) *For a <u>novice</u> chess player, she shows great patience and maturity.* *nova n. novitiate n.*

- **muted** (myōot´ əd) *adj.* weaker; less intense (p. 471) *The room was furnished in <u>muted</u> blues and greens.* *mute v. mute n.*

- **diffused** (di fyōozd´) *v.* spread out (p. 473) *The wind <u>diffused</u> the confetti over the field.* *diffuse v. diffusion n.*

- **extrapolating** (ek strap´ ə lāt´ iŋ) *v.* arriving at a conclusion by inferring from known facts (p. 474) *I decided I would like the whole CD by <u>extrapolating</u> from the first song.* *extrapolation n.*

Word Power

The **Latin root -nov-** means "new" or "recent."

Someone who is new to something is inexperienced. In this essay, Sally Ride describes herself as a **novice**. She feels as if she were an inexperienced geologist, new to the job.

Author of
Single Room, Earth View

Although best known as an astronaut, Sally Ride was also a talented athlete in her youth. She was a ranked player on the junior tennis circuit and considered turning professional before deciding to go to college instead.

The Right Stuff In 1978, Ride read a newspaper advertisement about NASA's search for astronauts. After extensive testing to be sure she had "the right stuff," NASA chose her as one of six women and twenty-five men accepted from among 8,000 applicants. Five years later, in 1983, she took her historic flight. Ride retired from NASA in 1987 and currently teaches physics at the University of California.

BACKGROUND FOR THE TEXT
History Connection

First American Woman in Space
On June 18, 1983, when she worked as a flight engineer and mission specialist aboard the shuttle *Challenger*, Sally Ride became the first American woman in space. Her historic mission allowed her to experience what she recounts in "Single Room, Earth View."

Did You Know?
Sally Ride holds four degrees from Stanford University, including a Master's and a Doctorate.

Single Room, Earth View

Sally Ride

Everyone I've met has a glittering, if vague, mental image of space travel. And naturally enough, people want to hear about it from an astronaut: "How did it feel . . . ?" "What did it look like . . . ?" "Were you scared?" Sometimes, the questions come from reporters, their pens poised and their tape recorders silently reeling in the words; sometimes, it's wide-eyed, ten-year-old girls who want answers. I find a way to answer all of them, but it's not easy.

Imagine trying to describe an airplane ride to someone who has never flown. An articulate traveler could describe the sights but would find it much harder to explain the difference in perspective provided by the new view from a greater distance, along with the feelings, impressions, and insights that go with that new perspective. And the difference is enormous: Spaceflight moves the traveler another giant step farther away. Eight and one-half thunderous minutes after launch, an astronaut is orbiting high above the Earth, suddenly able to watch typhoons form, volcanoes smolder, and meteors streak through the atmosphere below.

◀ **Critical Viewing**
Based on this photograph, how might travel in the space shuttle defy description? **[Connect]**

Vocabulary
articulate (är tik´ yo͞o lit) *adj.* able to express oneself clearly and easily

Vocabulary
surreal (sər rē´ əl) *adj.*
strange, like something
from a dream

Reading Skill
Main Idea
Explain how these details
help support Ride's main,
or controlling, idea—the
difficulties of describing
space travel.

Vocabulary
novice (näv´ is) *adj.*
new to an activity;
inexperienced

While flying over the Hawaiian Islands, several astronauts have marveled that the islands look just like they do on a map. When people first hear that, they wonder what should be so surprising about Hawaii looking the way it does in the atlas. Yet, to the astronauts it is an absolutely startling sensation: The islands really *do* look as if that part of the world has been carpeted with a big page torn out of Rand-McNally, and all we can do is try to convey the surreal quality of that scene.

In orbit, racing along at five miles per second, the space shuttle circles the Earth once every 90 minutes. I found that at this speed, unless I kept my nose pressed to the window, it was almost impossible to keep track of where we were at any given moment—the world below simply changes too fast. If I turned my concentration away for too long, even just to change film in a camera, I could miss an entire land mass. It's embarrassing to float up to a window, glance outside, and then have to ask a crewmate, "What continent is this?"

We could see smoke rising from fires that dotted the entire east coast of Africa, and in the same orbit only moments later, ice floes jostling for position in the Antarctic. We could see the Ganges River dumping its murky, sediment-laden water into the Indian Ocean and watch ominous hurricane clouds expanding and rising like biscuits in the oven of the Caribbean.

Mountain ranges, volcanoes, and river deltas appeared in salt-and-flour relief, all leading me to assume the role of a novice geologist. In such moments, it was easy to imagine the dynamic upheavals that created jutting mountain ranges and the internal wrenchings that created rifts and seas. I also became an instant believer in plate tectonics; India really *is* crashing into Asia, and Saudi Arabia and Egypt really *are* pulling apart, making the Red Sea wider. Even though their respective motion is really no more than mere inches a year, the view from overhead makes theory come alive. Spectacular as the view is from 200 miles up, the Earth is not the awe-inspiring "blue marble" made famous by the photos from the moon. From space shuttle height, we can't see the entire globe at a glance, but we can look down the entire boot of Italy, or up the East Coast of the United

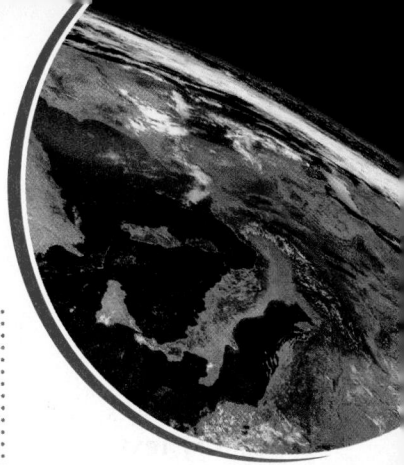

States from Cape Hatteras to Cape Cod. The panoramic view inspires an appreciation for the scale of some of nature's phenomena. One day, as I scanned the sandy expanse of Northern Africa, I couldn't find any of the familiar landmarks—colorful outcroppings of rock in Chad, irrigated patches of the Sahara. Then I realized they were obscured by a huge dust storm, a cloud of sand that enveloped the continent from Morocco to the Sudan.

Since the space shuttle flies fairly low (at least by orbital standards; it's more than 22,000 miles lower than a typical TV satellite), we can make out both natural and manmade features in surprising detail. Familiar geographical features like San Francisco Bay, Long Island, and Lake Michigan are easy to recognize, as are many cities, bridges, and airports. The Great Wall of China is not the only man-made object visible from space.

The signatures of civilization are usually seen in straight lines (bridges or runways) or sharp delineations (abrupt transitions from desert to irrigated land, as in California's Imperial Valley). A modern city like New York doesn't leap from the canvas of its surroundings, but its straight piers and concrete runways catch the eye—and around them, the city materializes. I found Salina, Kansas (and pleased my in-laws, who live there) by spotting its long runway amid the wheat fields near the city. Over Florida, I could see the launch pad where we had begun our trip, and the landing strip, where we would eventually land.

Some of civilization's more unfortunate effects on the environment are also evident from orbit. Oil slicks glisten on the surface of the Persian Gulf, patches of pollution-damaged trees dot the forests of central Europe. Some cities look out of focus, and their colors muted, when viewed through a pollutant haze. Not surprisingly, the effects are more noticeable now than they were a decade ago. An astronaut who has flown in both Skylab and the space shuttle reported that the horizon didn't seem quite as sharp, or the colors quite as bright, in 1983 as they had in 1973.

Of course, informal observations by individual astronauts are one thing, but more precise measurements are continually being made from space: The space shuttle has carried infrared film to document damage to citrus trees in Florida and in rain forests along the Amazon. It has carried even more sophisticated sensors in the payload bay. Here is one example: sensors used to measure atmospheric carbon monoxide levels, allowing scientists to study the environmental effects of city emissions and land-clearing fires.

Most of the Earth's surface is covered with water, and at first glance it all looks the same: blue. But with the right lighting conditions and a couple of orbits of practice, it's possible to make

Literary Analysis
Expository Text
What point about environmental change does Ride support with her descriptions in this paragraph?

Vocabulary
muted (myo͞ot´ əd) *adj.* weaker; less intense

Reading Check
What kinds of structures reveal the "signatures of civilization" from space?

Single Room, Earth View **471**

out the intricate patterns in the oceans—eddies and spirals become visible because of the subtle differences in water color or reflectivity.

Observations and photographs by astronauts have contributed significantly to the understanding of ocean dynamics, and some of the more intriguing discoveries prompted the National Aeronautics and Space Administration to fly an oceanographic observer for the express purpose of studying the ocean from orbit. Scientists' understanding of the energy balance in the oceans has increased significantly as a result of the discoveries of circular and spiral eddies tens of kilometers in diameter, of standing waves hundreds of kilometers long, and of spiral eddies that sometimes trail into one another for thousands of kilometers. If a scientist wants to study features on this scale, it's much easier from an orbiting vehicle than from the vantage point of a boat.

Believe it or not, an astronaut can also see the wakes of large ships and the contrails of airplanes. The sun angle has to be just right, but when the lighting conditions are perfect, you can follow otherwise invisible oil tankers on the Persian Gulf and trace major shipping lanes through the Mediterranean Sea. Similarly, when atmospheric conditions allow contrail formation, the thousand-mile-long condensation trails let astronauts trace the major air routes across the northern Pacific Ocean.

Literary Analysis
Expository Text
What relationship between space travel and ocean study does Ride discuss in this passage?

◄ Astronaut Sally Ride monitors control panels from the pilot's chair on the shuttle Columbia in June 1983.

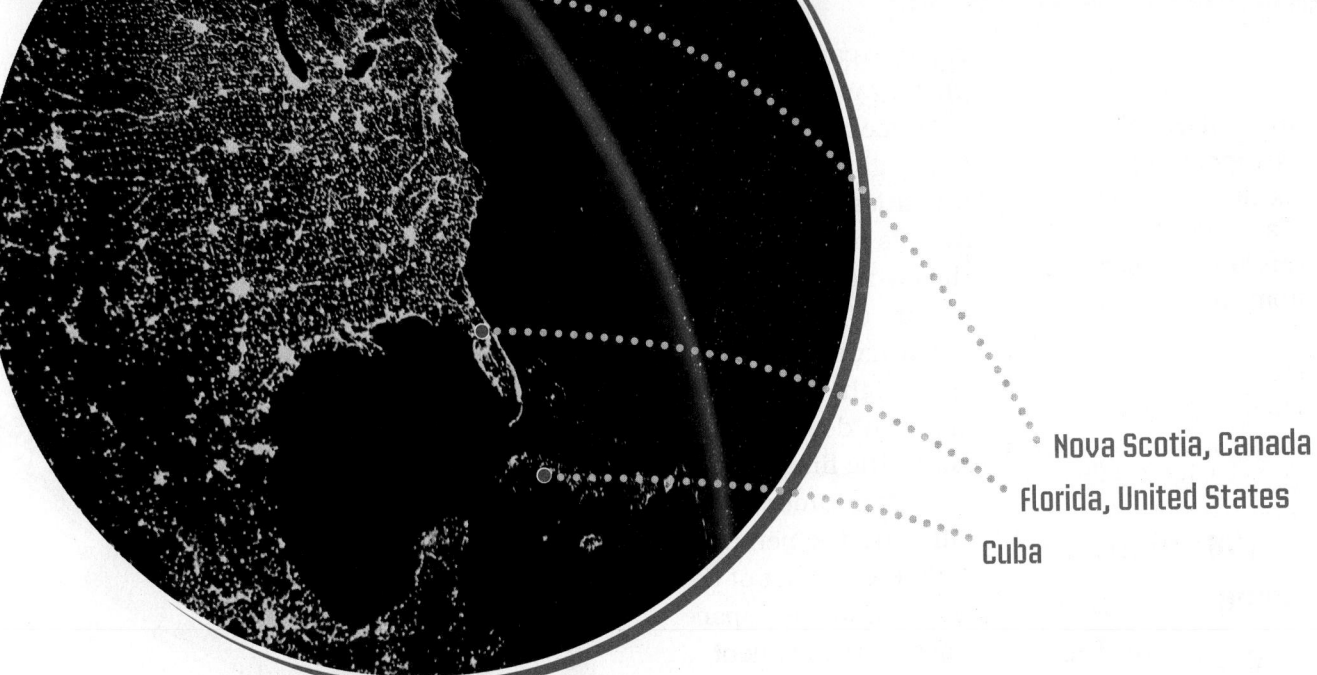

Nova Scotia, Canada
Florida, United States
Cuba

Part of every orbit takes us to the dark side of the planet. In space, night is very, very black—but that doesn't mean there's nothing to look at. The lights of cities sparkle; on nights when there was no moon, it was difficult for me to tell the Earth from the sky— the twinkling lights could be stars or they could be small cities. On one nighttime pass from Cuba to Nova Scotia, the entire East Coast of the United States appeared in twinkling outline.

When the moon is full, it casts an eerie light on the Earth. In its light, we see ghostly clouds and bright reflections on the water. One night, the Mississippi River flashed into view, and because of our viewing angle and orbital path, the reflected moonlight seemed to flow downstream—as if Huck Finn had tied a candle to his raft.

Of all the sights from orbit, the most spectacular may be the magnificent displays of lightning that ignite the clouds at night. On Earth, we see lightning from below the clouds; in orbit, we see it from above. Bolts of lightning are diffused by the clouds into bursting balls of light. Sometimes, when a storm extends hundreds of miles, it looks like a transcontinental brigade is tossing fireworks from cloud to cloud.

As the shuttle races the sun around the Earth, we pass from day to night and back again during a single orbit—hurtling into darkness, then bursting into daylight. The sun's appearance unleashes spectacular blue and orange bands along the horizon, a clockwork miracle that astronauts witness every 90 minutes. But I really can't describe a sunrise in orbit. The drama set against the black backdrop of space and the magic of the materializing colors

On one nighttime pass from Cuba to Nova Scotia, the entire East Coast of the United States appeared in twinkling outline.

Vocabulary
diffused (di fyoozd´)
v. spread out

Reading Check
What can astronauts see from space when the light is right?

Vocabulary
extrapolating
(ek strap´ ə lāt´ iŋ)
v. arriving at a
conclusion by inferring
from known facts

Part of the
fascination with
space travel is
the element of
the unknown...

can't be captured in an astronomer's equations or an astronaut's photographs.

I once heard someone (not an astronaut) suggest that it's possible to imagine what spaceflight is like by simply extrapolating from the sensations you experience on an airplane. All you have to do, he said, is mentally raise the airplane 200 miles, mentally eliminate the air noise and the turbulence, and you get an accurate mental picture of a trip in the space shuttle.

Not true. And while it's natural to try to liken spaceflight to familiar experiences, it can't be brought "down to Earth"— not in the final sense. The environment is different, the perspective is different. Part of the fascination with space travel is the element of the unknown— the conviction that it's different from earthbound experiences. And it is.

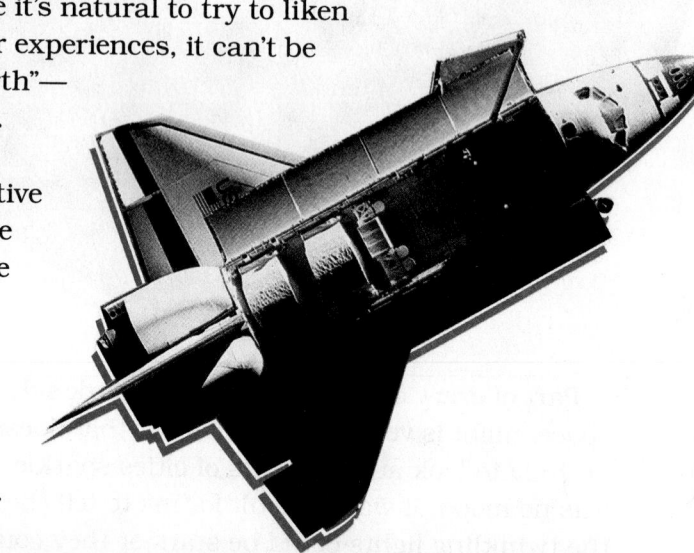

Critical Thinking

1. **Respond:** Based on Sally Ride's description of her experiences in space, would you like to be an astronaut? Why or why not?

2. **(a)** Which geological features did Ride observe from the shuttle in orbit? **(b) Interpret:** Why do you think Ride found it easier to imagine the workings of geological forces when she saw Earth from space?

3. **(a)** What "unfortunate effects" does Ride say she could see as she orbited Earth? **(b) Analyze:** Why would these effects make colors seen in 1983 seem not as bright as those seen ten years earlier?

4. **Assess:** Have Ride's descriptions of Earth changed the way you think about our planet? Explain your answer.

Is knowledge the same as understanding?
Does Ride's understanding of Earth change as a result of her experience on the space shuttle? Explain.

Support
your responses
with evidence
from the text.

After You Read

Single Room, Earth View

Literary Analysis: Expository Text

1. What is the purpose of Sally Ride's essay?

2. **(a)** What scientific data does Ride use to make her ideas clear to readers? **(b)** Does this text persuade you to have a certain opinion? Explain your response. **(c)** How might you extend or elaborate on Ride's ideas and share them with others?

3. **(a)** Using a chart like the one shown, analyze the text to identify passages in which Ride uses description, comparison and contrast, or cause and effect. Find one example of each technique.
(b) Explain how each example adds depth and context to the information Ride presents in that passage.

	Example	Effect
Description		
Comparison/Contrast		
Cause and Effect		

Reading Skill: Main Idea

4. Explain the **main, or controlling, idea** of the expository text, "Single Room, Earth View."

5. **(a)** List three **supporting details** that serve as evidence for the points that Sally Ride makes. **(b)** Do you think the author adequately supports her controlling idea with details? Explain.

Vocabulary

Practice Review the vocabulary list on page 466. Then, identify the word in each group that does not belong and explain your response.

1. articulate, eloquent, unclear
2. novice, expert, veteran
3. diffused, scattered, withheld
4. extrapolating, concluding, donating
5. surreal, odd, normal
6. muted, intense, vibrant

Word Power Use the context of the sentences and what you know about the **Latin root -nov-** to explain your answer to each question.

1. Is a *novel* idea common or unusual?
2. Why might a star that suddenly becomes much brighter be called a *nova*?

Word Power

The **Latin root -nov-** means "new" or "recent."

Apply It Explain how the root -nov- helps you determine the meanings of these words. Consult a dictionary if necessary.

novelty
innovation
renovate

Is *knowledge* the same as *understanding?*

The **News**

Neil Postman

Writing About the Big Question

In "The News," the author describes the pros and cons of television news. Use these sentence starters to develop your ideas about the Big Question.

We react in different ways to the presentation of news **information** on television and to the presentation in other media because _____.

Television news appeals to the viewers' **senses** by _____ and _____ .

As You Read Consider the writer's ideas about television news as a source of information. Then, determine whether he believes watching television news can lead to understanding.

Vocabulary

Read each word and its definition. Decide whether you know the word well, know it a little bit, or do not know it at all. After you read, see how your knowledge of each word has increased.

- **compensation** (käm´ pən sā´ shən) *n.* anything that makes up for a loss, damage, or debt (p. 478) *They ran out of prizes, so they gave free tickets as <u>compensation</u>. compensate v. compensatory adj.*

- **temporal** (tem´ pə rəl) *adj.* having to do with time (p. 478) *His persistent lateness suggests that he has no <u>temporal</u> sense. tempo n.*

- **medium** (mē´ dē əm) *n.* a particular way of communicating information and news to people, such as a newspaper or a television broadcast (p. 480) *Politicians prefer to use the <u>medium</u> of television. media n. pl.*

- **imposition** (im´ pə zish´ ən) *n.* the introduction of something such as a rule, tax, or punishment (p. 482) *The <u>imposition</u> of the tax on tea caused many colonists to rebel. imposing adj. impose v.*

- **revered** (ri vird´) *adj.* regarded with great respect and awe (p. 483) *Many students came to the retirement party for the <u>revered</u> teacher. revere v. reverence n.*

- **daunting** (dônt´ iŋ) *adj.* intimidating (p. 484) *Climbing Mount Everest is a <u>daunting</u> task. daunt v. dauntless adj.*

Word Power

The **Latin root -temp-** means "time."

In this selection, the author comments that film alone cannot accurately show the **temporal,** or time, aspects of events.

Meet
Neil Postman
(1931–2003)

Author of
The News

Neil Postman was a media critic and a revered professor of communications at New York University, where he taught for more than forty years. He called his field "media ecology," and his great concern was the effect of television on Americans.

Teachings on Television Born in New York, Postman received a doctorate in education from Columbia University. He also wrote twenty books and hundreds of articles. One of his most intense arguments is set forth in *The Disappearance of Childhood* (1982), in which he asserts that television exposes children to adult concerns far too early in their lives.

BACKGROUND FOR THE TEXT

(Social Studies Connection)

Television News

In 1948, only 400,000 American homes had a television. By 1960, more than 46 million American homes had a television, and TV began to take over as the news medium of choice. Today, television news is one of the most influential institutions in American culture.

Did You Know?

Postman once said, "You have to understand, what Americans do is watch television. I am not saying that's who they are. But that is what they do. Americans . . . watch . . . television."

The News

Neil Postman

Vocabulary

compensation
(käm´ pən sā´ shən)
n. anything that
makes up for a loss,
damage, or debt

temporal
(tem´ pə rəl) *adj.* having
to do with time

The whole problem with news on television comes down to this: all the words uttered in an hour of news coverage could be printed on one page of a newspaper. And the world cannot be understood in one page. Of course, there is a compensation: television offers pictures, and the pictures move. It is often said that moving pictures are a kind of language in themselves, and there is a good deal of truth in this. But the language of pictures differs radically from oral and written language, and the differences are crucial for understanding television news.

To begin with, the grammar of pictures is weak in communicating past-ness and present-ness. When terrorists want to prove to the world that their kidnap victims are still alive, they photograph them holding a copy of a recent newspaper. The dateline on the newspaper provides the proof that the photograph was taken on or after that date. Without the help of the written word, film and videotape cannot portray temporal dimensions with any precision. Consider a film clip showing an aircraft carrier at sea. One might be able to identify the ship as Soviet[1] or American, but there would be no way of telling where in the world the carrier was, where it was headed, or when the pictures were taken. It is only through language—words spoken over the pictures or reproduced in them—that the image of the aircraft carrier takes on meaning as a portrayal of a specific event.

---

1. Soviet (sō´ vē et´) *adj.* belonging to the Soviet Union, the formerly socialist nation of which the main part was Russia.

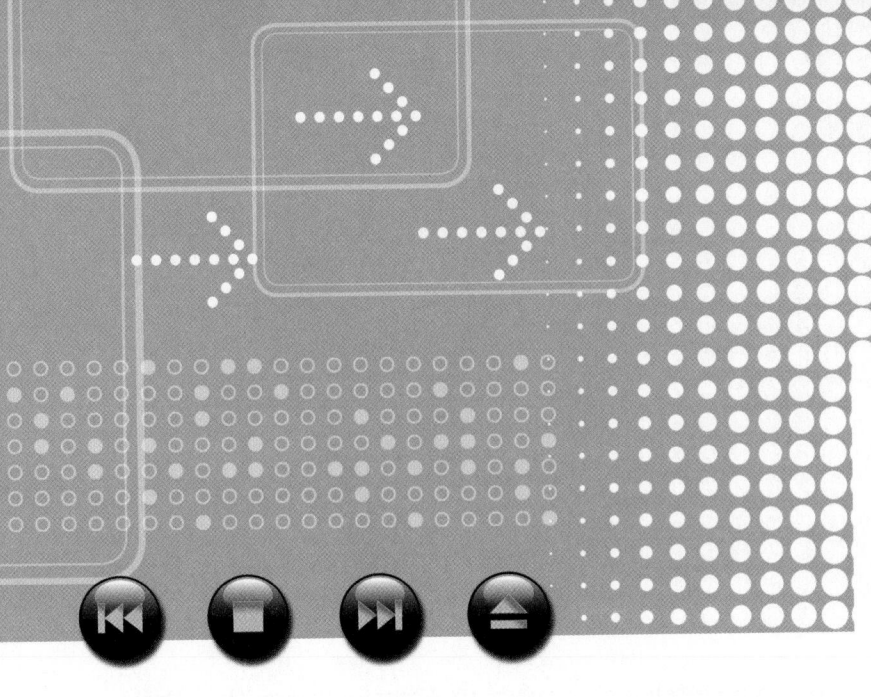

> But the language of pictures differs radically from oral and written language, and the differences are crucial for understanding television news.

Still, it is possible to enjoy the image of the carrier for its own sake. One might find the hugeness of the vessel interesting; it signifies military power on the move. There is a certain drama in watching the planes come in at high speeds and skid to a stop on the deck. Suppose the ship were burning: that would be even more interesting. This leads to a second point about the language of pictures. The grammar of moving pictures favors images that change. That is why violence and destruction find their way onto television so often. When something is destroyed violently its constitution is altered in a highly visible way: hence the entrancing power of fire. Fire gives visual form to the ideas of consumption, disappearance, death—the thing which is burned is actually taken away by fire. It is at this very basic level that fires make a good subject for television news. Something was here, now it's gone, and the change is recorded on film.

Earthquakes and typhoons have the same power: before the viewer's eyes the world is taken apart. If a television viewer has relatives in Mexico City and an earthquake occurs there, then she may take an interest in the images of destruction as a report from a specific place and time. That is, she may look to television news for information about an important event. But film of an earthquake can still be interesting if the viewer cares nothing about the event itself. Which is only to say that there is another way of participating in the news—as a spectator who desires to be entertained. Actually to see buildings topple is exciting, no matter where the buildings are. The world turns to dust before our eyes.

Literary Analysis
Expository Text
How do details about airplanes and fire support Postman's point that television favors change?

☑ Reading Check

What does Postman mean by the "grammar" of pictures?

Vocabulary
medium (mē´ dē əm)
n. a particular way
of communicating
information and news
to people, such as
a newspaper or a
television broadcast

Those who produce television news in America know that their
medium favors images that move. That is why they despise "talking
heads," people who simply appear in front of a camera and speak.
When talking heads appear on television, there is nothing to record
or document, no change in process. In the cinema the situation is
somewhat different. On a movie screen, close-ups of a good actor
speaking dramatically can sometimes be interesting to watch.
When Clint Eastwood narrows his eyes and challenges his rival
to shoot first, the spectator sees the cool rage of the Eastwood
character take visual form, and the narrowing of the eyes is
dramatic. But much of the effect of this small movement depends
on the size of the movie screen and the darkness of the theater,
which make Eastwood and his every action "larger than life."

The television screen is smaller than life. It occupies about 15
percent of the viewer's visual field (compared to about 70 percent for
the movie screen). It is not set in a darkened theater closed off from
the world but in the viewer's ordinary living space. This means that
visual changes must be more extreme and more dramatic to be
interesting on television. A narrowing of the eyes will not do. A car
crash, an earthquake, a burning factory are much better.

With these principles in mind, let us examine more closely the
structure of a typical newscast. In America, almost all news shows
begin with music, the tone of which suggests important events
about to unfold. (Beethoven's Fifth Symphony would be entirely
appropriate.) The music is very important, for it equates the news
with various forms of drama and ritual—the opera, for example,
or a wedding procession—in which musical themes underscore the
meaning of the event. Music takes us immediately into the realm

Literary Analysis
Expository Text
What topic will Postman
analyze more closely in
this text?

of the symbolic, a world that is not to be taken literally. After all, when events unfold in the real world, they do so without musical accompaniment. More symbolism follows. The sound of teletype machines can be heard in the studio, not because it is impossible to screen this noise out, but because the sound is a kind of music in itself. It tells us that data are pouring in from all corners of the globe, a sensation reinforced by the world map in the background (or clocks noting the time on different continents).

Already, then, before a single news item is introduced, a great deal has been communicated. We know that we are in the presence of a symbolic event, a form of theater in which the day's events are to be dramatized. This theater takes the entire globe as its subject, although it may look at the world from the perspective of a single nation. A certain tension is present, like the atmosphere in a theater just before the curtain goes up. The tension is represented by the music, the staccato beat of the teletype machines, and the sight of newsworkers scurrying around typing reports and answering phones. As a technical matter, it would be no problem to build a set in which the newsroom staff remained off camera, invisible to the viewer, but an important theatrical effect would be lost. By being busy on camera, the workers help communicate urgency about the events at hand, which it is suggested are changing so rapidly that constant revision of the news is necessary.

**Reading Skill
Main Idea**
Explain how these descriptive details support Postman's main, or controlling, idea—that a newscast is a form of theater.

The staff in the background also helps signal the importance of the person in the center, the anchorman (or -woman) "in command" of both the staff and the news. The anchorman plays the role of host. He welcomes us to the newscast and welcomes us back from the different locations we visit during filmed reports. His voice, appearance, and manner establish the mood of the broadcast. It would be unthinkable for the anchor to be ugly, or a nervous sort who could not complete a sentence. Viewers must be able to believe in the anchor as a person of authority and skill, a person who would not panic in a crisis—someone to trust.

> This theater takes the entire globe as its subject, although it may look at the world from the perspective of a single nation.

This belief is based not on knowledge of the anchorman's character or achievements as a journalist, but on his presentation of self while on the air. Does he look the part of a trusted man? Does he speak firmly and clearly? Does he have a warm smile? Does he project confidence without seeming arrogant? The value the anchor must communicate above all else is control. He must be in control of himself, his voice, his emotions. He must know what is coming next in the broadcast, and he must move smoothly and

**Reading
Check**
What are "talking heads" and why do television producers despise them?

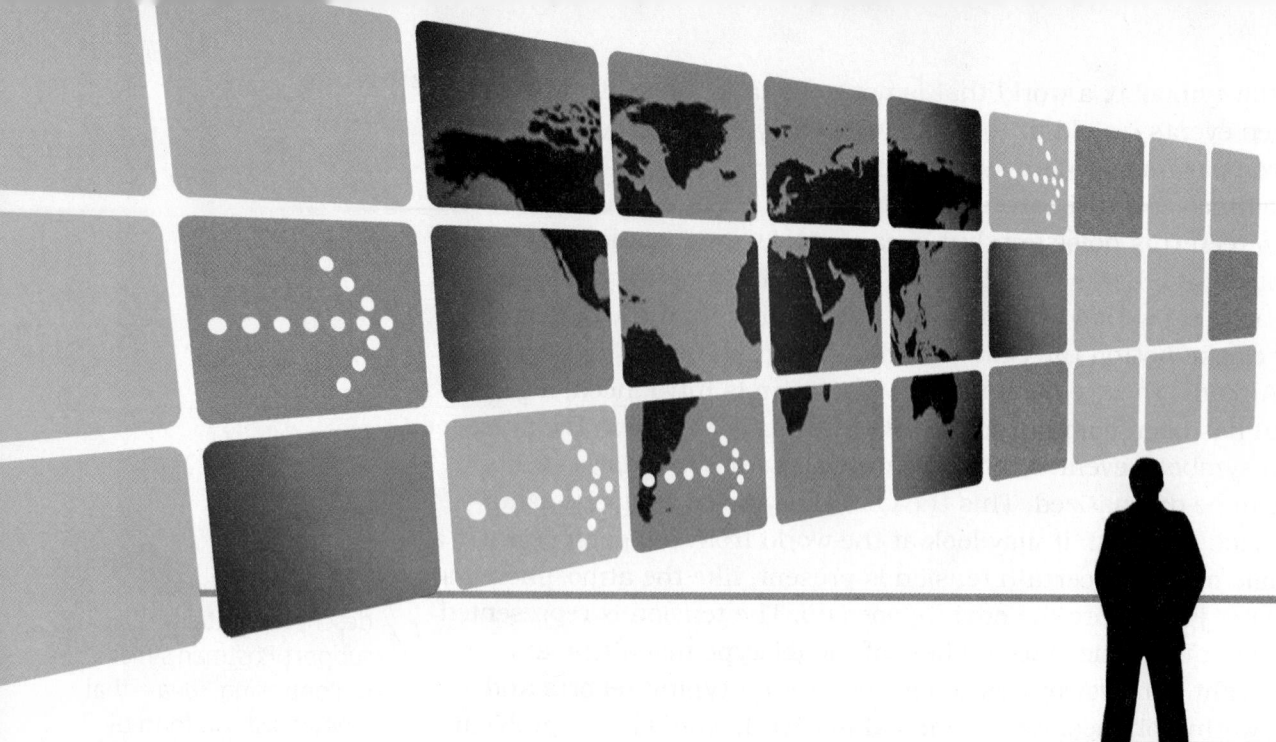

▲ **Critical Viewing**
How does this image relate to the idea of people connecting to their world through the news? **[Interpret]**

Vocabulary
imposition (im´ pə zish´ ən) *n.* the introduction of something such as a rule, tax, or punishment

confidently from segment to segment. Again, it would be unthinkable for the anchor to break down and weep over a story, or laugh uncontrollably on camera, no matter how "human" these responses may be.

Many other features of the newscast help the anchor to establish the impression of control. These are usually equated with professionalism in broadcasting. They include such things as graphics that tell the viewer what is being shown, or maps and charts that suddenly appear on the screen and disappear on cue, or the orderly progression from story to story, starting with the most important events first. They also include the absence of gaps or "deadtime" during the broadcast, even the simple fact that the news starts and ends at a certain hour. These common features are thought of as purely technical matters, which a professional crew handles as a matter of course. But they are also symbols of a dominant theme of television news: the imposition of an orderly world—called "the news"—upon the disorderly flow of events.

While the form of a news broadcast emphasizes tidiness and control, its content can best be described as chaotic. Because time is so precious on television, because the nature of the medium favors dynamic visual images, and because the pressures of a commercial structure require the news to hold its audience above all else, there is rarely any attempt to explain issues in depth or place events in their proper context. The news moves nervously from a warehouse fire to a court decision, from a guerrilla war to a World Cup match, the quality of the film often determining the length of the story. Certain stories show up only because they offer dramatic pictures. Bleachers collapse in South America: hundreds of people are crushed—a perfect television news story, for the cameras can record the face of disaster in all its anguish. Back in Washington, a new budget is approved by Congress. Here there is nothing to photograph because a budget is not a physical event; it is a document full of language and numbers. So the producers of the news will show a photo of the document itself, focusing on the cover where it says: "Budget of the United States of America." Or sometimes they will send a camera crew to the government printing plant where copies of the budget are produced. That evening, while the contents of the budget are summarized by a voice-over, the viewer sees stacks of documents being loaded into boxes at the government printing plant. Then a few of the budget's more important provisions will be flashed on the screen in written form, but this is such a time-consuming process—using television as a printed page—that the producers keep it to a minimum. In short, the budget is not televisable, and for that reason its time on the news must be brief. The bleacher collapse will get more minutes that evening.

With priorities of this sort, it is almost impossible for the news to offer an adequate account of important events. Indeed, it is the trivial event that is often best suited for television coverage. This is such a commonplace that no one even bothers to challenge it. Walter Cronkite, a revered figure in television and anchorman of the CBS Evening News for many years, has acknowledged several times that television cannot be relied on to inform the citizens of a democratic nation. Unless they also read newspapers and magazines, television viewers are helpless to understand their world, Cronkite has said. No one at CBS has ever disagreed with his conclusion, other than to say, "We do the best we can."

Of course, it is a tendency of journalism in general to concentrate on the surface of events rather than underlying conditions; this is as true for the newspaper as it is for the newscast. But several features of television undermine whatever efforts journalists may make to give sense to the world. One is that a television broadcast is a series of events that occur in sequence, and the sequence is the same for all viewers. This is not true for a newspaper page, which displays many items simultaneously, allowing readers to choose the order in which they read them. If a newspaper reader wants only a summary of the latest tax bill, he can read the headline and the first paragraph of an article, and if he wants more, he can keep reading. In a sense, then, everyone reads a different newspaper, for no two readers will read (or ignore) the same items.

Vocabulary
revered (ri vird´) *adj.* regarded with great respect and awe

Literary Analysis
Expository Text
According to Postman, how are newspaper and television journalism similar and different?

Reading
Check
According to Postman, why must a news anchorperson convey *control* above all other values?

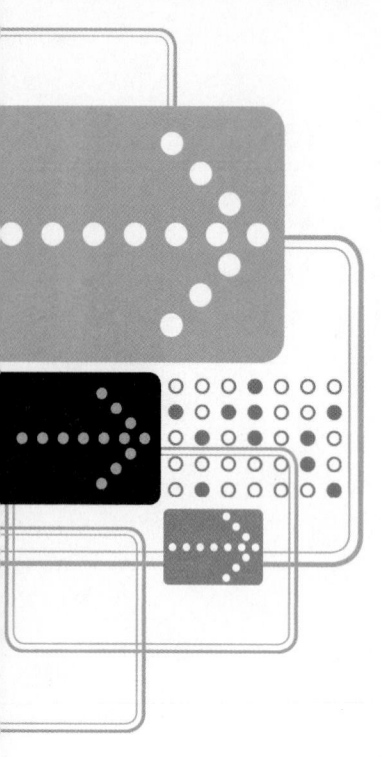

But all television viewers see the same broadcast. They have no choices. A report is either in the broadcast or out, which means that anything which is of narrow interest is unlikely to be included. As NBC News executive Reuven Frank once explained:

> A newspaper, for example, can easily afford to print an item of conceivable interest to only a fraction of its readers. A television news program must be put together with the assumption that each item will be of some interest to everyone that watches. Every time a newspaper includes a feature which will attract a specialized group it can assume it is adding at least a little bit to its circulation. To the degree a television news program includes an item of this sort . . . it must assume that its audience will diminish.

The need to "include everyone," an identifying feature of commercial television in all its forms, prevents journalists from offering lengthy or complex explanations, or from tracing the sequence of events leading up to today's headlines. One of the ironies of political life in modern democracies is that many problems which concern the "general welfare" are of interest only to specialized groups. Arms control, for example, is an issue that literally concerns everyone in the world, and yet the language of arms control and the complexity of the subject are so daunting that only a minority of people can actually follow the issue from week to week and month to month. If it wants to act responsibly, a newspaper can at least make available more information about arms control than most people want. But commercial television cannot afford to do so.

This illustrates an important point in the psychology of television's appeal. Many of the items in newspapers and magazines are not, in a strict sense, demanded by a majority of readers. They are there because some readers might be interested or because the editors think their readers should be interested. On commercial television, "might" and "should" are not the relevant words. The producers attempt to make sure that "each item will be of some interest to everyone that watches," as Reuven Frank put it. What this means is that a newspaper or magazine can challenge its audience in a way that television cannot. Print media have the luxury of suggesting or inviting interest, whereas television must always concern itself with conforming to existing interests. In a way, television is more strictly responsive to the demands of its huge audience. But there is one demand it cannot meet: the desire to be challenged, to be told "this is worth attending to," to be surprised by what one thought would not be of interest.

Vocabulary
daunting (dônt´ iŋ)
adj. intimidating

Another severe limitation on television is time. There is simply not enough of it. The evening news programs at CBS, NBC, and ABC all run for thirty minutes, eight of which are taken up by commercials. No one believes that twenty-two minutes for the day's news is adequate. For years news executives at ABC, NBC, and CBS have suggested that the news be expanded to one hour. But by tradition the half-hour after the national evening news is given over to the hundreds of local affiliate stations around the country to use as they see fit. They have found it a very profitable time to broadcast game shows or half-hour situation comedies, and they are reluctant to give up the income they derive from these programs.

The evening news produced by the three networks is profitable for both the networks and the local stations. The local stations are paid a fee by the network to broadcast the network news, and they profit from this fee since the news—produced by the network—costs them nothing. It is likely that they would also make money from a one-hour newscast, but not as much, they judge, as they do from the game shows and comedies they now schedule.

> The result is that the evening news must try to do what cannot reasonably be done: give a decent account of the day's events in twenty-two minutes.

The result is that the evening news must try to do what cannot reasonably be done: give a decent account of the day's events in twenty-two minutes. What the viewer gets instead is a series of impressions, many of them purely visual, most of them unconnected to each other or to any sense of a history unfolding. Taken together, they suggest a world that is fundamentally ungovernable, where events do not arise out of historical conditions but rather explode from the heavens in a series of disasters that suggest a permanent state of crisis. It is this crisis—highly visual, ahistorical, and unsolvable—which the evening news presents as theater every evening.

The audience for this theater is offered a contradictory pair of responses. On the one hand, it is reassured by the smooth presentation of the news itself, especially the firm voice and steady gaze of the trusty anchorman. Newscasts frequently end with a "human-interest story," often with a sentimental or comic touch.

Literary Analysis
Expository Text
What sense of the world does television news cause?

Reading Check
According to Postman, why are television news broadcasts so short?

Example: a little girl in Chicago writes Gorbachev a letter, and he answers her, saying that he and President Reagan are trying to work out their differences. This item reassures viewers that all is well, leaders are in command, we can still communicate with each other, and so on. But—and now we come to the other hand—the rest of the broadcast has told a different story. It has shown the audience a world that is out of control and incomprehensible, full of violence, disaster, and suffering. Whatever authority the anchorman may project through his steady manner is undermined by the terror inspired by the news itself.

This is where television news is at its most radical—not in giving publicity to radical causes, but in producing the impression of an ungovernable world. And it produces this impression not because the people who work in television are leftists or anarchists.[2] The anarchy in television news is a direct result of the commercial structure of broadcasting, which introduces into news judgments a single-mindedness more powerful than any ideology: the overwhelming need to keep people watching.

---

2. **leftists . . . anarchists** (an´ ər kists´) leftists desire to change the existing political order in the name of greater freedom for all; anarchists oppose any political authority.

Critical Thinking

1. **Respond:** Do you agree with Postman about the limitations of television? Why or why not?

2. **(a)** According to Postman, what elements make a news broadcast like a form of theater? **(b) Make Inferences:** What problem does Postman see in the similarity between television news and theater?

3. **(a)** What type of role is an anchorperson supposed to play while broadcasting? **(b) Draw Conclusions:** How does the impression created by the anchor relate to the "radical" nature of television?

Support your responses with evidence from the text.

4. **(a)** How long do people in the news business feel the evening news broadcast should have to present the news?
(b) Cause and Effect: What effects do time limits have on television news?

Is knowledge the same as understanding?
(a) What does the writer believe about television news as a source of information? **(b)** How does our knowledge of the news affect our understanding of the world? **(c)** How does the changing nature of the news affect this understanding?

Literary Analysis: **Expository Text**

1. What is the purpose of Neil Postman's essay?

2. **(a)** What quotations does Postman use to make his ideas clear to readers? **(b)** Does this text persuade you to have a certain opinion? Explain your response. **(c)** How might you extend or elaborate on Postman's ideas and share them with others?

3. **(a)** Using a chart like the one shown, analyze the text to identify passages in which Postman uses description, comparison and contrast, or cause and effect. Find one example of each technique. **(b)** Explain how each example adds depth and context to the information Postman presents in that passage.

	Example	Effect
Description		
Comparison/Contrast		
Cause and Effect		

Reading Skill: **Main Idea**

4. Explain the **main, or controlling, idea** of the expository text, "The News."

5. **(a)** List three **supporting details** that serve as evidence for the points that Neil Postman makes. **(b)** Do you think the author adequately supports his controlling idea with details? Explain.

Vocabulary

Practice Review the vocabulary list on page 476. Then, identify the word in each group that does not belong and explain your response.

1. compensation, repayment, donation

2. temporal, timed, severe

3. revered, scorned, ridiculed

4. daunting, challenging, tempting

5. medium, magazine, memory

6. law, imposition, stamp

Word Power Use the context of the sentences and what you know about the **Latin root -*temp*-** to explain your answer to each question.

1. Why is it essential for a musician to keep a *tempo*?

2. For how long might a *temporary* job last?

Word Power

The **Latin root -*temp*-** means "time."

Apply It Explain how the root -*temp*- helps you determine the meanings of these words. Consult a dictionary if necessary.

temporize
extemporaneous
contemporary

Integrated Language Skills

Single Room, Earth View • The News

Conventions: Predicate Nominatives and Predicate Adjectives

A **subject** is the word or group of words that tell whom or what a sentence is about.

A **predicate** is the verb or verb phrase that tells what the subject of a sentence does or is.

A **predicate nominative** renames the subject of a sentence.

The predicate nominative follows a linking verb and *renames, identifies, or explains* the subject of the sentence. In a sentence with a predicate nominative, the linking verb acts as an equal sign between the subject and the predicate nominative.

A **predicate adjective** is an adjective that appears with a linking verb and *describes* the subject of a sentence.

	Example	Explanation
Predicate Nominative	The winner of the tournament is our *team*.	*Team* renames *winner*.
	That player was the *star*.	*Star* renames *player*.
Predicate Adjective	The swimmer was *fast*.	*Fast* describes *swimmer*.
	Josh is very *clever*.	*Clever* describes *Josh*.

Practice A Identify the predicate nominatives and predicate adjectives in the following sentences.

1. Sally Ride was the first woman astronaut to join the NASA program.
2. The space shuttle is a plane capable of flying into space.
3. As seen from space, Earth is beautiful.
4. Space is a vast new frontier.

Reading Application In "Single Room, Earth View," find one sentence with a predicate nominative and one with a predicate adjective.

Practice B Add a predicate nominative or a predicate adjective as indicated to complete the sentence.

1. The news anchor is _____. (predicate nominative)
2. That film was _____. (predicate adjective)
3. Media, such as television, tend to be _____. (predicate adjective)

Writing Application Write four sentences about television. Use predicate nominatives in two of the sentences and use predicate adjectives in two of the sentences.

PH GRAMMAR HANDBOOK Further instruction and practice are available in the *Prentice Hall Grammar Handbook*.

Writing

Write a **script for a public service announcement** in which you highlight the rewards of a certain profession. If you read "Single Room, Earth View," write a script that NASA might use to attract candidates. If you read "The News," write a script that promotes careers in journalism.

As you prepare your script:

- Note details that contribute to a **definitive mood** or **tone** and an **explicit theme** or message.
- Describe visual elements that will help create a persuasive message.
- Structure your ideas to persuade people to take action.

Grammar Application Make sure to use predicate nominatives and predicate adjectives correctly as you draft your script.

Writing Workshop: *Work in Progress*

Prewriting for Business Letter From your writing portfolio, review the Questions List you generated. Answer each question using specific evidence from your experience. Save your Questions List in your portfolio.

Research and Technology

Using library and Internet resources, conduct research based on the following assignment choices and write two **journal entries.**

- If you read "Single Room, Earth View," research the training that astronauts undergo. Based on this information, write two journal entries that an astronaut might write while in training.
- If you read "The News," research the work television journalists do to prepare a news story. Then, write two journal entries a reporter might write while working on a story.

Consider these tips as you **formulate and follow a plan** for engaging in research on the many facets, or aspects, of your complex topic:

- Evaluate the **relevance** of the information. Then, use only the information that strongly relates to your topic.
- Examine the authority and objectivity of your sources, both on paper and from the Internet. Are they the best sources of information? Do they have points of view that might affect the information they provide? Use what you know about the sources to determine their **reliability, validity, and accuracy.**
- Choose a workable organization as you write your journal entries.

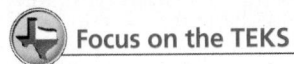 Focus on the TEKS

Writing
(14)(C) Write a script with an explicit theme and details that contribute to a definite mood or tone.

Research
(20)(B) Formulate a plan for engaging in research.
(22)(B) Evaluate the relevance of information to the topic and determine the reliability, validity, and accuracy of sources by examining their authority and objectivity.

Use this prewriting activity to prepare for the **Writing Workshop** on page 512.

www.PHLitOnline.com

- Interactive graphic organizers
- Grammar tutorial
- Interactive journals

Strategy for Success

Controlling Idea

Focus on the TEKS

Reading
(8) Explain the controlling idea and specific purpose of an expository text and distinguish the most important from the less important details that support the author's purpose.

Comprehension
RC-9(B) Make complex inferences about text.

The reading sections of Texas standardized tests may ask you to understand a text's controlling idea—the central message, insight, or main idea. You can use supporting details in the text to make complex inferences about the controlling idea of an expository text on standardized tests.

As you read, consider what the author wants you to learn. If a passage does not have a title, write one. Your title will point you toward the controlling idea. Distinguishing the most important details from the less important details will also help you to analyze the controlling idea. Look for common ideas or topics in the most important details to help you infer the controlling idea. The following examples show how you can determine the controlling idea on standardized tests.

Think of a Title

To monitor your comprehension, think of a title for the passage that describes its content clearly. The title should help you identify the controlling idea of the passage.

1   Every year about 300,000 bicycle accidents involve young people. Simple steps can help keep you safe. Wear a sturdy helmet and bright clothes.

   1 This selection is mainly about —
   A bicycling accidents
   B the right cycling clothes
   C how to wear a bicycle helmet correctly
   D the importance of bicycle safety

You might give this passage the title, "Preventing Biking Accidents." Because **A** is not supported by all of the sentences, it cannot be the controlling idea. **B** and **C** also refer to passage details, not to the controlling idea. **D,** the correct answer, is closest to the made-up title, and it expresses the overall message supported by the details in the text.

Distinguish Important Details

Identify the most important details and facts that explain or illustrate a particular idea. The most important details relate directly to the controlling idea.

1   Time management has many advantages. It can reduce stress and help you get more done. To manage your time, you can make to-do lists, and you can prioritize tasks.

   2 Which detail best supports the controlling idea of the paragraph?
   F *Time management has many advantages.*
   G *It can reduce stress and help you get more done.*
   H *You can make to-do lists.*
   J *You can prioritize tasks.*

Because **F** states the controlling idea, it is not a supporting detail. **H** and **J** do not directly support the idea. **G** lists some advantages of time management; it is an important supporting detail and the correct answer.

Texas Test Practice

Read this selection. Then answer the questions that follow it. Answer question 4 on a separate sheet of paper.

The New, Active Video Games

1   A gamer sits still, frantically pressing buttons on a hand-held controller: This is the traditional way video games are played. But this unhealthful style of gaming is changing, with new video games that get gamers moving, improving their fitness as they rack up points and unlock hidden levels.

2   In one popular fitness-oriented game, players don't hold a controller in their hands at all. Instead, they step back and forth on squares on a special floor mat, matching sequences flashed on a screen in time to music. Gamers work up a sweat as they move their feet.

3   Realizing the benefits of these active games, physical-education classes in schools across the nation are beginning to use them to teach students about fitness. Teachers say the video games are accessible because they appeal to a wide range of students, are easy to learn, and require no special skills. In addition, they are less competitive than traditional team sports. These teachers conclude that when students can easily participate in a fun game to try to top their own best scores, they truly enjoy their workouts and are encouraged to include fitness in their daily lives.

1 Paragraph 2 is mainly about —
   A why fitness is important
   B whether or not the new games get players moving
   C why video games are changing
   D how one particular fitness video game is played

2 Which detail supports the idea that fitness video games are not competitive?
   F The games appeal to a wide range of players.
   G Players only try to top their own scores.
   H The games help students enjoy exercise.
   J Gamers work up a sweat.

3 Which sentence best conveys the controlling idea of the selection?
   A Video games are an unhealthful activity.
   B Students prefer activities that are not competitive.
   C New video games improve players' fitness.
   D Schools are including video games in their classes.

4 Why are some schools using video games in their physical-education classes? Support your answer with evidence from the selection.

Informational Texts

Expository Texts

Technical Document
Space Shuttle Basics

News Article
Atlantis to Blast Off on First Flight. . .

Blog Entries
Live From Kennedy Space Center

 Focus on the TEKS

Reading

(9)(D) Synthesize and make logical connections between ideas and details in several texts selected to reflect a range of viewpoints on the same topic and support those findings with textual evidence.

(11)(B) Analyze technical data presented in multiple graphical sources.

(12)(C) Compare and contrast coverage of the same event in various media.

Writing

(13)(B) Develop drafts in timed situations that include transitions used to convey meaning.

Reading Skill: Connect and Synthesize Ideas

As you read texts on related topics, even if those texts are written from different viewpoints, you may find that the writers refer to some of the same information or ideas. You can **connect** and **synthesize** ideas and details from the texts to build your understanding. To connect ideas and details, read the various sources, including any **technical data** that may be included in **graphical sources.** Look for pieces of information that logically relate to each other. Then, synthesize those ideas and details by considering them as a group and combining them to form an over-arching idea that is not directly stated in any of the texts.

The three expository texts that follow reflect a range of viewpoints on the National Aeronautics and Space Administration's (NASA) space shuttle program.

As You Read Use a chart like the one shown to record ideas and details that appear across the texts. Be sure to include **technical data** presented in **graphical sources.** Use your completed chart to synthesize and make logical connections between ideas and details in the texts, supporting your ideas with textual evidence.

Information or Idea	Technical Document	News Article	Blog Entries
space shuttle fuel tank	paragraph 3, statistics chart, labeled diagram	paragraph 6	

This chart is a graphical source. **Analyze the technical data. What types of information are presented? Synthesize and make logical connections between these ideas and details about the shuttle's size and power and the descriptions of Atlantis in the news article.**

NATIONAL AERONAUTICS AND SPACE ADMINISTRATION

Features:

- technical language and data
- specifications and other facts
- diagrams and other graphical sources

Space Shuttle Basics

Shuttle Statistics

Length	
Space shuttle: 56.14 meters (184.2 feet) Orbiter: 37.23 meters (122.17 feet)	
Height	
Orbiter on runway: 17.27 meters (56.67 feet)	
Wingspan	
23.79 meters (78.06 feet)	
Weight*	
At liftoff: 2,041,166 kilograms (4.5 million pounds)	
End of mission: 104,326 kilograms (230,000 pounds)	
Maximum cargo to orbit	
28,803 kilograms (63,500 pounds)	
SRB separation	
Two minutes after launch	
External tank separation	
8.5 minutes after launch Altitude: 109.26 kilometers (59 nautical miles) Velocity: 28,067 kph (17,440 mph)	
Orbit	
185 to 643 kilometers (115 to 400 statute miles) Velocity: 27,875 kph (17,321 mph)	

*weight will vary depending on payloads and onboard consumables.

The space shuttle is the world's first reusable spacecraft, and the first spacecraft in history that can carry large satellites both to and from orbit. The shuttle launches like a rocket, maneuvers in Earth orbit like a spacecraft, and lands like an airplane. Each of the three space shuttle orbiters now in operation— *Discovery, Atlantis* and *Endeavour*— is designed to fly at least 100 missions. So far, altogether they have flown a combined total of less than one-fourth of that.

Columbia was the first space shuttle orbiter to be delivered to NASA's Kennedy Space Center, Fla., in March 1979. *Columbia* and the STS-107 crew were lost Feb. 1, 2003, during re-entry. The orbiter *Challenger* was delivered to KSC in July 1982 and was destroyed in an explosion during ascent in January 1986. *Discovery* was delivered in November 1983. *Atlantis* was delivered in April 1985. *Endeavour* was built as a replacement following the *Challenger* accident and was delivered to Florida in May 1991. An early space shuttle orbiter, the *Enterprise*, never flew in space but was used for approach and landing tests at the Dryden Flight Research Center and several launch-pad studies in the late 1970s.

The space shuttle consists of three major components: the orbiter, which houses the crew; a large external fuel tank that holds fuel for the main engines; and two solid rocket boosters, which provide most of the shuttle's lift during the first two minutes of flight. All of the components are reused except for the external fuel tank, which burns up in the atmosphere after each launch.

The technical document discusses the major components of a space shuttle. **Connect and synthesize these ideas and details with the content about the structure of Atlantis in the news article and support your findings with textual evidence.**

These diagrams are graphical sources. **Analyze and make logical connections between the ideas and details in the diagrams and those presented in other graphical sources in these texts. Then, synthesize the ideas and details in the diagrams with information from the other sources to write a brief description of Atlantis' main components.**

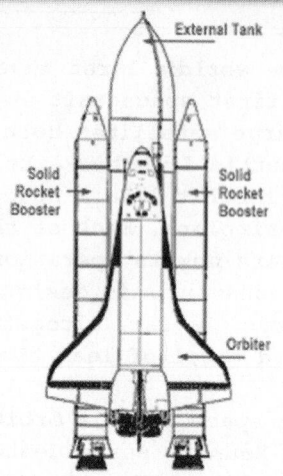

External Tank

Solid Rocket Booster

Solid Rocket Booster

Orbiter

Space Shuttle
(launch configuration)

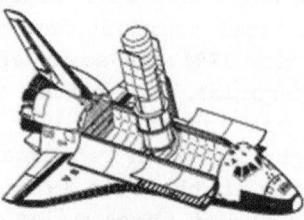

orbiter flight configuration
(w/satellite in payload bay)

The text discusses safety during shuttle launches. **Connect and synthesize these details and ideas with the content about safety in other texts. Support your findings with textual evidence.**

The longest the shuttle has stayed in orbit on any single mission is 17.5 days on mission STS-80 in November 1996. Normally, missions may be planned for anywhere from 5 to 16 days in duration. The smallest crew ever to fly on the shuttle numbered two people on the first few missions. The largest crew numbered eight people. Normally, crews may range in size from five to seven people. The shuttle is designed to reach orbits ranging from about 185 kilometers to 643 kilometers (115 statute miles to 400 statute miles) high.

The shuttle has the most reliable launch record of any rocket now in operation. Since 1981, it has boosted more than 1.36 million kilograms (3 million pounds) of cargo into orbit. More than 600 crew members have flown on its missions. Although it has been in operation for almost 20 years, the shuttle has continually evolved and is significantly different today than when it first was launched. NASA has made literally thousands of major and minor modifications to the original design that have made it safer, more reliable, and more capable today than ever before.

Since 1992 alone, NASA has made engine and system improvements that are estimated to have tripled the safety of flying the space shuttle, and the number of problems experienced while a space shuttle is in flight has decreased by 70 percent. During the same period, the cost of operating the shuttle has decreased by one and a quarter billion dollars annually—a reduction of more than 40 percent. At the same time, because of weight reductions and other improvements, the cargo the shuttle can carry has increased by 7.3 metric tons (8 tons).

NASA is prepared to continue flying the shuttle for at least the next decade and plans to continue to improve the shuttle during the next five years, with goals of increasing its safety by improving the highest-risk components. NASA will also be working with the Columbia Accident Investigation Board to correct any problems the board may find as it works to determine the cause of the *Columbia* accident.

In managing and operating the space shuttle, NASA holds the safety of the crew as its highest priority.

THE BIG

Is knowledge the same as understanding?
How does connecting and synthesizing ideas help you understand the work that goes into a shuttle launch? Explain.

News Article

Features:

- information on a current event
- background and quotations that clarify the topic
- text written for a general audience

El Paso Times

Atlantis to blast off on first flight of the year (4:10 P.M.)

June 8, 2007

CAPE CANAVERAL, Fla.—Seven astronauts today climbed aboard a patched-up Atlantis for the first space shuttle flight of 2007—a mission that was delayed by a damaging hailstorm.

The shuttle was set to blast off at 7:38 P.M. on a mission to continue building the international space station.

Astronaut Danny Olivas used sign language to say, "I love you" before crawling into the spacecraft and getting strapped in.

The forecast looked great and the countdown appeared trouble-free except for the discovery of a loose pipe clamp on the launch platform. Technicians considered trying to screw it down but ultimately decided it was safe to leave it alone.

During the 11-day flight, Atlantis' astronauts will deliver a new segment and a pair of solar panels to the orbiting outpost. They will also swap out a member of the space station's crew.

The mission was delayed for three months after a freak storm at the launch pad hurled golf-ball-size hail at Atlantis' 154-foot fuel tank, putting thousands of pockmarks in its vital insulating foam and one of the orbiter's wings.

Although the repaired burnt-orange tank was splotched with so many white patches today it looked like a beat-up old car that had undergone bodywork in someone's garage, officials said it was safe.

"We have done extensive tests and analysis," said LeRoy Cain, launch integration manager.

NASA has not had a shuttle launch since December.

After the hailstorm, Atlantis was rolled back to the hangar, and the space agency decided to sand down and patch the gouge marks with foam rather than swap out the entire tank.

The foam has been of paramount concern to NASA ever since the Columbia disaster in 2003, when a chunk of the insulating material broke off during liftoff and gashed a wing, allowing fiery gases to penetrate the shuttle during its return to Earth. All seven astronauts aboard were killed.

The hailstorm forced NASA to reduce the number of shuttle missions in 2007 from five to four.

The space agency hopes to fly at least 12 construction missions besides this one to the space station, and also plans to send a crew to repair the Hubble Space Telescope before the shuttle fleet is retired in 2010.

Atlantis' crew is led by commander Rick Sturckow. The other members are pilot Lee Archambault and mission specialists Patrick Forrester, Steven Swanson, Danny Olivas, James Reilly and Clayton Anderson. It is the first all-male crew at launch since 2002.

Anderson will replace astronaut Sunita Williams as the U.S. representative aboard the space station, and Williams will return to Earth aboard Atlantis after six months in orbit.

Danny Olivas, astronaut and El Paso native

Copyright © 2007 El Paso Times, a MediaNews Group Newspaper.

Both this news article and the technical document mention *Columbia*. **Write a brief paragraph in which you connect the writers' ideas about the accident.**

The article provides details about the crew. **Synthesize and make logical connections between these ideas and details and information in the technical document that focuses on the crew. Explain what the crew should expect on this mission and how this crew may differ from previous shuttle crews.**

THE BIG ? **Is knowledge the same as understanding?** How might understanding the dangers of space flight differ from having a knowledge of the dangers of space flight?

TEXAS

Features:

- journal-like entries (posts) published on a Web page
- text written for the public, especially readers with an interest in the topic
- mix of facts and personal thoughts

El Paso News

REPORTER'S NOTEBOOK:
Live From Kennedy Space Center

The following are thoughts from KFOX News Reporter Daniel Novick during his recent trip to Kennedy Space Center in Cape Canaveral, Fla. All times are in Eastern Standard Time.

Friday, June 8th, 2007—Launch Day

11:00 A.M. Joe and I didn't get to have breakfast, so by now we are starving. Off to the NASA cafeteria, a 10-minute walk from the press site. I can't emphasize enough how neat it is to be walking on the grounds of Kennedy Space Center, with a badge around my neck giving me access to this rare opportunity.

6:48 P.M. The weather is magnificent at Kennedy Space Center. I am told by the local news media that this is a rarity this time of year. The weather is not so good in Spain. Now why should I care about that? There are two places in Spain, Zaragosa and Moron, that if for one reason or another the space shuttle needs to abort its mission during the first critical few minutes of flight, they would be over Europe at that time, particularly Spain. But if the weather is bad in Spain, they can't abort there. No abort site, no go for launch.

7:36 P.M. John and Liz on the desk back in El Paso go back out to me one more time before the launch. I must now talk for the next two minutes without going over, because who really wants to see me talking while the space shuttle is lifting off behind me. Joe is counting me down, and faster then I realize, we are at T-minus 15 seconds. I stop talking, and become a viewer, just like you.

7:38 P.M. Lift off. From our vantage point, all we see a plume of smoke. Then the shuttle begins to appear above a fire that was brighter then I ever expected. This was the most vibrant yellow and orange I have ever seen in my life. Bright does not describe how bright it was. That was just one of the surprises of seeing it in person. The next was you see the huge smoke, and the shuttle beginning to rise, but you hear nothing. It is the serenity that you would find at any natural wildlife refuge like Kennedy Space Center is. Then you hear cheering from nearly every direction, which is quickly drowned out by the loudness of the shuttle launch. For about 15 seconds it sounds like a large number of jets all going at once, followed by a consistent popping sound. I described it like a million bags of popcorn setting off all at the same time. Even three miles away, the ground shakes like an earthquake, and that popping sound can be felt on your clothing. It is a wild experience.

I wish I could describe it to you more, but really it is indescribable. I am in the business of using words and talking, but there are just some things where words don't do justice. A space shuttle launch is one of those things.

> Here, the text mentions the launch. **Connect this entry to an earlier text. Synthesize the ideas and details presented to formulate an idea about the shuttle's "reliable launch record," mentioned in the technical document.**

> One of the other texts also describes a lift-off. **What idea about lift-offs can you synthesize by connecting the texts?**

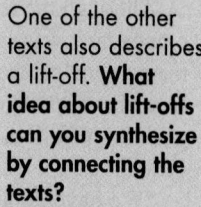

Is knowledge the same as understanding?
This writer shares some knowledge about shuttle flights. How well do you think he understands it? Explain.

TEXAS

Comparing Informational Texts

(a) Analyze: Compare and contrast the coverage of the shuttle launch in the news article and in the blog entries. **(b)** Think about the information in all three texts. Then, **connect and synthesize** those ideas and details into a new idea about the space shuttle program—one that did not occur to you before you read these texts. Write that idea in a single sentence.

 College Readiness | Timed Writing

Write an Explanatory Essay

Format
The prompt gives specific directions regarding the topic. It also offers guidance about using the texts to form and support your ideas.

Write an essay in which you explain the importance of safety in the building and launching of space shuttles. Consider the welfare of the astronauts as well as the timing of launches. In your essay, synthesize and make logical connections between the ideas and details in all three texts and support those findings with textual evidence. (35 minutes)

Academic Vocabulary
When you *support findings with textual evidence,* you use examples, ideas, and quotations from a text to prove or explain your conclusions.

 5-Minute Planner

Complete these steps before you begin to write:

1. Read the prompt carefully and completely.

2. Review the texts, making notes about ideas and details related to safety. **TIP** Be sure to **analyze any technical data presented in graphical sources** and include these details in your notes.

3. Review your notes. What main idea about safety do they suggest? Create a main idea statement for your essay.

4. Plan the organizing structure for your essay. For example, you might first discuss overall mission safety and then the safety of the astronauts. You might instead begin by discussing past challenges to safety and then NASA's improvements. Whichever structure you choose, make sure that when you develop your draft, you **include transitions that convey meaning**—helping readers to understand your logic.

5. Refer to your notes and organizational plans as you draft your essay.

Comparing Biographical Writing

Biographical writing is a form of nonfiction in which a writer tells the life story of another person. Biographies are often structured to focus on one or more of the aspects of a subject's life. Factual information is important, but a good biographer also interprets the facts, showing why an understanding of the subject's life is meaningful.

In biographical writing, the details that a writer chooses establish a **tone**—the writer's attitude toward the subject. The use of tone affects our impression of the subject, but a writer's tone is not stated as one piece of information. Therefore, when reading a biography, as well as other nonfiction works, take note of the details the author includes and consider how that information works together to reveal the author's tone.

As You Read Make a chart like this one to note details that describe specific aspects of each subject's life. Then, use your work to **make complex inferences** about each writer's tone, or attitude toward his subject. Use **textual evidence from the chart to support your understanding.**

Details about . . .	Lincoln	Ashe
Personality		
Upbringing		
Relationships		
Life events		
Role in major events		
Influence on others		
My inference about author's tone		

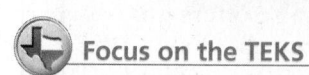
Focus on the TEKS

Comprehension
RC-9(B) Make complex inferences about text and use textual evidence to support understanding.

Writing
(13)(B) Develop drafts in timed situations that include transitions used to convey meaning.

TEXAS
PHLitOnline
www.PHLitOnline.com

- Vocabulary flashcards
- Interactive journals
- More about the authors
- Selection audio
- Interactive graphic organizers

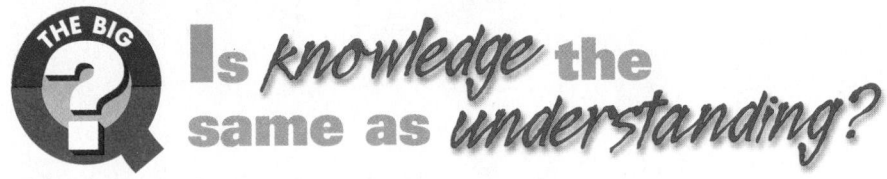

Is *knowledge* the same as *understanding?*

Writing About the Big Question

Each of these biographers provides factual details to help readers understand the essence of his subject. Use this sentence starter to develop your ideas about the Big Question.

When I read to learn about someone, I expect to find out _____, _____, and _____.

Meet the Authors

Carl Sandburg (1878–1967)

Author of *A Lincoln Preface*

Between the ages of thirteen and twenty, Carl Sandburg worked as a porter, scene changer, truck handler, dishwasher, and farm worker. Sandburg served briefly in Puerto Rico during the Spanish-American War, which brought on the strong antiwar feelings he would hold throughout his life.

Childhood Favorite Even as a child, Sandburg was fascinated by Abraham Lincoln. For thirty years, he collected material about Lincoln, and his single-mindedness paid off. Sandburg's six-volume work about Lincoln is considered the definitive biography.

John McPhee (b. 1931)

Author of "Arthur Ashe Remembered"

John McPhee's big break as a writer came in 1965, when *The New Yorker* magazine published his profile of Princeton basketball star Bill Bradley. That profile, which became the basis for McPhee's first book, combined two of the author's great loves: sports and his hometown of Princeton, New Jersey, where he still lives today.

Broader Interests McPhee continues to write about sports, but he has broadened his subject matter to include the natural world, with books on Alaska, whales, and North American geology. McPhee's extraordinary prose has won many important honors, including a Pulitzer Prize.

from A Lincoln Preface

Carl Sandburg

Courtesy of The Lincoln Museum, Fort Wayne, Indiana, (#983) – *Lincoln Proclaiming Thanksgiving*, Dean Cornwell

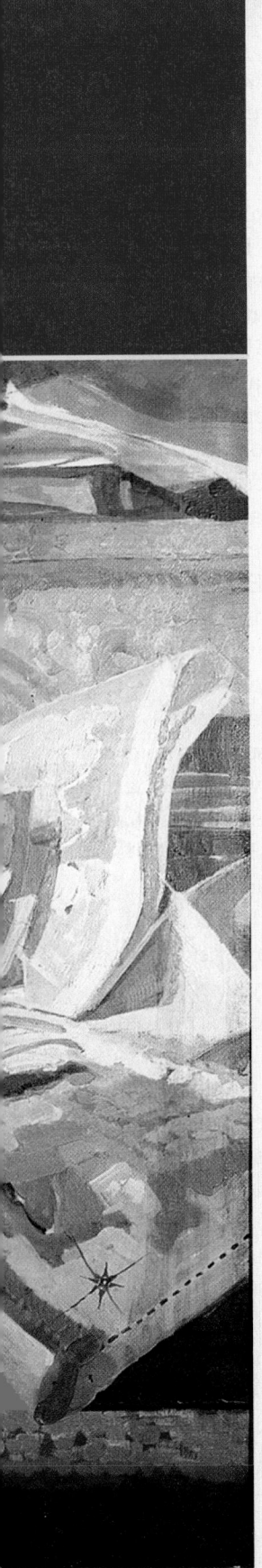

Background Ever since the birth of the
United States in 1776, the issue of slavery had troubled
the nation. Each time a new state entered the Union,
Congress debated fiercely over whether it would be
a slaveholding or free state. In 1860, when Abraham
Lincoln was elected president, he refused to support any
congressional proposal that would allow for new slave
states. The Southern slaveholding states resolved to fight
to keep new states open to slavery. This conflict led to
the outbreak of the Civil War in April 1861.

In the time of the April lilacs in the year
1865, a man in the City of Washington, D.C.,
trusted a guard to watch at a door, and the
guard was careless, left the door, and the man
was shot, lingered a night, passed away, was laid
in a box, and carried north and west a thousand
miles; bells sobbed; cities wore crepe;[1] people
stood with hats off as the railroad burial car
came past at midnight, dawn or noon.

During the four years of time before he gave up
the ghost, this man was clothed with despotic
power, commanding the most powerful armies
till then assembled in modern warfare, enforcing
drafts of soldiers, abolishing the right of habeas
corpus,[2] directing politically and spiritually the
wild, massive forces loosed in civil war.

Four billion dollars' worth of property was
taken from those who had been legal owners
of it, confiscated, wiped out as by fire, at his
instigation and executive direction; a class of

Vocabulary
despotic (des pät´ ik)
adj. like an absolute ruler
or tyrant

✓ Reading
  Check

What violent event
happened in April 1865?

---

1. **crepe** (krāp) *n.* thin, black cloth worn to show mourning.
2. **habeas corpus** (hā´ bē əs kôr´ pəs) *n.* right of an imprisoned
   person to have a court hearing.

◀ **Critical Viewing** Does this painting portray Lincoln
as a man of great power? Explain. **[Make a Judgment]**

Peculiarsome Abe, N.C. Wyeth, Courtesy of Children's Literature Research Collection, The Free Library of Philadelphia. Photography courtesy of the Brandywine River Museum

▲ **Critical Viewing**
What impression of Lincoln does this painting convey? **[Describe]**

chattel[3] property recognized as lawful for two hundred years went to the scrap pile.

When the woman who wrote *Uncle Tom's Cabin*[4] came to see him in the White House, he greeted her, "So you're the little woman who wrote the book that made this great war," and as they seated themselves at a fireplace, "I do love an open fire: I always had one at home." As they were finishing their talk of the days of blood, he said, "I shan't last long after it's over."

An Illinois Congressman looked in on him as he had his face lathered for a shave in the White House and remarked, "If anybody had told me that in a great crisis like this the people were going out to a little one-horse town and pick out a one-horse lawyer for president, I wouldn't have believed it." The answer was, "Neither would I. But it was a time when a man with a policy would have been fatal to the country. I never had a policy. I have simply tried to do what seemed best each day, as each day came."

"I don't intend precisely to throw the Constitution overboard, but I will stick it in a hole if I can," he told a Cabinet officer. The enemy was violating the Constitution to destroy the Union, he argued, and therefore, "I will violate the Constitution, if necessary, to save the Union." He instructed a messenger to the Secretary of the Treasury, "Tell him not to bother himself about the Constitution. Say that I have that sacred instrument here at the White House, and I am guarding it with great care."

When he was renominated, it was by the device of seating delegates from Tennessee, which gave enough added votes to seat favorable delegates from Kentucky, Missouri, Louisiana, Arkansas, and from one county in Florida. Until late in that campaign of 1864, he expected to lose the November election; military victories brought the tide his way; the vote was 2,200,000 for him and 1,800,000 against him. Among those who bitterly fought him politically, and

---

3. **chattel** (chat′′l) *n.* a movable item of personal property.
4. **woman . . . Cabin** Harriet Beecher Stowe (1811–1896), whose novel stirred up opinion against slavery.

accused him of blunders or crimes, were Franklin Pierce, a former president of the United States; Horatio Seymour, the Governor of New York; Samuel F. B. Morse, inventor of the telegraph; Cyrus H. McCormick, inventor of the farm reaper; General George B. McClellan, a Democrat who had commanded the Army of the Potomac; and the *Chicago Times*, a daily newspaper. In all its essential propositions the Southern Confederacy had the moral support of powerful, respectable elements throughout the North, probably more than a million votes believing in the justice of the cause of the South as compared with the North.

While propagandas raged, and the war winds howled, he sat in the White House, the Stubborn Man of History, writing that the Mississippi was one river and could not belong to two countries, that the plans for railroad connection from coast to coast must be pushed through and the Union Pacific[5] realized.

His life, mind and heart ran in contrasts. When his white kid gloves broke into tatters while shaking hands at a White House reception, he remarked, "This looks like a general bustification." When he talked with an Ohio friend one day during the 1864 campaign, he mentioned one public man, and murmured, "He's a thistle! I don't see why God lets him live." Of a devious Senator, he said, "He's too crooked to lie still!" And of a New York editor, "In early life in the West, we used to make our shoes last a great while with much mending, and sometimes, when far gone, we found the leather so rotten the stitches would not hold. Greeley is so rotten that nothing can be done with him. He is not truthful; the stitches all tear out." As he sat in the telegraph office of the War Department, reading cipher dispatches, and came to the words, Hosanna and Husband, he would chuckle, "Jeffy D.,"[6] and at the words, Hunter and Happy, "Bobby Lee."[7]

While the luck of war wavered and broke and came again, as generals failed and campaigns were lost, he held enough forces of the Union together to raise new armies and supply them, until generals were found who made war as victorious war has always been made, with terror, frightfulness, destruction, and valor and sacrifice past words of man to tell.

A slouching, gray-headed poet,[8] haunting the hospitals at Washington, characterized him as "the grandest figure on the crowded canvas of the drama of the nineteenth century—a Hoosier Michael Angelo."[9]

Literary Analysis
Biographical Writing
Which details here present Lincoln's strength in the face of opposition? Explain.

> His life, mind and heart ran in contrasts.

Reading Check
Under what circumstances was Lincoln willing to violate the Constitution?

---

5. **Union Pacific** railroad chartered by Congress in 1862 to form part of a transcontinental system.
6. **"Jeffy D."** Jefferson Davis (1808–1889), president of the Confederacy.
7. **"Bobby Lee"** Robert E. Lee (1807–1870), commander in chief of the Confederate army.
8. **slouching . . . poet** Walt Whitman (1819–1892).
9. **Michael Angelo** Michelangelo (mī´ kəl an´ jə lō´) (1475–1564), famous Italian artist.

His own speeches, letters, telegrams and official messages during that war form the most significant and enduring document from any one man on why the war began, why it went on, and the dangers beyond its end. He mentioned "the politicians," over and again "the politicians," with scorn and blame. As the platoons filed before him at a review of an army corps, he asked, "What is to become of these boys when the war is over?"

He was a chosen spokesman: yet there were times he was silent; nothing but silence could at those times have fitted a chosen spokesman; in the mixed shame and blame of the immense wrongs of two crashing civilizations, with nothing to say, he said nothing, slept not at all, and wept at those times in a way that made weeping appropriate, decent, majestic.

His hat was shot off as he rode alone one night in Washington; a son he loved died as he watched at the bed; his wife was accused of betraying information to the enemy, until denials from him were necessary; his best companion was a fine-hearted and brilliant son with a deformed palate and an impediment of speech; when a Pennsylvania Congressman told him the enemy had declared they would break into the city and hang him to a lamp-post, he said he had considered "the violent preliminaries" to such a scene; on his left thumb was a scar where an ax had nearly chopped the thumb off when he was a boy; over one eye was a scar where he had been hit with a club in the hands of a man trying to steal the cargo off a Mississippi River flatboat; he threw a cashiered[10] officer out of his room in the White House, crying, "I can bear censure, but not insult. I never wish to see your face again."

As he shook hands with the correspondent of the London *Times*, he drawled, "Well, I guess the London *Times* is about the greatest power on earth—unless perhaps it is the Mississippi River." He rebuked with anger a woman who got on her knees to thank him for a pardon that saved her son from being shot at sunrise; and when an Iowa woman said she had journeyed out of her way to Washington just for a look at him, he grinned, "Well, in the matter of looking at one another, I have altogether the advantage."

He asked his Cabinet to vote on the high military command, and after the vote, told them the appointment had already been made; one Cabinet officer, who had been governor of Ohio, came away personally baffled and frustrated from an interview, to exclaim, to a private secretary, "That man is the most cunning person I ever saw in my life"; an Illinois lawyer who had been sent on errands carrying his political secrets, said, "He is a trimmer[11] and such a trimmer as the world has never seen."

Literary Analysis
Biographical Writing
Make a complex inference about the writer's tone in this paragraph. Use textual evidence to support your understanding.

Vocabulary
censure (sen´ shər) *n.* strong disapproval

---

10. **cashiered** (ka shird´) *adj.* dishonorably discharged.
11. **trimmer** (trim´ ər) *n.* person who changes his or her opinion to suit the circumstances.

He manipulated the admission of Nevada as a state in the Union, when her votes were needed for the Emancipation Proclamation, saying, "It is easier to admit Nevada than to raise another million of soldiers." At the same time he went to the office of a former New York editor, who had become Assistant Secretary of War, and said the votes of three congressmen were wanted for the required three-quarters of votes in the House of Representatives, advising, "There are three that you can deal with better than anybody else. . . . Whatever promise you make to those men, I will perform it." And in the same week, he said to a Massachusetts politician that two votes were lacking, and, "Those two votes must be procured. I leave it to you to determine how it shall be done; but remember that I am President of the United States and clothed with immense power, and I expect you to procure those votes." And while he was thus employing every last resource and device of practical politics to constitutionally abolish slavery, the abolitionist[12] Henry Ward Beecher attacked him with javelins of scorn and detestation in a series of editorials that brought from him the single comment, "Is thy servant a dog?"

When the King of Siam sent him a costly sword of exquisite embellishment, and two elephant tusks, along with letters and a photograph of the King, he acknowledged the gifts in a manner as lavish as the Orientals. Addressing the King of Siam as "Great and Good Friend," he wrote thanks for each of the gifts, including "also two elephant's tusks of length and magnitude, such as indicate they could have belonged only to an animal which was a native of Siam." After further thanks for the tokens received, he closed the letter to the King of Siam with strange grace and humor, saying, "I appreciate most highly your Majesty's tender of good offices in forwarding to this Government a stock from which a supply of elephants might be raised on our soil. . . our political jurisdiction, however, does not reach a latitude so low as to favor the multiplication of the elephant, and steam on land as well as water has been our best agent of transportation . . . . Meantime, wishing for your Majesty a long and happy life, and, for

---

12. **abolitionist** (ab´ ə lish´ ən ist) *n.* person in favor of doing away with slavery in the United States.

LITERATURE IN CONTEXT

History Connection

The Emancipation Proclamation

On January 1, 1863, Lincoln signed the Emancipation Proclamation, freeing the slaves in all Confederate states. The proclamation was largely a symbolic document because the federal government had no means to enforce it. Nevertheless, it gave Southern blacks cause to hope. Eventually, as Union armies advanced, freeing thousands of slaves, the promise of the proclamation became a reality.

Connect to the Literature

How were Lincoln's efforts to admit Nevada into the Union related to the passage of the Emancipation Proclamation?

Reading Check

Who was Lincoln's best companion?

▲ Abraham Lincoln
in 1863

Literary Analysis
Biographical Writing
What do you learn
about Lincoln from the
statement overheard by
an Indiana man?

Vocabulary
droll (drōl) *adj.* funny in
an odd way

the generous and emulous people of Siam, the highest
possible prosperity, I commend both to the blessing of
Almighty God."

He sent hundreds of telegrams, "Suspend death
sentence" or "Suspend execution" of So-and-So, who
was to be shot at sunrise. The telegrams varied oddly
at times, as in one, "If Thomas Samplogh, of the First
Delaware Regiment, has been sentenced to death, and
is not yet executed, suspend and report the case to me."
And another, "Is it Lieut. Samuel B. Davis whose death
sentence is commuted? If not done, let it be done."

While the war drums beat, he liked best of all the
stories told of him, one of two Quakeresses[13] heard
talking in a railway car. "I think that Jefferson will
succeed." "Why does thee think so?" "Because Jefferson
is a praying man." "And so is Abraham a praying man."
"Yes, but the Lord will think Abraham is joking."

An Indiana man at the White House heard him say,
"Voorhees, don't it seem strange to you that I, who could never
so much as cut off the head of a chicken, should be elected, or
selected, into the midst of all this blood?"

A party of American citizens, standing in the ruins of the Forum
in Rome, Italy, heard there the news of the first assassination of the
first American dictator, and took it as a sign of the growing up and
the aging of the civilization on the North American continent. Far
out in Coles County, Illinois, a beautiful, gaunt old woman in a log
cabin said, "I knowed he'd never come back."

Of men taking too fat profits out of the war, he said, "Where the
carcass is there will the eagles be gathered together."

An enemy general, Longstreet, after the war, declared him to have
been "the one matchless man in forty millions of people," while one
of his private secretaries, Hay, declared his life to have been the most
perfect in its relationships and adjustments since that of Christ.

Between the days in which he crawled as a baby on the dirt floor
of a Kentucky cabin, and the time when he gave his final breath
in Washington, he packed a rich life with work, thought, laughter,
tears, hate, love.

With vast reservoirs of the comic and the droll, and
notwithstanding a mastery of mirth and nonsense, he delivered
a volume of addresses and letters of terrible and serious appeal,
with import beyond his own day, shot through here and there with

---

13. Quakeresses (kwā′ kər es əz) *n.* female members of the religious group known as the
Society of Friends, or Quakers.

far, thin ironics, with paragraphs having raillery[14] of the quality of the Book of Job,[15] and echoes as subtle as the whispers of wind in prairie grass.

Perhaps no human clay pot has held more laughter and tears.

The facts and myths of his life are to be an American possession, shared widely over the world, for thousands of years, as the tradition of Knute or Alfred, Lao-tse or Diogenes, Pericles or Caesar,[16] are kept. This because he was not only a genius in the science of neighborly human relationships and an artist in the personal handling of life from day to day, but a strange friend and a friendly stranger to all forms of life that he met.

He lived fifty-six years of which fifty-two were lived in the West—the prairie years.

---

14. **raillery** (rā´ lər ē) *n.* good-natured teasing.
15. **Book of Job** (jōb) *n.* book of the Old Testament in which Job is tested by God.
16. **Knute** (kno͞ot) **or Alfred, Lao-tse** (lou´ dzu´) **or Diogenes** (dī äj´ ə nēz´), **Pericles** (per´ ə klēz´) **or Caesar** (sē´ zər) well-known thinkers and leaders from different eras and places.

Literary Analysis
Biographical Writing
According to Sandburg, what personal qualities make Lincoln a great historical figure?

> P̲erhaps no human clay pot has held more laughter and tears.

Critical Thinking

1. **Respond:** Which story about Lincoln interested you the most? Why?

2. **(a)** To whom did Lincoln refer as "the little woman who wrote the book that made this great war"? **(b) Make Inferences:** Why do you think Lincoln wanted to meet this woman?
   (c) Draw Conclusions: What does Lincoln's interest in meeting this woman say about his character?

3. **(a)** How did Lincoln justify admitting Nevada to the Union?
   (b) Connect: What other examples of Lincoln's "practical" politics does the author note? **(c) Make a Judgment:** Does Sandburg seem to admire this aspect of Lincoln's character? Explain.

4. **(a)** According to Sandburg, what aspects of Lincoln's life will be "an American possession, shared widely over the world"?
   (b) Interpret: What does Sandburg mean by this comment?

Support your responses with evidence from the text.

Is knowledge the same as understanding?
Sandburg says that Lincoln "packed a rich life with work, thought, laughter, tears, hate, love." Do you believe this better demonstrates Sandburg's knowledge about Lincoln or his understanding of him? Explain.

Arthur Ashe
Remembered

John McPhee

Writing With Focus and Coherence

To be effective, the details in a business letter need to be focused and coherent, or connected in a logical way. Busy professionals respond well to concise letters that include only essential information presented in an appropriate, formal style. Using an appropriate voice can set the stage for a focused, coherent business letter.

Identifying the Needs of Your Audience If you were writing an e-mail to a close friend, you would likely use a loose format and informal language. Your friend would likely respond in a similar manner. However, when you are writing a business letter, you need to present information in an organized, focused way. The relationship between ideas should be clear. You are not simply chatting with a friend—you want to give or receive information. Every sentence should contribute to the development of your letter. The voice of a business letter, or the use of formal vocabulary and tone, can help you to express yourself clearly.

Maintaining Focus and Coherence Use these tips to maintain focus and coherence.

- Use an organizing structure appropriate to your purpose.
- Include only essential information needed to answer your question.
- As you develop your draft, **include transitions** that clearly **convey your meaning** to your audience.
- Reread your letter to be sure every detail is connected to your topic.
- Replace casual expressions with formal language.
- Follow reader-friendly formatting conventions.

These two letters request the same information, but they are structured quite differently.

Unfocused, Incoherent Letter	Focused, Coherent Letter
I love riding bicycles. I also love skateboarding. I have outgrown mine and want a new one really badly. My sister has my old bike now. Do you have any sisters? Anyway, which is the best kind for me? How much does it cost? It better be cheap!	I am planning on purchasing a new bicycle. I like riding on the street, but I mostly ride the bike trails with my parents. Would a mountain bike be best for me? Or would a hybrid better serve my needs? What is the price range for recreational bicycles like these?

Drafting Strategies

Select a reader-friendly format. Choose a standard business letter format, using a consistent font and spacing. This formatting technique will contribute to the readability and impact of your letter. You may use block format, in which each part of the letter begins at the left margin. Alternatively, you may use modified block format, in which the heading, closing, and signature are centered on the page. (For a sample business letter, see page R38.) Use this checklist as you draft:

Business Letter Elements

- ❑ **Heading**—the writer's address and organization (if any) and the date
- ❑ **Inside Address**—where the letter will be sent
- ❑ **Greeting**—a salutation always punctuated by a colon
- ❑ **Body**—a presentation of the writer's purpose
- ❑ **Closing**—an appropriate farewell
- ❑ **Signature**—a hand-signed name

Organize information. Keeping your information organized will allow your letter to be more easily understood. Make sure that any details you include in your letter are placed in the proper sections. Details related to a particular issue or topic should be mentioned near each other.

Write a memo or send an e-mail. To give information to a number of people, you might choose to send a memo instead of the more formal letter format. A memo has who wrote it, whom it is to, the date, and the subject at the top. The body contains the pertinent information.

E-mail can be an efficient way to request or present information. It can be speedier and provide direct access to information. When you write an e-mail, compose a short, clear subject line. Include a greeting, a body, a closing, and an electronic signature.

Revising Strategy

Highlight the active voice. A verb in the active voice expresses an action done by its subject. A verb in the passive voice expresses an action done to its subject. The active voice is preferable because it produces a more direct and forceful sentence than the passive voice.

Passive Voice: The vacuum cleaner *was broken* by the salesman.

Active Voice: The salesman *broke* the vacuum cleaner.

Review your draft to improve style and subtlety of meaning. Rethink how well you have addressed your purpose, audience, and genre. Highlight verbs written in the passive voice and rewrite sentences in the active voice where you think it would be more effective.

 Focus on the TEKS

Writing
(13)(C) Revise drafts to improve style, sentence variety, and subtlety of meaning after rethinking how well questions of purpose, audience, and genre have been addressed.
(15)(B)(i);(ii) Write work-related documents (e.g., correspondence) that include organized information; and reader-friendly formatting techniques.

WRITE GUY
Jeff Anderson, M.Ed.

What Do You Notice?

Active Voice

The following sentence is from Carl Sandburg's *A Lincoln Preface*. Read the sentence several times.

His own speeches, letters, telegrams and official messages during that war form the most significant and enduring document from any one man on why the war began, why it went on, and the dangers beyond its end.

Jot down what you find interesting about this sentence. Consider how you can use active voice in your letter to communicate clearly.

Revising to Combine Choppy Sentences

Revising to Combine Choppy Sentences Avoid choppy, disconnected sentences by combining two or more related ideas into a single sentence. There are several effective methods for sentence combining.

Use Compound Verbs. More than one verb linked to a single subject can be used to combine two short sentences.

> **Choppy:** I *disconnected* my phone. I *took* it in for service.

> **Compound Verb:** I *disconnected* my phone and *took* it in for service.

Use Compound Objects. More than one object linked to a single verb can help combine sentences.

> **Choppy:** I purchased *a scanner*. I purchased *a fax machine*.

> **Compound Object:** I purchased *a scanner and a fax machine*.

A third option is the use of **compound predicate nominatives** or **predicate adjectives**.

> **Choppy:** My newest device *is a printer*. It is also *a scanner*. It is also *a fax machine*.

> **Compound Predicative Nominative:** My newest device *is a printer, scanner, and fax machine*.

> **Choppy:** The fax is *automated*. It is *fast*.

> **Compound Predicative Adjective:** The fax is *automated and fast*.

PH GRAMMAR HANDBOOK

Further instruction and practice are available in the *Prentice Hall Grammar Handbook*.

Fixing Choppy Sentences Rethink how well your purpose, audience, and genre have been addressed. Then, **revise your draft to improve sentence variety.**

1. **Read your draft aloud.** Listen for overuse of short sentences.

2. **Identify sentences that can be combined.** Look for sentences that share a common subject or a common predicate element.

3. **Use a variety of sentence combining techniques.** Use compound verbs, compound direct objects, or compound predicate nominatives or predicate adjectives to create a wider variety of flowing sentences.

Grammar in Your Writing

Review your letter, highlighting central ideas or images. Look for opportunities to express related ideas or information in a single sentence. Combine these elements using one of the methods presented here.

Student Model: Myles Hardeman, Arlington, TX

 Focus on the TEKS

Myles Hardeman
123 Any Street
Arlington, TX 70000
October 8, 2008

Yamaha Electronics Corporation USA
6660 Orangethorpe Avenue
Buena Park, CA 90620

Dear Sir or Madam:

I am planning to purchase a new electric piano or keyboard. Therefore, I would like to obtain information about your products.

My current piano is a traditional, standard, upright piano. It is out of tune and has not been tuned for at least 5 years. My parents and I have decided it would be easier and less expensive to purchase a new electric piano or keyboard than to continue to have my current piano tuned in the future.

I would like an electric piano with many sound choices (like strings, guitar, drum kits, synthesized, brass instruments, voice, organ, etc.), a sustaining pedal, and synthesizer knobs. These features interest me because I play the keyboard in a band with my brothers and I need different sounds for the songs that we play together. I would rather the price be under $3000. I do not have much experience in piano shopping but, from my research, I believe $3000 is about the average price of an electric piano or keyboard of this type.

I have chosen to purchase one of your products because I have seen many of your products and they are very upstanding. Your pianos are durable and they sound great. I also noticed that your pianos have many ports in the back for audio input and output. Though I might not need all of the audio inputs and output outlets right now, our band might play publicly someday in the future and the extras could be useful. Purchasing one of your pianos soon would save me the time and money on a piano or keyboard later.

Thank you for your attention. Please send a catalog of the products you have to offer to the above address.

Sincerely,

Myles Hardeman
Myles Hardeman

Writing
(15)(B)(i) Write work-related documents (e.g., correspondence) that include accurately conveyed information.

Conventions
(18)(A) Use conventions of capitalization.
(19) Spell correctly, including using various resources to check correct spellings.

Myles uses modified block format.

Myles' purpose is stated clearly and concisely.

In this paragraph, the author provides details about the features and price of the product that interests him.

In his conclusion, Myles summarizes the request using concise and polite formal language.

TEXAS

Editing and Proofreading

Edit your draft for errors in grammar and mechanics, such as punctuation and capitalization. Use various resources, such as printed and electronic dictionaries, to check correct spellings.

Focus on Conveying Information Accurately: Make certain that the names of individuals and companies are spelled correctly and that the address is complete. Use the conventions of capitalization and check abbreviations to ensure they are correct.

Publishing and Presenting

Consider ways to publish your written work for appropriate audiences:

Send your letter. If your letter is written to an existing business, e-mail or mail it. When you get a response, share it with classmates.

Conduct a discussion. Use your letter to begin a class discussion about the role of communication skills in everyday life. Be open to the variety of ideas your classmates suggest. Make notes on their comments, and add your letter and notes to your writing portfolio.

Reflecting on Your Writing

Writer's Journal Jot down your answers to these questions:

How did writing a business letter help you learn about a topic?

How is business writing different from other types of writing?

Rubric for Self-Assessment

Find evidence in your writing to address each category. Then, use the rating scale to grade your work.

Spiral Review

Earlier in this unit, you learned about **direct and indirect objects** (p. 462) and **predicate nominatives and predicate adjectives** (p. 488). Check your business letter to be sure that you have used these elements of grammar correctly.

Written Composition Criteria	Rating Scale
	not very very
Focus and Coherence: How well do the details in the letter relate to your purpose and topic?	1 2 3 4
Organization: How thoroughly have you incorporated all the elements of a business letter, including reader-friendly formatting techniques?	1 2 3 4
Development of Ideas: How well have you organized your information and ideas?	1 2 3 4
Conventions: How correct is your grammar, especially your use of compound subjects, objects, and complements?	1 2 3 4
Voice: How well have you maintained a consistently formal and polite tone?	1 2 3 4

Selection Choices

Lian Dolan

▲ Read **"Carry Your Own Skis"** to discover the real benefits of taking care of yourself.

Libraries Face Sad Chapter
Pete Hamill

▲ Read **"Libraries Face Sad Chapter"** to learn why libraries are considered national treasures.

 TEXAS Focus on the TEKS

Meet these standards with either **"Carry Your Own Skis"** (p. 522) or **"Libraries Face Sad Chapter"** (p. 530).

Reading
(10) Analyze persuasive text and provide evidence from the text to support analysis. *(Literary Analysis: Persuasive Text)*

(10)(A) Analyze the relevance, quality, and credibility of evidence given to support or oppose an argument for a specific audience. *(Reading Skill: Analyze Persuasion)*

(1)(A) Determine the meanings of grade-level technical academic English words in multiple content areas derived from Latin roots. *(Word Power: Apply It)*

Writing
(15) Write expository texts to communicate ideas and information to specific audiences for specific purposes. *(Writing: Abstract)*

Listening and Speaking
(24)(C) Evaluate the effectiveness of a speaker's main and supporting ideas. *(Listening and Speaking: Persuasive Presentation)*

(25) Give presentations using informal and technical language effectively to meet the needs of audience, purpose, and occasion. *(Listening and Speaking: Persuasive Presentation)*

Literary Analysis: Persuasive Text

A **persuasive text** is a nonfiction work in which the author's purpose is to support or oppose an argument and convince a specific audience to agree with that position. Persuasive texts usually include the following:

- **Appeals to reason:** logical arguments based on verifiable evidence, such as facts, statistics, or expert testimony.

- **Appeals to emotion:** statements intended to affect listeners' feelings about a subject. These statements often include charged language—words with strong positive or negative associations.

As You Read Analyze the author's motive, or intent, in the persuasive text. Ask, "Why is this issue so important to the writer?"

Reading Skill: Analyze Persuasion

A persuasive argument is composed of a series of claims. To analyze and evaluate an author's argument in a persuasive text, identify passages in which the author makes a claim in support of his or her position. Then, reread those passages to **analyze the author's evidence.** Ask yourself:

- Is the evidence **relevant**—connected to the topic—and complete?

- Are all statements supported by **quality** evidence? Are they based on facts, based on research, or able to be proved?

- Is the author's argument supported by **credible**—reliable and believable—evidence, or is it based on faulty assumptions?

- How well does the evidence suit the **specific audience?**

Using the Strategy: Persuasion Analysis Diagram

As You Read Use a chart like this one to analyze the relevance, quality, and credibility of evidence given to **support** or **oppose arguments** for specific audiences.

Who is the audience?	
What is the argument and the evidence that supports it?	
Is the evidence relevant?	
Is the evidence of good quality?	
Is the evidence credible?	

TEXAS
PHLitOnline
www.PHLitOnline.com

Hear It!
- Selection summary audio
- Selection audio

See It!
- Get Connected video
- Background video
- More about the author
- Vocabulary flashcards

Do It!
- Interactive journals
- Interactive graphic organizers
- Self-test
- Internet activity
- Grammar tutorial
- Interactive vocabulary games

Carry Your Own Skis

Lian Dolan

Is *knowledge* the same as *understanding?*

Writing About the Big Question

In "Carry Your Own Skis," the author draws an analogy between carrying your own skis and taking responsibility for yourself. Use this sentence starter to develop your ideas about the Big Question.

Personal responsibility is a **concept** that many people do not truly understand because _____.

As You Read Look for details that illustrate the benefits of taking personal responsibility.

Vocabulary

Read each word and its definition. Decide whether you know the word well, know it a little bit, or do not know it at all. After you read, see how your knowledge of each word has increased.

- **entailed** (en tāld´) *v.* caused or required as a necessary consequence; involved; necessitated (p. 523) *The plan to repaint the house entailed a lot of work.* entail *v.* entailment *n.*

- **inevitability** (in ev´ i tə bil´ ə tē) *n.* quality of being certain to happen; certainty (p. 523) *The inevitability of losing did not keep the team from playing hard.* inevitable *adj.* inevitably *adv.*

- **collective** (kə lek´ tiv) *adj.* put together as a group; gathered into a whole (p. 523) *With our collective friends, we had enough people to get the group rate.* collect *v.* collection *n.* collectively *adv.*

- **forgo** (fôr gō´) *v.* do without; abstain from; give up (p. 523) *The coach said we could forgo practice tomorrow if we worked hard today.* forgone *v.*

- **potential** (pō ten´ shəl) *n.* possibility (p. 524) *She has the potential to be a good player, but she needs lots of practice.* potential *adj.*

- **riddled** (rid´ 'ld) *adj.* very full of something, especially something unpleasant (p. 525) *The old tree was riddled with wormholes.* riddle *v.*

Word Power

The **Latin root -potens-** means "able" or "having the essence of." The root relates to power and possibility.

When Dolan describes skiing as having the **potential** for fun, she means it has the possibility of being exciting.

Meet
Lian Dolan
(b. 1966)

Author of
Carry Your Own Skis

Lian Dolan is one of the "Satellite Sisters," a group of five sisters who host a radio show. Before helping launch the show, Dolan tried everything from working as a waitress to producing films. She also writes the column "The Chaos Chronicles" for *Working Mother* magazine.

"The Sassiest" Lian is known as the sassiest of the sisters, and she is not afraid to express her opinions on any topic. Even though Lian is the youngest of the five sisters, she directs all of their writing projects. She enjoys being the "Head Sister," giving orders to her older siblings.

Did You Know?
The Satellite Sisters live in four different cities on two continents. They link via satellite for their popular radio show.

BACKGROUND FOR THE ESSAY
Science Connection
Cold-Weather Clothing
Before the development of synthetic, lightweight, waterproof fabrics that "breathe" and keep the wearer dry, keeping warm on the ski slopes meant wearing heavy wool and cotton clothing. Garments made from these fabrics would become wet and cold in the snow, and they would stay wet and cold until removed.

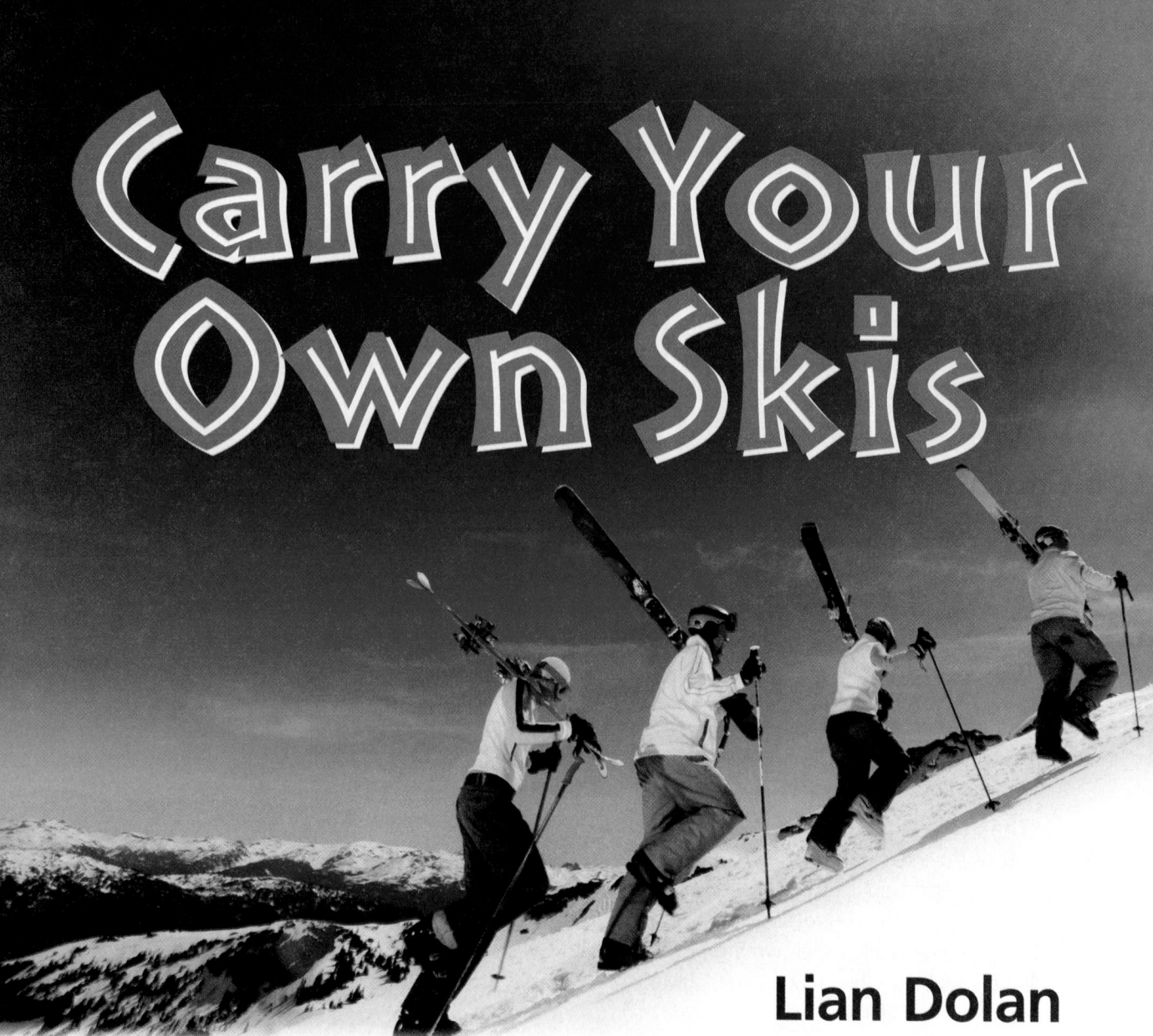

Carry Your Own Skis

Lian Dolan

▲ Critical Viewing
Based on this photo-
graph, does skiing look
like work or recreation?
Explain. [Analyze]

When my mother was forty, she took up skiing. Or, more
correctly, she and her twin sister took up skiing. They got on a bus,
went to ski camp for a week, and learned to ski. After that, they'd
get in the car and head up to Ladies Day at Powder Hill as often as
they could to practice their stem christies.[1] Don't let the name fool
you, Powder Hill (which later became the more Everest-like "Powder
Ridge") was no pushover bunny slope.[2]

---

1. **stem christies** turns made by angling one ski and then bringing the other into alignment.
2. **bunny slope** gently sloping hill used for practice by beginning skiers.

This was in the mid-sixties, when skiing was work—decades before valet parking, fondue lunches, and gear that actually keeps you dry, warm, and safe. My mother and my aunt took up the kind of skiing that entailed wooden skis, tie boots, and rope tows[3] that could jerk your arm out of its socket. This was the kind of skiing where skiers, not the Sno-Cats, groomed the hill[4] in the morning. Ticket buyers were expected to sidestep up and down slopes and herringbone the lift lines.[5] The typical A-frame lodge had a big fireplace, a couple of bathrooms, rows of picnic tables, and maybe some hot chocolate for sale. At the end of the day, there were no hot toddies by a roaring fire in furry boots or drinks in the hot tub of a slopeside condo. Instead, my mother and her sister faced the inevitability of a station wagon with a dead battery and the long, dark drive back home in wet clothes.

Why did they learn to ski? It wasn't to spend some quality time outdoors together away from their responsibilities at home. They learned to ski so that they could take their collective children skiing, all seventeen of us. My mother's eight children and my aunt's nine. And learn to ski we did, eagerly. There was, however, one rule my mother had about skiing: Carry your own skis.

My mother didn't teach us to ski until we could carry our own skis from the car to the lodge in the morning and—this is key—from the lodge back to the car at the end of the day. Even cold, wet, and tired, we had to get our skis, poles, and boots back to that station wagon on our own. No falling behind. No dragging. And no whining. My mother had the responsibility for her gear, the giant lunch, the car, and the occasional trip to the ER for broken legs. We were in charge of our own gear and meeting at the end of the day. These were the conditions to be allowed to accompany siblings and cousins to the slopes. Carry your own skis or sit in the lodge all day.

No one wanted to get left in the lodge. A cold, wet day on the ice-blue slopes of New England, freezing in leather boots and the generation of ski clothes before microfibers was far preferable to being left out of all that fun. Miss the lunches of soggy tuna fish sandwiches and mini chocolate bars? No way! Sit in the lodge instead of side-slipping your way down a sheet of ice disguised as a trail or tramping through three feet of snow to get the pole you dropped under the chair lift? Not me! Forgo that last run of the day in near darkness, cold and alone and crying because your siblings have skied on ahead without you? Who'd want to miss all that fun? Sitting in the

---

3. **rope tows** moving ropes that skiers hold to be pulled to the top of the hill.
4. **groomed the hill** packed and smoothed the snow.
5. **herringbone the lift lines** walk uphill to chair lift by stepping with skis pointed outward to avoid sliding back down the hill. The skis leave a "herringbone" pattern—a line of connected v-shapes—on the snow.

Vocabulary

entailed (en tāld´) *v.* caused or required as a necessary consequence; involved; necessitated

inevitability (in ev´ i tə bil´ ə tē) *n.* quality of being certain to happen; certainty

collective (kə lek´ tiv) *adj.* put together as a group; gathered into a whole

forgo (fôr gō´) *v.* do without; abstain from; give up

Literary Analysis
Persuasive Text
Which details in this paragraph appeal to the emotions? Explain.

Reading Check
Why did Dolan's mother and aunt learn to ski?

Vocabulary
potential (pō ten´ shəl)
n. possibility

lodge all day just wasn't an option once we reached ski age. We were expected to participate. We learned to carry our own skis.

The lesson was simple, really. Be responsible for yourself and your stuff or you miss out. No one wanted to miss out. Getting across the icy parking lot and back seemed a small price to pay for the potential of great fun. And even if you dropped your poles or the bindings cut into your hands or you fell on your rear end, that was part of the experience. The "carry your own skis" mentality filtered into almost every area of our life as we were growing up. Doing homework, getting to practice, applying to college—be responsible for yourself and your stuff or you miss out.

I began to notice the people who hadn't learned to carry their own skis when I was as young as eleven. I didn't have a name for this concept yet, but I had the notion that maybe other kids operated by a different set of rules. They thought that somewhere, somebody was going to take care of things for them. I remember the girls at summer

◀ **Critical Viewing**
How do you think the girl in this photograph feels about skiing?
[Speculate]

camp who never signed up to pack out or pack in for a camping trip, expecting that someone else would provide food or do all the cleanup for them. But me? I would sign up to make the PB&Js and to clean up the mess. I'd load the canoes onto the truck and take 'em off again. And the tent? I'd put it up and I'd take it down. I didn't know any different. As a result, I was invited to go on a lot of camping trips. The lodge and back, baby—that was my attitude.

In high school, the kids who didn't carry their own skis called their parents to bring in assignments they'd forgotten or to ask for a ride home instead of walking or taking the late bus. In college, the no-ski carriers all had pink T-shirts—a sure sign that they had never done laundry before—and they complained about how much work they had. Isn't that what college was about—doing your own laundry and finishing your work? Then you could get to the fun stuff.

The real world is riddled with people who have never learned to carry their own skis—the blame-shifters, the no-RSVPers, the coworkers who never participate in those painful group birthdays except if it's their own. I admit it: I don't really get these people.

I like the folks who clear the dishes, even when they're the guests. Or the committee members who show up on time, assignment completed and ready to pitch in on the next event. Or the neighbor who drives the carpool even though her kids are sick. I get these people. These people have learned to carry their own skis.

In early adulthood, carrying my own skis meant getting a job, paying off my student loans, and working hard for the company that was providing my paycheck. If I did those things, then I could enjoy the other areas of my life. Dull, yes, but freeing, too. When I wasn't responsible for myself or my stuff, I felt lousy. Sometimes I could get to the lodge, but I just couldn't get back to the station wagon at the end of the day. It was an unfamiliar feeling to let someone down by missing a deadline at work or not showing up for an early-morning run. . . . On days like that, the parking lot seemed bigger and icier than I had anticipated.

Now I have a life that includes a husband, two children, a dog, a house, friends, schools, and a radio show that involves lots of other people, including four sisters. The "stuff" of my life may seem much heavier than two skis, two boots, and two poles, but it isn't really—just a little bit trickier to carry. I have to do more balancing and let go of the commitments that I'd probably drop anyway. If I commit to more than I can handle, I miss out. That's when I think of Powder Hill.

Reading Skill
Analyze Persuasion
Here, the author mentions people who, she believes, would argue against "carrying their own skis." Analyze the evidence given to oppose this argument. Is the evidence relevant to, credible to, and of good quality for the text's specific audience?

Vocabulary
riddled (rid´ 'ld) *adj.* very full of something, especially something unpleasant

Be responsible for yourself and your stuff or you miss out.

Reading Check
How did Dolan adapt the "carry your own skis" idea to other areas of her life?

Carry Your Own Skis **525**

The funny thing is, some of the worst moments of my childhood were spent on skis or in pursuit of skiing. The truth is, I didn't really like skiing as a kid. And I wasn't a very good skier. Most days, skiing for me was about freezing rain and constantly trying to catch up to my older, faster, more talented siblings. The hard falls on the hard ice. I can still feel the damp long underwear and the wet wool during the endless ride home. But whether I liked to ski or not didn't really matter. I was expected to learn to ski, and I did. And I also learned that in life you need to be responsible for yourself and your stuff or you miss out. The lodge and back, baby.

Critical Thinking

1. **Respond:** What more would you like to know about Dolan's childhood? Explain your answer.

2. **(a)** What is the one rule that Dolan's mother had about skiing? **(b) Make Inferences:** Does Dolan think her mother's expectations of her own children were reasonable? Explain your response.

Support your responses with evidence from the text.

3. **(a)** What lesson does Dolan say she learned from carrying her own skis? **(b) Connect:** In what other aspects of life does the author say this lesson has guided her behavior?

4. **(a) Take a Position:** Do you agree or disagree with Dolan's claim that people who do not take responsibility miss out on things? Explain. **(b) Discuss:** Share your response with a partner, and then explain how the discussion has or has not changed your response to the question.

Is knowledge the same as understanding?
How do the author's family skiing experiences lead to a better understanding of her personal responsibility?

Literary Analysis: Persuasive Text

1. **(a)** In this text, what is the author trying to persuade readers to do? **(b)** What **evidence** does she use to support her **argument?**

2. **(a)** Using a chart like the one shown, identify three passages in which Dolan argues for "the 'carry your own skis' mentality." Indicate whether each passage is an appeal to reason or to emotion. **(b)** Which kind of appeals does the author seem to favor— appeals to reason or appeals to emotion? Explain.

Passage	Reason or Emotion

3. What do you think is the author's motive for trying to persuade readers to agree with her?

Reading Skill: Analyze Persuasion

4. Overall, is the evidence given to support and oppose arguments in this text **relevant, credible,** and of good **quality?** Explain.

5. Which passages are especially convincing for their specific audience? Explain.

Vocabulary

Practice In vocabulary study, **analogies** show the relationships between pairs of words. Use a word from the vocabulary list on page 520 to complete each analogy. In each, your choice should create a word pair that matches the relationship between the first two words given.

1. conflict : agreement :: uncertainty : _____
2. idea : reality :: _____ : actual
3. soaked : water :: _____ : dents
4. hidden : revealed : : individual : _____
5. accept : attend :: _____ : decline
6. began : started :: caused : _____

Word Power Use the context of the sentences and what you know about the **Latin root -potens-** to explain your answers to each question.

1. Is a *potent* smell difficult to notice?
2. Is a *potentate* likely to be a weak person?

Word Power

The **Latin root -potens-** means "able" or "having the essence of." The root relates to power and possibility.

Apply It Explain how the root -potens- helps you determine the meanings of these technical academic words from science. Consult a dictionary if necessary.

potency
equipotential

Is *knowledge* the same as *understanding?*

Libraries Face Sad Chapter

Pete Hamill

Writing About the Big Question

In "Libraries Face Sad Chapter," the author urges readers to contribute to a fund to support public libraries, a source of knowledge. Use these sentence starters to develop your ideas about the Big Question.

Libraries, as a **source** of **information** and a place for **research,** are still important because _____. They can help us **clarify** information we find on the Internet because _____.

As You Read Look for facts that support the author's opinion that libraries must be saved. Then, consider whether he has helped you understand the situation he describes.

Vocabulary

Read each word and its definition. Decide whether you know the word well, know it a little bit, or do not know it at all. After you read, see how your knowledge of each word has increased.

- **volumes** (väl´ yo͞omz) *n.* books that are either part of a set or combined into one. (p. 531) *My grandfather had random volumes of an old set of encyclopedias stored in the basement.*

- **presumed** (prē zo͞omd´) *adj.* accepted as true; supposed (p. 531) *Someone who has been arrested is presumed to be innocent until proven guilty. presume v. presumption n. presumptuous adj.*

- **curtailed** (kər tāld´) *v.* cut short; reduced (p. 532) *The game was curtailed by darkness. curtailing v.*

- **medium** (mē´ dē əm) *n.* means of communication (p. 532) *Television may be today's most popular medium. media n. pl.*

- **duration** (do͞o rā´ shən) *n.* length of time something lasts (p. 533) *The graduating class remained standing for the duration of the ceremony. durable adj. endure v.*

- **emulate** (em´ yo͞o lāt) *v.* imitate (a person or thing admired) (p. 534) *Josh tries to emulate his favorite rock star by dying his hair different colors. emulation n.*

Word Power

The **Latin root -sum-** means "to take."

Pete Hamill describes a shelf in the library that was **presumed** to be safe from children. The librarians took for granted that children would not get to the books placed there.

Meet
Pete Hamill
(b. 1935)

Author of
Libraries Face Sad Chapter

Pete Hamill has had two novels on *The New York Times* bestseller list, but he is first and foremost a journalist. After quitting school at sixteen to work in the Brooklyn Navy Yard, Hamill joined the U.S. Navy. He completed his high school education while in the navy.

"The work was everything." In 1960, Hamill went to work as a reporter for the *New York Post* newspaper. Although he would write for several other newspapers in his career, Hamill loved his job at the *Post*. He wrote, "Nothing before (or since) could compare with walking into the *New York Post* at midnight, being sent into the dark scary city on assignment and coming back to write a story."

BACKGROUND FOR THE ESSAY
(Social Studies Connection)
Public Libraries
Although the first American library was established in 1638, it was not until the 1800s that public libraries became common in the United States. Since then, Americans have come to rely on public libraries as a free source of education, entertainment, and community.

Did You Know?
During Hamill's long career as a reporter, he covered wars in a number of countries including Vietnam, Nicaragua, Lebanon, and Northern Ireland.

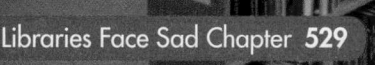

Libraries Face Sad Chapter

Pete Hamill

The library was four blocks from where we lived, on the corner of Ninth St. and Sixth Ave., and it was one of the treasure houses of our Brooklyn lives.

This was in the years before television, when we saw movies once a week at the Minerva or the Avon or the RKO Prospect, and fed our imaginations through radio and books. That is, it was in a time when *The Count of Monte Cristo* was as vivid in our minds, and talk, and dreams, as Jack Roosevelt Robinson. Dumas told the story of the count as vividly as Red Barber[1] recited the unfolding tale of No. 42.

We passed into that library between two mock-Corinthian columns that gave the building a majestic aura. For me, every visit was an astonishment. There was a children's room, first seen when I was 8, where I first read the wonderful Babar books, and then moved on to Howard Pyle's *Book of Pirates,* and all of Robert Louis Stevenson, with those rich, golden, mysterious illustrations by N.C. Wyeth.

There were bound volumes of a children's magazine called *St. Nicholas,* full of spidery drawings of animals that talked, and villains who didn't. There were picture books bursting with images of lost cities or the solar system. In that room, I learned that the world was larger than our neighborhood.

And then, at 10 or 11, I found my way into the adult stacks, to borrow books about the daily life of the Romans, the flight of Richard Hannay across Scotland, the conquests of Mexico and Peru, the cases of Sherlock Holmes. On a high shelf, presumed to be safe from the curious eyes of children, was a lavish (in memory) edition of *The Thousand and One Nights.*[2]

No teacher sent us to those leathery cliffs of books. Reading wasn't an assignment; it was a pleasure. We read for the combined thrills of villainy and heroism, along with knowledge of the vast world beyond the parish. Living in those other worlds, we could become other people: Jim Hawkins, or Edmund Dantes, or (most thrillingly) d'Artagnan, with his three musketeers.

We could live in the South Seas, or Paris, or the Rome of Caligula. It never occurred to us that we were inheriting our little share of civilization. But that's what was happening.

---

1. **The Count of Monte Cristo . . . Red Barber** *The Count of Monte Cristo* is a nineteenth-century novel by Alexandre Dumas. Jackie Robinson was the first African American major league baseball player. He joined the Brooklyn Dodgers in 1947 and wore number 42. Dodgers games were broadcast on the radio, and the action was described by announcer Red Barber.
2. **The Thousand and One Nights** collection of ancient tales also known as *The Arabian Nights.* Although many of the tales, including "Aladdin," are now retold as children's stories, the original tellings are full of violence, bloodshed, poisonings, and betrayals.

Literary Analysis
Persuasive Text
Which words here suggest that the author appeals to positive feelings about childhood and imagination?

Vocabulary
volumes (väl′ yo̅o̅mz) *n.* books that are either part of a set or combined into one

presumed (prē zo̅o̅md′) *adj.* accepted as true; supposed

◀ **Critical Viewing**
How might the young Pete Hamill have regarded this empty library? **[Speculate]**

Reading Check
According to Hamill, why did he read so much?

Built by Carnegie

Vocabulary
curtailed (kər tāld´) v.
cut short; reduced

The library of my childhood is still there, since 1975 known as the Park Slope Branch of the Brooklyn Public Library. It was built with grant money from my favorite capitalist, Andrew Carnegie, in 1906. But once again, as happened in 1992, the teeming imaginative life of libraries is in danger of being curtailed. Services might be cut. Hours trimmed. Staff reduced. The reason is the same: money, or the lack of it.

Such reductions are absolutely understandable. As we all know, Mayor Bloomberg has more than a $4 billion shortfall[3] that must be made up. Unlike the spend-more tax-less leaders of the federal government, the government of New York City can't print money to keep things going. In this season of post-September 11 austerities,[4] something must give. I hope it isn't the libraries.

Reading Skill
Analyze Persuasion
The author explains that library services are sometimes cut for budgetary reasons. Analyze the evidence given here to oppose that argument. Is the evidence relevant to, credible to, and of good quality for the essay's specific audience?

The reason is simple: In hard times, libraries are more important than ever. Human beings need what books give them better than any other medium. Since those ancient nights around prehistoric campfires, we have needed myth. And heroes. And moral tales. And information about the world beyond the nearest mountains or oceans.

---

3. **shortfall** (shôrt´ fôl´) n. the difference between the amount you have and the amount you need or expect.
4. **austerities** (ô ster´ ə tēz) n. acts of self-discipline and self-denial.

Vocabulary
medium (mē´ dē əm) n.
means of communication

▼ **Critical Viewing**
How does this photograph support Hamill's idea that a library is a "treasure house of the imagination"? **[Connect]**

In hard times, libraries are more important than ever.

Today, with books and movies more expensive than ever, and television entertainment in free fall to the lowest levels of stupidity, freely circulating books are an absolute necessity. They are quite simply another kind of food. We imagine, and then we live.

Hard times are also an opportunity. Parents and teachers all moan about the refusal of the young to read. Here is the chance to revive the power of the printed page. The Harry Potter books show that the audience for young readers is potentially immense. A child who starts with Harry Potter can find his or her way to Dumas and Arthur Conan Doyle, to Mark Twain and Walt Whitman, and, yes, to Tolstoy and Joyce and Proust.●

Immigrants' Appreciation

For those without money, the road to that treasure house of the imagination begins at the public library. When I was a boy, the rooms were crowded with immigrants and their children. That is, with people who came from places where there were no libraries for the poor. With their children, they built the New York in which we now live.

Today, the libraries of this city are still doing that work. The libraries of Brooklyn and Queens are jammed with the new immigrants and their astonishing children, the people who will build the New York of tomorrow. The older people want information about this new world, and how to get better jobs and green cards and citizenship. Their American children want to vanish into books their parents cannot afford, thus filling themselves with the endless possibilities of the future.

They are no different from the Irish, the Jews and the Italians of my childhood. My father only went to the eighth grade in Belfast. I remember my mother drilling him at our kitchen table for his citizenship test, and I know that he first read the Constitution in a book borrowed from the Prospect Branch of the Brooklyn Public Library. Lying in a darkened bed off that kitchen, I first heard the language of the Bill of Rights.

That process must go on in all the places where the poor now live. If it's impossible for the city to do it, then we must do it ourselves. Bloomberg can give us the hard numbers, explain the shortfall in the library budget and explain how much we need. Then we should try to make it up with the establishment of a private fund to maintain the libraries at full strength for the duration of the crisis.

Reading Skill
Analyze Persuasion
The author says that libraries are essential to the education of a city. Analyze the evidence given to support that argument. Is the evidence relevant to, credible to, and of good quality for the essay's specific audience?

Vocabulary
duration (dͦͦo rā´ shən)
n. length of time something lasts

Vocabulary
emulate (em´ yōō lāt)
v. imitate (a person
or thing admired)

All of us whose lives have been affected by the treasures of public libraries could contribute. The rich could emulate Carnegie, who used his wealth to create more than 1,600 public libraries, including 65 in New York. But the middle class could also send in small amounts from $10 to $50.

This would be a kind of voluntary tax. On one level, it would be a powerful pledge to maintain the life of the mind among all classes in this city. That is obviously in our own interest. But above all, it would be a means of honoring the labor of those men and women who got us here, and who paid taxes to buy books for all New Yorkers, and first took us by the hand and walked us into the treasure houses. We who dreamed of Ebbets Field and the Chateau d'If on the same American nights owe debts to New York that we can never pay. This is one that must be honored.

Critical Thinking

1. **Respond:** Do you share Hamill's feelings about public libraries? Why or why not?

2. **(a)** What books and magazines does Hamill remember from early visits to the library? **(b) Make Inferences:** What do these memories suggest about how Hamill felt about the library as a child?

3. **(a) Interpret:** What does Hamill mean by calling books "another kind of food"? **(b) Draw Conclusions:** What does this comparison suggest about the value he places on books?

4. **(a) Take a Position:** Do you agree with Hamill's claims about the importance of free public libraries? Explain. **(b) Discuss:** Share your response with a partner, and then explain how the discussion has or has not changed your response to the question.

Support your responses with evidence from the text.

Is knowledge the same as understanding?
(a) What does Hamill want you to know about the need for public libraries? **(b)** Do the facts he presents make you understand enough to want to act? Explain.

Literary Analysis: Persuasive Text

1. **(a)** In this essay, what is the author trying to persuade readers to do? **(b)** What **evidence** does he use to support his **argument?**

2. **(a)** Using a chart like the one shown, identify three passages in which Hamill asserts his position on public libraries. Indicate whether each passage is an appeal to reason or to emotion. **(b)** Which kind of appeals does the author seem to favor—appeals to reason or appeals to emotion? Explain.

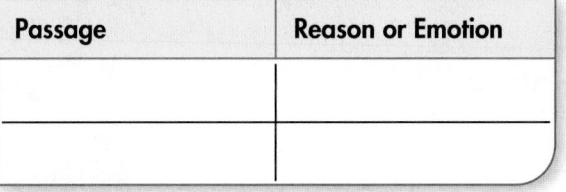

Passage	Reason or Emotion

3. What do you think is the author's motive for trying to persuade readers to agree with him?

Reading Skill: Analyze Persuasion

4. Overall, is the evidence given to support and oppose arguments in this text **relevant, credible,** and of good **quality?** Explain.

5. Which passages are especially convincing to their specific audience? Explain.

Vocabulary

Practice In vocabulary study, **analogies** show the relationships between pairs of words. Use a word from the vocabulary list on page 528 to complete each analogy. In each, your choice should create a word pair that matches the relationship between the first two words.

1. sugar : sweetness :: time : _____
2. bucket : water :: _____ : information
3. arrived : departed :: continued : _____
4. people : groups :: pages : _____
5. knew : guessed :: proved : _____
6. persuade: convince :: mimic : _____

Word Power Use the context of the sentences and what you know about the **Latin root -sum-** to explain your answer to each question.

1. If you *resume* an activity, do you stop doing it?
2. Is it wise to make a *presumption* about someone else's wishes?

Word Power

The **Latin root -sum-** means "to take."

Apply It Explain how the root *-sum-* helps you determine the meanings of these technical academic words from social studies. Consult a dictionary if necessary.

assumption
consume

Integrated Language Skills

Carry Your Own Skis • Libraries Face Sad Chapter

Conventions: Adjectives

An **adjective** is a word used to give a noun or pronoun a more specific meaning.

Adjectives modify, or change, nouns and pronouns by telling *what kind, which one, how many,* or *how much.*

Noun/Pronoun	Question	Adjective and Noun/Pronoun
school	What kind?	martial arts school
student	Which one?	involved student
cars	How many?/How much?	three cars

Usually an adjective comes before the noun it modifies. Sometimes, however, the adjective may follow the noun by coming after a linking verb.

Before   The *large, yellow* dog is next door.

After   The dog next door is *large and yellow.*

Practice A Identify the adjectives in the following sentences. Then, write a new sentence for each, replacing each adjective with a different adjective.

1. The little child carried the heavy skis.
2. The wet, brown sweater was uncomfortable.
3. Her soggy tuna fish sandwich was tasteless.
4. She smiled as she thought about her wonderful day.
5. The ski slope is long and icy.

Reading Application Find two sentences in "Carry Your Own Skis" in which an adjective comes before the noun it modifies. Find two sentences in which the adjective follows its noun.

Practice B Modify each noun in these sentences with one or more adjectives.

1. Most libraries contain books.
2. Children often make animal drawings.
3. The librarian is a lady.
4. Libraries use technology.
5. Libraries need money.

Writing Application Look at the image on page 532. Write four sentences describing what might be going on in this picture. Use at least two adjectives in each sentence and position them both before *and* after the noun.

PH GRAMMAR HANDBOOK Further instruction and practice are available in the *Prentice Hall Grammar Handbook*.

Writing

Both of these essays convey an overall main idea and message the reader can take away from the text. Write an **abstract** of "Carry Your Own Skis" or "Libraries Face Sad Chapter." An abstract is a type of summary that readers consult to see if an essay or article is relevant to their research.

- Keep in mind your specific **audience** and **purpose.**
- Clearly **communicate** the main ideas and information of the essay.
- Briefly convey important supporting details.

Grammar Application Make sure all adjectives in your abstract are properly placed.

Writing Workshop: *Work in Progress*

Prewriting for Editorial For an editorial you may write, identify, and list at least three specific elements of music, fashion, books, or movies that influence you and your friends. Put this Topic List in your writing portfolio.

Listening and Speaking

Do research. Then, prepare and give a **persuasive presentation.**

- If you read "Carry Your Own Skis," research today's popular winter sports. Persuade your audience to support one of the less popular sports, making it more visible.
- If you read "Libraries Face Sad Chapter," research the services offered by libraries. Persuade your audience to use these services.

Use these tips to effectively meet the needs of your **purpose, audience, and occasion:**

- Because you are addressing your peers about an "everyday" topic, use **informal language** in your presentation.
- While researching, you will encounter terms particular to your subject. When you use this **technical language** in your presentation, be sure to provide clear definitions and explanations for your audience.
- Employ **eye contact** and **purposeful gestures** to engage your audience.
- Use **speaking rate, volume, enunciation,** and the **conventions of language** to communicate ideas effectively.

After each presentation, hold a class discussion, evaluating the **effectiveness** of the speaker's **main** and **supporting ideas.**

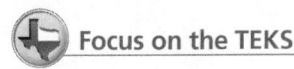 Focus on the TEKS

Writing
(15) Write expository texts to communicate ideas and information to specific audiences for specific purposes.

Listening and Speaking
(24)(C) Evaluate the effectiveness of a speaker's main and supporting ideas.

(25) Give presentations using informal and technical language effectively to meet the needs of audience, purpose, and occasion, employing eye contact, speaking rate, volume, enunciation, purposeful gestures, and conventions of language to communicate ideas effectively.

Use this prewriting activity to prepare for the **Writing Workshop** on page 582.

 **TEXAS**
PHLitOnline
www.PHLitOnline.com

- Interactive graphic organizers
- Grammar tutorial
- Interactive journals

Selection Choices

▲ Read **"I Have a Dream"** to discover the power of an idea and a speech.

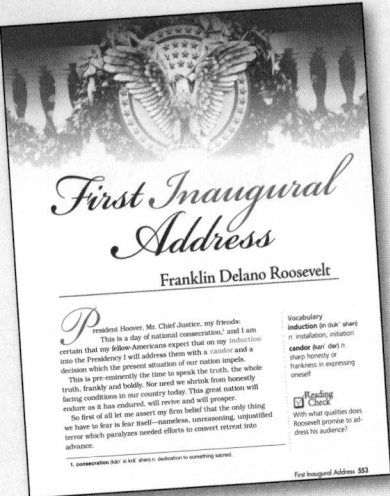

▲ Read **"First Inaugural Address"** to learn about a generation's determination to solve a national calamity.

 TEXAS Focus on the TEKS

Meet these standards with either **"I Have a Dream"** (p. 542) or **"First Inaugural Address"** (p. 552).

Reading
(10)(B) Analyze famous speeches for the rhetorical structures and devices used to convince the reader of the authors' propositions. *(Literary Analysis: Persuasive Speech)*

(10) Analyze persuasive text. *(Reading Skill: Analyze Persuasion)*

(10)(A) Analyze the relevance, quality, and credibility of evidence given to support or oppose an argument for a specific audience. *(Spiral Review: Analyze Persuasion)*

(1)(A) Determine the meaning of grade-level technical academic English words in multiple content areas derived from Latin roots. *(Word Power: Apply It)*

Writing
(15) Write expository text to communicate ideas and information. *(Writing: Essay)*

Listening and Speaking
(25) Give presentations using formal language effectively to meet the needs of audience, purpose, and occasion. *(Listening and Speaking: Television News Report)*

Literary Analysis: **Persuasive Speech**

In a **persuasive speech,** a speaker tries to convince listeners of a **proposition,** or an opinion. Persuasive speeches often include a call to action, an argument to convince people to take a particular action. Speakers often use **rhetorical structures and devices**—patterns of words and ideas that create emphasis and stir emotion, such as

- **Parallelism:** repeating a grammatical structure or an arrangement of words to create rhythm and momentum (*rhetorical structure*)

- **Repetition:** using the same words frequently to reinforce concepts and unify the speech (*rhetorical structure*)

- **Analogy:** drawing a comparison that shows a similarity between two unlike things (*rhetorical device*)

- **Restatement:** expressing the same idea in different words to clarify and stress key points (*rhetorical device*)

As You Read **Analyze the famous speech** for rhetorical structures and devices used to convince the reader of the author's propositions. Jot down notes about your findings.

Reading Skill: **Analyze Persuasion**

Persuasive techniques are devices used to influence the audience in favor of the author's argument. In addition to presenting evidence in a persuasive speech, a speaker may also use *emotionally charged language* and rhetorical devices, such as those described above.

To analyze persuasive techniques, **read aloud to hear the effect.** Notice the emotional impact of the words and of the rhythm created by specific word patterns. Consider the purpose of these techniques. Then, decide whether the speaker has supported his ideas with valid evidence.

Using the Strategy: Analysis Chart

As You Read Use a chart like this one to analyze the persuasive text. Note the purpose and effect of each persuasive technique the author employs.

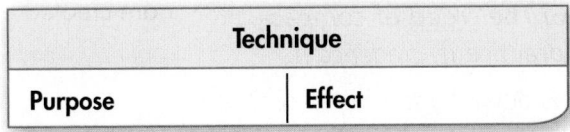

Technique	
Purpose	**Effect**

Hear It!
- Selection summary audio
- Selection audio

See It!
- Get Connected video
- Background video
- More about the author
- Vocabulary flashcards

Do It!
- Interactive journals
- Interactive graphic organizers
- Self-test
- Internet activity
- Grammar tutorial
- Interactive vocabulary games

Is *knowledge* the same as *understanding*?

"I Have a Dream"
Martin Luther King, Jr.

Writing About the Big Question

In "I Have a Dream," Martin Luther King, Jr., makes a logical and emotional speech to help listeners understand his dream of freedom and equality. Use these sentence starters to develop your ideas about the Big Question.

The **concept** of equality might be **ambiguous** to some people because _____.

To ensure equality exists in our country, we must make **connections** with each other because _____.

As You Read Look for the arguments and evidence King uses to help his listeners understand his experience.

Vocabulary

Read each word and its definition. Decide whether you know the word well, know it a little bit, or do not know it at all. After you read, see how your knowledge of each word has increased.

- **momentous** (mō men´ təs) *adj.* very important (p. 543) *The opening of the new library was a __momentous__ occasion in our town.* moment *n.* momentum *n.*

- **defaulted** (dē fôlt´ əd) *v.* failed to do something or be somewhere when required or expected; failed to make payment when due (p. 543) *The homeowners __defaulted__ on their loan and lost their house.* default *n.* default *v.*

- **hallowed** (hal´ ōd) *adj.* sacred (p. 544) *The old battlefield is considered by many to be __hallowed__ ground.* hallow *v.*

- **degenerate** (dē jen´ ər āt´) *v.* grow worse (p. 545) *Don't let this discussion __degenerate__ into a shouting match.* generate *v.*

- **creed** (krēd) *n.* statement of belief (p. 546) *The __creed__ of compassion is preached by many who do not practice it.* credence *n.*

- **oppression** (ə presh´ ən) *n.* keeping others down by the unjust use of power (p. 546) *The __oppression__ of the poor by the rich is the theme of many novels and plays.* oppress *v.* oppressive *adj.*

Word Power

The **Latin root -cred-** means "to trust; to believe."

In this speech, King refers to America's **creed,** or statement of belief, that all people are created equal.

Meet
Dr. Martin Luther King, Jr.
(1929–1968)

Author of
"I Have a Dream"

Born in Atlanta, Georgia, Dr. Martin Luther King, Jr., was one of the most charismatic leaders of the civil rights movement. During the 1950s and 1960s, King organized nonviolent protests to bring about equal rights for all Americans.

A Voice for the Oppressed King first came to national attention in 1956 in Montgomery, Alabama, when he organized a 382-day boycott by African Americans of the city's segregated buses. He went on to lead other protests and to speak out eloquently against poverty and social injustice. He was assassinated on April 4, 1968. His birthday, January 15, has since become a national holiday.

BACKGROUND FOR THE SPEECH

History Connection
The Civil Rights Movement

The U.S. Constitution guarantees certain rights to all Americans. The struggle of African Americans to have their rights recognized is known as the civil rights movement. Marked by demonstrations and legal challenges, this movement began in the 1950s and was led by figures like Martin Luther King, Jr.

Did You Know?

At thirty-five, King became the youngest man and only the third black man to be awarded a Nobel Peace Prize.

"I Have a Dream"

Martin Luther King, Jr.

Background Because speeches are written to be spoken aloud, they are a more fluid form of literature than most other nonfiction. A strong speaker will react to unspoken signals from his or her listeners and adjust a speech accordingly. He or she might change words or add whole phrases. This is the case with Dr. Martin Luther King, Jr., one of the greatest speakers of the modern age. The text that appears here represents the speech exactly as it was delivered by Dr. King on the steps of the Lincoln Memorial.

Five score years ago, a great American, in whose symbolic shadow we stand today, signed the Emancipation Proclamation. This momentous decree came as a great beacon light of hope to millions of Negro slaves who had been seared in the flames of withering injustice. It came as a joyous daybreak to end the long night of their captivity.

But one hundred years later, the Negro still is not free. One hundred years later, the life of the Negro is still sadly crippled by the manacles of segregation and the chains of discrimination. One hundred years later, the Negro lives on a lonely island of poverty in the midst of a vast ocean of material prosperity. One hundred years later, the Negro is still languished in the corners of American society and finds himself an exile in his own land. So we've come here today to dramatize a shameful condition.

In a sense we've come to our nation's Capital to cash a check. When the architects of our republic wrote the magnificent words of the Constitution and the Declaration of Independence, they were signing a promissory note[1] to which every American was to fall heir. This note was a promise that all men, yes, black men as well as white men, would be guaranteed the unalienable rights of life, liberty, and the pursuit of happiness.

It is obvious today that America has defaulted on this promissory note insofar as her citizens of color are concerned. Instead of honoring this sacred obligation, America has given the Negro people a bad check; a check which has come back marked "insufficient funds." But we refuse to believe that the bank of justice is bankrupt. We refuse to believe that there are insufficient funds in the great vaults of opportunity of this nation. And so we've come to cash this check—a check that will give us upon demand the riches of freedom and the security of justice. We have also come to

---

1. **promissory** (präm´ i sôr´ ē) **note** written promise to pay a specific amount.

◄ **Critical Viewing** Which details in this photograph demonstrate the importance of the event at which King gave his speech? **[Analyze]**

Vocabulary
momentous
(mō men´ təs) *adj.*
very important

defaulted (dē fôlt´ əd)
v. failed to do something or be somewhere when required or expected: failed to make payment when due

Literary Analysis
Persuasive Speech
Explain King's analogy between a financial transaction and the idea of justice. How might this rhetorical device help convince King's readers or listeners of the author's propositions?

Reading Check
What injustices are King and his listeners protesting?

"I Have a Dream" **543**

Literary Analysis
Persuasive Speech
What idea does King's repetition of the word "Now" help to emphasize?

this hallowed spot to remind America of the fierce urgency of *now*. This is no time to engage in the luxury of cooling off or to take the tranquilizing drug of gradualism.

Now is the time to make real the promises of Democracy.

Now is the time to rise from the dark and desolate valley of segregation to the sunlit path of racial justice.

Now is the time to lift our nation from the quicksands of racial injustice to the solid rock of brotherhood.

Now is the time to make justice a reality for all of God's children.

It would be fatal for the nation to overlook the urgency of the moment. This sweltering summer of the Negro's legitimate discontent will not pass until there is an invigorating autumn of freedom and equality. Nineteen sixty-three is not an end, but a beginning. Those who hope that the Negro needed to blow off steam and will now be content will have a rude awakening if the nation returns to business as usual. There will be neither rest nor tranquillity in America until the Negro is granted his citizenship rights. The whirlwinds of revolt will continue to shake the foundations of our nation until the bright day of justice emerges.

But there is something that I must say to my people who stand on the warm threshold which leads into the palace of justice. In the process of gaining our rightful place we must not be guilty of wrongful deeds. Let us not seek to satisfy our thirst for freedom

▼ **Critical Viewing**
Describe King's expression as he delivers his speech. **[Analyze]**

by drinking from the cup of bitterness and hatred. We must forever conduct our struggle on the high plane of dignity and discipline. We must not allow our creative protest to degenerate into physical violence. Again and again we must rise to the majestic heights of meeting physical force with soul force. The marvelous new militancy which has engulfed the Negro community must not lead us to a distrust of all white people, for many of our white brothers, as evidenced by their presence here today, have come to realize that their destiny is tied up with our destiny. And they have come to realize that their freedom is inextricably bound to our freedom. We cannot walk alone. ●

And as we walk, we must make the pledge that we shall always march ahead. We cannot turn back. There are those who are asking the devotees of civil rights, "When will you be satisfied?" We can never be satisfied as long as the Negro is the victim of the unspeakable horrors of police brutality. We can never be satisfied as long as our bodies, heavy with the fatigue of travel, cannot gain lodging in the motels of the highways and the hotels of the cities. We cannot be satisfied as long as the Negro's basic mobility is from a smaller ghetto to a larger one. We cannot be satisfied as long as a Negro in Mississippi cannot vote and a Negro in New York believes he has nothing for which to vote. No, no, we are not satisfied, and we will not be satisfied until justice rolls down like waters and righteousness like a mighty stream.

I am not unmindful that some of you have come here out of great trials and tribulations. Some of you have come fresh from narrow jail cells. Some of you have come from areas where your quest for freedom left you battered by the storms of persecution and staggered by the winds of police brutality. You have been the veterans of creative suffering. Continue to work with the faith that unearned suffering is redemptive.

Go back to Mississippi, go back to Alabama, go back to South Carolina, go back to Georgia, go back to Louisiana, go back to the slums and ghettos of our northern cities, knowing that somehow this situation can and will be changed. Let us not wallow in the valley of despair.

I say to you today, my friends, so even though we face the difficulties of today and tomorrow, I still have a dream. It is a dream deeply rooted in the American dream.

I have a dream that one day this nation will rise up and live out the true meaning of its creed: "We hold these truths to be self-evident; that all men are created equal."

I have a dream that one day on the red hills of Georgia the sons of former slaves and the sons of former slaveowners will be able to

Vocabulary
degenerate (dē jen´ ər āt´) *v.* grow worse

Spiral Review
Analyze Persuasion
In the paragraph that begins, "And as we walk…," King mentions an argument against his position. Is the evidence given against the argument relevant to, credible to, and of good quality for the text's specific audience?

Vocabulary
creed (krēd) *n.* statement of belief

Reading Check
According to King, how should his people react to physical force?

Vocabulary
oppression
(ə presh´ ən) *n.* keep-
ing others down by the
unjust use of power

Literary Analysis
Persuasive Speech
In this section, how
does the author use the
rhetorical structure of
parallelism to try to
convince the reader of
his proposition?

Reading Skill
Analyze Persuasion
What idea does King
reinforce using the
rhythm of repetition?

▶ **Critical Viewing**
Based on this image, in
what ways does King
use body language to
make his speech more
effective? **[Interpret]**

sit down together at the table of brotherhood.

I have a dream that one day even the state of Mississippi, a state sweltering with the heat of injustice, sweltering with the heat of **oppression**, will be transformed into an oasis of freedom and justice.

I have a dream that my four little children will one day live in a nation where they will not be judged by the color of their skin but by the content of their character.

I have a dream today.

I have a dream that one day down in Alabama, with its vicious racists, with its governor still having his lips dripping with the words of interposition and nullification,[2] one day right down in Alabama little black boys and black girls will be able to join hands with little white boys and white girls as sisters and brothers.

I have a dream today.

I have a dream that one day every valley shall be exalted, every hill and mountain shall be made low, the rough places will be made plains, and the crooked places will be made straight, and the glory of the Lord shall be revealed, and all flesh shall see it together.[3]

This is our hope. This is the faith that I go back to the South with. With this faith we will be able to hew out of the mountain of despair a stone of hope. With this faith we will be able to transform the jangling discords of our nation into a beautiful symphony of brotherhood. With this faith we will be able to work together, to pray together, to struggle together, to go to jail together, to stand up for freedom together, knowing that we will be free one day.

This will be the day when all of God's children will be able to sing with new meaning

My country, 'tis of thee,
Sweet land of liberty,
  Of thee I sing:
Land where my fathers died,
Land of the pilgrims' pride,
From every mountainside
  Let freedom ring.

And if America is to be a great nation this must become true. So let freedom ring from the prodigious hilltops of New Hampshire. Let freedom ring from the mighty mountains of New York. Let freedom ring from the heightening Alleghenies of Pennsylvania!

---

2. **interposition** (in´ tər pə zish´ ən) **and nullification** (nul´ ə fi kā´ shən) disputed doctrine that a state can reject federal laws considered to be violations of its rights. Governor George C. Wallace used this doctrine to reject federal civil rights legislation.

3. **every valley . . . all flesh shall see it together** reference to a biblical passage (Isaiah 40:4–5). King is likening the struggle of African Americans to the struggle of the Israelites.

I have a dream that one day this nation will rise up and live out the true meaning of its creed: "We hold these truths to be self-evident; that all men are created equal."

From every mountainside, let freedom ring.

Let freedom ring from the snowcapped Rockies of Colorado!

Let freedom ring from the curvacious slopes of California!

But not only that; let freedom ring from Stone Mountain of Georgia!

Let freedom ring from Lookout Mountain of Tennessee!

Let freedom ring from every hill and molehill of Mississippi. From every mountainside, let freedom ring.

And when this happens, when we allow freedom to ring, when we let it ring from every village and every hamlet, from every state and every city, we will be able to speed up that day when all of God's children, black men and white men, Jews and Gentiles, Protestants and Catholics, will be able to join hands and sing in the words of the old Negro spiritual, "Free at last! free at last! thank God almighty, we are free at last!"

Spiral Review
Main Idea
Explain the controlling idea of this speech. Remember to take into account the cultural and historical contexts surrounding it.

Critical Thinking

1. **Respond:** What feelings does Dr. King's "I Have a Dream" speech stir in you? Explain.

2. **(a)** Which words does King quote from "My Country 'Tis of Thee"? **(b) Draw Conclusions:** What message does he send to his audience by quoting these lines?

3. **(a)** Which different parts of the United States does King mention in his speech? **(b) Make Inferences:** How does the mention of all of these places tie in with the overall message of his speech?

4. **(a) Hypothesize:** Why do you think "I Have a Dream" has lived on as one of the best-known speeches in modern history? **(b) Make a Judgment:** Do you think it deserves this standing? Explain your response.

 Support your responses with evidence from the text.

 **Is knowledge the same as understanding?**
(a) What facts and information does King give to increase your knowledge of equality in America in the 1960s? **(b)** Do the experiences he shares help you understand the importance of his dream? Explain.

Literary Analysis: Persuasive Speech

1. Of what **proposition** is King trying to convince his readers?

2. (a) In what ways does King appeal to emotion in this speech? Explain. **(b)** In what ways does he appeal to reason? Explain.

3. (a) Using a chart, identify examples of rhetorical structures and devices in King's speech. **(b)** Describe the effect of each example.

	Example	Effect
Parallelism		
Repetition		
Restatement		
Analogy		

4. In this **famous persuasive speech,** does the author use **rhetorical structures** and **devices** effectively to convince the reader of his propositions? Explain your analysis.

Reading Skill: Analyze Persuasion

5. (a) Identify a passage in which King uses **emotionally charged language** as a **persuasive technique. (b)** What specific purpose do you think King had in using such language? Explain. **(c)** Does King use this technique effectively in this speech? Explain.

Vocabulary

Practice In vocabulary study, **analogies** show the relationships between words. Use a word from the list on page 540 to complete each analogy.

1. stumble : rise :: _____ : improve

2. oath : office :: _____ : religion

3. barren : desert :: _____ : church

4. dull : interesting :: trivial : _____

5. supportive : harmful :: assistance : _____

6. broken : promise :: _____ : agreement

Word Power Use the context of the sentences and what you know about the **Latin root -cred-** to explain your answer to each question.

1. Should a judge in a criminal trial have *credibility*?

2. How would you feel if someone tried to *discredit* you?

Word Power

The **Latin root -cred-** means "to trust; to believe."

Apply It Explain how the root -cred- helps you determine the meanings of these technical academic words from social studies. Consult a dictionary if necessary.

credit
creditor
accreditation

Is *knowledge* the same as *understanding*?

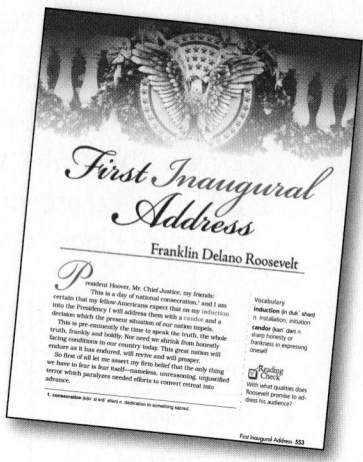

Writing About the Big Question

In "First Inaugural Address," President Roosevelt acknowledges the hard realities of the Great Depression and he promises to do whatever is necessary to help the nation recover. Use this sentence starter to develop your ideas about the Big Question.

For leaders to inspire confidence, they must **comprehend** _____ because _____.

As You Read Look for evidence that the President understands why people are suffering and also why they should have hope.

Vocabulary

Read each word and its definition. Decide whether you know the word well, know it a little bit, or do not know it at all. After you read, see how your knowledge of each word has increased.

- **induction** (in duk´ shən) *n.* installation; initiation (p.553) *At his official __induction__ into the school's honor society, Pedro gave a speech.* induct *v.* inductee *n.*

- **candor** (kan´ dər) *n.* sharp honesty or frankness in expressing oneself (p. 553) *Joanna spoke with great __candor__ about her feelings for her mother.* candid *adj.*

- **abdicated** (ab´ di kāt´ əd) *v.* gave up formally (p. 555) *The king __abdicated__ his throne and left the country.* abdicator *n.*

- **discipline** (dis´ ə plin´) *n.* training that develops self-control, character, or efficiency (p. 557) *Working from home requires a great deal of __discipline__.* discipline *v.* disciplinary *adj.*

- **feasible** (fē´ zə bəl) *adj.* capable of being done or carried out; practicable; possible (p. 559) *Solar heating is both technically and economically __feasible__.* feasibility *n.*

- **arduous** (är´ jo͞o əs) *adj.* difficult; laborious (p. 559) *Rebuilding the house by ourselves was an __arduous__ task.*

Word Power

The **Latin root -duct-** or **-duc-** means "to lead" or "to bring."

Roosevelt speaks during his **induction**—the ceremony that brought him into his role as president of the United States.

Author of

First Inaugural Address

Franklin Delano Roosevelt had a relatively easy life until he was stricken with polio at age 39. Ironically, Roosevelt realized his potential as a leader only after falling victim to this illness. He was twice elected governor of New York; then, in 1932, he defeated President Herbert Hoover to become the nation's thirty-second president. Roosevelt won an unprecedented four terms as president.

A Leader in Dark Times Franklin Roosevelt led the nation through two great challenges: the Great Depression and World War II. The war was almost over when the president died of a cerebral hemorrhage in 1945.

BACKGROUND FOR THE SPEECH
(History Connection)

The Great Depression

On March 4, 1933, newly elected President Franklin Delano Roosevelt delivered his inaugural address to a nation close to despair. The Great Depression had weighed down American life for more than three years. Americans sat by their radios to hear the new president's address, a speech he had written himself. In this speech, Roosevelt gave Americans hope.

Did You Know?
Roosevelt's wife, Eleanor, became one of the most active and widely admired first ladies in American history.

First Inaugural Address

Franklin Delano Roosevelt

President Hoover, Mr. Chief Justice, my friends:

This is a day of national consecration,[1] and I am certain that my fellow-Americans expect that on my induction into the Presidency I will address them with a candor and a decision which the present situation of our nation impels.

This is pre-eminently the time to speak the truth, the whole truth, frankly and boldly. Nor need we shrink from honestly facing conditions in our country today. This great nation will endure as it has endured, will revive and will prosper.

So first of all let me assert my firm belief that the only thing we have to fear is fear itself—nameless, unreasoning, unjustified terror which paralyzes needed efforts to convert retreat into advance.

---

1. **consecration** (kän´ si krā´ shən) *n.* dedication to something sacred.

Vocabulary
induction (in duk´ shən) *n.* installation; initiation

candor (kan´ dər) *n.* sharp honesty in expressing oneself

Literary Analysis
Persuasive Speech
In these first paragraphs, how does the author use the rhetorical device of restatement to try to convince the reader of his propositions?

Reading Skill
Analyze Persuasion
How do you think
Roosevelt wanted
listeners to respond to
the language here?

Spiral Review
Analyze Persuasion
Roosevelt mentions
the arguments of
"foolish optimists."
Is the evidence
given to oppose
their arguments
relevant to, credible
to, and of good
quality for the text's
specific audience?
Explain.

4 In every dark hour of our national life a leadership of frankness and vigor has met with that understanding and support of the people themselves which is essential to victory. I am convinced that you will again give that support to leadership in these critical days.

5 In such a spirit on my part and on yours we face our common difficulties. They concern, thank God, only material things. Values have shrunken to fantastic levels; taxes have risen; our ability to pay has fallen, government of all kinds is faced by serious curtailment of income; the means of exchange are frozen in the currents of trade; the withered leaves of industrial enterprise lie on every side; farmers find no markets for their produce; the savings of many years in thousands of families are gone.

6 More important, a host of unemployed citizens face the grim problem of existence, and an equally great number toil with little return. Only a foolish optimist can deny the dark realities of the moment.

7 Yet our distress comes from no failure of substance. We are stricken by no plague of locusts.[2] Compared with the perils which our forefathers conquered because they believed and were not afraid, we have still much to be thankful for. Nature still offers

---

2. **plague of locusts** According to Exodus 10:3–20, the plague of locusts was one of ten plagues inflicted by God on the Egyptians as punishment for enslaving the Israelites.

Only a foolish optimist can deny
the dark realities of the moment.

her bounty and human efforts have multiplied it. Plenty is at our doorstep, but a generous use of it languishes in the very sight of the supply.

8 Primarily, this is because the rulers of the exchange of mankind's goods have failed through their own stubbornness and their own incompetence, have admitted that failure and abdicated. Practices of the unscrupulous money changers stand indicted in the court of public opinion, rejected by the hearts and minds of men.

9 True, they have tried, but their efforts have been cast in the pattern of an outworn tradition. Faced by failure of credit, they have proposed only the lending of more money.

10 Stripped of the lure of profit by which to induce our people to follow their false leadership, they have resorted to exhortations, pleading tearfully for restored confidence. They know only the rules of a generation of self-seekers.

11 They have no vision, and when there is no vision the people perish.

12 The money changers have fled from their high seats in the temple[3] of our civilization. We may now restore that temple to the ancient truths. ●

---

3. **money changers . . . temple** allusion to Matthew 21:12–13, in which Jesus overturns the money changers' tables at the temple in Jerusalem. FDR is comparing those ancient money changers to modern bankers who took great risks with depositors' money and who charged excessive interest rates for loans.

Literary Analysis
Persuasive Speech
How might this description of national problems have changed people's minds about their troubles?

Vocabulary
abdicated (ab´ di kāt´ əd) v. gave up formally

Reading Check
On whom does Roosevelt place the largest blame for the Great Depression?

Spiral Review
Main Idea
Explain the controlling idea of this speech, remembering to take into account the cultural and historical contexts surrounding it.

13 The measure of the restoration lies in the extent to which we apply social values more noble than mere monetary profit.

14 Happiness lies not in the mere possession of money; it lies in the joy of achievement, in the thrill of creative effort.

15 The joy and moral stimulation of work no longer must be forgotten in the mad chase of evanescent profits. These dark days will be worth all they cost us if they teach us that our true destiny is not to be ministered unto but to minister to ourselves and to our fellow-men.

16 Recognition of the falsity of material wealth as the standard of success goes hand in hand with the abandonment of the false belief that public office and high political position are to be valued only by the standards of pride of place and personal profit; and there must be an end to a conduct in banking and in business which too often has given to a sacred trust the likeness of callous and selfish wrongdoing.

> Happiness lies not in the mere possession of money; it lies in the joy of achievement, in the thrill of creative effort.

17 Small wonder that confidence languishes, for it thrives only on honesty, on honor, on the sacredness of obligations, on faithful protection, on unselfish performance. Without them it cannot live.

18 Restoration calls, however, not for changes in ethics alone. This nation asks for action, and action now.

19 Our greatest primary task is to put people to work. This is no unsolvable problem if we face it wisely and courageously. . . .

20 I favor as a practical policy the putting of first things first. I shall spare no effort to restore world trade by international economic readjustment, but the emergency at home cannot wait on that accomplishment.

21 The basic thought that guides these specific means of national recovery is not narrowly nationalistic.

22 It is the insistence, as a first consideration, upon the interdependence of the various elements in, and parts of, the United States—a recognition of the old and permanently important manifestation of the American spirit of the pioneer.

23 It is the way to recovery. It is the immediate way. It is the strongest assurance that the recovery will endure.

24 In the field of world policy I would dedicate this nation to the policy of the good neighbor—the neighbor who resolutely respects himself and, because he does so, respects the rights of others—the

Literary Analysis
Persuasive Speech
Analyze the parallelism in the paragraph beginning "It is the way . . . ." How might this rhetorical structure help convince the reader of the author's propositions?

neighbor who respects his obligations and respects the sanctity of his agreements in and with a world of neighbors.

25 If I read the temper of our people correctly, we now realize as we have never before, our interdependence on each other; that we cannot merely take, but we must give as well; that if we are to go forward we must move as a trained and loyal army willing to sacrifice for the good of a common discipline, because, without such discipline, no progress is made, no leadership becomes effective.

26 We are, I know, ready and willing to submit our lives and property to such discipline because it makes possible a leadership which aims at a larger good. ●

Vocabulary

discipline (dis´ ə plin´) *n.* training that develops self-control, character, or efficiency

Reading Check

What does Roosevelt say is the "greatest primary task" facing the nation?

LITERATURE IN CONTEXT

Social Studies Connection

Getting Back to Work: FDR and the WPA
In 1935, President Roosevelt established the Works Progress Administration (WPA) to aid struggling Americans. At the height of its activity, the WPA provided jobs to one third of the unemployed, ranging from artists to construction workers.

▲ This mural painted by WPA artist William Gropper shows the building of a WPA project dam.

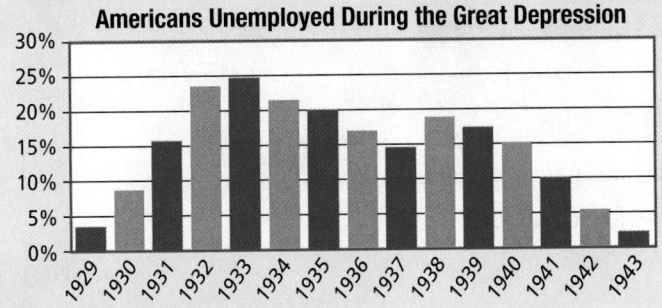

Americans Unemployed During the Great Depression

(Bar graph showing unemployment percentages from 1929 to 1943, with values approximately: 1929: 3%, 1930: 9%, 1931: 16%, 1932: 24%, 1933: 25%, 1934: 22%, 1935: 20%, 1936: 17%, 1937: 15%, 1938: 19%, 1939: 17%, 1940: 11%, 1941: 6%, 1942: 3%)

The WPA Projects

WPA workers produced:	650,000	miles of roads
	125,000	public buildings
	75,000	bridges
	8,000	parks
	800	airports
WPA artists created:	2,566	murals
	100,000	paintings
	17,700	sculptures
	300,000	fine prints

Connect to the Literature

President Roosevelt gave his First Inaugural Address in March of 1933. Basing your answer on the chart of unemployment, explain why this was a particularly hard time in American life.

27   This I propose to offer, pledging that the larger purposes will bind upon us all as a sacred obligation with a unity of duty hitherto evoked only in time of armed strife.

28   With this pledge taken, I assume unhesitatingly the leadership of this great army of our people, dedicated to a disciplined attack upon our common problems.

29   Action in this image and to this end is feasible under the forms of government which we have inherited from our ancestors.

30   Our Constitution is so simple and practical that it is possible always to meet extraordinary needs by changes in emphasis and arrangement without loss of essential form.

31   That is why our constitutional system has proved itself the most superbly enduring political mechanism the modern world has produced. It has met every stress of vast expansion of territory, of foreign wars, of bitter internal strife, of world relations. . . .

32   I am prepared under my constitutional duty to recommend the measures that a stricken nation in the midst of a stricken world may require.

33   These measures, or such other measures as the Congress may build out of its experience and wisdom, I shall seek, within my constitutional authority, to bring to speedy adoption.

34   But in the event that the Congress shall fail to take one of these two courses, and in the event that the national emergency is still critical, I shall not evade the clear course of duty that will then confront me.

35   I shall ask the Congress for the one remaining instrument to meet the crisis—broad executive power to wage a war against the emergency as great as the power that would be given me if we were in fact invaded by a foreign foe. ●

36   For the trust reposed in me I will return the courage and the devotion that befit the time. I can do no less.

37   We face the arduous days that lie before us in the warm courage of national unity; with the clear consciousness of seeking

Vocabulary
feasible (fē′ zə bəl)
adj. capable of being done or carried out; practicable; possible

> Our Constitution is so simple and practical that it is possible always to meet extraordinary needs by changes . . .

Literary Analysis
Persuasive Speech
What call to action does Roosevelt issue to Congress in this passage?

Vocabulary
arduous (är′ jōō əs)
adj. difficult; laborious

◀ **Critical Viewing**
This photograph of President Roosevelt in the Oval Office was taken on the day of his first inauguration. Do you think he projects an image of confidence? Explain. **[Analyze]**

old and precious moral values; with the clean satisfaction that comes from the stern performance of duty by old and young alike.

38 We aim at the assurance of a rounded and permanent national life.

39 We do not distrust the future of essential democracy. The people of the United States have not failed. In their need they have registered a mandate that they want direct, vigorous action.

40 They have asked for discipline and direction under leadership. They have made me the present instrument of their wishes. In the spirit of the gift I take it.

41 In this dedication of a nation we humbly ask the blessing of God. May He protect each and every one of us. May He guide me in the days to come.

Critical Thinking

1. **Respond:** What feelings does Roosevelt's speech stir in you? Explain your response.

2. **(a)** What words does Roosevelt use to describe the leaders who caused the country's financial problems? **(b) Draw Conclusions:** What message is sent by describing financial leaders this way?

3. **(a)** What does Roosevelt say about Americans from earlier periods in history? **(b) Speculate:** How do you think his listeners felt on hearing about earlier Americans?

4. **Make a Judgment:** Roosevelt's speech was made more than seventy years ago to a country in economic ruin. Which parts of the speech do you think would be most appealing to Americans today? Which parts might be less appealing? Explain.

Support your responses with evidence from the text.

Is knowledge the same as understanding?
(a) What information in this speech lets you know that Roosevelt understands the country he is about to lead?
(b) What is the main thing he wants his listeners to understand?

Literary Analysis: Persuasive Speech

1. Of what **proposition** is Roosevelt trying to convince his readers?

2. (a) In what ways does Roosevelt appeal to emotion in his speech? Explain. **(b)** In what ways does he appeal to reason? Explain.

3. (a) Using a chart, identify examples of rhetorical structures and devices in Roosevelt's speech. **(b)** Describe the effect of each example.

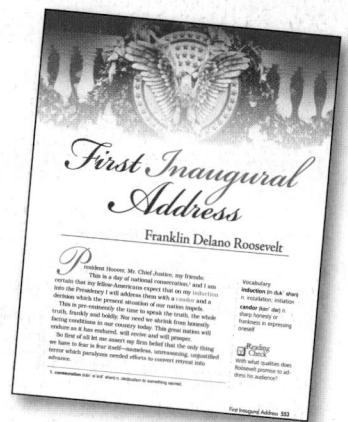

	Example	Effect
Parallelism		
Repetition		
Restatement		
Analogy		

4. In this **famous persuasive speech,** does the author use **rhetorical structures** and **devices** effectively to convince the reader of his propositions? Explain your analysis.

Reading Skill: Analyze Persuasion

5. (a) Identify a passage in which Roosevelt uses **emotionally charged language** as a **persuasive technique. (b)** What specific purpose do you think Roosevelt had in using such language? Explain. **(c)** Does Roosevelt use this technique effectively in this speech? Explain.

Vocabulary

Practice Vocabulary **analogies** show the relationships between pairs of words. Use a word from the list on page 550 to complete each analogy.

1. coach : resigned :: ruler : _____

2. vacation : relaxing :: labor : _____

3. insecurity : confidence :: deception : _____

4. vague : definite :: impossible : _____

5. initiation : fraternity :: _____ : military

6. left : right :: laxness : _____

Word Power Use the context of sentences and what you know about the **Latin root -duct-** or **-duc-** to explain your answer to each question.

1. If you *introduce* someone, do you help her meet other people?

2. Is a *conductor* someone who watches an orchestra?

Word Power

The **Latin root -duct-** or **-duc-** means "to lead" or "to bring."

Apply It Explain how the root *-duct-* or *-duc-* help you determine the meanings of these technical academic words from science. Consult a dictionary if necessary.

conduct
deduction
superconductor

Integrated Language Skills

"I Have a Dream" • First Inaugural Address

Conventions: Adverbs

Adverbs are words that modify verbs, adjectives, and other adverbs. They answer the questions *Where? When? In what way?* and *To what extent?* about the words they modify.

An adverb modifying a verb can answer any of the above questions. An adverb modifying an adjective or another adverb will only answer the question *To what extent?*

Modifying a verb:
Dave drove the car <u>smoothly.</u> (The adverb *smoothly* modifies the verb *drove*.)

Modifying an adjective:
He drove an <u>extremely</u> large car. (The adverb *extremely* modifies the adjective *large*.)

Modifying another adverb:
He drove the car <u>very</u> smoothly. (The adverb *very* modifies the adverb *smoothly*.)

Practice A Identify the adverbs in the following sentences. Then, tell what question each adverb answers.

1. King stood there waiting to speak.
2. King spoke clearly and passionately before the large audience.
3. The audience was especially attentive to King's words.
4. King spoke more forcefully than people remembered.

Reading Application Find three sentences in "I Have a Dream" that include an adverb. Identify the word modified as a verb, an adjective, or another adverb.

Practice B In each sentence, identify the adverb and the word it modifies. Then, write a related sentence using a different adverb.

1. Roosevelt spoke compassionately to his audience.
2. Roosevelt often spoke to the nation.
3. Roosevelt very clearly understood the needs of his listeners.
4. Roosevelt was calmly resolute.

Writing Application Choose one photo from "First Inaugural Address." Write three sentences to describe the photograph. Use adverbs to modify verbs, adjectives, and adverbs.

PH GRAMMAR HANDBOOK Further instruction and practice are available in the *Prentice Hall Grammar Handbook*.

Writing

Write an **expository essay** to analyze how foundational United States documents relate to the foundational work of American literature you read.

- If you read "I Have a Dream," analyze how the speech relates to the Bill of Rights of the U.S. Constitution.
- If you read "First Inaugural Address," analyze how the speech relates to the portion of the Emergency Relief Appropriation Act of 1935 that established the Works Progress Administration.

Use Internet and library sources to locate and research the document. Then, read it and draft a brief essay. In your essay, explain how the foundational document is relevant to the speech. Also, describe how each text helps you to better understand and appreciate the issues addressed in the other text.

Grammar Application Make sure to use adverbs correctly in your essay.

Writing Workshop: *Work in Progress*

Prewriting for Editorial Review the Topic List you have prepared. Identify one cultural factor that you feel has the greatest effect on you and your friends. In a two-column chart, jot down three positive and three negative aspects of this influence. Save this Positive/Negative Chart in your writing portfolio.

Listening and Speaking

With a partner, present a **television news report** that provides on-the-spot coverage of the speech you just read. Include excerpts from the speech, a description of the crowd's reaction, and appropriate background information.

- If you read "I Have a Dream," include information about the civil rights movement.
- If you read "First Inaugural Address," include information about the Great Depression.

Keep the needs of your audience, purpose, and occasion in mind as you consider these tips to make your presentation successful:

- Speak clearly and to the point.
- Use **formal language** effectively to share information with your listeners.
- Employ **eye contact** and **purposeful gestures** to keep the interest of your audience.
- Use **speaking rate** (e.g., pauses for effect), **volume, enunciation,** and **conventions of language** to communicate ideas effectively.

 Focus on the TEKS

Writing
(15) Write expository text to communicate ideas and information.

Listening and Speaking
(25) Give presentations using formal language effectively to meet the needs of audience, purpose, and occasion, employing eye contact, speaking rate (e.g., pauses for effect), volume, enunciation, purposeful gestures, and conventions of language to communicate ideas effectively.

Use this prewriting activity to prepare for the **Writing Workshop** on page 582.

PHLitOnline
www.PHLitOnline.com

- Interactive graphic organizers
- Grammar tutorial
- Interactive journals

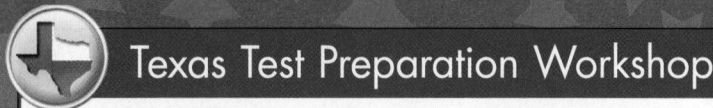
Strategy for Success

Analyze Evidence

The reading sections of the PSAT, the SAT, and Texas standardized tests may ask you to analyze evidence in text that is intended to persuade. Authors may base arguments on facts or expert testimony, or they may use faulty assumptions and emotional appeals. When you analyze the relevance, quality, and credibility of evidence given to support or oppose arguments on standardized tests, you will be prepared to evaluate the overall arguments to determine whether they are valid.

Consider each piece of evidence in the text to determine whether or not it is valid support for the author's argument. The following examples show how you can analyze evidence on standardized tests.

Focus on the TEKS

Reading
(10) Analyze the relevance, quality, and credibility of evidence given to support or oppose an argument for a specific audience.

Analyze Relevance

Not all details and evidence in a persuasive text are relevant, or central to the argument. Identify which statements are relevant and which are not.

5   Household chores teach kids valuable skills. Chores help children to be responsible. A child who helps at home learns how to take care of herself and to take pride in work. Paying kids for chores can help them learn to manage money. Some children even like having chores.

1. Which evidence is not relevant to the author's argument?
   (A) Chores teach responsibility.
   (B) Chores teach self-reliance.
   (C) Chores help children to take pride in their work.
   (D) Money from chores helps kids learn about finances.
   (E) Some kids enjoy having regular chores.

The author's controlling idea is that chores teach important skills. **A, B, C,** and **D** all support the idea that chores are good educational tools for children. **E** is the correct answer, because it does not relate to the argument that chores teach children skills.

Analyze Quality and Credibility

An author may support an argument with information from appropriate, credible sources, or he or she may appeal to emotion with words meant to affect readers' feelings. Arguments based on accurate facts are more likely to be more credible and of better quality than arguments based on emotional appeals.

5   Wild animals should never be captured. The sadness in the eyes of a wild animal looking through the bars of a cage is unmistakable.

2. The author uses which of the following to make his or her point?
   (A) logical reasoning
   (B) personal experience
   (C) expert testimony
   (D) emotional appeal
   (E) statistical data

The second sentence uses a sad image to appeal to readers' emotions. **D** is correct. The options listed in **A, B, C,** and **E** are examples of other types of appeals, but they are not modeled here.

SAT/PSAT Practice

Questions 1–4 are based on the following passage.

My career as a music teacher, drama director, and principal taught me that the arts are essential in helping students develop skills and character traits that will help them be successful throughout their lives.

Line
5
In one university's study of student development, music was the only subject in which students had to make four or five decisions every second and take responsibility for acting on those decisions to meet their goals.

Published reports show that students who participate in the arts are four times more likely to be recognized for academic achievement than their peers. They are likely to read for pleasure nearly twice as often and
10 volunteer for community service more than four times as often.

Involvement in artistic activities improves students' creativity, thinking skills, decision making, confidence, and work ethic. Business leaders say these are exactly the skills students will need to succeed in the working world as adults.

15 To help students acquire these important skills, schools must encourage students' interest in the arts and provide avenues for them to participate. By instilling the confidence to take risks and achieve goals, the arts are key to helping young people develop into successful adults.

1. In lines 1–3, the author lists his or her career history to prove that he or she is
(A) a methodical writer
(B) an expert on arts education
(C) an master of persuasion
(D) a leading recruiter of teachers
(E) a candidate for a promotion

2. In the second and third paragraphs, the author supports the argument by
(A) making generalizations about the arts
(B) presenting logical reasoning
(C) citing studies and reports
(D) quoting knowledgeable people
(E) giving personal opinions

3. The author cites business leaders to show that
(A) the arts matter to businesses
(B) experts agree with her argument
(C) many artists work in businesses
(D) business requires confidence
(E) the arts teach decision making

4. Which statement(s), if true, would weaken the claim of this passage?
   I Some schools have programs in the arts.
   II Music classes discourage ambition.
   III Some schools have more funding for arts education than other schools.
(A) I only
(B) II only
(C) III only
(D) I and II only
(E) I, II, and III

Informational Texts

Persuasive Texts

Historical Research Study	Speech
Nothing to Fear	**Radio Address**

Focus on the TEKS

Reading
(10)(A) Analyze the relevance, quality, and credibility of evidence given to support an argument for a specific audience.

(10)(B) Analyze famous speeches for the rhetorical structures and devices used to convince the reader of the authors' propositions.

Writing
(13)(B) Develop drafts in timed situations that include the rhetorical devices used to convey meaning.

Reading Skill: Analyze Evidence

When an author makes an argument, his or her purpose is to convince a specific audience to adopt a position. To determine whether the argument is valid, you must analyze the **relevance, quality,** and **credibility** of evidence the author gives to support the argument.

Authors may also use **rhetorical structures and devices** to appeal to listeners' or readers' feelings. Note whether the author has used any of the following techniques to convince listeners or readers of his or her propositions. Look out for rhetoric that hides a lack of evidence.

- **Repetition** and **parallelism** are the use of repeated words or language structures.

- **Analogies** compare one situation or relationship to another.

- **Restatement** is the repetition of the same idea in different words.

As You Read Use a checklist like this one to analyze the evidence, rhetorical structures, and rhetorical devices given to support arguments for specific audiences and convince readers of the authors' propositions.

		yes	no
Relevance	Is the evidence closely connected or related to the topic?	☐	☐
Quality	Does the evidence have value, merit, or worth?	☐	☐
Credibility	Is the evidence believable, logical, and from a reliable and unbiased, or impartial, source?	☐	☐
Rhetorical Structures and Devices	If rhetorical structures and devices are used, are they conveying valid evidence rather than simply evoking emotions?	☐	☐

Features:

- summary or excerpt of a historical document
- facts and opinions about the document
- explanations and interpretations
- text written for a specific audience

from **Nothing to Fear:**
Lessons in Leadership from FDR
by Alan Axelrod

"This great nation will endure as it has endured, will revive and will prosper. So, first of all, let me assert my firm belief that the only thing we have to fear is fear itself—nameless, unreasoning, unjustified terror which paralyzes needed efforts to convert retreat into advance."

—First inaugural address, March 4, 1933

The study begins with a quotation from a speech by Franklin Delano Roosevelt. It focuses the argument on the famous line, "The only thing we have to fear is fear itself." All evidence should be closely related to this topic.

In *Defending Your Life*, a charmingly provocative 1991 movie written and directed by its star, Albert Brooks, we discover that the only truly unforgivable sin in life is fear. Killed in a head-on crash with a bus, yuppie Brooks finds himself transported to Judgment City, where he must "defend his life" before a pair of judges who will decide whether he is to be returned to Earth for another crack at life or be permitted to progress to the next plane of existence. His attorney (for the benevolent managers of the universe provide defense assistance) explains to him the nature of fear, which is, he says, a "fog" that obscures everything and that makes intelligent, productive action impossible.

It is a stimulating thought—that fear is not so much the sensation accompanying the realization of danger, but a fog, an obscurer of truth, an interference with how we may productively engage reality. Certainly this is the way FDR saw it. In 1921 polio threatened first to kill him and then paralyzed him, subjected him to a life of relentless pain, and nearly ended his career in public service. He could then and there have given in to the fog of fear, but he chose not to. He chose instead to understand polio, to see clearly the extent of his disability, and then to assess—also clearly—his options for overcoming that disability. He did not blink at the odds. He looked at them, contemplated them, assessed them, and then acted on them.

Franklin D. Roosevelt with a local child, 1941.

Now, more than a decade later, assuming the office of president of the United States, he began by asking the American people to sweep aside the fog of fear, "nameless, unreasoning, unjustified terror which paralyzes needed efforts to convert retreat into advance." He didn't ask them to stop being afraid, but to stop letting fear obscure their vision of reality. He asked the people to confront what they feared, so that they could see clearly what needed to be done and thereby overcome (and the word is significant) the terror that paralyzes.

● In the second paragraph of his inaugural speech, FDR lifted the fog of fear. What did he reveal to his audience, the American people?

> Values have shrunken to fantastic levels; taxes have risen; our ability to pay has fallen; government of all kinds is faced by serious curtailment of income; the means of exchange are frozen in the currents of trade; the withered leaves of industrial enterprise lie on every side; farmers find no markets for their produce; the savings of many years in thousands of families are gone.

● There is no sugarcoating of reality here! The fog has lifted, the scene is sharply etched and downright frightening: "a host of unemployed citizens face the grim problem of existence, and an equally great number toil with little return. Only a foolish optimist can deny the dark realities of the moment."

FDR did not blink at reality and he did not allow his audience to do so either. He embarked on this catalog of economic disasters by defining them as "our common difficulties," which "concern, thank God, only material things."

The fog was lifted and the president's listeners could see the reality they already knew, a reality of poverty and despair, to be sure; yet with the fog of fear lifted, they could see it in a new light: Our common difficulties "concern, thank God, only material things."

Not one to blink at disaster, FDR also saw a way out of it:

> Yet our distress comes from no failure of substance. We are stricken by no plague of locusts. Compared with the perils which our forefathers conquered because they believed and were not afraid, we have still much to be thankful for. Nature still offers her bounty and human efforts have multiplied it. Plenty is at our doorstep. . .

Lift the fog of fear and you could see that the Great Depression was not of natural, supernatural, or inevitable origin. It was not a plague of biblical proportion. Our kind has conquered worse in the past.

 **Is knowledge the same as understanding?**
How has this research study affected your understanding of how FDR viewed fear? Explain your response.

Axelrod refers back to the "fog" described in the introduction. In later paragraphs, he continues to refer to the "fog of fear." This repetition gives structure to the text, and attempts to show the relevance of each piece of evidence he provides.

In this paragraph, the author makes a generalization about the speech. **Is the quote he uses as evidence to support his argument relevant, credible, and of good quality? Explain.**

from
Radio Address on Drought Conditions

by Franklin Delano Roosevelt
September 6, 1936

Features:

- text spoken aloud to an audience
- remarks that communicate an important message
- language intended to engage listeners and support the speaker's ideas

I have been on a journey of husbandry. I went primarily to see at first hand conditions in the drought states; to see how effectively Federal and local authorities are taking care of pressing problems of relief and also how they are to work together to defend the people of this country against the effects of future droughts.

I saw drought devastation in nine states.

I talked with families who had lost their wheat crop, lost their corn crop, lost their livestock, lost the water in their well, lost their garden and come through to the end of the summer without one dollar of cash resources, facing a winter without feed or food—facing a planting season without seed to put in the ground.

That was the extreme case, but there are thousands and thousands of families on western farms who share the same difficulties.

I saw cattlemen who because of lack of grass or lack of winter feed have been compelled to sell all but their breeding stock and will need help to carry even these through the coming winter. I saw livestock kept alive only because water had been brought to them long distances in tank cars. I saw other farm families who have not lost everything but who, because they have made only partial crops, must have some form of help if they are to continue farming next spring.

I shall never forget the fields of wheat so blasted by heat that they cannot be harvested. I shall never forget field after field of corn stunted, earless and stripped of leaves, for what the sun left the grasshoppers took. I saw brown pastures which would not keep a cow on fifty acres.

Yet I would not have you think for a single minute that there is permanent disaster in these drought regions, or that the picture I saw meant depopulating these areas. No cracked earth, no blistering sun, no burning wind, no grasshoppers, are a permanent match for the indomitable American farmers and stockmen and their wives and children who have carried on through desperate days, and inspire us with their self-reliance, their tenacity and their courage. It was their fathers' task to make homes; it is their task to keep those homes; it is our task to help them with their fight.

First let me talk for a minute about this autumn and the coming winter. We have the option, in the case of families who need actual subsistence, of putting them on the dole or putting them to work. They do not want to go on the dole and they are one thousand percent right. We agree, therefore, that we must put them to work for a decent wage, and when we reach that decision we

In this famous speech, Roosevelt repeats the word I to emphasize his personal experience. **How might this rhetorical structure help convince readers of the president's propositions?**

Here, Roosevelt restates a general idea several times in different ways. **How might this rhetorical device help convince readers of the author's propositions?**

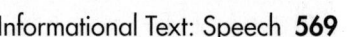

kill two birds with one stone, because these families will earn enough by working, not only to subsist themselves, but to buy food for their stock, and seed for next year's planting. Into this scheme of things there fit of course the government lending agencies which next year, as in the past, will help with production loans.

Every Governor with whom I have talked is in full accord with this program of doing work for these farm families, just as every Governor agrees that the individual states will take care of their unemployables but that the cost of employing those who are entirely able and willing to work must be borne by the Federal Government. . . .

Roosevelt gives evidence to support the argument he is making.

Spending like this is not waste. It would spell future waste if we did not spend for such things now. These emergency work projects provide money to buy food and clothing for the winter; they keep the livestock on the farm; they provide seed for a new crop, and, best of all, they will conserve soil and water in the future in those areas most frequently hit by drought.

If, for example, in some local area the water table continues to drop and the topsoil to blow away, the land values will disappear with the water and the soil. People on the farms will drift into the nearby cities; the cities will have no farm trade and the workers in the city factories and stores will have no jobs. Property values in the cities will decline. If, on the other hand, the farms within that area remain as farms with better water supply and no erosion, the farm population will stay on the land and prosper and the nearby cities will prosper too. Property values will increase instead of disappearing. That is why it is worth our while as a nation to spend money in order to save money.

. . . The very existence of the men and women working in the clothing factories of New York, making clothes worn by farmers and their families; of the workers in the steel mills in Pittsburgh, in the automobile factories of Detroit, and in the harvester factories of Illinois, depend upon the farmers' ability to purchase the commodities they produce. In the same way it is the purchasing power of the workers in these factories in the cities that enables them and their wives and children to eat more beef, more pork, more wheat, more corn, more fruit and more dairy products, and to buy more clothing made from cotton, wool and leather. In a physical and a property sense, as well as in a spiritual sense, we are members one of another.

. . . We are going to have a farm policy that will serve the national welfare. That is our hope for the future.

THE BIG ?

Is knowledge the same as understanding?

How successful is Roosevelt at helping his audience to understand his plan for dealing with drought conditions? Explain your response.

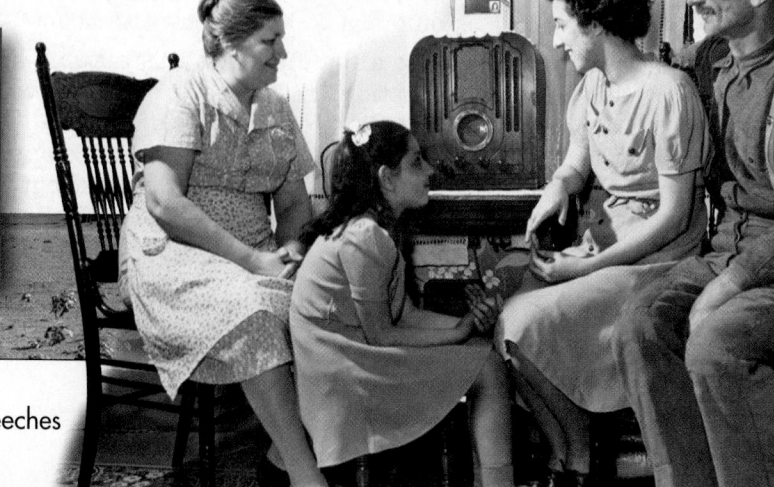

Comparing Informational Texts

(a) Analyze: Compare the **relevance, quality, and credibility of the evidence given to support the authors' arguments** in the historical research study and the speech. Be sure to consider the specific audience of each text in your analysis. **(b)** Compare the ways in which each author uses **rhetorical structures and devices** to convince the reader of his propositions. Provide evidence from the texts to support your ideas.

 College Readiness | Timed Writing

Write a Persuasive Essay

Format
The prompt directs you to write a persuasive essay. Therefore, you should consider and include techniques, devices, and language that will convince your audience that your ideas are logical and correct.

Write a persuasive essay in which you propose a solution to a problem in your school or community. In your essay, present an explanation of the problem as well as a description of your solution. Include rhetorical devices, such as analogy and restatement, to help convince readers of your proposition and clearly convey your meaning. (35 minutes)

Academic Vocabulary
When you *propose* an idea, you suggest it and then show that your plan is logical and sound. A well-written proposal provides facts and evidence as support.

 ### 5-Minute Planner

Complete these steps before you begin to write:

1. Read the prompt carefully and completely.

2. Jot down three problems that exist in your school or community. Then, choose the one you have the strongest feelings about as the topic of your essay.

3. Consider how the problem you have chosen might be solved. Make notes about your ideas.

4. Review your solutions and choose the strongest ideas as the ones you will include in your essay.

5. Reread the prompt.

6. Refer to your notes as you draft your essay. **TIP** Make sure you address all parts of the prompt in your response.

Comparing Literary Works

The Talk • Talk

Comparing Humorous Writing

Humor is an **element** of both **fiction** and **literary nonfiction.** Humorous writing is intended to make the reader laugh. It may also include a serious message or issue.

A **folk tale** is a story passed down from generation to generation that expresses the beliefs and values of its culture. Folk tales typically present simple characters and far-fetched situations. A humorous folk tale is meant to entertain and instruct. In humorous fiction, authors often include these figures of speech:

- **hyperbole:** intentional, sometimes outrageous, exaggeration—for example, describing a small patch of ice as a "vast, frozen wasteland"

- **understatement:** the presentation of an idea, a person, or an event to make it seem less than it is—for example, describing a huge loss as a "minor setback"

Besides these elements, the writer's comic diction, or word choice, may include informal, colloquial language; slang; or other verbal humor.

As You Read Use a graphic organizer like the one shown to identify the serious ideas in "The Talk" and "Talk." Then, explain why the authors may have chosen to use humorous elements of fiction and features of nonfiction to explore these issues. Use **evidence** from the text to support your understanding.

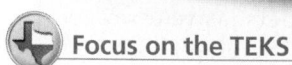 **Focus on the TEKS**

Reading
(5) Understand the elements of fiction and provide evidence from the text to support understanding.
(6) Understand the features of literary nonfiction and provide evidence from the text to support understanding.

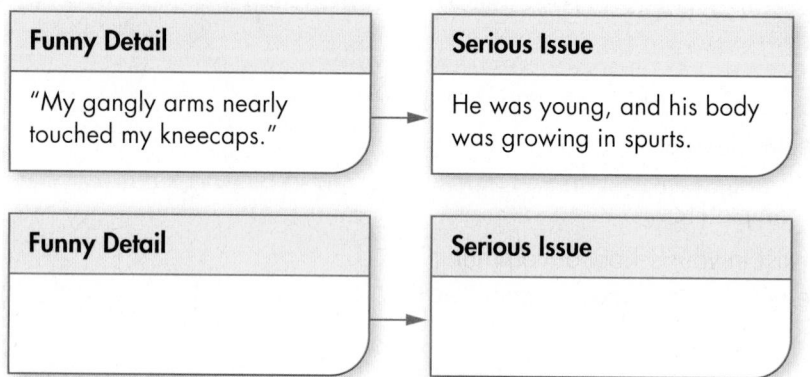

Funny Detail		Serious Issue
"My gangly arms nearly touched my kneecaps."	→	He was young, and his body was growing in spurts.

Funny Detail		Serious Issue
	→	

PHLitOnline
www.PHLitOnline.com

- Vocabulary flashcards
- Interactive journals
- More about the authors

- Selection audio
- Interactive graphic organizers

572 Types of Nonfiction: Essays, Articles, and Speeches

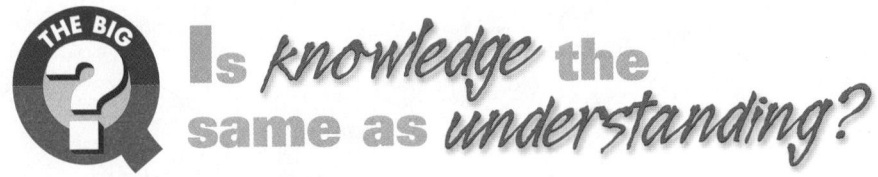

Is *knowledge* the same as *understanding?*

Writing About the Big Question

In both of these selections, the writers describe serious ideas or **insights** in a humorous way. Use this sentence starter to develop your ideas about the Big Question.

Humor can help **clarify** ideas and build understanding by _____.

Meet the Authors

Gary Soto (b. 1952)
Author of "The Talk"

Gary Soto grew up in a Mexican American section of Fresno, California. As a child, he wanted to be either a priest or a scientist. Then, in high school, he discovered great writers, including John Steinbeck and Robert Frost. In college, Soto started writing poetry.

Living Through Books Soto's favorite pastime is reading. He has said, "It appears these days I don't have much of a life because my nose is often stuck in a book. But I discovered that reading builds a life inside the mind."

Harold Courlander (1908–1996) and George Herzog (1901–1983)
Retellers of "Talk"

"Talk" is an Ashanti folk tale. The Ashanti live in what is now the West African country of Ghana. They have a history that dates back centuries. "Talk" is retold by Harold Courlander and George Herzog.

A Distinguished Career Courlander studied the history and folklore of African and other world cultures. He wrote more than thirty-five fiction and nonfiction books inspired by these studies.

Music and Culture Born in Budapest, Hungary, Herzog pioneered the study of the cultural aspects of music. He also taught linguistics and anthropology and published books on folk music.

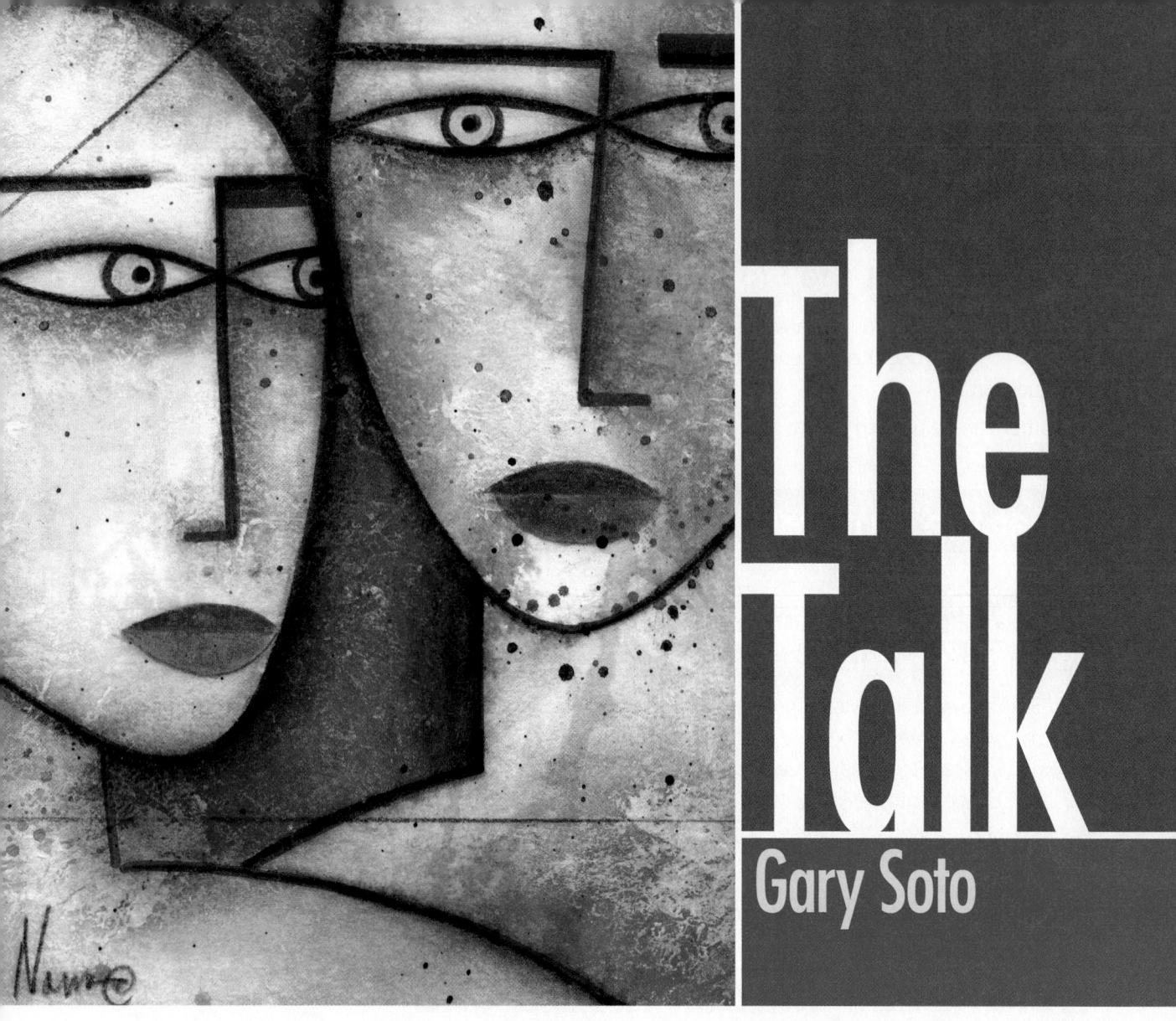

The Talk

Gary Soto

▲ **Critical Viewing**
Based on this image and
title, what topics do you
think the author of this
essay might discuss?
Explain. **[Predict]**

My best friend and I knew that we were going to grow up to be ugly.
On a backyard lawn—the summer light failing west of the mulberry
tree where the house of the most beautiful girl on the street stood—
we talked about what we could do: shake the second-base dirt from
our hair, wash our hands of frog smells and canal water, and learn
to smile without showing our crooked teeth. We had to stop spitting
when girls were looking and learn not to pile food onto a fork and
into a fat cheek already churning hot grub.

We were twelve, with lean bodies that were beginning to grow
in weird ways. First, our heads got large, but our necks wavered,
frail as crisp tulips. The eyes stayed small as well, receding into
pencil dots on each side of an unshapely nose that cast remarkable
shadows when we turned sideways. It seemed that Scott's legs

sprouted muscle and renegade veins, but his arms, blue with ink markings, stayed short and hung just below his waist. My gangly arms nearly touched my kneecaps. In this way, I was built for picking up grounders and doing cartwheels, my arms swaying just inches from the summery grass.

We sat on the lawn, with the porch light off, waiting for the beautiful girl to turn on her bedroom light and read on her stomach with one leg stirring the air. This stirred us, and our dream was a clean dream of holding hands and airing out our loneliness by walking up and down the block.

When Scott asked whom I was going to marry, I said a brown girl from the valley. He said that he was going to marry a strawberry blonde who would enjoy Millerton Lake, dirty as it was. I said mine would like cats and the sea and would think nothing of getting up at night from a warm, restless bed and sitting in the yard under the icy stars. Scott said his wife would work for the first year or so, because he would go to trade school[1] in refrigeration. Since our town was made with what was left over after God made hell, there was money in air conditioning, he reasoned.

I said that while my wife would clean the house and stir pots of nice grub, I would drive a truck to my job as a carpenter, which would allow me to use my long arms. I would need only a stepladder to hand a fellow worker on the roof a pinch of nails. I could hammer, saw, lift beams into place, and see the work I got done at the end of the day. Of course, she might like to work, and that would be okay, because then we could buy two cars and wave at each other if we should see the other drive by. In the evenings, we would drink Kool-Aid and throw a slipper at our feisty dog at least a hundred times before we went inside for a Pop-Tart and hot chocolate.

Scott said he would work hard too, but now and then he would find money on the street and the two of them could buy extra things like a second TV for the bedroom and a Doughboy swimming pool for his three kids. He planned on having three kids and a ranch house on the river, where he could dip a hand in the water, drink, and say, "Ahh, tastes good."

But that would be years later. Now we had to do something about our looks. We plucked at the grass and flung it into each other's faces.

"Rotten luck," Scott said. "My arms are too short. Look at 'em."

"Maybe we can lift weights. This would make up for our looks," I said.

"I don't think so," Scott said, depressed. "People like people with nice faces."

---

1. **trade school** school that specializes in teaching the skills needed to work in a particular job.

Vocabulary
renegade (ren´ ə gād´) *adj.* disloyal; traitorous

Literary Analysis
Humorous Writing
Which details of the boys' youthful dreams might seem funny later in life?

Vocabulary
feisty (fīs´ tē) *adj.* full of spirit; energetic

Reading Check
What are the boys worried they will be like when they grow up?

He was probably right. I turned onto my stomach, a stalk of grass in my mouth. "Even if I'm ugly, my wife's going to be good-looking," I said. "She'll have a lot of dresses and I'll have more shirts than I have now. Do you know how much carpenters make?"

Then I saw the bedroom light come on and the beautiful girl walk into the room drying her hair with a towel. I nudged Scott's short arm and he saw what I saw. We flicked the stalks of grass, stood up, and walked over to the fence to look at her scrub her hair dry. She plopped onto the bed and began to comb it, slowly at first because it was tangled. With a rubber band, she tied it back, and picked up a book that was thick as a good-sized sandwich.

Scott and I watched her read a book, now both legs in the air and twined together, her painted toenails like red petals. She turned the pages slowly, very carefully, and now and then lowered her face into the pillow. She looked sad but beautiful, and we didn't know what to do except nudge each other in the heart and creep away to the front yard.

"I can't stand it anymore. We have to talk about this," Scott said.

"If I try, I think I can make myself better looking," I said. "I read an article about a girl whitening her teeth with water and flour."

So we walked up the street, depressed. For every step I took, Scott took two, his short arms pumping to keep up. For every time Scott said, "I think we're ugly," I said two times, "Yeah, yeah, we're in big trouble."

> "I can't stand it anymore. We have to talk about this."

Critical Thinking

1. **Respond:** What were your feelings about the boys as you read this essay? Explain.

2. **(a)** What jobs do the boys hope to have when they get older? **(b) Make Inferences:** What do the boys' choices of future jobs suggest about their characters? Explain.

3. **(a) Make Inferences:** Do you think this is the first time the boys have watched the beautiful girl? Why or why not? **(b) Draw Conclusions:** What do you think the girl in the window represents for the two boys?

4. **Speculate:** What advice do you think an adult might give the two boys to help them feel better about themselves?

 Support your responses with evidence from the text.

 **Is knowledge the same as understanding?**
Soto presents the boys' expectations of the future in a humorous way. What impact does the use of humor have on your understanding of the characters and their plight?

·Talk·

retold by **Harold Courlander** and **George Herzog**

ONCE, not far from the city of Accra on the Gulf of Guinea, a country man went out to his garden to dig up some yams to take to market. While he was digging, one of the yams said to him:

"Well, at last you're here. You never weeded me, but now you come around with your digging stick. Go away and leave me alone!"

The farmer turned around and looked at his cow in amazement. The cow was chewing her cud and looking at him.

"Did you say something?" he asked.

The cow kept on chewing and said nothing, but the man's dog spoke up.

"It wasn't the cow who spoke to you," the dog said. "It was the yam. The yam says leave him alone."

The man became angry, because his dog had never talked before, and he didn't like his tone besides. So he took his knife and cut a branch from a palm tree to whip his dog. Just then the palm tree said:

"Put that branch down!"

The man was getting very upset about the way things were going, and he started to throw the palm branch away, but the palm branch said:

"Man, put me down softly!"

He put the branch down gently on a stone, and the stone said:

"Hey, take that thing off me!"

This was enough, and the frightened farmer started to run for his village. On the way he met a fisherman going the other way with a fish trap on his head.

"What's the hurry?" the fisherman asked.

"My yam said, 'Leave me alone!' Then the dog said, 'Listen to what the yam says!' When I went to whip the dog with a palm branch the tree said, 'Put that branch down!' Then the palm branch said, 'Do it softly!' Then the stone said, 'Take that thing off me!'"

"Is that all?" the man with the fish trap asked. "Is that so frightening?"

"Well," the man's fish trap said, "did he take it off the stone?"

"Wah!" the fisherman shouted. He threw the fish trap on the ground and began to run with the farmer, and on the trail they met a weaver with a bundle of cloth on his head.

"Where are you going in such a rush?" he asked them.

"My yam said, 'Leave me alone!'" the farmer said. "The dog said, 'Listen to what the yam says!' The tree said, 'Put that branch down!' The branch said, 'Do it softly!' And the stone said, 'Take that thing off me!'"

Literary Analysis
Humorous Writing
How do the authors use the element of understatement to add humor to this passage?

"And then," the fisherman continued, "the fish trap said, 'Did he take it off?'"

"That's nothing to get excited about," the weaver said, "no reason at all."

"Oh yes it is," his bundle of cloth said. "If it happened to you you'd run too!"

"Wah!" the weaver shouted. He threw his bundle on the trail and started running with the other men.

They came panting to the ford in the river and found a man bathing.

"Are you chasing a gazelle?" he asked them.

The first man said breathlessly:

"My yam talked at me, and it said, 'Leave me alone!' And my dog said, 'Listen to your yam!' And when I cut myself a branch the tree said, 'Put that branch down!' And the branch said, 'Do it softly!' And the stone said, 'Take that thing off me!'"

The fisherman panted:

"And my trap said, 'Did he?'"

The weaver wheezed:

"And my bundle of cloth said, 'You'd run too!'"

"Is that why you're running?" the man in the river asked.

"Well, wouldn't you run if you were in their position?" the river said.

The man jumped out of the water and began to run with the others. They ran down the main street of the village to the house of the chief. The chief's servants brought his stool out, and he came and sat on it to listen to their complaints. The men began to recite their troubles.

"I went out to my garden to dig yams," the farmer said, waving his arms. "Then everything began to talk! My yam said, 'Leave me alone!' My dog said, 'Pay attention to your yam!' The tree said, 'Put that branch down!' The branch said, 'Do it softly!' And the stone said, 'Take it off me!'"

"Wah!" the weaver shouted. He threw his bundle on the trail and started running with the other men.

Vocabulary

wheezed (wēzd´) *v.* breathed hard with a breathy sound

![Reading Check]Reading Check

What prompts the man in the river to start to run with the others?

Vocabulary

bulging (bulj iŋ) *adj.*
swelling

refrain (ri frān´) *v.* hold
back

Literary Analysis
Humorous Writing
How would this folk tale
be different if it ended
with the line "Nonsense
like that upsets the
community"?

"And my fish trap said, 'Well, did he
take it off?'" the fisherman said.

"And my cloth said, 'You'd run
too!'" the weaver said.

"And the river said the same,"
the bather said hoarsely, his
eyes bulging.

The chief listened to them
patiently, but he couldn't
refrain from scowling.

"Now this is really a wild
story," he said at last. "You'd
better all go back to your
work before I punish you for
disturbing the peace."

So the men went away, and
the chief shook his head and
mumbled to himself, "Nonsense
like that upsets the community."

"Fantastic, isn't it?" his stool
said. "Imagine, a talking yam!"

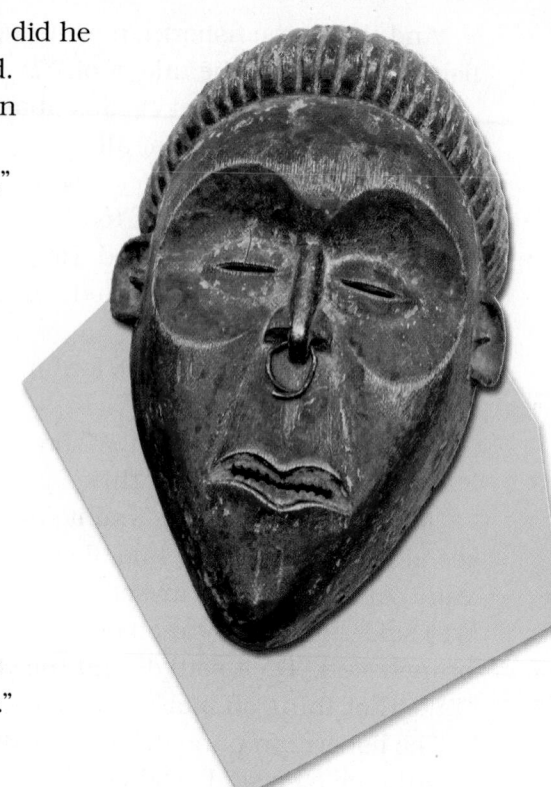

Critical Thinking

1. **Respond:** What were your feelings about the characters who
   heard the things talking? Explain.

2. **(a)** Why does the man cut a branch from the palm tree?
   (b) Interpret: Why does the man want to whip his dog?

Support
your responses
with evidence
from the text.

3. **(a)** What is the fisherman's first response when he hears the farmer's story? **(b) Draw Conclusions:** Why doesn't the fisherman
   become frightened when he hears the farmer's story?
   (c) Draw Conclusions: Why does the fisherman become frightened only after his fish trap talks to him?

4. **(a)** How does the chief react when the men tell him what happened to them? **(b) Speculate:** How do you think the chief
   reacted when he heard the stool talk?

   Is knowledge the same as understanding?
   (a) What serious message do you think this folk tale
   might convey? Explain. **(b)** Why might the author have
   chosen humorous writing to convey this message?

Comparing Humorous Writing

1. (a) Use a chart like the one shown to identify at least one example of each of the listed elements in each piece of humorous writing.
(b) Explain how each example adds to the humor of the writing.

Element	The Talk	Talk
Hyperbole		
Understatement		
Comic Diction		

2. (a) Compare the use of informal, colloquial language in the two stories. **(b)** How does this diction add to the humor?

3. Would you describe the humor of these selections as harsh or gentle? Use **evidence** from the texts to support your response.

 College Readiness | **Timed Writing**

Write to Compare Humorous Writing

In an essay, discuss and compare the serious ideas expressed in each of these selections. Consider why the authors chose to present these issues through humor. Provide evidence from the text to support your response. (25 minutes)

 5-Minute Planner

1. Read the prompt carefully and completely.

2. Gather your ideas by jotting down answers to these questions:

- What challenges do the characters in each selection face?

- What specific circumstances do you think may have added to those challenges? Note specific details from each selection that support your ideas.

- How are humor and seriousness featured alongside one another to convey the author's message?

- How does the use of humor help suggest that these challenges can be overcome?

3. Reread the prompt, and then draft your essay.

Persuasive Text: Editorial

Defining the Form An **editorial** is a brief argumentative essay that attempts to influence the attitudes or actions of a specific audience on a specific issue. You might use elements of this type of writing in letters to the editor, position papers, and speeches.

Assignment Write an editorial about an issue that confronts your school or community. Include these elements:

✔ a clear *thesis,* or *position,* based on logical reasons supported by precise and relevant evidence

✔ consideration of *a whole range of information* and *views* on the topic and accurate and honest representation of these views

✔ *counter-arguments* based on evidence to anticipate and address objections

✔ a *structure* appropriate to purpose, audience, and context

✔ an *analysis* of the relative value of specific data, facts, and ideas

✔ error-free grammar, including correct use of parallel structures

To preview the criteria on which your editorial may be judged, see the rubric on page 589.

 Writing Workshop: *Work in Progress*

Review the work you did on pages 537 and 563.

WRITE GUY
Jeff Anderson, M.Ed.

What Do You Notice?

Supporting Evidence

Read the following sentences from Pete Hamill's "Libraries Face Sad Chapter" several times.

For those without money, the road to that treasure house of the imagination begins at the public library. When I was a boy, the rooms were crowded with . . . people who came from places where there were no libraries for the poor. With their children, they built the New York in which we now live.

Discuss your ideas about the passage with a partner. Then, consider how you can use evidence to support the opinions in your editorial as Hamill did in this passage.

 Focus on the TEKS

Writing
(16)(A);(B);(C);(D);(E) Write an argumentative essay to the appropriate audience that includes: a clear thesis or position based on logical reasons supported by precise and relevant evidence; consideration of the whole range of information and views on the topic and accurate and honest representation of these views; counter-arguments based on evidence to anticipate and address objections; an organizing structure appropriate to the purpose, audience, and context; an analysis of the relative value of specific data, facts, and ideas.

Reading-Writing Connection

To get a feel for an editorial, read "Libraries Face Sad Chapter" by Pete Hamill on page 530.

Prewriting/Planning Strategies

Determine topics through background reading. Scan through a newspaper, looking for stories that interest you personally. Notice articles that describe situations that strike you as unfair, foolish, or harmful. Use one of these news stories as a topic for your editorial.

Discuss potential topics with a partner. Pair up with a classmate, and briefly discuss topics that are important to each of you, noting those that cause the most disagreement. Select an issue that has compelling arguments on both sides. Then, choose a position to support.

Consider the whole range of information and views. Gather a wide variety of evidence on your topic. Do not ignore information that contradicts or opposes your position. In a chart like the one shown, record evidence on both sides of your issue. Plan to include accurate and honest representations of all sides of the argument in your essay.

Apply It!

Support for school uniforms	Opposition to school uniforms
Reduce violence and discrimination	Take choice away from students
Create positive school image	Cause resentment among students

Develop a clear thesis statement. After reviewing the information you have gathered, decide which part of the issue to address. Write your opinion about the topic in one sentence. That sentence is your thesis statement, an expression of your **position** that should be based on logical reasons supported by precise and relevant evidence that you are prepared to defend.

Appeal to logic and emotion. Effective persuasion appeals to both logic and emotion—your audience's thoughts and feelings.

- *Logic:* Make a list of ideas, facts, and details that will make people think, analyze, and reason rather than feel.

- *Emotion:* Brainstorm for relevant anecdotes, or brief stories, descriptions, case studies, analogies, and personal examples that will affect readers' emotions. Quickly jot these down. As you work, experiment with language that carries strong emotional connotations, or words that generate positive or negative feelings in readers.

  - **Neutral connotation:** Megan continues to work.
  - **Strong connotation:** Megan soldiers on.

TEXAS
PHLitOnline
www.PHLitOnline.com
- Author video: Writing Process
- Author video: Rewards of Writing

Drafting Strategies

Plan an organizing structure for your draft. Present your ideas in a way that is appropriate to your **purpose, audience,** and **context.** Use an **outline** or a **graphic organizer,** like the one shown on this page, to structure your ideas in a sustained and persuasive way.

- **Evaluate your arguments.** Review all the points that support your thesis, and consider their impact on your intended audience. Then, rank arguments according to their persuasiveness.

- **Use an outline.** Use your ranking to write an outline showing order-of-importance organization. Start with your least important point and build toward your most persuasive point. In your outline, be sure to indicate where you will address counter-arguments. The chart shown demonstrates order-of-importance organization for an editorial.

Provide precise and relevant evidence. Support your thesis with convincing information. Precise and relevant evidence might include:

- **Statistics:** numbers that show the impact of an issue or a proposal
- **Expert opinions:** the viewpoints or advice of those who have relevant training and experience
- **Personal observations:** your own experiences with the topic
- **Testimonials:** statements from observers that reinforce an argument

Less convincing evidence might include errors in reasoning, or common fallacies, which should be avoided. Some common fallacies include:

- **Common opinion:** using the fact that many people hold a particular opinion as proof that the opinion must be true
  Some people say littering is wrong, but many people do it, so it must be acceptable.

- **False dilemma:** reasoning based on an incomplete set of options
  If I do not buy a computer, I will not be able to do my homework.

Analyze the relative value of evidence. Consider each piece of evidence—the specific data, facts, and ideas—that you may include as support in your essay. Decide which details are the strongest and most convincing, and which are less so. Data and facts—information that can be proved true—are the strongest evidence. Ideas, including opinions, tend to be weaker because they cannot usually be proved true or false. Keep this analysis in mind as you choose which evidence to include and in what order to present it.

Consult dictionaries and glossaries. Use printed or electronic resources to determine the correct spellings and meanings of unfamiliar words and phrases.

 Focus on the TEKS

Reading
(1)(E) Use a glossary (printed or electronic) to determine the meanings of words or phrases.

Writing
(13)(B) Structure ideas in a sustained and persuasive way (e.g., using outlines, graphic organizers).

(16)(A);(D);(E) Write an argumentative essay to the appropriate audience that includes: a clear thesis or position supported by precise and relevant evidence; an organizing structure appropriate to the purpose, audience, and context; an analysis of the relative value of specific data, facts, and ideas.

Organizing Structure

$\downarrow$

Present thesis statement.

$\downarrow$

Present arguments to support thesis.

$\downarrow$

Address counter-arguments.

$\downarrow$

Provide strongest argument in support of thesis.

$\downarrow$

Conclude by restating thesis and presenting a memorable final thought or quotation.

Rebecca Walker

On Choosing the Right Details

This excerpt is from the introductory essay to a book I edited about new perspectives on masculinity. I think about what I am going to write for a long time, maybe months, before committing my thoughts to the page. Long before I sat down to write, I knew I would prompt readers to think about masculinity in new ways by using this personal exchange between my son and me. What I didn't know was how I would finish the piece.

"Taking one's initial impulse to completion, that's the challenge . . ."
—Rebecca Walker

from *"What Makes a Man"*

After a big bowl of his favorite pasta, he sat on a sofa in my study and read his science textbook as I wrote at my desk. . . . As we worked under the soft glow of paper lanterns, . . . I could feel a shift as he began to remember, deep in his body, that he was home, that he was safe, that he didn't have to brace to protect himself from the expectations of the outside world.

An hour or so passed like this before he announced that he had a question. . . . "I've been thinking that maybe I should play sports at school."

. . . I cocked my head to one side. "What brought this on?"

"I don't know," he said. "Maybe girls will like me if I play sports."

Excuse me?

My boy is intuitive, smart, and creative . . . At the time he loved animals, Japanese anime, . . . and everything having to do with snowboarding. He liked to help both of his grandmothers in the garden. He read science fiction. . . . and was beginning what I thought would be a lifelong love affair with chess.

Maybe girls would like him if he played sports?

I wanted to convey a sense of peace and relaxation, so I added this detail to draw the reader into the tranquility of the "scene."

I used italics here to suggest my surprise and outrage, and to reinforce a direct and intimate connection with the reader.

I included actual things my son enjoyed to add authenticity and texture, and to provide a strong counterpoint to sports.

Revising Strategies

Revise to anticipate and address objections. Not all readers will agree with your perspective. Your editorial will be even more persuasive if you acknowledge and overcome opposing perspectives. Show readers that you have anticipated their potential questions, objections, and counterclaims and that you understand their concerns and points of view by addressing these objections.

- Review your draft and highlight controversial claims that a critic of your position would oppose.
- For each claim, develop **counter-arguments** with strong evidence.
- Find points in your essay where you can include this information.

Revise your draft to improve word choice. To be persuasive, your essay should include precise words that convey meaning and tone. Look at these examples:

Neutral: Some adults *dislike* today's students' fashions.
Powerful: Some adults *deplore* today's students' fashions.

Neutral: Joanna *did not want* to wear a uniform.
Powerful: Joanna *refused* to wear a uniform.

Rethink how well the words you have chosen in your letter address your **purpose, audience,** and **genre.** Revise your word choice to make your argument more effective. Here are some examples of powerful words you might use to replace ordinary ones. Also, consider consulting a printed or electronic **thesaurus** to find more word replacements.

Ordinary	Powerful
Walk	Pace, trudge, scramble, shuffle
Like	Be fond of, enjoy, appreciate, adore
Nice	Pleasant, kind, gentle, thoughtful
Boring	Uninteresting, tedious, dreary, dull, mind-numbing

Peer Feedback

Exchange drafts with a partner. Review each other's work, highlighting weak words that could be replaced by stronger ones. Then, in response to your peer's feedback, revise your final draft, replacing neutral language with words that will encourage your readers to feel and think. After you have made your revisions, exchange drafts with your partner again. Discuss whether the new word choices are more effective.

 **Focus on the TEKS**

Reading
(1)(E) Use a thesaurus (printed or electronic).

Writing
(13)(C) Revise drafts to improve word choice after rethinking how well questions of purpose, audience, and genre have been addressed.

(13)(E) Revise final drafts in response to feedback from peers.

(16)(C) Write an argumentative essay to the appropriate audience that includes counter-arguments based on evidence to anticipate and address objections.

Revising to Create Parallelism

Parallelism is the use of similar grammatical forms or patterns to express similar ideas. Effective use of parallelism adds rhythm and balance to your writing and strengthens connections among your ideas.

Identifying Nonparallel Constructions Parallel constructions place equal ideas in words, phrases, or clauses of similar types. Nonparallel constructions present equal ideas in an unnecessary mix of grammatical forms, producing awkward, distracting shifts for readers.

> **Nonparallel:** Dress codes are <u>less restrictive</u>, <u>less costly</u>, and <u>are not a controversial set of rules.</u>

> **Parallel:** Dress codes are <u>less restrictive</u>, <u>less costly</u>, and <u>less controversial.</u>

Fixing Nonparallel Constructions To revise faulty parallelism, follow these steps:

1. **Identify similar or equal ideas within a sentence.**

2. **Determine whether the ideas are expressed in the same form—for example, all nouns or all prepositional phrases.**

3. **Rewrite the sentence so that all the elements match the stronger pattern.** Choose forms that produce the smoothest rhythm or require the fewest words.

Sample Parallel Forms	
Nouns	sharp eyes, strong hands, deft fingers
Verbs	to ask, to learn, to share
Phrases	under a gray sky, near an icy river
Adverb clauses	when I am happy, when I am peaceful
Adjective clauses	those who read with care, those who act with concern

Grammar in Your Writing

Review several paragraphs in your editorial, highlighting any sentences in which you present a series of ideas. In each case, make sure the constructions are parallel. If they are not, revise them.

Student Model: Chloe Pham, Pflugerville, TX

Our Youth is Our Future

With the baby boomer generation growing old, the burden of national crises is going to fall upon the youth of today. But with young people only concerned about frivolous things, such as video games or the latest celebrity fashions, the degree of urgency is lacking to say the least. It is imperative for the youth to be educated on current events. Staying informed about the news enables us to have a voice in our society. In addition, gaining knowledge about the events happening in our world allows us to peek into the future and plan accordingly—not only to benefit ourselves, but also to benefit the world in which we live.

John Adams wrote, "Liberty cannot be preserved without a general knowledge among the people." When the next presidential election rolls around, wouldn't you like to take part in determining who will guide the next years of your life? Shouldn't you at least be aware of the next president's plan for the country? With knowledge on policies put forth in the campaign, you allow yourself the ability to make informed decisions on which candidate to support. What's happening now is going to shape what's going to happen in the future. Our future. With the power of understanding, you can take part in molding the years that lie ahead of you.

Learning about current events will provide an immediate benefit to your academic and social life. Many school subjects such as history and social sciences are based on past events that are similar to current happenings. Understanding current events now will help you to understand events from the past. Being well versed in current events also will help you to carry on intelligent conversations, and help you to have a more fulfilling social life.

Today's youth will face a career and economic landscape that is much more difficult than the previous generation's. Under these conditions, a radically different mindset and skill set will be required to be successful in the new global economy. Those who are not aware of global predicaments may face unpleasant surprises in the future. By being conscious of events currently taking place in our society, we safeguard ourselves from the difficult times that have yet to occur.

It seems that as generations pass, young people have become increasingly ignorant of the world around them. Trivialities are substituted for substantial knowledge. With today's technology, news can be effortlessly accessed and yet kids still remain uninformed. I urge the youth of today: stay informed and be active in your community. Develop an insatiable curiosity about the world around you. Knowledge is the roadmap to a healthier and happier future for humanity. It is our responsibility to take care of the world we've inherited from those who have preceded us.

Focus on the TEKS

Writing
(13)(D) Edit drafts for grammar, mechanics, and spelling.
(13)(E) Publish written work for appropriate audiences.
Conventions
(19) Spell correctly, including using various resources to check correct spellings.

Chloe includes a clear thesis statement.

The author supports her thesis with a famous quote.

Chloe offers relevant evidence that supports her position.

In the conclusion, the author restates her thesis and offers an additional insight.

TEXAS

Editing and Proofreading

Edit your draft for grammar and mechanics, such as punctuation. Use various resources, such as dictionaries and glossaries, to check correct spellings.

Focus on Spelling: An editorial that includes spelling errors loses its authority to convince. Check the spelling of each word. Look for words that you frequently misspell and make sure they are spelled correctly.

Publishing and Presenting

Consider ways to publish your written work for appropriate audiences:

Deliver an oral presentation. Use your editorial as the basis for an oral presentation about your topic. As you speak, be sensitive to your audience. If they seem confused or doubtful, modify your word choice to clarify your ideas.

Submit your essay to a newspaper or Web site. Send your editorial to a school or community newspaper—as a letter to the editor or posted online.

Reflecting on Your Writing

Writer's Journal Jot down your answer to this question:
How did writing about your topic help you understand it?

Rubric for Self-Assessment

Find evidence in your writing to address each category. Then, use the rating scale to grade your work.

Spiral Review
Earlier in this unit, you learned about **adjectives** (p. 536) and **adverbs** (p. 562). Check your editorial to be sure that you have used these parts of speech correctly.

Written Composition Criteria	Rating Scale not very / very
Focus and Coherence: How precise and relevant is the evidence you have used as support for your thesis?	1 2 3 4
Organization: How appropriate is your organizing structure to your purpose, audience, and context?	1 2 3 4
Development of Ideas: Have you developed an argument using a whole range of information and views on your topic, and represented those views in an accurate and honest way?	1 2 3 4
Conventions: How error-free is your grammar, especially your use of parallel structures?	1 2 3 4
Voice: How well does your word choice suit your audience and purpose?	1 2 3 4

Applying the Big Question

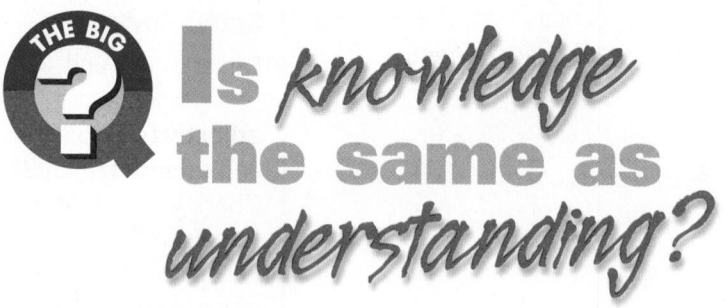 Is *knowledge the same as understanding?*

Think About It

Think about what you have read in this unit, and what you have learned about knowledge and understanding in your other classes and from your own experience. Copy and complete the chart below to apply what you have learned about knowledge and understanding. One row has been completed for you.

Example	What facts and information the author had	What knowledge the author gained	What the author came to understand	What I learned
From Literature	In "On Summer," the author's friend has cancer.	Her friend faced life courageously.	We understand life better when others share their knowledge and experience.	Taking the time to understand others gives life more meaning.
From Literature				
From Science				
From Social Studies				
From Your Life				

Talk About It

Choose one of the examples from your knowledge and understanding chart to develop a short **oral response** to the Big Question. Begin by preparing an outline of your ideas. Include examples, facts, and reasons to support your point of view. Present your speech to a small group of classmates. Invite questions and comments from the group when you have finished.

Write About It

At the beginning of Unit 3, you wrote a response to the Big Question. Now that you have completed the unit, write a new response, discussing how your initial ideas have either been changed or reinforced.

- ❏ Knowledge is the same as understanding.
- ❏ Knowledge and understanding are different ways of knowing.
- ❏ My own response: _____.

Support your answer with one or more of the examples in your chart.

Challenge What issues does the Big Question still raise for you? How could you continue your exploration?

★ Connecting to Citizenship

Group Discussion With a small team, discuss how having both knowledge and understanding is important to becoming a good and thoughtful citizen. Then, share key points from your discussion with the class. Consider these questions in your discussion:

- What knowledge should a responsible citizen have?
- What understanding should a responsible citizen have?
- Why might it be important for a community to value both knowledge and understanding?

During the discussion:

- Team members should take turns speaking.
- While one member is speaking, others should listen responsively, asking questions related to the content for **clarification** and **elaboration.**
- In your team, participate productively by **building on the ideas of others** and contributing **relevant information.**

When everyone has had a chance to speak, **develop a plan for consensus-building**—coming to a general group agreement. Follow your plan to choose three key points from your discussion to present to the class.

 Focus on the TEKS

Listening and Speaking
(24)(A) Listen responsively to a speaker by asking questions related to the content for clarification and elaboration.
(26) Participate productively in teams, building on the ideas of others, contributing relevant information, developing a plan for consensus-building.

Big Question Vocabulary

Use some of these words as you complete the activities on these pages.

- ambiguous
- comprehend
- concept
- clarify
- connection
- fact
- feeling
- information
- insight
- instinct
- interpret
- research
- senses/sensory
- sources
- statistics

This list includes academic vocabulary words, which are defined on pp. R1–R14.

Producing Analogies

An **analogy** is a type of comparison that shows relationships between words. Writers sometimes use analogies to help readers understand a concept they are unfamiliar with by comparing it to a concept they already know. In addition, analogies are a good way to develop your vocabulary.

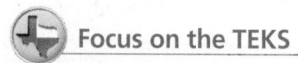

Focus on the TEKS

Reading
(1)(C) Produce analogies that describe a function of an object or its description.

Sometimes you will see analogies written with colons, in this format:

broom : sweep :: lamp : light

This example would be read "*Broom* is to *sweep* as *lamp* is to *light*." The relationship shown is one of *function.* In other words:

The function of a <u>broom</u> is to <u>sweep</u>.

The function of a <u>lamp</u> is to <u>light</u>.

Therefore, <u>broom</u> is to <u>sweep</u> as <u>lamp</u> is to <u>light</u>.

An analogy can also be explored using a graphic organizer like this one:

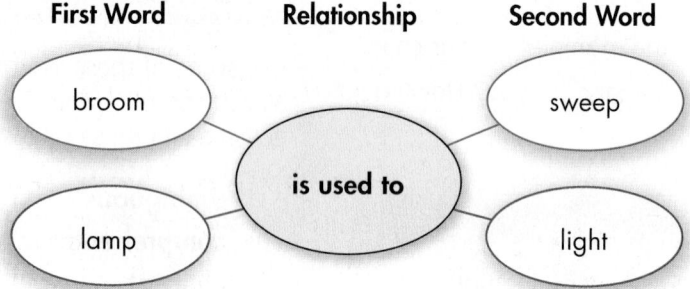

Common Analogy Patterns This chart lists some relationships that are common in analogies, along with examples.

Example	Relationship
tire : car	part to whole
fire : blaze	synonyms
good : bad	antonyms
orange : fruit	object to type
broom : sweep	object to function
plant : green	object to description

TEXAS
PHLitOnline
www.PHLitOnline.com

• Illustrated vocabulary words
• Interactive vocabulary games
• Vocabulary flashcards

Practice A Using each listed object, produce an analogy that describes a function of the object. Write the analogy as a full sentence with the four key words underlined. Here is an example for the word *pencil:*

<u>Pencil</u> is to <u>write</u> as <u>bicycle</u> is to <u>ride</u>.

1. spoon

2. backpack

3. flashlight

4. blanket

Practice B Using each listed description, produce an analogy that describes an object. Write the analogy as a full sentence with the four key words underlined. Here is an example for the word *pretty:*

<u>Flower</u> is to <u>*pretty*</u> as <u>cotton</u> is to <u>soft</u>.

1. yellow

2. smooth

3. light

4. sweet

Activity Using the colon format, produce analogies for these objects: *football, calculator, towel, eraser.*

- First, produce an analogy for each that describes a function of the object.
- Next, produce an analogy for each that describes the object itself.
- Write each analogy on the front of a notecard and write the word relationship on the back.
- Then, use your notecards to test a partner. Show your classmate the front of a card and ask him or her to identify the analogy's relationship. Turn the card over to see if your partner's answer is correct.

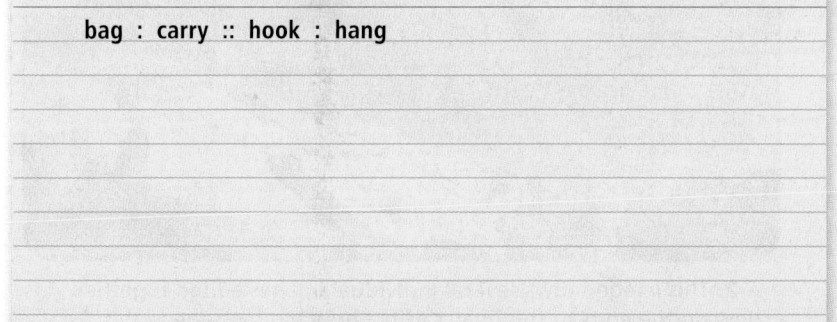

bag : carry :: hook : hang

Teamwork

Work with two classmates to write a technical statement describing the function of an object. For example, you might describe the function of a computer mouse, a solar panel, or a bicycle. Conduct research if necessary. Use analogies to help your reader understand the function of the object.

Analyzing Media Messages

Visual and audio techniques are tools used in media such as commercials and news broadcasts to convey messages. Develop your media literacy by analyzing the use of these techniques in different types of media.

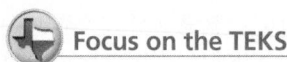 **Focus on the TEKS**

Reading
(12)(B) Analyze how messages in media are conveyed through visual and sound techniques (e.g., editing, reaction shots, sequencing, background music).

Learn the Skills

View a film or media clip and take notes about the response it generates in you. Then, identify the use of the following visual and sound techniques in the clip you viewed. Analyze how messages are conveyed through these visual and sound techniques.

Analyze editing. Visual and audio material can be edited by deleting, reorganizing, and altering images and sounds to have a specific effect on an audience. For example, an editor may include a slow motion sequence, an abrupt shift from scene to scene, or scene transitions. Special effects are examples of digital editing. When you notice edits in media, consider how they affect the message the audience receives.

Analyze sequencing. Reorganizing the order of visuals and sounds is a type of editing called sequencing. As you view or hear media, ask yourself:

- What does the sequence of images emphasize?
- How does the sequencing help convey a message?

Analyze reaction shots. In visual media, an image of a person or group of people reacting to a remark, an event, or an action is known as a reaction shot. When you see reaction shots, ask yourself:

- What caused this reaction?
- In what way will it affect the audience?
- How does the reaction shot help convey a message?

▲ **1.** How might this reaction shot affect an audience's perception of what the boy is seeing?

▲ **2.** This image shows several individual images edited together. How do the edits to this image affect how the message in the photo is conveyed?

Analyze background music. The sounds you hear in a film can be just as important as the images you see. Background music and special sound effects can set a tone or convey information. When you hear background music, ask yourself:

- How does the background music convey a message?
- How would the scene be different without the background music?

TEXAS PHLitOnline

www.PHLitOnline.com

Apply the skills you have learned in this workshop as you watch the videos on www.PHLitOnline.com.

Practice the Skills

Use what you have learned in this workshop to complete the following activity.

ACTIVITY: Analyze Media Messages

With your class, view a visual media production such as a commercial, a video montage, or a news segment. Take notes as you watch.
Answer the following questions in your notes:
- What is the video's main message?
- What role do reaction shots play in this video?
- What does the sequencing emphasize or express?
- What other visual and sound techniques do you notice?
- How does the editing support the video's message?

Use an Analysis Checklist like the one below to analyze how messages in media are conveyed through visual and sound techniques.

Analysis Checklist

Title:
What is the main message in the media production?

Visual and Sound Techniques
Describe how each of the following techniques is used in the media production.

Technique	Description of Use
Editing	_____
Reaction Shots	_____
Sequencing	_____
Background Music	_____
Other Techniques	_____

With a team of your classmates, analyze how the visual and sound techniques in the media production affect how the messages in the production are conveyed. Report your conclusions to the entire class.

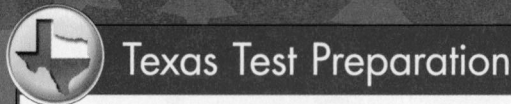
Cumulative Review

Reading

Read this selection. Then answer the questions that follow it.

TEKS Spiral Review

Reading
(10) Analyze persuasive text.
(10)(A) Analyze the relevance, quality, and credibility of evidence given to support or oppose an argument for a specific audience.
Comprehension
RC-9(B) Make complex inferences about text.

Remember Veterans on Memorial Day

by Danny Calhoun

1   John turned 17 years old on November 1, 1941. On December 7, 1941 John's world was torn apart when the attack on Pearl Harbor thrust the United States into World War II.

2   John and his family were devoutly religious. Even though he had some misgivings about the war, he had been taught to love his fellow man and that thou shall not kill. He knew that his destiny was to enter the service and defend his country and its freedoms, which had provided so much for him.

3   John spent the next four years of his young life fighting on what seemed like every island in the Pacific Ocean. His outfit always seemed to be the one sent in first. John, not quite 21 years old, had endured the horrors of war that most people could never imagine, even in their worst nightmares. As he continued to fight, his resolve to win, and his love for his country and comrades became stronger. He had seen first hand what happened when other countries lost their freedom.

4   On his last battlefield John was wounded by rifle fire four times as he attempted to remove his wounded comrades from the line of fire. He was awarded The Silver Star and a Purple Heart for his heroism that day.

5   He returned to the country he loved as a hero.

6   John's life as he knew it, and his dreams, ended that day. He had sustained such severe wounds that he would be confined to a lifetime of hospital beds and pain.

7   That was 56 years ago and he has lain in a hospital bed, mostly alone, with his thoughts and pain since that day.

8   He is well taken care of by the staff. However, he has never known the basic joys that give a man's life meaning: the love of a woman sharing your life, the love and pride in your children and grandchildren, the closeness of true friends, the ability to work toward a goal and someday to reap the rewards of having reached that goal.

9   John's thoughts went back to the first years of his confinement. He remembered how veterans' groups and others would come to visit him. They were such happy times for him. He would spend hours just talking with these guests. They don't come anymore though. I guess they are just too involved in their own lives, in this busy world, to find time for him.

10   John felt tears stinging his eyes as he reached to his nightstand and picked up his Silver Star and Purple Heart. He thought of the dreams of his youth, of the horrors of war, of his comrades and of his country, which he still loved so much.

11   John turned his head and looked out the window, into the courtyard, at the flag of his country waving so majestically in the afternoon breeze. The tears continued to flow from his eyes as he smiled and whispered the final thoughts of his life, "If I had the choice I would do it all over again."

12   John then passed into a place of peace, tranquility, serenity, and no pain; a place he had longed for so long.

13   There are tens of thousands of men like John in our VA Hospitals and nursing homes today. Men who have given and sacrificed so much out of love for their country and fellow men. Men of honor who ask for nothing more than a visit from someone and knowing that someone still cares and remembers. Men who not only served in World War II, but all our country's wars.

14   May 30th will be celebrated as Memorial Day. A special day set aside to commemorate and honor the memory of men like John, who sacrificed so much to ensure our right to live in freedom. That freedom did not come about without a cost. The cost was paid by many thousands of men like John—ordinary, but special men, who willingly placed honor, pride and a devout love of their country and its freedoms, above self, and proudly served their country to provide those freedoms to their fellow men.

15   Many of those men, like John, didn't die, but still sacrificed their lives and dreams for their beliefs. Many of these men, like John, are confined to hospitals and nursing homes, still paying for those freedoms.

16   With freedom comes responsibility. With responsibility comes obligation. We all carry the responsibility to take what these men have given us and never stop building upon it, constantly striving to ensure that our country is not only the greatest on earth, but also provides the most freedoms of any country. We also have the absolute obligation to honor and remember those men who have provided us with the foundation to accomplish this.

17   On this Memorial Day please take the time to remember and honor those veterans who have given so much of their lives to defend the rights, privileges and freedoms we as a free society love and enjoy so much. Take the time to honor those that served and returned, those who never returned and those still paying the price for freedom.

1 The introduction in paragraph *1* is most likely intended to —

   A describe what happened on John's birthday

   B list what has happened to John's friends and family

   C show the reader that John is an elderly man

   D give basic details about John's life

2 In paragraph *11,* the description of the flag and John's words —

   F emphasize his age

   G emphasize his patriotism

   H show he does not think about his military service

   J show he misses feeling the breeze outdoors

3 The author most likely includes John's final moments to —

   A gain the reader's sympathy

   B relate the facts objectively

   C show that John regretted his decisions

   D give an accurate, complete history of John's life

4 Read these sentences from paragraph *16.*

> With freedom comes responsibility. With responsibility comes obligation.

In the article, which argument do these generalizations support?

   F Veterans are responsible for fighting for freedom.

   G We must honor those who fought for our freedom.

   H Responsible people are those who feel truly free.

   J We have a responsibility to ensure our own freedom.

5 How does the author support the claim that John sacrificed for his country?

   A by describing how John's wounds affected his life

   B by quoting older veterans

   C by explaining that John enlisted as a young man

   D by explaining why people celebrate Memorial Day

6 The author's main argument in the article is that people should —

   F learn about World War II

   G feel grateful for freedom

   H listen to the stories told by veterans and soldiers

   J honor veterans and soldiers on Memorial Day

DIRECTIONS
Answer the following question on a separate sheet of paper.

7 How does the story of John's life support the argument for remembering veterans on Memorial Day? Support your answer with evidence from the selection.

Revising and Editing

DIRECTIONS
Read the following passage and mark your answers on your answer document. Remember that you are NOT permitted to use dictionaries or other reference material on this section of the test.

Derrick was asked to write a paper about a person who is a hero. Derrick plays the trumpet, so he wrote about jazz musician Wynton Marsalis. Read Derrick's rough draft and think about the corrections and improvements he should make. When you finish reading, answer the questions that follow.

 TEKS Spiral Review

Writing
(13)(C) Revise drafts to improve style and sentence variety.
(13)(D) Edit drafts for grammar, mechanics, and spelling.
Conventions
(18)(B)(iii) Use correct punctuation marks including dashes to emphasize parenthetical information.

Wynton Marsalis, Musician and Hero

(1) He is a trumpeter, composer, and jazz musician known throughout the world. (2) He dazzles audiences with his complex technique, intense emotion, and surprising improvisation. (3) He has made dozens of musical recordings and has been honored with nine Grammy Awards. (4) But Wynton Marsalis is a hero not because of his musical success but because of his dedication in giving back to the community he came from: New Orleans.

(5) When Hurricane Katrina hit New Orleans in 2005, Marsalis was working in New York City. (6) He was the artistic director of Jazz at Lincoln Center, one of the top jazz venues in the world. (7) To support people in his hometown who had been affected by Katrina, Marsalis immediately began planning performances to raise much-needed funds. (8) The biggest of these performances was a benefit concert produced by Jazz at Lincoln Center. (9) Through that concert alone, Marsalis helped raise more than $2 million to help people in the aftermath of the hurricane.

(10) The year 2005 was not the first time Marsalis had been involved in helping communities in New Orleans. (11) He had supported individual musicians from the area. (12) He had also supported summer music programs for students there. (13) But after Hurricane Katrina, he became even more involved. (14) Speaking with the city's leaders, he urged them to include all residents, whether they were wealthy or not, in restoring the city. (15) He believed that if everyone worked together, the people of the city could gain strength from their experiens.

(16) By using his musical talent and his love of his hometown to benefit those in need, Marsalis has shown that he is a true hero. (17) His actions have inspired many musicians to consider following in his footsteps.

1 What change, if any, should be made in sentence 2?

   A Change *dazzles* to **dazzle**

   B Change *technique* to **techniche**

   C Change *surprising* to **surprises**

   D Make no change

2 Which sentences, if any, should be combined?

   F Sentences 6 and 7

   G Sentences 9 and 10

   H Sentences 11 and 12

   J Make no change

3 What change, if any, should be made in sentence 14?

   A Change *Speaking* to **Spoke**

   B Change *whether* to **weather**

   C Insert a dash after *not*

   D Make no change

4 What change should be made in sentence 15?

   F Change *believed* to **beleived**

   G Change *strength* to **strenth**

   H Change *worked* to **works**

   J Change *experiens* to **experience**

STOP

Written Composition

Use blank pages to prewrite. Then write your composition on one or two lined pages.

Writing
(14) Students write literary texts to express their ideas and feelings about ideas.

> **Write about a time when you set a good example for others.**

> **REMEMBER—YOU SHOULD**
>
> ❏ write about the assigned topic
>
> ❏ make your writing thoughtful and interesting
>
> ❏ make sure that each sentence you write contributes to your composition as a whole
>
> ❏ make sure that your ideas are clear and easy for the reader to follow
>
> ❏ write about your ideas in depth so that the reader is able to develop a good understanding of what you are saying
>
> ❏ proofread your writing to correct errors in spelling, capitalization, punctuation, grammar, and sentence structure

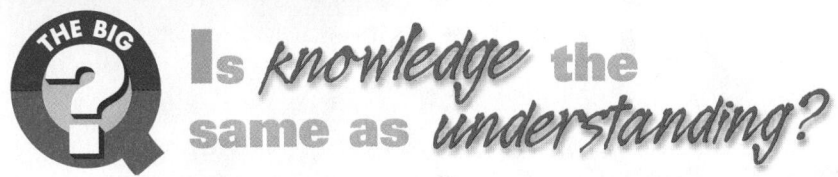

Is *knowledge* the same as *understanding?*

Focus on the TEKS

Reading
(12)(B) Analyze how messages in media are conveyed through sound techniques (e.g., background music).

Media Literacy

The use of **background music** is a **sound technique** used in media. Directors include background music to emphasize a mood or to reveal a historical or cultural context. This Viewing and Listening Guide will help you analyze how messages in media are conveyed through background music. Use the questions in the chart to guide your study of a Get Connected video, or any other video clip available to you.

www.PHLitOnline.com

Viewing and Listening Guide

Technique	Why it might be used	What you should think about
Background Music	To set the mood of a scene	• How does the music support the images? • How would the scene or clip affect you differently if it did not have background music?
	To give information or to reflect a specific historical or cultural context	• Does the music come from a particular time in history or cultural setting? If not, should it? Explain. • How does the background music affect the main message?

Independent Reading

Abraham Lincoln—DK Biography
Tanya Lee Stone
Dorling Kindersley Publishing, 2005
This biography tells the story of a revered American and the turbulent times in which he lived.

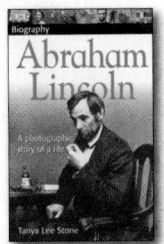

Biography and Autobiography
Prentice Hall, 2000
This collection invites readers into the lives of men and women from different times and places.

20,000 Leagues Under the Sea
Jules Verne   Signet, 1969
In this work of science fiction, characters embark on a quest for knowledge that leads them to new understandings.

Why We Can't Wait
Martin Luther King, Jr.   Signet, 2000
King's nonfiction text is both a description of the Civil Rights movement and a poetic testament to the wisdom and courage of the man who wrote it.

THE BIG ?

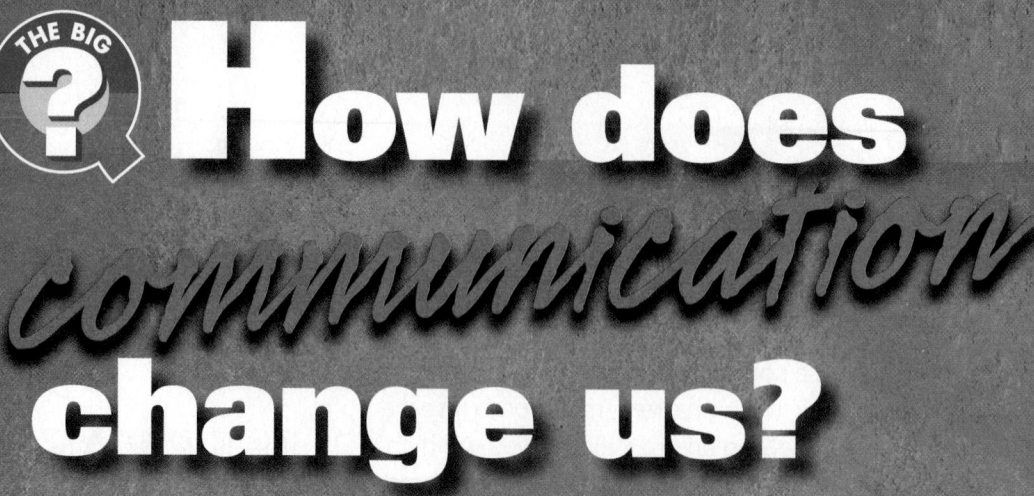

How does *communication* change us?

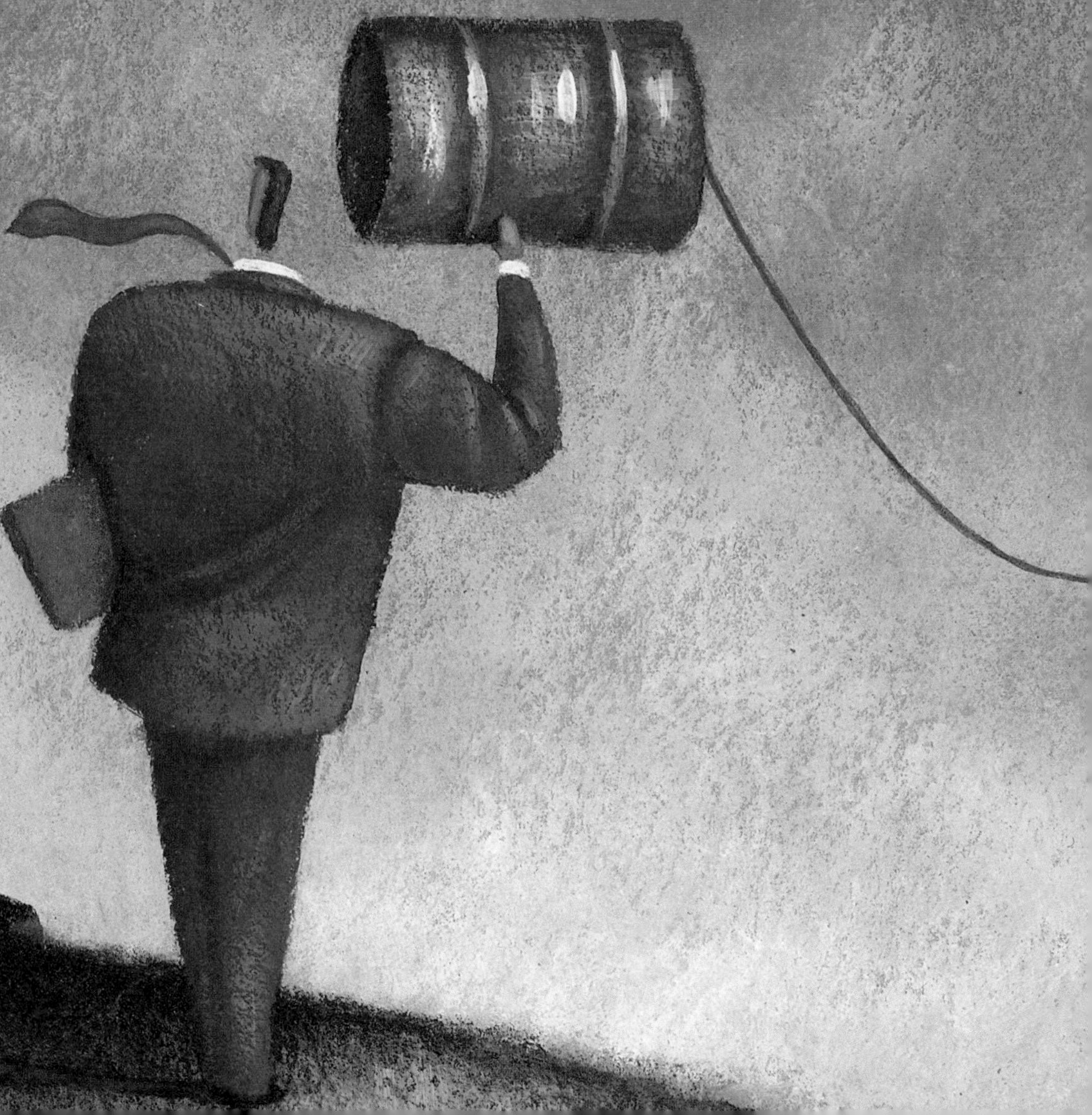

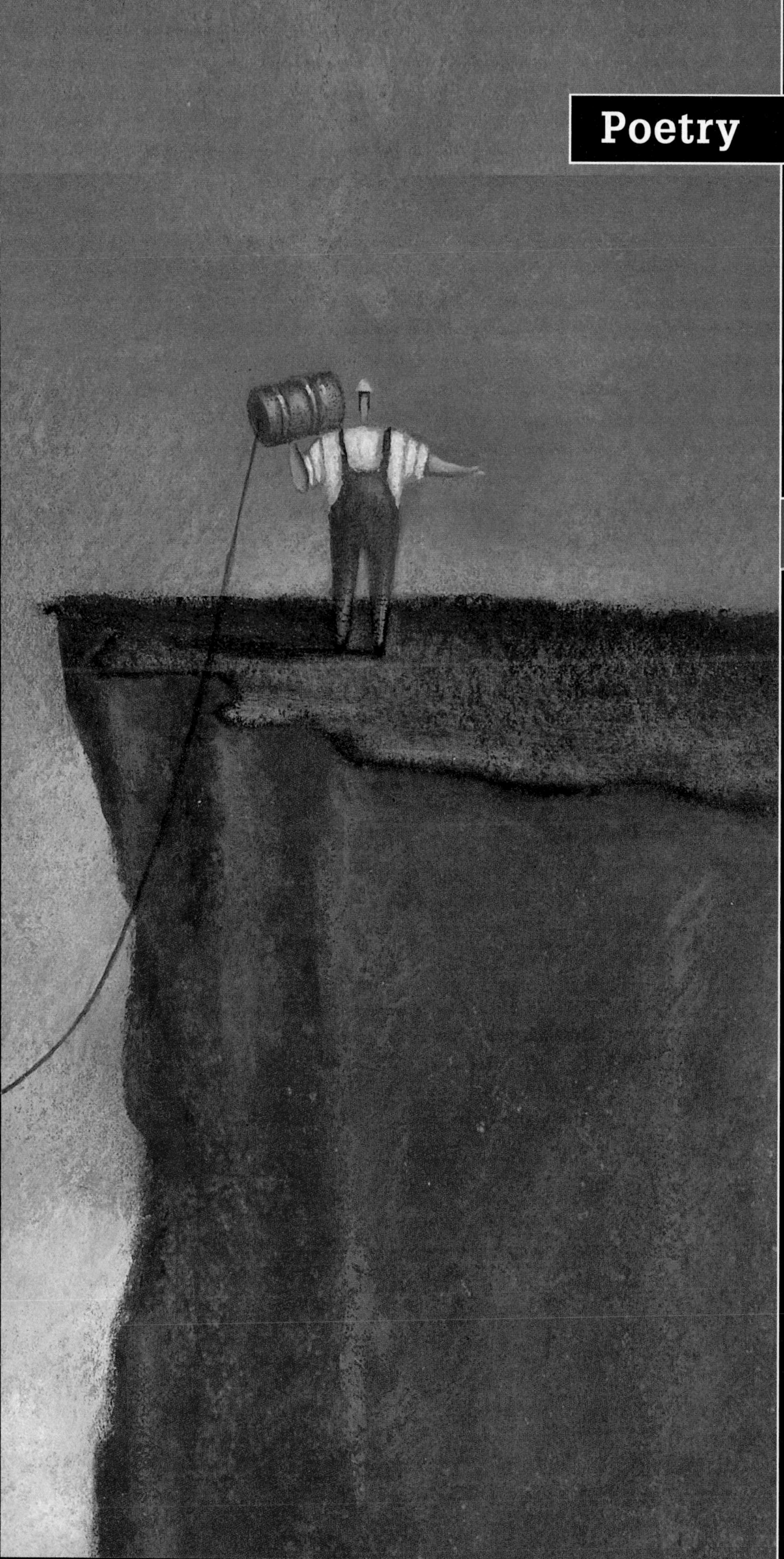

Poetry

Unit 4

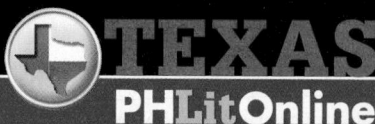

TEXAS PHLitOnline

www.PHLitOnline.com

Hear It!
- Selection summary audio
- Selection audio
- Big Question Tunes

See It!
- Penguin author video
- Big Question video
- Get Connected videos
- Background videos
- More about the authors
- Illustrated vocabulary words
- Vocabulary flashcards

Do It!
- Interactive journals
- Interactive graphic organizers
- Grammar tutorials
- Interactive vocabulary games
- Test practice

Introducing the Big Question

 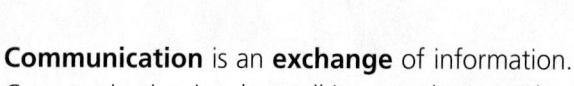 **How does communication change us?**

Communication is an **exchange** of information. Communication involves talking to other people and also listening to them and learning from them. It takes place when you **discuss** an issue with a friend, for example, or **react to** a piece of writing. Communication is the **understanding** you get when you read a poem. It is the **empathy** you feel for others after listening to a news interview with victims of a natural disaster. All of this communication may change us, but how? Does it make us smarter, wiser, kinder, angrier? Does it make us better people, or just more experienced?

Begin thinking about the Big Question by listing examples of the many ways that you communicate.

Tell What You Know

List situations in which you communicate. Describe an example from each of the following categories:

- A movie that moved you emotionally
- An argument you have had that still bothers you
- A speech or dramatic presentation you gave or heard
- A poem or story you will always remember
- An important conversation you have had
- A commercial or news story that moved you to take action
- A photograph, painting, or song that touched you deeply

Share your list with a partner. Talk about how these significant communications led to change. To practice your own communication skills, listen responsively to your partner. Ask questions related to the content of his or her comments for clarification and elaboration.

TEXAS
PHLitOnline
www.PHLitOnline.com

- Big Question video
- Illustrated vocabulary words
- Interactive vocabulary games
- Big Question Tunes

Explain What You Know

Use the examples and ideas you discussed with your partner to help complete these sentences about communication.

- Real communication only happens when _____.
- Communication requires two people who are interested not only in _____ but also in _____.
- Honest communication may result in _____.

Share your responses with a partner.

Write What You Think

Based on your discussions, decide what you think right now. Your answer may change as you read the selections in this unit. Develop your response to the Big Question using this beginning or write one of your own.

❑ Communication changes us by _____.

Connecting to the Literature

Each reading in this unit will give you insight into the Big Question. At the end of the unit, you will have the opportunity to see how your ideas have changed.

★ Connecting to Citizenship

Texas Profiles: Helen Cloud Austin

Award Winning Social Worker Helen Cloud Austin was the second African American student to attend the University of Louisville's Raymond A. Kent School of Social Work. When she initially applied for employment at the San Antonio State Hospital, she was denied a position because of her race. Despite this setback, Austin eventually became chief of the hospital's Social Services Department. Austin won national and local recognition and awards for her excellent work and dedication.

How does communication change us?

- What message did the hospital communicate when it did not hire Austin initially?
- Did that message change Austin's dedication to service?
- What can you learn from Austin's story that can help you become a thoughtful, active citizen?

 Focus on the TEKS

Listening and Speaking (24)(A) Listen responsively to a speaker by asking questions related to the content for clarification and elaboration.

Big Question Vocabulary

Use some of these words as you complete the activities on these pages.

aware
communication
comprehension
discuss
empathy
exchange
illuminate
informed
interpretation
meaning
react
relationship
resolution
respond
understanding

This list includes academic vocabulary words, which are defined on pp. R1–R14.

 # Introduction: Poetry

How does *communication* change us?

Words can change how we see the world and ourselves.

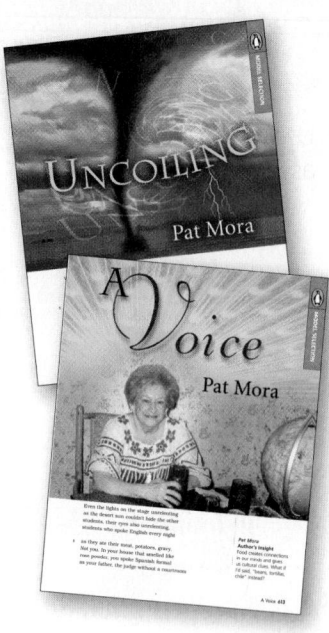

 **TEXAS**
PHLitOnline

www.PHLitOnline.com

- Penguin author video
- Interactive journals
- Interactive graphic organizers
- Selection audio
- Self-test

What Is Poetry?
by Pat Mora

I've lived near two rivers: the Rio Grande that separates my native state of Texas from Mexico and the Ohio River that separates Ohio from Kentucky. When I watch a river flowing by, I think about the journey it has made and where it's going. Rivers democratically gather branches and leaves as they move along. The sun and moon both travel on the ripples. Though water slips through our fingers, rivers carve canyons.

Poetry's River Includes You

As one of my favorite poets, Mary Oliver, says in the quotation on the next page, "Poetry is a river." You and I can be part of it. No one will compose the poem about popcorn or tennis shoes that you will. When you sit and bring all of yourself to the page, all you've seen, heard, read, and felt, and when you begin to play with words, you can eventually write a unique poem. You will choose your own **form; images,** words that appeal to the senses; and **speaker,** the person who says the words of the poem.

Paintings and music are unique in the same way. Many artists and musicians could see a teenager sitting alone at a party. Each artist would paint the scene differently; each musician would create different sounds to capture the scene, the mood.

A Poem Is Like a River in a Room

I like the spareness of poetry. It demands that I remove the unnecessary. For example, I could have a grand time filling a room with objects I like—flowers, folk art, books, family photos. Suppose, though, that I decided to focus my attention. What if I allowed myself less space and chose each detail carefully because I wanted to create surprises for visitors, to have you not just see the room but experience it. Suppose that I put one small river flowing through the middle of the room.

You walk in and stare and wonder, as readers sometimes wonder about poems, What's going on here? What's she trying to do? You listen to the river as I hope you listen to poems, and you hear something your neighbor or friend might miss. You connect with that river or that poem because you're you, and you're willing to risk releasing your imagination.

When I begin a poem, I sit with paper and pen. I try not to pressure myself to write a perfect first line. I write to get going, knowing I can discard whatever I write. The page is my landscape, and I'm like that river traveling along, exploring.

Poetry is a river; many voices travel in it; poem after poem moves along in the exciting crests and falls of the river waves.

from *A Poetry Handbook*

—Mary Oliver

Meet
Pat Mora (b. 1942)

Author of "Uncoiling" and "A Voice"

In her works, Pat Mora has explored the experience of being "American but hyphenated," that is, a bilingual and bicultural Mexican American. She stresses the importance of family and cultural heritage, often using Spanish words and phrases in her writing. She has also published some works in bilingual editions.

Her poetry is spare, yet rich in imagery and feeling. Mora encourages her readers to write their own poems and to "enjoy the word-play."

Did You Know?
Pat Mora was born in El Paso, Texas.

Exploring Poetry

Elements of Poetry

Poetry is a literary form that uses precise **diction,** or word choice, to evoke the emotions, sounds, and rhythms associated with language. Many poems are structured in **stanzas,** or groupings of lines. Specific stanza types include **couplets,** which have two lines, and **quatrains,** which have four lines.

LUCKY COW © 2003 Mark Pett. Dist. By UNIVERSAL PRESS SYNDICATE. Reprinted with permission. All rights reserved.

Poets use **figurative language,** such as metaphor, simile, personification, and onomatopoeia, to express ideas or feelings in a fresh way.

- Poets use **metaphors** to compare two apparently unlike things without using the words *like, as, than,* or *resembles,* as in "The sky is a patch-work quilt." Poets use **similes** to make such comparisons using connecting words, as in "The sky is like a patchwork quilt."
- **Personification** is language that attributes human qualities to non-human things, as in "The wind danced in the trees."
- **Onomatopoeia** is the use of a word whose sound imitates its meaning. Examples of such words are *buzz, hiss, thud,* and *sizzle.*

Imagery is descriptive language used to create word pictures. Images are created by **sensory language,** which provides details related to the senses.

Poets use a number of **sound devices** to achieve a musical quality.

- **Rhythm** is the pattern created by the stressed and unstressed syllables of words in sequence. A controlled pattern of rhythm is called **meter.**
- **Rhyme** is the repetition of identical or similar sounds in stressed syllables. A pattern of end rhymes is called a **rhyme scheme. Free verse** has no set meter or rhyme scheme.
- **Alliteration** is the repetition of the initial consonant sounds of words, as in the phrase *"dark days."* **Assonance** is the repetition of vowel sounds in nearby words, as in the phrase *"child of silence."* **Consonance** is the repetition of consonants within nearby words in which the separating vowels differ, as in the phrase *"give and love."*
- **Repetition** is the use of any language element more than once.

Types of Poetry

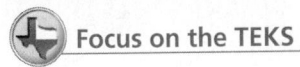 Focus on the TEKS

Reading
(3) Analyze the effects of diction and imagery in poetry.

There are three main types of poetry.
- In a **narrative poem,** the writer tells a story in verse. Narrative poems can take many forms. For example, an **epic** is a long narrative poem about gods or heroes. In contrast, a **ballad** is a songlike narrative about an adventure or a romance.
- In a **dramatic poem,** the writer tells a story using a character's own thoughts or statements.
- A **lyric** is a brief poem in which the author expresses the feelings of a single speaker, creating a single effect on the reader. Lyrics are notable for their musical qualities, achieved through rhyme and rhythm.

Forms of Poetry

Poems can also be categorized by form—their particular structural patterns of rhyme, rhythm, line structure, stanza format, or another element. The haiku and sonnet are two popular forms of poetry.
- A **haiku** is a poem containing three unrhymed lines of five, seven, and five syllables. This Japanese poetic form uses imagery to convey a single vivid emotion.
- A **sonnet** is a fourteen-line lyric poem with formal patterns of rhyme, rhythm, and line structure.

TEKS Check

Reread a poem or song that you already know. Which words and images from the work left an impression on you? Use a graphic organizer to analyze the effects of the work's diction, or word choice, and imagery. For example, you may find that the effect of a poem's diction is to set a mood, or to create a specific feeling. You may think that the effect of a certain image is to create a vivid emotion in a reader's mind.

Title	Diction or Imagery	Effect

Pat Mora Introduces
"Uncoiling" and "A Voice"

I am a writer because I'm a reader, and because I love words in English and Spanish, their pleasure and power. I'm also a writer because of my mother. Mom, a reader who knew both Spanish and English, was my first editor and gave me good advice on my writing assignments and speeches.

"Uncoiling": Using Language to See

If I use **figurative language** effectively, a phrase like "spunky as a peacock" or "lace lullabies" in the poem "Uncoiling" helps you see what I'm seeing or hearing. Poets spend time choosing words, sounds; poets play with possibilities. The desert is, like my mother, a powerful woman in my life. In "Uncoiling," I chose **personification** to create her on the page for you.

Poetry is a word journey. If I succeed, it's a word journey for you too. I discover and you discover as you read. Poetry asks us to use our imagination, to fill in the silences, to leap.

"A Voice": Exploring Mom's Power

When I became interested in spending more time writing, I interviewed my family. Have you done that? Every family has good stories to tell. I listened and wrote about the way Mom and Mexicans or people of Mexican descent felt. I wrote about her in the children's book *The Rainbow Tulip;* in my family memoir, *House of Houses;* and in poems such as "A Voice."

When I was a teacher, my students and I would sometimes discuss the **theme** of a poem. What was the poem really about? What did it mean? Sometimes people avoid poetry because they think it's a puzzle. I don't write poetry to confuse you or to preach. I'm exploring with words. Writing poetry is taking a word journey.

I wanted to tell the story of Mom, a high school student, attending a speech contest. She felt frightened at feeling different. We all know that feeling. I also wanted to explore Mom's power in the life of our family.

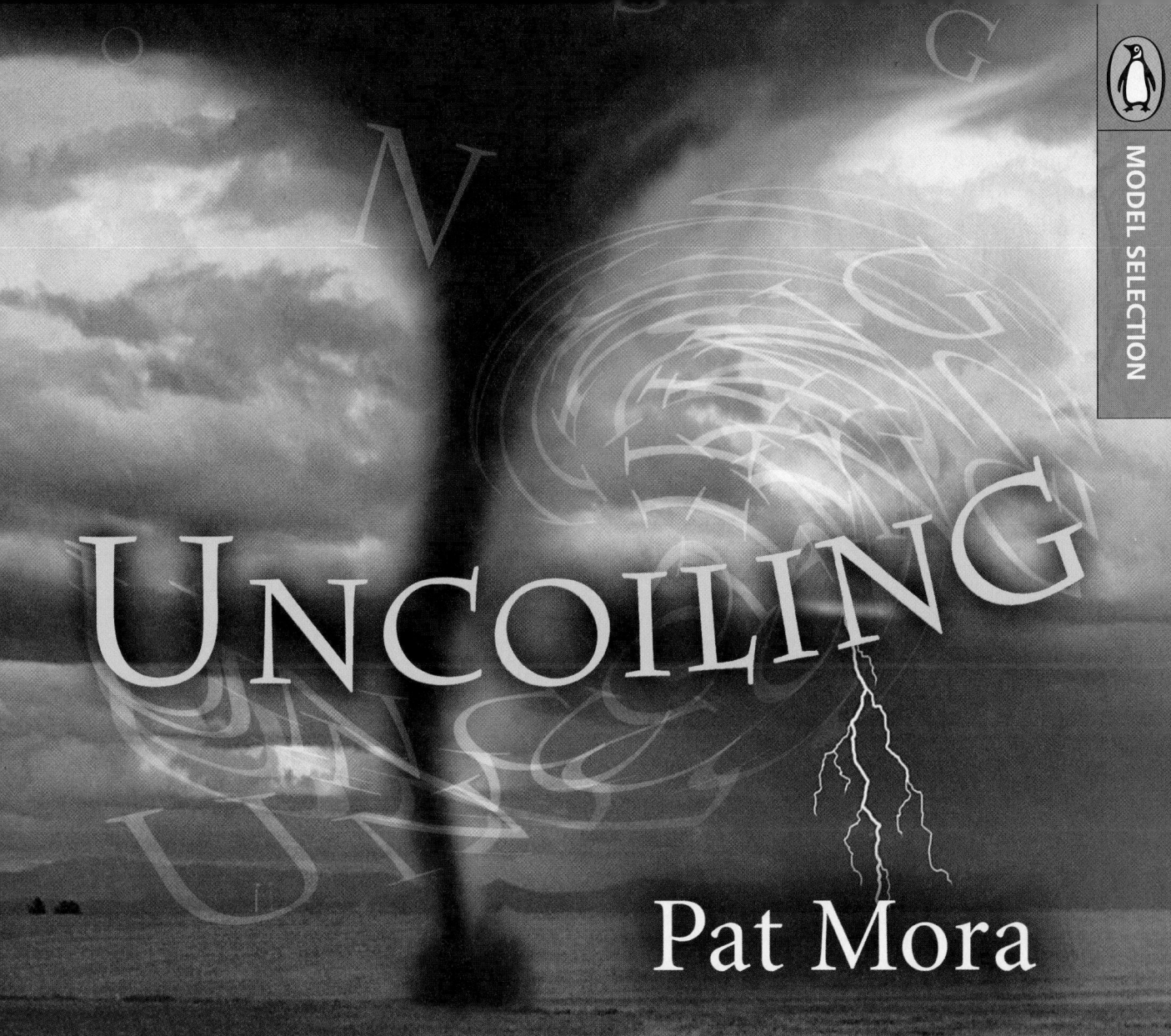

UNCOILING

Pat Mora

With thorns, she scratches
    on my window, tosses her hair dark with rain,
        snares lightning, cholla,[1] hawks, butterfly
            swarms in the tangles.
5   She sighs clouds,
      head thrown back, eyes closed, roars
                     and rivers leap,
boulders retreat like crabs
into themselves.

Pat Mora
Author's Insight
"The desert, nature,
is no wimp. It survives
through strength. I
chose verbs like 'roars'
to convey the desert's
energy and power."

---

1. cholla (chō′ yä) *n.* spiny cactus found in the southwestern United States and Mexico.

Poetry
Imagery Mora's vivid
images express both
the appearance and the
power of the storm.

10   She spews gusts and thunder,
            spooks pale women who scurry to
                  lock doors, windows
                        when her tumbleweed skirt starts its spin.

      They sing lace lullabies
15   so their children won't hear
                  her uncoiling
                        through her lips, howling
                              leaves off trees, flesh
                                    off bones, until she becomes

▼ **Critical Viewing**
What humanlike qualities
do you think a tornado
like the one shown here
exhibits? **[Interpret]**

20   sound, spins herself
            to sleep, sand stinging her ankles,
                  whirring into her raw skin like stars.

A Voice

Pat Mora

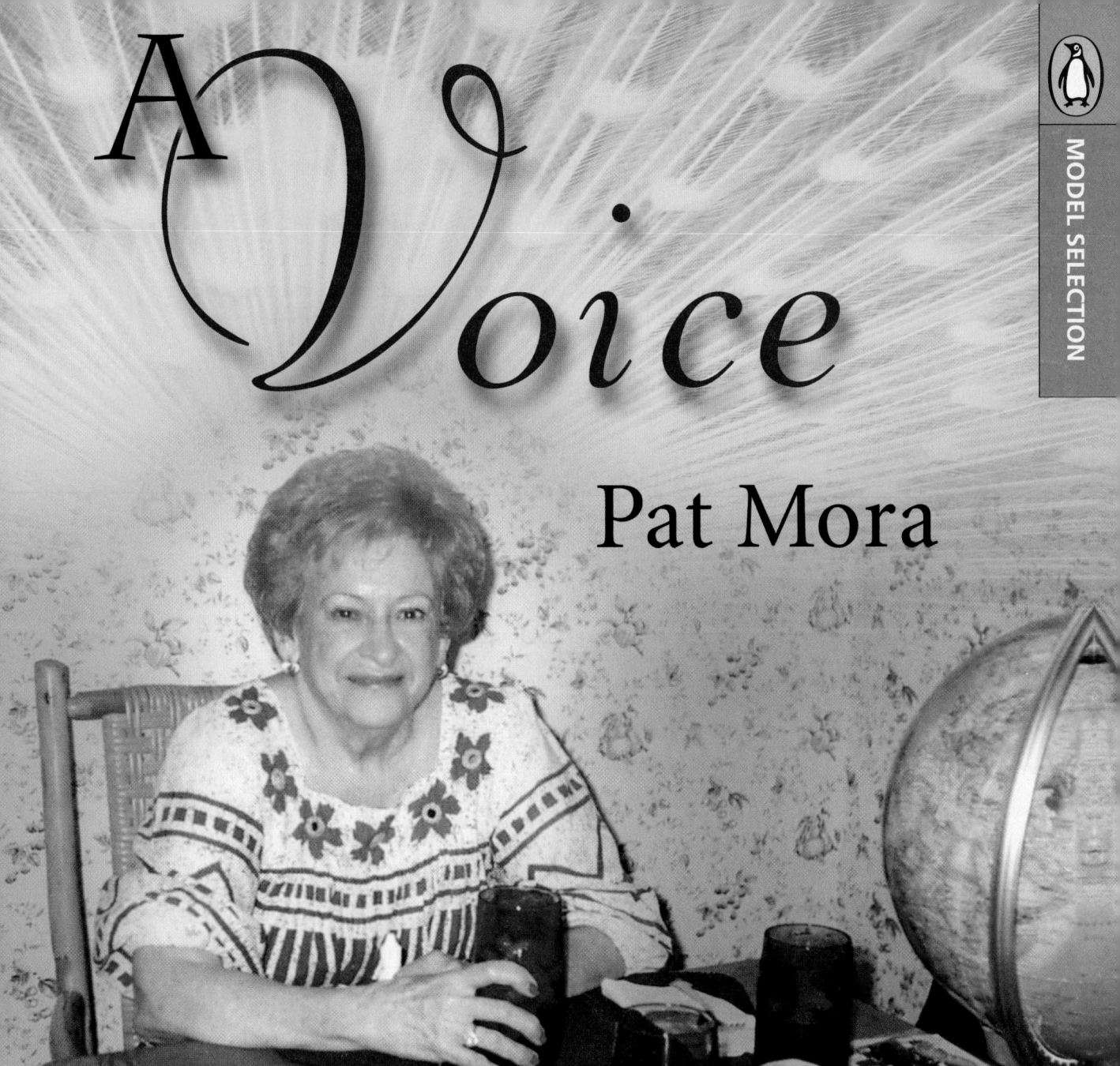

Even the lights on the stage unrelenting
as the desert sun couldn't hide the other
students, their eyes also unrelenting,
students who spoke English every night

5   as they ate their meat, potatoes, gravy.
Not you. In your house that smelled like
rose powder, you spoke Spanish formal
as your father, the judge without a courtroom

Pat Mora
Author's Insight
"Food creates
connections in our minds
and gives us cultural
clues. What if I'd said,
'beans, tortillas, chili'
instead?"

Poetry
Figurative Language
By comparing the father's walk to a "hot river," Mora suggests more than simply his rate of movement.

in the country he floated to in the dark
10 on a flatbed truck. He walked slow
as a hot river down the narrow hall
of your house. You never dared to race past him

to say, "Please move," in the language
you learned effortlessly, as you learned to run,
15 the language forbidden at home, though your mother
said you learned it to fight with the neighbors.

Poetry
Repetition Mora uses repetition in this stanza to create a rhythmic effect.

You like winning with words. You liked
writing speeches about patriotism and democracy.
You liked all the faces looking at you, all those eyes.
20 "How did I do it?" you ask me now. "How did I do it

Vocabulary
spunky (spuŋ´ kē) *adj.*
courageous; spirited

when my parents didn't understand?"
The family story says your voice is the voice
of an aunt in Mexico, spunky as a peacock.
Family stories sing of what lives in the blood.

25 You told me only once about the time you went
to the state capitol, your family proud as if
you'd been named governor. But when you looked
around, the only Mexican in the auditorium,

you wanted to hide from those strange faces.
30 Their eyes were pinpricks, and you faked
hoarseness. You, who are never at a loss
for words, felt your breath stick in your throat

like an ice cube. "I can't," you whispered.
"I can't." Yet you did. Not that day but years later.
35 You taught the four of us to speak up.
This is America, Mom. The undoable is done

in the next generation. Your breath moves
through the family like the wind
moves through the trees.

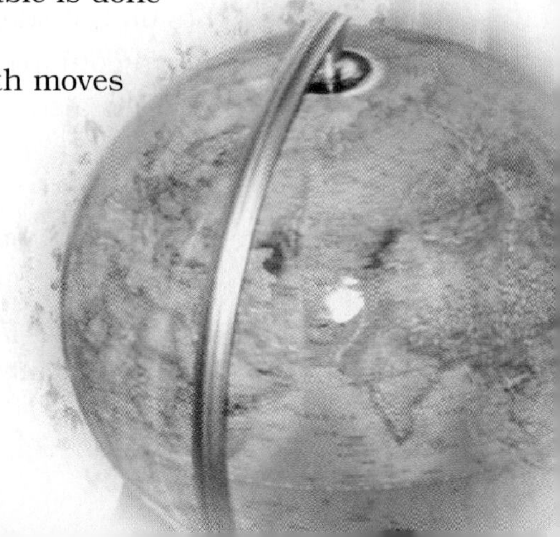

Critical Thinking

1. **Respond:** Which poem did you find more powerful? Why?

2. **(a) Make Inferences:** In "Uncoiling," what kind of storm does the speaker describe? **(b) Interpret:** Identify three actions the storm takes. **(c) Analyze:** How do the actions show the storm's violence?

3. **(a)** Who is the subject of "A Voice"? **(b) Interpret:** Which of this person's childhood accomplishments does the poet celebrate?

4. **(a) Summarize:** What happens to the person at the state capitol? **(b) Analyze:** According to the speaker, how is the failure of that day transformed later in the subject's life?

How does communication change us?
(a) How does nature communicate its strength and power in "Uncoiling"? **(b)** What power do you think Mora is describing when she says, "Your breath moves through the family like the wind moves through the trees" in "A Voice"?

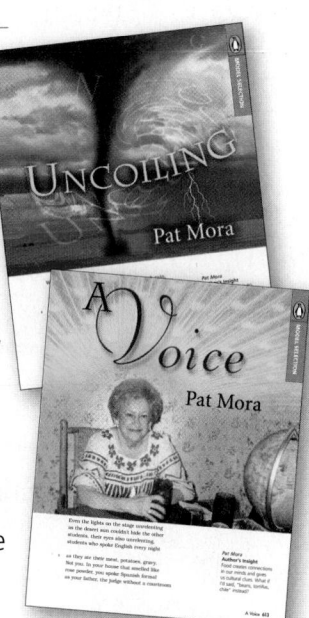

Poetry Review

5. In "Uncoiling," Mora uses **personification** to give the storm human attributes. **(a)** What qualities does the storm possess? **(b)** How does the storm's behavior compare with the women's actions in the poem?

6. **(a)** In the first column of a chart like the one shown, list **images** of breathing or speaking from the poems. In the second column, note the literal meaning of the image. In the third column, describe the image's effect—the word picture it conveys or feeling it expresses. **(b)** In a small group, discuss your findings.

What It Says	What It Means	Effect

Research the Author

Prepare a **report** in which you describe Pat Mora's views about her dual-language heritage and literary career. Follow these steps:

- Find biographical sources with comments on Mora's writing.
- Refer to poems in which Mora mentions her dual-language heritage.
- Share your report with your class.

Collection Choices

▲ **Poetry Collection 1** includes poems about dreams, the natural world, and love.

▲ The poems in **Poetry Collection 2** explore connections between physical and emotional worlds.

 TEXAS Focus on the TEKS

Meet these standards with either **Poetry Collection 1** (p. 620) or **Poetry Collection 2** (p. 632).

Reading
(7) Explain the role of paradox in literary works. (Literary Analysis: Figurative Language)
(1)(A) Determine the meaning of grade-level technical academic English words in multiple content areas derived from Latin roots. (Word Power: Apply It)

Writing
(13)(A) Plan a first draft by selecting the correct genre for conveying the intended meaning to multiple audiences. (Writing: Descriptive Essay, Poem)

Listening and Speaking
(25) Give presentations using informal language effectively to meet the needs of audience, purpose, and occasion, employing eye contact, speaking rate, volume, enunciation, purposeful gestures, and conventions of language to communicate ideas effectively. (Listening and Speaking: Informal Presentation)

Literary Analysis: **Figurative Language**

www.PHLitOnline.com

Hear It!
- Selection summary audio
- Selection audio

See It!
- Get Connected video
- Background video
- More about the author
- Vocabulary flashcards

Do It!
- Interactive journals
- Interactive graphic organizers
- Self-test
- Internet activity
- Grammar tutorial
- Interactive vocabulary games

Figurative language is language that is used imaginatively rather than literally, which can significantly impact the tone, mood, and theme of a poem. Figurative language includes one or more **figures of speech,** literary devices that make unexpected comparisons or change the usual meaning of words. The following are specific types of figures of speech:

- **Simile:** a comparison of two apparently unlike things using *like, as, than,* or *resembles:* "The morning sun is <u>like</u> a red rubber ball."
- **Metaphor:** a description of one thing as if it were another: "The morning sun <u>is</u> a red rubber ball."
- **Personification:** assignment of human characteristics to a non-human subject: "The <u>sea</u> was <u>angry</u> that day, my friends."
- **Paradox:** a statement, an idea, or a situation that seems contradictory but actually expresses a truth: "The more <u>things change</u>, the more <u>they stay the same</u>."

Using the Strategy: Figurative Language Chart

As You Read Use a chart like this one to record examples of figurative language (including paradox) in the poems. Then, explain the role of each example.

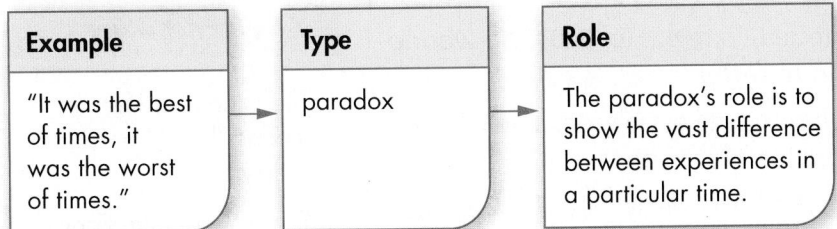

Example	Type	Role
"It was the best of times, it was the worst of times."	paradox	The paradox's role is to show the vast difference between experiences in a particular time.

Reading Skill: **Read Fluently**

When you **read fluently,** you read smoothly while also comprehending the text and appreciating the writer's artistry. To read poetry fluently, read in sentences or units of meaning. Line length is an important element of poetry, but punctuation can clarify meaning.

As You Read Use punctuation rather than the ends of lines to determine where to pause or stop reading.

How does *communication* change us?

Writing About the Big Question

The poets in this collection communicate ideas that help us think about the world in new ways. Use this sentence starter to develop your ideas about the Big Question.

When the speaker of a poem asks the audience to **respond** to a question, the reader is pushed to _____ and _____.

As You Read Think about what idea or ideas the speaker of each poem is sharing with us. Then, decide how you would respond to any questions the poetry raises.

Vocabulary

Read each word and its definition. Decide whether you know the word well, know it a little bit, or do not know it at all. After you read, see how your knowledge of each word has increased.

- **deferred** (dē fʉrd´) *adj.* put off until a future time (p. 620) *Jackie deferred her trip to Italy until she had more money.* *defer v. deferring v. deferral n. deference n.*

- **fester** (fes´ tər) *v.* become infected; form pus (p. 620) *The wound became infected and began to fester.* *festering adj.*

- **barren** (bar´ ən) *adj.* empty; having little or no vegetation (p. 621) *The hillside was barren after the fire.* *barrenness n.*

- **paradoxical** (par´ ə däk´ si kəl) *adj.* seemingly full of contradictions (p. 623) *I think it is paradoxical that people in cities could be lonely.* *paradox n.*

- **pensive** (pen´ siv) *adj.* deeply or seriously thoughtful (p. 628) *Everyone remembered the professor as a quiet and pensive man.* *pensively adv. pensiveness n.*

- **solitude** (säl´ ə to͞od´) *n.* the state of being solitary, or alone; seclusion, isolation, or remoteness (p. 628) *I enjoy a quiet moment of solitude before the guests arrive.* *solitary adj. sole adj.*

Word Power

The **Latin root -fer-** means "bring" or "carry."

The first poem in Poetry Collection 1 is about a dream that has been **deferred**—the dream may have been carried away, or put off until a future time.

Langston Hughes

(1902–1967)

Author of "Dream Deferred" • "Dreams" (pp. 620, 621)

Born in Joplin, Missouri, Langston Hughes was the first African American to earn a living by writing literary works. As a young man, he held a variety of jobs—teacher, ranch hand, and farmer, among others. He drew on all of these experiences, but primarily on his perspective as an African American, to create his great body of work.

Jean de Sponde

(1557–1595)

Author of "Sonnet on Love XIII" (p. 622)

The French poet Jean de Sponde was a true Renaissance man who served in the court of King Henry IV, dabbled in chemistry, and published scholarly editions of ancient Greek texts. "Sonnet on Love XIII" is part of his finest work, *Sonnets of Love and Death.*

Gabriela Mistral

(1889–1957)

Author of "Meciendo/Rocking" (p. 624)

Born in Chile as Lucila Godoy y Alcayaga, this writer formed her pen name from the names of her two favorite poets, the Italian Gabriele D'Annunzio and the French Frederic Mistral. Gabriela Mistral wrote many moving poems about children and motherhood. She was awarded the Nobel Prize in Literature in 1945.

William Wordsworth

(1770–1850)

Author of "I Wandered Lonely as a Cloud" (p. 626)

William Wordsworth was born in England's rural Lake District. In 1798, he and fellow poet Samuel Taylor Coleridge published *Lyrical Ballads*—poems that use simple language to exalt everyday life. Emphasizing nature and the imagination, Wordsworth ushered in the age of Romanticism.

Street Shadows, 1959, Jacob Lawrence, © ARS, NY/ Photo courtesy of: The Jacob and Gwendolyn Lawrence Foundation / Art Resource, NY

Dream *Deferred*

Langston Hughes

▲ **Critical Viewing**
Does the context of
this poem make the
image above seem
hopeless or hopeful?
Explain. **[Interpret]**

Vocabulary
deferred (dē fʉrdʹ)
adj. put off until
a future time
fester (fesʹ tər) *v.*
become infected;
form pus

Harlem

What happens to a dream deferred?

Does it dry up
like a raisin in the sun?
5   Or fester like a sore—
And then run?
Does it stink like rotten meat?
Or crust and sugar over—
like a syrupy sweet?

10   Maybe it just sags
like a heavy load.

Or does it explode?

Dreams
Langston Hughes

Hold fast to dreams
For if dreams die
Life is a broken-winged bird
That cannot fly.

5   Hold fast to dreams
For when dreams go
Life is a barren field
Frozen with snow.

Reading Skill
Read Fluently
How many sentences
are in the first stanza?

Vocabulary
barren (bar´ ən) *adj.*
empty; having little
or no vegetation

Sonnet on Love XIII

Jean de Sponde

translated by David R. Slavitt

Background Archimedes (är´ kə mē´ dēz´) (287?–212 B.C.) has been called the founder of theoretical mechanics. He was a brilliant Greek mathematician and inventor who once boasted that, given a place to stand in space and a long enough lever, he could move the Earth itself. Legend has it that when he made a great discovery, he jumped up and shouted "Eureka!" ("I have found it!")

"Give me a place to stand," Archimedes said,
"and I can move the world." Paradoxical, clever,
his remark which first explained the use of the lever
was an academic joke. But if that dead

5   sage could return to life, he would find a clear
demonstration of his idea, which is not
pure theory after all. That putative[1] spot
exists in the love I feel for you, my dear.

What could be more immovable or stronger?
10 What becomes more and more secure, the longer
it is battered by inconstancy and the stress

we find in our lives? Here is that fine fixed point
from which to move a world that is out of joint,
as he could have done, had he known a love like this.

---

1. **putative** (pyo͞ot´ ə tiv) *adj.* supposed; known by reputation.

Vocabulary
paradoxical (par´ ə däk´ si kəl) *adj.* seemingly full of contradictions

Reading Skill
Read Fluently
Where does the sentence that starts in line 10 end?

Literary Analysis
Figurative Language
Explain the role of paradox in lines 10–12.

◀ **Critical Viewing** Based on this depiction of Archimedes, how do you think he would have responded to de Sponde's poem? **[Speculate]**

Meciendo

Gabriela Mistral

▲ **Critical Viewing**
How well does this photograph illustrate the "loving sea" described in the poem? Explain. **[Evaluate]**

El mar sus millares de olas
mece, divino.
Oyendo a los mares amantes,
mezo a mi niño.

5   El viento errabundo en la noche
mece a los trigos.
Oyendo a los vientos amantes,
mezo a mi niño.

Diós Padre sus miles de mundos
10 mece sin ruido.
Sintiendo su mano en la sombra,
mezo a mi niño.

Rocking (Meciendo)

Gabriela Mistral

translated by Doris Dana

The sea rocks her thousands of waves.
The sea is divine.
Hearing the loving sea,
I rock my son.

5 The wind wandering by night
rocks the wheat.
Hearing the loving wind,
I rock my son.

God, the Father, soundlessly rocks
10 His thousands of worlds.
Feeling His hand in the shadow,
I rock my son.

Literary Analysis
Figurative Language
What human traits does
the wind show in the
second stanza?

I Wandered Lonely as a Cloud

William Wordsworth

I wandered lonely as a cloud
That floats on high o'er vales[1] and hills,
When all at once I saw a crowd,
A host, of golden daffodils;
5   Beside the lake, beneath the trees,
Fluttering and dancing in the breeze.

Continuous as the stars that shine
And twinkle on the milky way,
They stretched in never-ending line
10   Along the margin of a bay:
Ten thousand saw I at a glance,
Tossing their heads in sprightly dance.
The waves beside them danced; but they
Outdid the sparkling waves in glee;
15   A poet could not but be gay,
In such a jocund[2] company;

---

1. o'er vales over valleys.
2. jocund (jak´ ənd) *adj.* cheerful.

Vocabulary

pensive (pen´ siv)
adj. deeply or seriously thoughtful

solitude (säl´ ə tōōd´) *n.*
the state of being solitary, or alone; seclusion, isolation, or remoteness

I gazed—and gazed—but little thought
What wealth the show to me had brought:

20 For oft, when on my couch I lie
In vacant or in pensive mood,
They flash upon that inward eye
Which is the bliss of solitude;
And then my heart with pleasure fills,
And dances with the daffodils.

Critical Thinking

Support your responses with evidence from the text.

1. **Respond:** Which of these poems affected you the most? Explain your answer.

2. **(a)** To what two things does the speaker in "Dreams" compare life? **(b) Interpret:** Restate in your own words the advice that "Dreams" offers.

3. **(a)** How many questions does "Dream Deferred" ask? Explain. **(b) Analyze:** In what way is the last question different from the others? Explain your response.

4. **(a)** In "I Wandered Lonely as a Cloud," what natural sight does the speaker describe? **(b)** In "Meciendo/Rocking," what natural sights and sounds does the speaker describe? **(c) Compare and Contrast:** How do the natural sights and sounds affect each of the speakers? Explain how each poem reveals this.

5. **(a) Interpret:** In "Sonnet on Love XIII," to what does the speaker compare his love? **(b) Draw Conclusions:** What does this comparison suggest about the speaker's feelings? Explain your response.

 **How does communication change us?**
(a) How would you answer the main question posed by the speaker in "Dream Deferred"? Why? **(b)** How does your response to that question grow or change when you read "Dreams"? Explain.

Literary Analysis: Figurative Language

1. **(a)** Identify one **simile** in "Dream Deferred" and one **metaphor** in "Dreams." **(b)** Explain what each **figure of speech** contributes to the overall meaning of the poem in which it appears.
2. **(a)** Identify an example of **personification** in Poetry Collection 1. **(b)** Explain how this use of **figurative language** contributes to the overall effect of the poem in which it appears.
3. **(a)** Identify the **paradox** in lines 1 and 2 of "Sonnet on Love XIII." **(b)** Explain why it is a paradox and what role it plays in the poem.

Reading Skill: Read Fluently

4. **(a)** Using this chart as a model, rewrite one stanza in Poetry Collection 1 as a prose paragraph.

Stanza	Paragraph
God, the Father, soundlessly rocks His thousands of worlds. Feeling His hand in the shadow, I rock my son.	God, the Father, soundlessly rocks His thousands of worlds. Feeling His hand in the shadow, I rock my son.

(b) Read the stanza and the paragraph aloud. How does following the punctuation help you **read fluently?**

Vocabulary

Practice Vocabulary **analogies** show the relationships between pairs of words. Use a word from the vocabulary list on page 618 to make a word pair that matches the relationship between the first two given words.

1. active : exercise :: _____ : ponder
2. rainy : weather :: _____ : statement
3. empty : full :: _____ : fruitful
4. rushed : hurried :: _____ : delayed
5. multitude : many :: _____ : one
6. burn : blaze :: _____ : rot

Word Power Use the context of the sentences and what you know about the **Latin root -fer-** to explain your answer to each question.

1. If you *transfer* something, do you keep it in one place?
2. Does a *conference* bring people together?

Word Power

The **Latin root -fer-** means "bring" or "carry."

Apply It Explain how the root -fer- helps you determine the meanings of these technical academic words from science. Consult a dictionary if necessary.

refer
coniferous
fertile

Making Connections
Poetry Collection 2

All Watched Over... •
"Hope" is the thing... •
Much Madness is divinest... •
The War Against the Trees

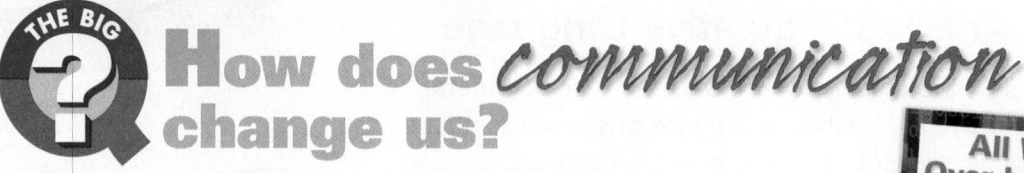

How does *communication* change us?

Writing About the Big Question

The poets in this collection share thoughts about how technology, war, and even ideas can change both us and the way we regard the world. Use this sentence starter to develop your ideas about the Big Question:

As a result of advances in computer technology, **relationships** between people have become _____ because _____.

As You Read Consider what each poem has to say about how people relate to each other and to the world around them.

Vocabulary

Read each word and its definition. Decide whether you know the word well, know it a little bit, or do not know it at all. After you read, see how your knowledge of each word has increased.

- **abash** (ə bash´) *v.* embarrass (p. 634) *The bully would continuously abash his peers to make himself feel more confident.* abashed *adj.* abashedly *adv.* bashful *adj.*

- **discerning** (di surn´ iŋ) *adj.* having good judgment or understanding (p. 635) *The discerning viewer will realize what a bad movie this is.* discern *v.* discernment *n.*

- **prevail** (prē vāl´) *v.* gain the advantage or mastery; be victorious; triumph (p. 635) *Good prevails over evil in this holiday movie.* prevailing *adj.*

- **preliminaries** (prē lim´ ə ner´ ēz) *n.* steps or events before the main one (p. 637) *The preliminaries, especially the national anthem, were more exciting than the game.* preliminary *adj.*

- **subverting** (səb vurt´ iŋ) *v.* overthrowing or destroying something established (p. 637) *By subverting the monarchy, the revolutionaries hoped to bring freedom.* subvert *v.* subversive *adj.* subversion *n.*

- **seizure** (sē´ zhər) *n.* a sudden and brief loss of consciousness and body control. (p. 637) *One of the customers in the store suffered a seizure and fell to the floor.* seize *v.*

Word Power

The **Latin root -vert-** means "turn."

In the poem "The War Against the Trees," the speaker describes the **subverting** of trees. Bulldozers dig into the roots of the trees and *turn* the trees over from underneath.

Richard Brautigan

(1935–1984)

Author of "All Watched Over by Machines of Loving Grace"
(p. 632)

With his 1967 novel *Trout Fishing in America,* Richard Brautigan became a spokesperson for the hippie generation. Ironically, he was at least fifteen years older than the hippies and a product of the Beat generation that preceded them. Nevertheless, his writing demonstrates his free spirit. His books present sketches of a counterculture that resists dependence on machines, industry, and business.

Emily Dickinson

(1830–1886)

**Author of "'Hope' is the thing with feathers—" •
"Much Madness is divinest Sense—"** (pp. 634, 635)

Despite her quiet, outward behavior, Emily Dickinson's inner life overflowed with energy. She produced at least 1,775 poems. Dickinson looked deeply into simple subjects—a fly buzzing, a bird on a walk, the changing seasons. She also made profound explorations of love, death, and the relationship between the human and the divine. She remains unquestionably one of America's finest poets.

Stanley Kunitz

(1905–2006)

Author of "The War Against the Trees" (p. 636)

Stanley Kunitz was born in Worcester, Massachusetts, and published his first book of poems in 1930. Kunitz worked as an editor on many small magazines and taught countless young poets. He was named the United States Poet Laureate in 2000.

All Watched Over by Machines of Loving Grace

Richard Brautigan

I like to think (and
the sooner the better!)
of a cybernetic meadow
where mammals and computers
5 live together in mutually
programming harmony
like pure water
touching clear sky.

I like to think
    (right now, please!)
10 of a cybernetic forest
filled with pines and electronics
where deer stroll peacefully
past computers
as if they were flowers
15 with spinning blossoms.

I like to think
    (it has to be!)
of a cybernetic ecology
where we are free of our labors
and joined back to nature,
20 returned to our mammal
brothers and sisters,
and all watched over
by machines of loving grace.

Literary Analysis
Figurative Language
What simile does the speaker use in lines 3–8 to describe the cybernetic meadow?

"Hope" is the thing with feathers—

EMILY DICKINSON

Reading Skill
Read Fluently
Where in the second stanza could you replace a dash with a period to signify the end of a sentence?

Vocabulary
abash (ə bash´)
v. embarrass

"Hope" is the thing with feathers—
That perches in the soul—
And sings the tune without the words—
And never stops—at all—

5   And sweetest—in the Gale[1]—is heard—
And sore must be the storm—
That could abash the little Bird
That kept so many warm—

I've heard it in the chillest land—
10 And on the strangest Sea—
Yet, never, in Extremity,
It asked a crumb—of Me.

---

1. Gale (gāl) *n.* strong wind.

▶ **Critical Viewing**
Why might someone associate birds with hope? **[Speculate]**

Much Madness is divinest Sense—

EMILY DICKINSON

Much Madness is divinest Sense—
To a discerning Eye—
Much Sense—the starkest Madness—
'Tis the Majority
5 In this, as All, prevail—
Assent[1]—and you are sane—
Demur[2]—you're straightway dangerous—
And handled with a Chain—

---

1. assent (ə sent´) v. agree.
2. demur (dē mʉr´) v. hesitate because of doubts or objections.

Vocabulary
discerning (di sʉrn´ iŋ)
adj. having good judgment or understanding
prevail (prē vāl´) v. gain the advantage or mastery; be victorious; triumph

THE WAR AGAINST THE TREES

STANLEY KUNITZ

The man who sold his lawn to standard oil
Joked with his neighbors come to watch the show
While the bulldozers, drunk with gasoline,
Tested the virtue of the soil
5   Under the branchy sky
By overthrowing first the privet-row.

Forsythia-forays and hydrangea-raids
Were but **preliminaries** to a war
Against the great-grandfathers of the town,
10 So freshly lopped and maimed.
They struck and struck again,
And with each elm a century went down.

All day the hireling engines charged the trees,
Subverting them by hacking underground
15 In grub-dominions, where dark summer's mole
Rampages through his halls,
Till a northern **seizure** shook
Those crowns, forcing the giants to their knees.

Vocabulary
preliminaries (prē lim´ ə ner´ ēz) *n.* steps or events before the main one

subverting (səb vurt´ iŋ) *v.* overthrowing or destroying something established

seizure (sē´ zhər) *n.* a sudden and brief loss of consciousness and body control

Literary Analysis
Figurative Language
What are the "giants" that are personified in line 18?

◄ **Critical Viewing** What does a tree like the one shown represent to the speaker of the poem? **[Connect]**

I saw the ghosts of children at their games
20 Racing beyond their childhood in the shade,
And while the green world turned its death-foxed page
And a red wagon wheeled,
I watched them disappear
Into the suburbs of their grievous age.

25 Ripped from the craters much too big for hearts
The club-roots bared their amputated coils,
Raw gorgons matted blind, whose pocks and scars
Cried Moon! on a corner lot
One witness-moment, caught
30 In the rear-view mirrors of the passing cars.

Critical Thinking

Support your responses with evidence from the text.

1. **(a) Respond:** Which of these poems affected you the most? Explain your answer. **(b) Take a Position:** In each poem in this collection, the author voices a strong point of view. What is your position on each of these points of view? Explain why you hold each of these positions.

2. **(a)** To what does the speaker compare computers in the imaginary world of "All Watched Over by Machines of Loving Grace"? **(b) Interpret:** What does this comparison suggest about the speaker's feelings about computers in the real world?

3. **(a)** In "'Hope' is the thing with feathers—," when does hope sing the sweetest? **(b) Interpret:** Why does hope sing so well at these times? Explain your response.

4. **(a) Interpret:** In "The War Against the Trees," who or what is at war with the trees? **(b) Draw Conclusions:** What does the image of war suggest about the speaker's feelings toward the trees and what is happening to them? Explain how the poem reveals this.

5. **(a) Interpret:** In "Much Madness is divinest Sense—," what kind of behavior is considered insane? **(b) Evaluate:** Do you agree with the speaker's ideas? Explain your answer.

THE BIG Q

How does communication change us?
(a) Describe the relationship that the speaker of "All Watched Over by Machines of Loving Grace" envisions between people and computers. **(b)** How might people change as a result of this new kind of relationship with computers? Explain.

After You Read
Poetry Collection 2

All Watched Over... •
"Hope" is the thing... •
Much Madness is divinest... •
The War Against the Trees

Literary Analysis: Figurative Language

1. **(a)** Identify a **simile** and a **metaphor** in Poetry Collection 2.
   (b) Explain what each **figure of speech** contributes to the overall meaning or effect of the poem in which it appears.
2. **(a)** Identify one example of **personification** in Collection 2.
   (b) Explain how this use of **figurative language** contributes to the overall effect of the poem in which it appears.
3. **(a)** Identify the **paradox** in "Much Madness is divinest Sense—."
   (b) Explain why it is a paradox and what role it plays in the poem.

Reading Skill: **Read Fluently**

4. **(a)** Using this chart as a model, rewrite one stanza in Poetry Collection 2 as a prose paragraph.

Stanza	Paragraph
I've heard it in the chillest land— And on the strangest Sea— Yet, never, in Extremity, It asked a crumb—of Me.	I've heard it in the chillest land and on the strangest Sea, yet never, in Extremity, it asked a crumb of me.

(b) Read the stanza and the paragraph aloud. How does following punctuation help you **read fluently?**

Vocabulary

Practice Vocabulary **analogies** show the relationships between pairs of words. Use a word from the Poetry Collection 2 list on page 630 that creates a word pair matching the relationship between the first two given words.

1. destroying : creating :: _____ : supporting
2. forgiving : fan :: _____ : expert
3. rehearsal : performance :: _____ : championship
4. lose : defeat :: _____ : victory
5. praise : confidence :: _____ : shame
6. house : home :: _____ : attack

Word Power Use the context of the sentence and what you know about the **Latin root -vert-** to explain your answer to this question.

Is someone who is *introverted* outgoing or shy?

Word Power

The **Latin root -vert-** means "turn."

Apply It Explain how the root -vert- helps you determine the meanings of these technical academic words from science. Consult a dictionary if necessary.

inversion
revert
vertical

Integrated Language Skills

Poetry Collections 1 and 2

Conventions: Prepositions

Poetry Collection 1

A **preposition** is a word that relates a noun or pronoun to another word in the sentence.

The **object of the preposition** is the noun or pronoun at the end of a **prepositional phrase.**

Although most prepositions, such as *at* and *with,* are single words, some prepositions are made up of two or three words. These prepositions are called **compound prepositions.** Some compound prepositions are spelled as a single word, such as *into* and *throughout.* Others, such as *because of* and *in addition to,* are spelled as separate words.

Poetry Collection 2

> **Common Prepositions:** about, above, across, below, beyond, by, down, except, for, from, in, like, of, on, over, past, through, to, under, until, up, with
>
> **Common Compound Prepositions:** without, underneath, outside, according to, along with, in front of, instead of, next to
>
> **Prepositional Phrase:** Mr. Johnson ate <u>at a good restaurant</u>.
> (*restaurant* is the *object of the preposition at*)

Practice A Identify the preposition and object of the preposition in each sentence.

1. Hold fast to dreams.
2. I wandered lonely as a cloud.
3. Feeling His hand in the shadow, I rock my son.
4. According to legend, Archimedes shouted "Eureka!" when he made a discovery.

Reading Application Find three sentences in "Dream Deferred" that contain a preposition. Identify both the preposition and the object of the preposition in each sentence.

Practice B Identify the preposition and object of the preposition in each sentence. Then, rewrite each sentence using a different prepositional phrase.

1. Deer stroll peacefully past computers.
2. I've heard it in the chillest land.
3. The bulldozers rolled across the yard.
4. People stood across the street and watched the bulldozers.

Writing Application Write three sentences about the image on page 636, using a compound preposition in each one.

PH **GRAMMAR HANDBOOK** | Further instruction and practice are available in the *Prentice Hall Grammar Handbook.*

Writing

Many of the poems in these collections connect nature with larger ideas. Using one of the scenes described in either Poetry Collection 1 or Poetry Collection 2 as a model, write about a scene in nature. **Choose a genre** that will best convey your intended meaning to multiple audiences—your teacher and classmates. For example, you may choose **a descriptive essay or a poem.** Using the language techniques of the author who wrote the original scene, develop your own descriptive word picture.

- Choose a scene that you know firsthand or from photographs.
- List details in the scene that appeal to one or more of the senses.
- Refer to your list of details as you draft in the genre of your choice.

Grammar Application Make sure you use prepositions correctly in your writing.

Writing Workshop: *Work in Progress*

Prewriting for Poem To prepare for a poem you may write, make a list of three places. For each place, write ten words that describe how the place looks. Then, choose the place that is most interesting to you and make a Sensory Word List of adjectives that describe other characteristics of the place, such as smells or sounds. Save your Sensory Word List in your portfolio.

Listening and Speaking

Use a poem from Poetry Collection 1 or Poetry Collection 2 as the basis for an **informal presentation** about dreams, nature, or love. Instead of writing a script or outline, jot down the central point you want to convey. Make concise notes to refer to during your delivery. Consider these tips as you plan and present:

- Choose interesting details, ideas, or viewpoints that will engage your audience, especially in your introduction and conclusion.
- Use **informal language** effectively to meet the needs of your **audience, purpose,** and **occasion.** Choose words and terms that your audience will understand, but be sure to maintain the **conventions of language** by following the rules of grammar and usage.
- Make your ideas memorable by using figurative language.
- Employ **eye contact** and **purposeful gestures** to enhance your ideas and to convey sincerity.
- Use **speaking rate, volume,** and **enunciation** to communicate ideas effectively.

 Focus on the TEKS

Writing
(13)(A) Plan a first draft by selecting the correct genre for conveying the intended meaning to multiple audiences.

Listening and Speaking
(25) Give presentations using informal language effectively to meet the needs of audience, purpose, and occasion, employing eye contact, speaking rate, volume, enunciation, purposeful gestures, and conventions of language to communicate ideas effectively.

Use this prewriting activity to prepare for the **Writing Workshop** on page 686.

 **TEXAS**
PHLitOnline
www.PHLitOnline.com
- Interactive graphic organizers
- Grammar tutorial
- Interactive journals

Collection Choices

▲ The poems in **Poetry Collection 3** use powerful language to make ordinary events extraordinary.

▲ The poems in **Poetry Collection 4** use sounds to add layers of meaning.

 TEXAS Focus on the TEKS

Meet these standards with either **Poetry Collection 3** (p. 646) or **Poetry Collection 4** (p. 654).

Reading
(3) Understand the elements of poetry and provide evidence from the text to support understanding. *(Literary Analysis: Sound Devices)*

(1)(A) Determine the meaning of grade-level technical academic English words in multiple content areas derived from Greek affixes. *(Word Power: Apply It)*

Reading/Comprehension Skills
RC-9(A) Reflect on understanding to monitor comprehension. *(Reading Skill: Read Fluently)*

Writing
(16)(D);(E) Write an argumentative essay to the appropriate audience that includes:

an organizing structure appropriate to the purpose, audience, and context; and an analysis of the relative value of specific data, facts, and ideas. *(Writing: Editorial)*

Listening and Speaking
(25) Give presentations using formal language effectively to meet the needs of audience, purpose, and occasion, employing eye contact, speaking rate, volume, enunciation, purposeful gestures, and conventions of language to communicate ideas effectively. *(Listening and Speaking: Formal Presentation)*

Literary Analysis: **Sound Devices**

An important element of poetry is the sound of the words the author uses. Poets use **sound devices** to emphasize sound relationships among words, which often bring fluidity and meaning to a text. These include:

- **Alliteration:** the repetition of initial consonant sounds in stressed syllables: "The fair <u>b</u>reeze <u>b</u>lew, the white <u>f</u>oam <u>f</u>lew . . ."
- **Consonance:** the repetition of final consonant sounds in stressed syllables with different vowel sounds, as in si<u>t</u> and ca<u>t</u>
- **Assonance:** the repetition of similar vowel sounds in stressed syllables that end with different consonants, as in s<u>ea</u>l and m<u>ee</u>t
- **Onomatopoeia:** the use of a word whose sound imitates its meaning, such as *pop* or *hiss*

All of these sound devices work to engage the reader's senses and create musical and emotional effects.

As You Read Analyze elements of poetry. Note evidence of the way in which each poet uses sound devices to engage the reader's senses.

Reading Skill: **Read Fluently**

When you **read fluently,** you read smoothly and continuously while also **reflecting on your understanding** to **monitor your comprehension** of text. Because poetry is a condensed form of language that employs figurative language, you may need to read poems several times to unlock layers of meaning.

Using the Strategy: **Multiple Reading Chart**

As You Read Use a multiple reading chart like the one shown to reflect on your understanding and monitor your comprehension of the poems.

	My Understanding
1st Reading • Read for basic meaning.	
2nd Reading • Read to unlock deeper meanings.	
3rd Reading • Read to recognize and appreciate poet's craft.	

TEXAS
PHLitOnline
www.PHLitOnline.com

Hear It!
- Selection summary audio
- Selection audio

See It!
- Get Connected video
- Background video
- More about the author
- Vocabulary flashcards

Do It!
- Interactive journals
- Interactive graphic organizers
- Self-test
- Internet activity
- Grammar tutorial
- Interactive vocabulary games

How does *communication* change us?

Writing About the Big Question

In "Analysis of Baseball," the speaker shares her impressions of "America's pastime." Use these sentence starters to develop your ideas about the Big Question.

Reading someone's **interpretation** of a common experience can **illuminate** one's **understanding** of that experience because

_____.

When people **exchange** stories about the past, they become more **aware** of the present because _____.

As You Read Notice when the speaker of a poem describes an experience with which you are familiar, and compare the speaker's response to your own.

Vocabulary

Read each word and its definition. Decide whether you know the word well, know it a little bit, or do not know it at all. After you read, see how your knowledge of each word has increased.

- **clasps** (klasps) *v.* grips (p. 647) *My mother <u>clasps</u> the steering wheel tightly whenever she approaches a sharp turn in the road. clasp n.*

- **azure** (azh´ ər) *adj.* sky blue (p. 647) *She painted the ceiling in her bedroom <u>azure</u> so that it would look like the sky.*

- **analysis** (ə nal´ ə sis) *n.* careful examination by studying something's elements or parts (p. 649) *After a careful <u>analysis</u> of the food sample, the pathologist determined that it had been poisoned. analyze v. analytical adj.*

- **disgrace** (dis grās´) *n.* loss of respect, honor, or esteem; shame (p. 649) *After scoring on themselves and losing to their rivals as a result, the team left the field in <u>disgrace</u>. disgraceful adj. disgraced v.*

Word Power

The **Greek prefix** *ana-* means "up," "back," or "against."

Translated directly from its Greek word parts, the word **analysis** means "a loosening up." In the poem "Analysis of Baseball," the speaker "loosens up" the subject of baseball by describing its most basic parts.

Walter Dean Myers

(b. 1937)

Author of "Summer" (p. 646)

Growing up poor in West Virginia and New York City, Walter Dean Myers never imagined himself becoming a writer. Although he was writing poems and stories by his early teens, he believed that his dream of a literary career would never be realized. Myers's dream was fulfilled, however, when he won a writing contest sponsored by the Council on Interracial Books for Children with his book *Where Does a Day Go?*

Alfred, Lord Tennyson

(1809–1892)

Author of "The Eagle" (p. 647)

The most popular British poet during his lifetime, Alfred, Lord Tennyson rose from humble beginnings to the position of poet laureate of England. Although he was enthralled by the technological advances of the Victorian Era, Tennyson remained a poet of nature, bringing both imagination and feeling to descriptions of the landscape and its inhabitants.

May Swenson

(1919–1989)

Author of "Analysis of Baseball" (p. 648)

May Swenson has been called "one of the surest poets, clear-eyed and absolute." She was born in Logan, Utah, and attended Utah State University. After working for a while as a newspaper reporter, she moved to New York City, where she worked as an editor and as a college lecturer. Her poems were published in such magazines as *The New Yorker, Harper's,* and *The Nation.* Swenson also served as a Chancellor of The Academy of American Poets from 1980 to 1989.

SUMMER

Walter Dean Myers

I like hot days, hot days
Sweat is what you got days
Bugs buzzin from cousin to cousin
Juices dripping
5   Running and ripping
Catch the one you love days

Birds peeping
Old men sleeping
Lazy days, daisies lay
10   Beaming and dreaming
Of hot days, hot days,
Sweat is what you got days

▼ **Critical Viewing**
How well does this photograph illustrate the speaker's feelings about summer? Explain. **[Evaluate]**

The Eagle

Alfred, Lord Tennyson

He **clasps** the crag[1] with crooked hands;
Close to the sun in lonely lands,
Ring'd with the **azure** world, he stands.

The wrinkled sea beneath him crawls;
5   He watches from his mountain walls,
And like a thunderbolt he falls.

---

1. crag (krag) *n.* steep, rugged rock that rises above others or projects from a rock mass.

Vocabulary
clasps (klasps) *v.* grips
azure (azh´ ər) *adj.*
sky blue

Analysis *Of* Baseball

May Swenson

It's about
the ball,
the bat,
and the mitt.
5 Ball hits
bat, or it
hits mitt.
Bat doesn't
hit ball, bat
10 meets it.
Ball bounces
off bat, flies
air, or thuds
ground (dud)
15 or it
fits mitt.

Bat waits
for ball
to mate.
20 Ball hates
to take bat's
bait. Ball
flirts, bat's
late, don't
25 keep the date.
Ball goes in
(thwack) to mitt,
and goes out
(thwack) back
30 to mitt.

Ball fits
mitt, but
not all
the time.
35 Sometimes
ball gets hit
(pow) when bat
meets it,
and sails
40 to a place
where mitt
has to quit
in disgrace.

Literary Analysis
Sound Devices What
final consonant sound is
repeated frequently in
the first ten lines?

Reading Skill
Read Fluently After
the first reading, reflect
on your understanding
to monitor your compre-
hension. What would
you say is the basic
meaning of the
first stanza?

Vocabulary
analysis (ə nal′ ə sis)
n. careful examination
by studying something's
elements or parts
disgrace (dis grās′) *n.*
loss of respect, honor,
or esteem; shame

That's about
45 the bases
loaded,
about 40,000
fans exploded.

It's about
50 the ball,
the bat,
the mitt,
the bases
and the fans.
55 It's done
on a diamond,
and for fun.
It's about
home, and it's
60 about run.

▲ **Critical Viewing**
Which words in the poem might describe the action in this image? **[Connect]**

Support your responses with evidence from the text.

Critical Thinking

1. **Respond:** How does each of these poems make you feel about its subject? Explain your answer.

2. **(a)** In lines 1–2 of "Summer," how does the speaker describe summer? **(b) Connect:** In what way is the image in line 4 a continuation of the one in line 2? Explain your response.

3. **(a) Make Inferences:** What is the eagle watching for in line 5 of "The Eagle"? **(b) Interpret:** What is the eagle doing when he "falls" in line 6?

4. **Make a Judgment:** Do you think the poem "Analysis of Baseball" can be appreciated by someone who is unfamiliar with the rules of baseball? Why or why not?

How does communication change us?
(a) How does "Analysis of Baseball" compare with your experience with the sport of baseball? **(b)** Does the poem change how you think about baseball? Why or why not?

Literary Analysis: **Sound Devices**

1. (a) For each poem in Poetry Collection 3, use a chart like the one shown to list one example of each **sound device** listed. **(b)** How does each example add to the musical feeling of each poem?

	Example	Effect
Alliteration		
Consonance		
Assonance		

2. (a) Identify an example of onomatopoeia in "Analysis of Baseball." **(b)** What sound does the word imitate? **(c)** How well does the word imitate the sound? Explain your answer.

3. (a) Which of these poems do you think makes the most effective use of sound devices? **(b)** Discuss your choice with a small group and decide on a single response.

Reading Skill: **Read Fluently**

4. How did your understanding of the poems deepen with each reading? Provide evidence from the texts to support your understanding.

5. (a) In what way does **reading fluently** help you to appreciate a poem's sound devices? **(b)** Which of your senses, other than your sense of hearing, were most engaged by each of these poems?

Vocabulary

Practice Identify the word in each group that does not belong with the others. Explain your response.

1. clasps, hands, blanket

2. azure, bread, green

3. analysis, study, recording

4. disgrace, pride, approval

Word Power Use the context of the sentences and what you know about the **Greek prefix ana-** to explain your answer to each question.

1. If something is an *anachronism,* is it in the correct time period?

2. Why is a study of *anatomy* important for doctors?

Word Power

The **Greek prefix ana-** means "up," "back," or "against."

Apply It Explain how the prefix *ana-* helps you determine the meanings of these technical academic words from language arts and social studies. Consult a dictionary if necessary.

anagram
anarchy

How does *communication* change us?

Writing About the Big Question

The speaker in "The Bells" describes a range of ideas associated with the sounds of different bells. Use this sentence starter to develop your ideas about the Big Question.

> By reading about the **meaning** that someone finds in certain sounds, a reader can learn to _____.

As You Read Notice when the speaker of a poem mentions a specific sound. Compare the speaker's response to that sound with your own reactions. Notice whether the speaker's response changes how you think about that sound.

Vocabulary

Read each word and its definition. Decide whether you know the word well, know it a little bit, or do not know it at all. After you have read the selection, see how your knowledge of each word has increased.

- **voluminously** (və lōō′ mə nəs lē) *adv.* fully; in great volume (p. 656) *Her coach praised her voluminously at the awards banquet.* volume *n.*

- **endeavor** (en dev′ ər) *n.* an earnest attempt or effort (p. 656) *My endeavor to stay up all night failed when I fell asleep at midnight.* endeavor *v.*

- **palpitating** (pal′ pə tāt′ iŋ) *v.* beating rapidly; throbbing (p. 656) *The palpitating drums of the pep band excited the fans.*

- **monotone** (män′ ə tōn′) *n.* uninterrupted repetition of the same tone; utterance of successive syllables or words without change of pitch or key (p. 659) *The actor spoke in a monotone, which did nothing to keep me awake during the play.* monotonous *adj.* monotony *n.*

- **metaphysical** (met′ ə fiz′ i kəl) *adj.* spiritual; beyond the physical (p. 661) *She says that songwriting is metaphysical—the songs come to her in dreams.*

- **jibed** (jībd) *v.* changed direction (p. 661) *As the wind shifted, the crew jibed to keep the sails full.*

Word Power

The **Greek prefix** *mono-* means "one."

In "The Bells," the speaker describes the "muffled **monotone**" of certain bells. He refers to a kind of ringing that has only one tone, or pitch, that repeats without changing.

Edgar Allan Poe

(1809–1849)

Author of "The Bells" (p. 654)

As poems like "The Bells" illustrate, Edgar Allan Poe was a master at using rhythm and sound devices to powerful effect. Many scholars believe that the idea for "The Bells" was suggested to Poe by Marie Louise Shew, a woman with medical training who treated Poe when his health began to fail.

Yusef Komunyakaa

(b. 1947)

Author of "Slam, Dunk, & Hook" (p. 660)

Yusef Komunyakaa grew up in Bogalusa, Louisiana. During the mid-1960s, he served in Vietnam as a reporter and an editor for the military newspaper *The Southern Cross*. Komunyakaa later turned his attention to poetry, winning a Pulitzer Prize for his book *Neon Vernacular: New and Selected Poems* (1993). Komunyakaa has said that he likes "connecting the abstract to the concrete."

Lewis Carroll

(1832–1898)

Author of "Jabberwocky" (p. 662)

Charles Lutwidge Dodgson was a professor of mathematics and a talented early photographer. Today, he is best remembered for two children's books he wrote under the pen name Lewis Carroll: *Alice's Adventures in Wonderland* (1865) and its sequel, *Through the Looking Glass* (1871). Huge bestsellers almost from the moment they appeared, the Alice books have been the basis of numerous stage plays and films.

The Bells

Edgar Allan Poe

I

Hear the sledges[1] with the bells—
Silver bells!
What a world of merriment their melody foretells!
How they tinkle, tinkle, tinkle,
In the icy air of night!
While the stars, that oversprinkle
All the heavens, seem to twinkle
With a crystalline delight;
Keeping time, time, time,
In a sort of Runic[2] rhyme,
To the tintinnabulation[3] that so musically wells
From the bells, bells, bells, bells,
Bells, bells, bells—
From the jingling and the tinkling of the bells.

5

10

II

Hear the mellow wedding bells,
Golden bells!
What a world of happiness their harmony foretells!
Through the balmy air of night
How they ring out their delight!
From the molten golden-notes,

15

20

---

1. sledges (slej´ əz) *n.* sleighs.
2. Runic (rōō´ nik) *adj.* songlike; poetical.
3. tintinnabulation (tin´ ti na´ byōō la´ shən) *n.* ringing sound of bells.

Reading
Check

What type of bells does section one describe?

And all in tune,
What a liquid ditty[4] floats
To the turtle-dove[5] that listens, while she gloats
On the moon!
25   Oh, from out the sounding cells,
What a gush of euphony[6] **voluminously** wells!
How it swells!
How it dwells
On the future! how it tells
30   Of the rapture that impels
To the swinging and the ringing
Of the bells, bells, bells,
Of the bells, bells, bells, bells
Bells, bells, bells—
35   To the rhyming and the chiming of the bells!

III

Hear the loud alarum[7] bells!
Brazen[8] bells!
What a tale of terror now their turbulency tells!
In the startled ear of night
40   How they scream out their affright!
Too much horrified to speak,
They can only shriek, shriek,
Out of tune,
In a clamorous appealing to the mercy of the fire,
45   In a mad expostulation[9] with the deaf and frantic fire
Leaping higher, higher, higher,
With a desperate desire,
And a resolute **endeavor**
Now—now to sit or never,
50   By the side of the pale-faced moon.
Oh, the bells, bells, bells!
What a tale their terror tells
Of Despair!
How they clang, and clash, and roar!
55   What a horror they outpour
On the bosom of the **palpitating** air!

---

4. ditty (dit´ ē) *n.* short, simple song.
5. turtle-dove (tʉrt´´l duv´) The turtle dove is traditionally associated with love.
6. euphony (yōō´ fə nē) *n.* pleasing sound.
7. alarum (ə ler´ əm) *adj.* sudden call to arms; alarm.
8. brazen (brā´ zən) *adj.* made of brass; having the ringing sound of brass.
9. expostulation (ek späs´ chə lā´ shən) *n.* objection; complaint.

Vocabulary
voluminously (və lōō´ mə nəs lē) *adv.* fully; in great volume

Literary Analysis
Sound Devices What quality of alarm bells might the alliteration of the *t* sound in line 38 imitate?

Vocabulary
endeavor (en dev´ ər) *n.* an earnest attempt or effort

palpitating (pal´ pə tāt´ iŋ) *v.* beating rapidly; throbbing

Yet the ear it fully knows,
By the twanging
And the clanging,
How the danger ebbs and flows;
Yet the ear distinctly tells,
In the jangling,
And the wrangling,
How the danger sinks and swells,
By the sinking or the swelling in the anger of the bells—
Of the bells—
Of the bells, bells, bells, bells,
Bells, bells, bells—
In the clamor and the clangor of the bells!

IV

Hear the tolling of the bells—
Iron bells!
What a world of solemn thought their monody[10] compels!

60

65

70

---

10. monody (mä´ nə dē) *n.* poem of mourning; a steady sound; music in which one instrument or voice is dominant.

Literary Analysis
Sound Devices What is the effect of the repetition in lines 67–68?

Reading Check
What kind of story do the alarm bells tell?

In the silence of the night,
How we shiver with affright
At the melancholy menace of their tone!
For every sound that floats
From the rust within their throats
Is a groan.
And the people—ah, the people—
They that dwell up in the steeple,
All alone,
And who tolling, tolling, tolling,
In that muffled monotone,
Feel a glory in so rolling
On the human heart a stone—
They are neither man nor woman—
They are neither brute nor human—
They are Ghouls:[11]
And their king it is who tolls;
And he rolls, rolls, rolls,
Rolls
A pæan from the bells!
And his merry bosom swells
With the pæan of the bells!
And he dances and he yells;
Keeping time, time, time,
In a sort of Runic rhyme,
To the pæan of the bells—
Of the bells:
Keeping time, time, time,
In a sort of Runic rhyme,
To the throbbing of the bells—
Of the bells, bells, bells—
To the sobbing of the bells;
Keeping time, time, time,
As he knells, knells, knells,
In a happy Runic rhyme,
To the rolling of the bells—
Of the bells, bells, bells—
To the tolling of the bells,
Of the bells, bells, bells, bells,
Bells, bells, bells—
To the moaning and the groaning of the bells.

75
80
85
90
95
100
105
110

Literary Analysis
Sound Devices What alliteration appears in lines 83–85?

Vocabulary
monotone (män´ ə tōn´) *n.* uninterrupted repetition of the same tone; utterance of successive syllables or words without change of pitch or key

Reading Skill
Read Fluently
Reflect on your understanding to monitor your comprehension. Which repeated words in this stanza might sound like the repetitive tolling of bells?

◀ **Critical Viewing**
Which kind of bells do you think this painting best illustrates? Why? **[Assess]**

---

11. Ghouls (gōōlz) *n.* evil spirits that rob graves.

Slam, Dunk, & Hook

Yusef Komunyakaa

Fast breaks. Lay ups. With Mercury's[1]
Insignia[2] on our sneakers,
We outmaneuvered the footwork
Of bad angels. Nothing but a hot
5　Swish of strings like silk
Ten feet out. In the roundhouse[3]
Labyrinth[4] our bodies
Created, we could almost
Last forever, poised in midair
10　Like storybook sea monsters.
A high note hung there
A long second. Off
The rim. We'd corkscrew
Up & dunk balls that exploded
15　The skullcap of hope & good
Intention. Bug-eyed, lanky,
All hands & feet . . . sprung rhythm.
We were metaphysical when girls
Cheered on the sidelines.
20　Tangled up in a falling,
Muscles were a bright motor
Double-flashing to the metal hoop
Nailed to our oak.
When Sonny Boy's mama died
25　He played nonstop all day, so hard
Our backboard splintered.
Glistening with sweat, we jibed
& rolled the ball off our
Fingertips. Trouble
30　Was there slapping a blackjack
Against an open palm.
Dribble, drive to the inside, feint,
& glide like a sparrow hawk.
Lay ups. Fast breaks.
35　We had moves we didn't know
We had. Our bodies spun
On swivels of bone & faith,
Through a lyric slipknot
Of joy, & we knew we were
40　Beautiful & dangerous.

◀ **Critical Viewing**
Which details in this
painting relate to lines
in "Slam, Dunk, &
Hook"? **[Connect]**

Vocabulary
metaphysical (met´ ə
fiz´ i kəl) *adj.* spiritual;
beyond the physical
jibed (jībd) *v.*
changed direction

Literary Analysis
Sound Devices What
sound does the poet
emphasize with the use
of assonance in lines 30
and 31?

---

1. **Mercury's** Mercury was the Roman god of travel, usually depicted with wings on his feet.
2. **insignia** (in sig´ nē ə) *n.* emblems or badges; logos.
3. **roundhouse** (round´ hous´) *n.* area on the court beneath the basket.
4. **labyrinth** (lab´ ə rin*th*´) *n.* maze.

Jabberwocky

Lewis Carroll

'Twas brillig, and the slithy toves
    Did gyre and gimble in the wabe;
All mimsy were the borogoves,
    And the mome raths outgrabe.

5   "Beware the Jabberwock, my son!
    The jaws that bite, the claws that catch!
Beware the Jubjub bird, and shun
    The frumious Bandersnatch!"

He took his vorpal sword in hand:
10   Long time the manxome foe he sought—
So rested he by the Tumtum tree,
    And stood awhile in thought.

And as in uffish thought he stood,
    The Jabberwock, with eyes of flame,
15   Came whiffling through the tulgey wood,
    And burbled as it came!

◀▼ **Critical Viewing**
Which aspects of these illustrations convey the fantastical quality of "Jabberwocky"?
[Analyze]

**Literary Analysis
Sound Devices** What sound or noise does the onomatopoeia *burbled* reflect?

LITERATURE IN CONTEXT

Language Connection

Carroll's Invented Language In the first chapter of *Through the Looking-Glass,* Alice encounters a creature called a Jabberwock. She cannot understand it, so Humpty Dumpty explains some of the words it uses, including these:

brillig: four o'clock in the afternoon, the time when you begin broiling things for dinner

toves: creatures that are something like badgers, something like lizards, and something like corkscrews

gyre: go round and round like a gyroscope

gimble: make holes like a gimlet (a hand tool that bores holes)

wabe: grass plot around a sundial

mome: having lost the way home

raths: something like green pigs

Connect to the Literature

What challenges do you think Carroll faced in writing a poem with invented language?

One, two! One, two! And through and through
    The vorpal blade went snicker-snack!
He left it dead, and with its head
20   He went galumphing back.

"And hast thou slain the Jabberwock?
    Come to my arms, my beamish boy!
O frabjous day! Callooh! Callay!"
    He chortled in his joy.

25 'Twas brillig, and the slithy toves
    Did gyre and gimble in the wabe;
All mimsy were the borogoves,
    And the mome raths outgrabe.

Critical Thinking

Support your responses with evidence from the text.

1. **Respond:** Which of these poems did you find most entertaining? Explain your choice.

2. **(a)** In lines 4–5 of "Slam, Dunk, & Hook," what sound does the speaker describe? **(b) Make Inferences:** What action causes this sound?

3. **(a)** In "Jabberwocky," what does the hero do after being warned about the Jabberwock? **(b) Evaluate:** Do you think the poem pokes fun at heroism? Explain your response.

4. **Take a Position:** The poet T. S. Eliot once said that poetry can be enjoyed before it is understood. Could "The Bells" be used as evidence to support this idea? Explain your answer.

 **How does communication change us?**
Do any of the poems in this collection make you think differently about sounds you hear every day? Explain.

Literary Analysis: **Sound Devices**

1. (a) For each poem in Poetry Collection 4, use a chart like the one shown to give one example of each **sound device** listed. **(b)** How does each example add to the musical feeling of each poem?

	Example	Effect
Alliteration		
Consonance		
Assonance		

2. (a) Identify an example of onomatopoeia in "The Bells." **(b)** What sound does the word imitate? **(c)** How well does the word imitate the sound? Explain your answer.

3. (a) Which of these poems do you think makes the most effective use of sound devices? **(b)** Discuss your idea with a small group and decide on a single response.

Reading Skill: **Read Fluently**

4. How did your understanding of the poems deepen with each reading? Provide evidence from the texts to support your understanding.

5. (a) In what way does **reading fluently** help you to appreciate a poem's sound devices? **(b)** Which of your senses, other than your sense of hearing, were most engaged by each of these poems?

Vocabulary

Practice Identify the word in each group that does not belong with the others. Explain your response.

1. metaphysical, concrete, bodily

2. jibed, turn, straight

3. voluminously, tiny, huge

4. palpitating, pulse, hum

5. endeavor, avoid, attempt

6. monotone, voice, flower

Word Power Use the context of the sentences and what you know about the **Greek prefix mono-** to explain your answer to each question.

1. If a painting is *monochromatic,* does it have one color or many?

2. If Joe is *monolingual,* how many languages does he speak?

Word Power

The **Greek prefix mono-** means "one."

Apply It Explain how the prefix *mono-* helps you determine the meanings of these technical academic words from mathematics and social studies. Consult a dictionary if necessary.

monomial
monotheism
monorail

Integrated Language Skills

Poetry Collections 3 and 4

Conventions: Prepositional Phrases

Poetry Collection 3

A **prepositional phrase** is a group of words beginning with a preposition and ending with a noun or pronoun, called the *object* of the preposition.

A prepositional phrase may function as either an adjective or an adverb, depending on the word it modifies. An adjective phrase modifies a noun or a pronoun by telling *what kind* or *which one*. An adverb phrase modifies a verb, an adjective, or an adverb by pointing out *where, when, in what way,* or *to what extent.*

Poetry Collection 4

Adjective phrase: The players <u>on their team</u> are more experienced. (modifies the noun *players*)

Adjective phrase: The flowers <u>with yellow petals</u> are my favorites. (modifies the noun *flowers*)

Adverb phrase: They played <u>with more skill</u>. (modifies the verb *played*)

Adverb phrase: My parents walked <u>through the door</u> <u>at that moment.</u> (both phrases modify the verb *walked*)

Practice A Identify the prepositional phrase in each sentence, and tell whether it functions as an adjective or an adverb.

1. Myers's poem describes the hot days of summer.
2. He clasps the crag with crooked hands.
3. He watches from his mountain walls.
4. Baseball is played on a diamond.
5. Tennyson's poem about the eagle is very descriptive.

Reading Application In "The Eagle," find one prepositional phrase that functions as an adjective and one that functions as an adverb.

Practice B Following the instructions in parentheses, use each prepositional phrase in a sentence of your own.

1. of joyful singing (adjective phrase)
2. in the woods (adverb phrase)
3. under the bridge (adjective phrase)
4. through the hoop (adverb phrase)

Writing Application Following these models, write four sentences. Identify which phrases are used as adjectives and which are used as adverbs.
  Running with a knife is not safe.
  The child's book was illustrated with animals of many kinds.

PH GRAMMAR HANDBOOK Further instruction and practice are available in the *Prentice Hall Grammar Handbook.*

Writing

Write an **editorial**—an argumentative text that presents one side of an issue—related to one of the poems you read. For example, if you read "The Eagle," you could write an editorial about the need to preserve the North American bald eagle. If you read "Slam, Dunk, & Hook," you might write about the need for funding for neighborhood sports.

- Include a clear thesis, or position, based on logical reasons supported by precise and relevant evidence.
- Consider a whole range of information and views on the topic, and accurately and honestly represent those views.
- Analyze the **relative value** of specific **data, facts,** and **ideas,** and choose the strongest items for your draft.
- Incorporate counter-arguments based on evidence to anticipate and address possible objections from your specific audience—classmates.
- Use an **organizing structure** appropriate to your purpose, audience, and context.

Grammar Application Make sure you have used prepositional phrases correctly in your editorial.

Writing Workshop: *Work in Progress*

Prewriting for Poem Using your Sensory Words List, name three emotions that you associate with the subject you chose. Then, jot down the reasons why you feel those emotions. Save this list in your portfolio.

Listening and Speaking

Give a **formal presentation** exploring one of the poems you read. Design a poster or other graphic representation inspired by the poem to display for your audience. Then, present a dramatic reading of the poem. Complete your presentation with a brief speech discussing how your display relates to the poem. Follow these guidelines:

- As you plan and deliver your presentation, consider how you will meet the needs of your **audience, purpose,** and **occasion.**
- During your presentation, employ **eye contact** and **purposeful gestures** to effectively communicate ideas.
- Use **speaking rate, volume,** and **enunciation** to engage your audience in what you are saying.
- During your speech, use **formal language.** Speak to your audience in a polite manner, using standard English and proper grammar—the **conventions of language.**

 **Focus on the TEKS**

Writing
(16)(D);(E) Write an argumentative essay to the appropriate audience that includes an organizing structure appropriate to the purpose, audience, and context; an analysis of the relative value of specific data, facts, and ideas.

Listening and Speaking
(25) Give presentations using formal language effectively, employing eye contact, speaking rate, volume, enunciation, purposeful gestures, and conventions of language.

Use this prewriting activity to prepare for the **Writing Workshop** on page 686.

 **TEXAS**
PHLitOnline
www.PHLitOnline.com

- Interactive graphic organizers
- Grammar tutorial
- Interactive journals

Strategy for Success

Monitor Comprehension

The reading sections of the Texas standardized tests may ask you to analyze the effects of diction, or word choice, and imagery to better understand poems. Considering the images in a poem and the phrasing the poet uses can help you monitor comprehension on standardized tests.

Begin by reading fluently, in sentences or units of meaning. Then, analyze the poet's diction by considering how the poet's use of words contributes to the tone and message of the poem. Is he or she using humor, exaggeration, or figurative language? The following examples show how you can monitor your comprehension by analyzing the effects of diction and imagery in poetry on standardized tests.

 Focus on the TEKS

Reading
(3) Analyze the effects of diction and imagery (e.g., figurative language, understatement, overstatement) in poetry.

Comprehension
RC-9(A) Reflect on understanding to monitor comprehension (e.g., asking questions).

Analyze Diction

Consider the poet's diction in individual stanzas or sentences in a poem.

1 I type each keyword hopefully
but never find the place
I earnestly seek; I must admit
I'm lost in cyberspace.

1 Based on the poet's diction, the stanza could best be described as —
  A casual and humorous
  B old-fashioned and dramatic
  C literary and good-natured
  D bored and cynical

The phrasing and language suggest that the narrator is discouraged but can still laugh about the situation. **A, B,** and **D** do not match this description. **C** is correct, as supported by such words and phrases as "earnestly seek," and "cyberspace."

Analyze Figurative Language

Look for the ways personification, similes, and metaphors contribute to meaning.

1 It hovers over the intersection,
Blinking its eye of red, yellow, green,
A conductor of an auto orchestra,
Cuing each section in turn.

2 The object referred to in the poem is a —
  F traffic light
  G musical instrument
  H stop sign
  J car

Clues such as the word *intersection*; the blinking colors of red, yellow, and green; and the act of cuing different groups of cars suggest that the poem is a metaphor about a stoplight. Choices **G, H,** and **J** do not describe stoplights; choice **F** is correct. Choice **G** suggests the musical instrument is literal. Choice **H,** a stop sign, and choice **J,** a car, are both literal responses that do not take into account all the figurative language of the stanza.

Texas Test Practice

Monitor Comprehension

> **Read this selection. Then answer the questions that follow it.**

The Choice

Dorothy Parker

1   He'd have given me rolling lands,
      Houses of marble, and billowing farms,
   Pearls, to trickle between my hands,
      Smoldering rubies, to circle my arms.
   You—you'd only a lilting song.
      Only a melody, happy and high,
   You were sudden and swift and strong,—
      Never a thought for another had I.

2   He'd have given me laces rare,
      Dresses that glimmered with frosty sheen,
   Shining ribbons to wrap my hair,
      Horses to draw me, as fine as a queen.
   You—you'd only to whistle low,
      Gaily I followed wherever you led.
   I took you, and I let him go—
      Somebody ought to examine my head!

1 In "The Choice," the poet uses exaggeration to —

  A contrast two people
  B convey surprise
  C accurately describe riches
  D justify her decision

2 The word "smoldering" in stanza 1 helps the reader picture —

  F anger in someone's eyes
  G the red glow of a fire
  H stylish clothing
  J the speaker's hair

3 What does the speaker mean when she says she would have been "as fine as a queen" in stanza 2?

  A She would have become a queen of a country.
  B She would have been able to meet a queen.
  C She would have looked beautiful.
  D She would have been very wealthy.

4 Do you think the poet regrets the choice she has made? Support your answer with details from the poem.

Informational Texts

Procedural Texts

Consumer Publication
How Podcasting Works

Instructions for Software
Presentation Software

Focus on the TEKS

Reading
(11)(A) Analyze the clarity of the objective(s) of procedural texts (e.g. consider reading instructions for software, consumer publications).

Reading Skill:
Analyze the Clarity of Objectives

The **objective,** or goal, of a procedural text is to explain to readers how to complete a task or how something works. In a well-written procedural text, the objective is clearly stated and explained. A key element in the explanation is the steps that need to be taken to complete the procedure. In order to fulfill his or her objective clearly, the author must include all the steps needed and explain them in a way that is understandable to readers.

As You Read Use a checklist like this one to **analyze the clarity of objectives** in the consumer publication and the instructions for software.

Objective:		
To introduce podcasting and explain how it is done		
Does the author clearly explain the objective?	☐ Yes	☐ No
Are all the steps included in the text?	☐ Yes	☐ No
Are the steps clearly and directly explained?	☐ Yes	☐ No
Are the steps logically organized?	☐ Yes	☐ No
Are common questions or problems addressed?	☐ Yes	☐ No
Does the author explain the process in a way that is understandable?	☐ Yes	☐ No

How Podcasting Works

by Stephanie Watson

Consumer Publication

Features:

- background about a topic
- some technical language
- step-by-step instructions

ON AIR

This heading indicates that this section will provide an introduction to the subject of podcasting.

Introduction to How Podcasting Works

Have you ever dreamed of having your own radio show? Are you a recording artist hoping to have your songs heard by the masses? Decades ago, you would have had to have a lot of connections—or a fortune—to get heard.

The text includes background information about podcasting and its purposes.

But now, thanks to the Internet and its instantaneous connection to millions of people, your dreams can become reality. Just as blogging has enabled almost anyone with a computer to become a bona fide reporter, a new technology called podcasting is allowing virtually anyone with a computer to become a radio disc jockey, talk show host or recording artist.

If you post it, they will come. Although podcasting is still primarily used by the techie set, it's beginning to catch on with the general public. Log onto one of several podcast sites on the Web, and you can download content ranging from music to philosophy. . . . Podcasting combines the freedom of blogging with the technology of MP3 to create an almost endless supply of content. Some say this new technology is democratizing the once corporate-run world of radio.

In this article, you'll learn how podcasting works, find out what tools you need to record and receive podcasts and hear what industry analysts have to say about the future of this burgeoning technology.

Podcasting is a free service that allows Internet users to pull audio files (typically MP3s) from a podcasting Web site to listen to on their computer or personal digital audio player. The name comes from a combination of the words **iPod** and **broadcasting**. Even though the name is derived from the iPod, you don't need an iPod to listen to a podcast. You can use virtually any MP3 player or your computer.

Boldface text highlights key technical words.

Unlike with Internet radio, users don't have to "tune in" to a particular broadcast; instead, they **subscribe** to a podcast, and the audio files are automatically downloaded to their computer via **RSS feed** as often as they request. The technology is similar to that used by TiVo, a personal video recorder that lets users set which programs they'd like to record and then automatically records those programs for later viewing.

Podcasting History

Podcasting was developed in 2004 by former MTV video jockey Adam Curry and software developer Dave Winer. Curry wrote a program, called iPodder, that enabled him to automatically download Internet radio broadcasts to his iPod. Several developers improved upon his idea, and podcasting was officially born. . . .

Right now, podcasting is free from government regulation. Podcasters don't need to buy a license to broadcast their programming, as radio stations do, and they don't need to conform to the the Federal Communication Commission's (FCC) broadcast decency regulations. . . .

Although several corporations and big broadcast companies have ventured into the medium, many podcasters are amateurs broadcasting from home studios. Because podcasters don't rely on ratings as radio broadcasters do, the subject matter of podcasts can range from the refined to the silly to the excruciatingly mundane. . . .

Several companies are trying to turn podcasting into a profitable business. Podcasting aggregators. . . are including advertising on their sites. The Podcast Network, based in Australia, runs commercials and sponsorships during its audio broadcasts. Television networks have gotten into the action. National Public Radio, the Canadian Broadcasting Corporation and the BBC have begun podcasting some of their shows. Corporations. . . have created their own podcasts to attract consumers.

Some experts say podcasting still has a long way to go before it catches on with the masses. But others believe it will eventually become as popular as text blogging, which grew from a few thousand blogs in the late '90s to more than 7 million today. Some podcasts are already providing thousands of downloads a day.

Creating and Listening to Podcasts

Virtually anyone with a computer and recording capabilities can create his or her own podcast. Podcasts may include music, comedy, sports, philosophy—even people's rants and raves. Here's how the process works.

To record a podcast:

1. Plug a USB headset with a microphone into your computer.

2. Install an MP3 recorder for Windows, Mac, or Linux.

3. Create an audio file by making a recording (you can talk, sing, or record music) and saving it as an MP3 file.

4. Finally, upload the MP3 audio file to one of the podcasting sites.

To listen to a podcast:

1. Go to a podcasting site and download the free software.

2. Click on the hyperlink for each podcast you want. You can listen right away on your computer (both Windows and Mac support podcasting) or download the podcast to your MP3 player.

3. You can also subscribe to one or more RSS feeds. Your podcasting software will check the RSS feeds regularly and automatically pull content that matches your playlist. When you dock your MP3 player to your computer, it automatically updates with the latest content.

> The subheads in this section help readers to find information. **Analyze the clarity of the objectives in this section of the procedural text.**

> Numbered lists provide step-by-step instructions.

How does communication change us?

How has podcasting changed the exchange of information?

Features:

- key elements and capabilities of the software
- information about how to use the software
- numbered steps or bulleted lists

THE UNIVERSITY OF TEXAS AT AUSTIN

University of Texas Libraries

Presentation Software

Remember the last PowerPoint presentation you slept through? If used correctly, presentation software can greatly enhance your session, but it is also often associated with boring and ineffective presentations.

When and why should you use it?

Presentation software can add to your session in the following ways:

- Help structure your presentation.
- Outline the main points you wish to make.
- Facilitate showing visual information such as graphs, tables, and charts.
- Display images or screen captures for demonstrating Web resources.
- Present bulleted lists to highlight key points.
- Display graphics, sound, and video clips.
- Easily make information available on the Web by posting it after the presentation.

Remember that if the slide show is not integrated into the session, or becomes more important than the rest of the session itself, it is actually a detriment to effective teaching.

The introductory text and the red headings help readers to navigate the instructions. **Analyze the clarity of the objectives in this section of the procedural text.**

What information should you include?

- Include a title page with your name, contact information, date, and session topic.
- Limit the number of slides you use—generally no more than one slide every 3–4 minutes is sufficient.
- Include only the main points.
- Include only one main concept per slide.
- Put text on the slides sparingly—you don't want students to read your slides while you are talking (try to limit your text to 6–7 words per line and 5–6 lines per slide).
- Sounds, color, animation, video clips, or other effects can be used minimally to support your presentation.
- Include a conclusion slide with a summary.

TEXAS

What are some design tips?

- Keep the presentation clean and simple.
- Use sans-serif fonts like Arial or Verdana if your visual will be projected on a screen.
- Use no more than 3 different fonts in a single presentation or slide.
- Text needs to be legible—the larger your classroom, the larger your font should be.
- Plan a color scheme for your full presentation, and then use other colors sparingly to highlight important text and to emphasize relationships between ideas or to set them apart.

Slide Section	Recommended Font Size
Titles	36–48
Subtitles/Subdivisions	30–36
Body	24–30

The chart presents information clearly and succinctly.

How can you avoid typical problems associated with using presentation software?

- Don't put your whole presentation on slides and then read it.
- Keep slides to a minimum.
- It's tempting to include many different colors, sound effects, clip art, and images, but they too often take away from the presentation. Keep them to a minimum, and include them only to enhance content.
- Make a practice run through the slide show before the presentation.
- Remember that technology sometimes doesn't work—save your presentation in several different formats.
- Finally, have a contingency plan in place if your presentation can't be accessed at all.

TEXAS

THE BIG ?

How does communication change us?

How might presentation software be used to communicate to and change the ideas of others?

Comparing Informational Texts

1. (a) Analyze: Review each text to analyze the clarity of its objectives.
(b) Evaluate: Which text was more successful in meeting its goal? Explain.

2. (a) Analyze: What methods did the authors of the texts use to present the specific procedures? **(b) Make Inferences:** Why might the authors have chosen to use these methods?

 **College Readiness** | **Timed Writing**

Write a Critique

Format
The prompt directs you to write a *critique*. Therefore, you should share your opinion about the strengths and weaknesses of a text. Your opinions must be supported with evidence from the text.

Write a critique in which you analyze the clarity of the objectives of the instructions for software. If you find that a particular objective is unclear, discuss how that objective might be clarified. Provide evidence from the text to support your response. (30 minutes)

Academic Vocabulary
When you *discuss* a topic, you give in-depth descriptions and observations in order to explain a point of view.

 ### 5-Minute Planner

Complete these steps before you begin to write:

1. Read the prompt carefully and completely.

2. Review the instructions for software, identifying the strengths and weaknesses of the text. Jot down evidence to support your opinions.

3. Draft a thesis, or statement of your opinion, about the clarity of objectives in the text.

4. Decide how you will structure your critique, and draft a quick outline.

5. Refer to your notes and outline as you draft your essay.

Comparing Imagery

Sensory language is language that appeals to one or more of the senses—sight, hearing, touch, taste, and smell. Sensory language creates **imagery**—mental pictures. The use of imagery allows writers to express their ideas with vividness and immediacy. Imagery helps readers to form mental pictures and to connect their own experiences to the worlds the writers describe.

Comparing imagery is important in analyzing the aesthetic qualities of a variety of selections. These are the stylistic qualities that make a poem's language beautiful. Writers, for example, often include patterns of images and **controlling images,** or central images. By recognizing image patterns, or motifs, and controlling images, you can better appreciate differences and similarities among selections.

As You Read Use a chart like the one shown to analyze the effects of imagery on the poem in which it appears.

 Focus on the TEKS

Reading
(3) Analyze the effects of imagery (e.g., controlling images) in poetry.

Poem: "There Is No Word For Goodbye"

Sensory Language	Imagery	Effect
"wind–tanned skin"	brownish, weathered skin	The reader can see and feel Sokoya's skin.

PHLitOnline
www.PHLitOnline.com

- Vocabulary flashcards
- Interactive journals
- More about the authors
- Selection audio
- Interactive graphic organizers

How does *communication* change us?

Writing About the Big Question

In these selections, the writers want you to see an experience as clearly as they do. Use this sentence starter to develop your ideas.

Seeing the world through someone else's eyes may help a person become **aware** of _____.

Meet the Authors

Mary Tall Mountain (1918–1991)
Author of "There Is No Word For Goodbye" (p. 678)

An Athabaskan Indian, Mary Tall Mountain was born in Alaska. When Tall Mountain was six, her mother died, and she was adopted by a family who removed her from her culture. In "There Is No Word For Goodbye," Tall Mountain reconnects with her Native American roots

Naomi Shihab Nye (b. 1952)
Author of "Daily" (p. 679)

Naomi Shihab Nye, a successful poet, was born to a Palestinian father and an American mother. Of poems, she has said, "I liked the space around them, and the way they took you to a deeper, quieter place, almost immediately."

David T. Hilbun (b. 1992)
Author of "Hope" (p. 680)

David T. Hilbun has been publishing his work since he was in the first grade. He wrote "Hope" after Hurricane Katrina for his eighth grade English class. "I'm not sure yet what I plan to do in the future," Hilbun says, "but I do want to continue writing in some fashion."

Tyroneca "Ty" Booker (b. 1987)
Author of "The Day of the Storm" (p. 682)

Tyroneca Booker resides in Louisiana. Booker's piece, "The Day of the Storm," was written in an English course when she was asked to reflect on Hurricane Katrina. She says, "I wrote from my heart, a very true account of what life was like during and after these powerful storms."

THERE IS NO WORD FOR GOODBYE

Mary Tall Mountain

Literary Analysis
Imagery What effect does the imagery in lines 1–4 of this poem have on your understanding of who Sokoya is?

Sokoya, I said, looking through
    the net of wrinkles into
    wise black pools
    of her eyes.

5   What do you say in Athabaskan
    when you leave each other?
    What is the word
    for goodbye?

Literary Analysis
Imagery Which details in lines 9–12 appeal to the sense of touch?

A shade of feeling rippled
10   the wind-tanned skin.
    Ah, nothing, she said,
    watching the river flash.

She looked at me close.
    We just say, Tlaa. That means,
15   See you.
    We never leave each other.
    When does your mouth
    say goodbye to your heart?

She touched me light
20   as a bluebell.
    You forget when you leave us,
    You're so small then.
    We don't use that word.

We always think you're coming back,
25   but if you don't,
    we'll see you some place else.
    You understand.
    There is no word for goodbye.

Sokoya: Aunt (mother's sister)

DAILY

Naomi Shihab Nye

These shriveled seeds we plant,
corn kernel, dried bean,
poke into loosened soil,
cover over with measured fingertips

5   These T-shirts we fold into
perfect white squares

These tortillas we slice and fry to crisp strips
This rich egg scrambled in a gray clay bowl

This bed whose covers I straighten
10   smoothing edges till blue quilt fits brown blanket
and nothing hangs out

This envelope I address
so the name balances like a cloud
in the center of the sky

15   This page I type and retype
This table I dust till the scarred wood shines
This bundle of clothes I wash and hang and wash again
like flags we share, a country so close
no one needs to name it

20   The days are nouns; touch them
The hands are churches that worship the world

Vocabulary
shriveled (shriv´ əld) *adj.*
shrunken and wrinkled

Literary Analysis
Imagery Analyze the effect on the poem of the imagery in lines 7 and 8.

Vocabulary
scarred (skärd) *adj.*
marked or dented

Critical Thinking

1. **Respond:** Which description did you find the most vivid? Explain.

2. **Make Inferences:** In "There Is No Word For Goodbye," why might the speaker want to know the word for goodbye?

3. **Make Inferences:** Does the speaker in "Daily" seem to take pleasure in doing the tasks described? Explain.

 **How does communication change us?**
(a) Explain each writer's message about life. **(b)** How might readers benefit from understanding these views?

Support your responses with evidence from the text.

Hope

David T. Hilbun
8th Grade, Paul Breaux Middle School, Lafayette, Louisiana

Literary Analysis
Imagery To which senses does the imagery in the first paragraph appeal?

"Adam, get behind me!" his dad called over the roaring winds and splashing waves. Adam's reply was cut off by the crash of a huge oak tree being ripped out of the dirt and slamming into the ground a few meters away with the force of a stick of dynamite. "Quick, into the storm cellar!" The storm cellar had been designed by Adam's dad years ago. It was made of 6-inch solid steel and had enough MRE's[1] to feed 12 hungry people for a week.

They made it to the door and were able to get inside. Fretful, cold, and frightened, they got out of the storm. In their "secret place," as Adam called it when he was littler, they felt strangely peaceful. Maybe it was the knowledge that they both were safe, maybe it was the comfort of the cellar, they didn't know, but at least they had each other.

Over time, the noise outside got worse and worse. At one point, it was so loud that it felt as if a huge gong were crashing inside their heads. Suddenly, the noise stopped.

---

1. MRE's: prepared foods; acronym for Meals Ready to Eat.

"What's going on, Dad?" Adam asked.

"I think the eyewall passed over us," he said. "We can probably go outside for a little while."

Outside was a scene of total destruction. Their house was gone, a few planks in its place.

The school was wrecked, the remains of an airliner strewn all over the football field. But worst, they saw a huge fallen tree. Sticking out from under it was a human arm.

Feeling sick, Adam turned to go underground when the eyewall passed over. Hundred-mile-an-hour winds lifted Adam into the air. Screaming, flipping over and over, he bid a mental farewell to his father and a mental hello to his mother. Crying, thinking all hope was lost, he was miraculously caught by his dad. Inch by inch, they made their way back to the cellar, where they waited out the storm.

Finally, it was over. They looked around at the scene surrounding them in awestruck silence. Luckily, there were no bodies this time.

Too shocked to cry, too scared to do anything but stand there, Adam and his dad looked at each other.

After a time, the shock wore off. They walked around. Adam motioned his dad over.

"Look," he said simply, smiling.

And there, amid all the destruction, was a single green plant.

Vocabulary

miraculously (mi rak´ yoo ləs le) *adv.* in an amazing way; as though by a miracle

awestruck (ô´ struk) *adj.* filled with wonder

amid (ə mid´) *prep.* among; in the middle of

Critical Thinking

1. Respond: What question would you like to ask the author?

2. (a) Where do Adam and his father go when the storm hits? **(b) Make Inferences:** Why do you think Adam's father had built the storm shelter?

3. (a) What do Adam and his father find when they leave the shelter the first time? **(b) Make Inferences:** What makes Adam feel sick?

4. (a) What do Adam and his father find when they emerge from the shelter the last time? **(b) Interpret:** Why is the plant so meaningful to Adam?

How does communication change us?
(a) Why might those who have experienced a tragic storm be interested in this narrative? **(b)** Does the story change the way you regard storms? Why or why not?

Support your responses with evidence from the text.

Hope **681**

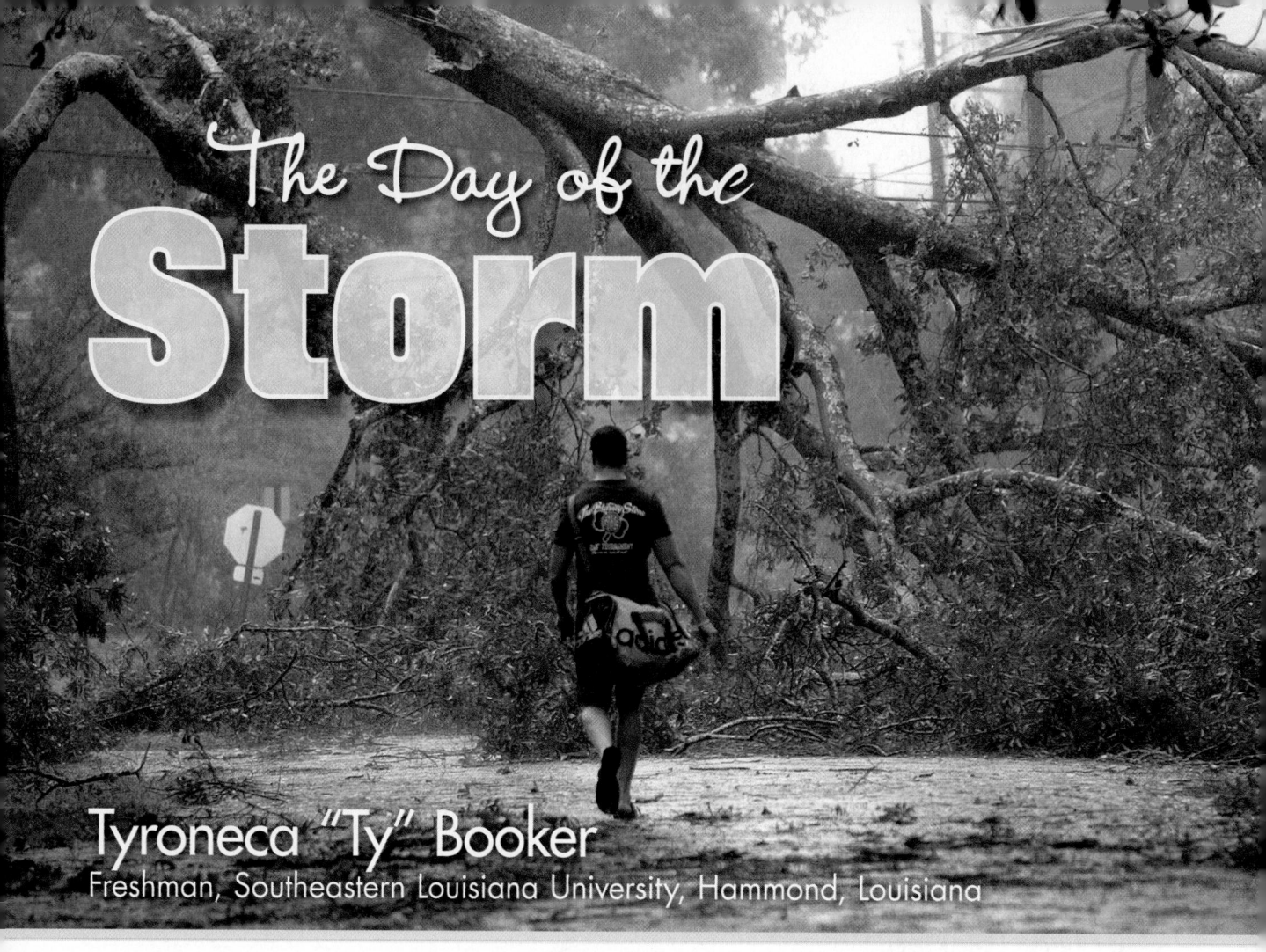

The Day of the Storm

Tyroneca "Ty" Booker

Freshman, Southeastern Louisiana University, Hammond, Louisiana

Vocabulary
emitting (e mit´ inj) *v.*
sending out

I don't watch much T.V., so to hear a hurricane was heading for Louisiana was a scare. Earlier in the week, I was talking to my sister and she had informed me a storm was brewing in the Gulf. I paid little to no attention because every storm since Andrew in '98 was supposedly due to hit Louisiana directly and didn't. As a matter of fact, Andrew is the only "big" storm I can remember. Vivid images come to mind—pine trees, emitting their signature smells from the freshly cracked wood, lie in the street like barricades. For about a week my family survived on Cheerios and Spam; it was all we had. Since then, a hurricane only meant a day or two off from school, and Louisiana dodging the bullet one more time. Friday, August 26th, my cousin and I drove to New Orleans to pick up another relative. We took for granted the scenery and simple pleasures of the city. We never realized what lay ahead.

I have always been a hard-headed person, so this particular weekend I'd decided to stay on campus. My cousin traveled back to Baton Rouge alone to go to work, while I stayed in Hammond, ignorant of the events ahead. On Saturday, the calls flooded my cell phone. Everyone called to tell me about Katrina. I finally, after 20 phone calls, decided to turn on the T.V. There she was: coming straight for New Orleans. I was only a city or two away. Every channel and every news bulletin carried the same, yet simple message: Get out while you can! As I watched her turn like a propeller, it all became grim reality—we were going to be hit and hit hard. I had nowhere to go. Here I was on the fourth floor of Livingston Hall in my room with a category five hurricane headed for a city only 52 miles away.

I knew I needed to stock up on food if I was going to be here to endure the storm. Cayman's was closed, and the Lion's Den wasn't an option. The only thing I had was my SLU ID, so I decided to make a "vending-machine run." After three trips to the electric snack havens, I'd figured that I had enough. The last time I walked across the barren, deserted parking lot, a man in Army fatigues caught my eye. Curiosity took over, and I went to inquire as to why he was on campus.

He proceeded to explain that the Kinesiology and Health Studies building was being used as shelter for ill people. As he continued to ramble on, my thoughts began to come into focus—this was serious. I pretended to listen, but only a few words stuck out in my mind: dorms closed. University Center, shelter. I thanked him, walked away, and those words formed themselves into two ton bricks, each falling upon me like rain: each one came faster than the one before. I realized he had just told me we had to evacuate the dorms, and take shelter in the University Center. I panicked, packed up my belongings as if it were check-out time, and waited for the all-call.[1] At about 5:15 p.m., the clouds couldn't take the pressure as they succumbed to the rain, surrendering themselves peacefully without a fight. The wind picked up, and here I was running to the University Center on North Campus with the few belongings that I could grab. The wind began to howl like a werewolf in the night—this was the one! Katrina was here, and she was as strong as two oxen.

I made it into the University Center, soaked but safe. I looked around, found a spot and made myself at home. I drifted off into a deep sleep, the last peaceful night of rest I would get for a while. When I did awake, I heard the University President, Randy Moffett, on the loudspeaker telling us that Katrina was in fact here, and she

---

1. all-call phone system used to contact students at Southeastern Louisiana University.

Literary Analysis
Imagery To which sense does the image "turn like a propeller" appeal?

Vocabulary
succumbed (sə kumd) v. gave way; yielded

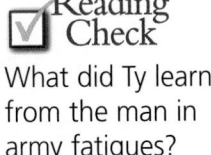
Reading Check

What did Ty learn from the man in army fatigues?

Literary Analysis
Imagery How does the writer's use of imagery in this paragraph help you understand her experience?

Vocabulary
submerged (səb murjd′) *adj.* covered with water or the like

was marking her territory all around us as he spoke. He told us we were in the worst two or three hours of the storm, and we had no water or lights, until the generators could be powered up. I went to the window looking out on University Avenue, and surveyed old oak trees thrown around as if they were small branches. As I took all this in, I couldn't help but think—this isn't the worst, this is only the beginning.

When we were let out of the University Center on Tuesday, August 30th, the water was on, but cold, and there was still no electricity. I came back to a dank, dark dorm room, but I was thankful to have survived and to have a place to call home to come to. Later in the day, my cousin came back to pick me up; I was relieved, and cried tears of joy. I was grateful to be back in Baton Rouge with my family, and out of harm's way. However, once I arrived, I realized the devastation Katrina's wrath caused along the Gulf Coast. When I turned on the T.V. I thought it was something unreal. I couldn't even have imagined what I saw—houses submerged to their roof, a whole city flooded. It was then that I thanked the heavens above allowing me to be fortunate, and it was then that I vowed never to take life's simple gifts for granted.

Critical Thinking

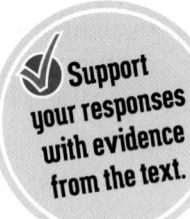
Support your responses with evidence from the text.

1. **Respond:** What do you think is the most interesting thing about the writer?

2. **(a)** How does the writer prepare for evacuating the dorm? **(b) Deduce:** Why does she take so few belongings with her to the University Center?

3. **(a)** What does the university president tell those gathered in the University Center during the height of the storm? **(b) Make Inferences:** What does the writer think about the president's announcement? **(c) Make a Judgment:** Was she correct about the president's prediction? Explain.

4. **(a) Interpret:** In the final paragraph, what does the writer mean when she says she "realized the devastation of Katrina's wrath?" **(b) Draw Conclusions:** What do you think the writer learned from her experiences? Share your response with a partner.

How does communication change us?
(a) How does the news coverage of Katrina affect the writer's thoughts and actions before, during, and after the storm? **(b)** How does reading this account change your own understanding of hurricanes?

Comparing Imagery

1. For each selection, use charts like the one below to identify examples of **imagery.** Build charts like the one below to list examples for each of the five senses. Then, analyze the effects of this imagery.

Selection	Image Appealing to Touch
"There Is No Word For Goodbye"	
"Daily"	
"Hope"	
"The Day of the Storm"	

2. (a) Analyze the selections and decide whether each author uses a **controlling image** in his or her work. Describe each controlling image. **(b)** Compare and contrast the effects of the controlling images.

 College Readiness | Timed Writing

Write to Compare Imagery

In an essay, compare and contrast the effects of the writers' use of imagery in each selection. Provide evidence from the texts to support your response. (35 minutes)

 5-Minute Planner

1. Read the prompt carefully and completely.

2. Consider these questions and jot down your responses:

- In "There Is No Word For Goodbye," how do the images of Sokoya help you understand the speaker's feelings for her aunt?
- In "Daily," how does the imagery help you understand the speaker's affection for ordinary things?
- In "Hope," how does the sound imagery help convey fear?
- In "The Day of the Storm," how does the writer use images to help convey a picture of the deserted campus?
- What effect does the imagery in these works have on the reader?

3. Reread the prompt, and then reference your notes as you draft your essay.

Literary Text: Poem

Defining the Form Poetry is a condensed form of language that uses precise diction, vivid images, descriptive and figurative language, and sound devices such as rhyme and rhythm to help the reader see an image or experience an emotion. You might use elements of poetry in descriptive essays, short stories, and journal entries.

Assignment Write a poem that expresses your ideas and feelings about a real or imagined person, event, or place. Include these **poetic techniques** and elements:

- ✔ a specific *poetic form,* such as a *sonnet*
- ✔ *structural elements,* such as rhyme or meter, that emphasize a particular tone
- ✔ diction that leaves an impression on the reader
- ✔ *figurative language* chosen to convey a distinct mood
- ✔ imagery that appeals to one or more of the senses
- ✔ sound devices that create a musical or emotional effect
- ✔ appropriate grammar and formatting

To preview the criteria on which your poem may be judged, see the rubric on page 691.

 Focus on the TEKS

Writing
(14)(B) Write a poem using a variety of poetic techniques (e.g., structural elements, figurative language) and a variety of poetic forms (e.g., sonnets).

 Writing Workshop: *Work in Progress*

Review the work you did on pages 641 and 667.

Prewriting/Planning Strategy

Use RAFT. Brainstorm the basics of your poem using the RAFT strategy: consider the **R**ole of the speaker, the **A**udience, the **F**ormat, and the **T**opic. Use a chart like the one shown here in your brainstorming session.

Role (Speaker) Who are you?	Audience To whom is this written?	Format What form will it take?	Topic What is the subject of this writing?
a teenager	a parent	free verse	enjoying a day in the park

Planning Poetic Form and Structure

Before you begin to write, consider the form and structure that would best suit your poem's topic.

Choosing a Form Narrative poetry tells a story. Lyric poetry expresses feelings and thoughts and has a musical quality that adds to its impact. Here are some forms of lyric poetry:

Type of Lyric Poetry	Characteristics of the Type
Free Verse	• no regular pattern of sound or rhythm • lines of irregular length
Haiku	• three unrhymed lines of five, seven, and five syllables each • imagery to convey a single, vivid emotion
Sonnet	• fourteen lines with a specific rhyme scheme • written in iambic pentameter

(See page 748 for more information on these forms.)

Think about what you want to convey in your poem, and choose a form you think best suits your purpose. For example, if you want to convey a single image and its associated feelings, haiku might be a good choice.

Using Rhyme and Meter The form you choose may require a pattern of rhyme and meter.

- Rhyme is the repetition of sounds at the ends of words. Rhyme can be exact (*grow, mow*) or slant (*day, rate*) and can be placed at the ends of lines or within lines (internal rhyme).

- Meter is the pattern of stressed and unstressed syllables within a line. Some forms of poetry are based on specific rhyme and meter. As its name implies, free verse does not require a specific rhyme or meter.

(For more information on rhyme and meter, see pages 719–720.)

Using Structure to Affect Tone The rhyme and meter of a poem can help establish the poem's tone. For example, in Poe's "The Raven" (page 711), the sound of the word *nevermore* and its many rhymes throughout the poem establish a mournful, dreary atmosphere.

Apply the Techniques As you prepare to draft your poem, consider:

- Does the form fit the subject of the poem?
- What mood and tone do I want to convey?
- How can rhyme and meter help convey that tone?

Drafting Strategies

Choose precise words. Your diction, or word choice, is important in making your poem memorable. Note the specific, vivid details used by these two poets, one using informal diction and the other using formal diction.

Informal	Formal
I like hot days, hot days Sweat is what you got days Bugs buzzin from cousin to cousin —*from* "Summer" by Walter Dean Myers (p. 646)	He clasps the crag with crooked hands; Close to the sun in lonely lands, Ring'd with the azure world, he stands. —*from* "The Eagle" by Alfred, Lord Tennyson (p. 647)

Words such as *sweat, bugs,* and *buzzin* in "Summer" convey a lighthearted feeling. In "The Eagle," phrases such as *lonely lands* and *azure world* are more formal, and they convey a sense of majesty. Both poems, though very different, use diction to create vivid images.

Using sound devices. In addition to rhyme and meter, poets can use other sound devices, such as alliteration, consonance, assonance, and onomatopoeia, to make a musical or emotional effect, and to emphasize images conveyed in poems. As you draft your poem, think about the effect you want to make. For example, if you are describing a stormy ocean, you might want to use words that emphasize the sounds of the waves crashing and slapping.

Revising Strategies

Listen to your poem. Read your poem aloud, focusing on the sound of rhyme, alliteration, or other sound devices. Check that the sound devices and images convey the mood or feeling that you intend.

Revise to improve word choice. Poems use condensed and concentrated language, so every word should serve a purpose. Think again about your purpose, audience, and genre. Then, work to strengthen the impression your poem makes by replacing vague and dull words with interesting, precise ones. Use a thesaurus to help with diction, or word choice.

Vague	Revise for Diction and Sound Devices
The insects were loud and annoying.	Mosquitoes murmured and buzzed, whizzing around my ears, flying fearlessly.

 Focus on the TEKS

Writing
(13)(C) Revise drafts to improve word choice and figurative language after rethinking how well questions of purpose, audience, and genre have been addressed.
(14)(B) Write a poem using a variety of poetic techniques (e.g., figurative language).
Reading
(1)(E) Use a thesaurus.

WRITE GUY
Jeff Anderson, M.Ed.

What Do You Notice?

Sounds in Poetry

The following passage is from May Swenson's poem "Analysis of Baseball." Read the passage several times.

It's about
the ball,
the bat,
and the mitt.
Ball hits
bat, or it
hits mitt.

Jot down what you notice about the passage. Discuss your responses with a partner. Then, as you draft your own poem, try to use diction and sound devices to convey your meaning.

Revising to Strengthen Use of Poetic Techniques

Voice is the "sound" of a poet on the page. You can make your voice engaging by using poetic techniques, such as figurative and sensory language.

Improving Figurative Language and Mood Figurative language, including similes, metaphors, and personification, can help set the mood of your poem. The figurative language you use to describe something can determine how your readers feel about that object. This chart shows how figures of speech can affect mood. Rethink how well you have served your purpose, audience, and genre. Then, revise your draft to improve your use of figurative language.

Object	Mood/Tone	Figure of Speech
the sun	harsh	The hot breath of the sun stung my skin. *(personification)*
	happy	The rays of warm sunlight were like golden drops spilling on the garden. *(simile)*
	foreboding	The sun was a dark red ball, sinking slowly below the horizon. *(metaphor)*

Using Vivid Sensory Language As you revise your poem, consider including language that paints a clear and colorful image by appealing to the senses. These examples show how the poet Pat Mora uses figures of speech and sensory language in her poems "Uncoiling" and "A Voice."

> **smell** "In your house that smelled like/rose powder. . . "
> **touch** ". . . felt your breath stick in your throat/like an ice cube. "
> **sound** ". . . howling/leaves off trees . . . "
> **sight** ". . . lights on the stage unrelenting/as the desert sun . . . "

Consider adding effective adjectives and adverbs to enhance your images and appeal to your readers' senses. Remember that creating a vivid image does not mean using a lot of words to describe something. Rather, it means choosing exact words to convey the image you want.

Using a Thesaurus A thesaurus can be a helpful reference tool for exploring word options. If you find a word in a thesaurus that you would like to include, be sure that you know its meaning before you use it.

Student Model: Drake LeSage, Lago Vista, TX

Writing
(13)(D) Edit drafts for grammar, mechanics, and spelling.
(13)(E) Revise final draft in response to feedback from peers and publish written work for appropriate audiences.

Football Fever

Running out under the Friday night lights,
The roar of the crowd vibrates through my ears.
Scoring a touchdown—six points take new heights.
The disappointment of the other team,
Making a tackle is accomplishing.
The impact of the hit, all bruised and scarred,
The big pick—oh, so exhilarating.
Give me the ball, I want to make that yard!
Highlights of the game make me scream for more.
Catching the football, getting a first down,
The beauty of the touchdown, one more score,
By morning I'll be the talk of the town.
The win, the rush, the glory of the team
Don't wake me up, don't let this be a dream.

Drake's poem is similar to a sonnet in many ways, but he has altered the rhyme and meter slightly to make the form his own.

Here, Drake uses sensory language to describe the physical action of the game.

Drake's diction, or word choice, emphasizes the joyous, victorious mood he is trying to convey.

Editing and Proofreading

Edit your draft for errors in grammar and mechanics—the use of capitalization and punctuation. Use a printed or electronic dictionary to check correct spellings.

Focus on Poetic Form and Structure: Check your poem against the form and structure you have chosen. For example, if you have chosen to write a Shakespearean sonnet, be sure that your lines are written in iambic pentameter and that the poem uses the correct rhyme scheme.

Publishing and Presenting

Consider ways to publish your written work for appropriate audiences:

Deliver an oral reading. Prepare an oral reading of your poem. Deliver your reading for the class, recording the reading on audiotape if possible. Hold a class discussion about your poem after the reading.

Publish an anthology. Meet with a small group of classmates to plan an anthology, or collection of poems. First, review and discuss one another's poems. Then, **revise your final draft in response to this feedback from your peers.** Publish your poem in an online or printed class poetry anthology.

Reflecting on Your Writing

Writer's Journal Jot down your answer to this question:
How did writing a poem help you understand elements of poetry?

Rubric for Self-Assessment

Find evidence in your writing to address each category. Then, use the rating scale to grade your work.

Spiral Review
Earlier in the unit, you learned about **prepositions** (p. 640) and **prepositional phrases** (p. 666). If you have included these parts of speech in your poem, make sure you have used them appropriately.

Written Composition Criteria	Rating Scale			
	not very			*very*
Focus and Coherence: How clear and vivid is the image or impression your diction creates?	1	2	3	4
Organization: How effectively do the poetic form and structure of your poem convey your idea?	1	2	3	4
Development of Ideas: How effective and appropriate are the sound devices employed in your poem?	1	2	3	4
Conventions: How appropriate is your grammar?	1	2	3	4
Voice: How well do poetic techniques, including figurative and sensory language, convey the tone and mood of your poem?	1	2	3	4

Collection Choices

▲ **Poetry Collection 5**
includes poems with a
unique mood or feeling.

▲ **Poetry Collection 6**
includes poems with a
thought-provoking setting.

 TEXAS Focus on the TEKS

Meet these standards with either **Poetry Collection 5** (p. 696) or
Poetry Collection 6 (p. 706).

Reading
(3) Analyze the effects of diction in poetry.
(Literary Analysis: Narrative Poetry)

**(1)(A) Determine the meaning of grade-level
technical academic English words in multiple
content areas derived from Latin affixes.** *(Word
Power: Apply It)*

(1)(E) Use a thesaurus. *(Writing: Poem)*

**(12)(B) Analyze how messages in media are
conveyed through visual and sound techniques
(e.g., editing, reaction shots, sequencing,
background music).** *(Listening and Speaking:
Report)*

Reading/Comprehension Skills
**RC-9(A) Reflect on understanding to monitor
comprehension.** *(Reading Skill: Paraphrase)*

Writing
**(14)(B) Write a poem using a variety of poetic
forms.** *(Writing: Poem)*

Literary Analysis: Narrative Poetry

Narrative poetry tells a story and includes the same literary elements as narrative prose: a plot, or sequence of events; specific settings; and people or characters who participate in the action.

Like short stories, narrative poems convey a **mood,** or atmosphere—an overall feeling expressed by many elements, including the setting, plot, and images. The mood of a poem can also be an effect of **diction,** or the words an author chooses to use. Diction, for example, can make a poem gloomy, joyous, or mysterious.

As You Read Analyze the effects of diction in poetry. Jot down examples of words that contribute to the overall mood of each poem.

Reading Skill: Paraphrase

When you **paraphrase,** you restate in your own words what someone else has written or said. A paraphrase retains the meaning of a text, but is simpler. Paraphrasing is especially useful in comprehending poems that contain **figurative language**—words that are used imaginatively rather than literally. To paraphrase a narrative poem, pause periodically while reading to **reflect on your understanding** by picturing the action.

- Based on details in the poem, form a mental image of the setting, the characters, and the characters' actions.

- To **monitor your comprehension,** consider which mental images are clear and which are confusing. Revisit the text to clarify its meaning.

- Then, use your own words to describe your mental image of the scene and the action taking place in it.

Using the Strategy: Paraphrase Chart

As You Read Reflect on your understanding to monitor comprehension. Use a paraphrase chart like the one shown to record your paraphrases.

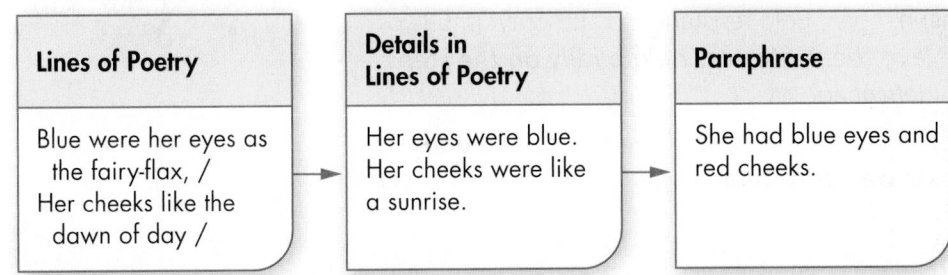

Lines of Poetry	Details in Lines of Poetry	Paraphrase
Blue were her eyes as the fairy-flax, / Her cheeks like the dawn of day /	Her eyes were blue. Her cheeks were like a sunrise.	She had blue eyes and red cheeks.

TEXAS
PHLitOnline
www.PHLitOnline.com

Hear It!
- Selection summary audio
- Selection audio

See It!
- Get Connected video
- Background video
- More about the author
- Vocabulary flashcards

Do It!
- Interactive journals
- Interactive graphic organizers
- Self-test
- Internet activity
- Grammar tutorial
- Interactive vocabulary games

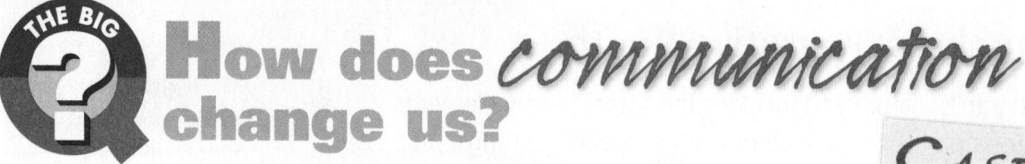

How does *communication* change us?

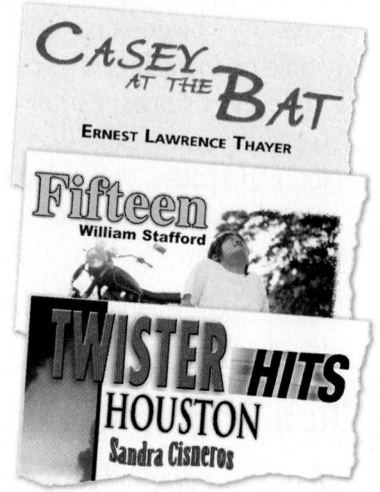

Writing About the Big Question

In "Casey at the Bat," the fans of a baseball team voice their enthusiastic support for their star player. Use this sentence starter to develop your ideas about the Big Question.

When a crowd communicates its support or disapproval, an athlete might **react** by _____.

As You Read Think about what effect the crowd's cheering has on Casey and his performance in "Casey at the Bat."

Vocabulary

Read each word and its definition. Decide whether you know the word well, know it a little bit, or do not know it at all. After you read, see how your knowledge of each word has increased.

- **pallor** (pal´ ər) *n.* unnatural paleness (p. 697) *His pallor made us realize just how ill he was.* pale *adj.* pallid *adj.*

- **preceded** (prē cēd´ əd) *v.* came before in time, place, order, rank, or importance (p. 697) *The police car preceded the floats in the annual parade.* precede *v.* preceding *adj.* precedence *n.*

- **multitude** (mul´ tə tōōd) *n.* a large number of persons or things, especially when gathered together or considered as a unit (p. 697) *I like to read books that have a multitude of characters.* multitudinous *adj.*

- **writhing** (rīth´ iŋ) *v.* twisting; turning (p. 698) *He struggled to hold the writhing cat still.* writhe *v.*

- **defiance** (dē fī´ əns) *n.* open, bold resistance to authority (p. 698) *In defiance of the law, the protestors held a rally on the steps of city hall.* defy *v.* defiant *adj.*

- **demure** (di myŏŏr´) *adj.* modest (p. 699) *The movie star's demure and proper behavior was refreshing.* demurely *adv.* demureness *n.*

Word Power

The **Latin prefix** *pre-* means "before."

In "Casey at the Bat," the speaker says that Flynn **preceded** Casey, meaning that Flynn went before Casey.

Ernest Lawrence Thayer

(1863–1940)

Author of "Casey at the Bat" (p. 696)

It is not surprising that "Casey at the Bat" reads like a sports story in verse. The poet, Ernest Lawrence Thayer, worked for many years as a sports reporter on the staff of newspapers in New York and California. "Casey at the Bat" first appeared in the *San Francisco Examiner* in 1888. It became so popular that in 1953 it inspired an operetta called *The Mighty Casey*.

William Stafford

(1914–1993)

Author of "Fifteen" (p. 699)

William Stafford was raised in Kansas. He did not publish his first book, *West of Your City,* until he was 46. However, he made up for lost time after that, publishing many collections, including *Traveling Through the Dark*. Fellow poet Robert Bly has said that Stafford's poems are "spoken like a friend over coffee."

Sandra Cisneros

(b. 1954)

Author of "Twister Hits Houston" (p. 700)

Sandra Cisneros was born in Chicago, but her family moved frequently between Chicago and Mexico City. She began her first novel, *The House on Mango Street,* while she was still a college student. Cisneros has worked with high-school students, serving as poet-in-residence in several schools. She has received many awards for her writing. Cisneros currently resides in San Antonio, Texas.

▲ **Critical Viewing** Compare and contrast the stance and attitude of the batter in this painting with Casey's stance and attitude in the poem. **[Compare and Contrast]**

CASEY AT THE BAT

ERNEST LAWRENCE THAYER

It looked extremely rocky for the Mudville nine that day;
The score stood two to four, with but an inning left to play.
So, when Cooney died at second, and Burrows did the same,
A pallor wreathed the features of the patrons of the game.

5   A straggling few got up to go, leaving there the rest,
With that hope which springs eternal within the human breast.
For they thought: "If only Casey would get a whack at that,"
They'd put even money now, with Casey at the bat.

But Flynn preceded Casey, and likewise so did Blake,
10 And the former was a pudd'n, and the latter was a fake.
So on that stricken multitude a deathlike silence sat;
For there seemed but little chance of Casey's getting to the bat.

But Flynn let drive a "single," to the wonderment of all.
And the much-despised Blakey "tore the cover off the ball."
15 And when the dust had lifted, and they saw what had occurred,
There was Blakey safe at second, and Flynn a-huggin' third.

Then from the gladdened multitude went up a joyous yell—
It rumbled in the mountaintops, it rattled in the dell;
It struck upon the hillside and rebounded on the flat;
20 For Casey, mighty Casey, was advancing to the bat.

There was ease in Casey's manner as he stepped into his place,
There was pride in Casey's bearing and a smile on Casey's face;
And when responding to the cheers he lightly doffed his hat,
No stranger in the crowd could doubt 'twas Casey at the bat.

Vocabulary
pallor (pal´ ər) *n.* unnatural paleness

preceded (prē cēd´ əd) *v.* came before in time, place, order, rank, or importance

Literary Analysis
Narrative Poetry
What is the setting of this narrative poem?

Vocabulary
multitude (mul´ tə tōōd) *n.* a large number of persons or things, especially when gathered together or considered as a unit

Reading Check

Where are Blakey and Flynn when Casey comes to bat?

Vocabulary

writhing (rīth´ iŋ) *v.*
twisting; turning

defiance (dē fī´ əns)
n. open, bold resistance to authority

25 Ten thousand eyes were on him as he rubbed his hands with
    dirt,
   Five thousand tongues applauded when he wiped them on his
    shirt;
   Then when the writhing pitcher ground the ball into his hip,
   Defiance glanced in Casey's eye, a sneer curled Casey's lip.

   And now the leather-covered sphere came hurtling through the
    air,
30 And Casey stood a-watching it in haughty grandeur there.
   Close by the sturdy batsman the ball unheeded sped;
   "That ain't my style," said Casey. "Strike one," the umpire said.

   From the benches, black with people, there went up a muffled
    roar,
   Like the beating of the storm waves on the stern and distant
    shore.
35 "Kill him! kill the umpire!" shouted someone on the stand;
   And it's likely they'd have killed him had not Casey raised his
    hand.

   With a smile of Christian charity great Casey's visage shone;
   He stilled the rising tumult, he made the game go on;
   He signaled to the pitcher, and once more the spheroid flew;
40 But Casey still ignored it, and the umpire said, "Strike two."

Literary Analysis
Narrative Poetry
Analyze the effects of
diction in the stanza that
begins with line 45. How
does the poet's word
choice contribute to the
change in mood?

   "Fraud!" cried the maddened thousands, and the echo
    answered "Fraud!"
   But one scornful look from Casey and the audience was awed;
   They saw his face grow stern and cold, they saw his muscles
    strain,
   And they knew that Casey wouldn't let the ball go by again.

Spiral Review
Main Idea What
complex inference
can you make
about the main,
or controlling, idea
of this poem? Use
textual evidence
to support your
understanding.

45 The sneer is gone from Casey's lips, his teeth are clenched in
    hate.
   He pounds with cruel vengeance his bat upon the plate:
   And now the pitcher holds the ball, and now he lets it go,
   And now the air is shattered by the force of Casey's blow.

   Oh, somewhere in this favored land the sun is shining bright,
50 The band is playing somewhere, and somewhere hearts are
    light:
   And somewhere men are laughing, and somewhere children
    shout,
   But there is no joy in Mudville: Mighty Casey has struck out.

Fifteen

William Stafford

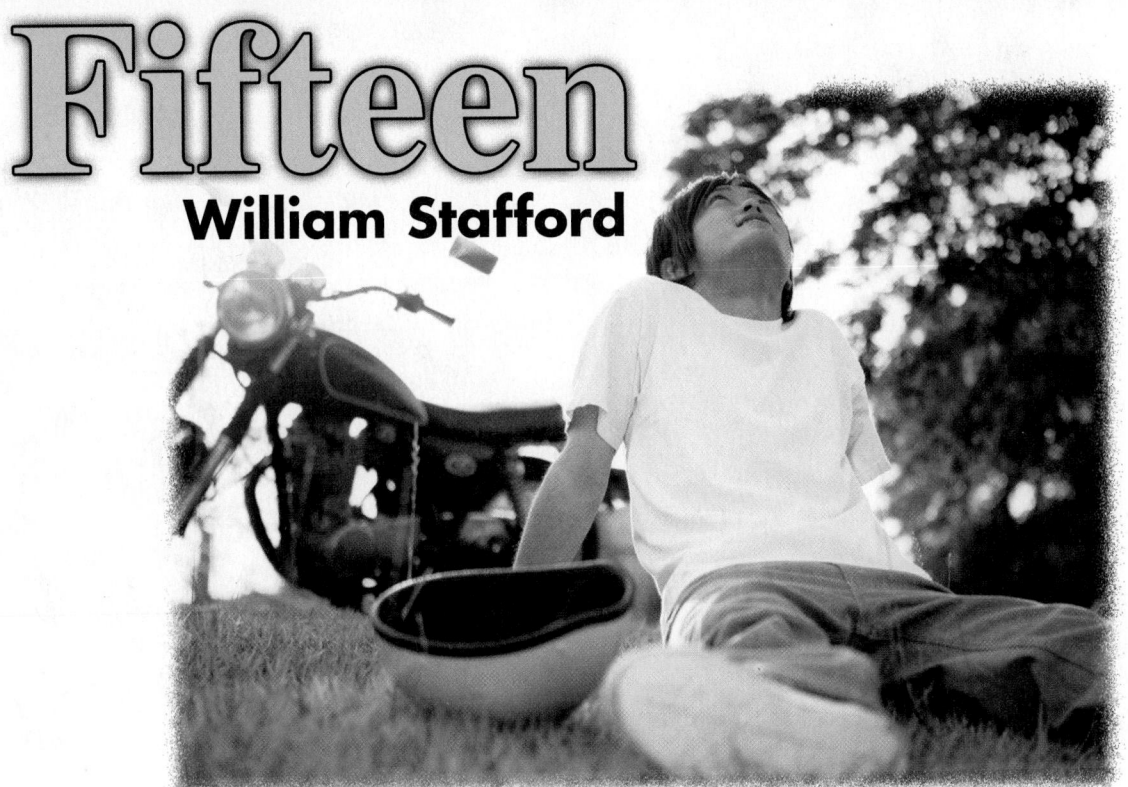

South of the bridge on Seventeenth
I found back of the willows one summer
day a motorcycle with engine running
as it lay on its side, ticking over
5   slowly in the high grass. I was fifteen.

I admired all that pulsing gleam, the
shiny flanks, the demure headlights
fringed where it lay; I led it gently
to the road and stood with that
10 companion, ready and friendly. I was fifteen.

We could find the end of a road, meet
the sky on out Seventeenth. I thought about
hills, and patting the handle got back a
confident opinion. On the bridge we indulged
15 a forward feeling, a tremble. I was fifteen.

Thinking, back farther in the grass I found
the owner, just coming to, where he had flipped
over the rail. He had blood on his hand, was pale—
I helped him walk to his machine. He ran his hand
20 over it, called me a good man, roared away.

I stood there, fifteen.

Vocabulary
demure (di myoor´)
adj. modest

Reading Skill
Paraphrase Pause to
reflect on your under-
standing by picturing the
action in lines 11 and
12. Then, monitor your
comprehension by restat-
ing the phrase "meet the
sky" in your own words.

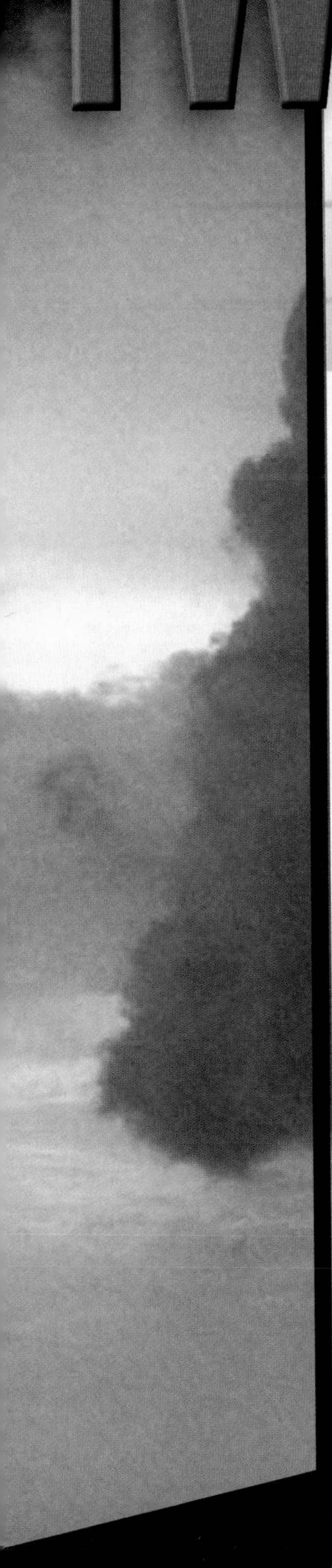

TWISTER *HITS* HOUSTON

Sandra Cisneros

Papa was on the front porch.
Mama was in the kitchen.
Mama was trying
to screw a lightbulb into a fixture.
5   Papa was watching the rain.
Mama, it's a cyclone for sure,
he shouted to his wife in the kitchen.
Papa who was sitting on his front porch
when the storm hit
10 said the twister ripped
the big black oak to splinter,

◀ **Critical Viewing**
How does the power
of the tornado in this
photograph add to your
understanding of the
poem? **[Connect]**

tossed a green sedan into his garden,
and banged the back door
like a mad cat wanting in.

15 Mama who was in the kitchen
said Papa saw everything,
the big oak ripped to kindling,[1]
the green sedan land out back,
the back door slam and slam.
20 I missed it.
Mama was in the kitchen Papa explained.
Papa was sitting on the front porch.
The light bulb is still sitting
where I left it. Don't matter now.
25 Got no electricity anyway.

---

1. **kindling** (kind´ liŋ) *n.* bits of dry wood used for starting fires.

Critical Thinking

1. **Respond:** Which of the poems in this collection do you think has the most exciting or interesting plot? Explain your answer.

2. **(a)** In "Casey at the Bat," what details does the speaker use to describe Casey? **(b) Make Inferences:** What does the description suggest about Casey's personality? **(c) Draw Conclusions:** How might his personality have affected the game's outcome?

3. **(a)** In the third stanza of "Fifteen," what does the speaker imagine doing with the motorcycle? **(b) Interpret:** What does the motorcycle represent to him? Explain your response.

4. **(a)** What does the speaker's father do throughout the storm in "Twister Hits Houston"? **(b) Make a Judgment:** Is his behavior appropriate for the situation? Explain your answer.

How does communication change us?
What role, if any, do you think the crowd played in Casey's performance in "Casey at the Bat"? Explain.

Literary Analysis: Narrative Poetry

1. (a) Using a chart like the one shown, identify and describe the story elements in each **narrative poem. (b)** Explain why you think each writer chose poetry to bring these elements to life.

	Setting	Characters	Plot
"Casey at the Bat"			
"Fifteen"			
"Twister Hits Houston"			

2. (a) In "Fifteen," how would you describe the speaker? **(b)** Analyze the **effects of diction** in "Fifteen" by identifying three words that contribute to the poem's **mood.** Explain each choice.

3. (a) Do you think a poem is an effective way to tell a story? Why or why not? **(b)** Share your response with a partner, and then explain whether his or her response changed your own.

Reading Skill: Paraphrase

4. (a) Paraphrase lines 29 through 32 of "Casey at the Bat."
(b) Explain how picturing the action helped you restate the lines.

Vocabulary

Practice In vocabulary study, **analogies** show the relationships between pairs of words. Use a word from the list on page 694 to make a word pair that matches the relationship between the first two given words.

1. flapping : bird :: _____ : snake
2. blush : red :: _____ : white
3. boastful : proud :: _____ : humble
4. approval : happy :: _____ : angry
5. club : member :: _____ : individual
6. early : late :: _____ : followed

Word Power Use the context of the sentences and what you know about the **Latin prefix _pre-_** to explain your answer to each question.

1. If you want to *prevent* a fire, when should you take action against it?
2. Are there any records of *prehistoric* events?

Word Power

The **Latin prefix _pre-_** means "before."

Apply It Explain how the prefix _pre-_ helps you determine the meanings of these technical academic words from language arts. Consult a dictionary if necessary.

predict
preview
preface

How does *communication* change us?

Writing About the Big Question

In "The Writer," a father is moved by the sound of his daughter typing a story. Use this sentence starter to develop your ideas about the Big Question.

> Having **empathy** for someone who is in a difficult situation might make a person realize that _____.

As You Read Consider how the speaker in "The Writer" is affected by his young daughter's attempt to write a story.

Vocabulary

Read each word and its definition. Decide whether you know the word well, know it a little bit, or do not know it at all. After you read, see how your knowledge of each word has increased.

- **impenetrable** (im pen´ i trə bəl) *adj.* that cannot be passed through; that cannot be solved or understood (p. 706) *I could not see my hand in front of my face in the <u>impenetrable</u> darkness of the cave.* impenetrability *n.* penetrate *v.*

- **archaic** (är kā´ ik) *adj.* from an earlier time; ancient (p. 707) *Some people say the old song is timeless; others say it is <u>archaic</u>.*

- **iridescent** (ir´ i des´ ənt) *adj.* showing colors that seem to change in different lights (p. 709) *The silvery scales of the fish were <u>iridescent</u> in the sunlight.* iridescence *n.*

- **pondered** (pän´ dərd) *v.* thought deeply about (p. 711) *After hearing the inspirational speaker, Ralph <u>pondered</u> the meaning of life.* ponder *v.* ponderous *adj.*

- **beguiling** (bē gīl´ iŋ) *v.* tricking; charming (p. 712) *The children's innocence was <u>beguiling</u> their parents.* guile *n.*

- **respite** (res´ pit) *n.* rest; relief (p. 713) *The rain provided a <u>respite</u> from the long dry spell.*

Word Power

The **Latin prefix im-** means "not."

In "The Horses," the speaker refers to an "**impenetrable** sorrow." If something is impenetrable, it cannot be penetrated, or pierced. An impenetrable sorrow is a deep sadness that cannot be relieved.

Edwin Muir

(1887–1959)

Author of "The Horses" (p. 706)

An author of numerous books of poetry as well as several novels, Edwin Muir had visions of the future that were rooted in his past. He spent his early years on a farm in the Orkney Islands, north of Scotland. Much of the imagery in his poetry comes from these islands.

Richard Wilbur

(b. 1921)

Author of "The Writer" (p. 708)

As a young man, Richard Wilbur planned to be a cartoonist. Instead, he became an award-winning poet. By the time he was thirty, Wilbur had published two collections of poetry and established himself as an important young writer. In 1987, Wilbur was appointed Poet Laureate of the United States.

Edgar Allan Poe

(1809–1849)

Author of "The Raven" (p. 710)

One of the first great American storytellers, Edgar Allan Poe often explored dark and bizarre events in his stories and poems. His inspiration may have come from his own life, which was often filled with sadness. He found some happiness in his marriage to Virginia Clemm, but after her death, Poe became depressed and antisocial. Many of his poems and stories focus on an ideal love that is lost.

THE HORSES

EDWIN MUIR

Barely a twelvemonth after
The seven days war that put the world to sleep,
Late in the evening the strange horses came.
By then we had made our covenant with silence,
5   But in the first few days it was so still
We listened to our breathing and were afraid.
On the second day
The radios failed; we turned the knobs; no answer.
On the third day a warship passed us, heading north,
10   Dead bodies piled on the deck. On the sixth day
A plane plunged over us into the sea. Thereafter
Nothing. The radios dumb;
And still they stand in corners of our kitchens,
And stand, perhaps, turned on, in a million rooms
15   All over the world. But now if they should speak,
If on a sudden they should speak again,
If on the stroke of noon a voice should speak,
We would not listen, we would not let it bring
That old bad world that swallowed its children quick
20   At one great gulp. We would not have it again.
Sometimes we think of the nations lying asleep,
Curled blindly in impenetrable sorrow,
And then the thought confounds us with its strangeness.

The tractors lie about our fields; at evening
25   They look like dank sea-monsters couched and waiting.
We leave them where they are and let them rust:

Literary Analysis
Narrative Poetry
Which details in the first stanza reveal that the poem takes place in the future?

Vocabulary
impenetrable (im pen´ i trə bəl) *adj.* that cannot be passed through; that cannot be solved or understood

▶ **Critical Viewing** Do these horses appear "stubborn and shy" like the ones described in the poem? Explain. **[Compare and Contrast]**

'They'll moulder away and be like other loam'.[1]
We make our oxen drag our rusty ploughs,
Long laid aside. We have gone back
30 Far past our fathers' land.
                    And then, that evening
Late in the summer the strange horses came.
We heard a distant tapping on the road,
A deepening drumming; it stopped, went on again
35 And at the corner changed to hollow thunder.
We saw the heads
Like a wild wave charging and were afraid.
We had sold our horses in our fathers' time
To buy new tractors. Now they were strange to us
40 As fabulous steeds set on an ancient shield
Or illustrations in a book of knights.
We did not dare go near them. Yet they waited,
Stubborn and shy, as if they had been sent
By an old command to find our whereabouts
45 And that long-lost archaic companionship.
In the first moment we had never a thought
That they were creatures to be owned and used.
Among them were some half-a-dozen colts
Dropped in some wilderness of the broken world,
50 Yet new as if they had come from their own Eden.[2]
Since then they have pulled our ploughs and borne our loads,
But that free servitude still can pierce our hearts.
Our life is changed; their coming our beginning.

---

1. **loam** (lōm) *n.* dark, rich soil.
2. **Eden** in the Bible, the garden where life began with Adam and Eve; paradise.

Reading Skill
Paraphrase Pause to reflect on your understanding by picturing the scene here. Then, monitor your comprehension by restating lines 31–35 in your own words.

Vocabulary
archaic (är kā′ ik) *adj.* from an earlier time; ancient

Spiral Review
Main Idea What complex inference can you make about the main, or controlling, idea of this poem? Use textual evidence to support your understanding.

The Writer

RICHARD WILBUR

Literary Analysis
Narrative Poetry
What details about the characters and setting are introduced in the first stanza?

In her room at the prow[1] of the house
Where light breaks, and the windows are tossed with linden,[2]
My daughter is writing a story.

I pause in the stairwell, hearing
5 From her shut door a commotion of typewriter-keys
Like a chain hauled over a gunwale.[3]

Young as she is, the stuff
Of her life is a great cargo, and some of it heavy:
I wish her a lucky passage.

10 But now it is she who pauses,
As if to reject my thought and its easy figure.
A stillness greatens, in which

The whole house seems to be thinking,
And then she is at it again with a bunched clamor
15 Of strokes, and again is silent.

---

1. prow (prou) *n.* front part of a ship or boat.
2. linden (lin´ dən) *n.* type of tree.
3. gunwale (gun´ əl) *n.* upper edge of the side of a ship or boat.

I remember the dazed starling [4]
Which was trapped in that very room, two years ago;
How we stole in, lifted a sash

And retreated, not to affright it;
20 And how for a helpless hour, through the crack of the door,
We watched the sleek, wild, dark

And iridescent creature
Batter against the brilliance, drop like a glove
To the hard floor, or the desk-top,

25 And wait then, humped and bloody,
For the wits to try it again; and how our spirits
Rose when, suddenly sure,

It lifted off from a chair-back,
Beating a smooth course for the right window
30 And clearing the sill of the world.

It is always a matter, my darling,
Of life or death, as I had forgotten. I wish
What I wished you before, but harder.

---

4. **starling** (stär´ liŋ) *n.* bird with black feathers that shine in a greenish or purplish way.

Reading Skill
Paraphrase Picture the action here and paraphrase lines 16–30.

Vocabulary
iridescent (ir´ i des´ ənt) *adj.* showing colors that seem to change in different lights

▼ **Critical Viewing**
Do you think a typewriter like this would allow a writer more or less creativity than a computer? **[Speculate]**

The Raven

Edgar Allan Poe

Once upon a midnight dreary, while I pondered, weak and weary,
Over many a quaint and curious volume of forgotten lore,
While I nodded, nearly napping, suddenly there came a tapping,
As of someone gently rapping, rapping at my chamber door.
5   "Tis some visitor," I muttered, "tapping at my chamber door—
      Only this, and nothing more."

Ah, distinctly I remember it was in the bleak December,
And each separate dying ember wrought its ghost upon the floor.
Eagerly I wished the morrow—vainly I had tried to borrow
10 From my books surcease[1] of sorrow—sorrow for the lost Lenore—
For the rare and radiant maiden whom the angels name Lenore—
      Nameless here for evermore.

And the silken, sad, uncertain rustling of each purple curtain
Thrilled me—filled me with fantastic terrors never felt before;
15 So that now, to still the beating of my heart, I stood repeating
"'Tis some visitor entreating entrance at my chamber door—
Some late visitor entreating entrance at my chamber door—
      This it is and nothing more."

Presently my soul grew stronger; hesitating then no longer,
20 "Sir," said I, "or Madam, truly your forgiveness I implore;
But the fact is I was napping, and so gently you came rapping,
And so faintly you came tapping, tapping at my chamber door,
That I scarce was sure I heard you"—here I opened wide the
    door;—
      Darkness there, and nothing more.

25 Deep into that darkness peering, long I stood there wondering,
    fearing,
Doubting, dreaming dreams no mortal ever dared to dream
    before;
But the silence was unbroken, and the darkness gave no token,
And the only word there spoken was the whispered word,
    "Lenore!"
This *I* whispered, and an echo murmured back the word,
    "Lenore!"
30   Merely this, and nothing more.

Then into the chamber turning, all my soul within me burning,
Soon I heard again a tapping somewhat louder than before.
"Surely," said I, "surely that is something at my window lattice;
Let me see, then, what thereat[2] is, and this mystery explore—

---

1. **surcease** (sʉr sēs´) *n.* end.
2. **thereat** (*th*er at´) *adv.* there.

The Raven **711**

Vocabulary
pondered (pän´ dərd) *v.*
thought deeply about

Literary Analysis
Narrative Poetry
Analyze the effects of
diction in this stanza.
What words in this
stanza help you picture
the setting? What mood
do those words convey?

Reading Skill
Paraphrase Pause to
reflect on your under-
standing by picturing
the action the speaker
describes. Then, monitor
your comprehension by
paraphrasing this stanza.

Literary Analysis
Narrative Poetry
How has the speaker's
emotional state changed
since the first stanza?

Reading Check

What sorrow is the
speaker hoping to ease
by reading?

Reading Skill
Paraphrase In your own words, describe how the raven behaved as it entered the chamber.

Vocabulary
beguiling (bē gīl´ iŋ)
v. tricking; charming

35 Let my heart be still a moment and this mystery explore—
  'Tis the wind, and nothing more!"
 Open here I flung the shutter, when, with many a flirt[3] and flutter,
 In there stepped a stately raven of the saintly days of yore;
 Not the least obeisance[4] made he; not an instant stopped or stayed he;
40 But, with mien[5] of lord or lady, perched above my chamber door—
 Perched upon a bust of Pallas just above my chamber door—
  Perched, and sat, and nothing more.

 Then this ebony bird beguiling my sad fancy[6] into smiling,
 By the grave and stern decorum of the countenance[7] it wore,
45 "Though thy crest be shorn and shaven, thou," I said, "art sure no craven,[8]
 Ghastly grim and ancient raven wandering from the Nightly shore—
 Tell me what thy lordly name is on the Night's Plutonian[9] shore!"
  Quoth[10] the raven, "Nevermore."

 Much I marveled this ungainly fowl to hear discourse so plainly,
50 Though its answer little meaning—little relevancy bore;
 For we cannot help agreeing that no sublunary[11] being
 Ever yet was blessed with seeing bird above his chamber door—
 Bird or beast upon the sculptured bust above his chamber door,
  With such name as "Nevermore."

55 But the raven, sitting lonely on the placid bust, spoke only
 That one word, as if his soul in that one word he did outpour.
 Nothing farther then he uttered—not a feather then he fluttered—
 Till I scarcely more than muttered, "Other friends have flown before—
 On the morrow *he* will leave me, as my hopes have flown before."
60 Quoth the raven, "Nevermore."

 Wondering at the stillness broken by reply so aptly spoken,
 "Doubtless," said I, "what it utters is its only stock and store,

---

3. **flirt** (flʉrt) *n.* quick, uneven movement.
4. **obeisance** (ō bā´ səns) *n.* bow or another sign of respect.
5. **mien** (mēn) *n.* manner.
6. **fancy** (fan´ sē) *n.* imagination.
7. **countenance** (kount´'n əns) *n.* facial appearance.
8. **craven** (krā´ vən) *n.* coward (usually an adjective).
9. **Plutonian** (ploo tō´ nē ən) *adj.* like the underworld, ruled by the ancient Roman god Pluto.
10. **quoth** (kwōth) *v.* said.
11. **sublunary** (sub loon´ ər ē) *adj.* earthly.

Caught from some unhappy master whom unmerciful Disaster
Followed fast and followed faster—so, when Hope he would
 adjure,[12]
65 Stern Despair returned, instead of the sweet Hope he dared
  adjure—
   That sad answer, 'Nevermore.'"

But the raven still beguiling all my sad soul into smiling,
Straight I wheeled a cushioned seat in front of bird, and
  bust, and door;
Then upon the velvet sinking, I betook myself to linking
70 Fancy unto fancy, thinking what this ominous bird of yore—
What this grim, ungainly, ghastly, gaunt, and ominous bird
  of yore
   Meant in croaking "Nevermore."

This I sat engaged in guessing, but no syllable expressing
To the fowl whose fiery eyes now burned into my bosom's core;
75 This and more I sat divining,[13] with my head at ease reclining
On the cushion's velvet lining that the lamplight gloated o'er,
But whose velvet violet lining with the lamplight gloating o'er,
   She shall press, ah, nevermore!

Then, methought, the air grew denser, perfumed from
  an unseen censer[14]
80 Swung by angels whose faint footfalls tinkled on the tufted floor.
"Wretch," I cried, "thy God hath lent thee—by these angels
  he hath sent thee
 Respite—respite and Nepenthe[15] from thy memories of Lenore!
Let me quaff this kind Nepenthe and forget this lost Lenore!"
   Quoth the raven, "Nevermore."

85 "Prophet!" said I, "thing of evil!—prophet still, if bird or devil!—
Whether Tempter sent, or whether tempest tossed thee here
  ashore,
Desolate, yet all undaunted, on this desert land enchanted—
On this home by Horror haunted—tell me truly, I
  implore—
Is there—is there balm in Gilead?[16]—tell me—tell me, I
  implore!"
90   Quoth the raven, "Nevermore."

---

12. adjure (ə joor´) *v.* appeal to; ask earnestly.
13. divining (də vīn´ iŋ) *v.* guessing.
14. censer (sen´ sər) *n.* container for burning incense.
15. Nepenthe (nē pen´ *th*ē) *n.* drug believed by the ancient Greeks to cause
 forgetfulness of sorrow.
16. balm (bäm) **in Gilead** (gil´ ē əd) cure for suffering; the Bible refers to a
 medicinal ointment, or balm, made in a region called Gilead.

Literary Analysis
Narrative Poetry What
two conflicts or problems
does the speaker face in
this stanza?

Vocabulary
respite (res´ pit)
n. rest; relief

Reading
Check

What one word does the
raven repeat?

"Prophet!" said I, "thing of evil!—prophet still, if bird or devil!
By that Heaven that bends above us—by that God we both
    adore—
Tell this soul with sorrow laden if, within the distant Aidenn,[17]
It shall clasp a sainted maiden whom the angels name Lenore—
95   Clasp a rare and radiant maiden whom the angels name Lenore."
        Quoth the raven, "Nevermore."

"Be that word our sign of parting, bird or fiend!" I shrieked,
    upstarting—
"Get thee back into the tempest and the Night's Plutonian shore!
Leave no black plume as a token of that lie thy soul hath spoken!
100 Leave my loneliness unbroken!—quit the bust above my door!
Take thy beak from out my heart, and take thy form from
    off my door!"
        Quoth the raven, "Nevermore."

And the raven, never flitting, still is sitting, still is sitting
On the pallid bust of Pallas just above my chamber door;
105 And his eyes have all the seeming of a demon that is dreaming,
And the lamplight o'er him streaming throws his shadow on
    the floor;
And my soul from out that shadow that lies floating on the floor
        Shall be lifted—nevermore!

17. Aidenn name meant to suggest Eden, or paradise.

Literary Analysis
Narrative Poetry How
does the mood here
compare with the mood
at the beginning of the
poem? Explain.

Critical Thinking

Support
your responses
with evidence
from the text.

1. **Respond:** Which of the poems in this collection do you think has
   the most exciting or interesting plot? Explain your answer.

2. **(a)** What happens to the tractors in "The Horses"? **(b) Interpret:**
   Why does the poet place the tractors and the horses side by side?

3. **Analyze:** Why does the speaker of "The Writer" recall the
   incident of the trapped starling? Explain your answer.

4. **(a)** In the first line of "The Raven," which two adjectives does the
   speaker use to describe his state of mind? **(b) Draw Conclusions:**
   How would you describe the speaker's state of mind at the end of
   the poem? **(c) Analyze Cause and Effect:** What has caused the
   speaker to change?

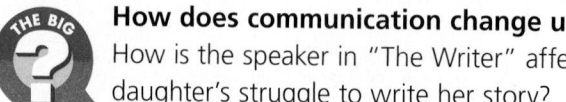

How does communication change us?
How is the speaker in "The Writer" affected by his
daughter's struggle to write her story?

Literary Analysis: Narrative Poetry

1. (a) Using a chart like the one shown, identify and describe the story elements in each **narrative poem. (b)** Explain why you think each writer chose poetry to bring these elements to life.

	Setting	Characters	Plot
"The Horses"			
"The Writer"			
"The Raven"			

2. (a) In "The Raven," how would you describe the speaker's personality? **(b)** Analyze the **effects of diction** in "The Raven" by identifying six words that contribute to the poem's mysterious and frantic **mood.** Explain each choice.

3. (a) Do you think a poem is an effective way to tell a story? Why or why not? **(b)** Share your response with a partner, and then explain if his or her response changed your own.

Reading Skill: Paraphrase

4. (a) Paraphrase lines 37 through 39 of "The Raven." **(b)** Explain how picturing the action helped you restate the lines.

Vocabulary

Practice In vocabulary study, **analogies** show the relationships between pairs of words. Use a word from the list on page 704 to make a word pair that matches the relationship between the first two given words.

1. stale : fresh :: _____ : modern

2. exercise : tiredness :: _____ : rest

3. teaching : professor :: _____ : trickster

4. clear : glass :: _____ : steel

5. kicked : foot :: _____ : mind

6. spicy : bland :: _____ : dull

Word Power Use the context of the sentences and what you know about the **Latin prefix im-** to explain your answer to each question.

1. Is it possible to move an *immovable* object?

2. How likely is it that an *improbable* event will occur?

Word Power

The **Latin prefix im-** means "not."

Apply It Explain how the prefix *im-* helps you determine the meanings of these technical academic words from science and social studies. Consult a dictionary if necessary.

immobile
immeasurable
impartial

Integrated Language Skills

Poetry Collections 5 and 6

Poetry Collection 5

Conventions: Appositive Phrases

An **appositive phrase** is a noun or pronoun with modifiers that functions as a noun and adds information to the noun or pronoun it follows.

An appositive phrase is usually set off with commas and functions as a unit that identifies, renames, or explains the noun or pronoun that comes before it. Notice that appositive phrases do not contain any verbs.

Using appositives is a good way to make your writing more concise. Notice how combining sentences using an appositive phrase (underlined) makes the revised version more concise than the original.

Poetry Collection 6

Less Concise	Revision With Appositive
"The Raven" is a poem by Edgar Allan Poe. Edgar Allan Poe was one of the first great American writers.	"The Raven" is a poem by Edgar Allan Poe, <u>one of the first great American writers</u>.

Practice A Identify each appositive phrase.

1. "Casey at the Bat" takes place in Mudville, a fictional town.
2. The crowd cheered for Casey, the best player on the team.
3. In "Fifteen," a poem by William Stafford, the speaker finds a motorcycle by the side of a road.
4. Houston, the largest city in Texas, is the setting for Cisneros's poem.

Reading Application Rewrite lines 9 and 10 of "Casey at the Bat" as two sentences. Use an appositive phrase in each one. Then, exchange sentences with a partner and read his or her sentences. Identify the appositive phrases.

Practice B For each item, combine the two sentences using an appositive phrase.

1. The raven perches on a bust of Pallas. Pallas was an ancient Greek goddess.
2. Muir grew up in Orkney. Orkney is a group of islands north of Scotland.
3. "The Writer" is one of Richard Wilbur's most famous poems. "The Writer" was published in 1969.
4. The speaker and his daughter watched as the bird tried to fly through the window. The bird was a starling.

Writing Application Write two sentences about an image in one of the poems you read. Use an appositive phrase in each one.

PH GRAMMAR HANDBOOK Further instruction and practice are available in the *Prentice Hall Grammar Handbook*.

Writing

The poems in both collections use precise diction to convey moods. Write a **poem** in which you use diction to develop a specific mood.

- Jot down details about the setting, action, and characters (if any). Consider the mood you want to set and note how details about characters, setting, and action can evoke this mood.
- Review your notes and list precise words to help you to build the mood in your poem. Use a **thesaurus** to help you choose words. Be sure you know the meanings of the words you choose.
- Choose a **poetic form,** or structure, that fits your mood and meaning. Consider the number of lines per stanza, and whether you will use a rhythm or rhyme scheme.

Grammar Application If you include appositive phrases in your poem, make sure you use them correctly.

Writing Workshop: *Work in Progress*

Prewriting for Interpretative Response To prepare for an interpretative response to literature you may write, review these poems. Identify a character in each poem that makes an impression. Jot down details that build that impression. Put your Character Descriptions in your portfolio.

Listening and Speaking

With a partner, analyze a media message and write a **report** detailing your analysis. If you read "Fifteen," analyze a motorcycle or automobile commercial. If you read "The Horses," analyze a commercial advertising a computer or other contemporary electronic device.

Analyze how **media messages** are conveyed through **visual** and **sound techniques** in the commercial. These techniques include:

- **editing,** or cutting and rearranging visual and audio elements
- **reaction shots,** or audio or visual portrayals of people reacting to something, such as an idea, an action, or an event
- **sequencing,** or the order of events in which visual and sound messages are presented
- **background music,** the music that is added to a scene to set a mood or to play on viewers' and listeners' emotions

If possible, watch the commercial several times before you begin your analysis. Consider the effect of each of these elements on the audience. Then, explain how the elements work together to convey a particular message. Present your completed report to the class.

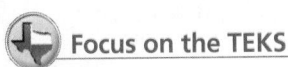 Focus on the TEKS

Writing
(14)(B) Write a poem using a variety of poetic forms.
Reading
(1)(E) Use a thesaurus.
(12)(B) Analyze how messages in media are conveyed through visual and sound techniques (e.g., editing, reaction shots, sequencing, background music).

Use this prewriting activity to prepare for the **Writing Workshop** on page 756.

PHLitOnline
www.PHLitOnline.com

- Interactive graphic organizers
- Grammar tutorial
- Interactive journals

Collection Choices

▲ **Poetry Collection 7** explores the nature of heroism and making crucial decisions.

▲ **Poetry Collection 8** explores the emotions and roles people take on in life.

 TEXAS Focus on the TEKS

Meet these standards with either **Poetry Collection 7** (p. 724) or **Poetry Collection 8** (p. 732).

Reading
(3) Understand the structure and elements of poetry and provide evidence from the text to support understanding. (Literary Analysis: Rhyme and Meter)

(1)(A) Determine the meaning of grade-level technical academic English words in multiple content areas derived from other linguistic affixes. (Word Power: Apply It)

Reading/Comprehension Skills
RC-9(A) Reflect on understanding to monitor comprehension. (Reading Skill: Paraphrase)

Oral and Written Conventions
(17)(A)(i) Use and understand the function of more complex verbals (infinitives) in the context of reading, writing, and speaking. (Conventions: Infinitives)

Writing
(14)(B) Write a poem using a variety of poetic techniques. (Writing: Poem)

Listening and Speaking
(26) Participate productively in teams, building on the ideas of others and developing a plan for consensus-building. (Listening and Speaking: Panel Discussion)

Literary Analysis: **Rhyme and Meter**

TEXAS
PHLitOnline
www.PHLitOnline.com

Hear It!
- Selection summary audio
- Selection audio

See It!
- Get Connected video
- Background video
- More about the author
- Vocabulary flashcards

Do It!
- Interactive journals
- Interactive graphic organizers
- Self-test
- Internet activity
- Grammar tutorial
- Interactive vocabulary games

Rhyme and meter are two literary devices often used in poetry. **Rhyme,** an important element in many types of poetry, is the repetition of sounds at the ends of words. There are several types of rhyme:

- **Exact rhyme:** the repetition of words that end with the same vowel and consonant sounds, as in *love* and *dove*
- **Slant rhyme:** the repetition of words that end with similar sounds but do not rhyme perfectly, as in *prove* and *glove*
- **End rhyme:** the rhyming of words at the ends of lines
- **Internal rhyme:** the rhyming of words within a line

A **rhyme scheme** is a regular pattern of end rhymes in a poem or stanza, in which a letter is assigned to each set of rhyming sounds. For example, in "Ring Out, Wild Bells," Alfred, Lord Tennyson uses the rhyme scheme *abba*:

Ring out, wild bells, to the wild sky,	a
The flying cloud, the frosty light:	b
The year is dying in the night;	b
Ring out, wild bells, and let him die.	a

Lewis Carroll opens "Jabberwocky" with the rhyme scheme *abab*:

'Twas brillig, and the slithy toves	a
Did gyre and gimble in the wabe;	b
All mimsy were the borogroves,	a
And the mome raths outgrabe.	b

Meter, a **structural element** of poetry, is the rhythmical pattern in a line of poetry that results from the arrangement of stressed (ˊ) and unstressed (˘) syllables. The stress goes on the syllable that is accented in natural speech. Reading the line aloud reveals the steady rhythmic pulse of the stressed syllables:

The flýǐng clóud, thĕ frósty̆ líght

Hálf ă leaǧue, hálf ă leaǧue, / Hálf ă leaǧue ońwărd

Each meter is named based on its length and rhythmical pattern. A common pattern uses *iambs,* beats in which the stress is on the second syllable, such as hĕllóor ălóud. In *iambic pentameter,* each line contains five iambs.

Shăll Í / cŏmpáre / thĕe tó / ă súm / mĕr's dáy?

Thŏu árt / mŏre lóve / Ĭy ánd / mŏre témp / ĕr áte.

(continued)

Literary Analysis: Rhyme and Meter (continued)

An *iambic dimeter* consists of two iambs, a *trimeter* consists of three iambs, a *tetrameter* consists of four iambs, and so on. See the chart below for examples of these metric groupings.

Iambic Meter	Example
Dimeter (2 beats per line)	And for / redress Of all / my pain,
Trimeter (3 beats per line)	We romped / until / the pans Slid from / the kitch / en shelf;
Tetrameter (4 beats per line)	I think / that I / shall ne / ver see a po / em love / ly as / a tree.

Not all poems include rhyme, a rhyme scheme, or a regular meter. Nonmetrical poetry, or poems that do not contain a regular pattern of meter, is known as **free verse.** These lines from "Uncoiling" by Pat Mora are written as free verse:

> With thorns she scratches
> on my window, tosses her hair dark with rain,
> snares lightning, cholla, hawks, butterfly
> swarms in the tangles.

Poems that do not rhyme but consist of iambic pentameter are known as **blank verse.** William Shakespeare wrote many of his plays in blank verse, as in this line from *Romeo and Juliet*:

> But soft! / What light / through yon / der win / dow breaks?
> It is / the east, / and Ju / liet is / the sun!

Poets often use one or more rhyming techniques to create musical effects and achieve a sense of unity in their poems.

As You Read Notice the structure and elements of each poem. Take notes about specific rhymes and meters and the effects of poetic devices in each poem. Include evidence from the text to support your understanding.

- Look for examples of different types of rhyme.
- Determine if the lines follow a rhyme scheme.
- Notice whether or not the lines follow a regular meter.

Reading Skill: Paraphrase

When you **paraphrase,** you restate in your own words what someone else has written or said. A paraphrase should retain the essential meaning and ideas of the original but should be simpler to read and to understand. Paraphrasing will help you to reflect on your understanding to monitor your comprehension. One way to simplify the text that you are paraphrasing is to break down long sentences. Follow these steps:

- Divide long sentences into parts and paraphrase those parts.
- If a sentence contains multiple subjects or verbs, see if it can be separated into smaller sentences that each contain one subject and one verb.
- If a sentence contains colons, semicolons, or dashes, create separate sentences by treating those punctuation marks as periods.
- If a sentence contains long phrases or long passages in parentheses, turn each phrase or parenthetical passage into a separate sentence.

Poets often write sentences that span several lines to give their poems fluidity. By breaking down and paraphrasing long sentences, you can monitor your comprehension while still enjoying a poem's fluid quality.

Paraphrasing can also help you synthesize content that comes from several works by the same author addressing a single issue. Analyzing the author's views from these various sources may become easier once the information is brought together in your own words. This strategy can give you a more comprehensive picture of the author.

www.PHLitOnline.com

Hear It!
- Selection summary audio
- Selection audio

See It!
- Get Connected video
- Background video
- More about the author
- Vocabulary flashcards

Do It!
- Interactive journals
- Interactive graphic organizers
- Self-test
- Internet activity
- Grammar tutorial
- Interactive vocabulary games

Using the Strategy: Paraphrase Chart

As You Read Reflect on your understanding to monitor comprehension. Break down long sentences, using a paraphrase chart like this one.

Original Lines	Lines in Smaller Sentences	Paraphrase
I celebrate myself and sing myself, / And what I assume you shall assume, / For every atom belonging to me as good belongs to you. —Walt Whitman	I celebrate myself. I sing myself. What I assume you shall assume. Every atom belonging to me as good belongs to you.	I celebrate myself and share my joy with you. What is mine is also yours.

How does *communication* change us?

Writing About the Big Question

In the last poem in Collection 7, the speaker claims that "We never know how high we are / Till we are asked to rise." Use this sentence starter to develop your ideas about the Big Question.

A person can make someone else **aware** of his or her potential by _____.

As You Read Consider whether it is true that people achieve more when more is asked of them.

Vocabulary

Read each word and its definition. Decide whether you know the word well, know it a little bit, or do not know it at all. After you read, see how your knowledge of each word has increased.

- **diverged** (dī vʉrjd´) v. branched out in different directions (p. 725) *When the highway <u>diverged</u>, we were not sure which way to go. diverge v. divergence n. diverging adj. diversity n.*

- **bafflement** (baf´ əl mənt) n. puzzlement; bewilderment (p. 726) *To the <u>bafflement</u> of many, the jet pilot was afraid of heights. baffle v. baffling adj.*

- **depravity** (dē prav´ ə tē) n. crookedness; corruption (p. 727) *The criminal's <u>depravity</u> was well known, and his arrest was cheered. depraved adj. deprave v.*

- **rifled** (rī´ fəld) v. ransacked and robbed; searched quickly through a cupboard or drawer (p. 727) *My little sister <u>rifled</u> through my drawer and took my favorite sweater. rifle v.*

- **disclosed** (dis klōzd´) v. revealed; made known (p. 727) *John <u>disclosed</u> the location of his hidden treasure. disclose v. disclosure n.*

- **warp** (wôrp) v. twist; distort (p. 728) *Skilled artists can <u>warp</u> wood into different shapes. warped adj.*

Word Power

The **suffix -ment,** meaning "act" or "resulting state of," comes to English through **Middle English** and **French.**

In "Macavity: The Mystery Cat," the speaker refers to Macavity as "the **bafflement** of Scotland Yard." Bafflement is the resulting state of being baffled, or puzzled. The speaker means that Macavity is the reason Scotland Yard is puzzled.

Robert Frost

(1874–1963)

"The Road Not Taken" (p. 724)

In January 1961, when John F. Kennedy became president of the United States, he called on fellow New Englander Robert Frost to recite two poems at the inauguration. At the time, Frost was America's most famous living poet. He became famous when *A Boy's Will* (1913) and *North of Boston* (1914) won wide praise in both the United Kingdom and the United States.

T. S. Eliot

(1888–1965)

"Macavity: The Mystery Cat" (p. 726)

A whimsical poem like "Macavity: The Mystery Cat" was a rarity in the writing of Thomas Stearns Eliot. He was better known for serious, philosophical poems. Born in the United States, Eliot settled in the United Kingdom. He became a highly influential poet and won the Nobel Prize in 1948.

Emily Dickinson

(1830–1886)

"We never know how high we are" (p. 728)

Emily Dickinson's life in Amherst, Massachusetts, seemed to be quiet and uneventful. Yet, the emotional power of her poems shows the wide range of her energy and imagination. She found profound meanings in simple subjects, and her poems still delight readers.

The Road Not Taken

Robert Frost

Two roads diverged in a yellow wood,
And sorry I could not travel both
And be one traveler, long I stood
And looked down one as far as I could
5 To where it bent in the undergrowth;

Then took the other, as just as fair,
And having perhaps the better claim,
Because it was grassy and wanted wear;
Though as for that, the passing there
10 Had worn them really about the same,

And both that morning equally lay
In leaves no step had trodden black.
Oh, I kept the first for another day!
Yet knowing how way leads on to way,
15 I doubted if I should ever come back.

I shall be telling this with a sigh
Somewhere ages and ages hence:
Two roads diverged in a wood, and I—
I took the one less traveled by,
20 And that has made all the difference.

Vocabulary
diverged (dī vʉrjd´) v.
branched out in different directions

Reading Skill
Paraphrase Pause to reflect on your understanding to monitor your comprehension. In your own words, restate the decision the speaker makes in lines 6–8.

Literary Analysis
Rhyme and Meter
What is the rhyme scheme of stanza four?

◀ **Critical Viewing** Based on this image, explain why the idea of a fork in a road is an effective symbol for a life choice. **[Support]**

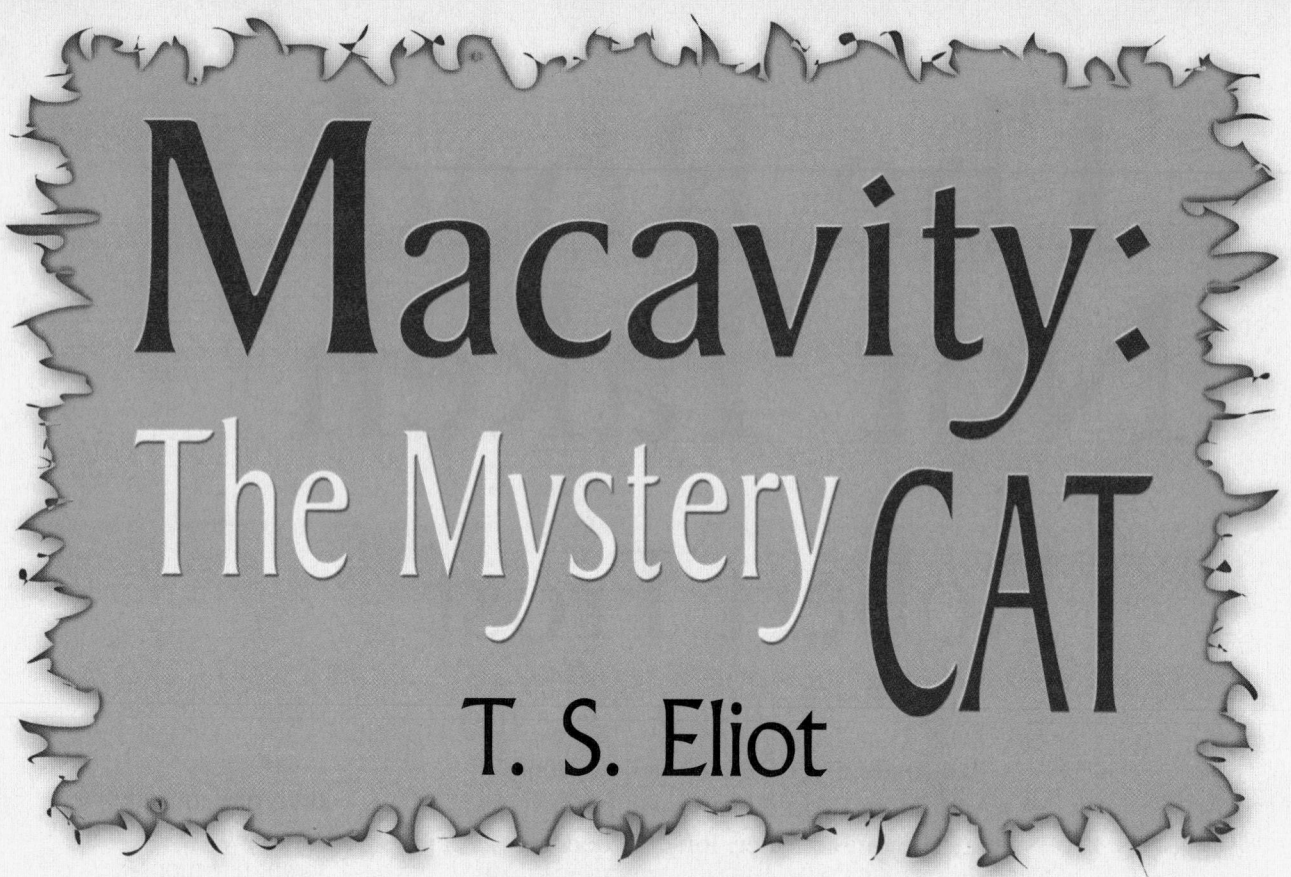

Macavity: The Mystery CAT

T. S. Eliot

Vocabulary
bafflement (baf´
əl mənt) *n.* puzzle-
ment; bewilderment

Macavity's a Mystery Cat: he's called the Hidden Paw—
For he's the master criminal who can defy the Law.
He's the bafflement of Scotland Yard,[1] the Flying Squad's[2]
    despair:
5 For when they reach the scene of crime—*Macavity's not
    there!*

Literary Analysis
Rhyme and Meter
What type of rhyme does
this stanza contain?

Macavity, Macavity, there's no one like Macavity,
He's broken every human law, he breaks the law of gravity.
His powers of levitation would make a fakir[3] stare,
10 And when you reach the scene of crime—*Macavity's not there!*
You may seek him in the basement, you may look up in the
    air—
But I tell you once and once again, *Macavity's not there!*

Macavity's a ginger cat, he's very tall and thin;
15 You would know him if you saw him, for his eyes are sunken in.

---

1. **Scotland Yard** London police.
2. **Flying Squad** criminal-investigation department.
3. **fakir** (fə kir´) *n.* Muslim or Hindu beggar who claims to perform miracles.

His brow is deeply lined with thought, his head is highly
      domed;
His coat is dusty from neglect, his whiskers are uncombed.
He sways his head from side to side, with movements like a
20   snake;
And when you think he's half asleep, he's always wide awake.

Macavity, Macavity, there's no one like Macavity,
For he's a fiend in feline shape, a monster of depravity.
You may meet him in a by-street, you may see him in the
25   square—
But when a crime's discovered, then *Macavity's not there!*

He's outwardly respectable. (They say he cheats at cards.)
And his footprints are not found in any file of Scotland Yard's.
And when the larder's looted, or the jewel-case is rifled,
30 Or when the milk is missing, or another Peke's⁴ been stifled,
Or the greenhouse glass is broken, and the trellis past repair—
Ay, there's the wonder of the thing! *Macavity's not there!*

And when the Foreign Office find a Treaty's gone astray,
Or the Admiralty lose some plans and drawings by the way,
35 There may be a scrap of paper in the hall or on the stair—
But it's useless to investigate—*Macavity's not there!*
And when the loss has been disclosed, the Secret Service say:
'It *must* have been Macavity!'—but he's a mile away.
You'll be sure to find him resting, or a-licking of his thumbs,
40 Or engaged in doing complicated long division sums.

Macavity, Macavity, there's no one like Macavity,
There never was a Cat of such deceitfulness and suavity.
He always has an alibi, and one or two to spare:
At whatever time the deed took place—MACAVITY WASN'T
45   THERE!
And they say that all the Cats whose wicked deeds are widely
      known
(I might mention Mungojerrie, I might mention Griddlebone)
Are nothing more than agents for the Cat who all the time
50 Just controls their operations: the Napoleon of Crime!⁵

Vocabulary
depravity (dē prav´
ə tē) *n.* crooked-
ness; corruption
rifled (rī´ fəld) *v.* ransacked and robbed;
searched quickly through
a cupboard or drawer

Vocabulary
disclosed (dis klōzd´) *v.*
revealed; made known

Reading Skill
Paraphrase Pause to
reflect on your under-
standing to monitor your
comprehension. Break
down the sentence in
lines 43–45 into three
smaller sentences. Re-
state each sentence in
your own words.

---

4. **Peke** short for Pekingese, a small dog with long, silky hair and a pug nose.
5. **the Napoleon of Crime** criminal mastermind; emperor of crime—just as Napoleon
   Bonaparte (1769–1821) was a masterful military strategist who had himself crowned
   emperor.

Bubbles, Watercolor, 39" x 29", by Scott Burdick, Courtesy of the artist

Vocabulary
warp (wôrp) *v.*
twist; distort

We never know how high we are

Emily Dickinson

We never know how high we are
Till we are asked to rise
And then if we are true to plan
Our statures touch the skies—
The Heroism we recite
Would be a normal thing
Did not ourselves the Cubits[1] warp
For fear to be a King—

---

1. **Cubits** (kyōō´ bitz) *n.* ancient measure using the length of the arm from the end of the middle finger to the elbow (about 18–22 inches).

Critical Thinking

1. **Respond:** Which poem sounds best when read aloud? Why?

2. **(a)** In "The Road Not Taken," what does the traveler do when faced with a divide in the road? **(b) Make Inferences:** What details tell you he is happy with his decision? **(c) Evaluate:** Do you think the poem has a lesson to teach? Explain.

Support your responses with evidence from the text.

3. **Speculate:** Which qualities of cats might have caused T. S. Eliot to associate them with criminal activities in "Macavity: The Mystery Cat"? Explain.

How does communication change us?
(a) According to "We never know how high we are," what happens when people are asked to rise to an occasion? **(b)** Do you agree with that claim? Why or why not?

Literary Analysis: Rhyme and Meter

1. Identify two lines in "The Road Not Taken" that illustrate both **exact rhyme** and **end rhyme.** Explain your choices.

2. Which two words in line 31 of "Macavity: The Mystery Cat" illustrate both **slant rhyme** and **internal rhyme?**

3. (a) Use letters to identify the **rhyme scheme** in "We never know how high we are." **(b)** In what way does the shift in rhyme scheme midway through the poem help to signal a turning point in the poem's message?

4. (a) Which poem has lines with a more regular **meter:** "The Road Not Taken" or "We never know how high we are"? Explain. **(b)** What effect does the meter of each poem have on the reader? Explain.

Reading Skill: Paraphrase

5. (a) Rewrite the first stanza of "The Road Not Taken" as a series of sentences. Then, **paraphrase** the stanza. **(b)** In what way does breaking down long sentences make this poem's meaning clearer?

Vocabulary

Practice Decide if each statement is true or false. Then, explain your answer.

1. Reporters are taught to *warp* the facts of events they cover.

2. Two people whose opinions *diverged* would be in disagreement.

3. *Bafflement* is a likely reaction to a bizarre event.

4. Laws are written to encourage *depravity* in society.

5. A closet is tidier after it has been *rifled.*

6. Information that has been *disclosed* is no longer secret.

Word Power Use the context of the sentences and what you know about the **suffix -ment** to explain your answer to each question.

1. Would an *amusement* park entertain you?

2. When you make an *improvement,* do you make something better or worse?

Word Power

The **suffix -*ment,*** meaning "act" or "resulting state of," comes to English through **Middle English** and **French.**

Apply It Explain how the suffix -*ment* helps you determine the meanings of these technical academic words from the arts. Consult a dictionary if necessary.

**accompaniment
entertainment
arrangement**

How does *communication* change us?

Writing About the Big Question

The speaker of "The Seven Ages of Man" compares the people of the world to actors in a play. Use this sentence starter to develop your ideas about the Big Question.

Communication between two people can seem like action in a play when _____.

(**As You Read**) Look for ways in which people's lives and interactions can resemble actors playing roles. Then, consider how this knowledge might offer a useful way to look at life.

Vocabulary

Read each word and its definition. Decide whether you know the word well, know it a little bit, or do not know it at all. After you have read the selection, see how your knowledge of each word has increased.

- **stranded** (strand´ əd) *adj.* in a place or situation which one needs help to leave (p. 732) *The stranded airline passengers had to spend the night in the terminal.* strand *v.*

- **languid** (laŋ´ gwid) *adj.* drooping; weak (p. 732) *The heat of the summer afternoon made us all feel languid.* languish *v.*

- **woeful** (wō´ fəl) *adj.* full of sorrow (p. 735) *His woeful story brought us to tears.* woe *n.* woefully *adv.*

- **treble** (treb´ əl) *n.* high-pitched voice or sound (p. 735) *The harsh treble of her alarm clock woke everyone in the house.*

- **oblivion** (ə bliv´ ē ən) *n.* forgetfulness; the state of being unconscious or unaware (p. 735) *While sleeping, most people are in a state of total oblivion.* oblivious *adj.*

- **suffice** (sə fīs´) *v.* be enough (p. 736) *Five tables will suffice for a party of this size.* sufficient *adj.*

Word Power

The **suffix -ion,** meaning "act" or "condition of," comes to English through **Middle English** and **French.** It usually indicates a noun.

Someone who is oblivious is unaware. In "The Seven Ages of Man," the speaker refers to a man's final stage as "mere **oblivion**," a condition of complete unawareness.

E. E. Cummings

(1894–1962)

"maggie and milly and molly and may" (p. 732)

Born in Cambridge, Massachusetts, Edward Estlin Cummings graduated from Harvard University. Both as poet and playwright, Cummings became notorious for his unconventional style, which reflects his individualistic outlook. Much of his work is playful and lyrical, and he often disregarded rules of grammar, spelling, and punctuation.

William Shakespeare

(1564–1616)

"The Seven Ages of Man" (p. 734)

William Shakespeare forged a perfect blend of high drama and exalted language. He wrote more than three dozen plays, and because of the timelessness of his themes and the beauty of his language, lines from his plays are quoted more often than those of any other writer. "The Seven Ages of Man" from the play *As You Like It,* is considered one of his best monologues. (For more on William Shakespeare, see p. 802.)

Robert Frost

(1874–1963)

"Fire and Ice" (p. 736)

Like the title of his poem "Fire and Ice," Robert Frost seemed warm to some people, cold to other people. All agreed, however, that poetry came first in his life. Frost produced a large body of work and became the most popular American poet of his time, winning four Pulitzer Prizes.

maggie and milly and molly and may

E. E. Cummings

maggie and milly and molly and may
went down to the beach (to play one day)

and maggie discovered a shell that sang
so sweetly she couldn't remember her troubles, and

5 milly befriended a stranded star
whose rays five languid fingers were;

and molly was chased by a horrible thing
which raced sideways while blowing bubbles: and

may came home with a smooth round stone
10 as small as a world and as large as alone.

For whatever we lose (like a you or a me)
it's always ourselves we find in the sea

Vocabulary
stranded (strand´ əd) *adj.* in a place or situation which one needs help to leave
languid (laŋ´ gwid) *adj.* drooping; weak

Literary Analysis
Rhyme and Meter
What type of rhyme does Cummings use in the first and last stanzas?

▶ **Critical Viewing**   How well does this photograph illustrate the "stranded star" in the poem? **[Evaluate]**

The Seven Ages of Man, Folger Shakespeare Library, Washington, D.C.

The Seven Ages of Man

William Shakespeare

All the world's a stage,
And all the men and women merely players:[1]
They have their exits and their entrances;
And one man in his time plays many parts,
His acts being seven ages. At first the infant,
Mewling[2] and puking in the nurse's arms.
And then the whining schoolboy, with his satchel,
And shining morning face, creeping like snail
Unwillingly to school. And then the lover,
Sighing like furnace, with a **woeful** ballad
Made to his mistress' eyebrow. Then a soldier,
Full of strange oaths, and bearded like the pard,[3]
Jealous in honor,[4] sudden and quick in quarrel,
Seeking the bubble reputation
Even in the cannon's mouth. And then the justice,[5]
In fair round belly with good capon[6] lined,
With eyes severe and beard of formal cut,
Full of wise saws and modern instances;[7]
And so he plays his part. The sixth age shifts
Into the lean and slippered pantaloon,[8]
With spectacles on nose and pouch on side,
His youthful hose[9] well saved, a world too wide
For his shrunk shank;[10] and his big manly voice,
Turning again toward childish **treble**, pipes
And whistles in his sound. Last scene of all,
That ends this strange eventful history,
Is second childishness, and mere **oblivion**,
Sans[11] teeth, sans eyes, sans taste, sans everything.

---

1. **players** actors.
2. **Mewling** (myōōl′ iŋ) *v.* whimpering; crying weakly.
3. **pard** (pärd) *n.* leopard or panther.
4. **Jealous in honor** very concerned about his honor.
5. **justice** judge.
6. **capon** (kā′ pän′) *n.* roasted chicken.
7. **wise saws and modern instances** sayings, and examples that show the truth of the sayings.
8. **pantaloon** (pan′ tə lōōn′) *n.* thin, foolish old man who is a character in old comedies.
9. **hose** (hōz) *n.* stockings.
10. **shank** (shaŋk) *n.* leg.
11. **sans** (sanz) *prep.* without; lacking.

Literary Analysis
Rhyme and Meter What is the pattern of stressed and unstressed syllables in lines 2–4?

Reading Skill
Paraphrase Pause to reflect on your understanding to monitor your comprehension. Paraphrase the first sentence of the poem.

Vocabulary
woeful (wō′ fəl) *adj.* full of sorrow

Vocabulary
treble (treb′ əl) *n.* high-pitched voice or sound

oblivion (ə bliv′ ē ən) *n.* forgetfulness; the state of being unconscious or unaware

◀ Critical Viewing
How do the images in this stained-glass window add to your understanding of the poem? **[Relate]**

FIRE AND ICE
Robert Frost

Some say the world will end in fire,
Some say in ice.
From what I've tasted of desire
I hold with those who favor fire.
5   But if it had to perish twice,
I think I know enough of hate
To say that for destruction ice
Is also great
And would suffice.

Vocabulary
suffice (sə fīs´)
v. be enough

Critical Thinking

1. **Respond:** Which poem sounds best when read aloud? Why?

2. **(a)** In "maggie and milly and molly and may," what experience does each character have? **(b) Analyze:** How does each character's experience support the conclusion in the poem's final line?

3. **(a)** In "Fire and Ice," which emotions does the speaker associate with fire and ice? **(b) Interpret:** Why are fire and ice fitting metaphors for these emotions? **(c) Discuss:** Share your answers with a partner or group, and explain how the poem's message applies to teenagers.

Support your responses with evidence from the text.

How does communication change us?
Does "The Seven Ages of Man" in any way change your perspective on the stages of life and the "roles" people play? Explain your response.

Literary Analysis: Rhyme and Meter

1. Identify two lines in "maggie and milly and molly and may" that illustrate both **exact rhyme** and **end rhyme.** Explain your choices.

2. Which two words in line 17 of "The Seven Ages of Man" illustrate both **slant rhyme** and **internal rhyme?**

3. **(a)** Use letters to identify the **rhyme scheme** in "Fire and Ice." **(b)** In what way does the shift in rhyme scheme midway through the poem help signal a turning point in the poem's message?

4. **(a)** Which poem has lines with a more regular **meter:** "Fire and Ice" or "The Seven Ages of Man"? Explain. **(b)** What effect does the meter of each poem have on the reader? Explain.

Reading Skill: Paraphrase

5. **(a)** Rewrite the first ten lines of "maggie and milly and molly and may" as a series of sentences. Then, **paraphrase** the lines. **(b)** In what way does breaking down long sentences make this poem's meaning more clear?

Vocabulary

Practice Decide if each statement is true or false. Then, explain your answer.

1. If something will *suffice*, it will be satisfactory.
2. A captain should avoid letting his ship become *stranded*.
3. Coaches hope their players will be *languid* during a game.
4. A *woeful* sight is likely to inspire pity.
5. A *treble* is a deep sound like a foghorn.
6. Sleep is a kind of *oblivion*.

Word Power Use the context of the sentences and what you know about the **suffix -ion** to explain your answer to each question.

1. Could complicated directions lead to *confusion*?
2. Is *precision* a good quality for a surgeon to possess?

Word Power

The **suffix -ion,** meaning "act" or "condition of," comes to English through **Middle English** and **French.** It usually indicates a noun.

Apply It Explain how the suffix -ion helps you determine the meanings of these technical academic words from science and social studies. Consult a dictionary if necessary.

erosion
rebellion
coercion

Integrated Language Skills

Poetry Collections 7 and 8

Conventions: Infinitives

Poetry Collection 7

An **infinitive** is a verb form that generally appears with the word *to* and acts as a noun, adjective, or adverb.

An **infinitive phrase** is an infinitive with modifiers, complements, or a subject. Like infinitives, infinitive phrases can function as nouns, adjectives, or adverbs.

Infinitive	Infinitive Phrase
Used as a Noun *To write* requires dedication.	**Used as a Noun** *To win a Pulitzer Prize* is an honor.
Used as an Adjective E. E. Cummings is a good poet *to study.*	**Used as an Adjective** Cummings had a desire *to write unconventional poetry.*
Used as an Adverb When Shakespeare sat down *to work,* he used a quill dipped in ink.	**Used as an Adverb** Shakespeare wrote his plays *to be performed on a stage.*

Poetry Collection 8

Avoid this possible point of confusion: Infinitives include *to* and a verb as in *to hear.* Prepositional phrases include *to* and a noun or pronoun, as in *to the house.*

Practice A Identify the infinitive or infinitive phrase and its function in each sentence.

1. It is important to learn about these poets.
2. One needs confidence to be a king.
3. The speaker of "The Road Not Taken" chose to take the more difficult path.
4. The police have failed to catch Macavity.

Speaking Application Find two sentences that include infinitives or infinitive phrases in "Macavity: The Mystery Cat." With a partner, read these sentences and explain each infinitive's function.

Practice B Identify the infinitive or infinitive phrase in each sentence. Then, rewrite the sentence using a different infinitive or infinitive phrase.

1. Maggie went down to the beach to play.
2. Frost uses ice to represent hate.
3. To pass through seven ages is man's destiny.
4. "The Seven Ages of Man" is not the only speech to be quoted by other writers.

Writing Application Write two sentences about the beach image on page 733. Use an infinitive or an infinitive phrase in each one.

PH GRAMMAR HANDBOOK Further instruction and practice are available in the *Prentice Hall Grammar Handbook.*

Writing

Write a **poem** using the same poetic techniques of rhyme scheme and form as a poem in Collection 7 or Collection 8.

- Choose a poem and identify its rhyme scheme and form.
- Decide on a subject for your poem.
- Brainstorm for a list of images, precise details, phrases, or vivid words.
- Draft your lines, but focus on rhyme only after you have expressed your ideas and feelings.

Share your poem with a classmate. Ask him or her to identify the poem's rhyme scheme and discuss the way the rhythm and word choice affect the mood of the poem.

Grammar Application If you include infinitives and infinitive phrases, make sure you use them correctly in your poem.

Writing Workshop: *Work in Progress*

Prewriting for Interpretative Response Review your Character Descriptions, and write a one-sentence conclusion about each character. Save this Draft Thesis in your writing portfolio.

Listening and Speaking

With a team of classmates, hold a **panel discussion** about possible interpretations of a Robert Frost poem. If you read Poetry Collection 7, discuss "The Road Not Taken." If you read Collection 8, discuss "Fire and Ice."

To prepare for the discussion, conduct research about the poet's extensive works. As a group, assemble an electronic database of texts by and about Robert Frost. Consider these questions to guide your research:

- What topics and themes does Frost's work often address?
- What style does he most frequently use?
- What have others said about his works?

Write concise notes that you can refer to during the discussion. Then, as part of a team, **participate productively** in the panel discussion by sharing your ideas and by building on the ideas of others.

Before you begin the discussion, **develop a plan for consensus-building.** In other words, decide how you will work together as a team to come to a general understanding at the close of the discussion. Then, at the close of the panel, when you have reached a consensus that is acceptable to most panelists, present a position statement to the class.

 Focus on the TEKS

Conventions
(17)(A)(i) Use and understand the function of more complex verbals (infinitives) in the context of reading, writing, and speaking.

Writing
(14)(B) Write a poem using a variety of poetic techniques.

Listening and Speaking
(26) Participate productively in teams, building on the ideas of others and developing a plan for consensus-building.

Use this prewriting activity to prepare for the **Writing Workshop** on page 756.

www.PHLitOnline.com

- Interactive graphic organizers
- Grammar tutorial
- Interactive journals

Strategy for Success

Paraphrase

To perform well on the reading sections of the ACT and the Texas standardized tests, monitor your comprehension by paraphrasing as you read. One way to help yourself paraphrase is by creating mental images from the text.

As you read, form a detailed mental image of what is happening in the text. Use sensory details and figurative words and phrases to picture what the author is describing. Then, paraphrase what you have read by restating the text in your own words while keeping the same meaning. The following examples show how you can paraphrase on standardized tests.

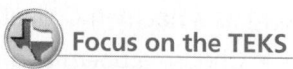 **Focus on the TEKS**

Comprehension
RC-9(A) Reflect on understanding to monitor comprehension (e.g., creating sensory images)..

Picture the Action

Make sure your mental picture includes all the details used to describe a scene.

> 1 Waving his mighty sword in the air, the knight bellowed, "I challenge you to a duel!" Then, he paused, sighed, and turned to the director sheepishly. "I'm sorry," he muttered, "I forgot my next line."
>
> **1.** The scene in the passage portrays a:
> **A.** historically accurate sword fight.
> **B.** scene in a play or movie.
> **C.** real sword fight.
> **D.** man learning how to duel.

A and **C** represent the reader's mental picture after the first sentence: an actual sword fight. However, this image quickly changes to that of an actor in a scene. A man would not need to know lines to duel, so **D** is not correct. **B** is the correct answer.

Paraphrase Figurative Language

Consider how similes, metaphors, and other figurative language can be restated.

> 1 My first car wasn't exactly the sleek new sports car I'd dreamed of for years; it was a rusty antique.
>
> **2.** The author uses the word *antique* in line 3 to suggest that the car:
> **F.** once belonged to his or her grandparent.
> **G.** is expensive and sporty.
> **H.** seems outdated.
> **J.** is trendy and modern.

The author is not referring to a literal antique, as in **F.** Instead, he or she is saying that the car is similar to an antique because it is old. **G** and **J** do not relate to antiques. **H** relates to the characteristics of an antique and is correct.

ACT Practice

DIRECTIONS: The passage in this test is followed by several questions. After reading the passage, choose the best answer to each question and fill in the corresponding oval on your answer document. You may refer to the passage as often as necessary.

HUMANITIES

We are step dancers; we dance to our own music, moving to the beat of our own hands slapping and clapping together and our feet stomping the floor. We are tribal drums echoing over the African savannahs; we are the thumping bass of a stereo playing hip hop; we are the clattering of all the
5 drums in the marching band that make you want to sway with them.

We walk on the stage with military precision, standing tall, the steady thud-thud-thud of our boots setting our pace. We face the audience, waiting, counting silently until that moment we crash our hands together above our heads to start the dance. Then we move together, like a reflection
10 repeated to infinity in a series of mirrors, with hands up—hands down—turn around—dodge to the side, gradually accelerating the pace of our steps.

The energy of each moment carries us to the next, as our hearts beat faster and adrenaline pumps through our bodies. We are different bodies,
15 but we are of one mind; the hours of practice preparing have paid off in the layers of rhythms we make as we move in perfect synchronization.

Now we have one more eight-count left in our routine, eight beats for our final, fastest rhythm. Then with one last stomp we stand triumphant, breathing hard, basking in waves of elation as the cheers wash over us.

1. In lines 3–5, the author uses metaphors to convey the idea that the group's members:
  A. play musical instruments.
  B. make a variety of rhythms.
  C. dance to recorded music.
  D. are from varied backgrounds.

2. The image of military precision in lines 6–7 suggests that the step dancers:
  F. are members of the military.
  G. pretend to be soldiers.
  H. march together in formation.
  J. receive military training.

3. Which phrase best restates the simile in lines 9 and 10 of the passage?
  A. in unison
  B. individually
  C. in opposite directions
  D. concerned about appearance

4. The images in the last three paragraphs of the passage help the reader picture a:
  F. step-dancing team practice.
  G. step-dancing performance.
  H. group learning to step dance.
  J. person observing step dancers.

Informational Texts

Expository Texts

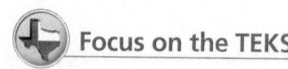
Case Study
Careers in Robotics

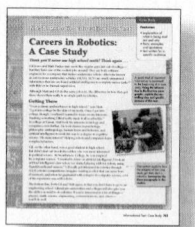

News Article
Team Builds 'Sociable' Robot

Reading
(8) Explain the controlling idea and specific purpose of an expository text and distinguish the most important from the less important details that support the author's purpose.
(9)(A) Summarize text.
Writing
(13)(B) Develop drafts in timed situations that include rhetorical devices used to convey meaning.

Reading Skill: Summarize Text: Controlling Idea and Details

In a well-written expository text, an author's main, or **controlling,** idea is supported by a variety of details. An author chooses the types of details to use according to a **specific purpose** for writing. For example, if an author is writing to describe a scientific discovery, he or she might use technical data and quotes from experts. Some of these details will be more significant than others.

As you read expository texts, it is important to understand the controlling idea and specific purpose of the essay. Then, you can **distinguish the most important from the less important details** that support the author's purpose. In turn, you can use this understanding to help you summarize a text. When you **summarize,** you briefly state the controlling idea and most important details of a text in your own words.

As You Read Use a graphic organizer to explain the controlling idea, specific purpose, and supporting details of the following texts. Mark the most important details with a star to distinguish them from the less important details.

NASA Robotic Education Project

Features:

- explanation of what is being studied and why
- facts, examples, and quotations
- text written for a specific audience

Careers in Robotics: A Case Study

Think you'll never use high school math? Think again . . .

Gil Jones and Matt Zucker may seem like regular guys just out of college—but they have one of the coolest jobs around! They are both software engineers for a company that makes underwater robots, otherwise known as autonomous underwater vehicles (AUVs). AUVs are small, unmanned submarines that use on-board artificial intelligence to complete survey tasks with little or no human supervision.

Although Matt and Gil do the same job now, the difference in how they got there shows there really is no single path to robotics.

Important information is contained in the beginning of a case study. **Using the information in the first two paragraphs, explain the controlling idea and specific purpose of this text.**

Getting There

"I was a classic underachiever in high school," says Matt. "I got into college by the skin of my teeth. Once I got into college, though, I realized I wanted to focus on my interests. Studying something I liked really made it all worthwhile." In college at Vassar, Matt took his interests in biology and computers even further. He took classes in psychology, philosophy, anthropology, human brain and behavior, and artificial intelligence to work his way to a degree in cognitive science. His main interest? Helping robots and computers learn complex behaviors.

Gil, on the other hand, was a good student in high school, but didn't start out in robotics either—he was more interested in political science. At Swarthmore College, he was inspired by computer science. "I wanted to focus on artificial intelligence. I took an artificial intelligence class where we started playing with toy robots, using Handyboards and sensors." Gil really got interested in robotics through AAAI robotics competitions (imagine creating a robot that can serve hors d'oeuvres!), and when he graduated with a degree in computer science, a lot of his experience was with robots.

This section explains how the subjects of this case study got their start in robotics. **Summarize the three paragraphs in this section.**

The bottom line, both Gil and Matt agree, is that you don't have to go to an engineering school. Liberal arts universities and colleges will also give you the skills you need to do robotics. If you're interested in a lot of things—physics, math, science, engineering, communications, and others—you'll do well.

Landing the Job

Both Gil and Matt did summer internships during college that provided them with work experience and an idea of how to get a job in robotics. During one summer, Gil worked for the Naval Research Laboratory doing software artificial intelligence research and then, after graduating, spent the summer preparing for another AAAI competition. When one of his friends got a job at a robotics company, Gil learned about the company and then applied to be a software engineer. Matt got an internship at the same company during the summer between his junior and senior years and was then offered a job following graduation. What's their best advice for getting internships and jobs? Perseverance! "Just find someone who works in robotics and ask them for advice," says Matt. Gil adds, "Sometimes it's difficult to get in, but keep trying. Think about doing an internship for free. Often internships are the first step through the door."

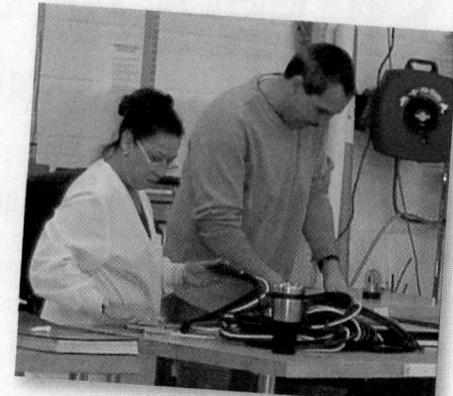

Research, Programming, and . . . Cruising(?)

One of the great things about this job is the variety. Sometimes they spend all day reading up on robotics research, sometimes they spend all day in front of a computer . . . and sometimes they spend all day hanging out on a boat testing the robot in the ocean! "You're making something that has a purpose, something that's part of a bigger project," says Gil. "You get to see if what you did worked. Of course, that means you're entirely responsible." Another perk, according to Matt, is that "you usually get to learn something big and new every few weeks." One warning: Pay attention in high school math classes. "You'll use trigonometry like crazy!"

Next Steps

Both Matt and Gil plan on going back to school sometime to do graduate work. Matt wants to study computer science, focusing on computer graphics and computer-human interfaces. Eventually, he wants to be a professor. Gil plans to go back to school specifically in robotics. He finds underwater robotics exciting because it requires autonomy, but there are a lot of other cool areas of robotics he'd like to explore. The draw for both of them is that robotics is a quickly changing and very open field. As they point out, "You can do new stuff in any of the related areas and that's exciting!"

> The final paragraph of the text often contains important information. **What is the author's purpose here? Identify one of the most important details and one of the least important details presented.**

How does communication change us?

(a) According to this article, what changes are taking place in the way humans must communicate with robots in order to accomplish tasks? **(b)** How might this change affect our world?

Features:

- information on current events
- descriptions, examples, and quotations
- text written for a general or specific audience

TEAM BUILDS 'SOCIABLE' ROBOT

Elizabeth A. Thompson, News Office

February 14, 2001

"Hello, Kismet," said Cynthia Breazeal in a singsong voice. Leaning closer to the object of her attention, she asked, "Are you going to talk to me?"

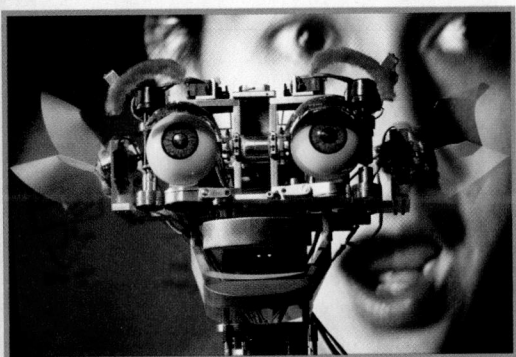

The exchange could be familiar to any parent, but Kismet is not a child. It's a robotic head that can interact with humans in a human-like way via myriad facial expressions, head positions, and tones of voice. "The goal is to build a socially intelligent machine that learns things as we learn them, through social interactions," said Dr. Breazeal, a postdoctoral associate at MIT's Artificial Intelligence Laboratory and leader of the Kismet team.

Building a sociable machine, she believes, is also key to building a smarter machine. Most current robots are programmed to be very good at a specific task—say, navigating a room—but they can't do much more. "Can we build a much more open-ended

> Here, an expert on the article's subject is quoted. **How important do you think this detail is in supporting the author's purpose?**

learning system?" asks Dr. Breazeal.

"I'm building a robot that can leverage off the social structure that people already use to help each other learn. If we can build a robot that can tap into that system, then we might not have to program in every piece of its behavior."

> This article includes complex, technical information. **Summarize complex ideas like the ones in this paragraph to monitor your comprehension.**

INSPIRED BY KIDS

The work, which began in 1997, is heavily inspired by child developmental psychology. "The robot starts off in a rather helpless and primitive condition, and requires the help of a sophisticated and benevolent caretaker to learn and develop," Dr. Breazeal said. Even Kismet's physical features—which include big blue eyes, lips, ears and eyebrows—are patterned after features known to elicit a caregiving response from human adults.

The eyes, in particular, are actually sensors that allow the robot to glean information from its environment, such as whether something is being jiggled next to its face. Kismet can then respond to such stimuli—by moving its head back if an object gets too close, for example—and communicate a number of emotion-like processes (such as happiness, fear and disgust).

A human wears a microphone to talk to the robot, which also has microphones in its ears. The latter will eventually be used for sound localization.

The robot's features, behavior and "emotions" work together so it can "interact with humans in an intuitive, natural way," Dr. Breazeal said. For example, if an object is too close for the robot's cameras to see well, Kismet backs away. "This behavior, by itself, aids the cameras somewhat by increasing the distance between Kismet and the human," Dr. Breazeal said. "But the behavior can have a secondary and greater effect through social amplification. A withdrawal response is a strong social cue for the human to back away."

Kismet, she noted, is the exact opposite of HAL, the menacing robot in the movie *2001: A Space Odyssey*. "HAL is simply a glowing red light with no feedback as to what the machine is thinking. That's why it's so eerie. Kismet, on the other hand, both gives and takes feedback to communicate."

"I think people are often afraid that technology is making us less human. Kismet is a counterpoint to that; it really celebrates our humanity. This is a robot that thrives on social interactions."

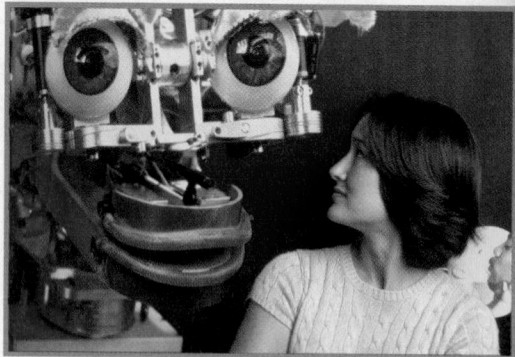

MAKING IT LIFELIKE

To make Kismet as lifelike as possible, Dr. Breazeal and colleagues have not only incorporated findings from developmental psychology, but have also invited the comments of cartoon animators. "How do you make something that's not alive appear lifelike? That's what animators do so well," Dr. Breazeal explained.

The proverbial wizard behind the curtain (or in this case, wall) is a bank of some 15 computers. These process software programs that allow the robot to perceive its environment, analyze what it finds and react.

In experiments over the last year or so, the researchers have been exploring how the robot interacts with people who aren't familiar with it. Are Kismet's actions and emotions understandable? Do people use those actions as feedback to adjust their own

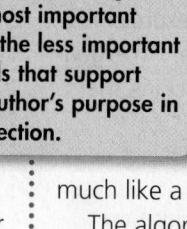

This section discusses making a robot seem lifelike. **Keeping in mind the reason for the article, distinguish the most important from the less important details that support the author's purpose in this section.**

responses? Conversely, is the robot correctly "reading" its visitors?

Results to date are encouraging. For example, many of the people who've met Kismet have told Dr. Breazeal that the robot has a real presence. "It seems to really impact them on an emotional level, to the point where they tell me that when I turn Kismet off, it's really jarring. That's powerful. It means that I've really captured something in this robot that's special. That kind of reaction is also critical to the robot's design and purpose."

Once Kismet's social skills are optimized, "we can move on to other forms of learning," Dr. Breazeal said. In early work to that end, the researchers are teaching Kismet how to use its voice to negotiate the social world. "We want it to be able to get people to do things for it, much like a very young child."

The algorithms that are crucial to this will allow the robot to "learn" by trial and error. When it first attempts a task, it won't be very good. The robot will "remember" its mistakes, however, and make incremental improvements as it goes along. It can then apply what it's learned to completing the same task under different conditions.

How does communication change us?
How does Dr. Breazeal use common forms of communication to build a "smart" machine?

Comparing Informational Texts

(a) Summarize both the case study and the news article. **(b)** Using your summaries as references, explain the controlling ideas and specific purposes of both texts. **(c) Analyze:** Compare and contrast the authors' purposes in the texts.

College Readiness | **Timed Writing**

Write a Persuasive Essay

Format
The prompt directs you to write a persuasive essay. Therefore, be sure your response includes an introduction, body paragraphs with strong supporting details, and a conclusion.

Robert Collier said, "Success is the sum of small efforts, repeated day in and day out." Write a persuasive essay in response to this quote. Support or refute it using the most important details from both texts. Use rhetorical devices, such as repetition and anecdotes, to strengthen your argument and better convey your meaning. (30 minutes)

Academic Vocabulary
When you *support* a statement, you provide evidence to show that it is true. When you *refute* a statement, you prove that it is not true.

5-Minute Planner

Complete these steps before you begin to write:

1. Read the prompt carefully and completely.

2. Determine whether you agree or disagree with the quotation.

3. Review the case study and the news article to find support for your opinion. Distinguish the **most important from the less important details** that support the author's purpose in each text. To provide the strongest support for your argument, use only the most important details in your essay. **TIP Summarizing** short sections of texts can make connections between ideas easier to notice.

4. Plan how you will employ **rhetorical devices** in your essay to strengthen your argument and make it more persuasive. Look for words to stress through repetition, and consider what anecdotes or stories can help you communicate your ideas.

5. Decide the order in which you will present your supporting details. Then, create a brief outline for your essay.

6. Refer to your notes and outline as you draft your persuasive essay.

Comparing Forms of Lyric Poetry

Lyric poetry has a musical quality that expresses the thoughts and feelings of a speaker. It does not tell a complete story, but it does describe an emotion or a mood, often by using vivid imagery. A lyric poem is relatively short and produces a single effect. Poets can use a variety of **lyric forms,** or **structures,** to explore topics and themes, and create different effects.

- A **haiku** is a classical form of literature with roots in the non-English-speaking literary tradition of Japan. Haiku is an unrhymed verse form arranged into three lines of five, seven, and five syllables. The author of a haiku often uses a striking image from nature to convey a strong emotion.

- A **free verse** poem does not follow a regular pattern of rhythm or rhyme. The poet may use sound and rhythmic devices and even rhyme—but not in a regular pattern.

- A **sonnet** is a fourteen-line poem that is usually written in iambic pentameter and often rhymes. Two common sonnet types are the Italian, or Petrarchan, and the English, or Shakespearean, sonnet. This chart shows the structure of a Shakespearean sonnet.

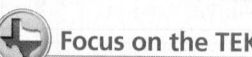

Focus on the TEKS

Reading
(3) Understand the structure of poetry and provide evidence from the text to support understanding.
(5)(D) Demonstrate familiarity with works by authors from non-English-speaking literary traditions with emphasis on classical literature.

Shakespearean Sonnet	
Formatting: usually presented with no spaces between the stanzas, which are unified by their distinct ideas and rhyme schemes	**Three quatrains:** (four-line stanzas) each explores a different aspect of the poem's theme
Final couplet: the two lines at the end of a sonnet, which present a concluding comment	**Rhyme scheme:** the lines in each quatrain follow a regular pattern of *abab cdcd efef gg*

As You Read Consider how the poet's choice of a particular lyric form adds to the poem's meaning. Use the information on this page to help you understand how each poem's structure enhances its message.

TEXAS
PHLitOnline
www.PHLitOnline.com

- Vocabulary flashcards
- Interactive journals
- More about the authors
- Selection audio
- Interactive graphic organizers

How does *communication* change us?

Writing About the Big Question

In few words, the speakers in these poems communicate intense thoughts and feelings. Use this sentence starter to develop your ideas.

A powerful piece of writing can make readers **aware** of _____.

Meet the Authors

Walt Whitman (1819–1892)

Author of "I Hear America Singing" (p. 750)

American poet Walt Whitman celebrated individual freedom. He published his first book of poetry, *Leaves of Grass*, at his own expense. Now, *Leaves of Grass* is known as a very influential volume in American literature.

Bashō and Chiyojo
(1644–1694)   (1703–1775)

Authors of "Three Haiku" (p. 751)

One of the greatest Japanese poets, Bashō raised the haiku from a comic form to a high art. Chiyojo was the wife of a samurai's servant. After her husband died, she became a nun and studied poetry. Both Bashō and Chiyojo are considered classical writers: Their haiku are admired and emulated even centuries after being written.

◄ Bashō

Alice Walker (b. 1944)

Author of "Women" (p. 752)

From the age of eight, Alice Walker kept a journal and wrote poems. Today, Walker is an acclaimed novelist, essayist, and poet. Her novel *The Color Purple* was made into a movie and a play.

William Shakespeare (1564–1616)

Author of "Sonnet 30" (p. 754)

English poet and playwright William Shakespeare is one of the most beloved writers of all time. Experts believe he possessed the largest vocabulary of any writer in history. His many plays are still performed around the world.

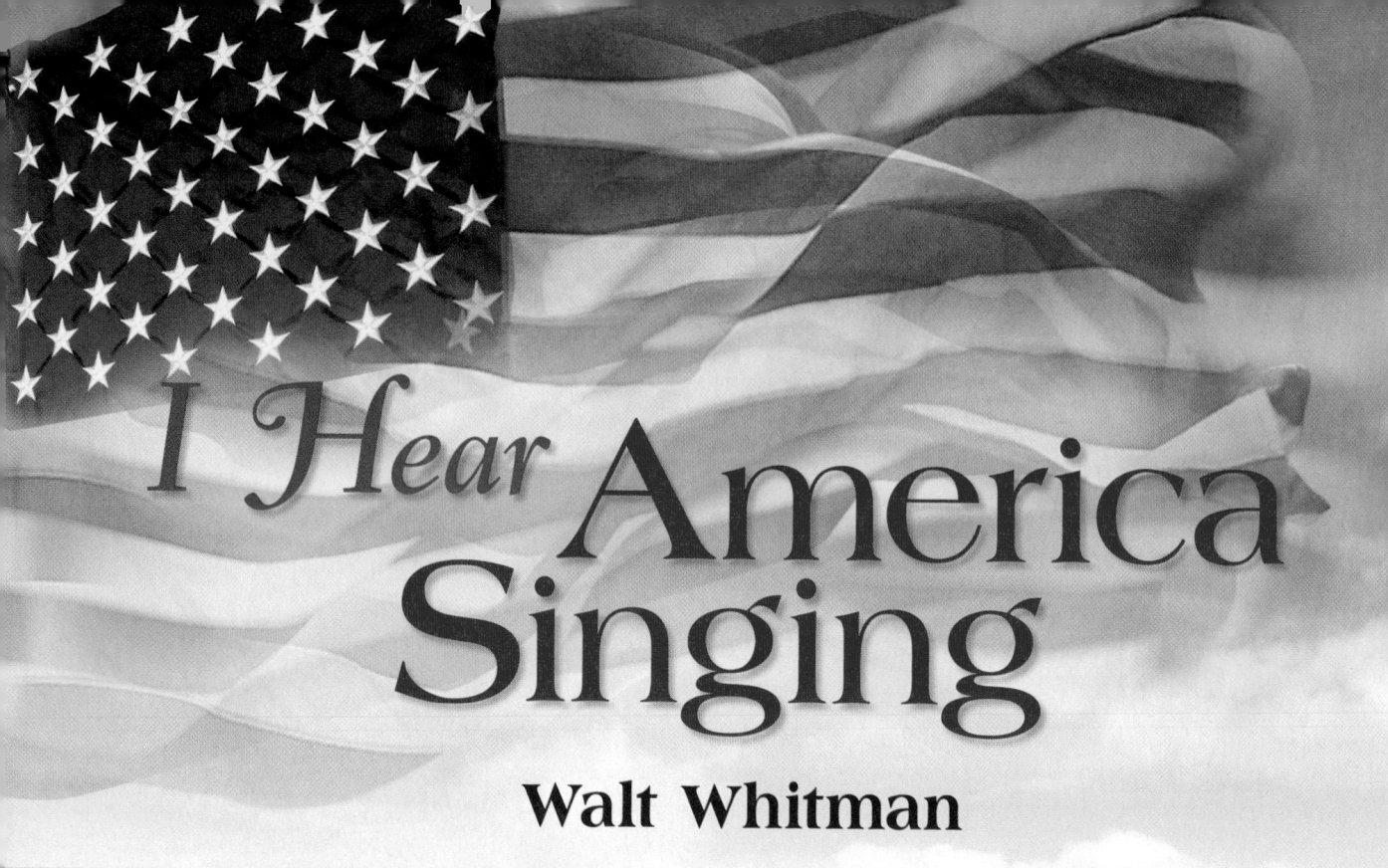

I Hear America Singing

Walt Whitman

Literary Analysis
Lyric Poetry Which word in the opening line helps identify this as a lyric poem?

I hear America singing, the varied carols I hear,
Those of mechanics, each one singing his as it should be blithe and strong,
The carpenter singing his as he measures his plank or beam,
The mason singing his as he makes ready for work, or leaves off work,
5   The boatman singing what belongs to him in his boat, the deckhand singing on the steamboat deck,
The shoemaker singing as he sits on his bench, the hatter singing as he stands,
The wood-cutter's song, the ploughboy's on his way in the morning, or at noon intermission or at sundown,
The delicious singing of the mother, or of the young wife at work, or of the girl sewing or washing,
Each singing what belongs to him or her and to none else,
10   The day what belongs to the day—at night the party of young fellows, robust, friendly,
Singing with open mouths their strong melodious songs.

Vocabulary

intermission (in´ tər mish´ ən) *n.* any kind of break; more specifically, a break during a performance

Three Haiku

translated by Daniel C. Buchanan

Temple bells die out.
The fragrant blossoms remain.
A perfect evening!

—Bashō

Dragonfly catcher,
How far have you gone today
In your wandering?

—Chiyojo

Bearing no flowers,
I am free to toss madly
Like the willow tree.

—Chiyojo

Literary Analysis
Lyric Poetry In the last haiku, what impression does the speaker convey by comparing herself to a willow tree?

Critical Thinking

1. **Respond:** Which of these four poems do you like the best? Why?

2. **(a)** Identify three singers Whitman names. **(b) Interpret:** What does Whitman mean when he says he hears their songs?

3. **Generalize:** How does the language of haiku, works from non-English-speaking literary traditions, differ from the language in poems you have read that are from English-speaking literary traditions?

4. **(a)** In Bashō's haiku, what dies out and what remains?
   (b) Interpret: To which senses does Bashō's haiku appeal?
   (c) Analyze: Why are these senses most appropriate in a poem about evening?

5. **Assess:** Would the first haiku by Chiyojo be as effective if it had been written as a statement rather than as a question? Explain.

Support your responses with evidence from the text.

How does communication change us?
Which of these poems causes you to see something from a different or more intense point of view?

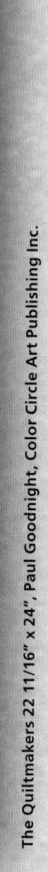

The Quiltmakers 22 11/16" x 24", Paul Goodnight, Color Circle Art Publishing Inc.

Women ALICE WALKER

Background In "Women," the speaker praises African American women who fought for public school desegregation in the American South. Until the 1950s, African American and white students attended different schools in the South. In 1954, the U.S. Supreme Court ruled that segregated public schooling was unconstitutional.

They were women then
My mama's generation
Husky of voice—Stout of
Step
5   With fists as well as
Hands
How they battered down
Doors
And ironed
10 Starched white
Shirts
How they led
Armies
Headragged Generals
15 Across mined
Fields
Booby-trapped
Kitchens
To discover books
20 Desks
A place for us
How they knew what we
Must know
Without knowing a page
25 Of it
Themselves.

Vocabulary
stout (stout) *adj.* sturdy

Literary Analysis
Lyric Poetry What emotion or feeling does the phrase "Headragged Generals" evoke?

◀ **Critical Vewing**
Is the artist's attitude toward these women similar to the one expressed by the poet? **[Compare]**

Critical Thinking

1. **Respond:** What question would you ask the speaker? Why?

2. **(a)** List three images in the poem that convey the women's determination to help their children. **(b) Assess:** Which image did you find the most powerful? Why?

3. **(a)** What do the women want to "discover" and for whom? **(b) Draw Conclusions:** In lines 22–26, why is the women's knowledge so remarkable?

How does communication change us?
(a) What message about education do the women communicate with their actions? Use details to support your answer. **(b)** What impact do you think this message had on their children? Explain your answer.

Support your responses with evidence from the text.

SONNET 30

WILLIAM SHAKESPEARE

Vocabulary

woes (wōz) *n.* great sorrows

wail (wāl)) *n.* lament; cry of deep sorrow

When to the sessions of sweet silent thought
I summon up remembrance of things past,
I sigh the lack of many a thing I sought,
And with old woes new wail my dear times waste:[1]

5 Then can I drown an eye, unused to flow,
For precious friends hid in death's dateless[2] night,
And weep afresh love's long since cancelled woe,
And moan the expense[3] of many a vanished sight:
Then can I grieve at grievances foregone,[4]

10 And heavily from woe to woe tell o'er[5]
The sad account of fore-bemoanèd moan,[6]
Which I new pay as if not paid before.
But if the while I think on thee, dear friend,
All losses are restored and sorrows end.

1. **And . . . waste** and by grieving anew for past sorrows, ruin the precious present.
2. **dateless** endless.
3. **expense** loss.
4. **foregone** past and done with.
5. **tell o'er** count up.
6. **fore-bemoanèd moan** sorrows suffered in the past.

Critical Thinking

1. **Respond:** Would you want the speaker as a friend? Explain.

2. **(a) Make Inferences:** In line 5, what does "drown an eye" mean? **(b) Analyze Cause and Effect:** What causes the speaker to "drown an eye"? Why?

3. **(a) Clarify:** What is the speaker describing in lines 10–12? **(b) Relate:** Why might someone spend time doing this?

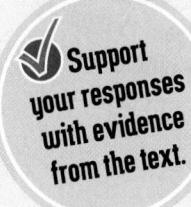

Support your responses with evidence from the text.

How does communication change us?
In what ways could the speaker's words change a person's response to a disappointment or personal loss?

Comparing Forms of Lyric Poetry

1. Both "I Hear America Singing" and "Women" are **free verse,** with a **structure** imposed by the poet. **(a)** Compare the emotions conveyed in these poems. **(b)** Which poem follows more of a pattern? Explain.

2. In his **sonnet,** Shakespeare presents an idea in the first quatrain (four lines), explores the idea in the next two quatrains, and reaches a conclusion in the final couplet. Use a chart like the one shown to analyze the structure of "Sonnet 30."

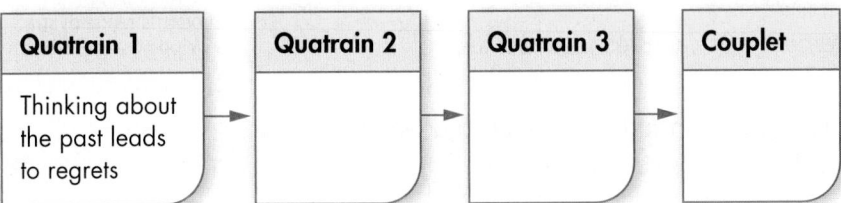

Quatrain 1	Quatrain 2	Quatrain 3	Couplet
Thinking about the past leads to regrets			

3. The three **haiku** are classical poems from the Japanese tradition. Compare and contrast the subjects and structures of these poems with those of the other three poems from English-speaking traditions.

College Readiness |Timed Writing

Write to Compare Forms of Lyric Poetry

In an essay, compare the ways the structure of the different lyric forms affect the meanings of these poems. Choose two poems and structures to discuss. Provide evidence from the texts to support your response. (30 minutes)

🕐 5-Minute Planner

1. Read the prompt carefully and completely.

2. Gather your ideas by jotting down answers to these questions:

- How does the free verse structure of Whitman's and Walker's poems help the strength of each poem's message?

- How does the strict form of the haiku help to capture the feeling of a brief moment in time?

- How would the meaning of "Sonnet 30" be different without the final two lines?

3. Reread the prompt. Then, refer to your notes as you draft your essay.

Expository Text: Interpretative Response

Defining the Form An **interpretative response to literature** gives you an opportunity to explore and explain the effects of a specific work. In doing so, you deepen your understanding of the work and also gain a greater appreciation of literary technique in general. You might use elements of this type of writing in critical reviews and literary analysis.

Assignment Write an interpretative response to a literary text that:

✔ *includes an analysis of the work* that extends beyond a summary and literal analysis

✔ addresses the writing skills for an *analytical essay*

✔ features a *thesis statement* that captures the main idea of your response

✔ *provides evidence from the text,* including using embedded quotations to support the opinions you present

✔ *analyzes the aesthetic effects* of an author's use of stylistic or rhetorical devices

✔ employs error-free grammar, including properly formatted and punctuated quotations

To preview the criteria on which your interpretative response may be judged, see the rubric on page 763.

Writing Workshop: *Work in Progress*

Review the work you did on pages 717 and 739.

WRITE GUY
Jeff Anderson, M.Ed.

What Do You Notice?

Direct Quotations

The following excerpt is from *Nothing to Fear: Lessons in Leadership from FDR* by Alan Axelrod. Read the excerpt several times.

There is no sugarcoating of reality here! The fog has lifted, the scene is sharply etched and downright frightening: "a host of unemployed citizens face the grim problem of existence, and an equally great number toil with little return."

Jot down what you find effective about the use of a quotation in this excerpt. As you work on your interpretative response to literature, think of ways you can best use direct quotations as evidence to support your ideas.

 Focus on the TEKS

Writing
(15)(C)(i);(ii);(iii) Write an interpretative response to a literary text that extends beyond a summary and literal analysis; addresses the writing skills for an analytical essay and provides evidence from the text using embedded quotations; and analyzes the aesthetic effects of an author's use of stylistic or rhetorical devices.

(13)(A) Plan a first draft by determining appropriate topics through a range of strategies and developing a thesis or controlling idea.

Reading-Writing Connection

To get a feel for interpretative responses, read the excerpt from *Nothing to Fear: Lessons in Leadership from FDR* by Alan Axelrod on page 567.

Prewriting/Planning Strategies

Use strategies to determine an appropriate topic. Think of stories, poems, or other works of literature that you found memorable. Then, narrow that list using a "top-ten" strategy—creating a top-ten list of titles and authors. Next to each entry, briefly note your initial reactions to the work. Finally, review your list and notes and choose one work as your topic.

Clarify your purpose. Determine the specific purpose of your essay. For example, you may want to share your enthusiasm for a new writer or analyze the meaning of a short story. Write a statement of purpose for your essay. Use both the title and the author's name in your statement:

> **Example of statement of purpose:** *In this essay, I will analyze the character of General Zaroff in Richard Connell's short story "The Most Dangerous Game."*

Develop your thesis. Your essay should feature a clear thesis statement that you will develop and support throughout your essay. Review your notes to draft a single sentence that combines the statement of purpose you wrote earlier with the ideas and evidence you have accumulated. The sentence should clearly capture the main idea of the response you intend to convey about the work of literature you have chosen as your topic. You will use this thesis statement to direct the writing of your essay.

Find supporting evidence. Return to the work of literature you have selected to find examples, excerpts, and direct quotations that relate to your topic. Prepare a series of notecards, with one card for every idea you want to prove. Write your main point or idea across the top of the card. Underneath, write your notes on the details you gathered from the text to support that point or idea.

By breaking down the details and referring them back to your purpose, you will be able to present complex ideas in a sustained and compelling manner.

Identifying Supporting Evidence

Thesis: What I want to prove:
General Zaroff's civilized exterior conceals a ruthless, heartless murderer.

How I can prove it:
His elegant castle is also a prison.

Explain in detail:
Zaroff makes Rainsford comfortable in the castle in order to make him healthy and, therefore, the hunt more intriguing.

www.PHLitOnline.com

- Author video: Writing Process
- Author video: Rewards of Writing

Drafting Strategies

Extend beyond a summary and literal analysis. As you draft, keep in mind that you should include enough background information so that a reader who may not have read the work you are analyzing will understand your key points. You should provide summaries of key sections of the work. However, an interpretative response must be more than a summary and literal analysis. You should explore your own responses and ideas about the literary work you are analyzing.

Organize your ideas. Use a graphic organizer like this one to structure your ideas in a sustained and persuasive way. Your introduction should include your thesis, and every body paragraph should provide its support.

Focus on the TEKS

Writing
(15)(C)(i);(ii);(iii) Write an interpretative response to a literary text that: extends beyond a summary and literal analysis; provides evidence from the text using embedded quotations; and analyzes the aesthetic effects of an author's use of stylistic or rhetorical devices.

Organize Your Ideas

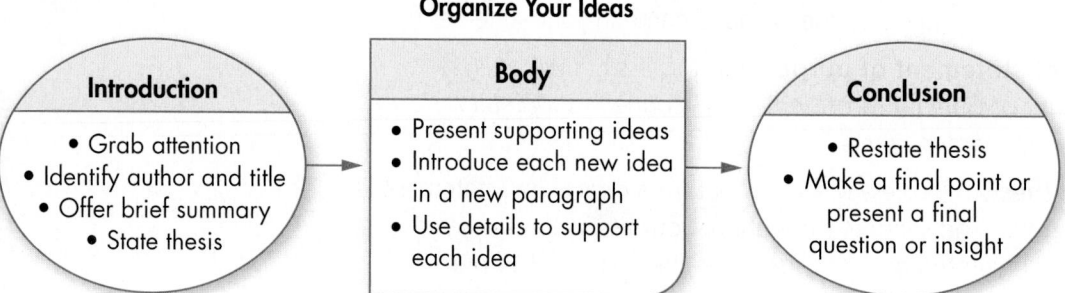

Introduction
- Grab attention
- Identify author and title
- Offer brief summary
- State thesis

Body
- Present supporting ideas
- Introduce each new idea in a new paragraph
- Use details to support each idea

Conclusion
- Restate thesis
- Make a final point or present a final question or insight

Analyze aesthetics. A writer's craft is more than just the words he or she puts on a page. Poets and authors use many tools and techniques to convey their ideas and feelings, and these elements contribute greatly to the effect a work has on a reader. As you draft, consider not only *what* the author said in the literary work, but *how* he or she said it. Analyze the aesthetic—or artistic—effects of an author's use of stylistic or rhetorical devices.

Provide evidence from the text. Include evidence from the literary work to support the opinions you present in your essay.

- **Quotations** can illustrate a character's attitude, a writer's word choice, or an essayist's opinion. Be sure that quotations, including embedded quotations, are exact and enclosed in quotation marks.

- **Examples** of a character's actions or of a specific literary element can enhance your analysis.

- **Paraphrases,** or restatements in your own words, can help you explain a writer's theme, discuss the conflict, analyze a character, or clarify key ideas. Paraphrases must accurately reflect the original text.

Avoid padding your draft with irrelevant passages. Focus on conveying the point of your essay and work to tell readers why you have included each quotation.

Pat Mora

On Responding to Literature

Many of my best teachers are authors I will never meet. In the essay "Unseen Teachers," I explore how authors help me experience the world more intensely. Literature and all forms of art can make us more human.

This passage from the essay was inspired by a quotation from Southwest artist Georgia O'Keeffe saying that she was trying to prompt the viewer to notice. As I tried to show, writers who see their work as part of a group's struggle for justice do the same.

"I love words and their interweavings."
—Pat Mora

from "Unseen Teachers," from *Nepantla*

I still smile at her [Georgia O'Keeffe's] laughing confession that by painting huge flowers, she forced us to notice. . . .

We too seek to force a society to notice the bitter and the sweet. Often we both participate in our communities and are solitary writers, a tension. The mere cover of Denise Levertov's *The Poet in the World* reminds me of her firm conviction: "Both life and poetry fade, wilt, shrink when they are divorced." Lorna Dee Cervantes, Sandra Cisneros, Alice Walker, Lucille Clifton, Amy Tan, Joy Harjo, and Linda Hogan are thick in the struggle of their people, and their writing is part of that struggle. Though the daily realities—high dropout rates, low per capita income, high unemployment—continue, these women teach me that the arrangement and rearrangement of work on the page is neither elitist nor irrelevant. It is the appropriate task of the person who weaves words for people's use.

I love art and often get ideas in museums. Many readers know O'Keeffe's paintings of flowers. Here, they make my thesis colorful and concrete.

I debated what names to include and what realities to list. These authors support the diversity that's a theme for the book.

Braids or weaves I wondered? Both, like writing, are hand activities. I chose *weaves* because weavers create both basic items of clothing and beautiful art pieces.

Revising Strategies

Revise to eliminate unnecessary information. Make your writing precise by reviewing your draft to eliminate extra details. Identify instances in which the information you provide may not support your main idea, and may actually distract from it. Follow these steps to revise your work:

- Underline your thesis and the main ideas of each paragraph.

- Highlight sentences that do not support your thesis.

- Consider revising details to make a tighter connection to your main idea.

- As you develop your draft, be sure you have included **transitions** that connect your ideas and help convey your meaning clearly. If you have trouble adding a transition, consider whether your ideas are truly related.

- Eliminate any paragraphs or details that do not clearly contribute to your analysis.

Revise to address writing skills for an analytical essay. Certain elements are common to all well-written analytical essays, including interpretative responses. Using these elements of good writing will strengthen your essay and enable readers to better understand the ideas and opinions you are trying to communicate.

Use a checklist like this one to be sure you have included all the basic elements required.

Writing Skills for an Analytical Essay

- ❑ Sufficient length
- ❑ Effective introductory and concluding paragraphs
- ❑ A variety of sentence structures
- ❑ Rhetorical devices
- ❑ Transitions between paragraphs
- ❑ A controlling idea or thesis
- ❑ An organizing structure appropriate to purpose, audience, and context
- ❑ Relevant information and valid inferences

Teacher Feedback

Ask your teacher to review your final draft, paying special attention to how well you have addressed the writing skills for an analytical essay. Review and consider any suggestions or guidance you receive, and revise your final draft in response to this feedback from your teacher.

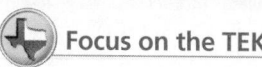

Focus on the TEKS

Writing

(13)(B) Develop drafts in open-ended situations that include transitions used to convey meaning.

(15)(C)(ii) Write an interpretative response to a literary text that addresses the writing skills for an analytical essay and provides evidence from the text using embedded quotations.

(13)(E) Revise final draft in response to feedback from teacher.

Using Quotations

One of the strongest pieces of evidence you can use when supporting an idea about a literary text is a quotation from that text. **Direct quotations** are passages from a work of literature taken word for word. **Indirect quotations** are paraphrases of the words from literature.

Punctuating Direct Quotations All direct quotations that are included in the running text, or **embedded,** must be enclosed in quotation marks. A direct quotation is usually preceded by a comma and sometimes by a colon. It is followed by its page number enclosed in parentheses. The period or comma from the quotation follows the page number.

Example of direct embedded quotation:

Rainsford is horrified when he realizes the truth of his situation: "The Cossack was the cat; he was the mouse" (232).

When you quote a passage from the text that runs more than four lines, set it off from the text by indenting it ten spaces. In this case, do not use quotation marks. This type of quotation is often preceded by a colon. Also, the end punctuation comes before the page-number citation.

Example of block indented quotation:

As Rainsford awaits Zaroff's discovery of him, he breathes a sigh of relief when Zaroff leaves. Then the horror of the situation hits him:

> *Rainsford did not want to believe what his reason told him was true, but the truth was as evident as the sun that had by now pushed through the morning mists. The general was playing with him! The general was saving him for another day's sport! (231)*

Zaroff's true character becomes apparent to Rainsford in this moment.

Punctuating Indirect Quotations Because indirect quotations are paraphrases of the text, you do not need to put them in quotation marks.

Example of indirect embedded quotation:

When Rainsford realizes that Zaroff is playing a game of cat and mouse, he is horrified. (232)

Grammar in Your Writing

Scan your essay for direct quotations—embedded and block indented—that you have used as evidence. Make sure you have accurately quoted the original text and used proper punctuation. Revise if necessary.

> **PH GRAMMAR HANDBOOK**
>
> Further instruction and practice are available in the *Prentice Hall Grammar Handbook*.

Student Model: Jeff Rutherford, Broken Arrow, OK

 Focus on the TEKS

Writing
(13)(D) Edit drafts for grammar, mechanics, and spelling.
(13)(E) Publish written work for appropriate audiences.
Conventions
(19) Spell correctly, including using various resources to check correct spellings.

Characterization of General Zaroff

What lies at the heart of a refined man? In Richard Connell's short story "The Most Dangerous Game," the deranged, yet cunning and elegant, General Zaroff shares his taste for hunting with an unsuspecting visitor. Although he is civilized in his dress and habits, Zaroff's beliefs reveal a murderous mind behind the illusion of a charming, charismatic man.

When we first encounter General Zaroff, our initial reaction is one of delight and admiration for his wealth and charm. Zaroff lives in a massive castle, feasts on the finest delicacies, and wears expensive clothes. His luxurious surroundings and lifestyle reflect a highly civilized, eloquent, and proper gentleman. As readers soon learn, however, there is more to Zaroff than food and elegance.

Beneath Zaroff's fine qualities lies an overwhelming attitude of arrogance. This attitude comes from his firm belief that his way of thinking is superior to that of the average person. Zaroff also fancies himself a phenomenal hunter: "My hand was made for the trigger," he claims (223). It is this deadly mixture of arrogance, superior hunting skills, and belief that it is natural for the strong to prevail over the weak that makes him disregard the value of human life.

Zaroff's extreme beliefs lead him to conclude that only the intelligent mind of a human being can provide him with the dangerous game he desires. Rationalizing that "the weak of the world were put here to give the strong pleasure," he chooses to hunt humans instead of animals (225). Unfortunately, Rainsford steps into this situation. The major conflicts in "The Most Dangerous Game" demonstrate what happens during such an inhumane hunt.

However, the general's arrogance and disregard for human life blind him to the fear and desperation of his prey. His attitude leads to his own demise at the hands of Rainsford, his prey. The characterization of Zaroff as a murderer hiding behind a mask of civility shows that beneath even the most beautiful rose can lie a sharp and deadly thorn.

The title indicates that the essay will focus on a single character.

Jeff uses strong language to state his thesis clearly.

Embedded quotations provide evidence for this understanding of Zaroff.

Jeff's essay extends beyond a summary and literal analysis of the work.

Editing and Proofreading

Edit your draft for errors in grammar and mechanics—the use of punctuation. Use various resources to check correct spellings.

Correcting Common Usage Problems: *Among* implies three or more elements, whereas *between* is usually used with only two elements. *Like, as, as if,* and *as though* are not interchangeable. *Like* is a preposition meaning "similar to" or "such as." It should not be used in place of *as, as if,* or *as though,* which are conjunctions that introduce clauses.

Publishing and Presenting

Consider ways to publish your written work for appropriate audiences:

Participate in a panel review. Work with a team of your classmates to read and review each other's written work. Then, discuss the most effective techniques in each paper.

Publish a collection of interpretative responses. Organize several of your classmates' essays into a collection for posting online or displaying in the school library.

Reflecting on Your Writing

Writer's Journal Jot down your answer to this question:

How did writing about the work help you to understand it?

Rubric for Self-Assessment

Find evidence in your writing to address each category. Then, use the rating scale to grade your work.

Spiral Review

Earlier in this unit, you learned about **appositive phrases** (p. 716) and **infinitives** (p. 738). Make sure you have used these parts of speech properly in your interpretative response.

Written Composition Criteria	Rating Scale *not very* *very*
Focus and Coherence: How relevant is the evidence provided from the original text to the opinions presented?	1 2 3 4
Organization: How well are the writing skills for an analytical essay, including an appropriate organizing structure, addressed?	1 2 3 4
Development of Ideas: How far beyond a summary and literal analysis does the analysis of the work extend?	1 2 3 4
Conventions: How error free is your grammar, especially the formats and punctuation of quotations?	1 2 3 4
Voice: How well are rhetorical devices and transitions between paragraphs used?	1 2 3 4

Applying the Big Question

How does *communication* change us?

Think About It

Think about what you have read in this unit, and what you have learned about communication in your other classes and from your own experience. Copy and complete the chart below to apply what you have learned about communication. One row has been completed for you.

Example	The subject	What happens	The writer's response	How my ideas changed
From Literature	Making decisions in "The Road Not Taken"	The speaker makes a decision about a small matter.	The decision may change his life forever.	I realize that small decisions may affect my entire life.
From Literature				
From Science				
From Social Studies				
From Your Life				

Talk About It

Choose one of the examples from your communication chart to develop for a **discussion** about the Big Question. Begin by preparing notecards about the example you have chosen. If the example is from something you have read, include images, figures of speech, quotations, and other details that helped you understand the writer's feelings and experiences. If the example is from your own experience, cite details, examples, and facts and tell how they affected you. Then, talk about your examples with a small team of classmates. **Participate productively** in the team by **building on the ideas of others** and **contributing relevant information** to the discussion.

Write About It

At the beginning of Unit 4, you wrote a response to the Big Question. Now that you have completed the unit, write a new response, discussing how your initial ideas have either been changed or reinforced. You may use this sentence starter to begin your response.

❑ Communication changes us by _____.

Support your answer with one or more examples from your chart.

Challenge What issues does the Big Question still raise for you? How could you continue your exploration?

 Focus on the TEKS

Listening and Speaking
(26) Participate productively in teams, building on the ideas of others, contributing relevant information, and setting ground rules for decision-making.

★ Connecting to Citizenship

Group Discussion With a small team, discuss how communication can help you to be a thoughtful and active citizen. Then, share key points from your discussion with the class. Consider these questions in your discussion:

- What forms of communication might affect citizens in a community?
- How might communication change a citizen in a positive way?
- How might communication change a citizen in a negative way?
- Is honest communication an important part of thoughtful, active citizenship? Explain your response.

At the conclusion of your discussion about communication, talk with your team about **setting ground rules for decision-making.** Agree on a way to choose main points from your discussion. Then, use this method to select three key ideas to share with the class. Elect a member of your group to represent your team in presenting those ideas. Be sure to listen politely and attentively as other teams share their ideas.

Big Question Vocabulary

Use some of these words as you complete the activities on these pages.

aware
communication
comprehension
discuss
empathy
exchange
illuminate
informed
interpretation
meaning
react
relationship
resolution
respond
understanding

This list includes academic vocabulary words, which are defined on pp. R1–R14.

Connotation and Denotation

The **denotation** of a word is its direct, dictionary meaning. A word's **connotations** include the ideas, images, and feelings that are associated with the word. Consider the words *fragrance, smell,* and *stench.* These words are **synonyms,** which means they share a similar denotation—having a scent or odor. However, their connotations are very different.

The connotation of *smell* is about the same as its denotation. It has a neutral connotation and can be defined as "the quality that you recognize by using your nose." The connotation of *fragrance* is positive, suggesting a pleasant, sweet smell or scent. *Stench* has negative connotations, suggesting a foul, unpleasant odor. The following graphic shows the positive, neutral, and negative connotations of some synonyms.

Sometimes a word does not carry a particular connotation, but an author may still intend for the reader to attach a connotation to that word. In these cases, you need to analyze the **textual context**—the sentence or larger section of text—in which the word appears in order to distinguish between its denotative and connotative meanings.

Focus on the TEKS

Reading
(1)(B) Analyze textual context (within a sentence and in larger sections of text) to distinguish between the denotative and connotative meanings of words.

(1)(E) Use a dictionary to determine the meanings of words and phrases, including their connotations and denotations.

Positive →	Neutral →	Negative
modest	shy	mousy
inquisitive	curious	nosy
home	house	shack

Practice A Analyze the textual context of each italicized word. Then, distinguish between the denotative and connotative meaning of each word by stating the two meanings and explaining the difference. Finally, identify if the connotation is positive, negative, or neutral.

1. "Can we finish this *astronomical* amount of cleaning?" Danny said with concern.

2. "Is that *odor* coming from your omelet?" my uncle asked as he pinched his nose.

3. The crowd *roared* with laughter at the comedian's final joke.

4. The inventor's *novel* idea impressed her audience.

Practice B Analyze the textual context of each italicized word. Then, distinguish between the denotative and connotative meaning of each word by writing the two meanings and explaining the difference. Finally, use a dictionary to confirm the meanings of the words, including their connotations and denotations.

> When your days seem *overcast* and bad days feel *infinite,* try your best to keep a positive attitude. It may seem impossible to stay *buoyant* in tough times. If you make an effort to look on the bright side, though, even the most *lackluster* week can get a little better. Soon, you may find your *disposition* has truly changed and you can easily find one aspect of every day to *cherish.*

Activity Working with a partner, prepare three notecards, each with the headings shown on the card below. Then, with one team member working with List 1, and the other working with List 2, use a dictionary to determine the denotations of each word on your list. On each of your cards, write a word and its denotation. Then, write a sentence in which context clues can be used to determine the word's connotation. When you have completed your three cards, exchange cards with your partner. Analyze the textual context of each of your partner's words to distinguish the connotative meaning from the denotative meaning. Write down your conclusions. Then, discuss the sentences with your partner.

List 1	List 2
startled	proud
tricky	notorious
confident	shrewd

Word:

Denotation:

Sentence:

www.PHLitOnline.com

- Illustrated vocabulary words
- Interactive vocabulary games
- Vocabulary flashcards

Teamwork

With a small team, review "The Day of the Storm" on pages 682–684. Find the following terms on page 683, and write down their denotations: *hard-headed, flooded, howl, drifted,* and *rest.* Then, analyze textual context (within sentences and larger sections of text) to distinguish between the denotative and connotative meanings of the words. Next, as a team, classify each term's connotation as positive, negative, or neutral. Finally, work as a team to use a dictionary to confirm the meanings of the words and phrases, including their connotations and denotations.

Comparing Media Coverage

Both visual images and non-visual texts present events and communicate information. Comparing and contrasting how the media uses images and text to communicate will help you to develop your media literacy skills.

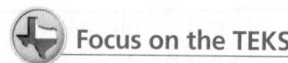

Focus on the TEKS

Reading
(12)(A) Compare and contrast how events are presented and information is communicated by visual images (e.g., graphic art, illustrations, news photographs) versus non-visual texts.

Learn the Skills

Analyze and then compare and contrast the ways in which events and information are conveyed in various types of media.

Compare and Contrast How Events Are Presented News events can be described with words or with images, or both. As you look at media coverage, compare and contrast the way in which text and/or images such as graphics, illustrations, and photographs bring events to life for readers.

- *When examining non-visual texts, ask:* In what order are the events described? What event, if any, is identified as most important or critical? What words or phrases indicate the importance of the event?

- *When viewing visual images, ask:* What event does the image capture? Why was this particular image chosen? What point of view does the image reveal?

Compare and Contrast How Information Is Communicated Once you have analyzed the presentation of events, compare and contrast the ways in which the information is communicated. Ask:

- In what ways is the information in the text and the visual similar and different?

- Which treatment, the text or visual, gives more detailed information?

- Which treatment, the text or visual, has more impact? Why?

Twin Pandas Reach Critical Milestone

Veterinarians at the Beijing Zoo have announced that twin pandas born in September are now expected to survive. Their mother, Yong Yong, was unable to nurse them from birth. The zoo staff quickly intervened, but the future of the young pandas was uncertain. Now that the pandas have survived their first seven weeks, veterinarians are optimistic that the pandas will survive.

When asked how long the pandas will require care

▲ **1.** This article describes an event. Compare and contrast how this article and the photograph present the event.

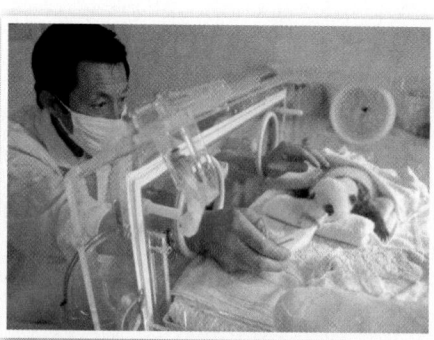

▲ **2.** This photograph shows a scene that is part of the event the text describes. Compare and contrast how the photograph and the text communicate information.

TEXAS
PHLitOnline
www.PHLitOnline.com

Apply the skills you have
learned in this workshop as
you watch the videos on
www.PHLitOnline.com.

ACTIVITY: Compare and Contrast Text and Visuals

With a partner, examine the encyclopedia entry below. Take notes
on ways in which the visual and the text present events and
communicate information. In your notes, point out similarities
and differences between the text and the visual. Then write and
present a summary of your findings to your class.

Practice the Skills

Use what you've learned and the discussion guide to complete
the activity.

San Francisco Earthquake

Damage from the San Francisco Earthquake

The San Francisco earthquake of 1906 had its epicenter near San
Francisco, but the effects of the quake reached from southern Oregon
to Los Angeles. Those who experienced the quake described it as
about a minute of forceful shaking and powerful shocks.

The conditions of the earthquake challenged the views of contemporary scientists and resulted in extensive studies by scientists of the
time. The insights that resulted from their research are the basis for

Use a **discussion guide** like this to compare and contrast how events
are presented and information is communicated in visual images and
non-visual texts.

1. **Compare:** What event is depicted both in the visual and in the text?

2. **Contrast:** What aspect of the event does the text describe that the
   visual does not? What aspect of the event does the visual bring to life
   that the text does not?

3. **Compare and contrast:** What overall information, or main idea,
   is communicated by the visual alone? What overall information is
   communicated by the text alone?

4. **Evaluate:** Would the encyclopedia entry be as effective if it contained
   text only? Why or why not?

Discuss your responses with a partner. Then, write a brief paragraph to
summarize the similarities and differences you observed and to make
generalizations about the kinds of information that are best conveyed
with visuals and the kinds of information that seem better suited to text.

Cumulative Review
Reading

Read this selection. Then answer the questions that follow it.

 TEKS Spiral Review

Reading
(3) Analyze the effects of diction and imagery (e.g., understatement, overstatement, irony, paradox) in poetry.
(7) Explain the role of paradox in literary works.
Comprehension
RC-9(A) Reflect on understanding to monitor comprehension (e.g., creating sensory images).

Mushrooms
by Sylvia Plath

1   Overnight, very
    Whitely, discreetly,
    Very quietly

2   Our toes, our noses
    Take hold on the loam,
    Acquire the air.

3   Nobody sees us,
    Stops us, betrays us;
    The small grains make room.

4   Soft fists insist on
    Heaving the needles,
    The leafy bedding,

5   Even the paving.
    Our hammers, our rams,
    Earless and eyeless,

6   Perfectly voiceless,
      Widen the crannies,
      Shoulder through holes. We

7   Diet on water,
      On crumbs of shadow,
      Bland-mannered, asking

8   Little or nothing.
      So many of us!
      So many of us!

9   We are shelves, we are
      Tables, we are meek,
      We are edible,

10   Nudgers and shovers
      In spite of ourselves.
      Our kind multiplies:

11   We shall by morning
      Inherit the earth.
      Our foot's in the door.

GO ON ▶

1 In "Mushrooms," the poet uses personification to portray —

  A growth from mushrooms' point of view
  B reactions to fast-growing mushrooms
  C people who are moving around by night
  D the environment in which mushrooms grow

2 Stanza 2 of the poem mainly helps the reader picture the speaker —

  F testing unfamiliar soil
  G collecting natural resources
  H inhaling fragrant night air
  J coming up from underneath the ground

3 The image of "Soft fists . . . Heaving the needles" suggests the mushrooms are —

  A being harvested by people
  B battling against one another
  C soft hands carefully avoiding sharp metal objects
  D growing through pine needles on the forest floor

4 In stanza 7, the statement that the mushrooms eat "crumbs of shadow" is an —

  F objective observation about their typical diet
  G understatement that shows they are undemanding
  H overstatement that shows their aggressiveness
  J interesting fact to grab the reader's attention

5 Read these lines from stanzas 9 and 10.

> . . . we are meek,
> We are edible.
>
> Nudgers and shovers
> In spite of ourselves.

With this paradox, the poet suggests that mushrooms are —

  A loud and pushy
  B not rude
  C quietly pushing ahead
  D too shy to move forward

6 The last line of the poem recalls which description of mushrooms given earlier in the poem?

  F multiplying
  G dieting on water
  H asking little or nothing
  J shouldering through holes

DIRECTIONS

Answer the following question on a separate sheet of paper.

7 How does the poet use imagery in the poem to suggest that the mushrooms are secretive? Use textual evidence to support your answer.

Revising and Editing

DIRECTIONS

Read the following passage and mark your answers on your answer document. Remember that you are NOT permitted to use dictionaries or other reference material on this section of the text.

Writing
(13)(C) Revise drafts to improve sentence variety.
(13)(D) Edit drafts for grammar, mechanics, and spelling.

Josh is writing a paper about his experience learning a new sport. He would like you to read his paper and think about the corrections and improvements he should make. When you finish reading, answer the questions that follow.

Kayaking the Rapids

(1) My parents first took me canoeing when I was six years old. (2) I was too small to paddle, so I sat in the middle of the canoe just staring, amazed, at the clear, flowing water of the river. (3) After that, I wanted to go canoeing all the time. (4) Then, when I was older, I learned about the rapids upriver that could only be explored kayak. (5) From the moment I heard about those rapids, I knew I wanted to learn whitewater kayaking.

(6) A month later, I joined a class that would certify me. (7) Then I would negotiate the rapids safely. (8) We started on a Friday evening with paddling drills at a kayak training facility on the San Marcos River. (9) The instructor had set up several gates in the flowing river, and our task was to take our individual kayaks through each gate. (10) I'd thought canoeing had taught me all I needed to know about paddling, but the technique for kayaking was very different! (11) Eventually, though, I managed to make my way through all the gates.

(12) The next morning, we met at the San Marcos River headwaters for a drill in river rescue. (13) We learned how to "roll" back up if our kayaks flipped over as well as how to safely rescue someone who had fallen into the water. (14) After a few hours of practice, we were all soaking wet, but we could roll and maneuver with confidence.

(15) On Sunday the final day of the class we had a chance to test the skills we had learned. (16) We all went kayaking on the Comal River in New Braunfels. (17) Guiding my kayak through the swirling, splashing rapids was the highlight of my weekend. (18) When we finally returned to the training center to be gave our certification, all I could think was that I could not wait to get back out there in the rapids.

GO ON

1 Which preposition, if any, should be added in sentence 4?

   A Add **until** before *older*

   B Add **outside** after *upriver*

   C Add **by** before *kayak*

   D Make no change

2 What change, if any, should be made to sentence 15?

   F Add commas after *Sunday* and *class*

   G Change *final* to **Final**

   H Change *the skills we had learned* to *we had learnt skills*

   J Make no change

3 What change should be made to sentence 18?

   A Change *returned* to **return**

   B Insert a comma after *returned*

   C Change *gave* to **given**

   D Change *could not* to **can't**

4 Which is the best way to combine sentences 6 and 7?

   F A month later, I joined a class that would certify me, I would negotiate the rapids safely.

   G A month later, I joined a class that would certify me to negotiate the rapids safely.

   H A month later, I joined a class that would certify me and negotiate the rapids safely.

   J A month later, I joined a class that would certify me for negotiate the rapids safely.

Written Composition

Use blank pages to prewrite. Then write your composition on one or two lined pages.

TEKS Spiral Review

Writing
(14) Write literary texts to express ideas and feelings about real people, events, and ideas.

> Write a composition about an accomplishment that made you proud.

REMEMBER—YOU SHOULD

❏ write about the assigned topic

❏ make your writing thoughtful and interesting

❏ make sure that each sentence you write contributes to your composition as a whole

❏ make sure that your ideas are clear and easy for the reader to follow

❏ write about your ideas in depth so that the reader is able to develop a good understanding of what you are saying

❏ proofread your writing to correct errors in spelling, capitalization, punctuation, grammar, and sentence structure

How does *communication* change us?

Focus on the TEKS

Reading
(12)(B) Analyze how messages in media are conveyed through visual and sound techniques (e.g., editing, reaction shots, sequencing).

Media Literacy

Editing is the act of altering video and sound recordings. Media editors use **visual and sound techniques** to communicate with audiences and to appeal to, or change, an audience's emotional response.

- A **reaction shot,** or a quick close-up of someone responding to something, might be included to gain an audience's sympathy.
- A specific image **sequence,** or order, may suggest that a character has grown.

This chart will help you analyze editing as you view the Big Question videos, or as you view any video clip.

TEXAS
PHLitOnline
www.PHLitOnline.com

Viewing and Listening Guide

Editing technique	What it is	What you should think about
Reaction shot	quick close-up to reveal a reaction	• What examples of this technique do you notice? • What do you think the media editor wants to communicate in these instances?
Sequencing	chosen order of images and sounds	• Would you expect the use of this technique to change or influence the audience's thoughts or feelings? Why or why not?

Independent Reading

Trouble the Water: 250 Years of African American Poetry
Jerry W. Ward, Editor
Penguin Putnam, 1997
This volume spans many aspects of the African American experience.

Poems by Robert Frost: A Boy's Will and North of Boston
Robert Frost
Signet, 1990
This collection of poems captures the human spirit with an authentic New England voice.

Reflections on a Gift of Watermelon Pickle
Scott Foresman Anthology
Scott Foresman, 1995
Voices from a variety of backgrounds and cultures blend in this collection of modern poetry.

The Canterbury Tales
Geoffrey Chaucer
Penguin Classics, 2003
A storytelling competition among a diverse group of pilgrims sets the stage for tales of humor, romance, and fantasy.

THE BIG ?

Do our *differences* define us?

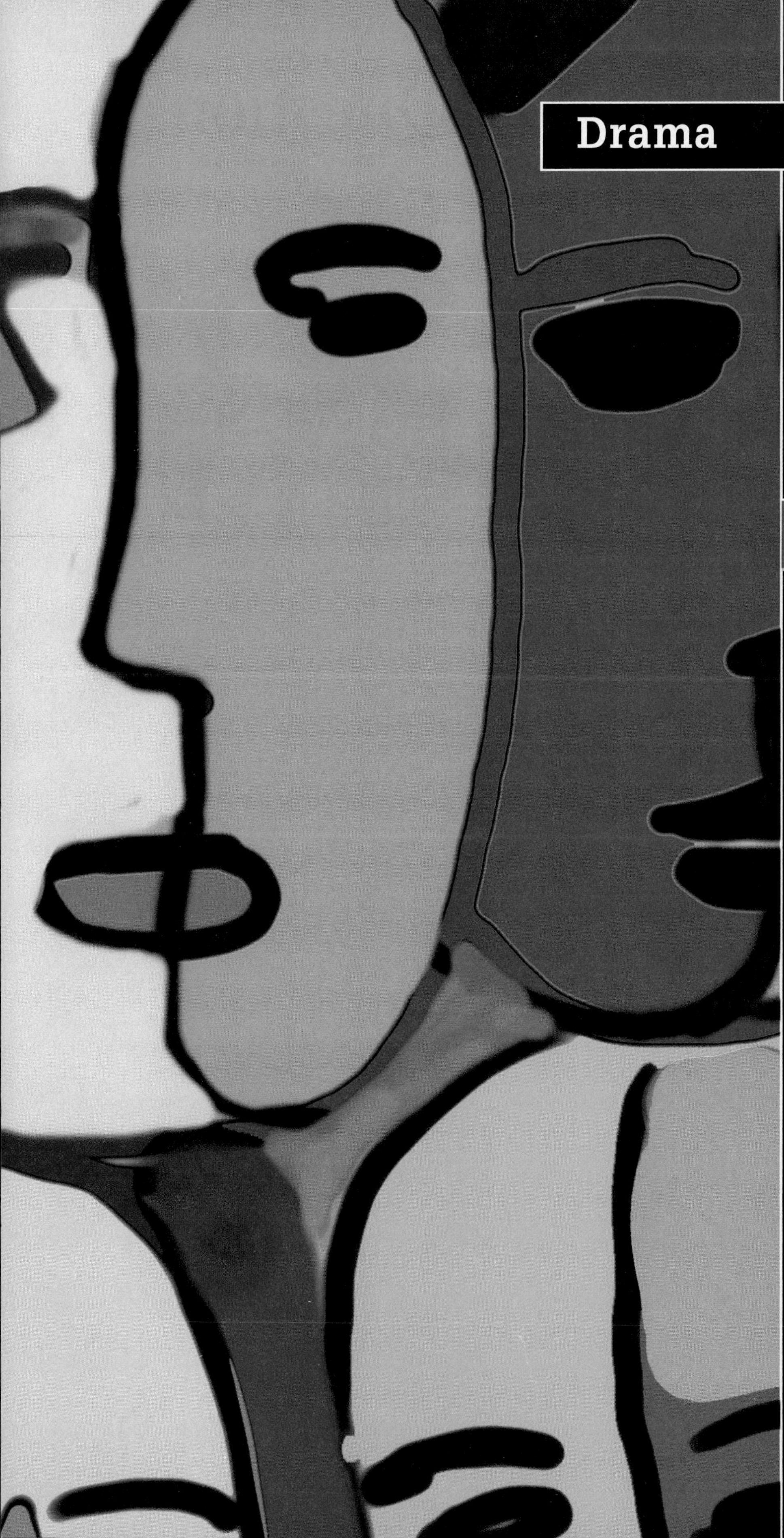

Drama

www.PHLitOnline.com

Hear It!
- Selection summary audio
- Selection audio
- Big Question Tunes

See It!
- Penguin author video
- Big Question video
- Get Connected videos
- Background videos
- More about the authors
- Illustrated vocabulary words
- Vocabulary flashcards

Do It!
- Interactive journals
- Interactive graphic organizers
- Grammar tutorials
- Interactive vocabulary games
- Test practice

Introducing the Big Question

 Do our *differences* define us?

We are all different. The **differences** may be obvious, like the color of our hair, how tall we are, and the accent that marks our speech. Other differences are more subtle and may be noticed only when we get to know others. These differences might show up in our **values** and in the mannerisms and traditions that stem from our **culture.** The differences, large and small, make each of us **unique.** They may also put us at odds with each other and even result in conflicts. Do they define who we are?

Start thinking about the Big Question by listing examples of ways in which people may differ.

Tell What You Know

List differences that you have observed or read about among people. Describe one specific example of each of these **differences.**

- Physical appearance
- **Culture** or family traditions
- Personal style, such as the way people dress and talk
- **Values** and opinions
- Ability to **accept** others
- Interests, sports, or hobbies

Share your list with a small team. Discuss whether the **differences** you each listed help to define the people around you. Participate productively in the team by

- listening respectfully as others speak
- **building on the ideas of others**
- **contributing relevant information**

TEXAS PHLitOnline
www.PHLitOnline.com

- Big Question video
- Illustrated vocabulary words
- Interactive vocabulary games
- Big Question Tunes

Explain What You Know

Use the ideas and examples you discussed with your partner to help you complete these sentences about differences.

- The biggest differences among people are _____.
- Differences in culture affect how people respond to one another because _____.
- When people have strong but different values or opinions, it is _____.
- Our personal style reveals _____ but it also _____.

Share your responses with a partner.

Write What You Think

Based on your discussions, decide what you think right now. Your answer may change as you read the selections in this unit. Choose one of these responses to the Big Question or write one of your own.

- ❏ Differences define who we are.
- ❏ Differences do not define who we are.

Connecting to the Literature

Each reading in this unit will give you insight into the Big Question. At the end of the unit, you will have an opportunity to see how your ideas have changed.

Connecting to Citizenship

Texas Profiles: Hector Garcia

Doctor and Activist Hector Garcia studied medicine at the University of Texas Medical School, which accepted only one Mexican American student a year. In addition to practicing medicine, Garcia devoted his life to helping Mexican Americans gain rights. As a war veteran, he was also active in veteran affairs, including organizing the American G.I. Forum in 1948. The forum, dedicated to improving veteran benefits, is still active today.

Do our differences define us?

- Did Garcia allow differences to define him? Explain.
- What can you learn from Garcia's story that can help you become a thoughtful, active citizen?

Focus on the TEKS

Listening and Speaking
(26) Participate productively in teams, building on the ideas of others and contributing relevant information.

Big Question Vocabulary

Use some of these words as you complete the activities on these pages.

background
differentiate
similarity
understanding
accept
discriminate
individuality
unique
conformity
values
determine
differences
culture
defend
assimilated

This list includes academic vocabulary words, which are defined on pp. R1–R14.

Do our *differences* define us?

Like many other literary forms, drama explores our differences.

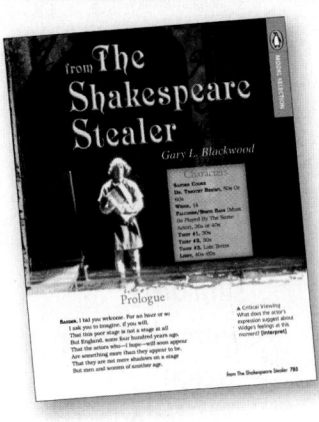

PHLitOnline

www.PHLitOnline.com

- Penguin author video
- Interactive journals
- Interactive graphic organizers
- Selection audio
- Self-test

What Is Drama?
by Gary L. Blackwood

I consider myself, in all modesty, fairly successful as a playwright. Yet, even in a good year, only about ten percent of the money I make comes from productions of my plays; the other ninety percent is from my novels and nonfiction books.

So why, you may ask—as my wife often does—do I bother writing **drama** at all? Why not just devote all my time and effort to books?

When the House Lights Go Down

The short answer is, "Because I love the theater." During high school and college, and for several years afterward, I was mainly interested in **acting.** But when my first play was produced, I discovered that performing in someone else's play wasn't nearly as much fun as watching other people perform my play. (Actually, I ended up acting in my own play when the lead got sick, but that's another story.)

It's a great feeling, of course, to see a new book in print for the first time or to get a glowing review or an enthusiastic fan letter. But it doesn't compare to the feeling you get when the house lights go down and the stage lights come up and **actors** start saying **dialogue** that you created and the **audience** responds with laughter or, better yet, with rapt silence.

Drama: **Actual People Doing Actual Things**

I experience that same sort of excitement even when the drama or comedy I'm watching isn't mine. As indispensable as books and movies are, the theater offers something they don't: No matter how skimpy the set is, no matter how much the dialogue differs from everyday speech, you still get the sensation that what's taking place onstage is real. And it is. It's not just images projected on a screen or letters printed on a page. It's actual people doing actual things and actually speaking, with no quotation marks, no description, no exposition, no soundtrack.

Never the Same

Because it's live, not printed or recorded, you can never see the same play twice. Each **performance** is different. And a large part of what makes it different is the audience. Our reaction to the play actually contributes to it, influences it.

Another reason I love the theater is that it tends to challenge its audience more than books and movies do. I think most playwrights—including Israel Horovitz, who is quoted here—are less interested in offering an escape from real life than they are in reflecting real life and commenting on it.

After you experience any work of art, you have that moment of asking yourself, "From this I've learned . . . what?". . . That's the bottom line question, and I believe that artists have a responsibility to address that—of course, not giving an answer, but at least giving an audience comfort with the realization that we're all wrestling with the same questions.

from an interview in *The Dramatist*
—Israel Horovitz

Meet
Gary L. Blackwood (b. 1945)

Author of *The Shakespeare Stealer*

Before Gary L. Blackwood adapted his popular novel *The Shakespeare Stealer* for the stage, he had written some notable plays: *Dark Horse,* a prizewinning courtroom drama, and *The Count of One,* a drama about the use of hypnotism. One of his books of historical fiction, *The Year of the Hangman,* is set in colonial America. *Beyond the Door,* one of his science-fiction and fantasy novels, deals with an alternate world beyond a door in the library.

Did You Know?
Blackwood sold his first story when he was nineteen.

Exploring Drama

Elements of Drama

A drama, or play, is a story written to be performed by actors. It features **characters** facing a **conflict,** or struggle, that propels the sequence of events called the **plot.** The conflict reaches a **climax,** the point of greatest tension, and is then resolved. The **dialogue,** or speeches of the characters, tells the story, unlike in fiction, where the voice of a narrator tells the story.

These elements are specific to drama:

- **Acts** and **scenes** are the basic structures of drama. A drama may consist of one or more acts, each of which may contain any number of scenes.
- The author of a play, called the **playwright,** provides the **script,** or text, of a play. The script contains both dialogue and stage directions.
- **Stage directions** tell how the work is to be performed, or staged. Providing details about sets, lighting, sound effects, props, costumes, and acting, stage directions are often printed in italics and set off in brackets. Some playwrights use abbreviations to provide additional direction about where on or offstage a speech may be delivered. These include *O.S.* for offstage; *D.S.* for downstage, or closer to the audience; and *U.S.* for upstage, or farther from the audience.

Drama coach.

IN THE BLEACHERS © 1999 Steve Moore. Reprinted with permission of UNIVERSAL PRESS SYNDICATE. All rights reserved.

- **Sets** are the constructions that set the scene for the drama. They may represent the historical period of the play or they may simply create a mood with scenic elements and lighting. A set may include elements such as painted backdrops, wooden frames, and trap doors.
- **Props** are movable objects, like swords, that actors use onstage.

All the elements of drama combine in performance to produce the vivid illusion of reality known as **dramatic effect.** Through this effect, the dramatist explores a **theme,** or insight into life.

Types of Drama and Dramatic Conventions

 **Focus on the TEKS**

Reading
(4) Explain how dramatic conventions enhance dramatic text.

Throughout the history of drama, playwrights have used certain dramatic **conventions,** or methods, to enhance their texts, which can usually be categorized by type. The ancient Greeks, who developed drama, created two types of plays:

- A **tragedy** shows the downfall or death of the **tragic hero,** or main character. In ancient Greek drama, the hero was an outstanding person brought low by a **tragic flaw,** a mistaken action or defect in character. In modern tragedy, the hero can be an ordinary person destroyed by an evil force in society. Greek tragedy included a **chorus,** a group of performers who commented on the action. William Shakespeare sometimes used a single actor in the role of the chorus. **Dramatic irony,** when the audience knows something that a certain character onstage does not, is another convention of tragedy.

- A **comedy** has a happy ending, usually after an amusing series of predicaments. While tragedy emphasizes human greatness, comedy stresses the weaknesses of ordinary people or of society itself. In some cases, the comedy of a scene relies on irony.

Dialogue in a play helps to develop characters and further the plot. In addition to dialogue involving conversations between two or more characters, dramatists use these types of **dramatic speech:**

- A **monologue** is a long, uninterrupted speech delivered by a character to other characters who are onstage but remain silent.
- A **soliloquy** is a speech in which a character who is usually alone on-stage reveals private thoughts that the audience is allowed to overhear.
- An **aside** is a brief remark in which a character expresses private thoughts to the audience rather than to other characters.

TEKS Check

Recall or revisit a dramatic text you have read or seen performed. Use the graphic organizer below to explain how dramatic conventions (e.g., mono-logues, soliloquies, dramatic irony) enhance the text.

Dramatic Convention	Example from Drama	Enhances the Text by…

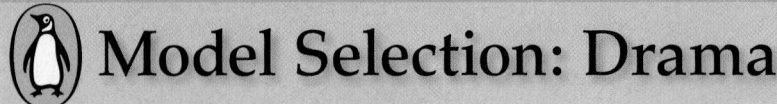
Model Selection: Drama

Gary L. Blackwood Introduces
The Shakespeare Stealer

Adapting my young-adult novel *The Shakespeare Stealer* for the stage was a whole new experience for me. I'd written plenty of original plays, and even turned novels by other authors into plays, but I'd never tried to dramatize one of my own books.

From the Page to the Stage

It's not an easy thing to do. When you're the author of the book, your tendency is to try to put as much of it as possible into the play. My first draft was over two hours long and had roughly twenty **characters.** The problem was, the theater that initially produced it wanted a one-hour play that could be performed by nine actors.

So I set to work cutting cherished **scenes** (including the sword battle with the thieves, which appears in the first **act** of the play), giving the boot to beloved characters, and doubling—having each actor play several roles. I kept on cutting right up until opening night.

No Horses or Rivers on the Set!

The second theater to produce it wanted a full-length play. Back went most of the deleted scenes, plus some new ones. Naturally, even in a longer version, I couldn't keep everything from the novel. I couldn't very well have the actors on horseback, for example, or practically drowning in the Thames River, as they do in the book.

To simplify matters and make the play move quickly, I kept the number of scene changes to a minimum and let a single **set**—called a unit set— represent several different locations.

Historical Context: Creating Another Time

Despite all this, the play is very demanding technically. The **historical context** is just as important as it is in the book. In the book, however, I could get away with an occasional brief description of the clothing, the Globe Theatre, the sword-fighting moves, etc. On the stage, all that has to actually be re-created from brief **stage directions** included in the **script.** So the actors have to cope with early seventeenth-century costumes and **props,** learn Elizabethan sword-fighting techniques, and approximate London and Yorkshire accents.

from The Shakespeare Stealer

Gary L. Blackwood

Characters

SANDER COOKE
DR. TIMOTHY BRIGHT, 50s
or 60s
WIDGE, 14
FALCONER/SIMON BASS
(Must Be Played By The
Same Actor), 30s or 40s
THIEF #1, 30s
THIEF #2, 30s
THIEF #3, Late Teens
LIBBY, 40s–60s

Prologue

SANDER. I BID YOU WELCOME. FOR AN HOUR OR SO
    I ask you to imagine, if you will,
    That this poor stage is not a stage at all
    But England, some four hundred years ago.
    That the actors who—I hope—will soon appear
    Are something more than they appear to be,
    That they are not mere shadows on a stage
    But men and women of another age.

▲ **Critical Viewing**
What does the actor's
expression suggest
about his character's
feelings at this
moment? **[Interpret]**

Act I

At the rear of the playing area is a shallow, two-story set with a narrow flight of steps leading to the upper story. In the center of the upper story is a single wide doorway draped with a curtain. The lower story has two smaller openings, one at Left and one at Right, also covered by curtains. At various times, this set will represent DR. TIMOTHY BRIGHT'S *apothecary, with* WIDGE'S *living quarters upstairs;* SIMON BASS'S *house; and the backstage area at the Globe Theatre.*

At Lights Up, it is DR. BRIGHT'S *apothecary in Berwick-in-Elmet, Yorkshire, c. 1601. A table at Center contains glass and earthenware jars and beakers. One of the containers bubbles over a pot filled with burning pitch.* WIDGE *sits on a stool at the table, copying something from a small bound notebook onto loose sheets of paper, using a plumbago pencil—a stick of graphite wrapped in paper, similar to a grease pencil or charcoal pencil.* WIDGE *is a slight boy of fourteen with a "pudding basin," or bowl, haircut. He wears a working-class tunic.*

All is quiet and peaceful for a long moment. Then the audience is startled by the entrance of DR. TIMOTHY BRIGHT, *a florid, overweight man in his forties or fifties, who is slightly deaf. He strides on brandishing a walking stick, and roaring—but he is nearly as comical as he is menacing.*

BRIGHT. You! . . . clod-pated drivel! (WIDGE *reacts, knocking a beaker to the floor, where it shatters, enraging* BRIGHT *even more*) You . . . halfwitted hoddypeak! Do you know what you've done?!

WIDGE. (*Puts the table between himself and* BRIGHT) I—I didn't mean to! I'll clean it up at once!

BRIGHT. Not *that*, you simpleton! This! (*He waves a paper about*) It's from the bishop's secretary. I've been accused of stealing sermons from my fellow rectors! How in heaven's name did the bishop get wind of this? Have you let a hint drop to anyone of what you were up to? Anyone at all?

WIDGE. Nay, I never! So help me God and halidom!

BRIGHT. Has anyone shown any signs of suspecting you?

WIDGE. Nay, no one.

BRIGHT. You're lying. No, don't bother to deny it. I've the proof here. The rector at Leeds caught you red-handed. Isn't that so? Isn't that so?

WIDGE. (*murmurs*) Aye.

BRIGHT. What's that? Speak up, boy!

Drama
Stage Directions
Blackwood's detailed descriptions of the set and props reinforce the time setting of the play.

▶ **Critical Viewing**
How does the costume of the actor playing Dr. Bright suggest a man who is "nearly as comical as he is menacing"? **[Connect]**

WIDGE. Aye! It was a fortnight ago. 'A spotted me scribbling away, and afore I could make me escape, 'a collared me and snatched away me table-book!

BRIGHT. Why did you not tell me this sooner?

WIDGE. I was afeared. I kenned you'd be angry.

BRIGHT. You were right. But . . . if he took away your transcription of his sermon, then . . . then whose sermon was it that I . . . (*he doesn't want to say "stole"*) . . . used as my model last Sunday?

WIDGE. Well . . . I—I wrote it all out as best I could remember . . .

BRIGHT. *You?* I delivered a sermon composed by my idle-headed apprentice? You deceitful little whelp! When will you learn not to lie to me? Well, by St. Pintle, I'll teach you right from wrong! Come here! (WIDGE *dodges the man's grasp, circling the table, but then he slips on the contents of the broken beaker, and is caught.* BRIGHT *raises the stick as if to strike;* WIDGE *cowers and flinches. But then* BRIGHT *tosses him aside and, puffing with the exertion, plops down on the stool*) Ahh, what's the use of it? If I haven't beaten some sense into you by now, I never will. (*shakes his head*) When I think of all I've done for you, all the years I've invested in you. When I took you in five years ago—

WIDGE. Seven.

Gary L. Blackwood
Author's Insight
"Unless you use a narrator, everything in a play has to be conveyed through dialogue. In the book, the information in this scene is revealed through exposition, an explanation of background material."

Reading Check

What has Dr. Bright been accused of stealing?

Vocabulary
feckless (fek´ lis) *adj.*
careless; irresponsible

Drama
Dramatic Effect The
author's instruction to
actors about how to
react to specific events
or dialogue adds to the
play's illusion of reality.

Drama
Staging A detailed
description of Falconer
provides valuable
information for both
costumers and actors
when staging the play.

Vocabulary
spectral (spek´ trəl) *adj.*
like a phantom or ghost

BRIGHT. Eh? What's that?

WIDGE. It's been seven years, sir.

BRIGHT. That's beside the point. When I took you in, you were a feckless illiterate orphan with no prospects whatever in the world. I taught you to read and cipher, taught you about medicine, even taught you my system of swift writing, and this is what I get in return? (*waves the paper*) If someone were to offer it, I'd sell your services for a farthing; it's far more than you're worth. Yes, and I expect you'd jump at the chance to change masters, wouldn't you? Eh? (*The way* WIDGE *hangs his head makes it clear that he would*) Well, all I can say is, be careful what you wish for, boy. There are far worse places than this, believe me, and far worse masters than me.

WIDGE. (*aside*) Aye, the Devil, for one.

BRIGHT. What's that?

WIDGE. Nothing. (*He sets about cleaning up the broken beaker, while* BRIGHT *checks his boiling potion. The silence is broken by the sound of an iron door knocker pounding O.S. Right*)

BRIGHT. Yes, yes, coming. Bloody patients. Why can't they be sick in the daytime? (*He crosses to Left, reaches O.S. to open a door, then backs up as* FALCONER *enters, a tall figure in a hooded cloak, looking as grim as Death. Beneath the cloak he carries a rapier. We seldom see his face, but when he does reveal a glimpse of it, we see that he has a bushy, dark beard and a hooked nose. A nasty scar disfigures one side of his face*) G-good evening, sir. How may I serve you?

FALCONER. (*seems to reach for his rapier, but instead takes a leather-bound book from beneath his cloak. In a deep, almost spectral voice*) This is yours, is it not?

BRIGHT. (*moves hesitantly closer to the man*) Why, yes. Yes, it is. It's a copy of my book on charactery.

FALCONER. Does it work?

BRIGHT. I beg your pardon?

FALCONER. Your system of charactery. Does it work?

BRIGHT. Of course it works. Using my system of swift writing, one may without effort transcribe the written or the spoken word—

FALCONER. How long does it take?

Culture Connection

Shorthand and Speedwriting

Dr. Timothy Bright was a real person who developed a "swift-writing" system in 1588. Efforts to create a fast way of recording speech go back more than 2,000 years.

- In 63 B.C., Marcus Tiro invented a system of abbreviations to transcribe speeches. His ampersand (&) is still used today.
- 19th century writer Charles Dickens used Gurney's system, developed in 1707.
- Both the Pitman and Gregg systems, invented during the 1800s, are still in use.

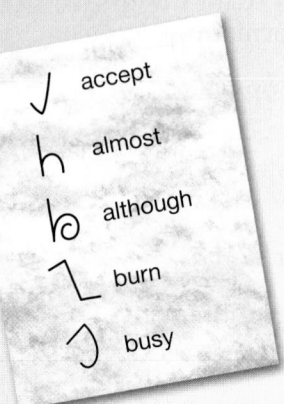
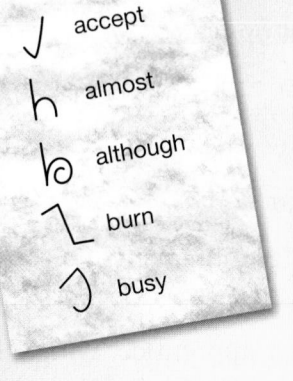
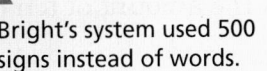

accept

almost

although

burn

busy

▲ Bright's system used 500 signs instead of words.

▲ Court reporters today use stenograph machines to record testimony at the speed of speech.

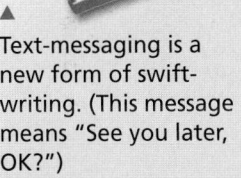

▲ Text-messaging is a new form of swift-writing. (This message means "See you later, OK?")

Connect to the Literature

In an age when books were scarce, why might Widge's swift-writing skills be highly valued?

BRIGHT. As I was about to say, one may set down speech as rapidly as it is spoken—

FALCONER. (*impatient*) Yes, yes, but how long to learn it?

BRIGHT. Well, that depends upon the aptitude of the—

FALCONER. How *long*?

BRIGHT. (*nervously, stretching the truth*) Oh, two months, perhaps three. Well, let's say four. Five, at the outside.

FALCONER. (*tosses the book rather contemptuously onto the table*) To how many have you taught this system of yours?

BRIGHT. Let me see . . . There's my apprentice, here, and then . . .

FALCONER. How many?

BRIGHT. Well . . . one, actually.

FALCONER. And how proficient is he?

BRIGHT. Oh, quite proficient. Extremely. (WIDGE *is surprised to hear this*)

Gary L. Blackwood
Author's Insight
"Since dialogue comes more easily to me than narrative and description, there are long passages of it in my novels. Scenes like this one are taken almost directly from the book."

Reading Check

What kind of system has Dr. Bright invented?

FALCONER. Show me.

BRIGHT. (*to* WIDGE) Are you deaf, boy? The gentleman wishes a demonstration of your skill.

WIDGE. (*picks up notebook and pencil*) What must I write?

FALCONER. Write this: "I hereby convey to the bearer of this paper the services of my former apprentice—"

WIDGE. Go on. I've kept up wi' you.

FALCONER. Your name.

WIDGE. Pardon?

FALCONER. What is your *name*?

BRIGHT. Widge. It's Widge. (*laughs as if to show that he realizes how odd it sounds*)

FALCONER. "—my former apprentice, Widge, in consideration of which I have accepted the amount of ten pounds sterling."

BRIGHT. (*staggered*) Ten p—?!

WIDGE. Is that all, then?

FALCONER. Let me see it. (WIDGE *hands him the notebook. Skeptical*) You've copied down every word?

WIDGE. Aye.

FALCONER. Read it back.

WIDGE. (*takes notebook*) "I hereby convey to the bearer of this paper the services of my former apprentice, Widge, in consideration—" (*the meaning of the words finally sinks in*) Do you—does this mean—?

FALCONER. Copy it out, now, in a normal hand.

BRIGHT. (*when* WIDGE *hesitates*) Go on. Do as he says! (*While* WIDGE *copies it out,* FALCONER *takes out a purse and counts out ten sovereigns onto the table, with* BRIGHT *watching greedily*)

FALCONER. If there's anything you want to take along, you'd best fetch it now, boy. I'll be outside. (*to* BRIGHT) Where can I water my horse?

BRIGHT. On the north side of the house, there's a trough. (*to* WIDGE) Go on, lad. (*through the following* WIDGE *goes upstairs, collects his meager belongings, including a leather wallet on a strap. To* FALCONER) I hope you'll keep a close eye on the boy. (*The concern*

this implies is belied by BRIGHT'S *next line*) He can be sluggish if you don't stir him from time to time with a stick. (FALCONER *exits*) Move your bones, boy, before he changes his mind. (WIDGE *descends the stairs reluctantly*)

WIDGE. Must I go with him, then?

BRIGHT. (*busy fondling the sovereigns*) Eh? Of course you must. He's paid for you, and far more handsomely than I would have dreamed.

WIDGE. Will you not bid me farewell, at least, sir?

BRIGHT. (*perfunctorily*) Of course, of course. Fair 'chieve you, boy, fair 'chieve you.

Transition

(FALCONER *enters at Down Right, looking about warily, trailed by* WIDGE, *who is rubbing his backside*)

WIDGE. Gog's blood, I'm glad to be off that horse.

FALCONER. It won't be for long. Here. (*Hands* WIDGE *a journey cake, nibbles at one himself, still looking about alertly. They pass a flask of something back and forth*)

WIDGE. When will we be at our destination?

FALCONER. When we get there.

WIDGE. These woods are much more . . . wild than around Berwick, and more dense. It feels almost as though they're closing in on us. (*shivers*)

FALCONER. Stop your wagging tongue. You'll have every cutpurse within a league down upon us.

WIDGE. Cutpurse? (*looks about even more fearfully*) You mean . . . there are thieves in these woods? (*realizes he's still talking*) Sorry.

(*Horse whinnies O.S. Right.* FALCONER *reacts, abruptly puts away the flask and loosens his rapier in its sheath, looking about and listening intently.* THREE THIEVES *enter at Left, one armed with a pistol, two with swords*)

THIEF #1. Don't move, if you value your life.

FALCONER. (*unexpectedly amiable*) God rest you, gentlemen.

THIEF #1. God, is it? Don't tell me you're a parson.

FALCONER. No, no. Far from it.

Drama
Stage Directions
By simply indicating "Transition," Blackwood lets the director devise the best way to show a change of scene.

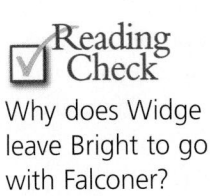
Reading Check
Why does Widge leave Bright to go with Falconer?

Vocabulary
parsimonious
(pär´ sə mō´ nē əs)
adj. miserly; stingy

Gary L. Blackwood
Author's Insight
"Shakespeare was very fond of puns—humorous plays on words that sound alike—so I made liberal use of them, too. Since they depend on words sounding alike, they work even better in a play than in a book."

Drama
Dialogue Falconer's awful pun on the word *told* restores a humorous tone to the scene after a violent struggle.

▶ **Critical Viewing**
Based on this photograph of Widge with Libby, do you think his new life will be better than his old one? **[Predict]**

THIEF #1. Good. I don't like doing business with parsons. They're too parsimonious. (*Laughs*) All right, let's have it, then.

FALCONER. Have what?

THIEF #1. (*Laughs again*) Have what, 'a says! Have what? Why, have a pot of ale wi' us, of course. (*More soberly*) Come now, enough pleasantries. Let's have your purse, man.

FALCONER. (*Pulls out his hefty purse. Still amiable*) Ah. Forgive me for not taking your meaning.

THIEF #1. Oh, aye, an you forgive *me* for taking your purse.

(FALCONER *steps to the man, who holds out a hand for the purse. Instead of handing it over,* FALCONER *swings it swiftly upward, catching thief #1 alongside the head. The man cries out, crumples to the ground; his pistol goes off wildly. The other thieves spring forward.* FALCONER *draws his rapier, parries an ineffectual blow, kicks the man in the groin.* WIDGE *picks up a rock, but has no chance to use it.* FALCONER *grasps the third man's blade in his cloak-wrapped hand, yanks it away, and slices the man's ribs with his own sword. With the thieves lying about groaning,* FAL-CONER *lifts his purse with the point of his sword, flips it in the air, catches it, then shakes a single coin from it and throws it at the men's feet*)

FALCONER. If this is a toll road, you might simply have *tolled* me.

THIEF #1. (*laughs, then groans in pain*) Would that you had been a parson after all.

FALCONER. (*to* WIDGE) Come. (*starts Off Right*)

WIDGE. What you did back there—I've never seen the like of it.

FALCONER. Yes, well, you haven't seen much, have you?

Transition

(*A bed has been brought on upstairs, and a writing desk and two chairs downstairs.* FALCONER *and* WIDGE *enter at Right.* WIDGE *is walking stiffly, wincing*)

WIDGE. Are we in London, then?

FALCONER. (*scoffing*) Hardly. This is Leicester.

(LIBBY, *a sympathetic, plain woman in a maid's garb, emerges from one of the downstairs doorways*)

LIBBY. Welcome back, sir.

FALCONER. The boy will be staying the night. Show him to the garret. (*Exits upstage*)

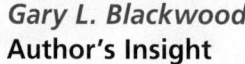

LIBBY. Yes, sir. (*looking* WIDGE *over*) Where you from, then?

WIDGE. Berwick-in-Elmet.

LIBBY. Where's *that*?

WIDGE. Up Yorkshire way. Near Leeds.

LIBBY. I see. Well, come. We'd best get you to your room. (*Leads him up the steps*) I'll bring you some food up in a bit. Here you are. It's not much.

WIDGE. More than I'm used to. Mind you, it could be a pit of snakes for all I care, I'm that exhausted. (*sinks down on the bed*) You didn't seem surprised at all, that 'a came back wi' *me* in tow.

LIBBY. Nothing the master does surprises me. Have a good rest.

Transition

(WIDGE *wakes up, rubs eyes, looks around at the unfamiliar surroundings then hobbles downstairs.* LIBBY *is at the bottom of the steps*)

LIBBY. I was just coming to wake you. The master said to bring you to him as soon as you were up. I don't think he expected you to sleep so late. (*They cross to where* SIMON BASS *sits at the writing desk. He is played by the same actor who plays* FALCONER, *minus the hooded cloak, the curly black wig, the hooked nose, the swarthy skin, the beard, the scar, and the high boots that make him several inches taller.* BASS *is much more approachable and genial,*

MODEL SELECTION

Gary L. Blackwood
Author's Insight
"It's hard to change costume and makeup this quickly. To give the actor enough time, I created a conversation between Widge and Libby."

Reading Check

Where does Falconer bring Widge?

but a prickliness lurks beneath the surface)

WIDGE. Will 'a be cross wi' me, do you wis?

LIBBY. I can't say. He's a queer one, the master is. (*sotto voce*) Not to tell him I said so, now. (*Leaning into desk area*) I've brought the boy, sir.

BASS. (*without turning; we still assume it's* FALCONER *sitting there*) Come in, Widge. (WIDGE *enters the "room," clearly awed by the furnishings*) Sit down.

WIDGE. Eh? Oh. (*sits*) Sorry. It's just that I've never seen such a grand room, with so many books, not even at Squire Cheyney's.

BASS. Wait until you see the houses in London. (*He turns, rises. We and* WIDGE *get our first good look at him.* WIDGE *is obviously bewildered*)

WIDGE. Who—who are you?

BASS. My name is Simon Bass. I'm your new master.

WIDGE. But—but I thought—

BASS. You thought the one who brought you here was to be your master.

WIDGE. Aye.

BASS. (*shrugs*) Falconer is not the most communicative of men, I warrant, nor the most genial. But he is reliable and effective. I could not go to Yorkshire myself . . . for various reasons. He got you here safe and sound, it appears.

WIDGE. (*squirming on his sore rear end*) Well, *safe*, at any rate.

BASS. Let's get down to business. You'll want to know what's expected of you.

WIDGE. Aye.

BASS. Very well. The first thing I expect is for you to say "yes," rather than *"aye."* I'd just as soon you did not sound like a complete **rustic**. Understood?

WIDGE. Aye—I mean, yes.

BASS. Excellent. Now, when you go to London—

WIDGE. London?

BASS. Yes. It's a large city to the south.

◄ **Critical Viewing** Which details in this photograph show that Bass, at left, is more sophisticated than Widge? **[Compare and Contrast]**

Drama
Dialogue Here and throughout the play, Blackwood uses words like *aye* to reinforce the setting in time and place.

Vocabulary
rustic (rus´ tik) *n.* unsophisticated person

Reading Check
Why does Bass want Widge to say "yes" instead of "aye"?

from The Shakespeare Stealer **795**

WIDGE. I ken that, but—

BASS. Let me finish, then ask questions. You will be attending a play called *The Tragedy of Hamlet, Prince of Denmark.* You will copy down the play, every word of it, in Dr. Bright's charactery, and then you will deliver it to me. (WIDGE *looks uncomfortable*) Do you have some objection to that?

WIDGE. Nay, not especially. It's only words, after all. It's just that— Well, when a wight back home caught me copying his sermons, 'a got very upset wi' me.

BASS. Then you'll have to make certain you don't get caught, won't you? You will use a small tablebook, easily concealed . . . (*rummages through his desk*) You see how easily it's concealed? Even I can't find it. Ah, here it is. (*hands it to* WIDGE) Keep it in your wallet. You have a plumbago pencil?

WIDGE. Ay—Yes. An I might ask—for what purpose am I to do this?

BASS. Does it matter?

WIDGE. Nay; I was only curious. The only plays I've ever seen are the ones the church does at Easter and Yuletide, and those certainly didn't seem worth stealing.

BASS. (*being prickly now*) I would prefer it if you did not use that term. I am not a thief. I am a man of business, and one of my more profitable ventures is a company of players. They are not so successful as the Lord Chamberlain's Men or the Admiral's Men, of course, but they draw a sizable audience here in the Midlands. If we could stage a current work, by a well-known poet, we could double our profits. Now, sooner or later someone will pry this *Tragedy of Hamlet* from the grasp of its author, Mr. Shakespeare, just as they have his earlier plays. I would like that someone to be me. If I wait for others to do it, they will do a botched job, cobbled together from various sources, none of them very reliable. Mr. Shakespeare deserves better. He is a poet of quality, perhaps of genius, and if his work is to be borrowed, it should be done properly. That is your mission. If you fulfill it satisfactorily, the reward will be considerable.

WIDGE. And . . . what an I do not?

BASS. Falconer will make certain that you do.

WIDGE. Oh. I didn't ken that 'a would go wi' me.

BASS. Did you suppose I would send you off to London on your own? I might as well send you to Guiana. Go and rest now, or soak your haunches, or whatever you will. You'll be leaving for London early in the morning. (*He exits.* WIDGE *shuffles downstage as* LIBBY *enters at Left*)

Drama

Conflict With this speech, Blackwood lays out the central elements of his plot. Readers can link the title of the play with Bass's information to predict how the play will develop.

After You Read

Critical Thinking

1. **Respond:** Do you think Bass's assignment to Widge is unethical or wrong? Why or why not?

2. **(a)** What special skill has Widge been taught by Dr. Bright? **(b) Summarize:** What happened when the rector at Leeds caught Widge transcribing a sermon? **(c) Make Inferences:** What does this episode show about Widge's talent as a writer?

3. **(a) Make Inferences:** How did Falconer learn about Dr. Bright's swift-writing system? Explain.

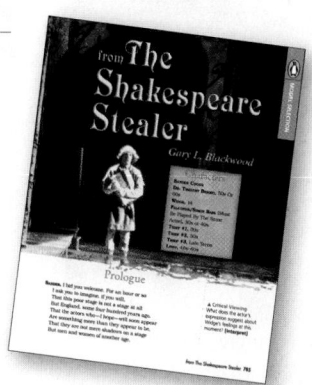

4. **(a)** How does Bass plan to profit from Widge's skill? **(b) Take a Position:** Do you see any similarities between Bass's plan and modern-day practices involving music or movies? Explain.

Do our differences define us?
(a) What skill does Widge have that other servants do not?
(b) Why might someone argue that this difference defines him? **(c)** What details in the selection could refute, or disprove, this argument?

Drama Review

1. **(a)** Note three details in the **stage directions** that establish the setting of the **drama** in Shakespearean England. **(b)** Note three examples of **dialogue** that reinforce that setting.

2. **(a)** Use a chart like the one shown to explore how characters use **props** to reveal their personalities. **(b)** In the first column, list props that are used by Dr. Bright, Widge, and Falconer. In the second column, record how the characters use each prop. In the third column, describe what their actions show about their personalities.

Prop	How It Is Used	What It Shows

Research the Author

Gary Blackwood has written several books that continue Widge's adventures. Write the **foreword,** or introductory material, to a collection of these works. Write to interest your peers in reading these works.

- Use the Internet and your library to locate Blackwood works that feature Widge and Shakespeare. Gather information about the plots.

- Write your foreword and share it with the class.

ROMEO *and* JULIET

Of all the love stories ever written, that of Romeo and Juliet is one of the most famous. To many people, Shakespeare's tragic lovers represent the essence of romantic love. When Shakespeare wrote *The Tragedy of Romeo and Juliet,* he was a young man, and the play is about young love.

▲ Hollywood's modern-day adaptation of *The Tragedy of Romeo and Juliet.*

The Theater in Shakespeare's Day

The Tragedy of Romeo and Juliet, like most of Shakespeare's plays, was produced in a public theater. Public theaters were built around roofless courtyards without artificial light. Performances, therefore, were given only during daylight hours. Surrounding the courtyard were three levels of galleries with benches on which wealthier playgoers sat. Less wealthy spectators, called groundlings, stood and watched a play from the courtyard, which was called the pit.

Most of Shakespeare's plays were performed in the Globe theater. No one is certain exactly what the Globe looked like, though Shakespeare tells us it was round or octagonal. We know that it was open to the sky and held between 2,500 and 3,000 people. Scholars disagree about its actual dimensions and size. The discovery of its foundation in 1990 was exciting because the eventual excavation would reveal clues about the plays, the actors, and the audience. The tiny part of the foundation initially uncovered yielded a great number of hazelnut shells. Hazelnuts were Elizabethan popcorn; people munched on them throughout the performance.

The stage was a platform that extended into the pit. Actors entered and left the stage from doors located behind the platform. The portion of the galleries behind and above the stage was used primarily as dressing and storage rooms. The second-level gallery right above the stage, however, was used as an upper stage. It would have been here that the famous balcony scene in *The Tragedy of Romeo and Juliet* was enacted.

There was no scenery in the theaters of Shakespeare's day. Settings were indicated by references in the dialogue. As a result, one scene could follow another in rapid succession. The actors wore elaborate clothing. It was, in fact, typical Elizabethan clothing, not costuming. Thus, the plays produced in Shakespeare's day were fast-paced, colorful productions. Usually, a play lasted two hours.

One other difference between Shakespeare's theater and today's is that acting companies in the sixteenth century were made up only of men and boys. Women did not perform on the stage because it was not considered proper. As a general rule, boys of eleven, twelve, or thirteen—before their voices changed—performed the female roles.

The Globe Today

Building a replica of Shakespeare's Globe was the dream of American actor Sam Wanamaker. After long years of fundraising and construction, the theater opened in London to its first full season on June 8, 1997, with a production of *Henry V*. Like the earlier Globe, this one is made of wood, with a thatched roof and lime plaster covering the walls. The stage and the galleries are covered, but the "bear pit," where the modern-day groundlings stand, is open to the skies, exposing the spectators to the weather.

▼ **Critical Viewing**
What do you think it would be like to be an audience member at the Globe theater? **[Speculate]**

Drama Selection

The Tragedy of
ROMEO *and* JULIET
William Shakespeare

806 Drama

▲ Read **The Tragedy of Romeo and Juliet** to learn about the tragedy of a passionate love torn apart by conflict.

 TEXAS Focus on the TEKS

Meet these standards with **The Tragedy of Romeo and Juliet, Act I** (p. 806).

Reading
(4) Understand the structure and elements of drama. *(Literary Analysis: Dialogue and Stage Directions)*

(7) Explain the role of paradox in literary works. *(Spiral Review: Figurative Language)*

(1)(A) Determine the meaning of grade-level technical academic English words in multiple content areas (e.g., science) derived from Latin affixes. *(Word Power: Apply It)*

Reading/Comprehension Skills
RC-9(A) Reflect on understanding to monitor comprehension. *(Reading Skill: Summarize)*

For more TEKS, see pages 932–935.

Literary Analysis:
Dialogue and Stage Directions

Some of the structures and elements found in drama are common to many forms of literature—for instance, character and plot—while others are unique to drama.

Acts divide a play into parts. A major plot point or event usually occurs in each act. **Scenes** divide acts, usually signaling a change in setting.

Dialogue is conversation between characters. In prose, dialogue is usually set off with quotation marks. In drama, it generally follows the name of the speaker, as in this example:

> **BENVOLIO.** My noble uncle, do you know the cause?
> **MONTAGUE.** I neither know it nor can learn of him.

Dialogue reveals the personalities and relationships of the characters and advances the action of the play. Dialogue captures the language of the time and place in which a play is set.

Stage directions are notes that describe how a play should be performed, describing scenes, lighting, sounds, and character actions. They are usually set in italics and put in brackets or parentheses. For example:

> [*Enter* FRIAR LAWRENCE *alone, with a basket.*]

As You Read Note the structure and elements of drama at work in this act. Notice how the dialogue and stage directions work together to help you "see" and "hear" the play in your mind.

Reading Skill: **Summarize**

Summarizing is briefly stating the main points of a text. Pausing to summarize as you read helps you monitor your comprehension. To be sure that you understand Shakespeare's language before you summarize, use **text aids**—the numbered explanations that appear with the text.

- If you are confused by a passage, check to see if there is a footnote or side note and read the corresponding explanation.
- **Reread** the passage, using the information from the note to be sure you grasp the meaning of the passage.

Using the Strategy: Summarizing Chart

As You Read Pause to **reflect on your understanding. Monitor your comprehension** by using a chart to summarize each scene.

www.PHLitOnline.com

Hear It!
- Selection summary audio
- Selection audio

See It!
- Get Connected video
- Background video
- More about the author
- Vocabulary flashcards

Do It!
- Interactive journals
- Interactive graphic organizers
- Self-test
- Internet activity
- Grammar tutorial
- Interactive vocabulary games

Summary of Action in Act I
Scene I
Scene II
Scene III
Scene IV
Scene V

Meet
William Shakespeare
(1564–1616)

Author of

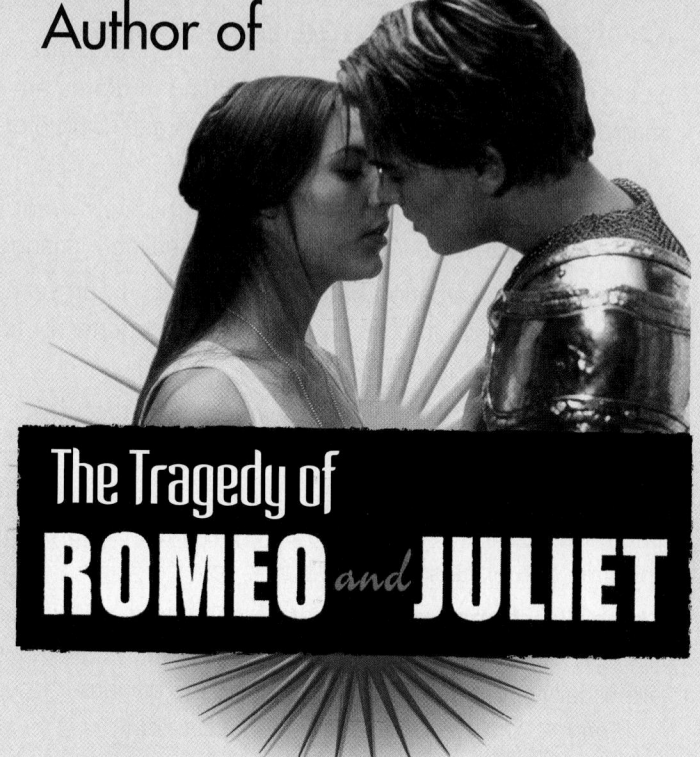

The Tragedy of
ROMEO *and* JULIET

Almost 400 years after William Shakespeare's death, his thirty-seven plays continue to be read widely and produced frequently throughout the world. They have as powerful an impact on audiences today as when they were first staged.

Starting in Stratford Not much is known about Shakespeare's early life. One reason for this lack of information is that playwrights during Shakespeare's time were not considered very important people socially. Therefore, no biographies were written about him until many years after his death. Church and town records in his hometown of Stratford-on-Avon—a busy market town about seventy-five miles northwest of London—provide some clues about Shakespeare's beginnings, however. His mother, whose maiden name was Mary Arden, was the daughter of his father's landlord. His father, John, was a prosperous merchant in Stratford and even served a term as the town's mayor. John Shakespeare's social standing made it possible for William to attend Stratford Grammar School free of charge until the age of fourteen. There, he studied Latin and Greek, as well as British and world history. Shakespeare would later put all of these lessons to use in his plays about historical figures such as Julius Caesar, Pericles, Macbeth, Richard III, and Henry IV.

Building a Love of Theater Because Stratford was a commercial center, traveling companies of professional actors visited several times a year. Young William probably attended many of these performances, which inspired his interest in the stage. In 1582, at the age of eighteen, Shakespeare married and was soon the father of three children. It is uncertain how Shakespeare spent the next few years, but he did not settle down in Stratford. His heart was set on London and the theater, so he followed his heart there sometime before 1592, leaving his patient family behind. Stratford nevertheless remained an important part of Shakespeare's life, and he visited often. Once he had achieved success in London, Shakespeare purchased one of Stratford's nicest homes for his family, and he retired there after his playwriting career ended.

Stage Celebrity By 1594, William Shakespeare, now a Londoner, had developed a reputation as an actor, had written several plays, and had become the principal playwright of the Lord Chamberlain's Men, a successful London theater company. He was also a part owner of the company, which meant that he earned money in three ways—from fees for his plays, from his acting salary, and from his share of the profits of the company. In 1599, the company built the famous Globe theater, where most of Shakespeare's plays were performed. When James I became king in 1603, Shakespeare and his partners renamed the company The King's Men. Shakespeare stayed with the company until 1610, when he retired to Stratford-on-Avon.

When Were They Written? Because Shakespeare wrote his plays to be performed, not published, no one knows exactly when each play was written. However, scholars have charted several distinct periods in Shakespeare's development as a playwright. During his early years, he wrote a number of comedies, several histories, and two tragedies. *Romeo and Juliet*—inspiration for the musical *West Side Story* as well as ballets, songs, stories, and movies—was written around 1595. Between that date and the turn of the 17th century, Shakespeare wrote several of his finest romantic comedies (*As You Like It, Twelfth Night,* and *Much Ado About Nothing*). During the first decade of the 17th century, Shakespeare created his greatest tragedies (*Hamlet, Othello, King Lear, Macbeth, Antony and Cleopatra,* and *Coriolanus*). Finally, toward the end of his career, Shakespeare wrote several plays referred to as romances or tragicomedies. Shakespeare's plays were finally published in a one-volume edition in 1623, seven years after his death. More than 1,000 copies of the first printing were sold for the considerable sum of one pound each—more than $50 per copy in today's currency.

Do our *differences* define us?

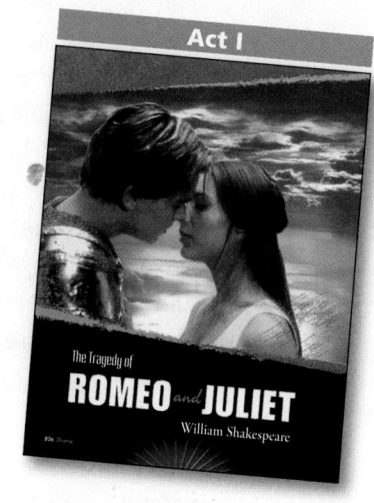

Act I

The Tragedy of
ROMEO *and* **JULIET**
William Shakespeare

Writing About the Big Question

In *The Tragedy of Romeo and Juliet,* two young people from families locked in a deadly feud fall in love. That difference defines their relationship and forces the plot toward tragic consequences. Use this sentence starter to develop your ideas about the Big Question.

When family **differences** stand between two people, it can be destructive because _____.

As You Read Look for ways in which family background influences the love between Romeo and Juliet.

Vocabulary

Read each word and its definition. Decide whether you know the word well, know it a little bit, or do not know it at all. After you read, see how your knowledge of each word has increased.

- **pernicious** (pər nish′ əs) *adj.* causing great injury or ruin (p. 811) *The spy's activities had a* pernicious *effect on the top-secret project.* perniciously *adv.*

- **adversary** (ad′ vər ser′ ē) *n.* a person who opposes or fights against another (p. 811) *Standing tall and trying to look brave, Pam faced her* adversary *in fencing.* adverse *adj.* adversarial *adj.*

- **augmenting** (ôg ment′ iŋ) *v.* increasing; enlarging (p. 812) *With small deposits each week, our family is* augmenting *its savings.* augmentable *adj.* augmentation *n.*

- **grievance** (grēv′ əns) *n.* injustice; complaint (p. 813) *The board investigated the worker's* grievance *against his supervisor.*

- **oppression** (ə presh′ ən) *n.* feeling of being weighed down with worries or problems (p. 813) *He could not pay all of his bills, and this caused a feeling of* oppression. oppress *v.* oppressive *adj.*

- **transgression** (trans gresh′ ən) *n.* wrongdoing; sin (p. 813) *Stealing from the poor is a* transgression *against humanity.* transgress *v.* transgressor *n.*

Word Power

The **Latin prefix** *trans-* means "across," "over," or "through."

In the play, Romeo describes his friend's sympathy for him as love's **transgression.** The word suggests that love has crossed a boundary and unfairly involved his friend.

Background for the Play

(History Connection)

Shakespeare's Source

Shakespeare based his play on a poem published in 1562 by Arthur Brooke. Brooke's 3,000-line poem—about star-crossed lovers from feuding Italian families—has a highly moral tone: Disobedience, as well as fate, leads to the deaths of the two lovers. While he borrowed a story line, Shakespeare portrayed the young lovers more sympathetically. He also elevated these everyday characters by presenting their tale in a tragedy—a serious type of drama that traditionally involved kings, emperors, or other characters of great importance.

Elizabethan Language

The Tragedy of Romeo and Juliet is written in Elizabethan English—the English spoken in the 17th century. Most of the unfamiliar words are explained in footnotes. However, the following words appear so frequently that learning them now will make your reading of the play easier.

against for; in preparation for

alack alas (an exclamation of sorrow)

anon soon

aye yes

but only; except

e'en even

e'er ever

haply perhaps

happy fortunate

hence away; from here

hie hurry

hither here

marry indeed

whence where

wherefore why

wilt will

withal in addition; notwithstanding

would wish

The Tragedy of

ROMEO *and* JULIET

William Shakespeare

Characters

CHORUS
ESCALUS, Prince of Verona
PARIS, a young count, kinsman to the Prince
MONTAGUE
CAPULET
AN OLD MAN, of the Capulet family
ROMEO, son to Montague
MERCUTIO, kinsman to the Prince and
    friend to Romeo
BENVOLIO, nephew to Montague and
    friend to Romeo
TYBALT, nephew to Lady Capulet
FRIAR LAWRENCE, Franciscan
FRIAR JOHN, Franciscan
BALTHASAR, servant to Romeo

SAMPSON, servant to Capulet
GREGORY, servant to Capulet
PETER, servant to Juliet's nurse
ABRAM, servant to Montague
AN APOTHECARY
THREE MUSICIANS
AN OFFICER
LADY MONTAGUE, wife to Montague
LADY CAPULET, wife to Capulet
JULIET, daughter to Capulet
NURSE TO JULIET
CITIZENS OF VERONA, Gentlemen
    and Gentlewomen of both houses,
    Maskers, Torchbearers, Pages, Guards,
    Watchmen, Servants, and Attendants

Prologue

Scene: Verona; Mantua

[Enter CHORUS.*]*

    CHORUS. Two households, both alike in dignity.[1]
        In fair Verona, where we lay our scene,
    From ancient grudge break to new mutiny,[2]
        Where civil blood makes civil hands unclean.[3]
5   From forth the fatal loins of these two foes
        A pair of star-crossed[4] lovers take their life;
    Whose misadventured piteous overthrows[5]
        Doth with their death bury their parents' strife.
    The fearful passage of their death-marked love,
10   And the continuance of their parents' rage,
    Which, but[6] their children's end, naught could remove,
        Is now the two hours' traffic[7] of our stage;
    The which if you with patient ears attend,
    What here shall miss, our toil shall strive to mend.[8] *[Exit.]*

1. **dignity** high social rank.
2. **mutiny** violence.
3. **Where . . . unclean** in which the blood of citizens stains citizens' hands.
4. **star-crossed** ill-fated by the unfavorable positions of the stars.
5. **Whose . . . overthrows** whose unfortunate, sorrowful destruction.
6. **but** except.
7. **two hours' traffic** two hours' business.
8. **What . . . mend** What is not clear in this prologue we actors shall try to clarify in the course of the play.

ACT I

Scene i. Verona. A public place.

[*Enter* SAMPSON *and* GREGORY, *with swords and bucklers,*[1] *of the house of Capulet.*]

SAMPSON. Gregory, on my word, we'll not carry coals.[2]

GREGORY. No, for then we should be colliers.[3]

SAMPSON. I mean, an we be in choler, we'll draw.[4]

GREGORY. Ay, while you live, draw your neck out of collar.[5]

5   **SAMPSON.** I strike quickly, being moved.

GREGORY. But thou art not quickly moved to strike.

SAMPSON. A dog of the house of Montague moves me.

GREGORY. To move is to stir, and to be valiant is to stand. Therefore, if thou art moved, thou run'st away.

10   **SAMPSON.** A dog of that house shall move me to stand. I will take the wall[6] of any man or maid of Montague's.

GREGORY. That shows thee a weak slave; for the weakest goes to the wall.

SAMPSON. 'Tis true; and therefore women, being the weaker
15   vessels, are ever thrust to the wall. Therefore I will push Montague's men from the wall and thrust his maids to the wall.

GREGORY. The quarrel is between our masters and us their men.

20   **SAMPSON.** Tis all one. I will show myself a tyrant. When I have fought with the men, I will be civil with the maids—I will cut off their heads.

GREGORY. The heads of the maids?

SAMPSON. Ay, the heads of the maids or their maidenheads.
25   Take it in what sense thou wilt.

GREGORY. They must take it in sense that feel it.

---

1. bucklers small shields.
2. carry coals endure insults.
3. colliers sellers of coal.
4. an . . . draw If we are angered, we'll draw our swords.
5. collar hangman's noose.

6. take the wall assert superiority by walking nearer the houses and therefore farther from the gutter.

**Literary Analysis
Dialogue and Stage Directions** What does this conversation among servants reveal about the Montagues?

SAMPSON. Me they shall feel while I am able to stand;
and 'tis known I am a pretty piece of flesh.

30 **GREGORY.** Tis well thou art not fish; if thou hadst, thou hadst
been Poor John. Draw thy tool!⁷ Here comes two of the
house of Montagues.

[Enter two other Servingmen, ABRAM *and* BALTHASAR.*]*

SAMPSON. My naked weapon is out. Quarrel! I will back thee.

GREGORY. How? Turn thy back and run?

SAMPSON. Fear me not.

35 **GREGORY.** No, marry. I fear thee!

SAMPSON. Let us take the law of our sides;⁸ let them begin.

GREGORY. I will frown as I pass by, and let them take it as they
list.⁹

SAMPSON. Nay, as they dare. I will bite my thumb¹⁰ at them,
40 which is disgrace to them if they bear it.

ABRAM. Do you bite your thumb at us, sir?

SAMPSON. I do bite my thumb, sir.

ABRAM. Do you bite your thumb at us, sir?

SAMPSON. *[Aside to* GREGORY*]* Is the law of our side if I say ay?

45 **GREGORY.** *[Aside to* SAMPSON*]* No.

SAMPSON. No, sir, I do not bite my thumb at you, sir; but I bite
my thumb, sir.

GREGORY. Do you quarrel, sir?

ABRAM. Quarrel, sir? No, sir.

50 **SAMPSON.** But if you do, sir, I am for you. I serve as good a man
as you.

ABRAM. No better.

SAMPSON. Well, sir.

[Enter BENVOLIO.*]*

55 **GREGORY.** *[Aside to* SAMPSON*]* Say "better." Here comes one of
my master's kinsmen.

SAMPSON. Yes, better, sir.

ABRAM. You lie.

7. **tool** weapon.

Reading Skill
Summarize How does
footnote 8 help you un-
derstand Sampson's logic
in line 36?

8. **take . . . sides** make sure
the law is on our side.
9. **list** please.
10. **bite . . . thumb** make an
insulting gesture.

Literary Analysis
Dialogue and Stage
Directions Which words
in the stage directions
in line 44 clarify that
Sampson is not speaking
to Abram?

 **Reading**
Check

With which family are
the quarreling servants
affiliated?

11. **swashing** hard downward swordstroke.

12. **heartless hinds** cowardly servants. *Hind* also means "a female deer."

SAMPSON. Draw, if you be men. Gregory, remember thy
swashing[11] blow.   [*They fight.*]

60 **BENVOLIO.** Part, fools!
Put up your swords. You know not what you do.

[*Enter* TYBALT.]

TYBALT. What art thou drawn among these heartless hinds?[12]
Turn thee, Benvolio; look upon thy death.

BENVOLIO. I do but keep the peace. Put up thy sword,
65   Or manage it to part these men with me.

TYBALT. What, drawn, and talk of peace? I hate the word
As I hate hell, all Montagues, and thee.
Have at thee, coward!   [*They fight.*]

[*Enter an* OFFICER, *and three or four* CITIZENS *with clubs or partisans.*[13]]

13. **partisans** spearlike weapons with broad blades.

14. **bills** weapons consisting of hook-shaped blades with long handles.

OFFICER. Clubs, bills,[14] and partisans! Strike! Beat them down!
70   Down with the Capulets! Down with the Montagues!

[*Enter old* CAPULET *in his gown, and his* WIFE.]

CAPULET. What noise is this? Give me my long sword, ho!

LADY CAPULET. A crutch, a crutch! Why call you for a sword?

CAPULET. My sword, I say! Old Montague is come
And flourishes his blade in spite[15] of me.

15. **spite** defiance.

[*Enter old* MONTAGUE *and his* WIFE.]

LITERATURE IN CONTEXT

History Connection

Prince of Verona

When Prince Escalus intervenes in the fight between the Capulets and the Montagues, he does so under his authority as the podesta, or "chief magistrate," of Verona. The powers and duties of the podesta combined those of a modern mayor, chief of police, and head of the local militia. Scholars believe that Shakespeare based the character of Prince Escalus on Bartolomeo della Scala, who ruled the northern Italian city of Verona during the early fourteenth century.

Connect to the Literature

Which part of his authority is Prince Escalus exercising in this scene—mayor, police chief, or head of the army? Explain.

75 **MONTAGUE.** Thou villain Capulet!—Hold me not; let me go.

LADY MONTAGUE. Thou shalt not stir one foot to seek a foe.

[*Enter* PRINCE ESCALUS, *with his Train.*[16]]

PRINCE. Rebellious subjects, enemies to peace,
Profaners[17] of this neighbor-stainèd steel—
Will they not hear? What, ho! You men, you beasts,
80 That quench the fire of your pernicious rage
With purple fountains issuing from your veins!
On pain of torture, from those bloody hands
Throw your mistempered[18] weapons to the ground
And hear the sentence of your moved prince.
85 Three civil brawls, bred of an airy word
By thee, old Capulet, and Montague,
Have thrice disturbed the quiet of our streets
And made Verona's ancient citizens
Cast by their grave beseeming ornaments[19]
90 To wield old partisans, in hands as old,
Cank'red with peace, to part your cank'red hate.[20]
If ever you disturb our streets again,
Your lives shall pay the forfeit of the peace.
For this time all the rest depart away.
95 You, Capulet, shall go along with me;
And, Montague, come you this afternoon,
To know our farther pleasure in this case,
To old Freetown, our common judgment place.
Once more, on pain of death, all men depart.

[*Exit all but* MONTAGUE, *his* WIFE, *and* BENVOLIO.]

100 **MONTAGUE.** Who set this ancient quarrel new abroach?[21]
Speak, nephew, were you by when it began?

BENVOLIO. Here were the servants of your adversary
And yours, close fighting ere I did approach.
I drew to part them. In the instant came
105 The fiery Tybalt, with his sword prepared;
Which, as he breathed defiance to my ears,
He swung about his head and cut the winds,
Who, nothing hurt withal, hissed him in scorn.
While we were interchanging thrusts and blows,
110 Came more and more, and fought on part and part,[22]
Till the Prince came, who parted either part.

LADY MONTAGUE. O, where is Romeo? Saw you him today?
Right glad I am he was not at this fray.

16. **Train** attendants.
17. **Profaners** those who show disrespect or contempt.

Vocabulary
pernicious (pər nish´ əs)
adj. causing great injury or ruin

18. **mistempered** hardened for a wrong purpose; bad-tempered.

19. **Cast . . . ornaments** put aside their dignified and appropriate clothing.
20. **Cank'red . . . hate** rusted from lack of use, to put an end to your malignant feuding.

Reading Skill
Summarize Summarize the warning that the Prince issues to the Montagues and Capulets in this speech.

21. **Who . . . abroach?** Who reopened this old fight?

Vocabulary
adversary (ad´ vər ser´ ē)
n. a person who opposes or fights against another

22. **on . . . part** on one side and the other.

Reading Check

Who stops the brawl between the Montagues and the Capulets?

Spiral Review
Characterization
In this section, how does the author develop the complex character of Romeo through the dialogue of others?

23. **ware** aware; wary.
24. **covert** hidden place.
25. **measuring . . . affections** judging his feelings.
26. **Which . . . found** which wanted to be where there was no one else.
27. **Pursued . . . his** followed my own mind by not following after Romeo.

Vocabulary

augmenting (ôg ment´ iŋ) *v.* increasing; enlarging

28. **heavy** sad; moody.

29. **portentous** promising bad fortune.

30. **importuned** questioned deeply.

31. **sounding** understanding.

BENVOLIO. Madam, an hour before the worshiped sun
115 Peered forth the golden window of the East,
A troubled mind drave me to walk abroad:
Where, underneath the grove of sycamore
That westward rooteth from this city side,
So early walking did I see your son.
120 Towards him I made, but he was ware[23] of me
And stole into the covert[24] of the wood.
I, measuring his affections[25] by my own,
Which then most sought where most might not be found,[26]
Being one too many by my weary self,
125 Pursued my humor not pursuing his,[27]
And gladly shunned who gladly fled from me.

MONTAGUE. Many a morning hath he there been seen,
With tears augmenting the fresh morning's dew,
Adding to clouds more clouds with his deep sighs;
130 But all so soon as the all-cheering sun
Should in the farthest East begin to draw
The shady curtains from Aurora's bed,
Away from light steals home my heavy[28] son
And private in his chamber pens himself,
135 Shuts up his windows, locks fair daylight out,
And makes himself an artificial night.
Black and portentous[29] must this humor prove
Unless good counsel may the cause remove.

BENVOLIO. My noble uncle, do you know the cause?

140 **MONTAGUE.** I neither know it nor can learn of him.

BENVOLIO. Have you importuned[30] him by any means?

MONTAGUE. Both by myself and many other friends;
But he, his own affections' counselor,
Is to himself—I will not say how true—
145 But to himself so secret and so close,
So far from sounding[31] and discovery,
As is the bud bit with an envious worm
Ere he can spread his sweet leaves to the air
Or dedicate his beauty to the sun.
150 Could we but learn from whence his sorrows grow,
We would as willingly give cure as know.

[*Enter* ROMEO.]

BENVOLIO. See, where he comes. So please you step aside;
I'll know his grievance, or be much denied.

MONTAGUE. I would thou wert so happy by thy stay
155   To hear true shrift.[32] Come, madam, let's away.

                                        [*Exit* MONTAGUE *and* WIFE.]

BENVOLIO. Good morrow, cousin.

ROMEO.   Is the day so young?

BENVOLIO. But new struck nine.

ROMEO.   Ay me! Sad hours seem long.
Was that my father that went hence so fast?

BENVOLIO. It was. What sadness lengthens Romeo's hours?

160   **ROMEO.** Not having that which having makes them short.

BENVOLIO. In love?

ROMEO. Out—

BENVOLIO. Of love?

ROMEO. Out of her favor where I am in love.

165   **BENVOLIO.** Alas that love, so gentle in his view,[33]
Should be so tyrannous and rough in proof![34]

ROMEO. Alas that love, whose view is muffled still,[35]
Should without eyes see pathways to his will!
Where shall we dine? O me! What fray was here?
170   Yet tell me not, for I have heard it all.
Here's much to do with hate, but more with love.[36]
Why then, O brawling love, O loving hate,
O anything, of nothing first created!
O heavy lightness, serious vanity,
175   Misshapen chaos of well-seeming forms,
Feather of lead, bright smoke, cold fire, sick health,
Still-waking sleep, that is not what it is!
This love feel I, that feel no love in this.
Dost thou not laugh?

BENVOLIO.   No, coz,[37] I rather weep.

ROMEO. Good heart, at what?

180   **BENVOLIO.**   At thy good heart's oppression.

ROMEO. Why, such is love's transgression.
Griefs of mine own lie heavy in my breast,

Vocabulary
grievance (grēv´ əns)
n. injustice; complaint

32. I . . . shrift I hope you are
lucky enough to hear him
confess the truth.

Literary Analysis
**Dialogue and Stage
Directions** What does
this conversation reveal
about Romeo's state of
mind?

33. **view** appearance.
34. **in proof** when
experienced.
35. **whose . . . still** Cupid is
traditionally represented
as blindfolded.
36. **but . . . love** loyalty to
family and love of fighting.
In the following lines,
Romeo speaks of love as a
series of contradictions—a
union of opposites.
37. **coz** cousin.

Vocabulary
oppression (ə presh´ ən)
n. feeling of being
weighed down with
worries or problems

transgression
(trans gresh´ ən) *n.*
wrongdoing; sin

Reading Check

What reason for his
sadness does Romeo
give to Benvolio?

38. **Which . . . thine** which griefs you will increase by adding your own sorrow to them.
39. **discreet** intelligently sensitive.

40. **gall** a bitter liquid.

41. **Soft!** Wait!

42. **in sadness** seriously.

43. **Dian's wit** the mind of Diana, goddess of chastity.
44. **proof** armor.
45. **stay** endure; put up with.
46. **That . . . store** in that her beauty will die with her if she does not marry and have children.

Spiral Review
Figurative
Language Explain the role of paradox in line 204.

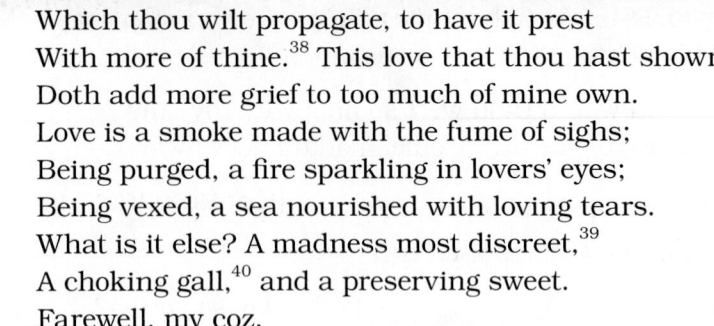

Which thou wilt propagate, to have it prest

185 With more of thine.³⁸ This love that thou hast shown
Doth add more grief to too much of mine own.
Love is a smoke made with the fume of sighs;
Being purged, a fire sparkling in lovers' eyes;
Being vexed, a sea nourished with loving tears.
What is it else? A madness most discreet,³⁹
190 A choking gall,⁴⁰ and a preserving sweet.
Farewell, my coz.

BENVOLIO.   Soft!⁴¹ I will go along.
And if you leave me so, you do me wrong.

ROMEO. Tut! I have lost myself; I am not here;
This is not Romeo, he's some other where.

195 **BENVOLIO.** Tell me in sadness,⁴² who is that you love?

ROMEO. What, shall I groan and tell thee?

BENVOLIO.   Groan? Why, no;
But sadly tell me who.

ROMEO. Bid a sick man in sadness make his will.
Ah, word ill urged to one that is so ill!
200 In sadness, cousin, I do love a woman.

BENVOLIO. I aimed so near when I supposed you loved.

ROMEO. A right good markman. And she's fair I love.

BENVOLIO. A right fair mark, fair coz, is soonest hit.

ROMEO. Well, in that hit you miss. She'll not be hit
205 With Cupid's arrow. She hath Dian's wit,⁴³
And, in strong proof⁴⁴ of chastity well armed,
From Love's weak childish bow she lives uncharmed.
She will not stay⁴⁵ the siege of loving terms,
Nor bide th' encounter of assailing eyes,
210 Nor ope her lap to saint-seducing gold.
O, she is rich in beauty; only poor
That, when she dies, with beauty dies her store.⁴⁶

BENVOLIO. Then she hath sworn that she will still live chaste?

ROMEO. She hath, and in that sparing make huge waste;
215 For beauty, starved with her severity,

◄ **Critical Viewing** What does this photograph reveal about Romeo's feelings? **[Analyze]**

Cuts beauty off from all posterity.[47]
She is too fair, too wise, wisely too fair
To merit bliss by making me despair.[48]
She hath forsworn to[49] love, and in that vow
220   Do I live dead that live to tell it now.

BENVOLIO. Be ruled by me; forget to think of her.

ROMEO. O, teach me how I should forget to think!

BENVOLIO. By giving liberty unto thine eyes.
   Examine other beauties.

ROMEO.   'Tis the way
225   To call hers, exquisite, in question more.[50]
These happy masks that kiss fair ladies' brows,
Being black puts us in mind they hide the fair.
He that is strucken blind cannot forget
The precious treasure of his eyesight lost.
230   Show me a mistress that is passing fair:
What doth her beauty serve but as a note
Where I may read who passed that passing fair?[51]
Farewell. Thou canst not teach me to forget.

BENVOLIO. I'll pay that doctrine, or else die in debt.[52]   [*Exit all.*]

Scene ii. A street.

[*Enter* CAPULET, COUNTY PARIS, *and the* CLOWN, *his servant.*]

CAPULET. But Montague is bound as well as I,
   In penalty alike; and 'tis not hard, I think,
   For men so old as we to keep the peace.

PARIS. Of honorable reckoning[1] are you both,
5   And pity 'tis you lived at odds so long.
   But now, my lord, what say you to my suit?

CAPULET. But saying o'er what I have said before:
   My child is yet a stranger in the world,
   She hath not seen the change of fourteen years;
10   Let two more summers wither in their pride
   Ere we may think her ripe to be a bride.

PARIS. Younger than she are happy mothers made.

CAPULET. And too soon marred are those so early made.
   Earth hath swallowed all my hopes[2] but she;
15   She is the hopeful lady of my earth.[3]
   But woo her, gentle Paris, get her heart;
   My will to her consent is but a part.

47. in . . . posterity By denying herself love and marriage, she wastes her beauty, which will not live on in future generations.

48. She . . . despair She is being too good—she will earn happiness in heaven by dooming me to live without her love.

49. forsworn to sworn not to.

50. 'Tis . . . more That way will only make her beauty more strongly present in my mind.

51. who . . . fair who surpassed in beauty that very beautiful woman.

52. I'll . . . debt I will teach you to forget, or else die trying.

1. reckoning reputation.

2. hopes children.

3. She . . . earth My hopes for the future rest in her; she will inherit all that is mine.

Reading Check

What advice does Benvolio give to Romeo about the woman he loves?

4. **An . . . voice** If she agrees, I will consent to and agree with her choice.

5. **Earth-treading stars** young ladies.

6. **Which . . . none** If you look at all the young girls, you may see her as merely one among many, and not worth special admiration.
7. **stay** await.

Reading Skill

Summarize Reflect on your understanding of lines 38–41. Then, monitor your comprehension by summarizing the servant's remarks.

8. **shoemaker . . . nets** The servant is confusing workers and their tools. He intends to say that people should stick with what they know.
9. **In good time!** Just in time! The servant has seen Benvolio and Romeo, who can read.
10. **Turn . . . turning** If you are dizzy from turning one way, turn the other way.
11. **plantain leaf** leaf used to stop bleeding.

An she agree, within her scope of choice
Lies my consent and fair according voice,[4]
20 This night I hold an old accustomed feast,
Whereto I have invited many a guest,
Such as I love; and you among the store,
One more, most welcome, makes my number more.
At my poor house look to behold this night
25 Earth-treading stars[5] that make dark heaven light.
Such comfort as do lusty young men feel
When well-appareled April on the heel
Of limping Winter treads, even such delight
Among fresh fennel buds shall you this night
30 Inherit at my house. Hear all, all see,
And like her most whose merit most shall be;
Which, on more view of many, mine, being one,
May stand in number, though in reck'ning none.[6]
Come, go with me. [*To* SERVANT, *giving him a paper*]
    Go, sirrah, trudge about
35 Through fair Verona; find those persons out
Whose names are written there, and to them say
My house and welcome on their pleasure stay.[7]

[*Exit with* PARIS.]

SERVANT. Find them out whose names are written here? It is
    written that the shoemaker should meddle with his yard and
40 the tailor with his last, the fisher with his pencil and the
    painter with his nets;[8] but I am sent to find those persons
    whose names are here writ, and can never find what names
    the writing person hath here writ. I must to the learned.
    In good time![9]

[*Enter* BENVOLIO *and* ROMEO.]

45 **BENVOLIO.** Tut, man, one fire burns out another's burning;
    One pain is less'ned by another's anguish;
    Turn giddy, and be holp by backward turning;[10]
    One desperate grief cures with another's languish.
    Take thou some new infection to thy eye,
50 And the rank poison of the old will die.

ROMEO. Your plantain leaf[11] is excellent for that.

BENVOLIO. For what, I pray thee?

ROMEO.   For your broken shin.

BENVOLIO. Why, Romeo, art thou mad?

ROMEO. Not mad, but bound more than a madman is;
55   Shut up in prison, kept without my food,
      Whipped and tormented and—God-den,[12] good fellow.

SERVANT. God gi' go-den. I pray, sir, can you read?

ROMEO. Ay, mine own fortune in my misery.

SERVANT. Perhaps you have learned it without book.
60   But, I pray, can you read anything you see?

ROMEO. Ay, if I know the letters and the language.

SERVANT. Ye say honestly. Rest you merry.[13]

ROMEO. Stay, fellow; I can read. [*He reads the letter.*]
      "Signior Martino and his wife and daughters;
65   County Anselm and his beauteous sisters;
      The lady widow of Vitruvio;
      Signior Placentio and his lovely nieces;
      Mercutio and his brother Valentine;
      Mine uncle Capulet, his wife and daughters;
70   My fair niece Rosaline; Livia;
      Signior Valentio and his cousin Tybalt;
      Lucio and the lively Helena."
      A fair assembly. Whither should they come?

SERVANT. Up.

75 **ROMEO.** Whither? To supper?

SERVANT. To our house.

ROMEO. Whose house?

SERVANT. My master's.

ROMEO. Indeed I should have asked you that before.

80 **SERVANT.** Now I'll tell you without asking. My master is the
      great rich Capulet; and if you be not of the house of
      Montagues, I pray come and crush a cup of wine. Rest you
      merry.   [*Exit.*]

BENVOLIO. At this same ancient[14] feast of Capulet's
85   Sups the fair Rosaline whom thou so loves;
      With all the admirèd beauties of Verona.
      Go thither, and with unattainted[15] eye
      Compare her face with some that I shall show,
      And I will make thee think thy swan a crow.

90 **ROMEO.** When the devout religion of mine eye
      Maintains such falsehood, then turn tears to fires;

12. God-den good afternoon; good evening.

13. Rest you merry May God keep you happy—a way of saying farewell.

Literary Analysis
Dialogue and Stage Directions What important information in the stage directions clarifies Romeo's speech here?

14. ancient long-established; traditional.
15. unattainted unprejudiced.

Reading
Check

Why does Capulet's servant talk to Romeo and Benvolio?

And these, who, often drowned, could never die,
  Transparent heretics, be burnt for liars![16]
 One fairer than my love? The all-seeing sun
95 Ne'er saw her match since first the world begun.

  BENVOLIO. Tut! you saw her fair, none else being by,
  Herself poised with herself in either eye;[17]
  But in that crystal scales[18] let there be weighed
  Your lady's love against some other maid
100 That I will show you shining at this feast,
  And she shall scant show well that now seems best.

  ROMEO. I'll go along, no such sight to be shown,
  But to rejoice in splendor of mine own.[19]   *[Exit all.]*

Scene iii. A room in Capulet's house.

[Enter CAPULET's WIFE, *and* NURSE.]

  LADY CAPULET. Nurse, where's my daughter? Call her forth to
  me.

  NURSE. Now, by my maidenhead at twelve year old,
  I bade her come. What, lamb! What, ladybird!
  God forbid, where's this girl? What, Juliet!

[Enter JULIET.]

5 **JULIET.** How now? Who calls?

  NURSE.   Your mother.

  JULIET.   Madam, I am here.
  What is your will?

  LADY CAPULET. This is the matter—Nurse, give leave[1] awhile;
  We must talk in secret. Nurse, come back again.
  I have rememb'red me; thou's hear our counsel.[2]
10 Thou knowest my daughter's of a pretty age.

  NURSE. Faith, I can tell her age unto an hour.

  LADY CAPULET. She's not fourteen.

  NURSE.   I'll lay fourteen of my teeth—
  And yet, to my teen[3] be it spoken, I have but four—
  She's not fourteen. How long is it now
  To Lammastide?[4]

15 **LADY CAPULET.** A fortnight and odd days.[5]

  NURSE. Even or odd, of all days in the year,
  Come Lammas Eve at night shall she be fourteen.

---

16. When . . . liars! When I see Rosaline as just a plain-looking girl, may my tears turn to fire and burn my eyes out!

17. Herself . . . eye Rosaline compared with no one else.

18. crystal scales your eyes.

19. mine own my own love, Rosaline.

1. give leave Leave us alone.

2. thou's . . . counsel You shall hear our conference.

3. teen sorrow.

4. Lammastide August 1, a holiday celebrating the summer harvest.

5. A fortnight and odd days two weeks plus a few days.

Susan and she (God rest all Christian souls!)
Were of an age.[6] Well, Susan is with God;

20 She was too good for me. But, as I said,
On Lammas Eve at night shall she be fourteen;
That shall she, marry; I remember it well.
'Tis since the earthquake now eleven years,
And she was weaned (I never shall forget it),

25 Of all the days of the year, upon that day;
For I had then laid wormwood to my dug,
Sitting in the sun under the dovehouse wall.
My lord and you were then at Mantua.
Nay, I do bear a brain. But, as I said,

30 When it did taste the wormwood on the nipple
Of my dug and felt it bitter, pretty fool,
To see it tetchy and fall out with the dug!
Shake, quoth the dovehouse! 'Twas no need, I trow,
To bid me trudge.

35 And since that time it is eleven years,
For then she could stand high-lone; nay, by th' rood,
She could have run and waddled all about;
For even the day before, she broke her brow;
And then my husband (God be with his soul!

40 'A was a merry man) took up the child.
"Yea," quoth he, "dost thou fall upon thy face?
Thou wilt fall backward when thou hast more wit;
Wilt thou not, Jule?" and, by my holidam,
The pretty wretch left crying and said, "Ay."

45 To see now how a jest shall come about!
I warrant, and I should live a thousand years,
I never should forget it. "Wilt thou not, Jule?" quoth he,
And, pretty fool, it stinted and said, "Ay."

LADY CAPULET. Enough of this. I pray thee hold thy peace.

50 **NURSE.** Yes, madam. Yet I cannot choose but laugh
To think it should leave crying and say, "Ay."
And yet, I warrant, it had upon it brow
A bump as big as a young cock'rel's stone;
A perilous knock; and it cried bitterly.

55 "Yea," quoth my husband, "fall'st upon thy face?
Thou wilt fall backward when thou comest to age,
Wilt thou not, Jule?" It stinted and said, "Ay."

JULIET. And stint thou too, I pray thee, nurse, say I.

NURSE. Peace, I have done. God mark thee to His grace!

6. **Susan . . . age** Susan, the Nurse's child, and Juliet were the same age.

Literary Analysis
Dialogue and Stage Directions What do the Nurse's words here reveal about her devotion to Juliet?

Literary Analysis
Dialogue and Stage Directions What does this conversation reveal about the Nurse's personality?

Reading Check

How old is Juliet?

60   Thou wast the prettiest babe that e'er I nursed.
      And I might live to see thee married once,
      I have my wish.

LADY CAPULET. Marry, that "marry" is the very theme
      I came to talk of. Tell me, daughter Juliet,
65   How stands your dispositions to be married?

JULIET. It is an honor that I dream not of.

NURSE. An honor? Were not I thine only nurse,
      I would say thou hadst sucked wisdom from thy teat.

LADY CAPULET. Well, think of marriage now. Younger than you,
70   Here in Verona, ladies of esteem,
      Are made already mothers. By my count,
      I was your mother much upon these years
      That you are now a maid.[7] Thus then in brief;
      The valiant Paris seeks you for his love.

75 **NURSE.** A man, young lady! Lady, such a man
      As all the world—Why, he's a man of wax.[8]

LADY CAPULET. Verona's summer hath not such a flower.

NURSE. Nay, he's a flower, in faith—a very flower.

LADY CAPULET. What say you? Can you love the gentleman?
80   This night you shall behold him at our feast.
      Read o'er the volume of young Paris' face,
      And find delight writ there with beauty's pen;
      Examine every married lineament,
      And see how one another lends content;[9]
85   And what obscured in this fair volume lies
      Find written in the margent[10] of his eyes.
      This precious book of love, this unbound lover,
      To beautify him only lacks a cover.[11]
      The fish lives in the sea, and 'tis much pride
90   For fair without the fair within to hide.
      That book in many's eyes doth share the glory,
      That in gold clasps locks in the golden story;
      So shall you share all that he doth possess,
      By having him making yourself no less.

95 **NURSE.** No less? Nay, bigger! Women grow by men.

LADY CAPULET. Speak briefly, can you like of Paris' love?

JULIET. I'll look to like, if looking liking move;[12]
      But no more deep will I endart mine eye

---

7. I . . . maid I was your mother when I was as old as you are now.

8. he's . . . wax He's a model of a man.

Reading Skill

Summarize Reflect on your understanding to monitor your comprehension. Use the information in footnote 8 and the dialogue to help you summarize the Nurse's opinion of Paris.

9. Examine . . . content Examine every harmonious feature of his face, and see how each one enhances every other. Throughout this speech, Lady Capulet compares Paris to a book.

10. margent margin. Paris's eyes are compared to the margin of a book, where whatever is not clear in the text (the rest of his face) can be explained by notes.

11. cover metaphor for wife.

12. I'll . . . move If looking favorably at someone leads to liking him, I will look at Paris in a way that will lead to liking him.

Than your consent gives strength to make it fly.[13]

[*Enter* SERVINGMAN.]

100 **SERVINGMAN.** Madam, the guests are come, supper served up, you called, my young lady asked for, the nurse cursed in the pantry, and everything in extremity. I must hence to wait. I beseech you follow straight.   [*Exit.*]

LADY CAPULET. We follow thee. Juliet, the County stays.[14]

105 **NURSE.** Go, girl, seek happy nights to happy days.   [*Exit all.*]

Scene iv. A street.

[*Enter* ROMEO, MERCUTIO, BENVOLIO, *with five or six other* MASKERS; TORCHBEARERS.]

ROMEO. What, shall this speech[1] be spoke for our excuse?
Or shall we on without apology?

BENVOLIO. The date is out of such prolixity.[2]
We'll have no Cupid hoodwinked with a scarf,
5   Bearing a Tartar's painted bow of lath,
Scaring the ladies like a crowkeeper,
Nor no without-book prologue, faintly spoke
After the prompter, for our entrance;
But, let them measure us by what they will,
10   We'll measure them a measure and be gone.

ROMEO. Give me a torch. I am not for this ambling.
Being but heavy,[3] I will bear the light.

MERCUTIO. Nay, gentle Romeo, we must have you dance.

ROMEO. Not I, believe me. You have dancing shoes
15   With nimble soles; I have a soul of lead
So stakes me to the ground I cannot move.

MERCUTIO. You are a lover. Borrow Cupid's wings
And soar with them above a common bound.

ROMEO. I am too sore enpiercèd with his shaft
20   To soar with his light feathers; and so bound
I cannot bound a pitch above dull woe.
Under love's heavy burden do I sink.

MERCUTIO. And, to sink in it, should you burden love—
Too great oppression for a tender thing.

Literary Analysis
Dialogue and Stage Directions What does the dialogue reveal about Juliet's attitude toward marriage and Paris?

13. **But . . . fly** But I will not look harder than you want me to.
14. **the County stays** The Count, Paris, is waiting.

1. **this speech** Romeo asks whether he and his companions, being uninvited guests, should follow custom by announcing their arrival in a speech.
2. **The . . . prolixity** Such wordiness is outdated. In the following lines, Benvolio says, in sum, "Let us forget about announcing our entrance with a show. The other guests can look over as they see fit. We will dance a while, then leave."
3. **heavy** weighed down with sadness.

Reading Check

Why has Lady Capulet come to talk to Juliet?

25 **ROMEO.** Is love a tender thing? It is too rough,
Too rude, too boist'rous, and it pricks like thorn.

MERCUTIO. If love be rough with you, be rough with love.
Prick love for pricking, and you beat love down.
Give me a case to put my visage[4] in.
30 A visor for a visor![5] What care I
What curious eye doth quote deformities?[6]
Here are the beetle brows shall blush for me.

BENVOLIO. Come, knock and enter; and no sooner in
But every man betake him to his legs.[7]

35 **ROMEO.** A torch for me! Let wantons light of heart
Tickle the senseless rushes[8] with their heels;
For I am proverbed with a grandsire phrase,[9]
I'll be a candleholder and look on;
The game was ne'er so fair, and I am done.[10]

40 **MERCUTIO.** Tut! Dun's the mouse, the constable's own word![11]
If thou art Dun,[12] we'll draw thee from the mire
Of this sir-reverence love, wherein thou stickest
Up to the ears. Come, we burn daylight, ho!

ROMEO. Nay, that's not so.

MERCUTIO.   I mean, sir, in delay
45 We waste our lights in vain, like lights by day.
Take our good meaning, for our judgment sits
Five times in that ere once in our five wits.[13]

ROMEO. And we mean well in going to this masque,
But 'tis no wit to go.

MERCUTIO.   Why, may one ask?

ROMEO. I dreamt a dream tonight.

50 **MERCUTIO.**   And so did I.

ROMEO. Well, what was yours?

MERCUTIO.   That dreamers often lie.

ROMEO. In bed asleep, while they do dream things true.

MERCUTIO. O, then I see Queen Mab[14] hath been with you.
She is the fairies' midwife, and she comes
55 In shape no bigger than an agate stone
On the forefinger of an alderman,
Drawn with a team of little atomies[15]
Over men's noses as they lie asleep;

4. **visage** mask.
5. **A visor . . . visor!** A mask
   for a mask—which is what
   my real face is like!
6. **quote deformities** notice
   my ugly features.
7. **betake . . . legs** start
   dancing.
8. **Let . . . rushes** Let fun-
   loving people dance on
   the floor coverings.
9. **proverbed . . . phrase**
   directed by an old saying.
10. **The game . . . done**
    No matter how much
    enjoyment may be had, I
    will not have any.
11. **Dun's . . . word!** Lie low
    like a mouse—that is what
    a constable waiting to
    make an arrest might say.
12. **Dun** proverbial name for a
    horse.

Literary Analysis
Dialogue and Stage
Directions What con-
trast between Mercutio
and Romeo does the
dialogue reveal?

13. **Take . . . wits** Understand
    my intended meaning.
    That shows more
    intelligence than merely
    following what your
    senses perceive.

14. **Queen Mab** the queen of
    fairyland.

15. **atomies** creatures.

60 Her wagon spokes made of long spinners'[16] legs,
The cover, of the wings of grasshoppers;
Her traces, of the smallest spider web;
Her collars, of the moonshine's wat'ry beams;
Her whip, of cricket's bone; the lash, of film;[17]
Her wagoner, a small gray-coated gnat,
65 Not half so big as a round little worm
Pricked from the lazy finger of a maid;
Her chariot is an empty hazelnut,
Made by the joiner squirrel or old grub,[18]
Time out o' mind the fairies' coachmakers.
70 And in this state she gallops night by night
Through lovers' brains, and then they dream of love;
On courtiers' knees, that dream on curtsies straight;
O'er lawyers' fingers, who straight dream on fees;
O'er ladies' lips, who straight on kisses dream,
75 Which oft the angry Mab with blisters plagues,
Because their breath with sweetmeats[19] tainted are.
Sometimes she gallops o'er a courtier's nose,
And then dreams he of smelling out a suit;[20]
And sometime comes she with a tithe pig's[21] tail
80 Tickling a parson's nose as 'a lies asleep,
Then he dreams of another benefice.[22]
Sometime she driveth o'er a soldier's neck,
And then dream he of cutting foreign throats,
Of breaches, ambuscadoes,[23] Spanish blades,
85 Of healths[24] five fathom deep; and then anon

16. **spinners** spiders.
17. **film** spider's thread.

18. **old grub** insect that bores holes in nuts.
19. **sweetmeats** candy.

20. **smelling . . . suit** finding someone who has a petition (suit) for the king and who will pay the courtier to gain the king's favor for the petition.
21. **tithe pig** pig donated to a parson.
22. **benefice** church appointment that included a guaranteed income.
23. **ambuscadoes** ambushes.
24. **healths** toasts ("To your health!").

Reading Check

How does Romeo feel about going to the Capulets' feast?

Drums in his ear, at which he starts and wakes,
And being thus frighted, swears a prayer or two
And sleeps again. This is that very Mab
That plats[25] the manes of horses in the night
90   And bakes the elflocks[26] in foul sluttish hairs,
Which once untangled much misfortune bodes.
This is the hag, when maids lie on their backs,
That presses them and learns them first to bear,
Making them women of good carriage.[27]
This is she—

95   **ROMEO.**   Peace, peace, Mercutio, peace!
Thou talk'st of nothing.

MERCUTIO.   True, I talk of dreams;
Which are the children of an idle brain,
Begot of nothing but vain fantasy;
Which is as thin of substance as the air,
100 And more inconstant than the wind, who woos
Even now the frozen bosom of the North
And, being angered, puffs away from thence,
Turning his side to the dew-dropping South.

BENVOLIO. This wind you talk of blows us from ourselves.
105 Supper is done, and we shall come too late.

ROMEO. I fear, too early; for my mind misgives
Some consequence yet hanging in the stars
Shall bitterly begin his fearful date
With this night's revels and expire the term
110 Of a despisèd life, closed in my breast,
By some vile forfeit of untimely death.[28]
But he that hath the steerage of my course
Direct my sail! On, lusty gentlemen!

BENVOLIO. Strike, drum.

[*They march about the stage, and retire to one side.*]

Scene v. A hall in Capulet's house.

[SERVINGMEN *come forth with napkins.*]

FIRST SERVINGMAN. Where's Potpan, that he helps not to
take away? He shift a trencher![1] He scrape a trencher!

SECOND SERVINGMAN. When good manners shall lie all in one
or two men's hands, and they unwashed too, 'tis a foul thing.

Reading Skill

Summarize Review Mercutio's speech and summarize his ideas about Queen Mab.

Literary Analysis

Dialogue and Stage Directions What do Mercutio's comments about dreams reveal about his character?

Reading Skill

Summarize Use footnote 28 to help you summarize Romeo's response to Benvolio.

28. **my mind . . . death** My mind is fearful that some future event, fated by the stars, shall start to run its course tonight and cut my life short.

1. **trencher** wooden platter.

5   **FIRST SERVINGMAN.** Away with the joint-stools, remove the
     court cupboard, look to the plate. Good thou, save me a
     piece of marchpane,[2] and, as thou loves me, let the porter
     let in Susan Grindstone and Nell. Anthony and Potpan!

     SECOND SERVINGMAN. Ay, boy, ready.

10 **FIRST SERVINGMAN.** You are looked for and called for,
     asked for and sought for, in the great chamber.

     THIRD SERVINGMAN. We cannot be here and there too.
     Cheerly, boys! Be brisk awhile, and the longest liver
     take all.   [*Exit.*]

[*Enter* CAPULET, *his* WIFE, JULIET, TYBALT, NURSE, *and all the* GUESTS
and GENTLEWOMEN *to the* MASKERS.]

15 **CAPULET.** Welcome, gentlemen! Ladies that have their toes
     Unplagued with corns will walk a bout[3] with you.
     Ah, my mistresses, which of you all
     Will now deny to dance? She that makes dainty,[4]
     She I'll swear hath corns. Am I come near ye now?
20   Welcome, gentlemen! I have seen the day
     That I have worn a visor and could tell
     A whispering tale in a fair lady's ear,
     Such as would please. 'Tis gone, 'tis gone, 'tis gone.
     You are welcome, gentlemen! Come, musicians,
        play.
                          [*Music plays, and they dance.*]
25   A hall,[5] a hall! Give room! And foot it, girls.
     More light, you knaves, and turn the tables up,
     And quench the fire; the room is grown too hot.
     Ah, sirrah, this unlooked-for sport comes well.
     Nay, sit; nay, sit, good cousin Capulet;
30   For you and I are past our dancing days.
     How long is't now since last yourself and I
     Were in a mask?

     SECOND CAPULET. By'r Lady, thirty years.

     CAPULET. What, man? 'Tis not so much, 'tis not so
        much;
     'Tis since the nuptial of Lucentio,
35   Come Pentecost as quickly as it will,
     Some five-and-twenty years, and then we masked.

     SECOND CAPULET. 'Tis more, 'tis more. His son is elder, sir;
     His son is thirty.

2. **marchpane** marzipan, a
   confection made of sugar
   and almonds.

3. **walk a bout** dance a turn.
4. **makes dainty** hesitates;
   acts shy.

5. **A hall** clear the floor, make
   room for dancing.

Reading Check

What does Romeo fear
might happen in the near
future?

The Tragedy of Romeo and Juliet, Act I **825**

▲ ▶ **Critical Viewing**
What can you tell
about Romeo and
Juliet's feelings for
each other at this point
from these images?
[Draw Conclusions]

Literary Analysis
Dialogue and Stage
Directions What do
the stage direction in
line 40 and the dialogue
that follows reveal about
Romeo?

6. **ward** minor.
7. **Forswear** deny.
8. **antic face** strange,
   fantastic mask.
9. **fleer** mock.

CAPULET.   Will you tell me that?
His son was but a ward[6] two years ago.

40 **ROMEO.** [*To a* SERVINGMAN] What lady's that which doth
          enrich the hand
      Of yonder knight?

SERVINGMAN. I know not, sir.

ROMEO. O, she doth teach the torches to burn bright!
      It seems she hangs upon the cheek of night
45   As a rich jewel in an Ethiop's ear—
      Beauty too rich for use, for earth too dear!
      So shows a snowy dove trooping with crows
      As yonder lady o'er her fellows shows.
      The measure done, I'll watch her place of stand
50   And, touching hers, make blessèd my rude hand.
      Did my heart love till now? Forswear[7] it, sight!
      For I ne'er saw true beauty till this night.

TYBALT. This, by his voice, should be a Montague.
      Fetch me my rapier, boy. What! Dares the slave
55   Come hither, covered with an antic face,[8]
      To fleer[9] and scorn at our solemnity?
      Now, by the stock and honor of my kin,
      To strike him dead I hold it not a sin.

CAPULET. Why, how now, kinsman? Wherefore storm you so?

60 **TYBALT.** Uncle, this is a Montague, our foe,
      A villain, that is hither come in spite

To scorn at our solemnity this night.

CAPULET. Young Romeo is it?

TYBALT.   'Tis he, that villain Romeo.

CAPULET. Content thee, gentle coz,[10] let him alone.
65   'A bears him like a portly gentleman,[11]
       And, to say truth, Verona brags of him
       To be a virtuous and well-governed youth.
       I would not for the wealth of all this town
       Here in my house do him disparagement.[12]
70   Therefore be patient; take no note of him.
       It is my will, the which if thou respect,
       Show a fair presence and put off these frowns,
       An ill-beseeming semblance[13] for a feast.

TYBALT. It fits when such a villain is a guest.
       I'll not endure him.

75 **CAPULET.**   He shall be endured.
       What, goodman[14] boy! I say he shall. Go to![15]
       Am I the master here, or you? Go to!
       You'll not endure him, God shall mend my soul![16]
       You'll make a mutiny among my guests!
80   You will set cock-a-hoop.[17] You'll be the man!

TYBALT. Why, uncle, 'tis a shame.

CAPULET.   Go to, go to!
       You are a saucy boy. Is't so, indeed?
       This trick may chance to scathe you.[18] I know what.
       You must contrary me! Marry, 'tis time—
85   Well said, my hearts!—You are a princox[19]—go!
       Be quiet, or—more light, more light!—For shame!
       I'll make you quiet. What!—Cheerly, my hearts!

10. **coz** Here, "coz" is used as a term of address for a relative.
11. **'A . . . gentleman** He behaves like a dignified gentleman.
12. **disparagement** insult.
13. **ill-beseeming semblance** inappropriate appearance.
14. **goodman** term of address for someone below the rank of gentleman.
15. **Go to!** expression of angry impatience.
16. **God . . . soul!** expression of impatience, equivalent to "God save me!"
17. **You will set cock-a-hoop** You want to swagger like a barnyard rooster.

Literary Analysis
Dialogue and Stage Directions What does the dialogue between Capulet and Tybalt show about their relationship?

18. **This . . . you** This trait of yours may turn out to hurt you.
19. **princox** rude youngster; wise guy.

Reading Check

How does Capulet respond when Tybalt says he does not want Romeo at the party?

20. **Patience . . . meeting**
enforced self-control
mixing with strong anger.

TYBALT. Patience perforce with willful choler meeting[20]
      Makes my flesh tremble in their different greeting.
90   I will withdraw; but this intrusion shall,
      Now seeming sweet, convert to bitt'rest gall.   [*Exit.*]

ROMEO. If I profane with my unworthiest hand
      This holy shrine,[21] the gentle sin is this:
      My lips, two blushing pilgrims, ready stand
95   To smooth that rough touch with a tender kiss.

21. **shrine** Juliet's hand.

JULIET. Good pilgrim, you do wrong your hand too much,
      Which mannerly devotion shows in this;
      For saints have hands that pilgrims' hands do touch
      And palm to palm is holy palmers'[22] kiss.

22. **palmers** pilgrims who
at one time carried palm
branches from the Holy
Land.
23. **move** initiate involvement
in earthly affairs.

100 **ROMEO.** Have not saints lips, and holy palmers too?

JULIET. Ay, pilgrim, lips that they must use in prayer.

ROMEO. O, then, dear saint, let lips do what hands do!
      They pray; grant thou, lest faith turn to despair.

JULIET. Saints do not move,[23] though grant for prayers' sake.

105 **ROMEO.** Then move not while my prayer's effect I take.
      Thus from my lips, by thine my sin is purged.   [*Kisses her.*]

Literary Analysis
Dialogue and Stage
Directions What do
the dialogue and stage
directions in this passage
reveal about Romeo's
and Juliet's feelings?

JULIET. Then have my lips the sin that they have took.

ROMEO. Sin from my lips? O trespass sweetly urged![24]
      Give me my sin again.   [*Kisses her.*]

24. **O . . . urged!** Romeo is
saying, in substance, that
he is happy. Juliet calls his
kiss a sin, for now he can
take it back—by another
kiss.
25. **by th' book** as if you were
following a manual of
courtly love.

JULIET.   You kiss by th' book.[25]

110 **NURSE.** Madam, your mother craves a word with you.

ROMEO. What is her mother?

NURSE.   Marry, bachelor,
      Her mother is the lady of the house,
      And a good lady, and a wise and virtuous.
      I nursed her daughter that you talked withal.
115   I tell you, he that can lay hold of her
      Shall have the chinks.[26]

26. **chinks** cash.

ROMEO.   Is she a Capulet?
      O dear account! My life is my foe's debt.[27]

BENVOLIO. Away, be gone; the sport is at the best.

ROMEO. Ay, so I fear; the more is my unrest.

27. **My life . . . debt** Since
Juliet is a Capulet,
Romeo's life is at the
mercy of the enemies of
his family.

CAPULET. Nay, gentlemen, prepare not to be gone; 120
We have a trifling foolish banquet towards.[28]
Is it e'en so?[29] Why then, I thank you all.
I thank you, honest gentlemen. Good night.
More torches here! Come on then; let's to bed.
Ah, sirrah, by my fay,[30] it waxes late; 125
I'll to my rest.   [*Exit all but* JULIET *and* NURSE.]

JULIET. Come hither, nurse. What is yond gentleman?

NURSE. The son and heir of old Tiberio.

JULIET. What's he that now is going out of door?

NURSE. Marry, that, I think, be young Petruchio. 130

JULIET. What's he that follows here, that would not dance?

NURSE. I know not.

JULIET. Go ask his name—If he is married,

28. **towards** being prepared.
29. **Is . . . so?** Is it the case that you really must leave?

30. **fay** faith.

Literary Analysis
Dialogue and Stage Directions How can you tell that the dialogue that follows line 126 is a private conversation?

Reading Check
How does Romeo get Juliet to kiss him?

My grave is like to be my wedding bed.

135 **NURSE.** His name is Romeo, and a Montague,
    The only son of your great enemy.

JULIET. My only love, sprung from my only hate!
    Too early seen unknown, and known too late!
    Prodigious³¹ birth of love it is to me
140   That I must love a loathèd enemy.

NURSE. What's this? What's this?

JULIET.   A rhyme I learnt even now.
    Of one I danced withal.   [*One calls within,* "JULIET."]

NURSE.   Anon, anon!
    Come, let's away; the strangers all are gone.   [*Exit all.*]

**Spiral Review
Figurative
Language** Explain
the role of paradox
in line 137.

31. Prodigious monstrous;
foretelling misfortune.

Critical Thinking

1. **Respond:** If you were Romeo or Juliet, would you pursue a relationship with the other? Explain your answer.

2. **(a)** Based on Act I, what do you know about Romeo's and Juliet's lives? **(b) Compare and Contrast:** Use details from the text to show how their personalities are similar and different.

3. **(a)** What information about the two households is presented in the Prologue? **(b) Connect:** How does Juliet's comment in Act I, Scene v, lines 137–138, echo the Prologue? Explain your response.

4. **Analyze:** How do the comments of Mercutio and Benvolio add to your understanding of Romeo's character? Explain your answer.

5. **(a) Analyze:** What threats to Romeo and Juliet's love already exist in Act I? **(b) Speculate:** How do you think Romeo and Juliet will react to these threats? Explain your response.

6. **Evaluate:** Based on Romeo's behavior in Act I, do you think Shakespeare accurately portrays a teenager in love? Explain.

Support your responses with evidence from the text.

Do our differences define us?
How do the differences between Romeo and Juliet define their relationship? Explain.

Literary Analysis:
Dialogue and Stage Directions

1. Using a chart like the one shown, explain what the **dialogue** involving the Nurse, Juliet, and Lady Capulet in Act I, Scene iii, reveals about each character.

Act I

The Tragedy of
ROMEO and JULIET
William Shakespeare

Character	Dialogue		Reveals
		→	

2. Most of the **stage directions** in Act I mark the characters' entrances and exits. **(a)** Identify three examples of stage directions that do more than simply dictate characters' movements on and off stage. **(b)** Explain what each of these directions tells us about the characters and the action.

Reading Skill: Summarize

3. Use **text aids** to restate Capulet's scolding of Tybalt in Act I, Scene v, lines 77–87, in your own words.

4. (a) Using text aids to clarify her meaning, explain the play on words in Juliet's speech in Act I, Scene v, lines 96–99.
(b) Summarize Juliet's speech in a few sentences.

Vocabulary

Practice An **oxymoron** is a phrase combining contradictory or opposing ideas, often used as a figure of speech for poetic effect. Review the vocabulary list on page 804. Then, explain the meaning of each phrase and tell why each one is an oxymoron.

1. pernicious blessing

2. augmenting scarcity

3. flattering grievance

4. honorable transgression

5. cooperative adversary

6. cheerful oppression

Word Power Use the context of the sentences and what you know about the **Latin prefix *trans-*** to explain your answer to each question.

1. Can you *transfer* information from the Internet to a computer?

2. If the operation of a government office is *transparent,* will people know what is going on?

Word Power

The **Latin prefix *trans-*** means "across," "over," or "through."

Apply It Explain how the prefix *trans-* helps you determine the meanings of these technical academic words from science. Consult a dictionary if necessary.

transfusion
translucent
transition

Do our *differences* define us?

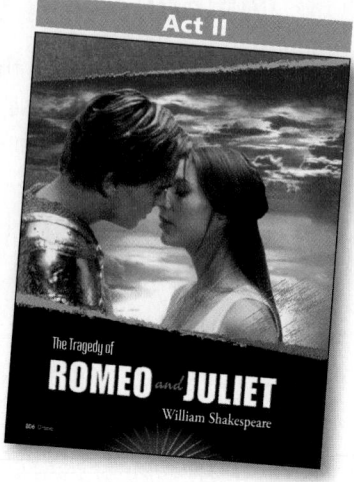

Act II

The Tragedy of
ROMEO *and* **JULIET**
William Shakespeare

As You Read Continue to notice the differences between Romeo and Juliet. Decide whether these differences have a strong effect on the way their relationship develops.

TEXAS Focus on the TEKS

Meet these standards with **The Tragedy of Romeo and Juliet, Act II** (p. 834).

Reading
(9)(A) Distinguish between a summary that captures the main ideas and elements of a text and a critique that takes a position and expresses an opinion. (*Critical Thinking: Analyze*)

(1)(A) Determine the meaning of grade-level technical academic English words in multiple content areas (e.g., social studies) derived from Latin affixes. (*Word Power: Apply It*)

Reading/Comprehension Skills
RC-9(A) Reflect on understanding to monitor comprehension. (*Reading Skill: Summarize*)

For more TEKS, see pages 932–935.

Vocabulary

Read each word and its definition. Decide whether you know the word well, know it a little bit, or do not know it at all. After you read, see how your knowledge of each word has increased.

- **procure** (prō kyoor´) *v.* get; obtain (p. 843) *The hungry man tried to procure food.* procurement *n.* procurable *adj.*

- **predominant** (prē däm´ ə nənt) *adj.* of or having stronger influence (p. 845) *Despite some disagreement, the predominant tone of the meeting was one of unity.* predominantly *adv.* dominant *adv.* dominate *v.*

- **intercession** (in´ tər sesh´ ən) *n.* act of pleading on another's behalf (p. 846) *Thanks to the intercession by Andy and Paula, Jim was allowed into the concert without a ticket.* intercede *v.*

- **sallow** (sal´ ō) *adj.* of a sickly, pale-yellowish hue (p. 846) *When her sickness passed, her face no longer looked sallow.* sallowness *n.*

- **lamentable** (lam´ ən tə bəl) *adj.* distressing; sad (p. 848) *His lack of concern about his health is lamentable.* lament *v.* lamentably *adv.*

- **unwieldy** (un wēl´ dē) *adj.* awkward; clumsy (p. 854) *Joe's sprained ankle made him unwieldy on the dance floor.* wield *v.*

Word Power

The **Latin prefix pro-** means "before," "forward."

In this play, Juliet promises to **procure** the opportunity to come to Romeo, if his intentions are to marry her. She means she will take steps beforehand so that she can see him.

Literary Analysis: Blank Verse

Blank verse is unrhymed poetry written in a meter called iambic pentameter. A line of iambic pentameter has five stressed syllables, each preceded by an unstressed syllable, as in the following example:

- Bŭt sóft! Whăt líght thrŏŭgh yónděr wíndŏw bréaks?
- Ĭt ís thĕ eást, ănd Júliĕt ís thĕ sún!

Much of *The Tragedy of Romeo and Juliet* is written in blank verse. Shakespeare uses its formal meter to reinforce character rank. Important or aristocratic characters typically speak in blank verse. Minor or comic characters often do not speak in verse. This deliberate change in style has an impact on the tone and mood of the character's interactions.

As You Read Notice the effect the use of blank verse has on your impression of the characters who use it in their dialogue.

Reading Skill: Summarize

Summarizing is briefly stating the main points in a piece of writing. Stopping periodically to summarize what you have read helps you to check your comprehension before you read further.

Summarizing is especially useful when reading a play that has long passages of blank verse. When you encounter one of these passages, read in sentences—just as if you were reading a poem. Pause according to the punctuation instead of at the end of each line. As you become more accustomed to the form, you will be able to increase your speed.

Once you have grasped the meanings of individual sentences in blank verse, you can more easily and accurately summarize long passages.

Using the Strategy: Summarizing Chart

As You Read **Reflect on your understanding.** Use a chart like this one to **monitor your comprehension** by summarizing passages in this act of the drama.

Passage	Sentences	Summary
What's Montague? It is nor hand, nor foot, / Nor arm, nor face, nor any other part / Belonging to a man. O, be some other name! / What's in a name? That which we call a rose / By any other name would smell as sweet.	① What's Montague? ② It is nor hand, nor foot, Nor arm, nor face, nor any other part Belonging to a man. ③ O, be some other name! ④ What's in a name? ⑤ That which we call a rose By any other name would smell as sweet.	Montague is just a name; it's not who Romeo physically is, but Juliet wishes he had another name because of what she knows it represents.

Hear It!
- Selection summary audio
- Selection audio

See It!
- Get Connected video
- Background video
- More about the author
- Vocabulary flashcards

Do It!
- Interactive journals
- Interactive graphic organizers
- Self-test
- Internet activity
- Grammar tutorial
- Interactive vocabulary games

www.PHLitOnline.com

ACT II

Reflect "The fourfold of Juliet, Mercutio, the Nurse, and Romeo ... *Romeo and Juliet* matters, as a play, because of these four exuberantly realized characters."

from *Shakespeare: The Invention of the Human* by Harold Bloom

Recall Act I reveals a bitter, long-standing feud between the Montagues and the Capulets. It also introduces the play's title characters, who meet at a feast and immediately fall in love, only to discover that they come from opposing sides of the feud.

Anticipate Based on what you have learned about the personalities of Romeo and Juliet, how do you expect them to respond to their love for each other and to the problems it poses? How do you think their families will react?

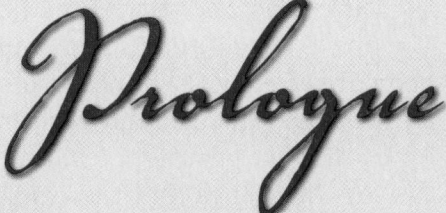

Prologue

[*Enter* CHORUS.]

   CHORUS. Now old desire[1] doth in his deathbed lie,
      And young affection gapes to be his heir;[2]
  That fair[3] for which love groaned for and would die,
      With tender Juliet matched, is now not fair.
5 Now Romeo is beloved and loves again,
      Alike bewitchèd[4] by the charm of looks;
  But to his foe supposed he must complain,[5]
      And she steal love's sweet bait from fearful hooks.

1. **old desire** Romeo's love for Rosaline.
2. **young . . . heir** Romeo's new love for Juliet is eager to replace his love for Rosaline.
3. **fair** beautiful woman (Rosaline).
4. **Alike bewitchèd** Both Romeo and Juliet are enchanted.
5. **complain** address his words of love.

Being held a foe, he may not have access
10   To breathe such vows as lovers use to swear,
      And she as much in love, her means much less
            To meet her new belovèd anywhere;
      But passion lends them power, time means to meet,
      Temp'ring extremities with extreme sweet.[6]
[Exit.]

Scene i. Near Capulet's orchard.

[Enter ROMEO alone.]

ROMEO. Can I go forward when my heart is here?
Turn back, dull earth,[1] and find thy center[2] out.

[Enter BENVOLIO with MERCUTIO. ROMEO retires.]

BENVOLIO. Romeo! My cousin Romeo! Romeo!

MERCUTIO.   He is wise.
And, on my life, hath stol'n him home to bed.

5   **BENVOLIO.** He ran this way and leapt this orchard wall.
Call, good Mercutio.

MERCUTIO.   Nay, I'll conjure[3] too.
Romeo! Humors! Madman! Passion! Lover!
Appear thou in the likeness of a sigh;
Speak but one rhyme, and I am satisfied!
10   Cry but "Ay me!" Pronounce but "love" and "dove";
Speak to my gossip[4] Venus one fair word,
One nickname for her purblind son and heir,
Young Abraham Cupid, he that shot so true
When King Cophetua loved the beggar maid!
15   He heareth not, he stirreth not, he moveth not;
The ape is dead,[5] and I must conjure him.
I conjure thee by Rosaline's bright eyes,
By her high forehead and her scarlet lip,
By her fine foot, straight leg, and quivering thigh,
20   And the demesnes that there adjacent lie,
That in thy likeness thou appear to us!

BENVOLIO. And if he hear thee, thou wilt anger him.

MERCUTIO. This cannot anger him. 'Twould anger him
To raise a spirit in his mistress' circle
25   Of some strange nature, letting it there stand
Till she had laid it and conjured it down.

---

6. Temp'ring . . . sweet easing their difficulties with great delights.

1. dull earth lifeless body.
2. center heart, or possibly soul (Juliet).

3. conjure recite a spell to make Romeo appear.

4. gossip merry old lady.

5. The ape is dead Romeo, like a trained monkey, seems to be playing.

Literary Analysis
Blank Verse Based on the meter of this speech, how can you tell that Mercutio is an aristocratic character?

That were some spite; my invocation
Is fair and honest; in his mistress' name,
I conjure only but to raise up him.

30 **BENVOLIO.** Come, he hath hid himself among these trees
To be consorted[6] with the humorous[7] night.
Blind is his love and best befits the dark.

MERCUTIO. If love be blind, love cannot hit the mark.
Now will he sit under a medlar[8] tree
35 And wish his mistress were that kind of fruit
As maids call medlars when they laugh alone.
O, Romeo, that she were, O that she were
An open *et cetera,* thou a pop'rin pear!
Romeo, good night. I'll to my truckle bed;[9]
40 This field bed is too cold for me to sleep.
Come, shall we go?

BENVOLIO.   Go then, for 'tis in vain
To seek him here that means not to be found.

                              [*Exit with others.*]

Scene ii. Capulet's orchard.

ROMEO. [*Coming forward*] He jests at scars that never felt a
          wound.

[*Enter* JULIET *at a window.*]

But soft! What light through yonder window breaks?
It is the East, and Juliet is the sun!
Arise, fair sun, and kill the envious moon,
5 Who is already sick and pale with grief
That thou her maid art far more fair than she.
Be not her maid, since she is envious.
Her vestal livery[1] is but sick and green,
And none but fools do wear it. Cast it off.
10 It is my lady! O, it is my love!
O, that she knew she were!
She speaks, yet she says nothing. What of that?
Her eye discourses; I will answer it.
I am too bold; 'tis not to me she speaks.
15 Two of the fairest stars in all the heaven,
Having some business, do entreat her eyes
To twinkle in their spheres[2] till they return.
What if her eyes were there, they in her head?

6. **consorted** associated.
7. **humorous** humid; moody,
   like a lover.

8. **medlar** applelike fruit.

9. **truckle bed** trundlebed,
   placed under a larger bed
   when not in use.

Literary Analysis
Blank Verse Which
line in Romeo's speech
breaks the pattern of
five stressed syllables per
line?

1. **livery** clothing or costume
   worn by a servant.

2. **spheres** orbits.

 Reading
Check

Whom does Romeo see
at the window?

Spiral Review
Imagery Explain the imagery and figurative language that Shakespeare uses here.

The brightness of her cheek would shame those stars
20 As daylight doth a lamp; her eyes in heaven
Would through the airy region stream so bright
That birds would sing and think it were not night.
See how she leans her cheek upon that hand,
O, that I were a glove upon that hand,
That I might touch that cheek!

JULIET.   Ay me!

25 **ROMEO.**   She speaks.
O, speak again, bright angel, for thou art
As glorious to this night, being o'er my head,
As is a wingèd messenger of heaven
Unto the white-upturnèd wond'ring eyes
30 Of mortals that fall back to gaze on him
When he bestrides the lazy puffing clouds
And sails upon the bosom of the air.

JULIET. O Romeo, Romeo! Wherefore art thou Romeo?[3]
Deny thy father and refuse thy name;
35 Or, if thou wilt not, be but sworn my love,
And I'll no longer be a Capulet.

▼ **Critical Viewing**
Which line of dialogue in this scene might this photograph capture? **[Connect]**

3. **Wherefore . . . Romeo?**
Why are you Romeo—a Montague?

ROMEO. [*Aside*] Shall I hear more, or shall I speak at this?

JULIET. 'Tis but thy name that is my enemy.
 Thou art thyself, though not⁴ a Montague.
40 What's Montague? It is nor hand, nor foot,
 Nor arm, nor face, nor any other part
 Belonging to a man. O, be some other name!
 What's in a name? That which we call a rose
 By any other name would smell as sweet.
45 So Romeo would, were he not Romeo called,
 Retain that dear perfection which he owes⁵
 Without that title. Romeo, doff⁶ thy name;
 And for thy name, which is no part of thee,
 Take all myself.

ROMEO.   I take thee at thy word.
50 Call me but love, and I'll be new baptized;
 Henceforth I never will be Romeo.

JULIET. What man art thou, thus bescreened in night,
 So stumblest on my counsel?⁷

ROMEO.   By a name
 I know not how to tell thee who I am.
55 My name, dear saint, is hateful to myself
 Because it is an enemy to thee.
 Had I it written, I would tear the word.

JULIET. My ears have yet not drunk a hundred words
 Of thy tongue's uttering, yet I know the sound.
60 Art thou not Romeo, and a Montague?

ROMEO. Neither, fair maid, if either thee dislike.

JULIET. How camest thou hither, tell me, and wherefore?
 The orchard walls are high and hard to climb,
 And the place death, considering who thou art,
65 If any of my kinsmen find thee here.

ROMEO. With love's light wings did I o'erperch⁸ these walls;
 For stony limits cannot hold love out,
 And what love can do, that dares love attempt.
 Therefore thy kinsmen are no stop to me.

70 **JULIET.** If they do see thee, they will murder thee.

ROMEO. Alack, there lies more peril in thine eye
 Than twenty of their swords! Look thou but sweet,
 And I am proof⁹ against their enmity.

4. though not even if you were not.

Reading Skill
Summarize Briefly summarize Juliet's speech about Romeo's name.

5. owes owns; possesses.
6. doff remove.

7. counsel secret thoughts.

Literary Analysis
Blank Verse How do the stressed syllables in line 57 reinforce Romeo's meaning?

8. o'erperch fly over.

9. proof protected, as by armor.

Reading
Check

Why does Romeo say his name is hateful to him?

JULIET. I would not for the world they saw thee here.

75 **ROMEO.** I have night's cloak to hide me from their eyes;
And but[10] thou love me, let them find me here.
My life were better ended by their hate
Than death proroguèd,[11] wanting of thy love.

JULIET. By whose direction found'st thou out this place?

80 **ROMEO.** By love, that first did prompt me to inquire.
He lent me counsel, and I lent him eyes.
I am no pilot; yet, wert thou as far
As that vast shore washed with the farthest sea,
I should adventure[12] for such merchandise.

85 **JULIET.** Thou knowest the mask of night is on my face;
Else would a maiden blush bepaint my cheek
For that which thou hast heard me speak tonight.
Fain would I dwell on form[13]—fain, fain deny
What I have spoke; but farewell compliment![14]
90 Dost thou love me? I know thou wilt say "Ay";
And I will take thy word. Yet, if thou swear'st,
Thou mayst prove false. At lovers' perjuries,
They say Jove laughs. O gentle Romeo,
If thou dost love, pronounce it faithfully.
95 Or if thou thinkest I am too quickly won,
I'll frown and be perverse[15] and say thee nay,
So thou wilt woo; but else, not for the world.
In truth, fair Montague, I am too fond,[16]
And therefore thou mayst think my havior light;[17]
100 But trust me, gentleman, I'll prove more true
Than those that have more cunning to be strange.[18]
I should have been more strange, I must confess,
But that thou overheard'st, ere I was ware,
My truelove passion. Therefore pardon me,
105 And not impute this yielding to light love,
Which the dark night hath so discoverèd.[19]

ROMEO. Lady, by yonder blessèd moon I vow,
That tips with silver all these fruit-tree tops—

JULIET. O, swear not by the moon, th' inconstant moon,
110 That monthly changes in her circle orb,
Lest that thy love prove likewise variable.

10. **And but** unless.

11. **proroguèd** postponed.

12. **adventure** risk a long journey, like a sea adventurer.
13. **Fain . . . form** eagerly would I follow convention (by acting reserved).
14. **compliment** conventional behavior.

15. **be perverse** act contrary to my true feelings.
16. **fond** affectionate.
17. **my havior light** my behavior immodest or unserious.
18. **strange** distant and cold.

19. **discoverèd** revealed.

ROMEO. What shall I swear by?

JULIET.   Do not swear at all;
Or if thou wilt, swear by thy gracious self,
Which is the god of my idolatry,
And I'll believe thee.

115 **ROMEO.** If my heart's dear love—

JULIET. Well, do not swear. Although I joy in thee,
I have no joy of this contract[20] tonight.
It is too rash, too unadvised, too sudden;
Too like the lightning, which doth cease to be
120 Ere one can say it lightens. Sweet, good night!
This bud of love, by summer's ripening breath,
May prove a beauteous flow'r when next we meet.
Good night, good night! As sweet repose and rest
Come to thy heart as that within my breast!

125 **ROMEO.** O, wilt thou leave me so unsatisfied?

JULIET. What satisfaction canst thou have tonight?

ROMEO. Th'exchange of thy love's faithful vow for mine.

Literary Analysis
Blank Verse The five stressed syllables of both lines 112 and 115 are split between the two speakers. What does this weaving together of dialogue suggest about the speakers' relationship?

20. contract betrothal.

Reading
Check

Why does Juliet tell Romeo not to swear his love by the moon?

JULIET. I gave thee mine before thou didst request it;
And yet I would it were to give again.

130 **ROMEO.** Wouldst thou withdraw it? For what purpose, love?

JULIET. But to be frank[21] and give it thee again.
And yet I wish but for the thing I have.
My bounty[22] is as boundless as the sea,
My love as deep; the more I give to thee,
135 The more I have, for both are infinite,
I hear some noise within. Dear love, adieu!

[NURSE *calls within.*]

Anon, good nurse! Sweet Montague, be true.
Stay but a little, I will come again.   [*Exit.*]

21. **frank** generous.

22. **bounty** what I have to give.

LITERATURE IN CONTEXT

Culture Connection

Falconry

When Juliet longs for "a falc'ners voice," she is referring to someone who practices falconry, the sport of hunting with falcons. Falcons are swift, hawk-like birds of prey. The falconer trains the bird to respond to a combination of physical and vocal commands.

During Shakespeare's time, one's rank in society determined the kind of bird one could own:

Rank	Type of Bird
King	Gyr falcon
Prince	Peregrine falcon (male)
Knight	Saker falcon
Squire	Lanner falcon
Lady	Merlin (female)
Yeoman (landowner)	Goshawk
Servants, children	Kestrel

◄ Falconry began as a way to obtain food but gradually evolved into the "sport of kings."

Thick leather gloves protect the falconer from the bird's talons. ►

Connect to the Literature

Why do you think Juliet wishes Romeo would respond to her voice as a falcon does to the falconer's commands?

ROMEO. O blessèd, blessèd night! I am afeard,

140   Being in night, all this is but a dream,

     Too flattering-sweet to be substantial.[23]

[*Enter* JULIET *again.*]

JULIET. Three words, dear Romeo, and good night indeed.

     If that thy bent[24] of love be honorable,

     Thy purpose marriage, send me word tomorrow,

145   By one that I'll procure to come to thee,

     Where and what time thou wilt perform the rite;

     And all my fortunes at thy foot I'll lay

     And follow thee my lord throughout the world.

NURSE. [*Within*] Madam!

150 **JULIET.** I come anon.—But if thou meanest not well,

     I do beseech thee—

NURSE.   [*Within*] Madam!

JULIET.   By and by[25] I come.—

     To cease thy strife[26] and leave me to my grief.

     Tomorrow will I send.

ROMEO.   So thrive my soul—

JULIET. A thousand times good night!   [*Exit.*]

155 **ROMEO.** A thousand times the worse, to want thy light!

     Love goes toward love as schoolboys from their books;

     But love from love, toward school with heavy looks.

[*Enter* JULIET *again.*]

JULIET. Hist! Romeo, hist! O for a falc'ner's voice

     To lure this tassel gentle[27] back again!

160   Bondage is hoarse[28] and may not speak aloud,

     Else would I tear the cave where Echo[29] lies

     And make her airy tongue more hoarse than mine

     With repetition of "My Romeo!"

ROMEO. It is my soul that calls upon my name.

165   How silver-sweet sound lovers' tongues by night,

     Like softest music to attending ears!

JULIET. Romeo!

ROMEO.   My sweet?

JULIET.   What o'clock tomorrow

     Shall I send to thee?

---

23. substantial real.
24. bent purpose; intention.

Vocabulary
procure (prō kyoor´)
v. get; obtain

25. By and by at once.
26. strife efforts.

Literary Analysis
Blank Verse Based on the fact that Romeo and Juliet speak in blank verse, what can you conclude about their characters' ranks?

27. tassel gentle male falcon.
28. Bondage is hoarse Being bound in by my family restricts my speech.
29. Echo In classical mythology, the nymph Echo, unable to win the love of Narcissus, wasted away in a cave until nothing was left of her but her voice.

Reading Check

Why can't Juliet speak loudly to Romeo?

ROMEO. By the hour of nine.

JULIET. I will not fail. 'Tis twenty year till then.
170   I have forgot why I did call thee back.

ROMEO. Let me stand here till thou remember it.

JULIET. I shall forget, to have thee still stand there,
      Rememb'ring how I love thy company.

ROMEO. And I'll stay, to have thee still forget,
175   Forgetting any other home but this.

JULIET. 'Tis almost morning. I would have thee gone—
      And yet no farther than a wanton's[30] bird,
      That lets it hop a little from his hand,
      Like a poor prisoner in his twisted gyves,[31]
180   And with a silken thread plucks it back again,
      So loving-jealous of his liberty.

ROMEO. I would I were thy bird.

JULIET. Sweet, so would I.
      Yet I should kill thee with much cherishing.
      Good night, good night! Parting is such sweet sorrow
185   That I shall say good night till it be morrow.   [*Exit.*]

ROMEO. Sleep dwell upon thine eyes, peace in thy breast!
      Would I were sleep and peace, so sweet to rest!
      Hence will I to my ghostly friar's[32] close cell,[33]
      His help to crave and my dear hap[34] to tell.   [*Exit.*]

Scene iii. Friar Lawrence's cell.

[*Enter* FRIAR LAWRENCE *alone, with a basket.*]

FRIAR. The gray-eyed morn smiles on the frowning night,
      Check'ring the eastern clouds with streaks of light;
      And fleckèd[1] darkness like a drunkard reels
      From forth day's path and Titan's burning wheels.[2]
5   Now, ere the sun advance his burning eye
      The day to cheer and night's dank dew to dry,
      I must upfill this osier cage[3] of ours
      With baleful[4] weeds and precious-juicèd flowers.
      The earth that's nature's mother is her tomb.
10   What is her burying grave, that is her womb;
      And from her womb children of divers kind[5]
      We sucking on her natural bosom find,
      Many for many virtues excellent,

---

30. **wanton's** spoiled, playful child's.
31. **gyves** (jīvz) chains.

32. **ghostly friar's** spiritual father's.
33. **close cell** small room.
34. **dear hap** good fortune.

Reading Skill

Summarize Pause to reflect on your understanding of lines 1–30. Then, monitor your comprehension by briefly stating the main points of the Friar's speech.

1. **fleckèd** spotted.
2. **Titan's burning wheels** wheels of the sun god's chariot.
3. **osier cage** willow basket.
4. **baleful** poisonous.
5. **divers kind** different kinds.

15 None but for some, and yet all different.
    O, mickle[6] is the powerful grace[7] that lies
    In plants, herbs, stones, and their true qualities;
    For naught so vile that on the earth doth live
    But to the earth some special good doth give;
20 Nor aught so good but, strained[8] from that fair use,
    Revolts from true birth,[9] stumbling on abuse.
    Virtue itself turns vice, being misapplied,
    And vice sometime by action dignified.

[*Enter* ROMEO.]

    Within the infant rind[10] of this weak flower
    Poison hath residence and medicine power;[11]
25 For this, being smelt, with that part cheers each part;[12]
    Being tasted, stays all senses with the heart.[13]
    Two such opposèd kings encamp them still[14]
    In man as well as herbs—grace and rude will;
    And where the worser is predominant,
30 Full soon the canker[15] death eats up that plant.

ROMEO. Good morrow, father.

FRIAR.   *Benedicite*![16]
    What early tongue so sweet saluteth me?
    Young son, it argues a distemperèd head[17]
    So soon to bid good morrow to thy bed.
35 Care keeps his watch in every old man's eye,
    And where care lodges, sleep will never lie;
    But where unbruisèd youth with unstuffed[18] brain
    Doth couch his limbs, there golden sleep doth reign,
    Therefore thy earliness doth me assure
40 Thou art uproused with some distemp'rature;[19]
    Or if not so, then here I hit it right—
    Our Romeo hath not been in bed tonight.

ROMEO. That last is true. The sweeter rest was mine.

FRIAR. God pardon sin! Wast thou with Rosaline?

45 **ROMEO.** With Rosaline, my ghostly father? No.
    I have forgot that name and that name's woe.

FRIAR. That's my good son! But where hast thou been then?

ROMEO. I'll tell thee ere thou ask it me again.
    I have been feasting with mine enemy,
50 Where on a sudden one hath wounded me
    That's by me wounded. Both our remedies

6. **mickle** great.
7. **grace** divine power.
8. **strained** turned away.
9. **Revolts . . . birth** conflicts with its real purpose.
10. **infant rind** tender skin.
11. **and medicine power** and medicinal quality has power.
12. **with . . . part** with that quality—odor—revives each part of the body.
13. **stays . . . heart** kills (stops the working of the five senses along with the heart).
14. **still** always.
15. **canker** destructive caterpillar.

Vocabulary
predominant (prē däm´ ə nənt) *adj.* of or having stronger influence

16. *Benedicite*! God bless you!
17. **distemperèd head** troubled mind.

18. **unstuffed** not filled with cares.
19. **distemp'rature** illness.

Literary Analysis
Blank Verse What sets the Friar's lines apart from normal blank verse?

Reading Check

What plan do Romeo and Juliet make for the following day?

Vocabulary

intercession (in´ tər sesh´ ən) *n.* act of pleading on another's behalf

20. **physic** (fiz´ ik) medicine.
21. **My . . . foe** my plea also helps my enemy (Juliet, a Capulet).
22. **and . . . drift** and simple in your speech.
23. **Riddling . . . shrift** A confusing confession will get you uncertain forgiveness. The Friar means that unless Romeo speaks clearly, he will not get clear and direct advice.
24. **And . . . save** and we are united in every way, except for (save).
25. **brine** salt water (tears).

Vocabulary

sallow (sal´ ō) *adj.* of a sickly, pale-yellowish hue

26. **fall** be weak or inconstant.
27. **strength** constancy; stability.
28. **doting** being infatuated.
29. **badst** urged.

30. **grace** favor.
31. **allow** give.
32. **Thy . . . spell** your love recited words from memory with no understanding of them.

Within thy help and holy physic[20] lies.
I bear no hatred, blessèd man, for, lo,
My intercession likewise steads my foe.[21]

55 **FRIAR.** Be plain, good son, and homely in thy drift.[22]
Riddling confession finds but riddling shrift.[23]

ROMEO. Then plainly know my heart's dear love is set
On the fair daughter of rich Capulet;
As mine on hers, so hers is set on mine,
60 And all combined, save[24] what thou must combine
By holy marriage. When and where and how
We met, we wooed, and made exchange of vow,
I'll tell thee as we pass; but this I pray,
That thou consent to marry us today.

65 **FRIAR.** Holy Saint Francis! What a change is here!
Is Rosaline, that thou didst love so dear,
So soon forsaken? Young men's love then lies
Not truly in their hearts, but in their eyes.
Jesu Maria! What a deal of brine[25]
70 Hath washed thy sallow cheeks for Rosaline!
How much salt water thrown away in waste
To season love, that of it doth not taste!
The sun not yet thy sighs from heaven clears,
Thy old groans ring yet in mine ancient ears.
75 Lo, here upon thy cheek the stain doth sit
Of an old tear that is not washed off yet.
If e'er thou wast thyself, and these woes thine,
Thou and these woes were all for Rosaline.
And art thou changed? Pronounce this sentence then:
80 Women may fall[26] when there's no strength[27] in men.

ROMEO. Thou chidst me oft for loving Rosaline.

FRIAR. For doting,[28] not for loving, pupil mine.

ROMEO. And badst[29] me bury love.

FRIAR.   Not in a grave
To lay one in, another out to have.

85 **ROMEO.** I pray thee chide me not. Her I love now
Doth grace[30] for grace and love for love allow.[31]
The other did not so.

FRIAR.   O, she knew well
Thy love did read by rote, that could not spell.[32]

But come, young waverer, come go with me.
In one respect I'll thy assistant be;
For this alliance may so happy prove
To turn your households' rancor[33] to pure love.

ROMEO. O, let us hence! I stand on[34] sudden haste.

FRIAR. Wisely and slow. They stumble that run fast.   [*Exit all.*]

90 (line marker)

33. **rancor** hatred.
34. **stand on** insist on.

Scene iv. A street.

[*Enter* BENVOLIO *and* MERCUTIO.]

MERCUTIO. Where the devil should this Romeo be? Came he not
home tonight?

BENVOLIO. Not to his father's. I spoke with his man.

MERCUTIO. Why, that same pale hardhearted wench, that
Rosaline,
torments him so that he will sure run mad.

BENVOLIO. Tybalt, the kinsman to old Capulet,
Hath sent a letter to his father's house.

MERCUTIO. A challenge, on my life.

BENVOLIO. Romeo will answer it.

MERCUTIO. Any man that can write may answer a letter.

BENVOLIO. Nay, he will answer the letter's master, how he dares,
being dared.

MERCUTIO. Alas, poor Romeo, he is already dead: stabbed
with a white wench's black eye; run through the ear
with a love song; the very pin of his heart cleft with the
blind bow-boy's butt-shaft;[1] and is he a man to encounter
Tybalt?

BENVOLIO. Why, what is Tybalt?

MERCUTIO. More than Prince of Cats.[2] O, he's the courageous
captain of compliments.[3] He fights as you sing
pricksong[4]—keeps time, distance, and proportion; he
rests his minim rests,[5] one, two, and the third in your
bosom! The very butcher of a silk button,[6] a duelist, a
duelist! A gentleman of the very first house,[7] of the first
and second cause.[8] Ah, the immortal *passado*! The
punto reverso! The hay![9]

BENVOLIO. The what?

MERCUTIO. The pox of such antic, lisping, affecting

Literary Analysis
Blank Verse In what
way is Mercutio's and
Benvolio's speech in this
scene different from
what it was earlier in
Act II?

1. **blind bow-boy's butt-shaft** Cupid's blunt arrow.
2. **Prince of Cats** Tybalt, or a variation of it, is the name of the cat in medieval stories of Reynard the Fox.
3. **captain of compliments** master of formal behavior.
4. **as you sing pricksong** with attention to precision.
5. **rests . . . rests** observes all formalities.
6. **button** exact spot on his opponent's shirt.
7. **first house** finest school of fencing.
8. **the first and second cause** reasons that would cause a gentleman to challenge another to a duel.
9. *passado! . . . punto reverso! . . . hay!* lunge . . . backhanded stroke . . . home thrust.

Reading
Check

What does the Friar think
Romeo and Juliet's love
will do for the Capulets
and Montagues?

10. The pox . . . accent May the plague strike these absurd characters with their phony manners.

Vocabulary
lamentable (lam´ ən tə bəl) *adj.* distressing; sad

11. these pardon-me's these men who are always saying "Pardon me."
12. Without . . . herring worn out.
13. numbers verses of love poems.

14. slip escape. *Slip* is also a term for a counterfeit coin.

30 fantasticoes—these new tuners of accent![10] "By Jesu, a very good blade! A very tall man! A very good whore!" Why, is not this a lamentable thing, grandsir, that we should be thus afflicted with these strange flies, these fashionmongers, these pardon-me's,[11] who stand so 35 much on the new form that they cannot sit at ease on the old bench? O, their bones, their bones!

[*Enter* ROMEO.]

BENVOLIO. Here comes Romeo! Here comes Romeo!

MERCUTIO. Without his roe, like a dried herring.[12] O flesh, flesh, how art thou fishified! Now is he for the numbers[13] 40 that Petrarch flowed in. Laura, to his lady, was a kitchen wench (marry, she had a better love to berhyme her), Dido a dowdy, Cleopatra a gypsy, Helen and Hero hildings and harlots, Thisbe a gray eye or so, but not to the purpose. Signior Romeo, *bonjour*! 45 There's a French salutation to your French slop. You gave us the counterfeit fairly last night.

ROMEO. Good morrow to you both. What counterfeit did I give you?

MERCUTIO. The slip,[14] sir, the slip. Can you not conceive?

LITERATURE IN CONTEXT

(History Connection)

Mercutio's Allusions

The women Mercutio names as he taunts Romeo are famous figures in European literature and history. Laura was the name of a woman to whom the Italian poet Petrarch addressed much of his love poetry. Dido, according to Roman mythology, was the queen of Carthage and love interest of Aeneas, the founder of Rome. Cleopatra was the famed Egyptian queen with whom Julius Caesar and later Mark Antony fell in love. Helen, Hero, and Thisbe are all legendary beauties in Greek mythology. Mercutio mocks Romeo by saying that Romeo thinks none of them compare with Rosaline.

Connect to the Literature

Why is Mercutio's use of grand references and exaggerated language a fitting way to tease Romeo?

ROMEO. Pardon, good Mercutio. My business was great, 50
and in such a case as mine a man may strain courtesy.

MERCUTIO. That's as much as to say, such a case as yours
constrains a man to bow in the hams.[15]

15. **hams** hips.

ROMEO. Meaning, to curtsy.

MERCUTIO. Thou hast most kindly hit it. 55

ROMEO. A most courteous exposition.

MERCUTIO. Nay, I am the very pink of courtesy.

ROMEO. Pink for flower.

MERCUTIO. Right.

ROMEO. Why, then is my pump[16] well-flowered. 60

16. **pump** shoe.

MERCUTIO. Sure wit, follow me this jest now till thou hast
worn out thy pump, that, when the single sole of it is
worn, the jest may remain, after the wearing, solely
singular.[17]

17. **when . . . singular** The
jest will outwear the shoe
and will then be all alone.
18. **O . . . singleness!** O thin
joke, unique for only one
thing—weakness!
19. **Swits . . . match** Drive
your wit harder to beat me
or else I will claim victory
in this match of wordplay.

ROMEO. O single-soled jest, solely singular for the singleness![18] 65

MERCUTIO. Come between us, good Benvolio! My wits faints.

ROMEO. Swits and spurs, swits and spurs; or I'll cry a
match.[19]

MERCUTIO. Nay, if our wits run the wild-goose chase, I
am done; for thou hast more of the wild goose in one of
thy wits than, I am sure, I have in my whole five. Was I 70
with you there for the goose?

ROMEO. Thou wast never with me for anything when thou
wast not there for the goose.

MERCUTIO. I will bite thee by the ear for that jest.

ROMEO. Nay, good goose, bite not! 75

MERCUTIO. Thy wit is a very bitter sweeting;[20] it is a most sharp
sauce.

ROMEO. And is it not, then, well served in to a sweet goose?

MERCUTIO. O, here's a wit of cheveril,[21] that stretches from an
inch narrow to an ell broad! 80

ROMEO. I stretch it out for that word "broad," which added
to the goose, proves thee far and wide a broad goose.

Literary Analysis
Blank Verse Why do
you think Romeo does
not speak in blank verse
in this conversation with
his friends?

20. **sweeting** kind of apple.
21. **cheveril** easily stretched
kid leather.

Reading
Check

How does Romeo
respond when Mercutio
says that Romeo gave
his friends "the slip" the
night before?

22. **natural** idiot.
23. **lolling** with tongue hanging out.
24. **bauble** toy.
25. **the hair** natural inclination.

MERCUTIO. Why, is not this better now than groaning for
love? Now art thou sociable, now art thou Romeo; now
art thou what thou art, by art as well as by nature. For
this driveling love is like a great natural[22] that runs
lolling[23] up and down to hide his bauble[24] in a hole.

85

BENVOLIO. Stop there, stop there!

MERCUTIO. Thou desirest me to stop in my tale against the
hair.[25]

90

BENVOLIO. Thou wouldst else have made thy tale large.

26. **occupy the argument** talk about the matter.
27. **goodly gear** good stuff for joking (Romeo sees Nurse approaching).
28. **A shirt and a smock** a man and a woman.

MERCUTIO. O, thou art deceived! I would have made it
short; for I was come to the whole depth of my tale,
and meant indeed to occupy the argument[26] no longer.

ROMEO. Here's goodly gear![27]

[*Enter* NURSE *and her Man,* PETER.]

95

A sail, a sail!

MERCUTIO. Two, two! A shirt and a smock.[28]

NURSE. Peter!

PETER. Anon.

NURSE. My fan, Peter.

100

MERCUTIO. Good Peter, to hide her face; for her fan's the
fairer face.

NURSE. God ye good morrow, gentlemen.

MERCUTIO. God ye good-den, fair gentlewoman.

NURSE. Is it good-den?

Literary Analysis
Blank Verse How does Shakespeare reveal Romeo and Mercutio's intelligence even when they are not speaking in blank verse?

105

MERCUTIO. 'Tis no less, I tell ye; for the bawdy hand of the
dial is now upon the prick of noon.

NURSE. Out upon you! What a man are you!

ROMEO. One, gentlewoman, that God hath made, himself to mar.

NURSE. By my troth, it is well said. "For himself to mar,"
110   quoth 'a? Gentlemen, can any of you tell me where I
may find the young Romeo?

ROMEO. I can tell you; but young Romeo will be older
when you have found him than he was when you sought
him. I am the youngest of that name, for fault[29] of a
115   worse.

29. **fault** lack.

NURSE. You say well.

MERCUTIO. Yea, is the worst well? Very well took,[30] i' faith! Wisely, wisely.

NURSE. If you be he, sir, I desire some confidence[31] with you.

120 **BENVOLIO.** She will endite him to some supper.

MERCUTIO. A bawd, a bawd, a bawd! So ho!

ROMEO. What hast thou found?

MERCUTIO. No hare, sir; unless a hare, sir, in a lenten pie, that is something stale and hoar ere it be spent.

[*He walks by them and sings.*]

125   An old hare hoar,
          And an old hare hoar,
              Is very good meat in Lent;
          But a hare that is hoar
          Is too much for a score
130   When it hoars ere it be spent.

30. **took** understood.

31. **confidence** Nurse means "conference."

Reading Check

Who interrupts Romeo and his friends to ask about Romeo?

Romeo, will you come to your father's? We'll to dinner thither.

ROMEO. I will follow you.

MERCUTIO. Farewell, ancient lady. Farewell, [*singing*] "Lady, lady, lady."[32]

[*Exit* MERCUTIO, BENVOLIO.]

135   **NURSE.** I pray you, sir, what saucy merchant was this that was so full of his ropery?[33]

ROMEO. A gentleman, nurse, that loves to hear himself talk and will speak more in a minute than he will stand to in a month.

140   **NURSE.** And 'a[34] speak anything against me, I'll take him down, and 'a were lustier than he is, and twenty such Jacks; and if I cannot, I'll find those that shall. Scurvy knave! I am none of his flirt-gills;[35] I am none of his skainsmates.[36] And thou must stand by too, and suffer
145   every knave to use me at his pleasure!

PETER. I saw no man use you at his pleasure. If I had, my weapon should quickly have been out, I warrant you. I dare draw as soon as another man, if I see occasion in a good quarrel, and the law on my side.

150   **NURSE.** Now, afore God, I am so vexed that every part about me quivers. Scurvy knave! Pray you, sir, a word; and, as I told you, my young lady bid me inquire you out. What she bid me say, I will keep to myself; but first let me tell ye, if ye should lead her in a fool's paradise, as
155   they say, it were a very gross kind of behavior, as they say; for the gentlewoman is young; and therefore, if you should deal double with her, truly it were an ill thing to be off'red to any gentlewoman, and very weak[37] dealing.

160   **ROMEO.** Nurse, commend[38] me to thy lady and mistress. I protest unto thee—

NURSE. Good heart, and i' faith I will tell her as much. Lord, Lord, she will be a joyful woman.

ROMEO. What wilt thou tell her, nurse? Thou dost not
165   mark me.

NURSE. I will tell her, sir, that you do protest, which, as I take it, is a gentlemanlike offer.

---

32. **"Lady . . . lady"** line from an old ballad, "Chaste Susanna."
33. **ropery** Nurse means "roguery," the talk and conduct of a rascal.

34. **'a** he.

35. **flirt-gills** common girls.
36. **skainsmates** criminals; cutthroats.

37. **weak** unmanly.

38. **commend** convey my respect and best wishes.

ROMEO. Bid her devise
Some means to come to shrift[39] this afternoon;
170 And there she shall at Friar Lawrence' cell
Be shrived and married. Here is for thy pains.

NURSE. No, truly, sir; not a penny.

ROMEO. Go to! I say you shall.

NURSE. This afternoon, sir? Well, she shall be there.

175 **ROMEO.** And stay, good nurse, behind the abbey wall.
Within this hour my man shall be with thee
And bring thee cords made like a tackled stair.[40]
Which to the high topgallant[41] of my joy
Must be my convoy[42] in the secret night.
180 Farewell. Be trusty, and I'll quit[43] thy pains.
Farewell. Commend me to thy mistress.

NURSE. Now God in heaven bless thee! Hark you, sir.

ROMEO. What say'st thou, my dear nurse?

NURSE. Is your man secret? Did you ne'er hear say,
185 Two may keep counsel, putting one away?[44]

ROMEO. Warrant thee my man's as true as steel.

NURSE. Well, sir, my mistress is the sweetest lady. Lord,
Lord! When 'twas a little prating[45] thing—O, there is a
nobleman in town, one Paris, that would fain lay knife
190 aboard;[46] but she, good soul, had as lieve[47] see a toad,
a very toad, as see him. I anger her sometimes, and tell
her that Paris is the properer man; but I'll warrant
you, when I say so, she looks as pale as any clout[48]
in the versal world.[49] Doth not rosemary and Romeo
195 begin both with a letter?

ROMEO. Ay, nurse; what of that? Both with an R.

NURSE. Ah, mocker! That's the dog's name.[50] R is for the—
No; I know it begins with some other letter; and she
hath the prettiest sententious[51] of it, of you and rosemary,
200 that it would do you good to hear it.

ROMEO. Commend me to thy lady.

NURSE. Ay, a thousand times. [*Exit* ROMEO.] Peter!

PETER. Anon.

205 **NURSE.** Before, and apace.[52]   [*Exit, after* PETER.]

39. **shrift** confession.

Reading Skill
Summarize Read in sentences to summarize Romeo's instructions to the Nurse in lines 175–181.

40. **tackled stair** rope ladder.
41. **topgallant** summit.
42. **convoy** conveyance.
43. **quit** reward; pay you back for.

44. **Two . . . away** Two can keep a secret if one is ignorant, or out of the way.
45. **prating** babbling.
46. **fain . . . aboard** eagerly seize Juliet for himself.
47. **had as lieve** would as willingly.
48. **clout** cloth.
49. **versal world** universe.
50. **dog's name** *R* sounds like a growl.
51. **sententious** Nurse means "sentences"—clever, wise sayings.
52. **Before, and apace** Go ahead of me, and quickly.

Literary Analysis
Blank Verse What is the effect of hearing Romeo's blank verse after long passages of prose?

Reading Check
What does Romeo ask the Nurse to tell Juliet?

Scene v. Capulet's orchard.

[*Enter* JULIET.]

JULIET. The clock struck nine when I did send the nurse;
    In half an hour she promised to return.
    Perchance she cannot meet him. That's not so.
    O, she is lame! Love's heralds should be thoughts,
5   Which ten times faster glides than the sun's beams
    Driving back shadows over low'ring[1] hills.
    Therefore do nimble-pinioned doves draw Love,[2]
    And therefore hath the wind-swift Cupid wings.
    Now is the sun upon the highmost hill
10   Of this day's journey, and from nine till twelve
    Is three long hours; yet she is not come.
    Had she affections and warm youthful blood,
    She would be as swift in motion as a ball;
    My words would bandy her[3] to my sweet love,
15   And his to me.
    But old folks, many feign[4] as they were dead—
    Unwieldy, slow, heavy and pale as lead.

[*Enter* NURSE *and* PETER.]

    O God, she comes! O honey nurse, what news?
    Hast thou met with him? Send thy man away.

20 **NURSE.** Peter, stay at the gate.   [*Exit* PETER.]

JULIET. Now, good sweet nurse—O Lord, why lookest thou sad?
    Though news be sad, yet tell them merrily;
    If good, thou shamest the music of sweet news
    By playing it to me with so sour a face.

25 **NURSE.** I am aweary, give me leave[5] awhile.
    Fie, how my bones ache! What a jaunce[6] have I!

JULIET. I would thou hadst my bones, and I thy news.
    Nay, come, I pray thee speak. Good, good nurse, speak.

NURSE. Jesu, what haste? Can you not stay a while?
30   Do you not see that I am out of breath?

JULIET. How art thou out of breath when thou hast breath
    To say to me that thou art out of breath?
    The excuse that thou dost make in this delay
    Is longer than the tale thou dost excuse.
35   Is thy news good or bad? Answer to that.

1. low'ring darkening.
2. Therefore . . . Love therefore, doves with quick wings pull the chariot of Venus, goddess of love.

3. bandy her send her rapidly.

Vocabulary
unwieldy (un wēl′ dē)
adj. awkward; clumsy

4. feign act.

5. give me leave excuse me; give me a moment's rest.
6. jaunce rough trip.

Say either, and I'll stay the circumstance.[7]
Let me be satisfied, is't good or bad?

NURSE. Well, you have made a simple[8] choice; you know
40 not how to choose a man. Romeo? No, not he. Though
his face be better than any man's, yet his leg excels all
men's; and for a hand and a foot, and a body, though
they be not to be talked on, yet they are past compare.
He is not the flower of courtesy, but, I'll warrant him,
as gentle as a lamb. Go thy ways, wench; serve God.
45 What, have you dined at home?

JULIET. No, no. But all this I did know before.
What says he of our marriage? What of that?

NURSE. Lord, how my head aches! What a head have I!
It beats as it would fall in twenty pieces.
50 My back a[9] t'other side—ah, my back, my back!
Beshrew[10] your heart for sending me about
To catch my death with jauncing up and down!

JULIET. I' faith, I am sorry that thou art not well.
Sweet, sweet, sweet nurse, tell me, what says my love?

55 **NURSE.** Your love says, like an honest gentleman, and a
courteous, and a kind, and a handsome, and, I warrant,
a virtuous—Where is your mother?

JULIET. Where is my mother? Why, she is within.
Where should she be? How oddly thou repliest!
60 "Your love says, like an honest gentleman,
'Where is your mother?'"

NURSE.   O God's Lady dear!
Are you so hot?[11] Marry come up, I trow.[12]
Is this the poultice[13] for my aching bones?
Henceforward do your messages yourself.

65 **JULIET.** Here's such a coil![14] Come, what says Romeo?

NURSE. Have you got leave to go to shrift today?

JULIET. I have.

NURSE. Then hie you hence to Friar Lawrence' cell;
There stays a husband to make you a wife.
70 Now comes the wanton[15] blood up in your cheeks:
They'll be in scarlet straight at any news.
Hie you to church: I must another way,

7. **stay the circumstance**
   wait for the details.
8. **simple** foolish;
   simpleminded.

9. **a** on.
10. **Beshrew** shame on.

Literary Analysis
Blank Verse What
might Shakespeare
be indicating about
the Nurse's character
by having her switch
between prose and blank
verse?

11. **hot** impatient; hot-
    tempered.
12. **Marry . . . trow** Indeed,
    cool down, I say.
13. **poultice** remedy.
14. **coil** disturbance.
15. **wanton** excited.

Reading
Check

How does the Nurse
describe Romeo?

To fetch a ladder, by the which your love
Must climb a bird's nest soon when it is dark.
75 I am the drudge, and toil in your delight:
But you shall bear the burden soon at night.
Go; I'll to dinner; hie you to the cell.

JULIET. Hie to high fortune! Honest nurse, farewell.

[*Exit all.*]

Scene vi. Friar Lawrence's cell.

[*Enter* FRIAR LAWRENCE *and* ROMEO.]

FRIAR. So smile the heavens upon this holy act
That afterhours with sorrow chide us not![1]

ROMEO. Amen, amen! But come what sorrow can,
It cannot countervail[2] the exchange of joy
5 That one short minute gives me in her sight.
Do thou but close our hands with holy words,
Then love-devouring death do what he dare—
It is enough I may but call her mine.

FRIAR. These violent delights have violent ends
10 And in their triumph die, like fire and powder,[3]
Which, as they kiss, consume. The sweetest honey

1. **That . . . not!** that the future does not punish us with sorrow.
2. **countervail** equal.
3. **powder** gunpowder.

▶ **Critical Viewing**
Which details in this picture reflect the feelings Romeo and Juliet have for each other? **[Interpret]**

Is loathsome in his own deliciousness
And in the taste confounds[4] the appetite.
Therefore love moderately: long love doth so;
15　Too swift arrives as tardy as too slow.

[*Enter* JULIET.]

Here comes the lady. O, so light a foot
Will ne'er wear out the everlasting flint.[5]
A lover may bestride the gossamers[6]
That idles in the wanton summer air,
20　And yet not fall; so light is vanity.[7]

JULIET. Good even to my ghostly confessor.

FRIAR. Romeo shall thank thee, daughter, for us both.

4. **confounds** destroys.

5. **flint** stone.
6. **gossamers** spider webs.
7. **vanity** foolish things that cannot last.

8. As . . . him the same greeting to him.

9. and . . . it and if you are better able to proclaim it.

10. Conceit . . . ornament Understanding does not need to be dressed up in words.

JULIET. As much to him,[8] else is his thanks too much.

ROMEO. Ah, Juliet, if the measure of thy joy
25 Be heaped like mine, and that thy skill be more
    To blazon it,[9] then sweeten with thy breath
    This neighbor air, and let rich music's tongue
    Unfold the imagined happiness that both
    Receive in either by this dear encounter.

30 **JULIET.** Conceit, more rich in matter than in words,
    Brags of his substance, not of ornament.[10]
    They are but beggars that can count their worth;
    But my true love is grown to such excess
    I cannot sum up sum of half my wealth.

35 **FRIAR.** Come, come with me, and we will make short work;
    For, by your leaves, you shall not stay alone
    Till Holy Church incorporate two in one.   [*Exit all.*]

Critical Thinking

1. **Respond:** Is Friar Lawrence wise to agree to marry Romeo and Juliet? Explain.

2. **(a)** Where do Romeo and Juliet first mutually declare their love? **(b) Interpret:** What role does darkness play in the scene?

3. **(a)** What weakness in Romeo does the Friar point out before agreeing to help? **(b) Compare and Contrast:** How do the Friar's motives differ from the couple's motives? Explain your response.

4. **(a)** For whom does Juliet wait in Act II, Scene v? **(b) Analyze:** What are her feelings as she waits? Explain.

5. **(a) Analyze:** Review the *Reflect* and *Recall* features on page 835. Which is a summary that captures the main ideas and elements of a text, and which is a critique that takes a position and expresses an opinion? **(b)** Explain how you distinguished between the two.

Support your responses with evidence from the text.

Do our differences define us?
Have the differences between Romeo and Juliet affected their relationship? Explain.

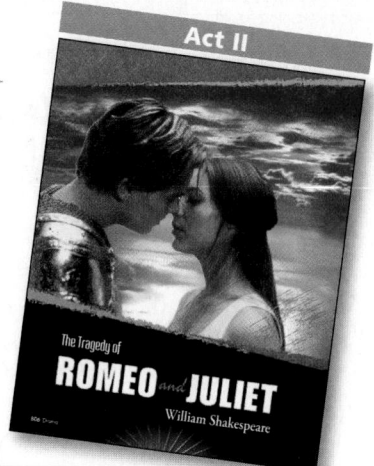

Literary Analysis: Blank Verse

1. Copy the following passages of **blank verse.** Then, indicate the pattern of accented (´) and unaccented (˘) syllables in each line. **(a)** Act II, Scene ii, lines 43–51 **(b)** Act II, Scene vi, lines 3–8

2. Using a chart, rewrite the following lines, marking stressed and unstressed syllables. Then, identify the key words stressed in each line, and explain what meaning is conveyed by this emphasis.
   (a) ROMEO. Can I go forward when my heart is here?
   (b) JULIET. But my true love is grown to such excess.

Blank Verse Pattern	Key Words	Significance

3. **(a)** Identify the aristocratic and common people in Acts I and II based on whether or not they speak in blank verse. **(b)** Why do you think Shakespeare chose to have aristocratic characters speak in blank verse instead of ordinary prose?

Reading Skill: Summarize

4. **(a)** How many sentences are in lines 1–8 of Act II, Scene v?
   (b) Write a **summary** of these lines.

Vocabulary

Practice Answer each question. Then, explain your answer.

1. Where would you go to _procure_ groceries?
2. What is the _predominant_ feeling at a celebration?
3. How many people are needed for an _intercession_ to occur?
4. Is a _sallow_ complexion a sign of good health?
5. If a situation is _lamentable_, are people likely to be happy about it?
6. Is an _unwieldy_ package something you would want to carry far?

Word Power Use the context of the sentences and what you know about the **Latin prefix pro-** to explain your answer to each question.

1. If you make a _proposal,_ have you suggested a course of action?
2. If you are _proactive,_ are you waiting for something to occur?

Word Power

The **Latin prefix pro-** means "before," "forward."

Apply It Explain how the prefix pro- helps you determine the meanings of these technical academic words from social studies. Consult a dictionary if necessary.
pro bono
prohibition

Before You Read

The Tragedy of Romeo and Juliet, Act III

 Do our *differences* define us?

(**As You Read**) Look for the steps that Romeo and Juliet try to take to overcome their differences—and think about the new separations they are developing among friends and family.

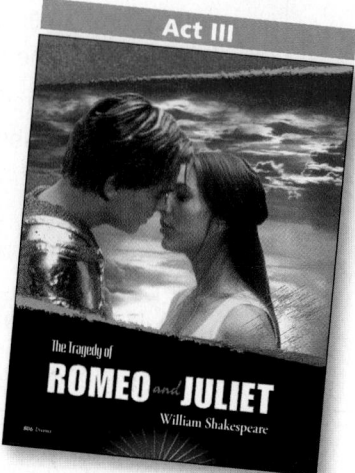

TEXAS Focus on the TEKS

Meet these standards with *The Tragedy of Romeo and Juliet,* **Act III** (p. 862).

Reading

(4) Explain how dramatic conventions (e.g., monologues, soliloquies) enhance dramatic text. *(Literary Analysis: Dramatic Speeches)*

(5)(B) Analyze how authors develop complex yet believable characters in works of fiction through a range of literary devices, including character foils. *(Literary Analysis: Dramatic Speeches)*

(9)(A) Distinguish between a summary that captures the main idea and elements of a text and a critique that takes a position and expresses an opinion. *(Critical Thinking: Analyze)*

Reading/Comprehension Skills

RC-9(A) Reflect on understanding to monitor comprehension. *(Reading Skill: Summarize)*

For more TEKS, see pages 932–935.

Vocabulary

Read each word and its definition. Decide whether you know the word well, know it a little bit, or do not know it at all. After you read, see how your knowledge of each word has increased.

- **gallant** (gal´ ənt) *adj.* brave and noble (p. 868) *We called the firefighters <u>gallant</u>, but they said they were just doing their job.* gallantly *adv.* gallantry *n.*

- **fray** (frā) *n.* noisy fight (p. 869) *The crew argued, but the captain stayed above the <u>fray</u>.* fray *v.* frayed *adj.*

- **martial** (mär´ shəl) *adj.* military; warlike (p. 869) *The band played <u>martial</u> music to honor the soldiers.* martialist *n.*

- **exile** (eks´ īl´) *v.* banish (p. 870) *Years ago, rulers would <u>exile</u> criminals to faraway places.* exiler *n.*

- **eloquence** (el´ ə kwəns) *n.* speech that is graceful and persuasive (p. 871) *The <u>eloquence</u> of her speech moved the audience.* eloquent *adj.* eloquently *adv.*

- **fickle** (fik´ əl) *adj.* changeable (p. 884) *His <u>fickle</u> sense of style made buying clothes for him difficult.* fickleness *n.*

Word Power

The **Latin root -*loque*-** means "talk," "speak," or "say."

In Act III, Juliet says that everyone who speaks Romeo's name speaks **eloquence.** She means that the name itself is a graceful, vivid expression.

Literary Analysis: Dramatic Speeches

In most plays, the dramatic action takes place through **dialogue**—the conversations between characters. Playwrights may also make use of **dramatic conventions,** including **speeches,** to enhance text. Here are some examples:

- **Monologue:** a lengthy speech by one character. Unlike a soliloquy, a monologue is addressed to other characters.
- **Soliloquy:** a lengthy speech in which a character—usually alone on-stage—expresses his or her true thoughts or feelings. Soliloquies are unheard by other characters.
- **Aside:** a character revealing his or her true thoughts or feelings in a remark that is unheard by other characters.

Authors often use dialogue and action to emphasize the differences between characters. Another way authors convey differences is through **foils**—characters whose words and actions show personality contrasts.

As You Read Analyze the speeches and character foils in Act III, and how Shakespeare uses these elements to develop **complex yet believable characters.** Jot down notes explaining how these **dramatic conventions** and literary devices enhance the text.

Reading Skill: Summarize

Summarizing is briefly stating the main points in a piece of writing. Before you summarize a passage of a play by Shakespeare, **paraphrase** it, or restate the lines in your own words. Once you have paraphrased small portions of text, you can more easily and accurately summarize an entire passage.

Using the Strategy: Summarizing Chart

As You Read Reflect on your understanding. Monitor your comprehension by using a chart like this one to paraphrase and summarize the text.

TEXAS
PHLitOnline
www.PHLitOnline.com

Hear It!
- Selection summary audio
- Selection audio

See It!
- Get Connected video
- Background video
- More about the author
- Vocabulary flashcards

Do It!
- Interactive journals
- Interactive graphic organizers
- Self-test
- Internet activity
- Grammar tutorial
- Interactive vocabulary games

Text	Paraphrase	Summary
"I pray thee, good Mercutio, let's retire. The day is hot, the Capulets abroad, And, if we meet, we shall not 'scape a brawl, For now, these hot days, is the mad blood stirring."	Please, Mercutio, let's leave. It's hot out, and the Capulets are around. And if we meet up with them, we will most likely fight, because on these hot days we have fight in us.	Benvolio is trying to convince Mercutio to leave the public place they are meeting in, because he is afraid a brawl with the Capulets is inevitable.

Act III

Reflect "The two fatal figures in the play are its two liveliest comics, Mercutio and the Nurse."

from *Shakespeare: The Invention of the Human*
by Harold Bloom

Recall In Act II, Romeo and Juliet express their mutual love and enlist the aid of Juliet's nurse and Friar Lawrence to arrange a secret marriage ceremony. As the act closes, the young couple is about to be married. Before performing the ceremony, the Friar warns, "These violent delights have violent ends. . . ."

Anticipate How might the Friar's warning hint at events that will occur in Act III or later in the play?

Scene i. A public place.
[*Enter* MERCUTIO, BENVOLIO, *and* MEN.]

> **BENVOLIO.** I pray thee, good Mercutio, let's retire.
> The day is hot, the Capulets abroad,
> And, if we meet, we shall not 'scape a brawl,
> For now, these hot days, is the mad blood stirring.

> 5 **MERCUTIO.** Thou art like one of these fellows that, when he enters the confines of a tavern, claps me his sword upon the table and says, "God send me no need of thee!" and by the operation of the second cup draws him on the drawer,[1] when indeed there is no need.

> 10 **BENVOLIO.** Am I like such a fellow?

> **MERCUTIO.** Come, come, thou art as hot a Jack in thy mood as any in Italy; and as soon moved to be moody, and as soon moody to be moved.[2]

1. **and . . . drawer** and by the effect of the second drink, draws his sword against the waiter.
2. **and . . . moved** and as quickly stirred to anger as you are eager to be so stirred.

Reading Check

Why does Benvolio want to get off the street?

Literary Analysis
Dramatic Speeches
Mercutio's speech is a monologue. Explain how this dramatic convention helps the reader better understand the situation and enhances the text.

3. **addle** scrambled; crazy.

4. **doublet** jacket.
5. **riband** ribbon.
6. **tutor . . . quarreling** instruct me not to quarrel.
7. **fee simple** complete possession.
8. **an hour and a quarter** length of time that a man with Mercutio's fondness for quarreling may be expected to live.
9. **O simple!** O stupid!

Reading Skill
Summarize How would you paraphrase the exchange between Tybalt and Mercutio?

10. **occasion** cause; reason.
11. **consortest** associate with.
12. **Consort** associate with; "consort" also meant a group of musicians.
13. **discords** harsh sounds.
14. **Zounds** exclamation of surprise or anger ("By God's wounds").

Literary Analysis
Dramatic Speeches
How does the author develop the complex, yet believable, characters of Mercutio and Benvolio using the literary device of character foils?

BENVOLIO. And what to?

15 **MERCUTIO.** Nay, and there were two such, we should have none shortly, for one would kill the other. Thou! Why, thou wilt quarrel with a man that hath a hair more or a hair less in his beard than thou hast. Thou wilt quarrel with a man for cracking nuts, having no other reason but because thou

20 hast hazel eyes. What eye but such an eye would spy out such a quarrel? Thy head is as full of quarrels as an egg is full of meat; and yet thy head hath been beaten as addle[3] as an egg for quarreling. Thou hast quarreled with a man for coughing in the street, because he hath wakened thy dog

25 that hath lain asleep in the sun. Didst thou not fall out with a tailor for wearing his new doublet[4] before Easter? With another for tying his new shoes with old riband?[5] And yet thou wilt tutor me from quarreling![6]

BENVOLIO. And I were so apt to quarrel as thou art, any man

30 should buy the fee simple[7] of my life for an hour and a quarter.[8]

MERCUTIO. The fee simple? O simple![9]

[*Enter* TYBALT, PETRUCHIO, *and* OTHERS.]

BENVOLIO. By my head, here comes the Capulets.

MERCUTIO. By my heel, I care not.

35 **TYBALT.** Follow me close, for I will speak to them.
Gentlemen, good-den. A word with one of you.

MERCUTIO. And but one word with one of us? Couple it with something; make it a word and a blow.

TYBALT. You shall find me apt enough to that, sir, and you will

40 give me occasion.[10]

MERCUTIO. Could you not take some occasion without giving?

TYBALT. Mercutio, thou consortest[11] with Romeo.

MERCUTIO. Consort?[12] What, dost thou make us minstrels?
And thou make minstrels of us, look to hear nothing but

45 discords.[13] Here's my fiddlestick; here's that shall make you dance. Zounds,[14] consort!

BENVOLIO. We talk here in the public haunt of men.
Either withdraw unto some private place,
Or reason coldly of your grievances,

50 Or else depart. Here all eyes gaze on us.

MERCUTIO. Men's eyes were made to look, and let them gaze.
    I will not budge for no man's pleasure, I.

[*Enter* ROMEO.]

TYBALT. Well, peace be with you, sir. Here comes my man.[15]

MERCUTIO. But I'll be hanged, sir, if he wear your livery.[16]
55   Marry, go before to field,[17] he'll be your follower!
    Your worship in that sense may call him man.

TYBALT. Romeo, the love I bear thee can afford
    No better term than this: thou art a villain.[18]

ROMEO. Tybalt, the reason that I have to love thee
60   Doth much excuse the appertaining[19] rage
    To such a greeting. Villain am I none.
    Therefore farewell. I see thou knowest me not.

15. **man** man I am looking for; "man" also meant "manservant."
16. **livery** servant's uniform.
17. **field** dueling place.
18. **villain** low, vulgar person.
19. **appertaining** appropriate.

Reading Check

What are Mercutio and Benvolio arguing about?

TYBALT. Boy, this shall not excuse the injuries
    That thou hast done me; therefore turn and draw.

65 **ROMEO.** I do protest I never injured thee,
    But love thee better than thou canst devise[20]
    Till thou shalt know the reason of my love;
    And so, good Capulet, which name I tender[21]
    As dearly as mine own, be satisfied.

70 **MERCUTIO.** O calm, dishonorable, vile submission!
    Alla stoccata[22] carries it away.   *[Draws.]*
    Tybalt, you ratcatcher, will you walk?

TYBALT. What wouldst thou have with me?

MERCUTIO. Good King of Cats, nothing but one of your
75   nine lives. That I mean to make bold withal,[23] and, as
    you shall use me here-after, dry-beat[24] the rest of the
    eight. Will you pluck your sword out of his pilcher[25]
    by the ears? Make haste, lest mine be about your
    ears ere it be out.

80 **TYBALT.** I am for you.   *[Draws.]*

ROMEO. Gentle Mercutio, put thy rapier up.

MERCUTIO. Come, sir, your *passado*!   *[They fight.]*

ROMEO. Draw, Benvolio; beat down their weapons.
    Gentlemen, for shame! Forbear this outrage!
85   Tybalt, Mercutio, the Prince expressly hath

20. **devise** understand; imagine.
21. **tender** value.

22. *Alla stoccata* at the thrust—an Italian fencing term that Mercutio uses as a nickname for Tybalt.

23. **make bold withal** make bold with; take.
24. **dry-beat** thrash.
25. **pilcher** scabbard.

▼▶ **Critical Viewing**
Which details in these photographs suggest that a duel is about to take place? **[Analyze]**

Forbid this bandying in Verona streets.
Hold, Tybalt! Good Mercutio!

[TYBALT *under* ROMEO'S *arm thrusts* MERCUTIO *in, and flies.*]

MERCUTIO.   I am hurt.
A plague a²⁶ both houses! I am sped.²⁷
Is he gone and hath nothing?

BENVOLIO.   What, art thou hurt?

90 **MERCUTIO.** Ay, ay, a scratch, a scratch. Marry, 'tis enough.
Where is my page? Go, villain, fetch a surgeon.   [*Exit* PAGE.]

ROMEO. Courage, man. The hurt cannot be much.

MERCUTIO. No, 'tis not so deep as a well, nor so wide as
a church door; but 'tis enough, 'twill serve. Ask for
95 me tomorrow, and you shall find me a grave man. I
am peppered,²⁸ I warrant, for this world. A plague a
both your houses! Zounds, a dog, a rat, a mouse, a

26. **a** on.
27. **sped** wounded; done for.

28. **peppered** finished off.

Reading
Check

What is the outcome of
the duel between Tybalt
and Mercutio?

29. **by . . . arithmetic** by
formal rules.

Reading Skill
Summarize
Paraphrase Mercutio's
line "A plague a both
your houses!" and
summarize his reasons
for uttering this curse.

30. **I have it** I have got my
deathblow.
31. **ally** relative.

Vocabulary
gallant (gal′ ənt) *adj.*
brave and noble

32. **aspired** climbed to.
33. **moe** more.
34. **depend** hang over.

35. **respective lenity**
thoughtful mercy.
36. **conduct** guide.

cat, to scratch a man to death! A braggart, a rogue,
a villain, that fights by the book of arithmetic![29] Why

100 the devil came you between us? I was hurt under
your arm.

ROMEO. I thought all for the best.

MERCUTIO. Help me into some house, Benvolio,
Or I shall faint. A plague a both your houses!

105 They have made worms' meat of me. I have it,[30]
And soundly too. Your houses! [*Exit* MERCUTIO *and* BENVOLIO.]

ROMEO. This gentleman, the Prince's near ally,[31]
My very friend, hath got his mortal hurt
In my behalf—my reputation stained

110 With Tybalt's slander—Tybalt, that an hour
Hath been my cousin. O sweet Juliet,
Thy beauty hath made me effeminate
And in my temper soft'ned valor's steel!

[*Enter* BENVOLIO.]

BENVOLIO. O Romeo, Romeo, brave Mercutio is dead!

115 That gallant spirit hath aspired[32] the clouds,
Which too untimely here did scorn the earth.

ROMEO. This day's black fate on moe[33] days doth depend;[34]
This but begins the woe others must end.

[*Enter* TYBALT.]

BENVOLIO. Here comes the furious Tybalt back again.

120 **ROMEO.** Alive in triumph, and Mercutio slain?
Away to heaven respective lenity,[35]
And fire-eyed fury be my conduct[36] now!
Now, Tybalt, take the "villain" back again
That late thou gavest me; for Mercutio's soul

125 Is but a little way above our heads,
Staying for thine to keep him company.
Either thou or I, or both, must go with him.

TYBALT. Thou, wretched boy, that didst consort him here,
Shalt with him hence.

ROMEO. This shall determine that.
[*They fight.* TYBALT *falls.*]

130 **BENVOLIO.** Romeo, away, be gone!

The citizens are up, and Tybalt slain.
Stand not amazed. The Prince will doom thee death
If thou art taken. Hence, be gone, away!

ROMEO. O, I am fortune's fool!³⁷

BENVOLIO.   Why dost thou stay?

                                        [*Exit* ROMEO.]

[*Enter* CITIZENS.]

135 **CITIZEN.** Which way ran he that killed Mercutio?
Tybalt, that murderer, which way ran he?

BENVOLIO. There lies that Tybalt.

CITIZEN.   Up, sir, go with me.
I charge thee in the Prince's name obey.

[*Enter* PRINCE, OLD MONTAGUE, CAPULET, *their* WIVES, *and all.*]

PRINCE. Where are the vile beginners of this fray?

140 **BENVOLIO.** O noble Prince, I can discover³⁸ all
The unlucky manage³⁹ of this fatal brawl.
There lies the man, slain by young Romeo,
That slew thy kinsman, brave Mercutio.

LADY CAPULET. Tybalt, my cousin! O my brother's child!
145   O Prince! O cousin! Husband! O, the blood is spilled
Of my dear kinsman! Prince, as thou art true,
For blood of ours shed blood of Montague.
O cousin, cousin!

PRINCE. Benvolio, who began this bloody fray?

150 **BENVOLIO.** Tybalt, here slain, whom Romeo's hand did slay.
Romeo, that spoke him fair, bid him bethink
How nice⁴⁰ the quarrel was, and urged withal
Your high displeasure. All this—utterèd
With gentle breath, calm look, knees humbly bowed—
155   Could not take truce with the unruly spleen⁴¹
Of Tybalt deaf to peace, but that he tilts⁴²
With piercing steel at bold Mercutio's breast;
Who, all as hot, turns deadly point to point,
And, with a martial scorn, with one hand beats
160   Cold death aside and with the other sends
It back to Tybalt, whose dexterity
Retorts it. Romeo he cries aloud,
"Hold, friends! Friends, part!" and swifter than his tongue,
His agile arm beats down their fatal points,

37. fool plaything.

Vocabulary
fray (frā) *n.* noisy fight

38. discover reveal.
39. manage course.

40. nice trivial.

41. spleen angry nature.
42. tilts thrusts.

Vocabulary
martial (mär´ shəl)
adj. military; warlike

Reading
Check
Who does Benvolio say
started the brawl?

Literary Analysis
Dramatic Speeches
Which details of Benvolio's speech suggest that he is trying to portray Romeo favorably?

43. **envious** full of hatred.
44. **entertained** considered.

165 And 'twixt them rushes; underneath whose arm
An envious[43] thrust from Tybalt hit the life
Of stout Mercutio, and then Tybalt fled;
But by and by comes back to Romeo,
Who had but newly entertained[44] revenge,
170 And to't they go like lightning; for, ere I
Could draw to part them, was stout Tybalt slain;
And, as he fell, did Romeo turn and fly.
This is the truth, or let Benvolio die.

LADY CAPULET. He is a kinsman to the Montague;
175 Affection makes him false, he speaks not true.
Some twenty of them fought in this black strife,
And all those twenty could but kill one life.
I beg for justice, which thou, Prince, must give.
Romeo slew Tybalt; Romeo must not live.

180 **PRINCE.** Romeo slew him; he slew Mercutio.
Who now the price of his dear blood doth owe?

MONTAGUE. Not Romeo, Prince; he was Mercutio's friend;
His fault concludes but what the law should end,
The life of Tybalt.[45]

45. **His fault . . . Tybalt** by killing Tybalt, he did what the law would have done.

185 **PRINCE.**   And for that offense
Immediately we do exile him hence.
I have an interest in your hate's proceeding.
My blood[46] for your rude brawls doth lie a-bleeding;
But I'll amerce[47] you with so strong a fine
190 That you shall all repent the loss of mine.
I will be deaf to pleading and excuses;
Nor tears nor prayers shall purchase out abuses.
Therefore use none. Let Romeo hence in haste,
Else, when he is found, that hour is his last.
195 Bear hence this body and attend our will.[48]
Mercy but murders, pardoning those that kill.

[*Exit with others.*]

Vocabulary
exile (eks´ īl´) *v.* banish

46. **My blood** Mercutio was related to the Prince.
47. **amerce** punish.

48. **attend our will** await my decision.

Scene ii. Capulet's orchard.
[*Enter* JULIET *alone.*]

JULIET. Gallop apace, you fiery-footed steeds,[1]
Towards Phoebus' lodging![2] Such a wagoner
As Phaëton[3] would whip you to the west
And bring in cloudy night immediately.

1. **fiery-footed steeds** horses of the sun god, Phoebus.
2. **Phoebus' lodging** below the horizon.
3. **Phaëton** Phoebus' son, who tried to drive his father's horses but was unable to control them.

5   Spread thy close curtain, love-performing night,
      That runaways' eyes may wink,⁴ and Romeo
      Leap to these arms untalked of and unseen.
      Lovers can see to do their amorous rites,
      And by their own beauties; or, if love be blind,
10   It best agrees with night. Come, civil night,
      Thou sober-suited matron all in black,
      And learn me how to lose a winning match,
      Played for a pair of stainless maidenhoods.
      Hood my unmanned blood, bating in my cheeks,⁵
15   With thy black mantle till strange⁶ love grow bold,
      Think true love acted simple modesty,
      Come, night; come, Romeo; come, thou day in night;
      For thou wilt lie upon the wings of night
      Whiter than new snow upon a raven's back.
20   Come, gentle night; come, loving, black-browed night;
      Give me my Romeo; and when I shall die,
      Take him and cut him out in little stars,
      And he will make the face of heaven so fine
      That all the world will be in love with night
25   And pay no worship to the garish sun.
      O, I have bought the mansion of a love,
      But not possessed it; and though I am sold,
      Not yet enjoyed. So tedious is this day
      As is the night before some festival
30   To an impatient child that hath new robes
      And may not wear them. O, here comes my nurse,

[*Enter* NURSE, *with cords.*]

      And she brings news; and every tongue that speaks
      But Romeo's name speaks heavenly **eloquence**.
      Now, nurse, what news? What hast thou there, the cords
      That Romeo bid thee fetch?

35   **NURSE.**   Ay, ay, the cords.

      JULIET. Ay me! What news? Why dost thou wring thy hands?

      NURSE. Ah, weraday!⁷ He's dead, he's dead, he's dead!
      We are undone, lady, we are undone!
      Alack the day! He's gone, he's killed, he's dead!

      JULIET. Can heaven be so envious?

40   **NURSE.**   Romeo can,
      Though heaven cannot. O Romeo, Romeo!
      Who ever would have thought it? Romeo!

> **Literary Analysis**
> **Dramatic Speeches**
> How can you tell that Juliet's speech is a soliloquy?
>
> **4. That runaways' eyes may wink** so that the eyes of busybodies may not see.
> **5. Hood . . . cheeks** Hide the untamed blood that makes me blush.
> **6. strange** unfamiliar.

> **Vocabulary**
> **eloquence** (el′ ə kwəns) *n.* speech that is graceful and persuasive

> **7. Ah, weraday!** alas!

>
> **Reading Check**
> What punishment does the Prince order for Romeo?

The Tragedy of Romeo and Juliet, Act III **871**

History Connection

Cockatrice

In a play on words, Juliet links "Ay" with the dangerous "eye" of a cockatrice (Act III, Scene ii, line 47). The cockatrice is a serpent that, according to myth, could kill with a look or transform people into stone. The creature resembles a snake with the head and yellow feathers of a rooster. It feared the song of the rooster and its own reflection in a mirror.

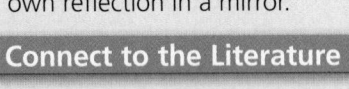

Connect to the Literature

How does Juliet's allusion to a cockatrice reinforce the nature of her conversation with the Nurse?

JULIET. What devil art thou that dost torment me thus?
This torture should be roared in dismal hell.

45 Hath Romeo slain himself? Say thou but "Ay,"
And that bare vowel "I" shall poison more
Than the death-darting eye of cockatrice.
I am not I, if there be such an "Ay,"[8]
Or those eyes' shot[9] that makes thee answer "Ay."

50 If he be slain, say "Ay"; or if not, "No."
Brief sounds determine of my weal or woe.

NURSE. I saw the wound, I saw it with mine eyes,
(God save the mark![10]) here on his manly breast.
A piteous corse,[11] a bloody piteous corse;

55 Pale, pale as ashes, all bedaubed in blood,
All in gore-blood. I sounded[12] at the sight.

JULIET. O, break, my heart! Poor bankrout,[13] break at once!
To prison, eyes; ne'er look on liberty!
Vile earth, to earth resign;[14] end motion here,

60 And thou and Romeo press one heavy bier![15]

NURSE. O Tybalt, Tybalt, the best friend I had!
O courteous Tybalt! Honest gentleman!
That ever I should live to see thee dead!

JULIET. What storm is this that blows so contrary?[16]

65 Is Romeo slaught'red, and is Tybalt dead?
My dearest cousin, and my dearer lord?
Then, dreadful trumpet, sound the general doom![17]

---

8. "Ay" yes.
9. eyes' shot the Nurse's glance.

10. God save the mark! May God save us from evil!
11. corse corpse.
12. sounded swooned; fainted.
13. bankrout bankrupt.

14. Vile . . . resign Let my body return to the earth.
15. bier platform on which a corpse is displayed before burial.

16. contrary in opposite directions.
17. dreadful . . . doom Let the trumpet that announces doomsday be sounded.

For who is living, if those two are gone?

NURSE. Tybalt is gone, and Romeo banishèd;
70   Romeo that killed him, he is banishèd.

JULIET. O God! Did Romeo's hand shed Tybalt's blood?

NURSE. It did, it did! Alas the day, it did!

JULIET. O serpent heart, hid with a flow'ring face!
        Did ever dragon keep so fair a cave?
75   Beautiful tyrant! Fiend angelical!
        Dove-feathered raven! Wolvish-ravening lamb!
        Despisèd substance of divinest show!
        Just opposite to what thou justly seem'st—
        A damnèd saint, an honorable villain!
80   O nature, what hadst thou to do in hell
        When thou didst bower the spirit of a fiend
        In mortal paradise of such sweet flesh?
        Was ever book containing such vile matter
        So fairly bound? O, that deceit should dwell
        In such a gorgeous palace!

85 **NURSE.**   There's no trust,
        No faith, no honesty in men; all perjured,
        All forsworn,[18] all naught, all dissemblers.[19]
        Ah, where's my man? Give me some aqua vitae.[20]
        These griefs, these woes, these sorrows make me old.
        Shame come to Romeo!

90 **JULIET.**   Blistered be thy tongue
        For such a wish! He was not born to shame.
        Upon his brow shame is ashamed to sit;
        For 'tis a throne where honor may be crowned
        Sole monarch of the universal earth.
95   O, what a beast was I to chide at him!

NURSE. Will you speak well of him that killed your cousin?

JULIET. Shall I speak ill of him that is my husband?
        Ah, poor my lord, what tongue shall smooth thy name
        When I, thy three-hours wife, have mangled it?
100   But wherefore, villain, didst thou kill my cousin?
        That villain cousin would have killed my husband.
        Back, foolish tears, back to your native spring!
        Your tributary[21] drops belong to woe,
        Which you, mistaking, offer up to joy.
105   My husband lives, that Tybalt would have slain;

Spiral Review
Figurative Language Explain the role of paradox in lines 75–79.

Reading Skill
Summarize Briefly summarize Juliet's remarks about Romeo in lines 73–84.

18. **forsworn** are liars.
19. **dissemblers** hypocrites.
20. **aqua vitae** brandy.

21. **tributary** in tribute.

Reading Check
What is Juliet's initial reaction to Romeo's involvement in Tybalt's death?

**Literary Analysis
Dramatic Speeches**
What makes this speech
a monologue but not a
soliloquy?

110

115

120

125

And Tybalt's dead, that would have slain my husband.
All this is comfort; wherefore weep I then?
Some word there was, worser than Tybalt's death,
That murd'red me. I would forget it fain;
But O, it presses to my memory
Like damnèd guilty deeds to sinners' minds!
"Tybalt is dead, and Romeo—banishèd."
That "banishèd," that one word "banishèd,"
Hath slain ten thousand Tybalts. Tybalt's death
Was woe enough, if it had ended there;
Or, if sour woe delights in fellowship
And needly will be ranked with[22] other griefs,
Why followed not, when she said "Tybalt's dead,"
Thy father, or thy mother, nay, or both,
Which modern[23] lamentation might have moved?
But with a rearward[24] following Tybalt's death,
"Romeo is banishèd"—to speak that word
Is father, mother, Tybalt, Romeo, Juliet,
All slain, all dead. "Romeo is banishèd"—
There is no end, no limit, measure, bound,
In that word's death; no words can that woe sound.
Where is my father and my mother, nurse?

NURSE. Weeping and wailing over Tybalt's corse.
Will you go to them? I will bring you thither.

130 **JULIET.** Wash they his wounds with tears? Mine shall be spent,
When theirs are dry, for Romeo's banishment.
Take up those cords. Poor ropes, you are beguiled,
Both you and I, for Romeo is exiled.
He made you for a highway to my bed;
135 But I, a maid, die maiden-widowèd.
Come, cords; come, nurse. I'll to my wedding bed;
And death, not Romeo, take my maidenhead!

NURSE. Hie to your chamber. I'll find Romeo
To comfort you. I wot[25] well where he is.
140 Hark ye, your Romeo will be here at night.
I'll to him; he is hid at Lawrence' cell.

JULIET. O, find him! Give this ring to my true knight
And bid him come to take his last farewell. [*Exit with* NURSE.]

22. **needly . . . with** must be
accompanied by.

23. **modern** ordinary.
24. **rearward** follow up;
literally, a rear guard.

25. **wot** know.

Scene iii. Friar Lawrence's cell.
[*Enter* FRIAR LAWRENCE.]

FRIAR. Romeo, come forth; come forth, thou fearful man.
    Affliction is enamored of thy parts,[1]
    And thou art wedded to calamity.

[*Enter* ROMEO.]

ROMEO. Father, what news? What is the Prince's doom?[2]
5   What sorrow craves acquaintance at my hand
    That I yet know not?

FRIAR.   Too familiar
    Is my dear son with such sour company.
    I bring thee tidings of the Prince's doom.

ROMEO. What less than doomsday[3] is the Prince's doom?

10 **FRIAR.** A gentler judgment vanished[4] from his lips—
    Not body's death, but body's banishment.

ROMEO. Ha, banishment? Be merciful, say "death";
    For exile hath more terror in his look,
    Much more than death. Do not say "banishment."

15 **FRIAR.** Here from Verona art thou banishèd.
    Be patient, for the world is broad and wide.

ROMEO. There is no world without[5] Verona walls,
    But purgatory, torture, hell itself.
    Hence banishèd is banished from the world,
20   And world's exile is death. Then "banishèd"
    Is death mistermed. Calling death "banishèd,"
    Thou cut'st my head off with a golden ax
    And smilest upon the stroke that murders me.

FRIAR. O deadly sin! O rude unthankfulness!
25   Thy fault our law calls death;[6] but the kind Prince,
    Taking thy part, hath rushed[7] aside the law,
    And turned that black word "death" to "banishment."
    This is dear mercy, and thou seest it not.

ROMEO. 'Tis torture, and not mercy. Heaven is here,
30   Where Juliet lives; and every cat and dog
    And little mouse, every unworthy thing,
    Live here in heaven and may look on her;
    But Romeo may not. More validity,[8]
    More honorable state, more courtship lives
35   In carrion flies than Romeo. They may seize

1. **Affliction . . . parts**
misery is in love with your
attractive qualities.

2. **doom** final decision.

3. **doomsday** my death.
4. **vanished** escaped; came
forth.

5. **without** outside.
6. **Thy fault . . . death** for
what you did our law
demands the death
penalty.
7. **rushed** pushed.
8. **validity** value.

**Reading Skill
Summarize**
Paraphrase Romeo's
complaint in lines 29–33,
and then summarize
his reaction to his
banishment.

**Reading
Check**

What punishment does
the Friar say Romeo
could have received for
his crime?

On the white wonder of dear Juliet's hand
And steal immortal blessing from her lips,
Who, even in pure and vestal modesty,
Still blush, as thinking their own kisses sin;
40　But Romeo may not, he is banishèd.
Flies may do this but I from this must fly;
They are freemen, but I am banishèd.
And sayest thou yet that exile is not death?
Hadst thou no poison mixed, no sharp-ground knife,
45　No sudden mean[9] of death, though ne'er so mean,[10]
But "banishèd" to kill me—"banishèd"?
O friar, the damnèd use that word in hell;
Howling attends it! How hast thou the heart,
Being a divine, a ghostly confessor,
50　A sin-absolver, and my friend professed,
To mangle me with that word "banishèd"?

FRIAR. Thou fond mad man, hear me a little speak.

ROMEO. O, thou wilt speak again of banishment.

FRIAR. I'll give thee armor to keep off that word;
55　Adversity's sweet milk, philosophy,
To comfort thee, though thou art banishèd.

9. mean method.
10. mean humiliating.

Romeo and Juliet Through the Years

These illustrations and images from various productions of *The Tragedy of Romeo and Juliet* mark the timelessness of Shakespeare's most dramatized piece. The core qualities of the play, including its theme and language, have moved forward into the present with updated costumes and props, diverse casts, and new technology.

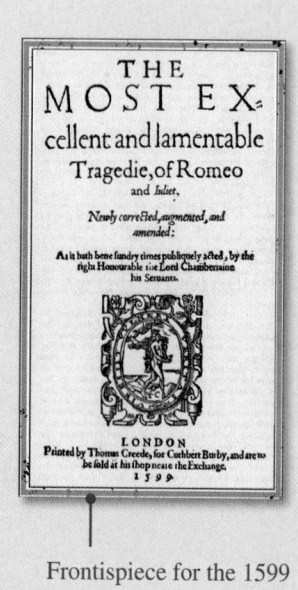

THE
MOST EX:
cellent and lamentable
Tragedie, of Romeo
and Juliet.

Newly corrected, augmented, and
amended:

As it hath been sundry times publiquely acted, by the
right Honourable the Lord Chamberlaine
his Seruants.

LONDON
Printed by Thomas Creede, for Cuthbert Burby, and are to
be sold at his shop neare the Exchange.
1599

Frontispiece for the 1599 edition

Movie – 1916
Romeo and Juliet.
(Directors: Maxwell Karger and J. Gordon Edwards
Actors: Harry Hilliard and Theda Bara)

Book illustration – 1905

ROMEO. Yet "banishèd"? Hang up philosophy!
    Unless philosophy can make a Juliet,
    Displant a town, reverse a prince's doom,
60   It helps not, it prevails not. Talk no more.

FRIAR. O, then I see that madmen have no ears.

ROMEO. How should they, when that wise men have no eyes?

FRIAR. Let me dispute[11] with thee of thy estate.[12]

ROMEO. Thou canst not speak of that thou dost not feel.
65   Wert thou as young as I, Juliet thy love,
    An hour but married, Tybalt murderèd,
    Doting like me, and like me banishèd,
    Then mightst thou speak, then mightst thou tear thy hair,
    And fall upon the ground, as I do now,
70   Taking the measure of an unmade grave.

[*Knock.*]

FRIAR. Arise, one knocks. Good Romeo, hide thyself.

ROMEO. Not I; unless the breath of heartsick groans
    Mistlike infold me from the search of eyes. [*Knock.*]

Reading Skill
Summarize
Summarize Romeo's ideas in lines 57–60. What do they suggest about his state of mind?

11. **dispute** discuss.
12. **estate** condition; situation.

Reading Check
How does Romeo view his banishment?

Movie – 1936
Poster and balcony scene.
(Director: George Cukor
Actors: Norma Shearer and Leslie Howard)

Movie – 1968
Balcony scene.
(Director: Franco Zeffirelli
Actors: Leonard Whiting and Olivia Hussey)

FRIAR. Hark, how they knock! Who's there? Romeo, arise;

75   Thou wilt be taken.—Stay awhile!—Stand up; [*Knock.*]

    Run to my study.—By and by![13]—God's will,

    What simpleness[14] is this.—I come, I come! [*Knock.*]

    Who knocks so hard? Whence come you? What's your will?

[*Enter* NURSE.]

NURSE. Let me come in, and you shall know my errand.

    I come from Lady Juliet.

80 **FRIAR.**   Welcome then.

NURSE. O holy friar, O, tell me, holy friar,

    Where is my lady's lord, where's Romeo?

FRIAR. There on the ground, with his own tears made drunk.

NURSE. O, he is even in my mistress' case,

85   Just in her case! O woeful sympathy!

    Piteous predicament! Even so lies she,

    Blubb'ring and weeping, weeping and blubb'ring.

    Stand up, stand up! Stand, and you be a man.

    For Juliet's sake, for her sake, rise and stand!

90   Why should you fall into so deep an O?[15]

13. By and by! In a minute! (said to the person knocking).

14. simpleness silly behavior (Romeo does not move).

Literary Analysis
Dramatic Speeches
What does this brief speech by the Nurse reveal about her relationship with Romeo?

15. O cry of grief.

Stage production – 1990s
Royal Shakespeare Company
Romeo and Juliet.

Stage production – 2004
Royal Shakespeare Company
Friar and Juliet.

Ballet – 2001
Kirov Ballet of St. Petersburg,
Russia.

ROMEO. [*Rises.*] Nurse—

NURSE. Ah sir, ah sir! Death's the end of all.

ROMEO. Spakest thou of Juliet? How is it with her?
Doth not she think me an old murderer,
95   Now I have stained the childhood of our joy
With blood removed but little from her own?
Where is she? And how doth she? And what says
My concealed lady[16] to our canceled love?

NURSE. O, she says nothing, sir, but weeps and weeps;
100   And now falls on her bed, and then starts up,
And Tybalt calls; and then on Romeo cries,
And then down falls again.

ROMEO.   As if that name,
Shot from the deadly level[17] of a gun,
Did murder her; as that name's cursèd hand
105   Murdered her kinsman. O, tell me, friar, tell me,
In what vile part of this anatomy
Doth my name lodge? Tell me, that I may sack[18]
The hateful mansion.

[*He offers to stab himself, and* NURSE *snatches the dagger away.*]

16. **concealed lady** secret bride.

17. **level** aim.
18. **sack** plunder.

> ### Reading Check
>
> What does Romeo nearly do before the Nurse stops him?

Stage production – 2004 Royal Shakespeare Company Fight scene.

Verona, Italy Balcony and Juliet.

Illustration – 2006

FRIAR.   Hold thy desperate hand.
Art thou a man? Thy form cries out thou art;
Thy tears are womanish, thy wild acts denote
The unreasonable fury of a beast.
Unseemly[19] woman in a seeming man!
And ill-beseeming beast in seeming both![20]
Thou hast amazed me. By my holy order,
I thought thy disposition better tempered.
Hast thou slain Tybalt? Wilt thou slay thyself?
And slay thy lady that in thy life lives,
By doing damnèd hate upon thyself?
Why railest thou on thy birth, the heaven, and earth?
Since birth and heaven and earth, all three do meet
In thee at once; which thou at once wouldst lose.
Fie, fie, thou shamest thy shape, thy love, thy wit,[21]
Which, like a usurer,[22] abound'st in all,
And usest none in that true use indeed
Which should bedeck[23] thy shape, thy love, thy wit.
Thy noble shape is but a form of wax,
Digressing from the valor of a man;
Thy dear love sworn but hollow perjury,
Killing that love which thou hast vowed to cherish;
Thy wit, that ornament to shape and love,
Misshapen in the conduct[24] of them both,
Like powder in a skilless soldier's flask,[25]
Is set afire by thine own ignorance,
And thou dismemb'red with thine own defense.[26]
What, rouse thee, man! Thy Juliet is alive,
For whose dear sake thou wast but lately dead.[27]
There art thou happy.[28] Tybalt would kill thee,
But thou slewest Tybalt. There art thou happy.
The law, that threat'ned death, becomes thy friend
And turns it to exile. There art thou happy.
A pack of blessings light upon thy back;
Happiness courts thee in her best array;
But, like a misbehaved and sullen wench,[29]
Thou puts up[30] thy fortune and thy love.
Take heed, take heed, for such die miserable.
Go get thee to thy love, as was decreed,
Ascend her chamber, hence and comfort her.
But look thou stay not till the watch be set,[31]
For then thou canst not pass to Mantua,
Where thou shalt live till we can find a time
To blaze[32] your marriage, reconcile your friends,

110

115

120

125

130

135

140

145

150

19. Unseemly inappropriate (because unnatural).
20. And . . . both! Romeo has inappropriately lost his human nature because he seems like a man and woman combined.

21. wit mind; intellect.
22. Which, like a usurer who, like a rich moneylender.
23. bedeck do honor to.

24. conduct management.
25. flask powder flask.
26. And thou . . . defense The friar is saying that Romeo's mind, which is now irrational, is destroying rather than aiding him.
27. but lately dead only recently declaring yourself dead.
28. happy fortunate.

29. wench low, common girl.
30. puts up pouts over.

31. watch be set watchmen go on duty.

32. blaze announce publicly.

Beg pardon of the Prince, and call thee back
With twenty hundred thousand times more joy
Than thou went'st forth in lamentation.
155 Go before, nurse. Commend me to thy lady,
And bid her hasten all the house to bed,
Which heavy sorrow makes them apt unto.³³
Romeo is coming.

NURSE. O Lord, I could have stayed here all the night
160 To hear good counsel. O, what learning is!
My lord, I'll tell my lady you will come.

ROMEO. Do so, and bid my sweet prepare to chide.³⁴
[NURSE *offers to go in and turns again.*]

NURSE. Here, sir, a ring she bid me give you, sir.
Hie you, make haste, for it grows very late.   [*Exit.*]
165 **ROMEO.** How well my comfort is revived by this!

FRIAR. Go hence; good night; and here stands all your state:³⁵
Either be gone before the watch be set,
Or by the break of day disguised from hence.
Sojourn³⁶ in Mantua. I'll find out your man,
170 And he shall signify³⁷ from time to time
Every good hap to you that chances here.
Give me thy hand. 'Tis late. Farewell; good night.

ROMEO. But that a joy past joy calls out on me,
It were a grief so brief to part with thee.
175 Farewell.   [*Exit all.*]

Scene iv. A room in Capulet's house.
[*Enter old* CAPULET, *his* WIFE, *and* PARIS.]

CAPULET. Things have fall'n out, sir, so unluckily
That we have had no time to move¹ our daughter.
Look you, she loved her kinsman Tybalt dearly,
And so did I. Well, we were born to die.
5 'Tis very late; she'll not come down tonight.
I promise you, but for your company,
I would have been abed an hour ago.

PARIS. These times of woe afford no times to woo.
Madam, good night. Commend me to your daughter.

10 **LADY.** I will, and know her mind early tomorrow;
Tonight she's mewed up to her heaviness.²

Reading Skill
Summarize Briefly state
the main points of the
Friar's speech to Romeo.

33. **apt unto** likely to do.

34. **chide** rebuke me (for
slaying Tybalt).

35. **here . . . state** this is your
situation.

36. **Sojourn** remain.
37. **signify** let you know.

1. **move** discuss your
proposal with.
2. **mewed . . . heaviness**
locked up with her sorrow.

Reading
Check
What reason do the
Capulets give Paris to
explain why Juliet
cannot see him?

CAPULET. Sir, Paris, I will make a desperate tender³
    Of my child's love. I think she will be ruled
    In all respects by me; nay more, I doubt it not.
15   Wife, go you to her ere you go to bed;
    Acquaint her here of my son⁴ Paris' love
    And bid her (mark you me?) on Wednesday next—
    But soft! What day is this?

PARIS.   Monday, my lord.

CAPULET. Monday! Ha, ha! Well, Wednesday is too soon.
20   A⁵ Thursday let it be—a Thursday, tell her,
    She shall be married to this noble earl.
    Will you be ready? Do you like this haste?
    We'll keep no great ado⁶—a friend or two;
    For hark you, Tybalt being slain so late,
25   It may be thought we held him carelessly,⁷
    Being our kinsman, if we revel much.
    Therefore we'll have some half a dozen friends,
    And there an end. But what say you to Thursday?

PARIS. My lord, I would that Thursday were tomorrow.

30 **CAPULET.** Well, get you gone. A Thursday be it then.
    Go you to Juliet ere you go to bed;
    Prepare her, wife, against⁸ this wedding day.
    Farewell, my lord.—Light to my chamber, ho!
    Afore me,⁹ it is so very late
35   That we may call it early by and by.
    Good night.   *[Exit all.]*

Scene v. Capulet's orchard.
[Enter ROMEO *and* JULIET *aloft.]*

JULIET. Wilt thou be gone? It is not yet near day.
    It was the nightingale, and not the lark,
    That pierced the fearful hollow of thine ear.
    Nightly she sings on yond pomegranate tree.
5   Believe me, love, it was the nightingale.

ROMEO. It was the lark, the herald of the morn;
    No nightingale. Look, love, what envious streaks
    Do lace the severing¹ clouds in yonder East.
    Night's candles² are burnt out, and jocund day
10   Stands tiptoe on the misty mountaintops.
    I must be gone and live, or stay and die.

---

3. desperate tender risky offer.
4. son son-in-law.

5. A on.

6. We'll . . . ado We will not make a great fuss.
7. held him carelessly did not respect him enough.

Reading Skill
Summarize
Summarize Lord Capulet's remarks about the timing of Juliet's marriage to Paris.

8. against for.
9. Afore me indeed (a mild oath).

1. severing parting.
2. Night's candles stars.

Literature Connection

The Nightingale and the Lark

The nightingale and the lark are two birds that appear frequently in literature, particularly in poetry. Both birds are admired for their beautiful singing, and they also have symbolic associations. The nightingale and its song are traditionally associated with night; the lark and its song with dawn. Shakespeare draws on these associations in this exchange between Romeo and Juliet.

Connect to the Literature

Why do Romeo and Juliet have negative associations with the lark at this point in the play?

Lark

JULIET. Yond light is not daylight; I know it, I.
It is some meteor that the sun exhales³
To be to thee this night a torchbearer
15   And light thee on thy way to Mantua.
Therefore stay yet; thou need'st not to be gone.

ROMEO. Let me be ta'en, let me be put to death.
I am content, so thou wilt have it so.
I'll say yon gray is not the morning's eye,
20   'Tis but the pale reflex of Cynthia's brow;⁴
Nor that is not the lark whose notes do beat
The vaulty heaven so high above our heads.
I have more care to stay than will to go.
Come, death, and welcome! Juliet wills it so.
25   How is't, my soul? Let's talk; it is not day.

JULIET. It is, it is! Hie hence, be gone, away!
It is the lark that sings so out of tune,
Straining harsh discords and unpleasing sharps.⁵
Some say the lark makes sweet division;⁶
30   This doth not so, for she divideth us.
Some say the lark and loathèd toad change eyes;⁷
O, now I would they had changed voices too,
Since arm from arm that voice doth us affray,⁸
Hunting thee hence with hunt's-up⁹ to the day.
35   O, now be gone! More light and light it grows.

ROMEO. More light and light—more dark and dark our woes.

3. **exhales** sends out.

4. **reflex . . . brow** reflection of the moon (Cynthia was a name for the moon goddess).

5. **sharps** shrill high notes.
6. **division** melody.
7. **change eyes** exchange eyes (because the lark has a beautiful body with ugly eyes and the toad has an ugly body with beautiful eyes).
8. **affray** frighten.
9. **hunt's-up** morning song for hunters.

Reading Check

What do the Capulets plan for Juliet on Thursday?

[*Enter* NURSE.]

NURSE. Madam!

JULIET. Nurse?

NURSE. Your lady mother is coming to your chamber.
40   The day is broke; be wary, look about.   [*Exit.*]

JULIET. Then, window, let day in, and let life out.

ROMEO. Farewell, farewell! One kiss, and I'll descend.

[*He goeth down.*]

Reading Skill
Summarize Identify the key points of the farewell conversation between Romeo and Juliet.

JULIET. Art thou gone so, love-lord, ay husband-friend?
    I must hear from thee every day in the hour,
45   For in a minute there are many days.
    O, by this count I shall be much in years[10]
    Ere I again behold my Romeo!

10. **much in years** much older.

ROMEO. Farewell!
    I will omit no opportunity
50   That may convey my greetings, love, to thee.

JULIET. O, think'st thou we shall ever meet again?

ROMEO. I doubt it not; and all these woes shall serve
    For sweet discourses[11] in our times to come.

11. **discourses** conversations.

12. **ill-divining** predicting evil.

JULIET. O God, I have an ill-divining[12] soul!
55   Methinks I see thee, now thou art so low,
    As one dead in the bottom of a tomb.
    Either my eyesight fails, or thou lookest pale.

13. **Dry sorrow . . . blood** It was once believed that sorrow drained away the blood.

14. **dost thou** do you have to do.

ROMEO. And trust me, love, in my eye so do you.
    Dry sorrow drinks our blood.[13] Adieu, adieu!   [*Exit.*]

60 **JULIET.** O Fortune, Fortune! All men call thee fickle.
    If thou art fickle, what dost thou[14] with him
    That is renowned for faith? Be fickle, Fortune,
    For then I hope thou wilt not keep him long
    But send him back.

Vocabulary
fickle (fik´ əl) *adj.*
changeable

[*Enter* MOTHER.]

65 **LADY CAPULET.** Ho, daughter! Are you up?

15. **Is she . . . late** Has she stayed up so late?

16. **What . . . hither?** What unusual reason brings her here?

JULIET. Who is't that calls? It is my lady mother.
    Is she not down so late,[15] or up so early?
    What unaccustomed cause procures her hither?[16]

LADY CAPULET. Why, how now, Juliet?

JULIET. Madam, I am not well.

70 **LADY CAPULET.** Evermore weeping for your cousin's death?
What, wilt thou wash him from his grave with tears?
And if thou couldst, thou couldst not make him live.
Therefore have done. Some grief shows much of love;
But much of grief shows still some want of wit.

75 **JULIET.** Yet let me weep for such a feeling[17] loss.

17. **feeling** deeply felt.

LADY CAPULET. So shall you feel the loss, but not the friend
Which you weep for.

JULIET. Feeling so the loss,
I cannot choose but ever weep the friend.

LADY CAPULET. Well, girl, thou weep'st not so much for his death
80 As that the villain lives which slaughtered him.

JULIET. What villain, madam?

LADY CAPULET. That same villain Romeo.

18. **asunder** apart.

JULIET. [*Aside*] Villain and he be many miles asunder.[18]—
God pardon him! I do, with all my heart;
And yet no man like he doth grieve my heart.

**Literary Analysis
Dramatic Speeches**
What qualities of an aside do you find in line 82?

85 **LADY CAPULET.** That is because the traitor murderer lives.

JULIET. Ay, madam, from the reach of these my hands.
Would none but I might venge my cousin's death!

LADY CAPULET. We will have vengeance for it, fear thou not.
Then weep no more. I'll send to one in Mantua,
90 Where that same banished runagate[19] doth live,
Shall give him such an unaccustomed dram[20]
That he shall soon keep Tybalt company;
And then I hope thou wilt be satisfied.

19. **runagate** renegade; runaway.
20. **unaccustomed dram** unexpected dose of poison.

JULIET. Indeed I never shall be satisfied
95 With Romeo till I behold him—dead[21]—
Is my poor heart so for a kinsman vexed.
Madam, if you could find out but a man
To bear a poison, I would temper[22] it;
That Romeo should, upon receipt thereof,
100 Soon sleep in quiet. O, how my heart abhors
To hear him named and cannot come to him,
To wreak[23] the love I bore my cousin
Upon his body that hath slaughtered him!

21. **dead** Juliet is deliberately ambiguous here. Her mother thinks *dead* refers to Romeo. But Juliet is using the word with the following line, in reference to her heart.
22. **temper** mix; weaken.
23. **wreak** (rēk) avenge; express.

Reading Check
What are Lady Capulet's plans for Romeo?

LADY CAPULET. Find thou the means, and I'll find such a man.
105   But now I'll tell thee joyful tidings, girl.

JULIET. And joy comes well in such a needy time.
    What are they, I beseech your ladyship?

24. careful considerate.

LADY CAPULET. Well, well, thou hast a careful[24] father, child;
    One who, to put thee from thy heaviness,

25. sorted out selected.

110   Hath sorted out[25] a sudden day of joy
    That thou expects not nor I looked not for.

26. in happy time just in time.

JULIET. Madam, in happy time![26] What day is that?

Literary Analysis
Dramatic Speeches
Analyze Lady Capulet's
dialogue. How is the
author developing
Romeo as a complex,
yet believable, charac-
ter through the literary
device of character foils?

LADY CAPULET. Marry, my child, early next Thursday morn
    The gallant, young, and noble gentleman,
115   The County Paris, at Saint Peter's Church,
    Shall happily make thee there a joyful bride.

JULIET. Now by Saint Peter's Church, and Peter too,
    He shall not make me there a joyful bride!
    I wonder at this haste, that I must wed
120   Ere he that should be husband comes to woo.
    I pray you tell my lord and father, madam,
    I will not marry yet; and when I do, I swear
    It shall be Romeo, whom you know I hate,
    Rather than Paris. These are news indeed!

125 **LADY CAPULET.** Here comes your father. Tell him so yourself,
    And see how he will take it at your hands.

[*Enter* CAPULET *and* NURSE.]

CAPULET. When the sun sets the earth doth drizzle dew,
    But for the sunset of my brother's son
    It rains downright.

27. conduit water pipe.

28. bark boat.

Reading Skill
Summarize
Summarize the
comparison Lord Capulet
makes in lines 130–138.

130   How now? A conduit,[27] girl? What, still in tears?
    Evermore show'ring? In one little body
    Thou counterfeits a bark,[28] a sea, a wind:
    For still thy eyes, which I may call the sea,
    Do ebb and flow with tears; the bark thy body is,
135   Sailing in this salt flood; the winds, thy sighs,
    Who, raging with thy tears and they with them,
    Without a sudden calm will overset
    Thy tempest-tossèd body. How now, wife?
    Have you delivered to her our decree?

29. she will none . . . thanks
She will have nothing to do
with it, thank you.

140 **LADY CAPULET.** Ay, sir; but she will none, she gives you
    thanks.[29]
    I would the fool were married to her grave!

CAPULET. Soft! Take me with you,[30] take me with you, wife.
How? Will she none? Doth she not give us thanks?
Is she not proud?[31] Doth she not count her blest,
145 Unworthy as she is, that we have wrought[32]
So worthy a gentleman to be her bride?

JULIET. Not proud you have, but thankful that you have.
Proud can I never be of what I hate,
But thankful even for hate that is meant love.

150 **CAPULET.** How, how, how, how, chopped-logic?[33] What is this?
"Proud"—and "I thank you"—and "I thank you not"—
And yet "not proud"? Mistress minion[34] you,
Thank me no thankings, nor proud me no prouds,
But fettle[35] your fine joints 'gainst Thursday next
155 To go with Paris to Saint Peter's Church,
Or I will drag thee on a hurdle[36] thither.
Out, you greensickness carrion![37] Out, you baggage![38]
You tallow-face![39]

LADY CAPULET.   Fie, fie! What, are you mad?

JULIET. Good father, I beseech you on my knees,
160 Hear me with patience but to speak a word.

CAPULET. Hang thee, young baggage! Disobedient wretch!
I tell thee what—get thee to church a Thursday
Or never after look me in the face.
Speak not, reply not, do not answer me!
165 My fingers itch. Wife, we scarce thought us blest
That God had lent us but this only child;
But now I see this one is one too much,
And that we have a curse in having her.
Out on her, hilding![40]

NURSE.   God in heaven bless her!
170 You are to blame, my lord, to rate[41] her so.

CAPULET. And why, my Lady Wisdom? Hold your tongue,
Good Prudence. Smatter with your gossips, go![42]

NURSE. I speak no treason.

CAPULET.   O, God-i-god-en!

NURSE. May not one speak?

CAPULET.   Peace, you mumbling fool!
175 Utter your gravity[43] o'er a gossip's bowl,
For here we need it not.

---

30. **Soft! Take . . . you** Wait a minute. Let me understand you.
31. **proud** pleased.
32. **wrought** arranged.

33. **chopped-logic** contradictory, unsound thought and speech.
34. **Mistress minion** Miss Uppity; overly proud.
35. **fettle** prepare.
36. **hurdle** sled on which prisoners were taken to their execution.
37. **greensickness carrion** anemic lump of flesh.
38. **baggage** naughty girl.
39. **tallow-face** wax-pale face.

Literary Analysis
Dramatic Speeches
What feelings and personality traits does Lord Capulet reveal in this brief speech?

40. **hilding** worthless person.

41. **rate** scold; berate.

42. **Smatter . . . go!** Go chatter with the other old women.
43. **gravity** wisdom.

Reading Check

Rather than Paris, whom does Juliet threaten to marry?

LADY CAPULET. You are too hot.

CAPULET. God's bread![44] It makes me mad.
    Day, night; hour, tide, time; work, play;
    Alone, in company; still my care hath been
180 To have her matched; and having now provided
    A gentleman of noble parentage,
    Of fair demesnes,[45] youthful, and nobly trained,
    Stuffed, as they say, with honorable parts,[46]
    Proportioned as one's thought would wish a man—
185 And then to have a wretched puling[47] fool,
    A whining mammet,[48] in her fortune's tender,[49]
    To answer "I'll not wed, I cannot love;
    I am too young, I pray you pardon me"!
    But, and you will not wed, I'll pardon you!
190 Graze where you will, you shall not house with me.
    Look to't, think on't; I do not use to jest.
    Thursday is near; lay hand on heart, advise:[50]
    And you be mine, I'll give you to my friend;
    And you be not, hang, beg, starve, die in the streets,
195 For, by my soul, I'll ne'er acknowledge thee,
    Nor what is mine shall never do thee good.
    Trust to't. Bethink you. I'll not be forsworn.[51]   [*Exit.*]

JULIET. Is there no pity sitting in the clouds
    That sees into the bottom of my grief?
200 O sweet my mother, cast me not away!
    Delay this marriage for a month, a week;
    Or if you do not, make the bridal bed
    In that dim monument where Tybalt lies.

LADY CAPULET. Talk not to me, for I'll not speak a word.
205 Do as thou wilt, for I have done with thee.   [*Exit.*]

JULIET. O God!—O nurse, how shall this be prevented?
    My husband is on earth, my faith in heaven.[52]
    How shall that faith return again to earth
    Unless that husband send it me from heaven
210 By leaving earth?[53] Comfort me, counsel me.

---

44. **God's bread!** By the holy Eucharist!

45. **demesnes** property.
46. **parts** qualities.
47. **puling** whining.

48. **mammet** doll.
49. **in . . . tender** when good fortune is offered her.

50. **advise** consider.

51. **forsworn** made to violate my promise.

Reading Skill
Summarize
Summarize the threat that Lord Capulet makes to Juliet in this monologue.

52. **my faith in heaven** my marriage vow is recorded in heaven.
53. **leaving earth** dying.

Alack, alack, that heaven should practice stratagems[54]
Upon so soft a subject as myself!
What say'st thou? Hast thou not a word of joy?
Some comfort, nurse.

215 **NURSE.**   Faith, here it is.
Romeo is banished; and all the world to nothing[55]
That he dares ne'er come back to challenge[56] you;
Or if he do, it needs must be by stealth.
Then, since the case so stands as now it doth,
I think it best you married with the County.
220 O, he's a lovely gentleman!
Romeo's a dishclout to him.[57] An eagle, madam,
Hath not so green, so quick, so fair an eye
As Paris hath. Beshrew my very heart,
I think you are happy in this second match,
225 For it excels your first; or if it did not,
Your first is dead—or 'twere as good he were
As living here and you no use of him.

JULIET. Speak'st thou from thy heart?

NURSE. And from my soul too; else beshrew them both.

230 **JULIET.** Amen!

▶ **Critical Viewing** In what ways
does this picture suggest Juliet's
vulnerability? Explain. **[Interpret]**

54. **stratagems** tricks; plots.

55. **all . . . nothing** the odds
are overwhelming.
56. **challenge** claim.

57. **a dishclout to him** a
dishcloth compared with
him.

Reading
Check
How do the Capulets
respond to the Nurse's
attempts to defend
Juliet?

58. be absolved receive forgiveness for my sins.

59. Ancient damnation! Old devil!

60. Thou . . . twain You will from now on be separated from my trust.

Literary Analysis
Dramatic Speeches
Here, Juliet delivers a soliloquy. Explain how this dramatic convention enhances the text.

NURSE. What?

JULIET. Well, thou hast comforted me marvelous much.
Go in; and tell my lady I am gone,
Having displeased my father, to Lawrence' cell,
235   To make confession and to be absolved.⁵⁸

NURSE. Marry, I will; and this is wisely done.   [*Exit.*]

JULIET. Ancient damnation!⁵⁹ O most wicked fiend!
Is it more sin to wish me thus forsworn,
Or to dispraise my lord with that same tongue
240   Which she hath praised him with above compare
So many thousand times? Go, counselor!
Thou and my bosom henceforth shall be twain.⁶⁰
I'll to the friar to know his remedy.
If all else fail, myself have power to die.   [*Exit.*]

Critical Thinking

Support your responses with evidence from the text.

1. **Respond:** What would you do if you were in Romeo's or Juliet's situation? Explain your answer.

2. **(a)** Make a three-column chart. In the first column, write the remark regarding the Montagues and Capulets that Mercutio makes three times as he is dying. **(b) Make Inferences:** In the second column, explain what Mercutio means by this exclamation. **(c) Interpret:** In the third column, explain how his remark reinforces ideas set forth in the play's Prologue.

3. **(a)** How and why does Romeo kill Tybalt? **(b) Interpret:** What does Romeo mean when he says, "I am fortune's fool"?

4. **Resolve:** How might Tybalt's death have been avoided?

5. **(a) Analyze:** Review the *Reflect* and *Recall* features on page 863. Which is a summary that captures the main ideas and elements of a text, and which is a critique that takes a position and expresses an opinion? **(b)** Explain how you distinguished between the two.

 **Do our differences define us?**
How have the differences between Romeo and Juliet returned to threaten their future together? Explain.

Literary Analysis: Dramatic Speeches

1. (a) What thoughts and feelings does Juliet express in the **soliloquy** that opens Scene ii of Act III? **(b)** Explain how this **dramatic convention** enhances the text.

2. What criticisms of Romeo does the Friar address in his Scene iii **monologue** beginning, "Hold thy desperate hand"?

3. (a) In Act III, Scene v, when her mother refers to Romeo as a villain, Juliet utters the **aside,** "Villain and he be many miles asunder." What does Juliet mean? **(b)** Why is it important that the audience, but not Lady Capulet, hears Juliet's remark?

4. (a) Describe the personalities of each of the following characters: Romeo, Tybalt, Benvolio, Mercutio. **(b)** Which of these characters are **foils** to each other? **(c)** Analyze these pairs. Explain how Shakespeare develops them as complex, yet believable, characters through the literary device of character foils.

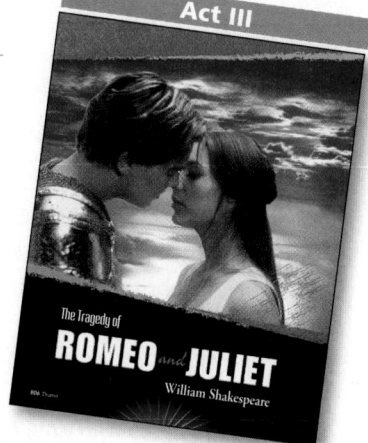

Reading Skill: Summarize

5. (a) Paraphrase lines 29–51 in Act III, Scene iii. **(b)** Based on your paraphrase, write a few sentences that **summarize** what Romeo is saying to the Friar in these lines.

6. Summarize the events of Act III.

Vocabulary

Practice Identify which two words in each group are **synonyms** and which one is an **antonym** of the other two. Explain your response.

1. gallant, courageous, cowardly

2. fray, truce, brawl

3. exile, banishment, welcome

4. martial, peaceful, warlike

5. eloquence, expressiveness, awkwardness

6. fickle, unpredictable, constant

Word Power Use the context of the sentences and what you know about the **Latin root -loque-** to explain your answer to each question.

1. Would a *colloquialism* be out of place when used among friends?

2. What would you expect to occur at a *colloquium* on Shakespeare?

Word Power

The **Latin root -loque-** means "talk," "speak," or "say."

Apply It Explain how the root -loque- helps you determine the meanings of these words. Consult a dictionary if necessary.

ventriloquist
soliloquy
loquacious

Do our *differences* define us?

As You Read Look for the ways that the feud between the Montagues and the Capulets continues to drive the young lovers apart. Then, decide whether the actions they take are wise or foolish.

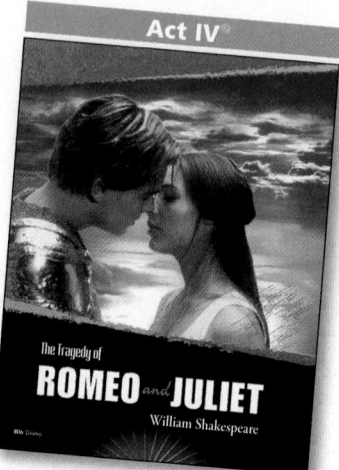

Act IV

The Tragedy of
ROMEO and JULIET
William Shakespeare

🏴 TEXAS Focus on the TEKS

Meet these standards with *The Tragedy of Romeo and Juliet,* **Act IV** (p. 894).

Reading

(4) Explain how dramatic conventions (e.g., dramatic irony) enhance dramatic text. *(Literary Analysis: Dramatic Irony)*

(7) Explain the role of irony in literary works. *(Literary Analysis: Dramatic Irony)*

(1)(B) Analyze textual context to distinguish between the denotative and connotative meanings of words. *(Spiral Review: Connotation and Denotation)*

(9)(A) Distinguish between a summary and a critique. *(Critical Thinking: Analyze)*

Reading/Comprehension

RC-9(A) Reflect on understanding to monitor comprehension. *(Reading Skill: Summarize)*

For more TEKS, see pages 932–935.

Vocabulary

Read each word and its definition. Decide whether you know the word well, know it a little bit, or do not know it at all. After you read, see how your knowledge of each word has increased.

- **pensive** (pen´ siv) *adj.* deeply thoughtful (p. 896) *She listened intently, looking* <u>pensive</u>. *pensively adv. pensiveness n.*

- **vial** (vī´ əl) *n.* small bottle containing medicine or other liquids (p. 898) *The* <u>vial</u> *was filled with expensive perfume.*

- **enjoined** (en joind´) *v.* ordered (p. 900) *The jurors were* <u>enjoined</u> *not to discuss the case. enjoin v. enjoinment n.*

- **wayward** (wā´ wərd) *adj.* headstrong (p. 900) *The* <u>wayward</u> *boy did not listen to anyone and insisted on working alone. waywardly adv. waywardness n.*

- **dismal** (diz´ məl) *adj.* causing gloom or misery (p. 901) *The* <u>dismal</u> *sight of his abandoned house made the old man sad. dismally adv.*

- **loathsome** (lōth´ səm) *adj.* disgusting; detestable (p. 903) *The* <u>loathsome</u> *smell of rotten eggs filled the laboratory. loathe v.*

Word Power

The **Latin prefix en-** means "in," "into," or "within."

In Act IV, Juliet says she is **enjoined** by Friar Lawrence to be ruled by her father. She means that Friar Lawrence wants her to join with her father by obeying his wishes.

Literary Analysis: Dramatic Irony

Dramatic irony is a contradiction between what a character thinks and what the audience knows to be true. The role of the **dramatic convention** of irony is to engage the audience emotionally; tension and suspense build as the audience waits for the truth to be revealed to the characters.

Shakespeare understood the importance of providing a balance of tragic and comic elements in his plays. Injecting **humor** into an otherwise tragic plot lets the audience experience a range of reactions to the events unfolding. These comic elements appear throughout the play:

- **Comic relief:** the introduction of a humorous character or situation into an otherwise tragic scene.

- **Puns:** plays on words using a word with multiple meanings or two words that sound alike but have different meanings. For example, the dying Mercutio makes a pun using the word *grave:* "Ask for me tomorrow, and you shall find me a grave man."

As You Read Jot down notes that explain how Shakespeare uses the dramatic conventions of irony and humor to enhance the text. Then, explain the role of irony in the literary work.

Reading Skill: Summarize

To **summarize** long passages of Shakespearean dialogue, you should break down long sentences into shorter units of meaning.

- If a sentence contains multiple subjects or verbs, separate it into smaller sentences with one subject and one verb.

- If a sentence contains colons, semicolons, or dashes, treat these marks as periods in order to make shorter sentences.

Using the Strategy: Summarizing Chart

As You Read Pause periodically to **reflect on your understanding. Monitor your comprehension** by using a chart like this one to help you break down long sentences.

Line of Dialogue	Line in Smaller Sentences	Summary
Immoderately she weeps for Tybalt's death, / And therefore have I little talked of love; / For Venus smiles not in a house of tears.	1. Immoderately she weeps for Tybalt's death. 2. Therefore have I little talked of love. 3. Venus smiles not in a house of tears.	Paris has not talked of love with Juliet because she is crying over Tybalt's death.

TEXAS

PHLitOnline

www.PHLitOnline.com

Hear It!
- Selection summary audio
- Selection audio

See It!
- Get Connected video
- Background video
- More about the author
- Vocabulary flashcards

Do It!
- Interactive journals
- Interactive graphic organizers
- Self-test
- Internet activity
- Grammar tutorial
- Interactive vocabulary games

ACT IV

Reflect "A bemused audience, unless the director is shrewd, is likely to become skeptical that event after event arrives in the untimeliest way possible."

from *Shakespeare: The Invention of the Human*
by Harold Bloom

Recall Romeo and Juliet are married for only a few hours when disaster strikes. In Act III, Juliet's cousin Tybalt kills Mercutio, and then Romeo kills Tybalt. This leads to Romeo's banishment from Verona. To make matters worse, Juliet's parents are determined to marry her to Paris.

Anticipate Will Romeo and Juliet ever be able to live together as husband and wife? What, if anything, can the lovers now do to preserve their relationship?

Scene i. Friar Lawrence's cell.

[*Enter* FRIAR LAWRENCE *and* COUNTY PARIS.]

    FRIAR. On Thursday, sir? The time is very short.

    PARIS. My father[1] Capulet will have it so,
        And I am nothing slow to slack his haste.[2]

    FRIAR. You say you do not know the lady's mind.
5   Uneven is the course;[3] I like it not.

    PARIS. Immoderately she weeps for Tybalt's death,
        And therefore have I little talked of love;
        For Venus smiles not in a house of tears.
        Now, sir, her father counts it dangerous

1. **father** future father-in-law.
2. **I . . . haste** I will not slow him down by being slow myself.
3. **Uneven . . . course** irregular is the plan.

Reading Check

What is the Friar's complaint to Paris about the impending wedding?

4. **inundation** flood.
5. **minded** thought about.

Literary Analysis
Dramatic Irony
In what way does Paris's comment show that he does not understand the real reason that Juliet is crying? What is the role of this irony?

6. **That's . . . text** That is a certain truth.

7. **price** value.

8. **before their spite** before the harm that the tears did.

Vocabulary
pensive (pen´ siv) *adj.* deeply thoughtful

9. **entreat . . . alone** ask to have this time to ourselves.

10   That she do give her sorrow so much sway,
    And in his wisdom hastes our marriage
    To stop the inundation[4] of her tears,
    Which, too much minded[5] by herself alone,
    May be put from her by society.
15   Now do you know the reason of this haste.

    FRIAR. [*Aside*] I would I knew not why it should be slowed.—
        Look, sir, here comes the lady toward my cell.

[*Enter* JULIET.]

    PARIS. Happily met, my lady and my wife!

    JULIET. That may be, sir, when I may be a wife.

20   **PARIS.** That "may be" must be, love, on Thursday next.

    JULIET. What must be shall be.

    FRIAR.   That's a certain text.[6]

    PARIS. Come you to make confession to this father?

    JULIET. To answer that, I should confess to you.

    PARIS. Do not deny to him that you love me.

25   **JULIET.** I will confess to you that I love him.

    PARIS. So will ye, I am sure, that you love me.

    JULIET. If I do so, it will be of more price,[7]
        Being spoke behind your back, than to your face.

    PARIS. Poor soul, thy face is much abused with tears.

30   **JULIET.** The tears have got small victory by that,
        For it was bad enough before their spite.[8]

    PARIS. Thou wrong'st it more than tears with that report.

    JULIET. That is no slander, sir, which is a truth;
        And what I spake, I spake it to my face.

35   **PARIS.** Thy face is mine, and thou hast sland'red it.

    JULIET. It may be so, for it is not mine own.
        Are you at leisure, holy father, now,
        Or shall I come to you at evening mass?

    FRIAR. My leisure serves me, pensive daughter, now.
40   My lord, we must entreat the time alone.[9]

PARIS. God shield[10] I should disturb devotion!
    Juliet, on Thursday early will I rouse ye.
    Till then, adieu, and keep this holy kiss.   [*Exit.*]

JULIET. O, shut the door, and when thou hast done so,
45   Come weep with me—past hope, past care, past help!

FRIAR. O Juliet, I already know thy grief;
    It strains me past the compass of my wits.[11]
    I hear thou must, and nothing may prorogue[12] it,
    On Thursday next be married to this County.

50 **JULIET.** Tell me not, friar, that thou hearest of this,
    Unless thou tell me how I may prevent it.
    If in thy wisdom thou canst give no help,
    Do thou but call my resolution wise
    And with this knife I'll help it presently.[13]
55   God joined my heart and Romeo's, thou our hands;
    And ere this hand, by thee to Romeo's sealed,
    Shall be the label to another deed,[14]
    Or my true heart with treacherous revolt
    Turn to another, this shall slay them both.
60   Therefore, out of thy long-experienced time,
    Give me some present counsel; or, behold,
    'Twixt my extremes and me[15] this bloody knife
    Shall play the umpire, arbitrating[16] that
    Which the commission of thy years and art
65   Could to no issue of true honor bring.[17]
    Be not so long to speak. I long to die
    If what thou speak'st speak not of remedy.

FRIAR. Hold, daughter. I do spy a kind of hope,
    Which craves[18] as desperate an execution
70   As that is desperate which we would prevent.
    If, rather than to marry County Paris,
    Thou hast the strength of will to slay thyself,
    Then is it likely thou wilt undertake
    A thing like death to chide away this shame,
75   That cop'st with death himself to scape from it;[19]
    And, if thou darest, I'll give thee remedy.

JULIET. O, bid me leap, rather than marry Paris,
    From off the battlements of any tower,
    Or walk in thievish ways,[20] or bid me lurk

---

10. **shield** forbid.

11. **past . . . wits** beyond the ability of my mind to find a remedy.
12. **prorogue** delay.

13. **presently** at once.
14. **Shall . . . deed** shall give the seal of approval to another marriage contract.
15. **'Twixt . . me** between my misfortunes and me.
16. **arbitrating** deciding.
17. **Which . . . bring** which the authority that derives from your age and ability could not solve honorably.

Literary Analysis
Dramatic Irony Which two meanings of the word "long" does Juliet use to make a pun in line 66?

18. **craves** requires.
19. **That cop'st . . . it** that bargains with death itself to escape from it.
20. **thievish ways** roads where criminals lurk.

Reading Check
What does Juliet threaten to do to avoid marrying Paris?

21. **charnel house** vault for bones removed from graves to be reused.
22. **reeky** foul-smelling.
23. **chapless** jawless.

Vocabulary
vial (vī´ əl) *n.* small bottle containing medicine or other liquids

24. **humor** fluid; liquid.
25. **native** natural.
26. **surcease** stop.
27. **wanny ashes** to the color of pale ashes.
28. **eyes' windows** eyelids.
29. **supple government** ability for maintaining motion.

30. **uncovered on the bier** displayed on the funeral platform.
31. **against** before.
32. **drift** purpose; plan.

80 Where serpents are; chain me with roaring bears,
    Or hide me nightly in a charnel house,[21]
    O'ercovered quite with dead men's rattling bones,
    With reeky[22] shanks and yellow chapless[23] skulls;
    Or bid me go into a new-made grave
85 And hide me with a dead man in his shroud—
    Things that, to hear them told, have made me tremble—
    And I will do it without fear or doubt,
    To live an unstained wife to my sweet love.

FRIAR. Hold, then. Go home, be merry, give consent
90 To marry Paris. Wednesday is tomorrow.
    Tomorrow night look that thou lie alone;
    Let not the nurse lie with thee in thy chamber.
    Take thou this vial, being then in bed,
    And this distilling liquor drink thou off;
95 When presently through all thy veins shall run
    A cold and drowsy humor;[24] for no pulse
    Shall keep his native[25] progress, but surcease;[26]
    No warmth, no breath, shall testify thou livest;
    The roses in thy lips and cheeks shall fade
100 To wanny ashes,[27] thy eyes' windows[28] fall
    Like death when he shuts up the day of life;
    Each part, deprived of supple government,[29]
    Shall, stiff and stark and cold, appear like death;
    And in this borrowed likeness of shrunk death
105 Thou shalt continue two-and-forty hours,
    And then awake as from a pleasant sleep.
    Now, when the bridegroom in the morning comes
    To rouse thee from thy bed, there art thou dead.
    Then, as the manner of our country is,
110 In thy best robes uncovered on the bier[30]
    Thou shalt be borne to that same ancient vault
    Where all the kindred of the Capulets lie.
    In the meantime, against[31] thou shalt awake,
    Shall Romeo by my letters know our drift;[32]
115 And hither shall he come; and he and I

Will watch thy waking, and that very night
Shall Romeo bear thee hence to Mantua.
And this shall free thee from this present shame,
If no inconstant toy[33] nor womanish fear
120 Abate thy valor[34] in the acting it.

    JULIET. Give me, give me! O, tell not me of fear!

    FRIAR. Hold! Get you gone, be strong and prosperous
In this resolve. I'll send a friar with speed
To Mantua, with my letters to thy lord.

125 **JULIET.** Love give me strength, and strength shall help afford.
    Farewell, dear father.   [*Exit with* FRIAR.]

Scene ii. *Hall in Capulet's house.*

[*Enter* FATHER CAPULET, MOTHER, NURSE, *and* SERVINGMEN, *two or three.*]

    CAPULET. So many guests invite as here are writ.
             [*Exit a* SERVINGMAN.]

    Sirrah, go hire me twenty cunning[1] cooks.

    SERVINGMAN. You shall have none ill, sir; for I'll try[2] if they can
    lick their fingers.

5 **CAPULET.** How canst thou try them so?

    SERVINGMAN. Marry, sir, 'tis an ill cook that cannot lick his own
    fingers.[3] Therefore he that cannot lick his fingers goes not
    with me.

    CAPULET. Go, begone.
            [*Exit* SERVINGMAN.]

    We shall be much unfurnished[4] for this time.
10 What, is my daughter gone to Friar Lawrence?

    NURSE. Ay, forsooth.[5]

    CAPULET. Well, he may chance to do some good on her.
    A peevish self-willed harlotry it is.[6]

[*Enter* JULIET.]

    NURSE. See where she comes from shrift with merry look.

15 **CAPULET.** How now, my headstrong? Where have you been
    gadding?

---

33. **inconstant toy** passing whim.
34. **Abate thy valor** Lessen your courage.

Literary Analysis
Dramatic Irony
What information does Juliet now have that Romeo does not? How does the dramatic convention of dramatic irony enhance the text?

1. **cunning** skillful.

2. **try** test.

3. **'tis . . . fingers** It is a bad cook who will not taste his own cooking.

4. **unfurnished** unprepared.
5. **forsooth** in truth.
6. **A peevish . . . it is** It is the ill-tempered, selfish behavior of a woman without good breeding.

Reading
Check
According to the Friar, how will Romeo learn of Juliet's plan to meet him?

Vocabulary
enjoined (en joind´)
v. ordered

7. **behests** requests.

8. **fall prostrate** lie face down in humble submission.

9. **becomèd** suitable; proper.

Literary Analysis
Dramatic Irony What is ironic about Lord Capulet's relief in this scene?

10. **bound** indebted.
11. **closet** private room.
12. **ornaments** clothes.

13. **short . . . provision** lacking time for preparation.

14. **deck up her** dress her; get her ready.
15. **What, ho!** Capulet is calling for his servants.

Vocabulary
wayward (wā´ wərd)
adj. headstrong

JULIET. Where I have learnt me to repent the sin
  Of disobedient opposition
  To you and your behests,[7] and am enjoined
  By holy Lawrence to fall prostrate[8] here
20 To beg your pardon. Pardon, I beseech you!
  Henceforward I am ever ruled by you.

CAPULET. Send for the County. Go tell him of this.
  I'll have this knot knit up tomorrow morning.

JULIET. I met the youthful lord at Lawrence' cell
25 And gave him what becomèd[9] love I might,
  Not stepping o'er the bounds of modesty.

CAPULET. Why, I am glad on't. This is well. Stand up.
  This is as't should be. Let me see the County.
  Ay, marry, go, I say, and fetch him hither.
30 Now, afore God, this reverend holy friar,
  All our whole city is much bound[10] to him.

JULIET. Nurse, will you go with me into my closet[11]
  To help me sort such needful ornaments[12]
  As you think fit to furnish me tomorrow?

35 **LADY CAPULET.** No, not till Thursday. There is time enough.

CAPULET. Go, nurse, go with her. We'll to church tomorrow.

[*Exit* JULIET *and* NURSE.]

LADY CAPULET. We shall be short in our provision.[13]
  'Tis now near night.

CAPULET.   Tush, I will stir about,
  And all things shall be well, I warrant thee, wife.
  Go thou to Juliet, help to deck up her.[14]
40 I'll not to bed tonight; let me alone.
  I'll play the housewife for this once. What, ho![15]
  They are all forth; well, I will walk myself
  To County Paris, to prepare up him
45 Against tomorrow. My heart is wondrous light,
  Since this same wayward girl is so reclaimed.

[*Exit with* MOTHER.]

Scene iii. Juliet's chamber.

[*Enter* JULIET *and* NURSE.]

JULIET. Ay, those attires are best; but, gentle nurse,
I pray thee leave me to myself tonight;
For I have need of many orisons¹
To move the heavens to smile upon my state,²
5   Which, well thou knowest, is cross³ and full of sin.

[*Enter* MOTHER.]

LADY CAPULET. What, are you busy, ho? Need you my help?

JULIET. No, madam; we have culled⁴ such necessaries
As are behoveful⁵ for our state tomorrow.
So please you, let me now be left alone,
10   And let the nurse this night sit up with you:
For I am sure you have your hands full all
In this so sudden business.

LADY CAPULET.   Good night.
Get thee to bed, and rest: for thou hast need.

[*Exit* MOTHER *and* NURSE.]

JULIET. Farewell! God knows when we shall meet again.
15   I have a faint cold fear thrills through my veins
That almost freezes up the heat of life.
I'll call them back again to comfort me.
Nurse!—What should she do here?
My dismal scene I needs must act alone.
20   Come, vial.
What if this mixture do not work at all?
Shall I be married then tomorrow morning?
No, no! This shall forbid it. Lie thou there.

[*Lays down a dagger.*]

What if it be a poison which the friar
25   Subtly hath minist'red⁶ to have me dead,
Lest in this marriage he should be dishonored
Because he married me before to Romeo?
I fear it is; and yet methinks it should not,
For he hath still been tried⁷ a holy man.
30   How if, when I am laid into the tomb,
I wake before the time that Romeo
Come to redeem me? There's a fearful point!

1. orisons prayers.
2. state condition.
3. cross selfish; disobedient.

4. culled chosen.
5. behoveful desirable; appropriate.

Reading Skill
Summarize Briefly state the reasons Juliet gives for why she should be alone.

Vocabulary
dismal (diz´ məl) *adj.* causing gloom or misery

6. minist'red given me.

7. tried proved.

Reading
Check
How does Juliet regain her parents' favor?

The Tragedy of Romeo and Juliet, Act IV **901**

Shall I not then be stifled in the vault,
To whose foul mouth no healthsome air breathes in,
35 And there die strangled ere my Romeo comes?
Or, if I live, is it not very like
The horrible conceit[8] of death and night,
Together with the terror of the place—
As in a vault, an ancient receptacle
40 Where for this many hundred years the bones
Of all my buried ancestors are packed;
Where bloody Tybalt, yet but green in earth,[9]
Lies fest'ring in his shroud; where, as they say,
At some hours in the night spirits resort—
45 Alack, alack, is it not like[10] that I,
So early waking—what with loathsome smells,
And shrieks like mandrakes[11] torn out of the earth,
That living mortals, hearing them, run mad—
O, if I wake, shall I not be distraught,[12]
50 Environèd[13] with all these hideous fears,
And madly play with my forefathers' joints,
And pluck the mangled Tybalt from his shroud,
And, in this rage, with some great kinsman's bone
As with a club dash out my desp'rate brains?
55 O, look! Methinks I see my cousin's ghost
Seeking out Romeo, that did spit his body
Upon a rapier's point. Stay, Tybalt, stay!
Romeo, Romeo, Romeo, I drink to thee.
                [*She falls upon her bed within the curtains.*]

8. **conceit** idea; thought.

9. **green in earth** newly entombed.

10. **like** likely.

Vocabulary
loathsome (lō*th*ˊ səm)
adj. disgusting;
detestable

11. **mandrakes** plants with forked roots that resemble human legs. The mandrake was believed to shriek when uprooted and cause the hearer to go mad.

12. **distraught** insane.

13. **Environèd** surrounded.

Reading Skill
Summarize Summarize the fears that Juliet expresses in this soliloquy.

Reading
Check

What does Juliet do after her mother and the Nurse leave her chambers?

◀ **Critical Viewing** In what way do the colors in this photograph enhance the mood of the scene? **[Analyze]**

Scene iv. Hall in Capulet's house.

[*Enter* LADY OF THE HOUSE *and* NURSE.]

LADY CAPULET. Hold, take these keys and fetch more spices, nurse.

NURSE. They call for dates and quinces[1] in the pastry.[2]

[*Enter old* CAPULET.]

CAPULET. Come, stir, stir, stir! The second cock hath crowed,
    The curfew bell hath rung, 'tis three o'clock.
5   Look to the baked meats, good Angelica;[3]
    Spare not for cost.

NURSE.   Go, you cotquean,[4] go,
    Get you to bed! Faith, you'll be sick tomorrow
    For this night's watching.[5]

CAPULET. No, not a whit. What, I have watched ere now
10   All night for lesser cause, and ne'er been sick.

LADY CAPULET. Ay, you have been a mouse hunt[6] in your time;
    But I will watch you from such watching now.

                  [*Exit* LADY *and* NURSE.]

CAPULET. A jealous hood,[7] a jealous hood!

[*Enter three or four* FELLOWS *with spits and logs and baskets.*]
                  Now, fellow,

    What is there?

15 **FIRST FELLOW.** Things for the cook, sir; but I know not what.

CAPULET. Make haste, make haste. [*Exit* FIRST FELLOW.] Sirrah,
    fetch drier logs.
    Call Peter; he will show thee where they are.

SECOND FELLOW. I have a head, sir, that will find out logs
    And never trouble Peter for the matter.

20 **CAPULET.** Mass,[8] and well said; a merry whoreson, ha!
    Thou shalt be loggerhead.[9]

                  [*Exit* SECOND FELLOW, *with the others.*]
            Good faith, 'tis day.
    The County will be here with music straight,
    For so he said he would.   [*Play music.*]
           I hear him near.
    Nurse! Wife! What, ho! What, nurse, I say!

---

1. **quinces** golden, apple-shaped fruits.
2. **pastry** baking room.
3. **Angelica** This is probably the Nurse's name.
4. **cotquean** (kat´ kwēn´) man who does housework.
5. **watching** staying awake.
6. **mouse hunt** woman chaser.
7. **jealous hood** jealousy.
8. **Mass** by the Mass (an oath).
9. **loggerhead** blockhead.

Literary Analysis
Dramatic Irony Reread lines 16–21. In what way does Capulet's pun in line 21 contribute to the mood of Scene iv?

[*Enter* NURSE.]

25   Go waken Juliet; go and trim her up.
     I'll go and chat with Paris. Hie, make haste,
     Make haste! The bridegroom he is come already:
     Make haste, I say.   [*Exit.*]

Scene v. Juliet's chamber.

NURSE. Mistress! What, mistress! Juliet! Fast,[1] I warrant her,
          she.
     Why, lamb! Why, lady! Fie, you slugabed.[2]
     Why, love, I say! Madam; Sweetheart! Why, bride!
     What, not a word? You take your pennyworths now;
5   Sleep for a week; for the next night, I warrant,
     The County Paris hath set up his rest
     That you shall rest but little. God forgive me!
     Marry, and amen. How sound is she asleep!
     I needs must wake her. Madam, madam, madam!
10   Ay, let the County take you in your bed;
     He'll fright you up, i' faith. Will it not be?
                              [*Draws aside the curtains.*]
     What, dressed, and in your clothes, and down again?[3]
     I must needs wake you. Lady! Lady! Lady!
     Alas, alas! Help, help! My lady's dead!
15   O weraday that ever I was born!
     Some aqua vitae, ho! My lord! My lady!

[*Enter* MOTHER.]

LADY CAPULET. What noise is here?

NURSE.   O lamentable day!

LADY CAPULET. What is the matter?

NURSE.   Look, look! O heavy day!

LADY CAPULET. O me, O me! My child, my only life!
20   Revive, look up, or I will die with thee!
     Help, help! Call help.

[*Enter* FATHER.]

CAPULET. For shame, bring Juliet forth; her lord is come.

NURSE. She's dead, deceased; she's dead, alack the day!

LADY CAPULET. Alack the day, she's dead, she's dead, she's
          dead!

1. **Fast** fast asleep.
2. **slugabed** sleepyhead.

Literary Analysis
Dramatic Irony
Explain how the dramatic convention of irony enhances the Nurse's dialogue at the beginning of Scene v.

3. **down again** back in bed.

Reading Check
What does the Nurse find when she draws aside the curtains in Juliet's chamber?

25 **CAPULET.** Ha! Let me see her. Out alas! She's cold,
Her blood is settled, and her joints are stiff;
Life and these lips have long been separated.
Death lies on her like an untimely frost
Upon the sweetest flower of all the field.

NURSE. O lamentable day!

30 **LADY CAPULET.**   O woeful time!

CAPULET. Death, that hath ta'en her hence to make me wail,
Ties up my tongue and will not let me speak.

[*Enter* FRIAR LAWRENCE *and the* COUNTY PARIS, *with* MUSICIANS.]

**Literary Analysis
Dramatic Irony**

In what way does the Friar's question add to the dramatic irony of the scene?

FRIAR. Come, is the bride ready to go to church?

CAPULET. Ready to go, but never to return.
35 O son, the night before thy wedding day
Hath Death lain with thy wife. There she lies,
Flower as she was, deflowerèd by him.
Death is my son-in-law, Death is my heir;
My daughter he hath wedded. I will die
40 And leave him all. Life, living, all is Death's.

PARIS. Have I thought, love, to see this morning's face,
And doth it give me such a sight as this?

LADY CAPULET. Accursed, unhappy, wretched, hateful day!
Most miserable hour that e'er time saw
45 In lasting labor of his pilgrimage!
But one, poor one, one poor and loving child,
But one thing to rejoice and solace[4] in,
And cruel Death hath catched it from my sight.

4. solace find comfort.

NURSE. O woe! O woeful, woeful, woeful day!
50 Most lamentable day, most woeful day
That ever ever I did yet behold!
O day, O day, O day! O hateful day!
Never was seen so black a day as this.
O woeful day! O woeful day!

5. Beguiled cheated.

55 **PARIS.** Beguiled,[5] divorcèd, wrongèd, spited, slain!
Most detestable Death, by thee beguiled,
By cruel, cruel thee quite overthrown.
O love! O life!—not life, but love in death!

6. Uncomfortable painful, upsetting.

7. solemnity solemn rites.

CAPULET. Despised, distressèd, hated, martyred, killed!
60 Uncomfortable[6] time, why cam'st thou now
To murder, murder our solemnity?[7]

Culture Connection

Rosemary

When the Capulets discover Juliet apparently dead, the Friar advises, "Dry up your tears and stick your rosemary / On this fair corse." Rosemary is an evergreen herb that traditionally signifies remembrance, loyalty, and love. Shakespeare often included references to herbs in his plays for symbolic purposes, and rosemary is one herb that turned up often in his works. *Hamlet, King Lear, The Winter's Tale,* and *Pericles* all include references to rosemary as a symbol of remembrance.

Connect to the Literature

Why do you think the Friar tells the Capulets to lay a sprig of rosemary on Juliet's body?

O child, O child! My soul, and not my child!
Dead art thou—alack, my child is dead,
And with my child my joys are burièd!

65   **FRIAR.** Peace, ho, for shame! Confusion's cure lives not
In these confusions.[8] Heaven and yourself
Had part in this fair maid—now heaven hath all,
And all the better is it for the maid.
Your part in her you could not keep from death,

70   But heaven keeps his part in eternal life.
The most you sought was her promotion,
For 'twas your heaven she should be advanced;
And weep ye now, seeing she is advanced
Above the clouds, as high as heaven itself?

75   O, in this love, you love your child so ill
That you run mad, seeing that she is well.[9]
She's not well married that lives married long,
But she's best married that dies married young.
Dry up your tears and stick your rosemary[10]

80   On this fair corse, and, as the custom is,
And in her best array bear her to church:
For though fond nature[11] bids us all lament,
Yet nature's tears are reason's merriment.[12]

8. **Confusion's . . . confusions** The remedy for this calamity is not to be found in these outcries.

9. **well** blessed in heaven.

10. **rosemary** evergreen herb signifying love and remembrance.

11. **fond nature** mistake-prone human nature.

12. **Yet . . . merriment** While human nature causes us to weep for Juliet, reason should cause us to be happy (since she is in heaven).

Reading Check

What does the Friar recommend that the Capulets do when they discover Juliet and believe she is dead?

CAPULET. All things that we ordainèd festival[13]
85   Turn from their office to black funeral—
    Our instruments to melancholy bells,
    Our wedding cheer to a sad burial feast;
    Our solemn hymns to sullen dirges[14] change;
    Our bridal flowers serve for a buried corse;
90   And all things change them to the contrary.

FRIAR. Sir, go you in; and, madam, go with him;
    And go, Sir Paris. Everyone prepare
    To follow this fair corse unto her grave.
    The heavens do low'r[15] upon you for some ill;
95   Move them no more by crossing their high will.

[*Exit, casting rosemary on her and shutting the curtains.
The* NURSE *and* MUSICIANS *remain.*]

FIRST MUSICIAN. Faith, we may put up our pipes and be gone.

NURSE. Honest good fellows, ah, put up, put up!
    For well you know this is a pitiful case.[16]   [*Exit.*]

FIRST MUSICIAN. Ay, by my troth, the case may be amended.

[*Enter* PETER.]

100 **PETER.** Musicians, O, musicians, "Heart's ease," "Heart's ease"!
    O, and you will have me live, play "Heart's ease."

FIRST MUSICIAN. Why "Heart's ease"?

PETER. O, musicians, because my heart itself plays "My heart is full."
    O, play me some merry dump[17] to comfort me.

105 **FIRST MUSICIAN.** Not a dump we! 'Tis no time to play now.

PETER. You will not then?

FIRST MUSICIAN. No.

PETER. I will then give it you soundly.

FIRST MUSICIAN. What will you give us?

110 **PETER.** No money, on my faith, but the gleek.[18] I will give you[19] the minstrel.[20]

---

13. **ordainèd festival** planned to be part of a celebration.
14. **dirges** funeral hymns.

Literary Analysis
Dramatic Irony In what way does the dramatic irony of the Friar's words heighten the play's suspense?

15. **low'r** frown.

16. **case** situation; instrument case.

17. **dump** sad tune.

18. **gleek** scornful speech.
19. **give you** call you.
20. **minstrel** a contemptuous term (as opposed to "musician").

FIRST MUSICIAN. Then will I give you the serving-creature.

PETER. Then will I lay the serving-creature's dagger on
   your pate.
   I will carry no crotchets.[21] I'll *re* you, I'll *fa* you. Do you
   note me?

115 **FIRST MUSICIAN.** And you *re* us and *fa* us, you note us.

SECOND MUSICIAN. Pray you put up your dagger, and put out
   your wit.
   Then have at you with my wit!

PETER. I will dry-beat you with an iron wit, and put up my iron
   dagger. Answer me like men.
120 "When griping grief the heart doth wound,
      And doleful dumps the mind oppress,
   Then music with her silver sound"—
   Why "silver sound"? Why "music with her silver sound"?
   What say you, Simon Catling?

125 **FIRST MUSICIAN.** Marry, sir, because silver hath a sweet sound.

PETER. Pretty! What say you, Hugh Rebeck?

21. **crotchets** whims; quarter
   notes.

Spiral Review
Connotation and
Denotation Analyze
the textual context
of the word *men* in
line 119. Write the
word's denotation
and connotation. Tell
how you distinguished
between the denota-
tive and connotative
meanings of the word.

Literary Analysis
Dramatic Irony What kind of mood does the pun in line 127 help to create in this scene?

22. **cry you mercy** beg your pardon.

SECOND MUSICIAN. I say "silver sound" because musicians sound for silver.

PETER. Pretty too! What say you, James Soundpost?

130 **THIRD MUSICIAN.** Faith, I know not what to say.

PETER. O, I cry you mercy,²² you are the singer. I will say for you. It is "music with her silver sound" because musicians have no gold for sounding.
   "Then music with her silver sound
135   With speedy help doth lend redress." [*Exit.*]

FIRST MUSICIAN. What a pestilent knave is this same!

SECOND MUSICIAN. Hang him, Jack! Come, we'll in here, tarry for the mourners, and stay dinner. [*Exit with others.*]

Critical Thinking

Support your responses with evidence from the text.

1. **(a) Respond:** Should Romeo and Juliet have followed Friar Lawrence's advice? Why or why not? **(b)** Discuss your response with a partner.

2. **(a)** What is Friar Lawrence's plan for Juliet? **(b) Analyze:** Why does Juliet trust the Friar? Explain using details from the text.

3. **(a)** What three fears does Juliet reveal in her Act IV, Scene iii, soliloquy? **(b) Interpret:** What does the soliloquy reveal about her personality? Explain your response.

4. **(a) Evaluate:** Do you think drinking the potion is a brave act or a foolish act? Explain. **(b) Draw Conclusions:** How has Juliet changed in the course of the play? Give details to explain your response.

5. **(a) Analyze:** Review the *Reflect* and *Recall* features on page 895. Which is a summary that captures the main ideas and elements of a text, and which is a critique that takes a position and expresses an opinion? **(b)** Explain how you distinguished between the two.

Do our differences define us?
(a) In what way do Juliet's ideas about love differ from her parents' ideas? **(b)** What do Juliet's rebellious actions reveal about her?

Literary Analysis: **Dramatic Irony**

1. Review Juliet's encounter with Paris in Friar Lawrence's cell.
   (a) Explain how Shakespeare uses the **dramatic convention** of **irony** to enhance the text in this section. **(b)** What is the role of this irony?

2. Complete a chart like this one to demonstrate why Capulet's statement in Act IV, Scene iv, line 25, is an example of dramatic irony.

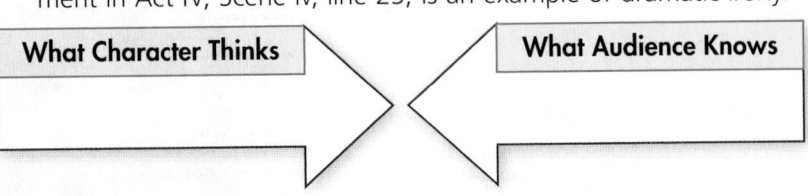

What Character Thinks   **What Audience Knows**

3. Explain how Capulet's encounter with the fellows in Act IV, Scene iv, represents an example of **comic relief.**

4. **(a)** Explain the **pun** in the Nurse's exchange with the First Musician in Act IV, Scene v, lines 97–98. **(b)** How is the conversation that follows among the musicians and Peter an example of comic relief?

Reading Skill: **Summarize**

5. **(a) Summarize** lines 50–59 of Act IV, Scene i by breaking down this long sentence into smaller ones. **(b)** How does breaking this long sentence into smaller ones make Juliet's speech clearer?

6. Summarize the events of Act IV.

Vocabulary

Practice Indicate whether each of the following statements is *True* or *False*. Revise the sentences that are false to make them true.

1. Clowns make children laugh by appearing *pensive*.

2. If you have been *enjoined* to attend an event, you should not go.

3. A *wayward* person would probably dislike orders.

4. If you were in a *dismal* mood, you would be good company.

5. A *loathsome* meal is not likely to be eaten quickly.

6. A *vial* would be a good container for a cough syrup.

Word Power Use the context of the sentences and what you know about the **Latin prefix en-** to explain your answer to each question.

1. Would a terrible insult *enrage* you?

2. What happens when someone *enlists* in the armed forces?

Word Power

The **Latin prefix en-** means "in," "into," "within."

Apply It Explain how the prefix en- helps you determine the meanings of these words. Consult a dictionary if necessary.

encage
entrap
entreat

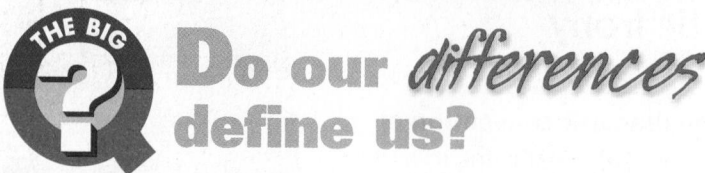

Do our *differences* define us?

As You Read Consider the ways differences in this drama lead to a tragic end. Then, decide if the events had to happen this way.

TEXAS Focus on the TEKS

Meet these standards with *The Tragedy of Romeo and Juliet*, **Act V** (p. 914).

Reading
(4) Explain how dramatic conventions enhance dramatic text. *(Literary Analysis: Tragedy and Motive)*

(9)(A) Distinguish between a summary and a critique. *(Critical Thinking: Analyze)*

Reading/Comprehension Skills
RC-9(A) Reflect on understanding to monitor comprehension. *(Reading Skill: Summarize)*
For more TEKS, see pages 932–935.

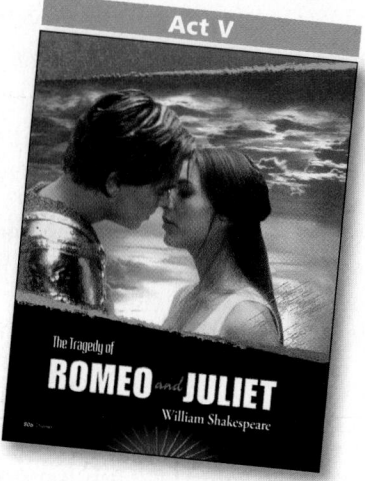

Vocabulary

Read each word and its definition. Decide whether you know the word well, know it a little bit, or do not know it at all. After you read, see how your knowledge of each word has increased.

- **remnants** (rem´ nənts) *n.* what is left over; remainders (p. 917) *The remnants of the house still stood after the fire.*

- **penury** (pen´ yōō rē) *n.* extreme poverty (p. 917) *His choice was either to find work or to live in penury. penurious adj.*

- **disperse** (di spʉrs´) *v.* to break up and scatter in all directions; spread about (p. 918) *Our group will disperse flyers about the fundraiser in the mall. dispersal n. dispersion n. dispersible adj.*

- **haughty** (hôt´ ē) *adj.* arrogant (p. 921) *He acts haughty onstage but humble offstage. haughtily adv. haughtiness n.*

- **ambiguities** (am´ bə gyōō´ ə tēz) *n.* statements or events whose meanings are unclear (p. 927) *Voters were confused by the ambiguities in the candidate's speech. ambiguous adj.*

- **scourge** (skʉrj) *n.* instrument for inflicting punishment (p. 929) *Longer practices were the scourge that the coach used to punish the players for their laziness.*

Word Power

The **Latin prefix ambi-** means "both."

In this drama, the Prince says he wants to clear up the **ambiguities** and learn the truth. He means that the facts are uncertain and can be understood from two or more points of view.

Literary Analysis: Tragedy and Motive

A **tragedy** is a drama in which the major character, who is of noble stature, meets with disaster or great misfortune. The tragic hero's downfall is usually the result of one of the following elements, or conventions:

- *fate,* or the idea of a pre-planned destiny
- a serious character flaw
- some combination of both

Motive is an important element of a tragic hero's character. A character's motives guide his or her thoughts or actions. Often, the hero's motives are basically good but misguided. As a result, the hero suffers a tragic fate that may seem undeserved.

Although tragedies are sad, they can also be uplifting. They show the greatness and nobility of the human spirit when faced with grave challenges.

As You Read Consider what positive message is conveyed by the drama's tragic events. Jot down notes explaining how the use of dramatic conventions enhances the final act of the play.

Reading Skill: Summarize

Summarizing is briefly stating the main points in a piece of writing. In summarizing the action of a play, it is useful to first identify causes and effects.

- A *cause* is an event, action, or emotion that produces a result.
- An *effect* is the result produced by the cause.

Tragedies often involve a chain of causes and effects that advance the plot and lead to the tragic outcome. Recognizing the sequence will help you summarize and understand plots like the one in this play.

Using the Strategy: Cause-and-Effect Chart

As You Read Pause periodically to **reflect on your understanding.** Use a chart like this one to **monitor your comprehension** by summarizing the causes and effects in the final act of *The Tragedy of Romeo and Juliet.*

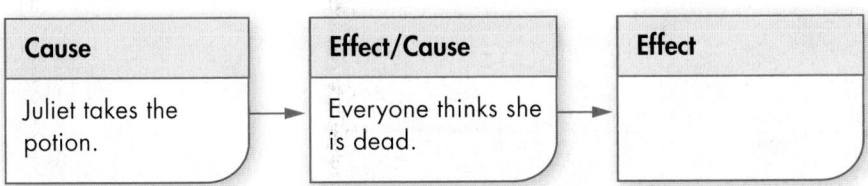

Cause	Effect/Cause	Effect
Juliet takes the potion.	Everyone thinks she is dead.	

Hear It!
- Selection summary audio
- Selection audio

See It!
- Get Connected video
- Background video
- More about the author
- Vocabulary flashcards

Do It!
- Interactive journals
- Interactive graphic organizers
- Self-test
- Internet activity
- Grammar tutorial
- Interactive vocabulary games

ACT V

Reflect "Tragedy did not come easily to Shakespeare, yet all this play's lyricism and comic genius cannot hold off the dawn that will become a destructive darkness."

from *Shakespeare: The Invention of the Human*
by Harold Bloom

Recall To prevent her marriage to Paris, Juliet has taken the Friar's potion and is in a temporary deathlike sleep. Her unsuspecting family plans her funeral. Meanwhile, the Friar has sent a messenger to Mantua to tell Romeo of the ruse, so that he may return and rescue Juliet from her family tomb.

Anticipate What do you think might go wrong with the Friar's plan?

Scene i. MANTUA. *A STREET.*

[*Enter* ROMEO.]

    ROMEO. If I may trust the flattering truth of sleep,[1]
        My dreams presage[2] some joyful news at hand.
        My bosom's lord[3] sits lightly in his throne,
        And all this day an unaccustomed spirit
5   Lifts me above the ground with cheerful thoughts.
        I dreamt my lady came and found me dead
        (Strange dream that gives a dead man leave to think!)
        And breathed such life with kisses in my lips
        That I revived and was an emperor.
10   Ah me! How sweet is love itself possessed,
        When but love's shadows[4] are so rich in joy!

[*Enter* ROMEO'S MAN, BALTHASAR, *booted.*]
        News from Verona! How now, Balthasar?

1. **flattering . . . sleep** pleasing illusions of dreams.
2. **presage** foretell.
3. **bosom's lord** heart.

4. **shadows** dreams; unreal images.

Reading Check

Why is Romeo in a good mood?

Dost thou not bring me letters from the friar?
How doth my lady? Is my father well?
15 How fares my Juliet? That I ask again,
For nothing can be ill if she be well.

MAN. Then she is well, and nothing can be ill.
Her body sleeps in Capels' monument,[5]
And her immortal part with angels lives.
20 I saw her laid low in her kindred's vault
And presently took post[6] to tell it you.
O, pardon me for bringing these ill news,
Since you did leave it for my office,[7] sir.

ROMEO. Is it e'en so? Then I defy you, stars!
25 Thou knowest my lodging. Get me ink and paper
And hire post horses. I will hence tonight.

5. Capels' monument the Capulets' burial vault.
6. presently took post immediately set out on horseback.
7. office duty.

Literary Analysis
Tragedy and Motive In what way does Romeo's remark in line 24 reinforce fate's role in the tragedy?

MAN. I do beseech you, sir, have patience.
Your looks are pale and wild and do import
Some misadventure.[8]

ROMEO.   Tush, thou art deceived.
30   Leave me and do the thing I bid thee do.
Hast thou no letters to me from the friar?

MAN. No, my good lord.

ROMEO.   No matter. Get thee gone.
And hire those horses. I'll be with thee straight.

[*Exit* BALTHASAR.]

Well, Juliet, I will lie with thee tonight.
35   Let's see for means. O mischief, thou art swift
To enter in the thoughts of desperate men!
I do remember an apothecary,[9]
And hereabouts 'a dwells, which late I noted
In tatt'red weeds, with overwhelming brows,
40   Culling of simples.[10] Meager were his looks,
Sharp misery had worn him to the bones;
And in his needy shop a tortoise hung,
An alligator stuffed, and other skins
Of ill-shaped fishes; and about his shelves
45   A beggarly account[11] of empty boxes,
Green earthen pots, bladders, and musty seeds,
Remnants of packthread, and old cakes of roses[12]
Were thinly scatterèd, to make up a show.
Noting this penury to myself I said,

8. **import / Some
   misadventure** suggest
   some misfortune.

9. **apothecary** one who
   prepares and sells drugs
   and medicines.
10. **In tatt'red . . . simples**
    in torn clothing, with
    overhanging eyebrows,
    sorting out herbs.
11. **beggarly account** small
    number.
12. **cakes of roses** pressed
    rose petals (used for
    perfume).

Vocabulary
remnants (rem´
nənts) *n.* what is left
over; remainders

penury (pen´ yoo̅ rē)
n. extreme poverty

Reading
Check

What does Romeo learn
from Balthasar?

The Tragedy of Romeo and Juliet, Act V **917**

Vocabulary
disperse (di spurs´) v.
to break up and scatter
in all directions; spread
about; distribute widely

50 "And if a man did need a poison now
Whose sale is present death in Mantua,
Here lives a caitiff[13] wretch would sell it him."
O, this same thought did but forerun my need,
And this same needy man must sell it me.
55 As I remember, this should be the house.
Being holiday, the beggar's shop is shut.
What, ho! Apothecary!

[*Enter* APOTHECARY.]

APOTHECARY. Who calls so loud?

ROMEO. Come hither, man. I see that thou art poor.
Hold, there is forty ducats.[14] Let me have
60 A dram of poison, such soon-speeding gear[15]
As will disperse itself through all the veins
That the life-weary taker may fall dead,
And that the trunk[16] may be discharged of breath
As violently as hasty powder fired
65 Doth hurry from the fatal cannon's womb.

APOTHECARY. Such mortal drugs I have; but Mantua's law
Is death to any he that utters[17] them.

13. **caitiff** miserable.

14. **ducats** (duk´ əts) gold coins.
15. **soon-speeding gear** fast-working stuff.

16. **trunk** body.
17. **utters** sells.

LITERATURE IN CONTEXT

History Connection

Plague Searchers
The Black Plague, or Black Death, was a disease that swept through Europe, Asia, and the Middle East during the 1300s, with outbreaks continuing until 1400. It is thought that as much as a third of Europe's population died of the disease between 1347 and 1351. During an outbreak of plague, officials would appoint plague searchers to quarantine people infected with the disease and dispose of victims' remains. In *Romeo and Juliet*, Friar John is quarantined by plague searchers who fear he has been infected. As a result, he is unable to deliver Friar Lawrence's letter to Romeo.

Connect to the Literature

In what way does the Black Death contribute to the tragedy in *Romeo and Juliet*?

ROMEO. Art thou so bare and full of wretchedness
　　　And fearest to die? Famine is in thy cheeks,
70　　Need and oppression starveth in thy eyes,
　　　Contempt and beggary hangs upon thy back:
　　　The world is not thy friend, nor the world's law;
　　　The world affords no law to make thee rich;
　　　Then be not poor, but break it and take this.

75　**APOTHECARY.** My poverty but not my will consents.

　　ROMEO. I pay thy poverty and not thy will.

　　APOTHECARY. Put this in any liquid thing you will
　　　And drink it off, and if you had the strength
　　　Of twenty men, it would dispatch you straight.

80　**ROMEO.** There is thy gold—worse poison to men's souls,
　　　Doing more murder in this loathsome world,
　　　Than these poor compounds[18] that thou mayst not sell.
　　　I sell thee poison; thou hast sold me none.
　　　Farewell. Buy food and get thyself in flesh.
85　　Come, cordial[19] and not poison, go with me
　　　To Juliet's grave; for there must I use thee.　　　[*Exit all.*]

Scene ii. Friar Lawrence's cell.

[*Enter* FRIAR JOHN, *calling* FRIAR LAWRENCE.]

　　JOHN. Holy Franciscan friar, brother, ho!

[*Enter* FRIAR LAWRENCE.]

　　LAWRENCE. This same should be the voice of Friar John.
　　　Welcome from Mantua. What says Romeo?
　　　Or, if his mind be writ, give me his letter.

5　**JOHN.** Going to find a barefoot brother out,
　　　One of our order, to associate[1] me
　　　Here in this city visiting the sick,
　　　And finding him, the searchers of the town,
　　　Suspecting that we both were in a house
10　　Where the infectious pestilence did reign,
　　　Sealed up the doors, and would not let us forth,
　　　So that my speed to Mantua there was stayed.

　　LAWRENCE. Who bare my letter, then, to Romeo?

　　JOHN. I could not send it—here it is again—
15　　Nor get a messenger to bring it thee,
　　　So fearful were they of infection.

Literary Analysis
Tragedy and Motive What is the apothecary's motive for selling Romeo the poison?

18. **compounds** mixtures.

19. **cordial** health-giving drink.

Reading Skill
Summarize Briefly state the causes and effects of Friar John's failure to deliver Friar Lawrence's letter.

1. **associate** accompany.

Reading Check

What does Romeo plan to do with the apothecary's help?

2. **nice** trivial.
3. **full of charge, / Of dear import** urgent and important.

4. **beshrew** blame.
5. **accidents** happenings.

LAWRENCE. Unhappy fortune! By my brotherhood,
　The letter was not nice,[2] but full of charge,
　Of dear import;[3] and the neglecting it
20　May do much danger. Friar John, go hence,
　Get me an iron crow and bring it straight
　Unto my cell.

JOHN.　　　　　Brother, I'll go and bring it thee.　*[Exit.]*

LAWRENCE. Now must I to the monument alone.
　Within this three hours will fair Juliet wake.
25　She will beshrew[4] me much that Romeo
　Hath had no notice of these accidents;[5]
　But I will write again to Mantua,
　And keep her at my cell till Romeo come—
　Poor living corse, closed in a dead man's tomb!　*[Exit.]*

Scene iii. A churchyard; in it a monument belonging to the Capulets.

[Enter PARIS *and his* PAGE *with flowers and sweet water.]*

1. **aloof** apart.

2. **lay . . . along** lie down flat.

PARIS. Give me thy torch, boy. Hence, and stand aloof.[1]
　Yet put it out, for I would not be seen.
　Under yond yew trees lay thee all along,[2]
　Holding thy ear close to the hollow ground.
5　So shall no foot upon the churchyard tread
　(Being loose, unfirm, with digging up of graves)
　But thou shalt hear it. Whistle then to me,
　As signal that thou hearest something approach.
　Give me those flowers. Do as I bid thee, go.

3. **adventure** chance it.

10　**PAGE.** *[Aside]* I am almost afraid to stand alone
　Here in the churchyard; yet I will adventure.[3]　*[Retires.]*

4. **sweet** perfumed.

5. **obsequies** memorial ceremonies.
6. **cross** interrupt.

PARIS. Sweet flower, with flowers thy bridal bed I strew
　　(O woe! thy canopy is dust and stones)
　Which with sweet[4] water nightly I will dew;
15　　Or, wanting that, with tears distilled by moans.
　The obsequies[5] that I for thee will keep
　Nightly shall be to strew thy grave and weep.　**[BOY** *whistles.]*
　The boy gives warning something doth approach.
　What cursèd foot wanders this way tonight
20　To cross[6] my obsequies and true love's rite?
　What, with a torch? Muffle me, night, awhile.　*[Retires.]*

[Enter ROMEO, *and* BALTHASAR *with a torch, a mattock, and a crow of iron.]*

ROMEO. Give me that mattock and the wrenching iron.
    Hold, take this letter. Early in the morning
    See thou deliver it to my lord and father.
25   Give me the light. Upon thy life I charge thee,
    Whate'er thou hearest or seest, stand all aloof
    And do not interrupt me in my course.
    Why I descend into this bed of death
    Is partly to behold my lady's face,
30   But chiefly to take thence from her dead finger
    A precious ring—a ring that I must use
    In dear employment.[7] Therefore hence, be gone.
    But if thou, jealous,[8] dost return to pry
    In what I farther shall intend to do,
35   By heaven, I will tear thee joint by joint
    And strew this hungry churchyard with thy limbs.
    The time and my intents are savage-wild,
    More fierce and more inexorable[9] far
    Than empty[10] tigers or the roaring sea.

40 **BALTHASAR.** I will be gone, sir, and not trouble ye.

ROMEO. So shalt thou show me friendship. Take thou that.
    Live, and be prosperous; and farewell, good fellow.

BALTHASAR. [*Aside*] For all this same, I'll hide me hereabout.
    His looks I fear, and his intents I doubt.   [*Retires.*]

45 **ROMEO.** Thou detestable maw,[11] thou womb of death,
    Gorged with the dearest morsel of the earth,
    Thus I enforce thy rotten jaws to open,
    And in despite[12] I'll cram thee with more food.

                  [ROMEO *opens the tomb.*]

PARIS. This is that banished haughty Montague
50   That murd'red my love's cousin—with which grief
    It is supposed the fair creature died—
    And here is come to do some villainous shame
    To the dead bodies. I will apprehend[13] him.
    Stop thy unhallowèd toil, vile Montague!
55   Can vengeance be pursued further than death?
    Condemnèd villain, I do apprehend thee.
    Obey, and go with me; for thou must die.

ROMEO. I must indeed; and therefore came I hither.
    Good gentle youth, tempt not a desp'rate man.

Literary Analysis
Tragedy and Motive What different motives do Paris and Romeo have for visiting Juliet's tomb?

7. **dear employment** important business.
8. **jealous** curious.

9. **inexorable** uncontrollable.
10. **empty** hungry.

11. **maw** stomach.

12. **despite** scorn.

Vocabulary
haughty (hôt´ ē) *adj.* arrogant

13. **apprehend** seize; arrest.

Reading Check

How does Paris react to seeing Romeo at Juliet's tomb?

Reading Skill
Summarize
Summarize the causes that you think will produce a tragic effect in the confrontation between Romeo and Paris.

14. **conjurations** solemn appeals.
15. **felon** criminal.

60 Fly hence and leave me. Think upon these gone;
Let them affright thee. I beseech thee, youth,
Put not another sin upon my head
By urging me to fury. O, be gone!
By heaven, I love thee better than myself,
65 For I come hither armed against myself.
Stay not, be gone. Live, and hereafter say
A madman's mercy bid thee run away.

PARIS. I do defy thy conjurations.[14]
And apprehend thee for a felon[15] here.

70 **ROMEO.** Wilt thou provoke me? Then have at thee, boy!
[*They fight.*]

PAGE. O Lord, they fight! I will go call the watch.

[*Exit.* PARIS *falls.*]

PARIS. O, I am slain! If thou be merciful,
Open the tomb, lay me with Juliet.   [*Dies.*]

16. **peruse** look over.
17. **betossèd** upset.
18. **attend** give attention to.

ROMEO. In faith, I will. Let me peruse[16] this face.
75 Mercutio's kinsman, noble County Paris!
What said my man when my betossèd[17] soul
Did not attend[18] him as we rode? I think
He told me Paris should have married Juliet.
Said he not so, or did I dream it so?
80 Or am I mad, hearing him talk of Juliet,
To think it was so? O, give me thy hand,
One writ with me in sour misfortune's book!
I'll bury thee in a triumphant grave.

19. **lanthorn** windowed structure on top of a room to admit light; also, a lantern.
20. **feasting presence** chamber fit for celebration.
21. **keepers** jailers.
22. **ensign** banner.

A grave? O, no, a lanthorn,[19] slaught'red youth,
85 For here lies Juliet, and her beauty makes
This vault a feasting presence[20] full of light.
Death, lie thou there, by a dead man interred.

[*Lays him in the tomb.*]
How oft when men are at the point of death
Have they been merry! Which their keepers[21] call
90 A lightning before death. O, how may I
Call this a lightning? O my love, my wife!
Death, that hath sucked the honey of thy breath,
Hath had no power yet upon thy beauty.
Thou art not conquered. Beauty's ensign[22] yet
95 Is crimson in thy lips and in thy cheeks,
And death's pale flag is not advancèd there.

Literary Analysis
Tragedy and Motive What tragic mistake does Romeo make regarding Juliet's appearance?

Tybalt, liest thou there in thy bloody sheet?
O, what more favor can I do to thee
Than with that hand that cut thy youth in twain
100　To sunder[23] his that was thine enemy?
Forgive me, cousin! Ah, dear Juliet,
Why art thou yet so fair? Shall I believe
That unsubstantial Death is amorous,[24]
And that the lean abhorrèd monster keeps
105　Thee here in dark to be his paramour?
For fear of that I still will stay with thee
And never from this pallet[25] of dim night
Depart again. Here, here will I remain
With worms that are thy chambermaids. O, here
110　Will I set up my everlasting rest
And shake the yoke of inauspicious[26] stars
From this world-wearied flesh. Eyes, look your last!

23. **sunder** cut off.

24. **amorous** full of love.

25. **pallet** bed.
26. **inauspicious** promising misfortune.

What happens to Paris at Juliet's tomb?

27. **dateless** eternal.
28. **engrossing** all-encompassing.
29. **conduct** guide (poison).
30. **pilot** captain (Romeo himself).

Arms, take your last embrace! And, lips, O you
The doors of breath, seal with a righteous kiss
115   A dateless²⁷ bargain to engrossing²⁸ death!
Come, bitter conduct;²⁹ come, unsavory guide!
Thou desperate pilot,³⁰ now at once run on
The dashing rocks thy seasick weary bark!
Here's to my love! [*Drinks.*] O true apothecary!
120   Thy drugs are quick. Thus with a kiss I die.   [*Falls.*]

[*Enter* FRIAR LAWRENCE, *with lanthorn, crow, and spade.*]

FRIAR. Saint Francis be my speed!³¹ How oft tonight
Have my old feet stumbled³² at graves! Who's there?

BALTHASAR. Here's one, a friend, and one that knows you well.

FRIAR. Bliss be upon you! Tell me, good my friend,
125   What torch is yond that vainly lends his light
To grubs³³ and eyeless skulls? As I discern,
It burneth in the Capels' monument.

BALTHASAR. It doth so, holy sir; and there's my master,
One that you love.

FRIAR.   Who is it?

31. **speed** help.
32. **stumbled** stumbling was thought to be a bad omen.
33. **grubs** worms.

▼ **Critical Viewing**
What feelings in the scene does this image convey? **[Analyze]**

BALTHASAR.   Romeo.

FRIAR. How long hath he been there?

130   **BALTHASAR.**   Full half an hour.

FRIAR. Go with me to the vault.

BALTHASAR.   I dare not, sir.
    My master knows not but I am gone hence,
    And fearfully did menace me with death
    If I did stay to look on his intents.

135   **FRIAR.** Stay then; I'll go alone. Fear comes upon me.
    O, much I fear some ill unthrifty[34] thing.

BALTHASAR. As I did sleep under this yew tree here,
    I dreamt my master and another fought,
    And that my master slew him.

FRIAR.   Romeo!
140   Alack, alack, what blood is this which stains
    The stony entrance of this sepulcher?
    What mean these masterless[35] and gory swords
    To lie discolored by this place of peace?   *[Enters the tomb.]*
    Romeo! O, pale! Who else? What, Paris too?
145   And steeped in blood? Ah, what an unkind[36] hour
    Is guilty of this lamentable chance!
    The lady stirs.   *[JULIET rises.]*

JULIET. O comfortable[37] friar! Where is my lord?
    I do remember well where I should be,
150   And there I am. Where is my Romeo?

FRIAR. I hear some noise. Lady, come from that nest
    Of death, contagion, and unnatural sleep.
    A greater power than we can contradict
    Hath thwarted our intents. Come, come away.
155   Thy husband in thy bosom there lies dead;
    And Paris too. Come, I'll dispose of thee
    Among a sisterhood of holy nuns.
    Stay not to question, for the watch is coming.
    Come, go, good Juliet. I dare no longer stay.

160   **JULIET.** Go, get thee hence, for I will not away.   *[Exit FRIAR.]*
    What's here? A cup, closed in my truelove's hand?
    Poison, I see, hath been his timeless[38] end.
    O churl![39] Drunk all, and left no friendly drop
    To help me after? I will kiss thy lips.

Literary Analysis
Tragedy and
Motive In what way
is Friar Lawrence's late
arrival another example
of chance contributing to
this tragedy?

34. **unthrifty** unlucky.

35. **masterless** discarded
(without masters).

36. **unkind** unnatural.

37. **comfortable** comforting.

38. **timeless** untimely; too
soon.
39. **churl** rude fellow.

Literary Analysis
Tragedy and
Motive Why do you
think Friar Lawrence
wants to "dispose of
Juliet" in a sisterhood of
nuns?

**Reading
Check**

How does Juliet react
when she wakes up?

40. restorative medicine.

165   Haply some poison yet doth hang on them
To make me die with a restorative.[40]   *[Kisses him.]*
Thy lips are warm!

CHIEF WATCHMAN. *[Within]* Lead, boy. Which way?

41. happy convenient; opportune.

JULIET. Yea, noise? Then I'll be brief. O happy[41] dagger!
                   [Snatches ROMEO'S *dagger.]*
170   This is thy sheath; there rust, and let me die.
                   [She stabs herself and falls.]

[Enter PARIS' BOY *and* WATCH.]

BOY. This is the place. There, where the torch doth burn.

CHIEF WATCHMAN. The ground is bloody. Search about the
      churchyard.

42. attach arrest.

Go, some of you; whoe'er you find attach.[42]
                   [Exit some of the WATCH.]
Pitiful sight! Here lies the County slain;
175   And Juliet bleeding, warm, and newly dead,
Who here hath lain this two days burièd.
Go, tell the Prince; run to the Capulets;
Raise up the Montagues; some others search.
                   [Exit others of the WATCH.]
We see the ground whereon these woes do lie,

43. ground cause.
44. without circumstance descry see clearly without details.

180   But the true ground[43] of all these piteous woes
We cannot without circumstance descry.[44]

[Enter some of the WATCH, *with* ROMEO'S MAN, BALTHASAR.]

SECOND WATCHMAN. Here's Romeo's man. We found him in the
      churchyard.

CHIEF WATCHMAN. Hold him in safety till the Prince come
      hither.

[Enter FRIAR LAWRENCE *and another* WATCHMAN.]

Literary Analysis
Tragedy and
Motive How might the tragic ending have been averted if Paris, Romeo, and the Friar had come to Juliet's tomb in a different order?

THIRD WATCHMAN. Here is a friar that trembles, sighs and
      weeps.
185   We took this mattock and this spade from him
As he was coming from this churchyard's side.

CHIEF WATCHMAN. A great suspicion! Stay the friar too.

[Enter the PRINCE *and* ATTENDANTS.]

PRINCE. What misadventure is so early up,
That calls our person from our morning rest?

[*Enter* CAPULET *and his* WIFE *with others.*]

190 **CAPULET.** What should it be, that is so shrieked abroad?

LADY CAPULET. O, the people in the street cry "Romeo,"
Some "Juliet," and some "Paris"; and all run
With open outcry toward our monument.

PRINCE. What fear is this which startles in your ears?

195 **CHIEF WATCHMAN.** Sovereign, here lies the County Paris slain;
And Romeo dead; and Juliet, dead before,
Warm and new killed.

PRINCE. Search, seek, and know how this foul murder comes.

CHIEF WATCHMAN. Here is a friar, and slaughtered Romeo's man,
200 With instruments upon them fit to open
These dead men's tombs.

CAPULET. O heavens! O wife, look how our daughter bleeds!
This dagger hath mista'en, for, lo, his house[45]
Is empty on the back of Montague,
205 And it missheathèd in my daughter's bosom!

> 45. **house** sheath.

LADY CAPULET. O me, this sight of death is as a bell
That warns my old age to a sepulcher.

[*Enter* MONTAGUE *and others.*]

PRINCE. Come, Montague; for thou art early up
To see thy son and heir more early down.

210 **MONTAGUE.** Alas, my liege,[46] my wife is dead tonight!
Grief of my son's exile hath stopped her breath.
What further woe conspires against mine age?

PRINCE. Look, and thou shalt see.

MONTAGUE. O thou untaught! What manners is in this,
215 To press before thy father to a grave?

PRINCE. Seal up the mouth of outrage[47] for a while,
Till we can clear these ambiguities
And know their spring, their head, their true descent;
And then will I be general of your woes[48]
220 And lead you even to death. Meantime forbear,
And let mischance be slave to patience.[49]
Bring forth the parties of suspicion.

> 46. **liege** (lēj) lord.
> 47. **mouth of outrage** violent cries.
> 48. **general . . . woes** leader in your sorrow.
> 49. **let . . . patience** be patient in the face of misfortune.

Vocabulary
ambiguities (am′ bə gyōō′ ə tēz) *n.* statements or events whose meanings are unclear

Reading Check

What effect did Romeo's exile have on his mother?

FRIAR. I am the greatest, able to do least,
　　Yet most suspected, as the time and place
225　Doth make against me, of this direful[50] murder;
　　And here I stand, both to impeach and purge[51]
　　Myself condemnèd and myself excused.

PRINCE. Then say at once what thou dost know in this.

FRIAR. I will be brief, for my short date of breath[52]
230　Is not so long as is a tedious tale.
　　Romeo, there dead, was husband to that Juliet;
　　And she, there dead, that's Romeo's faithful wife.
　　I married them; and their stol'n marriage day
　　Was Tybalt's doomsday, whose untimely death
235　Banished the new-made bridegroom from this city;
　　For whom, and not for Tybalt, Juliet pined.
　　You, to remove that siege of grief from her,
　　Betrothed and would have married her perforce
　　To County Paris. Then comes she to me
240　And with wild looks bid me devise some mean
　　To rid her from this second marriage,
　　Or in my cell there would she kill herself.
　　Then gave I her (so tutored by my art)
　　A sleeping potion; which so took effect
245　As I intended, for it wrought on her
　　The form of death. Meantime I writ to Romeo
　　That he should hither come as[53] this dire night
　　To help to take her from her borrowed grave,
　　Being the time the potion's force should cease,
250　But he which bore my letter, Friar John,
　　Was stayed by accident, and yesternight
　　Returned my letter back. Then all alone
　　At the prefixèd hour of her waking
　　Came I to take her from her kindred's vault;
255　Meaning to keep her closely[54] at my cell
　　Till I conveniently could send to Romeo.
　　But when I came, some minute ere the time
　　Of her awakening, here untimely lay
　　The noble Paris and true Romeo dead.
260　She wakes; and I entreated her come forth
　　And bear this work of heaven with patience;
　　But then a noise did scare me from the tomb,
　　And she, too desperate, would not go with me,
　　But, as it seems, did violence on herself.
265　All this I know, and to the marriage

50. **direful** terrible.
51. **impeach and purge** accuse and declare blameless.
52. **date of breath** term of life.

Literary Analysis
Tragedy and
Motive What examples of fate or character flaws do you find in the tragic events that the Friar recounts?

53. **as** on.

54. **closely** hidden; secretly.

Her nurse is privy;[55] and if aught in this
Miscarried by my fault, let my old life
Be sacrificed some hour before his time
Unto the rigor[56] of severest law.

270 **PRINCE.** We still have known thee for a holy man.
Where's Romeo's man? What can he say to this?

BALTHASAR. I brought my master news of Juliet's death;
And then in post he came from Mantua
To this same place, to this same monument.
275 This letter he early bid me give his father,
And threat'ned me with death, going in the vault,
If I departed not and left him there.

PRINCE. Give me the letter. I will look on it.
Where is the County's page that raised the watch?
280 Sirrah, what made your master[57] in this place?

BOY. He came with flowers to strew his lady's grave;
And bid me stand aloof, and so I did.
Anon comes one with light to ope the tomb;
And by and by my master drew on him;
285 And then I ran away to call the watch.

PRINCE. This letter doth make good the friar's words,
Their course of love, the tidings of her death;
And here he writes that he did buy a poison
Of a poor 'pothecary and therewithal
290 Came to this vault to die and lie with Juliet.
Where be these enemies? Capulet, Montague,
See what a scourge is laid upon your hate,
That heaven finds means to kill your joys with love.
And I, for winking at[58] your discords too,
295 Have lost a brace[59] of kinsmen. All are punished.

CAPULET. O brother Montague, give me thy hand.
This is my daughter's jointure,[60] for no more
Can I demand.

MONTAGUE.   But I can give thee more;
For I will raise her statue in pure gold,
300 That whiles Verona by that name is known,
There shall no figure at such rate[61] be set
As that of true and faithful Juliet.

CAPULET. As rich shall Romeo's by his lady's lie—
Poor sacrifices of our enmity![62]

55. **privy** secretly informed about.

56. **rigor** strictness.

57. **made your master** was your master doing.

Vocabulary
scourge (skʉrj) *n.*
instrument for inflicting
punishment

58. **winking at** closing my eyes to.
59. **brace** pair (Mercutio and Paris).
60. **jointure** wedding gift; marriage settlement.
61. **rate** value.
62. **enmity** hostility.

Reading
Check

How does the Friar
explain his role in the fate
of Romeo and Juliet?

63. **glooming** cloudy; gloomy.

Literary Analysis

Tragedy and

Motive What might be Lord Montague's motive for the promise he makes to Lord Capulet?

305 **PRINCE.** A glooming[63] peace this morning with it brings.
　　The sun for sorrow will not show his head.
　　Go hence, to have more talk of these sad things;
　　Some shall be pardoned, and some punishèd;
　　For never was a story of more woe
310　Than this of Juliet and her Romeo.　　　　　[*Exit all.*]

Critical Thinking

1. **Respond:** Were you surprised by the way this play ends? Why or why not?

2. **(a)** In Act V, Scene i, what causes Romeo to exclaim, "Then I defy you, stars"? **(b) Connect:** In what way are Romeo's words consistent with what you know of his character?

3. **(a)** Identify at least three events that cause the Friar's scheme to fail. **(b) Analyze:** Why is it not surprising that the scheme fails?

4. **(a)** How does the relationship between the feuding families change at the end of the play? **(b) Draw Conclusions:** Were Romeo and Juliet's deaths necessary for this change to occur? Explain. **(c) Make a Judgment:** Is the end of long-term violence between their families a fair exchange for the deaths of Romeo and Juliet? Explain your response.

5. **(a) Analyze:** Review the *Reflect* and *Recall* features on page 915. Which is a summary that captures the main ideas and elements of a text, and which is a critique that takes a position and expresses an opinion? **(b)** Explain how you distinguished between the two.

Do our differences define us? Did Romeo and Juliet have any control over the differences that separated them and led to their tragic end? Explain.

Support your responses with evidence from the text.

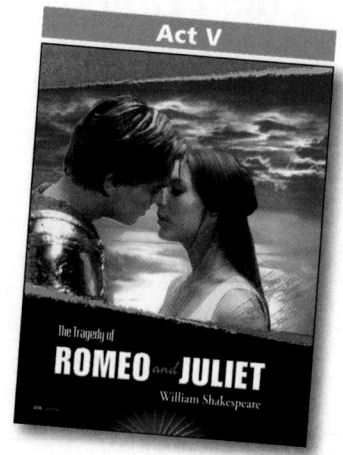

Act V

Literary Analysis: Tragedy and Motive

1. (a) Use a chart like the one shown to identify the elements that contribute to the play's tragic ending. **(b)** Using these details as examples, explain how Shakespeare uses **dramatic conventions** to enhance the text of his play.

Romeo's and Juliet's Personalities	Fate or Chance	Other Causes

2. (a) What is the Friar's **motive** for helping Romeo and Juliet? **(b)** To what extent is he responsible for their tragedy? Explain.

3. What theme or message does Shakespeare convey through the tragic events in the play?

4. What positive message about the human spirit, if any, does this tragic play offer? Explain.

Reading Skill: Summarize

5. (a) What events cause Romeo and Paris to arrive at Juliet's tomb at the same time? **(b)** What is the effect of this? Explain your answer.

6. (a) **Analyze** the chain of causes and effects that leads to the tragic ending. **(b)** **Summarize** the events that occur at the tomb.

Vocabulary

Practice Identify the word in each group that does not belong with the others. Explain your response.

1. remnants, future, past

2. penury, poor, wealthy

3. haughty, proud, insecure

4. ambiguities, absolute, uncertain

5. scourge, pleasure, happiness

6. disperse, scatter, collect

Word Power Use the context of the sentences and what you know about the **Latin prefix ambi-** to explain your answer to each question.

1. Would you know how to respond if someone asked an *ambiguous* question?

2. Is an *ambivalent* person unsure of what he or she wants in life?

Word Power

The **Latin prefix ambi-** means "both."

Apply It Explain how the prefix *ambi-* helps you determine the meanings of these words. Consult a dictionary if necessary.

ambient
ambidextrous
ambition

Integrated Language Skills

The Tragedy of Romeo and Juliet

Conventions: Participles and Participial Phrases, Gerunds and Gerund Phrases

A **participle** is a verb form that is used as an adjective.

A **present participle** ends in *-ing.* The past participle of a regular verb ends in *-ed.* A **participial phrase** is a group of words that functions as an adjective in the sentence and contains a participle.

Present Participle	*growing* child
Past Participle	*troubled* child
Participial Phrase	*Focusing intently,* the driver stopped in time.

A **gerund** is a verb form that acts as a noun.

It can function as a subject, an object, a predicate noun, or the object of a preposition. A **gerund phrase** is a gerund and its modifiers. A gerund phrase also acts as a noun.

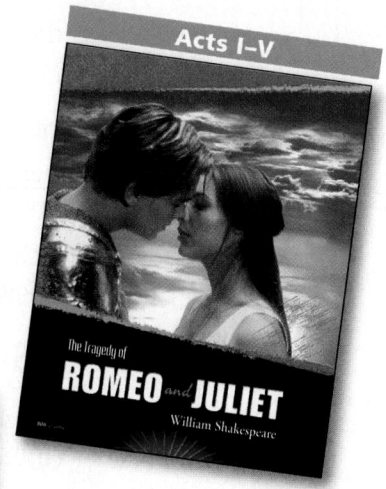

Subject	*Remodeling the building's style* was a good idea.
Direct Object	Michael enjoys *painting.*
Predicate Noun	His favorite sport is *fishing.*
Object of the Preposition	Lucille never gets tired of *singing.*
Gerund Phrase	The *loud, shrill howling* continued all morning.

Practice A Read the following sentences and identify the participle or gerund in each.

1. Suffering greatly, Romeo emptied the vial.
2. The young men seemed to enjoy fighting.
3. Loud weeping spread through Verona.

Speaking Application Use sentences with participles and gerunds to tell a partner about the scene in *The Tragedy of Romeo and Juliet* that you liked the most. Ask your partner to identify the participles and gerunds as you speak. Then, switch roles with your partner.

Practice B In each sentence, change one of the verbs to a participle or a gerund. Then, use that word or phrase to combine the two sentences.

1. Juliet felt great sorrow. She held the knife.
2. Capulet wanted his daughter married. He gave her to Paris.
3. He thought of Juliet. It was his greatest joy.

Writing Application Write two sentences that use participles and two sentences that use gerunds. Then, describe the function of these two parts of speech.

PH GRAMMAR HANDBOOK Further instruction and practice are available in the *Prentice Hall Grammar Handbook.*

Writing

Editorial Imagine that you are the editor of a newspaper in Verona at the time of the play. Write an editorial addressing the Prince's response to the deaths of Tybalt and Mercutio. Before you draft this **argumentative essay,** use these steps to plan.

- Review Act III, Scenes i–iii.
- Explain whether you agree or disagree with the Prince's sentence.

After you have finished planning, draft your editorial.

- Summarize the text leading up to the Prince's sentence so that your audience understands the background of the event.
- Provide a **clear position** based on **logical reasons.**
- Support your position with **precise and relevant evidence.**

Persuasive Letter As Friar Lawrence, write a persuasive letter to Lords Capulet and Montague. This **argumentative essay** should urge them to end their feud.

- Make a list of facts and emotional pleas that might persuade the families. Consider appealing to their sense of logic and ethical beliefs.
- Be sure to consider the **whole range of information and views** on the feud, and accurately and honestly represent those views.
- Include **counter-arguments** based on evidence to anticipate and address possible objections the lords might have.

Ask a classmate to read your draft from the point of view of both families. Revise your letter if it appears to favor one side or contains bias.

Grammar Application Make sure to use participles, participial phrases, gerunds, and gerund phrases correctly in your editorial and persuasive letter.

Writing Workshop: *Work in Progress*

Prewriting for Script For a script you may write, make a Character Profiles List for your writing portfolio. To do this, follow these steps:

1. Make a chart with three columns.
2. In the first column, jot down five names. Do not choose the names of people you know.
3. In the next column, beside each name, write two colorful personality traits that a person might have. For example, a person might be *charming, sensitive, worldly,* or *devious.*
4. In the third column, beside each trait, write two interesting things that a person might want. For example, a person might want *money, fame, adventure,* or *love.*

 Focus on the TEKS

Conventions
(17)(A)(i) Use and understand the function of verbals (gerunds, participles) in the context of reading, writing, and speaking.

Writing
(16)(A);(B);(C) Write an argumentative essay to the appropriate audience that includes: a clear position based on logical reasons supported by precise and relevant evidence; consideration of the whole range of information and views on the topic and accurate and honest representation of these views; counter-arguments based on evidence to anticipate and address objections.

Use this prewriting activity to prepare for the **Writing Workshop** on page 960.

Integrated Language Skills

Listening and Speaking

Staged Performance Each member of a small team should select a scene to direct from *The Tragedy of Romeo and Juliet* and plan a performance. The other members of the team will be your performers, and you will be performing in their scenes. During rehearsal, as the director, you should:

- **Give complex oral instructions** to the team to perform the specific tasks involved in the scene.

- Answer performers' questions about the scene.

- Solve any problems that may occur during rehearsal.

- Give team members oral instructions and coaching on how to complete the rehearsal process in a timely and orderly manner.

As a performer, make sure you listen carefully and **follow the complex oral instructions** given by the director. When you are ready, perform the scenes for the class, and invite comments and feedback.

Mock Trial As a class, conduct a **mock trial** to investigate the causes of the tragedy in *The Tragedy of Romeo and Juliet*. Follow these steps:

- Assign roles: the main characters of the play, the lawyers, and the judge. The rest of the class should serve in a team as the jury.

- Take depositions, or statements in which each character tells the story from his or her perspective. Lawyers should follow up the statements with questions to clarify and expand on the witnesses' stories.

- All participants should choose language—formal or informal—that fits the social, cultural, and professional status of each character.

After evidence is presented, the jury will deliberate, or consider the evidence to deliver a judgment. During deliberation, team members should **participate productively** by:

- **developing a plan for consensus-building**—formulating a plan for carrying out your discussion in an orderly fashion

- **building on the ideas of others** during discussions

- **contributing relevant information** for consideration

- **setting ground rules for decision-making**—discussing how you will decide upon a verdict, or decision

When the trial is completed, the jury should present their verdict, explaining which characters bear the most blame for the tragedy.

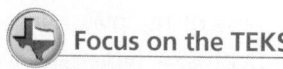 **Focus on the TEKS**

Listening and Speaking
(24)(B) Follow and give complex oral instructions to perform specific tasks, answer questions, solve problems, and complete processes.

(26) Participate productively in teams, building on the ideas of others, contributing relevant information, developing a plan for consensus-building, and setting ground rules for decision-making.

Research and Technology

Annotated Organization Chart Conduct research on the structure of the nobility in 16th century Verona. Then, **organize the information you gathered from multiple sources** to create a graphic organization chart. The chart should show the relative positions of the Prince, Count Paris, the Montagues, and the Capulets.

- **Evaluate the relevance of information** to your topic.
- **Determine the reliability, validity, and accuracy of sources** by examining their **authority and objectivity.**
- **Accurately cite all researched information** according to a standard format. (For more on citing sources, see page R40.)

Present and explain your organization to the class.

Film Review View a film of the ballet *Romeo and Juliet* with music by Russian composer Sergei Prokofiev. Take notes on the **aesthetic effects**—effects that contribute to the beauty or artistry of the film. Also analyze how the messages in this media are conveyed through **visual techniques** such as editing, reaction shots, and sequencing. Explain how the dance, music, and camerawork combine to communicate the play's ideas.

Locate a review of the film and compare it to your own opinion. Then, use your notes to present a film review for the rest of the class. If possible, use recorded excerpts to illustrate your comments.

Multimedia Presentation With a partner, produce a multimedia presentation on Renaissance music. Use library or Internet resources to collect information and details on the music that would have been played by the musicians in Act IV, Scene v.

- **Convey a distinctive point of view** on your topic by choosing details that particularly interest you and providing personal insights and ideas about those details.
- Be sure your presentation appeals to your **specific audience,** such as your classmates, by concentrating your research on aspects of the topic that you think would most interest them.
- **Use images—graphics and illustrations**—that add visual interest and help explain concepts where appropriate.
- **Incorporate sound** in the form of voice-overs, background music, and examples of Renaissance music.
- **Accurately cite all researched information** according to a standard format. (For more on citing sources, see page R40.)

Present your findings in class using available props, visual aids, and electronic media.

Focus on the TEKS

Reading
(12)(B) Analyze how messages in media are conveyed through visual techniques (e.g., editing, reaction shots, sequencing).

Writing
(15)(D) Produce a multimedia presentation with graphics, images, and sound that conveys a distinctive point of view and appeals to a specific audience.

Research
(21)(B) Organize information gathered from multiple sources to create a variety of graphics and forms.

(21)(C) Accurately cite all researched information according to a standard format.

(22)(B) Evaluate the relevance of information to the topic and determine the reliability, validity, and accuracy of sources by examining their authority and objectivity.

(23)(C) Synthesize research into a written or oral report that uses graphics and illustrations to help explain concepts where appropriate.

TEXAS
PHLitOnline
www.PHLitOnline.com

- Interactive graphic organizers
- Grammar tutorial
- Interactive journals

Strategy for Success

Summarize

Summarizing text on Texas standardized tests will help you to monitor your comprehension as you read. If you are able to summarize a text easily, your comprehension is probably strong. However, if you notice that a text is difficult to summarize, it may be helpful to check your comprehension and reread difficult sections.

To summarize text, briefly state the main points in a piece of writing. Paraphrase small portions of the text as you read rather than trying to summarize an entire passage at once. Focus on the most important ideas as you summarize, but also include critical details. For example, when you read a text that describes a sequence of events, include each major event in your summary. The following examples show how you can summarize on standardized tests.

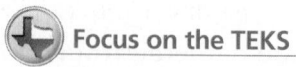 **Focus on the TEKS**

Comprehension
RC-9(A) Reflect on understanding to monitor comprehension (e.g., summarizing).

Identify Important Ideas

A summary should include all the important ideas but not the minor details.

1 After a touchdown by the home team tied the score, their kicker, a freshman from my town whom I've known all my life, made the extra point to win the game.

  1 What are the most important points in the passage?
    A The kicker was a freshman from my town.
    B The team would have won even without the extra point.
    C A freshman kicker played in the game.
    D The home team's touchdown tied the game, and the kicker's extra point won it.

A and **C** include minor details about the kicker's age and hometown. **B** is not supported by the text. **D** includes the important ideas and is the correct choice.

Follow Sequences of Events

For text that lists a sequence of events, the summary should include each main event.

1 If your clothes catch fire, you should first stop, then drop to the ground, and finally roll back and forth until the flames are out.

  2 Which of the following is the best summary of the passage?
    F You can put out flames on your clothes by stopping, dropping, and rolling.
    G It is important to know how to stop, drop, and roll.
    H If your clothes are on fire, you should first stop and then drop down to the ground.
    J Roll back and forth to put out flames on your clothes.

H and **J** do not include all the steps in the sequence "stop, drop, and roll." **G** is a conclusion the reader could draw but is not a summary of the passage. **F,** the correct answer, is a complete, accurate summary.

Texas Test Practice

Read this selection. Then answer the questions that follow it.

Safe, Secure Social Networking

1   Social networking Web sites are popular places to communicate online. Many teens use them to meet people and to keep in touch with friends. However, they are not without risk. Making private information public can lead to embarrassing situations or worse. Follow these simple steps to ensure that your online social networking is safe and secure.

2   When you register on a social networking site, you will first need to enter a name and an e-mail address. To protect your identity, do not give your full name, and be sure to use an e-mail address that does not reveal your full name. Second, you will need to select a password. Choose a combination of letters and numbers. The more random the characters, the harder it is for other people to guess or steal your password. Third, the site will prompt you to enter address information. Do not enter your street address or phone number. Fourth, the site will ask you to enter additional biographical information. Entering details about your age or school might seem like a good way to tell people about yourself, but it is safer to avoid giving out this information. Finally, the site will ask you to select your privacy preferences. These preferences let you control who can see your profile. The safest option is to limit profile access to people you know already.

3   Once you have followed steps to protect yourself, you will need to take steps to protect your computer. Be careful about clicking on links or downloading attachments in e-mails. They could cause viruses or spyware to harm your files or steal personal information kept on your computer. Consider using a spam filter or anti-virus software that scans messages.

1 What information from this passage is the most important?

   A Teens use Web sites to keep in touch.

   B Social networking Web sites will ask you to select privacy preferences.

   C Spam filters scan messages.

   D You can protect yourself online by limiting the information you share.

2 Which piece of information would be least useful to someone who wants to register on a networking Web site safely?

   F Do not give your full name.

   G Do not enter your phone number.

   H Using networking sites can help teens keep in touch with friends.

   J Entering details about your school should be avoided.

3 Which of the following is the best summary of the passage?

   A It is important to take steps to help ensure that your financial information is safe and secure.

   B You can safely use social networks by not giving out personal details and by protecting your computer.

   C To use social networks more safely, you can avoid giving personal information to people you meet online.

   D To make social networking more safe and secure, install a spam filter or anti-virus software.

Informational Texts

Expository Texts

Web Site
About the Event

Newspaper Article
A&M students help out . . .

Magazine Article
The Big Event

Focus on the TEKS

Reading
(12)(A) Compare and contrast how events are presented and information is communicated by visual images versus non-visual texts.

(12)(C) Compare and contrast coverage of the same event in various media.

Reading Skill: Analyze Media Coverage

Much of the information we gather comes from the media such as print or online newspapers, magazines, and radio and television broadcasts. Different media sources can focus on different aspects of an event. Therefore, it is important to compare and contrast coverage of the same event in various media to get the whole story. First, consider the sources each form of media uses. Next, think about the audience and purpose of the coverage, which can have an impact on how an event is portrayed. Also, look for **bias,** a prejudice or leaning toward one side or another.

Photographs and other images can also provide information and prompt emotional responses. As you consider and analyze media coverage, remember to pay attention to its **visual** impact and how the impact may have been different if the coverage had been **non-visual.**

As You Read Use a chart like the one shown to **compare and contrast coverage** of "The Big Event" in various media. Also, compare and contrast how information is communicated by visual images versus non-visual texts.

The Big Event

Web Site	Newspaper Article	Magazine Article
Content: Gives the history and purpose of the event	**Content:**	**Content:**
Sources:	**Sources:**	**Sources:**
Audience and Purpose:	**Audience and Purpose:**	**Audience and Purpose:**
Visuals:	**Visuals:**	**Visuals:**

Home
About the Event
For Participants
For Community Residents
Conference
Expansion
Contact

Web Site

Features:

- headings and sub-headings
- links to further information
- visuals that support the information

ABOUT THE EVENT

In 1982 Joe Nussbaum, then Vice President of the Student Government Association at Texas A&M University, started The BIG Event as a way for students to say "Thank You" to the surrounding community. Nussbaum envisioned a one-day service project where residents of Bryan and College Station would be shown appreciation for their continued support of Texas A&M University students during their college careers. Mr. Nussbaum viewed The BIG Event as a means for students to show their gratitude by completing various tasks at area residents' homes. Joe believed that it was the least the students could do to give one big thanks to their community on one big day each year.

The photograph gives information about The BIG Event. **Compare and contrast what you learn from the photograph with what you learn from the text.**

Mission Statement

Through service-oriented activities, The BIG Event promotes campus and community unity as students come together for one day to express their gratitude for the support from the surrounding community.

Core Values

The BIG Event at Texas A&M University is an organization which strives to uphold the ideals of unity and service. This one-day event is not based on socioeconomic need, but rather a way for the student body to express their gratitude to the entire community which supports Texas A&M. It is important to remember The BIG Event is not about the number of jobs completed or the number of students who participate each year. Instead, it is the interaction between students and residents, and the unity that results throughout the community that makes The BIG Event such a unique project.

The BIG Event is the largest, one-day, student-run service project in the nation where students of Texas A&M University come together to say 'thank you' to the residents of Bryan and College Station. For the past 26 years, Aggie students have participated in this annual event to show their appreciation to the surrounding community by completing service projects such as yard work, window washing, and painting for community members. Although The BIG Event has become the largest one-day, student-run service project in the nation, our message and our mission remains the same— to simply say "thank you."

The BIG Event is a proud member of the Student Government Association at Texas A&M and a recognized student organization of Texas A&M University.

The Mission Statement tells the goal of The BIG Event. The Core Values section of the text gives specific details about the event.

Do our differences define us?

How does The BIG Event work to support unity within the community?

TEXAS

Features:
- attention-grabbing title
- facts and details
- quotations from witnesses or participants

A&M students help out in 'big' way

By JOHN BRADEN
Eagle Staff Writer

With 10,600 students signed up for 1,000 jobs Saturday, Texas A&M University's Big Event was the largest in the program's history.

Big Event director Anna Rash said she was proud of everybody for reaching that milestone.

"This was the first time we were able to break 1,000 jobs," Rash said.

Since the Big Event began in 1982, student volunteers have logged more than 500,000 hours of community service, making it the largest one-day collegiate community service project in the nation, according to the Texas A&M Student Government Association.

College Station resident Poppy Capehart, who graduated from Texas A&M in 1975, and his wife, Tracey, class of 2005, said this was the first time the Big Event had come to their home.

> The writer quotes participants in order to present a personal view of the Big Event.

"It's a great chance for us to meet students, and I thought I could make a great contribution," Poppy Capehart said. "My daughter, class of 2006, was in the Aggie Band and participated in Big Event every year she was a student, and I'm glad that we get to participate now also."

Senior Kajay Rainey, site leader for Delta Zeta at the Capehart residence, said the main goal of the Big Event was to better the community in any way possible.

"This is just a great way for us to show everyone that we, as a Greek organization, do other things besides stereotypical Greek life," Rainey said. "It helps give A&M a good name and shows that the students care about this city and want to help out."

Meghan LePage was the freshman Delta Zeta job site leader at the Wellborn Cemetery, where the teams were responsible for cleaning up and pulling weeds around the graves.

"Everybody needs help of some kind, no matter what they do or where they work," LePage said.

Fellow Delta Zeta freshman Hanna Skinner said her interest in the volunteer project started when she came to visit A&M on Big Event weekend last year.

"My friends at other schools wouldn't believe we are doing stuff like this, and my parents loved the idea of me getting out and volunteering,"
Skinner said. "I think they got a kick out of me doing manual labor."

Andrew Garcia, sophomore Pi Kappa Phi site leader at the Wellborn Cemetery, said it was an interesting place to work.

"It's different, and a little creepy, but it works," Garcia said. "Even though all the work may seem hard and waking up early on a Saturday may be hard to do, it's worth it in the end. Just knowing that a whole bunch of people got together on one day and were able to accomplish something this huge is a moving experience, even if your job is cleaning a graveyard."

Teams spent all morning and most of the afternoon volunteering at locations all over Bryan, College Station, and neighboring communities.

Members of the coed service fraternity Alpha Pi Omega spent the day working at a daycare center in a Bryan home.

Marsha Mason, the owner of Precious Moments Daycare, expressed appreciation for the hard work A&M students do for the community.

"I have had Big Event students help me for three years, and the thing I like is that they are all volunteers," Mason said. "It is important to have this effort in the community, because a lot of residents can't get out and do the yard work themselves. Our society really appreciates the hard work they do."

> The writer gives a volunteer's perspective of the event's effects.

Sophomore Stephanie Taylor said that with 50,000 college students in the Bryan-College Station area, it's great that they get to give back at least once a year by doing good for the community.

"I would tell anybody considering to participate next year that it is definitely worth it," Taylor said. "When you walk out to start your day and there's 10,000 people standing there, ready to work, you just kind of get it. It's an overwhelming sight."

THE BIG Q

Do our differences define us?

According to a volunteer, "Everybody needs help . . . no matter what they do or where they work." How does this statement show that perhaps it is our similarities, not our differences, that define us?

TEXAS

AmericanProfile

Features:
- information from a variety of sources
- friendly or informal tone
- heads and sub-heads that organize information

The Big Event

by Marti Attoun

> This article opens with a vivid description of the beginning of the Big Event. **How might this information have been expressed visually?**

Running amid stacks of shovels and paint pans, ladders and limb loppers, Blaine Brawley, 21, and Bryan Alldredge, 22, help distribute tools to students at Texas A&M University in College Station. Within 15 minutes, 10,600 students are geared up and ready to tackle chores at more than a thousand local homes, churches, and schools.

"It's our way of saying thank-you to the community for supporting the college," says Anna Rash, 22, who directed this year's army of weed whackers and window washers as they fanned out March 29 across College Station (pop. 67,980) and Bryan (pop. 65,660).

The Big Event, billed as the largest, one-day, student-run service project in the nation, began at Texas A&M in 1982 and has been adopted by 71 colleges across the United States. Every year, tens of thousands of students hold the day of gratitude for the towns that they call home during their college years.

Ready, set, hoe

College Station residents eagerly await student workers each year. They've submitted job requests for everything from porch painting to drainage-ditch digging and have been visited by a student from The Big Event committee to see how many workers and what tools are needed for the job. Power tools aren't allowed, so trimming trees and sawing logs require muscle, sweat, and hand tools.

"I'm always happy to see this help," says Raymond Olson, 52, as he greets 14 shovel-toting young men from Walton Hall dormitory. "Every year they get another piece of yard work done. They've moved rocks, cleaned flower beds, moved lumber, raked leaves."

> Here, the author includes direct quotations from a community member.

TEXAS

Olson has hauled in a mound of dirt for this year's landscaping project. "I'd like to make a gradual incline here. It's too steep to mow," Olson says as he directs the students to the slope behind his house. The students get busy shoveling dirt into wheelbarrows, hauling it to the slope and evening out the area.

William Cook, 18, still has a smile on his glistening face as he wheels his 11th load of dirt.

"You get a good feeling from helping out," he says.

A few miles away at the home of Laura Schuett, 48, students from Phi Beta Lamda business fraternity rake and bag leaves in a 1-acre yard. "It's fun and it's good to give back to the community," Janelle Colborne, 20, says while tying a trash bag loaded with leaves.

"These kids are doing a great job," Schuett says. "They brought rakes and they're using a snow shovel to scoop leaves. They're really helping people."

What sets The Big Event apart from most service projects is that residents aren't required to meet any age or income guidelines. On the contrary, every resident is invited to fill out a job request for the one big day of thanks. Still, older residents like Jean and Anita Donaho, both 82, may appreciate the help and the visit most.

Anita has had a stroke and needs a walker, while Jean, who has Parkinson's disease, uses an electric scooter. The Donahos have the students carry furniture upstairs at their home, straighten their garage, and clean flower beds flanking their front sidewalk.

"I've already thought of what I want them to do next year if we're still around," says Anita, who baked chocolate-chip cookies for her household helpers. "We'll have them move a compost pile." Tessa Thibodeau, 21, listens as she pulls iris bulbs from a flower bed. "This is something so simple to us, but it helps them a lot," she says. "I think we forget in a college town that there is a community outside us. This is a good way to help."

The author ends with a quotation from one of the event volunteers.

 **Do our differences define us?**

What do all the participants in The Big Event have in common? How are they different?

TEXAS

Comparing Informational Texts

(a) Analyze: Compare and contrast **coverage** of "The Big Event" in the **various media**—the Web site, the newspaper article, and the magazine article. **(b) Analyze:** Compare and contrast how information is communicated by the **visual images** of the Web site and magazine article versus the **non-visual text** of the newspaper article.

 College Readiness |Timed Writing

Write a Proposal

> **Format**
> A proposal begins with a general description of the intended project and follows with specific ideas and examples to support the argument.

Write a proposal to your school administration persuading them to consider organizing an event to help the community surrounding your school. Be sure to identify solutions to specific needs in the community that could be established as projects on which students could work. Provide evidence and examples from the Web site, newspaper article, and magazine article to support your ideas. (20 minutes)

> **Academic Vocabulary**
> When you attempt to *persuade,* you try to convince an audience that your ideas are logical and correct by providing a convincing argument, supported by specific evidence.

 5-Minute Planner

Complete these steps before you begin to write:

1. Read the prompt carefully and completely.
2. Determine what kind of information you need to complete the task and where you can find that information.
3. Review the Web site, newspaper article, and magazine article, jotting down ideas and support for your proposal.
4. Next to those ideas, record projects that would benefit your specific community. Think about individuals as well as the community as a whole.
5. Make an informal outline of your proposal.
6. Refer to your notes and outline as you draft your proposal.

Comparing Literary Works

Comparing Archetypal Themes

An **archetype** is a plot, character, image, or setting that appears in
literature from around the world and throughout history. Archetypes
represent universal themes and truths about life and are said to mirror the
working of the human mind. Examples of common archetypes include

- characters: the hero; the outcast
- plot types: the quest, or search; the task
- symbols: water as a symbol of life; fire as a symbol of power

A **theme** is the central idea, message, or insight of a literary work.
Archetypal themes develop or explore fundamental, or archetypal, ideas.
Ill-fated love is one archetypal theme that appears in literature from all
over the world. Works of literature often differ in their presentations of
the same archetypal theme for many reasons, such as the values of the
work's era, the author's purpose, the author's culture and language, and
the genre in which the theme is conveyed. For example, playwrights often
rely on dialogue and character development to hint at theme. In fables and
myths, however, writers often state theme more directly, through the use
of a narrator who provides commentary on characters and events.

As You Read Consider an archetypal theme presented in two genres—a
myth and a play. **Analyze how the genre of texts with similar
themes shapes meaning.** Use a chart like this one to record observations about the way characters and events are presented in Ovid's
"Pyramus and Thisbe" (a myth) and Shakespeare's *The Tragedy of Romeo
and Juliet* (a tragedy) and *A Midsummer Night's Dream* (a comedy).

 **Focus on the TEKS**

Reading
(2)(A) Analyze how the genre of
texts with similar themes shapes
meaning.

	Tragedy	Myth	Comedy
How Characters Are Developed			
How Events Are Described			

PHLitOnline

www.PHLitOnline.com

- Vocabulary flashcards
- Interactive journals
- More about the authors

- Selection audio
- Interactive graphic organizers

Do our *differences* define us?

Writing About the Big Question

In these selections, the main characters fall in love despite the differences that separate them. Use this sentence starter to develop your ideas about the Big Question:

The **differences** between two people can be less important than _____.

Meet the Authors

Ovid (43 B.C.–A.D. 17)
Author of "Pyramus and Thisbe"

Educated in Rome, Ovid began his career writing poems about love and pleasure. However, the emperor Augustus wanted citizens to focus on morality and work toward an ideal Roman state. In response, Ovid decided to write about myths and traditional stories, such as "Pyramus and Thisbe."

Achievement and Exile After completing his masterpiece, *Metamorphoses,* in A.D. 8, Ovid was banished to a remote village. The reasons for his banishment are not entirely clear, but the emperor might have felt that Ovid's work endangered public morals. Although he continued to write, he was never allowed to return to Rome.

William Shakespeare (1564–1616)
Author of *A Midsummer Night's Dream*

Perhaps the greatest of all playwrights, William Shakespeare was born in the town of Stratford-on-Avon and gained his successes in the flourishing theatrical world of London. He worked as an actor, a playwright, and part owner of a theater company, earning enough to retire to Stratford in 1610.

Kings and Clowns, Lovers and Villains Shakespeare's 37 plays are populated with a wide range of characters who embody the depth and variety of human experience. No writer has played a more significant role in shaping the English language and English literature.

Pyramus and Thisbe

~ Ovid ~   retold by Edith Hamilton

Background

Background The tale of Pyramus and Thisbe appears in Book IV of *Metamorphoses,* Ovid's greatest achievement. A poem of nearly 12,000 lines, it tells a series of stories, beginning with the creation of the world and ending with the death of Julius Caesar. In each story, someone or something undergoes a change. Divided into fifteen books, the stories are linked by clever transitions, so that the entire work reads as one long, uninterrupted tale.

Once upon a time the deep red berries of the mulberry tree[1] were white as snow. The change in color came about strangely and sadly. The death of two young lovers was the cause.

Pyramus and Thisbe, he the most beautiful youth and she the loveliest maiden of all the East, lived in Babylon, the city of Queen Semiramis, in houses so close together that one wall was common to both. Growing up thus side by side they learned to love each other. They longed to marry, but their parents forbade. Love, however, cannot be forbidden. The more that flame is covered up, the hotter it burns. Also love can always find a way. It was impossible that these two whose hearts were on fire should be kept apart.

In the wall both houses shared there was a little chink.[2] No one before had noticed it, but there is nothing a lover does not notice. Our two young people discovered it and through it they were able to whisper sweetly back and forth. Thisbe on one side, Pyramus on the other. The hateful wall that separated them had become their means of reaching each other. "But for you we could touch, kiss," they would say. "But at least you let us speak together. You give a passage for loving words to reach loving ears. We are not ungrateful." So they would talk, and as night came on and they must part, each would press on the wall kisses that could not go through to the lips on the other side.

Every morning when the dawn had put out the stars, and the sun's rays had dried the hoarfrost on the grass, they would steal to the crack and, standing there, now utter words of burning love and now lament their hard fate, but always in softest whispers. Finally a day came when they could endure no longer. They decided that that very night they would try to slip away and steal out through the city into the open country where at last they could be together in freedom. They agreed to meet at a well-known place, the Tomb of Ninus, under a tree there, a tall mulberry full of snow-white berries, near which a cool spring bubbled up. The plan pleased them and it seemed to them the day would never end.

---

1. **mulberry** (mul´ ber´ rē) **tree** *n.* tree with an edible, purplish-red fruit.
2. **chink** (chiŋk) *n.* narrow opening; crack.

◀ **Critical Viewing**
What do you think the girl is feeling as she listens through the crack in the wall? **[Speculate]**

Literary Analysis
Archetypal Theme
What is the main obstacle the lovers face?

Vocabulary
lament (lə ment´) *v.*
express deep sorrow; mourn

Reading Check

How do Pyramus and Thisbe communicate with each other?

Literary Analysis
Archetypal Theme
What does Thisbe's "bold" behavior suggest about the power of love?

Vocabulary
inevitable (in ev´ i tə bəl)
adj. unavoidable; certain

At last the sun sank into the sea and night arose. In the darkness Thisbe crept out and made her way in all secrecy to the tomb. Pyramus had not come; still she waited for him, her love making her bold. But of a sudden she saw by the light of the moon a lioness. The fierce beast had made a kill; her jaws were bloody and she was coming to slake her thirst in the spring. She was still far enough away for Thisbe to escape, but as she fled she dropped her cloak. The lioness came upon it on her way back to her lair and she mouthed it and tore it before disappearing into the woods. That is what Pyramus saw when he appeared a few minutes later. Before him lay the bloodstained shreds of the cloak and clear in the dust were the tracks of the lioness. The conclusion was inevitable. He never doubted that he knew all. Thisbe was dead. He had let his love, a tender maiden, come alone to a place full of danger, and not been there first to protect her. "It is I who killed you," he said. He lifted up from the trampled dust what was left of the cloak and kissing it again and again carried it to the mulberry tree. "Now," he said, "you shall drink my blood too." He drew his sword and plunged it into his side. The blood spurted up over the berries and dyed them a dark red.

Thisbe, although terrified of the lioness, was still more afraid to fail her lover. She ventured to go back to the tree of the tryst, the mulberry with the shining white fruit. She could not find it. A tree was there, but not one gleam of white was on the branches. As she stared at it, something moved on the ground beneath. She started back shuddering. But in a moment, peering through the shadows, she

◄ **Critical Viewing**
Explain the similarities and differences between this lioness and the one Thisbe sees. **[Compare and Contrast]**

saw what was there. It was Pyramus, bathed in blood and dying. She flew to him and threw her arms around him. She kissed his cold lips and begged him to look at her, to speak to her. "It is I, your Thisbe, your dearest," she cried to him. At the sound of her name he opened his heavy eyes for one look. Then death closed them.

She saw his sword fallen from his hand and beside it her cloak stained and torn. She understood all. "Your own hand killed you," she said, "and your love for me. I too can be brave. I too can love. Only death would have had the power to separate us. It shall not have that power now." She plunged into her heart the sword that was still wet with his life's blood.

The gods were pitiful at the end, and the lovers' parents too. The deep red fruit of the mulberry is the everlasting memorial of these true lovers, and one urn holds the ashes of the two whom not even death could part.

Literary Analysis
Archetypal Theme
Compare the complexity of the plot in this myth to the complexity of the plot in *The Tragedy of Romeo and Juliet*. How is each work suited to its own genre? Analyze how the genres of these texts with similar themes shape their meanings.

Critical Thinking

1. **Respond:** What advice would you give to Pyramus and Thisbe as they whisper through the wall?

2. **(a)** How do the parents feel about the romance between Pyramus and Thisbe? **(b) Analyze Cause and Effect:** What actions do Pyramus and Thisbe take as a result of their parents' feelings?
   (c) Make a Judgment: Do you think Pyramus and Thisbe or their parents are more responsible for the tragic outcome?

3. **(a)** What does the chink in the wall enable the couple to do?
   (b) Speculate: How might the story be different if the chink did not exist?

4. **(a) Draw Conclusions:** What does the mulberry tree symbolize in this story? **(b) Analyze:** In what way does this symbol reinforce the story's theme?

5. **Speculate:** Do you think this story will continue to appeal to readers in the future? Why or why not?

Do our differences define us?
(a) How do Pyramus and Thisbe's wishes differ from those of their families?
(b) In what way did those differences lead to tragedy?

✔ **Support your responses with evidence from the text.**

from *A Midsummer Night's Dream*

William Shakespeare

Background In *A Midsummer Night's Dream,* Shakespeare creates comedy out of misunderstandings, magic transformations, and the interactions of characters from three different worlds: the noble class, the working class, and the realm of the fairy spirits. In this scene, several local craftsmen (the "Clowns") prepare to put on a play for the duke's wedding. Robin, the fairy king's jester, discovers the actors and decides to play a trick on one of them. All of this happens as Titania, the queen of the fairies, sleeps nearby. The actors do not know that Titania is under a spell that will cause her to fall in love with the first person she sees upon waking.

Act III, Scene i

With TITANIA *still asleep onstage, enter the* CLOWNS, BOTTOM, QUINCE, SNOUT, STARVELING, SNUG, *and* FLUTE.

BOTTOM. Are we all met?

QUINCE. Pat,[1] pat. And here's a marvels convenient place for our rehearsal. This green plot shall be our stage, this hawthorn brake[2] our tiring-house,[3] and we will do it in action as we will do it before the Duke.

BOTTOM. Peter Quince?

QUINCE. What sayest thou, bully[4] Bottom?

BOTTOM. There are things in this comedy of Pyramus and Thisbe that will never please. First, Pyramus must draw a sword to kill himself, which the ladies cannot abide. How answer you that?

SNOUT. By 'r lakin,[5] a parlous fear.

STARVELING. I believe we must leave the killing out, when all is done.[6]

◀ **Critical Viewing**
How would you describe Titania in the image shown here?

1. **pat** exactly; right on time.
2. **brake** thicket.
3. **tiring-house** room used for dressing, or attiring.
4. **bully** jolly fellow.
5. **By 'r lakin** shortened version of "By your ladykin (little lady)."
6. **when all is done** after all.

Reading Check

Who is asleep onstage when the Clowns enter?

15 **BOTTOM.** Not a whit! I have a device to make all well. Write me a prologue, and let the prologue seem to say we will do no harm with our swords, and that Pyramus is not killed indeed. And, for the more better assurance, tell them that I, Pyramus, am not Pyramus, but Bottom the weaver. This

20 will put them out of fear.

QUINCE. Well, we will have such a prologue, and it shall be written in eight and six.[7]

BOTTOM. No, make it two more. Let it be written in eight and eight.

25 **SNOUT.** Will not the ladies be afeard of the lion?

STARVELING. I fear it, I promise you.

BOTTOM. Masters, you ought to consider with yourself, to bring in God shield us! a lion among ladies is a most dreadful thing. For there is not a more fearful wildfowl than

30 your lion living, and we ought to look to it.

SNOUT. Therefore another prologue must tell he is not a lion.

BOTTOM. Nay, you must name his name, and half his face must be seen through the lion's neck, and he himself must speak through, saying thus, or to the same defect:

35 "Ladies," or "Fair ladies, I would wish you," or "I would request you," or "I would entreat you not to fear, not to tremble! My life for yours. If you think I come hither as a lion, it were pity of my life.[8] No, I am no such thing. I am a man as other men are." And there indeed let him name his

40 name and tell them plainly he is Snug the joiner.

7. eight and six ballad meter containing alternating eight- and six-syllable lines.

Literary Analysis
Archetypal Theme
How do the Clowns plan to soften their presentation of the lion?

8. it were . . . my life risky for me.

LITERATURE IN CONTEXT

(Science Connection)

Almanacs

When Bottom calls for an almanac, he is referring to a type of book that was very popular in Elizabethan times. The almanac was essentially a calendar, but it also provided lists of upcoming natural events, such as tides, full moons, and eclipses. The book was especially useful to farmers because it included gardening tips and weather predictions. Almanacs of various kinds are still published and consulted today.

Connect to the Literature

Do you think the Clowns are wise to rely on the accuracy of the almanac with regard to moonlight? Why or why not?

QUINCE. Well, it shall be so. But there is two hard things: that is, to bring the moonlight into a chamber, for you know Pyramus and Thisbe meet by moonlight.

SNOUT. Doth the moon shine that night we play our play?

45 **BOTTOM.** A calendar, a calendar! Look in the almanac. Find out moonshine, find out moonshine.

QUINCE *takes out a book.*

QUINCE. Yes, it doth shine that night.

BOTTOM. Why, then, may you leave a casement of the great chamber window, where we play, open, and the moon may

50 shine in at the casement.

QUINCE. Ay, or else one must come in with a bush of thorns[9] and a lantern and say he comes to disfigure[10] or to present the person of Moonshine. Then there is another thing: we must have a wall in the great chamber, for Pyramus and

55 Thisbe, says the story, did talk through the chink of a wall.

SNOUT. You can never bring in a wall. What say you, Bottom?

BOTTOM. Some man or other must present Wall. And let him have some plaster, or some loam, or some roughcast[11] about him to signify wall, or let him hold his fingers thus,

60 and through that cranny shall Pyramus and Thisbe whisper.

QUINCE. If that may be, then all is well. Come, sit down, every mother's son, and rehearse your parts. Pyramus, you begin. When you have spoken your speech, enter into

65 that brake, and so every one according to his cue.

Enter ROBIN *invisible to those onstage.*

ROBIN. *(aside)*
What hempen homespuns[12] have we swaggring
    here
So near the cradle[13] of the Fairy Queen?
What, a play toward?[14] I'll be an auditor—
An actor too perhaps, if I see cause.

70 **QUINCE.** Speak, Pyramus.—Thisbe, stand forth.

BOTTOM. *(as Pyramus)*
Thisbe, the flowers of odious savors sweet—

QUINCE. Odors, odors!

BOTTOM. *(as Pyramus)*
        . . . odors savors sweet.
So hath thy breath, my dearest Thisbe dear—

9. **a bush of thorns** according to legend, the man in the moon collected firewood on Sundays and was thus banished to the sky.
10. **disfigure** Quince means figure, as in "symbolize" or "stand for."
11. **plaster . . . roughcast** three different blended materials, each used for plastering walls.

12. **hempen homespuns** characters wearing clothing homemade from hemp, probably from the country.
13. **cradle** bower where Titania sleeps.
14. **toward** being rehearsed.

Reading Check

How do the Clowns plan to present the wall that separates Pyramus and Thisbe?

▶ Critical Viewing
How would Bottom feel if he knew how he looked to others? [Speculate]

But hark, a voice! Stay thou but here awhile.
75   And by and by I will to thee appear. *(He exits.)*

  ROBIN. *(aside)*
  A stranger Pyramus than e'er played here.

(He exits.)

FLUTE. Must I speak now?

QUINCE. Ay, marry, must you, for you must understand he goes
80   but to see a noise that he heard and is to come again.

FLUTE. *(as Thisbe)*
  Most radiant Pyramus, most lily-white of hue,
  Of color like the red rose on triumphant[15] brier,
  Most brisky juvenal[16] and eke[17] most lovely Jew,[18]
85 As true as truest horse, that yet would never tire.
  I'll meet thee, Pyramus, at Ninny's tomb.[19]

QUINCE. "Ninus tomb," man! Why, you must not speak that yet. That you answer to Pyramus. You speak all your part[20] at once, cues and all.— Pyramus, enter. Your cue is
90   past. It is "never tire."

FLUTE. O!

  (As Thisbe) As true as truest horse, that yet would never tire.

Enter ROBIN, *and* BOTTOM *as Pyramus with the ass-head.*[21]

BOTTOM. *(as Pyramus)*
  If I were fair, fair Thisbe, I were[22] only thine.

QUINCE. O monstrous! O strange! We are haunted. Pray,
95   masters, fly, masters! Help!

QUINCE, FLUTE, SNOUT, SNUG, *and* STARVELING *exit.*

ROBIN. I'll follow you. I'll lead you about a round,[23]
  Through bog, through bush, through brake, through brier.
  Sometime a horse I'll be, sometime a hound,
  A hog, a headless bear, sometime a fire.[24]

15. **triumphant** splendid; magnificent.
16. **juvenal** juvenile; a young person.
17. **eke** also.
18. **Jew** shortening of "jewel" to complete the rhyme.
19. **Ninny's tomb** refers to Ninus, legendary founder of biblical city of Nineveh.
20. **part** script containing stage cues, which Flute is accused of missing or misreading.
21. **with the ass-head** wearing an ass-head.
22. **were** would be.
23. **about a round** in a roundabout, like a circle dance.
24. **fire** will-o'-the-wisp.

100 And neigh, and bark, and grunt, and roar, and burn,
Like horse, hound, hog, bear, fire, at every turn.

(He exits.)

BOTTOM. Why do they run away? This is a knavery of them
to make me afeard.

Enter SNOUT.

SNOUT. O Bottom, thou art changed! What do I see on thee?

105 **BOTTOM.** What do you see? You see an ass-head of your
own, do you?

(SNOUT exits.)

Enter QUINCE.

QUINCE. Bless thee, Bottom, bless thee! Thou art
translated!²⁵

(He exits.)

BOTTOM. I see their knavery. This is to make an ass of me,
110 to fright me, if they could. But I will not stir from this
place, do what they can. I will walk up and down here,
and I will sing, that they shall hear I am not afraid.

(He sings.) The ouzel cock,²⁶ so black of hue,
115 *With orange-tawny bill,*
The throstle²⁷ with his note so true,
The wren with little quill—²⁸

TITANIA. *(waking up)*
What angel wakes me from my flow'ry bed?

BOTTOM. *(sings)*
The finch, the sparrow, and the lark,
120 *The plainsong cuckoo²⁹ gray,*
Whose note full many a man doth mark
And dares not answer "nay"—³⁰

for, indeed, who would set his wit to so foolish a bird? Who
would give a bird the lie³¹ though he cry "cuckoo" never so?³²

TITANIA.
125 I pray thee, gentle mortal, sing again.
Mine ear is much enamored of thy note,
So is mine eye enthralled to thy shape,
And thy fair virtue's force perforce doth move me³³
On the first view to say, to swear, I love thee.

130 **BOTTOM.** Methinks, mistress, you should have little reason
for that. And yet, to say the truth, reason and love keep little
company together nowadays. The more the pity that some

Literary Analysis
Archetypal Theme
How does Bottom's transformation make fun of the character of Pyramus?

25. **translated** changed; transformed.

26. **ouzel cock** male blackbird.

27. **throstle** thrush; a bird.

28. **quill** literally, a small reed pipe, but here meaning a tiny piping song.

29. **plainsong cuckoo** bird whose song is likened to church music called plainsong.

30. **Whose . . . "nay"** whose song married men listen to as a sign that their wives may be unfaithful, and who cannot deny that this may be so.

31. **Who would . . .the lie** who would use his intelligence to answer a foolish bird, yet who would dare to contradict the cuckoo's taunt?

32. **never so** over and over; ever so much.

33. **thy . . . move me** your beauty is so powerful it moves me whether I want it to or not.

Vocabulary
enamored (en am′ ərd)
v. filled with love and desire; charmed

enthralled (en *thr*ôld′)
v. held as in a spell; captivated

Reading Check

What physical change happens to Bottom?

▲ **Critical Viewing**
How do Titania and Bottom seem to feel about each other in this image? **[Describe]**

34. **gleek** jest; joke.

35. **rate** value; rank.

36. **still doth tend** still serves.

honest neighbors will not make them friends. Nay, I can gleek[34] upon occasion.

TITANIA.

135   Thou art as wise as thou art beautiful.

BOTTOM. Not so neither; but if I had wit enough to get out of this wood, I have enough to serve mine own turn.

TITANIA.

Out of this wood do not desire to go.
Thou shalt remain here whether thou wilt or no.
140   I am a spirit of no common rate.[35]
The summer still doth tend[36] upon my state,
And I do love thee. Therefore go with me.
I'll give thee fairies to attend on thee,
And they shall fetch thee jewels from the deep
145   And sing while thou on pressed flowers dost sleep.

And I will purge thy mortal grossness[37] so
That thou shalt like an airy spirit go.—
Peaseblossom, Cobweb, Mote,[38] and Mustardseed!

Enter four Fairies: PEASEBLOSSOM, COBWEB,
MOTE, *and* MUSTARDSEED.

PEASEBLOSSOM. Ready.

150 **COBWEB.** And I.

MOTE. And I.

MUSTARDSEED. And I.

ALL. Where shall we go?

TITANIA.
Be kind and courteous to this gentleman.
155 Hop in his walks and gambol in his eyes;
Feed him with apricocks and dewberries.[39]
With purple grapes, green figs, and mulberries;
The honey-bags steal from the humble-bees,
And for night-tapers crop their waxen thighs
160 And light them at the fiery glowworms' eyes
To have my love to bed and to arise;
And pluck the wings from painted butterflies
To fan the moonbeams from his sleeping eyes.
Nod to him, elves, and do him courtesies.

165 **PEASEBLOSSOM.** Hail, mortal!

COBWEB. Hail!

MOTE. Hail!

MUSTARDSEED. Hail!

BOTTOM. I cry your Worships mercy,[40] heartily.—I beseech
170 your Worship's name.

COBWEB. Cobweb.

BOTTOM. I shall desire you of more acquaintance, good
Master Cobweb. If I cut my finger, I shall make bold with
you.[41]—Your name, honest gentleman?

175 **PEASEBLOSSOM.** Peaseblossom.

BOTTOM. I pray you, commend me to Mistress Squash,[42]
your mother, and to Master Peascod,[43] your father. Good
Master Peaseblossom, I shall desire you of more
acquaintance, too.—Your name, I beseech you, sir?

180 **MUSTARDSEED**. Mustardseed.

---

37. **mortal grossness** the physical, mortal state of human beings.

38. **Mote** a speck, but also moth, as this word was pronounced similarly.

39. **apricocks and dewberries** apricots and blackberries.

Literary Analysis
Archetypal Theme
How do Titania's commands emphasize the absurdity of her feelings toward Bottom?

40. **cry . . . mercy** beg your pardon.

41. **Master . . . you** cobwebs were used to stop bleeding.

42. **squash** an unripe pea pod.

43. **peascod** a ripe pea pod.

Reading Check

How does Titania want the fairies to treat Bottom?

44. **your patience** your story;
your experience.

BOTTOM. Good Master Mustardseed, I know your patience[44]
well. That same cowardly, giantlike ox-beef hath devoured
many a gentleman of your house. I promise you, your
kindred hath made my eyes water ere now. I desire you of
185   more acquaintance, good Master Mustardseed.

TITANIA. Come, wait upon him. Lead him to my bower.
The moon, methinks, looks with a watery eye,
And when she weeps, weeps every little flower,
Lamenting some enforcèd chastity.[45]

45. **enforcèd chastity**
violation; requirement.

190   Tie up my lover's tongue. Bring him silently.

They exit.

Critical Thinking

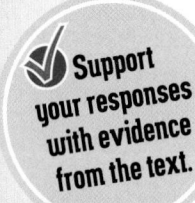

Support
your responses
with evidence
from the text.

1. **Respond:** Which aspect of this excerpt did you find funniest?
Explain.

2. **(a)** What are the Clowns trying to accomplish in this scene?
(b) Analyze Cause and Effect: What events prevent their
success? Explain.

3. **(a)** How is Bottom transformed? **(b) Make Inferences:** Is Bottom
aware of his transformation? Explain. **(c) Analyze:** Does the
transformation alter Bottom's personality as well as his appearance? Why or why not?

4. **(a)** Who is Titania? **(b) Analyze:** In what ways does the match
between Titania and Bottom mock typical portrayals of romantic
love?

5. **Analyze:** Does Bottom's transformation actually reveal a truth
about his character? Explain.

6. **(a) Summarize:** What alterations to script and costumes do the
Clowns plan in order to minimize the frightening aspects of their
play? **(b) Speculate:** Do you think the Clowns' eventual audience
will enjoy their production of "Pyramus and Thisbe"? Explain.

Do our differences define us?
(a) What are the major differences between Titania and
Bottom? **(b)** What similarities help them overcome their
differences? **(c)** Do you think their differences or their
similarities will matter more in the end? Explain.

Comparing Archetypal Themes

1. Use a chart like the one shown to identify the characters, obstacles, and main events in Shakespeare's *The Tragedy of Romeo and Juliet* and Ovid's "Pyramus and Thisbe."

Selection	Characters	Obstacles	Main Events
The Tragedy of Romeo and Juliet			
Pyramus and Thisbe			

2. Analyze how the genre of texts with similar themes shapes meaning. **(a)** Using your chart, explain similarities in the way both *The Tragedy of Romeo and Juliet* and "Pyramus and Thisbe" present the archetypal theme of ill-fated love. **(b)** What are the differences in the ways the two selections present this theme?

3. (a) In *A Midsummer Night's Dream*, why is Titania and Bottom's love ill-fated? **(b)** How do these reasons compare to the obstacles faced by Romeo and Juliet or Pyramus and Thisbe?

 College Readiness | Timed Writing

Write to Compare Archetypal Themes

In an essay, compare the way Shakespeare uses the characters and events from "Pyramus and Thisbe" in *The Tragedy of Romeo and Juliet* with the way he uses them in *A Midsummer Night's Dream*. Discuss why Shakespeare might explore the same story in both a tragedy and a comedy. (40 minutes)

5-Minute Planner

1. Read the prompt carefully and completely.

2. Gather your ideas by jotting down answers to these questions:

   • How do the different settings and characters in each of Shakespeare's plays affect the two presentations of the archetypal theme?

   • How do you think Shakespeare wanted audiences to feel about the ill-fated love in each play?

3. Reread the prompt, and then draft your essay.

Texas Writing Workshop

Literary Texts: Script

Defining the Form A **script** is the written dialogue, or conversation, between two or more actors that is meant to be performed. A script also contains stage directions, which are descriptions of how and where action happens. One of the most common uses of a script is for a play. Elements of scripts might also be used for television or movie productions, or sales calls and presentations.

Assignment Write a script for a play. Include these elements:

✔ a well-developed plot, including a conflict and resolution

✔ *an explicit or implicit theme*

✔ *details that contribute to a definite mood or tone*

✔ interesting and believable characters and dialogue

✔ descriptive stage directions

✔ error-free grammar and formatting

To preview the criteria on which your script may be judged, see the rubric on page 965.

📖 **Writing Workshop:** *Work in Progress*

Review the work you did on page 933.

Prewriting/Planning Strategy

Develop the plot. The plot of a play begins with the **exposition,** or the description of the setting and characters, and the basic **conflict** faced by the characters. The **rising action** shows the development of the conflict as it becomes more intense. The **climax** is the most intense moment of conflict. Following the climax, **falling action** leads to the **resolution** of the conflict, and the final insight gained by characters. Use a chart like the one below to sketch out the main events that will make up the plot of your script. Use as many lines as needed.

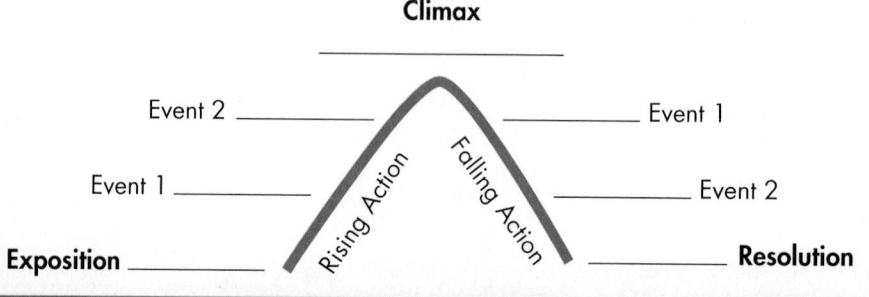

 Focus on the TEKS

Writing
(14)(C) Write a script with an explicit or implicit theme and details that contribute to a definite mood or tone.

Apply It!

Revealing the Theme

Theme refers to the central idea or insight provided by a literary work. Theme can be **explicit,** or stated directly, or it can be **implicit,** or implied. When a theme is implicit, readers have to think about the meaning of the events and what the events say about life or human nature. Use these tips to help you develop the theme of your script.

Stating the Theme Before you begin your script, think about what point you want to make in the play. What ideas or feelings about real or imagined people, events, or ideas do you want to express? You may have a theme in mind, or you may want to use a universal theme. Some themes that occur across world literature and throughout history, such as the theme of ill-fated love from *The Tragedy of Romeo and Juliet,* are **universal,** or archetypal, themes. These themes are repeated in a variety of stories, plays, and poems, and can take many forms. Following are just a few universal themes:

- Love is blind.
- Carrying a grudge harms the person who carries it.
- Love can overcome evil.
- Destroying your world leads to your own destruction.

Developing the Theme After deciding on a theme, think about whether you want to state the theme explicitly or implicitly. For example, in *The Tragedy of Romeo and Juliet,* the theme of "star-crossed lovers" is stated explicitly in the Prologue to the play. The chart below shows how a theme might be developed implicitly.

Theme	Characters	Events
Uncontrolled desire for power leads to destruction.	1. a king 2. a knight who serves as a general to the king 3. son of the king 4. other supporting characters	1. The king's army wins a war. 2. The king rewards the knight. 3. The knight imprisons the king and takes the throne. 4. The king's son raises an army and overthrows the knight.

Drafting Strategies

Format your script. A script for a play has specific elements and formatting rules. Refer to the chart below to format the various elements of a script.

Element	Example
a list and brief description of the cast of characters that includes name, position, and/or their relationship to other characters	*Henry,* King of England *Princess Elizabeth,* daughter of Henry
stage directions that include a description of the setting, characters present in the scene, and details about actions	***Scene i. the King's throne room*** [*Enter* PRINCESS ELIZABETH, *tiptoeing quietly*]
the name of each character preceding the dialogue he or she speaks, and the dialogue each character speaks	**PRINCESS ELIZABETH.** [*whispering to herself*] Where is my father?

Use dialogue to propel plot. Dialogue can be used to move the plot forward. As characters interact through conversation, their feelings, intentions, and motivations are revealed. You may also have characters' dialogue reveal actions that have taken place offstage, out of the view of the audience. Consider using these techniques as you draft dialogue to help to advance the action of the play.

Revising Strategies

Listen to your characters. Work in a group to read your script aloud, having each group member take the part of one character. Focus on the lines each character speaks, noting the tone and vocabulary. Make sure the dialogue is convincing and appropriate to each character.

Revise dialogue. Review your dialogue, underlining words and phrases that do not fit the character's personality. Consider revising your draft to improve word choice, choosing terms that might better fit each character. Check your changes by rereading the lines aloud.

Inappropriate: FIRST CHILD. The sun is setting and it will be dark soon.
SECOND CHILD. I am frightened of the dark.

Appropriate: FIRST CHILD. The sun's almost gone and it's getting dark.
SECOND CHILD. I'm really scared of the dark.

 **Focus on the TEKS**

Writing
(14)(C) Write a script with details that contribute to a definite mood or tone.

WRITE GUY
Jeff Anderson, M.Ed.

What Do You Notice?

Distinct Dialogue

The following passage is from William Shakespeare's *The Tragedy of Romeo and Juliet,* Act III, Scene i, lines 144–149. Read the passage several times.

LADY CAPULET. *Tybalt, my cousin! O my brother's child!*

O Prince! O cousin!
Husband! O, the blood is spilled

Of my dear kinsman!
Prince, as thou art true,

For blood of ours shed blood of Montague.

O cousin, cousin!

PRINCE. *Benvolio, who began this bloody fray?*

Jot down what you notice about this passage and share your thoughts with a partner. Consider how you can make each of your characters sound distinct and authentic.

TEXAS WRITER'S TOOLBOX

| Voice | Conventions | Focus and Coherence | Organization | Development of Ideas |

Finding the Right Voice

Voice in a play is the way a playwright expresses each character's unique sound or way of speaking. It is created through elements such as word choice and sentence structure, which in turn contribute to a mood or tone. Voice can be described as fast, slow, blunt, meandering, and so on. In a script, descriptive stage directions can help indicate mood and tone. Use the following tips to help you find the appropriate voice for each of your characters.

Consider the character. As you write dialogue, keep in mind the character who is speaking. Consider the character's personal traits. Is he or she timid, forceful, smart, irresponsible, or fun-loving? Then, think about how such a character would speak, his or her vocabulary (slang or formal language), and the sentence structure or phrasing the character might use.

Contribute to a definite mood or tone. As you draft, think about what is happening in the plot and what mood or tone you want to set. For example, if a group of friends is enjoying memories of good times, the tone of the dialogue might reflect the warmth and joy of the situation. Use details such as stage directions and dialogue to contribute to a definite mood or tone. Think of stage directions as descriptions that help the reader "see" the scene. The example script here shows how stage directions and dialogue can help set mood and tone.

Scene i. A warmly lit, comfortable room in a small cottage.
[EVA, ROSE, *and* ANNA *are seated around a coffee table, drinking from mugs*]

EVA. I certainly do remember that! [*all laugh*]

ROSE. But do you remember what happened afterwards? [*smiles*]

ANNA. I do. You ran. You ran out of the house so fast that you didn't realize you still had chocolate all over your face. The neighbors found you hiding in a bush with a cocoa mustache! [*giggles*]

ROSE. And we were left standing in the kitchen trying to explain the flour explosion and the jellybeans all over the floor!

EVA. No, I wouldn't call it an explosion . . .

ANNA. Of course you wouldn't! You ran out before the baking soda did its job. Rose and I were covered head to toe. Rose still had flour in her hair two days later [*pats* ROSE'S *head gently*] and her head gave off white puffs! [*all roll with laughter*]

Focus on the TEKS

Writing
(13)(D) Edit drafts for grammar, mechanics, and spelling.

Conventions
(19) Spell correctly, including using various resources to check correct spellings.

David

Scene i. A school locker room.

[DAVID *and the rest of the team are standing in a group.* COACH *stands addressing them.*]

COACH. I need a volunteer to work the concession stand tomorrow. The Varsity is hosting a basketball tournament and we are responsible for the afternoon shift. Whoever volunteers will need to be here from 11 until 2.

DAVID. [*raises his hand and steps forward*] Sure Coach, I'll work the afternoon shift.

COACH. [*gives* DAVID *a friendly slap on the back*] Thanks David, I really appreciate you stepping up to the plate. Practice is dismissed.

Scene ii. Saturday morning at 9 A.M., DAVID's *bedroom.*

[*An alarm clock rings.* DAVID *rolls over drowsily and silences the alarm.*]

MOM. [*walking into* DAVID'S *room*] David, what time do we need to leave to get to your shift on time?

DAVID. [*pondering*] Uh, 10:50 will work.

MOM. [*leaving the room*] OK, just make sure that you're ready so you're not late.

[*Phone rings and* DAVID *answers.*]

DAVID. Hello. [*listens for a few seconds*] The new James Bond movie this afternoon? Yeah, sure. Let me call you back just as soon as I talk to my mom.

[DAVID *walks into the living room calling for his mom; finds her sitting, reading*]

DAVID. Do you mind working my shift at the concession stand this afternoon?

MOM. [*looking at* DAVID *suspiciously*] Now why would I need to do that?

DAVID. Well, Jeff called and a bunch of the guys are going to the movies . . .

MOM. Did you tell them that you had a job to do?

DAVID. [*angrily, but looking toward his feet*] Well, I was kind of hoping that you would work my shift. If you can't, it's not a big deal. Who really cares if the concession stand is open? Besides that, it's a volunteer job.

MOM. [*sternly*] Is that really how you feel, David?

DAVID. [*shrugs*] I don't know. I guess I made a commitment and I need to see it through.

Talia indicates a scene change whenever the setting changes dramatically.

The author crafts dialogue that is convincing for each character.

Talia includes details that contribute to a definitive mood and tone.

The author expresses an explicit theme.

TEXAS

Editing and Proofreading

Edit your draft for errors in grammar and mechanics, such as punctuation. Use a printed or electronic dictionary to check correct spellings.

Focus on Formatting: Check the various elements of your script for appropriate formatting. Make sure each scene is labeled and the stage directions are correctly formatted. Be sure that each of the stage directions at the beginning of a scene includes the names of the characters present in that scene. Check the formatting of dialogue. Remember that as each character speaks in turn, that character's name must be identified and correctly formatted.

Spiral Review

Earlier in the unit, you learned about **participles and participial phrases, geruds and gerund phrases** (p. 932). Make sure you have used these parts of speech properly in your script.

Publishing and Presenting

Consider one of the following ways to share your writing.

Give a theatrical performance. Perform your script as a stage play, having classmates take the parts of the different characters. Use simple stage props. If possible, videotape your production.

Present a round-table reading. With a group of classmates, perform a round-table reading of your script for the class. Have a class discussion following the reading. Ask for feedback on the effectiveness of dialogue and stage directions.

Reflecting on Your Writing

Jot down your answer to this question:

How did writing a script help you understand the importance of stage directions and dialogue?

Rubric for Self-Assessment

Find evidence in your writing to address each category. Then, use the rating scale to grade your work.

Written Composition Criteria	Rating Scale not very very
Focus and Coherence: How necessary and descriptive are your stage directions?	1 2 3 4
Organization: How well-developed is your plot, including your conflict and resolution?	1 2 3 4
Development of Ideas: How well is your explicit or implicit theme expressed?	1 2 3 4
Conventions: How error-free is your grammar and formatting?	1 2 3 4
Voice: How well do your details contribute to a definitive mood or tone?	1 2 3 4

Drama Selection

▲ Read ***The Inspector-General*** to learn how it might feel to travel about in disguise and hear what people have to say about you.

 TEXAS Focus on the TEKS

Meet these standards with ***The Inspector-General*** (p. 970).

Reading

(4) Explain how dramatic conventions (e.g., dramatic irony) enhance dramatic text. *(Literary Analysis: Comedy)*

(5)(D) Demonstrate familiarity with works by authors from non-English speaking literary traditions with emphasis on classical literature. *(Critical Thinking: Analyze)*

(1)(A) Determine the meanings of grade-level technical academic English words in multiple-content areas derived from Greek roots. *(Word Power: Apply It)*

Oral and Written Conventions

(17)(A)(ii) Use and understand the function of restrictive and nonrestrictive relative clauses. *(Conventions: Restrictive and Nonrestrictive Clauses)*

(18)(B)(ii) Use correct punctuation marks including comma placement in clauses. *(Conventions: Restrictive and Nonrestrictive Clauses)*

Writing

(14)(C) Write a script with an explicit or implicit theme. *(Writing: Script)*

Research

(20)(B) Formulate a plan for engaging in research on a complex, multi-faceted topic. *(Research and Technology: Informational Chart)*

(21)(C) Accurately cite all researched information according to a standard format. *(Research and Technology: Informational Chart)*

(23)(E) Use a style manual. *(Research and Technology: Informational Chart)*

Literary Analysis: Comedy

Comedy is a form of drama that is lighter in mood than tragedy, ends happily, and aims primarily to amuse. The humor in comic plays may arise from one or more of the following elements:

- funny character names and witty dialogue
- incongruous situations, such as a woman in high heels stomping grapes or a clown conducting a meeting
- character misunderstandings and mistaken identities

The humor of comic situations often relies on **dramatic irony,** which is a contradiction between what a character thinks and says and what the audience knows. In comedies, the audience often knows the truth whereas the characters remain unaware. As a result, the characters' statements and behavior are often misguided or inappropriate, provoking laughter from the knowing audience.

As You Read Note examples of comedy and dramatic irony. Jot down notes explaining how these **dramatic conventions** enhance the text.

Reading Skill: Draw Conclusions

A **conclusion** is a decision or an opinion that you reach based on details in a text. In drawing conclusions about a play, consider stated and implied information. To draw conclusions about characters in a play:

- Consider what the **dialogue** reveals about characters' personalities and circumstances.
- Read **stage directions** closely for details about the scene and about characters' appearances and behavior.
- Note other details that could prove essential to the plot or ideas.

Using the Strategy: Conclusion Chart

As You Read Record the conclusions you draw about characters.

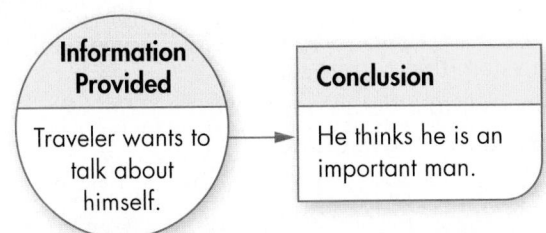

TEXAS
PHLitOnline
www.PHLitOnline.com

Hear It!
- Selection summary audio
- Selection audio

See It!
- Get Connected video
- Background video
- More about the author
- Vocabulary flashcards

Do It!
- Interactive journals
- Interactive graphic organizers
- Self-test
- Internet activity
- Grammar tutorial
- Interactive vocabulary games

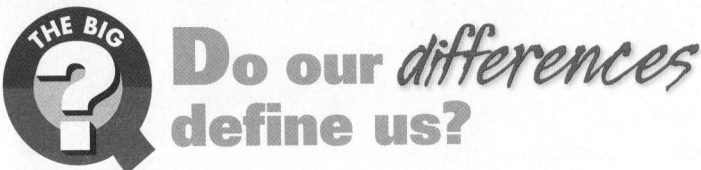

Do our *differences* define us?

Writing About the Big Question

In *The Inspector-General*, the Inspector-General dresses in disguise so people won't know he's on official business. He is different from those around him, though, and the truth is hard to conceal. Use this sentence starter to develop your ideas about the Big Question.

A person's **background** may be difficult to conceal because _____.

As You Read Look for clues about the Inspector-General's identity.

Vocabulary

Read each word and its definition. Decide whether you know the word well, know it a little bit, or do not know it at all. After you read, see how your knowledge of each word has increased.

- **incognito** (in´ käg nēt´ ō) *adj.* with true identity unrevealed or disguised; under an assumed name (p. 970) *The movie star was incognito because she hoped to have some privacy.*

- **anonymous** (ə nän´ ə məs) *adj.* without a known or acknowledged name (p. 970) *Wishing to remain anonymous, the writer sent an unsigned letter.* anonymously *adv.*

- **trundle** (trun´ dəl) *v.* roll along (p. 970) *While we were chatting, the shopping cart began to trundle down the aisle.* trundling *v.*

- **discreetly** (di skrēt´ lē) *adv.* without drawing attention (p. 972) *The candidate avoided embarrassment by discreetly straightening his crooked tie during the debate.* discreet *adj.* discreetness *n.*

- **cunning** (kun´ iŋ) *adj.* skilled in deception (p. 972) *The small but cunning animal is usually able to outwit and escape its predators.* cunningly *adv.*

- **telegraph** (tel´ ə graf´) *n.* an apparatus or system that converts a coded message into electric impulses and sends it to a distant receiver (p. 974) *The telegraph was invented to send messages quickly.* telegraph *v.* telegraphic *adj.* telegraphically *adv.*

Word Power

The **roots -nym-** and **-nom-** have their origins in the **Greek** word **onoma,** meaning "name."

In this selection, the Inspector-General receives an **anonymous** letter, summoning him to a small town. The letter was *anonymous* because there was no name on it.

Meet
Anton Chekhov
(1860–1904)

Author of

The Inspector-General

The grandson of a former serf who had purchased his freedom, Anton Chekhov grew up in a small Russian coastal town. He later attended medical school in Moscow, where he began writing humorous stories. Writing soon became his major focus. Chekhov wrote many short stories as well as several acclaimed plays, including *The Three Sisters* (1901).

The Russian Literary Tradition As is characteristic of the Russian literary tradition of the time, Chekhov's works explore the hardships of everyday life. His works also reflect these aspects of the Russian tradition:

- characters ranging from old peasants to society women
- portrayal of characters in great depth
- use of humor to make fun of authorities
- deep feeling for the Russian land
- knowledge of life in both small towns and big cities

All these qualities have helped make Chekhov a beloved Russian author.

BACKGROUND FOR THE PLAY

History Connection
Inspectors-General

The Inspector-General is set in imperial Russia, when the country was ruled by an emperor, or czar. To oversee the many officials in Russia's vast expanse, the czars employed inspectors-general. They observed how local schools, courts, and hospitals were functioning. Many citizens resented the czar's authority, however, and inspectors-general were often unwelcome.

Did You Know?
Chekhov married a famous actress, Olga Knipper.

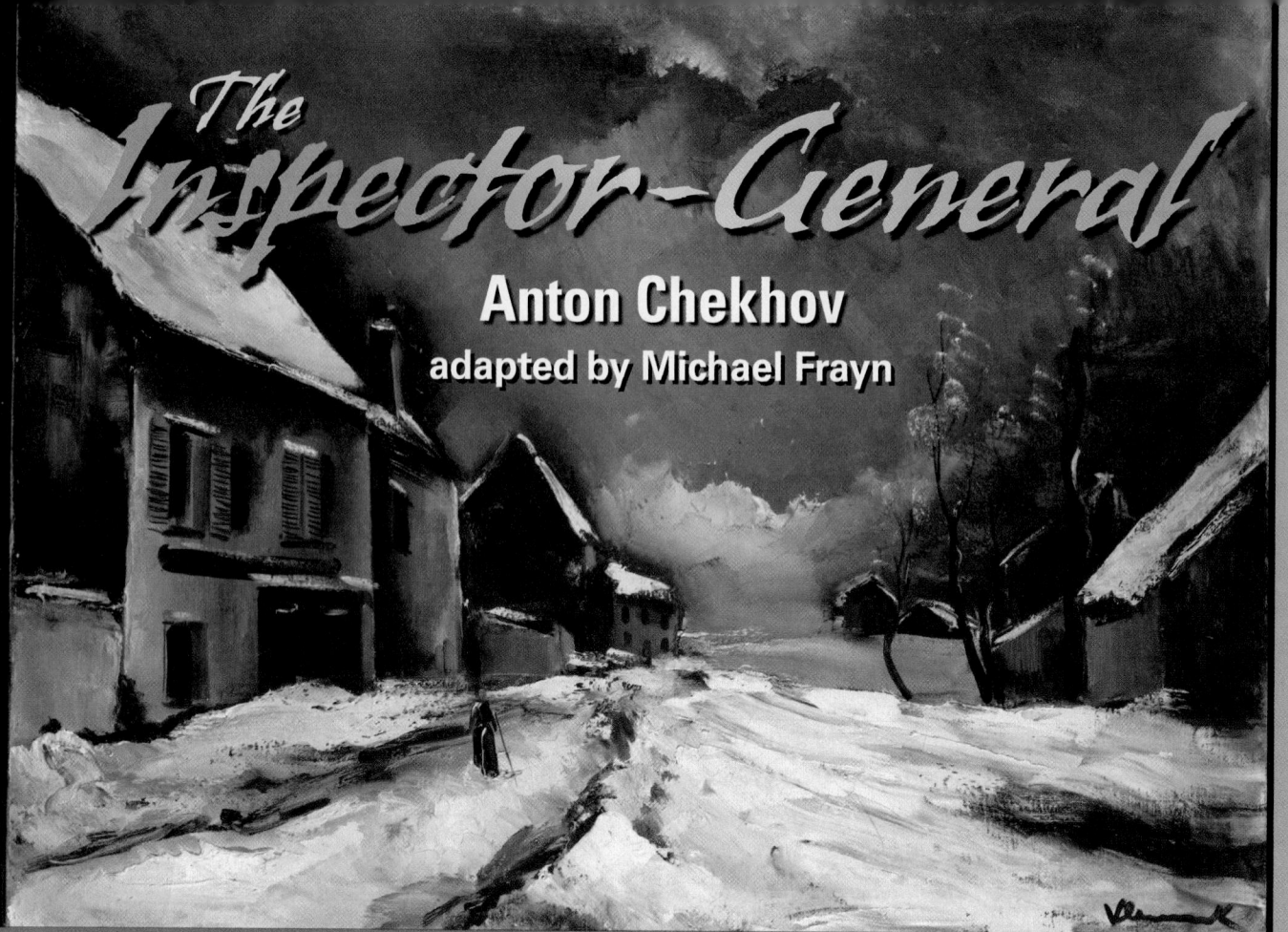

The Inspector-General

Anton Chekhov
adapted by Michael Frayn

The curtain goes up to reveal falling snow and a cart facing away from us. Enter the STORYTELLER, *who begins to read the story. Meanwhile, the* TRAVELER *enters. He is a middle-aged man of urban appearance, wearing dark glasses and a long overcoat with its collar turned up. He is carrying a small traveling bag. He climbs into the cart and sits facing us.*

Vocabulary

incognito (in´ käg nēt´ ō) *adj.* with true identity unrevealed or disguised; under an assumed name

anonymous (ə nän´ ə məs) *adj.* without a known or acknowledged name

trundle (trun´ dəl) *v.* roll along

STORYTELLER. The Inspector-General. In deepest incognito, first by express train, then along back roads, Pyotr Pavlovich Posudin[1] was hastening toward the little town of N, to which he had been summoned by an anonymous letter. "I'll take them by surprise," he thought to himself. "I'll come down on them like a thunderbolt out of the blue. I can just imagine their faces when they hear who I am . . ." [*Enter the* DRIVER, *a peasant, who climbs onto the cart, so that he is sitting with his back to us, and the cart begins to trundle slowly away from us.*] And when he'd thought to himself for long enough, he fell into conversation with the driver of the cart. What did he talk about? About himself, of course. [*Exit the* STORYTELLER.]

---

1. **Pyotr Pavlovich Posudin** (pyō´ tər päv lō´ vich pō syōō´ dən)

TRAVELER. I gather you've got a new Inspector-General in these parts.

DRIVER. True enough.

TRAVELER. Know anything about him? [*The driver turns and looks at the* TRAVELER, *who turns his coat collar up a little higher.*]

DRIVER. Know anything about him? Of course we do! We know everything about all of them up there! Every last little clerk—we know the color of his hair and the size of his boots! [*He turns back to the front, and the* TRAVELER *permits himself a slight smile.*]

TRAVELER. So, what do you reckon? Any good, is he? [*The* DRIVER *turns around.*]

DRIVER. Oh, yes, he's a good one, this one.

TRAVELER. Really?

DRIVER. Did one good thing straight off.

TRAVELER. What was that?

DRIVER. He got rid of the last one. Holy terror he was! Hear him coming five miles off! Say he's going to this little town. Somewhere like we're going, say. He'd let all the world know about it a month before. So now he's on his way, say, and it's like thunder and lightning coming down the road. And when he gets where he's going he has a good sleep, he has a good eat and drink—and then he starts. Stamps his feet, shouts his head off. Then he has another good sleep, and off he goes.

TRAVELER. But the new one's not like that?

DRIVER. Oh, no, the new one goes everywhere on the quiet, like. Creeps around like a cat. Don't want no one to see him, don't want no one to know who he is. Say he's going to this town down the road here. Someone there sent him a letter on the sly, let's say. "Things going on here you should know about." Something of that kind. Well, now, he creeps out of his office, so none of them up there see him go. He hops on a train just like anyone else, just like you or me. Then when he gets off he don't go jumping into a cab or nothing fancy. Oh, no. He wraps himself up from head to toe so you can't see his face, and he wheezes away like an old dog so no one can recognize his voice.

TRAVELER. Wheezes? That's not wheezing! That's the way he talks! So I gather.

◀ **Critical Viewing**
How might the people of a small town like this react to the arrival of an inspector? **[Speculate]**

Reading Skill
Draw Conclusions
Demonstrate your familiarity with Russian literary traditions to draw a conclusion about the characters in this scene.

Spiral Review
Characterization
What method of characterization does the author use here to develop the Inspector-General as a complex character?

Reading
Check
Why is the Inspector-General traveling to the town?

Literary Analysis
Comedy Explain how
the use of dramatic
conventions enhances
the text in this section.

DRIVER. Oh, is it? But the tales they tell about him. You'd laugh till you burst your tripes![2]

TRAVELER. [*sourly.*] I'm sure I would.

DRIVER. He drinks, mind!

TRAVELER. [*startled.*] Drinks?

DRIVER. Oh, like a hole in the ground. Famous for it.

TRAVELER. He's never touched a drop! I mean, from what I've heard.

DRIVER. Oh, not in public, no. Goes to some great ball—"No thank you, not for me." Oh, no, he puts it away at home! Wakes up in the morning, rubs his eyes, and the first thing he does, he shouts, "Vodka!" So in runs his valet with a glass. Fixed himself up a tube behind his desk, he has. Leans down, takes a pull on it, no one the wiser.

TRAVELER. [*offended.*] How do you know all this, may I ask?

Vocabulary
discreetly (di skrēt´ lē)
adv. without drawing
attention

DRIVER. Can't hide it from the servants, can you? The valet and the coachman have got tongues in their heads. Then again, he's on the road, say, going about his business, and he keeps the bottle in his little bag. [*The* TRAVELER *discreetly pushes the traveling bag out of the* DRIVER'S *sight.*] And his housekeeper . . .

TRAVELER. What about her?

DRIVER. Runs circles around him, she does, like a fox round his tail. She's the one who wears the trousers.[3] The people aren't half so frightened of him as they are of her.

TRAVELER. But at least he's good at his job, you say?

DRIVER. Oh, he's a blessing from heaven, I'll grant him that.

cunning (kun´ iŋ) *adj.*
skilled in deception

TRAVELER. Very cunning—you were saying.

DRIVER. Oh, he creeps around all right.

TRAVELER. And then he pounces, yes? I should think some people must get the surprise of their life, mustn't they?

DRIVER. No, no—let's be fair, now. Give him his due. He don't make no trouble.

TRAVELER. No, I mean, if no one knows he's coming . . .

DRIVER. Oh, that's what he thinks, but we all know.

---

2. **tripes** (trīps) *n.* parts of the stomach, usually of an ox or a sheep, when used as food.
3. **wears the trousers** has the greatest authority; is really in charge.

White Night, 1901, Edvard Munch. Photo: J. Lathion ©Nasjonalgalleriet 1997, ©2003 The Munch Museum/The Munch-Ellingsen Group/Artists Rights Society (ARS), NY

TRAVELER. You know?

DRIVER. Oh, some gentleman gets off the train at the station back there with his greatcoat up to his eyebrows and says, "No, I don't want a cab, thank you, just an ordinary horse and cart for me." Well, we'd put two and two together, wouldn't we! Say it was you, now, creeping along down the road here. The lads would be down there in a cab by now! By the time you got there the whole town would be as regular as clockwork! And you'd think to yourself, "Oh, look at that! As clean as a whistle! And they didn't know I was coming!" No, that's why he's such a blessing after the other one. This one believes it!

TRAVELER. Oh, I see.

▲ **Critical Viewing**
How does the countryside depicted in this painting compare to the setting of the play? **[Compare and Contrast]**

The Inspector-General **973**

Vocabulary
telegraph (tel´ ə graf´)
n. an apparatus or system that converts a coded message into electric impulses and sends it to a distant receiver

Reading Skill
Drawing Conclusions
What conclusion can you draw based on the Traveler's sudden order to turn around?

DRIVER. What, you thought we wouldn't know him? Why, we've got the electric telegraph these days! Take today, now. I'm going past the station back there this morning, and the fellow who runs the buffet comes out like a bolt of lightning. Arms full of baskets and bottles. "Where are you off to?" I say. "Doing drinks and refreshments for the Inspector-General!" he says, and he jumps into a carriage and goes flying off down the road here. So there's the old Inspector-General, all muffled up like a roll of carpet, going secretly along in a cart somewhere—and when he gets there, nothing to be seen but vodka and cold salmon!

TRAVELER. [*shouts.*] Right—turn around, then . . . !

DRIVER. [*to the horse.*] Whoa, boy! Whoa! [*To the* TRAVELER.] Oh, so what's this, then? Don't want to go running into the Inspector-General, is that it? [*The* TRAVELER *gestures impatiently for the* DRIVER *to turn the cart around.* DRIVER *to the horse.*] Back we go, then, boy. Home we go. [*He turns the cart around, and the* TRAVELER *takes a swig from his traveling bag.*] Though if I know the old devil, he's like as not turned around and gone home again himself. [*Blackout.*]

Critical Thinking

1. **(a) Respond:** What questions do you still have after reading *The Inspector-General?* Write your questions in the first column of a three-column chart. **(b) Discuss:** Trade lists with a partner. In the second column of the chart, try to answer your partner's questions. Then, discuss the questions and answers. **(c) Assess:** In the third column, explain how your understanding of the work has or has not changed based on the discussion.

Support your responses with evidence from the text.

2. **(a)** What does the Traveler do when the Driver mentions that the Inspector-General keeps a flask of vodka? **(b) Make Inferences:** What does this action tell you about the Traveler?

3. **Analyze:** Review the information on page 969 about the Russian literary tradition and about Chekhov, who wrote within this non-English-speaking tradition. In what ways does *The Inspector-General* reflect the classic Russian literary tradition to which Chekhov belongs?

Do our differences define us? (a) Why did the Inspector-General want to hide his background? **(b)** How was the driver able to determine the Inspector-General's identity?

Literary Analysis: Comedy

1. Note specific ways in which *The Inspector-General* uses the **dramatic conventions** of **comedy** to enhance the text. Explain and support your response with evidence from the text.

2. **(a)** What information, conveyed by the Storyteller, sets up the **dramatic irony** in *The Inspector-General?* **(b)** Identify an exchange between the Driver and the Traveler that highlights the dramatic irony of the situation.

Reading Skill: Draw Conclusions

3. What **conclusions** can you draw about the character of the Traveler based on the stage directions *sourly, startled,* and *offended* that precede three of his lines?

4. What conclusions can you draw about the character of the Driver based on his dialogue with the Traveler? Explain your answer.

5. Who do you think is the wiser and cleverer man, the Driver or the Traveler? Explain.

Vocabulary

Practice Indicate whether each statement is *True* or *False*. Explain your answers. Then, revise false sentences to make them true.

1. Someone making an *anonymous* donation wants recognition.
2. A tricycle is something that might *trundle.*
3. The best way to send a message *discreetly* is to shout.
4. If a man is *cunning,* he may not always tell the truth.
5. Movie stars sometimes travel *incognito* so they can escape notice.
6. People once used the *telegraph* to send packages and letters.

Word Power Use the context of the sentences and what you know about the **Latin root *-nym-*** or ***-nom-*** to explain your answer to each question.

1. Is scientific *nomenclature* for different animals hard to remember?
2. Do you think someone who is only the *nominal* Inspector-General would fulfill the responsibilities of the job?

Word Power

The **roots -*nym*- and -*nom*-** have their origin in the **Greek** word **onoma** meaning "name."

Apply It Explain how the roots -*nym*- and -*nom*- help you determine the meanings of these technical academic words from social studies and the arts. Consult a dictionary if necessary.

patronym
nominate
pseudonym

Integrated Language Skills

The Inspector-General

Conventions: Restrictive and Nonrestrictive Relative Clauses

A **clause** is a group of words that contains a subject and a verb. A **main clause** can stand alone as a complete sentence. A **subordinate clause** cannot. A subordinate clause that modifies a noun or a pronoun is called a **relative clause.**

When a relative clause is needed for the basic meaning of the sentence, it is called **restrictive,** and it is not set off by commas. When a relative clause is not necessary to the meaning, it is called **nonrestrictive,** and it is set off by commas.

Restrictive Relative Clause	Nonrestrictive Relative Clause
The man who is driving the cart might be wiser than we think.	The Inspector-General, who is wearing a disguise, gets in the cart.
The mode of transportation that the traveler chooses is a cart.	Chekhov wrote this play, which contains irony.

Practice A Identify the relative clause in each sentence and tell whether it is restrictive or nonrestrictive.

1. The Inspector-General, who likes to sneak into town, thinks he is clever.
2. The glasses that the traveler wears are dark.
3. Most officials would take a cab, which is a fancier way to travel.
4. The cart driver might be suspicious of the man who gets off the train.

Speaking Application Summarize *The Inspector-General* for a partner. Use at least one restrictive relative clause and one nonrestrictive relative clause as you tell your classmate about the play.

Practice B Add a relative clause to complete each sentence. If the clause is nonrestrictive, be sure to use correct comma placement.

1. The cart _____ is drawn by one horse.
2. The mysterious traveler _____ is the Inspector-General.
3. The Inspector-General cannot fool the towns-people _____.
4. The letter _____ is anonymous.

Writing Application Write two sentences the Inspector-General might include in his report. Use a restrictive relative clause in one sentence and a nonrestrictive relative clause in the other. Then, describe the function of each type of clause.

PH GRAMMAR HANDBOOK Further instruction and practice are available in the *Prentice Hall Grammar Handbook.*

Writing

Write a brief **script** for a play in which students outwit a bully. Create dramatic irony by including scenes in which the audience knows something the bully does not know.

- Write to entertain and teach without being cruel, even to the character of the bully.
- Include an **explicit** (stated) or **implicit** (not plainly stated) **theme.**
- Choose a **definitive mood** or **tone** for your play and include **details** in your script that contribute to that mood or tone.

Rehearse your play with classmates and perform it for your class. Use any available props within the classroom to bring your setting to life.

Grammar Application Make sure you use restrictive and nonrestrictive relative clauses properly in your script, including correct comma placement.

Writing Workshop: Work in Progress

Prewriting for Research Report For a research report you may be asked to write, list and discuss the details in *The Inspector-General* that seem drawn from historical research—for example, note details about language, dress, writing, materials, or theatrical practices of the day. Keep these Historical Research Notes in your writing portfolio.

Research and Technology

Use various resources to research life in Russia during the rule of the czars, including the role of inspectors-general. **Organize the information** you gather from multiple sources to create an **informational chart.**

- **Decide upon topics** to include in your report. For example, typical jobs, freedoms, or the role of government.
- Consider the resources available to you and **formulate a plan** for engaging in research on this complex, multi-faceted topic.
- To finalize your work, write an introductory paragraph that explains the purpose of your chart. Then, include a list of your sources, accurately **citing all researched information** according to a standard format. **Use a style manual** (e.g., *Modern Language Association, Chicago Manual of Style*) for assistance with documenting sources. (For information on citing sources, see page R40.)

 **Focus on the TEKS**

Conventions
(17)(A)(ii) Use and understand the function of restrictive and nonrestrictive relative clauses.
(18)(B)(ii) Use correct comma placement in clauses.
Writing
(14)(C) Write a script with an explicit or implicit theme and details that contribute to a definite mood or tone.
Research
(20)(B) Formulate a plan for engaging in research.
(21)(B) Organize information gathered from multiple sources.
(21)(C) Accurately cite all researched information.
(23)(E) Use a style manual.

Use this prewriting activity to prepare for the **Writing Workshop** on page 1002.

www.PHLitOnline.com

- Interactive graphic organizers
- Grammar tutorial
- Interactive journals

Strategy for Success

Draw Conclusions

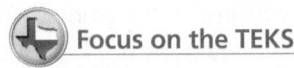

Focus on the TEKS

Reading/Comprehension Skills
(6) Draw conclusions about the features of literary nonfiction.

The reading sections of the PSAT, the SAT, and the Texas standardized tests ask you to draw conclusions about the text that you read. Drawing conclusions means using the information in the text as well as what you already know to come to a new understanding.

As you draw conclusions based on literary nonfiction texts, consider the facts and personal examples that are directly stated as well as information that is implied. Then, develop a statement of your new understanding that is based on the information in the text. The following examples show how you can draw conclusions on standardized tests.

Focus on Key Details

Base your conclusion on important details in the text.

> 5 When I was young, I wanted to play the clarinet. But my family couldn't afford one, so I never learned. Now that I am an adult, I have started a fund for local children who would like to learn to play musical instruments but who cannot afford to buy their own instruments.

1. Based on the information in the passage, one could conclude that the narrator believes
   (A) everyone should learn to play an instrument well
   (B) clarinets are more expensive than other instruments
   (C) learning to play music can be valuable
   (D) all children love music
   (E) most children's families cannot afford instruments

The narrator focuses only on people who are interested in learning to play music, so **A** and **D** are incorrect. **B** and **E** are not supported by the text. The narrator consistently shows that he or she values learning to play music, so **C** is correct.

Consider Implied Information

Draw conclusions based not only on what is stated but also on what is implied.

> 5 I congratulated my opponent on winning the competition and held out my hand. But she ignored the gesture and brushed past me toward the crowds of reporters waiting outside.

2. The information in the passage suggests that the winner of the competition is
   (A) arrogant about her success
   (B) considerate of her opponent
   (C) more polite than the narrator
   (D) less outgoing than the narrator
   (E) anxious about meeting reporters

The winner takes more interest in reporters than sportsmanlike gestures, such as responding to her competition's congratulations. **B, C, D,** and **E** each describe character traits that the winner does not demonstrate. The description in **A** is correct.

SAT/PSAT Practice

Questions 1–4 are based on the following passage.

It was Saturday, March 3, 1913, the day before Woodrow Wilson was to be inaugurated as president of the United States. I had arrived in Washington, D.C., just in time for the inaugural weekend, and that Saturday I rose early and donned my best hat
Line and dress. But I wasn't setting off to any of the inaugural events; as a woman, I hadn't
5 even had the right to cast my vote for or against our new president. Instead, I would be marching right down Pennsylvania Avenue—along with nearly 5,000 other women—in a demonstration for suffrage, the right to vote.

During our march we walked quietly and with dignity, wearing sashes and carrying purple and gold banners to show our support for women's suffrage. The crowds that
10 had come to Washington for the inauguration gathered to watch our march—and some of them jeered. But we knew that if we could walk past the unfriendly crowds with our heads held high, our march would bring national publicity to our cause.

I didn't see President Wilson that weekend, but I often wonder if perhaps our march left a lingering impression in his mind. Six long years later, the Nineteenth Amendment
15 was approved by both houses of Congress. When it was ratified by all the states in 1920, it immediately gave 26 million American women—half the nation's population—the right to vote. And the president who approved it, just before the end of his second term, was Woodrow Wilson.

1. Based on the purpose of the march and the statement that the women were marching with their "heads held high," it is reasonable to conclude that the women
(A) felt frightened of the watching crowds
(B) were looking for President Wilson
(C) felt angry at the people jeering at them
(D) were proud to march for their cause
(E) did not notice people watching them

2. The narrator was probably not planning to watch the inaugural events because she was
(A) not on the list of invited spectators
(B) not interested in politics
(C) upset that she was not allowed to vote
(D) not in Washington, D.C., at the time
(E) angry that Wilson had been elected

3. The passage suggests that the women's demonstration was
(A) peaceful
(B) private
(C) unplanned
(D) disrespectful
(E) not newsworthy

4. Based on the passage, one could conclude that the narrator believes the march in which she participated may have
(A) been quickly forgotten by spectators
(B) contributed to President Wilson's decision to sign the amendment
(C) encouraged others to demand suffrage
(D) been stopped by political officials
(E) caused President Wilson to ignore the issue of women's suffrage

Informational Texts

Expository Texts

Web Site
Tornadoes

Web Encyclopedia Entry
Tropical Cyclone

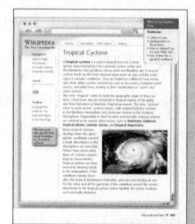

Focus on the TEKS

Reading
(9)(C) Draw complex conclusions about the ideas in text.

Research
(22)(B) Evaluate the relevance of information to the topic and determine the reliability, validity, and accuracy of sources (including Internet sources) by examining their authority and objectivity.

Reading Skill: Evaluate Sources

Many factors can affect the **reliability** (trustworthiness), **validity** (appropriateness or effectiveness), and **accuracy** (correctness) of an informational text. These factors include an author's or sponsor's personal interests and feelings, the method in which information was gathered, and the age of the source. When you read informational texts, **evaluate the source.** Consider how the source of the information might affect the content.

Evaluating sources is especially important on the Internet. Many Web sites include information that is unreliable, invalid, or inaccurate. **Drawing complex conclusions** about the quality of the information you find online is a key part of performing research on the Web.

As You Read Use a chart like this one to determine the reliability, validity, and accuracy of Internet sources by examining their authority and objectivity. Then, use this analysis to draw complex conclusions about the quality of the sources and the information and ideas presented.

Authority	
Is the main idea fully supported by the evidence? *(validity)*	
Are the author's arguments logical and valid? *(validity)*	
Can the evidence presented be verified? *(reliability, accuracy)*	
Is the source current? *(reliability, validity, accuracy)*	
Objectivity	
Is the material presented in an impartial way? *(validity, objectivity)*	
Who is the author or sponsor of the site? (For Web sites, URLs ending in *.edu* and *.gov* tend to be the most reliable.) *(reliability)*	

Web Site

Features:

- home page with links to other pages
- informative text for research or leisure reading
- photos or other images

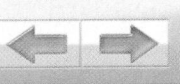

National Oceanic and Atmosphere Administration

NOAA is a government agency, so the information here should be reliable.

Home	Contacts	Media	Search

Weather Page
Fujita Tornado Damage Scale

Category F0: Light Damage (<73 mph); Some damage to chimneys and sign boards, branches broken off trees, shallow-rooted trees pushed over.

Category F1: Moderate Damage (73–112 mph); Peels surface off roofs; mobile homes pushed off foundations or overturned; moving autos blown off road.

Category F2: Considerable Damage (113–157 mph); Roofs torn off frame houses; mobile homes demolished; boxcars over-turned; large trees snapped or uprooted; light-object missiles generated; cars lifted off ground.

Category F3: Severe Damage (158–206 mph); Roofs and some walls torn off well-constructed houses, trains overturned; most trees in forest uprooted; heavy cars lifted off ground and thrown.

Category F4: Devastating Damage (207–260 mph); Well-constructed houses leveled; structure with weak foundations blown off some distance; cars thrown and large missiles generated.

Category F5: Incredible Damage (261–318 mph); Strong frame houses lifted off foundations and swept away; automobile sized missiles fly through the air in excess of 100 meters (109 yards); trees debarked.

Tornadoes

Tornadoes are one of nature's most violent storms. In an average year, about 1,000 tornadoes are reported across the United States, resulting in 80 deaths and over 1,500 injuries. A tornado is a violently rotating column of air extending from a thunderstorm to the ground. The most violent tornadoes are capable of tremendous destruction with wind speeds of 250 mph or more. Damage paths can be in excess of one mile wide and 50 miles long.

The main idea of this paragraph is fully supported by specific facts.

Tornadoes come in all shapes and sizes and can occur anywhere in the U.S. at any time of the year. In the southern states, peak tornado season is March through May, while peak months in the northern states are during the summer.

Preparedness Guides

- Are you prepared for <u>Nature's Most Violent Storms</u>? A preparedness guide including safety information for schools prepared by the National Weather Service, FEMA and the American Red Cross.
- <u>Thunderstorms and Camping Safety</u>
- <u>Weather Safety for Kids</u> — Owlie Skywarn's Weather Book about Tornadoes

More Info

- <u>Weather Glossary for Storm Spotters</u>
- <u>Storm Reports</u> — includes monthly tornado statistics, deadly tornadoes, current severe weather reports and more from the National Weather Service's Storm Prediction Center.
- <u>Tornadoes of the 20th Century</u> — a list of the more notable tornado outbreaks that occurred in the U.S. during the 20th century.

**Owlie's
Front Page**

View My Safety
Tips About . . .

Tornadoes
   Watches
   Warnings

Lightning

Flash Floods

Hurricanes

Winter Weather

Carbon Monoxide

National Weather Service
Owlie Skywarn's Weather Book
Watch Out...Storms Ahead!

TORNADO!

If you ever see a big black cloud with a funnel-like extension beneath it, watch out. It could be a tornado.

A tornado looks like a funnel with the fat part at the top. Inside it, winds may be swirling around at 3,000 miles per hour. If it goes through a town, the tornado could flatten houses and buildings, lift up cars and trucks, shatter mobile homes into splinters. Sometimes the path is narrow, but everything in the path gets wrecked. But you don't always see the funnel. It may be raining too hard. Or the tornado may come at night. Listen for the tornado's roar. Some people say it sounds like a thousand trains.

What to do if. . .

You are in your house	**You are downtown or in a shopping mall**	**You are outside**
You are in school	**You are in a mobile home**	**In Conclusion…**

Last updated June 22, 20__●───────

> The Web site indicates how recently its information was updated.

Educators and students should send their questions to the NOAA outreach team.

Do our differences define us?

How might daily life in an area where tornadoes often strike differ from daily life where tornadoes rarely strike?

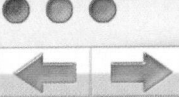

Web Encyclopedia Entry

Features:

- online access
- photographs or illustrations
- links to related topics and Web sites
- text written for a general audience

WIKIPEDIA
The Free Encyclopedia

Navigation

- Main Page
- Contents
- Current Events
- Random Article

Search

GO

Toolbox

- Upload File
- Add to File
- Special Pages
- Cite this Page

The entry presents specific facts about the behavior of tropical cyclones.

| Article | Discussion | Edit Article | History |

Tropical Cyclone

A **tropical cyclone** is a meteorological term for a storm system characterized by a low pressure system center and thunderstorms that produces strong wind and flooding rain. A tropical cyclone feeds on the heat released when moist air rises and the water vapor it contains condenses. They are fueled by a different heat mechanism than other cyclonic windstorms such as nor'easters, European windstorms, and polar lows, leading to their classification as "warm core" storm systems.

The term "tropical" refers to both the geographic origin of these systems, which form almost exclusively in tropical regions of the globe, and their formation in Maritime Tropical air masses. The term "cyclone" refers to such storms' cyclonic nature, with counterclockwise rotation in the Northern Hemisphere and clockwise rotation in the Southern Hemisphere. Depending on their location and strength, tropical cyclones are referred to by various other names, such as **hurricane, typhoon, tropical storm, cyclonic storm,** and **tropical depression.**

Many tropical cyclones develop when the atmospheric conditions around a weak disturbance in the atmosphere are favorable. Others form when other types of cyclones acquire tropical characteristics. Tropical systems are then moved by steering winds in the troposphere; if the conditions remain favor-

able, the tropical disturbance intensifies, and can even develop an eye. On the other end of the spectrum, if the conditions around the system deteriorate or the tropical cyclone makes landfall, the system weakens and eventually dissipates.

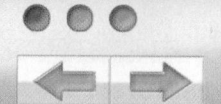

Wikipedia: Verifiability

This section describes the criteria the sponsors use to judge what entry information is included in this Web encyclopedia.

The threshold for inclusion in Wikipedia is **verifiability, not truth.** "Verifiable" in this context means that readers should be able to check that material added to Wikipedia has already been published by a reliable source. Editors should provide a reliable source for quotations and for any material that is challenged or is likely to be challenged, or it may be removed.

Burden of evidence

The burden of evidence lies with the editor who adds or restores material. All quotations and any material **challenged or likely to be challenged** should be attributed to a reliable, published source using an inline citation. The source should be cited clearly and precisely to enable readers to find the text that supports the article content in question.

Sources

This section discusses the Web site's policies about how evidence is to be verified and how to present material in an impartial way.

Articles should rely on reliable, third-party published sources with a reputation for fact-checking and accuracy. Reliable sources are necessary both to substantiate material within articles and to give credit to authors and publishers in order to avoid plagiarism and copyright violations. Sources should directly support the information as it is presented in an article and should be appropriate to the claims made: exceptional claims require exceptional sources.

All articles must adhere to Wikipedia's neutrality policy, fairly representing all majority and significant-minority viewpoints that have been published by reliable sources, in rough proportion to the prominence of each view. Tiny-minority views and fringe theories need not be included, except in articles devoted to them.

In general, the most reliable sources are peer-reviewed journals and books published in university presses; university-level textbooks; magazines, journals, and books published by respected publishing houses; and mainstream newspapers.

Do our differences define us?

How might living in an area that is prone to tropical cyclones define or affect a person's life?

Comparing Informational Texts

(a) Examine the **authority** and **objectivity** of the Web site and the Web encyclopedia entry. Determine and then compare the **reliability, validity, and accuracy** of these Internet sources. **(b) Draw Conclusions:** Which source is more reliable? Explain how you drew this conclusion.

 **College Readiness** | **Timed Writing**

Write an Evaluation

Format
The prompt directs you to write an essay. Therefore, your response should include an introduction, body paragraphs, and a conclusion.

> Write an essay evaluating the relevance of the Web encyclopedia entry as a source of information about the topic of tropical cyclones. Assess the usefulness of the information and ideas presented, and draw conclusions about their validity and reliability. Provide evidence from the text to support your evaluations and conclusions. (35 minutes)

Academic Vocabulary
When you *assess*, you make a determination about something's value.

 5-Minute Planner

Complete these steps before you begin to write:

1. Read the prompt carefully and completely.

2. Review the Web encyclopedia entry on tropical cyclones. Note details that help you understand the subject. Decide how useful the information in the entry would be if you were researching tropical cyclones.

3. Review the Web encyclopedia's statement regarding the verifiability of information on the site. Based on that statement, decide whether you think the information in the entry is completely reliable.
   TIP Consider whether information in the entry could be verified using another reliable source. Make notes about the verifiability of the information provided.

4. Use your notes to create a rough outline for your evaluation.

5. Refer to your notes and outline as you draft your essay.

Comparing Literary Works

Comparing Satire

Satire is writing that exposes and makes fun of the foolishness and faults of an individual, an institution, a society, or a situation. Although a satire may make readers laugh, it may also aim to correct the flaws that it criticizes. Some satires address serious social problems, while others explore less important subjects. Satirical writings vary in style and tone, level of *subtlety,* and the writer's attitude toward the subject and the audience. A satire may have the following characteristics:

- It might use **verbal irony**—language that means the opposite of what it says.

- It might use **situational irony**—when events turn out to be the opposite of what is expected.

- It might include **sarcasm**—the use of irony to make fun of someone or something.

- It may be gentle and sympathetic or angry and bitter in tone.

- It may exaggerate faults to make them both funny and obvious.

In addition, the perspective of the satirist plays a key role. Some satirists write as outside onlookers, while others include themselves as objects of the satire. Skilled satirists reveal their targets with subtleties in the text rather than elements that are overly obvious.

 **Focus on the TEKS**

Reading
(7) Explain the role of irony and sarcasm in literary works.

As You Read Use a chart like this one to explain the roles of irony and sarcasm in setting the tone of each satirical literary work.

The Importance of Being Earnest		
Characteristic of Satire	**Example of Characteristic**	**Role in this Literary Work**
irony		
sarcasm		
Big Kiss		
Characteristic of Satire	**Example of Characteristic**	**Role in this Literary Work**
irony		
sarcasm		

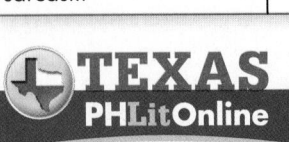
PHLitOnline
www.PHLitOnline.com

- Vocabulary flashcards
- Interactive journals
- More about the authors
- Selection audio
- Interactive graphic organizers

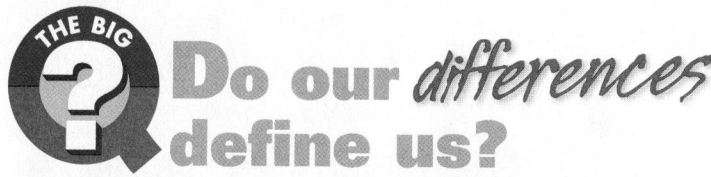

Do our *differences* define us?

Writing About the Big Question

Both these selections use people's differences to satirize an element of life or society. Use this sentence starter to develop your ideas about the Big Question.

When writers expose what is foolish in society, we can learn that our **differences** _____.

Meet the Authors

Oscar Wilde (1854–1900)

Author of *The Importance of Being Earnest*

Oscar Wilde was educated in Dublin and at Oxford University, where he became notorious for his wit. While he wrote poems and celebrated works of fiction, it was in his plays that Wilde's genius found its voice.

The Importance of Being Funny In a series of brilliant comedies, including *A Woman of No Importance* and *An Ideal Husband*, Wilde targeted the strait-laced manners and hypocrisy of English society in the 1890s. His masterpiece is *The Importance of Being Earnest*, a drama about Victorian values that still entertains audiences today.

Henry Alford (b. 1962)

Author of *Big Kiss*

Henry Alford calls himself an "investigative humorist," a comic journalist who unearths humor wherever it hides. Armed with dry wit and charm, he uncovers what makes popular culture funny, amazing, or outrageous.

Comic Escapades *Big Kiss: One Actor's Desperate Attempt to Claw His Way to the Middle* chronicles Alford's adventures as he tries to become an actor. He faces humiliation at the hands of acting teachers and directors, but he relishes his minor victory as an extra in *Godzilla*.

from

The Importance of Being Earnest

Oscar Wilde

The following excerpt is from Act I of *The Importance of Being Earnest*. The play takes place in England in the 1890s, during the reign of Queen Victoria, a time when elegance, manners, and social status were of great importance. In this scene, John Worthing, nicknamed Jack, visits the London apartment of his friend Algernon. Jack loves Algernon's cousin, Gwendolen. In order to maintain his spotless reputation at his home in the country, Jack takes on a different identity when he is in the city. When he is out in the country, he pretends to have a brother named Ernest, and when he visits London, Jack pretends to be Ernest. Gwendolen knows nothing about Jack's real name or his double identity.

CHARACTERS

John Worthing, JP   Algernon
Lady Bracknell
Hon. Gwendolen Fairfax

LADY BRACKNELL *and* ALGERNON *go into the music room,*
GWENDOLEN *remains behind.*

JACK. Charming day it has been, Miss Fairfax.

GWENDOLEN. Pray don't talk to me about the weather, Mr
Worthing. Whenever people talk to me about the weather, I
always feel quite certain that they mean something else. And
that makes me so nervous.

JACK. I do mean something else.

GWENDOLEN. I thought so. In fact, I am never wrong.

JACK. And I would like to be allowed to take advantage of Lady
Bracknell's temporary absence. . . .

GWENDOLEN. I would certainly advise you to do so. Mamma has a
way of coming back suddenly into a room that I have often had to
speak to her about.

JACK. *(nervously)* Miss Fairfax, ever since I met you I have admired
you more than any girl . . . I have ever met since . . . I met you.

GWENDOLEN. Yes, I am quite aware of the fact. And I often wish
that in public, at any rate, you had been more demonstrative. For
me you have always had an irresistible fascination. Even before
I met you I was far from indifferent to you. *(Jack looks at her in
amazement)* We live, as I hope you know, Mr Worthing, in an age
of ideals. The fact is constantly mentioned in the more expensive
monthly magazines, and has reached the provincial pulpits I am
told; and my ideal has always been to love someone of the name
of Ernest. There is something in that name that inspires absolute
confidence. The moment Algernon first mentioned to me that he
had a friend called Ernest, I knew I was destined to love you.

JACK. You really love me, Gwendolen?

GWENDOLEN. Passionately!

JACK. Darling! You don't know how happy you've made me.

Literary Analysis
Satire Which words
here make fun of
Gwendolen's
haughtiness?

**Reading
Check**

What is Gwendolen's
"ideal"?

◄ **Critical Viewing** Judging from the actor playing Jack in this photograph,
what do you think Jack will be like? **[Predict]**

GWENDOLEN. My own Ernest!

JACK. But you don't really mean to say that you couldn't love me if my name wasn't Ernest?

GWENDOLEN. But your name is Ernest.

JACK. Yes, I know it is. But supposing it was something else? Do you mean to say you couldn't love me then?

GWENDOLEN. *(glibly)* Ah! that is clearly a metaphysical speculation, and like most metaphysical speculations has very little reference at all to the actual facts of real life, as we know them.

JACK. Personally, darling, to speak quite candidly, I don't much care about the name Ernest. . . . I don't think the name suits me at all.

GWENDOLEN. It suits you perfectly. It is a divine name. It has music of its own. It produces vibrations.

JACK. Well, really, Gwendolen, I must say that I think there are lots of other much nicer names. I think Jack, for instance, a charming name.

GWENDOLEN. Jack? . . . No, there is very little music in the name Jack, if any at all, indeed. It does not thrill. It produces absolutely no vibrations. . . . I have known several Jacks, and they all, without exception, were more than usually plain. Besides, Jack is a notorious domesticity for John! And I pity any woman who is married to a man called John. She would probably never be allowed to know the entrancing pleasure of a single moment's solitude. The only really safe name is Ernest.

JACK. Gwendolen, I must get christened at once—I mean we must get married at once. There is no time to be lost.

GWENDOLEN. Married, Mr Worthing?

JACK. *(astounded)* Well . . . surely. You know that I love you, and you led me to believe, Miss Fairfax, that you were not absolutely indifferent to me.

Literary Analysis
Satire Explain the role of irony in the comedy surrounding Gwendolen's fascination with the name Ernest and her feelings for Jack.

▶ **Critical Viewing**
How would you describe the expression on Jack's face in the image at right? **[Describe]**

GWENDOLEN. I adore you. But you haven't proposed to me yet. Nothing has been said at all about marriage. The subject has not even been touched on.

JACK. Well . . . may I propose to you now?

GWENDOLEN. I think it would be an admirable opportunity. And to spare you any possible disappointment, Mr Worthing, I think it only fair to tell you quite frankly beforehand that I am fully determined to accept you.

JACK. Gwendolen!

GWENDOLEN. Yes, Mr Worthing, what have you got to say to me?

JACK. You know what I have got to say to you.

GWENDOLEN. Yes, but you don't say it.

JACK. Gwendolen, will you marry me? *(Goes on his knees)*

GWENDOLEN. Of course I will, darling. How long you have been about it! I am afraid you have had very little experience in how to propose.

JACK. My own one, I have never loved anyone in the world but you.

GWENDOLEN. Yes, but men often propose for practice. I know my brother Gerald does. All my girlfriends tell me so. What wonderfully blue eyes you have, Ernest! They are quite, quite blue. I hope you will always look at me just like that, especially when there are other people present.

(Enter LADY BRACKNELL*)*

LADY BRACKNELL. Mr Worthing! Rise, sir, from this semi-recumbent posture. It is most indecorous.

GWENDOLEN. Mamma! *(He tries to rise; she restrains him)* I must beg you to retire. This is no place for you. Besides, Mr Worthing has not quite finished yet.

LADY BRACKNELL. Finished what, may I ask?

GWENDOLEN. I am engaged to Mr Worthing, mamma.

(They rise together)

LADY BRACKNELL. Pardon me, you are not engaged to anyone. When you do become engaged to someone, I, or your father, should his health permit him, will inform you of the fact. An engagement should come on a young girl as a surprise, pleasant or unpleasant, as the case may be. It is hardly a matter that she could be allowed to arrange for herself. . . . And now I have a few questions to put to you, Mr Worthing. While I am making these inquiries, you, Gwendolen, will wait for me below in the carriage.

GWENDOLEN. *(reproachfully)* Mamma!

Literary Analysis
Satire What does Lady Bracknell's use of elaborate expressions suggest about her character?

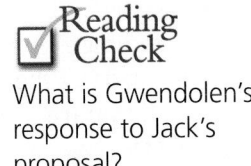
Reading Check
What is Gwendolen's response to Jack's proposal?

LADY BRACKNELL. In the carriage, Gwendolen!

> GWENDOLEN *goes to the door. She and* JACK *blow kisses to each other behind* LADY BRACKNELL'S *back.* LADY BRACKNELL *looks vaguely about as if she could not understand what the noise was. Finally turns round*

Gwendolen, the carriage!

GWENDOLEN. Yes, mamma.

> *Goes out, looking back at* JACK

LADY BRACKNELL. *(sitting down)* You can take a seat, Mr Worthing. *(Looks in her pocket for note-book and pencil)*

JACK. Thank you, Lady Bracknell, I prefer standing.

LADY BRACKNELL. *(pencil and note-book in hand)* I feel bound to tell you that you are not down on my list of eligible young men, although I have the same list as the dear Duchess of Bolton has. We work together, in fact. However, I am quite ready to enter your name, should your answers be what a really affectionate mother requires. How old are you?

JACK. Twenty-nine.

LADY BRACKNELL. A very good age to be married at. I have always been of opinion that a man who desires to get married should know either everything or nothing. Which do you know?

JACK. *(after some hesitation)* I know nothing, Lady Bracknell.

LADY BRACKNELL. I am pleased to hear it. I do not approve of anything that tampers with natural ignorance. Ignorance is like a delicate exotic fruit; touch it and the bloom is gone. The whole theory of modern education is radically unsound. Fortunately in England, at any rate, education produces no effect whatsoever. If it did, it would prove a serious danger to the upper classes, and probably lead to acts of violence in Grosvenor Square. What is your income?

JACK. Between seven and eight thousand a year.

LADY BRACKNELL. *(makes a note in her book)* In land, or in investments?

JACK. In investments, chiefly.

LADY BRACKNELL. That is satisfactory. What between the duties expected of one during one's lifetime, and the duties exacted from one after one's death, land has ceased to be either a profit or a pleasure. It gives one position, and prevents one from keeping it up. That's all that can be said about land.

JACK. I have a country house with some land, of course, attached to it, about fifteen hundred acres, I believe; but I don't depend

Literary Analysis
Satire Is Lady Bracknell truly "a really affectionate mother"? Explain.

Vocabulary
ignorance (ig´ nə rəns) *n.* lack of knowledge

▶ **Critical Viewing**
How do these actresses' portrayals of Lady Bracknell and Gwendolen compare to your mental image of the characters? **[Compare and Contrast]**

on that for my real income. In fact, as far as I can make out, the poachers are the only people who make anything out of it.

LADY BRACKNELL. A country house! How many bedrooms? Well, that point can be cleared up afterwards. You have a town house, I hope? A girl with a simple, unspoiled nature, like Gwendolen, could hardly be expected to reside in the country.

JACK. Well, I own a house in Belgrave Square, but it is let by the year to Lady Bloxham. Of course, I can get it back whenever I like, at six months' notice.

LADY BRACKNELL. Lady Bloxham? I don't know her.

JACK. Oh, she goes about very little. She is a lady considerably advanced in years.

LADY BRACKNELL. Ah, nowadays that is no guarantee of respectability of character. What number in Belgrave Square?

JACK. 149.

LADY BRACKNELL. *(shaking her head)* The unfashionable side. I thought there was something. However, that could easily be altered.

JACK. Do you mean the fashion, or the side?

LADY BRACKNELL. *(sternly)* Both, if necessary, I presume. What are your politics?

JACK. Well, I am afraid I really have none. I am a Liberal Unionist.

LADY BRACKNELL. Oh, they count as Tories. They dine with us. Or come in the evening, at any rate. Now to minor matters. Are your parents living?

JACK. I have lost both my parents.

LADY BRACKNELL. Both? . . . That seems like carelessness. Who was your father?

Literary Analysis
Satire Does Gwendolen really have a "simple, unspoiled nature"? Explain.

Reading Check
What kind of list does Lady Bracknell keep?

He was evidently a man of some wealth. Was he born in what the Radical papers call the purple of commerce, or did he rise from the ranks of the aristocracy?

JACK. I am afraid I really don't know. The fact is, Lady Bracknell, I said I had lost my parents. It would be nearer the truth to say that my parents seem to have lost me. . . . I don't actually know who I am by birth. I was . . . well, I was found.

LADY BRACKNELL. Found!

JACK. The late Mr Thomas Cardew, an old gentleman of a very charitable and kindly disposition, found me, and gave me the name of Worthing, because he happened to have a first-class ticket for Worthing in his pocket at the time. Worthing is a place in Sussex. It is a seaside resort.

LADY BRACKNELL. Where did the charitable gentleman who had a first-class ticket for this seaside resort find you?

JACK. *(gravely)* In a hand-bag.

LADY BRACKNELL. A hand-bag?

JACK. *(very seriously)* Yes, Lady Bracknell. I was in a hand-bag— a somewhat large, black leather handbag, with handles to it— an ordinary hand-bag in fact.

LADY BRACKNELL. In what locality did this Mr James, or Thomas, Cardew come across this ordinary hand-bag?

JACK. In the cloak-room at Victoria Station. It was given to him in mistake for his own.

LADY BRACKNELL. The cloak-room at Victoria Station?

JACK. Yes. The Brighton line.

LADY BRACKNELL. The line is immaterial. Mr Worthing, I confess I feel somewhat bewildered by what you have just told me. To be born, or at any rate bred, in a hand-bag, whether it had handles or not, seems to me to display a contempt for the ordinary decencies of family life that reminds one of the worst excesses of the French Revolution. And I presume you know what that unfortunate movement led to? As for the particular locality in which the hand-bag was found, a cloak-room at a railway station might serve to conceal a social indiscretion—has probably, indeed, been used for that purpose before now—but it could hardly be regarded as an assured basis for a recognized position in good society.

JACK. May I ask you then what you would advise me to do? I need hardly say I would do anything in the world to ensure Gwendolen's happiness.

Literary Analysis
Satire How does Jack's explanation of being "found" make fun of the Victorian value of proper lineage and family ties?

Literary Analysis
Satire Explain how Lady Bracknell's use of exaggeration adds to the satire.

LADY BRACKNELL. I would strongly advise you, Mr Worthing, to try and acquire some relations as soon as possible, and to make a definite effort to produce at any rate one parent, of either sex, before the season is quite over.

JACK. Well, I don't see how I could possibly manage to do that. I can produce the hand-bag at any moment. It is in my dressing-room at home. I really think that should satisfy you, Lady Bracknell.

LADY BRACKNELL. Me, sir! What has it to do with me? You can hardly imagine that I and Lord Bracknell would dream of allowing our only daughter—a girl brought up with the utmost care—to marry into a cloak-room, and form an alliance with a parcel? Good morning, Mr Worthing!

Lady Bracknell sweeps out in majestic indignation

JACK. Good morning! (ALGERNON, *from the other room, strikes up the Wedding March.* JACK *looks perfectly furious, and goes to the door)* For goodness' sake don't play that ghastly tune, Algy! How idiotic you are!

Literary Analysis
Satire How does Lady Bracknell's final demand add to the satire?

Critical Thinking

1. **Respond:** Would you like to spend time with the characters in this play? Why or why not?

2. **(a)** How does Gwendolen respond to Jack's proposal?
   (b) Make Inferences: How would you describe Gwendolen's feelings for Jack?

3. **(a)** According to Lady Bracknell, how should a young girl learn she is engaged? **(b) Make Inferences:** What do Lady Bracknell's remarks suggest about Victorian attitudes toward marriage and family?

4. **(a) Summarize:** Write a summary of the personal information that Lady Bracknell needs from Jack. **(b) Interpret:** In what ways does Lady Bracknell find Jack both acceptable and unacceptable as a possible husband? **(c) Assess:** Based on her judgment of Jack, describe Lady Bracknell's character.

5. **(a) Interpret:** What values does Lady Bracknell hold dear? Explain. **(b) Compare and Contrast:** How do you think Lady Bracknell's values compare to the values of most people today?

Do our differences define us?
(a) Which qualities in Jack are most important to Gwendolen and her mother? **(b)** What do you think the author suggests is more important than these differences?

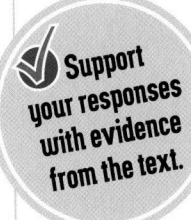
Support your responses with evidence from the text.

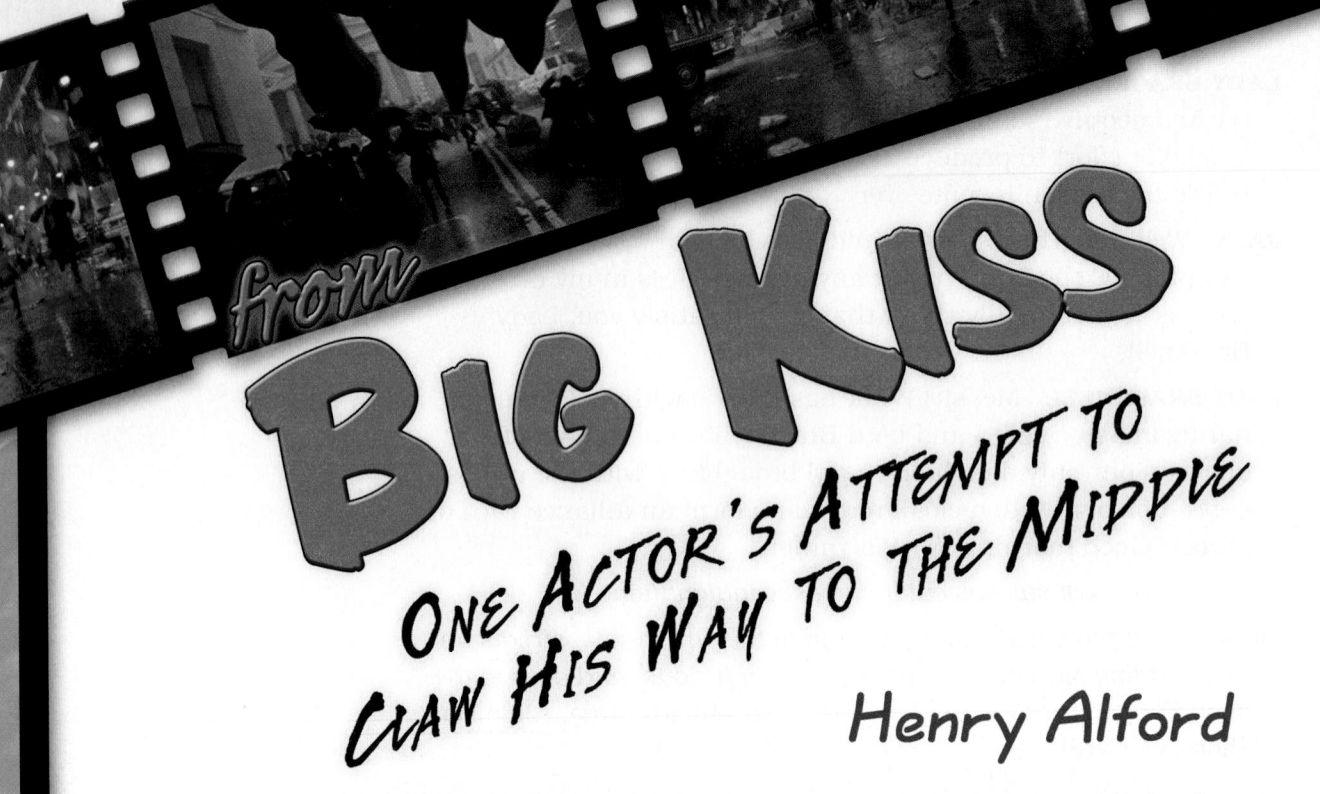

from BIG KISS
ONE ACTOR'S ATTEMPT TO CLAW HIS WAY TO THE MIDDLE

Henry Alford

In the acting profession, as in life, you must make the most of your tiny allotment. He who waits until he has been cast as Othello to pull out all the stops is setting himself up for disappointment—it will be Othello, not Desdemona,[1] who is strangled in this production. So when a classmate told me she was helping to cast extras for the remake of *Godzilla*, I quickly recommended myself for duty. I clearly had not slayed them at improv camp in Wisconsin; here was an opportunity to channel my feelings of disappointment into bravura acting. And perhaps, in so doing, to achieve every extra's dream: to be awarded a line of dialogue.

My classmate called me two days later and said that the filming, to be done that Sunday, would involve prodigious amounts of stage rain. I assured her that I was no stranger to adverse meteorological conditions, natural and man-made, and, as such, could "play wet." The pay for non-Screen Actors Guild[2] talent was seventy-five dollars; I needed to be available all day and night. I was to wear a raincoat and carry a black umbrella.

The harbinger[3] of location shooting in a metropolitan area is a table on the sidewalk, heaped high with haggard bagels. When

Literary Analysis
Satire Which details make Alford's role as an extra sound important?

---

1. **Othello . . . Desdemona** In Shakespeare's play, Othello kills his wife, Desdemona, because he believes she had an affair. He later discovers she had been faithful, and his grief causes him to kill himself.
2. **Screen Actors Guild** (SAG) labor union for performers.
3. **harbinger** (här´ bin jər) *n.* something that comes before to give an indication of what follows.

I arrived at the appointed location in the Financial District that Sunday morning at six-thirty, although the chaos I found there—Teamsters[4] bickering over sports scores, thick black cables veining the streets as if to depict the late stages of arteriosclerosis—had all the earmarks of filmmaking, I did not see the telltale breadstuffs and so was moved to ask the first walkie-talkie-wielding individual I saw, "Where are the bagels?"

"Are you SAG or non-SAG?" she asked.

"Non."

"You're in the tent."

She pointed to a huge, dun-colored tent around which loitered hundreds of men and women, many of whom were also wearing raincoats and carrying umbrellas. "My people," I exclaimed. I walked over to the tent and, seeing a line formed at one of the twenty or so tables thereunder, queued up. Four minutes later the casting people had checked my name off on a list and I had been given a voucher, the form by which I would be paid.

All was actor-clogged; I could barely find an empty seat at a table. I was glad I finally did—we proceeded to wait for two hours. During this time, small groups of us were presented to a young, unshaven man from Wardrobe who was, by turns, exhausted and sniffy. He looked at the camouflage cap that the fortysomething gentleman ahead of me in line was wearing and said, "I don't know anyone who would wear that cap." Then he scanned me—that is to say, my tan raincoat, my black umbrella, and my wingtips encased in black rubbers—and yawned, "You're fine."

Shortly thereafter we were herded down to the set in groups of thirty or forty. The set was Federal Hall, the majestic site of George Washington's inauguration, rich in Corinthian columns and impressive stairways, which dead-ends Broad Street in the manner of a lion's gaping jaws. Halfway up its main stairs was a podium, festooned with red, white, and blue bunting and a sign reading RE-ELECT MAYOR EBERT. I wondered aloud, "Where's the reptile?"

The self-appointed expert in my group explained, "They're gonna blue-screen[5] him in later."

We lined up on the sidewalk and then, one by one, walked through a small, cordoned-off area where a sweet, pale, bespectacled man was handing out props. It looked like about a third of the extras were being given still cameras and two thirds were being given placards reading RE-ELECT EBERT.

"I hope I get a camera," the woman standing behind me in line said.

Literary Analysis
Satire What does the word "herded" convey about the experience of extras?

Reading Check
What instructions does Alford's friend give him?

---

4. **Teamsters** (tēm′ stərz) *n.* members of a large labor union for truck drivers and other occupations.

5. **blue-screen** *v.* filming against a blue background, in order to apply special effects later.

Eager to be filmed shooting at Godzilla, I responded, "I hope I get a Taser."

Moments later I was handed three props—a fake 35-millimeter camera, a fanny pack, and a press badge. I looked at the badge. The first thing I noticed was that the photo on it was of the man who had just handed it to me. Hovering over the photo was the name Sean Haworth and the call letters WAQR. These call letters sounded more like radio than TV to me; but then why was I carrying a still camera?

Rather than let this seeming contradiction bother me, I decided to base my character interpretation on it. What if Sean Haworth labored under the impression that if he took a good enough photograph it would be aired on the radio? Wouldn't this, character-wise, raise the stakes, and imbue him with the driven quality that makes for an interesting dramatic character? Poor Sean, you can almost hear the editorial staff at WAQR whispering over the water cooler. If only he understood that ours is an aural medium.

But five minutes later an assistant director who had assembled about a hundred of us in front of Federal Hall took away my camera.

"I based my character interpretation on that!" I exclaimed, hoping that this would translate to him as "Serious actor. Could handle a line of dialogue."

"I need it for up front," he reported tersely, then walked to the front of the crowd.

One of my fellow colleagues—a vivacious English as a Second Language tutor and sometime actress in her early thirties with whom I had fallen into conversation back in the tent—witnessed my loss of camera and counseled, "You were probably overpropped anyway."

"Yes," I responded, "my work was getting proppy."

We proceeded to work for almost eleven hours, lunch break included, on variations of a single shot. In it, about four hundred of us New Yorkers are standing in the rain, listening to Mayor Ebert (Michael Lerner) give a speech. All of a sudden, we hear a thump. Some of the crowd—those born between January and April, to be precise—look behind them, down Broad Street, whence the sound originates. The mayor continues to netter on when thump! May through August now look down the street, too, expressing restlessness, a sense of discomfort, the vague possibility that this little piece of earth they call their own will soon be rent asunder.

Media Connection

Recipe for a Monster

He's big, he's green, he's mean, and his breath is radioactive. Godzilla—named "Gojira" in his native Japan—has been stomping on Tokyo since 1954, when he made his movie debut. A dinosaur transformed into a giant monster as the result of atomic testing, Godzilla's appearance was created by scientists and sculptors using the ingredients below.

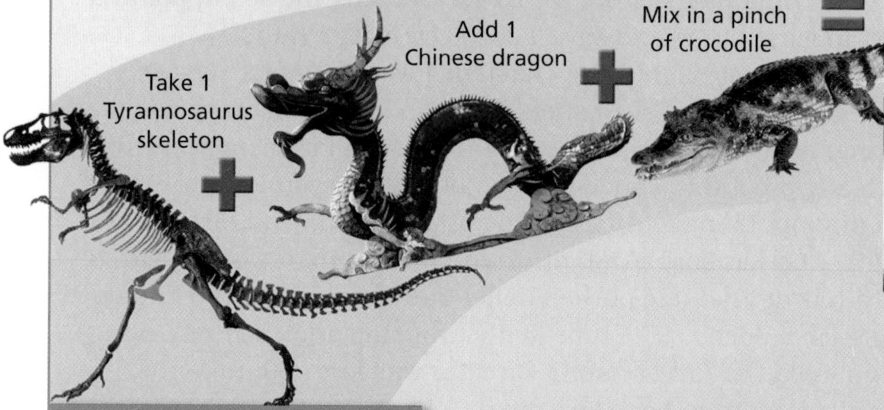

Take 1 Tyrannosaurus skeleton

Add 1 Chinese dragon

Mix in a pinch of crocodile

Raise the heat. Serve with a heaping portion of special effects.

Connect to the Literature

How do you think Alford's performance might have changed if Godzilla had been played by an actor instead of being a special effect?

Then seconds later a third THUMP!: Godzilla appears, causing the crowd, regardless of natal season, to shriek with abandon, perhaps to drop umbrellas or placards, and to run off in a prescribed direction.

Since I was born in February, my prescribed direction was straight ahead, up the thirty or so stairs of Federal Hall. So, hearing my thump, I would look behind me down Broad Street in highly nuanced, ever-burgeoning panic; erupt into a despair-tinged, Edvard Munch-calibre scream[6] on hearing the third thump; run northward, negotiating my way through what was, by now, a very festival of bad acting; ascend the stairs two at a time; look behind me again while closing my umbrella (note the elegant adherence to decorum, even in the face of apocalypse); and then hurl my body against Federal Hall's massive stone doors in an attempt to gain entry.

I loved this work. I would be hard-pressed to recount any event from my personal or professional life that more accurately typified the phrase crazy fun. Yes, my colleagues and I encountered much wetness; the rain machines were assiduous in their ministrations. Moreover, no lines of dialogue were being doled out by the director

Vocabulary
assiduous (ə sij´ ōō əs)
adj. done with constant and careful attention

Reading Check

How do the film-makers divide the crowd of extras into groups?

---

6. **Edvard Munch-calibre scream** an outcry with the intensity of *The Scream*, a famous painting by Norwegian artist Edvard Munch [munk] (1863–1944), which shows a person screaming.

from Big Kiss **999**

or assistant directors. But the acting task at hand wedded blitzkrieg-strength drama with stuntman-strength athleticism and, as such, was wholly engaging. Screaming at full force in the canyons of Wall Street on a Sunday morning was particularly liberating. On the first few takes (by the end of the day we would do more than twenty) I would yell, "There he is!" By the eighth take I was screaming, "Here comes trouble!" By the late afternoon, punchy, I was shrieking, in an accent vaguely Caribbean, vaguely Cockney, "'Zilla monster ate me baby!" causing the self-appointed expert to glare at me and say, "Let's keep it real, huh?"

This statement might have chastened were it not for the other extras. Seldom have I seen such a preponderance of scenery-chewing; my colleagues' every utterance and movement seemed to offer ready proof that vaudeville[7] is not dead. Several of the extras, in an attempt to make themselves noticed, would run directly at the camera. Another one, a tall, fiftysomething woman who appeared to be a recent graduate of the Lucille Ball School of Clown Makeup, made such a spectacle of repeatedly dropping and then retrieving her umbrella that an assistant director was forced to take the umbrella away from her; the woman, divested of her gimmick, then devoted her energies to shrieking.

"That woman just screamed right in my eardrum," the ESL tutor told me between takes, motioning with her head toward the offender.

"Yes," I acknowledged, "her work is particularly broad."

Literary Analysis
Satire Explain the role of irony in the comedy surrounding the extras' hopes to be noticed and their actual experiences.

Literary Analysis
Satire Explain the role of sarcasm in the last line of the text.

---

7. **vaudeville** (vôd′ vil) old-fashioned stage shows of mixed specialty acts, including songs, dances, and comic skits.

Critical Thinking

1. **Respond:** Would you want to be an extra in a movie? Explain.

2. **(a)** According to Alford's opening paragraph, what is every extra's dream? **(b) Analyze:** Even though his dream does not come true, does he still feel his experience was worthwhile? Explain.

3. **(a)** What are Alford and the other extras required to do during the scene? **(b) Generalize:** What do they actually do? **(c) Analyze:** Why do they do so much more than required?

Do our differences define us?
(a) What tricks do the extras try to make themselves "different" for the camera? **(b)** How do these tricks backfire? **(c)** What or whom do you think the author is mocking, or making fun of? Explain.

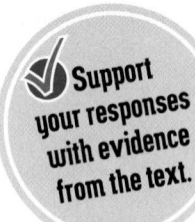
Support your responses with evidence from the text.

Comparing Satire

1. (a) Use a chart like the one shown to identify elements of satire in both *The Importance of Being Earnest* and *Big Kiss*. **(b)** Explain specific ways in which both selections use humor to expose people's foolishness or flaws. **(c)** Explain the roles of **irony** and **sarcasm** in these literary works.

Selection	Subject of the Satire	Foolishness or Faults Exposed	Irony or Sarcasm
The Importance of Being Earnest			
Big Kiss			

2. (a) Which selection satirizes serious social issues, and which one satirizes trivial or lighthearted issues? **(b)** Which selection is harsher toward the people it satirizes? Explain.

 College Readiness | **Timed Writing**

Write to Compare Satire

The perspective, or vantage point, of the writer helps shape the satire. In *The Importance of Being Earnest*, Wilde is not part of the events he satirizes. In the excerpt from *Big Kiss*, Alford is a participant in the action. In an essay, discuss how these different perspectives affect the satire. (35 minutes)

 5-Minute Planner

1. Read the prompt carefully and completely.

2. Note your answers to the following questions:

   • What purpose do you think Wilde had in writing this play about Victorian society?

   • What subtle hints in the text reveal Wilde's view of his characters?

   • Does Alford's point of view make him more, or less, sympathetic to the other actors he satirizes?

   • How do Alford's inner thoughts add to the humor of the satire?

   • Which text clues suggest Alford's level of seriousness about his topic?

   • Which satire do you think is more successful? Why?

3. Reread the prompt. Then, refer to your notes as you draft your essay.

Research Writing: Research Report

Defining the Form A **research report** presents and interprets information gathered through the extensive study of a subject. You might use elements of research in writing lab reports, documentaries, and histories.

Assignment Gather ideas and information on a subject that is both interesting and worth exploring in depth. Then, **synthesize,** or bring together, your research in a research report of a length specified by your teacher that includes:

✔ *evidence* in support of a clear thesis statement and related claims

✔ an *analysis* for the audience that reflects a logical progression of ideas and a clearly stated point of view

✔ *graphics and illustrations* that help explain concepts where appropriate

✔ proper *documentation of sources* and *formatting* of written materials according to a style manual

✔ error-free grammar, including correct use of adverb clauses

To preview the criteria on which your report may be judged, see the rubric on page 1013.

 Texas Writing Workshop: *Work in Progress*

Review the work you did on page 977.

WRITE GUY
Jeff Anderson, M.Ed.

What Do You Notice?

Examples that Build an Argument

This excerpt is from Alan Axelrod's historical research study *Nothing To Fear: Lessons in Leadership from FDR*. Read it several times.

He could then and there have given in to the fog of fear, but he chose not to. He chose instead to understand polio, to see clearly the extent of his disability, and then to assess—also clearly—his options for overcoming that disability.

What do you notice about these sentences? Discuss your observations with a partner. Consider how you can use examples to build an argument in your research report.

Focus on the TEKS

Research

(20)(A) Brainstorm, consult with others, decide upon a topic, and formulate a major research question to address the major research topic.

(20)(B) Formulate a plan for engaging in research on a complex, multi-faceted topic.

(21)(A) Follow the research plan to compile data from authoritative sources in a manner that identifies the major issues and debates within the field of inquiry.

(23)(A);(B);(C);(E) Synthesize the research into a written presentation that: marshals evidence in support of a clear thesis statement and related claims; provides an analysis for the audience that reflects a logical progression of ideas and a clearly stated point of view; uses graphics and illustrations to help explain concepts where appropriate; and uses a style manual to document sources and format written materials.

Reading-Writing Connection

To get a feel for research writing, read the excerpt from *Nothing To Fear* by Alan Axelrod on page 567.

Prewriting/Planning Strategies

Use the following strategies to decide upon a topic for research:

Brainstorm for a topic. Identify an area of general interest and list specific related categories. For example, from the area of art, you might list the following: sculpture, painting, and ceramics. Repeat the process: from painting, you might list Impressionism, Cubism, and Pop Art. Continue listing categories until you find a topic to research.

Consult with others. With a partner, discuss topics you are considering for your research. Ask your partner for feedback about your ideas including whether the topics may be too narrow or too broad to adequately cover in a single research report.

Formulate a major research question. Before you begin, compose a question about your topic. The question should be open-ended, allowing you to explore many areas of your topic while researching answers. It should however, also be limited enough so that the amount of research required is reasonable to accomplish. This question may become your thesis statement, or it may lead up to it.

> **Sample Question:** *How did the school of painting called Impressionism begin?*

Formulate a plan. In order to engage in research on a **complex, multi-faceted topic,** first formulate a plan. Your plan might include places to conduct research such as the library and Internet. It may also include types of sources to consult such as encyclopedias, newspapers, or individuals. Be sure to consider the reliability of sources as you plan.

Gathering Sources and Details

Follow your research plan. Compile data from authoritative sources in a manner that identifies the major issues and debates within your field of inquiry. Use a variety of primary and secondary sources to get a full view of your topic. Use **primary sources** (firsthand or original accounts, such as interview transcripts and newspaper articles) and **secondary sources** (accounts that are not original, such as encyclopedia entries).

Find appropriate sources. Analyze and assess your sources to be sure they are appropriate to the purpose of your report and your audience. You may find the information you need in specialized resources such as almanacs, government publications, and information services. Also, consider consumer, workplace, and public documents. Consult your librarian on the best sources to use.

TEXAS
PHLitOnline
www.PHLitOnline.com

- Author video: Writing Process
- Author video: Rewards of Writing

Gathering Sources and Details *(continued)*

You can find sources of specific information through an online search, a card catalog, or these more complex resources:

- **Databases:** Access databases of information to find appropriate sources. For example, the Modern Language Association (MLA) database indexes articles on humanities topics.

- **Indexes:** Locate magazine or newspaper articles by consulting the *Readers' Guide to Periodical Literature.*

Sample *Readers' Guide* Entry

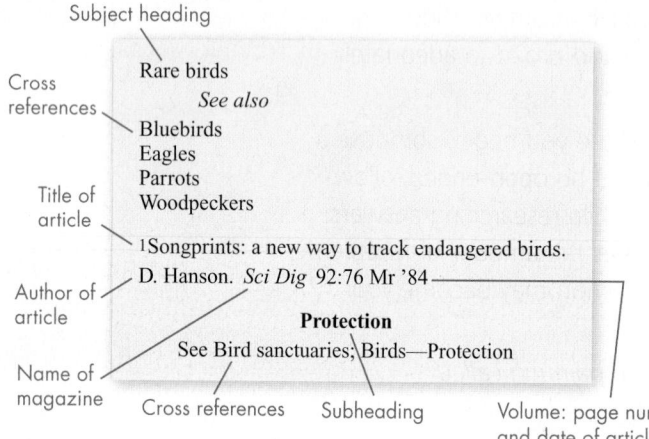

Subject heading

Cross references

Title of article

Author of article

Name of magazine

Cross references   Subheading

Rare birds
  See also
Bluebirds
Eagles
Parrots
Woodpeckers
¹Songprints: a new way to track endangered birds.
D. Hanson. *Sci Dig* 92:76 Mr '84

Protection
See Bird sanctuaries; Birds—Protection

Volume: page numbers and date of article

Evaluate the relevance of information. The information in your report should be closely related to your topic. In each source you consider, analyze the **relevance, quality,** and **credibility** of evidence given to support or oppose an argument for a specific audience.

Organize the information you gather. Take notes and keep a reference list of the multiple sources you use. This will help you to analyze and **make distinctions** between the relative value and significance of specific **data, facts,** and **ideas.** Consider these **forms:**

- **Source Cards** Make a card that identifies the author, title, publisher, city, date of publication, and page number of each source you consult. For Internet sources, record the name and Web address of the site, and the date you accessed the information.

- **Note Cards** For each item of information, make a card that includes both the fact or idea and its source. You may also use **electronic note-taking software.**

Source Card   [A]

Marsh, Peter, M.D. *Eye to Eye: How People Interact.* Topsfield, MA: Salem House Publishers, 1988.

(p. 54)

Note Card

Gestures vary from culture to culture. The American "OK" symbol (thumb and forefinger) is considered insulting in Greece and Turkey.

Source Card: A

Apply It!

Focus on the TEKS

Reading
(10)(A) Analyze the relevance, quality, and credibility of evidence given to support or oppose an argument for a specific audience.

Writing
(16)(E) Write an argumentative essay that includes an analysis of the relative value of specific data, facts, and ideas.

Research
(21)(B) Organize information gathered from multiple sources to create a variety of forms.

(21)(C) Paraphrase, summarize, and quote researched information.

(22)(A);(B);(C) Modify the major research question as necessary to refocus the research plan. Evaluate the relevance of information to the topic. Critique the research process at each step to implement changes as the need occurs and is identified.

(23)(A);(B);(C) Synthesize the research into a written presentation that: marshals evidence in support of a clear thesis statement and related claims; provides an analysis for the audience that reflects a logical progression of ideas and a clearly stated point of view; and uses graphics and illustrations to help explain concepts where appropriate.

Drafting Strategies

Modify the major research question as necessary. Before you begin drafting, revisit your open-ended research question. If the information you have gathered does not adequately answer the question, consider modifying the question to **refocus** the research plan. Then, return to gathering sources and information, following your revised plan.

Propose a clear thesis. Write a sentence that takes a position and can be supported by most of your research. A **thesis statement** is a controlling idea that gives your essay coherence.

- **Sample Thesis Statement:** *Claude Monet's use of light in his water-lily paintings typifies Impressionist techniques.*

Marshal evidence in support of your thesis statement. Include details and information in your essay that directly support your thesis statement as well as any **related claims.** Use these options to incorporate facts, examples, and quotations that support your proposition:

- **Direct Quotation:** Enclose a writer's exact words in quotation marks. Omissions should not alter the intent of the passage. Indicate omitted words with **ellipses,** or dots.
- **Paraphrase:** Restate a writer's specific ideas in your own words, accurately reflecting the writer's meaning.
- **Summary:** Condense an extended idea into a brief statement in your own words to introduce background information or review key ideas.

Provide an analysis for the audience. A well-written research report interprets facts for readers. Be sure your report reflects a **logical progression of ideas** and a **clearly stated point of view.**

Credit your sources. To avoid **plagiarism**—presenting another's work as your own—include documentation every time you use another writer's ideas. Note the author's last name and the page numbers of material used. Later, use these notes to create formal citations.

Quote accurately. Responsible research begins with the first note you take. Be sure to paraphrase, summarize, and quote your sources accurately so you can identify these sources later. In your notes, circle all quotes and paraphrases to distinguish them from your own comments. When photo-copying from a source, include the copyright information. Also, remember to include the Web addressess of printouts from online sources.

Use graphics and illustrations. Where appropriate, include visual aids to help explain concepts.

Critique the research process. Evaluate your plan at each step and implement changes as the need occurs and is identified. Good research techniques often include returning to earlier steps and improving plans.

Revising Strategies

Determine the reliability, validity, and accuracy of sources. Once you have a first draft, read it to improve your work. Evaluate your sources (including **Internet sources**) by examining their **authority,** or ability to supply reliable information, and **objectivity,** or lack of bias. Note any fact in your draft that may not have a trustworthy source. Try to confirm this information in a more reliable source, such as an established encyclopedia, a scholarly Web site, or a reputable newspaper. If you cannot verify the fact, consider removing it from the draft.

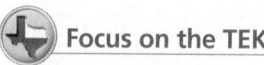 **Focus on the TEKS**

Reading
(1)(E) Use a thesaurus.

Writing
(13)(E) Revise final drafts in response to feedback from peers.

Research
(22)(B) Determine the reliability, validity, and accuracy of sources (including Internet sources) by examining their authority and objectivity.

> **Model: Evaluating Sources**
> A good way for people to convey a positive message is to avoid certain movements. ~~When people cross their arms it is always a sign of panic.~~

> This claim was supported by only one source. Since it was not important to her basic argument, the writer chose to delete it.

Use a thesaurus to vary word choice. Except for specific terminology required by your topic, avoid overuse of words and expressions. Review your draft to identify words that you may have overused. For each word, use a thesaurus (printed or electronic) to generate a list of possible synonyms, and substitute them as appropriate.

Example Synonym Banks

invention: innovation, development, contrivance, device

theory: belief, policy, system, position, idea, supposition

Peer Feedback

Exchange drafts with a partner. As you read each other's reports, circle or highlight words that recur repeatedly. Consider revising your final draft in response to this feedback from your peer by identifying word replacements to improve variety in your writing.

Revise to follow a consistent research format. As you finalize your report, be sure that it meets your teacher's criteria for length, format, and documentation of sources. The Modern Language Association (MLA) requires standardized parenthetical citations of sources and a works-cited list that includes only the sources used in the report.

Gary L. Blackwood

On Showing, Not Telling

To me, research is as much fun as beachcombing: You never know what fascinating items you're going to find. Since books are generally more reliable than the Internet, I do most of my beachcombing in libraries. I know that some people consider nonfiction dull, but I find good nonfiction more compelling than a novel, because I know the events really happened. Who could invent a story as singular and mysterious as that of Kaspar Hauser, which I came upon while researching my four-volume work *Unsolved History*?

"It helps to read sentences aloud."
—Gary L. Blackwood

---

from *"Perplexing People,"*
a volume in the *Unsolved History* series published by Benchmark Books (Marshall Cavendish) Sept. 2005

~~Sometime in the afternoon of~~ On May 26, 1828, a peculiar boy of about sixteen appeared, seemingly from nowhere, on a street in the German city of Nuremberg. His clothing was shabby and ill-fitting and he walked with a ~~peculiar~~ strange waddling gait, as though intoxicated. His face wore a vacant expression; he spoke and understood only a few words. Within a year he would become one of the ~~best known and most discussed~~ most celebrated and controversial people in Europe. . . .

The police questioned the boy, but his replies consisted of two phrases in ungrammatical German: "Don't know" and "I want to be a horseman as my father is." When they gave him paper and a pen ~~and asked to write his name and address,~~ he produced a series of scribbles, of which only two were intelligible: "cavalryman" and "Kaspar Hauser."

Writing can be factual without also being sleep-inducing. I try to liven things up by using vivid adjectives.

To add interest and a feeling of authenticity, I use a lot of quotes from primary sources—people who actually witnessed or participated in the events or chroniclers of the time.

Good prose—whether it's fiction or nonfiction—is clear and concise. I do a lot of cutting of superfluous words and phrases, and I may reword a sentence half a dozen times before I'm satisfied with it.

Documenting Sources

You must give proper credit to the people whose ideas and words you have borrowed. Failing to do this raises legal and ethical issues. Libel, slander, copyright infringement, and plagiarism are serious accusations. Good writers **accurately cite all researched information.**

Use a style manual. When **documenting sources,** follow a specific **standard format.** Modern Language Association (MLA) style calls for citations in parentheses directly following the material being cited.

- For print works, provide the author's or editor's name followed by a page number. If the work does not have an author, use a keyword or phrase from the title.

  Citing a Print Work: . . . body language makes up approximately 65 percent of human communication (Aylesworth 3).

- For Web sources, give the author's name and the title of the article or site.

  Citing a Web Source: Pearson.com refers to the novel as a literary masterpiece ("Fleming Wins Award").

At the end of your report, give information for each source you cite. The MLA style guide calls for you to format this material into an alphabetical *Works-Cited* list.

- For books, give the author's name (first name last), the title of the work, the city of publication, the name of the publisher, and the year of publication.

  Entry for a Book: Aylesworth, Thomas G. *Understanding Body Talk.* New York: F. Watts, 1979.

- For articles in periodicals, give the author's last name, first name, title of the article, the name of the magazine, the date of the issue, the volume and issue number, and the pages of the article. For any month with more than four letters, abbreviate the month by using the first three letters followed by a period.

  Entry for a Periodical Article: Kreisler, Kristin V. "Why We Dream What We Dream." *Reader's Digest.* Feb. 1995: 28.

- For Web sites, give all information that is available, in this order: author, page title, site title, date of last update, and name of the sponsor. Give the date you consulted the site and its full URL, or Web address.

  Entry for a Web Page: "Fleming Wins Award." *Pearson.* 2009. Pearson PLC. 3 Mar. 2010 <http://pearson.com>.

For more information on citing sources using MLA style, see page R40.

 **Focus on the TEKS**

Research
(21)(C) Accurately cite all researched information according to a standard format.
(23)(E) Use a style manual (e.g., *Modern Language Association*) to document sources and format written materials.

Revising to Combine Sentences Using Adverb Clauses

Identifying Adverb Clauses A clause is any group of words with a subject and a verb. An *independent clause* can stand by itself as a complete sentence; a *subordinate clause* is not complete because it does not express a full idea. An *adverb clause* is a subordinate clause that modifies a verb, an adjective, or another adverb in a sentence. It begins with a subordinating conjunction that tells *where, when, in what way, to what extent, under what condition,* or *why.*

When:	*After I read the report,* I agreed with the mayor.
Condition:	Dan will ask for a refund *if you will go with him.*
In what way:	The bulldog yawned *as if he were utterly bored.*
Why:	I drew a map *so that they would not get lost.*

Adverb clauses can be used to combine information from two sentences into one sentence. Often, the revised sentence will make the intended meaning more obvious.

Two sentences:	I joined the panel. Jay is the leader.
Combined:	I joined the panel because Jay is the leader.

Combining Sentences When combining two short sentences using adverb clauses, follow these steps:

1. **Look for a relationship between the ideas of the two clauses.**

2. **Select the appropriate subordinate conjunction to show that relationship.** Place the adverb clause at the beginning or end of the combined sentence—wherever it conveys your intent more clearly.

3. **Use a comma to separate a subordinate clause only when it begins a sentence.**

PH GRAMMAR HANDBOOK

Further instruction and practice are available in the *Prentice Hall Grammar Handbook*.

Grammar in Your Writing
Review your report and highlight any consecutive short sentences that you find. Look for a possible adverbial relationship (*where, when, in what way,* and so on) in two of the sentences. Following the steps outlined here, combine the sentences using an appropriate subordinating conjunction.

Common Subordinate Conjunctions			
after	because	since	when
although	before	so that	whenever
as	even though	unless	whether
as soon as	if	until	while

Student Model: Lyndsey Regan, Canyon Country, CA

Body Language

When we speak to other people, they are not only listening to our actual words, but sensing our facial expression, tone of voice, gestures, level of eye contact, posture, and movements as well. Nonverbal communication, or body language, makes up approximately 65 percent of human communication (Aylesworth 3). Body language has a major impact on how others perceive what we say. It can also be a tool for miscommunication when the speaker and listener are from different cultures or are communicating through technology that deprives them of visual cues. In fact, we often realize the importance of body language only when we cannot interpret someone else's body language correctly.

In *Eye to Eye: How People Interact*, Dr. Peter Marsh explains that before we speak, our gestures, posture, and facial expressions are already broadcasting messages to those around us. While we are speaking, these gestures continue to communicate messages—usually clarifying what we are saying, but sometimes contradicting us in telltale ways (Marsh 116–119).

Often, body language is an unconscious act that triggers the most developed senses in other people—hearing and sight (Aylesworth 18). That is why body language is such a great way to emphasize words and ideas. Many people take advantage of this. Advertisers, for example, cast actors in their commercials who use body language that appeals to viewers.

Studies have shown that people's body language changes when they are not telling the truth (Vrij, Edward, Roberts, and Bull 239–263). If someone's body language is inconsistent with what he or she is saying, people tend to believe what the body is telling them. A good way for people to convey a positive message is to avoid certain movements, like fidgeting or letting your eyes wander. Instead, good communicators maintain steady eye contact, nod in agreement, and smile. You may notice that people on television, like hosts of infomercials and talk-shows, generally display this positive body language when speaking.

Body language is usually learned, but it can also be inherited. It is affected by age, gender, background, and situation. The meaning of body language can change

The opening line captures the reader's attention by presenting a surprising perspective.

Lyndsey expresses her thesis statement clearly and concisely.

Lyndsey smoothly introduces a research source and explains the ideas it provided.

depending on cultural context. According to Dr. Marsh, each culture has developed its own repertoire of symbolic gestures, many with original associations that have now long been forgotten (Marsh 53–54). This causes people to be alarmed by foreign visitors or nervous around people when they visit new countries.

In the United States, people have a wide variety of regional influences because the country is a melting pot of diverse cultures. A gesture that means the same thing throughout the Unite States is the "OK" sign made with the thumb and forefinger. This gesture is interpreted similarly in some European countries, but if you were to perform this sign in Greece or Turkey, it would be considered very insulting (Marsh 54).

There are other cultural differences in body language within Europe. In Germany, body language often reflects social status, and Germans often use body language for emphasis. Italian gestures are often passionate, emotional expressions communicated with the face, arms, and shoulders. Italians often use body language to clarify themselves or to express urgency. In France, people tend to use more formal gestures. They are generally not as expressive or insistent as Italians. The body language of the French is not nearly as casual as we are used to in America (Ruesch and Kees 23–25). As you can see by exploring a few examples from different cultures, there are many differences in body language. Therefore, when you communicate with people from other countries, take special care in your use of body language.

Technological advancements in our society affect the way we communicate. For example, when we speak on the telephone, we are unable to see the person on the other end of the line. The message that a person may be trying to convey may be misinterpreted without the additional visual information provided by his or her body language. With electronic mail, there is no visual or verbal communication whatsoever. As a result, people cannot completely understand the meaning of what is being communicated. Therefore, people using e-mail should be careful about what they write. To avoid miscommunication, communicating the old-fashioned way—in person—may be the best approach.

Whenever Lyndsey presents a specific piece of evidence that is not her own idea or common knowledge, she cites it using the appropriate format.

Here, Lyndsey makes a claim and then provides evidence in support of that claim.

In conclusion, body language is a significant component of communication, even though we are often not aware of it. Body language, like facial expression and gestures, frequently enables people to clearly understand one another, but we must remember that people cannot always be read like a book. With cultural differences, body language can take on different meanings, and this allows for potential miscommunication. Changes in technology present a different kind of problem, but with a similar result. When body language cannot be seen, people may misinterpret the meaning of the communicator, making them angry or confused. As you can see, the additional information we provide with our body language plays a major role in how we communicate our thoughts and ideas.

Works-Cited List

Aylesworth, Thomas G. *Understanding Body Talk.* New York: F. Watts, 1979.

Marsh, Peter, M.D. *Eye to Eye: How People Interact.* Topsfield, MA: Salem House Publishers, 1988.

Ruesch, Jurgen, and Weldon Kees. *Nonverbal Communication: Notes on the Visual Perception of Human Relations.* Berkeley, CA: University of California Press, 1969.

Vrij, Aldert, Katherine Edward, Kim P. Roberts, and Ray Bull. "Detecting Deceit via Analysis of Verbal and Nonverbal Behavior." *Journal of Nonverbal Behavior,* Winter 2000: 239–263.

 Focus on the TEKS

Writing
(13)(D) Edit drafts for grammar, mechanics, and spelling.
(15)(D) Produce a multimedia presentation with graphics, images, and sound that conveys a distinctive point of view and appeals to a specific audience.

Conventions
(18)(A) Use conventions of capitalization.
(19) Spell correctly, including using various resources to check correct spellings.

Research
(23)(D) Synthesize the research into a written or an oral presentation that uses a variety of evaluative tools to examine the quality of the research.

After her conclusion, Lyndsey presents the complete information for the works cited in her report using MLA, a common style for citation.

Editing and Proofreading

Edit your draft for errors in grammar and mechanics, such as punctuation. Use various resources as you edit to check correct spellings.

Focus on Format: Follow the manuscript requirements by including an appropriate title page, pagination, spacing and margins, and citations. Make sure you have used the preferred system for crediting sources in your paper and for bibliographical sources at the end. Double-check that you have used the **conventions** of punctuation and **capitalization** correctly.

Publishing and Presenting

Research is an ongoing, cyclical process. Consider one of the following ways to share your writing. Ask for your audience's feedback, and use it, along with your own thoughts and assessments, as an **evaluative tool** with which to examine the quality of your research.

Produce a multimedia presentation. Read your research report aloud to your class, or consider producing the report as a multimedia presentation. Add appropriate graphics, images, and sound that convey a specific point of view and appeal to your intended audience.

Organize a panel discussion. If several of your classmates have written on a similar topic, plan a discussion to compare and contrast your findings. Speakers can summarize their research before opening the panel to questions from the class.

Reflecting on Your Writing

Jot down your answer to this question:

How did writing a research report affect your understanding of your topic?

Rubric for Self-Assessment

Find evidence in your writing to address each category. Then, use the rating scale to grade your work.

Spiral Review
Earlier in this unit you learned about **restrictive** and **nonrestrictive relative clauses** (p. 976). Make sure you use these parts of speech correctly in your research report.

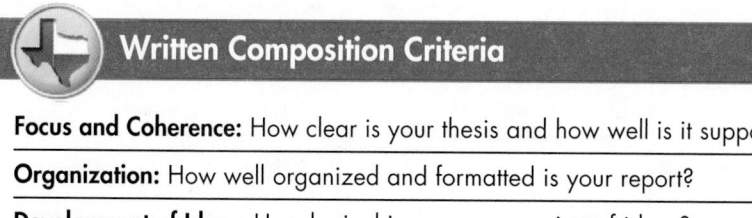

Written Composition Criteria	Rating Scale
	not very very
Focus and Coherence: How clear is your thesis and how well is it supported by evidence?	1 2 3 4
Organization: How well organized and formatted is your report?	1 2 3 4
Development of Ideas: How logical is your progression of ideas?	1 2 3 4
Conventions: How complete and correct is your source documentation?	1 2 3 4
Voice: How clearly is your point of view stated?	1 2 3 4

Applying the Big Question

Do our differences define us?

Think About It

Think about what you have read in this unit and what you have learned about whether people are defined by their differences. Also think about what you have learned about differences in your other classes and from your own experience. Copy and complete the chart below to apply what you have learned about differences. One row has been completed for you.

Example	Kinds of differences	The effect of the differences	What I learned
From Literature	Differences in authority and position in "The Inspector-General"	The peasant outsmarts the powerful inspector-general.	Differences in authority and position don't define how clever someone is.
From Literature			
From Science			
From Social Studies			
From Your Life			

Talk About It

Choose one of the examples from your communication chart to develop in a **persuasive speech** about the Big Question. Begin by preparing notecards about the example. Write quotations and other details that support your position. Add additional reasons you can give. Then, organize your notecards in the order you will present the ideas. As you plan your speech, remember to clearly state your position in your introduction. Then, present your arguments and supporting details. In your conclusion, summarize your arguments and restate your position. As you give your presentation, employ **eye contact, speaking rate, volume, enunciation, purposeful gestures,** and **conventions of language,** or proper grammar, to communicate ideas effectively.

Write About It

At the beginning of Unit 5, you wrote a response to the Big Question. Now that you have completed the unit, write a new response, discussing how your initial ideas have either been changed or reinforced.

- ❏ Differences define who we are.
- ❏ Differences do not define who we are.
- ❏ My own response: _____.

Support your answer with one or more of the examples in your chart.

Challenge What issues does the Big Question still raise for you? How could you continue your exploration?

 **Connecting to Citizenship**

Group Discussion With a small team, discuss how understanding differences between people can help you become a thoughtful and active citizen. Then, share key points from your discussion with the class. Consider these questions in your discussion:

- How might differences affect citizens in a community?
- Why might it be important to understand the reasons for particular differences between people?
- How might your own differences bring you closer to other members of your community?
- How can understanding the differences between people in your community make you a more thoughtful, active citizen?

During your discussion, remember to listen attentively to your teammates as they speak. Also, be sure to participate productively by building on the ideas of others and contributing relevant information to the team discussion.

 **Focus on the TEKS**

Listening and Speaking
(25) Give presentations employing eye contact, speaking rate, volume, enunciation, purposeful gestures, and conventions of language to communicate ideas effectively.
(26) Participate productively in teams, building on the ideas of others and contributing relevant information.

Big Question Vocabulary

Use some of these words as you complete the activities on these pages.

background
differentiate
similarity
understanding
accept
discriminate
individuality
unique
conformity
values
determine
differences
culture
defend
assimilated

This list includes academic vocabulary words, which are defined on pp. R1–R14.

Vocabulary Workshop

Borrowed and Foreign Words

English has more words than any other language. Many of these words are taken directly from other languages. At first, these new words are treated as **foreign words.**

Over time, as the words become common in everyday speech, most are accepted into the language and considered to be English. These words are called **borrowed words.** This chart shows some common borrowed words that are now part of the English language.

Borrowed Words	Original Language
ballet, cavalry, infantry, bigot	French
cargo, canyon, ranch, tornado	Spanish
chipmunk (Algonquian), pecan (Illinois), raccoon (Virginia Algonquian), moccasin (Algonquian)	Native American
bandanna, pajamas, thug, shampoo	Hindi
kindergarten, hamburger, dollar, vandal	German

Some words are not fully adopted into the language and are always treated as foreign words. Some of these words are written in italics. Dictionaries often indicate words that should be italicized. This chart describes the origins and meanings of some foreign words and phrases used frequently in written English.

au courant	French	up-to-date, informed on current affairs
mot juste	French	the exact, appropriate word
carpe diem	Latin	seize the day, or live for the day
nom de plume	French	a pen name
verboten	German	forbidden, prohibited

Practice A Use a dictionary to determine and describe the origins (or etymologies) and meanings (or denotations) of these foreign words and phrases used frequently in written English.

1. caveat emptor
2. *carte blanche*
3. tete a tete
4. pas de deux
5. *quid pro quo*
6. *Wanderjahr*

Focus on the TEKS

Reading
(1)(D) Describe the origins and meanings of foreign words or phrases used frequently in written English (e.g., *caveat emptor, carte blanche, tete a tete, pas de deux, bon appetit, quid pro quo*).

(1)(E) Use a dictionary to determine the meanings of words and phrases, including their denotations and their etymology.

Practice B Use a dictionary to determine the meanings (or denotations) of these borrowed and foreign words and phrases used frequently in written English. Then, complete each sentence with the correct term. Finally, describe the origins (or etymologies) of each word or phrase.

TEXAS
PHLitOnline
www.PHLitOnline.com

• Illustrated vocabulary words
• Interactive vocabulary games
• Vocabulary flashcards

mesa	*bon appétit*	*mano a mano*
algebra	RSVP	sushi
Weltschmerz	*fait accompli*	

1. After turning in his report, Alexis declared it a _____ .

2. Joshua really enjoyed eating the _____ until someone told him it was raw fish.

3. It was a steep climb to the top of the _____ , but then the ground became level.

4. I usually do well in _____ , but that one equation puzzled me.

5. "Tyler," said the smaller boy, "I challenge you to a game of basketball _____ ."

6. The card said _____ , so I immediately called Megan and accepted the invitation.

7. The chef served his famous dish, saying, "_____ " to his guests.

8. Each haunting line of the novel revealed the author's _____ .

Activity Prepare four notecards like the one shown. Write one of these foreign phrases on each card: *hoi polloi, savoir faire, vis-à-vis, ad hoc.* Then, use a dictionary to describe the origins and meanings of each foreign phrase used frequently in written English. Finally, write a sentence in which you correctly use each phrase.

Teamwork
Use a dictionary to determine and describe the origins (or etymologies), meanings (or denotations), and pronunciations of these foreign phrases used frequently in written English: *persona non grata, voilà, coup de grace, per se.* Then, use the words in a paragraph. Finally, meet with a partner and critique each other's word usage. Read the paragraphs aloud, being careful to pronounce the words correctly.

Phrase: _____

Origin: _____

Meaning: _____

Sentence: _____

Evaluating Formality and Tone

Focus on the TEKS

Reading
(12)(D) Evaluate changes
in formality and tone within
the same medium for specific
audiences and purposes.

Messages in media have specific purposes and are targeted for particular audiences. Examples from the same media, or method of communication, may use varying levels of formality and tone to appeal to different audiences or to achieve different purposes.

Learn the Skills

Use the skills below to evaluate the examples on this page for changes in formality and tone for specific audiences and purposes. Record your observations and conclusions in your notes.

Identify and Analyze Formality A communication's level of formality may give you clues about its intended audience and its purpose. Ask yourself these questions about the communication:

- How formal or specialized are the words? What audience would be most likely to use or appreciate this kind of language?

- How does the formality help to reinforce the purpose?

Identify and Analyze Tone An author's tone can give more information about audience and purpose. Ask yourself these questions about the communication:

- What is the overall tone of the communication? How do the words and images contribute to this tone?

- Which audience would respond well to this tone? How might the tone help this audience listen to the message?

- How does the tone help the communication to achieve its purpose?

Nutritionists Praise Texas Schools

Your child's school cafeteria now offers healthier meals than ever before. School lunches are required by law to comply with the Dietary Guidelines for Americans that were released by the Department of Health and Human Services in 2005. Nutritionists have praised recent efforts in Texas school districts to meet these guidelines.

Some schools have replaced deep fryers with salad bars to cut saturated fats in students' diets. . . .

Food That Will Actually Fill You Up!

Does your stomach always growl in your last class of the day? If so, skip the chocolate cookies at lunch and eat some real food! Many students don't realize that the empty calories in soda and cookies can leave you hungry later in the day. Schools across Texas have added more fruits and veggies to their lunch menus, so you may have more options than you think. Chow down on some carrot sticks or a grilled chicken salad, and you'll feel great for the rest of the day!

Practice the Skills

Use the skills you've learned to complete the activity.

TEXAS
PHLitOnline
www.PHLitOnline.com

Apply the skills you have
learned in this workshop as
you watch the videos on
www.PHLitOnline.com.

ACTIVITY: Evaluate Formality and Tone

Compare the blogs below. Evaluate changes in formality and tone
between these communications of the same medium. Consider how
word choice enables the blogs' writers to reach specific audiences and
achieve particular purposes.

Driving Lessons

Becoming an Instructor

December 30

Because I own a driving school, I am often
approached by people who want to become driving
instructors. I have decided to post answers to some
frequently asked questions.

Q: How much does it cost to become a driving
instructor?

A: The cost of training varies based on the
provider. The application fee is $75.

Q: Does the license allow me to teach driving
wherever I want to?

A: You must teach in a licensed program.

My Life in Alpine, TX

I passed the test!

December 30

I finally got my license, and I feel like
I need to share all my new driving know-
how with all you other driving hopefuls out there!
Here are my tips for taking (and passing) that test:

1. First, you can't drive at all before you have your
   permit. Don't believe your friends if they tell you
   something different. You could get in tons of
   trouble.
2. You have to start a driving course before you get
   your permit.

Use the points below to analyze each blog.

- Who is the audience?
- What is the purpose?
- Rate the formality on a scale of 1 (very casual) to 10 (very formal).
    What elements of the communication helped you rate the formality?
    How well does this level of formality fit the audience and the purpose?
- How would you describe the tone?
    What elements of the communication helped you describe the tone?
    How well does this tone fit the audience and the purpose?

Share your notes with a partner. Then, work with your partner to select two
new pieces from another form of media. Look for pieces that seem to be aimed
at different audiences or that have different purposes. Use the points above to
analyze those pieces. Write a brief paragraph evaluating the changes in formality
and tone within the same medium for specific audiences and purposes.

Cumulative Review

DIRECTIONS Read the two selections and the viewing and representing piece. Then answer the questions that follow.

from Summer on Wheels

by Gary Soto

Hector and his friend Mando have been watching a film crew make a commercial in their neighborhood for bandages. The director casts Hector in the commercial.

1   "All you have to do is listen for 'Camera, speed, action.'"

2   "Camera, speed, action," Hector repeated. "Camera, speed, action."

3   "That's right. When I say 'action,' just give yourself two or three seconds, and then walk around the corner and fall."

4   The director turned to talk with the camera operator.

5   "I got it, I think," Hector whispered to himself. His heart was bloated like a frog from excitement.

6   A woman approached Hector. She powdered his face and combed his hair. She added a touch of color to his cheeks and for the fun of it, added a dab on Mando, who was watching with his mouth hanging open.

7   "We look like clowns," Mando remarked with a frown.

8   "We are," Hector said and hurried over to the director when he heard his name called.

9   The director put his arm around Hector. "Just be natural, Hector." He looked up at the sky for lighting. He took a reading with the light meter. He called for a wider lens. To Hector, the director cooed, "Go around, trip, and go through the routine. You got it?"

10   "I learned to trip in kindergarten. It's a piece of cake."

11   The director walked away from Hector, who was nervous and itchy. He wanted to scratch his nose, but he was worried about peeling off some of his makeup. Minutes passed. Bystanders looked at him. Some were eating popcorn and slurping on sodas. Then he heard, "Camera, speed, action!"

12   Hector breathed in a rush of dusty city air, muttered, "Here goes," and rounded the corner almost skipping. He took a few steps and threw himself into the air. He saw his life flash before his eyes. He saw his mom and dad and his three cats, plus Smiley, his lazy dog. He saw Mando and Mando's parents. He saw his dead grandfather, and each of his aunts and uncles, all of them gathered strangely around a backyard barbecue. He felt his whole life fly like a ghost into the air, including the hundred dollars, all in ones—crisp as autumn leaves. He landed with two skips on his belly, smack against the cement. Immediately, tears leaked from his eyes, blurring his vision. He hurt, but not so much that he forgot his role. He reached into his pocket for the bandages, blew on his scraped knee, and smiled through his tears for the camera.

13   "Cut," the director yelled with a swishing ponytail. He clapped his hands together, clapped and clapped, he was so happy. "Perfect! Perfect! Let's do it again."

TEKS Spiral Review

Reading

(1)(E) Use a dictionary to determine or confirm the meanings of words.

(2)(A) Analyze how the genre of texts with similar themes shapes meaning.

(5)(B) Analyze how authors develop complex yet believable characters in works of fiction through a range of literary devices.

(5)(C) Analyze the way in which a work of fiction is shaped by the narrator's point of view.

(6) Draw conclusions about the features of literary nonfiction.

(7) Explain the role of irony in literary works.

(12) Use comprehension skills to analyze how words, images, graphics, and sounds work together in various forms to impact meaning.

Reading/Comprehension Skills

RC-9(A) Reflect on understanding to monitor comprehension (e.g., summarizing).

RC-9(B) Make complex inferences about text.

Fly Away *by Ralph Helfer*

Expert animal trainer Ralph Helfer tells how he managed to "train" 5,000 flies for a movie— with the help of a capsule of harmless insect tranquilizer provided by a professor friend who specializes in insects.

1   The director, a big, friendly sort, came over to me with a suspicious look in his eyes. "Is it true?"

2   "What?"

3   "That you can put 5,000 flies on something and they'll crawl around, but you can guarantee they won't fly right off?"

4   "It's true."

5   "Then when I tell you to let them go, they'll all fly away immediately?"

6   "Give or take a few."

7   "A few what?"

8   "Flies that won't fly away."

9   "If you pull this off, I'll double your fee," he said in disbelief.

10   "Ready whenever you are," I said, and headed for my fly house.

11   The camera was set. The "dead thing" turned out to be a special-effects monster baby that had supposedly died a while back and was now to be swarming with flies. Somebody was to walk by, and the flies would then have to fly away.

12   Everything was ready.

13   The skeptical assistant director yelled for the "fly man." One of my trainers and I carried the fly house over and set it near the camera. The loud buzzing of an enormous number of flies was obvious. Sheets of heavy paper prevented anyone from seeing into the box.

14   "Now, Ralph, I'll roll the camera whenever you say—okay?" asked the director.

15   "Sure, but everything has to be ready. I've only got 10,042 flies—just enough for two shots."

16   His look told me he wasn't sure whether I was putting him on or not.

17   "10,042—really!" he mumbled, and walked over to the camera.

18   With everything set, I opened the small door of the fly house. Hiding the gas capsule in the palm of my hand and reaching inside, I broke it open, closed the door, and waited for fifteen seconds. To everybody's amazement, the buzzing stopped. Next, I opened the door and scooped out three or four handfuls of flies. I shook them out as one would when counting a pound of peanuts. Putting the little sleeping flies all over the "body," I began to dramatically count the last few: "Five-thousand twenty, five-thousand twenty-one, five-thousand twenty-one . . . that makes it half!"

19   I told everyone to hold still, then I gave the flies a verbal cue:

20   "Okay, guys—Jack, Bill, Mary—come on, up and at 'em!"

21   Slowly the flies started to awaken, then move around. In a few moments the whole mass of them was swarming all over the "thing," but they were still too drowsy to fly, as my professor friend had told me they would be.

22   "Okay, roll!" yelled the director. The camera rolled on to the fly swarm, and I shot a look at the crew. They appeared to be in shock. Then, having gotten enough footage, the director shouted, "Okay, Ralph, *now*!"

23   My great moment.

24   "Okay, group," I said to the flies. "Get ready: on the count of three, all of you take off."

25   The crew, absolutely bug-eyed (forgive the pun), was hypnotized.

26   "One," I counted. They looked from the flies to me.

27   "Two."

28   "Three!" I yelled, clapping my hands and stamping my foot at the same time. Five thousand twenty-one flies flew up, up, around and around. The camera hummed until the director, rousing himself from his amazed state, said, "Cut!"

29   The entire crew was silent for a moment, and then they burst into applause and delighted laughter.

30   "You did it, you really did it!" said the director, slapping me heartily on the back. "I'm not even going to ask you how. I don't even want to know. But if I ever need a trained *anything,* you're the man I'll call!"

GO ON ▶

Open Casting Call!

Do you have a special talent or unique skill?

Audition for a new documentary about talented teens!

Bring your scripts, music, or whatever you need to impress our talent scouts!

April 10 • **Long Center for the Performing Arts**

Use "Summer on Wheels" (p. 1020) to answer questions 1–3.

1 The author includes details of how Hector's life flashes before his eyes mainly to —

   A show that Hector sees his fall as very dramatic

   B reveal what Hector has been thinking during the filming

   C explain what onlookers see as Hector falls

   D provide background details about Hector's family

2 The reader can infer that the reason Hector scrapes his knee is that he is —

   F moving too quickly

   G wearing too much makeup

   H following the routine the director asked him to do

   J feeling nervous about performing in front of people

3 Which of the following is the best summary of the passage?

   A Hector talks with the director and his friend Mando; he has to bandage his knee after he falls.

   B Hector gets instructions and makeup. On cue, he falls, then bandages his knee; the happy director yells, "Cut!"

   C Hector feels nervous and excited. Thinking about his family helps him do what the director has asked.

   D Hector talks with the director. Later, Mando says they look like clowns, and Hector agrees with him.

Use "Fly Away" (p. 1021) to answer questions 4–6.

4 Read the following dictionary entry for the word *roll*.

roll \rōl\ *v* **1.** to move forward by turning over and over **2.** to cause to begin operating *n* **3.** an official list **4.** something that is rolled up into a cylinder

Which of these definitions matches the word *roll* as it appears in paragraph 14 of the story?

   F Definition 1

   G Definition 2

   H Definition 3

   J Definition 4

5 The crew and director are amazed at what the flies do because —

   A they know exactly how Helfer achieved the effect

   B the flies do not perform as Helfer predicts they will

   C the flies seem to be trained to respond to Helfer's commands

   D they are shocked to see so many flies at once

6 The way Helfer carries out his "training" of the flies suggests —

   F he does not know how to do his job

   G he is an expert who also enjoys surprising people

   H movie crews and directors are easily fooled

   J he always uses a scientific approach to train animals

GO ON

Use "Summer on Wheels" and "Fly Away" to answer questions 7 and 8.

7 Unlike the director in "Summer on Wheels," the director in "Fly Away" is —

A happy with the end result

B confident that the scene will be done perfectly

C concerned about lighting

D skeptical that the effect he wants can be achieved

8 Hector's actions in "Summer on Wheels" and Helfer's actions in "Fly Away" could both be considered examples of —

F an impossible task

G a successful performance

H technical expertise

J failure to follow directions

Use the visual representation on page 1022 to answer questions 9 and 10.

9 The photographs were probably chosen to —

A convince people to watch the documentary

B provide examples of people already in the movie

C illustrate the types of talent the scouts are looking for

D show popular people in the photographer's hometown

10 Based on the flyer, which of the following people would most likely qualify for the casting call?

F someone who is good at acrobatics

G someone who has just learned how to play tennis

H someone who watches documentaries

J someone who is better at math than science

DIRECTIONS

Answer the following questions on a separate sheet of paper.

11 Why is it ironic that the director in "Summer on Wheels" tells Hector to "just be natural"? Support your answer with details from the selection.

12 How are Helfer's actions in "Fly Away" dramatic? Explain your answer and support it with evidence from the selection.

13 How is the goal of achieving a dramatic moment important in both "Summer on Wheels" and "Fly Away"? Support your answer with details from **both** selections.

Do our *differences* define us?

Focus on the TEKS

Reading
(12)(D) Evaluate changes in formality within the same medium for specific audiences and purposes.

Media Literacy

The media uses differences between people to define audiences, or groups of people with similar interests. Media may customize presentations for different audiences by adjusting the formality of the communication. Identifying the level of formality in media can indicate the audience the presentation is trying to reach and the presentation's purpose. Use the graphic organizer below to evaluate changes in levels of formality within the same medium when viewing media such as the videos for this unit or other videos available to you.

TEXAS
PHLitOnline
www.PHLitOnline.com

Viewing and Listening Guide	
What to look for	**What you should think about**
Visual clues (graphics, colors)	• What visual elements stand out? • What level of formality do the visual elements suggest? • What does the formality indicate about the audience and purpose?
Auditory clues (type of music, word choice)	• What do the auditory elements tell me about the level of formality? • How well does this level of formality support the communication's purpose and target a specific audience?

Independent Reading

The Prince and the Pauper: A Pacemaker Classic
Mark Twain
Penguin Putnam, 1997
When a poor boy and the heir to the English throne swap places, both get a new perspective on themselves.

Twentieth-Century American Drama
Prentice Hall, 2000
These plays capture the experiences that define us as Americans and as people.

The Giant's House
Elizabeth McCracken
Dial, 2007
When a lonely librarian falls for a gigantic young man, the two start to see the world through one another's eyes.

The Strange Case of Dr. Jekyll and Mr. Hyde
Robert Louis Stevenson
Prentice Hall, 2000
As you read this novel of ambition and science gone wrong, you may redefine your own ideas about responsibility.

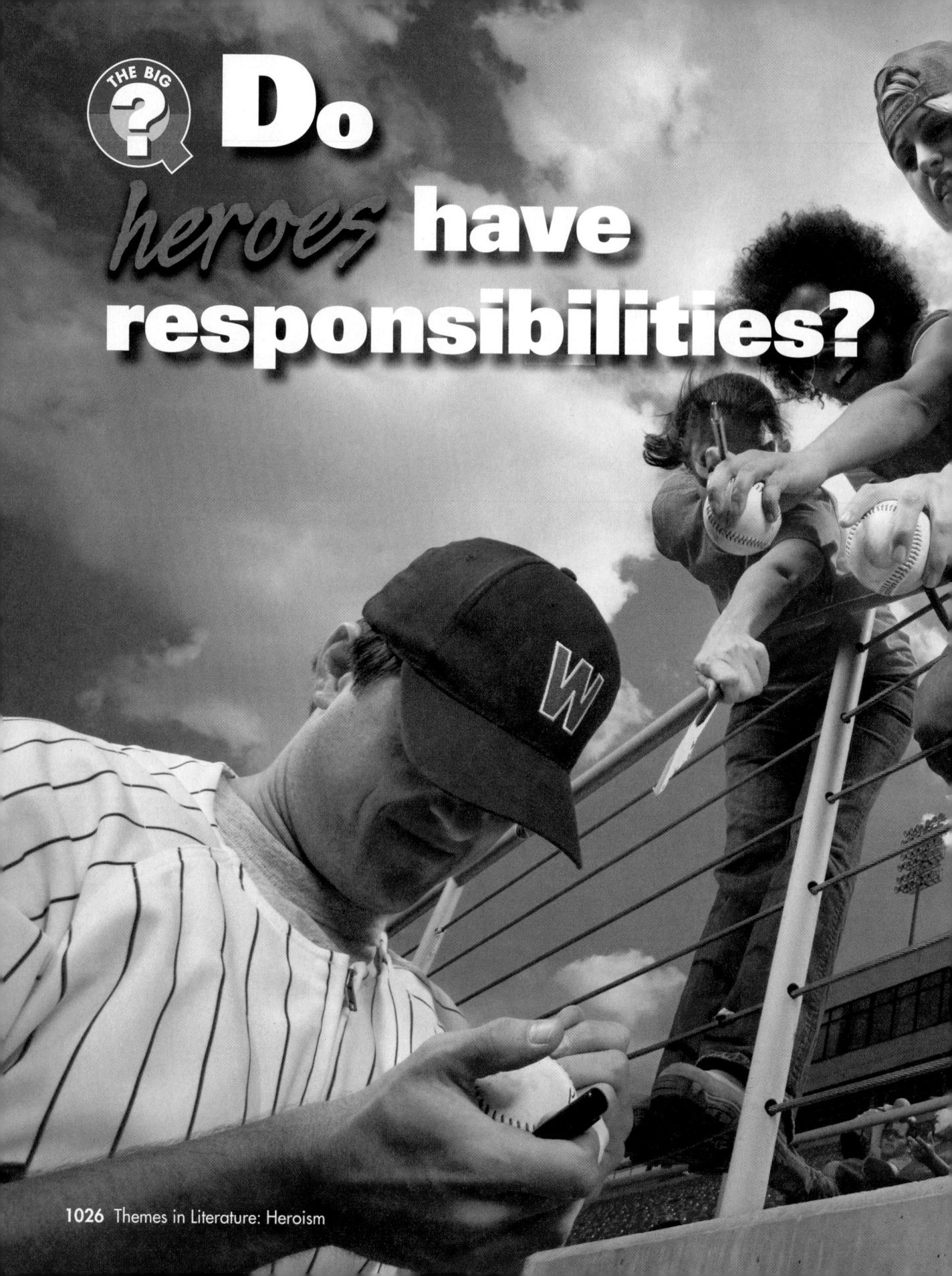

Do *heroes* have responsibilities?

Themes in Literature: Heroism

www.PHLitOnline.com

Hear It!
- Selection summary audio
- Selection audio
- Big Question Tunes

See It!
- Penguin author video
- Big Question video
- Get Connected videos
- Background videos
- More about the authors
- Illustrated vocabulary words
- Vocabulary flashcards

Do It!
- Interactive journals
- Interactive graphic organizers
- Grammar tutorials
- Interactive vocabulary games
- Test practice

Introducing the Big Question

 **Do** *heroes* **have responsibilities?**

Heroes are all around us. We find them in literature and in the real world. Heroes sometimes show strength of **character** and an unusual depth of **wisdom.** They make important **choices** and selflessly get **involved** when others might stand back. Heroes may **serve** others and fight for **justice.** Often, they exhibit outstanding courage, **honesty,** and leadership, but sometimes they do not have any of these qualities. They are just ordinary, unassuming people who somehow stand up in a crisis and act in heroic ways. Think about who these heroes are and what makes them act. Is it **character**? Is it a sense of **responsibility**?

Begin thinking about the Big Question by analyzing what you know and how you know it.

Tell What You Know

List heroes that you know about. They might be people you know personally or have read about in literature, history books, or the newspaper. They might be people you have watched on TV shows or in movies. Describe a **hero** from each of these categories.

- A hero whose **courageous** act saves or protects those who are in danger
- A hero who chooses **honesty** or integrity over self-interest
- A leader who guides others to success
- A hero who sacrifices himself or herself in order to **serve** others

Share your list with a small team. Talk about whether a sense of responsibility motivated these heroes to act. When a classmate speaks, listen responsively by asking questions related to the content of his or her comments for clarification or elaboration. Consider your own views in light of what your classmates have said. As you talk with your team, participate productively by building on the ideas of others when you speak.

TEXAS
PHLitOnline
www.PHLitOnline.com

- Big Question video
- Illustrated vocabulary words
- Interactive vocabulary games
- Big Question Tunes

Explain What You Know

Use the examples and ideas you discussed with your partner to help complete these sentences about heroes and responsibility.

- Most heroes act because they _____.
- The **choices** a hero makes involve _____.
- A **hero** may feel **responsibility** to _____.
- A hero thinks of himself or herself _____ and others _____.
- Someone who becomes a hero confronts danger because _____.

Share your responses with a partner.

Write What You Think

Based on the discussions, decide what you think right now. Your answer may change as you read the selections in this unit. Choose one of these responses to the Big Question or write one of your own:

- ❑ Heroes have responsibilities.
- ❑ Heroes do not have responsibilities.

Connecting to the Literature

Each reading in this unit will give you insight into the Big Question. At the end of the unit, you will have an opportunity to see how your ideas have changed.

★ Connecting to Citizenship

Texas Profiles: George Campbell Childress

Author of the Texas Declaration of Independence George Campbell Childress chaired the committee that wrote the Texas Declaration of Independence at the convention of 1836, and he is almost universally acknowledged as its main author. Childress also served as a diplomat for the Republic of Texas. In 1876, Childress County was formed and named to honor the memory of George Childress.

Do heroes have responsibilities?

- What responsibilities might Childress have had as the main author of the Texas Declaration of Independence?
- What can you learn from Childress's story about becoming a thoughtful, active citizen?

Focus on the TEKS

Listening and Speaking
(24)(A) Listen responsively to a speaker by asking questions related to the content for clarification or elaboration.

(26) Participate productively in teams, building on the ideas of others.

Big Question Vocabulary

Use some of these words as you complete the activities on these pages.

identify
obligation
honesty
responsibility
hero
character
morality
wisdom
choices
involvement
justice
serve
intentions
standard
imitate

This list includes academic vocabulary words, which are defined on pp. R1–R14.

THE BIG ?

Do *heroes* have responsibilities?

Fiction, nonfiction, and folk literature depict many different kinds of heroes.

Dean Smith, the legendary basketball coach, has collaborated with John Kilgo on a book about coaching and leadership.

TEXAS
PHLitOnline
www.PHLitOnline.com

• Penguin author video
• Interactive journals
• Interactive graphic organizers
• Selection audio
• Self-test

What Are Leadership and Heroism?

by Coach Dean Smith with John Kilgo

Before I agreed to write a book on the **theme of leadership,** I had to be convinced that a college basketball coach qualified as a true leader. I wondered whether all leaders have something in common, from heroic political figures like Nelson Mandela to mythic heroes like Odysseus down to coaches of winning teams.

Does Coaching Qualify as Leadership?

Each season, as North Carolina's basketball coach, I led thirteen to fifteen dedicated, talented young men who loved playing the sport. I knew as I began my career in coaching that I had to motivate, teach, and discipline fairly, and to care deeply about those I led, just as all effective leaders do. Experts in leadership later proved to me that coaching is leadership.

If a coach is a leader and teacher, the game of basketball itself could teach our society some important lessons. The game reflects the ideals of our culture. In college basketball, we begin the game 0–0. There's no advantage for being rich, no disadvantage for being poor. Basketball teaches us that people of all races and nationalities, holding various political and religious beliefs, can excel when given a fair and equal chance.

True Heroes Help Others

For me, the true heroes of basketball are not the players out for themselves, but those who help their team and their community. Before each practice at North Carolina, a Thought for the Day, which had nothing to do with basketball, was given to each player. He was expected to memorize it and be able to recite it if called upon.

One day's thought was: "Do something every day for someone who can't pay you back." We wanted our players to be involved with their community, take part in campus politics, make friends on campus with non-athletes, and experience the fulfillment one receives from helping someone in need, with no desire to be recognized publicly for the good works. I required this not for the sport, but to teach players about our culture and its values.

The inspiration for my belief in helping others came not only from the example set by my parents but also from literature, the novel *Magnificent Obsession,* which I quote from here.

Granpere, while you're over in that neighborhood, I noticed that Jim Abbot's ten year old boy is dragging his leg in a brace that didn't look right to me. . . . Why don't you hop into your car tomorrow and have Stephen drive you through the district? You'll be amazed what it does to you to make connections with people who need you. . . .

from *Magnificent Obsession*
—Lloyd C. Douglas

This novel is the story of a wealthy doctor who gives away his fortune to people in need who cannot pay him back. This passage, in which a character encourages his wealthy grandfather to help the poor, shows that true leaders, true heroes, are givers, not takers.

Meet **Dean Smith** (b. 1931) and **John Kilgo** (b. 1935)

Dean Smith, who spent thirty-six years as head coach of the University of North Carolina's Tar Heels, has been called the greatest college basketball coach who ever lived. He has the most wins for coaching in college basketball history: 879. **John Kilgo,** who has spent forty years writing about North Carolina sports, publishes a magazine called *Carolina Blue.* For fifteen years, he was a cohost of Smith's TV show.

Did You Know?
Smith was named "Sportsman of the Year" by *Sports Illustrated* in 1997.

Exploring Themes in Literature

Universal Themes in the Oral Tradition

Written literature grew out of the **oral tradition,** the passing of stories, poems, and sayings by word of mouth. Around campfires and at other gatherings, people told tales about love, ambition, and friendship. Expressing their human concerns in stories, they explored **universal themes,** insights into life that are true for many different times and cultures. The following are examples of common universal themes:

- the importance of heroism
- the strength of loyalty
- the power of love
- the dangers of greed

Storytellers explored such themes by means of **archetypes,** the situations, characters, images, and symbols that appear in the tales of various cultures. Archetypes appear across time and are recognizable even with different cultural variations. Here are some important archetypes:

- the **hero's quest,** in which a brave or clever person undergoes tests or trials while searching for something of great value

- the struggle between the **protagonist,** the main character, and the **antagonist,** a person or force that opposes the protagonist

- the **monster,** a nonhuman or semihuman creature that menaces human society and must be destroyed by the hero

- the **trickster,** a clever character who can fool others but often gets into trouble through curiosity

- the **circle** as a symbol of loyalty, completion, or protection

Beyond these key characters and symbols, the culture that created a story is also an important driving force in the oral tradition. The **historical and cultural setting,** also known as context, is the beliefs, traditions, and customs that reflect the particular time and place in which a tale was written. This context can influence many aspects of a story, including specific figurative language and the way in which universal archetypes are presented.

Cornered by Mike Baldwin

BALdwin

TALL TALES

SHORT STORIES

CORNERED © 2004 Mike Baldwin. Reprinted with permission of UNIVERSAL PRESS SYNDICATE. All rights reserved.

Forms That Express Universal Themes

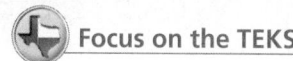
Anonymous storytellers developed various forms to express universal themes and archetypes. At first, these forms lived only in the memory, and a tale would probably vary with every telling. **Traditional literature** developed as stories were written down and individual authors emerged.

- **Myths** explain the actions of gods and the humans who interact with them. Myths also explain the causes of natural phenomena.

- **Folk tales** focus on human or animal heroes and, unlike myths, are not primarily concerned with gods or creation.

- **Legends** are folk tales that recount the adventures of a human hero and are usually based on a historical truth. A legend told in an exaggerated way is a tall tale.

- **Epics** are long narrative poems that describe the exploits of larger-than-life heroes. The hero usually engages in a dangerous journey or quest that is important to the history of a group or culture.

These narrative forms express the values, ideals, and behaviors cherished by a society. In many cases, the ideals of a particular society or culture are embodied in that culture's **classical literature**—works recognized as enduring and masterful. Although classic works are characteristic of the time and place in which they were written, they have broad appeal because of their artistry and the themes they explore.

As with many art forms, literary works of a particular time can be heavily influenced by the works that came before, either in form or content. The influence of mythic, classical, and traditional literature can often be found in more modern literature—works from the 20th and 21st centuries.

 TEKS Check

Review a 20th-century work you read in an earlier unit. Use a chart like the one shown here to analyze the influence of mythic, classical, and traditional literature on this work.

20th-Century Title	Archetype or Theme from Mythic, Classical, or Traditional Literature

Dean Smith and John Kilgo
Introduce "The Carolina Way"

Both of my parents were schoolteachers in my hometown of Emporia, Kansas. I developed a passion for athletics at an early age, but my parents insisted that sports not interfere with my studies, and if they did, sports took a backseat.

My parents received much joy and fulfillment from helping students learn and develop into good citizens, and were the major influences that led me to a career of teaching and coaching.

Creating a Culture of Unselfishness

At the University of North Carolina, I wanted to build a program in which all the players on the team, regardless of their backgrounds, respected each other, and highly talented players saw the wisdom of putting team goals in front of individual awards.

The Brightest Statistic

While a winning basketball program is very important at UNC, we established from the start that academics came first. Thanks to our players, we won 879 games and many championships in my thirty-six years as UNC's coach, but the statistic that stands brightest is that 96.6 percent of our players graduated, and more than a third of those went on to professional and graduate school.

Success Means Building Character

The university administration supported our efforts to build a program that emphasized education first, and the fact that we won almost eighty percent of our games says much about the players we had in our program. Thanks to them, some now refer to our method as "The Carolina Way."

That is also the title of the book I wrote about my coaching experience and philosophy. My purpose in writing this book was to demonstrate the methods we used to promote unselfish play and dedication to scholarship. And I was writing for an audience that I hoped would include not only athletes and sports fans but anyone who plays or works with others. As you read this excerpt from the book, you may be surprised to learn that I rarely talked to my players about winning!

Play Hard;
Play Together;
Play Smart

from **The Carolina Way**

Dean Smith with John Kilgo

I never went into a season as North Carolina's head coach thinking we'd just plug things into the previous year's plan and duplicate ourselves. As I said, we never had the same team return, and there were any number of other variables from one year to the next. We couldn't have had the long run of success that we enjoyed if we'd been too stubborn to change and come up with new ideas and different ways to play the game.

Themes in Literature
Values Smith introduces flexibility and willingness to change as values that contributed to his coaching success.

I will repeat this several times in this book: Don't fear change. Sometimes change can refresh a stale team; sometimes it's mandated by changing personnel; sometimes the rules of the game change. We adapted each year to hide our weaknesses and accentuate our strengths.

Although we didn't have a system at North Carolina, we certainly had a philosophy. We believed in it strongly and didn't stray very far from it. It pretty much stayed the same from my first year as head coach. It was our mission statement; our strategic plan, our entire approach in a nutshell: Play hard; play smart; play together.

Hard meant with effort, determination, and courage; *together* meant unselfishly, trusting your teammates, and doing everything possible not to let them down; *smart* meant with good execution and poise, treating each possession as if it were the only one in the game.

That was our philosophy; we believed that if we kept our focus on those tenets, success would follow. Our North Carolina players seldom heard me or my assistants talk about winning. Winning would be the by-product of the process. There could be no shortcuts.

Making winning the ultimate goal usually isn't good teaching. Tom Osborne, the great former football coach of the University of Nebraska, said that making winning the goal can actually get in the way of winning. I agree. So many things happened in games that were beyond our control: the talent and experience of the teams; bad calls by officials; injuries; bad luck.

By sticking to our philosophy, we asked realistic things from our players. A player could play hard. He could play unselfishly and do things to help his teammates succeed. He could play intelligently if we did the job in practice as coaches. We measured our success by how we did in those areas.

When we put these elements together, the players had fun, one of my goals as their coach. I wanted our players to enjoy the experience of playing basketball for North Carolina. Each player on our team knew he was important. Each did a terrific job of sharing the ball, which also made the game enjoyable for more players. All won and lost as a team.

Of course it is easier to talk about playing hard, playing smart, and playing together than it is to do all three. It begins by the recruiting of unselfish players, who subscribe to the philosophy of team over individual. In a summer physical education class I once taught at the Air Force Academy there was one young man who shot every time he touched the ball. Exasperated from watching him, I pulled his four teammates off the court. He asked who

---

Dean Smith
Author's Insight "A system signifies being rigid and unwilling to accept change. Our philosophy welcomed new and better ways of doing things."

Vocabulary
tenets (ten´ itz) *n.* principles or beliefs

Dean Smith
Author's Insight "We asked our players to concentrate only on those things within their control. This philosophy also eliminates excuse-making."

Themes in Literature
Leadership Smith describes his ideas about successful coaching.

would throw the ball inbounds to him. "You understand that it takes at least one more player," I said to him.

Playing Hard

Maybe a player wasn't the fastest, the tallest, or the most athletic person on the court. In the course of any given game that was out of his control. But each of them could control the effort with which he played. "Never let anyone play harder than you," I told them. "That is part of the game you can control." If another team played harder than we did, we had no excuse for it. None. We worked on it in every practice. If a player didn't give maximum effort, we dealt with it right then. We stopped practice and had the entire team run sprints for the offending player. We played a style of basketball that was physically exhausting and made it impossible for a player to go full throttle for forty minutes. When he got tired, he flashed the tired signal, a raised fist, and we substituted for him. He could put himself back in the game once he had rested. We didn't want tired players on the court because they usually tried to rest on defense. That wouldn't work in our plan. Therefore we watched closely in practice and in games to make sure players played hard. If they slacked off, it was important to catch them and get them out of the game, or if it occurred in practice, to have the entire team run.

Playing Together

One of the first things I did at the beginning of preseason practice was to spell out for our players the importance of team play. Basketball is a game that counts on togetherness. I pointed out that seldom, if ever, did the nation's leading scorer play on a ranked team. He certainly didn't play on a championship team. I made them understand that our plan would fall apart if they didn't take care of one another: set screens; play team defense; box out; pass to the open man. One man who failed to do his job unselfishly could undermine the efforts of the four other players on the court.

MODEL SELECTION

Dean Smith
Author's Insight
"Basketball is fun for the players when everyone on the team is treated equally and with respect. Players savor team accomplishments long after individual ones are forgotten."

▼ **Critical Viewing**
What does this picture tell you about the way Coach Dean Smith works with his players? **[Analyze]**

Reading Check
According to Coach Smith, what can a player always control?

▶ **Critical Viewing**
How does this photograph show that Coach Smith emphasizes the whole team, not just the "star" player? **[Analyze]**

Themes in Literature
Cultural Setting
Details here show the values and behaviors that lead to success.

Playing Smart

We taught and drilled until we made the things we wanted to see become habits. The only way to have a smart team is to have one that is fundamentally sound. We didn't skimp on fundamentals. We worked on them hard in practice and repeated them until they were down cold. We didn't introduce something and then move away from it before we had nailed it. Our entire program was built around practice, which we will talk more about in a later chapter. Practice, competitive games, late-game situations, and my relationship with our players are what I've missed most since I retired from coaching. We expected our team to execute well and with precision. If we practiced well and learned, we could play smart. It was another thing we could control. . . .

I stay in touch with many members of my extended family, former Carolina basketball players. These men have brought great happiness to my life. Ninety-six percent of them earned their college degrees, and one-third of those continued their studies at graduate and professional schools. It's the way a teacher's career should be judged. Our former players are doing great things for people in all walks of life.

The Carolina Way isn't the only way, that's for certain. But playing hard, playing smart, playing together certainly worked well for us.

Our trophy case is full, but far more important, our Museum of Good Memories runneth over.

After You Read — *from* **The Carolina Way**

Critical Thinking

1. **Respond:** Do you agree that playing a sport the right way is more important than winning? Explain.

2. **(a)** According to Smith, which factors in sports are beyond a team's control? **(b) Draw Conclusions:** How does Smith's philosophy provide a response to the unexpected in sports?

3. **(a)** According to Smith, how should a teacher's career be judged? **(b) Evaluate:** By his standards, is Smith's lifework meaningful because he was a teacher or because he was a coach? Explain.

Do heroes have responsibilities?
(a) How do Smith's players live up to their responsibilities as team members? **(b)** Is Smith a hero, or is he just living up to his responsibilities as a coach? Are these the same? Explain.

Reviewing Themes in Literature

4. Using a chart like the one shown, analyze the **values** that Smith emphasized as a basketball coach. **(a)** In the first column, list the three values that Smith taught. In the second column, give an example of how Smith promoted each value among his players. In the third column, suggest ways that Smith's values could apply to other areas of life. **(b)** Discuss your ideas in a small group, and add new insights to your chart.

Value	Specific Example	Application to Life

5. Do you think sports are an essential part of the **cultural setting** of the United States? Support your answer with details from the excerpt.

Research the Author

Many of Dean Smith's players have achieved great success in life. Use comments from Smith's former players to design a **testimonial poster** that shows the positive results of Smith's coaching beliefs.

- Identify athletes, coaches, or leaders who have played for Smith.

- Collect comments about Smith made by these former players. Focus on statements relating to values that have aided their success.

- Present the comments on a poster. Include graphics and illustrations.

Epic Selection

from the **ODYSSEY**

HOMER

translated by ROBERT FITZGERALD

1044 Themes in Literature: Heroism

▲ Read the **Odyssey** to learn about a hero of the ancient world, his long journey home, and the choices he made.

 TEXAS Focus on the TEKS

Meet these standards with Part 1 of the **Odyssey** (p. 1044).

Reading

(5)(A) Analyze non-linear plot development (e.g., flashbacks) and compare it to linear plot development. *(Literary Analysis: Epic Hero)*

(2)(C) Relate the figurative language of a literary work to its historical and cultural setting. *(Reading Skill: Historical and Cultural Context)*

(5)(D) Demonstrate familiarity with works by authors from non-English-speaking literary traditions with emphasis on classical literature. *(Critical Thinking: Analyze)*

(12)(C) Compare and contrast coverage of the same event in various media (e.g., newspapers, television, documentaries, blogs, Internet). *(Listening and Speaking: Media Analysis)*

Oral and Written Conventions

(17)(C) Use a variety of correctly structured sentences (e.g., compound). *(Conventions: Simple and Compound Sentences)*

Writing

(14)(A) Write an engaging story with interesting and believable characters. *(Writing: Everyday Epic)*

Literary Analysis: **Epic Hero**

An **epic hero** is the larger-than-life character in an **epic**—a long narrative poem about important events in the history or folklore of a culture. The epic hero possesses traits that are highly valued by his or her society. The epic hero's traits are developed by what he or she says in narration and dialogue and by his or her actions.

Many epics begin *in medias res* ("in the middle of things"), meaning that major events occurred before events in the poem begin. The hero's adventures are often recounted in a **flashback,** a nonlinear plot development technique in which a scene interrupts a narrative to relate earlier events.

As You Read Analyze linear and nonlinear plot developments in Part 1. In what way do Odysseus' actions reveal that he is an epic hero?

Reading Skill: **Historical and Cultural Context**

The **historical and cultural context, or setting,** of a literary work is the time and place in which the work is set or written and the themes and issues important at that time and place. When you read a work with a historical or cultural setting that differs from your own experiences, use background information and prior knowledge to analyze how context influences the work.

- Read the author biography, footnotes, and other text aids.
- Note how characters' actions and beliefs are affected by the setting.
- Analyze how figurative language—such as similes, metaphors, and personification—reflects a particular time and place.

Using the Strategy: Setting Influence Chart

As You Read **Relate the figurative language** and details of Homer's *Odyssey* to the work's historical and cultural setting in ancient Greece.

Figurative Language or Detail	Relationship	Historical/Cultural Setting
"Cyclops...lay down like a mast."	Homer's comparison emphasizes Cyclops' huge size and his stiff movements.	The main characters are sailors, who would be familiar with a mast—a huge, wooden pole on a ship.

Hear It!
- Selection summary audio
- Selection audio

See It!
- Get Connected video
- Background video
- More about the author
- Vocabulary flashcards

Do It!
- Interactive journals
- Interactive graphic organizers
- Self-test
- Internet activity
- Grammar tutorial
- Interactive vocabulary games

Do *heroes* have responsibilities?

Writing About the Big Question

In Part 1 of the *Odyssey*, Homer describes the hero Odysseus' long and dangerous journey home. Use these sentence starters to develop your ideas about the Big Question.

A **hero** has an **obligation** to _____ because _____.

The **choices** he or she makes are scrutinized because _____.

As You Read Look for characteristics that define the epic hero, and take note of the ways in which Odysseus looks after his men.

Vocabulary

Read each word and its definition. Decide whether you know the word well, know it a little bit, or do not know it at all. After you read, see how your knowledge of each word has increased.

- **plundered** (plun´ dərd) *v.* took goods by force; looted (p. 1045) *The fierce pirates captured the merchant ship and plundered it.* *plunderous adj. plunderer n.*

- **dispatched** (di spacht´) *v.* finished quickly (p. 1053) *Remarkably, she dispatched the assignment an hour before anyone else did.*

- **assuage** (ə swāj´) *v.* calm; pacify (p. 1065) *Gentle words may assuage their anger. assuaged v. assuagement n.*

- **bereft** (bē reft´) *adj.* deprived (p. 1068) *Bereft of sleep, she struggled to stay awake during the movie. bereavement n.*

- **ardor** (är´ dər) *n.* passion; enthusiasm (p. 1073) *The audience cheered their favorite characters with ardor. ardent adj.*

- **insidious** (in sid´ ē əs) *adj.* characterized by craftiness and betrayal (p. 1077) *The traitor's insidious actions led to the city's downfall. insidiously adv. insidiousness n.*

Word Power

The **Old English prefix be-** means "around," "make," or "covered with."

In this selection, Tiresias warns Odysseus that he will be **bereft** of his companions. Tiresias means that Odysseus will lose his companions. **Bereft** is a form of **bereave**, which means "made to suffer a loss."

Meet
Homer
(ca. 800 B.C.)

Author of
the Odyssey

Homer is the legendary poet credited with writing the *Iliad* and the *Odyssey*. As is characteristic of the ancient Greek literary tradition, Homer's works tell stories of heroes, gods, and monsters and explore themes of fate and destiny. These classical epics, known for their length and scope, gripping stories, imagery, and style have captured readers' imaginations for almost 3,000 years.

Did Homer Exist? Scholars disagree about whether the *Iliad* and the *Odyssey* were really written by Homer. According to tradition, Homer was born in western Asia Minor and was blind. However, many scholars feel confident that the *Iliad* and the *Odyssey* are the result of generations of oral poetic composition, masterpieces to which numerous ancient singers contributed. If Homer existed, he may have been the greatest in a long line of Greek epic storytellers.

DID YOU KNOW?

Homer's stories have been the basis for many Hollywood movies, including *Troy* in 2004.

BACKGROUND FOR THE EPIC

(Social Studies Connection)

The Trojan War

The *Odyssey* describes the experiences of the Greek hero Odysseus as he makes his way home after the Trojan War. According to legend, the Trojan War was sparked when Paris, a prince of Troy, ran off with Helen, the wife of the king of Sparta. A Greek force attacked Troy (in modern-day Turkey) to recapture her and was finally victorious after ten years of fighting.

from the
Odyssey
HOMER
translated by ROBERT FITZGERALD

PART 1

The Adventures of Odysseus

In the opening verses, Homer addresses the muse of epic poetry. He asks her help in telling the tale of Odysseus.

Sing in me, Muse,[1] and through me tell the story
of that man skilled in all ways of contending,
the wanderer, harried for years on end,
after he plundered the stronghold

5 on the proud height of Troy.[2]
                              He saw the townlands
and learned the minds of many distant men,
and weathered many bitter nights and days
in his deep heart at sea, while he fought only
to save his life, to bring his shipmates home.

10 But not by will nor valor could he save them,
for their own recklessness destroyed them all—
children and fools, they killed and feasted on
the cattle of Lord Helios,[3] the Sun,
and he who moves all day through heaven

15 took from their eyes the dawn of their return.
Of these adventures, Muse, daughter of Zeus,[4]
tell us in our time, lift the great song again.

> Note: In translating the *Odyssey*, Fitzgerald spelled Greek names to suggest the sound of the original Greek. In these excerpts, more familiar spellings have been used. For example, Fitzgerald's "Kirkê," "Kyklops," and "Seirênês" are spelled here as "Circe," "Cyclops," and "Sirens."

1. **Muse** (myōōz) any one of the nine goddesses of the arts, literature, and sciences; the spirit that is thought to inspire a poet or other artist.
2. **Troy** (trɔi) city in northwest Asia Minor; site of the Trojan War.

Vocabulary
plundered (plun´ dərd) *v.* took goods by force; looted

3. **Helios** (hē´ lē äs´) sun god.
4. **Zeus** (zōōs) king of the gods.

CHARACTERS

Alcinous (al sin´ ō əs)—king of the Phaeacians, to whom Odysseus tells his story

Odysseus (ō dis´ ē əs)—king of Ithaca

Calypso (kə lip´ sō)—sea goddess who loved Odysseus

Circe (sʉr´ sē)—enchantress who helped Odysseus

Zeus (zo͞os)—king of the gods

Apollo (ə päl´ ō)—god of music, poetry, prophecy, and medicine

Agamemnon (ag´ ə mem´ nän´)—king and leader of Greek forces

Poseidon (pō sī´ dən)—god of sea, earthquakes, horses, and storms at sea

Athena (ə thē´ nə)—goddess of wisdom, skills, and warfare

Polyphemus (päl´ i fē´ məs)—the Cyclops who imprisoned Odysseus

Laertes (lā ʉr´ tēz´)—Odysseus' father

Cronus (krō´ nəs)—Titan ruler of the universe; father of Zeus

Perimedes (per´ ə mē´ dēz)—member of Odysseus' crew

Eurylochus (yo͞o ril´ ə kəs)—another member of the crew

Tiresias (tī rē´ sē əs)—blind prophet who advised Odysseus

Persephone (pər sef´ ə nē)—wife of Hades

Telemachus (tə lem´ ə kəs)—Odysseus and Penelope's son

Sirens (sī´ rənz)—creatures whose songs lure sailors to their deaths

Scylla (sil´ ə)—sea monster of gray rock

Charybdis (kə rib´ dis)—enormous and dangerous whirlpool

Lampetia (lam pē´ shə)—nymph

Hermes (hʉr´ mēz´)—herald and messenger of the gods

Eumaeus (yo͞o mē´ əs)—old swineherd and friend of Odysseus

Antinous (an tin´ ō əs)—leader among the suitors

Eurynome (yo͞o rin´ ə mē)—housekeeper for Penelope

Penelope (pə nel´ ə pē)—Odysseus' wife

Eurymachus (yo͞o ri´ mə kəs)—suitor

Amphinomus (am fin´ ə məs)—suitor

Sailing from Troy

Ten years after the Trojan War, Odysseus departs from the goddess Calypso's island. He arrives in Phaeacia, ruled by Alcinous. Alcinous offers a ship to Odysseus and asks him to tell of his adventures.

"I am Laertes'[5] son, Odysseus.
                                        Men hold me
    formidable for guile[6] in peace and war:
20   this fame has gone abroad to the sky's rim.

    My home is on the peaked sea-mark of Ithaca[7]
    under Mount Neion's wind-blown robe of leaves,
    in sight of other islands—Dulichium,
    Same, wooded Zacynthus—Ithaca
25   being most lofty in that coastal sea,
    and northwest, while the rest lie east and south.
    A rocky isle, but good for a boy's training;
    I shall not see on earth a place more dear,
    though I have been detained long by Calypso,[8]
30   loveliest among goddesses, who held me
    in her smooth caves, to be her heart's delight,
    as Circe of Aeaea,[9] the enchantress,
    desired me, and detained me in her hall.
    But in my heart I never gave consent.
35   Where shall a man find sweetness to surpass
    his own home and his parents? In far lands
    he shall not, though he find a house of gold.

    What of my sailing, then, from Troy?
                                        What of those years
    of rough adventure, weathered under Zeus?
40   The wind that carried west from Ilium[10]
    brought me to Ismarus, on the far shore,
    a strongpoint on the coast of Cicones.[11]
    I stormed that place and killed the men who fought.
    Plunder we took, and we enslaved the women,
45   to make division, equal shares to all—
    but on the spot I told them: 'Back, and quickly!
    Out to sea again!' My men were mutinous,[12]
    fools, on stores of wine. Sheep after sheep

5. **Laertes** (lā ʉr´ tēz´)
6. **guile** (gīl) *n.* craftiness; cunning.
7. **Ithaca** (ith´ ə kə) island off the west coast of Greece.

Literary Analysis
Epic Hero For what quality does Odysseus say he is famous?

8. **Calypso** (kə lip´ sō) sea goddess who loved Odysseus.
9. **Circe** (sʉr´ sē) **of Aeaea** (ē´ ē ə)
10. **Ilium** (il´ ē əm) Troy.

11. **Cicones** (si kō´ nēz)
12. **mutinous** (myo͞ot´'n əs) *adj.* rebellious.

Reading Check

Who has asked Odysseus to tell his tale?

they butchered by the surf, and shambling cattle,
feasting,—while fugitives went inland, running
to call to arms the main force of Cicones.
This was an army, trained to fight on horseback
or, where the ground required, on foot. They came
with dawn over that terrain like the leaves
and blades of spring. So doom appeared to us,
dark word of Zeus for us, our evil days.
My men stood up and made a fight of it—
backed on the ships, with lances kept in play,
from bright morning through the blaze of noon
holding our beach, although so far outnumbered;
but when the sun passed toward unyoking time,
then the Achaeans,[13] one by one, gave way.
Six benches were left empty in every ship
that evening when we pulled away from death.
And this new grief we bore with us to sea:
our precious lives we had, but not our friends.
No ship made sail next day until some shipmate
had raised a cry, three times, for each poor ghost
unfleshed by the Cicones on that field.

The Lotus-Eaters

Now Zeus the lord of cloud roused in the north
a storm against the ships, and driving veils
of squall moved down like night on land and sea.
The bows went plunging at the gust; sails
cracked and lashed out strips in the big wind.
We saw death in that fury, dropped the yards,
unshipped the oars, and pulled for the nearest lee:[14]
then two long days and nights we lay offshore
worn out and sick at heart, tasting our grief,
until a third Dawn came with ringlets shining.
Then we put up our masts, hauled sail, and rested,
letting the steersmen and the breeze take over.

I might have made it safely home, that time,
but as I came round Malea the current
took me out to sea, and from the north
a fresh gale drove me on, past Cythera.
Nine days I drifted on the teeming sea
before dangerous high winds. Upon the tenth

50

55

60

65

70

75

80

85

13. Achaeans (ə kē´ ənz) *n.*
Greeks; here, Odysseus'
men.

Reading Skill
Historical and Cultural
Context What beliefs
and values are reflected
in lines 65–69?

14. lee (lē) *n.* area sheltered
from the wind.

Literary Analysis
Epic Hero Analyze the
nonlinear plot develop-
ment in this section.
What words in line 82
remind you that this part
of the text is a flashback?

we came to the coastline of the Lotus-Eaters,
who live upon that flower. We landed there
90 to take on water. All ships' companies
mustered alongside for the mid-day meal.
Then I sent out two picked men and a runner
to learn what race of men that land sustained.
They fell in, soon enough, with Lotus-Eaters,
95 who showed no will to do us harm, only
offering the sweet Lotus to our friends—
but those who ate this honeyed plant, the Lotus,
never cared to report, nor to return:
they longed to stay forever, browsing on
100 that native bloom, forgetful of their homeland.
I drove them, all three wailing, to the ships,
tied them down under their rowing benches,
and called the rest: 'All hands aboard;
come, clear the beach and no one taste
105 the Lotus, or you lose your hope of home.'
Filing in to their places by the rowlocks
my oarsmen dipped their long oars in the surf,
and we moved out again on our sea faring.

Spiral Review
Narrative
Poetry Analyze diction. What effect do the words *longed* and *wailing* in lines 99 and 101 have on your understanding of the men's situation?

Literary Analysis
Epic Hero Which characteristics of an epic hero does Odysseus display in this episode?

Critical Thinking

1. **Respond:** What is your first impression of Odysseus? Which of his qualities do you admire? Explain.

2. **(a)** While on Ismarus, in what ways do Odysseus' men disobey orders? **(b) Analyze:** What is the result of this disobedience? **(c) Speculate:** What lesson might Odysseus take away from this experience?

3. **(a)** What happens to the men who eat the Lotus? **(b) Make Inferences:** What does this episode suggest about the main problem that Odysseus has with his men? **(c) Evaluate:** Do you think Odysseus responds appropriately to the three men who long to stay with the Lotus-Eaters? Why or why not?

Support your responses with evidence from the text.

4. **(a)** Note two points at which Odysseus mentions a desire to return home. **(b) Make Inferences:** What significant role might his longing for home play in Odysseus' epic journey?

Do heroes have responsibilities?
(a) In this episode, does Odysseus prove himself to be a hero?
(b) What responsibilities does he demonstrate, if any?

The Cyclops

15. Cyclopes (sī klō′ pēz′) *n.* plural form of Cyclops (sī′ kläps′); race of giants with one eye in the middle of the forehead.

Reading Skill
Historical and Cultural Context Based on Odysseus' criticism of the Cyclopes, what kind of society do you think the Greeks valued?

In the next land we found were Cyclopes,[15]
110   giants, louts, without a law to bless them.
In ignorance leaving the fruitage of the earth in mystery
to the immortal gods, they neither plow
nor sow by hand, nor till the ground, though grain—
wild wheat and barley—grows untended, and
115   wine-grapes, in clusters, ripen in heaven's rains.
Cyclopes have no muster and no meeting,
no consultation or old tribal ways,
but each one dwells in his own mountain cave
dealing out rough justice to wife and child,
120   indifferent to what the others do. . . .

As we rowed on, and nearer to the mainland,
at one end of the bay, we saw a cavern
yawning above the water, screened with laurel,
and many rams and goats about the place
125   inside a sheepfold—made from slabs of stone
earthfast between tall trunks of pine and rugged
towering oak trees.
                     A prodigious[16] man

16. prodigious (prō dij′ əs) *adj.* enormous.

Reading Skill
Historical and Cultural Context How might the figurative language "he seemed rather a shaggy mountain reared in solitude" relate to this work's historical and cultural setting?

slept in this cave alone, and took his flocks
to graze afield—remote from all companions,
130   knowing none but savage ways, a brute
so huge, he seemed no man at all of those
who eat good wheaten bread; but he seemed rather
a shaggy mountain reared in solitude.
We beached there, and I told the crew
135   to stand by and keep watch over the ship:
as for myself I took my twelve best fighters
and went ahead. I had a goatskin full
of that sweet liquor that Euanthes' son,
Maron, had given me. He kept Apollo's[17]

17. Apollo (ə päl′ ō) god of music, poetry, prophecy, and medicine.

140   holy grove at Ismarus; for kindness
we showed him there, and showed his wife and child,
he gave me seven shining golden talents[18]
perfectly formed, a solid silver winebowl,
and then this liquor—twelve two-handled jars
145   of brandy, pure and fiery. Not a slave
in Maron's household knew this drink; only
he, his wife and the storeroom mistress knew;

18. talents units of money in ancient Greece.

and they would put one cupful—ruby-colored,
honey-smooth—in twenty more of water,
150   but still the sweet scent hovered like a fume
over the winebowl. No man turned away
when cups of this came round.

                                    A wineskin full
I brought along, and victuals[19] in a bag,
for in my bones I knew some towering brute
155   would be upon us soon—all outward power,
a wild man, ignorant of civility.

We climbed, then, briskly to the cave. But Cyclops
had gone afield, to pasture his fat sheep,
so we looked round at everything inside:
160   a drying rack that sagged with cheeses, pens
crowded with lambs and kids,[20] each in its class:
firstlings apart from middlings, and the 'dewdrops,'
or newborn lambkins, penned apart from both.
And vessels full of whey[21] were brimming there—
165   bowls of earthenware and pails for milking.
My men came pressing round me, pleading:

                                    'Why not
take these cheeses, get them stowed, come back,
throw open all the pens, and make a run for it?
We'll drive the kids and lambs aboard. We say
170   put out again on good salt water!'

                            Ah,
how sound that was! Yet I refused. I wished
to see the cave man, what he had to offer—
no pretty sight, it turned out, for my friends.
We lit a fire, burnt an offering,
175   and took some cheese to eat; then sat in silence
around the embers, waiting. When he came
he had a load of dry boughs[22] on his shoulder
to stoke his fire at suppertime. He dumped it
with a great crash into that hollow cave,
180   and we all scattered fast to the far wall.
Then over the broad cavern floor he ushered
the ewes he meant to milk. He left his rams
and he-goats in the yard outside, and swung
high overhead a slab of solid rock

19. victuals (vit´ əlz) *n.* food or
other provisions.

20. kids (kidz) *n.* young goats.

21. whey (hwā) *n.* thin, watery
part of milk separated
from the thicker curds.

Literary Analysis
Epic Hero
What character flaw
does Odysseus reveal
by refusing to leave the
cave?

22. boughs (bouz) *n.* tree
branches.

Reading
Check

Where is Cyclops when
Odysseus and his men
enter the cave?

185 to close the cave. Two dozen four-wheeled wagons,
     with heaving wagon teams, could not have stirred
     the tonnage of that rock from where he wedged it
     over the doorsill. Next he took his seat
     and milked his bleating ewes. A practiced job
190 he made of it, giving each ewe her suckling;
     thickened his milk, then, into curds and whey,
     sieved out the curds to drip in withy[23] baskets,
     and poured the whey to stand in bowls
     cooling until he drank it for his supper.
195 When all these chores were done, he poked the fire,
     heaping on brushwood. In the glare he saw us.

     'Strangers,' he said, 'who are you? And where from?
     What brings you here by seaways—a fair traffic?
     Or are you wandering rogues, who cast your lives
200 like dice, and ravage other folk by sea?'

     We felt a pressure on our hearts, in dread
     of that deep rumble and that mighty man.
     But all the same I spoke up in reply:
     'We are from Troy, Achaeans, blown off course
205 by shifting gales on the Great South Sea;
     homeward bound, but taking routes and ways
     uncommon; so the will of Zeus would have it.
     We served under Agamemnon,[24] son of Atreus—
     the whole world knows what city
210 he laid waste, what armies he destroyed.
     It was our luck to come here; here we stand,
     beholden for your help, or any gifts
     you give—as custom is to honor strangers.
     We would entreat you, great Sir, have a care
215 for the gods' courtesy; Zeus will avenge
     the unoffending guest.'

                                        He answered this
     from his brute chest, unmoved:

                                        'You are a ninny,
     or else you come from the other end of nowhere,
     telling me, mind the gods! We Cyclopes
220 care not a whistle for your thundering Zeus
     or all the gods in bliss; we have more force by far.

23. withy (with´ ē) *adj.* made from tough, flexible twigs.

Reading Skill
Historical and Cultural
Context How might the figurative language "cast your lives like dice" relate to this work's historical and cultural setting?

24. Agamemnon (ag´ ə mem´ nän´) king who led the Greek army during the Trojan War.

Reading Skill
Historical and Cultural
Context What ancient Greek beliefs regarding the gods, military might, and respect for strangers does Odysseus express in his words to the Cyclops?

I would not let you go for fear of Zeus—
you or your friends—unless I had a whim[25] to.
Tell me, where was it, now, you left your ship—
225   around the point, or down the shore, I wonder?'

He thought he'd find out, but I saw through this,
and answered with a ready lie:

                            'My ship?
Poseidon[26] Lord, who sets the earth a-tremble,
broke it up on the rocks at your land's end.
230   A wind from seaward served him, drove us there.
We are survivors, these good men and I.'

Neither reply nor pity came from him,
but in one stride he clutched at my companions
and caught two in his hands like squirming puppies
235   to beat their brains out, spattering the floor.
Then he dismembered them and made his meal,
gaping and crunching like a mountain lion—
everything: innards, flesh, and marrow bones.
We cried aloud, lifting our hands to Zeus,
240   powerless, looking on at this, appalled;
but Cyclops went on filling up his belly
with manflesh and great gulps of whey,
then lay down like a mast among his sheep.
My heart beat high now at the chance of action,
245   and drawing the sharp sword from my hip I went
along his flank to stab him where the midriff
holds the liver. I had touched the spot
when sudden fear stayed me: if I killed him
we perished there as well, for we could never
250   move his ponderous doorway slab aside.
So we were left to groan and wait for morning.

When the young Dawn with fingertips of rose
lit up the world, the Cyclops built a fire
and milked his handsome ewes, all in due order,
255   putting the sucklings to the mothers. Then,
his chores being all dispatched, he caught
another brace[27] of men to make his breakfast,
and whisked away his great door slab

25. whim (hwim) *n.* sudden thought or wish to do something.

26. Poseidon (pō sī´ dən) god of the sea, earthquakes, horses, and storms at sea.

Literary Analysis
Epic Hero In what way does Odysseus' response show that he is "formidable for guile"?

Literary Analysis
Epic Hero How do lines 244–250 show Odysseus' ability to think ahead?

Vocabulary
dispatched (di spacht´) *v.* finished quickly

27. brace (brās) *n.* pair.

Reading Check

What does Odysseus tell the Cyclops happened to his ship?

28. **cap a quiver** (kwiv´ ər)
close a case holding
arrows.

28. **cap a quiver** (kwiv´ ər)
close a case holding
arrows.
29. **din** (din) *n.* loud,
continuous noise; uproar.
30. **Athena** (ə thē´ nə)
goddess of wisdom, skills,
and warfare.
31. **felled green and left to
season** chopped down
and exposed to the
weather to age the wood.
32. **lugger** (lug´ ər) *n.* small
sailing vessel.

Literary Analysis
Epic Hero What heroic
qualities does Odysseus
reveal as he plots against
the Cyclops?

Literary Analysis
Epic Hero What plan do
you think Odysseus has
in mind by offering the
Cyclops the wine?

to let his sheep go through—but he, behind,
260 reset the stone as one would cap a quiver.[28]
There was a din[29] of whistling as the Cyclops
rounded his flock to higher ground, then stillness.
And now I pondered how to hurt him worst,
if but Athena[30] granted what I prayed for.
265 Here are the means I thought would serve my turn:

a club, or staff, lay there along the fold—
an olive tree, felled green and left to season[31]
for Cyclops' hand. And it was like a mast
a lugger[32] of twenty oars, broad in the beam—
270 a deep-sea-going craft—might carry:
so long, so big around, it seemed. Now I
chopped out a six foot section of this pole
and set it down before my men, who scraped it;
and when they had it smooth, I hewed again
275 to make a stake with pointed end. I held this
in the fire's heart and turned it, toughening it,
then hid it, well back in the cavern, under
one of the dung piles in profusion there.
Now came the time to toss for it: who ventured
280 along with me? whose hand could bear to thrust
and grind that spike in Cyclops' eye, when mild
sleep had mastered him? As luck would have it,
the men I would have chosen won the toss—
four strong men, and I made five as captain.

285 At evening came the shepherd with his flock,
his woolly flock. The rams as well, this time,
entered the cave: by some sheepherding whim—
or a god's bidding—none were left outside.
He hefted his great boulder into place
290 and sat him down to milk the bleating ewes
in proper order, put the lambs to suck,
and swiftly ran through all his evening chores.
Then he caught two more men and feasted on them.
My moment was at hand, and I went forward
295 holding an ivy bowl of my dark drink,
looking up, saying:

'Cyclops, try some wine.
Here's liquor to wash down your scraps of men.
Taste it, and see the kind of drink we carried

under our planks. I meant it for an offering
300   if you would help us home. But you are mad,
unbearable, a bloody monster! After this,
will any other traveler come to see you?'

He seized and drained the bowl, and it went down
so fiery and smooth he called for more:

305   'Give me another, thank you kindly. Tell me,
how are you called? I'll make a gift will please you.
Even Cyclopes know the wine grapes grow
out of grassland and loam in heaven's rain,
but here's a bit of nectar and ambrosia!'³³

310   Three bowls I brought him, and he poured them down.
I saw the fuddle and flush come over him,
then I sang out in cordial tones:

▲ **Critical Viewing**
What traits does this
image of the Cyclops
illustrate? **[Interpret]**

33. **nectar** (nek´ tər) and
ambrosia (am brō´ zhə)
drink and food of the
gods.

Reading
Check

What does Odysseus
plan to do with the
stake that he and his
men make?

                'Cyclops,
you ask my honorable name? Remember
the gift you promised me, and I shall tell you.

315 My name is Nohbdy: mother, father, and friends,
everyone calls me Nohbdy.'

                And he said:
'Nohbdy's my meat, then, after I eat his friends.
Others come first. There's a noble gift, now.'

Even as he spoke, he reeled and tumbled backward,
320 his great head lolling to one side; and sleep
took him like any creature. Drunk, hiccuping,
he dribbled streams of liquor and bits of men.

Reading Skill
Historical and Cultural
Context What cultural
values are represented in
Odysseus' reference to
"the gods" in line 323?

Now, by the gods, I drove my big hand spike
deep in the embers, charring it again,
325 and cheered my men along with battle talk
to keep their courage up: no quitting now.
The pike of olive, green though it had been,
reddened and glowed as if about to catch.
I drew it from the coals and my four fellows
330 gave me a hand, lugging it near the Cyclops
as more than natural force nerved them; straight
forward they sprinted, lifted it, and rammed it
deep in his crater eye, and leaned on it
turning it as a shipwright turns a drill
335 in planking, having men below to swing
the two-handled strap that spins it in the groove.
So with our brand we bored[34] that great eye socket
while blood ran out around the red-hot bar.
Eyelid and lash were seared; the pierced ball
340 hissed broiling, and the roots popped.

34. bored (bôrd) *v.* made a
    hole in.

Reading Skill
Historical and Cultural
Context How might the
figurative language in
lines 340–345 relate to
this work's historical and
cultural setting?

                In a smithy
one sees a white-hot axehead or an adze
plunged and wrung in a cold tub, screeching steam—
the way they make soft iron hale and hard—:
just so that eyeball hissed around the spike.
345 The Cyclops bellowed and the rock roared round him,
and we fell back in fear. Clawing his face
he tugged the bloody spike out of his eye,
threw it away, and his wild hands went groping;

then he set up a howl for Cyclopes
who lived in caves on windy peaks nearby.
Some heard him; and they came by divers[35] ways
to clump around outside and call:

                          'What ails you,
Polyphemus?[36] Why do you cry so sore
in the starry night? You will not let us sleep.
Sure no man's driving off your flock? No man
has tricked you, ruined you?'

                                Out of the cave
the mammoth Polyphemus roared in answer:

'Nohbdy, Nohbdy's tricked me, Nohbdy's ruined me!'

To this rough shout they made a sage[37] reply:

'Ah well, if nobody has played you foul
there in your lonely bed, we are no use in pain
given by great Zeus. Let it be your father,
Poseidon Lord, to whom you pray.'

                              So saying
they trailed away. And I was filled with laughter
to see how like a charm the name deceived them.
Now Cyclops, wheezing as the pain came on him,
fumbled to wrench away the great doorstone
and squatted in the breach with arms thrown wide
for any silly beast or man who bolted—
hoping somehow I might be such a fool.
But I kept thinking how to win the game:
death sat there huge; how could we slip away?
I drew on all my wits, and ran through tactics,
reasoning as a man will for dear life,
until a trick came—and it pleased me well.
The Cyclops' rams were handsome, fat, with heavy
fleeces, a dark violet.

                           Three abreast
I tied them silently together, twining
cords of willow from the ogre's bed;
then slung a man under each middle one
to ride there safely, shielded left and right.

350
355
360
365
370
375
380

35. **divers** (dī´ vərz) *adj.*
several; various.

36. **Polyphemus** (päl´ i fē´
məs)

37. **sage** (sāj) *adj.* wise.

Literary Analysis
Epic Hero What does
Odysseus' gleeful
response to his successful
trick reveal about his
character?

Reading Check

What do the other
Cyclopes think Polyphe-
mus is saying when he
says, "Nohbdy's tricked
me"?

So three sheep could convey each man. I took
the woolliest ram, the choicest of the flock,
and hung myself under his kinky belly,
385 pulled up tight, with fingers twisted deep
in sheepskin ringlets for an iron grip.
So, breathing hard, we waited until morning.

When Dawn spread out her fingertips of rose
the rams began to stir, moving for pasture,
390 and peals of bleating echoed round the pens
where dams with udders full called for a milking.
Blinded, and sick with pain from his head wound,
the master stroked each ram, then let it pass,
but my men riding on the pectoral[38] fleece
395 the giant's blind hands blundering never found.
Last of them all my ram, the leader, came,
weighted by wool and me with my meditations.
The Cyclops patted him, and then he said:

'Sweet cousin ram, why lag behind the rest
400 in the night cave? You never linger so,
but graze before them all, and go afar
to crop sweet grass, and take your stately way
leading along the streams, until at evening
you run to be the first one in the fold.
405 Why, now, so far behind? Can you be grieving
over your Master's eye? That carrion rogue[39]
and his accurst companions burnt it out
when he had conquered all my wits with wine.
Nohbdy will not get out alive, I swear.
410 Oh, had you brain and voice to tell
where he may be now, dodging all my fury!
Bashed by this hand and bashed on this rock wall
his brains would strew the floor, and I should have
rest from the outrage Nohbdy worked upon me.'

415 He sent us into the open, then. Close by,
I dropped and rolled clear of the ram's belly,
going this way and that to untie the men.
With many glances back, we rounded up
his fat, stiff-legged sheep to take aboard,
420 and drove them down to where the good ship lay.

38. pectoral (pek′ tə rəl) *adj.*
located in or on the chest.

Literary Analysis
Epic Hero What details of this speech show that Polyphemus is far less clever than Odysseus?

39. carrion (kar′ ē ən) **rogue** (rōg) repulsive scoundrel.

◄ **Critical Viewing**
How does this image compare with your mental picture of the Cyclops? **[Analyze]**

Reading Check

How do the men escape from the Cyclops' cave?

► **Critical Viewing**
Odysseus and his sur-
viving men escape in
their ship as the blinded
Cyclops hurls boulders
and curses. How does
this illustration compare
to your mental image of
the scene? **[Analyze]**

We saw, as we came near, our fellows' faces
shining; then we saw them turn to grief
tallying those who had not fled from death.
I hushed them, jerking head and eyebrows up,
425 and in a low voice told them: 'Load this herd;
move fast, and put the ship's head toward the breakers.'
They all pitched in at loading, then embarked
and struck their oars into the sea. Far out,
as far off shore as shouted words would carry,
430 I sent a few back to the adversary:
'O Cyclops! Would you feast on my companions?
Puny, am I, in a cave man's hands?
How do you like the beating that we gave you,
you damned cannibal? Eater of guests
435 under your roof! Zeus and the gods have paid you!'

The blind thing in his doubled fury broke
a hilltop in his hands and heaved it after us.
Ahead of our black prow it struck and sank
whelmed in a spuming geyser, a giant wave
440 that washed the ship stern foremost back to shore.
I got the longest boathook out and stood
fending us off, with furious nods to all
to put their backs into a racing stroke—
row, row, or perish. So the long oars bent
445 kicking the foam sternward, making head
until we drew away, and twice as far.
Now when I cupped my hands I heard the crew
in low voices protesting:

'Godsake, Captain!
Why bait the beast again? Let him alone!'

Literary Analysis
Epic Hero Despite his
heroism, what human
weaknesses does
Odysseus reveal as he
sails away?

450 'That tidal wave he made on the first throw
all but beached us.'

'All but stove us in!'
'Give him our bearing with your trumpeting,
he'll get the range and lob a boulder.'

'Aye
He'll smash our timbers and our heads together!'
455 I would not heed them in my glorying spirit,

Polyphemus, The Cyclops N. C. Wyeth, Brandywine River Museum

but let my anger flare and yelled:

'Cyclops,

if ever mortal man inquire
how you were put to shame and blinded, tell him
Odysseus, raider of cities, took your eye:
460   Laertes' son, whose home's on Ithaca!'

At this he gave a mighty sob and rumbled:
'Now comes the weird[40] upon me, spoken of old.
A wizard, grand and wondrous, lived here—Telemus,[41]
a son of Eurymus;[42] great length of days
465   he had in wizardry among the Cyclopes,
and these things he foretold for time to come:
my great eye lost, and at Odysseus' hands.
Always I had in mind some giant, armed
in giant force, would come against me here.
470   But this, but you—small, pitiful and twiggy—
you put me down with wine, you blinded me.
Come back, Odysseus, and I'll treat you well,
praying the god of earthquake[43] to befriend you—
his son I am, for he by his avowal
475   fathered me, and, if he will, he may
heal me of this black wound—he and no other
of all the happy gods or mortal men.'

Few words I shouted in reply to him:

'If I could take your life I would and take
480   your time away, and hurl you down to hell!
The god of earthquake could not heal you there!'

At this he stretched his hands out in his darkness
toward the sky of stars, and prayed Poseidon:

'O hear me, lord, blue girdler of the islands,
485   if I am thine indeed, and thou art father:
grant that Odysseus, raider of cities, never
see his home: Laertes' son, I mean,
who kept his hall on Ithaca. Should destiny
intend that he shall see his roof again
490   among his family in his father land,
far be that day, and dark the years between.

40. weird (wird) *n.* fate or destiny.
41. Telemus (tel´ e mǝs)
42. Eurymus (yōō rim´ ǝs)

43. god of earthquake Poseidon.

Reading Skill
Historical and Cultural Context What do lines 472–494 suggest about ancient Greek beliefs about the gods' involvement in the mortal world?

Let him lose all companions, and return
under strange sail to bitter days at home.'
In these words he prayed, and the god heard him.
495 Now he laid hands upon a bigger stone
and wheeled around, titanic for the cast,
to let it fly in the black-prowed vessel's track.
But it fell short, just aft the steering oar,
and whelming seas rose giant above the stone
500 to bear us onward toward the island.

                                    There
as we ran in we saw the squadron waiting,
the trim ships drawn up side by side, and all
our troubled friends who waited, looking seaward.
We beached her, grinding keel in the soft sand,
505 and waded in, ourselves, on the sandy beach.
Then we unloaded all the Cyclops' flock
to make division, share and share alike,
only my fighters voted that my ram,
the prize of all, should go to me. I slew him
510 by the seaside and burnt his long thighbones
to Zeus beyond the stormcloud, Cronus'[44] son,
who rules the world. But Zeus disdained my offering:
destruction for my ships he had in store
and death for those who sailed them, my companions.
515 Now all day long until the sun went down
we made our feast on mutton and sweet wine,
till after sunset in the gathering dark
we went to sleep above the wash of ripples.

When the young Dawn with fingertips of rose
520 touched the world, I roused the men, gave orders
to man the ships, cast off the mooring lines;
and filing in to sit beside the rowlocks
oarsmen in line dipped oars in the gray sea.
So we moved out, sad in the vast offing,[45]
525 having our precious lives, but not our friends.

Literary Analysis
Epic Hero What
admirable quality
does Odysseus show
by dividing the sheep
among his men?

44. Cronus (krō´ nəs)
Titan who was ruler
of the universe until
he was overthrown
by his son Zeus.

45. offing (ôf´ iŋ) *n.* distant
part of the sea visible from
the shore.

Reading
Check

What does the Cyclops
ask for in his prayer to
Poseidon?

The Land of the Dead

46. Aeolia (ē ō´ lē ə) . . .
   Aeolus (ē´ ə ləs)

Odysseus and his men sail to Aeolia, where Aeolus,[46] king of the winds, sends Odysseus on his way with a gift: a sack contain-ing all the winds except the favorable west wind. When they are near home, Odysseus' men open the sack, letting loose a storm that drives them back to Aeolia. Aeolus casts them out, having decided that they are detested by the gods. They sail for seven days and arrive in the land of the Laestrygonians,[47] a race of cannibals. These creatures destroy all of Odysseus' ships except the one he is sailing on. Odysseus and his reduced crew escape and reach Aeaea, the island ruled by the sorceress-goddess Circe. She transforms half of the men into swine. Protected by a magic herb, Odysseus demands that Circe change his men back into human form. Before Odysseus departs from the island a year later, Circe informs him that in order to reach home he must journey to the land of the dead, Hades, and consult the blind prophet Tiresias.

47. Laestrygonians
   (les tri gō´ nē ənz)

48. singing nymph . . . hair
   Circe.

**Reading Skill
Historical and Cultural
Context** What details
here suggest that the
source of wind was
mysterious to ancient
Greeks?

We bore down on the ship at the sea's edge
and launched her on the salt immortal sea,
stepping our mast and spar in the black ship;
embarked the ram and ewe and went aboard
530 in tears, with bitter and sore dread upon us.
But now a breeze came up for us astern—
a canvas-bellying landbreeze, hale shipmate
sent by the singing nymph with sunbright hair;[48]
so we made fast the braces, took our thwarts,
535 and let the wind and steersman work the ship
with full sail spread all day above our coursing,
till the sun dipped, and all the ways grew dark
upon the fathomless unresting sea.

                              By night
our ship ran onward toward the Ocean's bourne,
540 the realm and region of the Men of Winter,
hidden in mist and cloud. Never the flaming
eye of Helios lights on those men
at morning, when he climbs the sky of stars,
nor in descending earthward out of heaven;
545 ruinous night being rove over those wretches.
We made the land, put ram and ewe ashore,

and took our way along the Ocean stream
to find the place foretold for us by Circe.
There Perimedes and Eurylochus[49]
550 pinioned[50] the sacred beasts. With my drawn blade
I spaded up the votive[51] pit, and poured
libations[52] round it to the unnumbered dead:
sweet milk and honey, then sweet wine, and last
clear water; and I scattered barley down.
555 Then I addressed the blurred and breathless dead,
vowing to slaughter my best heifer for them
before she calved, at home in Ithaca,
and burn the choice bits on the altar fire;
as for Tiresias, I swore to sacrifice
560 a black lamb, handsomest of all our flock.
Thus to assuage the nations of the dead
I pledged these rites, then slashed the lamb and ewe,
letting their black blood stream into the wellpit.
Now the souls gathered, stirring out of Erebus,[53]
565 brides and young men, and men grown old in pain,
and tender girls whose hearts were new to grief;
many were there, too, torn by brazen lanceheads,
battle-slain, bearing still their bloody gear.
From every side they came and sought the pit
570 with rustling cries; and I grew sick with fear.
But presently I gave command to my officers
to flay those sheep the bronze cut down, and make
burnt offerings of flesh to the gods below—
to sovereign Death, to pale Persephone.[54]
575 Meanwhile I crouched with my drawn sword to keep
the surging phantoms from the bloody pit
till I should know the presence of Tiresias.[55]

One shade came first—Elpenor, of our company,
who lay unburied still on the wide earth
580 as we had left him—dead in Circe's hall,
untouched, unmourned, when other cares compelled us.
Now when I saw him there I wept for pity
and called out to him:
               'How is this, Elpenor,
how could you journey to the western gloom
585 swifter afoot than I in the black lugger?'
He sighed, and answered:

49. **Perimedes** (per´ ə mē´ dēz) and **Eurylochus** (yōō ril´ ə kəs)
50. **pinioned** (pin´ yənd) *v.* confined or shackled.
51. **votive** (vōt´ iv) *adj.* done to fulfill a vow or express thanks.
52. **libations** (lī bā´ shənz) *n.* wine or other liquids poured upon the ground as a sacrifice or offering.

Vocabulary
assuage (ə swāj´)
v. calm; pacify

53. **Erebus** (er´ ə bəs) dark region under the earth through which the dead pass before entering the realm of Hades.

54. **Persephone** (pər sef´ ə nē) wife of Hades.

55. **Tiresias** (tī rē´ sē əs)

Reading Check

What does Circe say that Odysseus must do in order to reach home?

Odysseus in the Land of the Dead from Homer's The Odyssey, N.C. Wyeth, Brandywine River Museum

                                        'Son of great Laertes,
Odysseus, master mariner and soldier,
bad luck shadowed me, and no kindly power;
ignoble death I drank with so much wine.
590 I slept on Circe's roof, then could not see
the long steep backward ladder, coming down,
and fell that height. My neckbone, buckled under,
snapped, and my spirit found this well of dark.
Now hear the grace I pray for, in the name
595 of those back in the world, not here—your wife
and father, he who gave you bread in childhood,
and your own child, your only son, Telemachus,[56]
long ago left at home.

                              When you make sail
and put these lodgings of dim Death behind,
600 you will moor ship, I know, upon Aeaea Island;
there, O my lord, remember me, I pray,
do not abandon me unwept, unburied,
to tempt the gods' wrath, while you sail for home;
but fire my corpse, and all the gear I had,
605 and build a cairn[57] for me above the breakers—
an unknown sailor's mark for men to come.
Heap up the mound there, and implant upon it
the oar I pulled in life with my companions.'

He ceased, and I replied:

                              'Unhappy spirit,
610 I promise you the barrow and the burial.'

So we conversed, and grimly, at a distance,
with my long sword between, guarding the blood,
while the faint image of the lad spoke on.
Now came the soul of Anticlea, dead,
615 my mother, daughter of Autolycus,[58]
dead now, though living still when I took ship
for holy Troy. Seeing this ghost I grieved,
but held her off, through pang on pang of tears,
till I should know the presence of Tiresias.
620 Soon from the dark that prince of Thebes[59] came forward
bearing a golden staff; and he addressed me:

◄ **Critical Viewing**
What can you infer about ancient Greek beliefs concerning death and the afterlife from lines 555–577 on page 1065 and from this illustration? **[Infer]**

56. **Telemachus** (tə lem′ ə kəs)

57. **cairn** (kern) *n.* conical heap of stones built as a monument.

58. **Autolycus** (ô täl′ i kəs)

59. **Thebes** (thēbz)

Reading Skill
Historical and Cultural Context What ancient Greek values and beliefs are suggested by Elpenor's requests?

Reading Check

What does Elpenor's spirit ask of Odysseus?

Spiral Review
Narrative
Poetry Analyze diction. What effect do the words *cold*, *dead*, and *joyless* have on your understanding of the place Elpenor describes?

Reading Skill
Historical and Cultural Context What ancient Greek value is reflected in the "narrow strait" that Tiresias describes (lines 637–638)?

60. **kine** (kīn) *n.* cattle.

Vocabulary
bereft (bē reft´)
adj. deprived

'Son of Laertes and the gods of old,
Odysseus, master of landways and seaways,
why leave the blazing sun, O man of woe,
625   to see the cold dead and the joyless region?
Stand clear, put up your sword;
let me but taste of blood, I shall speak true.'

At this I stepped aside, and in the scabbard
let my long sword ring home to the pommel silver,
630   as he bent down to the somber blood. Then spoke
the prince of those with gift of speech:

                         'Great captain,

a fair wind and the honey lights of home
are all you seek. But anguish lies ahead;
the god who thunders on the land prepares it,
635   not to be shaken from your track, implacable,
in rancor for the son whose eye you blinded.
One narrow strait may take you through his blows:
denial of yourself, restraint of shipmates.
When you make landfall on Thrinacia first
640   and quit the violet sea, dark on the land
you'll find the grazing herds of Helios
by whom all things are seen, all speech is known.
Avoid those kine,[60] hold fast to your intent,
and hard seafaring brings you all to Ithaca.
645   But if you raid the beeves, I see destruction
for ship and crew. Though you survive alone,
bereft of all companions, lost for years,
under strange sail shall you come home, to find
your own house filled with trouble: insolent men
650   eating your livestock as they court your lady.
Aye, you shall make those men atone in blood!
But after you have dealt out death—in open
combat or by stealth—to all the suitors,
go overland on foot, and take an oar,
655   until one day you come where men have lived
with meat unsalted, never known the sea,
nor seen seagoing ships, with crimson bows
and oars that fledge light hulls for dipping flight.
The spot will soon be plain to you, and I
660   can tell you how: some passerby will say,
"What winnowing fan is that upon your shoulder?"

Halt, and implant your smooth oar in the turf
and make fair sacrifice to Lord Poseidon:
a ram, a bull, a great buck boar; turn back,
665　and carry out pure hecatombs[61] at home
to all wide heaven's lords, the undying gods,
to each in order. Then a seaborne death
soft as this hand of mist will come upon you
when you are wearied out with rich old age,
670　your country folk in blessed peace around you.
And all this shall be just as I foretell.'

61. hecatombs (hek´ ə tōmz´) *n.* large-scale sacrifices to the gods in ancient Greece; often, the slaughter of 100 cattle at one time.

Critical Thinking

1. **Respond:** What do you think of Odysseus' plan for escaping from Polyphemus? Explain.

2. **(a)** Before the meeting with the Cyclops, what had Odysseus received from Maron at Ismarus? **(b) Generalize:** What does the encounter with Maron reveal about ancient Greek attitudes regarding hospitality?

3. **(a)** How do Odysseus and his companions expect to be treated by the Cyclops? **(b) Make Inferences:** What "laws" of behavior and attitude does Polyphemus violate?

4. **(a) Summarize:** How do Odysseus and his crew escape from the Cyclops? **(b) Evaluate:** What positive and negative character traits does Odysseus demonstrate in his adventure with the Cyclops?

5. **(a) Compare and Contrast:** Compare and contrast Odysseus' reactions to the three ghosts he meets in the Land of the Dead—Elpenor, Anticlea, and Tiresias. **(b) Analyze:** What character trait does Odysseus display in the Land of the Dead that he did not reveal earlier?

6. **(a) Summarize:** What difficulty does Tiresias predict for the journey to come? **(b) Speculate:** Why would Odysseus continue, despite the grim prophecies?

7. **Assess:** Judging from Tiresias' prediction, which heroic qualities will Odysseus need to rely upon as he continues his journey? Explain.

Do heroes have responsibilities?
(a) What are Odysseus' responsibilities as he reaches the land of the Cyclopes? **(b)** How well does he fulfill these responsibilities?

Support your responses with evidence from the text.

Circe Meanwhile Had Gone Her Ways..., 1924, William Russell Flint Collection of the New York Public Library, Special Collections/ Art Resources

The Sirens

Odysseus returns to Circe's island. The goddess reveals his course to him and gives advice on how to avoid the dangers he will face: the Sirens, who lure sailors to their destruction; the Wandering Rocks, sea rocks that destroy even birds in flight; the perils of the sea monster Scylla and, nearby, the whirlpool Charybdis;[62] and the cattle of the sun god, which Tiresias has warned Odysseus not to harm.

62. **Charybdis** (kə rib´ dis)

As Circe spoke, Dawn mounted her golden throne,
and on the first rays Circe left me, taking
her way like a great goddess up the island.
675   I made straight for the ship, roused up the men
to get aboard and cast off at the stern.
They scrambled to their places by the rowlocks
and all in line dipped oars in the gray sea.
But soon an offshore breeze blew to our liking—
680   a canvas-bellying breeze, a lusty shipmate
sent by the singing nymph with sunbright hair.
So we made fast the braces, and we rested,
letting the wind and steersman work the ship.
The crew being now silent before me, I
685   addressed them, sore at heart:

                        'Dear friends,
more than one man, or two, should know those things
Circe foresaw for us and shared with me,
so let me tell her forecast: then we die
with our eyes open, if we are going to die,
690   or know what death we baffle if we can. Sirens
weaving a haunting song over the sea
we are to shun, she said, and their green shore
all sweet with clover; yet she urged that I
alone should listen to their song. Therefore
695   you are to tie me up, tight as a splint,
erect along the mast, lashed to the mast,
and if I shout and beg to be untied,
take more turns of the rope to muffle me.'

I rather dwelt on this part of the forecast,
700   while our good ship made time, bound outward down
the wind for the strange island of Sirens.

◀ Critical Viewing
The sorceress Circe both helps and hinders Odysseus on his journey home. What can you tell about Circe from this illustration? **[Deduce]**

Literary Analysis
Epic Hero What does Odysseus reveal about his character by sharing information with his men?

Reading Check

What instructions does Odysseus give his ship-mates as they prepare to deal with the Sirens?

Then all at once the wind fell, and a calm
came over all the sea, as though some power
lulled the swell.

                              The crew were on their feet
705   briskly, to furl the sail, and stow it; then,
each in place, they poised the smooth oar blades
and sent the white foam scudding by. I carved
a massive cake of beeswax into bits
and rolled them in my hands until they softened—
710   no long task, for a burning heat came down
from Helios, lord of high noon. Going forward
I carried wax along the line, and laid it
thick on their ears. They tied me up, then, plumb
amidships, back to the mast, lashed to the mast,
715   and took themselves again to rowing. Soon,
as we came smartly within hailing distance,
the two Sirens, noting our fast ship
off their point, made ready, and they sang:

This way, oh turn your bows,
720   *Achaea's glory,*
As all the world allows—
              Moor and be merry.

Sweet coupled airs we sing.
              No lonely seafarer
725   *Holds clear of entering*
              Our green mirror.

Pleased by each purling note
              Like honey twining
From her throat and my throat,
730   *Who lies a-pining?*

Sea rovers here take joy
              Voyaging onward,
As from our song of Troy
Graybeard and rower-boy
735   *Goeth more learnèd.*

All feats on that great field
              In the long warfare,
Dark days the bright gods willed,
              Wounds you bore there,

Reading Skill
Historical and Cultural Context What does Odysseus' mention of Helios reveal about ancient Greek beliefs regarding astronomical events?

Literary Analysis
Epic Hero Which details in the Sirens' song are designed to flatter the epic hero?

740　　　　*Argos' old soldiery*[63]
　　　　　　On Troy beach teeming,
　　　　　Charmed out of time we see.
　　　　　No life on earth can be
　　　　　　Hid from our dreaming.

745　The lovely voices in ardor appealing over the water
　　　made me crave to listen, and I tried to say
　　　'Untie me!' to the crew, jerking my brows;
　　　but they bent steady to the oars. Then Perimedes
　　　got to his feet, he and Eurylochus,
750　and passed more line about, to hold me still.
　　　So all rowed on, until the Sirens
　　　dropped under the sea rim, and their singing
　　　dwindled away.

　　　　　　　　　　　My faithful company
　　　rested on their oars now, peeling off
755　the wax that I had laid thick on their ears;
　　　then set me free.

Scylla and Charybdis

　　　But scarcely had that island
　　　faded in blue air than I saw smoke
　　　and white water, with sound of waves in tumult—
　　　a sound the men heard, and it terrified them.
760　Oars flew from their hands; the blades went knocking
　　　wild alongside till the ship lost way,
　　　with no oar blades to drive her through the water.
　　　Well, I walked up and down from bow to stern,
　　　trying to put heart into them, standing over
765　every oarsman, saying gently,

　　　　　　　　　　　　　　'Friends,
　　　have we never been in danger before this?
　　　More fearsome, is it now, than when the Cyclops
　　　penned us in his cave? What power he had!
　　　Did I not keep my nerve, and use my wits
770　to find a way out for us?

63. Argos' old soldiery
　　soldiers from Argos, a city
　　in ancient Greece.

Vocabulary
ardor (är´ dər) *n.*
passion; enthusiasm

Reading Check

How does Odysseus keep his shipmates from hearing the Sirens sing?

Literary Analysis

Epic Hero What parts of Odysseus' speech demonstrate his strength as a leader?

by hook or crook this peril too shall be
something that we remember.

                                Heads up, lads!
We must obey the orders as I give them.
Get the oar shafts in your hands, and lay back

775   hard on your benches; hit these breaking seas.
Zeus help us pull away before we founder.
You at the tiller, listen, and take in
all that I say—the rudders are your duty;
keep her out of the combers and the smoke;[64]

780   steer for that headland; watch the drift, or we
fetch up in the smother, and you drown us.'

64. the combers (kōm′ ərs) **and the smoke** the large waves that break on the beach and the ocean spray.

That was all, and it brought them round to action.
But as I sent them on toward Scylla,[65] I
told them nothing, as they could do nothing.

65. Scylla (sil′ ə)

785   They would have dropped their oars again, in panic,
to roll for cover under the decking. Circe's
bidding against arms had slipped my mind,
so I tied on my cuirass[66] and took up
two heavy spears, then made my way along

66. cuirass (kwi ras′) *n.* armor for the upper body.

790   to the foredeck—thinking to see her first from there,
the monster of the gray rock, harboring
torment for my friends. I strained my eyes
upon the cliffside veiled in cloud, but nowhere
could I catch sight of her.

                            And all this time,

67. travail (trə vāl′) *n.* very hard work.

795   in travail,[67] sobbing, gaining on the current,
we rowed into the strait—Scylla to port
and on our starboard beam Charybdis, dire
gorge[68] of the salt seatide. By heaven! when she
vomited, all the sea was like a cauldron

68. gorge (gôrj) *n.* throat or gullet.

800   seething over intense fire, when the mixture
suddenly heaves and rises.

                         The shot spume
soared to the landside heights, and fell like rain.
But when she swallowed the sea water down
we saw the funnel of the maelstrom,[69] heard

69. maelstrom (māl′ strəm) *n.* large, violent whirlpool.

805   the rock bellowing all around, and dark
sand raged on the bottom far below.
My men all blanched against the gloom, our eyes

◀ **Critical Viewing**
How does this image
compare with the
description of Scylla in
the scene? **[Compare
and Contrast]**

were fixed upon that yawning mouth in fear
of being devoured.

                Then Scylla made her strike,
810   whisking six of my best men from the ship.
I happened to glance aft at ship and oarsmen
and caught sight of their arms and legs, dangling
high overhead. Voices came down to me
in anguish, calling my name for the last time.

815   A man surfcasting on a point of rock
for bass or mackerel, whipping his long rod
to drop the sinker and the bait far out,

☑ Reading
  Check
What demand does
Odysseus make of his
men as they approach
the rough waters?

from the Odyssey, Part 1 **1075**

will hook a fish and rip it from the surface
to dangle wriggling through the air:

                                      so these

820   were borne aloft in spasms toward the cliff.

She ate them as they shrieked there, in her den,
in the dire grapple, reaching still for me—
and deathly pity ran me through
at that sight—far the worst I ever suffered,
825   questing the passes of the strange sea.

                                      We rowed on.

The Rocks were now behind; Charybdis, too,
and Scylla dropped astern.

The Cattle of the Sun God

In the small hours of the third watch, when stars
that shone out in the first dusk of evening
830   had gone down to their setting, a giant wind
blew from heaven, and clouds driven by Zeus
shrouded land and sea in a night of storm;
so, just as Dawn with fingertips of rose
touched the windy world, we dragged our ship
835   to cover in a grotto, a sea cave
where nymphs had chairs of rock and sanded floors.
I mustered all the crew and said:

                              'Old shipmates,
our stores are in the ship's hold, food and drink;
the cattle here are not for our provision,
840   or we pay dearly for it.

                            Fierce the god is
who cherishes these heifers and these sheep:
Helios; and no man avoids his eye.'

To this my fighters nodded. Yes. But now
we had a month of onshore gales, blowing
845   day in, day out—south winds, or south by east.
As long as bread and good red wine remained
to keep the men up, and appease their craving,
they would not touch the cattle. But in the end,
when all the barley in the ship was gone,

Reading Skill
Historical and Cultural Context Which details here suggest that ancient Greeks believed the gods controlled the weather?

Reading Skill
Historical and Cultural Context How does this passage show that ancient Greeks believed their gods had human-like emotions?

850 hunger drove them to scour the wild shore
with angling hooks, for fishes and seafowl,
whatever fell into their hands; and lean days
wore their bellies thin.

                              The storms continued.
So one day I withdrew to the interior
855 to pray the gods in solitude, for hope
that one might show me some way of salvation.
Slipping away, I struck across the island
to a sheltered spot, out of the driving gale.
I washed my hands there, and made supplication
860 to the gods who own Olympus,⁷⁰ all the gods—
but they, for answer, only closed my eyes
under slow drops of sleep.

                      Now on the shore Eurylochus
made his **insidious** plea:

                              'Comrades,' he said,
'You've gone through everything; listen to what I say.
865 All deaths are hateful to us, mortal wretches,
but famine is the most pitiful, the worst
end that a man can come to.

                              Will you fight it?

Come, we'll cut out the noblest of these cattle
for sacrifice to the gods who own the sky;
870 and once at home, in the old country of Ithaca,
if ever that day comes—
we'll build a costly temple and adorn it
with every beauty for the Lord of Noon.⁷¹
But if he flares up over his heifers lost,
875 wishing our ship destroyed, and if the gods
make cause with him, why, then I say: Better
open your lungs to a big sea once for all
than waste to skin and bones on a lonely island!'

Thus Eurylochus; and they murmured 'Aye!'
880 trooping away at once to round up heifers.
Now, that day tranquil cattle with broad brows
were gazing near, and soon the men drew up
around their chosen beasts in ceremony.
They plucked the leaves that shone on a tall oak—
885 having no barley meal—to strew the victims,
performed the prayers and ritual, knifed the kine

70. Olympus (ō lim´ pəs)
Mount Olympus, home of
the gods.

Vocabulary
insidious (in sid´ ē əs)
adj. characterized by
craftiness and betrayal

71. Lord of Noon Helios.

Literary Analysis
Epic Hero How are
the values of Eurylochus
different from those of
Odysseus?

**Reading
Check**
Who owns the heifers
and sheep on the island?

Geography Connection

Real Places and Imaginary Events in the *Odyssey*

Odysseus' journey carries him to real places, including Troy, Sparta, and the Strait of Gibraltar. However, in the story, many of these real places are populated by imaginary creatures, such as the Cyclops and the Sirens. The combination of real places and fantastic events is part of the story's appeal.

Connect to the Literature   How does the inclusion of real places make the story's imaginary events more believable?

and flayed each carcass, cutting thighbones free
to wrap in double folds of fat. These offerings,
with strips of meat, were laid upon the fire.

890   Then, as they had no wine, they made libation
with clear spring water, broiling the entrails first;
and when the bones were burnt and tripes shared,
they spitted the carved meat.

                                        Just then my slumber
left me in a rush, my eyes opened,

895   and I went down the seaward path. No sooner
had I caught sight of our black hull, than savory
odors of burnt fat eddied around me;
grief took hold of me, and I cried aloud:

'O Father Zeus and gods in bliss forever,

900   you made me sleep away this day of mischief !
O cruel drowsing, in the evil hour!
Here they sat, and a great work they contrived.'⁷²

72. contrived (kən trīvd´) *v.*
thought up; devised.

Lampetia[73] in her long gown meanwhile
had borne swift word to the Overlord of Noon:
905 'They have killed your kine.'

And the Lord Helios

burst into angry speech amid the immortals:

'O Father Zeus and gods in bliss forever,
punish Odysseus' men! So overweening,
now they have killed my peaceful kine, my joy
910 at morning when I climbed the sky of stars,
and evening, when I bore westward from heaven.
Restitution or penalty they shall pay—
and pay in full—or I go down forever
to light the dead men in the underworld.'

915 Then Zeus who drives the stormcloud made reply:
'Peace, Helios: shine on among the gods,
shine over mortals in the fields of grain.
Let me throw down one white-hot bolt, and make
splinters of their ship in the winedark sea.'

920 —Calypso later told me of this exchange,
as she declared that Hermes[74] had told her.
Well, when I reached the sea cave and the ship,
I faced each man, and had it out; but where
could any remedy be found? There was none.
925 The silken beeves[75] of Helios were dead.
The gods, moreover, made queer signs appear:
cowhides began to crawl, and beef, both raw
and roasted, lowed like kine upon the spits.

Now six full days my gallant crew could feast
930 upon the prime beef they had marked for slaughter
from Helios' herd; and Zeus, the son of Cronus,
added one fine morning.

All the gales

had ceased, blown out, and with an offshore breeze
we launched again, stepping the mast and sail,
935 to make for the open sea. Astern of us
the island coastline faded, and no land
showed anywhere, but only sea and heaven,
when Zeus Cronion piled a thunderhead
above the ship, while gloom spread on the ocean.

73. **Lampetia** (lam pē´ shə)
a nymph.

74. **Hermes** (hʉr´ mēz´) *n.* god
who serves as herald and
messenger of the other
gods.

75. **beeves** (bēvz) *n.* alternate
plural form of "beef."

Literary Analysis
Epic Hero Analyze
the nonlinear plot
development in this
section. What details
in lines 920–921 clarify
the flashback presented
here?

Reading
Check

What do Odysseus'
shipmates do while he
is sleeping?

La Nef de Telemachus (The Ship of Telemachus), New York Public Library Picture Collection

940　We held our course, but briefly. Then the squall
　　 struck whining from the west, with gale force, breaking
　　 both forestays, and the mast came toppling aft
　　 along the ship's length, so the running rigging
　　 showered into the bilge.

　　　　　　　　　　　　　　　　　　On the afterdeck
945　the mast had hit the steersman a slant blow
　　 bashing the skull in, knocking him overside,
　　 as the brave soul fled the body, like a diver.
　　 With crack on crack of thunder, Zeus let fly
　　 a bolt against the ship, a direct hit,
950　so that she bucked, in reeking fumes of sulphur,
　　 and all the men were flung into the sea.
　　 They came up 'round the wreck, bobbing awhile
　　 like petrels[76] on the waves.

　　　　　　　　　　　　　　　　No more seafaring
　　 homeward for these, no sweet day of return;
955　the god had turned his face from them.

　　　　　　　　　　　　　　　　　　　I clambered
　　 fore and aft my hulk until a comber
　　 split her, keel from ribs, and the big timber
　　 floated free; the mast, too, broke away.
　　 A backstay floated dangling from it, stout
960　rawhide rope, and I used this for lashing
　　 mast and keel together. These I straddled,
　　 riding the frightful storm.

　　　　　　　　　　　　　　　　　　Nor had I yet
　　 seen the worst of it: for now the west wind
　　 dropped, and a southeast gale came on—one more
965　twist of the knife—taking me north again,
　　 straight for Charybdis. All that night I drifted,
　　 and in the sunrise, sure enough, I lay
　　 off Scylla mountain and Charybdis deep.
　　 There, as the whirlpool drank the tide, a billow
970　tossed me, and I sprang for the great fig tree,
　　 catching on like a bat under a bough.
　　 Nowhere had I to stand, no way of climbing,
　　 the root and bole[77] being far below, and far
　　 above my head the branches and their leaves,
975　massed, overshadowing Charybdis pool.
　　 But I clung grimly, thinking my mast and keel
　　 would come back to the surface when she spouted.

◄ **Critical Viewing**
In the *Odyssey*, Odysseus'
son Telemachus searches
for his father in a ship
like this one. From what
you observe in the
painting, how does this
ship compare with
modern ships? **[Compare
and Contrast]**

76. **petrels** (pe′ trəlz) *n.* small,
　　 dark sea birds.

Literary Analysis
Epic Hero Which of
Odysseus' heroic qualities
does he demonstrate in
this passage?

Reading Skill
**Historical and Cultural
Context** How might the
figurative language "one
more twist of the knife"
relate to this work's
historical and cultural
setting?

77. **bole** (bōl) *n.* tree trunk.

Reading
Check
How is Odysseus' ship
destroyed?

And ah! how long, with what desire, I waited!
till, at the twilight hour, when one who hears
980 and judges pleas in the marketplace all day
between contentious men, goes home to supper,
the long poles at last reared from the sea.

Now I let go with hands and feet, plunging
straight into the foam beside the timbers,
985 pulled astride, and rowed hard with my hands
to pass by Scylla. Never could I have passed her
had not the Father of gods and men,[78] this time,
kept me from her eyes. Once through the strait,
nine days I drifted in the open sea
990 before I made shore, buoyed up by the gods,
upon Ogygia[79] Isle. The dangerous nymph
Calypso lives and sings there, in her beauty,
and she received me, loved me.

                                                      But why tell
the same tale that I told last night in hall
995 to you and to your lady? Those adventures
made a long evening, and I do not hold
with tiresome repetition of a story."

78. Father . . . men Zeus.

79. Ogygia (o jij′ ĭ ə)

Literary Analysis
Epic Hero In what way do lines 994–997 remind you that Odysseus is telling his story to an audience?

Critical Thinking

Support your responses with evidence from the text.

1. **Respond:** If you were one of Odysseus' crew, how would you feel about having him as your leader? Explain your response.

2. **(a)** In the episode of the Lotus-Eaters, how does Odysseus handle the men who ate the lotus? **(b) Interpret:** What does Odysseus understand that his men do not?

3. **(a)** In the episode of the Cattle of the Sun God, why does the crew kill the cattle? **(b) Analyze:** What does Odysseus' reaction to this act show about the importance of the gods to him?

4. **(a) Evaluate:** Why do you think the *Odyssey* has endured as a great literary work? **(b) Discuss:** In a group, share your ideas.

5. **Analyze:** Review the information provided about Homer on page 1043. In what ways is the *Odyssey* typical of the non-English-speaking, classical, ancient Greek literary tradition?

Do heroes have responsibilities?
Could Odysseus have prevented his men from eating the cattle of Helios and so saved their lives? Explain.

Literary Analysis: Epic Hero

1. (a) Use a chart to identify three actions that the **epic hero** Odysseus performs. **(b)** For each action, list the trait that it reveals. **(c)** Then, explain which traits the ancient Greeks admired most.

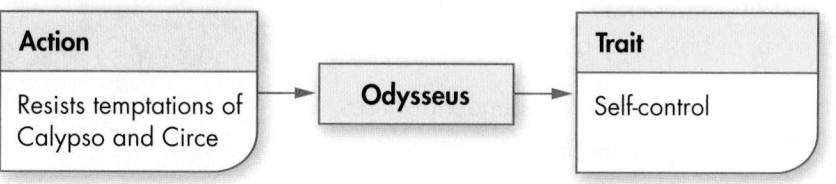
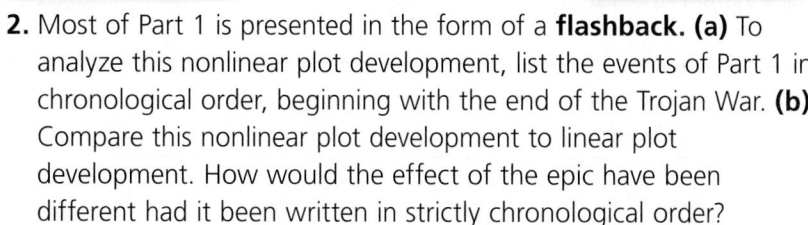

Action		Trait
Resists temptations of Calypso and Circe	**Odysseus**	Self-control

2. Most of Part 1 is presented in the form of a **flashback. (a)** To analyze this nonlinear plot development, list the events of Part 1 in chronological order, beginning with the end of the Trojan War. **(b)** Compare this nonlinear plot development to linear plot development. How would the effect of the epic have been different had it been written in strictly chronological order?

Reading Skill: Historical and Cultural Context

3. Consider the **cultural and historical context, or setting,** of Homer's *Odyssey*. What role do ancient Greek religious beliefs play in the epic? Provide examples from the text to support your response.

4. What forms of modern technology could have helped Odysseus?

Vocabulary

Practice Identify the word in each group that does not belong with the others. Explain your response.

1. plundered, robbed, donated
2. dispatched, hesitated, completed
3. assuage, soothe, increase
4. bereft, after, without
5. ardor, emotion, apathy
6. insidious, traitorous, friendly

Word Power Use the context of the sentences and what you know about the **Old English prefix be-** to explain your answer to each question.

1. If people *begrudge* your success, are they happy for you?
2. What might happen if a sailing ship were *becalmed*?

Word Power

The **Old English prefix be-** means "around," "make," or "covered with."

Apply It Explain how the root *be-* helps you determine the meanings of these words. Consult a dictionary if necessary.

bemuse
belittle
befriend

Integrated Language Skills

from the **Odyssey, Part 1**

Conventions: Simple and Compound Sentences

A **simple sentence** consists of a single independent clause.

Although a simple sentence is just one independent clause with one subject and one verb, the subject, verb, or both may be compound.

A **compound sentence** consists of two or more independent clauses.

The clauses can be joined by a comma and a coordinating conjunction or by a semicolon. The coordinating conjunctions are *and, but, or, nor, for, yet,* and *so.*

Simple sentence	He remembered an old story.
Simple sentence with compound subject	He and she remembered an old story.
Compound sentence	They laughed together, and they remembered an old story.

Practice A Read the following sentences and identify each as simple or compound. For compound sentences, identify the coordinating conjunction.

1. Odysseus led his ship through the perils of Scylla and Charybdis.

2. The Cyclops captured the Greeks, and he ate some of them.

3. The men were starving, but Odysseus commanded them not to eat Helios' cattle.

4. Calypso and Circe both helped and hindered Odysseus.

5. The crew was in peril, and they looked to the captain to save them.

Speaking Application Tell a partner about a trip you have taken. Use at least two correctly structured compound sentences in your telling.

Practice B Read each pair of simple sentences. Then, combine each pair to form a correctly structured compound sentence. Use a comma and coordinating conjunction or a semicolon to separate the clauses.

1. Odysseus yelled insults at Polyphemus. The Cyclops hurled a rock at the ship.

2. The Sirens sang. The ship sailed on.

3. Scylla swooped down on the ship. She grabbed six men.

4. The men screamed for help. Odysseus stood by helplessly.

5. Odysseus is Laertes' son. Odysseus is Penelope's husband.

Writing Application Write four sentences in response to the *Odyssey*. Use two correctly structured simple sentences and two correctly structured compound sentences.

PH GRAMMAR HANDBOOK Further instruction and practice are available in the *Prentice Hall Grammar Handbook*.

Writing

Write an **everyday epic.** Choose an ordinary daily event, and write an account that makes it seem larger than life. Write an engaging story with **interesting and believable characters.**

- Outline the plot of your story, adding points in the action where you can demonstrate your hero's traits, such as generosity and bravery. Include extreme challenges and plan appearances by gods and monsters.

- Use multiple points of view. Begin with the voice of a speaker outside the story, and then have one of the characters tell the tale.

- Use the models you find in the *Odyssey* to help you incorporate figurative language to accurately describe scenes for your reader.

- Reveal the emotions of your characters through dialogue.

Grammar Application Make sure you use correctly structured simple and compound sentences in your epic.

Writing Workshop: *Work in Progress*

Prewriting for Procedural Document To choose a topic for a Procedural Document you may write, list tasks that you do well. For example, you may be good at using a computer program, you might know how to use an outdated tool that not many people can work anymore, or you might be a skilled party planner. Save this Task List in your portfolio.

Listening and Speaking

With two teammates, complete and present a **media analysis.** Decide upon a recent travel-related news event. Find various forms of media (e.g., newspapers, television, documentaries, blogs, Internet) that report on the event. **Compare and contrast coverage of the event in the various media.** Consider your answers to the following questions:

- What is the purpose of each report, and how might the purpose affect the coverage?

- What is the intended audience of each report, and how might the audience affect the type of information that is presented?

- What effect might visuals, sound, and other tools and techniques have on the audience of each report?

After you have completed your analysis, present your findings to the class. If possible, show the different forms of media you analyzed to the audience during your presentation.

 Focus on the TEKS

Conventions
(17)(C) Use a variety of correctly structured sentences (e.g., compound).

Writing
(14)(A) Write an engaging story with interesting and believable characters.

Reading
(12)(C) Compare and contrast coverage of the same event in various media (e.g., newspapers, television, documentaries, blogs, Internet).

Use this prewriting activity to prepare for the **Writing Workshop** on page 1138.

www.PHLitOnline.com
- Interactive graphic organizers
- Grammar tutorial
- Interactive journals

Epic Selection

▲ Read the **Odyssey** to learn about Odysseus' return to Ithaca and the battle he must wage to regain his home.

 TEXAS Focus on the TEKS

Meet these standards with Part 2 of the **Odyssey** (p. 1089).

Reading
(3) Understand elements of poetry. *(Literary Analysis: Epic Simile)*
(2)(C) Relate the figurative language of a literary work to its historical and cultural setting. *(Reading Skill: Historical and Cultural Context)*

Oral and Written Conventions
(17)(C) Use a variety of correctly structured sentences (e.g., complex, compound-complex). *(Conventions: Complex and Compound-Complex Sentences)*

Writing
(15) Write expository texts to communicate ideas and information to specific audiences for specific purposes. *(Writing: Biography)*

Listening and Speaking
(26) Participate productively in teams, developing a plan for consensus-building, and setting ground rules for decision-making. *(Listening and Speaking: Debate)*
(24)(C) Evaluate the effectiveness of a speaker's main and supporting ideas. *(Listening and Speaking: Debate)*

Literary Analysis: Epic Simile

An **epic simile** is an elaborate comparison that may extend for several lines and that may use the words *like, as, just as,* or *so.* Unlike a typical simile, which draws a comparison to a single image, an epic simile might recall an entire place or story. In Part 1, lines 268–271, Odysseus uses an epic simile to describe the size of the tree from which he creates a weapon.

> And it was like a mast / a lugger of twenty oars, broad in the
> beam— / a deep-sea-going craft—might carry: / so long, so big
> around, it seemed.

As You Read Notice how Homer uses the poetic element of epic similes—often called Homeric similes—to bring descriptions to life.

Reading Skill: Historical and Cultural Context

The **historical and cultural context, or setting,** of a work is the time and place in which the work is set or was written. This context can include the events, beliefs, or customs of the time period. The historical and cultural setting of a work often influences many aspects of the work, including the figurative language used to convey ideas.

When you identify influences on your own reading and responses, the cultural context of a work becomes more apparent. Follow these steps:

- Keep your own beliefs and customs in mind.
- Notice the ways in which your reactions to ideas and situations in the work differ from the reactions of the characters.
- Consider whether your reactions reflect your cultural values.

Using the Strategy: Cultural Influences Chart

As You Read Use a chart like this one to note differences between your own cultural influences and those reflected in the *Odyssey.*

> **Detail in Text**
>
> Odysseus says he and his crew plundered Ismarus.

> **Meaning for Characters**
>
> Winners can take valuables from the defeated.

> **Meaning in My Culture**
>
> Looting is shameful.

TEXAS
PHLitOnline
www.PHLitOnline.com

Hear It!
- Selection summary audio
- Selection audio

See It!
- Get Connected video
- Background video
- More about the author
- Vocabulary flashcards

Do It!
- Interactive journals
- Interactive graphic organizers
- Self-test
- Internet activity
- Grammar tutorial
- Interactive vocabulary games

Do *heroes* have responsibilities?

Writing About the Big Question

In Part 2 of the *Odyssey,* Homer describes Odysseus' arrival home and the confrontation with suitors who are there to marry his wife and steal his lands. Use this sentence starter to develop your ideas about the Big Question.

The true **character** of a **hero** can be seen when _____.

As You Read Look for Odysseus' reactions to the challenges he faces. Also, note examples of the responsibilities Odysseus may have and what he does to fulfill them.

Vocabulary

Read each word and its definition. Decide whether you know the word well, know it a little bit, or do not know it at all. After you read, see how your knowledge of each word has increased.

- **dissemble** (di sem´ bəl) *v.* conceal under a false appearance; disguise (p. 1090) *The spy was able to dissemble and seem like a patriot.* *dissemblance n. resemble v.*

- **incredulity** (in´ krə d o͞o´ lə tē) *n.* unwillingness or inability to believe (p. 1092) *During the eclipse, they were silent with incredulity.* *incredulous adj. incredible adj.*

- **bemusing** (bē my o͞o z´ iŋ) *v.* stupefying or muddling (p. 1095) *After bemusing the audience, the speaker received little applause.* *bemusement n. amuse v.*

- **equity** (ek´ wit ē) *n.* fairness; justice (p. 1100) *Laws are meant to treat everyone with equity.* *equitable adj. inequity n.*

- **maudlin** (môd´ lin) *adj.* tearfully and foolishly sentimental (p. 1101) *The scene in which the lost dog finally returned home evoked maudlin responses from the audience.* *maudlinly adv. maudlinness n.*

- **contempt** (kən tempt´) *n.* disdain or scorn (p. 1108) *A good athlete shows respect, not contempt, for an opponent.* *contemptible adj.*

Word Power

The **Latin prefix *dis-*** means "away," "apart," or "not."

In this selection, the goddess Athena tells Odysseus not to **dissemble** to, or not disguise himself from, his son Telemachus.

from the

Odyssey

HOMER

translated by ROBERT FITZGERALD

PART 2

The Return of Odysseus

Review and Anticipate

In Part 1 of the Odyssey, *Odysseus and his companions face many perils on their voyage from Troy to Ithaca. At some moments, they are tempted to forsake their voyage; at others, their lives are endangered by powerful enemies. Ultimately, Odysseus' men bring about their own destruction at the hand of Zeus when they kill the cattle belonging to Helios.*

As Part 2 begins, Odysseus is alone when he reaches Ithaca after a twenty-year absence. What do you predict will happen when Odysseus arrives home?

"Twenty years gone, and I am back again . . ."

Odysseus has finished telling his story to the Phaeacians. The next day, young Phaeacian noblemen conduct him home by ship. He arrives in Ithaca after an absence of twenty years. The goddess Athena appears and informs him of the situation at home. Numerous suitors, believing Odysseus to be dead, have been continually seeking the hand of his wife, Penelope, in marriage, while overrunning Odysseus' palace and enjoying themselves at Penelope's expense. Moreover, they are plotting to murder Odysseus' son, Telemachus, before he can inherit his father's lands. Telemachus, who, like Penelope, still hopes for his father's return, has journeyed to Pylos and Sparta to learn what he can about his father's fate. Athena disguises Odysseus as a beggar and directs him to the hut of Eumaeus,[1] his old and faithful swineherd. While Odysseus and Eumaeus are eating breakfast, Telemachus arrives. Athena then appears to Odysseus.

1. Eumaeus (yōō mē′ əs)

               . . . From the air
she walked, taking the form of a tall woman,
handsome and clever at her craft, and stood

1000 beyond the gate in plain sight of Odysseus,
unseen, though, by Telemachus, unguessed,
for not to everyone will gods appear.
Odysseus noticed her; so did the dogs,
who cowered whimpering away from her. She only

1005 nodded, signing to him with her brows,
a sign he recognized. Crossing the yard,
he passed out through the gate in the stockade
to face the goddess. There she said to him:
"Son of Laertes and the gods of old,

1010 Odysseus, master of landways and seaways,
dissemble to your son no longer now.
The time has come: tell him how you together
will bring doom on the suitors in the town.
I shall not be far distant then, for I

1015 myself desire battle."

                      Saying no more,
she tipped her golden wand upon the man,
making his cloak pure white, and the knit tunic
fresh around him. Lithe and young she made him,
ruddy with sun, his jawline clean, the beard

▶ Critical Viewing
What can you tell about Eumaeus from this illustration? **[Infer]**

Vocabulary
dissemble (di sem′ bəl)
v. conceal under a false appearance; disguise

Reading Skill
**Historical and Cultural
Context** What do lines
1021–1029 suggest
about the way ancient
Greeks responded to the
presence of a god?

1020   no longer gray upon his chin. And she
       withdrew when she had done.
                                   Then Lord Odysseus
       reappeared—and his son was thunderstruck.
       Fear in his eyes, he looked down and away
       as though it were a god, and whispered:

                                              "Stranger,
1025   you are no longer what you were just now!
       Your cloak is new; even your skin! You are
       one of the gods who rule the sweep of heaven!
       Be kind to us, we'll make you fair oblation[2]
       and gifts of hammered gold. Have mercy on us!"

1030   The noble and enduring man replied:

       "No god. Why take me for a god? No, no.
       I am that father whom your boyhood lacked
       and suffered pain for lack of. I am he."

       Held back too long, the tears ran down his cheeks
1035   as he embraced his son.
                               Only Telemachus,
       uncomprehending, wild
       with incredulity, cried out:
                                   "You cannot
       be my father Odysseus! Meddling spirits
       conceived this trick to twist the knife in me!
1040   No man of woman born could work these wonders
       by his own craft, unless a god came into it
       with ease to turn him young or old at will.
       I swear you were in rags and old,
       and here you stand like one of the immortals!"

1045   Odysseus brought his ranging mind to bear
       and said:
                 "This is not princely, to be swept
       away by wonder at your father's presence.
       No other Odysseus will ever come,
       for he and I are one, the same; his bitter
1050   fortune and his wanderings are mine.
       Twenty years gone, and I am back again
       on my own island.

2. oblation (äb lā′ shən) *n.*
offering to a god.

**Vocabulary
incredulity** (in′ krə do͞o′
lə tē) *n.* unwillingness
or inability to believe

                    As for my change of skin,
that is a charm Athena, Hope of Soldiers,
uses as she will; she has the knack
1055 to make me seem a beggar man sometimes
and sometimes young, with finer clothes about me.
It is no hard thing for the gods of heaven
to glorify a man or bring him low."

When he had spoken, down he sat.
                              Then, throwing
1060 his arms around this marvel of a father
Telemachus began to weep. Salt tears
rose from the wells of longing in both men,
and cries burst from both as keen and fluttering
as those of the great taloned hawk,
1065 whose nestlings farmers take before they fly.
So helplessly they cried, pouring out tears,
and might have gone on weeping so till sundown,
had not Telemachus said:

                    "Dear father! Tell me
what kind of vessel put you here ashore
1070 on Ithaca? Your sailors, who were they?
I doubt you made it, walking on the sea!"

Then said Odysseus, who had borne the barren sea:

"Only plain truth shall I tell you, child.
Great seafarers, the Phaeacians, gave me passage
1075 as they give other wanderers. By night
over the open ocean, while I slept,
they brought me in their cutter,[3] set me down
on Ithaca, with gifts of bronze and gold
and stores of woven things. By the gods' will
1080 these lie all hidden in a cave. I came
to this wild place, directed by Athena,
so that we might lay plans to kill our enemies.
Count up the suitors for me, let me know
what men at arms are there, how many men.
1085 I must put all my mind to it, to see
if we two by ourselves can take them on
or if we should look round for help."

Reading Skill
Historical and Cultural Context Lines 1063–1065 contain an epic simile. How might this figurative language relate to the historical and cultural setting of the text?

3. **cutter** (kut´ər) *n.* small, swift ship or boat carried aboard a large ship to transport personnel or supplies.

Reading
Check

Why is Telemachus initially doubtful that the man before him is Odysseus, his father?

4. **in their prime** in the best or most vigorous stage of their lives.

Telemachus
replied:

"O Father, all my life your fame
as a fighting man has echoed in my ears—
1090 your skill with weapons and the tricks of war—
but what you speak of is a staggering thing,
beyond imagining, for me. How can two men
do battle with a houseful in their prime?⁴
For I must tell you this is no affair
1095 of ten or even twice ten men, but scores,
throngs of them. You shall see, here and now.
The number from Dulichium alone
is fifty-two picked men, with armorers,
a half dozen; twenty-four came from Same,
1100 twenty from Zacynthus; our own island
accounts for twelve, high-ranked, and their retainers,
Medon the crier, and the Master Harper,
besides a pair of handymen at feasts.
If we go in against all these
1105 I fear we pay in salt blood for your vengeance.
You must think hard if you would conjure up
the fighting strength to take us through."

Odysseus
who had endured the long war and the sea
answered:

"I'll tell you now.
1110 Suppose Athena's arm is over us, and Zeus
her father's, must I rack my brains for more?"

Clearheaded Telemachus looked hard and said:

"Those two are great defenders, no one doubts it,
but throned in the serene clouds overhead;
1115 other affairs of men and gods they have
to rule over."

And the hero answered:
"Before long they will stand to right and left of us
in combat, in the shouting, when the test comes—
our nerve against the suitors' in my hall.
1120 Here is your part: at break of day tomorrow
home with you, go mingle with our princes.
The swineherd later on will take me down

Reading Skill
Historical and Cultural Context What does Odysseus' statement in lines 1109–1111 suggest about ancient Greek beliefs about the gods' interest in human affairs?

the port-side trail—a beggar, by my looks,
hangdog and old. If they make fun of me
1125 in my own courtyard, let your ribs cage up
your springing heart, no matter what I suffer,
no matter if they pull me by the heels
or practice shots at me, to drive me out.
Look on, hold down your anger. You may even
1130 plead with them, by heaven! in gentle terms
to quit their horseplay—not that they will heed you,
rash as they are, facing their day of wrath.
Now fix the next step in your mind.

                                        Athena,
counseling me, will give me word, and I
1135 shall signal to you, nodding: at that point
round up all armor, lances, gear of war
left in our hall, and stow the lot away
back in the vaulted storeroom. When the suitors
miss those arms and question you, be soft
1140 in what you say: answer:

                        'I thought I'd move them
out of the smoke. They seemed no longer those
bright arms Odysseus left us years ago
when he went off to Troy. Here where the fire's
hot breath came, they had grown black and drear.
1145 One better reason, too, I had from Zeus:
suppose a brawl starts up when you are drunk,
you might be crazed and bloody one another,
and that would stain your feast, your courtship.
        Tempered
iron can magnetize a man.'
                                        Say that.
1150 But put aside two broadswords and two spears
for our own use, two oxhide shields nearby
when we go into action. Pallas Athena
and Zeus All-Provident will see you through,
bemusing our young friends.
                                Now one thing more.
1155 If son of mine you are and blood of mine,
let no one hear Odysseus is about.
Neither Laertes, nor the swineherd here,
nor any slave, nor even Penelope.

LITERATURE IN CONTEXT

Cultural Connection

Athena
Athena was the goddess of wisdom, skills, and warfare. When she helps Odysseus in this epic, it is not the first time that she offers assistance to a Greek hero. In Homer's *Iliad,* Athena helps the Greek hero Achilles defeat the Trojan warrior Hector. Athena favored Achilles for his unmatched skill in battle, but Odysseus was her favorite among the Greeks. He displayed not only skill in warfare, but also ingenuity and cunning.

Connect to the Literature

Which of Odysseus' deeds in the *Odyssey* might have helped him to earn Athena's favor? Explain.

Vocabulary
bemusing (bē myo͞oz′ iŋ) *v.* stupefying or muddling

Reading Check

How does Odysseus tell his son to respond if the suitors "practice shots" on Odysseus?

But you and I alone must learn how far
1160 the women are corrupted; we should know
how to locate good men among our hands,
the loyal and respectful, and the shirkers[5]
who take you lightly, as alone and young."

5. **shirkers** (shɜrk´ ərz) *n.*
people who get out of
doing what needs to be
done.

Argus

*Odysseus heads for town with Eumaeus. Outside the palace,
Odysseus' old dog, Argus, is lying at rest as his long-absent
master approaches.*

While he spoke
an old hound, lying near, pricked up his ears
1165 and lifted up his muzzle. This was Argus,
trained as a puppy by Odysseus,
but never taken on a hunt before
his master sailed for Troy. The young men, afterward,
hunted wild goats with him, and hare, and deer,
1170 but he had grown old in his master's absence.
Treated as rubbish now, he lay at last
upon a mass of dung before the gates—
manure of mules and cows, piled there until
fieldhands could spread it on the king's estate.
1175 Abandoned there, and half destroyed with flies,
old Argus lay.

But when he knew he heard
Odysseus' voice nearby, he did his best
to wag his tail, nose down, with flattened ears,
having no strength to move nearer his master.
1180 And the man looked away,
wiping a salt tear from his cheek; but he
hid this from Eumaeus. Then he said:

"I marvel that they leave this hound to lie
here on the dung pile;
1185 he would have been a fine dog, from the look of him,
though I can't say as to his power and speed
when he was young. You find the same good build
in house dogs, table dogs landowners keep
all for style."

▼ **Critical Viewing**
What can you infer
about the ancient Greeks
based on the fact that
they depicted their gods
on everyday objects
like this urn? **[Infer]**

And you replied, Eumaeus:

1190 "A hunter owned him—but the man is dead
in some far place. If this old hound could show
the form he had when Lord Odysseus left him,
going to Troy, you'd see him swift and strong.
He never shrank from any savage thing
1195 he'd brought to bay in the deep woods; on the scent
no other dog kept up with him. Now misery
has him in leash. His owner died abroad,
and here the women slaves will take no care of him.
You know how servants are: without a master
1200 they have no will to labor, or excel.
For Zeus who views the wide world takes away
half the manhood of a man, that day
he goes into captivity and slavery."

Eumaeus crossed the court and went straight forward
1205 into the megaron[6] among the suitors:
but death and darkness in that instant closed
the eyes of Argus, who had seen his master,
Odysseus, after twenty years.

The Suitors

Still disguised as a beggar, Odysseus enters his home.
He is confronted by the haughty[7] suitor Antinous.[8]

But here Antinous broke in, shouting:

                        "God!
1210 What evil wind blew in this pest?
                        Get over,
stand in the passage! Nudge my table, will you?
Egyptian whips are sweet
to what you'll come to here, you nosing rat,
making your pitch to everyone!
1215 These men have bread to throw away on you
because it is not theirs. Who cares? Who spares
another's food, when he has more than plenty?"

Reading Skill
Historical and Cultural Context How do Eumaeus' beliefs about servitude and slavery compare with those of your own culture?

6. **megaron** (meg´ ə rön) *n.* great, central hall of the house, usually containing a center hearth.

7. **haughty** (hôt´ ē) *adj.* arrogant.

8. **Antinous** (an tin´ ō əs)

Reading Check
How does Antinous react to Odysseus, who is disguised as a beggar?

With guile Odysseus drew away, then said:

"A pity that you have more looks than heart.
1220 You'd grudge a pinch of salt from your own larder
to your own handyman. You sit here, fat
on others' meat, and cannot bring yourself
to rummage out a crust of bread for me!"

Then anger made Antinous' heart beat hard,
1225 and, glowering under his brows, he answered:

                                        "Now!
You think you'll shuffle off and get away
after that impudence?[9] Oh, no you don't!"

The stool he let fly hit the man's right shoulder
on the packed muscle under the shoulder blade—
1230 like solid rock, for all the effect one saw.
Odysseus only shook his head, containing
thoughts of bloody work, as he walked on,
then sat, and dropped his loaded bag again
upon the door sill. Facing the whole crowd
1235 he said, and eyed them all:

                                        "One word only,
my lords, and suitors of the famous queen.
One thing I have to say.
There is no pain, no burden for the heart
when blows come to a man, and he defending
1240 his own cattle—his own cows and lambs.
Here it was otherwise. Antinous
hit me for being driven on by hunger—
how many bitter seas men cross for hunger!
If beggars interest the gods, if there are Furies[10]
1245 pent in the dark to avenge a poor man's wrong, then may
Antinous meet his death before his wedding day!"

Then said Eupeithes' son, Antinous:

                                        "Enough.
Eat and be quiet where you are, or shamble elsewhere,
unless you want these lads to stop your mouth
1250 pulling you by the heels, or hands and feet,
over the whole floor, till your back is peeled!"

**Reading Skill
Historical and Cultural
Context** What con-
flicting values does this
exchange between
Antinous and Odysseus
reveal?

9. **impudence** (im' pyoo
dəns) *n.* quality of being
shamelessly bold;
disrespectful.

**Reading Skill
Historical and Cultural
Context** What values
regarding the use of
physical force are evident
in this speech?

10. **Furies** (fyoor' ēz) *n.* three
terrible female spirits
who punish the doers of
unavenged crimes.

But now the rest were mortified, and someone
spoke from the crowd of young bucks to rebuke him:

"A poor show, that—hitting this famished tramp—
1255 bad business, if he happened to be a god.
You know they go in foreign guise, the gods do,
looking like strangers, turning up
in towns and settlements to keep an eye
on manners, good or bad."
                                    But at this notion
1260 Antinous only shrugged.
                                    Telemachus,
after the blow his father bore, sat still
without a tear, though his heart felt the blow.
Slowly he shook his head from side to side,
containing murderous thoughts.
                                    Penelope
1265 on the higher level of her room had heard
the blow, and knew who gave it. Now she murmured:

"Would god you could be hit yourself, Antinous—
hit by Apollo's bowshot!"

**Reading Skill
Historical and Cultural
Context** What ancient
Greek belief is conveyed
in this suitor's speech?

Reading
Check

How does Penelope
regard Antinous?

11. **Eurynome** (yōō rin´ əm ē)

And Eurynome[11]
her housekeeper, put in:

      "He and no other?

1270 If all we pray for came to pass, not one
would live till dawn!"

                               Her gentle mistress said:

      "Oh, Nan, they are a bad lot; they intend
ruin for all of us; but Antinous
appears a blacker-hearted hound than any.

1275 Here is a poor man come, a wanderer,
driven by want to beg his bread, and everyone
in hall gave bits, to cram his bag—only
Antinous threw a stool, and banged his shoulder!"

      So she described it, sitting in her chamber

1280 among her maids—while her true lord was eating.
Then she called in the forester and said:

      "Go to that man on my behalf, Eumaeus,
and send him here, so I can greet and question him.
Abroad in the great world, he may have heard

1285 rumors about Odysseus—may have known him!"

Penelope

In the evening, Penelope interrogates the old beggar.

      "Friend, let me ask you first of all:
who are you, where do you come from, of what nation
and parents were you born?"

                          And he replied:

      "My lady, never a man in the wide world

1290 should have a fault to find with you. Your name
has gone out under heaven like the sweet
honor of some god-fearing king, who rules
in equity over the strong: his black lands bear
both wheat and barley, fruit trees laden bright,

1295 new lambs at lambing time—and the deep sea
gives great hauls of fish by his good strategy,
so that his folk fare well.

Vocabulary
equity (ek´ wit ē) *n.*
fairness; justice

O my dear lady,
this being so, let it suffice to ask me
of other matters—not my blood, my homeland.
1300 Do not enforce me to recall my pain.
My heart is sore; but I must not be found
sitting in tears here, in another's house:
it is not well forever to be grieving.
One of the maids might say—or you might think—
1305 I had got maudlin over cups of wine."

And Penelope replied:

"Stranger, my looks,
my face, my carriage,[12] were soon lost or faded
when the Achaeans crossed the sea to Troy,
Odysseus my lord among the rest.
1310 If he returned, if he were here to care for me,
I might be happily renowned!
But grief instead heaven sent me—years of pain.
Sons of the noblest families on the islands,
Dulichium, Same, wooded Zacynthus,[13]
1315 with native Ithacans, are here to court me,
against my wish; and they consume this house.
Can I give proper heed to guest or suppliant
or herald on the realm's affairs?

How could I?

wasted with longing for Odysseus, while here
1320 they press for marriage.

Ruses[14] served my turn
to draw the time out—first a close-grained web
I had the happy thought to set up weaving
on my big loom in hall. I said, that day:
'Young men—my suitors, now my lord is dead,
1325 let me finish my weaving before I marry,
or else my thread will have been spun in vain.
It is a shroud I weave for Lord Laertes
when cold Death comes to lay him on his bier.
The country wives would hold me in dishonor
1330 if he, with all his fortune, lay unshrouded.'
I reached their hearts that way, and they agreed.
So every day I wove on the great loom,
but every night by torchlight I unwove it;
and so for three years I deceived the Achaeans.

Vocabulary
maudlin (môd´ lin)
adj. tearfully and foolishly sentimental

12. carriage (kar´ ij) *n.*
posture.

13. Zacynthus (za sin´ *th*us)

14. ruses (rōōz´ iz) *n.* tricks.

Reading Skill
**Historical and Cultural
Context** How do the
ancient Greek ideas in
Penelope's speech about
honoring the dead com-
pare to modern ideas?

Reading
Check
How was Penelope able
to delay marriage for
three years?

The Trial of the Bow from Homer's *The Odyssey*, N.C. Wyeth, Brandywine River Museum

1335 But when the seasons brought a fourth year on,
as long months waned, and the long days were spent,
through impudent folly in the slinking maids
they caught me—clamored up to me at night;
I had no choice then but to finish it.

1340 And now, as matters stand at last,
I have no strength left to evade a marriage,
cannot find any further way; my parents
urge it upon me, and my son
will not stand by while they eat up his property.

1345 He comprehends it, being a man full-grown,
able to oversee the kind of house
Zeus would endow with honor.

                                    But you too
confide in me, tell me your ancestry.
You were not born of mythic oak or stone."

*Penelope again asks the beggar to tell about himself. He
makes up a tale in which Odysseus is mentioned and
declares that Penelope's husband will soon be home.*

1350 "You see, then, he is alive and well, and headed
homeward now, no more to be abroad
far from his island, his dear wife and son.
Here is my sworn word for it. Witness this,
god of the zenith, noblest of the gods,[15]

1355 and Lord Odysseus' hearthfire, now before me:
I swear these things shall turn out as I say.
Between this present dark and one day's ebb,
after the wane, before the crescent moon,
Odysseus will come."

The Challenge

*Pressed by the suitors to choose a husband from among
them, Penelope says she will marry the man who can string
Odysseus' bow and shoot an arrow through twelve axhandle
sockets. The suitors try and fail. Still in disguise, Odysseus
asks for a turn and gets it.*

                          And Odysseus took his time,
1360 turning the bow, tapping it, every inch,
for borings that termites might have made

◀ **Critical Viewing**
The winner of the archery contest will win Penelope's hand in marriage. What details or artistic techniques capture the tension in this scene? **[Interpret]**

15. god of the zenith, noblest of the gods Zeus.

Reading Check

What means does Penelope decide she will use to choose a husband?

while the master of the weapon was abroad.
The suitors were now watching him, and some
jested among themselves:

"A bow lover!"

1365 "Dealer in old bows!"

"Maybe he has one like it
at home!"

"Or has an itch to make one for himself."

"See how he handles it, the sly old buzzard!"

And one disdainful suitor added this:
"May his fortune grow an inch for every inch he bends it!"

1370 But the man skilled in all ways of contending,
satisfied by the great bow's look and heft,
like a musician, like a harper, when
with quiet hand upon his instrument
he draws between his thumb and forefinger
1375 a sweet new string upon a peg: so effortlessly
Odysseus in one motion strung the bow.
Then slid his right hand down the cord and plucked it,
so the taut gut vibrating hummed and sang
a swallow's note.

In the hushed hall it smote the suitors
1380 and all their faces changed. Then Zeus thundered
overhead, one loud crack for a sign.
And Odysseus laughed within him that the son
of crooked-minded Cronus had flung that omen down.
He picked one ready arrow from his table
1385 where it lay bare: the rest were waiting still
in the quiver for the young men's turn to come.
He nocked[16] it, let it rest across the handgrip,
and drew the string and grooved butt of the arrow,
aiming from where he sat upon the stool.

▲ **Critical Viewing**
Does the hunter pictured
here show the same
grace as does Odysseus
in lines 1370–1392?
Explain. **[Compare
and Contrast]**

16. nocked (näkt) set an
arrow into the bowstring.

Now flashed

1390   arrow from twanging bow clean as a whistle
through every socket ring, and grazed not one,
to thud with heavy brazen head beyond.

Then quietly
Odysseus said:

"Telemachus, the stranger
you welcomed in your hall has not disgraced you.
1395   I did not miss, neither did I take all day
stringing the bow. My hand and eye are sound,
not so contemptible as the young men say.
The hour has come to cook their lordships' mutton—
supper by daylight. Other amusements later,
1400   with song and harping that adorn a feast."

He dropped his eyes and nodded, and the prince
Telemachus, true son of King Odysseus,
belted his sword on, clapped hand to his spear,
and with a clink and glitter of keen bronze
1405   stood by his chair, in the forefront near his father.

Spiral Review
Imagery How does the author use imagery in his description of the arrow being shot?

Critical Thinking

1. **Respond:** If you were Telemachus or Penelope, how would you react to the stranger's arrival? Explain your answer.

2. **(a)** Who does Telemachus think Odysseus is when they first reunite? **(b) Compare and Contrast:** Compare Odysseus' emotions with those of Telemachus at their reunion.

3. **(a)** Describe Antinous' treatment of Odysseus. **(b) Analyze Cause and Effect:** Why do you think Antinous treats Odysseus as he does?

4. **(a)** What does Odysseus tell Penelope about himself? **(b) Make Inferences:** Why do you think Odysseus chooses not to reveal his identity to his wife? **(c) Take a Position:** Is it wrong for Odysseus to deceive Penelope? Explain your response.

Do heroes have responsibilities?
(a) Which of Odysseus' responsibilities are revealed in this section? **(b)** Do you think he manages them heroically? Explain your response.

Support your responses with evidence from the text.

The Slaughter of the Suitors from Homer's The Odyssey, N.C. Wyeth, Licensed by ASAP Worldwide. Photo courtesy of the Archives of the American Illustrators Gallery, NYC. ©Copyright 2000 National Museum of American Illustration, Newport, RI. www.americanillustration.org

Odysseus' Revenge

Now shrugging off his rags the wiliest[17] fighter of the islands
leapt and stood on the broad doorsill, his own bow in his
   hand.
He poured out at his feet a rain of arrows from the quiver
and spoke to the crowd:

          "So much for that. Your clean-cut game is over.
1410 Now watch me hit a target that no man has hit before,
if I can make this shot. Help me, Apollo."

He drew to his fist the cruel head of an arrow for Antinous
just as the young man leaned to lift his beautiful drinking
   cup,
embossed, two-handled, golden: the cup was in his fingers:
1415 the wine was even at his lips: and did he dream of death?
How could he? In that revelry[18] amid his throng of friends
who would imagine a single foe—though a strong foe
   indeed—
could dare to bring death's pain on him and darkness on his
   eyes?
Odysseus' arrow hit him under the chin
1420 and punched up to the feathers through his throat.

Backward and down he went, letting the winecup fall
from his shocked hand. Like pipes his nostrils jetted
crimson runnels, a river of mortal red,
and one last kick upset his table
1425 knocking the bread and meat to soak in dusty blood.
Now as they craned to see their champion where he lay
the suitors jostled in uproar down the hall,
everyone on his feet. Wildly they turned and scanned
the walls in the long room for arms; but not a shield,
1430 not a good ashen spear was there for a man to take and
   throw.
All they could do was yell in outrage at Odysseus:

"Foul! to shoot at a man! That was your last shot!"
"Your own throat will be slit for this!"
          "Our finest lad is down!
You killed the best on Ithaca."
         "Buzzards will tear your eyes out!"

17. wiliest (wīl´ ē əst) *adj.*
craftiest; slyest.

◀ **Critical Viewing** Do
you think this illustration
presents the slaughter
of the suitors accurately?
Explain. **[Evaluate]**

18. revelry (rev´ əl rē) *n.* noisy
festivity.

Reading Skill
Historical and Cultural
Context Does the man-
ner in which Odysseus
kills Antinous agree
with your idea of a "fair
fight"? Explain.

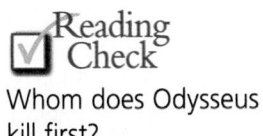
Reading
Check

Whom does Odysseus
kill first?

1435 For they imagined as they wished—that it was a wild shot,
an unintended killing—fools, not to comprehend
they were already in the grip of death.
But glaring under his brows Odysseus answered:

"You yellow dogs, you thought I'd never make it
1440 home from the land of Troy. You took my house to
        plunder. . .
You dared bid for my wife while I was still alive.
Contempt was all you had for the gods who rule wide
        heaven,
contempt for what men say of you hereafter.
Your last hour has come. You die in blood."

1445 As they all took this in, sickly green fear
pulled at their entrails, and their eyes flickered
looking for some hatch or hideaway from death.
Eurymachus[19] alone could speak. He said:

"If you are Odysseus of Ithaca come back,
1450 all that you say these men have done is true.
Rash actions, many here, more in the countryside.
But here he lies, the man who caused them all.
Antinous was the ringleader, he whipped us on
to do these things. He cared less for a marriage
1455 than for the power Cronion has denied him
as king of Ithaca. For that
he tried to trap your son and would have killed him.
He is dead now and has his portion. Spare
your own people. As for ourselves, we'll make
1460 restitution of wine and meat consumed,
and add, each one, a tithe of twenty oxen
with gifts of bronze and gold to warm your heart.
Meanwhile we cannot blame you for your anger."

Odysseus glowered under his black brows
1465 and said:
                "Not for the whole treasure of your fathers,
all you enjoy, lands, flocks, or any gold
put up by others, would I hold my hand.
There will be killing till the score is paid.
You forced yourselves upon this house. Fight your way out,
1470 or run for it, if you think you'll escape death.

Vocabulary
contempt (kən tempt′)
n. disdain or scorn

Reading Skill
**Historical and Cultural
Context** What cultural
values are revealed by
Odysseus' explanation
for his anger in lines
1441–1443?

19. Eurymachus
    (yoo ri′ mə kəs)

I doubt one man of you skins by."

They felt their knees fail, and their hearts—but heard
Eurymachus for the last time rallying them.
"Friends," he said, "the man is implacable.
1475 Now that he's got his hands on bow and quiver
he'll shoot from the big doorstone there
until he kills us to the last man.
                    Fight, I say,
let's remember the joy of it. Swords out!
Hold up your tables to deflect his arrows.
1480 After me, everyone: rush him where he stands.
If we can budge him from the door, if we can pass
into the town, we'll call out men to chase him.
This fellow with his bow will shoot no more."

He drew his own sword as he spoke, a broadsword of fine
          bronze,
1485 honed like a razor on either edge. Then crying hoarse and
          loud
he hurled himself at Odysseus. But the kingly man let fly
an arrow at that instant, and the quivering feathered butt
sprang to the nipple of his breast as the barb stuck in his
          liver.
The bright broadsword clanged down. He lurched and fell
          aside,
1490 pitching across his table. His cup, his bread and meat,
were spilt and scattered far and wide, and his head slammed
          on the ground.
Revulsion, anguish in his heart, with both feet kicking out,
he downed his chair, while the shrouding wave of mist closed
          on his eyes.

Amphinomus now came running at Odysseus,
1495 broadsword naked in his hand. He thought to make
the great soldier give way at the door.
But with a spear throw from behind Telemachus hit him
between the shoulders, and the lancehead drove
clear through his chest. He left his feet and fell
1500 forward, thudding, forehead against the ground.
Telemachus swerved around him, leaving the long dark
          spear
planted in Amphinomus. If he paused to yank it out

Literary Analysis
Epic Simile Why is the comparison of Eurymachus' sharp sword to a razor only a simile and not an epic simile?

Reading Check

What does Eurymachus offer Odysseus to try to calm his anger?

someone might jump him from behind or cut him down with
        a sword
at the moment he bent over. So he ran—ran from the tables
1505 to his father's side and halted, panting, saying:

"Father let me bring you a shield and spear,
a pair of spears, a helmet.
I can arm on the run myself; I'll give
outfits to Eumaeus and this cowherd.
1510 Better to have equipment."

                                        Said Odysseus:
"Run then, while I hold them off with arrows
as long as the arrows last. When all are gone
if I'm alone they can dislodge me."

                                        Quick
upon his father's word Telemachus
1515 ran to the room where spears and armor lay.
He caught up four light shields, four pairs of spears,
four helms of war high-plumed with flowing manes,
and ran back, loaded down, to his father's side.
He was the first to pull a helmet on
1520 and slide his bare arm in a buckler strap.
The servants armed themselves, and all three took their
        stand
beside the master of battle.

                                        While he had arrows
he aimed and shot, and every shot brought down
one of his huddling enemies.
1525 But when all barbs had flown from the bowman's fist,
he leaned his bow in the bright entryway
beside the door, and armed: a four-ply shield
hard on his shoulder, and a crested helm,
horsetailed, nodding stormy upon his head,
1530 then took his tough and bronze-shod spears. . . .

*Aided by Athena, Odysseus, Telemachus, Eumaeus, and
other faithful herdsmen kill all the suitors.*

And Odysseus looked around him, narrow-eyed,
for any others who had lain hidden
while death's black fury passed.

**Reading Skill
Historical and Cultural
Context** What cultural
values are reflected in
Telemachus' behavior
toward his father?

In blood and dust
he saw that crowd all fallen, many and many slain.

1535 Think of a catch that fishermen haul in to a half-moon bay
in a fine-meshed net from the whitecaps of the sea:
how all are poured out on the sand, in throes for the salt sea,
twitching their cold lives away in Helios' fiery air:
so lay the suitors heaped on one another.

Penelope's Test

Penelope tests Odysseus to prove he really is her husband.

1540 Greathearted Odysseus, home at last,
was being bathed now by Eurynome
and rubbed with golden oil, and clothed again
in a fresh tunic and a cloak. Athena
lent him beauty, head to foot. She made him
1545 taller, and massive, too, with crisping hair
in curls like petals of wild hyacinth
but all red-golden. Think of gold infused
on silver by a craftsman, whose fine art
Hephaestus[20] taught him, or Athena: one
1550 whose work moves to delight: just so she lavished
beauty over Odysseus' head and shoulders.
He sat then in the same chair by the pillar,
facing his silent wife, and said:

"Strange woman,
the immortals of Olympus made you hard,
1555 harder than any. Who else in the world
would keep aloof as you do from her husband
if he returned to her from years of trouble,
cast on his own land in the twentieth year?

Nurse, make up a bed for me to sleep on.
1560 Her heart is iron in her breast."

Penelope
spoke to Odysseus now. She said:

"Strange man,
if man you are . . . This is no pride on my part

Reading Skill
Historical and Cultural Context Lines 1535–1539 contain an epic simile. How might this figurative language relate to the historical and cultural setting of the text?

Literary Analysis
Epic Simile Which details in the epic simile in lines 1547–1551 compare Odysseus' hair to a work of art?

20. **Hephaestus** (hē fes′ təs) god of fire and metalworking.

Reading
Check

Who helps Odysseus defeat the suitors?

nor scorn for you—not even wonder, merely.
I know so well how you—how he—appeared
1565 boarding the ship for Troy. But all the same . . .

Make up his bed for him, Eurycleia.
Place it outside the bedchamber my lord
built with his own hands. Pile the big bed
with fleeces, rugs, and sheets of purest linen."

1570 With this she tried him to the breaking point,
and he turned on her in a flash raging:

"Woman, by heaven you've stung me now!
Who dared to move my bed?
No builder had the skill for that—unless
1575 a god came down to turn the trick. No mortal
in his best days could budge it with a crowbar.
There is our pact and pledge, our secret sign,
built into that bed—my handiwork
and no one else's!

                                    An old trunk of olive
1580 grew like a pillar on the building plot,
and I laid out our bedroom round that tree,
lined up the stone walls, built the walls and roof,
gave it a doorway and smooth-fitting doors.
Then I lopped off the silvery leaves and branches,
1585 hewed and shaped that stump from the roots up
into a bedpost, drilled it, let it serve
as model for the rest. I planed them all,
inlaid them all with silver, gold and ivory,
and stretched a bed between—a pliant web
1590 of oxhide thongs dyed crimson.
                                    There's our sign!
I know no more. Could someone else's hand
have sawn that trunk and dragged the frame away?"

Their secret! as she heard it told, her knees
grew tremulous and weak, her heart failed her.
1595 With eyes brimming tears she ran to him,
throwing her arms around his neck, and kissed him,
murmuring:
                                    "Do not rage at me, Odysseus!

Literary Analysis
Epic Simile Explain why the simile comparing the olive trunk to a pillar is not an epic simile.

◄ **Critical Viewing**
How does this image
convey the events in
the text? **[Connect]**

No one ever matched your caution! Think
what difficulty the gods gave: they denied us
1600   life together in our prime and flowering years,
kept us from crossing into age together.
Forgive me, don't be angry. I could not
welcome you with love on sight! I armed myself
long ago against the frauds of men,
1605   impostors who might come—and all those many
whose underhanded ways bring evil on! . . .
But here and now, what sign could be so clear
as this of our own bed?
No other man has ever laid eyes on it—
1610   only my own slave, Actoris, that my father
sent with me as a gift—she kept our door.
You make my stiff heart know that I am yours."

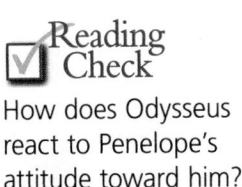

Reading
Check

How does Odysseus
react to Penelope's
attitude toward him?

21. **abyss** (ə bis´) *n.* ocean depths.

Now from his breast into his eyes the ache
of longing mounted, and he wept at last,
1615   his dear wife, clear and faithful, in his arms,
longed for as the sunwarmed earth is longed for by a
     swimmer
spent in rough water where his ship went down
under Poseidon's blows, gale winds and tons of sea.
Few men can keep alive through a big surf
1620   to crawl, clotted with brine, on kindly beaches
in joy, in joy, knowing the abyss[21] behind:
and so she too rejoiced, her gaze upon her husband,
her white arms round him pressed as though forever.

The Ending

Odysseus is reunited with his father. Athena commands that peace prevail between Odysseus and the relatives of the slain suitors. Odysseus has regained his family and his kingdom.

Critical Thinking

Support your responses with evidence from the text.

1. **Respond:** Who do you think faced greater hardships—Odysseus or Penelope? Compare your response with that of a classmate.

2. **(a)** When Odysseus returns to his home, who helps him?
   (b) Interpret: What does the varying social status of Odysseus' helpers suggest about his character?

3. **(a)** What planning does Odysseus do before he battles the suitors? **(b) Analyze:** How does his planning help him defeat his opponents?

4. **(a)** What is Penelope's test, and how does Odysseus pass it?
   (b) Make Inferences: Why does Penelope feel the need to test Odysseus even though he has abandoned his disguise?
   (c) Interpret: Is the mood after the test altogether happy? Explain.

5. **(a) Connect:** Are Odysseus' actions in dealing with the suitors consistent with his actions in earlier episodes of the epic?

   Do heroes have responsibilities?
   (a) Do you think Odysseus kills the suitors to fulfill his responsibilities? Explain. **(b)** Is Odysseus' revenge justified? Why or why not?

After You Read — *from the* **Odyssey, Part 2**

Literary Analysis: Epic Simile

1. (a) Using a chart like the one shown, analyze the **epic simile** in lines 1613–1624.

Items Being Compared	Details of Epic Simile	Purpose

(b) Why is this simile a powerful and fitting image for the conclusion of the *Odyssey?*

Reading Skill: **Historical and Cultural Context**

2. (a) What attitudes and values are reflected in Odysseus' actions toward the suitors? **(b)** What do his actions suggest about the **cultural and historical setting** of Homer's *Odyssey* and the attitudes and values of ancient Greeks? Explain your answer.

3. (a) Name one of Odysseus' cultural beliefs, attitudes, or practices that is similar to an idea or a tradition in your own culture. **(b)** Name one that is significantly different. **(c)** Are Odysseus' values unique to his culture, or are they universal? Explain.

Vocabulary

Practice Indicate whether each statement is *True* or *False*. Explain your answers. Then, revise false sentences to make them true.

1. People sometimes *dissemble* in order to hide their true feelings.

2. An event that is common and predictable evokes *incredulity*.

3. If road signs are *bemusing* drivers, the signs are working well.

4. A good judge is one with a strong sense of *equity*.

5. A pep band should play *maudlin* songs if it wants to excite fans.

6. Successful salespeople always show *contempt* for customers.

Word Power Use the context of the sentences and what you know about the **Latin prefix dis-** to explain your answer to each question.

1. If a reporter *discloses* the source of information, has she told where she got the information?

2. If you are *disheartened* by some news, do you feel better?

Word Power

The **Latin prefix dis-** means "away," "apart," or "not."

Apply It Explain how the prefix *dis-* helps you determine the meanings of these words. Consult a dictionary if necessary.

dispute
dishevel
disembark

Integrated Language Skills

from the Odyssey, Part 2

Conventions: Complex and Compound-Complex Sentences

Sentences can be classified by the number of dependent and independent clauses they contain. An *independent clause* contains a subject and a verb and can stand alone as a sentence. A *dependent* or *subordinate clause* contains a subject and a verb but cannot stand as a sentence. It begins with a subordinate conjunction such as *when, although, because, before, since,* and *while.*

A **complex sentence** consists of one independent clause.
A **compound-complex sentence** consists of two or more independent clauses and one or more subordinate clauses.

The independent clauses in compound-complex sentences usually connect with a comma and a coordinating conjunction.

Complex sentence	Compound-complex sentence
When the lights came on, he saw the audience.	When the lights came on, he saw the audience, and he waved to his parents.

Practice A Identify each sentence as complex or compound-complex. Identify the independent clauses and the subordinate clauses.

1. Because Odysseus was disguised, Penelope did not recognize her husband.
2. When Odysseus strung the bow, the suitors were amazed, and they stopped laughing.
3. Telemachus grabbed a sword, and he stood by his father while they fought.
4. Although there were many suitors, Odysseus killed every one of them.

Speaking Application Tell a partner the story of a hero, real or imagined. Use at least three correctly structured complex and compound-complex sentences in your telling.

Practice B Combine the simple sentences to form one new correctly structured sentence, as directed by the sentence type indicated in parentheses.

1. Argus recognized Odysseus. He died. (complex)
2. Odysseus strung the bow. Telemachus looked on. (complex)
3. Odysseus tested the bow. The suitors mocked him. Some of them called him names. (compound-complex)
4. He shot the arrow. It passed through each ring. The suitors were awed. (compound-complex)

Writing Application Write six simple sentences about the *Odyssey.* Choose from among your sentences to build two complex sentences and two compound-complex sentences.

PH GRAMMAR HANDBOOK Further instruction and practice are available in the *Prentice Hall Grammar Handbook.*

Writing

Write a short **biography** of Odysseus based on details in the *Odyssey*. In this expository text, present the basic facts of his life and adventures, and hold your readers' attention by describing the dramatic situations with gripping detail.

- List events in the *Odyssey* that are suitable for your biography. Focus on events that reveal the character of Odysseus.

- As you draft, summarize important sections of the text. Also, include quotations from the epic to add detail and depth.

- Share your biography with an audience of your classmates, and compare the events you each chose to include.

Grammar Application Make sure that any compound and compound-complex sentences in your biography are correctly structured.

Writing Workshop: *Work in Progress*

Prewriting for Procedural Document From your Task List, choose a topic for your Procedural Document. Think about the steps in the task and the order in which the instructions should be presented. Make an outline to plan your document. Save this Organizational Outline in your portfolio.

Listening and Speaking

Form two opposing teams and conduct a **debate** to decide whether Odysseus should be prosecuted for the murders of Penelope's suitors. To help you participate productively in your team and plan your strategy for debate, follow these steps:

- **Set ground rules for decision-making.** Discuss how your team will deal with disagreements that may come up during planning.

- **Develop a plan for consensus-building,** or coming to a generally agreed upon conclusion. This will allow you to more quickly move forward as a group should your team be unable to agree on a point unanimously.

- **Contribute relevant information** during team discussions. Your input into group planning sesssions should be focused and polite.

- **Build on the ideas of others.** Listen carefully and add to team-mates' thoughts when appropriate.

After planning, present your arguments before the class. Then, ask your audience to **evaluate the effectiveness** of each speaker's main and supporting ideas, deciding which team was more persuasive overall.

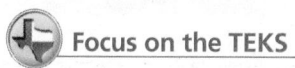 **Focus on the TEKS**

Conventions
(17)(C) Use a variety of correctly structured sentences (e.g., complex, compound-complex).

Writing
(15) Write expository texts to communicate ideas and information.

Listening and Speaking
(26) Participate productively in teams, building on the ideas of others, contributing relevant information, developing a plan for consensus-building, and setting ground rules for decision-making.

(24)(C) Evaluate the effectiveness of a speaker's main and supporting ideas.

Use this prewriting activity to prepare for the **Writing Workshop** on page 1138.

 **TEXAS PHLitOnline**
www.PHLitOnline.com

- Interactive graphic organizers
- Grammar tutorial
- Interactive journals

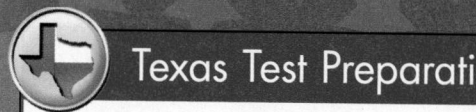

Strategy for Success

Use Context Clues

To perform well on the reading sections of the Texas standardized tests, you can analyze textual context to better understand the meanings of words. Consider both the denotative, or literal, meaning of a word and also the connotative meaning, which is made up of the ideas and emotions associated with the word. Using textual context to distinguish between these two meanings can help you to excel on standardized tests.

To analyze textual context, consider how the sentence in which the word appears and the text surrounding that sentence hint at the word's meaning. Use the text's historical and cultural backdrop as well as the behaviors and attitudes the text expresses to better understand a word's connotation. The following examples provide strategies for analyzing textual context on standardized tests.

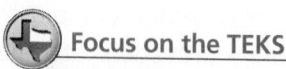 **Focus on the TEKS**

Reading/Comprehension Skills (1)(B) Analyze textual context (within a sentence and in larger sections of text) to distinguish between the denotative and connotative meanings of words.

Analyze Textual Details

Use details in the text to identify the historical and cultural context and to determine a word's meaning.

1 Suddenly the princess's lady-in-waiting burst out laughing. The stern, disciplined faces of the royal council turned in her direction. "Madam," said the prime minister coldly, "we cannot allow such frivolity here."

> **1** Which of the following expresses the connotation of *frivolity* as it is used in paragraph 1?
> **A** joy
> **B** happiness
> **C** deep sadness
> **D** lack of self-control

The cultural context of this scene is different from everyday life, so the speakers may not use everyday language. The royal council is not criticizing the lady-in-waiting for feeling happy, as in **A** or **B**. The lady-in-waiting does not feel sad, so **C** cannot be correct. Instead, the council is faulting her for her lack of self-control, so **D** is correct.

Analyze Attitude and Tone

The tone of the passage and the attitudes expressed in the text can provide clues to a word's connotative meaning.

1 It's lurking there, on the calendar, and I try not to dread it. It's the day that I can expect either that fat acceptance package or the skinny rejection letter in the mail.

> **2** Which words from paragraph 1 best convey the narrator's feelings about the upcoming day?
> **F** *fat, skinny*
> **G** *lurking, dread*
> **H** *acceptance, rejection*
> **J** *calendar, appearance*

The passage conveys the narrator's nervousness while waiting for either acceptance or rejection. **F**, **H**, and **J** do not reflect this anxiety. The words *lurking* and *dread* do have this connotation, so **G** is correct.

Texas Test Practice

Read this selection. Then, answer the questions that follow it.

Planning the Wedding

1   Jeremy turned his head left and right as first his mother and then his sister spoke, each in turn. He felt as if he were watching a frustratingly long tennis match, but with opinions, rather than tennis balls, flying back and forth interminably. It had been like this ever since his sister had started planning her wedding for the following year.

2   "I know it will be a large group," said his sister, "but we don't want to leave anyone out!"

3   "Two hundred is such a crowd," said his mother. "How can we afford so many?"

4   "If we invite fewer people," said his sister, changing tactics quickly, "maybe we'll have more money to buy the perfect dress for me. A long train would be so elegant!"

5   "So extravagant," said his mother. "When your father and I were married, I wore my best dress and hat. We were happy with the inexpensive things we had."

6   Jeremy's sister smiled sheepishly. "And you and Dad are still so happy together, Mom. I know that's more important than showy clothes."

7   Their mother smiled, too. "I'm sure you want to look lovely. Perhaps you could ask your Aunt Eva about your dress. Maybe she could even sew a train as her wedding gift to you."

8   The women nodded happily at each other, and Jeremy sighed and sat back in his chair. It was going to be a very long year.

1 Which phrase from paragraph 1 helps the reader understand the meaning of the word *interminably?*

  A *each in turn*

  B *back and forth*

  C *frustratingly long*

  D *for the following year*

2 Although Jeremy's sister calls the guests a "group," his mother calls them a "crowd" to —

  F suggest that the size of the group is excessive

  G avoid using the same word as her daughter

  H hint that some of the guests may be troublesome

  J show that she does not know any of the guests

3 Which words from the passage show Jeremy's sister's change of heart about the importance of her dress?

  A *perfect dress*

  B *showy clothes*

  C *inexpensive things*

  D *so extravagant*

4 Which of these words from the selection is an antonym for the word *extravagant* as it is used in paragraph 5?

  F *best*

  G *happy*

  H *elegant*

  J *inexpensive*

Informational Texts

Expository Texts

Magazine Article
The Sticker Bur

Magazine Article
The Tumbleweed

 **Focus on the TEKS**

Reading
(9)(B) Differentiate between opinions that are substantiated and unsubstantiated in the text.

Reading Skill: Evaluate Opinions

An **opinion** is a statement of a person's belief. An opinion may be identified in writing with an introduction, such as "I believe" or "In my opinion." However, this is not always the case. Sometimes writers state opinions as if they were facts. When a writer expresses an opinion in an essay or article, it is his or her job to provide evidence to support that opinion. When you evaluate opinions, you must differentiate between opinions that are **substantiated,** or supported, and **unsubstantiated,** or not supported.

As You Read Use a chart like this one to identify opinions and the support the author includes for those opinions. Then, evaluate each opinion, differentiating between opinions that are substantiated and unsubstantiated in the text.

Opinion	Support	Substantiated or unsubstantiated?
The author refers to the sandbur as "the loathsome sticker." She must hate sandburs.	The author recalls how sandburs hurt her when she was a child.	Substantiated

Features:
- title and byline
- friendly, relaxed tone
- text written for a general audience

The Sticker Bur

Into each and every barefoot Texas childhood a little sticker bur must fall.

Mimi Schwartz

I was in my early teens before I realized that children in other parts of the country could run barefoot through tall grass without fear. Any child who attempted to do so in Central Texas—or in most parts of the state, for that matter—was either very brave or just plain foolish. For Texas fields and lawns had little in common with the velvety expanses of, say, Massachusetts or Northern California. Here defenseless children had to contend with grass that concealed chiggers, mesquite thorns, hackberry branches, and, grizzliest of all, a small brown barb known to connoisseurs[1] as the sticker bur, land mine of the backyard. No instep, no matter how proudly toughened on sizzling pavement, could endure it.

The sticker bur served notice to suburban children that the Texas landscape, however well fenced, watered, graveled, or gardened, remained untamed and inhospitable. As part of a roving band of neighborhood kids, I learned to survey yards like a point man heading into dangerous territory. A dry, patchy lawn was best avoided, though a healthy-looking turf of Bermuda grass held no promise of safety either. Sticker grass was usually paler and spinier than Bermuda, but that difference was discernible only at very close range.

Our gang may not have known where stickers came from (I believed they were prickly pear burs, blown in from the desert), but we knew full well what they could do. When little Stan Shaw, one of our bravest members, would show off by racing up the street through the grass, the rest of us would wait to hear his strangled yelp—akin to that of a betrayed cocker spaniel. Then we knew the sticker had struck, and another yard was off-limits. Those were tragic moments for us because alternate routes were scarce: Even in October the asphalt was searing, and armies of red ants patrolled the curbs. Of course, no self-respecting Texas child would be caught dead doing the sensible thing, which was to put on a pair of shoes.

> The author expresses the opinion that children who ran through tall grass were "brave or just plain foolish." **Is this opinion substantiated or unsubstantiated? Explain.**

> Here, the author expresses an opinion about Stan Shaw and substantiates the opinion with examples as support.

---

1. **connoisseurs** (kän´ə surs´) n., pl. people who have expert knowledge and keen discrimination in some field.

TEXAS

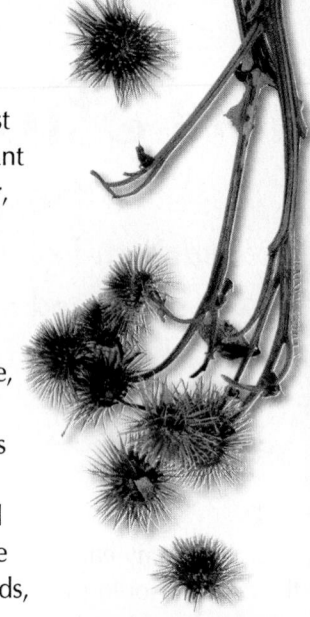

The sticker comes from a lateral and low-growing grasslike weed called the sandbur, which has been causing trouble for quite some time. It was first identified in the eighteenth century by Swedish botanist Carolus Linnaeus, author of *Species Plantarum*, the seminal work in plant taxonomy. The burs are actually spiny seeds that mature in the summer, just in time to torture tiny feet. "No other grassy plant has this…lance-armed bur, and a description therefore is almost useless," writes Edwin Rollin Spencer in *All About Weeds*. "He who finds a sandbur does not have to be told what it is."

Today there are several kinds of sandbur, including southern, longspine, and field sandbur (whose Latin name, *Cenchrus incertus*, is particularly apt). The most cursory study of a botanical map will reveal why the plants are so familiar to Texans. Sandburs prefer the sandy soil of the southern U.S., especially that beside highways and baseball diamonds, where sand containing sandbur seeds is dumped as fill. Some infested states may have one kind of sandbur but not another, but Texas has all three common kinds, and they all thrive here. In this case, more is clearly not better.

It's hard to find anyone who doesn't hate the sandbur. Weed specialists use words like "nuisance," "pernicious," "noxious," and "hateful" to describe it. "It's considered one of the real bad grasses," says Texas A&M extension weed specialist Rupert Palmer. Cows and sheep dislike sandbur because it is painful to eat; commercial stockmen hate sandbur because it contaminates wool and mohair and is grounds for docking at time of sale. Suburbanites hate sandbur because it hides and breeds in their Bermuda grass.

> The author presents opinions about the sandbur from a range of sources. **Are these opinions substantiated or unsubstantiated? Explain.**

Herbicides can be used to keep the seeds from germinating, but the best ways to get rid of sandbur are (a) mow and water your Bermuda grass frequently, (b) plant St. Augustine grass, which shades and crowds out sandbur, or (c) pull the sandbur out. One A&M specialist confessed that it took him three years to get his yard sticker-free using the last method, but it worked.

Still, there's one thing to be said for the loathsome sticker. It breeds cautiousness, a quality not widely admired here but useful in a state that features both jellyfish and rattlesnakes. The wise Texan learns to pick and choose his fights with the landscape. Nowadays, for instance, I do run through moderately high grass. But only with my boots on.

Do heroes have responsibilities?
The author mentions that the sticker "breeds cautiousness." Do you think this sort of carefulness encourages personal responsibility? Explain.

Magazine Article

Features:

- photos or other graphics
- focused subject
- facts and opinions on a topic

The Tumbleweed

It's only a humble thistle, but when you see one, it's sure to put you in a lonely, rambling, Western frame of mind.

Stephen Harrigan

Much that is haunting and inhospitable about the Texas prairie finds its image in the tumbleweed. "Lonely but free I'll be found," sing the Sons of the Pioneers, "drifting along with the tumbling tumbleweeds." A person would have to be unusually resistant to cowboy hokum not to feel some plaintive[1] stirring within himself when he hears that song or when he encounters its subject on a gusty fall day out on the range. The tumbleweed is as much a visual trademark of Western romance as the moonlit silhouette of a coyote.

Taxonomically,[2] though, the tumbleweed is a difficult thing to get a grip on. The term is casually applied to half a dozen different plants that all have the facility of dispersing their seeds as they are blown about by the wind. Only one of these, *Amaranthus albus*, or tumbling pigweed, is indigenous to Texas. But *Amaranthus* is rare and probably not the plant that the Sons of the Pioneers mean. The archetypal[3] tumbleweed is more likely Russian thistle, or *Salsola kali*, which did not appear in the United States until the 1870's, when its seeds were inadvertently carried over along with the flax seeds of some Russian immigrants.

The stowaway seeds thrived in the harsh, barren soil of the plains. The tumbleweed is a tough, aggressive plant, needing little water to support itself and yet requiring a good deal of open space to send out its shallow roots and grow into its globular form, which can reach five feet in diameter. It was perfectly at home in the loose, played-out soil of the Dust Bowl and in the vast overgrazed domains of West Texas.

What opinion does the author express in the first sentence? **Is this opinion substantiated or unsubstantiated? Explain.**

---

1. **plaintive** (plān′ tiv) *adj.* expressing sorrow or melancholy; mournful; sad.
2. **taxonomically** (tak sə näm′ ik lē) *adv.* having to do with the science of classification; laws and principles covering the classifying of objects.
3. **archetypal** (är′ kə tīp′ əl) *adj.* having the characteristics of an original pattern or model.

TEXAS

Tumbleweed is an annual that germinates in the spring and produces a verdant[4] ground-cover plant ornamented with tiny flowers. In early life its leaves are tender enough to provide sustenance for livestock, but they soon grow spiny and inedible. By the time it is full-grown, the tumbleweed holds tens of thousands of ripening seeds. Many of them fall where the plant is rooted, but many more are still attached when the first sustained winds of fall come and break the tumbleweed off its thin stalk and send it drifting across the plains. These remaining seeds will either be deposited along the way or remain with the tumbleweed when it falls into a ditch where the wind cannot reach it or snags against a fence or some other obstruction.

Early settlers regarded tumbleweeds as a menace. They tended to leach away soil nutrients that might otherwise have gone to desirable crops, and in a grass fire they could become bounding fireballs, extending the front of an advancing conflagration[5] for a hundred yards or more. They are not exactly prized today either. They are officially regarded as pests, and county extension agents are ready with instructions about how to poison them. If left uncontrolled, they can still crowd out a rancher's forage grass and pile up against a fence line in such numbers that they provide a foundation for a mound of dust that will someday obscure the fence completely.

But even as pests, tumbleweeds do not seem to generate much excitement. They are, in the great scheme of things, a minor component in the ecology. It is in the imagination, where their lonesome desolation continues to strike a sympathetic chord, that tumbleweeds loom large.

> In each of these paragraphs, the author expresses opinions about the tumbleweed. **Identify the opinions and differentiate between those that are substantiated and those that are unsubstantiated in the text.**

---

4. **verdant** (vur´dənt) *adj.* green.
5. **conflagration** (kän´flə grā´ shən) *n.* a big, destructive fire.

TEXAS

Do heroes have responsibilities?
Why was it early ranchers' and settlers' responsibility to try to control tumbleweeds?

Comparing Informational Texts

(a) Analyze: Review the chart you completed and compare and contrast the types of support used to substantiate the opinions in each magazine article. **(b) Make Inferences:** What makes each author's particular kind of support effective within the text?

 **College Readiness** | **Timed Writing**

Write a Critique

Format
The prompt directs you to write a *critique*. Therefore, your response should offer your judgments and opinions about the articles, supported by evidence and examples.

Write a critique of the opinions presented in either magazine article. Analyze one of the articles and differentiate between opinions that are substantiated and unsubstantiated in the text. For unsubstantiated opinions, explain how the writer could have better supported his or her position. Provide evidence from the text to support your ideas. (40 minutes)

Academic Vocabulary
When you *analyze* a text, you examine it in detail, looking for particular elements or characteristics.

🕐 5-Minute Planner

1. Read the prompt carefully and completely.

2. Revisit each article, looking for the opinions expressed and making notes about the details that support them.

3. Consider the support provided for each opinion and decide which opinions are well supported, or substantiated, and which are not well supported, or unsubstantiated.

4. Choose the article that you will use as the focus of your critique.
   TIP Only refer to the article you have chosen as you plan and draft your response.

5. Jot down notes about how unsubstantiated opinions could be better supported.

6. Make a brief outline to organize the information for your critique.

7. Refer to your outline and notes as you draft your essay.

Comparing Literary Works

Comparing Literary Influences

Older literary works sometimes affect, or influence, a newer piece of writing. These **literary influences** may be apparent in the characters, plot, symbols, and other elements of the later work. However, even when literary works are influenced by the same older work, they may differ widely in purpose and theme. Each writer's cultural and historical backgrounds, attitudes, and beliefs affect his or her perceptions of the older work and influence the new piece.

Many 20th and 21st century writers have been influenced by the timeless and universal appeal of the characters and events of Homer's *Odyssey*, written near the end of the eighth century B.C. Readers who have experienced Homer's ancient words will have particular insight into the later works his epic has influenced.

The epic form is a traditional form of the ancient world, and Homer's works are all considered to be classical because of their artistry and the time period in which they were written. Therefore, the *Odyssey*, like few other works, is considered not only mythic literature, but also a fine example of both classical and traditional literature.

The four poems that follow—"An Ancient Gesture," "Siren Song," "To a Lost Lover," and "Ithaca"—are 20th and 21st century works that have all been influenced by parts I and II of the *Odyssey*.

As You Read Use a chart like the one shown to **analyze the influence** of the *Odyssey*—mythic, classical, and traditional literature—on these works of 20th and 21st century literature.

Poem	Detail from the poem	Influence of the *Odyssey*
"An Ancient Gesture"		
"Siren Song"		
"To a Lost Lover"		
"Ithaca"		

Focus on the TEKS

Reading
(2)(B) Analyze the influence of mythic, classical and traditional literature on 20th and 21st century literature.

TEXAS
PHLitOnline
www.PHLitOnline.com

- Vocabulary flashcards
- Interactive journals
- More about the authors
- Selection audio
- Interactive graphic organizers

Do *heroes* have responsibilities?

Writing About the Big Question

In these poems, the heroic characters have different ways of living up to their responsibilities. Use these sentence starters to develop your ideas about the Big Question.

In my own life, I know I am **responsible** for _____.

If I do not live up to this **obligation,** one consequence might be _____.

When I make **responsible choices,** one positive result is _____.

Meet the Authors

Edna St. Vincent Millay (1892–1950)

Author of "An Ancient Gesture" (p. 1128)

Edna St. Vincent Millay is remembered for her artistic experimentation and rebelliousness. Her poetry collection *The Harp Weaver and Other Poems* earned her a Pulitzer Prize. "An Ancient Gesture" was written in 1954.

Margaret Atwood (b. 1939)

Author of "Siren Song" (p. 1130)

Much of Margaret Atwood's writing is about what it means to be a woman in a period of social change. In "Siren Song," which was written in 1976, Atwood presents another of her themes—the role of mythology in people's lives.

Marie Delgado Travis (b. 1949)

Author of "To a Lost Lover" (p. 1132)

A bilingual poet who writes in both Spanish and English, Marie Delgado Travis has won awards for her work in both languages. She was born in New York and now lives in Houston, Texas. "To a Lost Lover" was written in 2006.

Constantine Cavafy (1863–1933)

Author of "Ithaca" (p. 1135)

Constantine Cavafy was born to Greek parents in Alexandria, Egypt. "Ithaca," written in 1911, showcases his creative method: using Greek mythology to speak to the modern reader.

An Ancient Gesture

Edna St. Vincent Millay

I thought, as I wiped my eyes on the corner of my apron:
Penelope did this too.
And more than once: you can't keep weaving all day
And undoing it all through the night;
5   Your arms get tired, and the back of your neck gets tight;
And along towards morning, when you think it will never
    be light,
And your husband has been gone, and you don't know
    where, for years,
Suddenly you burst into tears;
There is simply nothing else to do.

10 And I thought, as I wiped my eyes on the corner of my apron:
This is an ancient gesture, authentic, antique,
In the very best tradition, classic, Greek;
Ulysses[1] did this too.
But only as a gesture,—a gesture which implied
15 To the assembled throng that he was much too moved
    to speak.
He learned it from Penelope . . .
Penelope, who really cried.

---

1. **Ulysses** Latin name for Odysseus.

Literary Analysis
Literary Influences
Analyze lines 1–9. How has the *Odyssey*, a piece of mythic, classical, and traditional literature, influenced these lines from a piece of 20th century literature?

Vocabulary
authentic (ô then´ tik) *adj.* genuine

◀ **Critical Viewing**
What is Penelope's attitude toward the suitors? How can you tell? **[Infer; Support]**

Critical Thinking

1. **Respond:** What do you think it means to "really cry"? Explain.

2. **(a)** How is the speaker similar to Penelope? **(b) Summarize:** According to the speaker, what caused Penelope to use this ancient gesture? **(c) Make Inferences:** Why might the speaker have made a similar gesture?

3. **(a)** According to the speaker, who else made this ancient gesture? **(b) Compare and Contrast:** How did this gesture differ from Penelope's? **(c) Analyze:** What do the different qualities of their gestures reveal about these characters?

4. **(a) Assess:** What questions about the speaker are left unanswered? **(b) Analyze Cause and Effect:** What effect do these unanswered questions create?

 **Do heroes have responsibilities?**
(a) According to this interpretation, does Odysseus live up to his responsibility as a husband? Explain.
(b) Who do you think the author felt was the hero in the *Odyssey*—Penelope or Odysseus? Explain.

 **Support your responses with evidence from the text.**

SIREN SONG

Margaret Atwood

This is the one song everyone
would like to learn: the song
that is irresistible:

the song that forces men
5 to leap overboard in squadrons
even though they see the beached skulls

the song nobody knows
because anyone who has heard it
is dead, and the others can't remember.

10 Shall I tell you the secret
and if I do, will you get me
out of this bird suit?[1]

---

1. bird suit Sirens are usually represented as half bird and half woman.

Literary Analysis
Literary Influences
Analyze lines 4–9. How has the *Odyssey,* a piece of mythic, classical, and traditional literature, influenced these lines from a piece of 20th century literature?

I don't enjoy it here
squatting on this island
15 looking picturesque and mythical

with these two feathery maniacs,
I don't enjoy singing
this trio, fatal and valuable.

I will tell the secret to you,
20 to you, only to you.
Come closer. This song

is a cry for help: Help me!
Only you, only you can,
you are unique

25 at last. Alas
it is a boring song
but it works every time.

Vocabulary
picturesque (pik´ chər
esk´) *adj.* attractive and
interesting

Literary Analysis
Literary Influences
What does the contem-
porary Siren say to flatter
and lure the listener?

Critical Thinking

1. **Respond:** Do you like the speaker in this poem? Why or why not?

2. **(a)** In the first stanza, what song does the speaker say everyone wants to learn? **(b) Analyze:** What does this song have the
power to do?

3. **(a)** What does the speaker want in exchange for revealing the
song's secret? **(b) Interpret:** Why does the speaker want to make
this deal?

4. **(a) Analyze:** Why do you think the speaker's compliment in lines
23 and 24 is so effective? **(b) Make Generalizations:** What
might the speaker be saying about the relationships between men
and women?

5. **(a) Make Inferences:** How does the speaker feel about her song
and its purpose? **(b) Draw Conclusions:** How much influence
has the *Odyssey* had on "Siren Song," and how much is due to
Atwood's own imagination?

Support
your responses
with evidence
from the text.

Do heroes have responsibilities?
(a) How does the Siren affect heroes? Explain.
(b) Do you think the Siren should be held responsible
for her effect on heroes? Why or why not?

To a Lost Lover

Marie Delgado Travis

I lingered on
The shore alone,
Hair tousled softly
By the ocean breeze.

5   The opal sea
—Jealous,
No doubt, of the
Blue depths
Of his eyes—
10   Had claimed
My lover
As her own
Many years
Before.

15   Invoking his spirit,
I asked if he still
Remembered.

And the sea
Began to churn
20   In beveled colors.

Vocabulary
opal (ō´ pəl) *adj.*
like an opal; being
semi-transparent and
reflecting light to give
the appearance of many
colors

Vocabulary
beveled (bev´əld´) *adj.*
sloped; cut at a slant

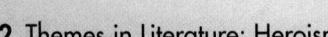

Blind Homer himself
Would have been
Dazzled by the
Foam-white and
25 Wine orchids
Shimmering
In the rosy
Sunset.

I knew then
30 For certain.

My Odysseus
Never left me.

And I remain
His true
35 Penelope.

Literary Analysis
Literary Influences
Analyze the last two stanzas. How has the *Odyssey*, a piece of mythic, classical, and traditional literature, influenced the theme of this poem, a piece of 21st century literature?

Critical Thinking

1. **Respond:** What is your opinion of the speaker? Explain.

2. **(a)** What is the speaker doing? **(b) Assess:** What is the speaker's state of mind?

3. **(a)** What was the sea jealous of? **(b) Draw Conclusions:** What has happened to Odysseus? How do you know?

4. **(a) Summarize:** How does the sea respond to the speaker's question in lines 16–17? **(b) Analyze:** How does this description evoke the language and feeling of the *Odyssey*? **(c) Draw Conclusions:** How do the allusions to the *Odyssey* add meaning to the poem?

5. **(a) Make Inferences:** How does the speaker know that Odysseus never left her? **(b) Interpret:** What does the speaker mean in the final lines?

Do heroes have responsibilities?
(a) Who is the hero in this poem? Explain. **(b)** Does this hero have responsibilities? If so, to whom?

Support your responses with evidence from the text.

Ithaca

Constantine Cavafy

When you start on your journey to Ithaca,
then pray that the road is long,
full of adventure, full of knowledge.
Do not fear the Lestrygonians[1]
5   and the Cyclopes and the angry Poseidon.
You will never meet such as these on your path,
if your thoughts remain lofty, if a fine
emotion touches your body and your spirit.
You will never meet the Lestrygonians,
10 the Cyclopes and the fierce Poseidon,
if you do not carry them within your soul,
if your soul does not raise them up before you.

Then pray that the road is long.
That the summer mornings are many,
15 that you will enter ports seen for the first time
with such pleasure, with such joy!
Stop at Phoenician markets,
and purchase fine merchandise,
mother-of-pearl and corals, amber and ebony,
20 and pleasurable perfumes of all kinds,
buy as many pleasurable perfumes as you can;
visit hosts of Egyptian cities,
to learn and learn from those who have knowledge.

---

1. **Lestrygonians** (les tri gō′ nē ənz) *n.* cannibals who destroy all of Odysseus' ships except his own and kill the crews.

◄ **Critical Viewing**
Which aspects of this image relate to Odysseus' journey? **[Connect]**

Vocabulary
lofty (lôf′ tē) *adj.* very high; noble

Literary Analysis
Literary Influences
Analyze lines 1–12. How has the *Odyssey,* a piece of mythic, classical, and traditional literature, influenced these lines in a piece of 20th century literature?

Reading Check

What advice does the speaker give about meeting the Lestrygonians?

Always keep Ithaca fixed in your mind.
25   To arrive there is your ultimate goal.
But do not hurry the voyage at all.
It is better to let it last for long years;
and even to anchor at the isle when you are old,
rich with all that you have gained on the way,
30   not expecting that Ithaca will offer you riches.

Ithaca has given you the beautiful voyage.
Without her you would never have taken the road.
But she has nothing more to give you.

And if you find her poor, Ithaca has not defrauded you.
35   With the great wisdom you have gained, with so much
          experience,
You must surely have understood by then what Ithaca
          means.

Literary Analysis
Literary Influences
How does Odysseus' desire for an end to his journey differ from the contemporary poet's attitude toward the journey?

Vocabulary
defrauded (dē frôd´ əd)
v. cheated

Critical Thinking

Support your responses with evidence from the text.

1. **Respond:** Does the journey in this poem appeal to you? Explain.
2. **(a) Analyze:** How is the role played by the Lestrygonians, the Cyclopes, and Poseidon in "Ithaca" different than their role in the *Odyssey?* **(b) Make Inferences:** Why might a person carry such terrors as these in his or her soul?
3. **(a)** What three things does the speaker say you should pray for on the journey to Ithaca? **(b) Connect:** What activities and pleasures are linked to these prayers?
4. **(a)** According to the speaker, why is Ithaca important? **(b) Make Inferences:** What might Ithaca symbolize for the poet?
5. **(a) Interpret:** What message is conveyed in the last three lines of the poem? **(b) Assess:** Do you agree with this message? Explain.
6. **(a) Speculate:** What advice might the speaker have given to Odysseus during his long journey? **(b) Take a Position:** Do you agree with this advice? Explain.

Do heroes have responsibilities?
(a) What does the "journey to Ithaca" symbolize?
(b) Do you think people have a responsibility to take a "journey to Ithaca" in their own lives? Why or why not?

Comparing Literary Influences

1. Analyze the four poems from the 20th and 21st centuries. In what ways has the *Odyssey,* an example of mythic, classical, and traditional literature, influenced different aspects of each of these poems?

2. Make charts like the one shown to compare and contrast each of the four 20th and 21st century poems with Homer's *Odyssey.*

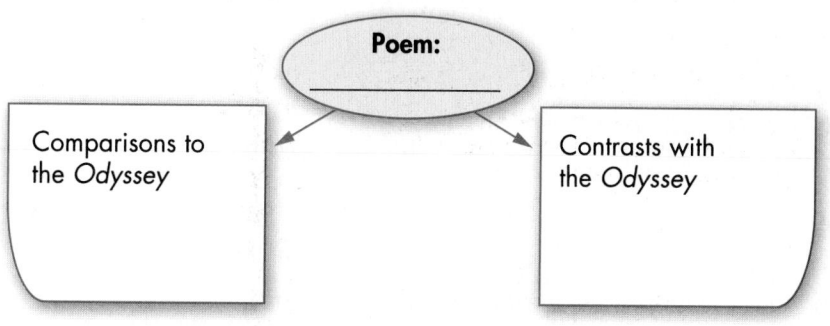

 **College
Readiness** | **Timed Writing**

Write to Compare Literary Influences

Compare and contrast the influence of the *Odyssey* on the themes of "An Ancient Gesture," "Siren Song," "To a Lost Lover," and "Ithaca." In a brief essay, discuss how each of the poems' themes compare to the themes in the *Odyssey* and to each other. Support your ideas with evidence from the texts. (40 minutes)

🕐 5-Minute Planner

1. Read the prompt carefully and completely.

2. Think about these questions and jot down ideas for your essay.

   • What is the theme of each poem? Does the *Odyssey* share a similar message or insight?

   • If the poet had written without having read the *Odyssey,* how might the poem have been different?

3. Choose and plan an organizational strategy for your essay.

4. Reread the prompt. Then, refer to your notes as you draft your essay.

Procedural Document: Instructions

Defining the Form Procedural documents communicate ideas and information to specific audiences for specific purposes. Instructions identify the steps to take to complete a task. You might use elements of this type of writing in manuals, rule books, and assembly directions.

Assignment Write instructions for others to use to complete a task, such as wrapping a gift, establishing an exercise routine, taking meeting minutes, or working together to resolve conflicts. Include these elements:

✔ *organized information*

✔ *accurately conveyed information*

✔ definitions and visuals to aid reader comprehension

✔ *reader-friendly formatting techniques*

✔ error-free grammar, especially correct sentence forms, without sentence fragments or run-ons

To preview the criteria on which your manual may be evaluated, see the rubric on page 1143.

Writing Workshop: *Work in Progress*

Review the work you did on pages 1085 and 1117.

Prewriting/Planning Strategy

Identify the information you will need to share. Before you write, think about how someone would successfully complete the task you will explain. Consider your audience and what they need to learn the task you have chosen. List the necessary materials and any specific skills you may need to detail. Complete a chart like the one shown to help you prepare to write your manual. If necessary, conduct research to learn more about your topic.

Task:			
Materials:	**Steps:**		**Special Skills:**

Apply It!

Focus on the TEKS

Writing
(15)(B)(i);(ii) Write procedural documents (e.g., instructions) that include organized and accurately conveyed information; and reader-friendly formatting techniques.

Expressing Your Ideas

Ideas are the basis for any form of writing, even procedural writing. To provide instruction on how to accomplish a task, you must express your ideas clearly and organize them logically. Think about the obvious steps you take to complete the process, record them logically, and then review them to make sure you did not miss anything.

Teach your audience. The main purpose behind instructions is to teach your specific audience how to accomplish a task. Begin by laying the groundwork for the task you will explain. Consider the needs of your audience as you write. For example, you may need to define any vocabulary that may be unfamiliar to them. Provide examples, scenarios, and clarifications to help your audience learn a new skill and complete the task in a variety of situations.

Use visual aids. Remember that visual aids can be helpful tools to convey basic information. It may be helpful to provide diagrams, charts, or maps. A labeled illustration like the one shown would be very helpful in a manual on bicycle repair.

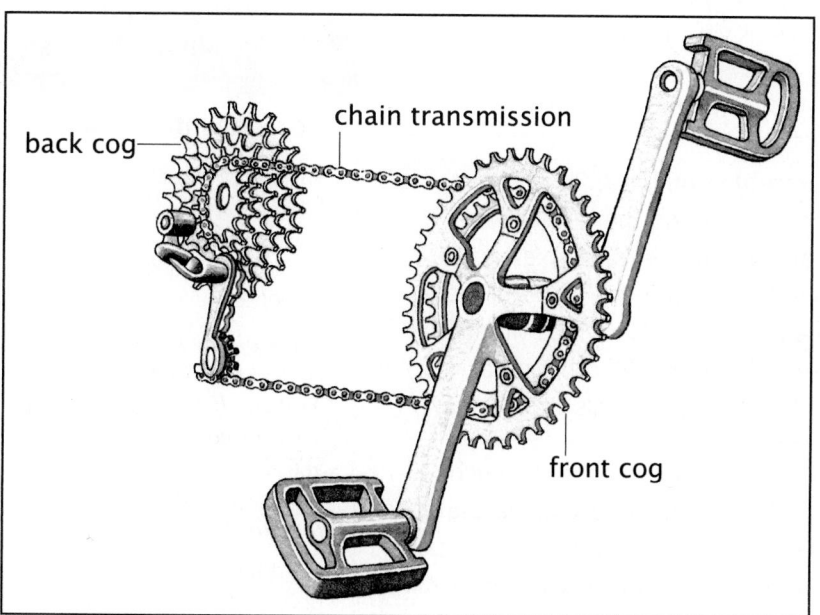

Drafting Strategies

Organize your information. Choose a logical organizing structure that will help you to present your information to an audience. Because most instructions describe a process that takes place over time, chronological order is often the most effective organizing structure.

Choose reader-friendly formatting techniques. Paragraphs are not always the best way to present information meant to instruct or explain. Your readers will have different needs at different times:

- A reader who is considering doing the activity outlined in your manual will want a quick overview of materials and steps.

- A reader who is in the middle of following your instructions will need to locate a step quickly.

- A reader who is looking for special tips or background information will want additional information.

To meet the needs of each of these readers, consider these formatting possibilities as you draft:

- Present essential steps as a series of numbered points or in a bulleted list for ease of reading.

- Provide additional information in separate sections, such as boxes set alongside your instructions. You may decide to build a trouble-shooting chart to help with problems your reader may encounter.

Revising Strategies

Be sure your information is accurately conveyed. To ensure that your readers can be successful in completing the task you are explaining, make sure the information you provide is completely accurate. Factual or technical errors in instructions can hinder a reader's progress and, in some cases, cause a potentially dangerous situation. Review your draft, checking facts, specifications, and other data. Revise as necessary to accurately and clearly convey this information.

Evaluate repeated words. Instructions should not include much figurative or flowery language. However, you should avoid overuse of words that may dull your writing. Review your draft to find and circle words you have used several times. Consider the words you have circled to decide whether you should replace a word with a synonym or even rephrase the sentence. **Use a dictionary or thesaurus** to determine the meanings of words—both their denotations and connotations, or emotional impact. Then, select the words that most accurately convey your intended meaning.

 Focus on the TEKS

Writing
(15)(B)(i);(ii) Write procedural documents (e.g., instructions) that include: organized and accurately conveyed information; and reader-friendly formatting techniques.

Reading
(1)(E) Use a dictionary or a thesaurus (printed or electronic) to determine the meanings of words, including their connotations and denotations.

WRITE GUY
Jeff Anderson, M.Ed.

What Do You Notice?

Accurate Information

The following sentences are from Stephanie Watson's technical directions "How Podcasting Works." Read the sentences several times.

Click on the hyperlink for each podcast you want. You can listen right away on your computer (both Windows and Mac support podcasting) or download the podcast to your MP3 player.

Jot down what you notice about this passage and share your thoughts with a partner. Consider how you can use technical language in your instructions.

Revising to Correct Fragments and Run-ons

A **fragment** is a group of words that does not express a complete thought but is punctuated as if it were a sentence. A **run-on** is two or more complete sentences that are not properly joined or separated.

Identifying and Correcting Fragments Fragments express incomplete thoughts. Often, they offer information that belongs to a nearby sentence. Correct fragments by attaching them to sentences.

> **Fragment:** They waited at the bus stop. *Huddled under an umbrella.*

> **Revised:**   They waited at the bus stop, huddled under an umbrella.

Other fragments can be corrected through expansion—adding the words needed to make a complete sentence.

> **Fragment:**   *As long as you agree to help.*

> **Expanded:** I will wash the car as long as you agree to help.

Identifying and Correcting Run-ons Run-ons include sentences that are fused with no punctuation at all or that are linked by only a comma.

> **Fused:**   She speaks Spanish fluently she does not speak Italian at all.

> **Comma splice:**   She speaks Spanish fluently, she does not speak Italian at all.

Three Ways to Correct a Run-on Sentence	
Use an appropriate end mark to separate a run-on into two sentences. Begin the second sentence with a capital letter.	She speaks Spanish fluently. She does not speak Italian at all.
Use a comma and a coordinating conjunction, such as *and, but, or, for,* and *nor,* to combine two related independent clauses.	She speaks Spanish fluently, but she does not speak Italian at all.
Use a semicolon to connect two closely related ideas.	She speaks Spanish fluently; she does not speak Italian at all.

PH GRAMMAR HANDBOOK

Further instruction and practice are available in the *Prentice Hall Grammar Handbook*.

Grammar in Your Writing

Scan your instructions for fragments and run-ons by looking for sentences that seem too short or too long. Neatly correct any sentence problems you find by using the strategies that have been presented.

Student Model: Alden Warr, Flint, TX

Focus on the TEKS

Writing
(13)(D) Edit drafts for grammar, mechanics, and spelling.
(13)(E) Publish written work for appropriate audiences.
Conventions
(19) Spell correctly, including using various resources to check correct spellings.

How to Do a Load of Laundry

I remember the time when, to my dismay, an entire load of laundry came out of the dryer different shades of pink because I had included my red shirt. After I had destroyed a fair share of valuable clothes, my mother decided it was time for me to learn how to wash clothes properly. Washing your clothes is a valuable skill to acquire and can be quick and easy if you know the basic steps and some helpful tricks to avoid disaster. You just need to remember three sets of three steps each to successfully wash a load.

The first step, sorting, can make the whole process more efficient. As you sort your clothes into piles, the first variable that must be considered is color. Divide the colors into three basic categories: darks, lights, and reds. Also to be considered is the degree of dirtiness. If clothes are especially dirty or stained, then a sub-pile must be formed within the color group so that it can be washed on a different cycle. For instance, if you wash a white dress shirt with muddy, white socks, your dress shirt will come out of the wash dirtier than it went in. The last variable is fabric type. Again, sub-piles must be formed to separate delicates, such as blouses or dress shirts, from sturdier fabrics, such as jeans. When the piles are formed, you can begin the washing cycle.

Washing is the most important step in laundry, but the exact steps are often overlooked. Again, three variables combine to create the ideal cycle for the load. Your first decision is load size. Depending upon the size of the pile, you will simply choose the "small," "medium," or "large" setting on your washing machine. Next, you must set your water temperature. The clothes that you set aside as dirtier or stained will require a higher temperature, while a cooler wash is adequate for your cleaner clothes. Also check the washing instructions in the pieces you are about to wash. These instructions may specify the temperatures that are safe for the pieces. Finally, the agitation level, or wash cycle, must be selected. Choosing "high," "medium," or "low" agitation depends upon the durability of the fabric. A higher agitation level would be appropriate for the sturdiest of fabrics while a lower setting would be best for the finer, more delicate fabric types. When this cycle has been completed, you may move on to the drying phase.

Now the final phase, drying, begins. After putting your wet clothes into the dryer, set the estimated time you think is required for the load size. For example, a large load of towels will take more time than a small load of delicates. Next, select the temperature for the drying cycle. It is best to dry clothing on a lower setting to prevent shrinking and to improve its longevity. The third step is to remove the clothes from the dryer while they are still slightly damp and lay them flat, smoothing out any wrinkles. This will give your clothes a pressed appearance. As soon as the clothes are dry, they are ready to be worn.

In summary, laundry can be simple if you just remember three sets of three steps. The steps will help you prevent shrunken shirts, ripped fabrics, and pink socks.

In the opening paragraph, Alden introduces the topic he will discuss.

The writer uses words and phrases that clarify the order in which the steps of the instructions must be followed.

Alden lists and clearly explains the reader's options during this step of the process.

The writer uses a conclusion to tie the steps together as an essay.

Editing and Proofreading

Edit your draft for errors in grammar and mechanics, such as punctuation.

Spell correctly. When you edit and proofread your writing, make sure you spell correctly. Review common errors in usage and use various resources such as print or online dictionaries or usage handbooks to check words you often confuse. Confirm word formation rules, such as adding prefixes and suffixes, and changing spellings.

Focus on legibility. Make sure revisions are clear and readable. Draw a single line through a word to delete it. Use a caret (^) to show where words or letters need to be added. Underline letters three times to show that they need to be capitalized.

Spiral Review

Earlier in the unit, you learned about **simple and compound sentences** (p. 1084) and **complex and compound-complex sentences** (p. 1116). Make sure you have properly constructed these sentence types in your instructions.

Publishing and Presenting

Consider these ways to publish your written work for appropriate audiences:

Print a manual. Make a clean copy of your final draft. Enter your instructions into a word-processing program and print out a manual for others to consult.

Produce a podcast. Use your instructions as the basis for a podcast script. Record your podcast, making sure you express your organization clearly.

Reflecting on Your Writing

Writer's Journal Jot down your answer to this question:

How did writing directions help you understand a process better?

Rubric for Self-Assessment

Find evidence in your writing to address each category. Then, use the rating scale to grade your work.

Written Composition Criteria	Rating Scale
	not very ⟶ *very*
Focus and Coherence: How reader-friendly are your formatting techniques?	1 2 3 4
Organization: How organized is your information?	1 2 3 4
Development of Ideas: How well have you used definitions and visual aids to aid reader comprehension?	1 2 3 4
Conventions: How error-free is your grammar, especially your revision of sentence fragments and run-ons?	1 2 3 4
Voice: How clearly and accurately conveyed is your information?	1 2 3 4

Selection Choices

▲ Read **"Three Skeleton Key"** to experience life at an isolated lighthouse and the unexpected dangers that lurk there.

▲ Read **"The Red-headed League"** to learn how a brilliant detective's mind works and to discover the hidden trail of a thief.

 TEXAS Focus on the TEKS

Meet these standards with either **"Three Skeleton Key"** (p. 1148) or **"The Red-headed League"** (p. 1166).

Reading

(5)(B) Analyze how authors develop complex yet believable characters in works of fiction. *(Literary Analysis: Protagonist and Antagonist)*

(1)(B) Analyze textual context (within a sentence) to distinguish between the denotative and connotative meanings of words. *(Spiral Review: Connotation and Denotation)*

(1)(A) Determine the meaning of grade-level technical academic English words in multiple content areas derived from Latin roots. *(Word Power: Apply It)*

Reading/Comprehension Skills
RC-9(A) Reflect on understanding to monitor comprehension (e.g., asking questions). *(Reading Skill: Comparing and Contrasting Characters)*

Oral and Written Conventions

(18)(B)(ii);(iii) Use correct punctuation marks including: comma placement in nonrestrictive phrases and contrasting expressions; and dashes to emphasize parenthetical information. *(Conventions: Commas and Dashes)*

Research

(20)(A) Formulate a major research question to address the major research topic. *(Research and Technology: Oral Report)*

(21)(B) Organize information gathered from multiple sources to create a variety of graphics. *(Research and Technology: Oral Report)*

(23)(C);(D) Use graphics and illustrations to help explain concepts where appropriate; use a variety of evaluative tools to examine the quality of research. *(Research and Technology: Oral Report)*

Literary Analysis:
Protagonist and Antagonist

TEXAS
PHLitOnline
www.PHLitOnline.com

The **protagonist** is the chief character in a literary work. Most literary works also have an **antagonist**—a character or force that opposes the protagonist. The antagonist is often another character, but may also be an external force, such as nature. These character types are literary devices that allow the author to develop complex, yet believable, characters while using the conflict that develops between the two characters to drive the plot of the story.

Hear It!
• Selection summary audio
• Selection audio

See It!
• Get Connected video
• Background video
• More about the author
• Vocabulary flashcards

Do It!
• Interactive journals
• Interactive graphic organizers
• Self-test
• Internet activity
• Grammar tutorial
• Interactive vocabulary games

- The protagonist's motives may be universally understood feelings and goals, such as curiosity or the search for love.
- The protagonist's conflict with the antagonist may represent a universal struggle, such as the conflict between good and evil.

Using the Strategy: Protagonist and Antagonist Chart

As You Read Use a chart to analyze the conflicts and motives of the protagonist and antagonist. Then, look for ways in which the characters' motives and conflicts are complex, yet believable.

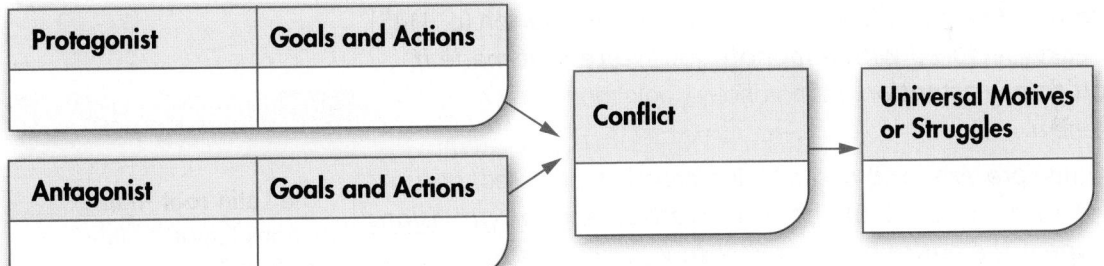

Protagonist	Goals and Actions

Antagonist	Goals and Actions

Conflict

Universal Motives or Struggles

Reading Skill:
Comparing and Contrasting Characters

To **compare and contrast characters,** analyze their similarities and differences. You can compare and contrast different characters in a work, characters from different works, or a single character at different points.

As You Read **Reflect on your understanding** of the characters. **Monitor your comprehension** by asking the same questions about each character and using the answers to compare and contrast the characters.

Do *heroes* have responsibilities?

Writing About the Big Question

In "Three Skeleton Key," three men who are staying on a tiny island confront an unexpected and dangerous enemy. Use this sentence starter to develop your ideas about the Big Question.

Some people often **choose** to take on the **responsibility** that can come with the role of **hero** because _____.

As You Read Look for choices the protagonist makes for his group and think about his responsibility for their situation.

Vocabulary

Read each word and its definition. Decide whether you know the word well, know it a little bit, or do not know it at all. After you read, see how your knowledge of each word has increased.

- **monotonous** (mə nät´ ´n əs) *adj.* having little or no variation (p. 1148) *The speaker lectured with a monotonous voice that made it difficult to pay attention.* monotonously *adv.* monotony *n.* monotone *n.*

- **provisions** (prə vizh´ ənz) *n.* something provided, prepared, or supplied for the future (p. 1150) *The scouts carried enough provisions to last them the entire hike.* provisioned *v.* provide *v.*

- **lurched** (lʉrcht) *v.* moved awkwardly and suddenly (p. 1152) *The newborn calf lurched forward as it tried to stand.*

- **diminution** (dim´ ə noo͞´ shən) *n.* lessening (p. 1156) *The players' diminution of enthusiasm caused them to play poorly.* diminutive *adj.*

- **incessantly** (in ses´ ənt lē) *adv.* continuing in a way that seems endless; continually; unceasingly (p. 1156) *The wind blew so incessantly during the storm that the streets were covered with toppled garbage cans when it was over.* incessant *adj.* cease *v.*

- **derisive** (di rī´ siv) *adj.* mocking (p. 1159) *The critic's derisive laugh offended the artist.* derisively *adv.* derisiveness *n.*

Word Power

The **Latin root -min-** means "small," "little," or "less."

In this selection, the narrator says there were so many rats, they could not see any **diminution**, or lessening, of their numbers when some were eaten by sharks.

Author of

Three Skeleton Key

BACKGROUND FOR THE STORY

Social Studies Connection

Lighthouses

A lighthouse, or "light," is a tower built on an island or other prominent point to warn ships away from treacherous areas near a coast. The tower is usually several stories high, with a large, bright, movable light at the top. Most lighthouses are now automated, but they used to be occupied by people who maintained and operated the light, moving the beam across the water when a ship approached. A lighthouse is often located on a key, which is a small island or a reef near a larger land mass.

The award-winning writer, editor, and scholar George Gustave Toudouze was born in Paris, France.

Writer of the Sea A maritime expert, Toudouze wrote nineteen books about the ocean and served as chief editor of *The French Maritime and Colonial League.* He also earned a doctorate of letters at the Sorbonne, one of the oldest and most distinguished universities in the world. He went on to become a professor of history and dramatic literature at the Paris Conservatory. His claim to fame, however, rests entirely upon one story, "Three Skeleton Key," which was published in 1937 in *Esquire* magazine.

DID YOU KNOW?

"Three Skeleton Key" is the only one of Toudouze's stories to appear in English.

Three Skeleton Key

George G. Toudouze

Vocabulary

monotonous (mə nät´ 'n əs) *adj.* having little or no variation

My most terrifying experience? Well, one does have a few in thirty-five years of service in the Lights, although it's mostly monotonous routine work—keeping the light in order, making out the reports.

When I was a young man, not very long in the service, there was an opening in a lighthouse newly built off the coast of Guiana,[1] on a small rock twenty miles or so from the mainland. The pay was high, so in order to reach the sum I had set out to save before I married, I volunteered for service in the new light.

---

1. Guiana (gē an´ ə) region on the northern coast of South America.

Three Skeleton Key, the small rock on which the light stood, bore a bad reputation. It earned its name from the story of the three convicts who, escaping from Cayenne[2] in a stolen dugout canoe, were wrecked on the rock during the night, managed to escape the sea but eventually died of hunger and thirst. When they were discovered, nothing remained but three heaps of bones, picked clean by the birds. The story was that the three skeletons, gleaming with phosphorescent light,[3] danced over the small rock, screaming. . . .

Reading Check

How did Three Skeleton Key get its name?

---

2. **Cayenne** (kī en´) capital city of French Guiana.
3. **phosphorescent** (fäs´ fə res´ ənt) **light** a glowing light produced by certain natural chemical reactions.

Literary Analysis
Protagonist and Antagonist Which details in the story's first four paragraphs suggest that the narrator is the central character in this story?

Vocabulary
provisions (prə vizh´ ənz) *n.* something provided, prepared, or supplied for the future

Reading Skill
Contrasting Characters What difference in the characters' ages does the narrator point out?

But there are many such stories, and I did not give the warnings of the old-timers at the Isle de Sein[4] a second thought. I signed up, boarded ship, and in a month I was installed at the light.

Picture a gray, tapering cylinder, welded to the solid black rock by iron rods and concrete, rising from a small island twenty odd miles from land. It lay in the midst of the sea, this island, a small, bare piece of stone, about one hundred fifty feet long, perhaps forty wide. Small, barely large enough for a man to walk about and stretch his legs at low tide.

This is an advantage one doesn't find in all lights, however, for some of them rise sheer from the waves, with no room for one to move save within the light itself. Still, on our island, one must be careful, for the rocks were treacherously smooth. One misstep and down you would fall into the sea—not that the risk of drowning was so great, but the waters about our island swarmed with huge sharks who kept an eternal patrol around the base of the light.

Still, it was a nice life there. We had enough provisions to last for months, in the event that the sea should become too rough for the supply ship to reach us on schedule. During the day we would work about the light, cleaning the rooms, polishing the metalwork and the lens and reflector of the light itself, and at night we would sit on the gallery and watch our light, a twenty thousand candle-power lantern, swinging its strong, white bar of light over the sea from the top of its hundred-twenty-foot tower. Some days, when the air would be very clear, we could see the land, a thread-like line to the west. To the east, north and south stretched the ocean. Landsmen, perhaps, would soon have tired of that kind of life, perched on a small island off the coast of South America for eighteen weeks, until one's turn for leave ashore came around. But we liked it there, my two fellow-tenders and myself—so much so that, for twenty-two months on end with the exception of shore leaves, I was greatly satisfied with the life on Three Skeleton Key.

I had just returned from my leave at the end of June, that is to say mid-winter in that latitude, and had settled down to the routine with my two fellow-keepers, a Breton[5] by the name of Le Gleo and the head-keeper, Itchoua, a Basque[6] some dozen years or so older than either of us.

Eight days went by as usual, then on the ninth night after my return, Itchoua, who was on night duty, called Le Gleo

---

4. **Isle de Sein** (ēl´ də sen´) island off the northwestern coast of France.
5. **Breton** (bret´ 'n) person born or living in Brittany, a region on the northwestern coast of France.
6. **Basque** (bask) member of a people who inhabit a region between Spain and France on the Bay of Biscay.

and me, sleeping in our rooms in the middle of the tower, at two in the morning. We rose immediately and, climbing the thirty or so steps that led to the gallery, stood beside our chief.

Itchoua pointed, and following his finger, we saw a big three-master, with all sail set, heading straight for the light. A queer course, for the vessel must have seen us, our light lit her with the glare of day each time it passed over her.

Now, ships were a rare sight in our waters, for our light was a warning of treacherous reefs, barely hidden under the surface and running far out to sea. Consequently we were always given a wide berth, especially by sailing vessels, which cannot maneuver as readily as steamers.

No wonder that we were surprised at seeing this three-master heading dead for us in the gloom of early morning. I had immediately recognized her lines, for she stood out plainly, even at the distance of a mile, when our light shone on her.

▲ **Critical Viewing**
How does this photograph of a Dutch sailing ship help establish the time period of the story? **[Connect]**

She was a beautiful ship of some four thousand tons, a fast sailor that had carried cargoes to every part of the world, plowing the seas unceasingly. By her lines she was identified as Dutch-built, which was understandable as Paramaribo and Dutch Guiana are very close to Cayenne.

Watching her sailing dead for us, a white wave boiling under her bows, Le Gleo cried out:

"What's wrong with her crew? Are they all drunk or insane? Can't they see us?"

Itchoua nodded soberly, looked at us sharply as he remarked: "See us? No doubt—if there is a crew aboard!"

"What do you mean, chief?" Le Gleo had started, turned to the Basque, "Are you saying that she's the Flying Dutchman?"[7]

His sudden fright had been so evident that the older man laughed:

"No, old man, that's not what I meant. If I say that no one's aboard, I mean she's a derelict."

Then we understood his queer behavior. Itchoua was right. For some reason, believing her doomed, her crew had abandoned her.

One misstep and down you would fall into the sea...

Reading Check

In the middle of the night, what surprising sight does Itchoua show his companions?

---

7. **Flying Dutchman** fabled ghost ship doomed to sail forever.

Vocabulary
lurched (lurcht) *v.* moved awkwardly and suddenly

Then she had righted herself and sailed on, wandering with the wind.

The three of us grew tense as the ship seemed about to crash on one of our numerous reefs, but she suddenly lurched with some change of the wind, the yards swung around, and the derelict came clumsily about and sailed dead away from us.

In the light of our lantern she seemed so sound, so strong, that Itchoua exclaimed impatiently:

"But why the devil was she abandoned? Nothing is smashed, no sign of fire—and she doesn't sail as if she were taking water."

Le Gleo waved to the departing ship:

"Bon voyage!"[8] he smiled at Itchoua and went on. "She's leaving us, chief, and now we'll never know what—"

"No she's not!" cried the Basque. "Look! She's turning!"

As if obeying his words, the derelict three-master stopped, came about and headed for us once more. And for the next four hours the vessel played around us—zigzagging, coming about,[9] stopping, then suddenly lurching forward. No doubt some freak of current and wind, of which our island was the center, kept her near us.

Then suddenly, the tropic dawn broke, the sun rose and it was day, and the ship was plainly visible as she sailed past us. Our light extinguished, we returned to the gallery with our glasses and inspected her.

The three of us focused our glasses on her poop,[10] saw standing out sharply, black letters on the white background of a life-ring, the stenciled name:

"*Cornelius-de-Witt*, Rotterdam."

We had read her lines correctly, she was Dutch. Just then the wind rose and the *Cornelius-de-Witt* changed course, leaned to port and headed straight for us once more. But this time she was so close that we knew she would not turn in time.

Reading Skill
Contrasting Characters
In what ways are Le Gleo's and the narrator's reactions to the doomed ship similar and different?

"Thunder!" cried Le Gleo, his Breton soul aching to see a fine ship doomed to smash upon a reef, "She's going to pile up! She's gone!"

I shook my head:

"Yes, and a shame to see that beautiful ship wreck herself. And we're helpless."

There was nothing we could do but watch. A ship sailing with all sail spread, creaming the sea with her forefoot as she runs before the wind, is one of the most beautiful sights in the world—but this time I could feel the tears stinging my eyes as I saw this fine ship headed for her doom.

---

8. **Bon voyage** (bän′ vɔi äzh′) French for "pleasant journey"; a farewell to a traveler.
9. **coming about** changing direction according to the direction of the wind.
10. **poop** (po͞op) *n.* raised deck at the rear of a sailing ship.

All this time our glasses were riveted on her, and we suddenly cried out together:

"The rats!"

Now we knew why this ship, in perfect condition, was sailing without her crew aboard. They had been driven out by the rats. Not those poor specimens of rats you see ashore, barely reaching the length of one foot from their trembling noses to the tip of their skinny tails, wretched creatures that dodge and hide at the mere sound of a footfall.

No, these were ships' rats, huge, wise creatures, born on the sea, sailing all over the world on ships, transferring to other, larger ships as they multiply. There is as much difference between the rats of the land and these maritime rats as between a fishing smack and an armored cruiser.

The rats of the sea are fierce, bold animals. Large, strong and intelligent, clannish and seawise, able to put the best of mariners to shame with their knowledge of the sea, their uncanny ability to foretell the weather.

And they are brave, these rats, and vengeful. If you so much as harm one, his sharp cry will bring hordes of his fellows to swarm over you, tear you and not cease until your flesh has been stripped from the bones.

The ones on this ship, the rats of Holland, are the worst, superior to other rats of the sea as their brethren are to the land rats. There is a well-known tale about these animals.

A Dutch captain, thinking to protect his cargo, brought aboard his ship—not cats—but two terriers, dogs trained in the hunting,

Reading Skill
Contrasting Characters
In what way are the rats on the *Cornelius-de-Witt* different from other rats in the world?

Reading
Check
What detail do the men notice that shows that the crew of the *Cornelius-de-Witt* did not abandon ship?

The rats of the sea are fierce, bold animals.

fighting and killing of vicious rats. By the time the ship, sailing from Rotterdam, had passed the Ostend light, the dogs were gone and never seen again. In twenty-four hours they had been overwhelmed, killed and eaten by the rats.

At times, when the cargo does not suffice, the rats attack the crew, either driving them from the ship or eating them alive. And studying the *Cornelius-de-Witt*, I turned sick, for her small boats were all in place. She had not been abandoned.

Over her bridge, on her deck, in the rigging, on every visible spot, the ship was a writhing mass—a starving army coming towards us aboard a vessel gone mad!

Our island was a small spot in that immense stretch of sea. The ship could have grazed us, passed to port or starboard with its ravening cargo—but no, she came for us at full speed, as if she were leading the regatta at a race, and impaled herself on a sharp point of rock.

There was a dull shock as her bottom stove in, then a horrible crackling as the three masts went overboard at once, as if cut down with one blow of some gigantic sickle. A sighing groan came as the water rushed into the ship, then she split in two and sank like a stone.

But the rats did not drown. Not these fellows! As much at home in the sea as any fish, they formed ranks in the water, heads lifted, tails stretched out, paws paddling. And half of them, those from the forepart of the ship, sprang along the masts and onto the rocks in the instant before she sank. Before we had time even to move, nothing remained of the three-master save some pieces of wreckage floating on the surface and an army of rats covering the rocks left bare by the receding tide.

Thousands of heads rose, felt the wind and we were scented, seen! To them we were fresh meat, after possible weeks of starving. There came a scream, composed of innumerable screams, sharper than the howl of a saw attacking a bar of iron, and in the one motion, every rat leaped to attack the tower! We barely had time to leap back, close the door leading onto the gallery, descend the stairs and shut every window tightly. Luckily the door at the base of the light, which we never could have reached in time, was of bronze set in granite and was tightly closed.

Literary Analysis
Protagonist and Antagonist What details in this section help develop the protagonist as a complex yet believable character? Explain.

▼ **Critical Viewing** Which details in the photograph make these rats appear fearsome, like the ones in "Three Skeleton Key"? **[Analyze]**

The horrible band, in no measurable time, had swarmed up and over the tower as if it had been a tree, piled on the embrasures of the windows, scraped at the glass with thousands of claws, covered the lighthouse with a furry mantle and reached the top of the tower, filling the gallery and piling atop the lantern.

Their teeth grated as they pressed against the glass of the lantern-room, where they could plainly see us, though they could not reach us. A few millimeters of glass, luckily very strong, separated our faces from their gleaming, beady eyes, their sharp claws and teeth. Their odor filled the tower, poisoned our lungs and rasped our nostrils with a pestilential, nauseating smell. And there we were, sealed alive in our own light, prisoners of a horde of starving rats.

That first night, the tension was so great that we could not sleep. Every moment, we felt that some opening had been made, some window given away, and that our horrible besiegers were pouring through the breach. The rising tide, chasing those of the rats which had stayed on the bare rocks, increased the numbers clinging to the walls, piled on the balcony—so much so that clusters of rats clinging to one another hung from the lantern and the gallery.

With the coming of darkness we lit the light, and the turning beam completely maddened the beasts. As the light turned, it successively blinded thousands of rats crowded against the glass, while the dark side of the lantern-room gleamed with thousands of points of light, burning like the eyes of jungle beasts in the night.

All the while we could hear the enraged scraping of claws against the stone and glass, while the chorus of cries was so loud that we had to shout to hear one another. From time to time, some of the rats fought among themselves and a dark cluster would detach itself, falling into the sea like a ripe fruit from a tree. Then we would see phosphorescent streaks as triangular fins slashed the water— sharks, permanent guardians of our rock, feasting on our jailors.

The next day we were calmer, and amused ourselves by teasing the rats, placing our faces against the glass which separated us. They could not fathom the invisible barrier which separated them from us, and we laughed as we watched them leaping against the heavy glass.

But the day after that, we realized how serious our position was. The air was foul; even the heavy smell of oil within our stronghold could not dominate the fetid odor of the beasts massed around us, and there was no way of admitting fresh air without also admitting the rats.

The morning of the fourth day, at early dawn, I saw the wooden framework of my window, eaten away from the outside, sagging

Spiral Review
Connotation and Denotation Analyze the context in which *pestilential* appears. Distinguish between the denotative and connotative meanings of the word.

Literary Analysis
Protagonist and Antagonist With what external force are the narrator, Le Gleo, and Itchoua now in conflict?

Reading Skill
Comparing Characters In what way do the sharks and the rats behave similarly?

Reading Check
What do the rats do almost immediately after landing on the island?

inwards. I called my comrades and the three of us fastened a sheet of tin in the opening, sealing it tightly. When we had completed the task, Itchoua turned to us and said dully:

"Well—the supply boat came thirteen days ago, and she won't be back for twenty-nine." He pointed at the white metal plate sealing the opening through the granite—"If that gives way—" he shrugged—"they can change the name of this place to Six Skeletons Key."

The next six days and seven nights, our only distraction was watching the rats whose holds were insecure fall a hundred and twenty feet into the maws of the sharks—but they were so many that we could not see any diminution in their numbers.

Thinking to calm ourselves and pass the time, we attempted to count them, but we soon gave up. They moved incessantly, never still. Then we tried identifying them, naming them.

One of them, larger than the others, who seemed to lead them in their rushes against the glass separating us, we named "Nero";[11] and there were several others whom we had learned to distinguish through various peculiarities.

But the thought of our bones joining those of the convicts was always in the back of our minds. And the gloom of our prison fed these thoughts, for the interior of the light was almost completely

11. **Nero** (nir´ ō) (A.D. 37–68) Roman emperor who was notoriously cruel.

Vocabulary
diminution (dim´ ə noō´ shən) *n.* lessening

incessantly (in ses´ ənt lē) *adv.* continuing in a way that seems endless; continually; unceasingly

▼ **Critical Viewing**
Why are even the fierce ship rats no match for a school of sharks like these? **[Assess]**

—"they can change the name of this place to Six Skeletons Key."

dark, as we had to seal every window in the same fashion as mine, and the only space that still admitted daylight was the glassed-in lantern-room at the very top of the tower.

Then Le Gleo became morose and had nightmares in which he would see the three skeletons dancing around him, gleaming coldly, seeking to grasp him. His maniacal, raving descriptions were so vivid that Itchoua and I began seeing them also.

It was a living nightmare, the raging cries of the rats as they swarmed over the light, mad with hunger; the sickening, strangling odor of their bodies—

True, there is a way of signaling from light-houses. But to reach the mast on which to hang the signal we would have to go out on the gallery where the rats were.

There was only one thing left to do. After debating all of the ninth day, we decided not to light the lantern that night. This is the greatest breach of our service, never committed as long as the tenders of the light are alive; for the light is something sacred, warning ships of danger in the night. Either the light gleams, a quarter hour after sundown, or no one is left alive to light it.

Well, that night, Three Skeleton Light was dark, and all the men were alive. At the risk of causing ships to crash on our reefs, we left it unlit, for we were worn out—going mad!

Literary Analysis
Protagonist and Antagonist In addition to the rats, what other problems do the men face?

Reading Check

What happens in Le Gleo's nightmares?

Literary Analysis
Protagonist and Antagonist What do you think motivates the narrator and Le Gleo to risk their own lives to help Itchoua?

At two in the morning, while Itchoua was dozing in his room, the sheet of metal sealing his window gave way. The chief had just time enough to leap to his feet and cry for help, the rats swarming over him.

But Le Gleo and I, who had been watching from the lantern-room, got to him immediately, and the three of us battled with the horde of maddened rats which flowed through the gaping window. They bit, we struck them down with our knives—and retreated.

We locked the door of the room on them, but before we had time to bind our wounds, the door was eaten through and gave way, and we retreated up the stairs, fighting off the rats that leaped on us from the knee-deep swarm.

I do not remember, to this day, how we ever managed to escape. All I can remember is wading through them up the stairs, striking them off as they swarmed over us; and then we found ourselves, bleeding from innumerable bites, our clothes shredded, sprawled across the trapdoor in the floor of the lantern-room—without food or drink. Luckily, the trapdoor was metal set into the granite with iron bolts.

The rats occupied the entire light beneath us, and on the floor of our retreat lay some twenty of their fellows, who had gotten in with us before the trapdoor closed, and whom we had killed with our knives. Below us, in the tower, we could hear the screams of the rats as they devoured everything edible that they found. Those on the outside squealed in reply, and writhed in a horrible curtain as they stared at us through the glass of the lantern-room.

Itchoua sat up, stared silently at his blood trickling from the wounds on his limbs and body, and running in thin streams on the floor around him. Le Gleo, who was in as bad a state (and so was I, for that matter) stared at the chief and me vacantly, started as his gaze swung to the multitude of rats against the glass, then suddenly began laughing horribly:

"Hee! Hee! The Three Skeletons! Hee! Hee! The Three Skeletons are now six skeletons! Six skeletons!"

He threw his head back and howled, his eyes glazed, a trickle of saliva running from the corners of his mouth and thinning the blood flowing over his chest. I shouted to him to shut up, but he did not hear me, so I did the only thing I could to quiet him—I swung the back of my hand across his face.

The howling stopped suddenly, his eyes swung around the room, then he bowed his head and began weeping softly, like a child.

Our darkened light had been noticed from the mainland, and as dawn was breaking, the patrol was there to investigate the failure of our light. Looking through my binoculars, I could see the horrified

Reading Skill
Contrasting Characters What differences between the narrator and Le Gleo do their reactions make clear?

expression on the faces of the officers and crew when, the daylight strengthening, they saw the light completely covered by a seething mass of rats. They thought, as I afterwards found out, that we had been eaten alive.

But the rats had also seen the ship, or had scented the crew. As the ship drew nearer, a solid phalanx[12] left the light, plunged into the water and, swimming out, attempted to board her. They would have succeeded, as the ship was hove to, but the engineer connected his steam to a hose on the deck and scalded the head of the attacking column, which slowed them up long enough for the ship to get under way and leave the rats behind.

Then the sharks took part. Belly up, mouths gaping, they arrived in swarms and scooped up the rats, sweeping through them like a sickle through wheat. That was one day that sharks really served a useful purpose.

The remaining rats turned tail, swam to the shore, and emerged dripping. As they neared the light, their comrades greeted them with shrill cries, with what sounded like a derisive note predominating. They answered angrily and mingled with their fellows. From the several tussles that broke out, they resented being ridiculed for their failure to capture the ship.

But all this did nothing to get us out of our jail. The small ship could not approach, but steamed around the light at a safe distance, and the tower must have seemed fantastic, some weird, many-mouthed beast hurling defiance at them.

Finally, seeing the rats running in and out of the tower through the door and the windows, those on the ship decided that we had perished and were about to leave when Itchoua, regaining his senses, thought of using the light as a signal. He lit it and, using a plank placed and withdrawn before the beam to form the dots and dashes, quickly sent out our story to those on the vessel.

Our reply came quickly. When they understood our position—how we could not get rid of the rats, Le Gleo's mind going fast, Itchoua and myself covered with bites, cornered in the lantern-room without food or water—they had a signalman send us their reply.

Vocabulary
derisive (di rī′ siv)
adj. mocking

Reading Check

What do the men do that results in the arrival of a patrol ship?

---

12. phalanx (fā′ laŋks′) *n.* group of individuals advancing in a close, compact formation.

His arms swinging like those of a windmill, he quickly spelled out: "Don't give up. Hang on a little longer! We'll get you out of this!"

Then she turned and steamed at top speed for the coast, leaving us little reassured.

She was back at noon, accompanied by the supply ship, two small coast guard boats, and the fire boat—a small squadron. At twelve-thirty the battle was on.

After a short reconnaissance,[13] the fire boat picked her way slowly through the reefs until she was close to us, then turned her powerful jet of water on the rats. The heavy stream tore the rats from their places, hurled them screaming into the water where the sharks gulped them down. But for every ten that were dislodged, seven swam ashore, and the stream could do nothing to the rats within the tower. Furthermore, some of them, instead of returning to the rocks, boarded the fire boat, and the men were forced to battle them hand to hand. They were true rats of Holland, fearing no man, fighting for the right to live!

---

13. reconnaissance (ri kän´ ə səns) *n.* exploratory survey or examination.

Reading Skill
Comparing Characters
What similarity between the rats and the men does the narrator's remark about the rats reveal?

▼ Critical Viewing
Based on this photograph, how easily do you think the sharks could attack the rats? Explain.
[Evaluate]

Nightfall came, and it was as if nothing had been done, the rats were still in possession. One of the patrol boats stayed by the island; the rest of the flotilla[14] departed for the coast. We had to spend another night in our prison. Le Gleo was sitting on the floor, babbling about skeletons, and as I turned to Itchoua, he fell unconscious from his wounds. I was in no better shape and could feel my blood flaming with fever.

Somehow the night dragged by, and the next afternoon I saw a tug, accompanied by the fire boat, coming from the mainland with a huge barge in tow. Through my glasses, I saw that the barge was filled with meat.

Risking the treacherous reefs, the tug dragged the barge as close to the island as possible. To the last rat, our besiegers deserted the rock, swam out and boarded the barge reeking with the scent of freshly cut meat. The tug dragged the barge about a mile from shore, where the fire boat drenched the barge with gasoline. A well placed incendiary shell from the patrol boat set her on fire.

The barge was covered with flames immediately, and the rats took to the water in swarms, but the patrol boat bombarded them with shrapnel from a safe distance, and the sharks finished off the survivors.

A whaleboat from the patrol boat took us off the island and left three men to replace us. By nightfall we were in the hospital in Cayenne.

---

14. **flotilla** (flō til′ ə) *n.* small fleet.

Literary Analysis
Protagonist and Antagonist In what way does human intelligence ultimately overcome the rats' brutality?

Reading Check
What does the fire boat do to attack the rats? What is the result?

They were true rats of Holland, fearing no man, fighting for the right to live!

Reading Skill
Contrasting Characters
How is Le Gleo changed
by the attack?

What became of my friends? Well, Le Gleo's mind had cracked and he was raving mad. They sent him back to France and locked him up in an asylum,[15] the poor devil; Itchoua died within a week; a rat's bite is dangerous in that hot, humid climate, and infection sets in rapidly.

As for me—when they fumigated[16] the light and repaired the damage done by the rats, I resumed my service there. Why not? No reason why such an incident should keep me from finishing out my service there, is there?

Besides—I told you I liked the place—to be truthful, I've never had a post as pleasant as that one, and when my time came to leave it forever, I tell you that I almost wept as Three Skeleton Key disappeared below the horizon.

---

15. asylum (ə sī ´ ləm) *n.* institution for the care of the mentally ill.
16. fumigated (fyōō´ mə gāt´ id) *v.* disinfected with fumes.

Critical Thinking

1. **Respond:** What feelings does this story stir in you, and why?

2. **(a)** How do the rats come to the lighthouse? **(b) Make Inferences:** What impression of the rats does this method of arrival create? **(c) Summarize:** Explain how the rescuers defeat the rats.

3. **(a)** What does Itchoua say about the name of the island and what will happen if the window seal gives way? **(b) Make Inferences:** What does he mean by this remark? **(c) Interpret:** How does this remark create suspense and add meaning to the story's title?

4. **(a) Categorize:** Which details portray the rats as intelligent and organized and which portray them as mindlessly vicious?
   (b) Evaluate: Does Toudouze make you believe that actual rats would be capable of the actions he describes? Explain.

   Do heroes have responsibilities?
   (a) Is the narrator a hero? Explain. **(b)** Does the narrator, acting as a hero, fulfill any responsibility toward the other characters?

Support your responses with evidence from the text.

Literary Analysis:
Protagonist and Antagonist

1. **(a)** Identify the **protagonist** in the narrative. **(b)** What is the protagonist's goal? **(c)** Why are readers interested in whether the protagonist achieves his goal?
2. **(a)** Identify the **antagonist. (b)** What is the antagonist's goal?
3. **(a)** In what ways are the story's characters complex? **(b)** Do you find the characters believable? Explain.

Reading Skill:
Comparing and Contrasting Characters

4. **(a)** Complete a Venn diagram like the one shown to **compare and contrast** the narrator's outlook at the beginning of the story with his outlook at the end of the story. **(b)** Explain whether the narrator has or has not changed as a result of his experience.

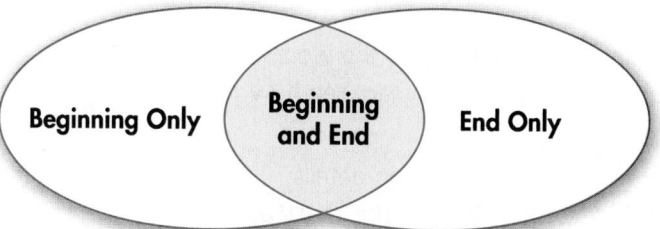

Beginning Only — **Beginning and End** — **End Only**

Vocabulary

Practice Analogies show the relationships between pairs of words. Use a word from the list on page 1146 to complete each analogy.

1. enlargement : increase :: _____ : decrease
2. glided : graceful :: _____ : clumsy
3. complimentary : praise :: _____ : ridicule
4. infrequently : rarely :: _____ : constantly
5. gasoline : automobile :: _____ : people
6. exciting : exhilarating :: _____ : boring

Word Power Use the context of the sentences and what you know about the **Latin root -min-** to explain your answer to each question.

1. Would a very hungry man want a *diminutive* sandwich?
2. Does exercise *minimize* the risk of heart attacks?

Word Power

The **Latin root -min-** means "small," "little," or "less."

Apply It Explain how the root -min- helps you determine the meanings of these technical academic words from social studies and the arts. Consult a dictionary if necessary.
minority
administer
miniaturist

Do *heroes* have responsibilities?

Writing About the Big Question

In "The Red-headed League," Sherlock Holmes sets out to solve a peculiar mystery involving men with brilliant red hair. Use these sentence starters to develop your ideas about the Big Question.

When a crime is being committed, a **hero** will _____.

The hero's **involvement** may show his or her **character** because

_____.

(As You Read) Look for Sherlock Holmes's motivations for solving the mystery and decide whether his actions make him a hero.

Vocabulary

Read each word and its definition. Decide whether you know the word well, know it a little bit, or do not know it at all. After you read, see how your knowledge of each word has increased.

- **embellish** (em bel´ ish) *v.* decorate or improve by adding details; ornament; adorn (p. 1167) *Max decided to embellish the story as he noticed his listeners losing interest halfway through.* *embellishment n.*

- **endeavored** (en dev´ ərd) *v.* made an earnest attempt to achieve or succeed; tried (p. 1168) *Jennifer endeavored to rank among the top ten students in her class.* *endeavor n./v.*

- **introspective** (in´ trə spek´ tiv) *adj.* having to do with looking into one's own thoughts and feelings (p. 1178) *The touching movie put me in an introspective mood.* *introspection n. introspectively adv.*

- **vex** (veks) *v.* annoy (p. 1180) *My allergies continued to vex me throughout the spring.* *vexing adj. vexation n. vexatiously adv.*

- **formidable** (fôr´ mə də bəl) *adj.* awe-inspiring (p. 1180) *Mt. Everest is a formidable sight.* *formidably adv. formidability n.*

- **tenacious** (tə nā´ shəs) *adj.* holding firmly to your point or beliefs; persistent; stubborn (p. 1183) *The tenacious man could not admit that he was wrong.* *tenacity n. tenaciousness n. tenaciously adv.*

Word Power

The **Latin root -spect-** means "see," "look," or "examine."

In this selection, Sherlock Holmes describes a German music program as **introspective** because it helps him look into his own thoughts.

Author of

The Red-Headed League

Sir Arthur Conan Doyle began his career as a doctor. He also pursued a career in writing. In a few years, he sold his first novel, *A Study in Scarlet*, which introduced Sherlock Holmes to the world.

The World's Favorite Detective It is likely that Conan Doyle modeled Sherlock Holmes on Dr. Joseph Bell, a professor of his who could diagnose illnesses from clues that other physicians had missed. Conan Doyle made the narrator of the Holmes mysteries Dr. John Watson. In the stories, Watson greatly admires Holmes but can never match his friend's powers of observation and reasoning.

Readers grew to love Sherlock Holmes. When Conan Doyle killed him off in a story in 1893, readers protested so strongly that the author was forced to bring back the beloved detective.

BACKGROUND FOR THE STORY

(Cultural Connection)

Sherlock Holmes

This story is one of many tales about the exploits of one of the world's most famous fictional detectives, Sherlock Holmes. Often depicted wearing a plaid cape and a deerstalker cap, Sherlock Holmes is widely recognized by people around the world.

DID YOU KNOW?

Although Holmes is often depicted in a plaid cape and a deerstalker hat, the stories never mention such clothing.

The Red-Headed League

Sir Arthur Conan Doyle

I had called upon my friend, Mr. Sherlock Holmes, one day in the autumn of last year and found him in deep conversation with a very stout, florid-faced, elderly gentleman with fiery red hair. With an apology for my intrusion, I was about to withdraw when Holmes pulled me abruptly into the room and closed the door behind me.

"You could not possibly have come at a better time, my dear Watson," he said cordially.

"I was afraid that you were engaged."

"So I am. Very much so."

"Then I can wait in the next room."

"Not at all. This gentleman, Mr. Wilson, has been my partner and helper in many of my most successful cases, and I have no doubt that he will be of the utmost use to me in yours also."

The stout gentleman half rose from his chair and gave a bob of greeting, with a quick little questioning glance from his small, fat-encircled eyes.

"Try the settee,"[1] said Holmes, relapsing into his armchair and putting his finger tips together, as was his custom when in judicial moods. "I know, my dear Watson, that you share my love of all that is bizarre and outside the conventions and humdrum routine of everyday life. You have shown your relish for it by the enthusiasm which has prompted you to chronicle, and, if you will excuse my saying so, somewhat to embellish so many of my own little adventures."

"Your cases have indeed been of the greatest interest to me," I observed.

"You will remember that I remarked the other day, just before we went into the very simple problem presented by Miss Mary Sutherland, that for strange effects and extraordinary combinations we must go to life itself, which is always far more daring than any effort of the imagination."

"A proposition which I took the liberty of doubting."

"You did, Doctor, but none the less you must come round to my view, for otherwise I shall keep on piling fact upon fact on you until your reason breaks down under them and acknowledges me to be right. Now, Mr. Jabez Wilson here has been good enough to call upon me this morning, and to begin a narrative which promises to be one of the most singular which I have listened to for some time. You have heard me remark that the strangest and most unique things are very often connected not with the larger but with the smaller crimes, and occasionally, indeed, where there is room for doubt whether any positive crime has been committed. As far as I have heard it is impossible for me to say whether the present case is an instance of crime or not, but the course of events is certainly among the most singular that I have ever listened to. Perhaps, Mr. Wilson, you would have the great kindness to recommence your

---

1. **settee** (se tē´) *n.* small sofa.

Reading Skill
Comparing Characters
According to Holmes, what do he and Watson have in common?

Vocabulary
embellish (em bel´ ish) *v.* decorate or improve by adding details; ornament; adorn

Literary Analysis
Protagonist and Antagonist Holmes's speech here suggests that he is a protagonist in this story. What details suggest this? How does the author use these details to develop Holmes as a complex yet believable character?

Reading Check
What interest do Watson and Holmes share?

narrative. I ask you not merely because my friend Dr. Watson has not heard the opening part but also because the peculiar nature of the story makes me anxious to have every possible detail from your lips. As a rule, when I have heard some slight indication of the course of events, I am able to guide myself by the thousands of other similar cases which occur to my memory. In the present instance I am forced to admit that the facts are, to the best of my belief, unique."

The portly client puffed out his chest with an appearance of some little pride and pulled a dirty and wrinkled newspaper from the inside pocket of his great coat. As he glanced down the advertisement column, with his head thrust forward and the paper flattened out upon his knee, I took a good look at the man and endeavored, after the fashion of my companion, to read the indications which might be presented by his dress or appearance.

I did not gain very much, however, by my inspection. Our visitor bore every mark of being an average commonplace British tradesman, obese, pompous, and slow. He wore rather baggy gray shepherd's check trousers, a not over-clean black frock coat, unbuttoned in the front, and a drab waistcoat with a heavy brassy Albert chain, and a square pierced bit of metal dangling down as an ornament. A frayed top hat and a faded brown overcoat with a wrinkled velvet collar lay upon a chair beside him. Altogether, look as I would, there was nothing remarkable about the man save his blazing red head, and the expression of extreme chagrin and discontent upon his features.

Sherlock Holmes's quick eye took in my occupation, and he shook his head with a smile as he noticed my questioning glances. "Beyond the obvious facts that he has at some time done manual labor, that he takes snuff,[2] that he is a Freemason,[3] that he has been in China, and that he has done a considerable amount of writing lately, I can deduce nothing else."

Vocabulary
endeavored (en dev´ ərd) *v.* made an earnest attempt to achieve or succeed; tried

Reading Skill
Contrasting Characters
How are Watson and Holmes different in terms of their powers of observation?

---

2. snuff (snuf) *n.* powdered tobacco.
3. Freemason member of a secret society.

Mr. Jabez Wilson started up in his chair, with his forefinger upon the paper, but his eyes upon my companion.

"How, in the name of good fortune, did you know all that, Mr. Holmes?" he asked. "How did you know, for example, that I did manual labor? It's as true as gospel, for I began as a ship's carpenter."

"Your hands, my dear sir. Your right hand is quite a size larger than your left. You have worked with it, and the muscles are more developed."

"Well, the snuff, then, and the Freemasonry?"

"I won't insult your intelligence by telling you how I read that, especially as, rather against the strict rules of your order, you use an arc-and-compass breastpin."

"Ah, of course, I forgot that. But the writing?"

"What else can be indicated by that right cuff so very shiny for five inches, and the left one with the smooth patch near the elbow where you rest it upon the desk?"

"Well, but China?"

"The fish that you have tattooed immediately above your right wrist could only have been done in China. I have made a small study of tattoo marks and have even contributed to the literature of the subject. That trick of staining the fishes' scales of a delicate pink is quite peculiar to China. When, in addition, I see a Chinese coin hanging from your watch-chain, the matter becomes even more simple."

Mr. Jabez Wilson laughed heavily. "Well, I never!" said he. "I thought at first that you had done something clever, but I see that there was nothing in it, after all."

"I begin to think, Watson," said Holmes, "that I make a mistake in explaining. 'Omne ignotum pro magnifico,'[4] you know, and my poor little reputation, such as it is, will suffer shipwreck if I am so candid. Can you not find the advertisement, Mr. Wilson?"

"Yes, I have got it now," he answered with his thick red finger planted halfway down the column. "Here it is. This is what began it all. You just read it for yourself, sir."

I took the paper from him and read as follows:

To THE RED-HEADED LEAGUE:

On account of the bequest of the late Ezekiah Hopkins, of Lebanon, Pennsylvania, U. S. A., there is now another vacancy open

Reading
Check

What facts about Mr. Wilson does Holmes deduce based on Wilson's appearance?

---

4. **Omne ignotum pro magnifico** (äm′ nā ig nō′ təm prō mag nē′ fē kō) Latin for "Whatever is unknown is magnified."

LITERATURE IN CONTEXT

(Math Connection)

Pound Conversions

The advertisement that concerns Mr. Wilson announces a salary of four pounds a week. The pound is the monetary unit of Great Britain. Its equivalency in American dollars fluctuates depending on current economic conditions. At the time Doyle wrote the story, one British pound equaled about $4.85, so four pounds would have equaled about $19.40. This was considered a large amount at the time in which the story is set, particularly for easy work.

Connect to the Literature

Why might an offer of a large sum of money "for purely nominal services" be cause for suspicion?

which entitles a member of the League to a salary of £4 a week for purely nominal services. All red-headed men who are sound in body and mind, and above the age of twenty-one years, are eligible. Apply in person on Monday, at eleven o'clock, to Duncan Ross, at the offices of the League, 7 Pope's Court, Fleet Street.

"What on earth does this mean?" I ejaculated after I had twice read over the extraordinary announcement.

Holmes chuckled and wriggled in his chair, as was his habit when in high spirits. "It is a little off the beaten track, isn't it?" said he. "And now, Mr. Wilson, off you go at scratch and tell us all about yourself, your household, and the effect which this advertisement had upon your fortunes. You will first make a note, Doctor, of the paper and the date."

"It is *The Morning Chronicle* of April 27, 1890. Just two months ago."

"Very good. Now, Mr. Wilson?"

"Well, it is just as I have been telling you, Mr. Sherlock Holmes," said Jabez Wilson, mopping his forehead; "I have a small pawnbroker's business at Coburg Square, near the City. It's not a very large affair, and of late years it has not done more than just give me a living. I used to be able to keep two assistants, but now I only keep one; and I would have a job to pay him but that he is willing to come for half wages so as to learn the business."

"What is the name of this obliging youth?" asked Sherlock Holmes.

"His name is Vincent Spaulding, and he's not such a youth, either. It's hard to say his age. I should not wish a smarter assistant, Mr. Holmes; and I know very well that he could better himself and earn twice what I am able to give him. But, after all, if he is satisfied, why should I put ideas in his head?"

"Why, indeed? You seem most fortunate in having an employee who comes under the full market price. It is not a common experience among employers in this age. I don't know that your assistant is not as remarkable as your advertisement."

"Oh, he has his faults, too," said Mr. Wilson. "Never was such a fellow for photography. Snapping away with a camera when he ought to be improving his mind, and then diving down into the cellar like a rabbit into its hole to develop his pictures. That is his main fault, but on the whole he's a good worker. There's no vice in him."

"He is still with you, I presume?"

Literary Analysis
Protagonist and Antagonist Which details in the description of Vincent Spaulding attract Holmes's notice?

"Yes, sir. He and a girl of fourteen, who does a bit of simple cooking and keeps the place clean—that's all I have in the house, for I am a widower and never had any family. We live very quietly, sir, the three of us; and we keep a roof over our heads and pay our debts, if we do nothing more.

"The first thing that put us out was that advertisement. Spaulding, he came down into the office just this day eight weeks, with this very paper in his hand, and he says:

"'I wish to the Lord, Mr. Wilson, that I was a red-headed man.'

"'Why that?' I asks.

"'Why,' says he, 'here's another vacancy on the League of the Red-headed Men. It's worth quite a little fortune to any man who gets it, and I understand that there are more vacancies than there are men, so that the trustees are at their wits' end what to do with the money. If my hair would only change color, here's a nice little crib all ready for me to step into.'

"'Why, what is it, then?' I asked. You see, Mr. Holmes, I am a very stay-at-home man, and as my business came to me instead of my having to go to it, I was often weeks on end without putting my foot over the doormat. In that way I didn't know much of what was going on outside, and I was always glad of a bit of news.

"'Have you never heard of the League of the Red-headed Men?' he asked with his eyes open.

"'Never.'

"'Why, I wonder at that, for you are eligible yourself for one of the vacancies.'

"'And what are they worth?' I asked.

"'Oh, merely a couple of hundred a year, but the work is slight, and it need not interfere very much with one's other occupations.'

"Well, you can easily think that that made me prick up my ears, for the business has not been over-good for some years, and an extra couple of hundred would have been very handy.

"'Tell me all about it,' said I.

"'Well,' said he, showing me the advertisement, 'you can see for

**Reading Skill
Contrasting Characters**
In what ways does Wilson's lack of awareness of the outside world present a contrast to Holmes and Watson?

☑ Reading Check
Who is eligible for the position in the advertisement?

The Red-headed League **1171**

yourself that the League has a vacancy, and there is the address where you should apply for particulars. As far as I can make out, the League was founded by an American millionaire, Ezekiah Hopkins, who was very peculiar in his ways. He was himself red-headed, and he had a great sympathy for all red-headed men; so when he died it was found that he had left his enormous fortune in the hands of trustees, with instructions to apply the interest to the providing of easy berths to men whose hair is of that color. From all I hear it is splendid pay and very little to do.

"'But,' said I, 'there would be millions of red-headed men who would apply.'

"'Not so many as you might think,' he answered. 'You see it is really confined to Londoners, and to grown men. This American had started from London when he was young, and he wanted to do the old town a good turn. Then, again, I have heard it is no use your applying if your hair is light red, or dark red, or anything but real bright, blazing, fiery red. Now, if you cared to apply, Mr. Wilson, you would just walk in; but perhaps it would hardly be worth your while to put yourself out of the way for the sake of a few hundred pounds.'

"Now, it is a fact, gentlemen, as you may see for yourselves, that my hair is of a very full and rich tint, so that it seemed to me that if there was to be any competition in the matter I stood as good a chance as any man that I had ever met. Vincent Spaulding seemed to know so much about it that I thought he might prove useful so I just ordered him to put up the shutters for the day and to come right away with me. He was very willing to have a holiday,[5] so we shut the business up and started off for the address that was given us in the advertisement.

"I never hope to see such a sight as that again, Mr. Holmes. From north, south, east, and west every man who had a shade of red in his hair had tramped into the city to answer the advertisement. Fleet Street was choked with red-headed folk, and Pope's Court looked like a coster's orange barrow.[6] I should not have thought there were so many in the whole country as were brought together by that single advertisement. Every shade of color they were—straw, lemon, orange, brick, Irish-setter, liver, clay; but, as Spaulding said, there were not many who had the real vivid flame-colored tint. When I saw how many were waiting, I would have given it up in despair; but Spaulding would not hear of it. How he did it I could not imagine, but he pushed and pulled and butted until he got me through the crowd, and right up to the steps which led to the office. There was a double stream upon the stair, some going up in hope, and some coming back dejected; but we wedged in as well as we could and soon found ourselves in the office."

5. **holiday** day off from work; vacation.
6. **coster's orange barrow** pushcart of a seller of oranges.

Reading Skill
Contrasting Characters
Who seems more invested in Wilson's joining the Red-headed League—Wilson or Spaulding? Explain.

Spiral Review
Connotation and Denotation Analyze the context in which *dejected* appears. Distinguish between the denotative and connotative meanings of the word.

"Your experience has been a most entertaining one," remarked Holmes as his client paused and refreshed his memory with a huge pinch of snuff. "Pray continue your very interesting statement."

"There was nothing in the office but a couple of wooden chairs and a deal table, behind which sat a small man with a head that was even redder than mine. He said a few words to each candidate as he came up, and then he always managed to find some fault in them which would disqualify them. Getting a vacancy did not seem to be such a very easy matter, after all. However, when our turn came the little man was much more favorable to me than to any of the others, and he closed the door as we entered, so that he might have a private word with us.

"'This is Mr. Jabez Wilson,' said my assistant, 'and he is willing to fill a vacancy in the League.'

"'And he is admirably suited for it,' the other answered. 'He has every requirement. I cannot recall when I have seen anything so fine.' He took a step backward, cocked his head on one side, and gazed at my hair until I felt quite bashful. Then suddenly he plunged forward, wrung my hand, and congratulated me warmly on my success.

"'It would be injustice to hesitate,' said he. 'You will, however, I am sure, excuse me for taking an obvious precaution.' With that he seized my hair in both his hands, and tugged until I yelled with the pain. 'There is water in your eyes,' said he as he released me. 'I perceive that all is as it should be. But we have to be careful, for we have twice been deceived by wigs and once by paint. I could tell you tales of cobbler's wax which would disgust you with human nature.' He stepped over to the window and shouted through it at the top of his voice that the vacancy was filled. A groan of disappointment came up from below, and the folk all trooped away in different directions until there was not a red head to be seen except my own and that of the manager.

"'My name,' said he, 'is Mr. Duncan Ross, and I am myself one of the pensioners upon the fund left by our noble benefactor. Are you a married man, Mr. Wilson? Have you a family?'

"I answered that I had not.

"His face fell immediately.

"'Dear me!' he said gravely, 'that is very serious indeed! I am sorry to hear you say that. The fund was, of course, for the propagation and spread of the red-heads as well as for their maintenance. It is exceedingly unfortunate that you should be a bachelor.'

"My face lengthened at this, Mr. Holmes, for I thought that I was not to have the vacancy after all; but after thinking it over for a few minutes he said that it would be all right.

Reading Skill
Contrasting Characters
In what way is the man's behavior toward Mr. Wilson different from his behavior toward the other candidates?

Reading Check
Who helps Wilson push through the crowd of men applying for the Red-headed League?

"'In the case of another,' said he, 'the objection might be fatal, but we must stretch a point in favor of a man with such a head of hair as yours. When shall you be able to enter upon your new duties?'

"'Well, it is a little awkward, for I have a business already,' said I.

"'Oh, never mind about that, Mr. Wilson!' said Vincent Spaulding. 'I should be able to look after that for you.'

"'What would be the hours?' I asked.

"'Ten to two.'

"Now a pawnbroker's business is mostly done of an evening, Mr. Holmes, especially Thursday and Friday evening, which is just before pay-day; so it would suit me very well to earn a little in the mornings. Besides, I knew that my assistant was a good man, and that he would see to anything that turned up.

"'That would suit me very well,' said I. 'And the pay?'

"'Is £4 a week.'

"And the work?'

"'Is purely nominal.'

"What do you call purely nominal?'

"'Well, you have to be in the office, or at least in the building, the whole time. If you leave, you forfeit your whole position forever. The will is very clear upon that point. You don't comply with the conditions if you budge from the office during that time.'

"'It's only four hours a day, and I should not think of leaving,' said I.

"'No excuse will avail,' said Mr. Duncan Ross; 'neither sickness nor business nor anything else. There you must stay, or you lose your billet.'[7]

"And the work?'

"'Is to copy out the Encyclopedia Britannica. There is the first volume of it in that press. You must find your own ink, pens, and blotting-paper, but we provide this table and chair. Will you be ready tomorrow?'

"'Certainly,' I answered.

"'Then, good-bye, Mr. Jabez Wilson, and let me congratulate you

Literary Analysis
Protagonist and Antagonist Which details in the description of Wilson's responsibilities make Ross seem like a suspicious character?

---

7. **billet** (bil' it) *n.* position; job.

once more on the important position which you have been fortunate enough to gain.' He bowed me out of the room, and I went home with my assistant, hardly knowing what to say or do, I was so pleased at my own good fortune.

"Well, I thought over the matter all day, and by evening I was in low spirits again; for I had quite persuaded myself that the whole affair must be some great hoax or fraud, though what its object might be I could not imagine. It seemed altogether past belief that anyone could make such a will, or that they would pay such a sum for doing anything so simple as copying out the Encyclopedia Britannica. Vincent Spaulding did what he could to cheer me up, but by bedtime I had reasoned myself out of the whole thing. However, in the morning I determined to have a look at it anyhow, so I bought a penny bottle of ink, and with a quill-pen, and seven sheets of foolscap paper, I started off for Pope's Court.

"Well, to my surprise and delight, everything was as right as possible. The table was set out ready for me, and Mr. Duncan Ross was there to see that I got fairly to work. He started me off upon the letter A, and then he left me; but he would drop in from time to time to see that all was right with me. At two o'clock he bade me good-day, complimented me upon the amount that I had written, and locked the door of the office after me.

"This went on day after day, Mr. Holmes, and on Saturday the manager came in and planked down four golden sovereigns for my week's work. It was the same next week, and the same the week after. Every morning I was there at ten, and every afternoon I left at two. By degrees Mr. Duncan Ross took to coming in only once of a morning, and then, after a time, he did not come in at all. Still, of course, I never dared to leave the room for an instant, for I was not sure when he might come, and the billet was such a good one, and suited me so well, that I would not risk the loss of it.

"Eight weeks passed away like this, and I had written about Abbots and Archery and Armor and Architecture and Attica, and hoped with diligence that I might get on to the B's before very long. It cost me something in foolscap, and I had pretty nearly filled a shelf with my writings. And then suddenly the whole business came to an end."

"To an end?"

"Yes, sir. And no later than this morning. I went to my work as

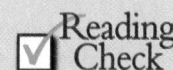

Reading Check

Who offers to look after Wilson's pawnbroker business while he is at his other job?

usual at ten o'clock, but the door was shut and locked, with a little square of cardboard hammered on to the middle of the panel with a tack. Here it is, and you can read for yourself."

He held up a piece of white cardboard about the size of a sheet of notepaper. It read in this fashion:

THE RED-HEADED LEAGUE IS DISSOLVED.
October 9, 1890.

Reading Skill
Contrasting Characters
How do the reactions of Watson and Holmes to the announcement compare with Mr. Wilson's? Explain.

Sherlock Holmes and I surveyed this curt announcement and the rueful face behind it, until the comical side of the affair so completely overtopped every other consideration that we both burst out into a roar of laughter.

"I cannot see that there is anything very funny," cried our client, flushing up to the roots of his flaming head. "If you can do nothing better than laugh at me, I can go elsewhere."

"No, no," cried Holmes, shoving him back into the chair from which he had half risen. "I really wouldn't miss your case for the world. It is most refreshingly unusual. But there is, if you will excuse my saying so, something just a little funny about it. Pray what steps did you take when you found the card upon the door?"

"I was staggered, sir. I did not know what to do. Then I called at the offices round, but none of them seemed to know anything about it. Finally, I went to the landlord, who is an accountant living on the ground floor, and I asked him if he could tell me what had become of the Red-headed League. He said that he had never heard of any such body. Then I asked him who Mr. Duncan Ross was. He answered that the name was new to him.

"'Well,' said I, 'the gentleman at No. 4.'

"'What, the red-headed man?'

"'Yes.'

Literary Analysis
Protagonist and Antagonist What does William Morris's dishonesty about his identity suggest about his character?

"'Oh,' said he, 'his name was William Morris. He was a solicitor[8] and was using my room as a temporary convenience until his new premises were ready. He moved out yesterday.'

"'Where could I find him?'

"'Oh, at his new offices. He did tell me the address. Yes, 17 King Edward Street, near St. Paul's.'

"I started off, Mr. Holmes, but when I got to that address it was a manufactory of artificial kneecaps, and no one in it had ever heard of either Mr. William Morris or Mr. Duncan Ross."

"And what did you do then?" asked Holmes.

"I went home to Saxe-Coburg Square, and I took the advice of my assistant. But he could not help me in any way. He could only say

---

8. solicitor (sə lis´ it ər) *n.* member of the legal profession.

that if I waited I should hear by post. But that was not quite good enough, Mr. Holmes. I did not wish to lose such a place without a struggle, so, as I had heard that you were good enough to give advice to poor folk who were in need of it, I came right away to you."

"And you did very wisely," said Holmes. "Your case is an exceedingly remarkable one, and I shall be happy to look into it. From what you have told me I think that it is possible that graver issues hang from it than might at first sight appear."

"Grave enough!" said Mr. Jabez Wilson. "Why, I have lost four pound a week."

"As far as you are personally concerned," remarked Holmes, "I do not see that you have any grievance against this extraordinary league. On the contrary, you are, as I understand, richer by some £30, to say nothing of the minute knowledge which you have gained on every subject which comes under the letter A. You have lost nothing by them."

"No, sir. But I want to find out about them, and who they are, and what their object was in playing this prank—if it was a prank—upon me. It was a pretty expensive joke for them, for it cost them two and thirty pounds."

"We shall endeavor to clear up these points for you. And, first, one or two questions, Mr. Wilson. This assistant of yours who first called your attention to the advertisement—how long had he been with you?"

"About a month then."

"How did he come?"

"In answer to an advertisement."

"Was he the only applicant?"

"No, I had a dozen."

"Why did you pick him?"

"Because he was handy and would come cheap."

"At half-wages, in fact."

"Yes."

"What is he like, this Vincent Spaulding?"

Literary Analysis
Protagonist and Antagonist What reason might Holmes have for being suspicious of Vincent Spaulding?

Reading Check

What reasons does Mr. Wilson give for hiring Vincent Spaulding?

"Small, stout-built, very quick in his ways. No hair on his face, though he's not short of thirty. Has a white splash of acid upon his forehead."

Holmes sat up in his chair in considerable excitement. "I thought as much," said he. "Have you ever observed that his ears are pierced for earrings?"

"Yes, sir. He told me that a gypsy had done it for him when he was a lad."

"Hum!" said Holmes, sinking back in deep thought. "He is still with you?"

"Oh, yes, sir; I have only just left him."

"And has your business been attended to in your absence?"

"Nothing to complain of, sir. There's never very much to do of a morning."

"That will do, Mr. Wilson. I shall be happy to give you an opinion upon the subject in the course of a day or two. Today is Saturday, and I hope that by Monday we may come to a conclusion."

"Well, Watson," said Holmes when our visitor had left us, "what do you make of it all?"

"I make nothing of it," I answered frankly. "It is a most mysterious business."

"As a rule," said Holmes, "the more bizarre a thing is the less mysterious it proves to be. It is your commonplace, featureless crimes which are really puzzling, just as a commonplace face is the most difficult to identify. But I must be prompt over this matter."

"What are you going to do, then?" I asked.

"To smoke," he answered. "It is quite a three pipe problem, and I beg that you won't speak to me for fifty minutes." He curled himself up in his chair, with his thin knees drawn up to his hawk-like nose, and there he sat with his eyes closed and his black clay pipe thrusting out like the bill of some strange bird. I had come to the conclusion that he had dropped asleep, and indeed was nodding myself, when he suddenly sprang out of his chair with the gesture of a man who has made up his mind and put his pipe down upon the mantelpiece.

"Sarasate[9] plays at the St. James's Hall this afternoon," he remarked. "What do you think, Watson? Could your patients spare you for a few hours?"

"I have nothing to do today. My practice is never very absorbing."

"Then put on your hat and come. I am going through the City first, and we can have some lunch on the way. I observe that there is a good deal of German music on the program, which is rather more to my taste than Italian or French. It is introspective, and I want to introspect. Come along!"

---

9. **Sarasate** (sä rä sä´ tä) Spanish violinist and composer.

Literary Analysis
Protagonist and Antagonist What does Holmes's expectation of reaching a conclusion in two days reveal about his character?

Vocabulary
introspective (in´ trə spek´ tiv) *adj.* having to do with looking into one's own thoughts and feelings

We traveled by the Underground as far as Aldersgate; and a short walk took us to Saxe-Coburg Square, the scene of the singular story which we had listened to in the morning. It was a poky, little, shabby-genteel place, where four lines of dingy two-storied brick houses looked out into a small railed-in enclosure, where a lawn of weedy grass and a few clumps of faded laurel bushes made a hard fight against a smoke-laden and uncongenial atmosphere. Three gilt balls and a brown board with "JABEZ WILSON" in white letters, upon a corner house, announced the place where our red-headed client carried on his business. Sherlock Holmes stopped in front of it with his head on one side and looked it all over, with his eyes shining brightly between puckered lids. Then he walked slowly up the street, and then down again to the corner, still looking keenly at the houses. Finally he returned to the pawnbroker's, and, having thumped vigorously upon the pavement with his stick two or three times, he went up to the door and knocked. It was instantly opened by a bright-looking, clean-shaven young fellow, who asked him to step in.

"Thank you," said Holmes, "I only wished to ask you how you would go from here to the Strand."

"Third right, fourth left," answered the assistant promptly, closing the door.

"Smart fellow, that," observed Holmes as we walked away. "He is, in my judgment, the fourth smartest man in London, and for daring I am not sure that he has not a claim to be third. I have known something of him before."

"Evidently," said I, "Mr. Wilson's assistant counts for a good deal in this mystery of the Red-headed League. I am sure that you inquired your way merely in order that you might see him."

"Not him."

"What then?"

"The knees of his trousers."

"And what did you see?"

"What I expected to see."

"Why did you beat the pavement?"

"My dear doctor, this is a time for observation, not for talk. We are spies in an enemy's country. We know something of Saxe-Coburg Square. Let us now explore the parts which lie behind it."

The road in which we found ourselves as we turned round the corner from the retired Saxe-Coburg Square presented as great a contrast to it as the front of a picture does to the back. It was one

Reading Skill
Comparing Characters
Based on Holmes's remark about Spaulding, what trait do the two men share? Explain.

Reading Check

Which aspect of Spaulding's appearance does Holmes want to observe?

of the main arteries which conveyed the traffic of the City to the north and west. The roadway was blocked with the immense stream of commerce flowing in a double tide inward and outward, while the footpaths were black with the hurrying swarm of pedestrians. It was difficult to realize as we looked at the line of fine shops and stately business premises that they really abutted on the other side upon the faded and stagnant square which we had just quitted.

"Let me see," said Holmes, standing at the corner and glancing along the line, "I should like just to remember the order of the houses here. It is a hobby of mine to have an exact knowledge of London. There is Mortimer's, the tobacconist, the little newspaper shop, the Coburg branch of the City and Suburban Bank, the Vegetarian Restaurant, and McFarlane's carriage-building depot. That carries us right on to the other block. And now, Doctor, we've done our work, so it's time we had some play. A sandwich and a cup of coffee, and then off to violin land, where all is sweetness and delicacy and harmony, and there are no red-headed clients to vex us with their conundrums."

My friend was an enthusiastic musician, being himself not only a very capable performer but a composer of no ordinary merit. All the afternoon he sat in the stalls wrapped in the most perfect happiness, gently waving his long, thin fingers in time to the music, while his gently smiling face and his languid, dreamy eyes were as unlike those of Holmes, the sleuthhound, Holmes the relentless, keen-witted, ready-handed criminal agent, as it was possible to conceive. In his singular character the dual nature alternately asserted itself, and his extreme exactness and astuteness represented, as I have often thought, the reaction against the poetic and contemplative mood which occasionally predominated in him. The swing of his nature took him from extreme languor to devouring energy; and, as I knew well, he was never so truly formidable as when, for days on end, he had been lounging in his armchair amid his improvisations and his black-letter editions. Then it was that the lust of the chase would suddenly come upon him, and that his brilliant reasoning power would rise to the level of intuition, until those who were unacquainted with his methods would look askance at him as on a man whose knowledge was not that of other mortals. When I saw him that afternoon so enwrapped in the music at St. James's Hall I felt that an evil time might be coming upon those whom he had set himself to hunt down.

"You want to go home, no doubt, Doctor," he remarked as we emerged.

Vocabulary

vex (veks) *v.* annoy

formidable (fôr´ mə də bəl) *adj.* awe-inspiring

"Yes, it would be as well."

"And I have some business to do which will take some hours. This business at Coburg Square is serious."

"Why serious?"

"A considerable crime is in contemplation. I have every reason to believe that we shall be in time to stop it. But today being Saturday rather complicates matters. I shall want your help tonight."

"At what time?"

"Ten will be early enough."

"I shall be at Baker Street at ten."

"Very well. And, I say, Doctor, there may be some little danger, so kindly put your army revolver in your pocket." He waved his hand, turned on his heel, and disappeared in an instant among the crowd.

I trust that I am not more dense than my neighbors, but I was always oppressed with a sense of my own stupidity in my dealings with Sherlock Holmes. Here I had heard what he had heard, I had seen what he had seen, and yet from his words it was evident that he saw clearly not only what had happened but what was about to happen, while to me the whole business was still confused and grotesque. As I drove home to my house in Kensington I thought over it all, from the extraordinary story of the red-headed copier of the Encyclopedia down to the visit to Saxe-Coburg Square, and the ominous words with which he had parted from me. What was this nocturnal expedition, and why should I go armed? Where were we going, and what were we to do? I had the hint from Holmes that this smooth-faced pawnbroker's assistant was a formidable man—a man who might play a deep game. I tried to puzzle it out, but gave it up in despair and set the matter aside until night should bring an explanation.

It was a quarter past nine when I started from home and made my way across the Park, and so through Oxford Street to Baker Street. Two hansoms were standing at the door, and as I entered the passage I heard the sound of voices from above. On entering his room I found Holmes in animated conversation with two men, one of whom I recognized as Peter Jones, the official police agent, while the other was a long, thin, sadfaced man, with a very shiny hat and oppressively respectable frock coat.

"Ha! our party is complete," said Holmes, buttoning up his

LITERATURE IN CONTEXT

Culture Connection

Hansoms

The hansom, also known as the hansom cab, is a two-wheeled covered carriage for two passengers that is pulled by one horse. The cab was named for its inventor, Joseph Hansom (1803–1882), a London architect. By the late 1850s, the hansom was popular in New York and Boston as well as in London. Customers could enjoy a scenic and romantic ride in private with an unobstructed view because the driver sat above and behind the passengers' cab. Today, updated hansom cabs are a popular tourist attraction in New York's Central Park. However, in this story, they are a common form of transportation.

Connect to the Literature

What problems would traveling by hansom pose for someone rushing to stop a crime?

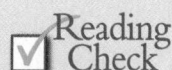

Reading Check

Where do the men plan to go in the evening?

peajacket and taking his heavy hunting crop from the rack. "Watson, I think you know Mr. Jones, of Scotland Yard? Let me introduce you to Mr. Merryweather, who is to be our companion in tonight's adventure."

"We're hunting in couples again, Doctor, you see," said Jones in his consequential way. "Our friend here is a wonderful man for starting a chase. All he wants is an old dog to help him to do the running down."

"I hope a wild goose may not prove to be the end of our chase," observed Mr. Merryweather gloomily.

"You may place considerable confidence in Mr. Holmes, sir," said the police agent loftily. "He has his own little methods, which are, if he won't mind my saying so, just a little too theoretical and fantastic, but he has the makings of a detective in him. It is not too much to say that once or twice, as in that business of the Sholto murder and the Agra treasure, he has been more nearly correct than the official force."

"Oh, if you say so, Mr. Jones, it is all right," said the stranger with deference. "Still, I confess that I miss my rubber.[10] It is the first Saturday night for seven-and-twenty years that I have not had my rubber."

"I think you will find," said Sherlock Holmes, "that you will play for a higher stake tonight than you have ever done yet, and that the play will be more exciting. For you, Mr. Merryweather, the stake will be some £30,000; and for you, Jones, it will be the man upon whom you wish to lay your hands."

Reading Skill
Comparing Characters
Despite their differences, in what ways are Sherlock Holmes and John Clay similar?

"John Clay, the murderer, thief, smasher, and forger. He's a young man, Mr. Merryweather, but he is at the head of his profession, and I would rather have my bracelets on him than on any criminal in London. He's a remarkable man, is young John Clay. His grandfather was a royal duke, and he himself has been to Eton[11] and Oxford.[12] His brain is as cunning as his fingers, and though we meet signs of him at every turn, we never know where to find the man himself. He'll crack a crib[13] in Scotland one week, and be raising money to build an orphanage in Cornwall the next. I've been on his track for years and have never set eyes on him yet."

"I hope that I may have the pleasure of introducing you tonight. I've had one or two little turns also with Mr. John Clay, and I agree with you that he is at the head of his profession. It is past ten, however, and quite time that we started. If you two will take the first hansom, Watson and I will follow in the second."

Sherlock Holmes was not very communicative during the long

---

10. rubber a term for a type of card game.
11. Eton famous British secondary school for boys.
12. Oxford oldest university in Great Britain.
13. crack a crib commit burglary.

drive and lay back in the cab humming the tunes which he had heard in the afternoon. We rattled through an endless labyrinth of gas-lit streets until we emerged into Farrington Street.

"We are close there now," my friend remarked. "This fellow Merryweather is a bank director, and personally interested in the matter. I thought it as well to have Jones with us also. He is not a bad fellow, though an absolute imbecile in his profession. He has one positive virtue. He is as brave as a bulldog and as tenacious as a lobster if he gets his claws upon anyone. Here we are, and they are waiting for us."

We had reached the same crowded thoroughfare in which we had found ourselves in the morning. Our cabs were dismissed, and, following the guidance of Mr. Merryweather, we passed down a narrow passage and through a side door, which he opened for us. Within there was a small corridor, which ended in a very massive iron gate. This also was opened, and led down a flight of winding stone steps, which terminated at another formidable gate. Mr. Merryweather stopped to light a lantern, and then conducted us down a dark, earth-smelling passage, and so, after opening a third door, into a huge vault or cellar, which was piled all round with crates and massive boxes.

"You are not very vulnerable from above," Holmes remarked as he held up the lantern and gazed about him.

"Nor from below," said Mr. Merryweather, striking his stick upon the flags which lined the floor. "Why, dear me, it sounds quite hollow!" he remarked, looking up in surprise.

"I must really ask you to be a little more quiet!" said Holmes severely. "You have already imperiled the whole success of our expedition. Might I beg that you would have the goodness to sit down upon one of those boxes, and not to interfere?"

The solemn Mr. Merryweather perched himself upon a crate, with a very injured expression upon his face, while Holmes fell upon his knees upon the floor and, with the lantern and a magnifying lens, began to examine minutely the cracks between the stones. A few seconds sufficed to satisfy him, for he sprang to his feet again and put his glass in his pocket.

"We have at least an hour before us," he remarked, "for they can hardly take any steps until the good pawnbroker is safely in bed. Then they will not lose a minute, for the sooner they do their work

Vocabulary
tenacious (tə nā´ shəs) *adj.* holding firmly to your point or beliefs; persistent; stubborn

Reading Check
Where does Mr. Merryweather lead Holmes and his companions?

Literary Analysis
Protagonist and
Antagonist What kind
of enemy does Holmes
anticipate he and his
companions will face?

the longer time they will have for their escape. We are at present, Doctor—as no doubt you have divined—in the cellar of the City branch of one of the principal London banks. Mr. Merryweather is the chairman of directors, and he will explain to you that there are reasons why the more daring criminals of London should take a considerable interest in this cellar at present."

"It is our French gold," whispered the director. "We have had several warnings that an attempt might be made upon it."

"Your French gold?"

"Yes. We had occasion some months ago to strengthen our resources and borrowed for that purpose 30,000 napoleons from the Bank of France. It has become known that we have never had occasion to unpack the money, and that it is still lying in our cellar. The crate upon which I sit contains 2,000 napoleons packed between layers of lead foil. Our reserve of bullion is much larger at present than is usually kept in a single branch office, and the directors have had misgivings upon the subject."

"Which were very well justified," observed Holmes.

"And now it is time that we arranged our little plans. I expect that within an hour matters will come to a head. In the meantime, Mr. Merryweather, we must put the screen over that dark lantern."

"And sit in the dark?"

"I am afraid so. I had brought a pack of cards in my pocket, and I thought that, as we were a *partie carrée*,[14] you might have your rubber after all. But I see that the enemy's preparations have gone so far that we cannot risk the presence of a light. And, first of all, we must choose our positions. These are daring men, and though we shall take them at a disadvantage, they may do us some harm unless we are careful. I shall stand behind this crate, and do you conceal yourselves behind those. Then, when I flash a light upon them, close in swiftly. If they fire, Watson, have no compunction about shooting them down."

I placed my revolver, cocked, upon the top of the wooden case behind which I crouched. Holmes shot the slide across the front of his lantern and left us in pitch darkness—such an absolute darkness as I have never before experienced. The smell of hot metal remained to assure us that the light was still there, ready to flash out at a moment's notice. To me, with my nerves worked up to a pitch of expectancy, there was something depressing and subduing in the sudden gloom, and in the cold dank air of the vault.

"They have but one retreat," whispered Holmes. "That is back through the house into Saxe-Coburg Square. I hope that you have done what I asked you, Jones?"

"I have an inspector and two officers waiting at the front door."

---

14. partie carrée (pär tē´ cä rā´) French for "group of four."

"Then we have stopped all the holes. And now we must be silent and wait."

What a time it seemed! From comparing notes afterwards it was but an hour and a quarter, yet it appeared to me that the night must have almost gone, and the dawn be breaking above us. My limbs were weary and stiff, for I feared to change my position; yet my nerves were worked up to the highest pitch of tension, and my hearing was so acute that I could not only hear the gentle breathing of my companions, but I could distinguish the deeper, heavier in-breath of the bulky Jones from the thin, sighing note of the bank director. From my position I could look over the case in the direction of the floor. Suddenly my eyes caught the glint of a light.

At first it was but a lurid spark upon the stone pavement. Then it lengthened out until it became a yellow line, and then, without any warning or sound, a gash seemed to open and a hand appeared; a white, almost womanly hand, which felt about in the center of the little area of light. For a minute or more the hand, with its writhing fingers, protruded out of the floor. Then it was withdrawn as suddenly as it appeared, and all was dark again save the single lurid spark which marked a chink between the stones.

Its disappearance, however, was but momentary. With a rending, tearing sound, one of the broad, white stones turned over upon its side and left a square, gaping hole, through which streamed the light of a lantern. Over the edge there peeped a clean-cut, boyish face, which looked keenly about it, and then, with a hand on either side of the aperture, drew itself shoulder-high and waist-high, until one knee rested upon the edge. In another instant he stood at the side of the hole and was hauling after him a companion, lithe and small like himself, with a pale face and a shock of very red hair.

"It's all clear," he whispered. "Have you the chisel and the bags? Great Scott! Jump, Archie, jump, and I'll swing for it."

Sherlock Holmes had sprung out and seized the intruder by the collar. The other dived down the hole, and I heard the sound of rending cloth as Jones clutched at his skirts. The light flashed upon the barrel of a revolver, but Holmes's hunting crop came down on the man's wrist, and the pistol clinked upon the stone floor.

"It's no use, John Clay," said Holmes blandly. "You have no chance at all."

"So I see," the other answered with the utmost coolness. "I fancy that my pal is all right, though I see you have got his coattails."

"There are three men waiting for him at the door," said Holmes.

"Oh, indeed! You seem to have done the thing very completely. I must compliment you."

"And I you," Holmes answered. "Your red-headed idea was very

Literary Analysis
Protagonist and Antagonist What details of Watson's account help build the suspense of the conflict?

Reading Skill
Comparing Characters In what ways is the first burglar's appearance similar to that of Vincent Spaulding?

Reading Check
What color is Clay's accomplice's hair?

new and effective."

"You'll see your pal again presently," said Jones. "He's quicker at climbing down holes than I am. Just hold out while I fix the derbies."[15]

"I beg that you will not touch me with your filthy hands," remarked our prisoner as the handcuffs clattered upon his wrists. "You may not be aware that I have royal blood in my veins. Have the goodness, also, when you address me always to say 'sir' and 'please.'"

"All right," said Jones with a stare and a snigger. "Well, would you please, sir, march upstairs, where we can get a cab to carry your Highness to the police station?"

"That is better," said John Clay serenely. He made a sweeping bow to the three of us and walked quietly off in the custody of the detective.

"Really, Mr. Holmes," said Mr. Merryweather as we followed them from the cellar, "I do not know how the bank can thank you or repay you. There is no doubt that you have detected and defeated in the most complete manner one of the most determined attempts at bank robbery that have ever come within my experience."

"I have had one or two little scores of my own to settle with Mr. John Clay," said Holmes. "I have been at some small expense over this matter, which I shall expect the bank to refund, but beyond that I am amply repaid by having had an experience which is in many ways unique, and by hearing the very remarkable narrative of the Red-headed League."

"You see, Watson," he explained in the early hours of the morning as we sat over a glass of whisky and soda in Baker Street, "it was perfectly obvious from the first that the only possible object of this rather fantastic business of the advertisement of the League, and the copying of the Encyclopedia, must be to get this not over-bright pawnbroker out of the way for a number of hours every day. It was a curious way of managing it, but, really, it would be difficult to

Reading Skill
Contrasting Characters
What difference between Holmes and Clay is revealed by Holmes's refusal to accept a reward?

15. **derbies** handcuffs.

suggest a better. The method was no doubt suggested to Clay's ingenious mind by the color of his accomplice's hair. The £4 a week was a lure which must draw him, and what was it to them, who were playing for thousands? They put in the advertisement, one rogue has the temporary office, the other rogue incites the man to apply for it, and together they manage to secure his absence every morning in the week. From the time that I heard of the assistant having come for half wages, it was obvious to me that he had some strong motive for securing the situation."

"But how could you guess what the motive was?"

"Had there been women in the house, I should have suspected a mere vulgar intrigue. That, however, was out of the question. The man's business was a small one, and there was nothing in his house which could account for such elaborate preparations, and such an expenditure as they were at. It must, then, be something out of the house. What could it be? I thought of the assistant's fondness for photography, and his trick of vanishing into the cellar. The cellar! There was the end of this tangled clue. Then I made inquiries as to this mysterious assistant and found that I had to deal with one of the coolest and most daring criminals in London. He was doing something in the cellar—something which took many hours a day for months on end. What could it be, once more? I could think of nothing save that he was running a tunnel to some other building.

Literary Analysis
Protagonist and Antagonist What was Clay's (Spaulding's) motivation in arranging for Wilson to be out of the house?

"So far I had got when we went to visit the scene of action. I surprised you by beating upon the pavement with my stick. I was ascertaining whether the cellar stretched out in front or behind. It was not in front. Then I rang the bell, and, as I hoped, the assistant answered it. We have had some skirmishes, but we had never set eyes upon each other before. I hardly looked at his face. His knees were what I wished to see. You must yourself have remarked how worn, wrinkled, and stained they were. They spoke of those hours of burrowing. The only remaining point was what they were burrowing for. I walked round the corner, saw that the City and Suburban Bank abutted on our friend's premises, and felt that I had solved my problem. When you drove home after the concert I called upon Scotland Yard and upon the chairman of the bank directors, with the result that you have seen."

"And how could you tell that they would make their attempt tonight?" I asked.

"Well, when they closed their League offices that was a sign that they cared no longer about Mr. Jabez Wilson's presence—in other words, that they had completed their tunnel. But it was essential

Reading Check

What was the motive behind the Red-headed League?

that they should use it soon, as it might be discovered, or the bullion might be removed. Saturday would suit them better than any other day, as it would give them two days for their escape. For all these reasons I expected them to come tonight."

"You reasoned it out beautifully," I exclaimed in unfeigned admiration. "It is so long a chain, and yet every link rings true."

"It saved me from ennui,"[16] he answered, yawning. "Alas! I already feel it closing in upon me. My life is spent in one long effort to escape from the commonplaces of existence. These little problems help me to do so."

"And you are a benefactor of the race," said I.

He shrugged his shoulders. "Well, perhaps, after all, it is of some little use," he remarked. "'*L'homme c'est rien—l'oeuvre c'est tout*,'[17] as Gustave Flaubert wrote to George Sand."[18]

Literary Analysis
Protagonist and Antagonist What does Holmes claim is his reason for solving crimes?

---

16. **ennui** (än´ wē´) *n.* boredom.
17. *L'homme c'est rien—l'oeuvre c'est tout* (lum sä rē en´ lʉvr sä tōō) French for "Man is nothing—the work is everything."
18. **Gustave Flaubert** (gōōs täv´ flō ber´) . . . **George Sand** notable French novelists of the nineteenth century.

Critical Thinking

1. **(a) Respond:** What did you think of Holmes's solution to the mystery? **(b)** Did you find it a satisfying ending? Explain.

2. **(a)** Why does Jabez Wilson visit Sherlock Holmes? **(b) Make Inferences:** Why does Holmes find Wilson's story interesting?

3. **(a)** What happens the night of the attempted burglary? **(b) Analyze Cause and Effect:** Which clues found at Saxe-Coburg Square lead to Holmes's solution of the mystery? **(c) Speculate:** What details could have been misinterpreted, leading to an incorrect conclusion? Explain your response.

4. **(a)** What remark does Holmes make about commonplace crimes? **(b) Make Inferences:** What does Holmes mean? **(c) Interpret:** What does his remark suggest about the qualities that make a great detective?

 **Do heroes have responsibilities?**
Would you call Holmes a hero? Why or why not?

Support your responses with evidence from the text.

| **The Red-headed League**

Literary Analysis:
Protagonist and Antagonist

1. (a) Identify the **protagonist** in the narrative. **(b)** What is the protagonist's goal? **(c)** Why are readers interested in whether the protagonist achieves his goal?

2. (a) Identify the **antagonist. (b)** What is the antagonist's goal?

3. (a) In what ways are the story's characters complex? **(b)** Do you find the characters believable? Explain.

Reading Skill:
Comparing and Contrasting Characters

4. (a) Use a Venn diagram to compare and contrast Holmes's character at the beginning and end of the story. **(b)** Explain whether Holmes changes during the story.

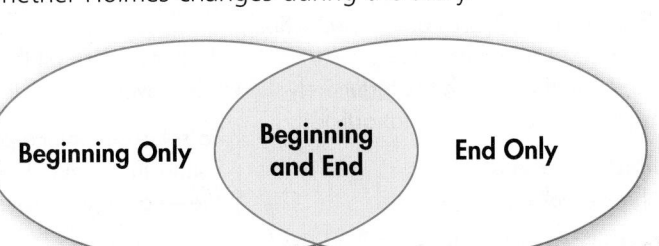

Beginning Only   Beginning and End   End Only

Vocabulary

Practice Analogies show the relationship between pairs of words. Use a word from the list on page 1164 to complete each analogy.

1. kind : gentle :: _____ : fearsome

2. burn : candle :: _____ : problem

3. descending : downward :: _____ : inward

4. lose : misplace :: _____ : exaggerate

5. brutal : kind :: _____ : indecisive

6. inquire : ask :: _____ : attempt

Word Power Use the context of the sentences and what you know about the **Latin root -spect-** to explain your answer to each question.

1. Might a *prospector* hope to find gold or silver?

2. If you take a new *perspective,* might you have new ideas?

Word Power

The **Latin root -spect-** means "see," "look," or "examine."

Apply It Explain how the root *-spect-* helps you determine the meanings of these technical academic words from science. Consult a dictionary if necessary.

spectacle
inspect
spectrometer

Integrated Language Skills

Three Skeleton Key •
The Red-headed League

Conventions: Commas and Dashes

Use **commas** when you need to indicate a short pause in your writing.

Use a **dash** to indicate an abrupt change of thought, a dramatic interruption, or a summary statement.

Use Commas to Separate...	Use Commas to Set Off...	Use Dashes to Indicate...
Two independent clauses joined by a coordinating conjunction to form a compound sentence I turned the ignition key, but the car did not start.	**An introductory word, phrase, or clause** Coincidentally, we all ended up at the same beach.	**Parenthetical information or an abrupt change of thought** The loss of the necklace—it had been in our family for years—was a shock.
Three or more words, phrases, or clauses in a series He spoke with passion, with gravity, and with sorrow.	**Nonrestrictive phrases and parenthetical or nonessential expressions** The magazine, which I unfortunately misplaced, had some great articles.	That man stole all that money—I don't even want to think about it.
Parts of dates, places, or certain titles We went to Sonoma, California, for the weekend.	**Direct quotations** Johanna yelled, "Stop!" **Contrasting expressions** I went to California, not Arizona, to visit my aunt.	**To set off an interrupting idea** John—his mom calls him Sweetie Pie—has a great sense of humor. **To set off a summary statement** Lemon, lime, or orange—deciding which flavor to pick was difficult.

Practice A Write each sentence, and add commas where they are necessary. Indicate which rule(s) you you are following.

1. The men called out "Rats!"
2. Incredibly the ship was covered with rats.
3. The rats which were on the ship leaped to the island.
4. The rats climbed squealed and chewed.
5. The men were most fearful of the rats not the sharks.

Reading Application In "Three Skeleton Key," find three sentences with commas that follow three different rules.

Practice B Write each sentence, and add dashes where they are necessary. Indicate which rule(s) you are following.

1. The crowd a large, rowdy group was full of red-headed men.
2. Blonde or red-headed which is preferable?
3. Holmes solved the case quickly the others were astonished.

Writing Application Write three sentences about stories of suspense that demonstrate the rules of using commas and dashes to punctuate nonrestrictive phrases, contrasting expressions, and parenthetical information.

PH GRAMMAR HANDBOOK Further instruction and practice are available in the *Prentice Hall Grammar Handbook*.

Writing

Imagine that you are one of the characters in the story you read. Choose a character other than the narrator in "Three Skeleton Key" or write as Dr. Watson in "The Red-headed League." Write three **journal entries** describing the events in the story as they unfold.

- Review the story and create a timeline for the major events.
- Decide which days you will record in your journal.
- As the character, write your thoughts about what happens each day.

As you write, stay in character, making sure that your journal reflects any changes that the character experiences in the story.

Grammar Application Make sure you have used commas and dashes correctly in your entries, especially in nonrestrictive phrases, contrasting expressions, and when emphasizing parenthetical information.

Writing Workshop: *Work in Progress*

Prewriting for Comparison-and-Contrast Essay For a comparison-and-contrast essay you may write, choose two places that you know well. For each, note the purpose, sound, and look of the place. Save this Comparison List in your writing portfolio.

Research and Technology

Prepare an **oral report** about a topic from the story you read.

- If you read "Three Skeleton Key," conduct research about ships' rats and how these rats differ from other rats.
- If you read "The Red-headed League," research the science of detective work. Investigate fingerprints, lie detectors, and police sketches.

During your research, refer to multiple sources, such as the Internet, encyclopedias, and other reference books. Compare what you learn to details presented about your topic in the story. Follow these steps to complete the assignment.

- Before you begin, **formulate a major research question** to address your major research topic. The question will direct you as you gather information.
- **Organize the information** into graphics and illustrations to help you explain concepts where appropriate.

Present your report to your class and invite questions and reviews from your teacher and peers. Use this feedback as an **evaluative tool** to examine the quality of your research. Consider revising your work if necessary.

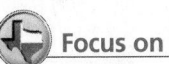 **Focus on the TEKS**

Conventions
(18)(B)(ii);(iii) Use correct punctuation marks including: comma placement in nonrestrictive phrases and contrasting expressions; and dashes to emphasize parenthetical information.

Research
(20)(A) Formulate a major research question to address the major research topic.
(21)(B) Organize information gathered from multiple sources to create a variety of graphics.
(23)(C);(D) Synthesize research into an oral presentation that uses graphics and illustrations to help explain concepts where appropriate; and uses a variety of evaluative tools to examine the quality of research.

Use this prewriting activity to prepare for the **Writing Workshop** on page 1244.

PHLitOnline
www.PHLitOnline.com

- Interactive graphic organizers
- Grammar tutorial
- Interactive journals

Selection Choices

▲ Read **"There Is a Longing"**
to learn about the dreams
and goals a Native American
leader had for his people.

▲ Read **"Glory and Hope"**
to see how the leader of
a reborn African nation
celebrated liberty and
promised to rebuild the
bridges between people.

 TEXAS Focus on the TEKS

Meet these standards with either **"There Is a Longing"** (p. 1196) or
"Glory and Hope" (p. 1202).

Reading
**(6) Understand the features of literary
nonfiction.** (Literary Analysis: Philosophical
Assumptions)

**(12)(D) Evaluate changes in formality and tone
within the same medium for specific audiences
and purposes.** (Listening and Speaking: Media
Analysis)

Reading/Comprehension Skills
**RC-9(A) Reflect on understanding to monitor
comprehension.** (Reading Skill: Comparing and
Contrasting)

Writing
**(15)(B) Write work-related documents (e.g.,
correspondence).** (Writing: Letter)
Research
**(23)(C) Use graphics to help explain concepts
where appropriate.** (Listening and Speaking:
Media Analysis)

Literary Analysis: Philosophical Assumptions

An **author's purpose,** or goal, is shaped by his or her **philosophical assumptions,** or basic beliefs. Philosophical assumptions are a key feature of literary nonfiction. They may be political ideologies, moral or ethical beliefs, or ideas about human nature. In some cases, the author may use these basic beliefs to support his or her argument. The response of the **audience,** or readers, depends on whether the audience shares the author's basic beliefs.

To read critically, identify the basic beliefs and assumptions in the work. Decide whether you accept them and whether the audience would be likely to accept them. Then, evaluate whether these assumptions help the author achieve his or her purpose.

Using the Strategy: Assumptions Chart

As You Read Use a chart like the one shown to record and evaluate the philosophical assumptions in the text.

Philosophical Assumptions	Evaluation
The basic beliefs included in the author's work	How basic beliefs do or do not support the author's purpose

Reading Skill: Comparing and Contrasting

When you **compare and contrast,** you recognize similarities and differences. In persuasive writing, authors often use a comparison-and-contrast organization to help readers see the similarities and differences between one point of view and another. These self-monitoring techniques will help you identify an author's use of comparison-and-contrast organization.

- Identify and list the things or ideas being compared.
- Restate the similarities and differences in your own words.
- Explain the significance of the similarities and differences.

If you cannot identify, restate, or explain the author's points, reread to clarify and to find words or phrases that were unclear.

As You Read Pause periodically to **reflect on your understanding.** Use the strategies listed here to **monitor your comprehension** of the comparisons the author makes.

TEXAS
PHLitOnline
www.PHLitOnline.com

Hear It!
- Selection summary audio
- Selection audio

See It!
- Get Connected video
- Background video
- More about the author
- Vocabulary flashcards

Do It!
- Interactive journals
- Interactive graphic organizers
- Self-test
- Internet activity
- Grammar tutorial
- Interactive vocabulary games

Do *heroes* have responsibilities?

THERE IS
A LONGING

Chief Dan George

Writing About the Big Question

In his speech, Chief Dan George says his power to make war is gone, but he longs to serve his people. Use these sentence starters to develop your ideas about the Big Question.

Not all **heroes** know they are heroes because _____.

A leader can be a true **hero** when he or she _____.

(As You Read) Look for ways in which Chief Dan George accepts the responsibilities of leadership. Consider whether he is a hero.

Vocabulary

Read each word and its definition. Decide whether you know the word well, know it a little bit, or do not know it at all. After you read, see how your knowledge of each word has increased.

- **longing** (lôn´ iŋ) *n.* a yearning, especially for something unattainable (p. 1197) *The passing dessert cart left the child longing for a piece of cake during the whole dinner.* long *v.* longingly *adv.*

- **determination** (dē tʉr´ mi nā´ shən) *n.* firm intention (p. 1197) *The runner's determination enabled him to win the race.* determined *adj.*

- **endurance** (en dʊr´ əns) *n.* ability to withstand hardship over time (p. 1197) *Surviving the hurricane required courage and endurance.* endure *v.* enduring *adj.*

- **emerge** (ē mʉrj´) *v.* come into existence; become visible or known (p. 1197) *Joe's parents hoped that after college he would emerge as a strong candidate for the business world.* emerging *adj.* emergent *adj.*

- **humbly** (hum´ blē) *adv.* in a manner that is not proud or arrogant; modestly (p. 1198) *Shannon accepted her award humbly, thanking everyone who helped her achieve it.* humble *adj.* humbled *v.*

- **segment** (seg´ mənt) *n.* a division or section (p. 1198) *Claire approached each segment of the test cautiously because the directions seemed to change with every one.* segmented *adj.*

Word Power

The **Latin root -merg-** means "dip" or "plunge."

In this selection, Chief Dan George says the young of his nation will **emerge** from years of study, as if rising up from the waters. They will take their place in society.

Meet
Chief Dan George
(1899–1981)

Author of
THERE IS
A LONGING

Chief Dan George had many careers, including actor and writer. Chief of a Salish Band of Native Americans in British Columbia, Canada, he was deeply concerned about improving the relationships between Native Americans and other North Americans.

Celebrity Activist Chief Dan George used the prominence he gained from his film and television roles to raise public awareness about the plight of Canada's native peoples. By the 1960s, he had become an unofficial spokesman for Native Americans and the environment. Throughout all of his endeavors against injustice, he always advocated peace over violence.

BACKGROUND FOR THE SPEECH

History Connection
The Struggle of Native Americans

When Europeans settled in the Americas, they encountered tribal peoples who had lived on the land for thousands of years. The Europeans' initial fear and prejudice led to violence, and many native tribes were destroyed. Nevertheless, Native American culture survived. Today, Native Americans continue to discover ways to succeed in the twenty-first century while maintaining their own cultural identity.

DID YOU KNOW?
Chief Dan George was nominated for an Academy Award as Best Supporting Actor for his role in the movie *Little Big Man*.

THERE IS
A LONGING

Chief Dan George

We the People, Kathy Morrow, Original scratchboard painting with hand-loomed beadwork. Courtesy of the artist.

▲ **Critical Viewing**
How does this painting reflect ideas found in the speech? **[Analyze]**

There is a longing in the heart of my people
to reach out and grasp that which is needed
for our survival. There is a longing among
the young of my nation to secure for themselves

5   and their people the skills that will
provide them with a sense of worth and
purpose. They will be our new warriors.
Their training will be much longer and
more demanding than it was in olden days.

10 The long years of study will demand more
determination; separation from home and
family will demand endurance. But they
will emerge with their hand held forward,
not to receive welfare, but to grasp the

15 place in society that is rightly ours.
I am a chief, but my power to make war
is gone, and the only weapon left to me
is speech. It is only with tongue and speech
that I can fight my people's war.

Vocabulary
longing (lôŋ´ iŋ) *n.* a yearning, especially for something unattainable

determination
(dē tʉr´ mi nā´ shən)
n. firm intention

endurance (en dʊr´ əns)
n. ability to withstand hardship over time

emerge (ē mʉrj´) *v.*
come into existence; become visible or known

Literary Analysis
Philosophical Assumptions What belief about the keys to success in the "new culture" does this passage reflect? Do you agree with the author?

Vocabulary
humbly (hum′ blē) *adv.* in a manner that is not proud or arrogant; modestly

segment (seg′ mənt) *n.* a division or section

20 Oh, Great Spirit![1] Give me back the courage
of the olden Chiefs. Let me wrestle with
my surroundings. Let me once again,
live in harmony with my environment.
Let me humbly accept this new culture
25 and through it rise up and go on. Like
the thunderbird[2] of old, I shall rise again
out of the sea; I shall grab the instruments
of the white man's success—his
education, his skills. With these new tools
30 I shall build my race into the proudest
segment of your society. I shall see our
young braves and our chiefs sitting in
the houses of law and government, ruling
and being ruled by the knowledge and
35 freedoms of our great land.

---

1. **Great Spirit** for many Native Americans, the greatest power or god.
2. **thunderbird** powerful supernatural creature that was thought to produce thunder by flapping its wings and to produce lightning by opening and closing its eyes. In the folklore of some Native American nations, the thunderbird is in constant warfare with the powers beneath the waters.

Critical Thinking

1. **(a) Respond:** Which statements in "There Is a Longing" affected you the most? Explain. **(b) Discuss:** Share your response with a partner. Explain how hearing someone else's response did or did not change your own.

2. **(a)** What does Chief Dan George say is his community's longing? **(b) Make Inferences:** What is his greatest fear?

3. **(a)** What training will the new warriors have to endure? **(b) Analyze:** Why does Chief Dan George believe that this training is necessary? **(c) Assess:** Do you agree? Why or why not?

4. **(a) Make Inferences:** In what way is Chief Dan George different from the "olden" chiefs? **(b) Interpret:** What does the chief mean when he refers to fighting "with tongue and speech"?

5. **Assess:** Do you think the chief's goal of achieving success through education and skills is the best means for improving his people's lives? Explain your response.

Support your responses with evidence from the text.

Do heroes have responsibilities?
Chief Dan George talks about fighting his people's war with "tongue and speech." Can someone who fights only with such weapons be a hero? Explain.

Literary Analysis: Philosophical Assumptions

1. **(a)** What is Chief Dan George's **purpose** in writing? **(b)** What are the **philosophical assumptions,** or basic beliefs, that help shape his purpose? **(c)** What argument could someone who disagreed with Chief Dan George use?

2. **(a)** For what **audience** did Chief Dan George originally write? **(b)** What details in the text indicate his intended audience? **(c)** Do you think his intended audience shared his basic beliefs?

3. Using Chief Dan George's speech as an example, explain how the audience for a speech can change over time.

THERE IS A LONGING

Chief Dan George

Reading Skill: Comparing and Contrasting

4. **(a)** Use a chart like the one shown to record the ideas Chief Dan George presents about the past, present, and future.

Past	Present	Future

(b) Explain the point Chief Dan George makes by **comparing and contrasting** the past, present, and future.

Vocabulary

Practice Indicate whether each statement is *True* or *False*. Explain your answers. Then, revise any sentences that are false to make them true.

1. Difficult tasks require *determination* to be completed.
2. Rock climbing requires less *endurance* than television watching.
3. When a winner responds *humbly* to a victory, he or she claims to be the world's greatest champion.
4. No one really wants to *emerge* from a time of pain or unpleasantness.
5. Only fortunate people have a *longing* to improve their lives.
6. Students are one *segment* of our society.

Word Power Use the context of the sentences and what you know about the **Latin root -merg-** to explain your answer to each question.

1. In an *emergency,* is someone in serious, unexpected trouble?
2. Is a *submersible* a ship built to float on the surface of the water?

Word Power

The **Latin root -merg-** means "dip" or "plunge."

Apply It Explain how the root -merg- helps you determine the meanings of these words. Consult a dictionary if necessary.
immerge
submerge
merger

Glory and Hope

Nelson Mandela

Do *heroes* have responsibilities?

Writing About the Big Question

In his speech, Nelson Mandela celebrates the liberty newly gained by his country and pleads for national reconciliation and liberty. Use these sentence starters to develop your ideas about the Big Question.

When a leader promises to **serve** his or her nation, he or she has an **obligation** to follow through because _____. The leader may become a **heroic** figure to many because _____.

As You Read Look for the values that Mandela celebrates and the goals that he has set. Consider whether you believe he is a hero.

Vocabulary

Read each word and its definition. Decide whether you know the word well, know it a little bit, or do not know it at all. After you read, see how your knowledge of each word has increased.

- **distinguished** (di stiŋ´ gwisht) *adj.* having an air of distinction; celebrated for excellence; renowned (p. 1202) *The distinguished gentleman stood and bowed to the crowd that acknowledged him. distinguish v. distinct adj.*

- **confer** (kən fʉr´) *v.* give (p. 1202) *The school will confer an honorary degree on the singer. conferable adj.*

- **intimately** (in´ tə mət lē) *adv.* in a close manner; familiarly (p. 1202). *Because they had worked together for years, Sandy and her colleagues knew each other intimately. intimate adj. intimacy n.*

- **pernicious** (pər nish´ əs) *adj.* destructive (p. 1203) *A pernicious insect destroyed the tree. perniciously adv. perniciousness n.*

- **covenant** (kuv´ ə nənt) *n.* agreement or contract, especially a sacred one (p. 1203) *They made a covenant to be friends forever.*

- **reconciliation** (rek´ ən sil´ ē ā´ shən) *n.* the settling of a conflict or argument; agreement; compromise (p. 1204) *Maryanne hoped she would come to some sort of reconciliation with her daughter after their terrible fight. reconcile v. reconcilable adj.*

Word Power

The **Latin root -fer-** means "carry" or "produce."

In this selection, Mandela says that by celebrating the change in South Africa, hope and glory will be **conferred** on, or carried onto, South Africa's new liberty.

Meet
Nelson Mandela
(b. 1918)

Author of
Glory and
Hope

Nelson Rolihlahla Mandela was born in South Africa, a nation whose white government maintained a strict policy of apartheid, or legal discrimination against blacks. In 1944, Mandela began protesting apartheid. Twenty years later, after several arrests, he was sentenced to life in prison for acts of protest.

Freedom for a Man and a Nation In 1990, after long years of imprisonment, Mandela was released. He continued to fight for equal rights for all South Africans. In 1991, apartheid was finally abolished and, in 1993, Mandela and South African president F. W. de Klerk shared the Nobel Prize for Peace. The next year, Mandela became the first black man to be elected president of South Africa. He retired from public life in 1999, and he currently lives in his birthplace, Qunu, Transkei.

Did You Know?
Robben Island, Mandela's prison for so many years, has now been turned into a learning center.

BACKGROUND FOR THE SPEECH

(History Connection)

Apartheid

In Afrikaans, one of the languages of South Africa, *apartheid* means "apartness." Apartheid is the policy of segregation and discrimination that was once practiced against nonwhites by the South African government. When apartheid became law in 1948, it affected housing, education, and transportation. In order to help end apartheid, many nations reduced trade with South Africa. Apartheid was finally abolished in 1991.

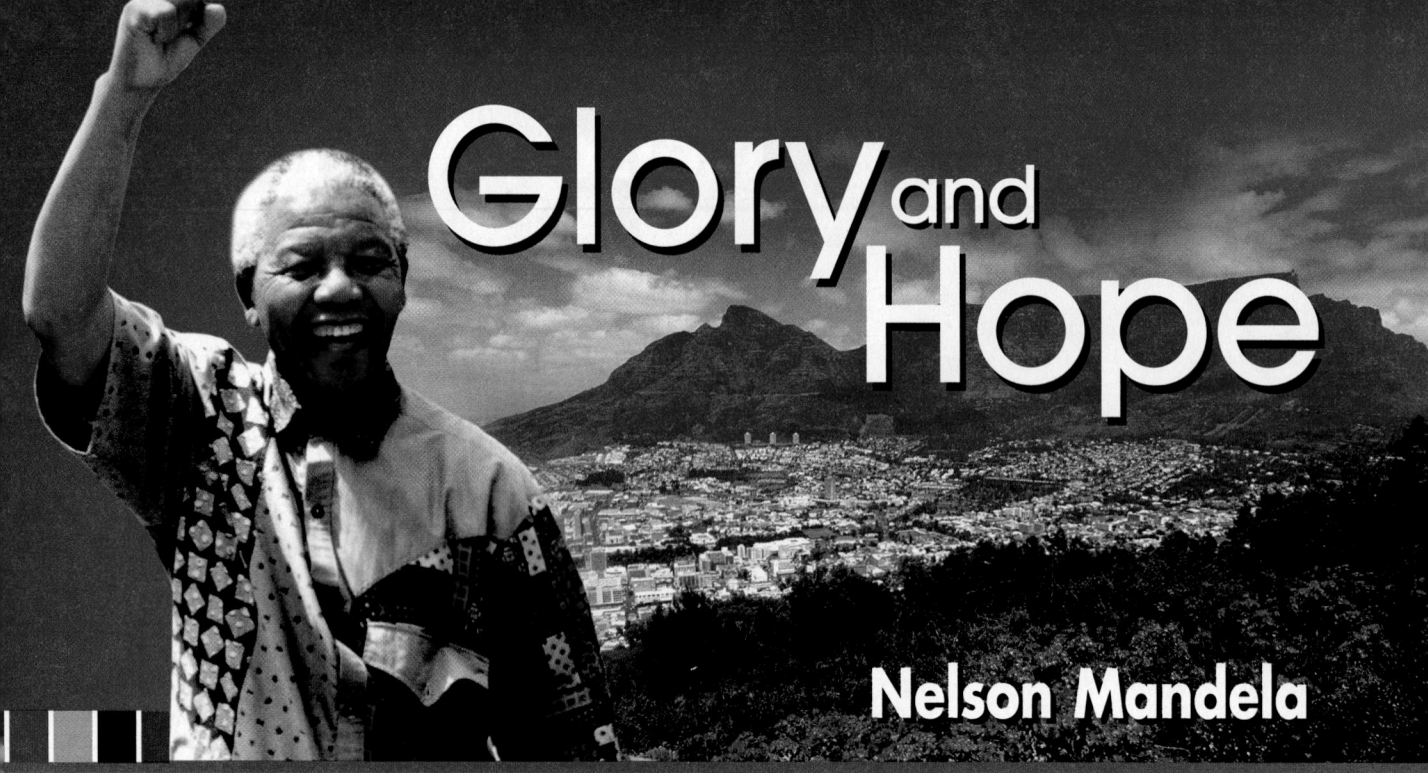

Glory and Hope

Nelson Mandela

Vocabulary

distinguished
(di stiŋ´ gwisht´) *adj.*
having an air of
distinction; celebrated
for excellence; renowned

confer (kən fur´) *v.* give

intimately
(in´ tə mət lē´) *adv.* in a
close manner; familiarly

Your majesties, your royal highnesses, distinguished guests, comrades and friends: Today, all of us do, by our presence here, and by our celebrations in other parts of our country and the world, confer glory and hope to newborn liberty.

Out of the experience of an extraordinary human disaster that lasted too long must be born a society of which all humanity will be proud.

Our daily deeds as ordinary South Africans must produce an actual South African reality that will reinforce humanity's belief in justice, strengthen its confidence in the nobility of the human soul and sustain all our hopes for a glorious life for all.

All this we owe both to ourselves and to the peoples of the world who are so well represented here today.

To my compatriots, I have no hesitation in saying that each one of us is as intimately attached to the soil of this beautiful country as are the famous jacaranda trees of Pretoria and the mimosa trees of the bushveld.[1]

Each time one of us touches the soil of this land, we feel a sense of personal renewal. The national mood changes as the seasons change.

We are moved by a sense of joy and exhilaration when the grass turns green and the flowers bloom.

That spiritual and physical oneness we all share with this common homeland explains the depth of the pain we all carried in

Reading Skill
Comparing and Contrasting What important difference does Mandela point out about South Africa's future as compared to its past?

---

1. **bushveld** (bʊʊsh´ velt) *n.* South African grassland with abundant shrubs and thorny vegetation.

our hearts as we saw our country tear itself apart in terrible conflict, and as we saw it spurned, outlawed and isolated by the peoples of the world, precisely because it has become the universal base of the pernicious ideology and practice of racism and racial oppression.

We, the people of South Africa, feel fulfilled that humanity has taken us back into its bosom, that we, who were outlaws not so long ago, have today been given the rare privilege to be host to the nations of the world on our own soil.

We thank all our distinguished international guests for having come to take possession with the people of our country of what is, after all, a common victory for justice, for peace, for human dignity.

We trust that you will continue to stand by us as we tackle the challenges of building peace, prosperity, nonsexism, nonracialism and democracy.

We deeply appreciate the role that the masses of our people and their democratic, religious, women, youth, business, traditional and other leaders have played to bring about this conclusion. Not least among them is my Second Deputy President, the Honorable F. W. de Klerk.

We would also like to pay tribute to our security forces, in all their ranks, for the distinguished role they have played in securing our first democratic elections and the transition to democracy, from bloodthirsty forces which still refuse to see the light.

The time for the healing of the wounds has come.

The moment to bridge the chasms that divide us has come.

The time to build is upon us.

We have, at last, achieved our political emancipation. We pledge ourselves to liberate all our people from the continuing bondage of poverty, deprivation, suffering, gender and other discrimination.

We succeeded to take our last steps to freedom in conditions of relative peace. We commit ourselves to the construction of a complete, just and lasting peace.

We have triumphed in the effort to implant hope in the breasts of the millions of our people. We enter into a covenant that we shall build the society in which all South Africans, both black and white, will be able to walk tall, without any fear in their hearts, assured of their inalienable right to human dignity—a rainbow nation at peace with itself and the world.

As a token of its commitment to the renewal of our country, the new Interim Government of National Unity will, as a matter of urgency, address the issue of amnesty for various categories of our people who are currently serving terms of imprisonment.

We dedicate this day to all the heroes and heroines in this country and the rest of the world who sacrificed in many ways and surrendered their lives so that we could be free.

Vocabulary
pernicious (pər nish′ əs)
adj. destructive

Vocabulary
covenant (kuv′ ə nənt)
n. agreement or contract, especially a sacred one

Reading
Check
What does Mandela say must be born "out of the experience of an extraordinary human disaster"?

Their dreams have become reality. Freedom is their reward.

We are both humbled and elevated by the honor and privilege that you, the people of South Africa, have bestowed on us, as the first President of a united, democratic, nonracial and nonsexist South Africa, to lead our country out of the valley of darkness.

We understand it still that there is no easy road to freedom.

We know it well that none of us acting alone can achieve success.

We must therefore act together as a united people, for national reconciliation, for nation building, for the birth of a new world.

Let there be justice for all.

Let there be peace for all.

Let there be work, bread, water and salt for all.

Let each know that for each the body, the mind and the soul have been freed to fulfill themselves.

Never, never and never again shall it be that this beautiful land will again experience the oppression of one by another and suffer the indignity of being the skunk of the world.

The sun shall never set on so glorious a human achievement!

Let freedom reign. God bless Africa!

Vocabulary
reconciliation
(rek′ ən sil′ ē ā′ shən) *n.*
the settling of a conflict or argument; agreement; compromise

Critical Thinking

1. **(a) Respond:** What do you admire most about the message in "Glory and Hope"? Explain. **(b) Discuss:** Share your response with a partner. Explain how hearing someone else's response did or did not change your own.

2. **(a)** What does Nelson Mandela say is "newborn" in his country? **(b) Analyze:** What emotion does the word "newborn" add to his remarks?

3. **(a)** Into what "covenant" does Mandela say the South African people are now entering? **(b) Generalize:** Which ideas in the speech are especially important for safeguarding the human rights of all people throughout today's world?

4. **(a) Interpret:** What do the words "glory" and "hope" mean? **(b) Connect:** How does the title of the speech connect with the ideas that Mandela conveys? Explain your response.

5. **Take a Position:** Basing your answer on Mandela's speech, what do you think was the new leader's greatest challenge? Explain.

 **Do heroes have responsibilities?**
Based on what you know about Nelson Mandela from his speech, would you call him a hero? Explain.

 Support your responses with evidence from the text.

Literary Analysis: Philosophical Assumptions

1. (a) What is Nelson Mandela's **purpose** in his speech? **(b)** What are the **philosophical assumptions,** or basic beliefs, that help shape his purpose? **(c)** What argument could someone who disagreed with Mandella use?

2. (a) For what **audience** did Nelson Mandela originally speak? **(b)** What details in the text indicate his intended audience? **(c)** Do you think his intended audience shared his basic beliefs?

3. Using Nelson Mandela's speech as an example, explain how the audience for a speech can change over time.

Reading Skill: Comparing and Contrasting

4. (a) Use a chart like the one shown to record the ideas Nelson Mandela presents about the past, present, and future.

Past	Present	Future

(b) Explain the point that Nelson Mandela makes by **comparing and contrasting** the past, present, and future.

Vocabulary

Practice Indicate whether each statement is *True* or *False*. Explain your answers. Then, revise any sentences that are false to make them true.

1. A signature serves to *confer* authenticity to a document.

2. A *pernicious* idea is always welcome at a team meeting.

3. Each party in a *covenant* hopes that the other party will break it.

4. A *distinguished* guest is well known to many people.

5. If you're *intimately* involved in an event, you know little about it.

6. If you make a *reconciliation* with a friend with whom you've quarreled, you might sit down together and talk things through.

Word Power Use the context of the sentences and what you know about the **Latin root -fer-** to explain your answer to each question.

1. Does an unhappy and *vociferous* shopper complain quietly?

2. Why might an employer ask for a *referral* from a teacher?

Word Power

The **Latin root -fer-** means "carry" or "produce."

Apply It Explain how the root -fer- helps you determine the meanings of these words. Consult a dictionary if necessary.

ferry
fertile
transfer

Integrated Language Skills

There Is a Longing • Glory and Hope

Conventions: Colons, Semicolons, and Ellipsis Points

Punctuation helps a writer clarify the meaning of a sentence.

A **colon** is used mainly to list items following an independent clause. A **semicolon** is used to join independent clauses that are closely related. A semicolon is also used to separate independent clauses or items in a series that already contain several commas.

Ellipsis points (. . .) are punctuation marks that show that something has not been expressed. Ellipsis points usually indicate the following:

- words that have been left out of a quotation
- a series that continues beyond the items mentioned
- time passing or action occurring in a narrative

Colon	Semicolon	Ellipsis Points
The flowers seemed human: nodding, bending, dancing.	The teacher lifted the desk herself; the sight greatly impressed the students.	He struck out... but the end of the game would surprise them all.

Practice A Explain the use of the colon, semicolon, or ellipsis points in each sentence.

1. Chief Dan George was a chief; he wanted to lead his people to a better future.
2. "I am a chief," he said, "but . . . the only weapon left to me is speech."
3. Chief Dan George expected great things for his people: education, participation in government, and freedom.
4. He spoke softly . . . and quietly sat down.

Reading Application Reread the fourth sentence of "There Is a Longing." Explain the use of a semicolon in this sentence.

Practice B Copy these sentences, adding colons, semicolons, or ellipsis points wherever necessary.

1. Nelson Mandela talked of the past, talked of the celebration in the present, and talked of.
2. Mandela had spent years working for liberty the years had brought him to this moment.
3. He wanted many things for his country justice, peace, work, and food for all.
4. The work was long the goal was liberty they celebrated the achievement.

Writing Application Write three sentences about Nelson Mandela's facial and bodily expressions in the opening image of "Glory and Hope." Use a colon, a semicolon, and ellipsis points in your writing.

PH **GRAMMAR HANDBOOK** Further instruction and practice are available in the *Prentice Hall Grammar Handbook*.

Writing

Both speeches present a vision for the future. Write a **letter** to the author of the speech you read. In your correspondence, express your feelings about the speech and identify passages that you found inspiring.

- List words that describe how the speech makes you feel. Next to each word, write the line or lines from the speech that evoke that emotion.
- Tell the author why you are writing and why you think the speech has a message for *all* readers.
- As you draft, use a friendly yet respectful tone, and maintain focus throughout your letter.
- Use formal business letter format. *(For an example, see page R38.)*

Grammar Application Make sure you have used colons, semicolons, and ellipsis points properly in your letter.

Writing Workshop: *Work in Progress*

Prewriting for Comparison and Contrast Review the Comparison List in your Writing Portfolio. Think about the two places you have listed. Next, jot down emotions you connect with each one. Then, use a Venn diagram to compare and contrast the two places. Save your Comparison work in your portfolio.

Listening and Speaking

In a small team, perform a **media analysis of Web sites.** Find one site intended to teach small children a message of empowerment. Next, find another site intended to inspire adults with a message similar to those in "There Is a Longing" or "Glory and Hope." Finally, perform a comparative analysis of these two sites.

- Identify the **specific audience and purpose** of each site.
- Evaluate **changes in formality and tone** between the two sites.
- Knowing the different audiences and purposes, consider the possible reasons for the changes in formality and tone within these two sources from the same medium (Internet). Why might each site present information in the manner it does?

As a team, prepare your analysis and present it to the class. **Use graphics,** such as screen shots, to help explain concepts where appropriate.

 **Focus on the TEKS**

Reading
(12)(D) Evaluate changes in formality and tone within the same medium for specific audiences and purposes.
Research
(23)(C) Use graphics to help explain concepts where appropriate.
Writing
(15)(B) Write work-related documents (e.g., correspondence).

Use this prewriting activity to prepare for the **Writing Workshop** on page 1244.

TEXAS
PHLitOnline
www.PHLitOnline.com

- Interactive graphic organizers
- Grammar tutorial
- Interactive journals

Strategy for Success

Analyze Context

The reading sections of the ACT and the Texas standardized tests ask you to analyze literary text set in different time periods and cultures. As you read these passages on standardized tests, analyze how the historical and cultural context relates to the theme and diction in the passage, including figurative language. For example, the references in a contemporary passage may be familiar to you. However, the theme of a passage set during the technology boom of the 1950s may be less familiar. The passage might include an idealized view of the future and of scientific aims as well as figurative language related to the technology of the time.

Take historical and cultural setting into consideration when you analyze literary text. Begin by identifying the setting and considering what you already know about it. Then, look at the theme and figurative language of the passage through the eyes of someone from that time and culture. Consider how this change in perspective affects your understanding.

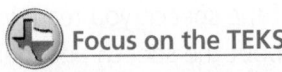 Focus on the TEKS

Reading/Comprehension Skills
(2) Analyze, make inferences and draw conclusions about theme in different cultural and historical contexts.
(2)(C) Relate the figurative language of a literary work to its historical and cultural setting.
RC-9(A) Reflect on understanding to monitor comprehension.

Analyze Figurative Language
Use historical and cultural setting to understand figurative language.

5   Bill threw the slop into the pig pen and thought over Bob's idea. Bob's ideas were usually as handy as hip pockets on a hog, but this time Bill wondered if Bob was on to something.

1. The phrase "as handy as hip pockets on a hog" suggests that
   A. Bill usually has the best ideas.
   B. Bill and Bob often share ideas.
   C. Bob rarely has good ideas.
   D. all ideas are like pockets.

It is unusual for Bill to think that Bob is "on to something," so **A** is incorrect. Sharing ideas is not related to the figurative language, so **B** is incorrect. The text refers only to Bob's ideas, so **D** is incorrect. The details suggest that Bill is familiar with pigs, so he knows that hogs have no use for hip pockets. Bob's ideas are just as useless. Based on this context, **C** is the correct choice.

Draw Conclusions About Theme
Use historical and cultural setting to draw conclusions about the passage's theme.

5   Ed steered the horses away from the rising sun while his family rode inside the wagon, cramped beside their only possessions. He missed his friends back home, but he had a responsibility to take care of his family in this new land.

2. What is the theme of the passage?
   F. Responsibilities are more important than interests.
   G. Perseverance helps people when others have abandoned them.
   H. Possessions are important, and so is family.
   J. Some people give up in tough times.

No one has been abandoned in the passage, and no one has given up, so **G** and **J** are incorrect. Ed values his family and their possessions, but he values his responsibility more, so **H** is incorrect. **F,** the correct choice, summarizes Ed's belief and states the theme of the passage.

ACT Practice

DIRECTIONS: The passage in this test is followed by several questions. After reading the passage, choose the best answer to each question and fill in the corresponding oval on your answer document. You may refer to the passage as often as necessary.

PROSE FICTION

Molly smoothed her homespun skirt and simple bonnet as she stood at the imposing door of the stately home. She always felt out of place in this elegant neighborhood, but she had to see her dearest friend, Abigail, especially with all that had happened in recent weeks. Burdened by unfair taxes from Britain, the American colonists had begun a

5   complete boycott of British goods. And she knew that Abigail, who was as attached to lovely things as a horse to a cart, must be suffering more than most.

"I'm so glad to see you!" Molly said as Abigail opened the door.

Abigail smiled. "Please come in, Molly. Won't you have a cup of tea?" She gestured toward a small table, where Molly was stunned to see a shiny new container of tea with the

10   unmistakable words *British East India Company* across the front.

"Abigail, surely your family's not buying British tea?"

"Why not?" said Abigail, tossing her head like an unbridled pony. "You know we always have the best things here—regardless of whether a few overexcited colonists here and there are trying to make a statement. In fact, this dress I'm wearing came in just

15   yesterday from the most wonderful shop in London. Do you like it?"

Molly paused. "It's nice," she said carefully. "But I thought we Americans were boycotting British goods until they lift the taxes they've put on us so unfairly. We all have to stand up for what's right—don't we?"

1. What is the setting of the passage?
   A. present-day Britain
   B. colonial America
   C. present-day East India
   D. colonial Britain

2. What is the main lesson Molly tries to convey to Abigail in the passage?
   F. No one should buy British tea.
   G. The taxes are unfair to colonists.
   H. Friendship is more important than anything else in life.
   J. People should join together to protest injustice.

3. If the story were taking place in modern times, Abigail's attachment to lovely things might be compared to
   A. a horse and a cart.
   B. a cup of tea and a cup of coffee.
   C. a satin dress and a tie.
   D. a magnet and a refrigerator.

4. The description of Abigail tossing her head "like an unbridled pony" is most likely included to
   F. suggest that Abigail likes horses.
   G. hint that Abigail dislikes Molly.
   H. contrast with Molly's hesitation and earnestness.
   J. show a similarity between Abigail and Molly.

Informational Texts

Expository Text

Almanac Entry
**Automobiles
in Texas**

Press Release
**Annual Study Shows
Traffic Congestion . . .**

Focus on the TEKS

Reading
(8) Explain the controlling idea and specific purpose of an expository text and distinguish the most important from the less important details that support the author's purpose.

Reading Skill: Analyze Author's Purpose

The **author's purpose** is his or her reason for writing. The general purposes for writing are to inform, to entertain, to persuade, and to describe. When you are analyzing author's purpose in a particular text, first identify the general purpose of the writing. Then, move to the more **specific purpose.** For example, a speech might have a general purpose to persuade and a specific purpose to convince others to participate in a recycling program.

To pinpoint the specific purpose of a text, take note of the author's **controlling, or main, idea** and the **details** he or she offers as support. These details should also support the author's purpose. To clarify the writer's purpose, follow these steps:

• Distinguish the **most important** from the **less important details** that support the author's message and purpose.

• Keep in mind the **cultural, historical, and contemporary contexts**—the time and place in which the author is writing. The issues, customs, and atmosphere that surround an author are often reflected in his or her specific purpose for writing.

As You Read Use a chart like this one to explain the specific purpose of each expository text.

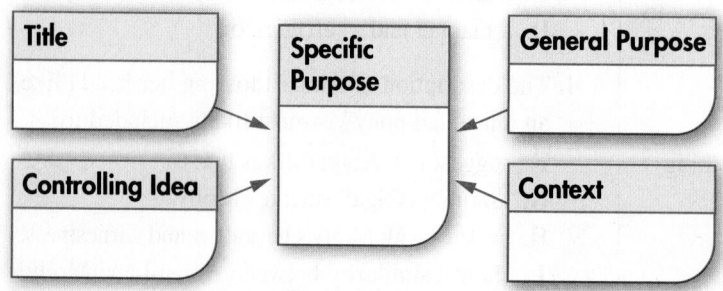

★ TEXAS ALMANAC ★

(from the 1911 Texas Almanac)

This attribution explains when the information was first published.

Features:
- yearly updates
- topic of general interest
- statistical information

➤ Automobiles in Texas ➤

Ten years ago an automobile was a curiosity in the leading cities of Texas. Five years ago the people in many counties had never seen what was then known as the horseless carriage. Today it is estimated that the number of automobiles in actual service in Texas will reach nearly 30,000 and that over $40,000,000 is invested in the machines. Reports, dated August 1, 1910, from 180 counties in the State show a total of 14,276 automobiles. A canvass by the Commercial Secretaries' Association places the number at 30,000, which, at an average value of $1,500 each, would make the investment $45,000,000. This number is constantly increasing, and counting the life of a machine at three years, the new machines purchased to take the place of old ones cost $15,000,000 annually.

Although the automobile is counted a luxury and in the majority of cases, is used for pleasure, or as a means of transportation from the home to the office, the automobile is found in practical everyday life in all parts of the State. In the cities it is taking the place of the hack and the carriage and in many instances of the truck and the delivery wagon.

Consider the information in this paragraph. **Explain the specific purpose of the paragraph. Then, distinguish the most important from the less important details that support the author's purpose.**

TEXAS

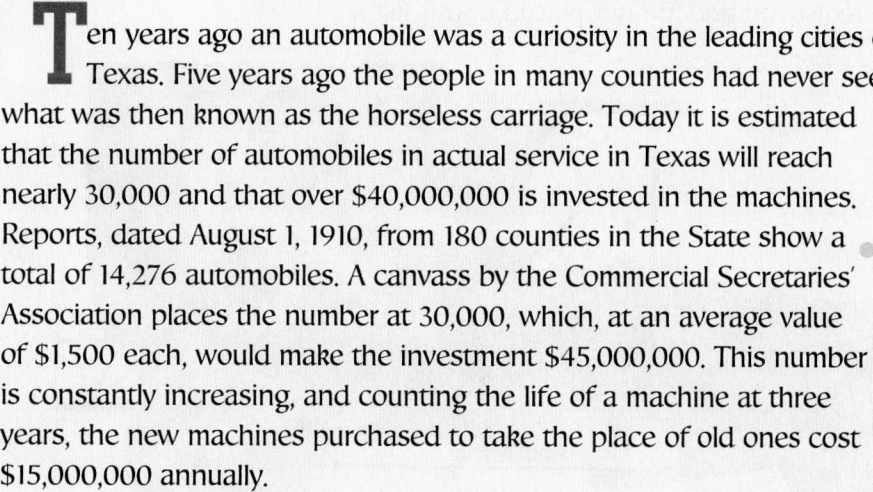

In the plains country the automobile is used to carry the mail and to cover long distances not traversed by railroads. Commercial travelers use them in making towns in their district or territory, saving time thereby, and in many other ways has the machine been adapted to commercial purposes.

According to the Almanac canvass, Dallas County led all other counties in the number of automobiles registered August 1, 1910. Since that date nearly 200 machines have been added to the list, but August 1 registry is used in comparison with other county statistics secured on that date.

On August 1, Dallas County reported 1,390 automobiles; Harris, 1,031; Bexar, 1,024; Tarrant, 852; McLennan, 546; El Paso, 506; Jefferson, 413; Travis, 375; Potter, 350; Williamson, 275; Galveston, 219; Hale, 200; Tom Green, 190; Taylor, 176; Hunt, 172; Bell, 171; Navarro, 146; Collins, 133; Runnels, 127; Cooke, 125; Lubbock, 125; Johnson, 110. Reports from other counties show less than 100 automobiles registered and are not placed in this list.

> Review the content of these sentences. **Explain the specific purpose of this paragraph.**

> The details in this paragraph support the author's purpose. The information directly reflects the cultural and historical contexts of the text.

Do heroes have responsibilities?

(a) How have the increasing numbers of automobiles added to the widespread effects of using them? **(b)** How have these increasing numbers and uses of automobiles added responsibility to both automakers and drivers?

Texas Transportation Institute

Texas A&M University System

Press Release

Press Release

Features:

- summary of technical information
- statistical data
- text written for a general audience

Annual study shows traffic congestion worsening in cities large and small

COLLEGE STATION, TX—Traffic congestion continues to worsen in American cities of all sizes, creating a $78 billion annual drain on the U.S. economy in the form of 4.2 billion lost hours and 2.9 billion gallons of wasted fuel—that's 105 million weeks of vacation and 58 fully-loaded supertankers.

These are among the key findings of the Texas Transportation Institute's *2007 Urban Mobility Report.* Improvements to the methodology used to measure congestion nationwide have produced the most detailed picture yet of a problem that is growing worse in all 437 of the nation's urban areas. The current report is based on 2005 figures, the most recent year for which complete data was available.

"There is no 'magic' technology or solution on the horizon because there is no single cause of congestion," noted study co-author Tim Lomax, a research engineer at TTI. "The good news is that there are multiple strategies involving traffic operations and public transit available right now that if applied together, can lessen this problem."

The 2007 mobility report notes that congestion causes the average peak period traveler to spend an extra 38 hours of travel time and consume an additional 26 gallons of fuel, amounting to a cost of $710 per traveler.

TEXAS

Sidebar annotations:

Review the title. **Explain what you think might be the controlling idea of the text.**

These paragraphs present facts and statistics to support the author's main idea and specific purpose. **Distinguish the most important from the less important details that support the author's purpose in these paragraphs.**

Along with expanding the estimates of the effect of congestion to all 437 U.S. urban areas, the study provides detailed information for 85 specific urban areas. The report also focuses on the problems presented by "irregular events"—crashes, stalled vehicles, work zones, weather problems, and special events—that cause unreliable travel times and contribute significantly to the overall congestion problem. Worsening congestion, the study notes, is reflected in several ways:

- Trips take longer
- Congestion affects more of the day
- Congestion affects weekend travel and rural areas
- Congestion affects more personal trips and freight shipments
- Trip travel times increasingly are unreliable

> The information in this section clearly reflects the cultural and contemporary contexts of the text.

Researchers spent two years revising the methodology using additional sources of traffic information, providing more—and higher quality—data on which to base the current study.

The report identifies multiple solutions to the congestion problem that, researchers say, must be used together to be effective. These include:

- Get as much service as possible from existing infrastructure
- Add road and transit system capacity in critical corridors
- Relieve chokepoints
- Change usage patterns
- Provide choices
- Diversify the development patterns
- Keep expectations realistic

> The author uses a bulleted list in this section of the text to organize details clearly. **Explain the controlling idea and specific purpose of this section.**

"Congestion is a far more complex problem than is apparent at first glance," Lomax said. "The better the data we use to define the problem, the more successful we will be in addressing its root causes."

TEXAS

Do heroes have responsibilities?

According to this article, what responsibility can individual drivers take concerning congestion?

Comparing Informational Texts

(a) Analyze: Compare and contrast each author's general purpose for writing. **(b) Analyze:** Compare and contrast the success of each author in achieving his or her general purpose. Provide details from the text to support your ideas.

 College Readiness | **Timed Writing**

Write an Essay

Format
The prompt directs you to write an essay. Therefore, you should include an introductory and concluding paragraph as well as several body paragraphs that provide details and support for your ideas.

Write an essay in which you explain and analyze the specific purposes of the almanac entry and press release. In your analysis, take into consideration the cultural, historical, and contemporary contexts—the times and places in which each author is writing and how these factors affect the authors' specific purposes. Provide evidence from the texts to support your ideas. (40 minutes)

Academic Vocabulary
When you *support* ideas, you give examples, facts, details, and explanations that prove that your ideas are valid and logical.

 5-Minute Planner

Complete these steps before you begin to write:

1. Read the prompt carefully and completely.
2. Review the almanac entry and press release. Jot down notes about the general and specific purposes of each text.
3. Briefly answer the following questions:
   - What culture does the text reflect?
   - What time period is represented in the text?
   - How might conditions in the culture and time period in which the author is writing have affected his or her purpose for writing?
4. Refer to your notes as you draft your essay.

Comparing Literary Works

Comparing Influences on Contemporary Literature

Contemporary writers' work is often influenced by the literary traditions of the past. Among these are the **mythic, classical** (of historical renown), and **traditional** literary traditions.

A **myth** is a story that explains the actions of gods or human heroes, the reasons for certain beliefs, or the causes of natural features and events. Mythic literature expresses the central values of a culture.

A **tall tale** is a type of traditional literature that has a larger-than-life hero, far-fetched situations and amazing feats, humor, and **hyperbole,** or exaggeration. Tall tales were especially popular on the American frontier.

The works of today's writers often show the influence of original myths and tall tales as well as the influence of more recent retellings. The following selections are examples of 20th and 21st century literature born out of older literary traditions. Consider how oral stories of a certain Texan legend may have influenced the tall tale "Pecos Bill: The Cyclone" (1958) and how traditional literature may have affected the writing of *Big Fish: Final Production Draft* (2004). Look also for the direct influence of the earlier myths on Edith Hamilton's "Perseus" (1942), and note how the mythic tradition influenced Geoffrey O'Brien's "From the Old Age of Perseus" (2002).

As You Read Use a chart like the one shown to analyze the influence of mythic and traditional literature on 21st century literature.

	Human or partly divine?	Performs amazing feats?	Receives divine aid?	Includes humor and exaggeration?
Edward in *Big Fish: Final Production Draft*				
Perseus in "From the Old Age of Perseus"				

Focus on the TEKS

Reading
(2)(B) Analyze the influence of mythic and traditional literature on 20th and 21st century literature.

TEXAS

PHLitOnline

www.PHLitOnline.com

- Vocabulary flashcards
- Interactive journals
- More about the authors
- Selection audio
- Interactive graphic organizers

Do *heroes* have responsibilities?

Writing About the Big Question

These selections present larger-than-life heroes who face great danger. Use these sentence starters to develop your ideas about the Big Question.

The level of danger in a situation is/is not important when assessing heroism because _____.

For someone to be heroic, his or her intentions must be _____.

Meet the Authors

Harold W. Felton (1902–1991)
Author of "Pecos Bill: The Cyclone"

Harold W. Felton practiced law and worked for the Internal Revenue Service, but he became increasingly interested in United States folklore. Over his life, he collected and retold hundreds of tales.

Daniel Wallace (b. 1959) and
John August (b. 1970)
Authors of *Big Fish: Final Production Draft*

Daniel Wallace, an author and illustrator, wrote the novel *Big Fish*. He teaches English at the University of North Carolina.

John August is a writer and director whose screenwriting credits include *Charlie and the Chocolate Factory*.

Edith Hamilton (1867–1963)
Author of "Perseus"

Edith Hamilton was a groundbreaking educator who helped found the Bryn Mawr School, the first college preparatory school for women. She taught young women not to limit their goals simply because they were not men.

Geoffrey O'Brien (b. 1948)
Author of "From the Old Age of Perseus"

Geoffrey O'Brien is editor-in-chief of the Library of America. He is a widely published author, book and film critic, and cultural historian whose credits include contributions to the *New York Review of Books*.

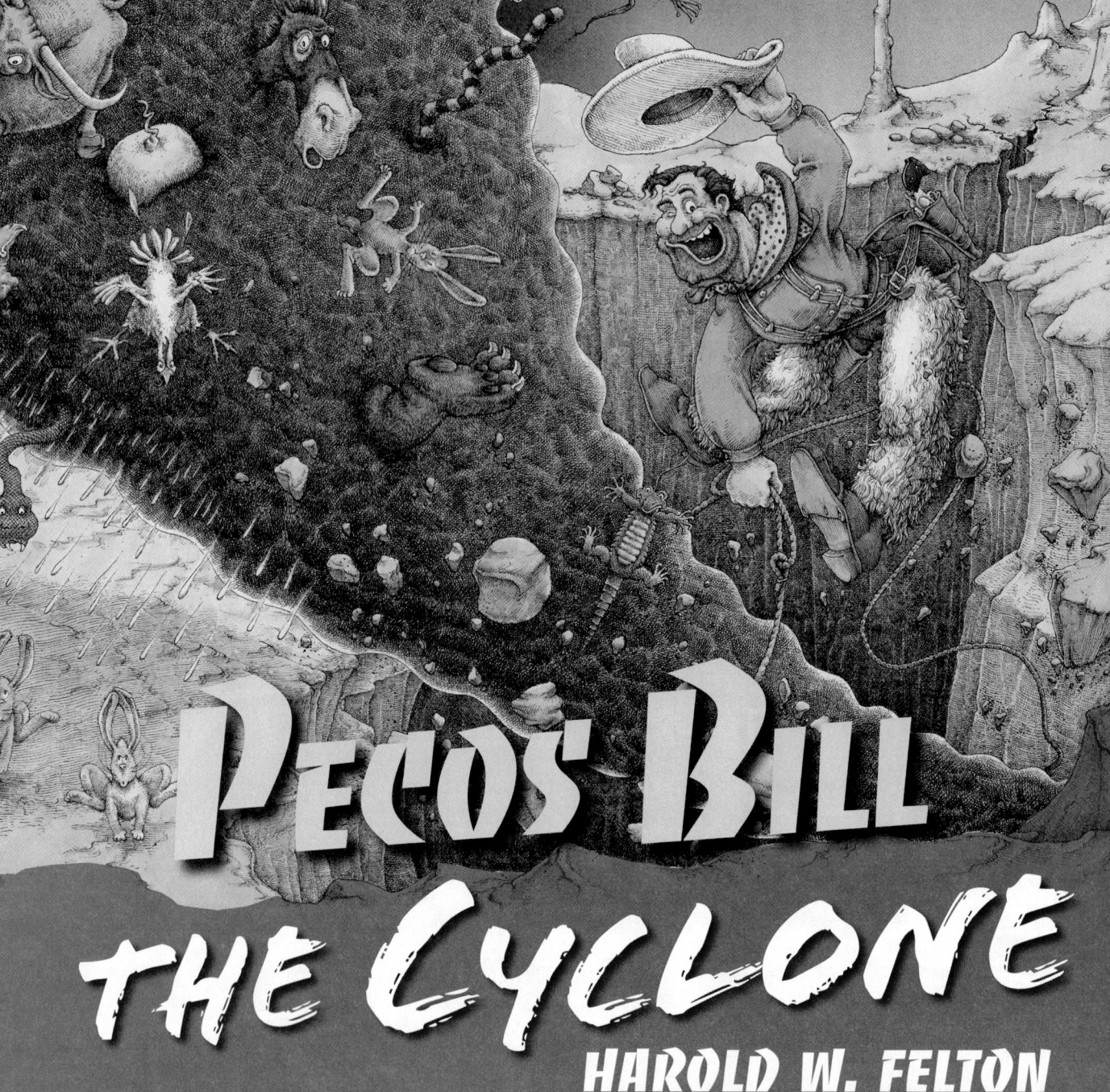

PECOS BILL

THE CYCLONE

HAROLD W. FELTON

One of Bill's greatest feats, if not the greatest feat of all time, occurred unexpectedly one Fourth of July. He had invented the Fourth of July some years before. It was a great day for the cowpunchers.[1] They had taken to it right off like the real Americans they were. But the celebration had always ended on a dismal note. Somehow it seemed to be spoiled by a cyclone.

One of Bill's greatest feats, if not the greatest feat of all time, occurred unexpectedly one Fourth of July. He had invented the Fourth of July some years before. It was a great day for the cowpunchers.[1] They had taken to it right off like the real Americans they were. But the celebration had always ended on a dismal note. Somehow it seemed to be spoiled by a cyclone.

Literary Analysis
Influences on Contemporary Literature
Which description in the first paragraph contains hyperbole?

---

1. **cowpunchers** (kou′ pun′ chərz) n. cowboys.

Bill had never minded the cyclone much. The truth is he rather liked it. But the other celebrants ran into caves for safety. He invented cyclone cellars for them. He even named the cellars. He called them "'fraid holes." Pecos wouldn't even say the word "afraid." The cyclone was something like he was. It was big and strong too. He always stood by musing pleasantly as he watched it.

The cyclone caused Bill some trouble, though. Usually it would destroy a few hundred miles of fence by blowing the postholes away. But it wasn't much trouble for him to fix it. All he had to do was to go and get the postholes and then take them back and put the fence posts in them. The holes were rarely ever blown more than twenty or thirty miles.

In one respect Bill even welcomed the cyclone, for it blew so hard it blew the earth away from his wells. The first time this happened, he thought the wells would be a total loss. There they were, sticking up several hundred feet out of the ground. As wells they were useless. But he found he could cut them up into lengths and sell them for postholes to farmers in Iowa and Nebraska. It was very profitable, especially after he invented a special posthole saw to cut them with. He didn't use that type of posthole himself. He got the prairie dogs to dig his for him. He simply caught a few gross[2] of prairie dogs and set them down at proper intervals. The prairie dog would dig a hole. Then Bill would put a post in it. The prairie dog would get disgusted and go down the row ahead of the others and dig another hole. Bill fenced all of Texas and parts of New Mexico and Arizona in this manner. He took a few contracts and fenced most of the Southern Pacific right of way too. That's the reason it is so crooked. He had trouble getting the prairie dogs to run a straight fence.

As for his wells, the badgers dug them. The system was the same as with the prairie dogs. The labor was cheap so it didn't make much difference if the cyclone did spoil some of the wells. The badgers were digging all of the time anyway. They didn't seem to care whether they dug wells or just badger holes.

One year he tried shipping the prairie dog holes up north, too, for postholes. It was not successful. They didn't keep in storage and they couldn't stand the handling in shipping. After they were installed they seemed to wear out quickly. Bill always thought the difference in climate had something to do with it.

---

2. gross (grōs) *n.* twelve dozen.

◀ **Critical Viewing**
Which details in this image suggest that this selection is a tall tale? Explain. **[Analyze]**

Literary Analysis
Influences on Contemporary Literature
Which realistic details in this passage add humor?

Reading Check

Where does Pecos Bill get the postholes he sells to farmers in Iowa and Nebraska?

It should be said that in those days there was only one cyclone. It was the first and original cyclone, bigger and more terrible by far than the small cyclones of today. It usually stayed by itself up north around Kansas and Oklahoma and didn't bother anyone much. But it was attracted by the noise of the Fourth of July celebration and without fail managed to put in an appearance before the close of the day.

On this particular Fourth of July, the celebration had gone off fine. The speeches were loud and long. The contests and games were hard fought. The high point of the day was Bill's exhibition with Widow Maker, which came right after he showed off Scat and Rat.[3] People seemed never to tire of seeing them in action. The mountain lion was almost useless as a work animal after his accident, and the snake had grown old and somewhat infirm, and was troubled with rheumatism in his rattles. But they too enjoyed the Fourth of July and liked to make a public appearance. They relived the old days.

Widow Maker had put on a good show, bucking as no ordinary horse could ever buck. Then Bill undertook to show the gaits[4] he had taught the palomino.[5] Other mustangs at that time had only two gaits. Walking and running. Only Widow Maker could pace. But now Bill had developed and taught him other gaits. Twenty-seven in all. Twenty-three forward and three reverse. He was very proud of the achievement. He showed off the slow gaits and the crowd was eager for more.

He showed the walk, trot, canter, lope, jog, slow rack, fast rack, single foot, pace, stepping pace, fox trot, running walk and the others now known. Both men and horses confuse the various gaits nowadays. Some of the gaits are now thought to be the same, such as the rack and the single foot. But with Widow Maker and Pecos Bill, each one was different. Each was precise and to be distinguished from the others. No one had ever imagined such a thing.

Then the cyclone came! All of the people except Bill ran into the 'fraid holes. Bill was annoyed. He stopped the performance. The remaining gaits were not shown. From that day to this horses have used no more than the gaits Widow Maker exhibited that day. It is unfortunate that the really fast gaits were not shown. If they were, horses might be much faster today than they are.

Bill glanced up at the cyclone and the quiet smile on his face faded into a frown. He saw the cyclone was angry. Very, very angry indeed.

---

3. **Widow Maker . . . Scat and Rat.** Widow Maker is a mustang, a type of wild horse. Scat is Bill's mountain lion, and Rat is Bill's pet rattlesnake.
4. **gaits** (gāts) *n.* foot movements of a horse.
5. **palomino** (pal′ ə mē′ nō) *n.* golden-tan or cream-colored horse that has a white, silver, or ivory tail and, often, white spots on the face and legs.

The cyclone had always been the center of attention. Everywhere it went people would look up in wonder, fear and amazement. It had been the undisputed master of the country. It had observed Bill's rapid climb to fame and had seen the Fourth of July celebration grow. It had been keeping an eye on things all right.

In the beginning, the Fourth of July crowd had aroused its curiosity. It liked nothing more than to show its superiority and power by breaking the crowd up sometime during the day. But every year the crowd was larger. This preyed on the cyclone's mind. This year it did not come to watch. It deliberately came to spoil the celebration. Jealous of Bill and of his success, it resolved to do away with the whole institution of the Fourth of July once and for all. So much havoc and destruction would be wrought that there would never be another Independence Day Celebration. On that day, in future years, it would circle around the horizon leering and gloating. At least, so it thought.

The cyclone was resolved, also, to do away with this bold fellow who did not hold it in awe and run for the 'fraid hole at its approach. For untold years it had been the most powerful thing in the land. And now, here was a mere man who threatened its position. More! Who had usurped its position!

When Bill looked at the horizon and saw the cyclone coming, he recognized the anger and rage. While a cyclone does not often smile, Bill had felt from the beginning that it was just a grouchy fellow who never had a pleasant word for anyone. But now, instead of merely an unpleasant character, Bill saw all the viciousness of which an angry cyclone is capable. He had no way of knowing that the cyclone saw its kingship tottering and was determined to stop this man who threatened its supremacy.

But Bill understood the violence of the onslaught even as the monster came into view. He knew he must meet it. The center of the cyclone was larger than ever before. The fact is, the cyclone had been training for this fight all winter and spring. It was in best form and at top weight. It headed straight for Bill intent on his destruction. In an instant it was upon him. Bill had sat quietly and silently on the great pacing mustang. But his mind was working rapidly. In the split second between his first sight of the monster and the time for action he had made his plans. Pecos Bill was ready! Ready and waiting!

Green clouds were dripping from the cyclone's jaws. Lightning flashed from its eyes as it swept down upon him. Its plan was to envelop Bill in one mighty grasp. Just as it was upon him, Bill turned Widow Maker to its left. This was a clever move for the cyclone was right-handed, and while it had been training hard to

Vocabulary

usurped (yo͞o sʉrpt´)
v. took power without right

Reading Check

Why is the cyclone angry with Bill?

Science Connection

Cyclones

A cyclone is an area of rapidly spinning winds that is associated with severe thunderstorms. The rotating winds can reach speeds of 250 miles per hour and are capable of lifting even very heavy objects into the column of circulating air. Cyclones develop when warm and cold masses of air collide, causing abrupt changes in wind speed and direction. Cyclones that were over a mile wide and that have spread damage along a fifty-mile path have been recorded. Unlike Pecos Bill, most people are smart enough to take shelter underground when they see a cyclone coming.

Connect to the Literature

Why might a literary character like Bill be especially beloved by people who live in areas affected by cyclones?

get its left in shape, that was not its best side. Bill gave rein to his mount. Widow Maker wheeled and turned on a dime which Pecos had, with great foresight and accuracy, thrown to the ground to mark the exact spot for this maneuver. It was the first time that anyone had thought of turning on a dime. Then he urged the great horse forward. The cyclone, filled with surprise, lost its balance and rushed forward at an increased speed. It went so fast that it met itself coming back. This confused the cyclone, but it did not confuse Pecos Bill. He had expected that to happen. Widow Maker went into his twenty-first gait and edged up close to the whirlwind. Soon they were running neck and neck.

At the proper instant Bill grabbed the cyclone's ears, kicked himself free of the stirrups and pulled himself lightly on its back. Bill never used spurs on Widow Maker. Sometimes he wore them for show and because he liked the jingling sound they made. They made a nice accompaniment for his cowboy songs. But he had not been singing, so he had no spurs. He did not have his rattlesnake for a quirt.[6] Of course there was no bridle. It was man against monster! There he was! Pecos Bill astride a raging cyclone, slick heeled and without a saddle!

The cyclone was taken by surprise at this sudden turn of events. But it was undaunted. It was sure of itself. Months of training had given it a conviction that it was invincible. With a mighty heave, it twisted to its full height. Then it fell back suddenly, twisting and turning violently, so that before it came back to earth, it had turned around a thousand times. Surely no rider could ever withstand such an attack. No rider ever had. Little wonder. No one had ever ridden a cyclone before. But Pecos Bill did! He fanned the tornado's ears with his hat and dug his heels into the demon's flanks and yelled, "Yipee-ee!"

The people who had run for shelter began to come out. The audience further enraged the cyclone. It was bad enough to be disgraced by having a man astride it. It was unbearable not to have thrown him. To have all the people see the failure was too much! It got down flat on the ground and rolled over and over. Bill retained his seat throughout this ruse. Evidence of this desperate but futile stratagem[7] remains today. The great Staked Plains, or as the Mexicans call it, Llano Estacado is

---

6. **quirt** (kwɜrt) *n.* riding whip with a braided lash and a short handle.
7. **futile** (fyo͞ot´´l) **stratagem** (strat´ ə jəm) useless or hopeless plan.

the result. Its small, rugged mountains were covered with trees at the time. The rolling of the cyclone destroyed the mountains, the trees, and almost everything else in the area. The destruction was so complete, that part of the country is flat and treeless to this day. When the settlers came, there were no landmarks to guide them across the vast unmarked space, so they drove stakes in the ground to mark the trails. That is the reason it is called "Staked Plains." Here is an example of the proof of the events of history by careful and painstaking research. It is also an example of how seemingly inexplicable geographical facts can be explained.

It was far more dangerous for the rider when the cyclone shot straight up to the sky. Once there, the twister tried the same thing it had tried on the ground. It rolled on the sky. It was no use. Bill could not be unseated. He kept his place, and he didn't have a sky hook with him either.

As for Bill, he was having the time of his life, shouting at the top of his voice, kicking his opponent in the ribs and jabbing his thumb in its flanks. It responded and went on a wild bucking rampage over the entire West. It used all the bucking tricks known to the wildest broncos as well as those known only to cyclones. The wind howled furiously and beat against the fearless rider. The rain poured. The lightning flashed around his ears. The fight went on and on. Bill enjoyed himself immensely. In spite of the elements he easily kept his place. . . .

The raging cyclone saw this out of the corner of its eye. It knew then who the victor was. It was twisting far above the Rocky Mountains when the awful truth came to it. In a horrible heave it disintegrated! Small pieces of cyclone flew in all directions. Bill still kept his seat on the main central portion until that rained out from under him. Then he jumped to a nearby streak of lightning and slid down it toward earth. But it was raining so hard that the rain put out the lightning. When it fizzled out from under him, Bill dropped the rest of the way. He lit in what is now called Death Valley. He hit quite hard, as is apparent from the fact that he so compressed the place that it is still two hundred and seventy-six feet below sea level. The Grand Canyon was washed out by the rain, though it must be understood that this happened after Paul Bunyan had given it a good start by carelessly dragging his ax behind him when he went west a short time before.

The cyclones and the hurricanes and the tornadoes nowadays are the small pieces that broke off of the big cyclone Pecos Bill rode. In fact, the rainstorms of the present day came into being in the same way. There are always **skeptics**, but even they will recognize

---

Literary Analysis
Influences on Contemporary Literature
In his encounter with the cyclone, which details show that Bill is a larger-than-life hero?

Vocabulary
skeptics (skep′ tiks) *n.* people who doubt accepted ideas

Literary Analysis
Influences on Contemporary Literature
According to the tale, how does Bill create a natural phenomenon?

Reading Check

What unusual feat does Bill complete with the cyclone?

the logic of the proof of this event. They will recall that even now it almost always rains on the Fourth of July. That is because the rainstorms of today still retain some of the characteristics of the giant cyclone that met its comeuppance at the hands of Pecos Bill.

Bill lay where he landed and looked up at the sky, but he could see no sign of the cyclone. Then he laughed softly as he felt the warm sand of Death Valley on his back. . . .

It was a rough ride though, and Bill had resisted unusual tensions and pressures. When he got on the cyclone he had a twenty-dollar gold piece and a bowie knife in his pocket. The tremendous force of the cyclone was such that when he finished the ride he found that his pocket contained a plugged nickel[8] and a little pearl-handled penknife. His two giant six-shooters were compressed and transformed into a small water pistol and a popgun.

It is a strange circumstance that lesser men have monuments raised in their honor. Death Valley is Bill's monument. Sort of a monument in reverse. Sunk in his honor, you might say. Perhaps that is as it should be. After all, Bill was different. He made his own monument. He made it with his hips, as is evident from the great depth of the valley. That is the hard way.

8. **plugged nickel** fake nickel.

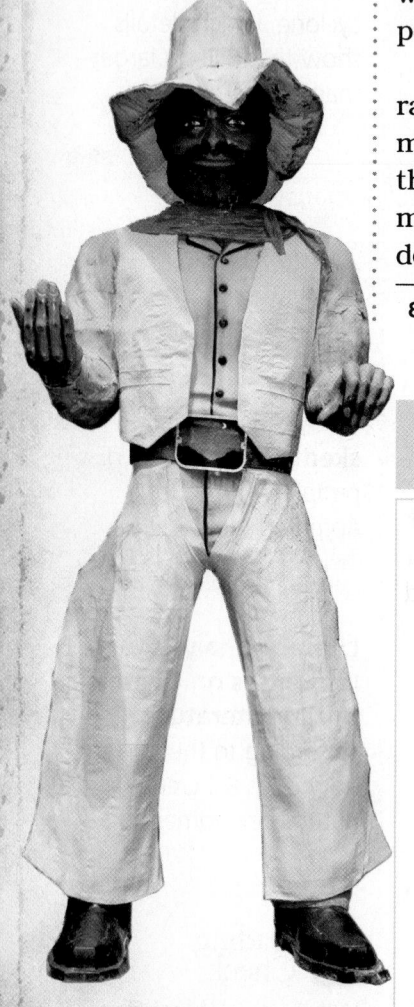

Literary Analysis
Influences on Contemporary Literature
Which details in this paragraph are examples of humorous exaggeration?

Critical Thinking

1. **Respond:** Which parts of the tale did you find funniest? Explain.

2. **(a)** What term does Bill use to refer to the cyclone cellars? **(b) Draw Conclusions:** What do you learn about the character of Pecos Bill from his reaction to the cellars?

3. **(a)** What word is Bill unwilling to say aloud? **(b) Draw Conclusions:** How does his resolve never to say this word explain, in part, why he is a folk hero?

4. **(a) Analyze:** What are three human characteristics of the cyclone? **(b) Compare and Contrast:** How does the cyclone resemble Pecos Bill himself?

Do heroes have responsibilities? (a) How does Pecos Bill ultimately show responsibility to his community? Explain. **(b)** Do you think Bill has a responsibility to use his special abilities to help his community, or can he choose not to? Explain.

From BIG FISH

Written by John August • Based on the novel by Daniel Wallace
Final Production Draft

INT.[1] WILL'S BEDROOM—DAY [FLASHBACK]

. . .where an eight-year old Will is propped up in bed, his face covered with chicken pox and pink calamine lotion. He's showing Edward how many bumps there are on his arm.

> **YOUNG WILL**
>
> Dr. Bennett says I'm going to have to be home for a week.

> **EDWARD**
>
> That's nothing. I once had to stay in bed for three years.

> **YOUNG WILL**
>
> Did you have chicken pox?

> **EDWARD**
>
> I wish.

CUT TO:[2]

INT. TINY CHURCH—DAY

Wearing a white shirt and tie, **YOUNG EDWARD**—still about 10—sings "Down to the River My Lord" along with the **CONGREGATION**. His voice is high and thin, but he gives it his all.

---

1. **INT.** abbreviation for "interior," a note to the crew that this scene will be filmed indoors.
2. **CUT TO** notes describing camera and film editing directions appear throughout.

from Big Fish: Final Production Draft **1225**

Vocabulary

chicken pox (chik´ ən päks) *n.* a highly contagious disease characterized by fever and a rash

Reading Check

What are the locations of the two scenes on this page?

Vocabulary
baritone (bar´ ə tōn´)
n. the tonal range of a
male voice that is deeper
than a tenor, higher than
a bass

Suddenly, his voice CRACKS and DROPS a half-octave. And then another. His friends Wilbur Freeley and Ruthie look over, wondering what's wrong. Embarrassed, Edward just keeps SINGING, trying to follow along with the baritone part.

He pulls at his collar. Then pulls again, his face getting red. Starting to panic, he loosens his tie. He's starting to undo the collar button when it POPS off by itself. Two more buttons fly off. One hits a CHUBBY WOMAN in the neck.

ON HIS SHOES
As we watch, Edward's pant cuffs rise inch by inch—that's how fast he's growing.

> EDWARD (V.O.)[3]
> Truth is, no one quite knew what was wrong. Most times, a person grows up gradually. I found myself in a hurry.

INT. YOUNG EDWARD'S BEDROOM—DAY
Young Edward lies in bed, his limbs connected to various pulleys and levers to support his weight. He has a dozen encyclopedias around him, and another dozen on the floor.

> EDWARD (V.O.)
> My muscles couldn't keep up with my bones, and my bones couldn't keep up with my body's ambition. So I spent the better part of three years confined to my bed, with the World Book Encyclopedia being my only means of exploration. I had made it all the way to the "G's," hoping to find an answer to my gigantificationism, when I uncovered an article about the common goldfish.

INSERT: The encyclopedia article, complete with drawings.

> YOUNG EDWARD (reading)
> "Kept in a small bowl, the goldfish will remain small. With more space, the fish can grow double, triple, or quadruple its size."

Young Edward thinks this through.

> EDWARD (V.O.)
> It occurred to me then, that perhaps the reason for my growth was that I was intended for larger things. After all, a giant man can't have an ordinary-sized life.

EXT.[4] BASEBALL FIELD—DAY
The CRACK of a bat announces the game-winning home run. The Crowd CHEERS the swing, and especially the batter as he rounds the bases.

Literary Analysis
Influences on Contemporary Literature How does this scene show the influence of traditional literature? Explain.

Spiral Review
Draw Conclusions
Consider familiar parts of the word *gigantificationism* as well as the context in which the word is used here. What conclusion can you draw about the meaning of this humorous, made-up word?

---

3. V.O. abbreviation for "voice-over," a voice commenting or narrating off camera.
4. EXT. abbreviation for "exterior," a note to the crew that this scene will be filmed outdoors.

Although we've seen him briefly before, this is our first real exposure to **GROWN-UP EDWARD**, who we'll follow from roughly the ages of 18 to 30.

> **EDWARD (V.O.)**
> As soon as my bones had settled in their adult configuration, I set upon my plan to make a bigger place for myself in Ashton.

EXT. SCHOOL FIELDS—DAY

SINGLE SHOTS: Football hero Edward leads his team to victory. On the sidelines, a **PRETTY GIRL** admits the name of her secret love:

> **GIRL**
> Edward Bloom!

The other **GIRLS SQUEAL** in agreement. Don Price looks over, glowers.

EXT. NEIGHBORHOOD—DAY

SINGLE SHOT: A lawnmower **ROARS** along the grass. We **LOOK UP** to see who's pushing it, but it's not Edward. It's one of his teenage **EMPLOYEES.**

Edward is back at the truck, which is painted to read, "Bloom Landscaping." He has workers on every lawn.

He signs an autograph for an **ADMIRING CUB SCOUT.**

INT. BASKETBALL COURT—DAY

Edward takes an impossible shot at the buzzer from the other end of the court. Naturally, he makes it, winning the game.

As the crowd goes wild for Edward, Don Price is the only teammate who doesn't mob him.

EXT. TOWN—DAY

Edward carries a dog out of a burning house.

INT. SCIENCE FAIR—DAY

Edward wins a blue ribbon for his invention, a machine labelled "Perpetual Motion." He and the **JUDGE** pose for a photograph. **A FLASH.**

Don Price throws his lima bean plants in the trash.

INT. HIGH SCHOOL STAGE—DAY

A dashingly handsome Edward leads the **CAST** out for a curtain call. He's the star of the show. Off to the side, we see Don Price is the back end of a horse costume.

▼ **Critical Viewing**
What is the mood in this image from the movie? Explain. **[Analyze]**

Literary Analysis
Influences on Contemporary Literature
How do these adventures show the influence of older tall tales?

Reading Check

Who is the hero in the scenes on the field, on the basketball court, and at the science fair?

Edward soaks in his applause, smiling and gracious.

EXT. GRADUATION STAGE—DAY

Edward accepts his diploma. The **PRINCIPAL** hugs him tight.

> **EDWARD (V.O.)**
> I was the biggest thing Ashton had ever seen. Until
> one day, a stranger arrived.

EXT. FARM—DAY

As two **FARMERS** shake their heads, we **REVERSE** to show a massive hole punched through the side of a barn. It's roughly the shape of man, but no human could be that large.

EXT. SHEEP PEN—DAY

Two fat ewes look up, a shadow falling across them. They BLEAT in panic as **TWO OVERSIZED HANDS** reach in and scoop them up. Their protests continue as they're carried away, one under each arm. We still haven't seen the full stranger.

EXT. COURT HOUSE—DAY

A **MOB** of about 50 have gathered. Amid the crowd we see Don Price.

> **SHARECROPPER**
> He ate an entire cornfield!

> **LITTLE GIRL**
> He ate my dog!

> **TOWNSPERSON**
> If you ain't gonna stop him Mayor, we will!

> **MAYOR**
> I won't have mob violence in this town. Now, has
> someone tried talking to him?

> **SOME FARMER**
> You can't reason with 'im!

> **SHEPHERD**
> He's a monster!

Agreement from the crowd. And then . . .

> **A VOICE (O.S.[5])**
> I'll do it.

Everyone turns to see who said that. The crowd parts to reveal none other than Edward Bloom. Don Price glowers.

---

5. O.S. abbreviation for "off stage," an indication that the audience hears the speaker but does not see him or her.

Vocabulary

ewes (yo͞oz) *n.* female sheep

bleat (blēt) *v.* to make the vocal sound characteristic of a sheep

EDWARD

I'll talk to him. See if I can get him to move on.

MAYOR

Son, that creature could crush you without trying.

EDWARD

Trust me, he'll have to try.

EXT. HILL OUTSIDE ASHTON—DAY

Edward climbs up the last bit of the steep hillside, reaching the mouth of a cave. Outside, buzzards squabble over the remains of the giant's feast: broken barrels, bones picked clean.

In his most serious voice, Edward calls out:

EDWARD

Hello!

There's no answer.

EDWARD

My name is Edward Bloom! I want to talk to you!

From deep in a cave, a thunderous voice:

VOICE (O.S.)

GO AWAY!

The giant's voice has such force, it blows Edward's hair back.

EDWARD

I'm not going anywhere until you show yourself.

A beat, then we hear a **RUMBLE**, like a train coming. Edward braces himself, fists ready for a fight, if that's what it's going to take.

As the **RUMBLE** gets louder, the ground starts to shake. Even Edward starts to worry. Just how big is this guy?

EDWARD (V.O.)

Armed with the foreknowledge of my own death,
I knew the giant couldn't kill me. All the same, I
preferred to keep my bones unbroken.

Edward picks up a stone, ready to play David to Goliath.

Then suddenly, the giant bursts forth. Hunched over, he slams into a stunned Edward, knocking him halfway down the hill.

KARL THE GIANT is bigger than any man you've ever seen. Not just tall, but massive. He's completely feral, with a beard to his elbow and skin scratched and blistered. What remains of his clothes

> # I'll talk to him. See if I can get him to move on.

Reading Check

What problem is the town facing?

from Big Fish: Final Production Draft **1229**

► **Critical Viewing**
How well does the giant in this image from the movie match the description given in the script? Explain.
[Analyze]

are ragged and muddy. Karl leans over Edward, blocking the sun. Edward throws his rock, but it just bounces off. The giant didn't even notice it.

> **KARL**
> Why are you here?

Edward ponders the best response, settling on . . .

> **EDWARD**
> So you can eat me. The town decided to send a human sacrifice, and I volunteered.

Karl's eyes narrow, confused. Edward stands up.

> **EDWARD**
> My arms are a little stringy, but there's some good eating on my legs. I mean, I'd be tempted to eat them myself. (beat) So I guess, just, if you could get it over with quick. Because I'm not much for pain, really.

Edward closes his eyes, hands at his side, ready to be eaten. Karl just stares at him, not sure what to do.

After a beat, Edward opens his eyes a tiny bit, just to see what the giant is doing. Relieved to see he's not licking his chops—

> **EDWARD**
> Look, I can't go back. I'm a human sacrifice. If I go back, everyone will think I'm a coward. And I'd rather be dinner than a coward.

Karl sits down with a BOOM, dejected.

> **EDWARD**
> Here, start with my hand. It'll be an appetizer.

Reaching up, Edward shoves his hand into Karl's mouth. But the giant spits it back out.

> **KARL**
> I don't want to eat you. I don't want to eat anybody. It's just I get so hungry. I'm too big.

And that's the sad truth. Karl is less a monster than a freak—a giant man, but in the end, just a man.

Edward takes a seat beside him.

> **EDWARD**
> Did you ever think maybe you're not too big? Maybe this town's just too small. I mean, look at it.

Vocabulary
dejected (dē jek´ tid)
adj. in low spirits; depressed

Literary Analysis
Influences on Contemporary Literature
In this confrontation with Karl, which details show Edward's great courage?

Circling behind them, we look down at Ashton—a tiny town in a tiny valley.

> **EDWARD**
> Hardly two stories in the whole place. Now I've heard in real cities, they've got buildings so tall you can't even see the tops of 'em.

> **KARL**
> Really?

> **EDWARD**
> Wouldn't lie to you. And they've got all-you-can-eat buffets. You can eat a lot, can't you?

> **KARL**
> I can.

> **EDWARD**
> So why are you wasting your time in a small town? You're a big man. You should be in the big city.

Karl smiles, but then it fades. A certain sad suspicion—

> **KARL**
> You're just trying to get me to leave, aren't you? That's why they sent you here.

> **EDWARD**
> What's your name, Giant?

> **KARL**
> Karl.

> **EDWARD**
> Mine's Edward. And truthfully, I do want you to leave, Karl. But I want to leave with you.
> (closer)
> You think this town is too small for you, well, it's too small for a man of my ambition. I can't see staying here a day longer.

> **KARL**
> You don't like it?

> **EDWARD**
> I love every square inch of it. But I can feel the edges closing in on me. A man's life can only grow to a certain size in a place like this.

Literary Analysis
Influences on Contemporary Literature
What details of this dialogue show the influence of traditional literature on this 21st century work?

Reading Check
Why does Edward go to Karl the Giant?

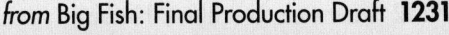

(beat)
So what do you say? Join me?

Karl thinks a moment. Then—

KARL
Okay.

EDWARD
Okay.

They shake on it.

EDWARD
Now first, we gotta get you ready for the city.

EXT. RIVER—DAY

IN A SINGLE SHOT, Karl cuts his hair with hedge clippers, while Edward cuts up a surplus army tent to make him a shirt.

EXT. MAIN STREET OF ASHTON—DAY

Spirits buoyed by the high school **MARCHING BAND,** all the good **CITIZENS** of Ashton are gathered to see off Edward and Karl.

There's a few tears amid the familiar faces.

MAYOR
(loudly, for the crowd)
Edward Bloom, first son of Ashton, it's with a heavy heart we see you go. But take with you this Key to the City, and know that any time you want to come back, all our doors are open to you.

Edward ducks a bit so the Mayor can put the key around his neck. The crowd **CHEERS.** And with that, Edward and Karl start walking, waving as they go.

Critical Thinking

1. Respond: Would you like to spend time with Edward? Why or why not?

2. (a) How does the information about goldfish influence Edward's later actions? **(b) Analyze:** In what way is Edward a larger-than-life hero?

3. (a) Who is Don Price? **(b) Make Inferences:** Why is Don Price angry when Edward volunteers to go talk to the giant, Karl?

Support your responses with evidence from the text.

Do heroes have responsibilities?
Do you think Edward's chief motivation for his actions is a sense of responsibility or something else? Explain.

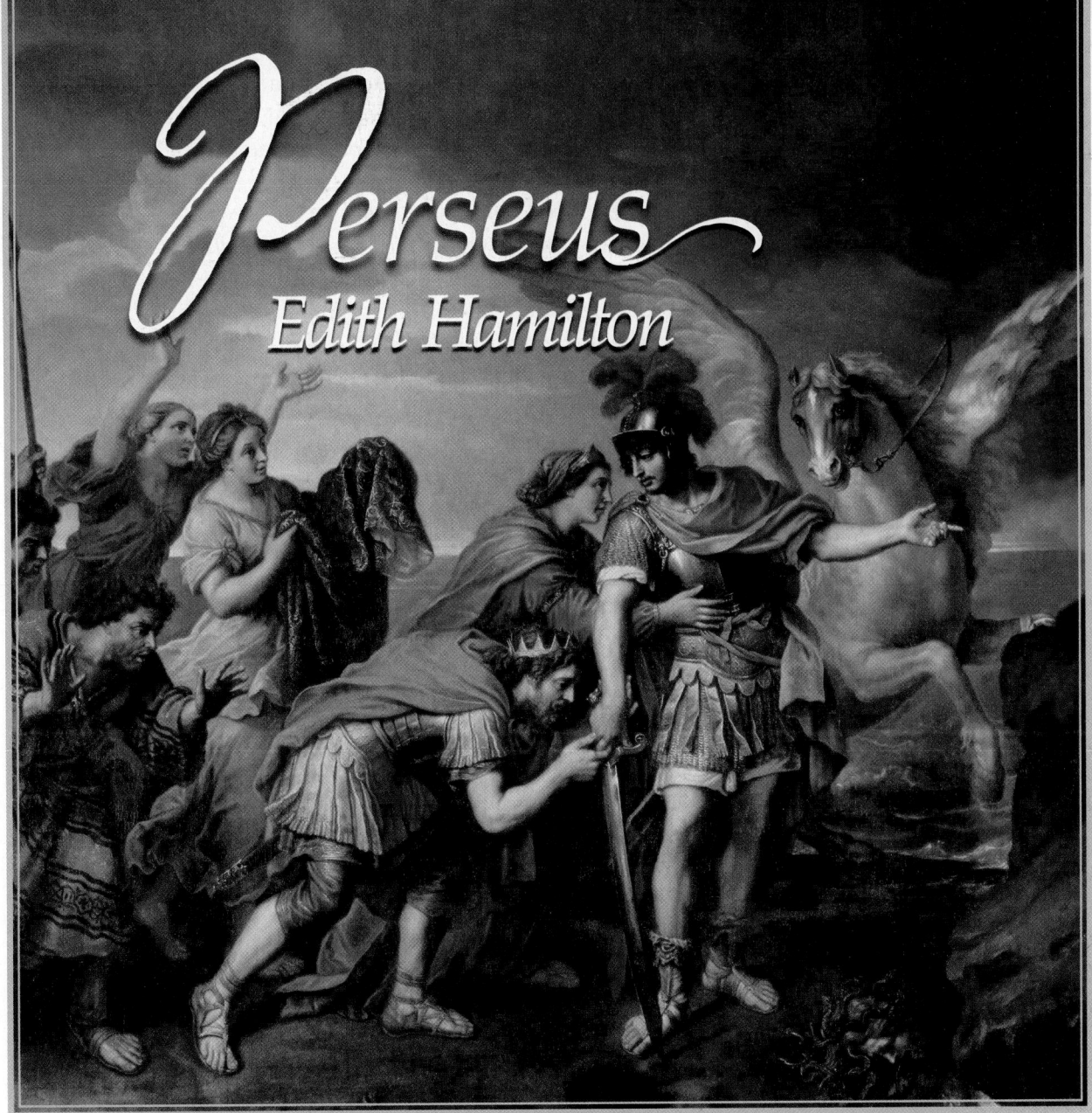

Perseus

Edith Hamilton

King Acrisius [a kris′ ē əs] of Argos had only one child, a daughter, Danaë [dan′ ā ē]. She was beautiful above all the other women of the land, but this was small comfort to the King for not having a son. He journeyed to Delphi to ask the god if there was any hope that some day he would be the father of a boy. The priestess told him no, and added what was far worse: that his daughter would have a son who would kill him.

The only sure way to escape that fate was for the King to have Danaë instantly put to death—taking no chances, but seeing to it himself. This Acrisius would not do. His fatherly affection was not strong, as events proved, but his fear of the gods was. They visited with terrible punishment those who shed the blood of kindred.

▲ **Critical Viewing**
The man with the sword is Perseus as an adult. Judging from this painting, how do you think others perceive him? **[Interpret]**

Acrisius did not dare slay his daughter. Instead, he had a house built all of bronze and sunk underground, but with part of the roof open to the sky so that light and air could come through. Here he shut her up and guarded her.

> So Danaë endured, the beautiful,
> To change the glad daylight for brass-bound walls,
> And in that chamber secret as the grave
> She lived a prisoner. Yet to her came
> Zeus in the golden rain.

As she sat there through the long days and hours with nothing to do, nothing to see except the clouds moving by overhead, a mysterious thing happened, a shower of gold fell from the sky and filled her chamber. How it was revealed to her that it was Zeus who had visited her in this shape we are not told, but she knew that the child she bore was his son.

For a time she kept his birth secret from her father, but it became increasingly difficult to do so in the narrow limits of that bronze house and finally one day the little boy—his name was Perseus—was discovered by his grandfather. "Your child!" Acrisius cried in great anger. "Who is his father?" But when Danaë answered proudly, "Zeus," he would not believe her. One thing only he was sure of, that the boy's life was a terrible danger to his own. He was afraid to kill him for the same reason that had kept him from killing her, fear of Zeus and the Furies who pursue such murderers. But if he could not kill them outright, he could put them in the way of tolerably certain death. He had a great chest made, and the two placed in it. Then it was taken out to sea and cast into the water.

In that strange boat Danaë sat with her little son. The daylight faded and she was alone on the sea.

> When in the carven chest the winds and waves
> Struck fear into her heart she put her arms,
> Not without tears, round Perseus tenderly
> She said, "O son, what grief is mine.
> But you sleep softly, little child,
> Sunk deep in rest within your cheerless home,
> Only a box, brass-bound. The night, this darkness visible,
> The scudding waves so near to your soft curls,
> The shrill voice of the wind, you do not heed,
> Nestled in your red cloak, fair little face."

Through the night in the tossing chest she listened to the waters that seemed always about to wash over them. The dawn came, but with no comfort to her for she could not see it. Neither could she see that around them there were islands rising high above the sea, many islands. All she knew was that presently a wave seemed to lift

Literary Analysis
Influences on Contemporary Literature
Which elements of Perseus' story so far suggest that he will be a mythic hero?

them and carry them swiftly on and then, retreating, leave them on something solid and motionless. They had made land; they were safe from the sea, but they were still in the chest with no way to get out.

Fate willed it—or perhaps Zeus, who up to now had done little for his love and his child—that they should be discovered by a good man, a fisherman named Dictys. He came upon the great box and broke it open and took the pitiful cargo home to his wife who was as kind as he. They had no children and they cared for Danaë and Perseus as if they were their own. The two lived there many years, Danaë content to let her son follow the fisherman's humble trade, out of harm's way. But in the end more trouble came. Polydectes [pol i dek′ tēz], the ruler of the little island, was the brother of Dictys, but he was a cruel and ruthless man. He seems to have taken no notice of the mother and son for a long time, but at last Danaë attracted his attention. She was still radiantly beautiful even though Perseus by now was full grown, and Polydectes fell in love with her. He wanted her, but he did not want her son, and he set himself to think out a way of getting rid of him.

▲ Critical Viewing
Which scene in the story does this art illustrate?
[Connect]

There were some fearsome monsters called Gorgons who lived on an island and were known far and wide because of their deadly power. Polydectes evidently talked to Perseus about them; he probably told him that he would rather have the head of one of them than anything else in the world. This seems practically certain from the plan he devised for killing Perseus. He announced that he was about to be married and he called his friends together for a celebration, including Perseus in the invitation. Each guest, as was customary, brought a gift for the bride-to-be, except Perseus alone. He had nothing he could give. He was young and proud and keenly mortified. He stood up before them all and did exactly what the King had hoped he would do, declared that he would give him a present better than any there. He would go off and kill Medusa and bring back her head as his gift. Nothing could have suited the King better. No one in his senses would have made such a proposal. Medusa was one of the Gorgons,

> And they are three, the Gorgons, each with wings
> And snaky hair, most horrible to mortals.
> Whom no man shall behold and draw again
> The breath of life,

Vocabulary
mortified (môrt′ ə fīd′) *adj.* extremely embarrassed

Reading Check
What does Perseus promise to give the king as a gift?

▼ Critical Viewing
Who is portrayed in this
art? Explain how you
know. [Connect]

for the reason that whoever looked at them were turned instantly into stone. It seemed that Perseus had been led by his angry pride into making an empty boast. No man unaided could kill Medusa.

But Perseus was saved from his folly. Two great gods were watching over him. He took ship as soon as he left the King's hall, not daring to see his mother first and tell her what he intended, and he sailed to Greece to learn where the three monsters were to be found. He went to Delphi, but all the priestess would say was to bid him seek the land where men eat not Demeter's golden grain, but only acorns. So he went to Dodona, in the land of oak trees, where the talking oaks were which declared Zeus's will and where the Selli lived who made their bread from acorns. They could tell him, however, no more than this, that he was under the protection of the gods. They did not know where the Gorgons lived.

When and how Hermes and Athena came to his help is not told in any story, but he must have known despair before they did so. At last, however, as he wandered on, he met a strange and beautiful person. We know what he looked like from many a poem, a young man with the first down upon his cheek when youth is loveliest, carrying, as no other young man ever did, a wand of gold with wings at one end, wearing a winged hat, too, and winged sandals. At sight of him hope must have entered Perseus' heart, for he would know that this could be none other than Hermes, the guide and the giver of good.

This radiant personage told him that before he attacked Medusa he must first be properly equipped, and that what he needed was in the possession of the nymphs of the North. To find the nymphs' abode, they must go to the Gray Women who alone could tell them the way. These women dwelt in a land where all was dim and shrouded in twilight. No ray of sun looked ever on that country, nor the moon by night. In that gray place the three women lived, all gray themselves and withered as in extreme old age. They were strange creatures, indeed, most of all because they had but one eye for the three, which it was their custom to take turns with, each removing it from her forehead when she had had it for a time and handing it to another.

All this Hermes told Perseus and then he unfolded his plan. He would himself guide Perseus to them. Once there Perseus must keep hidden until he saw one of them take the eye out of her forehead to pass it on. At that moment, when none of the three could see, he must rush forward and seize the eye and refuse to give it back until they told him how to reach the nymphs of the North.

He himself, Hermes said, would give him a sword to attack Medusa with—which could not be bent or broken by the Gorgon's scales, no matter how hard they were. This was a wonderful gift, no doubt, and yet of what use was a sword when the creature to be struck by it could turn the swordsman into stone before he was within striking distance? But another great deity was at hand to help. Pallas Athena stood beside Perseus. She took off the shield of polished bronze which covered her breast and held it out to him. "Look into this when you attack the Gorgon," she said. "You will be able to see her in it as in a mirror, and so avoid her deadly power."

Now, indeed, Perseus had good reason to hope. The journey to the twilight land was long, over the stream of Ocean and on to the very border of the black country where the Cimmerians dwell, but Hermes was his guide and he could not go astray. They found the Gray Women at last, looking in the wavering light like gray birds, for they had the shape of swans. But their heads were human and beneath their wings they had arms and hands. Perseus did just as Hermes had said, he held back until he saw one of them take the eye out of her forehead. Then before she could give it to her sister, he snatched it out of her hand. It was a moment or two before the three realized they had lost it. Each thought one of the others had it. But Perseus spoke out and told them he had taken it and that it would be theirs again only when they showed him how to find the nymphs of the North. They gave him full directions at once; they would have done anything to get their eye back. He returned it to them and went on the way they had pointed out to him. He was bound, although he did not know it, to the blessed country of the Hyperboreans [hī per bō´ rē anz], at the back of the North Wind, of which it is said: "Neither by ship nor yet by land shall one find the wondrous road to the gathering place of the Hyperboreans." But Perseus had Hermes with him, so that the road lay open to him, and he reached that host of happy people who are always banqueting and holding joyful revelry. They showed him great kindness: they welcomed him to their feast, and the maidens dancing to the sound of flute and lyre paused to get for him the

Literary Analysis

Influences on Contemporary Literature

Which details in this paragraph show Perseus' special status as a mythic hero?

Literary Analysis

Influences on Contemporary Literature

What heroic qualities does Perseus reveal in his encounter with the Gray Women?

Vocabulary

revelry (rev´ əl rē) *n.* noisy merrymaking

Reading Check

Who comes to Perseus' aid?

gifts he sought. These were three: winged sandals, a magic wallet which would always become the right size for whatever was to be carried in it, and, most important of all, a cap which made the wearer invisible. With these and Athena's shield and Hermes' sword Perseus was ready for the Gorgons. Hermes knew where they lived, and leaving the happy land the two flew back across Ocean and over the sea to the Terrible Sisters' island.

Literary Analysis
Influences on Contemporary Literature
What special knowledge helps Perseus kill Medusa?

By great good fortune they were all asleep when Perseus found them. In the mirror of the bright shield he could see them clearly, creatures with great wings and bodies covered with golden scales and hair a mass of twisting snakes. Athena was beside him now as well as Hermes. They told him which one was Medusa and that was important, for she alone of the three could be killed; the other two were immortal. Perseus on his winged sandals hovered above them, looking, however, only at the shield. Then he aimed a stroke down at Medusa's throat and Athena guided his hand. With a single sweep of his sword he cut through her neck and, his eyes still fixed on the shield with never a glance at her, he swooped low enough to seize the head. He dropped it into the wallet which closed around it. He had nothing to fear from it now. But the two other Gorgons had awakened and, horrified at the sight of their sister slain, tried to pursue the slayer. Perseus was safe; he had on the cap of darkness and they could not find him.

> So over the sea rich-haired Danaë's son,
> Perseus, on his winged sandals sped,
> Flying swift as thought.
> In a wallet of silver,
> A wonder to behold,
> He bore the head of the monster,
> While Hermes, the son of Maia,
> The messenger of Zeus,
> Kept ever at his side.

On his way back he came to Ethiopia and alighted there. By this time Hermes had left him. Perseus found, as Hercules was later to find, that a lovely maiden had been given up to be devoured by a horrible sea serpent. Her name was Andromeda and she was the daughter of a silly vain woman,

> That starred Ethiop queen who strove
> To set her beauty's praise above
> The sea-nymphs, and their power offended.

She had boasted that she was more beautiful than the daughters of Nereus, the Sea-god. An absolutely certain way in those days to draw down on one a wretched fate was to claim superiority

Literary Analysis
Influences on Contemporary Literature
Why do you think Hamilton included the verses within her story of Perseus?

in anything over any deity[1]; nevertheless people were perpetually doing so. In this case the punishment for the arrogance the gods detested fell not on Queen Cassiopeia [kas´ ē ō pē´ ə], Andromeda's mother, but on her daughter. The Ethiopians were being devoured in numbers by the serpent; and, learning from the oracle that they could be freed from the pest only if Andromeda were offered up to it, they forced Cepheus [sē fəs], her father, to consent. When Perseus arrived the maiden was on a rocky ledge by the sea, chained there to wait for the coming of the monster. Perseus saw her and on the instant loved her. He waited beside her until the great snake came for its prey; then he cut its head off just as he had the Gorgon's. The headless body dropped back into the water; Perseus took Andromeda to her parents and asked for her hand, which they gladly gave him.

With her he sailed back to the island and his mother, but in the house where he had lived so long he found no one. The fisherman Dictys' wife was long since dead, and the two others, Danaë and the man who had been like a father to Perseus, had had to fly and hide themselves from Polydectes, who was furious at Danaë's refusal to marry him. They had taken refuge in a temple, Perseus was told. He learned also that the King was holding a banquet in the palace and all the men who favored him were gathered there. Perseus instantly saw his opportunity. He went straight to the palace and entered the hall. As he stood at the entrance, Athena's shining buckler on his breast, the silver wallet at his side, he drew the eyes of every man there. Then before any could look away he held up the Gorgon's head; and at the sight one and all, the cruel King and his servile courtiers, were turned into stone. There they sat, a row of statues, each, as it were, frozen stiff in the attitude he had struck when he first saw Perseus.

When the islanders knew themselves freed from the tyrant it was easy for Perseus to find Danaë and Dictys. He made Dictys king of the island, but he and his mother decided that they would go back with Andromeda to Greece and try to be reconciled to Acrisius, to

---

1. **deity** (dē´ ə tē) *n.* a god.

▲ **Critical Viewing**
In what ways does this painting emphasize Perseus' physical strength and bravery? **[Interpret]**

Reading Check

Who does Perseus rescue from the sea serpent?

see if the many years that had passed since he had put them in the chest had not softened him so that he would be glad to receive his daughter and grandson. When they reached Argos, however, they found that Acrisius had been driven away from the city, and where he was no one could say. It happened that soon after their arrival Perseus heard that the King of Larissa, in the North, was holding a great athletic contest, and he journeyed there to take part. In the discus-throwing when his turn came and he hurled the heavy missile, it swerved and fell among the spectators. Acrisius was there on a visit to the King, and the discus struck him. The blow was fatal and he died at once.

So Apollo's oracle was again proved true. If Perseus felt any grief, at least he knew that his grandfather had done his best to kill him and his mother. With his death their troubles came to an end. Perseus and Andromeda lived happily ever after. Their son, Electryon, was the grandfather of Hercules.

Medusa's head was given to Athena, who bore it always upon the aegis, Zeus's shield, which she carried for him.

Critical Thinking

1. **Respond:** Which of Perseus' adventures would make the best action-adventure movie? Why?

2. **(a)** Why does Perseus set out to kill Medusa?
   (b) Make Inferences: What detail of Perseus' background might have led Athena and Hermes to help Perseus in his quest?

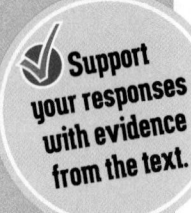

Support your responses with evidence from the text.

3. **(a) Analyze:** How much of Perseus' success resulted from the interference of the gods and how much resulted from his own prowess and courage? **(b) Hypothesize:** What might have happened to Perseus if he had not received help from the gods?

4. **(a) Interpret:** What lesson do you think this ancient myth taught its first audiences? **(b) Extend:** In what ways is this myth still relevant today?

Do heroes have responsibilities?
(a) How does Perseus' connection with the gods contribute to his stature as a hero? **(b)** How do his plans and deeds reflect his heroic responsibilities?

from FROM THE OLD AGE OF PERSEUS

Geoffrey O'Brien

2.

Sometimes I dream Medusa is still there
burrowing into that hillside
among the wreckage of sacred places.

She moves along the fringes of her territory
5   and the farmers run away. The hissing of serpents
is the sound of her thoughts.

And what thoughts does she have,
a creature with nobody to talk to,
10   who lives among shell and bone?

One look and the farmers are part of the landscape.
It is a kind of food for her,
that intercepted glance, the wetness in the eye,

the startled pupil quivering
15   toward a way out that no longer exists.
The moment of seeing is the moment of death.

They all try to pretend they don't see her—
jerk the head to show there was nothing to look at—
so the statuary exhibits a pattern of twisted necks,

20   the muscles distended in the pulling away,
or the arm raised as if by hiding his own face
he could abolish hers. There is a forest of them

and in the oldest the details are weathered out.
She is ancient and condemned to be ever more ancient.
25   Hideous sounds occasionally issue from her

and the farmers say she is praying
that someone might at length come close enough
to permit her to die.

3.

The gorgon, the gorgon. They are always going on
about the gorgon. I thought it would die down finally.
That was years ago. Yet only last week

Literary Analysis
Influences on Contemporary Literature
What details show the influence of mythic literature on this 21st century poem?

Vocabulary
burrowing (bʉr´ ō iŋ´)
v. digging
abolish (ə bäl´ ish) *v.* to do away with completely

gorgon (gôr´ gən) *n.* a mythic creature so horrible to look upon that the viewer is turned to stone

they dragged me to the main hall again, for one more
                    reenactment—
5   "Perseus, King of the Headhunters," with all new choruses—
and very beautifully phrased and performed it was.

The mask of the hero was truly flattering.
A dream: I was lost in a dream during it,
as I watched the story of the young man

who sliced off the monster's head
10 and used it to turn his enemies to stone,
until in the exact middle I remembered, Oh, it's me.

As for the gorgon head, that was of course
a different matter. They never get it remotely right.
My own efforts at description probably haven't helped much.

15 I never did see it full on, only in reflection
and (the first time only) at a tortuously *oblique* angle.
Afterwards I didn't see it at all, having by then

mastered the art of thrusting it toward my enemies
while steadfastly—with an air almost of indifference—
20 averting my gaze. I have to admit

that the most heroic episodes of my career
involved little more than a brief carefully calculated
restriction of my field of vision.

Literary Analysis
Influences on Contemporary Literature
What details from the story of Perseus' defeat of Medusa do readers need to know in order to understand this section of the poem?

Vocabulary
oblique (ō blēk´) *adj.*
indirect; not straight

Critical Thinking

1. **Respond:** Perseus asks "what thoughts does she [Medusa] have, / a creature with nobody to talk to . . . ."? How would you answer?

2. **(a)** When does this poem take place? **(b) Make Inferences:** How does Perseus feel about the reenactment of his encounter with the gorgon? **(c) Interpret:** What does Perseus mean when he says he remembered, in the middle of the play, "it's me"?

3. **Assess:** Does Perseus, as depicted in this poem, live up to the heroic figure you expect in mythic literature? Explain.

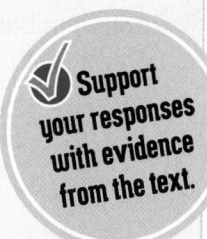

Support your responses with evidence from the text.

Do heroes have responsibilities?
In this poem, Perseus' heroic deeds happened long ago, and he is now in his old age. Does he still have responsibilities? Why or why not?

After You Read

Comparing Influences on Contemporary Literature

1. Think about how mythic and traditional literature have influenced these four works. Why do you think these influences are so powerful and enduring?

2. Make a chart like this one to analyze and compare the influence of mythic literature on elements of "Perseus" (a 20th century work) and "From the Old Age of Perseus" (a 21st century work).

	Element of mythic literature	Example from selection
Perseus		
From the Old Age of Perseus		

 **College Readiness** | Timed Writing

Write to Compare Influences

Write a brief essay in which you analyze and compare the influence of traditional literature on "Pecos Bill: The Cyclone" (a 20th century work) and *Big Fish: Final Production Draft* (a 21st century work). Support your ideas with evidence from both texts. (40 minutes)

 ### 5-Minute Planner

1. Read the prompt carefully and completely.

2. Jot down answers to these questions:
   - What elements of traditional literature can be found in each selection?
   - In what ways do the selections differ from traditional literature?
   - Why might each author have chosen to use elements of traditional literature in his or her writing?

3. List the main ideas you want to include in your essay. Then, number the ideas in the order you will discuss them.

4. Reread the prompt, and refer to your notes as you draft your essay.

Expository Text: Comparison-and-Contrast Essay

Defining the Form Whether you are considering foods, ideas, actions, or careers, comparative thinking is an underlying factor of almost every choice you make. A **comparison-and-contrast essay** is an analytical essay that explores the similarities and differences between or among two or more things. You may use elements of this type of writing in essays on historical figures and events, consumer reports, or essays on works of art, literature, or music.

Assignment Write a comparison-and-contrast essay of sufficient length about two events, ideas, or historical leaders. Include these elements:

- ✔ *a controlling idea or thesis,* including a purpose for the comparison
- ✔ accurate, factual details about each subject
- ✔ a balanced presentation of each subject using either subject-by-subject or point-by-point organization
- ✔ *rhetorical devices and transitions between paragraphs*
- ✔ error-free grammar, including a *variety of sentence structures* and lengths

To preview the criteria on which your comparison-and-contrast essay may be judged, see the rubric on page 1251.

 Writing Workshop: *Work in Progress*

Review the work you did on pages 1191 and 1207.

WRITE GUY
Jeff Anderson, M.Ed.

What Do You Notice?

Methods of Comparing and Contrasting

The following passage is from the 1911 Texas Almanac's "Automobiles in Texas." Read the passage several times.

Ten years ago an automobile was a curiosity in the leading cities of Texas. Five years ago the people in many counties had never seen what was then known as the horseless carriage. Today it is estimated that the number of automobiles in actual service in Texas will reach nearly 30,000 and that over $40,000,000 is invested in the machines.

Jot down what you notice about this passage and share your thoughts with a partner. Consider how you can use methods of comparing and contrasting in your essay.

Focus on the TEKS

Writing
(13)(A) Plan a first draft by determining appropriate topics through a range of strategies.
(15)(A)(i);(ii);(iii) Write an analytical essay of sufficient length that includes: a variety of sentence structures; rhetorical devices, and transitions between paragraphs; and a controlling idea or thesis.

Reading-Writing Connection

To get a feel for comparison-and-contrast writing, read "The News" by Neil Postman on page 478.

Prewriting/Planning Strategies

Explore categories. Plan a first draft by **determining appropriate topics** through the strategy of exploring categories. Working with a group, make a list of categories, such as famous athletes, famous artists, vacation spots, or favorite foods. Then, choose one category and discuss it in greater depth. Identify specific appropriate topics within the category that present clear similarities and differences.

Find related pairs. Explore topics in terms of clear opposites, clear similarities, or close relationships. Start with names of people, places, objects, or ideas. Note related subjects and relationships that interest you. Based on this strategy, choose one of these idea pairs to develop into a writing topic.

Specify your purpose. To identify a purpose for your essay, consider the following possibilities:

- To persuade—You may want readers to accept your opinion that one subject is preferable to another.

- To explain—You may want readers to understand something special about the subjects.

- To describe—You may want readers to understand the basic similarities and differences between your subjects.

Develop a controlling idea. Once you have specified your purpose, incorporate it into a controlling idea, or **thesis** statement. This statement will focus your essay and inform your reader of your main idea and purpose.

Use specific criteria. When you compare and contrast, you should examine specific criteria as a basis for your writing. Use a three-column chart like the one shown to identify criteria and the similarities and differences between subjects.

Criteria	Reading Literature	Listening to Music
Entertainment value	Very entertaining, requires you to use your imagination	Entertaining, helping change your mood or making you feel like dancing
Attention needed	Requires your full attention and concentration	Allows listener to do other things
Portability/ Necessary materials	Extremely portable, books can fit in most bags, light is always needed, batteries needed if flashlight is used	Portable if using a CD/Tape player or MP3 player, batteries or electricity may be needed

TEXAS
PHLitOnline
www.PHLitOnline.com
- Author video: Writing Process
- Author video: Rewards of Writing

Drafting Strategies

Structure your ideas in a sustained way. In preparation for comparing, look at your Criteria Chart. To organize your essay in this open-ended situation, use the details from your chart to fill in a Venn diagram, separating it into similarities and differences. Record similarities in the space where the circles overlap, and note differences in the outer sections of the circles.

Reading Literature
- requires concentration
- requires light
- silent

entertaining
portable, can be enjoyed anywhere

Listening to Music
- allows listener to do other things
- requires equipment and electricity
- audible

Choose an organization. Select an organization that suits your topic. Point-by-point and subject-by-subject plans are the most common types of organization used in comparison-and-contrast writing:

- **Point-by-point organization:** Move between your subjects as you discuss points of comparison. First, compare one element of both subjects, and then address another element of both subjects. Continue until you have covered all the features. This method allows you to sharpen your points of similarity and difference.

- **Subject-by-subject organization:** Compare your subjects as complete units. First, discuss all the features of one subject; then, discuss all the features of the other. This format allows you to focus on one subject at a time, but be sure to address the same features and devote equal time to each subject.

Support generalizations with specifics. Whatever your purpose, provide enough detail to fully develop your points. Support your comparison statements with facts, examples, and other evidence.

Use rhetorical devices to convey meaning. One such device is **parallelism**—the deliberate use of symmetry to show that two items are of equal importance. To employ this device, use similar wording or construction in several parts of a sentence or across sentences that express a comparison or a contrast between two things. Developing ideas in this way will help to maintain balance in your essay and to strengthen your comparisons.

Use words correctly. Use various resources—including printed and electronic dictionaries and glossaries—to confirm the **meanings** of unfamiliar words and phrases as you draft.

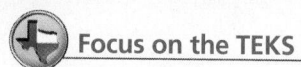 Focus on the TEKS

Writing
(13)(B) Structure ideas in a sustained way (e.g., using graphic organizers) and develop drafts in open-ended situations that include the rhetorical devices used to convey meaning.
(15)(A)(ii) Write an analytical essay that includes rhetorical devices.

Reading
(1)(E) Use a dictionary or glossary (printed or electronic) to confirm the meanings of words and phrases.

Point-by-Point Plan

Point 1
- Subject A
- Subject B
Point 2
- Subject A
- Subject B

Subject-by-Subject Plan

Subject A
- Point 1
- Point 2
Subject B
- Point 1
- Point 2

Coach Dean Smith with John Kilgo

On Word Choice

John Kilgo, my co-author, took notes of our conversations related to this book and put my ideas into written form. I have strong feelings about what I want my words to convey, which means we did extensive rewriting and revising. When we finally signed off on a chapter, it was always shorter, sharper in focus, and less repetitive than the original.

from *"The Carolina Way"*

A steady focus on taking care of the little things, attending diligently to the many details involved with building a team, helped us produce a mind-set that enhanced our ability to handle the big things. . . . Here are some of the so-called little things that we integrated into our program:

Punctuality: Players knew I arrived early for meetings and practices, and I expected everyone to be there and ready to go. . . . Tardiness is the ~~definition~~ height of arrogance. In effect, you're saying, "My time is more important than yours." Being on time is being considerate of others. . . .

Swearing: We discouraged it in our program. When a player cursed in practice, the entire team ran for him. . . . This is not an easy subject to talk about because it can sound ~~sanctimonious~~ pious. . . . However, I believe that anger can be expressed without using profanity.

Top priority: We checked on the class attendance of our players, as well as their grades and academic progress.

We used the phrase "produce a mind-set," because it's important for readers to know that our program had a strong philosophy concerning team-building techniques that we instilled in our players beginning with the first day they stepped on campus.

We first wrote that tardiness is the "definition" of arrogance, but changed it to "height of arrogance" on the rewrite. Using "height of arrogance" seemed to more strongly emphasize how unacceptable tardiness was in our program.

We first used "sanctimonious" in describing the difficulty in even discussing the subject of swearing, but changed it to "pious," which sounds less "preachy," or at least we thought so at the time. Also, words have a rhythm, and "pious" just seemed to fit better here.

Revising Strategies

Use transitions to make comparisons and contrasts clear. Using two different colors, mark your draft to distinguish between the two subjects you discuss. This color coding will reveal if you have developed a balanced presentation of both subjects. If necessary, you can expand or reduce coverage of one of your subjects to achieve balance. Next, evaluate the places where the two colors—and subjects—meet. Add **transitions between paragraphs** and sentences to make the shifts clear.

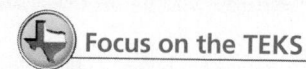 **Focus on the TEKS**

Writing
(13)(C) Revise drafts to improve subtlety of meaning after rethinking how well questions of purpose, audience, and genre have been addressed.
(13)(E) Revise final draft in response to feedback from teacher.
(15)(A)(i);(ii) Write an analytical essay that includes: a variety of sentence structures; and transitions between paragraphs.

Model: Revising for Clarity

Reading literature and listening to music are two of my favorite pastimes.

Reading literature is an excellent source of entertainment, taking me to worlds away from today. Listening to music is also fun. I can dance around the house while I do my chores.

Both
Reading and listening to music can be enjoyed most anywhere.
However,
It is better to have quiet when I try to read.

> The author uses the transitions "both" and "however" to move more fluidly from one idea to the next.

Revise to add specifics. To achieve your purpose and to help your readers understand the comparisons you make, add enough detail to explain the differences and similarities you see. Look for places where you can add information that strengthens your description or analysis.

Revise to be more precise. Rethink how well you have addressed the questions of purpose, audience, and genre and revise your draft to improve **subtlety of meaning,** making your essay sharper and more precise.

Vague: In contrast to literature, popular music forms a soundtrack for our lives.

Specific: In contrast to literature that we must read to enjoy, popular music, like the Top 40 tunes we hear on the radio, forms a soundtrack for our lives. We can enjoy it as we drive, shop, or even fall asleep at night.

Teacher Feedback

Submit your draft to your teacher. Ask him or her to circle any vague language. Then, discuss with your teacher specific details that would make your comparisions more vivid and convey your meaning more precisely. Revise your final draft in response to this feedback from your teacher.

Varying Sentence Structure and Length

A sequence of sentences of the same length and structural pattern can have a tedious effect on readers. You can make your paragraphs more interesting and readable by varying sentence length, introducing new sentence beginnings, and inverting subject-verb order.

Vary Sentence Length If you find an unbroken series of long sentences, look for an opportunity to include a short sentence. Since the short sentence will draw the reader's attention, use it to emphasize an important detail or idea. Be sure that it is a complete thought and not a fragment.

Original: Memories of long hours of practice, the brutal weather, and the aches and bruises of an endless season were erased by the single fact that we had won the championship.

Revised: Memories of long hours of practice, the brutal weather, and the aches and bruises of an endless season were erased by a single fact. We had won the championship.

Vary Sentence Beginnings If you have written a series of sentences beginning with a noun or pronoun, look for opportunities to start sentences with different parts of speech. Look at these techniques:

> **Adverb clause:** *Anywhere you go*, you will still find that most people care about others.
>
> **Prepositional phrase:** *After a long Saturday of work*, Sarah did not feel like going out.
>
> **Complement:** *Most interesting to me was* an electronic display of the battlefield. (complement of the verb *was*)
>
> **Direct object:** *Our report* I gave to the editor; my opinion I kept to myself. (object of the verb *gave*)

> **PH GRAMMAR HANDBOOK**
>
> Further instruction and practice are available in the *Prentice Hall Grammar Handbook*.

Vary Subject-Verb Order You can vary sentence beginnings by reversing the usual subject-verb order.

Original: The mystery guest is here at last.

Inverted: Here at last is the mystery guest.

Grammar in Your Writing

Examine the three longest paragraphs in your draft for the length and pattern of each sentence. Then, revise your draft to include a variety of sentence structures. Change sentence lengths, alter sentence beginnings, and invert subject-verb order to add interest to your writing.

Student Model: Morisa Jackson, Houston, TX

⊕ Focus on the TEKS

Writing
(13)(D) Edit drafts for grammar, mechanics, and spelling.
(13)(E) Publish written work for appropriate audiences.
(19) Spell correctly, including using various resources to check correct spellings.

Cars and Bikes

What would you most like to use as your major mode of transportation: cars or bikes? These days, it's certainly something to consider.

Because of the price of gasoline, people are trying to find new sources for conserving energy and money. Gas for cars has become expensive. As a result, bikes are now a little more popular because there is no gas requirement, just a little muscle power. Yes, using the bicycle as your primary mode of transportation will require more time to get to your destination, but it will save you money. There is also the benefit of the exercise you'll get along the way. The economic benefits of using a bicycle over a car are tremendous. Once purchased, the bike is paid off in full. There is no gas to buy, and there is usually minimal maintenance required. Every now and then, you may have to check your tires for sufficient air supply and maybe add some oil to your gear shaft for proper operation. With a bike, there is no need for a driver's license.

There are some disadvantages to using a bike for transportation. There is no AM/FM radio to listen to on your way to your destination. You also do not have the benefit of a cabin for your protection. Instead, bike riders must rely on protective gear: helmets and pads. Riding on the road with cars can be risky because not all drivers obey the rules of the road.

Cars are quite a bit different from bikes. Cars are much faster, of course, and can certainly get you to your destination quickly. However, cars require gasoline. Because of the price of gas these days, it can be hard for the average American to keep a full tank. Cars cost a significant amount more than bikes to purchase. The maintenance is usually very expensive, and with cars you are required to purchase insurance that protects others and yourself when there is an accident. The cost of cars can require that you make monthly payments. Some individuals pay for their automobiles for up to sixty months. Newer cars are usually pretty fancy, and they come with the latest technology. You can certainly listen to the radio, play your favorite CDs, or plug in your MP3 player. People may feel more protected because they are behind closed doors. Although you do not have to wear a helmet, it is advisable for you to wear a seat belt. Cars also come equipped with airbags for your protection. All drivers are required by law to have their cars registered in the state where they live, and they must have a valid driver's license.

Both modes of transportation have a number of similarities: they can get you to and from your destination, and they require you to go through a learning process and develop a certain level of expertise. The question is, which would you prefer: the car or the bicycle?

Morisa's essay will compare two modes of transportation: cars and bikes.

Morisa uses a subject-by-subject organization in order to discuss the benefits and disadvantages of cars and bikes.

In the conclusion, the writer summarizes her argument and presents her readers with a choice.

Editing and Proofreading

Edit your draft for errors in grammar and mechanics, such as capitalization and punctuation. Use a printed or electronic dictionary to check correct spellings.

Focus on Compound Sentences: Comparison-and-contrast essays often contain compound sentences—those with two independent clauses joined by a semicolon or a coordinating conjunction, such as *or*, *and*, or *but*. Check that you have correctly punctuated these sentences.

Conjunction:	I liked the chili, but it was spicy.
Semicolon:	I rushed out; I was late for the bus.

Spiral Review
Earlier in the unit, you learned about **commas and dashes** (p. 1190) and **colons, semicolons, and ellipsis points** (p. 1206). Make sure you have used these punctuation marks properly in your essay.

Publishing and Presenting

Consider ways to publish your written work for appropriate audiences:

Deliver an oral presentation. Read your essay aloud to your classmates. If possible, include props or visuals to enhance the reading.

Make a poster. Present your comparison-and-contrast findings visually in a poster. Use a graphic organizer, such as a Venn diagram, to show the similarities and differences of your subjects. If possible, add photographs and illustrations to show the distinctive elements of your subjects.

Reflecting on Your Writing

Writer's Journal Jot down your answer to this question:

How did writing about your topic help you understand it?

Rubric for Self-Assessment

Find evidence in your writing to address each category. Then, use the rating scale to grade your work.

Written Composition Criteria	Rating Scale
	not very — *very*
Focus and Coherence: How focused is your essay on your controlling idea, or thesis?	1 2 3 4
Organization: How well organized and balanced is your presentation of both subjects?	1 2 3 4
Development of Ideas: How well are your comparisons supported by accurate, factual details?	1 2 3 4
Conventions: To what extent have you used a variety of properly constructed sentence structures and lengths?	1 2 3 4
Voice: How well have you used rhetorical devices and transitions between paragraphs to effectively convey your ideas?	1 2 3 4

Applying the Big Question

Think About It

Think about what you have read in this unit, and what you know about heroes and their responsibilities from your other classes and from your own experience. Copy and complete the chart below to apply what you have learned about heroes and their responsibilities. One row has been completed for you.

Example	The heroic act	Motivation for the act	The hero's responsibilities	What I learned
From Literature	In "Odysseus' Revenge" in the Odyssey, Odysseus kills his wife's suitors	His sense of outrage and vengeance	To protect his wife, son, and the people of Ithaca	Heroes may have divided responsibilities and may give in to their emotions
From Literature				
From Science				
From Social Studies				
From Your Life				

Talk About It

Choose one of the examples from your chart to develop as a short **interpretive speech.** Begin by carefully analyzing your example. Then, interpret the hero's actions. Explain why the hero acted as he or she did and whether responsibilities did or should have motivated the hero. Present your speech to a small group of classmates. To effectively meet the needs of your audience, purpose, and occasion follow these steps:

- Use informal language in your presentation.
- Employ eye contact and purposeful gestures to communicate ideas effectively.
- When you have finished your presentation, invite comments and questions from your audience.

Write About It

At the beginning of Unit 6, you wrote a response to the Big Question. Now that you have completed the unit, see how your understanding has deepened. Write a new response, discussing how your initial ideas have either been changed or reinforced.

- ❏ Heroes have responsibilities.
- ❏ Heroes do not have responsibilities.
- ❏ My own response: _____.

Support your answer with one or more of the examples in your chart.

Challenge What issues does the Big Question still raise for you? How could you continue your exploration?

★ Connecting to Citizenship

Group Discussion With a small team, discuss how understanding heroes and their responsibilities can help you to become a thoughtful, active citizen. Use these questions to guide your discussion:

- What might prompt a hero to become involved in his or her community?
- How have you seen heroes serve your community?
- In what ways might the choices made by heroes influence choices made by other citizens?
- Does a community have obligations to its heroes? Explain.

As other team members speak, listen responsively by taking notes that highlight the speakers' most important ideas. Use your notes to critically reflect on the discussion.

🧭 **Focus on the TEKS**

Listening and Speaking
(24)(A) Listen responsively to a speaker by taking notes that highlight the speaker's ideas for critical reflection.

(25) Give presentations using informal language effectively to meet the needs of the audience, purpose, and occasion.

Big Question Vocabulary

Use some of these words as you complete the activities on these pages.

identify
obligation
honesty
responsibility
hero
character
morality
wisdom
choices
involvement
justice
serve
intentions
standard
imitate

This list includes academic vocabulary words, which are defined on pp. R1–R14.

Idioms, Jargon, and Technical Terms

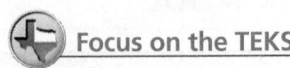 Focus on the TEKS

Listening and Speaking
(25) Give presentations using technical language effectively to meet the needs of audience, purpose, and occasion.
Reading
(1)(C) Produce analogies that describe a function of an object or its description.

An **idiom** is an expression that is characteristic of a language, region, community, or class of people. It cannot be understood literally. For example, *I'm all ears* does not mean "I am made of ears" but rather "I'm listening intently." *Throw in the towel* has nothing to do with fabric; instead, it refers to a boxer's act of forfeiting a match. Now, the phrase has reached past sports to become an idiom that is understood to mean "give up." Many dictionaries list idioms at the end of the entry for the main word in the idiom.

Many fields of study, work, and play have **technical terms.** These are words that may be familiar, but they have specialized meanings in the particular field. Examples from the field of computers include *software, hard drive, Internet,* and *USB port.* Technical terms help people who share knowledge of the field communicate more effectively. In some cases, analogies can be used to explain technical words and phrases to those outside of a field. For example, "A hard drive is to a computer as a brain is to a human."

Like technical terms, **jargon** is the specialized words and phrases used in a specific field. While it is frequently useful, jargon can sometimes appear to be scientific or technical but instead is vague and meaningless.

Jargon	Meaning
The vehicle's internal combustion engine became depleted of its distilled mixture of hydrocarbons.	The car ran out of gas.
This moisturizing cleansing bar is hot off the shelf.	This soap is brand new.
Stakeholders in our school environment need new text resources.	Students in our school need new textbooks.

Practice A Match the definition in the box with the underlined jargon in each sentence. Use context clues to figure out the meanings.

screen	clarinet	new sidewalks
car washer	black eye	

1. The baseball that hit me in the face gave me a <u>periorbital hematoma</u>.

2. On the large <u>monitor</u>, I can see more of the document at once.

3. The jazz musician put his <u>licorice stick</u> to his lips and played.

4. The <u>vehicle appearance operative</u> washed and dried the car.

5. <u>Public infrastructure upgrades</u> are needed so people can walk around more safely.

• Illustrated vocabulary words
• Interactive vocabulary games
• Vocabulary flashcards

Practice B Identify the idiom in each sentence and write a definition for each. If you are unsure of the meaning of the word or phrase, check your definition in a dictionary.

1. She let us down by not showing up for the game.

2. I am up to my ears in homework.

3. Marvin, please cool it and sit down over there.

4. It has been a long day, so I'm going to turn in.

5. Jurors must try to keep an open mind during the trial.

6. She should just nip this problem in the bud.

7. What are you driving at?

8. Your question has put the salesperson on the spot.

9. If you cheat in that game, I will blow the whistle on you.

10. I am going to whip this team into shape.

Activity Prepare four notecards like the one shown. Write each of the following words on a card:

      mouse   spare   snake   key

Look each word up in a dictionary and find both its common and a technical meaning. Write the common meaning, the profession or field the word comes from, and the technical meaning on the card. Finally, produce an analogy that describes the object and that would help a reader to better understand the item's function. An example is shown below.

Word: monitor

Common Definition: a person who observes or warns

Technical Definition: (technology) a video screen for displaying data, graphic images, and so on.

Analogy: A monitor is to a computer as a screen is to a television.

Teamwork

Work with a team to give a how-to presentation to your class using technical language. First, choose a specialized topic. You may, for example, explain how to use a resource in your school library. Use technical language effectively to meet the needs of your audience (your class), your occasion (a how-to presentation), and your purpose (to explain a skill). Plan to define terms that may be unfamiliar to your audience.

Delivering Technical Presentations

When you give a technical presentation, you explain specific and complex information to an audience. Effective technical presentations focus on the needs of the audience, purpose, and occasion.

Learn the Skills

Think of a technical topic that you know well. It might be related to a subject in school or a personal hobby. Use the language and communication skills on this page to plan a technical presentation on this topic and to deliver your presentation to a small team of your classmates. Then, use the listening strategies on the opposite page to evaluate your teammates' presentations.

Use Technical Language Effectively Include technical language that will be useful for your purpose and occasion, but avoid using technical language that seems unnecessarily complex. Ask yourself: Which technical words and concepts will my audience know? Which will I need to explain?

Use Strong Presentation Skills Employ the following strategies to meet the needs of your audience, purpose, and occasion and to communicate effectively:

- **Eye contact:** Use eye contact to connect with your audience.
- **Speaking rate:** Speak slowly when explaining new concepts. Pause to emphasize important ideas or for effect where useful.
- **Appropriate volume:** Project your voice so everyone in your audience can hear you.
- **Enunciation:** Pronounce words clearly, especially technical words that are unfamiliar to your audience.
- **Purposeful gestures:** Use gestures to illustrate ideas and emphasize important points. While you present, be aware of movements that may be distracting.
- **Conventions of language:** Follow conventions of language to ensure that your audience can understand you.

Focus on the TEKS

Listening and Speaking (24)(A) Listen responsively to a speaker by taking notes that summarize, synthesize, or highlight the speaker's ideas for critical reflection and by asking questions related to the content for clarification and elaboration.

(25) Give presentations using technical language effectively to meet the needs of audience, purpose, and occasion, employing eye contact, speaking rate (e.g., pauses for effect), volume, enunciation, purposeful gestures, and conventions of language to communicate ideas effectively.

Listen Responsively As you listen to a technical presentation, use these listening strategies:

- Summarize what you hear. Take notes that capture the speaker's main idea. Do not be afraid to ask for clarification or elaboration that will help you understand the content.

- Later, reflect critically on your notes. Highlight or underline key sentences, steps, or content.

- Synthesize the message with what you already know. Look for connections between your experience and the information the presentation shares.

Practice the Skills

Use what you've learned to complete the following activity.

ACTIVITY: Deliver Technical Presentations

Research a technical topic that interests you. Then, plan and deliver a technical presentation for your class. As you prepare, be sure that you have answered each of the following questions and addressed each of the items on the Technical Presentation Checklist.
- **What is the audience, purpose, and occasion of your presentation?**
- **How will you use technical language effectively to meet the needs of your audience, purpose, and occasion?**

As your classmates deliver their presentations, use the Technical Presentation Checklist to evaluate their effectiveness.

Technical Presentation Checklist

Technical Language
Rate the speaker's use of technical language on a scale of 1 (not successful) to 5 (very successful).
- The speaker's use of technical language meets the needs of the audience. _____
- The speaker's use of technical language meets the needs of the presentation's purpose. _____
- The speaker's use of technical language meets the needs of the occasion. _____

Speaking Strategies
Rate the speaker's use of each strategy on a scale of 1 (not successful) to 5 (very successful).

Eye contact _____   Volume _____   Purposeful gestures _____
Speaking rate _____   Enunciation _____   Conventions of language _____

Listener's Notes/Critical Reflection
- Summarize the presentation. Highlight at least two key ideas.
- Write one question you have that would provide clarification or elaboration of the topic.
- Synthesize the content of the presentation by linking it to something you already know.

Cumulative Review
Reading

Read this selection. Then answer the questions that follow it.

TEKS Spiral Review

Reading
(1)(B) Analyze textual context (within a sentence) to distinguish between the denotative and connotative meanings of words.

(2) Analyze, make inferences and draw conclusions about theme and genre in different cultural, historical, and contemporary contexts.

(2)(C) Relate the figurative language of a literary work to its historical and cultural setting.

(5)(A) Analyze non-linear plot development.

(5)(B) Analyze how authors develop complex yet believable characters in works of fiction through a range of literary devices.

Reading/Comprehension Skills
RC-9(A) Reflect on understanding to monitor comprehension.

Alamo Diary
from A Line in the Sand:
The Alamo Diary of Lucinda Lawrence
by Sherry Garland

Friday, March 11

1   I was in town around four in the afternoon when much excitement commenced over the arrival of Gen. Sam Houston. He is a giant in stature, standing a head higher than most others. His legs seemed too long for the horse he rode. Wearing a Cherokee coat, buckskin vest, and broad-brimmed hat with a feather in it, he would have looked more like a frontiersman than a commander in chief, were it not for his fine pistol and fancy sword.

2   Hardly had the general dismounted, when two Tejano[1] *rancheros* arrived from a *hacienda*[2] near San Antonio. The ranchers claimed they had witnessed the defeat of the Americans in the Alamo. Gen. Houston accused them of being spies for Santa Anna and had them promptly arrested. He told us not to spread the rumor for it had not been confirmed. When I got home Papa said not to let Mama know yet. No need to have her worry needlessly.

3   A deep, dark gloom has settled over the town. Even the restless men camped nearby are very quiet and speak only in whispers when they gather in little groups on street corners. Everyone is waiting for news of the Alamo. My common sense tells me all must be lost, but my heart still clings to hope.

4   Rumors are flying. If the Alamo has fallen, then four thousand Mexican soldiers are headed for Gonzales. Santa Anna has vowed to pillage and burn every Texian house and barn along the way. He will murder any Texian he finds and liberate the slaves. Such is the nature of Santa Anna. After destroying Gonzales, he will march onward to San Felipe and then to all the other colonies in Texas. We are counting heart and soul on Gen. Houston to stop Santa Anna at the Guadalupe River. But how can a few hundred poorly armed farmers defeat one of the largest and greatest armies in the world?

Saturday, March 12

5   The Roes left today. My heart ached with grief as we all hugged and said a tearful good-bye. Mittie gave me her red hair ribbon, and though I really

---

1. **Tejano** (tā hä′nō) a Texan of Hispanic descent (borrowed from Spanish).
2. **hacienda** (hä sē en′də) large estate.

do not care about ribbons anymore, I thanked her. We promised to keep in touch and reunite when this war is over.

6　　As there has been no bad news from Goliad, we believe that Uncle Henry is still alive and well. A few days ago, Captain Juan Seguin, who leads the Tejanos fighting for Texas, sent two of his scouts to find out about the Alamo. But they have been gone too long and it is feared they have been captured and put to death for being spies.

7　　Papa took apart his old pistol and oiled it. He has no more than five roughly made bullets and hardly enough powder. Such is the case with all the men. But they are determined to stop Santa Anna at the river. Even if the Alamo did fall, couldn't some of the men have escaped in the confusion?

Sunday, March 13

8　　My fingers tremble as I write, and I must pause to wipe the tears from my eyes. But I must record this most horrible of days; it is the least I can do to honor the dead. Late this evening our worst fears were confirmed. Willis is dead. Uncle Isaac is dead. Dear, sweet Galba, and those other boys, all dead. Nineteen-year-old Johnnie Kellog, whose young wife is due to deliver their first child any day; old Mr. Millsaps, whose blind widow has seven little children to raise all alone; Mr. Miller, owner of the general store—all are dead. Col. Travis will never write in his journal again; James Bowie will never twirl his knife; David Crockett will never play his fiddle, nor spin a yarn.

9　　Two of Houston's scouts met Susanna Dickinson and Angelina coming down the road today. Accompanying her was Joe, the black servant of William Travis, and Ben, a black servant of one of the Mexican generals, who carried a message from Santa Anna. Susanna's dress was sooty and grimy and her face was pale. She looked so old and tired, no longer a pretty young girl. Her blue eyes were full of the deepest pain one can imagine. She was taken straight away to Gen. Houston. A crowd gathered around while she told him what had happened.

10　　She said she and several Tejano women and children had hidden in the Alamo sacristy during the thirteen days of the siege. The final attack came before dawn on Sunday, March 6. Cannons bombarded the old mission walls and the smoke from guns made the air thick and hard to breathe. The screams of thousands of attacking Mexican soldiers and the groans of dying and wounded men surrounded her. She feared that even she and the children would be put to the sword. Her brave husband had but a few seconds to tell her good-bye before he returned to his post at a cannon, where he died.

11　　After the battle, when the survivors were discovered, they were taken to the governor's house and interrogated by Santa Anna himself. He was charmed by Angelina and wanted to adopt her, but Susanna refused. The general gave Susanna a silver peso and a blanket, and told her to inform Gen. Houston that death awaited all Texian traitors who defied him. He order the Texian bodies to be stacked into a large funeral pyre, layered with pieces of wood, and set ablaze. All the while Susanna told her story, Gen. Houston held her hand, and that old tough soldier wept like a little boy.

1 Read these lines from paragraph 1.

> He would have looked more like a frontiersman than a commander in chief, were it not for his fine pistol and fancy sword.

If the story were set in modern times, the word *frontiersman* could be replaced with which of the following words?

A governor
B civilian
C military man
D wealthy person

2 Which is a synonym for the word *restless* as it is used in paragraph 3?

F silent
G awake
H broken
J anxious

3 Which comment in the entry for March 12 indicates that the narrator has changed?

A "The Roes left today."
B "I really do not care about ribbons anymore."
C "I thanked her."
D "We promised to keep in touch and reunite when this war is over."

4 The author most likely relates the story of the battle through Susanna's account to —

F make the reader feel sympathy for Susanna
G give an objective account of the events of the battle
H organize the story by telling events in the order in which they happened in real life
J show what was occurring at the Alamo as the narrator's town was waiting for news

5 The author most likely mentions Santa Anna's attitude toward Angelina to —

A support other descriptions of the general's character
B show that the cruel general has a more human side
C demonstrate that Angelina is charming
D reflect Santa Anna's reputation

6 By the end of the selection, Gen. Houston becomes —

F suspicious and concerned
G saddened and sorrowful
H stronger but otherwise unchanged
J less like a general and more like a frontiersman

7 Which best states the theme of the diary entry on Sunday, March 13?

A People can honor the fallen by remembering their deeds.
B People show the most bravery during battles.
C It is better not to know the difficult details of a tragedy.
D The attack on the Alamo took place on March 6.

DIRECTIONS

Answer the following question on a separate sheet of paper.

8 How does the author's use of hope and grief enhance the story? Support your answer with details from the selection.

Revising and Editing

DIRECTIONS

Read the following passage and mark your answers on your answer document. Remember that you are NOT permitted to use dictionaries or other reference material on this section of the test.

Jacob has written about a memorable trip he took with his father. He has asked you to review his paper. As you read it, think about the corrections and improvements he might make. When you finish, answer the multiple-choice questions that follow.

TEKS Spiral Review

Conventions
(17)(A)(i) Use and understand the function of the following parts of speech in the context of reading, writing, and speaking: more complex active and passive tenses and verbals (gerunds, participles).

(17)(C) Use a variety of correctly structured sentences (e.g., compound, complex).

(18)(B)(ii) Use correct punctuation marks including: comma placement in nonrestrictive phrases, clauses, and contrasting expressions.

Seeing the Stars Along I-10

(1) My father and I have one thing in common: We love to watch the night sky. (2) When I was very young, my father used to wake me up in the middle of the night if there was a meteor shower or a comet passing by. (3) He always drove us far enough to leave the city lights behind so we could see the sky clearly. (4) I looked through the small telescope my father had given me to try and see more detail in the faraway shapes. (5) One summer, though, we got an even better view of the night sky by taking a road trip down highway I-10.

(6) Along I-10 are many astronomical observatories where both scientists and visitors can view the stars and planets. (7) Our first stop was the McDonald Observatory in the Davis Mountains. (8) During the day, we toured the research telescopes and met some of the astronomers worked there. (9) Then, at night, we observed the moon, stars, and even other planets. (10) They looked amazingly clear and close through the massive telescopes.

(11) Then we rode through southern New Mexico and into Arizona to visit one more observatory: the Kitt Peak National Observatory in Tucson. (12) At Kitt Peak which has the largest collection of optical telescopes in the world, we toured a few of the 24 optical telescopes as well as two radio telescopes designed to "see" even farther into outer space. (13) That night, we stood in a domed observatory and watched as the roof rolled back to reveal a stunning night sky. (14) With the help of the astronomers, we saw star clusters and galaxies we'd never seen before. (15) We were lucky to have a cool, clear night without a single cloud hide the stars.

(16) I still use my own small telescope, but I'll always remember the road trip. (17) I saw the stars "up close."

1 What change, if any, should be made in sentence 8?

   A Delete the comma after *day*

   B Insert a comma after *astronomers*

   C Change *worked* to **working**

   D Make no change

2 What change should be made in sentence 12?

   F Insert a comma after *Peak*

   G Change *which* to **that**

   H Delete the comma after *world*

   J Change *designed* to **design**

3 Which change should be made to sentence 15?

   A Change *were* to **are**

   B Remove the comma after *cool*

   C Add a comma after *clear*

   D Change *hide* to **hiding**

4 What is the BEST way to combine sentences 16 and 17?

   F I still use my own small telescope. I'll always remember the road trip. I saw the stars "up close."

   G I still use my own small telescope but I'll always remember the road trip and I saw the stars "up close."

   H I still use my own small telescope, but I'll always remember the road trip when I saw the stars "up close."

   J I still use my own small telescope. I'll always remember the road trip, but I saw the stars "up close."

Written Composition

Use blank pages to prewrite. Then write your composition on one or two lined pages.

Writing
(14) Write literary texts to express ideas and feelings about real or imagined people, events, and ideas.

> Write a composition about a time you solved a problem.

The information in the box below will help you remember what you should think about when you write your composition.

REMEMBER—YOU SHOULD

❑ write about the assigned topic

❑ make your writing thoughtful and interesting

❑ make sure that each sentence you write contributes to your composition as a whole

❑ make sure that your ideas are clear and easy for the reader to follow

❑ write about your ideas in depth so that the reader is able to develop a good understanding of what you are saying

❑ proofread your writing to correct errors in spelling, capitalization, punctuation, grammar, and sentence structure

---

Do *heroes* have responsibilities?

Focus on the TEKS

Reading
(12)(D) Evaluate changes in tone within the same medium for specific audiences and purposes.

Media Literacy

The tone of messages within the same medium—such as television, radio, or the Internet—may vary depending on each message's audience and purpose. For example, a radio message about a national figure delivered to an audience of citizens may have a serious tone that makes the subject seem heroic. However, a radio message for an audience of teens about an upcoming concert may have a more lighthearted tone that makes the event seem fun. Use the graphic organizer below to evaluate changes in tone within the same medium.

www.PHLitOnline.com

Viewing and Listening Guide: Tone	
What to look for	**What you should think about**
Language choices	• How do the words I hear contribute to the tone? • Is this tone appropriate for the audience? Explain. • Does this tone support the message's purpose? Explain.
Visual images	• What impression would the images give to most viewers? • How do the images support the tone?

Independent Reading

The Carolina Way
Dean Smith and Gerald Bell with John Kilgo
Penguin, 2004
Coach Dean Smith shares his strategies for leadership, teamwork, and winning with integrity.

Joan of Arc
Mary Gordon
Viking Penguin, 2000
This biography tells the remarkable story of Joan's rise as a knight and leader and how she lost her life, all before she was 20.

Nelson Mandela
Laaren Brown and Lenny Hort
DK Publishing, 2006
This biography describes Nelson Mandela's struggles against an unjust government.

The Odyssey
Homer, translated by Robert Fagles   Penguin, 1996
Set sail with Odysseus as he encounters man-eating monsters and vengeful gods. Read this epic tale to decide for yourself if Odysseus is the ultimate hero.

Resources

Glossary

Big Question vocabulary appears in **blue type**. High-utility Academic vocabulary is <u>underlined.</u>

A

abash (uh BASH) *v.* embarrass

abdicated (AB duh kayt uhd) *v.* gave up formally

abolish (uh BAWL ish) *v.* to do away with completely

absurdity (ab SUR duh tee) *n.* something ridiculous or nonsensical

accentuated (ak SEHN chu ayt uhd) *v.* emphasized; heightened the effect of

accept (ak SEHPT) *v.* take something that is given

accumulated (uh KYOO myuh layt uhd) *v.* piled up, collected, or gathered together, especially over a period of time

acquiesced (ak wee EHST) *v.* agreed or consented quietly without protest, but without enthusiasm

adversary (AD vuhr sehr ee) *n.* person who opposes or fights against another

afflicted (uh FLIHKT ihd) *v.* suffering or sickened

allotment (uh LOT muhnt) *n.* share; portion

aloofness (uh LOOF nehs) *n.* emotional distance

ambiguities (am buh GYOO uh teez) *n.* statements or events whose meanings are unclear

<u>ambiguous</u> (am BIHG yoo uhs) *adj.* having more than one meaning

amicably (AM uh kuh blee) *adv.* in a friendly manner

amid (uh MIHD) *prep.* among; in the middle of

analysis (uh NAL uh sis) *n.* careful examination by studying something's elements or parts

anguish (ANG gwihsh) *n.* great pain or suffering

anonymous (uh NON uh muhs) *adj.* without a known or acknowledged name

antagonize (an TAG uh nyz) *v.* make an enemy of

apex (AY pehks) *n.* highest point; peak

<u>appreciate</u> (uh PREE shee ayt) *v.* be aware of the value of

apprenticed (uh PRENT ehst) *v.* assigned to work a specified length of time in a craft or trade in return for instruction

archaic (ahr KAY ihk) *adj.* from an earlier time; ancient

ardor (AHR duhr) *n.* passion; enthusiasm

arduous (AHR joo uhs) *adj.* difficult; laborious

<u>argument</u> (AHR gyuh muhnt) *n.* discussion in which there is disagreement

<u>articulate</u> (ahr TIHK yuh layt) *v.* express an idea clearly

<u>articulate</u> (ahr TIHK yuh liht) *adj.* able to express oneself clearly

assiduous (uh SIHJ oo uhs) *adj.* done with constant and careful attention; diligent

assimilated (uh SIHM uh layt uhd) *v.* took in or absorbed

assimilated (uh SIHM uh layt uhd) *adj.* having been taken in fully

assuage (uh SWAYJ) *v.* calm; pacify

<u>assumption</u> (uh SUHMP shuhn) *n.* something taken for granted

atonement (uh TOHN muhnt) *n.* act of making up for a wrongdoing or an injury

attributes (AT rihb yoots) *n.* characteristics or qualities of a person or thing

augmenting (awg MEHNT ihng) *v.* increasing; enlarging

authentic (aw THEHN tihk) *adj.* genuine; true

aware (uh WAIR) *adj.* knowing something because you have experienced it or have been informed of it

awestruck (AW struhk) *adj.* filled with wonder

awry (uh RY) *adj.* not straight or in the right direction

azure (AZH uhr) *adj.* blue

B

background (BAK grownd) *n.* facts that cause or explain something

bafflement (BAF uhl muhnt) *n.* puzzlement; bewilderment

balmy (BAHL mee) *adj.* having the qualities of balm; soothing, mild, pleasant

baritone (BAR i tohn) *n.* the tonal range of a male voice that is deeper than a tenor, higher than a bass

barren (BAR uhn) *adj.* empty; having little or no vegetation

battle (BAT uhl) *n.* a fight between two opposing forces

battle (BAT uhl) *v.* fight or struggle

beguiling (bih GY lihng) *v.* tricking; charming

belief (bih LEEF) *n.* something accepted to be true

bemusing (bih MYOOZ ihng) *v.* stupefying; muddling

benevolently (buh NEHV uh luhnt lee) *adv.* in a well-meaning way

bereft (bih REHFT) *adj.* deprived

beveled (BE vuhld) *adj.* sloped, an inclined surface

bias (BY uhs) *n.* mental leaning or inclination; partiality

bilingual (by LIHNG gwuhl) *adj.* using two languages

bleat (bleet) *v.* to make the vocal sound characteristic of a sheep

blight (blyt) *n.* something that destroys or prevents growth

bulging (BUHLJ ihng) *adj.* swelling

burrowing (BER roh ing) *v.* digging

C

candor (KAN duhr) *n.* sharp honesty or frankness in expressing oneself

cascade (kas KAYD) *n.* small steep waterfall; anything suggesting such a waterfall

censure (SEHN shuhr) *n.* strong disapproval

character (KAR ihk tuhr) *n.* qualities that make a person unique

chicken pox (CHI ken pox) *n.* a highly-contagious disease, mainly of children, that is characterized by fever and a rash

choices (choys uhz) *n.* variety of things someone can choose from

circumstance (SUR kuhm stans) *n.* situation; event

clarify (KLAR uh fy) *v.* make something more clear or understandable

clasps (klasps) *v.* grips

collective (kuh LEHK tihv) *adj.* put together as a group; gathered into a whole

communication (kuh myoo nuh KAY shuhn) *n.* sharing information

compensation (kom puhn SAY shuhn) *n.* anything that makes up for a loss, damage, or debt

compete (kuhm PEET) *v.* try to win against an opponent

competition (kom puh TIHSH uhn) *n.* rivalry; act of competing

comprehend (kom prih HEHND) *v.* understand

comprehension (kom prih HEHN shuhn) *n.* act of understanding something

conceded (kuhn SEED uhd) *v.* admitted as true or valid; acknowledged

concept (KON sehpt) *n.* idea; notion

concessions (kuhn SEHSH uhnz) *n.* things given or granted as privileges

condolences (kuhn DOH luhns uhz) *n.* expressions of sympathy with another in grief

confer (kuhn FUR) *v.* give; bestow upon

confines (KON fynz) *n.* boundaries or bounded region; border; limit

conformity (kuhn FAWR muh tee) *n.* being in agreement with customs or rules

connection (kuh NEHK shuhn) *n.* joining of two or more things or ideas

conspicuous (kuhn SPIHK yoo uhs) *adj.* attracting attention by being unexpected, unusual, outstanding, or egregious; striking

contempt (kuhn TEHMPT) *n.* disdain or scorn

context (KON tehkst) *n.* parts of a sentence immediately next to or surrounding a word that determine its exact meaning

controversy (KON truh vur see) *n.* discussion of a question in which opposing opinions clash; debate; argument

convince (kuhn VIHNS) *v.* persuade by argument or evidence

cooperate (koh OP uh rayt) *v.* work together to achieve something

countenance (KOWN tuh nuhns) *n.* face

covenant (KUHV uh nuhnt) *n.* agreement or contract, especially a sacred one

credible (KREHD uh buhl) *adj.* believable

creed (kreed) *n.* statement of belief

culture (KUHL chuhr) *n.* ideas, customs, skills and arts of a group of people in a specific time in history

cunning (KUHN ihng) *adj.* skilled in deception

curtailed (kur TAYLD) *v.* cut short; reduced

D

daunting (DAWNT ihng) *adj.* intimidating

defaulted (dih FAWLT uhd) *v.* failed to do something or be somewhere when required or expected; failed to make payment when due

defend (dih FEHND) *v.* support a position with evidence or justifications

deferred (dih FURD) *adj.* put off until a future time

defiance (dih FY uhns) *n.* open, bold resistance to authority

defrauded (dih FRAWD uhd) *v.* cheated

degenerate (dih JEHN uh rayt) *v.* grow worse

dejected (dee JEKT id) *adj.* in low spirits; depressed

dejection (dih JEHK shuhn) *n.* lowness of spirits; depression

deleterious (dehl uh TIHR ee uhs) *adj.* harmful to health or well-being

demonstrative (dih MON struh tihv) *adj.* showing feelings openly

demure (dih MYUR) *adj.* modest

depravity (dih PRAV uh tee) *n.* crookedness; corruption

depreciate (dih PREE shee ayt) *v.* reduce in value

derisive (dih RY sihv) *adj.* showing contempt or ridicule; mocking

desolate (DEHS uh liht) *adj.* forlorn; wretched

despotic (dehs POT ihk) *adj.* like an absolute ruler or tyrant

desultory (DEHS uhl tawr ee) *adj.* aimless; random

determination (dih tur muh NAY shuhn) *n.* firm intention

determine (dih TUR muhn) *v.* cause something to happen in a certain way; control

differences (DIHF uhr uhns uhz) *n.* qualities that make things not the same; ways in which things are not the same

differentiate (dihf uh REHN shee ayt) *v.* see or express what makes two or more things different from each other

diffused (dih FYOOZD) *v.* spread out

dilapidated (duh LAP uh day tihd) *adj.* broken down

diminution (dihm uh NOO shuhn) *n.* lessening

discerning (duh ZUR nihng) *adj.* having good judgment or understanding

discipline (DIHS uh plihn) *n.* training that develops self-control, character, or orderliness and efficiency

disclosed (dihs KLOHZD) *v.* revealed; made known

disconsolately (dihs KON suh liht lee) *adv.* very unhappily

discreet (dihs KREET) *adj.* careful about what one says or does; prudent; keeping silent or preserving confidences when necessary

discreetly (dihs KREET lee) *adv.* without drawing attention

discriminate (dihs KRIHM uh nayt) *v.* see the differences between things; to act against someone because of prejudice

discuss (dihs KUHS) *v.* consider a topic in writing or speaking

disgrace (dihs GRAYS) *n.* loss of respect, honor, or esteem; shame

disheveled (dih SHEHV uhld) *adj.* untidy

dishevelment (dih SHEHV uhl muhnt) *n.* disorder; messiness

dismal (DIHZ muhl) *adj.* causing gloom or misery

dispatched (dihs PACHT) *v.* finished quickly

disperse (dihs PURS) *v.* break up and scatter in all directions; spread about; distribute widely

disputed (dihs PYOOT uhd) *adj.* contested; argued about

dissemble (dih SEHM buhl) *v.* conceal under a false appearance; disguise

distinguished (dihs TIHNG gwihsht) *adj.* having an air of distinction; celebrated for excellence; eminent; famous

distort (dihs TAWRT) *v.* twist out of shape

distraught (dihs TRAWT) *adj.* very troubled or confused

diverged (duh VURJD) *v.* branched out in different directions

droll (drohl) *adj.* funny in an odd or understated way

duration (du RAY shuhn) *n.* the time that a thing continues or lasts

E

elation (ih LAY shuhn) *n.* feeling of exultant joy; pride; high spirits

eloquence (EHL uh kwuhns) *n.* speech or writing that is graceful and persuasive

embellish (ehm BEHL ihsh) *v.* decorate or improve by adding details; ornament; adorn

emerge (ih MURJ) *v.* come into existence; become visible or known

emitting (ih MIHT ihng) *v.* sending out

empathy (EHM puh thee) *n.* ability to understand and share someone else's feelings

emulate (EHM yuh layt) *v.* imitate (a person or thing admired)

enamored (ehn AM uhrd) *v.* filled with love and desire; charmed

encroaching (ehn KROHCH ihng) *adj.* intruding in a sneaky way

endeavor (ehn DEHV uhr) *n.* an earnest attempt or effort

endeavored (ehn DEHV uhrd) *v.* made an earnest attempt to achieve or succeed; tried

endurance (ehn DUR uhns) *n.* ability to withstand hardship over time

enigma (ih NIHG muh) *n.* mystery

enjoined (ehn JOYND) *v.* ordered

entailed (ehn TAYLD) *v.* caused or required as a necessary consequence; involved; necessitated

enthralled (ehn THRAWLD) *v.* held as in a spell; captivated

enumerated (ih NOO muh rayt ihd) *v.* named one by one; specified, as in a list

equity (EHK wuh tee) *n.* quality of being fair; fairness; justice

esteem (ehs TEEM) *n.* favorable opinion; high regard; respect

evanescent (ehv uh NEHS uhnt) *adj.* temporary; tending to disappear

evidence (EHV uh duhns) *n.* proof

ewes (yooz) *n.* female sheep

exchange (ehks CHAYNJ) *n.* act of trading something

exchange (ehks CHAYNJ) *v.* trade

exile (EHG zyl) *v.* banish

explicit (ehk SPLIHS iht) *adj.* clearly stated

extrapolating (ehk STRAP uh layt ihng) *v.* arriving at a conclusion by inferring from known facts

F

fact (fakt) *n.* a thing that has actually happened or that is true

faltered (FAWL tuhrd) *v.* acted hesitantly; showed uncertainty; wavered; flinched

feasible (FEE zuh buhl) *adj.* capable of being done or carried out; practicable; possible

feeling (FEE lihng) *n.* emotion that a person is aware of

feisty (FYS tee) *adj.* full of spirit; energetic

fertile (FUR tuhl) *adj.* rich in nutrients that promote growth

fester (FEHS tuhr) *v.* become infected; form pus

feud (fyood) *n.* bitter, protracted, and violent quarrel, especially between clans or families

fickle (FIHK uhl) *adj.* changeable

forebears (FAWR bairz) *n.* ancestors

forgo (fawr GOH) *v.* do without; abstain from; give up

formality (fawr MAL uh tee) *n.* attention to established rules or customs

formidable (FAWR muh duh buhl) *adj.* awe-inspiring

fortitude (FAWR tuh tood) *n.* the strength to bear misfortune and pain calmly and patiently

fray (fray) *n.* noisy fight

furtive (FUR tihv) *adj.* sneaky; hidden

futile (FYOO tuhl) *adj.* useless; hopeless

G

gallant (GAL uhnt) *adj.* brave and noble

gorgon (GOYR gawn) *n.* one of three mythic creatures so horrible to look upon that the viewer is turned to stone

grievance (GREE vuhns) *n.* something that is thought to be unjust and a reason to feel resentment; complaint

grotesque (groh TEHSK) *adj.* having a strange, bizarre design; shocking or offensive

H

hallowed (HAL ohd) *adj.* sacred

haughty (HAW tee) *adj.* arrogant

hero (HIHR oh) *n.* someone who is admired for brave or noble actions

honesty (ON uh stee) *n.* quality of being truthful

humble (HUHM buhl) *adj.* modest; having humility

humbly (HUHM buh lee) *adv.* in a manner that is not proud or arrogant; modestly

I

identify (y DEHN tuh fy) *v.* say who someone or something is

ignorance (IHG nuhr uhns) *n.* lack of knowledge or education

illuminate (ih LOO muh nayt) *v.* light up; make something clearer

imitate (IHM uh tayt) *v.* copy the actions of another

immaculate (ih MAK yuh liht) *adj.* perfectly correct; without a flaw, fault or error

imminent (IHM uh nuhnt) *adj.* likely to happen soon

impassive (ihm PAS ihv) *adj.* showing no emotion

impenetrable (ihm PEHN uh truh buhl) *adj.* that cannot be passed through; that cannot be solved or understood; unfathomable

implications (ihm pluh KAY shuhnz) *n.* indirect results

imposition (ihm puh ZIHSH uhn) *n.* introduction of something such as a rule, tax, or punishment

incessantly (ihn SEHS uhnt lee) *adv.* continuing in a way that seems endless; continually; unceasingly

incognito (ihn kog NEE toh) *adj.* with true identity unrevealed or disguised; under an assumed name

incredulity (ihn kruh DOO luh tee) *n.* unwillingness or inability to believe

individuality (ihn duh vihj oo AL uh tee) *n.* state of being one of a kind

indolently (IHN duh luhnt lee) *adv.* lazily; idly

induction (ihn DUHK shuhn) *n.* installation; initiation

inevitability (ihn ehv uh tuh BIHL uh tee) *n.* quality of being certain to happen

inevitable (ihn EHV uh tuh buhl) *adj.* unavoidable; certain

infallibility (ihn fal uh BIHL uh tee) *n.* condition of not being likely to fail

information (ihn fuhr MAY shuhn) *n.* facts or knowledge about something

informed (ihn FAWRMD) *v.* gave someone information

informed (ihn FAWRMD) *adj.* having much knowledge, information, or education

inscrutable (ihn SKROO tuh buhl) *adj.* baffling; mysterious

insidious (ihn SIHD ee uhs) *adj.* characterized by craftiness and betrayal

insight (ihn syt) *n.* ability to have a deep understanding of something

insinuatingly (ihn SIHN yu ayt ihng lee) *adv.* suggesting indirectly; implying

insolent (IHN suh luhnt) *adj.* boldly disrespectful

instigates (IHN stuh gayts) *v.* urges on; stirs up

instinct (IHN stihngkt) *n.* behavior or response that one is born with

intentions (ihn TEHN shuhnz) *n.* aims or purposes of an action

intercession (ihn tuhr SEHSH uhn) *n.* act of pleading on another's behalf

interlopers (ihn tuhr LOHP erz) *n.* people who meddle in others' affairs; trespassers

interminably (ihn TUR muh nuh blee) *adv.* endlessly

intermission (ihn tuhr MIHSH uhn) *n.* any kind of break; more specifically, a break during a performance

interpret (ihn TUR priht) *v.* understand or explain the meaning of something

interpretation (ihn tur pruh TAY shuhn) *n.* explanation of the meaning of something

intimately (IHN tuh miht lee) *adv.* in a close manner; with a special or close knowledge; closely; jointly; familiarly

introspective (ihn truh SPEHK tihv) *adj.* having to do with looking into one's own thoughts and feelings

involvement (ihn VOLV muhnt) *n.* state of being included in something

iridescent (ihr uh DEHS uhnt) *adj.* showing colors that seem to change in different lights

issue (IHSH oo) *n.* subject for debate or discussion

J

jibed (jybd) *v.* changed direction

judicious (joo DIHSH uhs) *adj.* showing good judgment

justice (JUHS tihs) *n.* quality of fairness and impartiality

L

ladle (LAY duhl) *n.* long-handled, cup-like spoon for dipping out liquids

lament (luh MEHNT) *v.* express deep sorrow; mourn

lamentable (LAM uhn tuh buhl) *adj.* distressing; sad

languid (LANG gwihd) *adj.* drooping; weak

legacy (LEHG uh see) *n.* something handed down from an ancestor

lithe (lyth) *adj.* flexible

loathsome (LOHTH suhm) *adj.* disgusting; detestable

lofty (LAWF tee) *adj.* very high; noble

longing (lawng ihng) *n.* strong, persistent desire or craving, especially for something unattainable or distant; yearning

lurched (lurcht) *v.* moved awkwardly and suddenly

M

maladies (MAL uh deez) *n.* diseases

malodorous (mal OH duhr uhs) *adj.* having a bad smell

mammoth (MAM uhth) *adj.* enormous

manipulate (muh NIHP yuh layt) *v.* handle or control

martial (MAHR shuhl) *adj.* military; warlike

maudlin (MAWD luhn) *adj.* tearfully and foolishly sentimental

meaning (MEE nihng) *n.* what is referred to or understood

mediate (MEE dee ayt) *v.* bring about agreement between people who disagree

medium (MEE dee uhm) *n.* particular way of communicating information and news to people, such as a newspaper or a television broadcast

melancholy (MEHL uhn kol ee) *adj.* sad; gloomy

menacing (MEHN his ihng) *v.* threatening

metaphysical (meht uh FIHZ uh kuhl) *adj.* spiritual; beyond the physical

meticulously (muh TIHK yuh luhs lee) *adv.* very carefully and precisely

miraculously (muh RAK yuh luhs lee) *adv.* in an amazing way; as though by a miracle

momentous (moh MEHN tuhs) *adj.* very important

monotone (MON uh tohn) *n.* uninterrupted repetition of the same tone; utterance of successive syllables or words without change of pitch or key

monotonous (muh NOT uh nuhs) *adj.* going on in the same tone without variation

morality (muh RAL uh tee) *v.* principles that someone uses to decide if behavior is right or wrong

moribund (MAWR uh buhnd) *adj.* slowly dying

mortified (MAWR tuh fyd) *adj.* extremely embarrassed

multitude (MUHL tuh tood) *n.* large number of persons or things, especially when gathered together or considered as a unit

muted (myoot ihd) *adj.* weaker; less intense

N

naive (nah EEV) *adj.* unsophisticated; innocent

novice (NOV ihs) *adj.* new to an activity; inexperienced

nurturing (NUR chuhr ihng) *n.* the raising or promoting the development of; training, educating, fostering

O

obligation (ob luh GAY shuhn) *n.* something that must be done

oblique (uh BLEEK) *adj.* indirect; not straight

oblivion (uh BLIHV ee uhn) *n.* forgetfulness; the state of being unconscious or of not noticing what is happening

obstinacy (OB stuh nuh see) *n.* stubbornness

ominous (OM uh nuhs) *adj.* threatening

opal (OH pahl) *adj.* like an opal; being semi-transparent and reflecting light to give the appearance of many colors

oppression (uh PREHSH uhn) *n.* act of being weighed down or held back by worries or problems; keeping others down by the unjust use of power.

P

pallid (PAL ihd) *adj.* pale

pallor (PAL uhr) *n.* unnatural paleness

palpable (PAL puh buhl) *adj.* able to be felt; easily perceived

palpitating (PAL puh tayt ihng) *adj.* beating rapidly; throbbing

pandemonium (pan duh MOH nee uhm) *n.* any place or scene of wild disorder, noise, or confusion; chaos

paradoxical (PAR uh DOK suh kuhl) *adj.* seemingly full of contradictions

penetrated (PEHN uh trayt uhd) *v.* broke through

pensive (PEHN sihv) *adj.* thinking deeply or seriously; thoughtful

penury (PEHN yuhr ee) *n.* extreme poverty

perceive (puhr SEEV) *v.* become aware of

perennial (puh REHN ee uhl) *adj.* happening over and over; perpetual

permeate (PUR mee ayt) *v.* spread or flow throughout

pernicious (puhr NIHSH uhs) *adj.* causing great injury or ruin; destructive

perplexes (pehr PLEHKS uhz) *v.* confuses or puzzles

perspective (puhr SPEHK tihv) *n.* point of view

pertinent (PUR tuh nuhnt) *adj.* having some connection with the matter at hand; relevant; to the point

perverse (puhr VURS) *adj.* deviating from what is considered right

picturesque (pihk chuh REHSK) *adj.* like or suggesting a picture; lovely to look at; attractive and interesting

pious (PY uhs) *adj.* having or showing religious devotion

placidly (PLAS ihd lee) *adv.* calmly; quietly

plundered (PLUHN duhrd) *v.* took goods by force; looted

poignant (POY nuhnt) *adj.* emotionally touching

pondered (PON duhrd) *v.* thought deeply about

ponderously (PON duhr uhs lee) *adv.* in a labored and dull way; in a boring and serious way

potential (puh TEHN shuhl) *n.* possibility

precariously (prih KAIR ee uhs lee) *adv.* insecurely

preceded (pree SEED uhd) *v.* came before in time, place, order, rank, or importance

precipitous (prih SIHP uh tuhs) *adj.* steep; sheer

precluded (prih KLOOD ihd) *v.* prevented

predominant (prih DOM uh nuhnt) *adj.* having dominating influence over others

preliminaries (prih LIHM uh nehr eez) *n.* steps or events before the main one

preposterous (prih POS tuhr uhs) *adj.* so contrary to nature, reason, or common sense as to be laughable; absurd; ridiculous

presumed (prih ZOOMD) *adj.* taken for granted; accepted as true, lacking proof to the contrary; supposed

pretentious (prih TEHN shuhs) *adj.* grand in a showy way

prevail (prih VAYL) *v.* gain the advantage or mastery; be victorious; triumph

procure (pruh KYUR) *v.* get; obtain

prodigious (pruh DIHJ uhs) *adj.* enormous

prodigy (PROD uh jee) *n.* person who is amazingly talented or intelligent, especially a child of highly unusual talent or genius

profound (pruh FOWND) *adj.* deep; intense

profoundly (pruh FOWND lee) *adv.* deeply

provisions (pruh VIHZH uhnz) *n.* something provided, prepared, or supplied for the future

prudence (PROO duhns) *n.* a sensible and careful attitude; economy

pungent (PUHN juhnt) *adj.* producing a sharp smell

purged (purjd) *v.* cleansed

R

raggedy (RAG uh dee) *adj.* somewhat ragged and torn; tattered

raked (raykid) *v.* scratched or scraped, as with a rake

rancor (RANG kuhr) *n.* bitter hate

ravenous (RAV uh nuhs) *adj.* wildly hungry

react (ree AKT) *v.* do something in response to something else

reciprocate (rih SIHP ruh kayt) *v.* return

reckless (REHK lihs) *adj.* careless; rash

recoiling (rih KOYL ihng) *v.* staggering back

reconciliation (rehk uhn sihl ee AY shuhn) *n.* the settling of a conflict or argument; agreement; compromise

reels (reelz) *n.* frames or spools on which thread, wire, tape, film, or a net is wound

refrain (rih FRAYN) *v.* hold back

relationship (rih LAY shuhn shihp) *n.* connection between two or more people or things

remnants (REHM nuhnts) *n.* what is left over; remainders

renegade (REHN uh gayd) *adj.* disloyal; traitorous

research (rih SURCH) *n.* careful study in some field of knowledge

research (rih SURCH) *v.* perform careful study

resolution (rehz uh LOO shuhn) *n.* part of a narrative in which the plot is unraveled

respite (REHS piht) *n.* rest; relief

resplendent (rih SPLEHN duhnt) *adj.* shinning brightly

respond (rih SPOND) *v.* reply or react

responsibility (rih spon suh BIHL uh tee) *n.* having to answer to someone or something else; being accountable for success or failure

retort (rih TAWRT) *n.* sharp or clever reply

retribution (reht ruh BYOO shuhn) *n.* payback; punishment for a misdeed

revelry (REHV uhl ree) *n.* noisy merrymaking

revered (rih VIHRD) *adj.* regarded with great respect and awe

reverie (REHV uhr ee) *n.* dreamy thinking and imagining

revival (rih VY vuhl) *n.* a bringing or coming back into use, attention, or being after a decline

riddled (RIHD uhld) *adj.* affected throughout by something unpleasant

rifled (RY fuhld) *v.* ransacked and robbed; searched quickly through a cupboard or drawer

rueful (ROO fuhl) *adj.* feeling sorrow or regret

S

sallow (SAL oh) *adj.* of a sickly, pale-yellowish color

scarred (skahrd) *adj.* marked or dented

scourge (skurj) *n.* instrument for inflicting punishment

scruples (SKROO puhlz) *n.* misgivings about something one feels is wrong

segment (SEHG muhnt) *n.* division or section

seizure (SEE zhuhr) *n.* sudden and brief loss of consciousness and body control

senses (SEHNS uhz) *n.* physical ways in which a person or animal learns about the world: sight, hearing, touch, taste, and smell

sensory (SEHN suhr ee) *adj.* relating to the senses of sight, sound, taste, touch, or smell

serve (surv) *v.* work for; to be useful for

shriveled (SHRIHV uhld) *adj.* shrunken and wrinkled

siege (seej) *n.* encirclement of a fortified place by an opposing armed force intending to take it

similarity (sihm uh LAR uh tee) *n.* state of being alike

skeptics (SKEHP tihks) *n.* doubters; disbelievers

solitude (SOL uh tood) *n.* the state of being solitary, or alone; seclusion, isolation, or remoteness

sources (SAWRS uhz) *n.* places where things begin or are found

speculate (SPEHK yuh layt) *v.* think about or make up theories about a subject; guess at

spurn (spurn) *v.* reject with contempt or disdain

stalks (stawks) *v.* walks in a stiff, haughty, or grim manner

standard (STAN duhrd) *n.* idea to which other things are compared

standard (STAN duhrd) *adj.* normal; average

statistics (stuh TIHS tihks) *n.* science of collecting, analyzing, and using mathematical data

stout (stowt) *adj.* sturdy

stranded (STRAN dihd) *adj.* in a place or situation from which one needs help to leave

stupor (STOO puhr) *n.* mental dullness or insensibility

submerged (suhb MURJD) *adj.* covered with water or the like

subsided (suhb SYD ihd) *v.* settled down; became less active or intense

subverting (suhb VURT ihng) *v.* overthrowing or destroying something established

succumbed (suh KUHMD) *v.* gave way; yielded

suffice (suh FYS) *v.* be enough

surreal (suh REE uhl) *adj.* strange, like something from a dream

survival (suhr VY vuhl) *n.* the state of continuing to exist

T

tantalizingly (tan tuh LY zihng lee) *adv.* in a teasing way

telegraph (TEHL uh graf) *n.* an apparatus or system that converts a coded message into electric impulses and sends it to a distance receiver

temporal (TEHM puhr uhl) *adj.* having to do with time

tenacious (tih NAY shuhs) *adj.* holding firmly to beliefs; persistent; stubborn; adamant

tenement (TEHN uh muhnt) *n.* apartment house, often run-down

transgression (trans GREHSH uhn) *n.* wrongdoing; sin

treble (TREHB uhl) *n.* high-pitched voice or sound

trundle (TRUHN duhl) *v.* roll along

truth (trooth) *n.* corresponding with reality or fact

tumultuous (too MUHL chu uhs) *adj.* greatly disturbed; in an uproar

U

understanding (uhn duhr STAN dihng) *n.* ability to get the meaning of something; ability to think or learn

unique (yoo NEEK) *adj.* one of a kind

unpalatable (uhn PAL uh tuh buhl) *adj.* distasteful; unpleasant

unrequited (uhn rih KWY tuhd) *adj.* not returned or repaid

unwieldy (uhn WEEL dee) *adj.* awkward; clumsy

usurped (yoo SURPT) *v.* took power or position without right

V

values (VAL yooz) *n.* beliefs accepted by an individual

venture (VEHN chuhr) *n.* risky action

verify (VEHR uh fy) *v.* make sure something is true; confirm

vex (vehks) *v.* annoy

vial (vyl) *n.* small bottle containing medicine or other liquids

vigilant (VIHJ uh luhnt) *adj.* watchful

vile (vyl) *adj.* evil; wicked

volumes (VOL yuhmz) *n.* sets of the issues of a periodical over a fixed period of time, usually a year; books

voluminously (vuh LOO muh nuhs lee) *adv.* fully; in great volume

W

wail (wayl) *n.* lament; cry of deep sorrow

war (wawr) *n.* armed conflict between people

warp (wawrp) *v.* twist; distort

wayward (WAY wuhrd) *adj.* headstrong

wheezed (hweez) *v.* breathed hard with a breathy sound

wisdom (WIHZ duhm) *n.* ability to make good judgments based on knowledge and experience

woeful (WOH fuhl) *adj.* full of sorrow

woes (wohz) *n.* great sorrows

writhing (RYTH ihng) *v.* twisting; turning

Spanish Glossary

El vocabulario de Gran Pregunta aparece en **azul**. El vocabulario academico de alta utilidad esta **subraydo**.

A

abash / avergonzar *v.* apenar

abdicated / abdicó *v.* renunció formalmente

abolish / abolir *v.* acabar con algo por completo

absurdity / absurdo *s.* algo ridículo o un disparate

accentuated / acentuó *v.* enfatizó; realzó el efecto de

accept / aceptar *v.* recibir algo que se da

accumulated / acumuló *v.* amontonado, recopilado o reunido, especialmente durante algún lapso de tiempo

acquiesced / accedió *v.* consintió o se doblegó calladamente sin protestar, pero sin entusiasmo

adversary / adversario *s.* persona que se opone o lucha contra otra

afflicted / afligió *v.* que sufrió o padeció de

allotment / asignación *s.* parte; porción

aloofness / retraimiento *s.* calidad de estar distante o apartado

ambiguities / ambigüedades *s.* declaraciones o eventos cuyos significados no son claros

ambiguous / ambiguo *adj.* que tiene más de un significado

amicably / amigablemente *adv.* de manera amistosa

amicably / amistosamente *adv.* de manera amigable

amid / entre *prep.* en medio de; rodeado por

anguish / angustia *s.* gran dolor o sufrimiento

anonymous / anónimo *adj.* sin nombre conocido o reconocido

antagonize / contrariar *v.* enemistar

apex / cima *s.* punto más alto; cumbre

appreciate / apreciar *v.* reconocer el valor de algo

apprenticed / aprendiz *s.* persona que se ocupa por un tiempo específico de un oficio o arte a cambio de instrucción

archaic / arcaico *adj.* de épocas pasadas; antiguo

ardor / ardor *s.* pasión; entusiasmo

arduous / arduo *adj.* difícil; laborioso

argument / discusión *s.* intercambio de ideas cuando hay un desacuerdo

articulate / articulado *adj.* capaz de expresarse con claridad

articulate / elocuente *adj.* que se expresa con claridad y facilidad

assiduous / asiduo *adj.* hecho con atención constante y cuidadosa; diligente

assimilated / asimiló *v.* ingirió o absorbió

assimilated / asimilado *adj.* algo o alguien que ha sido completamente absorbido

assuage / apaciguar *v.* calmar; sosegar

assumption / suposición *s.* algo que se da por sentado

atonement / desagravio *s.* acción de enmendar algún agravio o perjuicio

attributes / atributos *s.* características o cualidades de una persona o cosa

augmenting / aumentando *v.* incrementando; haciendo más grande

authentic / auténtico *adj.* genuino; verdadero

aware / consciente *adj.* saber algo por haberlo experimentado o por haber sido informado de ello

awestruck / pasmado *adj.* maravillado

awry / ladeado *adj.* estar mal puesto o torcido

azure / azur *adv.* azul celeste

B

background / antecedentes *s.* hechos que causan o explican algo

bafflement / desconcierto *s.* perplejidad; dificultad de comprensión

balmy / balsámico *adj.* que tiene las cualidades del bálsamo; apacible, suave, agradable

baritone / barítono *s.* tono de la voz masculina que es más bajo que el de un tenor y más alto que el de un bajo

barren / árido *adj.* desértico; que tiene poca o ninguna vegetación

battle / batalla *s.* pelea entre fuerzas armadas

battle / combatir *v.* pelear o luchar

beguiling / cautivar *v.* engañar; encantar

belief / creencia *s.* algo que se acepta como cierto

bemusing / aturdiendo *v.* confundir; desconcertar

benevolently / benévolamente *adv.* de manera bien intencionada

bereft / desprovisto *adj.* despojado, privado de

beveled / biselado *adj.* superficie con un corte inclinado

bias / predisposición *s.* inclinación o tendencia mental; parcialidad

bilingual / bilingüe *adj.* que usa dos idiomas

bleat / balido *s.* sonido vocal que producen las ovejas

blight / plaga *s.* algo que destruye o impide el crecimiento

bulging / protuberante *adj.* abultado

burrowing / excavar *v.* abrir un hueco en una superficie

C

candor / franqueza *s.* marcada honestidad o sinceridad al expresarse

cascade / cascada *s.* pequeño salto de agua empinado; cualquier cosa que se asemeje a un salto de agua

censure / censura *s.* firme desaprobación

character / carácter *s.* cualidades que hacen única a una persona

chicken pox / varicela *s.* enfermedad altamente contagiosa que afecta principalmente a los niños y se caracteriza por causar fiebre y sarpullido

choices / elecciones *s.* variedad de cosas de donde uno puede seleccionar

circumstance / circunstancia *s.* situación; evento

clarify / aclarar *v.* hacer que algo sea más claro y comprensible

clasps / agarra *v.* sujeta con firmeza

collective / colectivo *adj.* conformado como grupo; reunido en uno solo

communication / comunicación *s.* intercambio de información

compensation / compensación *s.* cualquier cosa que sirve para subsanar una pérdida, daño o deuda

compete / competir *v.* tratar de ganar contra un adversario

competition / competencia *s.* rivalidad; acción de competir

comprehend / comprender *v.* entender

comprehension / comprensión *s.* acción de entender algo

comprehension / comprensión *s.* entendimiento

conceded / concedió *v.* admitió como cierto o válido; reconoció

concept / concepto *s.* idea; noción

concessions / concesiones *s.* cosas otorgadas o cedidas como privilegios

condolences / condolencias *s.* manifestaciones de compasión hacia otra persona que sufre

confer / conferir *v.* conceder; otorgar

confines / confines *s.* fronteras o zona fronteriza; borde; límite

conformity / conformidad *s.* estar de acuerdo con costumbres o normas

connection / conexión *s.* unión de dos o más cosas o ideas

conspicuous / conspicuo *adj.* que atrae la atención por ser inesperado, inusual, sobresaliente o notorio; impresionante

contempt / desprecio *s.* desdén o menosprecio

context / contexto *s.* partes de una oración cercanas a una palabra que determinan su significado exacto

controversy / controversia *s.* discusión de un asunto en el que chocan las opiniones divergentes

convince / convencer *v.* persuadir mediante argumentos o evidencia

cooperate / cooperar *v.* trabajar conjuntamente para lograr algo

countenance / semblante *s.* rostro

covenant / pacto *s.* convenio o acuerdo, especialmente uno sagrado

credible / creíble *adj.* verosímil

creed / credo *s.* declaración de creencias

culture / cultura *s.* ideas, costumbres, destrezas y arte de un grupo de personas de una época específica en la historia

cunning / astuto *adj.* hábil en el engaño

curtailed / restringió *v.* acortó; redujo

D

daunting / amedrentador *adj.* intimidante

defaulted / incumplió *v.* dejó de hacer algo o no compareció en alguna parte cuando era requerido o esperado; faltó a un pago a su vencimiento

defend / defender *v.* proteger contra ataques

deferred / difirió *v.* postergó a una fecha futura

defiance / desafío *s.* franca y descarada resistencia a la autoridad

defrauded / estafó *v.* engañó

degenerate / degenerar *v.* empeorar

dejection / desaliento *s.* desánimo; depresión

deleterious / nocivo *adj.* perjudicial para la salud o el bienestar

demonstrative / expresivo *adj.* que demuestra abiertamente los sentimientos

demure / reservado *adj.* modesto

depravity / depravación *s.* deshonestidad; corrupción

depreciate / depreciar *v.* disminuir su valor

derisive / burlón *adj.* que muestra desprecio o ridiculiza; mofador

desolate / desolado *adj.* afligido; desconsolado

despotic / despótico *adj.* como un gobernante absoluto o tirano

desultory / vago *adj.* sin rumbo; aleatorio

determination / determinación *s.* firme intención

determine / determinar *v.* ocasionar que algo ocurra de cierta forma

differences / diferencias *s.* características que hacen que las cosas sean disímiles; maneras en que las cosas no son iguales

differentiate / diferenciar *v.* ver o expresar lo que hace que dos o más cosas sean diferentes entre sí

diffused / difundió *v.* diseminó

dilapidated / desmoronado *adj.* ruinoso

diminution / disminución *s.* reducción

discerning / perspicaz *adj.* tener buen juicio o comprensión

discipline / disciplina *s.* entrenamiento que desarrolla el dominio de sí mismo, carácter, o el orden y eficiencia

disclosed / divulgó *v.* reveló; hizo público

disconsolately / desconsoladamente *adv.* muy desdichadamente

discreet / discreto *adj.* cuidadoso con lo que dice o hace; prudente; que calla o mantiene confidencias cuando es necesario

discreetly / discretamente *adv.* sin llamar la atención

discriminate / discriminar *v.* distinguir las diferencias entre las cosas; actuar en contra de alguien por prejuicio

discuss / discutir *v.* hablar sobre algo

disgrace / deshonra *s.* pérdida del respeto, honor, o estima; vergüenza

disheveled / desordenado *adj.* desarreglado

dishevelment / desorden *s.* desarreglo; desaseo

dismal / melancólico *adj.* que ocasiona tristeza o desolación

dispatched / despachó *v.* terminó con prontitud

disperse / dispersar *v.* romper y desparramar en todas direcciones; esparcir; distribuir ampliamente

disputed / disputado *adj.* en litigio; contencioso

dissemble / disimular *v.* ocultar bajo una falsa apariencia; disfrazar

distinguished / distinguido *adj.* que tiene un aire de distinción; reconocido por su excelencia; eminente; famoso

distort / distorsionar *v.* enredar hasta perder la forma original

distraught / afligido *adj.* muy alterado o confundido

diverged / bifurcó *v.* ramificó en diferentes direcciones

droll / gracioso *adj.* divertido de manera comedida

duration / duración *s.* el tiempo en que algo continúa o permanece

E

elation / entusiasmo *s.* sentimiento de júbilo; orgullo; alborozo

eloquence / elocuencia *s.* elegancia y persuasión en el discurso o la escritura

embellish / embellecer *v.* decorar o mejorar agregando detalles; ornamentar; adornar

emerge / surgir *v.* nacer como algo nuevo o mejorado; tornarse visible o conocido

emitting / emitir *v.* despedir

empathy / empatía *s.* capacidad de comprender y compartir los sentimientos de otra persona

emulate / emular *v.* imitar (a una persona o cosa que se admira)

enamored / enamoró *v.* lleno de amor y deseo; encantado

encroaching / de manera usurpadora *adj.* invadir de manera furtiva

endeavor / intento *s.* tentativa o esfuerzo formal

endeavored / intentó *v.* hizo un esfuerzo formal para conseguir o lograr algo; trató

endurance / resistencia *s.* capacidad para soportar adversidades

enigma / enigma *s.* misterio

enjoined / impuso *v.* exigió

entailed / implicó *v.* causó o requirió como consecuencia necesaria; involucró; obligó

enthralled / embelesó *v.* mantuvo como hechizado; cautivó

enumerated / enumeró *v.* nombró uno a uno; especificó, como en una lista

esteem / estima *s.* opinión favorable; aprecio; respeto

evanescent / evanescente *adj.* temporal; tendiente a desaparecer

evidence / evidencia *s.* prueba

ewes / oveja hembra *s.* oveja hembra

exchange / intercambio *s.* acción de comerciar algo

exchange / intercambiar *v.* comerciar

exile / exiliar *v.* desterrar

explicit / explícito *adj.* expresado con claridad

extrapolating / extrapolando *v.* llegando a una conclusión por deducción de hechos conocidos

F

fact / hecho *s.* algo que realmente ocurrió o que es cierto

faltered / titubeó *v.* actuó de forma vacilante; mostró incertidumbre; flaqueó; se acobardó

feasible / factible *adj.* capaz de hacerse o realizarse; viable; posible

feeling / sentimiento *s.* emoción de la que están conscientes las personas

feisty / determinado *adj.* lleno de coraje; vigoroso

fertile / fértil *adj.* rico en nutrientes que promueven el crecimiento

fester / enconar *v.* infectar; formar pus

feud / lucha encarnizada *s.* amargas, prolongadas y violentas disputas, especialmente entre clanes o familias

fickle / voluble *adj.* cambiante

forebears / antepasados *s.* ascendientes

forgo / privar *v.* contenerse de; abstenerse de; renunciar a

formality / formalidad *s.* atención a normas o costumbres establecidas

formidable / formidable *adj.* impresionante

fortitude / fortaleza *s.* fuerza para soportar el infortunio y el dolor con calma y paciencia

fray / refriega *s.* pelea escandalosa

furtive / furtivo *adj.* a hurtadillas; oculto

futile / fútil *adj.* inútil; sin remedio

G

gallant / gallardo *adj.* valiente y noble

gorgon / Gorgona *s.* una de tres criaturas míticas tan horribles que quien las mire se convierte en piedra

grotesque / grotesco *adj.* que tiene un diseño extraño, raro; extraño o inusual de manera tal que resulta repugnante u ofensivo

H

hallowed / santificado *adj.* sagrado

haughty / altanero *adj.* arrogante

hero / héroe *s.* alguien a quien se admira por sus acciones valientes o nobles

honesty / sinceridad *s.* calidad de ser veraz

humble / humilde *adj.* modesto; que tiene humildad

humbly / humildemente *adv.* de tal manera que no es soberbio ni arrogante; modestamente

I

identify / identificar *v.* describir lo que es una persona o cosa

ignorance / ignorancia *s.* falta de conocimiento o educación

illuminate / iluminar *v.* alumbrar; aclarar

imitate / imitar *v.* copiar las acciones de otro

immaculate / impecable *adj.* en perfectas condiciones; sin defectos, faltas o errores

imminent / inminente *adj.* que probablemente ocurrirá pronto

impassive / impasible *adj.* que no muestra emoción alguna

impenetrable / impenetrable *adj.* que no se puede atravesar; que no puede ser resuelto o entendido; insondable

implications / implicaciones *s.* consecuencias indirectas

imposition / imposición *s.* introducción de algo como una norma, impuesto o castigo

incessantly / incesantemente *adv.* que sigue de forma que pareciera interminable; continuamente; constantemente

incognito / incógnito *adj.* sin revelar la verdadera identidad; bajo un nombre ficticio

incredulity / incredulidad *s.* renuencia o incapacidad para creer

individuality / individualidad *s.* condición de ser único

indolently / indolentemente *adv.* con pereza; ociosamente

induction / instalación *s.* inclusión; iniciación

inevitability / inevitabilidad *s.* calidad de que ciertamente ocurrirá

inevitable / inevitable *adj.* ineludible; con seguridad

infallibility / infalibilidad *s.* condición de que no puede fallar

information / información *s.* hechos o conocimientos sobre algo

informed / informado *adj.* que tiene mucho conocimiento, información o educación

informed / informó *v.* le dio información a alguien

insight / perspicacia *s.* capacidad de tener una profunda comprensión sobre algo

inscrutable / inescrutable *adj.* desconcertante; misterioso

insidious / insidioso *adj.* que se caracteriza por su astucia y traición

insinuatingly / de manera insinuante *adv.* que sugiere indirectamente; que implica

insolent / insolente *adj.* descaradamente irrespetuoso

instigates / instiga *v.* fomenta; promueve

instinct / instinto *s.* conducta o respuesta con la que se nace

intentions / intenciones *s.* objetivos o propósitos de una acción

intercession / intercesión *s.* acción de abogar por otra persona

interlopers / intrusos *s.* personas que interfieren en los asuntos de otros; invasores

interminably / interminablemente *adv.* que no tiene fin

intermission / intermedio *s.* cualquier tipo de interrupción; más específicamente, el entreacto durante una función de teatro

interpret / interpretar *v.* entender o explicar el significado de algo

interpretation / interpretación *s.* explicación del significado de algo

intimately / íntimamente *adv.* de forma cercana; con conocimiento especial o estrecho; celosamente; conjuntamente; familiarmente

introspective / introspectivo *adj.* que tiene que ver con el análisis de sus propios pensamientos y sentimientos

involvement / participación *s.* condición de estar incluido en algo

iridescent / iridiscente *adj.* que muestra colores que parecen cambiar de acuerdo a los diferentes tipos de luz

issue / asunto *s.* tema para debate o discusión

J

jibed / viró *v.* cambió de dirección

judicious / juicioso *adj.* que muestra buen juicio

justice / justicia *s.* calidad de equidad e imparcialidad

L

ladle / cazo *s.* cucharón hondo de mango largo usado para servir líquidos

lament / lamentar *v.* expresar profunda tristeza; penar

lamentable / lamentable *adj.* angustioso; penoso

languid / lánguido *adj.* flojo; débil

legacy / legado *s.* algo heredado de un antepasado

lithe / ágil *adj.* flexible

loathsome / odioso *adj.* repugnante; detestable

lofty / elevado *adj.* muy alto; noble

longing / añoranza s. fuerte y persistente deseo o antojo, particularmente por algo inalcanzable o distante; nostalgia

lurched / sacudió v. se movió torpe y repentinamente

M

maladies / dolencias s. enfermedades

malodorous / maloliente adj. que tiene mal olor

mammoth / gigante adj. enorme

manipulate / manipular v. manejar o controlar

martial / marcial adj. de corte militar

maudlin / llorón adj. lloroso y tontamente sentimental

meaning / significado s. de qué trata o qué se entiende por algo

mediate / mediar v. interceder para que las partes que están en desacuerdo lleguen a un acuerdo

medium / medio s. manera particular de comunicar información y noticias a la gente, como un periódico o un programa de televisión

melancholy / melancolía s. tristeza; pesimismo

menacing / amenazar v. intimidar

metaphysical / metafísico adj. espiritual; que traspasa lo físico

meticulously / meticulosamente adv. de manera muy cuidadosa y precisa

miraculously / milagrosamente adv. de manera sorprendente; como por milagro

momentous / trascendental adj. muy importante

monotone / monotonía s. repetición ininterrumpida de un mismo tono; pronunciación de sílabas o palabras sucesivas sin cambiar el tono o tonalidad

monotonous / monótono adj. seguir en el mismo tono sin variación

morality / moralidad v. principios que sirven para decidir si el comportamiento es correcto o incorrecto

moribund / moribundo adj. que muere lentamente

mortified / avergonzado adj. extremadamente humillado

multitude / multitud s. gran cantidad de personas o cosas, especialmente cuando se juntan o se consideran una unidad

muted / silencioso adj. más débil; menos intenso

N

naive / ingenuo adj. poco sofisticado; inocente

novice / novato adj. nuevo en cualquier actividad; sin experiencia

nurturing / formación s. crianza o fomento del desarrollo; capacitación, educación, crianza

O

obligation / obligación s. algo que se debe hacer

oblique / oblicuo adj. que no es derecho

oblivion / olvido s. falta de memoria; condición de estar inconsciente o inadvertido de lo que ocurre

obstinacy / obstinación s. terquedad

ominous / siniestro adj. amenazante

opal / opalino adj. como el ópalo; de apariencia semi-transparente y que refleja la luz generado muchos colores

oppression / opresión s. sensación de estar agobiado o reprimido por preocupaciones, problemas o el uso injusto del poder

P

pallid / pálido adj. lívido

pallor / palidez s. lividez poco natural

palpable / palpable adj. capaz de sentirse; percibido con facilidad

palpitating / palpitante adj. que late rápidamente; que pulsa

pandemonium / pandemonio s. cualquier lugar o escena de desorden, ruido o confusión desenfrenada; caos

paradoxical / paradójico adj. aparentemente lleno de contradicciones

penetrated / penetró v. traspasó

pensive / pensativo adj. que reflexiona profunda o seriamente

penury / penuria s. extrema pobreza

perceive / percibir v. darse cuenta de

perennial / perenne adj. que ocurre una y otra vez; perpetuo

permeate / penetrar v. extenderse o fluir a través

pernicious / pernicioso adj. que causa gran perjuicio o ruina; destructivo

perplexes / desconcierta v. confunde o deja perplejo

perspective / perspectiva s. punto de vista

pertinent / pertinente adj. que tiene alguna conexión con el asunto entre manos; relevante; al grano

perverse / perverso adj. distinto de lo que se considera correcto o razonable

picturesque / pintoresco adj. que sugiere o que se parece a una pintura; hermoso a la vista

pious / piadoso adj. que tiene o muestra fervor religioso

placidly / plácidamente adv. tranquilamente; sosegadamente

plundered / saqueó v. que tomó mercancías por la fuerza; robó

poignant / conmovedor adj. que suscita emociones

pondered / sopesó v. consideró profundamente

ponderously / pesadamente adv. de manera forzada y monótona; de forma aburrida y seria

potential / potencial s. posibilidad; habilidades que se necesitan para triunfar

precariously / precariamente adv. de manera insegura

preceded / precedió v. que estaba antes en tiempo, lugar, orden, rango o importancia

precipitous / escarpado adj. abrupto; vertical

precluded / impidió v. imposibilitó

predominant / predominante *adj.* que tiene influencia dominante sobre otros

preliminaries / preparativos *s.* pasos o eventos antes del principal

preposterous / absurdo *adj.* tan contrario a la naturaleza, la razón o el sentido común que es irrisorio; ilógico; ridículo

presumed / supuesto *adj.* dado por sentado; aceptado como cierto, a falta de prueba de lo contrario; asumido

pretentious / pretencioso *adj.* magnífico de manera ostentosa

prevail / prevalecer *v.* obtener la ventaja o el dominio; salir victorioso; triunfar

procure / procurar *v.* lograr; obtener

prodigious / prodigioso *adj.* enorme

prodigy / prodigio *s.* persona que es increíblemente talentosa o inteligente, particularmente un niño de talento extraordinario; genio

profound / profundo *adj.* hondo; intenso

profoundly / profundamente *adv.* intensamente

provisions / suministros *s.* algo que se provee, prepara o suple para el futuro

prudence / prudencia *s.* actitud racional y cuidadosa; economía

pungent / acre *adj.* que produce un olor penetrante

purged / depuró *v.* purificó

R

raggedy / andrajoso *adj.* bastante harapiento y roto; hecho jirones

raked / rasgó *v.* rasguñó or raspó, como lo hace un rastrillo

rancor / rencor *s.* odio implacable

ravenous / voraz *adj.* con hambre desmesurada

react / reaccionar *v.* hacer algo en respuesta a otra cosa

reciprocate / corresponder *v.* devolver

reckless / temerario *adj.* descuidado; descabellado

recoiling / retrocediendo *v.* dando marcha atrás

reconciliation / reconciliación *s.* resolución de un conflicto o disputa; acuerdo; compromiso

reels / carretes *s.* marcos o rollos en los que se arrolla hilo, alambre, cinta o red

refrain / abstener *v.* contenerse

relationship / relación *s.* conexión entre dos o más personas o cosas

remnants / remanentes *s.* sobrantes; restos

renegade / renegado *adj.* desleal; traicionero

research / investigación *s.* estudio profundo en algún campo del conocimiento

research / investigar *v.* realizar estudio profundo

resolution / resolución *s.* parte de una narrativa en la que se desenmaraña la trama

respite / respiro *s.* descanso; alivio

resplendent / resplandeciente *adj.* radiantemente iluminado

respond / responder *v.* contestar o reaccionar

responsibility / responsabilidad *s.* tener que responder ante alguien o algo; tener que rendir cuentas por el éxito o el fracaso

retort / réplica *s.* respuesta cortante o astuta

retribution / castigo *s.* restitución; escarmiento por una falta cometida

revelry / parranda *s.* fiesta ruidosa

revered / venerado *adj.* tratado con gran respeto y admiración

reverie / ensueño *s.* pensamiento e imaginación soñadora

revival / restablecimiento *s.* traer o devolver al uso, atención o naturaleza después de un descenso

riddled / plagado *adj.* afectado completamente

rifled / desvalijó *v.* saqueó y robó; buscó rápidamente en un armario o gaveta

rueful / arrepentido *adj.* que siente tristeza o remordimiento

S

sallow / amarillento *adj.* de color enfermizo, pálido macilento

scarred / cicatrizado *adj.* marcado o abollado

scourge / azote *s.* instrumento para imponer un castigo

scruples / escrúpulos *s.* dudas sobre algo que uno siente que es incorrecto

segment / segmento *s.* división o sección

seizure / ataque *s.* breve y repentina pérdida del conocimiento y del control corporal

senses / sentidos *s.* formas físicas con las que una persona o animal aprende sobre el mundo: vista, oído, tacto, gusto y olfato

sensory / sensorial *adj.* relativo a los sentidos de la vista, oído, gusto, tacto y olfato

serve / servir *v.* trabajar para; ser útil para

shriveled / marchito *adj.* seco y arrugado

siege / sitio *s.* cercamiento de un lugar fortificado por fuerzas armadas opositoras con el fin de tomarlo

similarity / similitud *s.* condición de ser parecidos

skeptics / escépticos *s.* aquéllos que dudan; aquéllos que no creen

skeptics / escépticos *s.* personas que dudan y cuestionan las ideas generalmente aceptadas

solitude / soledad *s.* condición de estar solitario o solo; reclusión, aislamiento o alejamiento

sources / fuentes *s.* lugares en donde comienzan o se encuentran las cosas

speculate / especular *v.* pensar o inventar teor**ías sobre un tema; adivinar**

spurn / desdeñar *v.* rechazar con desprecio o desdén

stalks / taconea *v.* que camina de manera arrogante, ceremoniosa y severa

standard / norma *s.* concepto contra el que se comparan otras cosas

standard / estándar *adj.* normal; promedio

statistics / estadísticas *s.* ciencia de recoger, analizar y usar datos matemáticos

stout / sólido *adj.* robusto

stranded / varado *adj.* desamparado en un lugar o situación donde se necesita ayuda para salir

stupor / estupor *s.* insensibilidad or torpeza mental

submerged / sumergido *adj.* cubierto con agua o algo similar

subsided / disminuyó *v.* se calmó; se volvió menos activo o intenso

subverting / trastornando *v.* derribando o destruyendo algo establecido

succumbed / sucumbió *v.* se rindió; cedió

suffice / bastar *v.* ser suficiente

surreal / surrealista *adj.* extraño, como algo salido de un sueño

survival / supervivencia *s.* condición de continuar existiendo

T

tantalizingly / tentadoramente *adv.* de manera provocativa

telegraph / telégrafo *s.* aparato o sistema que convierte un mensaje codificado en impulsos eléctricos y lo envía a un receptor distante

temporal / temporal *adj.* que tiene que ver con el tiempo

tenacious / tenaz *adj.* que se mantiene firme en sus creencias; persistente; terco; decidido

tenement / casa de vecindad *s.* vivienda, a menudo en malas condiciones

transgression / transgresión *s.* infracción; pecado

treble / tiple *s.* voz o sonido muy agudo

trundle / rodar *v.* ir rodando

truth / verdad *s.* que corresponde a realidades o hechos

tumultuous / tumultuoso *adj.* muy agitado; en un alboroto

U

understanding / entendimiento *s.* capacidad de comprender el significado de algo; capacidad para pensar o aprender

unique / único *adj.* exclusivo

unpalatable / desagradable *adj.* repugnante; molesto

unrequited / no correspondido *adj.* no reciprocado ni devuelto

unwieldy / abultado *adj.* incómodo; torpe

usurped / usurpó *v.* tomó el poder o posición sin derecho

V

values / valores *s.* convicciones aceptadas por una persona

venture / ventura *s.* acción riesgosa

verify / verificar *v.* asegurarse de que algo es cierto; corroborar

vex / fastidiar *v.* irritar

vial / frasco *s.* envase pequeño que contiene medicamento u otros líquidos

vigilant / vigilante *adj.* alerta

vile / vil *adj.* malévolo; malvado

volumes / volúmenes *s.* conjuntos de ejemplares de periódicos que abarcan un lapso de tiempo fijo, generalmente un año; libros

voluminously / voluminosamente *adv.* completamente; de gran volumen

W

wail / gemido *s.* lamento; grito de profundo dolor

war / guerra *s.* conflicto armado entre pueblos

warp / torcer *v.* retorcer; distorsionar

wayward / avieso *adj.* caprichoso

wheezed / resolló *v.* respiró con silbido

wisdom / sabiduría *s.* capacidad de emitir buenos juicios con base en el conocimiento y la experiencia

woeful / afligido *adj.* lleno de dolor

woes / aflicciones *s.* grandes tristezas

writhing / retorcer *v.* contorsionar; serpentear

☆ **English Language Arts and Reading, English I
(One Credit), Begining with School Year 2009–2010.**

(a) Introduction.

(1) The English Language Arts and Reading Texas Essential Knowledge and Skills (TEKS) are orga-nized into the following strands: Reading, where students read and understand a wide variety of literary and informational texts; Writing, where students compose a variety of written texts with a clear controlling idea, coherent organization, and sufficient detail; Research, where students are expected to know how to locate a range of relevant sources and evaluate, synthesize, and present ideas and information; Listening and Speaking, where students listen and respond to the ideas of others while contributing their own ideas in conversations and in groups; and Oral and Written Conventions, where students learn how to use the oral and written conventions of the English language in speaking and writing. The standards are cumulative--students will continue to address earlier standards as needed while they attend to standards for their grade. In English I, students will engage in activities that build on their prior knowledge and skills in order to strengthen their reading, writing, and oral language skills. Students should read and write on a daily basis.

(2) For students whose first language is not English, the students' native language serves as a founda-tion for English language acquisition.

(A) English language learners (ELLs) are acquiring English, learning content in English, and learning to read simultaneously. For this reason, it is imperative that reading instruction should be comprehensive and that students receive instruction in phonemic awareness, phonics, decoding, and word attack skills while simultaneously being taught academic vocabulary and comprehension skills and strategies. Reading instruction that enhances ELL's ability to decode unfamiliar words and to make sense of those words in context will expedite their ability to make sense of what they read and learn from reading. Additionally, developing fluency, spelling, and grammatical conventions of academic language must be done in meaningful contexts and not in isolation.

(B) For ELLs, comprehension of texts requires additional scaffolds to support comprehensible input. ELL students should use the knowledge of their first language (e.g., cognates) to further vocabulary development. Vocabulary needs to be taught in the context of connected discourse so that language is meaningful. ELLs must learn how rhetorical devices in English differ from those in their native language. At the same time English learners are learning in English, the focus is on academic English, concepts, and the language structures specific to the content.

(C) During initial stages of English development, ELLs are expected to meet standards in a second language that many monolingual English speakers find difficult to meet in their native language. However, English language learners' abilities to meet these standards will be influ-enced by their proficiency in English. While English language learners can analyze, synthe-size, and evaluate, their level of English proficiency may impede their ability to demonstrate this knowledge during the initial stages of English language acquisition. It is also critical to understand that ELLs with no previous or with interrupted schooling will require explicit and strategic support as they acquire English and learn to learn in English simultaneously.

(3) To meet Public Education Goal 1 of the Texas Education Code, §4.002, which states, "The students in the public education system will demonstrate exemplary performance in the reading and writing of the English language," students will accomplish the essential knowledge, skills, and student expectations in English I as described in subsection (b) of this section.

(4) To meet Texas Education Code, §28.002(h), which states, ". . . each school district shall foster the continuation of the tradition of teaching United States and Texas history and the free enterprise system in regular subject matter and in reading courses and in the adoption of textbooks," students will be provided oral and written narratives as well as other informational texts that can help them to become thoughtful, active citizens who appreciate the basic democratic values of our state and nation.

(b) Knowledge and skills.

(1) **Reading/Vocabulary Development.** Students understand new vocabulary and use it when reading and writing. Students are expected to:

(A) determine the meaning of grade-level technical academic English words in multiple content areas (e.g., science, mathematics, social studies, the arts) derived from Latin, Greek, or other linguistic roots and affixes;

(B) analyze textual context (within a sentence and in larger sections of text) to distinguish between the denotative and connotative meanings of words;

(C) produce analogies that describe a function of an object or its description;

(D) describe the origins and meanings of foreign words or phrases used frequently in written English (e.g., *caveat emptor, carte blanche, tete a tete, pas de deux, bon appetit, quid pro quo*); and

(E) use a dictionary, a glossary, or a thesaurus (printed or electronic) to determine or confirm the meanings of words and phrases, including their connotations and denotations, and their etymology.

(2) **Reading/Comprehension of Literary Text/Theme and Genre.** Students analyze, make inferences and draw conclusions about theme and genre in different cultural, historical, and contemporary contexts and provide evidence from the text to support their understanding. Students are expected to:

(A) analyze how the genre of texts with similar themes shapes meaning;

(B) analyze the influence of mythic, classical and traditional literature on 20th and 21st century literature; and

(C) relate the figurative language of a literary work to its historical and cultural setting.

(3) **Reading/Comprehension of Literary Text/Poetry.** Students understand, make inferences and draw conclusions about the structure and elements of poetry and provide evidence from text to support their understanding. Students are expected to analyze the effects of diction and imagery (e.g., controlling images, figurative language, understatement, overstatement, irony, paradox) in poetry.

(4) **Reading/Comprehension of Literary Text/Drama.** Students understand, make inferences and draw conclusions about the structure and elements of drama and provide evidence from text to support their understanding. Students explain how dramatic conventions (e.g., monologues, soliloquies, dramatic irony) enhance dramatic text.

(5) **Reading/Comprehension of Literary Text/Fiction.** Students understand, make inferences and draw conclusions about the structure and elements of fiction and provide evidence from text to support their understanding. Students are expected to:

(A) analyze non-linear plot development (e.g., flashbacks, foreshadowing, sub-plots, parallel plot structures) and compare it to linear plot development;

(B) analyze how authors develop complex yet believable characters in works of fiction through a range of literary devices, including character foils;

(C) analyze the way in which a work of fiction is shaped by the narrator's point of view; and

(D) demonstrate familiarity with works by authors from non-English-speaking literary traditions with emphasis on classical literature.

(6) **Reading/Comprehension of Literary Text/Literary Nonfiction.** Students understand, make inferences and draw conclusions about the varied structural patterns and features of literary nonfiction and provide evidence from text to support their understanding. Students are expected to analyze how literary essays interweave personal examples and ideas with factual information to explain, present a perspective, or describe a situation or event.

(7) Reading/Comprehension of Literary Text/Sensory Language. Students understand, make inferences and draw conclusions about how an author's sensory language creates imagery in literary text and provide evidence from text to support their understanding. Students are expected to explain the role of irony, sarcasm, and paradox in literary works.

(8) Reading/Comprehension of Informational Text/Culture and History. Students analyze, make inferences and draw conclusions about the author's purpose in cultural, historical, and contemporary contexts and provide evidence from the text to support their understanding. Students are expected to explain the controlling idea and specific purpose of an expository text and distinguish the most important from the less important details that support the author's purpose.

(9) Reading/Comprehension of Informational Text/Expository Text. Students analyze, make inferences and draw conclusions about expository text and provide evidence from text to support their understanding. Students are expected to:

(A) summarize text and distinguish between a summary that captures the main ideas and elements of a text and a critique that takes a position and expresses an opinion;

(B) differentiate between opinions that are substantiated and unsubstantiated in the text;

(C) make subtle inferences and draw complex conclusions about the ideas in text and their organizational patterns; and

(D) synthesize and make logical connections between ideas and details in several texts selected to reflect a range of viewpoints on the same topic and support those findings with textual evidence.

(10) Reading/Comprehension of Informational Text/Persuasive Text. Students analyze, make inferences and draw conclusions about persuasive text and provide evidence from text to support their analysis. Students are expected to:

(A) analyze the relevance, quality, and credibility of evidence given to support or oppose an argument for a specific audience; and

(B) analyze famous speeches for the rhetorical structures and devices used to convince the reader of the authors' propositions.

(11) Reading/Comprehension of Informational Text/Procedural Texts. Students understand how to glean and use information in procedural texts and documents. Students are expected to:

(A) analyze the clarity of the objective(s) of procedural text (e.g., consider reading instructions for software, warranties, consumer publications); and

(B) analyze factual, quantitative, or technical data presented in multiple graphical sources.

(12) Reading/Media Literacy. Students use comprehension skills to analyze how words, images, graphics, and sounds work together in various forms to impact meaning. Students will continue to apply earlier standards with greater depth in increasingly more complex texts. Students are expected to:

(A) compare and contrast how events are presented and information is communicated by visual images (e.g., graphic art, illustrations, news photographs) versus non-visual texts;

(B) analyze how messages in media are conveyed through visual and sound techniques (e.g., editing, reaction shots, sequencing, background music);

(C) compare and contrast coverage of the same event in various media (e.g., newspapers, television, documentaries, blogs, Internet); and

(D) evaluate changes in formality and tone within the same medium for specific audiences and purposes.

(13) Writing/Writing Process. Students use elements of the writing process (planning, drafting, revising, editing, and publishing) to compose text. Students are expected to:

(A) plan a first draft by selecting the correct genre for conveying the intended meaning to multiple audiences, determining appropriate topics through a range of strategies (e.g., discussion, background reading, personal interests, interviews), and developing a thesis or controlling idea;

(B) structure ideas in a sustained and persuasive way (e.g., using outlines, note taking, graphic organizers, lists) and develop drafts in timed and open-ended situations that include transitions and the rhetorical devices used to convey meaning;

(C) revise drafts to improve style, word choice, figurative language, sentence variety, and subtlety of meaning after rethinking how well questions of purpose, audience, and genre have been addressed;

(D) edit drafts for grammar, mechanics, and spelling; and

(E) revise final draft in response to feedback from peers and teacher and publish written work for appropriate audiences.

(14) Writing/Literary Texts. Students write literary texts to express their ideas and feelings about real or imagined people, events, and ideas. Students are responsible for at least two forms of literary writing. Students are expected to:

(A) write an engaging story with a well-developed conflict and resolution, interesting and believable characters, and a range of literary strategies (e.g., dialogue, suspense) and devices to enhance the plot;

(B) write a poem using a variety of poetic techniques (e.g., structural elements, figurative language) and a variety of poetic forms (e.g., sonnets, ballads); and

(C) write a script with an explicit or implicit theme and details that contribute to a definite mood or tone.

(15) Writing/Expository and Procedural Texts. Students write expository and procedural or work-related texts to communicate ideas and information to specific audiences for specific purposes. Students are expected to:

(A) write an analytical essay of sufficient length that includes:

   (i) effective introductory and concluding paragraphs and a variety of sentence structures;

   (ii) rhetorical devices, and transitions between paragraphs;

   (iii) a controlling idea or thesis;

   (iv) an organizing structure appropriate to purpose, audience, and context; and

   (v) relevant information and valid inferences;

(B) write procedural or work-related documents (e.g., instructions, e-mails, correspondence, memos, project plans) that include:

   (i) organized and accurately conveyed information; and

   (ii) reader-friendly formatting techniques;

(C) write an interpretative response to an expository or a literary text (e.g., essay or review) that:

   (i) extends beyond a summary and literal analysis;

   (ii) addresses the writing skills for an analytical essay and provides evidence from the text using embedded quotations; and

   (iii) analyzes the aesthetic effects of an author's use of stylistic or rhetorical devices; and

(D) produce a multimedia presentation (e.g., documentary, class newspaper, docudrama, infomercial, visual or textual parodies, theatrical production) with graphics, images, and sound that conveys a distinctive point of view and appeals to a specific audience.

(16) Writing/Persuasive Texts. Students write persuasive texts to influence the attitudes or actions of a specific audience on specific issues. Students are expected to write an argumentative essay to the appropriate audience that includes:

(A) a clear thesis or position based on logical reasons supported by precise and relevant evidence;

(B) consideration of the whole range of information and views on the topic and accurate and honest representation of these views;

(C) counter-arguments based on evidence to anticipate and address objections;

(D) an organizing structure appropriate to the purpose, audience, and context; and

(E) an analysis of the relative value of specific data, facts, and ideas.

(17) Oral and Written Conventions/Conventions. Students understand the function of and use the conventions of academic language when speaking and writing. Students will continue to apply earlier standards with greater complexity. Students are expected to:

(A) use and understand the function of the following parts of speech in the context of reading, writing, and speaking:

   (i) more complex active and passive tenses and verbals (gerunds, infinitives, participles);

   (ii) restrictive and nonrestrictive relative clauses; and

   (iii) reciprocal pronouns (e.g., each other, one another);

(B) identify and use the subjunctive mood to express doubts, wishes, and possibilities; and

(C) use a variety of correctly structured sentences (e.g., compound, complex, compound-complex).

(18) Oral and Written Conventions/Handwriting, Capitalization, and Punctuation. Students write legibly and use appropriate capitalization and punctuation conventions in their compositions. Students are expected to:

(A) use conventions of capitalization; and

(B) use correct punctuation marks including:

   (i) quotation marks to indicate sarcasm or irony;

   (ii) comma placement in nonrestrictive phrases, clauses, and contrasting expressions; and

   (iii) dashes to emphasize parenthetical information.

(19) Oral and Written Conventions/Spelling. Students spell correctly. Students are expected to spell correctly, including using various resources to determine and check correct spellings.

(20) Research/Research Plan. Students ask open-ended research questions and develop a plan for answering them. Students are expected to:

(A) brainstorm, consult with others, decide upon a topic, and formulate a major research question to address the major research topic; and

(B) formulate a plan for engaging in research on a complex, multi-faceted topic.

(21) Research/Gathering Sources. Students determine, locate, and explore the full range of relevant sources addressing a research question and systematically record the information they gather. Students are expected to:

(A) follow the research plan to compile data from authoritative sources in a manner that identifies the major issues and debates within the field of inquiry;

(B) organize information gathered from multiple sources to create a variety of graphics and forms (e.g., notes, learning logs); and

(C) paraphrase, summarize, quote, and accurately cite all researched information according to a standard format (e.g., author, title, page number).

(22) Research/Synthesizing Information. Students clarify research questions and evaluate and synthesize collected information. Students are expected to:

(A) modify the major research question as necessary to refocus the research plan;

(B) evaluate the relevance of information to the topic and determine the reliability, validity, and accuracy of sources (including Internet sources) by examining their authority and objectivity; and

(C) critique the research process at each step to implement changes as the need occurs and is identified.

(23) Research/Organizing and Presenting Ideas. Students organize and present their ideas and information according to the purpose of the research and their audience. Students are expected to synthesize the research into a written or an oral presentation that:

(A) marshals evidence in support of a clear thesis statement and related claims;

(B) provides an analysis for the audience that reflects a logical progression of ideas and a clearly stated point of view;

(C) uses graphics and illustrations to help explain concepts where appropriate;

(D) uses a variety of evaluative tools (e.g., self-made rubrics, peer reviews, teacher and expert evaluations) to examine the quality of the research; and

(E) uses a style manual (e.g., *Modern Language Association, Chicago Manual of Style*) to document sources and format written materials.

(24) Listening and Speaking/Listening. Students will use comprehension skills to listen attentively to others in formal and informal settings. Students will continue to apply earlier standards with greater complexity. Students are expected to:

(A) listen responsively to a speaker by taking notes that summarize, synthesize, or highlight the speaker's ideas for critical reflection and by asking questions related to the content for clarification and elaboration;

(B) follow and give complex oral instructions to perform specific tasks, answer questions, solve problems, and complete processes; and

(C) evaluate the effectiveness of a speaker's main and supporting ideas.

(25) Listening and Speaking/Speaking. Students speak clearly and to the point, using the conventions of language. Students will continue to apply earlier standards with greater complexity. Students are expected to give presentations using informal, formal, and technical language effectively to meet the needs of audience, purpose, and occasion, employing eye contact, speaking rate (e.g., pauses for effect), volume, enunciation, purposeful gestures, and conventions of language to communicate ideas effectively.

(26) Listening and Speaking/Teamwork. Students work productively with others in teams. Students will continue to apply earlier standards with greater complexity. Students are expected to participate productively in teams, building on the ideas of others, contributing relevant information, developing a plan for consensus-building, and setting ground rules for decision-making.

RC-9 Reading/Comprehension Skills. Students use a flexible range of metacognitive reading skills in both assigned and independent reading to understand an author's message. Students will continue to apply earlier standards with greater depth in increasingly more complex texts as they become self-directed, critical readers. The student is expected to:

(A) reflect on understanding to monitor comprehension (e.g., asking questions, summarizing and synthesizing, making connections, creating sensory images); and

(B) make complex inferences about text and use textual evidence to support understanding.

Literary Terms

ACT See *Drama.*

ALLEGORY An *allegory* is a story or tale with two or more levels of meaning—a literal level and one or more symbolic levels. The events, setting, and characters in an allegory are symbols for ideas and qualities.

ALLITERATION *Alliteration* is the repetition of initial consonant sounds. Writers use alliteration to give emphasis to words, to imitate sounds, and to create musical effects. In the following line from Edgar Allan Poe's "The Raven" (p. 710), there is alliteration of the *w* sound: "Once upon a midnight dreary, while I pondered weak and weary, . . ."

ALLUSION An *allusion* is a reference to a well-known person, place, event, literary work, or work of art. In O. Henry's "The Gift of the Magi" (p. 260), the title and details of the story refer to the biblical account of the Magi, wise men who brought gifts to the baby Jesus.

ANALOGY An *analogy* makes a comparison between two or more things that are similar in some ways but otherwise unalike.

ANECDOTE An *anecdote* is a brief story about an interesting, amusing, or strange event told to entertain or to make a point. In the excerpt from "A Lincoln Preface" (p. 500), Carl Sandburg tells anecdotes about Abraham Lincoln. See also *Narrative*.

ANTAGONIST An *antagonist* is a character or force in conflict with a main character, or protagonist.

ANTICLIMAX Like a climax, an *anticlimax* is a turning point in a story. However, an anticlimax is always a letdown. It's the point at which you learn that the story will not turn out the way you had expected. In Thayer's "Casey at the Bat" (p. 696), the anticlimax occurs when Casey strikes out instead of hitting a game-winning run, as everyone had expected.

ARCHETYPE An *archetype* is a type of character, detail, image, or situation that appears in literature from around the world and throughout history. Some critics believe that archetypes reveal deep truths about human experience.

ASIDE An *aside* is a short speech delivered by a character in a play in order to express his or her true thoughts and feelings. Traditionally, the aside is directed to the audience and is presumed to be inaudible to the other actors.

ASSONANCE *Assonance* is the repetition of vowel sounds followed by different consonants in two or more stressed syllables. Assonance is found in the phrase "weak and weary" in Edgar Allan Poe's "The Raven" (p. 710).

ATMOSPHERE See *Mood.*

AUTOBIOGRAPHY An *autobiography* is a form of nonfiction in which a writer tells his or her own life story. An autobiography may tell about the person's whole life or only a part of it. An example of an autobiography is the excerpt from *A White House Diary* (p. 104).

See also *Biography* and *Nonfiction.*

See also *Oral Tradition.*

BIOGRAPHY A *biography* is a form of nonfiction in which a writer tells the life story of another person. Biographies have been written about many famous people, historical and contemporary, but they can also be written about "ordinary" people. An example of a biography is the excerpt from *Arthur Ashe Remembered* (p. 508).

See also *Autobiography* and *Nonfiction.*

BLANK VERSE *Blank verse* is poetry written in unrhymed iambic pentameter lines. This verse form was widely used by William Shakespeare.

See also *Meter.*

CHARACTER A *character* is a person or an animal that takes part in the action of a literary work. The main character, or protagonist, is the most important character in a story. This character often changes in some important way as a result of the story's events. In Richard Connell's "The Most Dangerous Game" (p. 214), Rainsford is the main character and General Zaroff is the antagonist, or character who opposes the main character.

Characters are sometimes classified as round or flat, dynamic or static. A *round character* shows many different traits—faults as well as virtues. A *flat character* shows only one trait. A *dynamic character* develops and grows during the course of the story; a *static character* does not change.

See also *Characterization* and *Motivation.*

CHARACTERIZATION *Characterization* is the act of creating and developing a character. In *direct characterization,* the author directly states a character's traits.

For example, at the beginning of "The Necklace" (p. 332), Maupassant directly characterizes Madame Loisel: "She was one of those pretty, charming young women. . . ."

In *indirect characterization,* an author provides clues about a character by describing what a character looks like, does, and says, as well as how other characters react to him or her. It is up to the reader to draw conclusions about the character based on this indirect information.

The most effective indirect characterizations usually result from showing characters acting or speaking.

See also *Character.*

CLIMAX The *climax* of a story, novel, or play is the high point of interest or suspense. The events that make up the rising action lead up to the climax. The events that make up the falling action follow the climax.

See also *Conflict, Plot,* and *Anticlimax.*

COMEDY A *comedy* is a literary work, especially a play, that has a happy ending. Comedies often show ordinary characters in conflict with society. These conflicts are resolved through misunderstandings, deceptions, and concealed identities, which result in the correction of moral faults or social wrongs. Types of comedy include *romantic comedy,* which involves problems among lovers, and the *comedy of manners,* which satirically challenges the social customs of a sophisticated society. Comedy is often contrasted with tragedy, in which the protagonist meets an unfortunate end.

COMIC RELIEF *Comic relief* is a technique that is used to interrupt a serious part of a literary work by introducing a humorous character or situation.

CONFLICT A *conflict* is a struggle between opposing forces. Characters in conflict form the basis of stories, novels, and plays.

There are two kinds of conflict: external and internal. In an *external conflict,* the main character struggles against an outside force. This force may be another character, as in Richard Connell's "The Most Dangerous Game" (p. 214), in which Rainsford struggles with General Zaroff. The outside force could also be the standards or expectations of a group, such as the family prejudices that Romeo and Juliet struggle against. Their story (p. 806) shows them in conflict with society. The outside force may be nature itself, a person-against-nature conflict. The two men who are trapped by a fallen tree in Saki's "The Interlopers" (p. 270) face such a conflict.

An *internal conflict* involves a character in conflict with himself or herself. In "Checkouts" (p. 82), two young people who meet by chance in a supermarket agonize over whether they should speak to each other.

See also *Plot.*

CONNOTATION The *connotation* of a word is the set of ideas associated with it in addition to its explicit meaning.

See also *Denotation.*

CONSONANCE *Consonance* is the repetition of final consonant sounds in stressed syllables with different vowel sounds, as in *hat* and *sit.*

CONTEMPORARY INTERPRETATION A *contemporary interpretation* is a literary work of today that responds to and sheds new light on a well-known, earlier work of literature. Such an interpretation may refer to any aspect of the older work, including plot, characters, settings, imagery, language, and theme. Edna St. Vincent Millay's poem "An Ancient Gesture" (p. 1128), for example, provides a modern perspective on the characters Penelope and Odysseus in the *Odyssey.*

COUPLET A *couplet* is a pair of rhyming lines, usually of the same length and meter. In the following couplet from a poem by William Shakespeare, the speaker comforts himself with the thought of his love:

> For thy sweet love remember'd such wealth brings
>
> That then I scorn to change my state with kings.

See also *Stanza.*

DENOTATION The *denotation* of a word is its dictionary meaning, independent of other associations that the word may have. The denotation of the word *lake,* for example, is an inland body of water. "Vacation spot" and "place where the fishing is good" are connotations of the word *lake.*

See also *Connotation.*

DESCRIPTION A *description* is a portrait in words of a person, a place, or an object. Descriptive writing uses sensory details, those that appeal to the senses: sight, hearing, taste, smell, and touch. Description can be found in all types of writing. Rudolfo Anaya's essay "A Celebration of Grandfathers" (p. 444) contains descriptive passages.

DIALECT *Dialect,* the form of language spoken by people in a particular region or group, may involve changes to the pronunciation, vocabulary, and sentence structure of standard English. An example from Mark Twain's "The Invalid's Story" (p. 362) is a character's use of the term *yourn* for *yours.*

DIALOGUE A *dialogue* is a conversation between characters that may reveal their traits and advance the action of a narrative. In fiction or nonfiction, quotation marks indicate a speaker's exact words, and a new paragraph usually indicates a change of speaker. Following is an exchange between the narrator and his frail younger brother, Doodle, in "The Scarlet Ibis" (p. 384):

> "Aw, come on Doodle," I urged. "You can do it. Do you want to be different from everybody else when you start school?"
>
> "Does it make any difference?"

Quotation marks are not used in a *script*, the printed copy of a play. Instead, the dialogue follows the name of the speaker, as in this example from Chekhov's *The Inspector General* (p. 970):

> **DRIVER.** Oh, yes, he's a good one, this one.

DICTION *Diction* refers to an author's choice of words, especially with regard to range of vocabulary, use of slang and colloquial language, and level of formality. These lines from Ernest Lawrence Thayer's poem "Casey at the Bat" (p. 696) are an example of colloquial, informal diction: "It looked extremely rocky for the Mudville nine that day; / The score stood two to four; with but an inning left to play."

See also **Connotation** and **Denotation.**

DIRECT CHARACTERIZATION See **Characterization.**

DRAMA A *drama* is a story written to be performed by actors. The script of a drama is made up of *dialogue*—the words the actors say—and *stage directions,* which are comments on how and where action happens.

The drama's *setting* is the time and place in which the action occurs. It is indicated by one or more sets, including furniture and backdrops, that suggest interior or exterior scenes. *Props* are objects, such as a sword or a cup of tea, that are used onstage.

At the beginning of most plays, a brief *exposition* gives the audience some background information about the characters and the situation. Just as in a story or novel, the plot of a drama is built around characters in conflict.

Dramas are divided into large units called *acts,* which are divided into smaller units called scenes. A long play may include many sets that change with the *scenes,* or it may indicate a change of scene with lighting.

See also **Dialogue, Genre, Stage Directions,** and **Tragedy.** *Romeo and Juliet* (p. 806) is a long play in five acts.

DRAMATIC IRONY See **Irony.**

DRAMATIC MONOLOGUE A *dramatic monologue* is a poem in which a character reveals himself or herself by speaking to a silent listener.

DRAMATIC POETRY *Dramatic poetry* is poetry that utilizes the techniques of drama. The dialogue used in Edgar Allan Poe's "The Raven" (p. 710) makes it dramatic dialogue. A *dramatic monologue* is a poem spoken by one person, addressing a silent listener.

END RHYME See **Rhyme.**

EPIC An *epic* is a long narrative poem about the deeds of gods or heroes. Homer's *Odyssey* (p. 1044) is an example of epic poetry. It tells the story of the Greek hero Odysseus, the king of Ithaca.

An epic is elevated in style and usually follows certain patterns. The poet begins by announcing the subject and asking a Muse—one of the nine goddesses of the arts, literature, and sciences—to help. An *epic hero* is the larger-than-life central character in an epic. Through behavior and deeds, the epic hero displays qualities that are valued by the society in which the epic originated.

See also **Epic Simile** and **Narrative Poem.**

EPIC SIMILE An *epic simile,* also called **Homeric simile,** is an elaborate comparison of unlike subjects. In this example from the *Odyssey* (p. 1044), Homer compares the bodies of men killed by Odysseus to a fisherman's catch heaped up on the shore:

> Think of a catch that fishermen haul in to a
> > half-moon bay
>
> in a fine-meshed net from the whitecaps of the sea:
> how all are poured out on the sand, in throes
> > for the salt sea,
>
> twitching their cold lives away in Helios' fiery air:
> > so lay the suitors heaped on one another.

See also **Figurative Language** and **Simile.**

EPIPHANY An *epiphany* is a character's sudden flash of insight into a conflict or situation. At the end of Judith

Ortiz Cofer's story "American History" (p. 240), for example, the central character experiences an epiphany.

ESSAY An *essay* is a short nonfiction work about a particular subject. While classification is difficult, four types of essays are sometimes identified.

A *descriptive essay* seeks to convey an impression about a person, place, or object. In "A Celebration of Grandfathers" (p. 444), Rudolfo Anaya describes the cultural values that his grandfather and other "old ones" from his childhood passed down.

A *narrative essay* tells a true story. In "The Washwoman" (p. 26), Isaac Bashevis Singer tells of his childhood in Poland.

An *expository essay* gives information, discusses ideas, or explains a process. In "Single Room, Earth View" (p. 468), Sally Ride explains what it is like to be in outer space.

A *persuasive essay* tries to convince readers to do something or to accept the writer's point of view. Pete Hamill's "Libraries Face Sad Chapter" (p. 530) is a persuasive essay.

See also *Description, Exposition, Genre, Narration, Nonfiction,* and *Persuasion.*

EXPOSITION *Exposition* is writing or speech that explains a process or presents information. In the plot of a story or drama, the exposition is the part of the work that introduces the characters, the setting, and the basic situation.

EXTENDED METAPHOR In an *extended metaphor,* as in regular metaphor, a writer speaks or writes of a subject as though it were something else. An extended metaphor sustains the comparison for several lines or for an entire poem.

See also *Figurative Language* and *Metaphor.*

EXTERNAL CONFLICT See *Conflict.*

FALLING ACTION See *Plot.*

FANTASY A *fantasy* is highly imaginative writing that contains elements not found in real life. Examples of fantasy include stories that involve supernatural elements, stories that resemble fairy tales, and stories that deal with imaginary places and creatures.

See also *Science Fiction.*

FICTION *Fiction* is prose writing that tells about imaginary characters and events. The term is usually used for novels and short stories, but it also applies to dramas and narrative poetry. Some writers rely on their imaginations alone to create their works of fiction. Others base their fiction on actual events and people, to which they add invented characters, dialogue, and plot situations.

See also *Genre, Narrative,* and *Nonfiction.*

FIGURATIVE LANGUAGE *Figurative language* is writing or speech not meant to be interpreted literally. It is often used to create vivid impressions by setting up comparisons between dissimilar things.

Some frequently used figures of speech are *metaphors, similes,* and *personifications.*

See also *Literal Language.*

FLASHBACK A *flashback* is a means by which authors present material that occurred earlier than the present tense of the narrative. Authors may include this material in a character's memories, dreams, or accounts of past events.

FOIL A *foil* is a character who provides a contrast to another character. In *Romeo and Juliet* (p. 806), the fiery temper of Tybalt serves as a foil to the good nature of Benvolio.

FOOT See *Meter.*

FORESHADOWING *Foreshadowing* is the use in a literary work of clues that suggest events that have yet to occur. This technique helps create suspense, keeping readers wondering about what will happen next.

See also *Suspense.*

FREE VERSE *Free verse* is poetry not written in a regular pattern of meter or rhyme. Like Whitman's "I Hear America Singing" (p. 750), however, it may use parallelism and various sound devices.

GENRE A *genre* is a category or type of literature. Literature is commonly divided into three major genres: poetry, prose, and drama. Each major genre is in turn divided into smaller genres, as follows:

1. Poetry: Lyric Poetry, Concrete Poetry, Dramatic Poetry, Narrative Poetry, and Epic Poetry

2. Prose: Fiction (Novels and Short Stories) and Nonfiction (Biography, Autobiography, Letters, Essays, and Reports)

3. Drama: Serious Drama and Tragedy, Comic Drama, Melodrama, and Farce

See also *Drama, Poetry,* and *Prose.*

HAIKU The *haiku* is a three-line verse form. The first and third lines of a haiku each have five syllables. The second line has seven syllables. A haiku seeks to convey a single vivid emotion by means of images from nature.

HOMERIC SIMILE See *Epic Simile.*

HYPERBOLE A *hyperbole* is a deliberate exaggeration or overstatement. In Mark Twain's "The Notorious Jumping Frog of Calaveras County," the claim that Jim Smiley would follow a bug as far as Mexico to win a bet is a hyperbole. As this example shows, hyperboles are often used for comic effect.

IAMB See *Meter.*

IDIOM An *idiom* is an expression that is characteristic of a language, region, community, or class of people. *Idiomatic expressions* often arise from figures of speech and therefore cannot be understood literally. In "The Invalid's Story" (p. 362), for example, a character uses the idiom *throw up the sponge,* meaning "surrender."

See also *Dialect.*

IMAGE An *image* is a word or phrase that appeals to one or more of the five senses—sight, hearing, touch, taste, or smell. Writers use images to re-create sensory experiences in words.

See also *Description.*

IMAGERY *Imagery* is the descriptive or figurative language used in literature to create word pictures for the reader. These pictures, or images, are created by details of sight, sound, taste, touch, smell, or movement.

INDIRECT CHARACTERIZATION See *Characterization.*

INTERNAL See *Conflict.*

INTERNAL RHYME See *Rhyme.*

IRONY *Irony* is the general term for literary techniques that portray differences between appearance and reality, or expectation and result. In *verbal irony,* words are used to suggest the opposite of what is meant. In *dramatic irony,* there is a contradiction between what a character thinks and what the reader or audience knows to be true. In *irony of situation,* an event occurs that directly contradicts the expectations of the characters, the reader, or the audience.

LEGEND See *Oral Tradition.*

LITERAL LANGUAGE *Literal language* uses words in their ordinary senses. It is the opposite of *figurative language.* If you tell someone standing on a diving board to jump in, you speak literally. If you tell someone on the street to jump in a lake, you are speaking figuratively.

See also *Figurative Language.*

LYRIC POEM A *lyric poem* is a highly musical verse that expresses the thoughts, observations, and feelings of a single speaker.

MAIN CHARACTER See *Character.*

METAPHOR A *metaphor* is a figure of speech in which one thing is spoken of as though it were something else. Unlike a simile, which compares two things using *like* or *as,* a metaphor implies a comparison between them. In "Dreams" (p. 621), Langston Hughes uses a metaphor to show what happens to a life without dreams:

> . . . if dreams die
>
> Life is a broken-winged bird
>
> That cannot fly.

See also *Extended Metaphor* and *Figurative Language.*

METER The *meter* of a poem is its rhythmical pattern. This pattern is determined by the number and types of stresses, or beats, in each line. To describe the meter of a poem, you must scan its lines. Scanning involves marking the stressed and unstressed syllables, as shown with the following two lines from "I Wandered Lonely as a Cloud" by William Wordsworth (p. 626):

> Ĭ wán|dĕřed lóne|lў ás| ă clóud
>
> Thăt floáts | ŏn hígh| o'ĕr váles| ănd hílls.

As you can see, each strong stress is marked with a slanted line (´) and each unstressed syllable with a horseshoe symbol (˘). The stressed and unstressed syllables are then divided by vertical lines (|) into groups called *feet.* The following types of feet are common in English poetry:

1. *Iamb:* a foot with one unstressed syllable followed by a stressed syllable, as in the word "again"

2. *Trochee:* a foot with one stressed syllable followed by an unstressed syllable, as in the word "wonder"

3. *Anapest:* a foot with two unstressed syllables followed by one strong stress, as in the phrase "on the beach"

4. *Dactyl:* a foot with one strong stress followed by two unstressed syllables, as in the word "wonderful"

5. *Spondee:* a foot with two strong stresses, as in the word "spacewalk"

Depending on the type of foot that is most common in them, lines of poetry are described as *iambic, trochaic, anapestic,* and so forth.

Lines are also described in terms of the number of feet that occur in them, as follows:

1. *Monometer:* verse written in one-foot lines
   All things
   Must pass
   Away.

2. *Dimeter:* verse written in two-foot lines
   Thomas | Jefferson
   What do | you say
   Under the | gravestone
   Hidden | away?

   —Rosemary and Stephen Vincent Benét, "Thomas Jefferson, 1743–1826"

3. *Trimeter:* verse written in three-foot lines
   I know | not whom | I meet
   I know | not where | I go.

4. *Tetrameter:* verse written in four-foot lines

5. *Pentameter:* verse written in five-foot lines

6. *Hexameter:* verse written in six-foot lines

7. *Heptameter:* verse written in seven-foot lines

Blank verse, used by Shakespeare in *Romeo and Juliet* (p. 806), is poetry written in unrhymed iambic pentameter.

Free verse, used by Walt Whitman in "I Hear America Singing" (p. 750), is poetry that does not follow a regular pattern of meter and rhyme.

MONOLOGUE A *monologue* in a play is a speech by one character that, unlike a *soliloquy,* is addressed to another character or characters. An example from Shakespeare's *Romeo and Juliet* (p. 806) is the speech by the Prince of Verona in Act 1, Scene i, lines 77–99.

See also *Soliloquy.*

MONOMETER See *Meter.*

MOOD *Mood,* or *atmosphere,* is the feeling created in the reader by a literary work or passage. The mood is often suggested by descriptive details. Often the mood can be described in a single word, such as *lighthearted, frightening,* or *despairing.* Notice how this passage from Edgar Allan Poe's "The Cask of Amontillado" (p. 60) contributes to an eerie, fearful mood:

"The niter!" I said; "see, it increases. It hangs like moss upon the vaults. We are below the river's bed. The drops of moisture trickle among the bones. Come, we will go back ere it is too late."

See also *Tone.*

MORAL A *moral* is a lesson taught by a literary work, especially a fable—many fables, for example, have a stated moral at the end. It is customary, however, to discuss contemporary works in terms of the themes they explore, rather than a moral that they teach.

MOTIVATION *Motivation* is a reason that explains or partially explains why a character thinks, feels, acts, or behaves in a certain way. Motivation results from a combination of the character's personality and the situation he or she must deal with. In "Checkouts" (p. 82), the main character is motivated by conflicting feelings.

See also *Character* and *Characterization.*

MYTH A *myth* is a fictional tale that describes the actions of gods and heroes or explains the causes of natural phenomena. Unlike legends, myths emphasize supernatural rather than historical elements. Many cultures have collections of myths, and the most familiar in the Western world are those of the ancient Greeks and Romans. "Perseus" (p. 1233) is a retelling of a famous ancient Greek myth.

See also *Oral Tradition.*

NARRATION *Narration* is writing that tells a story. The act of telling a story in speech is also called narration. Novels and short stories are fictional narratives. Nonfiction works—such as news stories, biographies, and autobiographies—are also narratives. A narrative poem tells a story in verse.

See also *Anecdote, Essay, Narrative Poem, Nonfiction, Novel,* and *Short Story.*

NARRATIVE A *narrative* is a story told in fiction, non-fiction, poetry, or drama.

See also *Narration.*

NARRATIVE POEM A *narrative poem* is one that tells a story. "Casey at the Bat" (p. 696) is a humorous narrative poem about the last inning of a baseball game. Edgar Allan Poe's "The Raven" (p. 710) is a serious narrative poem about a man's grief over the loss of a loved one.

See also *Dramatic Poetry, Epic,* and *Narration.*

NARRATOR A *narrator* is a speaker or character who tells a story. The writer's choice of narrator determines the story's *point of view,* which directs the type and amount of information the writer reveals.

When a character in the story tells the story, that character is a *first-person narrator*. This narrator may be a major character, a minor character, or just a witness. Readers see only what this character sees, hear only what he or she hears, and so on. The first-person narrator may or may not be reliable. We have reason, for example, to be suspicious of the first-person narrator of Edgar Allan Poe's "The Cask of Amontillado" (p. 60).

When a voice outside the story narrates, the story has a *third-person narrator*. An omniscient, or all-knowing, third-person narrator can tell readers what any character thinks and feels. For example, in Guy de Maupassant's "The Necklace" (p. 332), we know the feelings of both Monsieur and Madame Loisel. A limited third-person narrator sees the world through one character's eyes and reveals only that character's thoughts. In James Thurber's "The Secret Life of Walter Mitty" (p. 128), the narrator reveals only Mitty's experiences and feelings.

See also *Speaker.*

NONFICTION *Nonfiction* is prose writing that presents and explains ideas or that tells about real people, places, ideas, or events. To be classified as nonfiction, a work must be true. "Single Room, Earth View" (p. 468) is a nonfictional account of the view of Earth from space.

See also *Autobiography, Biography,* and *Essay.*

NOVEL A *novel* is a long work of fiction. It has a plot that explores characters in conflict. A novel may also have one or more subplots, or minor stories, and several themes.

NOVELLA A *novella* is a work of fiction that is longer than a short story but shorter than a novel.

OCTAVE See *Stanza.*

ONOMATOPOEIA *Onomatopoeia* is the use of words that imitate sounds. *Whirr, thud, sizzle,* and *hiss* are typical examples. Writers can deliberately choose words that contribute to a desired sound effect.

ORAL TRADITION The *oral tradition* is the passing of songs, stories, and poems from generation to generation by word of mouth. Many folk songs, ballads, fairy tales, legends, and myths originated in the oral tradition.

See also *Myth.*

OXYMORON An *oxymoron* is a combination of words, or parts of words, that contradict each other. Examples are "deafening silence," "honest thief," "wise fool," and "bittersweet." This device is effective when the apparent contradiction reveals a deeper truth, as in Act 2, Scene ii,

line 184, of *Romeo and Juliet* (p. 806) when Juliet bids goodbye to Romeo: "Parting is such *sweet sorrow.*"

PARADOX A *paradox* is a statement that seems contradictory but actually may be true. Because a paradox is surprising, it catches the reader's attention.

PARALLELISM See *Rhetorical Devices.*

PENTAMETER See *Meter.*

PERSONIFICATION *Personification* is a type of figurative language in which a nonhuman subject is given human characteristics. William Wordsworth personifies daffodils when he describes them as "Tossing their heads in sprightly dance" (p. 626).

See also *Figurative Language.*

PERSUASION *Persuasion* is writing or speech that attempts to convince the reader to adopt a particular opinion or course of action.

PLOT *Plot* is the sequence of events in a literary work. In most novels, dramas, short stories, and narrative poems, the plot involves both characters and a central conflict. The plot usually begins with an *exposition* that introduces the setting, the characters, and the basic situation. This is followed by the *inciting incident,* which introduces the central conflict. The conflict then increases during the *development* until it reaches a high point of interest or suspense, the *climax.* All the events leading up to the climax make up the *rising action.* The climax is followed by the *falling action,* which leads to the *denouement,* or *resolution,* in which a general insight or change is conveyed.

POETRY *Poetry* is one of the three major types of literature, the others being prose and drama. Most poems make use of highly concise, musical, and emotionally charged language. Many also make use of imagery, figurative language, and special devices of sound such as rhyme. Poems are often divided into lines and stanzas and often employ regular rhythmical patterns, or meters. However, some poems are written out just like prose, while others are written in free verse.

See also *Genre.*

POINT OF VIEW See *Narrator.*

PROSE *Prose* is the ordinary form of written language. Most writing that is not poetry, drama, or song is considered prose. Prose is one of the major genres of literature and occurs in two forms: fiction and nonfiction.

See also *Fiction, Genre,* and *Nonfiction.*

PROTAGONIST The protagonist is the main character in a literary work.

See also **Antagonist** and **Character.**

PUN A **pun** is a play on words involving a word with two or more different meanings or two words that sound alike but have different meanings. In *Romeo and Juliet* (p. 806), the dying Mercutio makes a pun involving two meanings of the word *grave,* "serious" and "burial site": "Ask for me tomorrow, and you shall find me a grave man" (Act 3, Scene i, lines 92–93).

QUATRAIN A **quatrain** is a stanza or poem made up of four lines, usually with a definite rhythm and rhyme scheme.

REPETITION **Repetition** is the use of any element of language—a sound, a word, a phrase, a clause, or a sentence—more than once.

Poets use many kinds of repetition. Alliteration, assonance, rhyme, and rhythm are repetitions of certain sounds and sound patterns. A refrain is a repeated line or group of lines. In both prose and poetry, repetition is used for musical effects and for emphasis.

See also **Alliteration, Assonance, Rhyme,** and **Rhythm.**

RESOLUTION See **Plot.**

RHETORICAL DEVICES **Rhetorical devices** are special patterns of words and ideas that create emphasis and stir emotion, especially in speeches or other oral presentations. **Parallelism,** for example, is the repetition of a grammatical structure in order to create a rhythm and make words more memorable. In his "I Have a Dream" speech (p. 542), Martin Luther King, Jr., uses parallel statements beginning, "I have a dream that . . ."

Other common rhetorical devices include *restatement,* expressing the same idea in different words, and *rhetorical questions,* questions with obvious answers.

RHYME **Rhyme** is the repetition of sounds at the ends of words. **End rhyme** occurs when the rhyming words come at the ends of lines, as in "The Desired Swan Song" by Samuel Taylor Coleridge:

> Swans sing before they die—'twere no bad thing
> Should certain persons die before they sing.

Internal rhyme occurs when the rhyming words appear in the same line, as in the first line of Edgar Allan Poe's "The Raven" (p. 710):

> Once upon a midnight *dreary,* while I pondered, weak and *weary,* . . .

Exact rhyme involves the repetition of words with the same vowel and consonant sounds, like *ball* and *hall. Slant rhyme* involves the repetition of words that sound alike but do not rhyme exactly, like *grove* and *love.*

See also **Repetition** and **Rhyme Scheme.**

RHYME SCHEME A **rhyme scheme** is a regular pattern of rhyming words in a poem. The rhyme scheme of a poem is indicated by using different letters of the alphabet for each new rhyme. In an *aabb* stanza, for example, line 1 rhymes with line 2 and line 3 rhymes with line 4. William Wordsworth's poem "I Wandered Lonely as a Cloud" (p. 626) uses an *ababcc* rhyme pattern:

> I wandered lonely as a cloud   a
> That floats on high o'er vales and hills,   b
> When all at once I saw a crowd,   a
> A host, of golden daffodils;   b
> Beside the lake, beneath the trees,   c
> Fluttering and dancing in the breeze.   c

Many poems use the same pattern of rhymes, though not the same rhymes, in each stanza.

See also **Rhyme.**

RHYTHM **Rhythm** is the pattern of *beats,* or *stresses,* in spoken or written language. Some poems have a very specific pattern, or meter, whereas prose and free verse use the natural rhythms of everyday speech.

See also **Meter.**

RISING ACTION See **Plot.**

ROUND CHARACTER See **Character.**

SATIRE A **satire** is a literary work that ridicules the foolishness and faults of individuals, an institution, society, or even humanity in general.

SCENE See **Drama.**

SCIENCE FICTION **Science fiction** is writing that tells about imaginary events involving science or technology. Many science-fiction stories are set in the future. Arthur C. Clarke's "If I Forget Thee, Oh Earth . . ." (p. 162) is set on the moon after a nuclear disaster on Earth.

See also **Fantasy.**

SENSORY LANGUAGE **Sensory language** is writing or speech that appeals to one or more of the senses.

See also **Image.**

SESTET See *Stanza.*

SETTING The *setting* of a literary work is the time and place of the action. Time can include not only the historical period—past, present, or future—but also a specific year, season, or time of day. Place may involve not only the geographical place—a region, country, state, or town—but also the social, economic, or cultural environment.

In some stories, setting serves merely as a backdrop for action, a context in which the characters move and speak. In others, however, setting is a crucial element.

See also *Mood.*

SHORT STORY A *short story* is a brief work of fiction. In most short stories, one main character faces a conflict that is resolved in the plot of the story. Great craftsmanship must go into the writing of a good story, for it has to accomplish its purpose in relatively few words.

See also *Fiction* and *Genre.*

SIMILE A *simile* is a figure of speech in which the words *like* or *as* are used to compare two apparently dissimilar items. The comparison, however, surprises the reader into a fresh perception by finding an unexpected likeness. In "Dream Deferred" (p. 620), Langston Hughes uses the simile "Does it dry up/like a raisin in the sun?" to discuss a dream deferred.

SOLILOQUY A *soliloquy* is a long speech expressing the thoughts of a character alone on stage. In William Shakespeare's *Romeo and Juliet* (p. 806), Romeo gives a soliloquy after the servant has fled and Paris has died (Act V, Scene iii, lines 74–120).

See also *Monologue.*

SONNET A *sonnet* is a fourteen-line lyric poem, usually written in rhymed iambic pentameter. The *English,* or *Shakespearean,* sonnet consists of three quatrains (four-line stanzas) and a couplet (two lines), usually rhyming *abab cdcd efef gg.* The couplet usually comments on the ideas contained in the preceding twelve lines. The sonnet is usually not printed with the stanzas divided, but a reader can see distinct ideas in each. See Sonnet 30 by William Shakespeare on page 754.

The *Italian,* or *Petrarchan,* sonnet consists of an octave (eight-line stanza) and a sestet (six-line stanza). Often, the octave rhymes *abbaabba* and the sestet rhymes *cdecde.* The octave states a theme or asks a question. The sestet comments on or answers the question.

See also *Lyric Poem, Meter,* and *Stanza.*

SOUND DEVICES A *sound device* is a technique used by a poet to emphasize the sound relationships among words in order to create musical and emotional effects and emphasize a poem's meaning. These devices include *alliteration, consonance, assonance, onomatopoeia,* and *rhyme.*

SPEAKER The *speaker* is the imaginary voice assumed by the writer of a poem. In many poems, the speaker is not identified by name. When reading a poem, remember that the speaker within the poem may be a person, an animal, a thing, or an abstraction. The speaker in the following stanza by Emily Dickinson is a person who has died:

> Because I could not stop for Death—
> He kindly stopped for me—
> The Carriage held but just Ourselves—
> And Immortality.

STAGE DIRECTIONS *Stage directions* are notes included in a drama to describe how the work is to be performed or staged. These instructions are printed in italics and are not spoken aloud. They are used to describe sets, lighting, sound effects, and the appearance, personalities, and movements of characters.

See also *Drama.*

STANZA A *stanza* is a repeated grouping of two or more lines in a poem that often share a pattern of rhythm and rhyme. Stanzas are sometimes named according to the number of lines they have—for example, a *couplet,* two lines; a *quatrain,* four lines; a *sestet,* six lines; and an *octave,* eight lines.

STATIC CHARACTER See *Character.*

STYLE *Style* refers to an author's unique way of writing. Elements determining style include diction; tone; characteristic use of figurative language, dialect, or rhythmic devices; and syntax, or typical grammatical structures and patterns.

See also *Diction* and *Tone.*

SURPRISE ENDING A *surprise ending* is a conclusion that violates the expectations of the reader but in a way that is both logical and believable.

O. Henry's "The Gift of the Magi" (p. 260) and Guy de Maupassant's "The Necklace" (p. 332) have surprise endings. Both authors were masters of this form.

SUSPENSE *Suspense* is a feeling of uncertainty about the outcome of events in a literary work. Writers create suspense by raising questions in the minds of their readers.

SYMBOL A *symbol* is anything that stands for something else. In addition to having its own meaning and reality, a symbol also represents abstract ideas. For example, a flag is a piece of cloth, but it also represents the idea of a country. Writers sometimes use conventional symbols like flags. Frequently, however, they create symbols of their own through emphasis or repetition. In James Hurst's "The Scarlet Ibis" (p. 384), for example, the ibis symbolizes the character named Doodle. Both are beautiful and other-worldly.

TALL TALE A *tall tale* is a type of folk tale that contains some or all of these features: humor, hyperbole, far-fetched situations, highly imaginative language, and a hero who performs outrageous feats. Tall tales originated during the development of the American frontier and are a particularly American form of folk tale. "Pecos Bill: The Cyclone" (p. 1218) is an example of a tall tale.

THEME A *theme* is a central message or insight into life revealed through a literary work.

The theme of a literary work may be stated directly or implied. When the theme of a work is implied, readers think about what the work suggests about people or life.

Archetypal themes are those that occur in folklore and literature across the world and throughout history. Ill-fated love, the theme of *Romeo and Juliet* (p. 806), is an example of such a theme.

TONE The *tone* of a literary work is the writer's attitude toward his or her audience and subject. The tone can often be described by a single adjective, such as *formal* or *informal, serious* or *playful, bitter* or *ironic.* When O. Henry discusses the young couple in "The Gift of the Magi" (p. 260), he uses a sympathetic tone.

See also *Mood.*

TRAGEDY A *tragedy* is a work of literature, especially a play, that results in a catastrophe, a disaster or great misfortune, for the main character, or *tragic hero.* In ancient Greek drama, the main character was always a significant person—a king or a hero—and the cause of the tragedy was a *tragic flaw,* or weakness, in his or her character. In modern drama, the main character can be an ordinary person, and the cause of the tragedy can be some evil in society itself. Tragedy not only arouses fear and pity in the audience but also, in some cases, conveys a sense of the grandeur and nobility of the human spirit.

Shakespeare's *Romeo and Juliet* (p. 806) is a tragedy. Romeo and Juliet both suffer from the tragic flaw of impulsiveness. This flaw ultimately leads to their deaths.

See also *Drama.*

UNDERSTATEMENT An *understatement* is a figure of speech in which the stated meaning is purposely less than (or "under") what is really meant. It is the opposite of *hyperbole,* which is a deliberate exaggeration.

UNIVERSAL THEME A *universal theme* is a message about life that can be understood by most cultures. Many folk tales and examples of classic literature address universal themes such as the importance of courage, the effects of honesty, or the danger of greed.

VERBAL IRONY See *Irony.*

VILLANELLE A *villanelle* is a nineteen-line lyric poem written in five three-line stanzas and ending in a four-line stanza. It uses two rhymes and repeats two refrain lines that appear initially in the first and third lines of the first stanza. These lines then appear alternately as the third line of subsequent three-line stanzas and, finally, as the last two lines of the poem.

VISUAL ESSAY A *visual essay* is an exploration of a topic that conveys its ideas through visual elements as well as language. Like a standard essay, a visual essay presents an author's views of a single topic. Unlike other essays, however, much of the meaning in a visual essay is conveyed through illustrations or photographs.

VOICE *Voice* is a writer's distinctive "sound" or way of "speaking" on the page. It is related to such elements as word choice, sentence structure, and tone. It is similar to an individual's speech style and can be described in the same way—fast, slow, blunt, meandering, breathless, and so on.

Voice resembles *style,* an author's typical way of writing, but style usually refers to a quality that can be found throughout an author's body of work, while an author's voice may sometimes vary from work to work.

See also *Style.*

Tips for Discussing Literature

As you read and study literature, discussion with other readers can help you understand, enjoy, and develop interpretations of what you read. Use the following tips to practice good speaking and listening skills while participating in group discussions of literature.

Understand the purpose of your discussion

When you discuss literature, your purpose is to broaden your understanding and appreciation of a work by testing your own ideas and hearing the ideas of others. Stay focused on the literature you are discussing, and keep your comments relevant to that literature. Starting with one focus question will help keep your discussion on track.

Communicate effectively

Effective communication requires thinking before speaking. Plan the points that you want to make, and decide how you will express them. Organize these points in logical order, and cite details from the work to support your ideas. Jot down informal notes to help keep your ideas focused.

Remember to speak clearly, pronouncing words slowly and carefully so that others can understand your points. Also, keep in mind that some literature touches readers deeply—be aware of the possibility of counterproductive emotional responses, and work to control them. Negative emotional responses can also be conveyed through body language, so work to demonstrate respect in your demeanor as well as in your words.

Encourage everyone to participate

While some people are comfortable participating in discussions, others are less eager to speak up in groups. However, everyone should work to contribute thoughts and ideas. To encourage the entire group's participation, try the following strategies:

- If you enjoy speaking, avoid monopolizing the conversation. After sharing your ideas, encourage others to share theirs.
- Try different roles. For example, have everyone take turns being the facilitator or host of the discussion.
- Use a prop, such as a book or gavel. Pass the prop around the group, allowing whomever is holding the prop to have the floor.

Make relevant contributions

Especially when responding to a short story, a poem, or a novel, avoid simply summarizing the plot. Instead, consider *what* you think might happen next, *why* events take place as they do, or *how* a writer provokes a response in you. Let your ideas inspire deeper thought or discussion about the literature.

Consider other ideas and interpretations

A work of literature can generate a wide variety of responses in different readers—and that can make your discussions exciting. Be open to the idea that many interpretations can be valid. To support your own ideas, point to the events, descriptions, characters, or other literary elements in the work that produced your interpretation. To consider someone else's ideas, decide whether details in the work support the interpretation he or she presents. Be sure to convey your criticism of the ideas of others in a respectful and supportive manner.

Ask questions and extend the contributions of others

Get in the habit of asking questions to help you clarify your understanding of another reader's ideas. You can also use questions to call attention to possible areas of confusion, to points that are open to debate, or to errors.

In addition, offer elaboration of the points that others make by providing examples and illustrations. To move a discussion forward, pause occasionally to summarize and evaluate tentative conclusions reached by the group members. Then, continue the discussion with a fresh understanding of the material and ideas you have already covered.

Manage differing opinions and views

Each participant brings his or her own personality, experiences, ideas, cultural background, likes and dislikes to the experience of reading, making disagreement almost inevitable. As differences arise, be sensitive to each individual's point of view. Do not personalize disagreements, but keep them focused on the literature or ideas under discussion.

When you meet with a group to discuss literature, use a chart like the one shown to analyze the discussion.

Work Being Discussed:	
Focus Question:	
Your Response:	Another Student's Response:
Supporting Evidence:	Supporting Evidence:

Literary Criticism

Criticism is writing that explores the meaning and techniques of literary works, usually in order to evaluate them. Writing criticism can help you think through your experience of a work of literature and can also help others deepen their own understanding. All literary criticism shares similar goals:

- *Making Connections* within or between works, or between a work of literature and its context
- *Making Distinctions* or showing differences between elements of a single work or aspects of two or more works
- *Achieving Insights* that were not apparent from a superficial reading
- *Making a Judgment* about the quality or value of a literary work

Critics use various *theories of literary criticism* to understand, appreciate, and evaluate literature. Some theories focus on the context of the work while others focus on the work itself. Sometimes critics combine one or more theories. These charts show a few examples of the many theories of criticism:

Focus on Contexts	
Human Experience	**Mythic Criticism** Explores universal situations, characters, and symbols called archetypes as they appear in a literary work.
Culture and History	**Historical Criticism** Analyzes how circumstances or ideas of an era influence a work
Author's Life	**Biographical Criticism** Explains how the author's life sheds light on the work

Focus on the Work Itself
Formal Criticism Shows how the work reflects characteristics of the genre, or literary type, to which it belongs

Examples of Literary Theories in Action

- *Mythic Criticism:* discussing how Robert Frost's "The Road Not Taken," p. 724, explores the archetypal situation of choice at a fork in the road
- *Historical Criticism:* showing how American frontier life led to the use of exaggeration in "Pecos Bill: The Cyclone," p. 1218
- *Biographical Criticism:* showing that Edgar Allan Poe's loss of his parents at an early age influenced the theme of "The Raven," p. 710
- *Formal Criticism:* showing how "The Scarlet Ibis," p. 384, displays short-story elements like plot, setting, character, symbol, and theme

Literary Movements

Our literary heritage has been shaped by a number of literary movements, directions in literature characterized by shared assumptions, beliefs, and practices. This chart shows, in chronological order, some important literary movements. While these movements developed at particular historical moments, all of them may still influence individual writers working today.

Movement	Beliefs and Practices	Examples
Classicism Europe during the Renaissance (c. 1300–1650)	• Looks to classical literature of ancient Greece and Rome as models • Values logic, clarity, balance, and restraint • Prefers "ordered" nature of parks and gardens	the clarity and restraint of Robert Frost's verse ("The Road Not Taken," p. 724)
Romanticism Europe during the late 1700s and the early 1800s	• Rebels against Classicism • Values imagination and emotion • Focuses on everyday life	the celebration of the natural world in Rachel Carson's writings ("Silent Spring," p. 167)
Realism Europe and America from the mid–1800s to the 1890s	• Rebels against Romanticism's search for the ideal • Focuses on everyday life	the faithful rendering of Pueblo life in Leslie Marmon Silko's fiction ("The Man to Send Rain Clouds," p. 292)
Naturalism Europe and America during the late 1800s and early 1900s	• Assumes people cannot choose their fate but are shaped by psychological and social forces • Views society as a competitive jungle	the portrayal of characters as victims of social pressures and psychology in Guy de Maupassant's fiction ("The Necklace," p. 332)
Modernism Worldwide between 1890 and 1945	• In response to WWI, questions human reason • Focuses on studies of the unconscious and the art of primitive peoples • Experiments with language and form	the experiments with language in E. E. Cummings's poetry ("maggie and milly and molly and may," p. 732)
Post-Modernism Worldwide after 1945; still prevalent today	• Includes an eclectic mix of styles, such as parody, magical realism, and dark humor. • Often rebels against reason.	the magical realism in Isabel Allende's fiction ("Uncle Marcos," p. 138)

Types of Writing

Writing is a process that begins with the exploration of ideas and ends with the presentation of a final draft. Often, the types of writing are grouped into modes according to form and purpose.

Narration

Whenever writers tell any type of story, they are using **narration.** Most narratives share certain elements, such as characters, a setting, a sequence of events, and, often, a theme. Following are some types of narration:

Autobiographical writing Autobiographical writing tells a true story about an important period, experience, or relationship in the writer's life. Effective autobiographical writing includes

- A series of events that involve the writer as the main character
- Details, thoughts, feelings, and insights from the writer's perspective
- A conflict or an event that affects the writer
- A logical organization that tells the story clearly
- Insights that the writer gained from the experience

Types of autobiographical writing include personal narratives, autobiographical sketches, reflective essays, eyewitness accounts, and memoirs.

Short story A short story is a brief, creative narrative. Most short stories include

- Details that establish the setting in time and place
- A main character who undergoes a change or learns something during the course of the story
- A conflict or a problem to be introduced, developed, and resolved
- A plot, the series of events that make up the action of the story
- A theme or message about life

Types of short stories include realistic stories, fantasies, historical narratives, mysteries, thrillers, science-fiction stories, and adventure stories.

Description

Descriptive writing is writing that creates a vivid picture of a person, place, thing, or event. Most descriptive writing includes

- Sensory details—sights, sounds, smells, tastes, and physical sensations

- Vivid, precise language
- Figurative language or comparisons
- Adjectives and adverbs that paint a word picture
- An organization suited to the subject

Types of descriptive writing include descriptions of ideas, observations, travel brochures, physical descriptions, functional descriptions, remembrances, and character sketches.

Persuasion

Persuasion is writing or speaking that attempts to convince people to accept a position or take a desired action. Following are some types of persuasion:

Persuasive essay A persuasive essay presents a position on an issue, urges readers to accept that position, and may encourage a specific action. An effective persuasive essay

- Explores an issue of importance to the writer
- Addresses an issue that is arguable
- Uses facts, examples, statistics, or personal experiences to support a position
- Tries to influence the audience through appeals to the readers' knowledge, experiences, or emotions
- Uses clear organization to present a logical argument

Forms of persuasion include editorials, position papers, persuasive speeches, grant proposals, advertisements, and debates.

Advertisements An advertisement is a planned communication meant to be seen, heard, or read. It attempts to persuade an audience to buy a product or service, accept an idea, or support a cause. Advertisements may appear in printed or broadcast form. An effective advertisement includes

- A memorable slogan to grab the audience's attention
- A call to action
- Persuasive and/or informative text
- Striking visual or aural images
- Informative details about price, location, date, and time

Several common types of advertisements are public-service announcements, billboards, merchandise ads, service ads, and political campaign literature.

Exposition

Exposition is writing that relies on facts to inform or explain. Effective expository writing reflects a well-thought-out organization—one that includes a clear introduction, body, and conclusion. Here are some types of exposition:

Comparison-and-contrast essay A comparison-and-contrast essay analyzes the similarities and differences between or among two or more things. An effective comparison-and-contrast essay

- Identifies a purpose for comparison and contrast
- Identifies similarities and differences between or among two or more things, people, places, or ideas
- Gives factual details about the subjects
- Uses an organizational plan suited to the topic and purpose

Cause-and-effect essay A cause-and-effect essay examines the relationship between events, explaining how one event or situation causes another. A successful cause-and-effect essay includes

- A discussion of a cause, event, or condition that produces a specific result
- An explanation of an effect, outcome, or result
- Evidence and examples to support the relationship between cause and effect
- A logical organization that makes the explanation clear

Problem-and-solution essay A problem-and-solution essay describes a problem and offers one or more solutions to it. It describes a clear set of steps to achieve a result. An effective problem-and-solution essay includes

- A clear statement of the problem, with its causes and effects summarized for the reader
- The most important aspects of the problem
- A proposal of at least one realistic solution
- Facts, statistics, data, or expert testimony to support the solution
- A clear organization that makes the relationship between problem and solution obvious

Research Writing

Research writing is based on information gathered from outside sources. A research paper—a focused study of a topic—helps writers explore and connect ideas, make discoveries, and share their findings with an audience. An effective research paper

- Focuses on a specific, narrow topic, which is usually summarized in a thesis statement
- Presents relevant information from a wide variety of sources
- Uses a clear organization that includes an introduction, body, and conclusion
- Includes a bibliography or works-cited list that identifies the sources from which the information was drawn

Other types of writing that depend on accurate and insightful research include multimedia presentations, statistical reports, annotated bibliographies, and experiment journals.

Response to Literature

When you write a **response-to-literature essay,** you give yourself the opportunity to discover *what, how,* and *why* a piece of writing affected you. An effective response

- Contains a reaction to a poem, story, essay, or other work of literature
- Analyzes the content of a literary work, its related ideas, or the work's effect on the reader
- Presents a thesis statement to identify the nature of the response
- Focuses on a single aspect of the work or gives a general overview
- Supports opinion with evidence from the work addressed

The following are just a few of the ways you might respond in writing to a literary work: reader's response journals, literary letters, and literary analyses.

Workplace Writing

Workplace writing is probably the format you will use most after you finish school. In general, workplace writing is fact-based and meant to communicate specific information in a structured format. Effective workplace writing

- Communicates information concisely
- Includes details that provide necessary information and anticipate potential questions
- Is error-free and neatly presented

Common types of workplace writing include business letters, memorandums, résumés, forms, and applications.

Writing Friendly Letters

Writing Friendly Letters

A friendly letter is much less formal than a business letter. It is a letter to a friend, a family member, or anyone with whom the writer wants to communicate in a personal, friendly way. Most friendly letters are made up of five parts:

- ✔ the heading
- ✔ the salutation, or greeting
- ✔ the body
- ✔ the closing
- ✔ the signature

The purpose of a friendly letter is often one of the following:

- ✔ to share personal news and feelings
- ✔ to send or to answer an invitation
- ✔ to express thanks

Model Friendly Letter

In this friendly letter, Betsy thanks her grandparents for a birthday present and gives them some news about her life.

---

11 Old Farm Road
Topsham, Maine 04011

April 14, 20—

Dear Grandma and Grandpa,

Thank you for the sweater you sent me for my birthday. It fits perfectly, and I love the color. I wore my new sweater to the carnival at school last weekend and got lots of compliments.

The weather here has been cool but sunny. Mom thinks that "real" spring will never come. I can't wait until it's warm enough to go swimming.

School is going fairly well. I really like my Social Studies class. We are learning about the U.S. Constitution, and I think it's very interesting. Maybe I will be a lawyer when I grow up.

When are you coming out to visit us? We haven't seen you since Thanksgiving. You can stay in my room when you come. I'll be happy to sleep on the couch. (The TV is in that room!!)

Well, thanks again and hope all is well with you.

Love,

Betsy

> The **heading** includes the writer's address and the date on which he or she wrote the letter.

> The **body** is the main part of the letter and contains the basic message.

> Some common **closings** for personal letters include "Best Wishes," "Love," "Sincerely," and "Yours Truly."

Writing Business Letters

Formatting Business Letters

Business letters follow one of several acceptable formats. In **block format,** each part of the letter begins at the left margin. A double space is used between paragraphs. In **modified block format,** some parts of the letter are indented to the center of the page. No matter which format is used, all letters in business format have a heading, an inside address, a salutation or greeting, a body, a closing, and a signature. These parts are shown and annotated on the model business letter below, formatted in modified block style.

Model Business Letter

In this letter, Yolanda Dodson uses modified block format to request information.

Students for a Cleaner Planet
c/o Memorial High School
333 Veteran's Drive
Denver, CO 80211

January 25, 20—

Steven Wilson, Director
Resource Recovery Really Works
300 Oak Street
Denver, CO 80216

Dear Mr. Wilson:

Memorial High School would like to start a branch of your successful recycling program. We share your commitment to reclaiming as much reusable material as we can. Because your program has been successful in other neighborhoods, we're sure that it can work in our community. Our school includes grades 9–12 and has about 800 students.

Would you send us some information about your community recycling program? For example, we need to know what materials can be recycled and how we can implement the program.

At least fifty students have already expressed an interest in getting involved, so I know we'll have the people power to make the program work. Please help us get started.

Thank you in advance for your time and consideration.

Sincerely,

Yolanda Dodson

Yolanda Dodson

The **heading** shows the writer's address and organization (if any) and the date.

The **inside address** indicates where the letter will be sent.

A **salutation** is punctuated by a colon. When the specific addressee is not known, use a general greeting such as "To whom it may concern:"

The **body** of the letter states the writer's purpose. In this case, the writer requests information.

The **closing** "Sincerely" is common, but "Yours truly" or "Respectfully yours" are also acceptable. To end the letter, the writer types her name and provides a **signature.**

Writing a Résumé

Writing a Résumé

A résumé summarizes your educational background, work experiences, relevant skills, and other employment qualifications. It also tells potential employers how to contact you. An effective résumé presents the applicant's name, address, and phone number. It follows an accepted résumé organization, using labels and headings to guide readers.

A résumé should outline the applicant's educational background, life experiences, and related qualifications using precise and active language.

Model Résumé

With this résumé, James, a college student, hopes to find a full-time job.

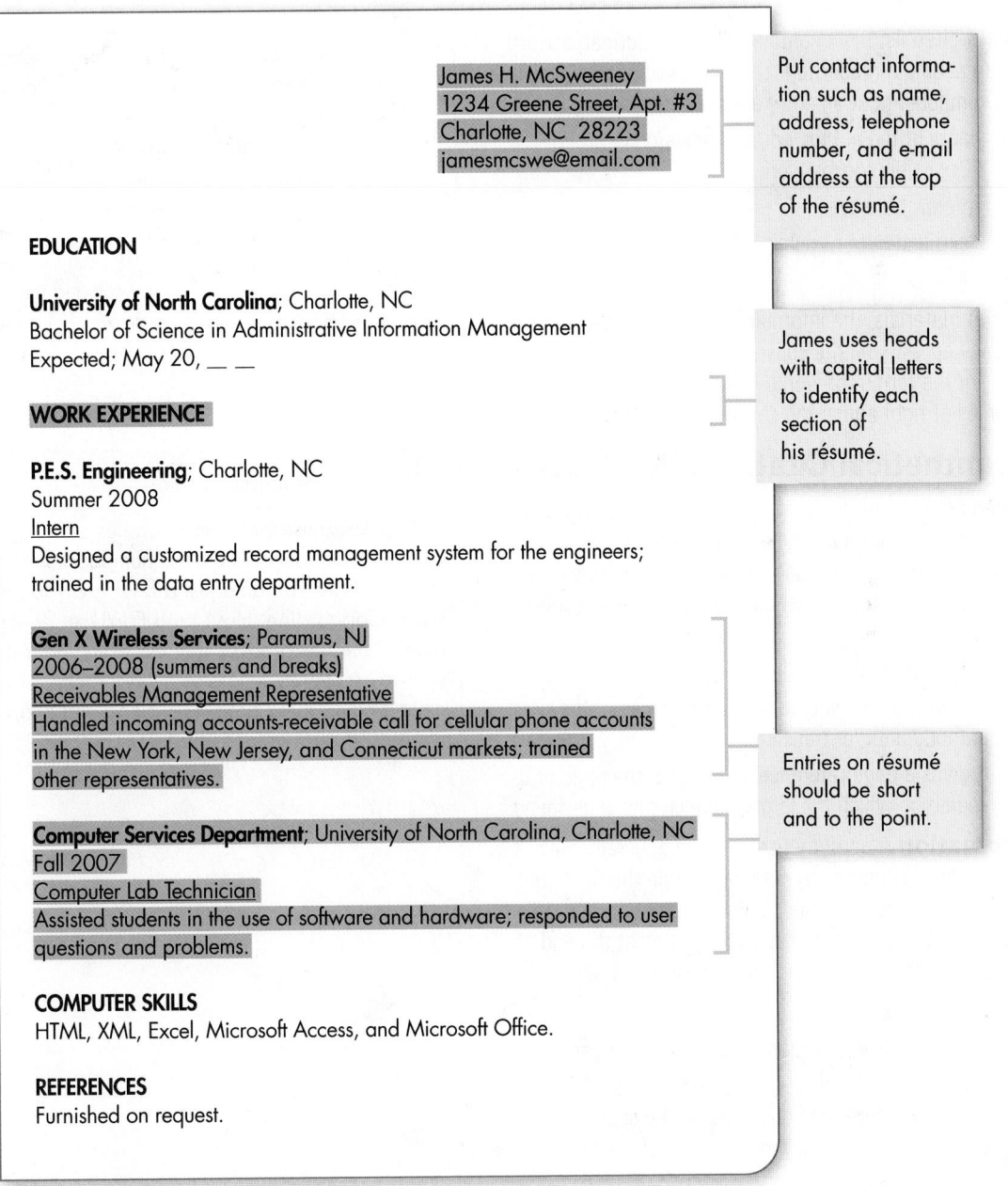

James H. McSweeney
1234 Greene Street, Apt. #3
Charlotte, NC 28223
jamesmcswe@email.com

> Put contact information such as name, address, telephone number, and e-mail address at the top of the résumé.

EDUCATION

University of North Carolina; Charlotte, NC
Bachelor of Science in Administrative Information Management
Expected; May 20, __ __

> James uses heads with capital letters to identify each section of his résumé.

WORK EXPERIENCE

P.E.S. Engineering; Charlotte, NC
Summer 2008
Intern
Designed a customized record management system for the engineers; trained in the data entry department.

Gen X Wireless Services; Paramus, NJ
2006–2008 (summers and breaks)
Receivables Management Representative
Handled incoming accounts-receivable call for cellular phone accounts in the New York, New Jersey, and Connecticut markets; trained other representatives.

Computer Services Department; University of North Carolina, Charlotte, NC
Fall 2007
Computer Lab Technician
Assisted students in the use of software and hardware; responded to user questions and problems.

> Entries on résumé should be short and to the point.

COMPUTER SKILLS
HTML, XML, Excel, Microsoft Access, and Microsoft Office.

REFERENCES
Furnished on request.

Citing Sources and Preparing Manuscript

In research writing, cite your sources. In the body of your paper, provide a footnote, an endnote, or a parenthetical citation, identifying the sources of facts, opinions, or quotations. At the end of your paper, provide a bibliography or a works-cited list, a list of all the sources you cite. Follow an established format, such as Modern Language Association (MLA) Style.

Works-Cited List (MLA Style)

A works-cited list must contain accurate information sufficient to enable a reader to locate each source you cite. The basic components of an entry are as follows:

- Name of the author, editor, translator, or group responsible for the work
- Title of the work
- Place and date of publication
- Publisher

For print materials, the information required for a citation generally appears on the copyright and title pages of a work. For the format of works-cited list entries, consult the examples at right and in the chart on page R41.

Parenthetical Citations (MLA Style)

A parenthetical citation briefly identifies the source from which you have taken a specific quotation, factual claim, or opinion. It refers the reader to one of the entries on your works-cited list. A parenthetical citation has the following features:

- It appears in parentheses.
- It identifies the source by the last name of the author, editor, or translator.
- It gives a page reference, identifying the page of the source on which the information cited can be found.

Punctuation A parenthetical citation generally falls outside a closing quotation mark but within the final punctuation of a clause or sentence. For a long quotation set off from the rest of your text, place the citation at the end of the excerpt without any punctuation following.

Special Cases

- If the author is an organization, use the organization's name, in a shortened version if necessary.
- If you cite more than one work by the same author, add the title or a shortened version of the title.

Sample Works-Cited Lists (MLA 7th Edition)

Carwardine, Mark, Erich Hoyt, R. Ewan Fordyce, and Peter Gill. *The Nature Company Guides: Whales, Dolphins, and Porpoises.* New York: Time-Life. 1998. Print.

"Discovering Whales." *Whales on the Net.* 1998. Whales in Danger Information Service. Web. 18 Oct. 1999.

Neruda, Pablo. "Ode to Spring." *Odes to Opposites.* Trans. Ken Krabbenhoft. Ed. and illus. Ferris Cook. Boston: Little, 1995. Print.

The Saga of the Volsungs. Trans. Jesse L. Byock. London: Penguin, 1990. Print.

> List an anonymous work by title.

> List both the title of the work and the collection in which it is found.

Sample Parenthetical Citations

It makes sense that baleen whales such as the blue whale, the bowhead whale, the humpback whale, and the sei whale (to name just a few) grow to immense sizes (Carwardine, Hoyt, and Fordyce 19–21). The blue whale has grooves running from under its chin to partway along the length of its underbelly. As in some other whales, these grooves expand and allow even more food and water to be taken in (Ellis 18–21).

> Author's last name

> Page numbers where information can be found

MLA Style for Listing Sources

Book with one author	Pyles, Thomas. *The Origins and Development of the English Language.* 2nd ed. New York: Harcourt, 1971. Print.
Book with two or three authors	McCrum, Robert, William Cran, and Robert MacNeil. *The Story of English.* New York: Penguin, 1987. Print.
Book with an editor	Truth, Sojourner. *Narrative of Sojourner Truth.* Ed. Margaret Washington. New York: Vintage, 1993. Print.
Book with more than three authors or editors	Donald, Robert B., et al. *Writing Clear Essays.* Upper Saddle River: Prentice, 1996. Print.
Single work in an anthology	Hawthorne, Nathaniel. "Young Goodman Brown." *Literature: An Introduction to Reading and Writing.* Ed. Edgar V. Roberts and Henry E. Jacobs. Upper Saddle River: Prentice, 1998. 376–385. Print. [Indicate pages for the entire selection.]
Introduction to a work in a published edition	Washington, Margaret. Introduction. *Narrative of Sojourner Truth.* By Sojourner Truth. Ed. Washington. New York: Vintage, 1993. v–xi. Print.
Signed article from an encyclopedia	Askeland, Donald R. "Welding." *World Book Encyclopedia.* 1991 ed. Print.
Signed article in a weekly magazine	Wallace, Charles. "A Vodacious Deal." *Time* 14 Feb. 2000: 63. Print.
Signed article in a monthly magazine	Gustaitis, Joseph. "The Sticky History of Chewing Gum." *American History* Oct. 1998: 30–38. Print.
Newspaper	Thurow, Roger. "South Africans Who Fought for Sanctions Now Scrap for Investors." *Wall Street Journal* 11 Feb. 2000: A1+. Print. [For a multipage article that does not appear on consecutive pages, write only the first page number on which it appears, followed by a plus sign.]
Unsigned editorial or story	"Selective Silence." Editorial. *Wall Street Journal* 11 Feb. 2000: A14. Print. [If the editorial or story is signed, begin with the author's name.]
Signed pamphlet or brochure	[Treat the pamphlet as though it were a book.]
Work from a library subscription service	Ertman, Earl L. "Nefertiti's Eyes." *Archaeology* Mar.–Apr. 2008: 28–32. *Kids Search.* EBSCO. New York Public Library. Web. 18 June 2008 [Indicate the date you accessed the information.]
Filmstrips, slide programs, videocassettes, DVDs, and other audiovisual media	*The Diary of Anne Frank.* Dir. George Stevens. Perf. Millie Perkins, Shelley Winters, Joseph Schildkraut, Lou Jacobi, and Richard Beymer. 1959. Twentieth Century Fox, 2004. DVD.
CD-ROM (with multiple publishers)	Simms, James, ed. *Romeo and Juliet.* By William Shakespeare. Oxford: Attica Cybernetics; London: BBC Education; London: Harper, 1995. CD-ROM.
Radio or television program transcript	"Washington's Crossing of the Delaware." *Weekend Edition Sunday.* Natl. Public Radio. WNYC, New York. 23 Dec. 2003. Television transcript.
Internet Web page	"Fun Facts About Gum." NACGM site. 1999. National Association of Chewing Gum Manufacturers. Web. 19 Dec. 1999 [Indicate the date you accessed the information.]
Personal interview	Smith, Jane. Personal interview. 10 Feb. 2000.

All examples follow the style given in the *MLA Handbook for Writers of Research Papers*, seventh edition, by Joseph Gibaldi.

Guide to Rubrics

What is a rubric?

A rubric is a tool, often in the form of a chart or a grid, that helps you assess your work. Rubrics are particularly helpful for writing and speaking assignments.

To help you or others assess, or evaluate, your work, a rubric offers several specific criteria to be applied to your work. Then, the rubric helps you or an evaluator indicate your range of success or failure according to those specific criteria. Rubrics are often used to evaluate writing for standardized tests.

Using a rubric will save you time, focus your learning, and improve the work you do. When you know what the rubric will be before you begin writing a persuasive essay, for example, you will be aware as you write of specific criteria that are important in that kind of essay. As you evaluate the essay before giving it to your teacher, you will focus on the specific areas that your teacher wants you to master—or on areas that you know present challenges for you. Instead of searching through your work randomly for any way to improve it or correct its errors, you will have a clear and helpful focus on specific criteria.

How are rubrics constructed?

Rubrics can be constructed in several different ways.

- Your teacher may assign a rubric for a specific assignment.
- Your teacher may direct you to a rubric in your textbook.
- Your teacher and your class may construct a rubric for a particular assignment together.
- You and your classmates may construct a rubric together.
- You may create your own rubric with criteria you want to evaluate in your work.

How will a rubric help me?

A rubric will help you assess your work on a scale. Scales vary from rubric to rubric but usually range from 6 to 1, 5 to 1, or 4 to 1, with 6, 5, or 4 being the highest score and 1 being the lowest. If someone else is using the rubric to assess your work, the rubric will give your evaluator a clear range within which to place your work. If you are using the rubric yourself, it will help you make improvements to your work.

What are the types of rubrics?

- A **holistic rubric** has general criteria that can apply to a variety of assignments. See p. R40 for an example of a holistic rubric.
- An **analytic rubric** is specific to a particular assignment. The criteria for evaluation address the specific issues important in that assignment. See p. R39 for examples of analytic rubrics.

Sample Analytic Rubrics

Rubric With a 4-point Scale

The following analytic rubric is an example of a rubric to assess a persuasive essay. It will help you evaluate focus, organization, support/elaboration, and style/convention.

	Focus	Organization	Support/Elaboration	Style/Convention
4	Demonstrates highly effective word choice; clearly focused on task.	Uses clear, consistent organizational strategy.	Provides convincing, well-elaborated reasons to support the position.	Incorporates transitions; includes very few mechanical errors.
3	Demonstrates good word choice; stays focused on persuasive task.	Uses clear organizational strategy with occasional inconsistencies.	Provides two or more moderately elaborated reasons to support the position.	Incorporates some transitions; includes few mechanical errors.
2	Shows some good word choices; minimally stays focused on persuasive task.	Uses inconsistent organizational strategy; presentation is not logical.	Provides several reasons, but few are elaborated; only one elaborated reason.	Incorporates few transitions; includes many mechanical errors.
1	Shows lack of attention to persuasive task.	Demonstrates lack of organizational strategy.	Provides no specific reasons or does not elaborate.	Does not connect ideas; includes many mechanical errors.

Rubric With a 6-point Scale

The following analytic rubric is an example of a rubric to assess a persuasive essay. It will help you evaluate presentation, position, evidence, and arguments.

	Presentation	Position	Evidence	Arguments
6	Essay clearly and effectively addresses an issue with more than one side.	Essay clearly states a supportable position on the issue.	All evidence is logically organized, well presented, and supports the position.	All reader concerns and counterarguments are effectively addressed.
5	Most of essay addresses an issue that has more than one side.	Essay clearly states a position on the issue.	Most evidence is logically organized, well presented, and supports the position.	Most reader concerns and counterarguments are effectively addressed.
4	Essay adequately addresses issue that has more than one side.	Essay adequately states a position on the issue.	Many parts of evidence support the position; some evidence is out of order.	Many reader concerns and counterarguments are adequately addressed.
3	Essay addresses issue with two sides but does not present second side clearly.	Essay states a position on the issue, but the position is difficult to support.	Some evidence supports the position, but some evidence is out of order.	Some reader concerns and counterarguments are addressed.
2	Essay addresses issue with two sides but does not present second side.	Essay states a position on the issue, but the position is not supportable.	Not much evidence supports the position, and what is included is out of order.	A few reader concerns and counterarguments are addressed.
1	Essay does not address issue with more than one side.	Essay does not state a position on the issue.	No evidence supports the position.	No reader concerns or counterarguments are addressed.

Sample Holistic Rubric

Holistic rubrics such as this one are sometimes used to assess writing assignments on standardized tests. Notice that the criteria for evaluation are focus, organization, support, and use of conventions.

Points	Criteria
6 Points	• The writing is strongly focused and shows fresh insight into the writing task. • The writing is marked by a sense of completeness and coherence and is organized with a logical progression of ideas. • A main idea is fully developed, and support is specific and substantial. • A mature command of the language is evident, and the writing may employ characteristic creative writing strategies. • Sentence structure is varied, and writing is free of all but purposefully used fragments. • Virtually no errors in writing conventions appear.
5 Points	• The writing is clearly focused on the task. • The writing is well organized and has a logical progression of ideas, though there may be occasional lapses. • A main idea is well developed and supported with relevant detail. • Sentence structure is varied, and the writing is free of fragments, except when used purposefully. • Writing conventions are followed correctly.
4 Points	• The writing is clearly focused on the task, but extraneous material may intrude at times. • Clear organizational pattern is present, though lapses may occur. • A main idea is adequately supported, but development may be uneven. • Sentence structure is generally fragment free but shows little variation. • Writing conventions are generally followed correctly.
3 Points	• Writing is generally focused on the task, but extraneous material may intrude at times. • An organizational pattern is evident, but writing may lack a logical progression of ideas. • Support for the main idea is generally present but is sometimes illogical. • Sentence structure is generally free of fragments, but there is almost no variation. • The work generally demonstrates a knowledge of writing conventions, with occasional misspellings.
2 Points	• The writing is related to the task but generally lacks focus. • There is little evidence of organizational pattern, and there is little sense of cohesion. • Support for the main idea is generally inadequate, illogical, or absent. • Sentence structure is unvaried, and serious errors may occur. • Errors in writing conventions and spellings are frequent.
1 Point	• The writing may have little connection to the task and is generally unfocused. • There has been little attempt at organization or development. • The paper seems fragmented, with no clear main idea. • Sentence structure is unvaried, and serious errors appear. • Poor word choice and poor command of the language obscure meaning. • Errors in writing conventions and spelling are frequent.
Unscorable	The paper is considered unscorable if: • The response is unrelated to the task or is simply a rewording of the prompt. • The response has been copied from a published work. • The student did not write a response. • The response is illegible. • The words in the response are arranged with no meaning. • There is an insufficient amount of writing to score.

Student Model

Persuasive Writing

This persuasive letter, which would receive a top score according to a persuasive rubric, is a response to the following writing prompt, or assignment:

With the increased use of technology in the workplace, the skills that high-school graduates must possess have changed. Write a letter to your principal advocating new technology courses that could give high-school graduates a competitive edge.

Dear Principal:

I am writing to alert you to an urgent need in our school's curriculum. We need computer graphics courses!

Although you would have to find funds to buy the equipment, I've concluded that setting up this course would well be worth it. By adding this course, you would be adding many high paying career options for students. Computer graphics is a type of art, and businesses all around us involve art in some form. You see computer graphics in commercials, movies, news broadcasts, weather broadcasts, architectural design, and business presentations. Workers with computer graphics skills are well paid because they are in such high demand.

You may argue that the school already has computer science classes. Good point! I'm in a computer science class and it is mainly programming. Once we did have an assignment to design a graphic of a pumpkin. You wouldn't believe how much coding it takes to get a simple, animated drawing. In order to get a really creative image with definite lines, shading, lifelike colors, and texture, you need to use computer graphics software designed especially for that purpose. With software, you can make images that move and talk smoothly and environments with realistic colors and lighting. This is the same graphics software that businesses use for commercials, movies, and brochures. Students should be learning how to use this software.

Most important, computer graphics is a subject area that allows students to express their creativity. Adding a computer graphics course would have a positive effect on students. Course participants would enjoy doing their assignments, so they would earn good grades and turn in creative work. The energy and enthusiasm they would bring to their projects would catch the attention of the community at large. As a result, they would make the school and the principal look good.

As you can see, adding a computer graphics course could be a very profitable idea for you, the students, and the community. You would be ensuring the success of the students who desire an art or computer career. You would be opening hundreds of different career pathways. Wouldn't it be great to know you were the reason for these students' success? Thanks for your time and consideration.

Sincerely,
Dawn Witherspoon

The letter begins with an engaging introduction that clearly states the persuasive focus.

The author effectively counters an opposing argument to increase the persuasive power of her own argument.

A positive argument that is well supported enhances the letter's persuasive appeal.

21st Century Skills

New technology has created many new ways to communicate. Today, it is easy to contribute information to the Internet and send a variety of messages to friends far and near. You can also share your ideas through photos, illustrations, video, and sound recordings. *21st Century Skills* gives you an overview of some ways you can use today's technology to create, share, and find information. Here are the topics you will find in this section.

- ✔ Blogs
- ✔ Multimedia Elements
- ✔ Social Networking
- ✔ Podcasts
- ✔ Widgets & Feeds
- ✔ Wikis

BLOGS

A **blog** is a common form of online writing. The word *blog* is a contraction of *Web log*. Most blogs include a series of entries known as *posts*. The posts appear in a single column and are displayed in reverse chronological order. That means that the most recent post is at the top of the page. As you scroll down, you will find earlier posts.

Blogs have become increasingly popular. Researchers estimate that 75,000 new blogs are launched every day. Blog authors are often called *bloggers*. They can use their personal sites to share ideas, songs, videos, photos, and other media. People who read blogs can often post their responses with a comments feature found in each new post.

Because blogs are designed so that they are easy to update, bloggers can post new messages as often as they like, often daily. For some people blogs become a public journal or diary, in which they share their thoughts about daily events.

Types of Blogs

Not all blogs are the same. Many blogs have a single author, but others are group projects. These are some common types of blog:

- ✔ Personal blogs often have a general focus. Bloggers post their thoughts on any topic they find interesting in their daily lives.

- ✔ Topical blogs focus on a specific theme, such as movie reviews, political news, class assignments, or health-care opportunities.

Web Safety

Always be aware that information you post on the Internet can be read by everyone with access to that page. Once you post a picture or text, it can be saved on someone else's computer, even if you later remove it.

Using the Internet safely means keeping personal information personal. Never include your address (e-mail or real), last name, or telephone numbers. Avoid mentioning places you can be frequently found. Never give out passwords you use to access other Web sites and do not respond to e-mails from people you do not know.

Anatomy of a Blog

Here are some of the features you can include in a blog.

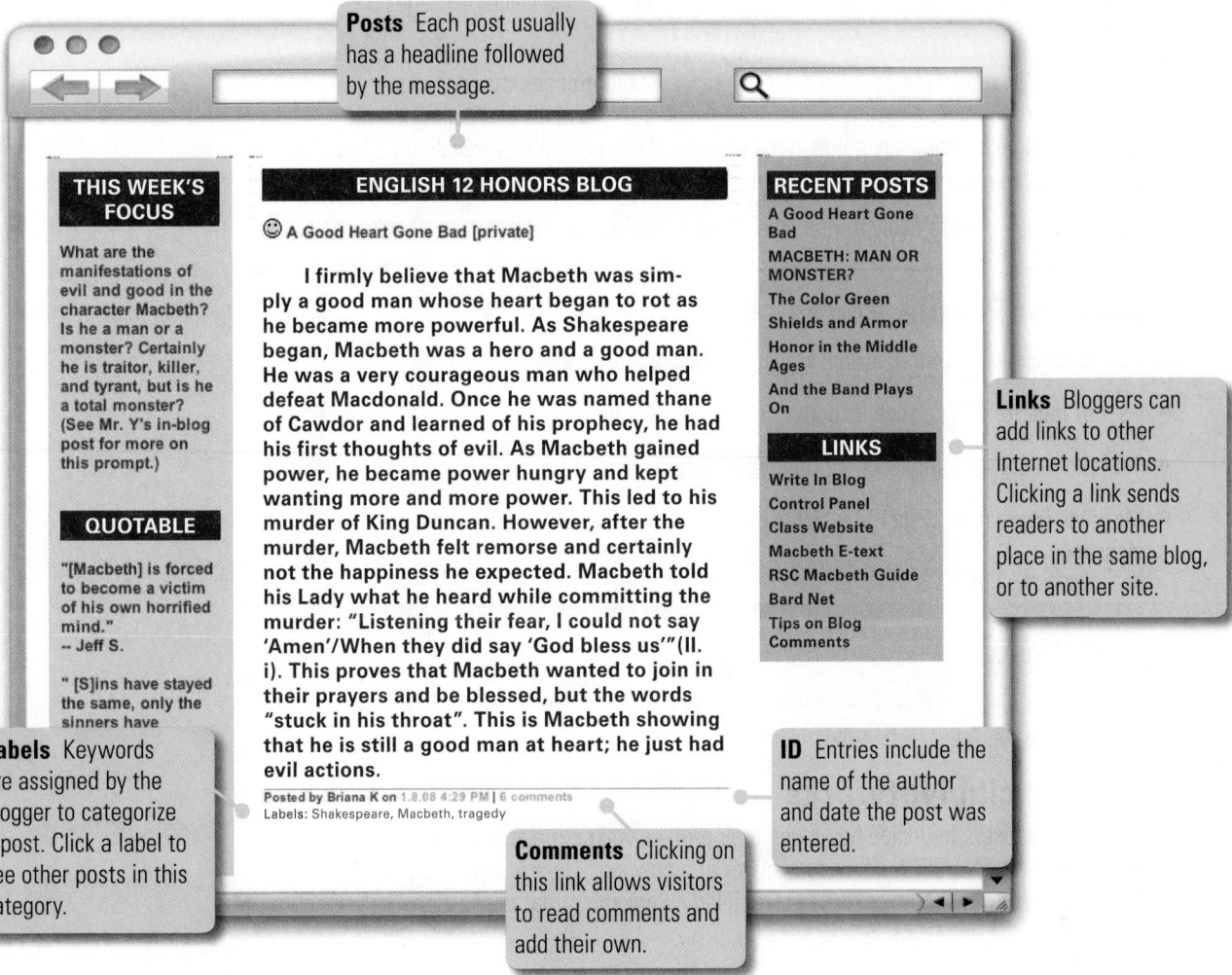

Posts Each post usually has a headline followed by the message.

THIS WEEK'S FOCUS

What are the manifestations of evil and good in the character Macbeth? Is he a man or a monster? Certainly he is traitor, killer, and tyrant, but is he a total monster? (See Mr. Y's in-blog post for more on this prompt.)

QUOTABLE

"[Macbeth] is forced to become a victim of his own horrified mind."
-- Jeff S.

" [S]ins have stayed the same, only the sinners have

ENGLISH 12 HONORS BLOG

A Good Heart Gone Bad [private]

I firmly believe that Macbeth was simply a good man whose heart began to rot as he became more powerful. As Shakespeare began, Macbeth was a hero and a good man. He was a very courageous man who helped defeat Macdonald. Once he was named thane of Cawdor and learned of his prophecy, he had his first thoughts of evil. As Macbeth gained power, he became power hungry and kept wanting more and more power. This led to his murder of King Duncan. However, after the murder, Macbeth felt remorse and certainly not the happiness he expected. Macbeth told his Lady what he heard while committing the murder: "Listening their fear, I could not say 'Amen'/When they did say 'God bless us'"(II. i). This proves that Macbeth wanted to join in their prayers and be blessed, but the words "stuck in his throat". This is Macbeth showing that he is still a good man at heart; he just had evil actions.

Posted by Briana K on 1.8.08 4:29 PM | 6 comments
Labels: Shakespeare, Macbeth, tragedy

RECENT POSTS

A Good Heart Gone Bad
MACBETH: MAN OR MONSTER?
The Color Green
Shields and Armor
Honor in the Middle Ages
And the Band Plays On

LINKS

Write In Blog
Control Panel
Class Website
Macbeth E-text
RSC Macbeth Guide
Bard Net
Tips on Blog Comments

Links Bloggers can add links to other Internet locations. Clicking a link sends readers to another place in the same blog, or to another site.

ID Entries include the name of the author and date the post was entered.

Labels Keywords are assigned by the blogger to categorize a post. Click a label to see other posts in this category.

Comments Clicking on this link allows visitors to read comments and add their own.

Creating a Blog

Keep these hints and strategies in mind to help you create an interesting and fair blog:

✔ Focus each blog entry on a single topic.

✔ Vary the length of your posts. Sometimes, all you need is a line or two to share a quick thought. Other posts will be much longer.

✔ Choose font colors and styles that can be read easily.

✔ Many people scan blogs rather than read them closely. You can make your main ideas pop out by using clear or clever headlines and boldfacing key terms.

✔ Give credit to other people's work and ideas. State the names of people whose ideas you are quoting or add a link to take readers to that person's blog or site.

✔ If you post comments, try to make them brief and polite.

SOCIAL NETWORKING

Social networking means any interaction between members of an online community. People can exchange many different kinds of information, from text and voice messages to video images.

Many social network communities allow users to create permanent pages that describe themselves. Users create home pages to express themselves, share ideas about their lives, and post messages to other members in the network. Each user is responsible for adding and updating the content on his or her profile page.

Here are some features you are likely to find on a social network profile:

Features of Profile Pages

- A biographical description, including photographs and artwork.

- Lists of favorite things, such as books, movies, music, and fashions.

- Playable media elements such as videos and sound recordings.

- Message boards, or "walls" in which members of the community can exchange messages.

You can create a social network page for an individual or a group, such as a school or special interest club. Many hosting sites do not charge to register, so you can also have fun by creating a page for a pet or a fictional character.

Privacy in Social Networks

Social networks allow users to decide how open their profiles will be. Be sure to read introductory information carefully before you register at a new site. Once you have a personal profile page, monitor your privacy settings regularly. Remember that any information you post will be available to anyone in your network.

Users often post messages anonymously or using false names, or *pseudonyms*. People can also post using someone else's name. Judge all information on the net critically. Do not assume that you know who posted some information simply because you recognize the name of the post author. The rapid speed of communication on the Internet can make it easy to jump to conclusions—be careful to avoid this trap.

Tips for Sending Effective Messages

Technology makes it easy to share ideas quickly, but writing for the Internet poses some special challenges, as well. The writing style for blogs and social networks is often very conversational. In blog posts and comments, instant messages, and e-mails, writers often express themselves very quickly, using relaxed language, short sentences, and abbreviations. However, in a conversation, we get a lot of information from a speaker's tone of voice and body language. On the Internet, those clues are missing. As a result, Internet writers often use italics or bracketed labels to indicate emotions. Another alternative is using emoticons—strings of characters that give visual clues to indicate emotion:

:-) smile (happy)	:-(frown (unhappy)	;-) wink (light sarcasm)

Use these strategies to communicate effectively when using technology:

✔ Reread your messages. Before you click *Send,* read your message through and make sure that your tone will be clear to the reader.

✔ Do not jump to conclusions—ask for clarification first. Make sure you really understand what someone is saying before you respond.

✔ Use abbreviations your reader will understand.

WIDGETS & FEEDS

A **widget** is a small application that performs a specific task. You might find widgets that give weather predictions, offer dictionary definitions or translations, provide entertainment such as games, or present a daily word, photograph, or quotation.

A **feed** is a special kind of widget. It displays headlines taken from the latest content on a specific media source. Clicking on the headline will take you to the full article.

Many social network communities and other Web sites allow you to personalize your home page by adding widgets and feeds.

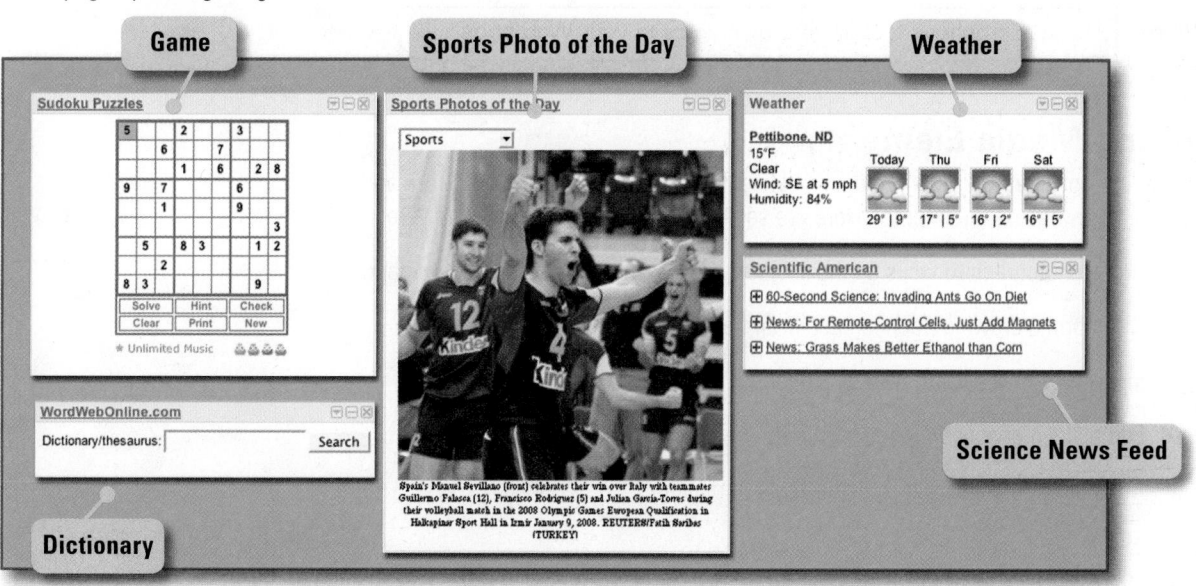

MULTIMEDIA ELEMENTS

One of the great advantages of communicating on the Internet is that you are not limited to using text only. When you create a Web profile or blog, you can share your ideas using a wide variety of media. In addition to widgets and feeds (see page R49), these media elements can make your Internet communication more entertaining and useful.

Graphics	
Photographs	You can post photos taken by digital cameras.
Illustrations	Artwork can be created using computer software. You can also use a scanner to post a digital image of a drawing or sketch.
Charts, Graphs, and Maps	Charts and graphs can make statistical information clear. Use spreadsheet software to create these elements. Use Internet sites to find maps of specific places.

Video	
Live Action	Digital video can be recorded by a camera or recorded from another media source.
Animation	Animated videos can also be created using software.

Sound	
Music	Many social network communities make it easy to share your favorite music with people who visit your page.
Voice	Use a microphone to add your own voice to your Web page.

Editing Media Elements

You can use software to customize media elements. Open source software is free and available to anyone on the Internet. Here are some things you can do with software:

- ✔ Crop a photograph to focus on the subject or brighten an image that is too dark.
- ✔ Transform a drawing's appearance from flat to three-dimensional.
- ✔ Insert a "You Are Here" arrow on a map.
- ✔ Edit a video or sound file to shorten its running time.
- ✔ Add background music or sound effects to a video.

PODCASTS

A **podcast** is a digital audio or video recording of a program that is made available on the Internet. Users can replay the podcast on a computer, or download it and replay it on a personal audio player. You might think of podcasts as radio or television programs that you create yourself. They can be embedded on a Web site or fed to a Web page through a podcast widget.

Creating an Effective Podcast

To make a podcast, you will need a recording device, such as a microphone or digital video camera, as well as editing software. Open source editing software is widely available and free of charge. Most audio podcasts are converted into the MP3 format. Here are some tips for creating a podcast that is clear and entertaining:

✔ Listen to several podcasts by different authors to get a feeling for the medium. Make a list of features and styles you like and also those you want to avoid.

✔ Test your microphone to find the best recording distance. Stand close enough to the microphone so that your voice sounds full, but not so close that you create an echo.

✔ Create an outline that shows your estimated timing for each element.

✔ Be prepared before you record. Rehearse, but do not create a script. Podcasts are best when they have a natural, easy flow.

✔ Talk directly to your listeners. Slow down enough so they can understand you.

✔ Use software to edit your podcast before publishing it. You can edit out mistakes or add additional elements.

WIKIS

A **wiki** is a collaborative Web site that lets visitors create, add, remove, and edit content. The term comes from the Hawaiian phrase *wiki wiki,* which means "quick." Web users at a wiki are both the readers and the writers of the site. Some wikis are open to contributions from anyone. Others require visitors to register before they can edit the content.

All of the text in these collaborative Web sites was written by people who use the site. Articles are constantly changing, as visitors find and correct errors and improve texts.

Wikis have both advantages and disadvantages as sources of information. They are valuable open forums for the exchange of ideas. The unique collaborative writing process allows entries to change over time. However, entries can also be modified incorrectly. Careless or malicious users can delete good content and add inappropriate or inaccurate information.

You can change the information on a wiki, but be sure your information is correct and clear before you add it. Wikis keep track of all changes, so your work will be recorded and can be evaluated by other users.

Rules of Debate

A **debate** is a structured contest based on a formal discussion of opinion. In essence, it is a battle of intellect and verbal skill. The goal is mastering the art of persuasion. Who can best express, argue, and support opinions on a given topic? Who can best refute an argument, showing that the opponent's points are invalid? Which team, in the end, can convince the judges that their argument is the most sound?

Teams

A **formal debate** is conducted with two teams—an Affirmation team and a Negative team. As the names suggest, the Affirmation team is responsible for presenting the "pro" side of an issue, while the Negative team presents the "con" side of the issue. Each team has a main purpose and will offer both constructive and rebuttal speeches, practicing the art of persuasion and debate.

Affirmation team The Affirmation team as a whole carries the burden of proof for the debate. They must prove there is a problem. To do so, they need to cite credible sources, include relevant details, and present and support valid points. Each team member has a specific job. The first speaker has the most responsibility. He or she must

- define the issue or problem

- introduce the team line—a one-line summary of the team's position on the issue

- identify the point of the argument each speaker will discuss

The remaining team members have the job of presenting and supporting the main points of the argument.

Negative team Though the Negative team does not carry the burden of proof, the team must show that there is no problem or that the Affirmation team's solutions are invalid. Though their purpose is to rebut an argument, the rebuttal technique calls for a formation of their own argument. They must argue against the Affirmation team. To construct their argument, they must use—like the Affirmation team—credible sources, relevant details, and valid points. They should incorporate any available statistics, pertinent facts, or applicable testimonies to bolster their argument. Even though the first speaker of the Affirmation team lays out each point of the argument, the Negative team speakers cannot address points that have not been thoroughly discussed by an Affirmation team member.

Structure

Just like most other contests, debates have a set structure. Debates are divided into halves. The first half begins with the constructive speeches from both teams, which last ten minutes each.

After the first half, there is a short intermission. Then, the second half begins with the Negative team. This half is reserved for the rebuttal speeches, which last five minutes each and include rebuttals and refutations. This is each team's chance to rebuild their arguments that the other team broke down (rebuttal), and put forth evidence to show the other team is wrong (refutation). Although the Negative team begins the argument in the second half, every debate begins and ends with the Affirmation team.

Structure of Debate

1st Half: Constructive Speeches (10 minutes each)	2nd Half: Rebuttal Speeches (5 minutes each)
1st Affirmative Team Speaker	1st Negative Team Speaker
1st Negative Team Speaker	1st Affirmative Team Speaker
2nd Affirmative Team Speaker	2nd Negative Team Speaker
2nd Negative Team Speaker	2nd Affirmative Team Speaker
3rd Affirmative Team Speaker	3rd Negative Team Speaker
3rd Negative Team Speaker	3rd Affirmative Team Speaker

Speeches—Content, Organization, and Delivery

Debate speeches are the result of practicing the art of persuasion. To be effective, speakers must include pertinent content, use clear and logical organization, and have a powerful delivery. These combined elements make a strong speech.

Content Debates often focus on concrete issues that can be proved or disproved. The basis for a debate speech is its content. The Affirmation team should first determine their position. They should be sure to include any facts and/or statistics that concretely support the argument. Speech writers should cite specific instances and occurrences that solidify their position. Writers might also include testimonies or ideas from professionals. Finally, the Affirmation team needs to propose possible solutions to the problem or issue and examine the costs and effects of those solutions.

Though the Negative team does not have to state a position—their position is automatically the opposing position—they still need to include facts, statistics, testimony, and descriptions of specific instances or occurrences to make their counterpoints. They need to analyze the Affirmation team's proposed solutions and explain why they will not work. In essence, the Negative team must construct an argument around the Affirmation team's argument.

Organization Debate speeches are organized like other speeches and essays. They should have an introduction, transitions, body, and conclusion. The speeches should have clear main points and supporting details for those points. Because a debate is a structured discussion, there will be a specific order of points and the speakers who present them must be identified. Speakers can use note cards to help them stick to the planned organization, but they should only use brief notes, never reading directly from the cards.

Delivery The manner in which a speech is delivered can make or break the argument. The impression the speaker makes on the audience, including the judges, is key. To make a good impression, the speaker must present the material with confidence. He or she can portray confidence by forming a connection with the audience through eye contact, glancing away only briefly to consult notes. A speaker should focus on his or her voice, varying the tone, volume, and pace appropriately. Body movements should not include fidgeting or nervous movement. They should only be used if they are deliberate and help express or underscore a point. Finally, speakers should be concise, focusing on vivid and clear word choice and using words that emphasize the point.

Scoring

Debates are scored much like other contests. Each side is judged on the content and delivery of their speeches. Judges contemplate different elements of content and delivery in order to determine the number of points to give each team. They might ask themselves the questions in the chart below in order to determine the score.

Finally, judges look at the observation of debate etiquette. Speakers are expected to be mature and respectful of their opponents. Speakers should never attack an opponent, but instead should attack the argument. Judges will deduct points for personal attacks.

Scoring Criteria

Content	Delivery
Were arguments convincing?	Were speakers able to speak extemporaneously?
Were arguments supported with credible, valid and relevant reasons?	Were body movements deliberate and effective?
Were refutations and rebuttals effective?	Did speakers make a connection with the audience?
Were speakers confident and knowledgeable?	Did speakers stay within their time limits?

Logic and Critical Thinking

Many works of nonfiction include content that appeals to readers' and viewers' emotions. Such content can be persuasive and powerful, but it may not always be factual or accurate. Likewise, some inaccurate or misleading content may be suggested or implied, rather than directly stated. Logic and critical thinking can help you to identify purely emotional responses and evaluate the validity of the content of persuasive and expository texts.

Most arguments include the following content elements:

- **Facts** are objective information that can be proved true.
- **Opinions** are the author's personal viewpoints.
- **Claims** are ideas or arguments that may or may not be true.
- **Premises** are basic concepts on which an argument is built. Premises may be explicit (directly stated) or implicit (implied, but not stated).
- **Evidence** is the facts, data, expert testimony, anecdotes, examples, and other information used to support a claim.
- **Conclusions** are the ultimate points that authors make.

Apply the following strategies to assess the content of persuasive and expository texts.

Strategy 1: Evaluate Evidence

The purpose of an argument is to prove a main claim or conclusion. Every argument should be supported by evidence, but not all evidence is equal. To evaluate an argument, analyze the evidence that supports or opposes it. Consider the quality and relevance of the information in your evaluation. Note that evidence may be stated directly, or it may be inferred or implied within an argument.

Evaluating Evidence

Types of Evidence	Quality	Relevance
Facts/Data Expert testimony Anecdotes Examples	• Are facts accurate? • Does information come from reliable, unbiased sources? • Are opinions supported by facts?	• Does the evidence help to prove the argument? • Is data accurately interpreted?

Consider the relationships among evidence, inferences, and claims when analyzing an argument. Types of relationships may include the following:

- **Causality:** cause-and-effect relationships between facts, events, or other information
- **Contradiction:** incompatible facts or ideas
- **Implication:** relationship in which one fact or idea proves the truth of another

Strategy 2: Assess Reasoning

Arguments may rely on various types of reasoning that rely on premises to support conclusions. The chart shown defines and gives examples of two types of reasoning, inductive and deductive.

Inductive and Deductive Reasoning

Type of Reasoning	Example
Deductive reasoning applies proven principles to draw a conclusion about a specific instance. An accurate deductive argument leads to a conclusion that must be true. **(Apply the rule)**	The dress code at my school requires students to wear uniforms. Jolene is a student at my school. Therefore, Jolene wears a uniform to school.
Inductive reasoning applies a specific observation to draw a general conclusion. An inductive argument leads to a conclusion that is probably true. **(Infer the rule)**	*Strong induction:* All students observed at my school wear uniforms. Therefore, the school has a dress code. *Weak induction:* Many accidents involve teenage drivers. Therefore, all teenagers are careless drivers.

To analyze reasoning, look for words that signal the writer is drawing a conclusion, such as *hence, consequently, given,* and *therefore.* These words are called explicit indicators, and may appear when writers use inductive and deductive reasoning.

Strategy 3: Identify Flaws in Arguments

Not all arguments are valid. If an argument is built on a **false premise,** any conclusions based on it are likely to be weak or untrue. A **logical fallacy** is an argument that is not accurate or logical. Types of logical fallacies include the following:

- **False Dilemma:** presentation that implies there are only two options when, in fact, more than two exist
- **Appeal to Common Opinion:** suggestion that something is right because it is popular
- **Appeal to Pity:** plea for sympathy used in place of reasoning
- **Personal Attack:** criticism of the person, rather than the ideas

A faulty argument may also include false statements, which are never valid evidence, or it may rely on opinions as though they were facts. To distinguish between facts and opinions, use established methods, such as relying on scientific or historical truths.

Strategy 4: Analyze Style and Rhetoric

Writers may use stylistic and rhetorical devices to persuade. These devices may not be logically connected to the argument. Examples of these devices include:

- **Loaded Terms:** language that has strong positive or negative connotations
- **Caricatures:** distortions of specific characteristics of people, things, or ideas
- **Leading Questions:** questions that "lead" an audience by suggesting their own answers
- **False Assumptions:** reasoning that is not logically correct

Strategy 5: Compare Arguments

Comparing arguments on the same topic can help you to understand the topic better. For example, an argument in favor of an idea may not discuss the idea's shortcomings. However, an opposing argument would include these shortcomings. To compare arguments, look for similarities and differences in their evidence, premises, and conclusions.

Parts of Speech

Nouns A noun names a person, place, or thing. Common nouns name any one of a class of people, places, or things. Proper nouns name specific people, places, or things.

Common Noun	*Proper Noun*
city	Washington, D.C.

Use *apostrophes* with nouns to show ownership. Add an apostrophe and *s* to show the **possessive case** of most singular nouns. Add just an apostrophe to show the possessive case of plural nouns ending in *s* or *es*. Add an apostrophe and s to show the possessive case of plural nouns that do not end in *s* or *es*.

Pronouns A **pronoun** is a word that stands for a noun or for a word that takes the place of a noun.

A **personal pronoun** refers to (1) the person speaking, (2) the person spoken to, or (3) the person, place, or thing spoken about.

	Singular	*Plural*
First Person	I, me, my, mine	we, us, our, ours
Second Person	you, your, yours	you, your, yours
Third Person	he, him, his,	they, them,
	she, her, hers, it, its	their, theirs

A **reflexive pronoun** ends in *-self* or *-selves* and adds information to a sentence by pointing back to a noun or pronoun earlier in the sentence.

As I said these words I busied *myself* among the pile of bones of which I have before spoken.
—"The Cask of Amontillado," p. 60

An **intensive pronoun** ends in *-self* or *-selves* and simply adds emphasis to a noun or a pronoun in the same sentence.

The best playground, however, was the dark alley *itself*.
—"Rules of the Game," p. 316

Reciprocal pronouns (*each other* and *one another*) indicate that a feeling or action is mutual.

Romeo and Juliet love *one another*.

The Capulets and the Montagues despised *each other*.

Demonstrative pronouns (*this, these, that,* and *those*) direct attention to a specific person, place, or thing.

These are the juiciest pears I have ever tasted.

A **relative pronoun** begins a subordinate (relative) clause and connects it to another idea in the sentence.

The poet *who* wrote "Fire and Ice" is Robert Frost.

The poet *whom* I admire is Frost.

An **interrogative pronoun** is used to begin a question. The five interrogative pronouns are *what, which, who, whom, whose*.

An **indefinite pronoun** refers to a person, place, or thing, often without specifying which one.

Some of the flowers were in bloom.

Everybody chose something.

Verbs A **verb** is a word that expresses time while showing an action, a condition, or the fact that something exists.

An **action verb** indicates the action of someone or something. An action verb is **transitive** if it directs action toward someone or something named in the same sentence.

Marcos accepted their bouquets . . .
—"Uncle Marcos," p. 138

An action verb is **intransitive** if it does not direct action toward something or someone named in the same sentence.

"He nodded and smiled a lot."
—"American History," p. 240

A **linking verb** is a verb that connects the subject of a sentence with a noun or pronoun that renames or describes the subject. All linking verbs are intransitive.

Life *is* a broken-winged bird . . .
—"Dreams," p. 621

A **helping verb** is a verb that can be added to another verb to make a verb phrase.

Nor *did* I suspect that these experiences could be part of a novel's meaning.

A **gerund** is a verb form that acts as a noun.

Running with our classmates on our small sports field. . .
—"The Girl Who Can," p. 90

An **infinitive** is a verb form that generally appears with the word *to* and acts as a noun, adjective, or adverb.

He looked ready *to leave*.
— *The Giant's House*, p. 15

A **participle** is a verb form that is used as an adjective.

Outdid the *sparkling* waves in glee;
—"I Wandered Lonely A Cloud," p. 627

Adjectives An **adjective** describes a noun or a pronoun or gives a noun or a pronoun a more specific meaning. Adjectives answer these questions:

What kind?	*blue* lamp, *large* tree
Which one?	*this* table, *those* books

| How many? | *five* stars, *several* buses |
| How much? | *less* money, *enough* votes |

The articles *the, a,* and *an* are adjectives. *An* is used before a word beginning with a vowel sound.

A noun may sometimes be used as an adjective.

diamond necklace   *summer* vacation

Adverbs An **adverb** modifies a verb, an adjective, or another adverb. Adverbs answer the questions *Where? When? In what way?* or *To what extent?*

He could stand *there*. (modifies verb *stand*)

He was *blissfully* happy. (modifies adjective *happy*)

It ended *too* soon. (modifies adverb *soon*)

Prepositions A **preposition** relates a noun or a pronoun that appears with it to another word in the sentence.

the scene *before* the end   stood *near* me

Conjunctions A **conjunction** connects other words or groups of words. A **coordinating conjunction** connects similar kinds or groups of words.

mother *and* father   simple *yet* stylish

Correlative conjunctions are used in pairs to connect similar words or groups of words.

both Sue *and* Meg   *neither* he *nor* I

A **subordinating conjunction** connects two complete ideas by placing one idea below the other in rank or importance.

You would know him *if* you saw him.

Interjections An **interjection** expresses feeling or emotion and functions independently of a sentence.

"*Oh*, my poor, poor, Mathilde!"
          —"The Necklace," p. 332

Sentences, Phrases, and Clauses

Sentences A **sentence** is a group of words with a subject and a predicate. Together, these parts express a complete thought.

I closed my eyes and pondered my next move.
          — "Rules of the Game," p. 316

A **fragment** is a group of words that does not express a complete thought.

The Swan Theater in London

A **run-on** is two or more complete sentences run together without punctuation.

Objects A **direct object** is a noun or pronoun that receives the action of a transitive verb.

An **indirect object** is a noun or pronoun that appears with a direct object and names the person or thing that something is given to or done for.

The Four Structures of Sentences There are two kinds of clauses: independent and subordinate. These can be used to form four basic sentence structures: *simple, compound, complex,* and *compound-complex.*

A **simple sentence** consists of a single independent clause.

A **compound sentence** consists of two or more independent clauses.

The clauses in a compound sentence can be joined by a comma and a coordinating conjunction (*and, but, for, not, or, so, yet*) or by a semicolon (;).

A **complex sentence** consists of one independent clause and one or more subordinate clauses.

The independent clause in a complex sentence is often called the *main clause* to distinguish it from the subordinate clause or clauses.

A **compound-complex sentence** consists of two or more independent clauses and one or more subordinate causes.

Phrases A **phrase** is a group of words, without a subject and a verb, that functions in a sentence as one part of speech.

A **prepositional phrase** is a group of words that includes a preposition and a noun or a pronoun that is the object of the preposition.

outside my window   below the counter

An **adjective phrase** is a prepositional phrase that modifies a noun or a pronoun by telling *what kind* or *which one.*

The wooden gates *of that lane* stood open.

An **adverb phrase** is a prepositional phrase that modifies a verb, an adjective, or an adverb by pointing out *where, when, in what way,* or *to what extent.*

". . . I could sleep without closing my eyes . . ."
          —"The Most Dangerous Game," p. 215

An **appositive phrase** is a noun or pronoun with modifiers, placed next to a noun or a pronoun to add information and details.

"It is a very great pleasure and honor to welcome Mr. Sanger Rainsford, *the celebrated hunter,* to my home."
          —"The Most Dangerous Game," p. 215

A **participial phrase** is a participle with its modifiers or complements. The entire phrase acts as an adjective.

"Try the settee," said Holmes, *relapsing into his armchair . . .*
          —"The Red-headed League," p. 1166

A **gerund phrase** is a gerund with modifiers or a complement, all acting together as a noun.

> *The baying of the hounds* drew nearer, . . .
> —"The Most Dangerous Game," p. 215

An **infinitive phrase** is an infinitive (*to* and a verb) with modifiers, complements, or a subject, all acting together as a single part of speech.

> I continued, as was my wont, *to smile in his face,* . . .
> —"The Cask of Amontillado," p. 60

Clauses A **clause** is a group of words with a subject and a verb.

An **independent clause** has a subject and a verb and can stand by itself as a complete sentence.

A **subordinate clause** has a subject and a verb but cannot stand by itself as a complete sentence; it can only be part of a sentence.

A **relative clause** is a subordinate clause that modifies a noun or pronoun. When it is needed for the basic meaning of a sentence, it is **restrictive** and is not set off by commas.

> I think the only children who thought he was the real thing were too young. . .
> — "Rules of the Game," p. 319

When the relative clause is not necessary, it is **nonrestrictive,** and it is set off by commas.

> The ones on this ship, the rats of Holland, are the worst. . .
> —"Three Skeleton Key," p. 1153

An **adjective clause** is a subordinate clause that modifies a noun or a pronoun by telling *what kind* or *which one.*

> Walter Mitty stopped the car in front of the building *where his wife went to have her hair done.*
> —"The Secret Life of Walter Mitty," p. 128

An **adverb clause** modifies a verb, an adjective, an adverb, or a verbal by telling *where, when, in what way, to what extent, under what condition,* or *why.*

> The hunter shook his head several times, *as if he was puzzled.*
> —"The Most Dangerous Game," p. 215

A **noun clause** is a subordinate clause that acts as a noun.

> . . . I discovered *that the intoxication had worn off* . . .
> —"The Cask of Amontillado," p. 60

Parallelism involves using similar grammatical structures to express similar ideas. Sentences with parallel structure contain repeated grammatical patterns or repeated types of phrases or clauses within a sentence.

> Marguerite has a great love *for art, for children,* and *for teaching.*

Verb Usage

The Four Principal Parts of Verbs Tenses are formed from principal parts and helping verbs.

A verb has four **principal parts:** the present, the present participle, the past, and the past participle.

Pronoun Case The **case** of a pronoun is the form it takes to show its use in a sentence. There are three pronoun cases: nominative, objective, and possessive.

The **nominative case** is used to rename the subject of the sentence. The nominative case pronouns are *I, you, he, she, it, we, you, they.*

> As the subject: *She* is brave.
> Renaming the subject: The leader is *she.*

The **objective case** is used as the direct object, indirect object, or object of the preposition. The objective case pronouns are *me, you, him, her, us, you, them.*

> **As a direct object:** Our manager praised her.
> **As an indirect object:** Give him the new product.
> **As an object of the preposition:** The coach gave pointers to me.

The **possessive case** is used to show ownership. The possessive pronouns are *my, you, his, her, its, our, their, mine, yours, his, hers, its, ours, theirs.*

Mood The mood of a verb may be indicative, imperative or subjunctive.

The **indicative mood** is used for factual statements.

> The library of my childhood is still there.
> —"Libraries Face Sad Chapter," p. 533

The **imperative mood** is used to give a direction or make a demand.

> "Listen to what the yam says!"
> —"Talk," p. 578

The **subjunctive mood** is used to express doubts and wishes. It is often used in clauses beginning with *if* and *that. That* clauses in the subjunctive mood frequently follow verbs such as *ask, wish, demand, insist, prefer, suggest,* and *require.*

> The lifeguard *asks that* children be careful when they walk around the pool.

Voice The voice of a verb depends on the relationship between the subject and the verb.

Active voice expresses an action done by a subject.

> I *dropped* and *rolled* clear of the ram's belly.
> —"The Odyssey, Part 1," p. 1059

Passive Voice expresses an action done to its subject.

> . . . a gum tree ahead of us *was shattered* by a bolt of lightening.
> —"The Scarlet Ibis," p. 394

Subject and Verb Agreement A singular verb must be used with a singular subject; a plural verb must be used with a plural subject.

> *Reegan is* going home now.
> Many *storms are* the cause of beach erosion.

In a sentence with combined singular and plural subjects, the verb should agree with the subject closest to it.

> Either the *cats* or the *dog is* hungry.
> Neither *Angie* nor her *sisters were* present.

Antecedents are the nouns (or the words that take the place of nouns) to which pronouns refer.

A personal pronoun must agree with its antecedent in number and gender. *Number* indicates whether a pronoun is singular or plural.

Some pronouns and nouns also indicate one of three *genders:* masculine, feminine, or neuter.

Use a singular personal pronoun to refer to two or more singular antecedents joined by *or* or *nor.*

Use a plural personal pronoun to refer to two or more antecedents joined by *and.*

Degrees of Comparison Most adjectives and adverbs have different forms to show degrees of comparison.

The three degrees of comparison are the *positive*, the *comparative*, and the *superlative*.

Use the comparative degree to compare two people, places, or things. Use the superlative degree to compare three or more people, places, or things.

Use *more* or *most* to form the comparative and superlative degrees of all modifiers with three or more syllables.

Memorize the irregular comparative and superlative forms of certain adjectives and adverbs. For instance, the modifiers *bad, badly,* and *ill* all have the same comparative and superlative forms (*worse, worst*).

Capitalization and Punctuation

Capitalization Capitalize the first word of a sentence and also the first word in a quotation if the quotation is a complete sentence.

> I said to him, "My dear Fortunato, you are luckily met."
> —"The Cask of Amontillado," p. 60

Capitalize all proper nouns and adjectives.

> O. Henry   Ganges River   Great Wall of China

Capitalize a person's title when it is followed by the person's name or when it is used in direct address.

> Madame   Dr. Mitty   General Zaroff

Capitalize titles showing family relationships when they refer to a specific person, unless they are preceded by a possessive noun or pronoun.

> Uncle Marcos   Granddaddy Cain   my mother

Capitalize the first word and all other key words in the titles of books, periodicals, poems, stories, plays, paintings, and other works of art.

> *Odyssey*   "I Wandered Lonely as a Cloud"

Punctuation

End Marks Use a **period** to end a declarative sentence, an imperative sentence, an indirect question, and most abbreviations.

> Mr. Jabez Wilson laughed heavily.
> —"The Red-headed League," p. 1166

Use a **question mark** to end a direct question, an incomplete question, or a statement that is intended as a question.

> "What do you expect me to do with that?"
> —"The Necklace," p. 332

Use an **exclamation mark** after a statement showing strong emotion, an urgent imperative sentence, or an interjection expressing strong emotion.

> Free at last! Free at last!
> Thank God almighty, we are free at last!
> —"I Have a Dream," p. 542

Commas Use a **comma** before the coordinating conjunction to separate two independent clauses in a compound sentence.

> All at once . . . she came upon a superb diamond necklace, and her heart started beating with overwhelming desire.
> —"The Necklace," p. 332

Use commas to separate three or more words, phrases, or clauses in a series.

> My brothers and I would peer into the medicinal herb shop, watching old Li dole out onto a stiff sheet of white paper the right amount of insect shells, saffron-colored seeds, and pungent leaves for his ailing customers.
>
> —"Rules of the Game," p. 316

Use commas to set off contrasting expressions.

> Danae wanted to save her son, not sacrifice him.

Use commas to separate adjectives of equal rank. Do not use commas to separate adjectives that must stay in a specific order.

> The big cottonwood tree stood apart from a small group of winterbare cottonwoods which grew in the wide, sandy arroyo.
>
> —"The Man to Send Rain Clouds," p. 292
>
> His present turned out to be a box of intricate plastic parts.
>
> —"Rules of the Game," p. 316

Use a comma after an introductory word, phrase, or clause.

> When Marvin was ten years old, his father took him through the long, echoing corridors . . .
>
> —"If I Forget Thee, Oh Earth . . . ," p. 162

Use commas to set off parenthetical and nonessential expressions, including nonrestrictive clauses and phrases.

> She had a rich friend, *a schoolmate from the convent she had attended,* but she didn't like to visit her. . .
>
> — "The Necklace," p. 334

Use commas with places, dates, and titles.

> Poe was raised in Richmond, Virginia.
>
> On September 1, 1939, World War II began.
>
> Dr. Martin Luther King, Jr., was born in 1929.

Use a comma to set off a direct quotation, to prevent a sentence from being misunderstood, and to indicate the omission of a common verb in a sentence with two or more clauses.

> Michele said, "I'm going to the game tonight."
>
> *Faulty:* She stifled the sob that rose to her lips and lay motionless.
>
> *Revised:* She stifled the sob that rose to her lips, and lay motionless.
>
> In the *Odyssey,* the Cyclops may symbolize brutishness; the Sirens, knowledge.

Semicolons Use a **semicolon** to join independent clauses that are not already joined by a conjunction.

> The lights of cities sparkle; on nights when there was no moon, it was difficult for me to tell the Earth from the sky. . . .
>
> —"Single Room, Earth View," p. 468

Use a semicolon to join independent clauses separated by either a conjunctive adverb or a transitional expression.

> Edward Way Teale wrote nearly thirty books; moreover, he was also an artist and a naturalist.

Use semicolons to avoid confusion when independent clauses or items in a series already contain commas.

> Unable to afford jewelry, she dressed simply; but she was as wretched as a *déclassée,* for women have neither caste nor breeding—in them beauty, grace, and charm replace pride of birth.
>
> —"The Necklace," p. 332

Colons Use a **colon** in order to introduce a list of items following an independent clause.

> The authors we are reading include a number of poets: Robert Frost, Lewis Carroll, and Emily Dickinson.

Use a colon to introduce a formal quotation.

> I have a dream that one day this nation will rise up and live out the true meaning of its creed: "We hold these truths to be self-evident; . . ."
>
> —"I Have a Dream," p. 542

Quotation Marks A **direct quotation** represents a person's exact speech or thoughts and is enclosed in quotation marks.

> "This great nation will endure as it has endured, will revive and will prosper," said President Franklin D. Roosevelt.
>
> —"First Inaugural Address," p. 552

An **indirect quotation** reports only the general meaning of what a person said or thought and does not require quotation marks.

> I went up to her, put my arms around her, and said something to her.
>
> —from *A White House Diary*, p. 104

Always place a comma or a period inside the final quotation mark.

> "There," he said, "there's something for you."
>
> —"The Necklace," p. 332

Place a question mark or an exclamation mark inside the final quotation mark if the end mark is part of the quotation; if it is not part of the quotation, place it outside the final quotation mark.

> "That pig will devour us, greedily!"
> —"The Golden Kite, the Silver Wind," p. 396
>
> Have you ever read the poem "Dreams"?

Use single quotation marks for a quotation within a quotation.

> " 'But,' said I, 'there would be millions of red-headed men who would apply.' "
> —"The Red-headed League," p. 1067

Use quotation marks around the titles of short written works, episodes in a series, songs, and titles of works mentioned as parts of a collection.

> "I Hear America Singing"   "Pride"

Use quotation marks to indicate sarcasm or irony.

> My "well-behaved" dog ate my homework.

Dashes Use **dashes** to emphasize parenthetical information such as an abrupt change of thought, a dramatic interrupting idea, or a summary statement.

> The streets were lined with people—lots and lots of people—the children all smiling, placards, confetti, people waving from windows.
> —from *A White House Diary*, p. 104

Parentheses Use **parentheses** to set off asides and explanations only when the material is not essential or when it consists of one or more sentences.

> One last happy moment I had was looking up and seeing Mary Griffith . . . (Mary for many years had been in charge of altering the clothes which I purchased) . . .
> —from *A White House Diary*, p. 104

Hyphens Use a **hyphen** with certain numbers, after certain prefixes, with two or more words used as one word, and with a compound modifier coming before a noun.

> seventy-six   Post-Modernist

Apostrophes Add an **apostrophe** and -*s* to show the possessive case of most singular nouns.

> Thurmond's wife   the playwright's craft

Add an apostrophe to show the possessive case of plural nouns ending in -*s* and -*es*.

> the sailors' ships   the Wattses' daughter

Add an apostrophe and -*s* to show the possessive case of plural nouns that do not end in -*s* or -*es*.

> the children's games   the people's friend

Use an apostrophe in a contraction to indicate the position of the missing letter or letters.

> You'll be lonely at first, they admitted, but you're so nice you'll make friends fast.
> —"Checkouts," p. 82

Glossary of Common Usage

among, between: *Among* is usually used with three or more items. *Between* is generally used with only two items.

> *Among* the poems we read this year, Margaret Walker's "Memory" was my favorite.
> Mark Twain's "The Invalid's Story" includes a humorous encounter *between* the narrator and a character named Thompson.

around: In formal writing, *around* should not be used to mean *approximately* or *about*. These usages are allowable, however, in informal writing or in colloquial dialogue.

> Shakespeare's *Romeo and Juliet* had its first performance in *approximately* 1595.
> Shakespeare was *about* thirty when he wrote this play.

as, because, like, as to: The word *as* has several meanings and can function as several parts of speech. To avoid confusion, use *because* rather than *as* when you want to indicate cause and effect.

> *Because* Cyril was interested in the history of African American poetry, he decided to write his report on Paul Laurence Dunbar.

Do not use the preposition *like* to introduce a clause that requires the conjunction as.

> Dorothy Parker conversed *as* she wrote—wittily.

The use of *as to* for *about* is awkward and should be avoided.

> Rosa has an interesting theory *about* E. E. Cummings's unusual typography in his poems.

beside, besides: *Beside* is a preposition meaning "at the side of" or "close to." Do not confuse *beside* with *besides*, which means "in addition to." *Besides* can be a preposition or an adverb.

> Lyndon Johnson was sworn in as president with Mrs. Kennedy *beside* him.
> There are many examples of mythological literature *besides* the *Odyssey*.

can, may: The verb *can* generally refers to the ability to do something. The verb *may* generally refers to permission to do something.

> Poe describes the sounds of the bells so vividly that most readers can hear them in their minds.

> The king's edict states that no one may disturb the peace.

different from, different than: The preferred usage is *different from.*

> The structure and rhyme scheme of a Shakespearean sonnet are *different from* the organization of a Petrarchan sonnet.

farther, further: Use *farther* when you refer to distance. Use *further* when you mean "to a greater degree" or "additional."

> The *farther* the rats travel, the more ominous and destructive they seem.

> Mercutio's curse *further* hints at the ominous deeds to come.

fewer, less: Use *fewer* for things that can be counted. Use *less* for amounts or quantities that cannot be counted.

> Poetry often uses *fewer* words than prose to convey ideas and images.

> It takes *less* time to perform a Greek tragedy than to perform a Shakespearean play.

good, well: Use the adjective *good* after linking verbs such as *feel, look, smell, taste,* and *seem.* Use *well* whenever you need an adverb or as an adjective describing health.

> By the end of the story, Mathilde does not look *good*; on the contrary, her appearance is "disheveled."

> Twain wrote especially *well* when he described eccentric characters.

hopefully: Do not attach this adverb to a sentence loosely, as in "*Hopefully*, the rain will stop by noon." Rewrite the sentence so that *hopefully* modifies a specific verb. Other possible ways of revising such sentences include using the adjective *hopeful* or a phrase such as *everyone hopes that.*

> Dr. Martin Luther King, Jr., wrote and spoke *hopefully* about his dream of racial harmony.

> The men of the town were *hopeful* that the rain would come.

> *Everyone hopes that* the class production of *The Inspector General* will be a big success.

its, it's: Do not confuse the possessive pronoun its with the contraction *it's,* used in place of "it is" or "it has."

> In *its* very first lines, "I Hear America Singing" establishes a hopeful mood.

> In *The Tragedy of Romeo and Juliet,* Romeo knows that *it's* dangerous to attend the party.

just, only: When you use *just* as an adverb meaning "no more than," be sure you place it directly before the word it logically modifies. Likewise, be sure you place *only* before the word it logically modifies.

> *Just* one missed phone call led to Daisy and Heron's tragic end.

> A short story can usually develop *only* a few characters, whereas a novel can include many.

kind of, sort of: In formal writing, you should not use these colloquial expressions. Instead, use a word such as *rather* or *somewhat.*

> Connell portrays General Zaroff as *rather* arrogant.

> The tone of the biography is *somewhat* harsh.

lay, lie: Do not confuse these verbs. *Lay* is a transitive verb meaning "to set or put something down." Its principal parts are *lay, laying, laid, laid. Lie* is an intransitive verb meaning "to recline." Its principal parts are *lie, lying, lay, lain.*

> Jim *laid* his gift for Della on the table.

> Juliet appears to be dead as she *lies* in her tomb.

leave, let: Be careful not to confuse these verbs. *Leave* means "to go away" or "to allow to remain." *Let* means "to permit."

> The entire town gathered to watch Uncle Marcos *leave* on his flying machine.

> Romeo and Juliet knew that their families would not *let* them marry.

raise, rise: *Raise* is a transitive verb that usually takes a direct object. *Rise* is an intransitive verb and never takes a direct object.

> Maya Angelou's "New Directions" *raises* issues of gender equity.

> In his inaugural address, Franklin Delano Roosevelt urged the American people to *rise* up and to leave fear behind.

set, sit: Do not confuse these verbs. *Set* is a transitive verb meaning "to put (something) in a certain place." Its principal parts are *set, setting, set, set. Sit* is an intransitive verb meaning "to be seated." Its principal parts are *sit, sitting, sat, sat.*

> Dolan's essay *sets* a high standard of personal responsibility for us.

> Lady Bracknell *sits* comfortably while she grills Jack for details about his background.

so, so that: Be careful not to use the coordinating conjunction *so* when your context requires *so that*. *So* means "accordingly" or "with the result that" and expresses a cause-and-effect relationship. *So that* expresses purpose—what someone intends to achieve.

He wanted to do well on the test, *so* he read "I Have a Dream" again.

Martin Luther King uses eloquent rhetoric to stir up the people *so that* they will take action.

than, then: The conjunction *than* is used to connect the two parts of a comparison. Do not confuse *than* with the adverb *then*, which usually refers to time.

I enjoyed "The News" more *than* other essays I've read recently.

Odysseus fought bravely in the war, and he *then* embarked on a treacherous journey home.

that, which, who: Use the relative pronoun *that* to refer to things. Use *which* only for things and *who* only for people.

The poem *that* Cheryl liked the most was "Much Madness is divinest Sense."

Haiku, *which* consists of only seventeen syllables, is often built around one or two vivid images.

The man *who* had been Ulrich's enemy was now trapped beneath a fallen tree with Ulrich himself.

unique: Because *unique* means "one of a kind," you should not use it carelessly to mean "interesting" or "unusual." Avoid such illogical expressions as "most unique," "very unique," and "extremely unique."

Emily Dickinson's bold experiments with form make her *unique* in the history of nineteenth-century American poetry.

when, where: Do not directly follow a linking verb with *when* or *where*. Be careful not to use *where* when your context requires *that*.

Faulty: The exposition is *when* an author provides the reader with important background information.

Revised: In the exposition, an author provides the reader with important background information.

Faulty: Burma is *where* Saki was born.

Revised: Saki was born in Burma.

Faulty: We read *where* the prizes were worth hundreds of dollars.

Revised: We read *that* the prizes were worth hundreds of dollars.

Index of Skills

Note: Page numbers in **boldface** refer to pages where terms are defined; *italicized* page numbers refer to writing applications.

Index of Features

Index of Authors and Titles

Notes: Page numbers in *italics* refer to biographical information; Nonfiction and informational text appears in red; Featured authors appear in **boldface** text.

Acknowledgments

Grateful acknowledgment is made to the following for copyrighted material:

Adams Media From *The Everything Tex-Mex Cookbook* by Linda Larsen. Copyright © 2006 F+W Publications, Inc. Used by permission of Adams Media, an F+W Company. All Rights Reserved.

Arte Publico Press, Inc. "A Voice" by Pat Mora from *Communion* by Pat Mora. Copyright © 1991 Arte Publico Press–University of Houston. Used by permission of the publisher.

The Associated Press "Atlantis to Blast Off on First Flight of the Year" by Times Wire Report from *El Paso Times*, June 8, 2007. Copyright © 2007 *El Paso Times*, a MediaNews Group Newspaper. Used by permission.

John August From "Big Fish: The Shooting Script" written by John August, based on the novel by Daniel Wallace. Copyright © 2003 Columbia Pictures. Used by permission of John August.

Ballantine Books "In the Presence of Dolphins" by Toni G. Frohoff from *Intimate Nature* by Linda Hogan, Deena Metzger and Brenda Peterson. Copyright © 1998 by Linda Hogan, Deena Metzger and Brenda Peterson (Introduction and Compilation). Used by permission of Ballantine Books, a division of Random House, Inc.

The Battalion Online "About The Big Event" from *http://bigevent.tamu.edu*. Used by permission.

Susan Bergholz Literary Services "Twister Hits Houston" from *My Wicked Wicked Ways* by Sandra Cisneros. Copyright © 1987 by Sandra Cisneros. Published by Third Woman Press and in hardcover by Alfred A. Knopf. From *A Celebration of Grandfathers* by Rudolfo Anaya. Copyright © 1983 by Rudolfo Anaya. First published in *New Mexico Magazine*, March 1983. "My English" by Julia Alvarez from *Something to Declare* by Julia Alvarez. Published by Plume, an imprint of Penguin Group (USA), in 1999 and originally in hardcover by Algonquin Books of Chapel Hill. Copyright © 1998 by Julia Alvarez. Used by permission of Third Woman Press and Susan Bergholz Literary Services, New York, NY and Lamy, NM. All Rights Reserved.

Gary L. Blackwood From *The Shakespeare Stealer* by Gary L. Blackwood. Copyright © 2003 by Gary I. Blackwood. Used by permission of the author.

Tyroneca Booker "The Day of the Storm" by Tyroneca Booker from *Katrina, In Their Own Words* edited by Richard Louth. All works copyrighted © 2006 by the individual authors. Southeastern Louisiana Writing Project, Publisher. Southeastern Louisiana University, Hammond, Louisiana, 70402. Used by permission of Tyroneca Booker.

BookStop Literary Agency, LLC From *Summer on Wheels* by Gary Soto. Copyright © 1995 by Gary Soto. Used with permission of the author and BookStop Literary Agency.

Brandt & Hochman Literary Agents, Inc. "The Most Dangerous Game" from *The Most Dangerous Game* by Richard Connell. Copyright © 1924 by Richard Connell. Copyright renewed © 1952 by Louise Fox Connell. "Sonata For Harp and Bicycle" from *The Green Flash and Other Tales of Horror* by Joan Aiken. Copyright © 1957, 1958, 1959, 1960, 1965, 1968, 1969, 1971 by Joan Aiken. Used by permission of Brandt & Hochman Literary Agents, Inc. Any copying or redistribution of the text is expressly forbidden.

Curtis Brown, Ltd. "Uncoiling" by Pat Mora. First appeared in *Daughters of the Fifth Sun*, published by Riverhead Press. Copyright © 1995. Used by permission of Curtis Brown, Ltd.

Bryan College Station Communications Inc. "A&M Students Help Out in a 'Big' Way" by John Braden from *http://www.theeagle.com/PrinterFriendly/A-amp-amp-M-students-help-out-in-a--big--way*. Copyright © 2008 The Bryan College Station Eagle. Used by permission.

The Bukowski Agency "The Jade Peony" by Wayson Choy. First published in the *UBC Alumni Chronicle*, Vol. 34, No. 4, Winter 1979. Copyright by Wayson Choy 1977. The novel *The Jade Peony*, based on this story, is published in the United States by The Other Press. Used by permission of The Bukowski Agency.

Marie Cloutier "The House on Mango Street, by Sandra Cisneros" by Marie Cloutier from *www.bostonbibliophile.com/2008/07/review-house-on-mango-street-by-sandra.html*. Used by permission of Marie Cloutier.

Jonathan Clowes Ltd. "The Red-headed League," from *The Adventures of Sherlock Holmes* by Sir Arthur Conan Doyle. Copyright © 1996 Sir Arthur Conan Doyle Copyright Holders. Used by kind permission of Jonathan Clowes Ltd., London, on behalf of Andrea Plunket, the Administrator of the Sir Arthur Conan Doyle Copyrights.

Commonwealth Journal "Remember Veterans on Memorial Day" by Danny Calhoun from *www.somerset-kentucky.com/editorials/local_story_136090754.html*. Copyright © 1999-2008 cnhi, Inc. Used by permission.

Don Congdon Associates, Inc. "The Golden Kite, the Silver Wind" by Ray Bradbury from *Epoch*, February 1953. Copyright © 1953 by Epoch Associates; renewed 1981 by Ray Bradbury. Used by permission of Don Congdon Associates, Inc.

Catherine Costello "There is No Word For Goodbye" by Mary Tall Mountain from *There Is No Word for Goodbye: Poems by Mary Tall Mountain*. Copyright © 1994 by Tall Mountain Estate. Used by permission of Catherine Costello. All Rights Reserved.

Richard Curtis Associates, Inc. "Fly Away," from *The Beauty of the Beasts: Tales of Hollywood's Wild Animal Stars* by Ralph Helfer. Copyright © 1990 by Ralph Helfer. Used by permission of Richard Curtis Associates, Inc.

Dell Publishing, a division of Random House, Inc. From *The Giant's House* by Elizabeth McCracken, copyright © 1996 by Elizabeth McCracken. Used by permission of The Dial Press/Dell Publishing, a division of Random House, Inc.

Dunow Carlson Lerner Agency "Desiderata" by Elizabeth McCracken from *http://www.randomhouse.com/boldtype/0397/mccracken/*. Copyright © 1996 by Elizabeth McCracken. Used by permission of Dunow Carlson Lerner Agency.

Eakin Press "Cornmeal Mush and Indian Cornmeal Cake Recipes" from *A Pinch of This and A Handful of That* by the Daughters of the Republic of Texas, District VIII. Copyright © 1988 by the Daughters of the Republic of Texas, District VIII. Used by permission of Eakin Press.

Stephen Edwards "Rock Climbing Equipment and Techniques" by Stephen Edwards from *http://alumnus.caltech.edu/~sedwards/climbing/techniques.html*. Used by permission of Stephen Edwards.

Faber and Faber Limited "The Horses" by Edwin Muir from *Collected Poems by Edwin Muir,* copyright © 1960 by Willa Muir. "Macavity: The Mystery Cat" by T. S. Eliot from *Old Possum's Book of Practical Cats* by T. S. Eliot. Copyright © 1939 by T. S. Eliot and renewed 1967 by Esme Valerie Eliot. Used by permission of Faber and Faber Limited.

Farrar, Straus & Giroux, LLC "The Washwoman" by Isaac Bashevis Singer from *A Day of Pleasure* by Isaac Bachevis Singer. Copyright © 1969 by Isaac Bashevis Singer. "Part 1: The Adventures of Odysseus" and "Part 2: The Return of Odysseus" from the *Odyssey* by Homer, translated by Robert Fitzgerald. Copyright © 1961, 1963 by Robert Fitzgerald. Copyright renewed 1989 by Benedict R. C. Fitzgerald, on behalf of the Fitzgerald children. Excerpt from "A Walk to the Jetty" from *Annie John* by Jamaica Kincaid. Copyright © 1985 by Jamaica Kincaid. Used with permission of Farrar, Straus and Giroux, LLC.

Florida Railroad Museum, Inc. Florida Gulf Coast Railroad Museum from *www.frrm.org/information.html.* Copyright © 2006 Florida Railroad Museum, Inc. Used by permission of Florida Railroad Museum, Inc.

Fresno State University Communications "iPods Join Educational Toolkit at Fresno State" by Megan Jacobsen from *FresnoStateNews* January 17, 2007, *www.fresnostatenews. com/2007/01/podcasts.htm.* Used courtesy of FresnoStateNews.com.

Graywolf Press "Fifteen" from *The Way It Is: New and Selected Poems* by William Stafford. Copyright © 1966, 1998 by the Estate of William Stafford. Used by permission of Graywolf Press, Saint Paul, MN.

Harcourt Education Limited "The Girl Who Can" by Ama Ata Aidoo from *Opening Spaces: An Anthology of Contemporary African Women's Writing,* edited by Yvonne Vera. Used by permission of Harcourt Education.

Harcourt, Inc. "The Writer" from *The Mind-Reader* by Richard Wilbur. Copyright © 1971 by Richard Wilbur. "Women" by Alice Walker from *Revolutionary Petunias & Other Poems,* copyright © 1970 and renewed 1998 by Alice Walker. From *A Lincoln Preface,* copyright 1953 by Carl Sandburg and renewed 1981 by Margaret Sandburg, Janet Sandburg, and Helga Sandburg Crile. "Macavity: The Mystery Cat" from *Old Possum's Book of Practical Cats* by T. S. Eliot. Copyright 1939 by T. S. Eliot and renewed 1967 by Esme Valerie Eliot. "Ithaca" by Constantine Cavafy from *The Complete Poems of Cavafy.* English translation copyright © 1961 and renewed 1989 by Rae Dalven. Used by permission of Harcourt, Inc. This material may not be reproduced in any form or by any means without the prior written permission of the publisher.

HarperCollins Publishers, Inc. "Summer" from *Brown Angels: An Album of Pictures and Verse* by Walter Dean Myers. Copyright © 1993 by Walter Dean Myers. Used by permission of HarperCollins Publishers.

Harvard University Press "Much madness is divinest sense" from *The Poems of Emily Dickinson,* Thomas H. Johnson, ed., Cambridge, Mass.: The Belknap Press of Harvard University Press, Copyright © 1951, 1955, 1979, 1983 by the President and Fellows of Harvard College. Used by permission of the publishers and the Trustees of Amherst College.

Hawaiian Lifeguard Association "Beach and Ocean Safety Signs" by Staff from *www.aloha.com.* Copyright © 1986, 2001 Hawaiian Lifeguard Association. All rights (and lefts) reserved. Used with permission.

David Hilbun "Hope" by David Hilbun from *Katrina, In Their Own Words* edited by Richard Louth. All works copyrighted © 2006 by the individual authors. Southeastern Louisiana Writing Project, Publisher. Southeastern Louisiana University, Hammond, Louisiana, 70402. Used by permission of David Hilbun.

Helmut Hirnschall "There is a Longing . . ." by Chief Dan George & Helmut Hirnschall from *My Heart Soars.* Copyright © 1974 by Chief Dan George and Helmut Hirnschall. Used by permission of Helmut Hirnschall.

The Barbara Hogenson Agency, Inc. "The Secret Life of Walter Mitty" by James Thurber from *My World-And Welcome To It.* Copyright © 1942 by James Thurber. Copyright © renewed 1970 by Rosemary A. Thurber. Used by permission from The Barbara Hogenson Agency, Inc.

Henry Holt and Company, Inc. "Talk" by Harold Courlander and George Herzog from *The Cow-Tail Switch and Other West African Stories* by Harold Courlander and George Herzog, © 1947, 1974 by Harold Courlander. "Fire and Ice" by Robert Frost from *The Poetry of Robert Frost,* edited by Edward Connery Lathem. Copyright © 1951 by Robert Frost. Used by permission of Henry Holt and Company, LLC.

Houghton Mifflin Company, Inc. "Siren Song" from *Selected Poems, 1965–1975* by Margaret Atwood. Copyright © 1976 by Margaret Atwood. Excerpt from "A Fable for Tomorrow" from *Silent Spring* by Rachel Carson. Copyright © 1962 by Rachel I. Carson, renewed 1990 by Roger Christie. "All Watched Over by Machines of Loving Grace" from *The Pill Versus the Springhill Mine Disaster* by Richard Brautigan. Copyright © 1968 by Richard Brautigan. Used by permission of Houghton Mifflin Company. All Rights Reserved.

Houghton Mifflin Harcourt Publishing Company From *The Window* by Jeanette Ingold. Copyright © 1996 by Jeanette Ingold. Used by permission of Houghton Mifflin Publishing Company.

HowStuffWorks, Inc. "How Podcasting Works" by Stephanie Watson from *http://computer.howstuffworks.com/podcasting.htm.* Copyright © 1998–2007 HowStuffWorks, Inc. Courtesy of How Stuff Works.com.

James R. Hurst "The Scarlet Ibis" by James Hurst, published in *The Atlantic Monthly,* July 1960. Copyright © 1988 by James Hurst. Used by permission of the author.

International Creative Management, Inc. "Libraries Face Sad Chapter" by Pete Hamill from *www.petehamill.com.* Copyright © 2002 by Pete Hamill. Used by permission of International Creative Management, Inc.

Japan Publications, Inc. "Temple bells die out" by Basho; and "Dragonfly catcher" and "Bearing no flowers" by Chiyojo, translated by Daniel C. Buchanan, from *One Hundred Famous Haiku* by Daniel C. Buchanan. Copyright © 1973 by Japan Publications. Used by permission of Japan Publications, Inc.

Lyndon B. Johnson Library From *A White House Diary* by Lady Bird Johnson. Used with permission of the Lyndon B. Johnson Library.

KFOX "Reporter's Notebook: Live From Kennedy Space Center" by Daniel Novick from *www.kfoxtv.com.* Copyright © 2007 KFOXTV. com. Used by permission.

The Estate of Dr. Martin Luther King, Jr. c/o Writer's House LLC "I Have a Dream" by Dr. Martin Luther King, Jr. from *The Words Of Martin Luther King, Jr.* Copyright © 1963 Martin Luther King, Jr., copyright renewed © 1991 Coretta Scott King. Used by arrangement with The Heirs to the Estate of Martin Luther King, Jr., c/o Writers House as agent for the proprietor New York, NY.

Alfred A. Knopf "Pecos Bill: The Cyclone" from *Pecos Bill: Texas Cowpuncher* by Harold W. Felton, illustrated by Aldren A. Watson, copyright © 1949 by Alfred A. Knopf, a division of Random House, Inc. Copyright © renewed 1976 by Harold W. Felton. "Dreams" from *The Collected Poems of Langston Hughes* by Langston Hughes. Copyright © 1994 by The Estate of Langston Hughes. "The News" from *Conscientious Objections* by Neil Postman, copyright © 1988 by Neil Postman. "Dream Deferred" from *The Collected Poems of Langston Hughes* by Langston Hughes. Copyright © 1994 by The Estate of Langston Hughes. "Uncle Marcos" by Isabel Allende, translated by Magda Bogin, from *The House of the Spirits* by Isabel Allende, copyright © 1985 by Alfred A. Knopf, a division of Random House, Inc. "What Happened During the Ice Storm" from *The One Room Schoolhouse* by Jim Heynen. Copyright © 1993 by Jim Heynen. "Mushrooms" from *The Colossus and Other Poems* by Sylvia Plath. Copyright © 1957, 1958, 1959, 1960, 1961, 1962 by Sylvia Plath. Used by permission of Alfred A. Knopf, a division of Random House, Inc.

Little, Brown and Company, Inc. "Pyramus and Thisbe" and "Perseus" from *Mythology* by Edith Hamilton. Copyright © 1942 by Edith Hamilton; Copyright © renewed 1969 by Dorian Fielding Reid and Doris Fielding Reid. Used by permission of Little Brown & Company.

Liveright Publishing Corporation "maggie and milly and molly and may" by E. E. Cummings from *Complete Poems, 1904–1962* by E.E. Cummings, edited by George J. Frimage. Copyright © 1956, 1984, 1991 by the Trustees for the E. E. Cummings Trust. Used by permission of Liveright Publishing Corporation.

Andrew MacAndrew "The Necklace" by Guy de Maupassant, translated by Andrew MacAndrew, from *Boule de Suif and Selected Stories* by Guy de Maupassant, New York, NAL, 1964, pp. 143–151. Translation copyright © 1964 by Andrew MacAndrew. Used by permission of Marie-Christine MacAndrew.

Massachusetts Institute of Technology "Team Builds 'Sociable' Robot" by Elizabeth A. Thomson from Massachusetts Institute of Technology News Office February 14, 2001, *http://web.mit.edu/newsoffice/2001/kismet-0214.html*. Copyright © 2001. Used by permission of MIT News Office.

John McPhee "Arthur Ashe Remembered" by John McPhee, first published in *The New Yorker*, March 1, 1993. Used by permission of the author.

Methuen Publishing, Ltd. "The Inspector-General" from *The Sneeze: Plays and Stories* by Anton Chekhov, translated and adapted by Michael Frayn, published by Methuen Drama. Originally from *An Awl in a Sack* by Anton Chekhov, 1885. Used by permission of Methuen Publishing, Ltd.

Edna St. Vincent Millay Society "An Ancient Gesture" by Edna St. Vincent Millay from *Collected Poems*, HarperCollins. Copyright © 1954, 1982 by Norma Millay Ellis. All Rights Reserved. Used by permission of Elizabeth Barnett, literary executor.

NASA Johnson Space Center "Space Shuttle Basics" by Staff from *www.nasa.gov*. "Robotics Education Project" by Staff from *http://robotics.arc.nasa.gov/*. Copyright © National Aeronautics and Space Administration.

Charles Neider "The Invalid's Story" by Mark Twain from *The Complete Sketches and Tales of Mark Twain*, edited by Charles Neider: Copyright © 1977 by Charles Neider. Used by permission of Charles Neider.

Northwestern University Press "Sonnets on Love XIII" from *Sonnets on Love and Death* by Jean de Sponde translated by David R. Slavitt. English translation copyright © 2001 by David R. Slavitt. Published 2001. Evanston: Northwestern University Press, 2001. Used by permission of Northwestern University Press. All Rights Reserved. *http://www.nupress.northwestern.edu*.

W. W. Norton & Company, Inc. "The War Against the Trees" from *The Collected Poems* by Stanley Kunitz. Copyright © 2000 by Stanley Kunitz. Used by permission of W. W. Norton & Company, Inc.

Naomi Shihab Nye "Daily" by Naomi Shihab Nye from *Hugging The Jukebox* by Naomi Shihab Nye. Copyright © 1982. All Rights Reserved. Used by permission of the author.

Geoffrey O'Brien From "From the Old Age of Perseus" by Geoffrey O'Brien from *Red Sky Café* (Cambridge, UK: Salt Publishing, 2005). Copyright © Geoffrey O'Brien. Used by permission of the author.

Orchard Books, an imprint of Scholastic Inc. "Checkouts" adapted from *A Couple of Kooks and Other Stories About Love* by Cynthia Rylant. Published by Scholastic Inc./Orchard Books. Copyright © 1990 by Cynthia Rylant. Used by permission of Scholastic, Inc.

Oxford University Press, Canada "Siren Song" by Margaret Atwood from *Selected Poems 1966–1984*. Copyright © Margaret Atwood 1990. Used by permission of Oxford University Press Canada.

Oxford University Press, Inc. "The Horses" by Edwin Muir from *Collected Poems* by Edwin Muir. Copyright © 1960 by Willa Muir. Used by permission of Oxford University Press, Inc.

The Penguin Press "Play Hard; Play Together; Play Smart" by Dean Smith and Gerald D. Bell with John Kilgo from *The Carolina Way: Leadership Lessons From A Life In Coaching*. Copyright © 2004 by Dean E. Smith. Used by permission of The Penguin Press, a division of Penguin Group (USA) Inc.

Playbill Magazine "On Summer" by Lorraine Hansberry, reprinted from *Playbill Magazine*, June 1960. Copyright © Playbill, Inc. All Rights Reserved. Used by permission of Playbill, Inc.

Portfolio (A Penguin Company) "The Only Thing We Have to Fear" from *Nothing to Fear: Lessons in Leadership from FDR*, by Alan Axelrod. Copyright © 2003 by Alan Axelrod. Used by permission of Portfolio, an imprint of Penguin Group (USA) Inc.

Publishing Group of America, Inc. "The Big Event" by Marti Attoun from American Profile, August 3, 2008 *http://www.americanprofile.com/article/28119.html*. Used courtesy of *American Profile Magazine*.

G.P. Putnam Sons From "Rules of the Game" from *The Joy Luck Club* by Amy Tan. Copyright © 1989 by Amy Tan. Used by permission of G.P. Putnam Sons, a division of Penguin Putnam, Inc.

Random House, Inc. "Blues Ain't No Mockin Bird" from *Gorilla, My Love* by Toni Cade Bambara. Copyright © 1971 by Toni Cade Bambara. "New Directions" from *Wouldn't Take Nothing For My Journey Now* by Maya Angelou. Copyright © 1993 by Maya Angelou. Used by permission of Random House, Inc.

Dr. Sally K. Ride c/o The Washington Speakers Bureau "Single Room, Earth View" by Sally Ride, published in the April/May 1986 issue of *Air & Space/Smithsonian Magazine*, published by The Smithsonian Institution. Used by permission of Dr. Sally K. Ride.

Riverhead Books "Carry Your Own Skis" by Lian Dolan, from *Satellite Sisters' Uncommon Sense* by Julie, Liz & Sheila Dolan and Monica & Lian Dolan. Copyright © 2001 by Satellite Sisters LLC. Used by permission of Riverhead Books, an imprint of Penguin Group (USA) Inc. From *Shakespeare: The Invention of the Human* [4 lines] by Harold Bloom. Copyright © 1998 by Harold Bloom.

Scholastic Inc. "A Line in the Sand" by Sherry Garland from *Dear America: A Line in the Sand—The Alamo Diary of Lucinda Lawrence* by Sherry Garland. Copyright © 1998 by Sherry Garland. Used by permission of Scholastic, Inc.

Scovil Chichak Galen Literary Agency, Inc. "If I Forget Thee, Oh Earth…" from *Expedition to Earth* by Arthur C. Clarke. Copyright © 1953, 1970 by Arthur C. Clarke; Copyright 1951 by Columbia Publications, Inc. Used by permission of the author and the author's agents, Scovil Chichak Galen Literary Agency, Inc.

Southeastern Railway Museum Southeastern Railway Museum: Georgia's Official Transportation History Museum from *www.srmduluth.org/Exhibits/diesel.htm*. Copyright © 1997–2006 Southeastern Railway Museum. All Rights Reserved. Used by permission of Southeastern Railway Museum.

St. Petersburg Times "New iPod mix: Jay-Z, Beyonce, Econ Lecture" by Shannon Colavecchio-Van Sickler from *http://www.sptimes.com/2006/08/05/Tampabay/New_iPod_mix__Jay_Z__.shtml*. Copyright © 2007 *St. Petersburg Times*. All Rights Reserved. Used by permission of *St. Petersburg Times*.

State Personnel Administration State of Georgia Application for Employment from *www.psc.state.ga.us/jobopenings/stateapp.doc*. Copyright © 1999 by the Georgia Merit System. Used by permission of the State Personnel Administration (formerly the Georgia Merit System).

Literary Estate of May Swenson "Analysis of Baseball" by May Swenson from *American Sports Poems* by R. R. Knudson and May Swenson. Copyright © 1989. Orchard Press. Used with permission of The Literary Estate of May Swenson.

Texas Cooking Online, Inc. "Early Texas Cuisine" by John Raven from *http://www.texascooking.com/features/jan98ravenbbq5.htm*. Copyright © 2008 Texas Cooking Online, Inc. All Rights Reserved. Used by permission.

Texas Monthly "The Sticker Bur" by Mimi Swartz from *Texas Monthly*, January 1985 issue. Copyright © 1973–2008 Texas Monthly, Inc. "The Tumbleweed" by Stephen Harrigan from *Texas Monthly*, March 1982 issue. Copyright © 1973–2008 Texas Monthly, Inc. Used by permission of *Texas Monthly*.

Texas State Railroad Official Website of the Texas State Railroad from *www.texasstaterr.com*. Copyright © Texas State Railroad. Used by permission.

Texas Transportation Institute "Annual study shows traffic congestion worsening in cities large and small" by Texas Transportation Institute from *http://mobility.tamu.edu/ums/media_information/press_release.stm*. Copyright © Texas Transportation Institute (TTI). Used by permission of Texas Transportation Institute.

The Texas State Historical Association (TSHA) "Automobiles in Texas" from *http://www.texasalmanac.com/history/early/1911Automobiles.pdf*. Copyright © 2008 The Texas State Historical Association. Used by permission.

Marie Delgado Travis "To a Lost Lover" by Marie Delgado Travis from *http://mariedelgadotravis.blogspot.com/2006/08/to-lost-lover.html*. Copyright © 2005 Marie Delgado Travis. Used by permission of the author.

The University of Georgia Press "American History" from *The Latin Deli: Prose and Poetry* by Judith Ortiz Cofer. Copyright © 1992 by Judith Ortiz Cofer. Used by permission of The University of Georgia Press.

University of Texas Libraries Presentation Software from *www.lib.utexas.edu/services/instruction/tips/tt/tt_present.html*. Used by permission of University of Texas Libraries.

University Press of New England "The Talk" by Gary Soto from *A Summer Life* by Gary Soto. Copyright © 1990 by University Press of New England, Hanover, NH. Reprinted with permission.

Viking Penguin, Inc. "The Choice" by Dorothy Parker from *The Portable Dorothy Parker*, edited by Marion Meade. Copyright © 1926, copyright renewed 1954 by Dorothy Parker. Used by permission of Viking Penguin, a division of Penguin Group (USA) Inc.

Villard Books From *Big Kiss* by Henry Alford, copyright © 2000 by Henry Alford. Used by permission of Villard Books, a division of Random House, Inc.

Vital Speeches of the Day "Glory and Hope" by Nelson Mandela, from *Vital Speeches of the Day*, June 1, 1994. Used by permission of *Vital Speeches of the Day*.

Wesleyan University Press "Slam, Dunk, & Hook" from *Magic City* by Yusef Komunyakaa. Copyright © 1992 by Yusef Komunyakaa. Used by permission of Wesleyan University Press.

Wikipedia.org "Hurricanes" retrieved from *http://en.wikipedia.org/wiki/Hurricane accessed on 07/23/07*. "Earthquakes" retrieved from http://en.wikipedia.org/wiki/Earthquake *accessed on 07/23/07*. "Wikipedia: Verifiability" retrieved from *http://en.wikipedia.org accessed on 07/23/07*.

Wiley Publishing, Inc. "The House on Mango Street" by CliffsNotes from *http://www.cliffsnotes.com*. Copyright © 2000–2008 by Wiley Publishing, Inc. Used by permission.

Writer's House, LLC "Meciendo" by Gabriela Mistral ("Rocking"), translated by Doris Dana from *Selected Poems Of Gabriela Mistral*, translated and edited by Doris Dana. Copyright © 1961, 1964, 1970, 1971 by Doris Dana. Used by permission of Writer's House, LLC.

The Wylie Agency, Inc. "The Man to Send Rain Clouds" from *Storyteller* by Leslie Marmon Silko. Copyright © 1981 by Leslie Marmon Silko. Used by permission of The Wylie Agency, Inc.

The *Texas Essential Knowledge and Skills for English Language Arts and Reading* reproduced by permission, Texas Education Agency, 1701 N. Congress Avenue, Austin, TX 78701.

Note: Every effort has been made to locate the copyright owner of material reproduced on this component. Omissions brought to our attention will be corrected in subsequent editions.

Credits

Photo Credits

xii–xiii: Sean Davey/CORBIS; xiv–xv: Sean Davey/CORBIS; xvi–xvii: Images.com/CORBIS; xviii–xix: Images.com/CORBIS; xx–xxi: Images. com/CORBIS; xxii–xxiii: Images.com/CORBIS; xxvi–xxvii: © Diana Ong/ SuperStock; xxviii–xxix: Nice One Productions/CORBIS; xxx–xxxi: Nice One Productions/CORBIS; xxxvi–xxxvii: Universal/Photofest; xxxviii: Aaron Horowitz/CORBIS; xxxix: tl. Denis Scott/CORBIS; tr. Paul Hardy/ CORBIS; m. istockphoto.com; b. istockphoto.com; xl: The Granger Collection, New York; xli: t. Time Life Pictures/Getty Images; b. The Art Archive/ Culver Pictures; Gr09 U1 1: © Catherine Cabrol/Kipa/CORBIS; 2: © Dave Cutler/Images.com; 3: © Johner/ Johner Images/ Getty Images; 5: Images.com/CORBIS; 6: CALVIN AND HOBBES © 1994 Watterson. Reprinted with permission of UNIVERSAL PRESS SYNDICATE. All Rights Reserved.; 9: Alberto Giacometti, *Man Pointing*, 1947. Bronze, 70 1/2 x 40 3/4 x 16 3/8". The Museum of Modern Art/Licensed by Scala-Art Resource, NY. Gift of Mrs. John D. Rockefeller 3rd. © 2004 Artists Rights Society (ARS), New York/ADAGP, Paris.; 10: © Lisa Haney / Images.com; 12: Christooph Wilhelm/Getty Images; 13: © Bob Winsett/ CORBIS; 15: *Library,* 2003 (acrylic on wood), Crook, P.J. (b. 1945) /Private Collection, /The Bridgeman Art Library International; 17: Michael S. Lewis/CORBIS; 17: bkgrnd. Nick Belton/ istockphoto.com; 18: Maria Ferrari/SuperStock; 18–19: bkgrnd. Nick Belton/ istockphoto. com; 20: akg-images; 20: bkgrnd. Nick Belton/ istockphoto.com; 25: t. Robert Maass/CORBIS; 25: b. Lee Snider/CORBIS; 26: *The Oldest Inhabitant,* 1876, Julian Alden Weir, oil on canvas, 65 1/2 x 32" Signed, upper left. Butler Institute of American Art, Youngstown, Ohio; 26: bkgrnd. Lee Snider/CORBIS; 29: Erich Lessing/Art Resource, NY; 30: *The Washerwomen*, from the 'Tableau de Paris' series, engraved by C. Motte, c.1830–1840 (colour litho), Delarue, Fortune (b. 1794) (after)/ Musee de la Ville de Paris, Musee Carnavalet, Paris, France, Archives Charmet/The Bridgeman Art Library International; 31: Lee Snider/ CORBIS; 32: *The Oldest Inhabitant* (detail), 1876, Julian Alden Weir, oil on canvas, 65 1/2 x 32" Signed, upper left. Butler Institute of American Art, Youngstown, Ohio; 35: t. Getty Images; 35: b. © Ashok Rodrigues/ istockphoto.com; 36: t. istockphoto.com; 36: b. © Ashok Rodrigues/ istockphoto.com; 37: CORBIS; 48: Royalty Free © Vladimir Piskunov/ Dreamtime.com; 49: John Heseltine/© Dorling Kindersley; 49: bkgrnd. istockphoto.com; 50: Canberra Bicycle Museum and Resource Centre, Australia; 52: © Dorling Kindersley; 54: Royalty Free/ PhotoDisc/ Getty Images; 55: tl. © Dorling Kindersley; 55: tr. istockphoto.com; 55: b. Canberra Bicycle Museum and Resource Centre, Australia; 56: rt. istockphoto.com; 56: tl. Royalty Free/ C Squared Studios/PhotoDisc/ Getty Images; 56: rb. istockphoto.com; 59: t. Bettmann/CORBIS; 60–61: © Held Collection/The Bridgeman Art Library International; 62: istockphoto. com; 62–63: border. istockphoto.com; 64: RF Digital Vision/ Getty Images; 64–65: border. istockphoto.com; 66: t. istockphoto.com; 66: b. istockphoto.com; 67: l. © Holton Collection/SuperStock; 67: r. istockphoto.com; 68: l. istockphoto.com; 68: r. istockphoto.com; 75–78: istockphoto.com; t. © GK Hart/Vikki Hart/ Getty Images; 78: b. © C.Fleurent/ photocuisine/ CORBIS; 81: © Precious Ngcobo; 82–83: istockphoto.com; 84: istockphoto.com; 85: RF © Tim Jones/ Digital Vision/ Getty Images; 86: © Ron Giling/Peter Arnold, Inc.; 88: © Ron Giling/Peter Arnold, Inc.; 90: Barnabas Kindersley/© Dorling Kindersley; 91: l. Corel Professional Photos CD-ROM™; 91: r. Corel Professional Photos CD-ROM™; 92: © Ron Giling/Peter Arnold, Inc.; 103: © Archive Photos; 104: Bettmann/ CORBIS; 104: bkgrnd. istockphoto.com; 105: l. Art Rickerby/Time & Life Pictures/Getty Images; 105: m. © CORBIS; 105: r. © Bettmann/ CORBIS; 106: tl. Audio Visual Archives at the John F. Kennedy Library; 106: tm. istockphoto.com; 106: tr. CORBIS Sygma; 106: m. Courtesy of The Peace Corps; 106: b. Bettmann/CORBIS; 107: l. © Randy Faris/ CORBIS; 107: m. © Bettmann/CORBIS; 107: r. © Bettmann/ CORBIS; 108: t. Loretta Hostettler/istockphoto.com; 108: bl. Art Rickerby/ Time & Life Pictures/ Getty Images; 108: bm. Bettmann/CORBIS; 108: br. © Wally McNamee/ CORBIS; 109: l. Bettmann/CORBIS; 109: m. Keystone/ Hulton Archive/ Getty images; 109: r. Lisa Svara/istockphoto.com; 110: istockphoto.com; 113: Copyright© by Julia Alvarez/Bill Eichner. Reprinted by permission of Susan Bergholz Literary Services, NY. All Rights Reserved.; 114: t. istockphoto.com; 114: b. RF Terry Vine/Blend Images/Getty Images; 114–115: istockphoto.com; 116: RF Medioimages/Photodisc/Getty Images; 119: l. istockphoto.com; 119: r. RF George Marks/Retrofile/Getty Images; 120: RF Terry Vine/Blend Images/Getty Images; 127: CORBIS; 128–129: istockphoto.com; 129: istockphoto.com; 130: © Ufuk Zivana/ istockphoto.com; 131: l. RF Tetra Images/Getty Images; 131: r. RF Joshua Ets-Hokin/ PhotoDisc/Getty Images; 132: l. Hulton-Deutsch/CORBIS; 132: r. Comstock Select/CORBIS; 132: inset. RF Rubberball/ Getty Images; 133: RF Joshua Ets-Hokin/ PhotoDisc/Getty Images; 134: istockphoto.com; 137: t. AFP/Getty Images; 137: m. RF © Brownie Harris/CORBIS; 137: b. RF PhotoDisc/ Jules Frazier/ Getty Images; 138: Images.com/CORBIS; 139: RF© Tom Grill/ CORBIS; 140: istockphoto.com; 141: istockphoto.com; 142: Bettmann/CORBIS; 142–143: istockphoto.com; 145: Bettmann/CORBIS; 147: l. RF © Brownie Harris/ CORBIS; 147: r. RF PhotoDisc/ Jules Frazier/ Getty Images; 148: Images.com/CORBIS; 156: Courtesy of NJ Transit; 157: l. istockphotocom; 157: Kim Todd/Stock Connection; 158: mr. © NRM/SSPL/The Image Works; 158: br. © Wolfgang Kaehler/ CORBIS; 158: istockphoto.com; 158: mr. courtesy of SouthEastern Railway Museum; 158: b. courtesy of SouthEastern Railway Museum; 161: t. AP/WideWorld Photos; 161: b. Photofest; 162: NASA; 164: t. NASA; 164: b. NASA; 165: © RF - ER Productions; 166: © RF - Natphotos/ DigitalVisions/ Getty Images; 167: © Momatiuk - Eastcott/ CORBIS; 168–169: © Ed Freeman/ Stone/Getty Images; 175: Prentice Hall; 182: © Michael Newman/Photo Edit; 184: l. Will Hart; r. Photo by Lynn Saville; Gr09 U2 192–193: Sean Davey/ CORBIS; 194: Associated Press; 197: © Images.com/CORBIS; 198: www.CartoonStock.com; 199: 20th Century Fox/Photofest; 201: © David Forbert/SuperStock; 201: border. istockphoto.com; 202: © Andrew Gunners/ Digital Vision/ Getty Images; 206: Pearson Education/PH School Division; 208: Alan Carey/Photo Researchers, Inc.; 213: The New York Times; 221: Sovfoto/Eastfoto; 233: bkgrnd. Hulton Archive/Getty Images Inc.; 233: t. Getty Images; 233: m. The Imperial War Museum London; 233: b. Jane Burton/© Dorling Kindersley; 239: Miriam Berkely/ Authorpix; 240: Ralph Fasanella, *Sunday Afternoon - Stickball Game* (1953). 40 X 36, oil on canvas. Courtesy A.C.A. Galleries, N.Y.; 249: CORBIS; 252: Robert Harding World Imagery; 259: l. Bettmann/CORBIS; 259: b. Corel Professional Photos CD-ROM™; 260: © Christie's Images; 262: *Hairdresser's Window,* 1907, John Sloan, oil on canvas, 1947.240, Wadsworth Atheneum, Hartford, Ct. The Ella Gallup Sumner and Mary Catlin Sumner Collection Fund; 263: Corel Professional Photos CD-ROM™; 269: t. E.O. Hoppe/Stringer/Time Life Pictures/Getty Images; 269: b. © Ingram Publishing/SuperStock; 270–271: © Ghislain & Marie David de Lossy/ Getty Images; 272: © Mel Curtis/ Stockbyte/ Getty Images; 273: © PhotoAlto/Ale Ventura/ Getty Images; 274–275: © Ken Redding/CORBIS; 276: © Ingram Publishing/SuperStock; 285: istockphoto.com; 287: © Adam Woolfitt/CORBIS; 290: istockphoto.com; 291: t. © Nancy Crampton; 291: b. Anne Katrine Senstad/Retna Ltd.; 295: *Feast Day,* San Juan Pueblo, 1921, William Penhallow Henderson, National Museum of American Art, Smithsonian Institution; Given in Memory of Joshua C. Taylor/Art Resource, New York; 298: MedioImages/CORBIS; 300: Richard Cummins/Getty Images; 302: Hughie Lee-Smith, *Vista II* (detail), 1987, oil on canvas. Art © Estate of Hughie Lee-Smith/Licensed by VAGA, New York, NY; 303: Arthur Morris/CORBIS; 315: © Gary Rhijnsburger/Masterfile; 316–317: Courtesy of Ryan Eastman; 318: ©1999, 2007 Kaihsu Tai; 321: © Gary Rhijnsburger/Masterfile; 322: Getty Images; 323: © Bob Krist/CORBIS; 325: Mary Grace Long /Asia Images/ Getty Images; 326: Red Chopsticks/ Getty Images; 328: David Muir/digital vision/Getty Images; **331:** Time Life Pictures/Getty Images; **332–333:** SuperStock, Inc./SuperStock; **333:** border. istockphoto.com; **333:** istockphoto.com; **334–335:** border. istockphoto.com; **337:** © Christie's Images/SuperStock; **338:** © SuperStock, Inc./SuperStock; **349:** Nikky Finney; **350:** Elizabeth Catlett, American, born 1915, *Sharecropper,* 1952, printed 1970, Color linocut on cream Japanese paper, 450 x 431 mm (block); 544 x 513 mm (sheet), Restricted gift of Mr. and Mrs. Robert S. Hartman, 1992.182, The Art Institute of Chicago. Photography © The Art Institute of Chicago.; **353:** *The Vegetable Garden,* Coombe, 1988, Riley, Paul (b. 1944) (Contemporary Artist)/Private Collection, © Chris Beetles, London, U.K./The Bridgeman Art Library International; **354:** t. Frank Greenaway/© Dorling Kindersley; **354:** b. Jim Zipp/Photo Researchers, Inc.; **361:** t. Bettmann/CORBIS; **361:** b. istockphoto.com; **362:** *Duchess in Defiance* (oil on canvas), Parrish, Kevin (Contemporary Artist) Guild of Railway Artist/Private Collection, The Bridgeman Art Library International; **364:** © Corey Hochachka/Design Pics/CORBIS; **368:** Foodpix; **369:** North Wind Picture Archives; **370:** istockphoto.com; **379:** istockphoto.com; **380:** Book design by Cathryn S. Aison, Random House, Inc. © 1984; **383:** t. Photo Courtesy James Hurst; **383:** b. Bassouls Sophie/CORBIS; **384:** © Biosphoto/BIOS; Bios - Auteurs (droits geres); Huguet Pierre;/Peter Arnold Inc.; **384–385:** © Panoramic Images/ Getty Images; **386:** © Robin Chittenden; Frank Lane Picture Agency/CORBIS; **387:** © Biosphoto/BIOS; Bios - Auteurs (droits geres); Huguet Pierre;/Peter Arnold Inc.; **389:** *Two Boys in a Punt,* 1915 - Cover Illustration, Popular Magazine N. C. Wyeth (1882–1945) Oil on Canvas, 37-1/2 x 26 1/2, Private Collection, Photography courtesy of Brandywine River Museum; **392:** © GERARD LACZ/*Animals Animals - Earth Scenes*; **394:** © Biosphoto/BIOS; Bios - Auteurs (droits geres); Huguet Pierre;/Peter Arnold Inc.; **396:** *Portrait of a Mandarin* (w/c) by Chinese School (19th century) Stapleton Collection, UK/ The Bridgeman Art Library; **398:** border. istockphoto.com; **398:** © Photographer:Rosmizan Abu Seman/Agency: Dreamstime.com; **400:** istockphoto.com; **402:** © Pierre Tremblay/Masterfile; **405:** Eric Cator; **410:** Associated Press; **412:** © Robert Recker/zefa/CORBIS; **414:** Pearson; **418:** istockphoto.com; **422–423:** Images.com/CORBIS; <u>Gr09 U3</u> **428:** *PEANUTS* reprinted by permission of United Feature Syndicate, Inc.; **429:** © Ryan McVay/ PhotoDisc/ Getty Images; **431:** tl. © aleksandar velasevic/ istockphoto.com; **431:** t. © Luis Bellagamba/ istockphoto.com; **433:** tr. © Manik Ratan/ istockphoto.com; **433:** t. istockphoto.com; **434:** © Brandon Laufenberg/ istockphoto.com; **434:** t. istockphoto.com; **437:** tr. istockphoto.com; **437:** tr. © Alexander Yakovlev/ istockphoto.com; **437:** t. istockphoto.com; **438:** b. istockphoto.com; **438:** b. © Sylwia Nowik/istockphoto.com; **443:** Courtesy of the author; **444:** © Prisma/SuperStock; **447:** Tom Lea, *Wood cutter and Burro* ("El Lenador"), 1934, Oil on Canvas 29"x42". on long term loan to the New Mexico Museum of Art from the U.S. General Services Administration, Works Project Administration. Photograph by Blair Clark (2833.23P); **448–449:** border. istockphoto.com; **448–449:** *Three Reds,* courtesy of Patrick Coffaro, Photography courtesy of Joan Cawley Licensing, Ltd.; **455:** CORBIS; **467:** b. Bettmann/CORBIS; **467:** m. NASA; **468–469:** NASA; **470:** istockphoto.com; **471:** istockphoto.com; **472:** AP/WideWorld Photos; **473:** istockphoto.com; **474:** NASA; **477:** t. AP/WideWorld Photos; **477:** b. Cartesia/ Photodisc/ Getty Images; **478:** Cartesia/ Photodisc/ Getty Images; **479:** istockphoto.com; **480:** t. istockphoto.com; **480:** t. Cartesia/ Photodisc/ Getty Images; **482:** t. istockphoto.com; **486:** istockphoto.com; **495–496:** Getty Images; **499:** b. Thomas Victor; **499:** r. Time Life Pictures/Getty Images; **500–501:** Courtesy of The Lincoln Museum, Fort Wayne, Indiana, (#983)- *Lincoln Proclaiming Thanksgiving,* Dean Cornwell; **502:** *Peculiarsome Abe,* N. C. Wyeth, Courtesy of Children's Literature Research Collection, The Free Library of Philadelphia, Photography courtesy of the Brandywine River Museum; **505:** Courtesy of the Library of Congress; **506:** © CORBIS; **508:** Focus on Sport/Getty Images; **509:** istockphoto.com; **510:** istockphoto.com; **521:** t. Photo Courtesy of ABC Radio Networks; **521:** b. Lambert/ Hulton Archive/ Getty Images; **522:** © Mike Powell/CORBIS; **524:** © Anthony Marsland/The Image Bank/ Getty Images; **526:** Lambert/Hulton

Archive/Getty Images; **529:** t. AP/WideWorld Photos; **529:** b. © Prisma/ SuperStock; **530:** © Prisma/SuperStock; **532:** © George Steinmetz/ CORBIS; **533:** The Granger Collection, New York; **534:** © Richard T. Nowitz/ CORBIS; **541:** Bettmann/CORBIS; **542:** Bettmann/CORBIS; **544:** CORBIS; **545:** © Flip Schulke/CORBIS; **547:** © Bob Adelman/Magnum Photos; **551:** t. CORBIS; **551:** b. Underwood & Underwood/CORBIS; **552:** CORBIS; **553:** Underwood & Underwood/CORBIS; **554:** Getty Images; **555:** Underwood & Underwood/CORBIS; **557:** t. Bettmann/CORBIS; **557:** b. National Collection of Fine Arts, Washington, DC; **558:** © Bettmann/ CORBIS; **560:** © Bettmann/ CORBIS; **569:** t. © Bettmann/ CORBIS; **569:** b. © CORBIS; **570:** © Bettmann/ CORBIS; **573:** t. Courtesy of the Author. Photo by Carolyn Soto.; **573:** m. © 1966 by Michael Courlander; **573:** b. Courtesy of Archives of Traditional Music; **574:** © Images.com/CORBIS; **577:** t. Images.com/CORBIS; **578:** l. istockphoto.com; **579:** r. istockphoto.com; **580:** r. istockphoto.com; **582:** b. Jose Luiz Pelaez, Inc. /CORBIS; **585:** Marion Ettlinger; **592:** Tony Freeman, PhotoEdit; **594:** istockphoto.com; **602–603:** Images.com/CORBIS; <u>Gr09 U4</u> **605:** © Colin Young-Wolff/Photo Edit; **607:** © Images.com/CORBIS; **608:** *LUCKY COW* ©2003 Mark Pett. Dist. By UNIVERSAL PRESS SYNDICATE. Reprinted with permission. All Rights Reserved.; **609:** © Bob Daemmrich/ PhotoEdit Inc.; **611:** Paul & Lindamarie Ambrose/Getty Images; **612:** Paul & Lindamarie Ambrose/ Getty Images; **613:** t. Photo courtesy of Pat Mora; **614:** b. Photo courtesy of Pat Mora; **619:** ml. Bettmann/CORBIS; **619:** t. Time Life Pictures/Getty Images; **619:** b. Getty Images; **619:** akg-images; **620:** t. Lawrence, Jacob (1917–2000), *Street Shadows,* 1959. Egg tempera on hardboard, 24 x 30". © ARS, NY/ Photo courtesy of: The Jacob and Gwendolyn Lawrence Foundation/Art Resource, NY; **621:** istockphoto.com; **622:** akg-images; **624:** t. Kathleen Brown/CORBIS; **625:** t. Kathleen Brown/CORBIS; **626:** © Ian Mckinnell/ Getty Images; **631:** m. Hulton Archive/Getty Images Inc.; **631:** b. Getty Images; **631:** t. Roger Ressmeyer/CORBIS; **632:** Charles O'Rear/CORBIS; **634:** b. McDonald Wildlife Photog./*Animals Animals*; **635:** m. Reza Estakhrian/ Getty Images; **636:** © Alamy Images; **645:** m. Alfred Lord Tennyson, © 1840, S. Laurence, by courtesy of the National Portrait Gallery, London; **645:** b. Oscar White/CORBIS; **645:** t. Miriam Berkley/Authorpix; **646:** b. Stewart Cohen/Digital Vision by Getty Images; **647:** t. © Antar Dayal/Illustration Works/CORBIS; **648–649:** © Lance Richbourg/SuperStock; **650:** t. © Lance Richbourg/SuperStock; **653:** m. Photo by Mandy Sayer; **653:** t. Bettmann/ CORBIS; **653:** b. Bettmann/CORBIS; **654:** *The Bells of Rostov,* 1983 (oil on canvas), Chepik, Sergei (b. 1953)/Private Collection, Roy Miles Fine Paintings/ The Bridgeman Art Library International; **657:** © Christie's Images/ SuperStock; **658:** The Bells, Edmund Dulac, New York Public Library; Astor, Lenox and Tilden Foundations; **660:** © Images.com/CORBIS; **662–663:** Illustrations copyright ©1977 by Jane Breskin Zalben from *Jabberwocky.* Published by Caroline House, Boyds Mills Press, Inc. Reprinted by permission.; **664:** Illustrations copyright ©1977 by Jane Breskin Zalben from *Jabberwocky.* Published by Caroline House, Boyds Mills Press, Inc. Reprinted by permission.; **671:** tl. Tetra Images/ CORBIS; **671:** mi. Stockbyte/Alamy; **672:** Michelangelo Gratton/ Photo Researchers, Inc.; **673:** Brand X/CORBIS; **674:** Tetra Images/Getty Images; **677:** rm. Photo by Robert Pedley; Courtesy of Kitty Costello; **677:** b. photo by James Evans; **677:** mb. © Bill Barksdale/CORBIS; **677:** mb. © Paul Buck/epa/CORBIS; **678:** bl. SuperStock; **680:** © Bill Barksdale/ CORBIS; **682:** © Paul Buck/epa/CORBIS; **695:** t. Bettmann/CORBIS; **695:** m. AP/WideWorld Photos; **695:** b. AP/WideWorld Photos; **696:** The Granger Collection, New York; **699:** © Cocoro Photos/CORBIS; **700:** Reuters/CORBIS; **705:** t. Mark Gerson Photography; **705:** m. Oscar White/ CORBIS; **705:** b. The Granger Collection, New York; **707:** Corel Professional Photos CD-ROM™; **708:** © Flip De Nooyer/Foto Natura/ Minden Pictures, Inc.; **709:** © Fred Carol/CORBIS Sygma; **710:** Aaron/ Horowitz/CORBIS; **713:** © Ed Reschke/Peter Arnold, Inc.; **723:** t. Eric Schaal/Time Life Pictures/Getty Images; **723:** m. Courtesy of the Library of Congress; **723:** b. The Granger Collection, New York; **724:** © The Stock Market/Alan Goldsmith; **728:** *Bubbles,* watercolor, 39" x 29", Courtesy of Scott Burdick; **731:** t. Courtesy of the Library of Congress; **731:** m.

SuperStock; **731:** b. Eric Schaal/Time Life Pictures/Getty Images; **736:** tl. Corel Professional Photos CD-ROM™; **736:** tr. Corel Professional Photos CD-ROM™; **742:** Photo courtesy of NASA, Ames Research Center; **743:** © George Steinmetz/ CORBIS; **744:** Sam Ogden/Photo Researchers, Inc.; **749:** The Granger Collection, New York; **749:** AP/WideWorld Photos; **749:** t. Bettmann/CORBIS; **749:** b. SuperStock; **750:** Ron Brown/SuperStock; **752:** *The Quiltmakers,* Paul Goodnight, 22 11/16" x 24" Color Circle Art Publishing Inc.; **756:** Jose Luiz Pelaez, Inc./Getty Images; **759:** t. Cheron Bayna; **766:** m. © Superstock; **766:** b. © image100/ CORBIS; **768:** AP/WideWorld Photos; **769:** Ted Streshinsky/CORBIS; **770–771:** istockphoto.com; **776–777:** © Diana Ong/SuperStock; **Gr09 U5 781:** istockphoto.com; **782:** *IN THE BLEACHERS* © 1999 Steve Moore. Reprinted with permission of UNIVERSAL PRESS SYNDICATE. All rights reserved.; **783:** © Inti St Clair/ Digital Vision/ Getty Images; **785:** Chris Bennion/Seattle Children's Theatre; **787:** Chris Bennion/Seattle Children's Theatre; **789:** tm. Michael Newman/PhotoEdit Inc.; **789:** tr. Getty Images; **793:** b. Chris Bennion/Seattle Children's Theatre; **794:** Chris Bennion/Seattle Children's Theatre; **798:** t. 20TH CENTURY FOX/THE KOBAL COLLECTION/MORTON, MERRICK; **798:** b. © Michel Porro/ Getty Images; **799:** © Andrea Pistolesi/ Getty Images; **802:** l. SuperStock; **802:** r. 20TH CENTURY FOX/THE KOBAL COLLECTION/MORTON, MERRIC; **805:** t. 20TH CENTURY FOX/THE KOBAL COLLECTION/MORTON, MERRICK; **805:** b. 20TH CENTURY FOX/THE KOBAL COLLECTION/MORTON, MERRICK; **806:** border. istockphoto.com; **806:** 20TH CENTURY FOX/THE KOBAL COLLECTION/MORTON, MERRICK; **810:** Alinari/Art Resource, NY; **814:** ™ and Copyright © 20th Century Fox Film Corp. All Rights Reserved. Courtesy: Everett Collection; **823:** ™ and Copyright © 20th Century Fox Film Corp. All Rights Reserved. Courtesy: Everett Collection; **826:** 20TH CENTURY FOX/THE KOBAL COLLECTION/MORTON, MERRICK; **827:** 20TH CENTURY FOX/THE KOBAL COLLECTION/MORTON, MERRICK; **829:** 20th Century Fox/Photofest; **834:** 20TH CENTURY FOX/THE KOBAL COLLECTION/MORTON, MERRICK; **838:** 20th Century Fox/Photofest; **841:** 20th Century Fox/Photofest; **842:** br. Michael Melford/Getty Images; **842:** m. akg-images; **848:** © Araldo de Luca/CORBIS; **851:** ™ and Copyright © 20th Century Fox Film Corp. All Rights Reserved. Courtesy: Everett Collection; **857:** 20TH CENTURY FOX/THE KOBAL COLLECTION/MORTON, MERRICK; **862:** 20TH CENTURY FOX/THE KOBAL COLLECTION/MORTON, MERRICK; **865:** ™ and Copyright © 20th Century Fox Film Corp. All Rights Reserved. Courtesy: Everett Collection; **866:** ™ and Copyright © 20th Century Fox Film Corp. All Rights Reserved. Courtesy: Everett Collection; **867:** 20TH CENTURY FOX/THE KOBAL COLLECTION/MORTON, MERRICK; **872:** Private Collecton/Bridgeman Art Library, London/New York; **876:** l. © Mary Evans Picture Library/The Image Works; **876:** m. © Mary Evans Picture Library/MARK FURNESS/The Image Works; **876:** r. THE KOBAL COLLECTION/ Picture- Desk; **877:** l. The Everett Collection; **877:** m. © MGM/ Photofest; **877:** r. © Paramount Pictures/ Photofest; **878:** l. © ArenaPal/Topham/The Image Works; **878:** m. © ArenaPal/Topham/The Image Works; **878:** r. © Royal Shakespeare Theatre/Lebre/Lebrecht Music & Arts; **879:** ml. © Tristram Kenton/ Lebrecht Music/Lebrecht Music & Arts; **879:** br. © Neale Osborne/ Lebrecht Music &/Lebrecht Music & Arts; **879:** bl. © Royal Shakespeare Theatre/Lebre/Lebrecht Music & Arts; **879:** br. © Maremagnum/ Getty Images; **883:** Rod Planck/Photo Researchers, Inc.; **889:** 20th Century Fox/Photofest; **894:** 20th Century Fox/Photofest; **902:** 20th Century Fox/Photofest; **907:** CORBIS; **909:** ™ and Copyright © 20th Century Fox Film Corp. All Rights Reserved. Courtesy: Everett Collection; **914:** 20TH CENTURY FOX/THE KOBAL COLLECTION/MORTON, MERRICK; **916:** ™ and Copyright © 20th Century Fox Film Corp. All Rights Reserved. Courtesy: Everett Collection; **918:** The Granger Collection, New York; **923:** 20TH CENTURY FOX/THE KOBAL COLLECTION/MORTON, MERRICK; **924:** 20TH CENTURY FOX/THE KOBAL COLLECTION/MORTON, MERRICK; **937:** © Michael Maslan Historic Photographs/CORBIS; **938:** © Michael Maslan Historic Photographs/CORBIS; **939:** Phillip Crowson/THE BATTALION; **941–942:** Phillip Crowson/THE

BATTALION; **945:** t. Archivo Iconografico, S.A/CORBIS; **945:** b. SuperStock; **946:** *Thisbe,* John William Waterhouse/The Bridgeman Art Library, London/New York; **946:** bkgrnd. © Helmut Meyer zur Capellen/ zefa/CORBIS; **948:** *Thisbe and the Lioness,* from *The Children's Hour: Stories from the Classics,* published by the Waverley Book Company (colour litho), Brock, Charles Edmund (1870–1938)/Private Collection/ The Bridgeman Art Library International; **949:** © Helmut Meyer zur Capellen/zefa/CORBIS; **950:** The Everett Collection, Inc; **951:** istockphoto.com; **952:** The Granger Collection, New York; **954:** The Everett Collection, Inc.; **956:** © CORBIS Sygma; **969:** Bettmann/CORBIS; **970:** Valmondois Sous La Neige, Maurice de Vlaminck, Superstock; **973:** *White Night,* 1901, Edvard Munch, oil on canvas, 45 1/2 x 43 1/2 in. (115.5 x 111 cm) Photo: J. Lathion © Nasjonalgalleriet 1997, ©2003 The Munch Museum/ The Munch-Ellingsen Group/Artists Rights Society (ARS), NY; **981:** © noneAA/CORBIS; **987:** t. Bettmann/CORBIS; **987:** b. Courtesy Henry Alford; **988:** bkgrnd. istockphoto.com; **988:** The Everett Collection, Inc; **989:** istockphoto.com; **990:** Photofest; **993:** Camera Press/Retna, LTD; **996:** Photofest; **998:** Photofest; **999:** tr. CORBIS; **999:** m. Lynton Gardiner/© Dorling Kindersley, Courtesy of The American Museum of Natural History; **999:** rm. Colin Keates/© Dorling Kindersley; **999:** mi. Paul Van Reil/Robert Harding World Imagery; **1002:** Kwame Zikomo/SuperStock; **1007:** Prentice Hall; **1016:** istockphoto.com; **1018:** istockphoto.com; **1019:** istockphoto.com; **1026–1027:** Nice One Productions/CORBIS; **1030:** istockphoto.com; **Gr09 U6 1031:** © Gerald Bustamante/Stock Illustration Source, Inc.; **1032:** *CORNERED* © 2004 Mike Baldwin. Reprinted with permission of UNIVERSAL PRESS SYNDICATE. All Rights Reserved.; **1037:** Getty Images; **1038:** Getty Images; **1043:** Bettmann/CORBIS; **1043:** l. © Kevin Fleming/CORBIS; **1043:** bkgrnd. istockphoto.com; **1043:** bkgrnd. istockphoto.com; **1044–1045:** l. © Kevin Fleming/CORBIS; **1044–1045:** bkgrnd. istockphoto.com; **1046:** Mary Evans Picture Library/EDWIN WALLACE/Everett Collection; **1055:** Mary Evans Picture Library/EDWIN WALLACE/Everett Collection; **1058:** Mary Evans Picture Library/EDWIN WALLACE/Everett Collection; **1061:** Polyphemus, *The Cyclop from Homer's The Odyssey,* N. C. Wyeth; **1066:** *Odysseus in the Land of the Dead from Homer's The Odyssey,* N. C. Wyeth, Brandywine River Museum; **1069:** Réunion des Musées Nationaux/Art Resource, NY; **1070:** *Circe Meanwhile Had Gone Her Ways...,* 1924, William Russell Flint, Collection of the New York Public Library; Astor, Lenox and Tilden Foundations; **1075:** Mary Evans Picture Library; **1080:** © Stapleton Collection/CORBIS; **1089:** © Kevin Fleming/CORBIS; **1089:** bkgrnd. istockphoto.com; **1089:** b. istockphoto.com; **1091:** *Eumaeus, the Swineherd from Homer's The Odyssey,* N. C. Wyeth, The Museum of Texas Tech University; **1095:** Scala/Art Resource, NY; **1096:** © Araldo de Luca/CORBIS; **1099:** Mary Evans Picture Library/EDWIN WALLACE/ Everett Collection; **1102:** *The Trial of the Bow from Homer's The Odyssey,* N. C. Wyeth, Brandywine River Museum; **1104:** Bridgeman Art Library, London/New York; **1106:** *The Slaughter of the Suitors from Homer's The Odyssey,* N. C. Wyeth, Licensed by ASaP Worldwide. Photo courtesy of the Archives of the American Illustrators Gallery, NYC. © Copyright 2000 National Museum of American Illustration, Newport, RI. www. americanillustration.org; **1113:** Erich Lessing/Art Resource, NY; **1119:** PARAMOUNT PICTURES/THE KOBAL COLLECTION; **1120:** b. AP/ WideWorld Photos; **1120:** bkgrnd. Frank Schwere/Getty Images; **1121:** t. Getty Images; b. Andrew McRobb/Dorling Kindersley; **1122:** t. Andrew McRobb/Dorling Kindersley; b. Scott Camazine/Photo Researchers, Inc.; **1123:** istockphoto.com; **1124:** Owaki/Kulla/CORBIS; **1127:** bl. The Granger Collection, New York; **1127:** tl. © Bassouls Sophie/CORBIS Sygma; **1127:** br. Getty Images; **1127:** Time Life Pictures/Getty Images; **1127:** br. Courtesy of Maria Delgado Travis; **1128:** *Penelope and the Suitors,* 1912, J.M. Waterhouse, 51 1/2 x 75 in. (131 x 191 cm) City of Aberdeen Art Gallery and Museums Collections, Scotland; **1130:** Herve Lewandowski/Reunion de Musees Nationaux/Art Resource; **1132:** Neil White/Trevillion Images; **1134–1135:** John Miller/Robert Harding Picture Library/Alamy; **1139:** Jason Lewis/© Dorling Kindersley; **1147:** t. © Agnew's, London, UK/ The Bridgeman Art Library; **1147:** b. istockphoto.

com; **1148–1149:** Paul Hardy/CORBIS; **1149:** inset. istockphoto.com; **1150:** istockphoto.com; **1151:** © Agnew's, London, UK/ The Bridgeman Art Library; **1153:** istockphoto.com; **1154:** istockphoto.com; **1156–1157:** Denis Scott/CORBIS; **1159:** istockphoto.com; **1160:** istockphoto.com; **1165:** t. Getty Images; **1165:** b. The Granger Collection, New York; **1166:** The Granger Collection, New York; **1168:** The Granger Collection, New York; **1170:** Simon Jauncey/Getty Images; **1171:** The Granger Collection, New York; **1174:** The Granger Collection, New York; **1175:** The Granger Collection, New York; **1177:** The Granger Collection, New York; **1179:** The Granger Collection, New York; **1180:** The Granger Collection, New York; **1181:** Historical Picture Archive/CORBIS; **1183:** The Granger Collection, New York; **1186:** The Granger Collection, New York; **1195:** Bettmann/CORBIS; **1196–1197:** *We the People,* Kathy Morrow, Original scratchboard painting with hand-loomed beadwork, Courtesy of the artist; **1201:** t. AP/WideWorld Photos; **1201:** b. © Tibor Bognar/CORBIS; **1202:** l. © BRAUCHLI DAVID/CORBIS SYGMA; **1202:** r. © Tibor Bognar/CORBIS; **1204:** © Reuters/ CORBIS; **1209:** AP/WideWorld Photos; **1209:** bkgrnd. AP/ WideWorld Photos; **1210:** Photo File/ MLB Photos via Getty Images; **1210:** bkgrnd. AP/WideWorld Photos; **1211:** Car Culture/CORBIS; **1212:** Hulton-Deutsch/CORBIS; **1213:** H.R. Bramaz/Peter Arnold, Inc; **1214:** Thinkstock/CORBIS; **1217:** t. AP/WideWorld Photos; b. Miriam Berkley/Author pix; **1218:** Illustration by Tim Raglin; **1220–1221:** border. istockphoto.com; **1222:** Jim Zuckerman/CORBIS; **1224:** Franck Fotos/Alamy; **1225:** Columbia/Tri-Star/The Kobal Collection; **1227–1232:** Columbia Pictures/Photofest; **1234:** Jose Luiz Pelaez, Inc. /CORBIS; **1237:** Getty Images; **1241:** Michael Trevillion/Trevillion Images

Staff Credits

The people who made up the Pearson Prentice Hall Literature team—representing design, editorial, editorial services, education technology, manufacturing and inventory planning, market research, marketing services, planning and budgeting, product planning, production services, project office, publishing processes, and rights and permissions—are listed below. Boldface type denotes the core team members.

Tobey Antao, Margaret Antonini, Rosalyn Arcilla, Penny Baker, James Ryan Bannon, Stephan Barth, **Tricia Battipede,** Krista Baudo, Rachel Beckman, Julie Berger, Lawrence Berkowitz, Melissa Biezin, **Suzanne Biron,** Rick Blount, **Marcela Boos, Betsy Bostwick,** Kay Bosworth, Jeff Bradley, Andrea Brescia, Susan Brorein, Lois Brown, **Pam Carey,** Lisa Carrillo, **Geoffrey Cassar,** Patty Cavuoto, Doria Ceraso, Jennifer Ciccone, Jaime Cohen, Rebecca Cottingham, Joe Cucchiara, Jason Cuoco, **Alan Dalgleish, Karen Edmonds, Irene Ehrmann,** Stephen Eldridge, Amy Fleming, Dorothea Fox, Steve Frankel, Cindy Frederick, Philip Fried, Diane Fristachi, Phillip Gagler, Pamela Gallo, Husain Gatlin, **Elaine Goldman,** Elizabeth Good, John Guild, Phil Hadad, Patricia Hade, Monduane Harris, Brian Hawkes, Jennifer B. Heart, Martha Heller, John Hill, Beth Hyslip, Mary Jean Jones, Grace Kang, Nathan Kinney, Roxanne Knoll, **Kate Krimsky,** Monisha Kumar, Jill Kushner, Sue Langan, Melisa Leong, Susan Levine, Dave Liston, **Mary Luthi, George Lychock, Gregory Lynch, Joan Mazzeo, Sandra McGloster,** Eve Melnechuk, Kathleen Mercandetti, Salita Metha, Artur Mkrtchyan, Karyn Mueller, Alison Muff, Christine Mulcahy, Kenneth Myett, Elizabeth Nemeth, Stefano Nese, Carrie O'Connor, April Okano, Kim Ortell, Sonia Pap, Raymond Parenteau, Dominique Pickens, Linda Punskovsky, **Sheila Ramsay,** Maureen Raymond, Mairead Reddin, **Erin Rehill-Seker, Renée Roberts, Laura Ross,** Bryan Salacki, Sharon Schultz, Jennifer Serra, **Melissa Shustyk,** Rose Sievers, Christy Singer, Yvonne Stecky, **Cynthia Summers,** Steve Thomas, Merle Uuesoo, Roberta Warshaw, Patricia Williams, Daniela Velez

Additional Credits

Lydie Bemba, Victoria Blades, Denise Data, Rachel Drice, Eleanor Kostyk, Jill Little, Loraine Machlin, Evan Marx, Marilyn McCarthy, Patrick O'Keefe, Shelia M. Smith, Lucia Tirondola, Laura Vivenzio, Linda Waldman, Angel Weyant